Street by Stree

MERSEY

Enlarged areas BIRKENHEAD, BOOTLE, ELLESMERE PORT, LIVERPOOL, RUNCORN, ST HELENS, SOUTHPORT, WARRINGTON, WIDNES

Plus Ashton-in-Makerfield, Bebington, Crosby, Formby, Heswall, Hoylake, Kirkby, Maghull, Neston, Ormskirk, Prescot, Skelmersdale, Wallasey, West Kirby

3rd edition November 2007

Original edition printed May 2001

Published by AA Publishing (a trading name of Automobile Association Developments Limited, whose registered office is Fanum House, Basing View, Basingstoke, Hampshire RG21 4EA. Registered number 1878835).

Produced by the Mapping Services Department of The Automobile Association. (A03390)

A CIP Catalogue record for this book is available from the British Library.

Printed by Oriental Press in Dubai

Ref: ML49y

Key to map pages ii-iii

Key to map symbols iv-1

Enlarged map pages 2-19

Main map pages 20-203

Index – towns & villages 204

Index – streets 205-247

Index – featured places 247-252

Acknowledgements 252

National Grid references are shown on the map frame of each page.
Red figures denote the 100 km square and blue figures the 1 km square.
Example, page 132 : Brewery 335 389

The reference can also be written using the National Grid two-letter prefix shown on this page, where 3 and 3 are replaced by SJ to give SJ3589.

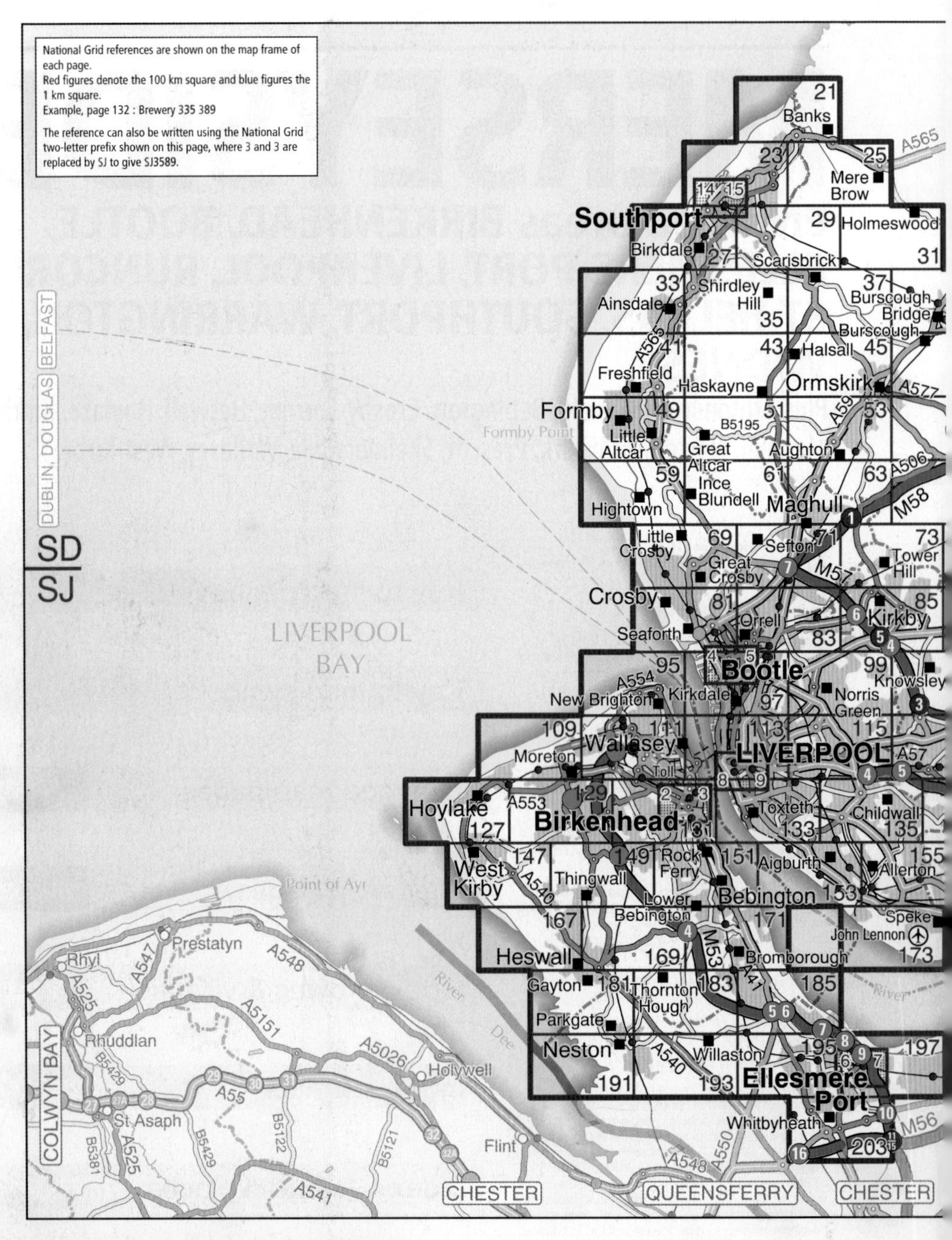

Scale of enlarged map pages **1:10,000** **6.3 inches to 1 mile**

0 1/4 miles 1/2

0 1/4 1/2 kilometres 3/4 1

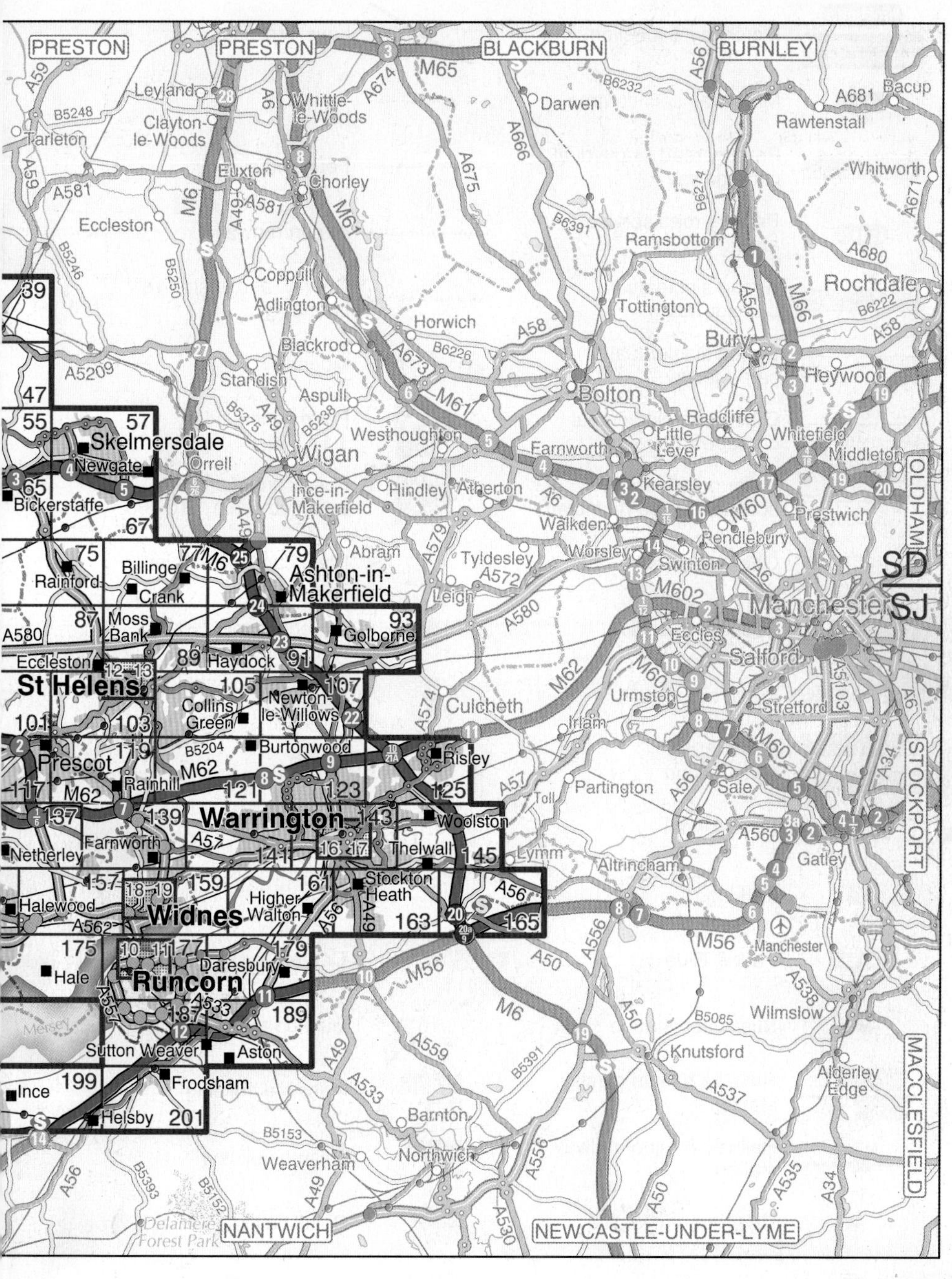

3.6 inches to 1 mile

Scale of main map pages **1:17,500**

0 1/2 miles 1

0 1/2 1 kilometres 1 1/2

Junction 9	Motorway & junction	LC	Level crossing
Services	Motorway service area		Tramway
	Primary road single/dual carriageway		Ferry route
Services	Primary road service area		Airport runway
	A road single/dual carriageway		County, administrative boundary
	B road single/dual carriageway		Mounds
	Other road single/dual carriageway	17	Page continuation 1:17,500
	Minor/private road, access may be restricted	3	Page continuation to enlarged scale 1:10,000
	One-way street		River/canal, lake, pier
	Pedestrian area		Aqueduct, lock, weir
	Track or footpath	465 Winter Hill	Peak (with height in metres)
	Road under construction		Beach
	Road tunnel		Woodland
P	Parking		Park
P+	Park & Ride		Cemetery
	Bus/coach station		Built-up area
	Railway & main railway station		Industrial building
	Railway & minor railway station		Leisure building
	Underground station		Retail building
	Light railway & station		Other building
	Preserved private railway	IKEA	IKEA store

	City wall
A&E	Hospital with 24-hour A&E department
PO	Post Office
	Public library
	Tourist Information Centre
	Seasonal Tourist Information Centre
	Petrol station, 24 hour Major suppliers only
	Church/chapel
	Public toilets
	Toilet with disabled facilities
PH	Public house AA recommended
	Restaurant AA inspected
Madeira Hotel	Hotel AA inspected
	Theatre or performing arts centre
	Cinema
	Golf course
	Camping AA inspected
	Caravan site AA inspected
	Camping & caravan site AA inspected
	Theme park
	Abbey, cathedral or priory

	Castle
	Historic house or building
Wakehurst Place (NT)	National Trust property
	Museum or art gallery
	Roman antiquity
	Ancient site, battlefield or monument
	Industrial interest
	Garden
	Garden Centre Garden Centre Association Member
	Garden Centre Wyevale Garden Centre
	Arboretum
	Farm or animal centre
	Zoological or wildlife collection
	Bird collection
	Nature reserve
	Aquarium
	Visitor or heritage centre
	Country park
	Cave
	Windmill
	Distillery, brewery or vineyard

2
CORPORATION ROAD
CORPORATION ROAD
A5030
B5146
CORPORATION ROAD
131
A
B
C
D
E
331
Price Street
Merritt
Smith Ave
Crutchley Av
Dawson Av
Our Lady And St Edwards RC Primary School
Cavendish St
Price Road
CLEVELAND STREET
DUKE STREET
A5027
Old Bidston Rd
Old Bidston St
Maddock St
Marshall Street
Cleveland Business Park
Braid St
Massey St
Vardon St
Berner St
Upr Beckwith St
Patten St
Street
Brill St
Brett Street
Bray St
Cavendish Medical Centre
Neston Gardens
Churchview Rd
St Edwards Cl
Price Street Bus Centre
Beckwith St
Price St
St Anne St
Annes Pl
St Annes Grove
Arthur St
Fieldway
Street
Brook St
A5030
Hilbre St
Lynas St
Neptune St
Works
Marcus St
Pool St
RENDEL STREET
A5027
Birkenhead Park Stn
St Annes Terrace
Beckwith St
Parkview Cl
Newhope Rd
Parkview Close
Court
Works
Brook Street
CH41
Cottage St
Charles St
Brook St
Brooklands
1
2
Park Drive
Cavendish Rd
PARK ROAD NORTH
Morley Av
Churchhill Av
Lloyd Av
Curzon Av
Hartington Av
Asquith Av
PO
DUKE STREET
Harcourt St
Arthur Street
Aspinall St
Newling St
Street
Livingstone St
Livingstone Gardens
Anne St
Price Street
Vittoria Medical Centre
Finch Ct
Anne St
Street
A5029
Watson St
Wood Close
PARK ROAD NORTH
Pr Edward St
The Priory CE Primary School
Aberdeen St
Trinity St
Vittoria St
Rosebank
Cathcart St
Cathcart Street Primary School
St Anne Way
WATSON STREET
Robert St
Park St
St Anne St
St Anne's Cl
Beckwith St E
Ashville Rd
Park Drive
Park Drive
A553
Newton Street
Banning Cl
Keightley St
Hope St
Dover Cl
Dover Cl
Edgar Ct
3
Ashville Road
Park Drive
CONWAY STREET
St Laurences RC Primary School
St L Cl
Laurence St
Kinmel Cl
130
89
East Road
Knowles St
Craven Cl
Bentinck St
Exmouth Way
Conway Dr
A5029
Birkenhead Park
Hilton Close
Street
Simpson St
Florence St
Parkfield Av
Park St
Europa Pool
A553
4
BIRKENHEAD
Birkenhead Park CC
Park Drive
Park Road
Paterson Street
Gladstone Cl
Bentinck Cl
Street
Exmouth Gdns
EXMOUTH STREET
Sisters Wy
Park Field Pl
Council Building
Hemingford St
Park Drive
Park Drive
Park Dr
Craven St
Park Cl
Fox St
Bright St
Gordon St
Bentinck St
Bright St
Ambulance Station
Fire Stn
Craven Business Centre
Sisters Wy
Cardigan Av
Pine Ct
Elm Ct
Superstore
Claughton
Cannon Hill
Park High School Sports
St Helen's Cl
Cole Street Primary School
Cloughton Rd
Catherine St
Coventry St
St John Street
Oliver St
5
St Hugh's Cl
Park Road South
Francis Av
Hawarden Av
Radnor Pl
Merton Pl
Alvanley Pl
Cole St
Cloughton Road
Bentinck Pl
Eastbourne Rd
Menai St
Oliver Road
St Andrew's Road
Slatey Road
Grange Road West
Grange Pl
Back Menai St
Charing Cross
River St
Grange
Pyramids Shopping Centre
The Gr Shoppi
Little Theatre
Grange Rd
Salisbury St
WHETSTONE LANE
BOROUGH ROAD A552
The Nook
Grosvenor Road
Grosvenor Court
Eaton Rd
Osborne Rd
Alexandra Rd
Ravenscroft Rd
Henthorne St
Barton St
Clayton St
Clayton Pl
Cook St
Grange Mount
Road
Warwick Cl
PO
6
Devonshire Road
Place
Palm
Caroline Pl
Devonshire Cl
Grange
Alfred Pl
The Lindens
Westbourne Rd
Clarendon Cl
Carlisle Mews
Quarrybank St
Wilkinson St
Health Cen
Zetland Rd
B5148
The Hollybank Rd
Hazel Rd
Fearnley Rd
Woodlands
Lowwood Grove
Brookland Rd
Lowwood Rd
Circular Rd
Lowwood Road
Grafton St
Slatey Rd
Reedville
Balfour Road
Euston Grove
Road
Ridley Street
Grange Vw
Town Vw
Belmont Grove
Oxton Rd
Oak Bank
Tetbury St
Canforth Cl
BOROUGH ROAD
Shaw St
Quarry Bank
Park Gv
Cedar Street
Maple St
Clifton
Charlesville
esford
Grove
7
Road
Mather Rd
Barnard Rd
Enfield Ter
Road
Devaney Medical Centre
James St
Princess Terrace
Ball's Road
Belmont
Penrith St
Ball's Road E
Mount Grove Place
Mount Gv
St Werburghs RC Primary School
Raffles Road
Willmer Road
Whalley Rd
Rawcliffe Rd
Tatton Rd
Mounsey Rd
Derby Rd
Council Building
Woodlands Primary School
WHETSTONE LANE
Wellington Ter
Wellington Ter
Rodney St
388
Larch Road
Christchurch CE Primary School
331
Elm Grove
Victoria Gardens
Lyndhurst
N Cl
Barren
Kings M
Road
131
Rd
Dingle Rd
Ash Rd
Beech Rd
Charlecombe St
Convent Cl
Rector Cl
Chesnut Grove
sbury Road
Jarrow Cl
Telford
Kent
Falc
Rd
Halcyon Road
Grove
Milton Road
Beech Court
Laurel Rd
Milton Rd E
Victoria
1 grid square represents 250 metres
CH42

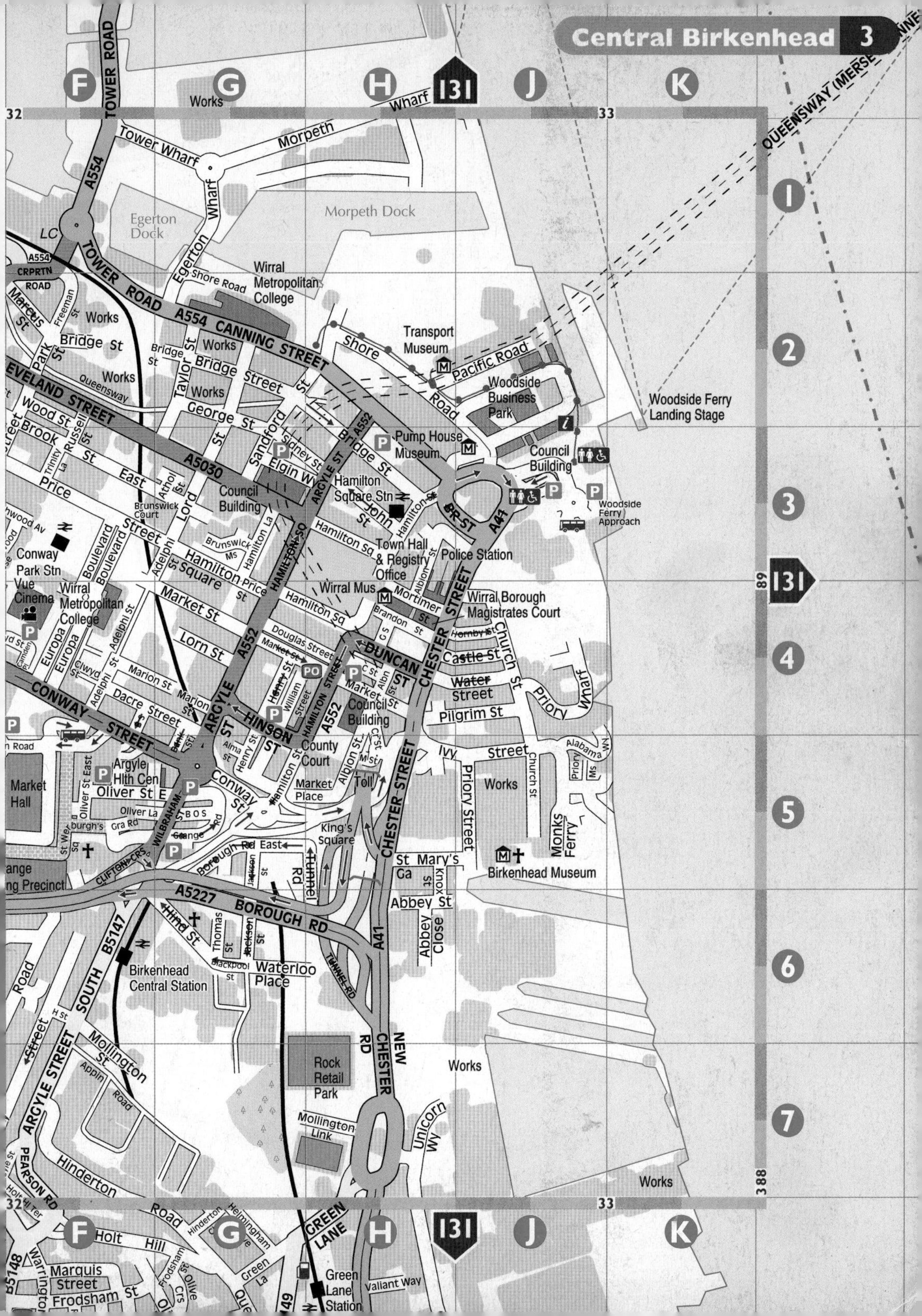

Central Birkenhead
3
F
G
H
131
J
K
32
33
Works
Tower Road
Tower Wharf
Morpeth
Wharf
A554
LC
Egerton Dock
Egerton
Wharf
Morpeth Dock
QUEENSWAY (MERSEY TUNNEL)
1
A554
CRPRTN ROAD
Tower Road
Shore Road
Wirral Metropolitan College
A554 Canning Street
Marcus St
Freeman St
Works
Bridge St
Park St
Bridge St
Taylor St
Works
Bridge Street
Queensway
Works
Cleveland Street
Wood St
Brook St
Russell St
George St
Sandford St
Shore Road
Transport Museum
Pacific Road
Woodside Business Park
2
Woodside Ferry Landing Stage
Sidney St
Argyle St
A552
Bridge St
Pump House Museum
Elgin Wy
A5030
Trinity La
Price St
East
Athol St
Council Building
Hamilton Square Stn
John St
Hamilton St
Council Building
BR ST
A41
Woodside Ferry Approach
3
Brunswick Court
Lord St
Brunswick Ms
Hamilton La
Hamilton Sq
Conway Park Stn
Boulevard
Street
Adelphi St
Hamilton Square
Price St
Hamilton Sq
Town Hall & Registry Office
Albion St
Police Station
Vue Cinema
Wirral Metropolitan College
Wirral Mus
Mortimer St
Chester Street
Wirral Borough Magistrates Court
89
131
Market St
Hamilton Sq
Brandon St
Hornby St
Church St
Europa
Adelphi St
Lorn St
A552
Douglas Street
Market St
Duncan St
Castle St
4
Camden Pl
Clwyd St
Marion St
Henry St
PO
Water Street
Priory Wharf
Conway Street
Adelphi St
Dacre Street
Marion St
William Street
Hamilton Street
Market St
Council Building
Pilgrim St
Argyle St
Hinson St
A552
Bank St
Alma St
Henry St
County Court
Albion St
M St
Ivy Street
Alabama Wy
Priory Ms
Market Hall
Argyle Hlth Cen
Oliver St East
Oliver St E
Oliver La
Wilbraham St
BOS
Conway St
Hamilton St
Market Place
Toll
Priory Street
Works
Church St
Monks Ferry
5
Gra Rd
Grange Rd
St Werburgh's Sq
Clifton Crs
Borough Rd East
Jackson St
Tunnel Rd
King's Square
Chester Street
St Mary's Ga
Knox St
Birkenhead Museum
Grange Shopping Precinct
A5227 Borough Rd
Hind St
Thomas St
Jackson St
Abbey St
Abbey Close
A41
Tunnel Rd
B5147
South
Road
Birkenhead Central Station
Blackpool St
Waterloo Place
6
H St
Street
Mollington St
Appin Road
Argyle Street
Rock Retail Park
New Chester Rd
Works
Mollington Link
Unicorn Wy
7
Pearson Rd
Hinderton Road
Works
388
Holt Hill
Hinderton
Helmingham
Green Lane
Green La
Green Lane Station
Valiant Way
B5148
Marquis Street
Frodsham St
Warrington
St Olive
Crs

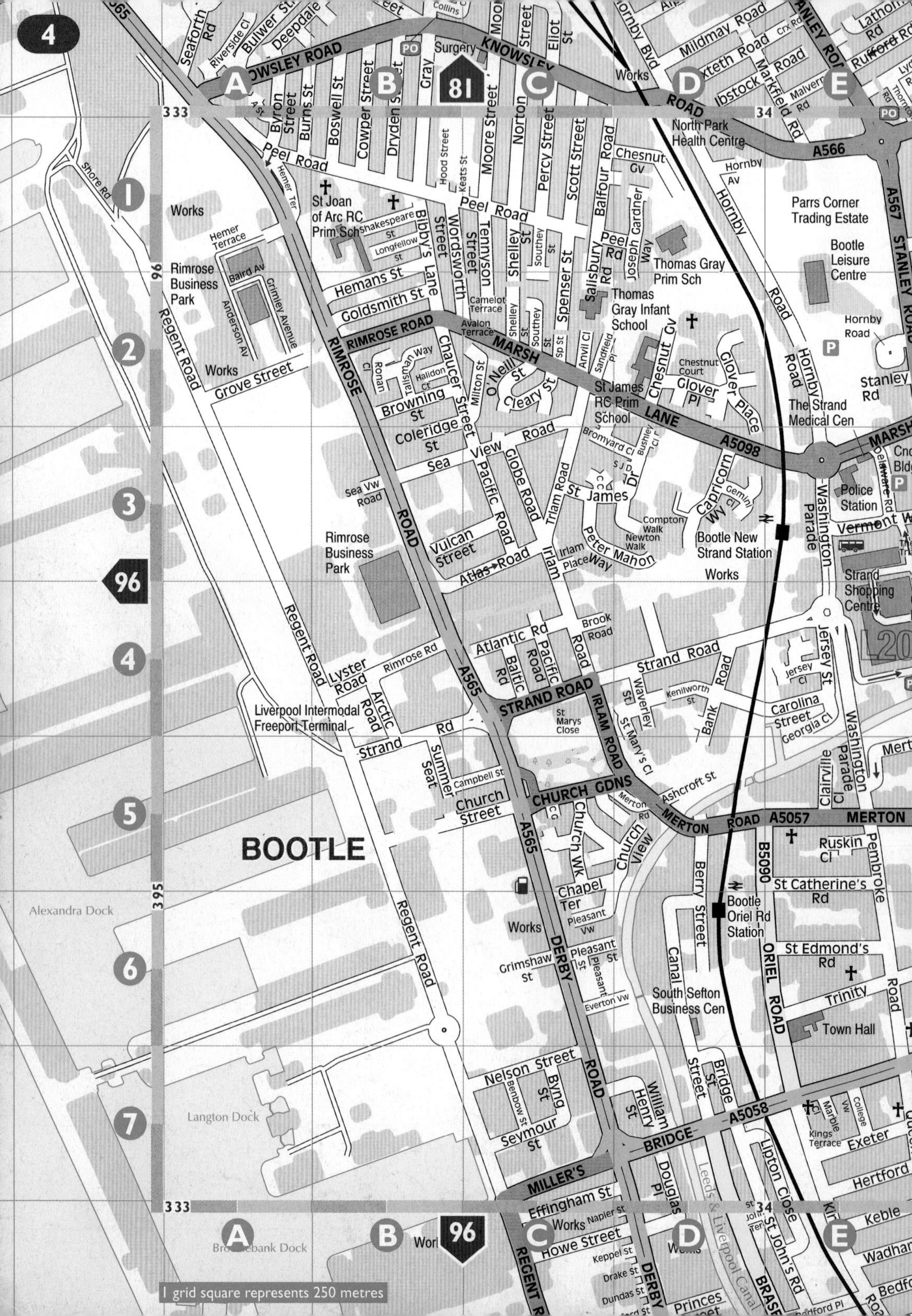

4
KNOWSLEY ROAD
Seaforth Rd
Riverside Cl
Bulwer St
Deepdale
Collins
PO
Surgery
81
Moor
Street
Elliot St
Hornby Blvd
Mildmay Road
Laxeth Road
Ibstock Road
Markfield Rd
Malvern Rd
Crx Rd
Lathom Rd
Rufford Rd
Works
A
B
C
D
E
333
34
Byron Street
Burns St
Boswell St
Cowper Street
Dryden Street
Gray
Hood Street
Keats St
Moore Street
Norton
Percy Street
Scott Street
Balfour Road
Chesnut Gv
North Park Health Centre
A566
Peel Road
Hemer Ter
Shore Rd
Hornby Av
Hornby Road
Parrs Corner Trading Estate
A567
STANLEY ROAD
1
Works
Hemer Terrace
St Joan of Arc RC Prim Sch
Shakespeare St
Longfellow St
Bibby's Lane
Wordsworth Street
Tennyson Street
Shelley St
Southey St
Spenser St
Salisbury Rd
Peel Rd
Joseph Gardner Way
Thomas Gray Prim Sch
Bootle Leisure Centre
96
Rimrose Business Park
Baird Av
Grimley Avenue
Anderson Av
Hemans St
Goldsmith St
Camelot Terrace
Avalon Terrace
Thomas Gray Infant School
Hornby Road
2
Regent Road
Works
Grove Street
RIMROSE ROAD
RIMROSE
Talisman Way
Halidon Ct
Ronan Cl
Chaucer Street
Milton St
O'Neill St
MARSH
Sp St
Anvil Cl
Sandfield Pl
Chesnut Gv
Chestnut Court
Glover Pl
Glover Place
P
Stanley Rd
Browning St
Cleary St
St James RC Prim School
LANE
The Strand Medical Cen
Coleridge St
Sea View Road
Bromyard Cl
Bushley Cl
A5098
MARSH
Cnc Bldg
Sea Vw Road
Pacific Road
Globe Road
Trlam Road
St James Dr
Capricorn Wy
Gemini Dr
Washington Parade
Police Station
3
ROAD
Compton Walk
Newton Walk
Bootle New Strand Station
Vermont W
Rimrose Business Park
Vulcan Street
Irlam Place
Peter Mahon Way
96
Atlas Road
Works
Strand Shopping Centre
Regent Road
Atlantic Rd
Baltic Rd
Pacific Road
Brook Road
L20
4
Lyster Road
Rimrose Rd
A565
Strand Road
Jersey Cl
Jersey St
Arctic Road
STRAND ROAD
Waverley St
Kenilworth St
Bank Road
Liverpool Intermodal Freeport Terminal
St Marys Close
IRLAM ROAD
St Mary's Cl
Carolina Street
Georgia Cl
Washington Parade
Strand Rd
Summer Seat
Campbell St
Ashcroft St
Clairville Cl
Mert
5
Church Street
CHURCH GDNS
Merton Rd
MERTON ROAD A5057 MERTON
BOOTLE
A565
Church Wk
Church View
Ruskin Cl
Pembroke
B5090
Berry Street
St Catherine's Rd
Chapel Ter
Bootle Oriel Rd Station
Alexandra Dock
395
Works
Pleasant Vw
Canal Street
ORIEL ROAD
St Edmond's Rd
6
Regent Road
Grimshaw St
DERBY
Pleasant St
Everton Vw
South Sefton Business Cen
Trinity
Road
Town Hall
Nelson Street
Benbow St
Byng St
ROAD
William Henry St
Bridge St
7
Langton Dock
Seymour St
A5058
BRIDGE
Lipton Close
Marble Vw
College
Kings Terrace
Exeter
MILLER'S
Douglas Pl
Leeds & Liverpool Canal
Hertford
333
Effingham St
Napier St
St John's Rd
Keble
Works
Howe Street
96
REGENT R
Keppel St
Drake St
Dundas St
DERBY
Princes
BRASE
Wadham
Bedford Pl
Bedfo
1 grid square represents 250 metres

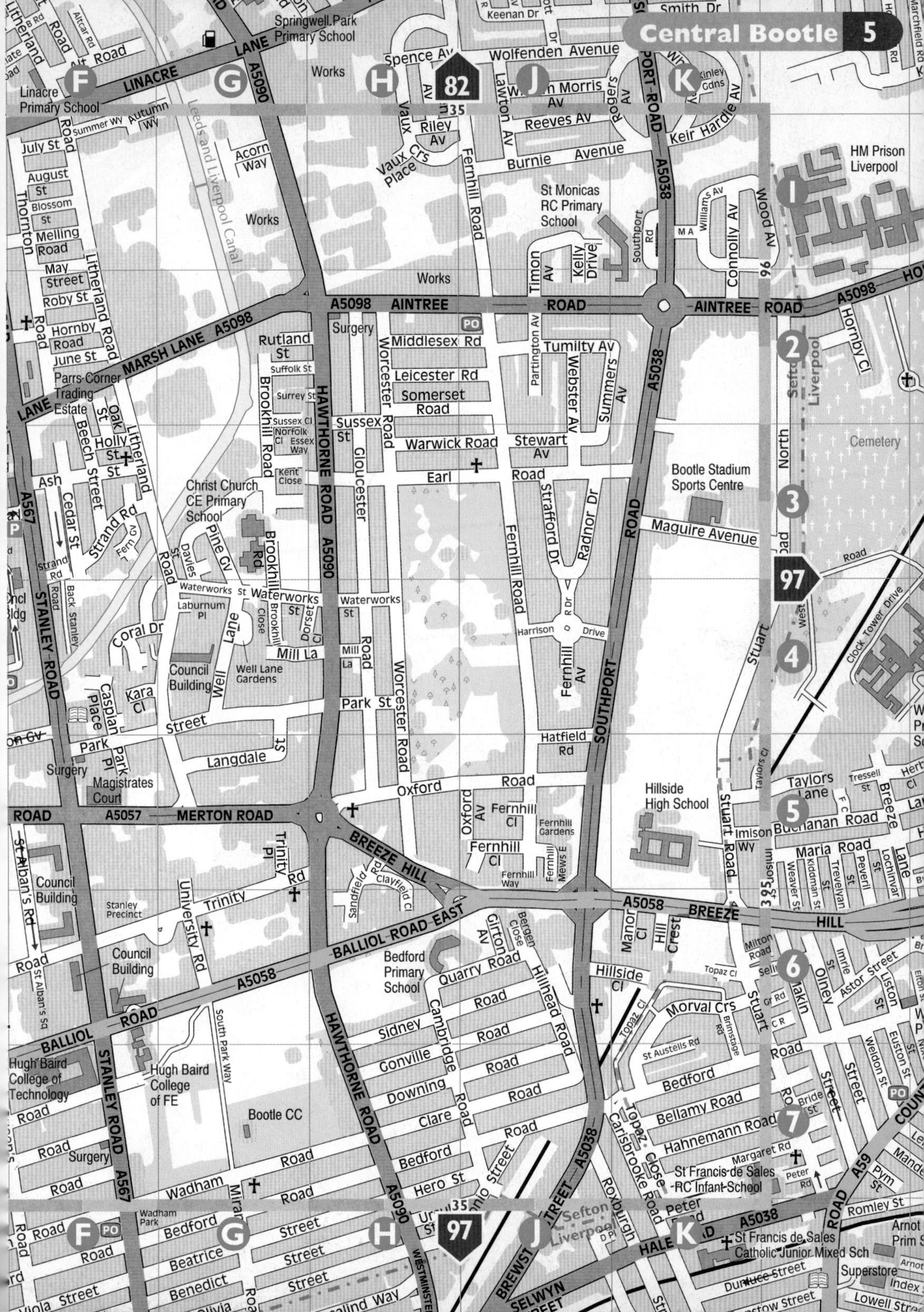
Springwell Park Primary School
Keenan Dr
Smith Dr
Litherland Road
Altcar Rd
Alt Road
Linacre Lane
Linacre Primary School
Works
Spence Av
82
Wolfenden Avenue
Kinley Gdns
William Morris Av
Rogers Av
Southport Road
Summer Wy
Autumn Wy
A5090
Vaux Av
Riley Av
Vaux Crs
Place
Lawton Av
Reeves Av
Keir Hardie Av
July St
August St
Blossom St
Melling Road
May Street
Roby St
Thornton Road
Hornby Road
June St
Litherland Road
Leeds and Liverpool Canal
Acorn Way
Burnie Avenue
Fernhill Road
HM Prison Liverpool
St Monicas RC Primary School
Williams Av
Connolly Av
Wood Av
Timon Av
Kelly Drive
Southport Rd
A5038
A5098 Aintree Road
Aintree Road
Marsh Lane
Lane
Parrs Corner Trading Estate
Rutland St
Suffolk St
Surrey St
Brookhill Road
Surgery
PO
Middlesex Rd
Leicester Rd
Somerset Road
Worcester Road
Partington Av
Tumilty Av
Webster Av
Summers Av
Hornby Cl
Sefton Liverpool Cemetery
Oak St
Holly St
Beech Street
Sussex Cl
Norfolk Cl
Essex Way
Sussex St
Warwick Road
Stewart Av
North Road
Ash
Cedar St
Kent Close
Earl Road
Christ Church CE Primary School
Gloucester
Bootle Stadium Sports Centre
A567
Strand Rd
Fern Gv
Pine Gv
Davies St
Brookhill Rd
Strafford Dr
Radnor Dr
Maguire Avenue
Strand Rd
Back Stanley Road
Waterworks St
Waterworks St
Laburnum Pl
Brookhill Close
Dorset Cl
Waterworks St
97
Clock Tower Drive
Stanley Road
Coral Dr
Well Lane
Mill La
Mill La
Harrison Drive
Fernhill Av
Stuart Road
West
Council Building
Well Lane Gardens
Kara Cl
Caspian Place
Street
Park St
Worcester Road
Hatfield Rd
Southport Road
Park Pl
Langdale St
Taylors Cl
Surgery
Magistrates Court
Oxford Road
Hillside High School
Taylors Lane
Tressell St
Breeze Lane
Road
A5057 Merton Road
Oxford Av
Fernhill Cl
Fernhill Gardens
Stuart Road
Imison Wy
Buchanan Road
Maria Road
St Alban's Rd
Council Building
Trinity Pl
Trinity Rd
Breeze Hill
Sandfield Rd
Clayfield Cl
Fernhill Cl
Fernhill Way
Fernhill Mews E
Imison St
Weaver St
Kiddman St
Trevelyan St
Peveril St
Lochinvar St
Stanley Precinct
University Rd
Balliol Road East
A5058
Girton Av
Bergen Close
Manor Cl
Hill Crest
A5058 Breeze Hill
Council Building
St Alban's Sq
Road
Bedford Primary School
Quarry Road
Hillhead Road
Hillside Cl
Milton Road
Topaz Cl
Makin
Olney
Imrie St
Astor Street
Liston St
Balliol Road
Hugh Baird College of Technology
Stanley Road
Hugh Baird College of FE
South Park Way
Sidney Road
Cambridge Road
Gonville Road
Downing Road
Clare Road
Topaz Cl
Morval Crs
Brimstage Rd
Stuart Road
Gr Rd
St Austells Rd
Bedford Road
Bellamy Road
Hahnemann Road
Topaz Close
Carisbrooke Road
Street
Weldon St
Euston St
Bride St
PO
Bootle CC
Surgery
Road
Bedford Road
Hero St
Road
Margaret Rd
St Francis de Sales RC Infant School
Peter Rd
A59
Pym St
Wadham Road
Mirar
A5090
Urmson St
97
Roxburgh
Peter Road
A5038
Romley St
Arnot Prim S
Wadham Park
Bedford Street
Beatrice Street
Benedict Street
Viola Street
Olivia
Westminster
Sefton Liverpool
Brewster Street
Selwyn Street
Hale Road
St Francis de Sales Catholic Junior Mixed Sch
Superstore
Dunluce Street
Index
Lowell Street

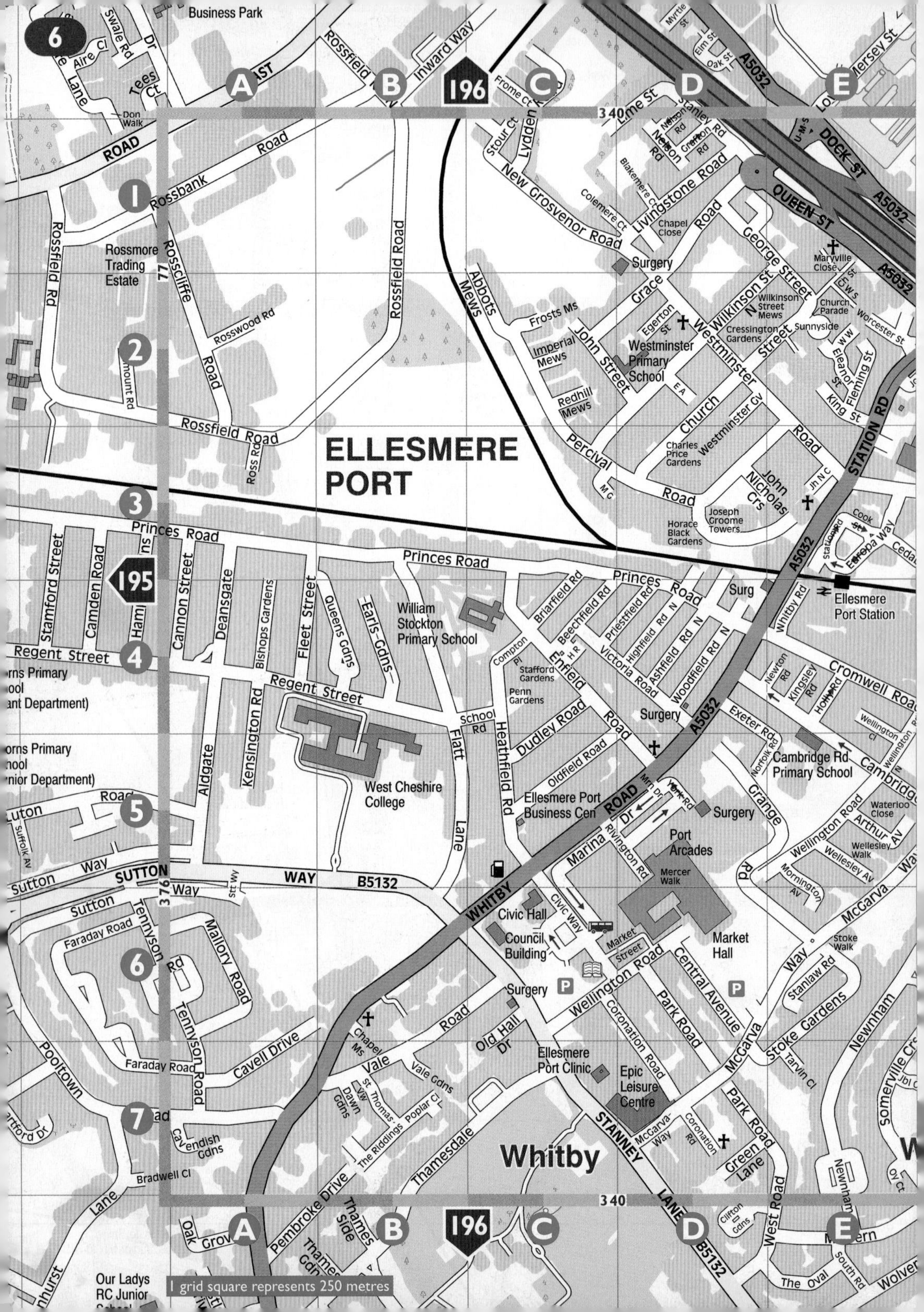
ELLESMERE PORT
Whitby
196
195
1 grid square represents 250 metres
Rossmore Trading Estate
Business Park
Westminster Primary School
William Stockton Primary School
West Cheshire College
Ellesmere Port Business Cen
Port Arcades
Mercer Walk
Market Hall
Civic Hall
Council Building
Ellesmere Port Clinic
Epic Leisure Centre
Cambridge Rd Primary School
Ellesmere Port Station
Surgery
Our Ladys RC Junior
Rossfield Road
Princes Road
Regent Street
Sutton Way
WHITBY ROAD
STANNEY LANE
STATION RD
QUEEN ST
DOCK ST
A5032
B5132
Westminster Road
Church Road
Grace Road
Percival Road
Wellington Road
Vale Road
Cavell Drive
Tennyson Road
Mallory Road
Faraday Road
Pooltown Road
Thamesdale
Pembroke Drive
Park Road
Central Avenue
Coronation Road
McCarva Way
Grange Rd
Cromwell Road
Enfield Road
Victoria Road
Dudley Road
Oldfield Road
Heathfield Rd
Flatt Lane
Kensington Rd
Aldgate
Deansgate
Cannon Street
Fleet Street
Stamford Street
Camden Road
Livingstone Road
New Grosvenor Road
George Street
John Street
Wilkinson St
Marina Dr
Civic Way
Market Street
Stoke Gardens
Newnham
West Road
Green Lane

F
G
H
196
J
K
41
Boat Museum
Pier Road
Manchester Ship Canal
Junction 9
Oil Sites Road
Canalside
Canalside Industrial Estate
CH65
M53
John Nicholas Crescent
Westminster Retail Park
Crescent Road
Dock Yard Road
Meadow Lane
Meadow Lane Industrial Park
Works
Oil Sites Road
Indigo Road
Bridges Road
Charterhouse Cl
Cloister Way
Cromwell Road
Garth Rd
Glebeway Rd
Lees Lane
South Road
New Bridge Road
Cambridge Road
Marchwiel Rd
Girton Cl
Girton Road
Lancing Road
Milton Road
Mltn Cl
Wolverham Primary School
Chesham Ct
Harrow Road
Eton Road
Wolverham Rd
Repton Road
Telford Road
Burnell Rd
Thornton Rd
Winchester Av
Wolverham
PO
Avenue
St Andrew's Rd
Braemar Court
Dundee Court
Stokesay Court
Ruskin Road
Ellesmere Port Stadium
Croft Court
Ludlow
Deans Rd
Cheltenham
I
2
3
4
5
6
7
376
77

LIVERPOOL
KINGSWAY
Superstore
Retail Park
King Edward Industrial Estate
King Edward Ind Est
Superstore
Radisson SAS Hotel
Princes Dock
Isle of Man Ferry Terminal
Crowne Plaza Hotel
George's Dock
Titanic Memorial
Royal Liver Building
Cunard Building
Mersey Ferries
War Memorial
Port of Liverpool Building
Museum of Liverpool (due to open 2010)
Canning Dock
HM Customs & Excise National Museum
Merseyside Maritime Museum & International Slavery Museum
Fingerprints of Elvis
Tate Gallery
Albert Dock Village
The Beatles Story
Albert Dock
Granada TV
Salthouse Dock
Premier Travel Inn
Wapping Basin
Kings Dock
Newspaper Office
Thistle Hotel
Council Building
Cabinet War Rooms
Town Hall
SAE Institute
Royal Coll of Nursing
James Street Stn
Queen Elizabeth II Law Courts
National Discovery Park
Fire Station
Merseyside Police HQ
Hotel Ibis
YHA
Liverpool Community College
Vauxhall Business Centre
Holy Cross Catholic Primary School
LJMU Hatton Garden Ind Est
Council Building
Co Fire HQ
Mag Court
Police Stn
Premier Travel Inn
Moorfields Station
Conservation Centre
Council Buildings
Met Quarter (under development)
Cavern Club
HM Coroners Court
Paradise Street Bus Station
BBC North & BBC Radio Merseyside
Police Station
Chadwick Court Industrial Centre
Atlantic Point
A B C D E
1 2 3 4 5 6 7
112
132
334
390
391
L3
1 grid square represents 250 metres

F
G
H
J
K
113
132
35
36
2
3
4
5
6
7
Whitley Gardens
Scotland Place
Byrom St
Great Richmond St
Richmond Row
Soho St
Field St
William
Birkett St
Christian Street
Police Station
St Anne Street
B5173
Mansfield St
Wakefield Street
Queen Anne Street
Harker St
Springfield
Trinity Walk
Soho Street
Bidder St
Langsdale St
Birchfield St
Canterbury St
Liverpool Hope University
Carver St
Langsdale Street
College St North
College St S
Islington House Medical Centre
Brunswick Road
A580
Trafalgar Way
Low Hill
A5049
Liverpool John Moores University
St Josephs Crs
Gerard St
Tom Mann Cl
New Islington
Hunter St
A57
Islington
Erskine Street
Erskine Street Industrial Estate
Moss St
A5048
Epworth St
Prospect St
Harper St
Devon Street
Council Building
Stafford St
Surgery
Kempston St
Constance St
Bayhorse La
Finch Pl
Prescot St
Roy Castle International Cen for Lung Research
A&E
Royal Liverpool University Hospital
Dental Hospital
University of Liverpool
Kensington
B5340
Sacred Heart RC Primary School
County Sessions Ho
Walker Art Gallery
Liverpool Mus
Lib
William Brown St
Commutation
Islington
Fraser St
Norton St
London Road
Audley St
London Road
Daulby St
Oakes St
Superstore
Pembroke Place
National Museums & Galleries Merseyside
St George's Hall
Odeon Cinema
Liverpool Empire Theatre
Lime St
A5038
Pudsey St
Hotham St
Back Bridport St
Bridport St
Ward St
Lord Nelson St
Seymour St
Academy
Greek St
Marquis St
Police Stn
Gill St
Great Newton Street
Pembroke St
Pembroke Gdns
Pembroke Place
A5047
West Derby Street
Crown Street
Mount Vernon St
Bengel St
Mount
Minshull St
Ltl Woolton St
St John's Lane
St George's Place
Queen Square
Hotel
Royal Court Theatre
Roe St
Uni Hall
Lime Street Station
Copperas Hill
Bronte St
Dansie St
St Andrew Street
Trowbridge St
Russell St
Sorting Office
Dover Street
Ashton Street
Brownlow St
Mkt
St John's Shop Cen
Radio City
St John's Beacon
Houghton St
Elliot St
Skelhorne St
Bolton St
Hawke St
Royal Mail St
Ainsworth St
Jones St
Newton Wy
Brownlow Hill
Archb CE Hi
Clayton Square Shopping Cen
Parker St
Leigh St
Ranelagh St
Central Stn
LJMU
Sch
Clarence St
St Nicholas Cath Primary School
Metropolitan Cathedral of Christ the King
Mount Pleasant
Peach Street
University of Liverpool
Crown St
Neptune Theatre
Bold Wood
Back Bold St
Renshaw St
Benson St
Cropper St
Newington
Pomona St
Cathedral Walk
Liverpool Community College
Mount Pleasant
Everyman Theatre
Oxford St
Univ
Chestnut St
Abercromby Square
Univ Sports Centre
Senate House
A5048
Grove Street
Oxford St
Concert St
Fleet St
Slater Street
Seel St
FACT
Wolstenholme Square
Parr St
Back Seel St
Duke Street
Colquitt St
Roscoe Pl
Berry St
Oldham Pl
Oldham St
Drug Dependency Clinic
Leece St
Hardman St
Maryland St
Health Cen
Arrad St
Cambridge St
Mulberry Street
Back Bedford St
Bedford St S
Cambridge St
University of Liverpool
Melville Place
Orphan
Henry
Works
Lydia Ann Street
Suffolk St
Kent Street
Bold Pl
Roscoe La
Roscoe St
Rodney Fertility Clinic
Surg
Unity Theatre
Rice St
Hope St
Philharmonic Hall
Caledonia St
Myrtle Street
Stowell St
Liverpool Community College
Community Cen
Myrtle Pde
Chatham Street
Bedford Cl
Bedford Walk
Vine St
Liverpool Community College
Myrtle St
Brampton Dr
St Vincent de Paul Cath Prim Sch
Vincent Ct
Liverpool Community College
Knight St
Back Knight St
Mount St
59 Rodney Street (NT)
Liverpool Institute for Performing Arts
Hope Street Natural Health Centre
Falkner St
Bickbrn Pl
Health Cen
Back Canning St
Catharine St
Falkner Street
Bedford
Toxteth Community College
Back Falkner St
South
Abercromby Health Centre
Pitt
Upr Pitt St
Frederick Street
Grenville Street
Cornwallis St
Kent St
Bailey St
Nelson St
Sankey St
Chinese Arch
Upper
Duke St
Mornington Business Centre
Surg
LJMU
Canning St
Little Bride St
Back Sir Howard St
Sandon St
Health Centre
Great George Square
Great George St
Street South
Hardy St
Cathedral Close
Dean Dillistone Court
Back Percy St
Percy St
Ltl Canning St
Street
Falkner Sq
Upper Huskisson Street
Falkner
Lowther Street
Nelson St
Cook St
Raffles St
St James
Hope Street
Huskisson
Back Egerton St N
Sandon St
Lady
L1
390

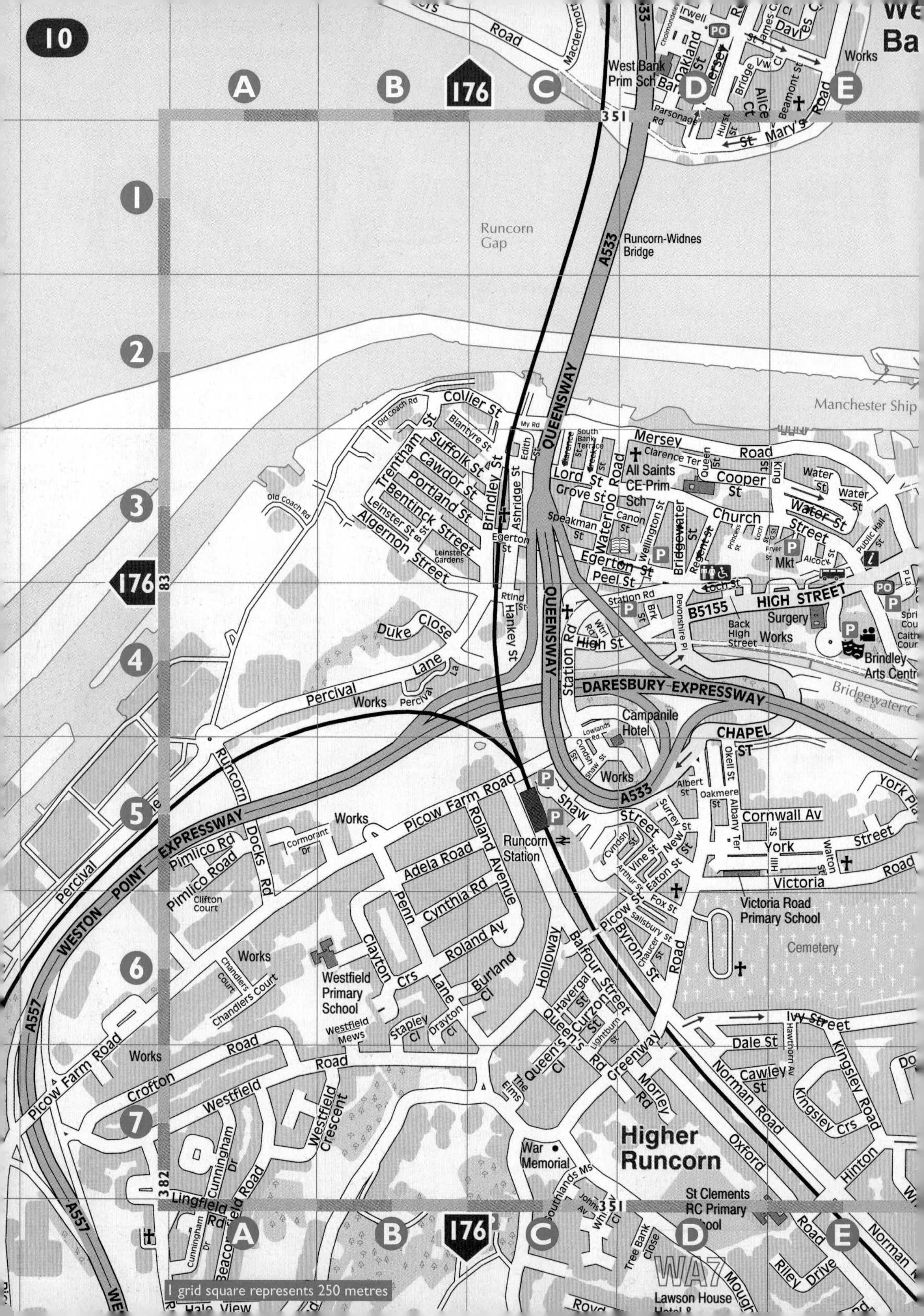

A
B
C
D
E
176
1
2
3
4
5
6
7
83
382
351
Runcorn Gap
Runcorn-Widnes Bridge
A533
QUEENSWAY
West Bank Prim Sch
Oakland St
Mersey
Parsonage Rd
Hurst St
St Mary's Road
Beamont St
Alice Ct
Bridge Vw
Works
Manchester Ship
Collier St
Old Coach Rd
Blantyre St
Suffolk St
Trentham St
Cawdor St
Portland St
Bentinck Street
Leinster St
Algernon Street
Leinster Gardens
Brindley St
Ashridge St
Edith St
Egerton St
My Rd
Mersey Road
Clarence Ter
All Saints CE Prim Sch
Lord St
Grove St
Waterloo Road
Speakman St
Canon St
Wellington St
Bridgewater St
Regent St
Church Street
Cooper St
Water St
Water Street
Public Hall St
Mkt
Alcock St
Egerton St
Peel St
Loch St
Station Rd
B5155
HIGH STREET
Surgery
Back High Street
Brindley Arts Centre
Devonshire Pl
High St
Station Rd
Hankey St
Duke Close
Percival Lane
Percival La
Works
DARESBURY EXPRESSWAY
Bridgewater C
Campanile Hotel
Lowlands Rd
CHAPEL ST
Okell St
Albert St
Oakmere St
Albany Ter
Runcorn
Picow Farm Road
Works
Shaw Street
Runcorn Station
Cornwall Av
York Street
Walton St
Hill St
Victoria Road
Victoria Road Primary School
Cemetery
Surrey St
New St
Vine St
Eaton St
Arthur St
Fox St
Salisbury St
Chaucer St
Byron St
Picow St
Road
WESTON POINT EXPRESSWAY
Pimlico Rd
Pimlico Road
Docks Rd
Cormorant Dr
Clifton Court
Adela Road
Roland Avenue
Cynthia Rd
Penn
Roland Av
Clayton Crs
Lane
Burland Cl
Holloway
Balfour Street
Westfield Primary School
Works
Chandlers Court
Westfield Mews
Stapley Cl
Drayton Cl
Havergal St
Curzon St
Queen's Rd
Queen's Cl
Lightburn St
Greenway
Morley Rd
The Elms
Ivy Street
Dale St
Cawley St
Hawthorn Av
Kingsley Road
Kingsley Crs
Norman Road
Oxford
Hinton
A557
Picow Farm Road
Crofton Road
Westfield
Westfield Crescent
Cunningham Dr
Lingfield Rd
Beaconsfield Road
War Memorial
Higher Runcorn
Southlands Ms
Johns Av
St Clements RC Primary School
Tree Bank Close
WA7
Lawson House
Riley Drive
1 grid square represents 250 metres

177
52
Canal
Works
Fredric Place
Old Quay St
Stanley St
Parker St
Pool Lane
Dover St
Thomas St
John's St
Ann St
Bold St
Fisher St
Irwell La
Grosvenor St
Norfolk St
Pinellas
St Edwards C Prim Sch
Wivern Pl
Runcorn AFC
B5155
BRIDGE STREET
Penketh Court
Ellesmere St
Howarth Court
Sutherland Court
Canal Street
Halton Rd
Windmill St
Victoria Rd
Wldg Av
Leiria Wy
HEATH ROAD
A533
Astmoor Road
Mason St
Linnets Pk
Lister Road
Jensen Court
Hardwick Road
Hardwick Rd
Astmoor Industrial Estate
Faraday Rd
Edison Rd
DARESBURY EXPRESSWAY
83
533
Needham Close
Needham Cl
Ringway Road
Stonehills Ct
Halton Road
Cambridge St
Robert St
Cartwright St
Vahler Ter
Grange Rd
Easby Cl
Grange Pk Rd
Porter St
Sewell St
Perrey St
Taylors Rw
Stonehills Lane
Wicksten Drive
Grange Pk Av
Holmfield Av
Saxon
Avenue
Malcolm St
Union St
Sutton St
PO
Claremont Road
Picton
Stenhills Crs
Stenhills Crescent
Marina Gv
LATHAM AV
Kent Gv
Duncan Av
Alexander Gv
The Grange Infant School
Works
Halton Ct
Ashley Rd
Dudley Av
Henley Ct
Fairfax Drive
Lane
Renton Av
Carlton Av
Manor Rd
Tenby Dr
Castle Rise
Ivychurch Ms
Quarry Cl
Boston Av
Langdale Road
Poolside Rd
Ivy Street
Harrop Rd
Coronation Dr
Woodall Dr
Heath Road
RUNCORN SPUR ROAD
Latham Avenue
Melford Dr
Adderley Close
Bickley Cl
Eccleston Dr
Lavender Cl
The Grange Junior School
The Grange Comprehensive School
Town Hall
B5155
Boston Avenue
Latham Av
Morval Crs
Morval Crescent
RUNCORN
Halton Brook Av
Halton Brook Avenue
The Winnows
The Penfolds
Fallowfield
Halton Brook
Leaside
Meadway
Fernhurst
382
Heath Road Medical Centre
Lyndon Gv
Heath Rd Crs
Boston Road
Birch
Festival
Elm Rd
Sycamore Road
Cotterill
The Holy Spirit RC Aided Primary Sch
Castleview Prim Sch

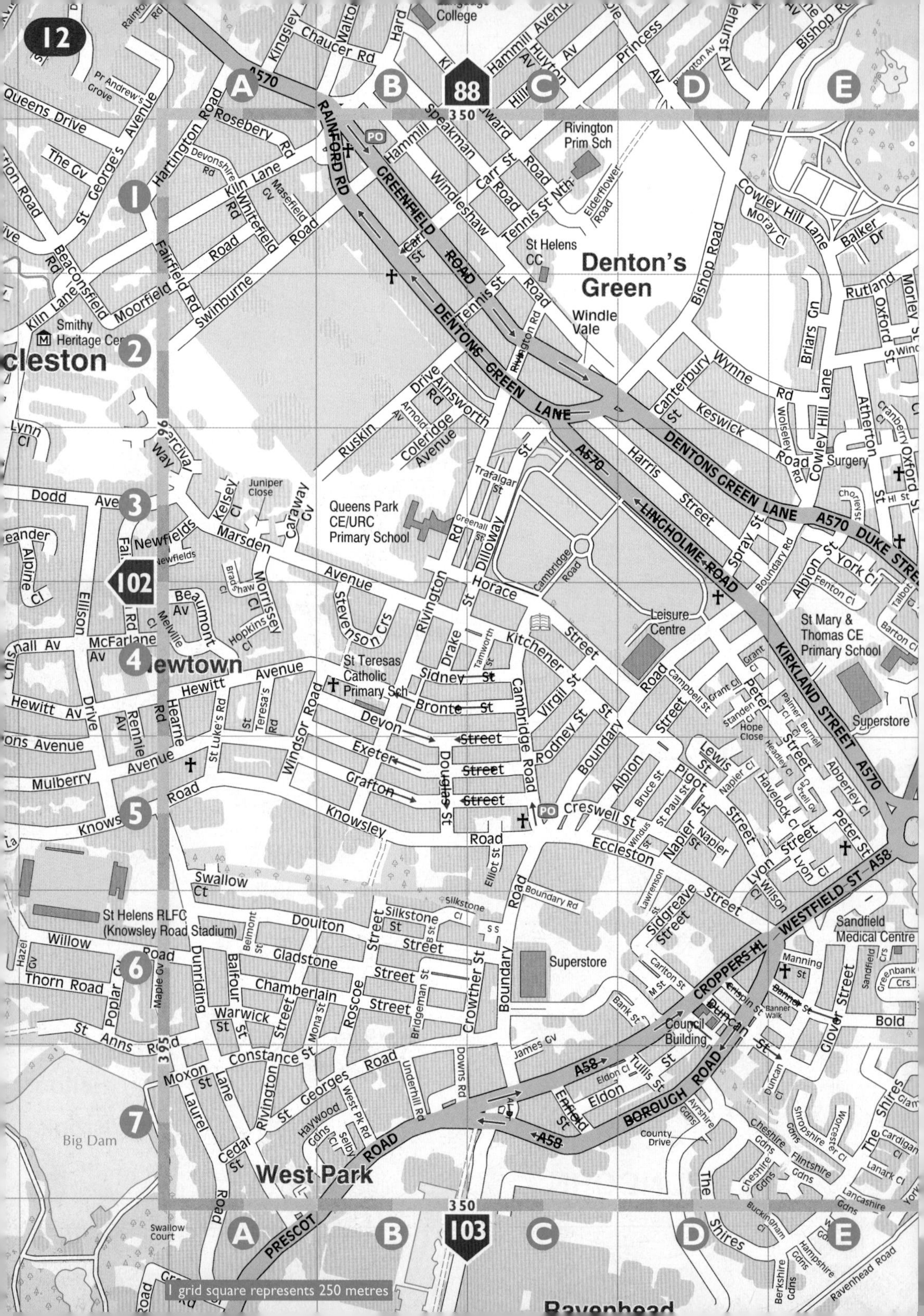
College
Chaucer Rd
Kingsley
Rosebery Rd
Hartington Road
Queens Drive
Pr Andrew's Grove
St George's Avenue
The Gv
Devonshire Rd
Kiln Lane
Whitefield Rd
Masefield Gv
Road
Beaconsfield Rd
Moorfield
Fairfield Rd
Swinburne
Kiln Lane
Smithy Heritage Cen
cleston
A570
RAINFORD RD
GREENFIELD ROAD
DENTONS GREEN LANE
Tennis St
Carr St
Hammill
Speakman
Windleshaw
Carr St
Road
Tennis St Nth
Elderflower Road
Rivington Prim Sch
Hammill Avenue
Huyton Av
Hill
Princess Av
Bishop Rd
St Helens CC
Denton's Green
Windle Vale
Bishop Road
Cowley Hill Lane
Moray Cl
Balker Dr
Rutland
Oxford St
Morley St
Briars Gn
Canterbury St
Wynne Rd
Keswick
Wolseley Rd
Cowley Hill Lane
Atherton St
Cranberry Cl
Oxford St
Surgery
Rivington Rd
Ruskin Drive
Arnold Av
Ainsworth Rd
Coleridge Avenue
Harris Street
DENTONS GREEN LANE
A570
DUKE STREET
LINGHOLME ROAD
Spray St
Boundary Rd
Albion St
York Cl
Fenton Cl
Talbot
Barton Cl
Lynn Cl
Percival Way
Dodd Ave
Kelsey Cl
Juniper Close
Caraway Gv
Queens Park CE/URC Primary School
Trafalgar St
Greenall St
Dilloway
Cambridge Road
Leisure Centre
St Mary & Thomas CE Primary School
Superstore
Leander
Alpine Cl
Newfields
Marsden Avenue
Bradshaw Cl
Morrissey Cl
Beaumont Av
Melville Cl
Hopkins Cl
Stevenson Crs
Rivington Rd
Drake St
Horace
Kitchener Street
Tamworth St
Ellison Drive
McFarlane Av
Chisnall Av
Newtown
Hewitt Avenue
Hewitt Av
Hearne Rd
Rennie Av
St Luke's Rd
Teresa's Rd
St Teresas Catholic Primary Sch
Sidney St
Bronte St
Devon Street
Exeter Street
Grafton Street
Douglas St
Windsor Road
Virgil St
Rodney St
Boundary St
Albion St
Road
Street
Campbell St
Grant Cl
Peter Street
Standen Cl
Hope Close
Lewis St
Palmer Cl
Burnell Cl
Headley Cl
Napier Cl
Havelock Cl
Cresswell Gv
Abberley Cl
KIRKLAND STREET
A570
Mulberry Avenue
Road
Knowsley Road
Creswell St
Bruce St
Pigot St
Windus St
St Paul St
Napier St
Lyon Street
Peter St
Lyon Cl
Eccleston Street
Swallow Ct
Elliot St
Boundary Rd
Lawrenson St
Sidgreave Street
Wilson Cl
WESTFIELD ST A58
CROPPERS HL
Sandfield Medical Centre
St Helens RLFC (Knowsley Road Stadium)
Hazel Gv
Willow Road
Thorn Road
Poplar Gv
Maple Gv
Dunriding Lane
Balfour St
Belmont St
Doulton Street
Silkstone St
B St
Silkstone Cl
Gladstone Street
Chamberlain Street
Bridgeman St
Crowther St
Boundary Road
Superstore
Carlton St
M St
Bank St
Council Building
Crispin St
Duncan St
Banner St
Banner Walk
Manning St
Glover Street
Sandfield Crs
Greenbank Crs
Bold
Warwick St
Roscoe
Mona St
St Anns Road
Constance St
Moxon St
Lane
Laurel Road
Rivington Rd
St Georges Road
Underhill Rd
Downs Rd
James Gv
A58
Eldon Cl
Tullis St
Eldon St
Enfield St
BOROUGH ROAD
Duncan Cl
The Shires
Glamis
Cardigan Cl
Lanark Cl
Worcester Cl
Shropshire Gdns
Flintshire Gdns
Cheshire Gdns
Ayrshire Gdns
County Drive
Haywood Gdns
West Pk Rd
Selby Cl
PRESCOT ROAD
Big Dam
Cedar St
West Park
Lancashire Gdns
Buckingham Cl
The Shires
Berkshire Gdns
Hampshire Gdns
Ravenhead Road
Swallow Court
Ravenhead
1 grid square represents 250 metres
A B C D E
1 2 3 4 5 6 7
88
102
103
350
395
PO

ST HELENS
F
G
H
88
J
K
51
52
1
2
3
4
5
6
7
104
103
96
395
Works
Albert St
Street
Stanhope St
Argyle
Chapel
North
Oldfield St
Road
Cowley Street
W Ter
Albert
Byron Cl
Victoria St
Lord Street
Lord St
Hill St
COLLEGE STREET
A571
HARESFINCH ROAD
Morello Close
Russet
Arnot Cl
Queen St
Peel Place
Swift St
Gleave St
Cooper Street
M Av
Morley Way
Halefield St
Norman Salisbury Court
Union St
Fox Place
PO
Register Office
Central Street
Crab Street
Surgery
Central Clinic
Lancaster House Medical Centre
North Road
Ward St
Mill St
Mill Street Medical Centre
Volunteer St
YMCA
Phoenix Medical Cen
Garswood St
Police Stn
Council Building
Birchley St
Brynn St
Hardshaw St
Vincent St
Clifton St
Charles St
Alfred St
Hospital St
Strickland St
Parish CE Primary School
Woodville Street
Standish Street
Holy Cross RC Primary School
Shaw Street
Cansfield Street
Tolver Street
Railway St
Waterside Court
Business Development Centre
Waterside
Lock Street
Merton Street
Holly Bank
Parlane St
Wood St
Pocket Nook
Varley Rd
Barber St
Vernon St
Nook
Earl St
Pitt St
Farnworth St
Graham St
Ivy Ct
Hgr Parr St
Traverse
Atlas Street
Ardwick St
Surgery
Randon Gv
Hamer St
Lingholme Health Centre
Henry St
Lowe St
KING STREET
A571
Corporation St
Mag & Co Courts
College St
Baldwin St
Ormskirk St
Claughton St
Surg
Victoria Square
Town Hall
Parade
Wesley House
Library & Rainford Gall
Theatre Royal
Hall St
Shaw St
Trading Estate
Woodville St
Alternative Med Centre
John St
North John St
Westfield Street
Cotham St
C St
Brook St
Barrow St
Bus Stn
Bickerstaffe St
Corporation Street
St Helens Central Station
Phoenix Brow
PARR ST
PARR STREET
A58
McCulloch St
Jackson Street
Langtree Street
Parr Mount Court
St Helens College
Waterloo St
Council Building
The Hardshaw Shopping Centre
Medical Centre
Haydock St
George St
Cineworld
Cross St
The Citadel
Church Square Shopping Centre
Church Square
Church St
Water St
Bridge St
Exchange St
Chalon Way W
Chalon Way West
Mkt St
Foundry St
St Marys' Market
Parr St
Todd Rd
Watts Clift Wy
Warrington New Road
Peasley Cross Lane
Warrington Old Road
A570
Bath St
Copperas St
Grove Street
Superstore
Chalon Way East
World of Glass
LINKWAY WEST
LINKWAY EAST
Chalon Way Industrial Estate
St Helens Retail Park
Canal Street
Works
West Side
Westside Industrial Estate
Peasley
Alma St
Hunter St
Clarence Cl
Manor Street
Milverny
ST

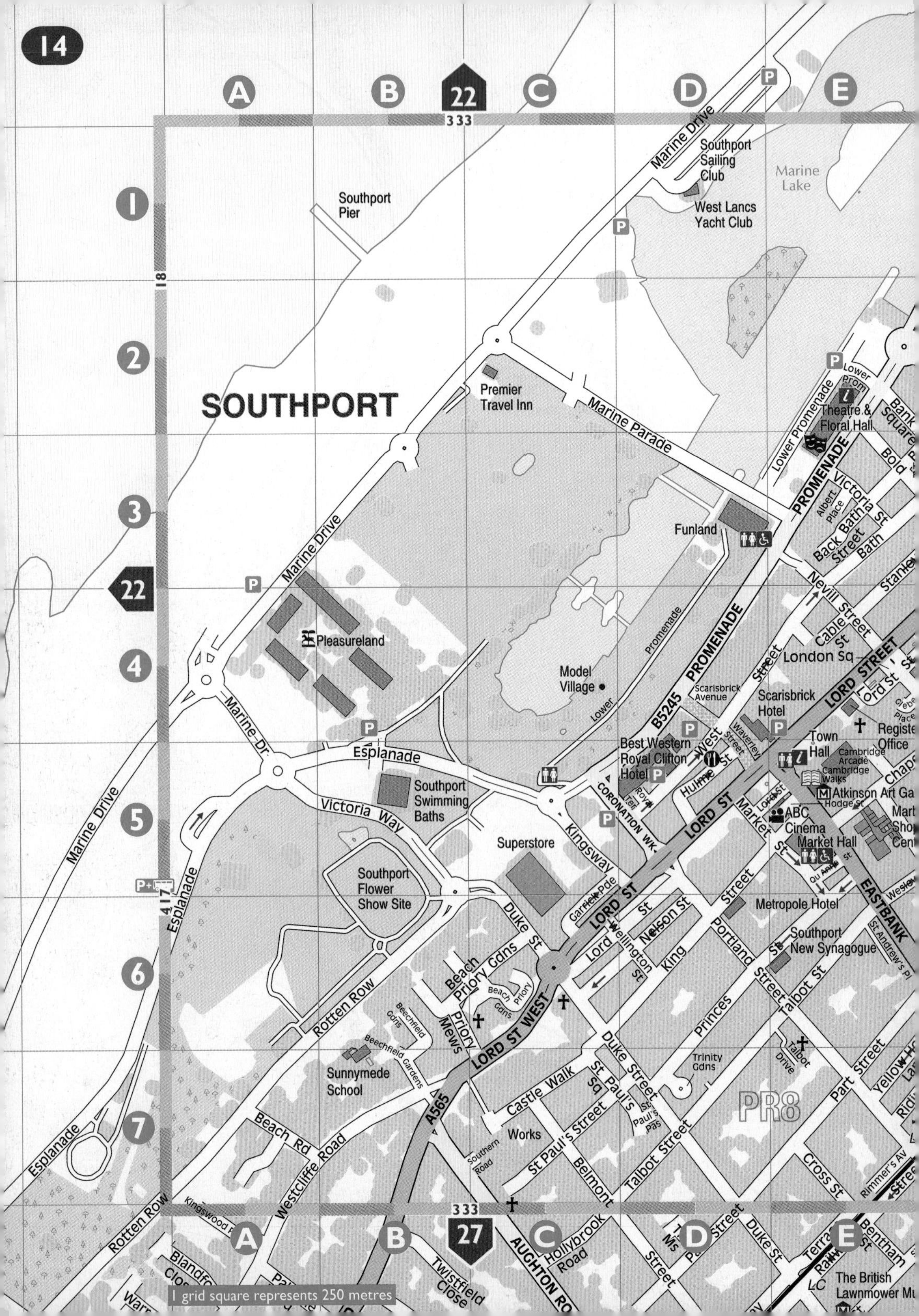
A
B
22
C
D
E
333
SOUTHPORT
Southport Pier
Marine Drive
Southport Sailing Club
West Lancs Yacht Club
Marine Lake
Premier Travel Inn
Marine Parade
Lower Promenade
Lower Prom
Theatre & Floral Hall
PROMENADE
Bank Square
Bold St
Victoria St
Albert Place
Back Bath Street
Bath Street
Funland
Nevill Street
Stanley
Cable St
London Sq
LORD STREET
Lord St
Glebe Place
Register Office
Pleasureland
Promenade
Model Village
Lower
B5245 PROMENADE
Scarisbrick Avenue
Scarisbrick Hotel
Town Hall
Cambridge Arcade
Cambridge Walks
Atkinson Art Gallery
Hodge St
Best Western Royal Clifton Hotel
West St
Waverley Street
Hulme St
Royal Terr
CORONATION WK
Esplanade
Marine Dr
Southport Swimming Baths
Victoria Way
Kingsway
Superstore
LORD ST
Market St
ABC Cinema
Market Hall
Market Shopping Centre
Chapel
EASTBANK
Weslo
Southport Flower Show Site
Garrick Pde
Duke St
Wellington St
Nelson St
King St
Portland Street
Metropole Hotel
Southport New Synagogue
St Andrew's Pl
Talbot St
Beach Priory Gdns
Priory Mews
Beach Priory Gdns
LORD ST WEST
Rotten Row
Beechfield Gdns
Beechfield Gardens
Sunnymede School
Duke Street
Princes Street
Trinity Gdns
Talbot Drive
Part Street
Yellow House Lane
PR8
Castle Walk
St Paul's Sq
St Paul's Pas
Works
A565
Beach Rd
Westcliffe Road
Southern Road
St Paul's Street
Belmont
Talbot Street
Cross St
Rimmer's Av
Riding
Kingswood
Rotten Row
Hollybrook Road
AUGHTON RO
Twistfield Close
Blandford Close
Paul St
Bentham St
Terrace
LC
The British Lawnmower Museum
27
18
417
1
2
3
4
5
6
7
1 grid square represents 250 metres

F
G
H
J
K
23
28
34
35
1
2
3
4
5
6
7
PR9
Southport Municipal Golf Club
Hesketh Centre (Hospital)
Best Western Stutelea Hotel
Cambridge House Hotel
Police Station & Mag Courts
Alexandra Mews
Balmoral Lodge Hotel
Fire Station
Sandringham Court
Bold Hotel
YMCA
Holy Trinity CE Primary School
Thistleton Mews
York Terrace
Halsall Buildings
Southport & Formby Hospital
Superstore
Health Clinic
Southport Business Centre
Little Theatre
Southport College of FE
Arden College
Southport Station
Works
Kensington Industrial Est
Rosehill Business Park
Surgery
St Philips CE Primary School
Holy Family Catholic Primary
Mount Terrace
Hart Street Bridge
Promenade
Albany
Chatham
Road
Leyland
Park Road West
Avondale Road North
Knowsley
Saunders
Irving Street
Gordon Av
Alexandra Rd
ALBERT ROAD
Park Road
Leyland Road
B5280 PARK CRESCENT
Morley
Brentwood
Rawlinson Rd
Avenue
Woodlands Close
Preston
PROMENADE
B5245
LEICESTER STREET
Avondale
Gordon
Seabank
Bath St North
North St
Court Road
QUEENS ROAD
Alexandra Road
Hawkshead St
Leyland Road
Park Road
Roe Park Mews
ROE
A5267
Irton Road
Grange Av
Kingfisher Ct
LORD STREET
Court Rd
Walton Street
Bradley Street
MANCHESTER ROAD
B5245
HARTWOOD ROAD
Castle St
Union Street
Hoghton Grove
Hill Street
Church Street
Hoghton
Arnside Rd
Trinity Mews
Arnside Terrace
Marlborough Road
Hope Square
Mount St
Hope St
Hawkshead Street
Ashley Road
East St
Zetland
Windsor Road
Hartwood Road
Grange
Mornington
Wright
Scarisbrick St
Vulcan Street
Hawesside Street
Derby Road
Hall Street
Sussex Road
Kensington Road
A5267 ST LUKE'S ROAD
Willow Grove
Beach Road
Laurel Gv
Olive Gv
Pine Grove
Tithebarn
Palm Gv
London Street
Tulketh Street
Bridge Street
STREET A570
Victoria Bridge Rd
Mill St
Hodson St
Hargreaves St
Virginia Street
Back Virginia Street
ROSE HILL
Tithebarn Rd
Hart Street
Maple Street
Back Forest Rd
Larkspur Cl
Ivy Street
Chambres Rd North
Forest Road
Arbour Street
Linaker St
Sefton Street
Hampton Road
Lime Street
Hart Street
Lansdowne Road
Blow
Portland St
St James St
Bridge Gv
SCARISBRICK
Southbank Road
Sefton St
Chambres Road
Lethbridge
Princes Gdn
Forest Road

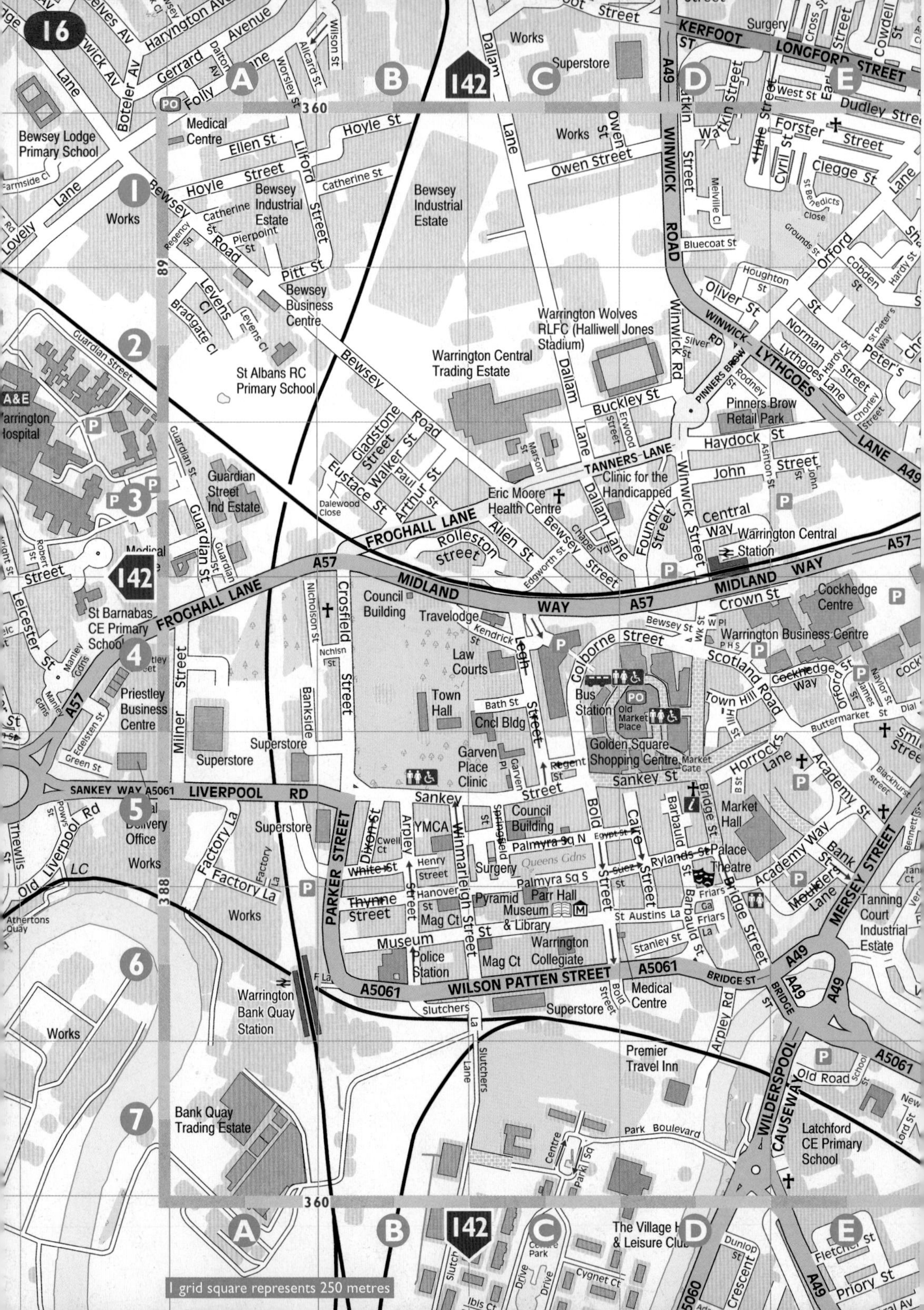
1 grid square represents 250 metres

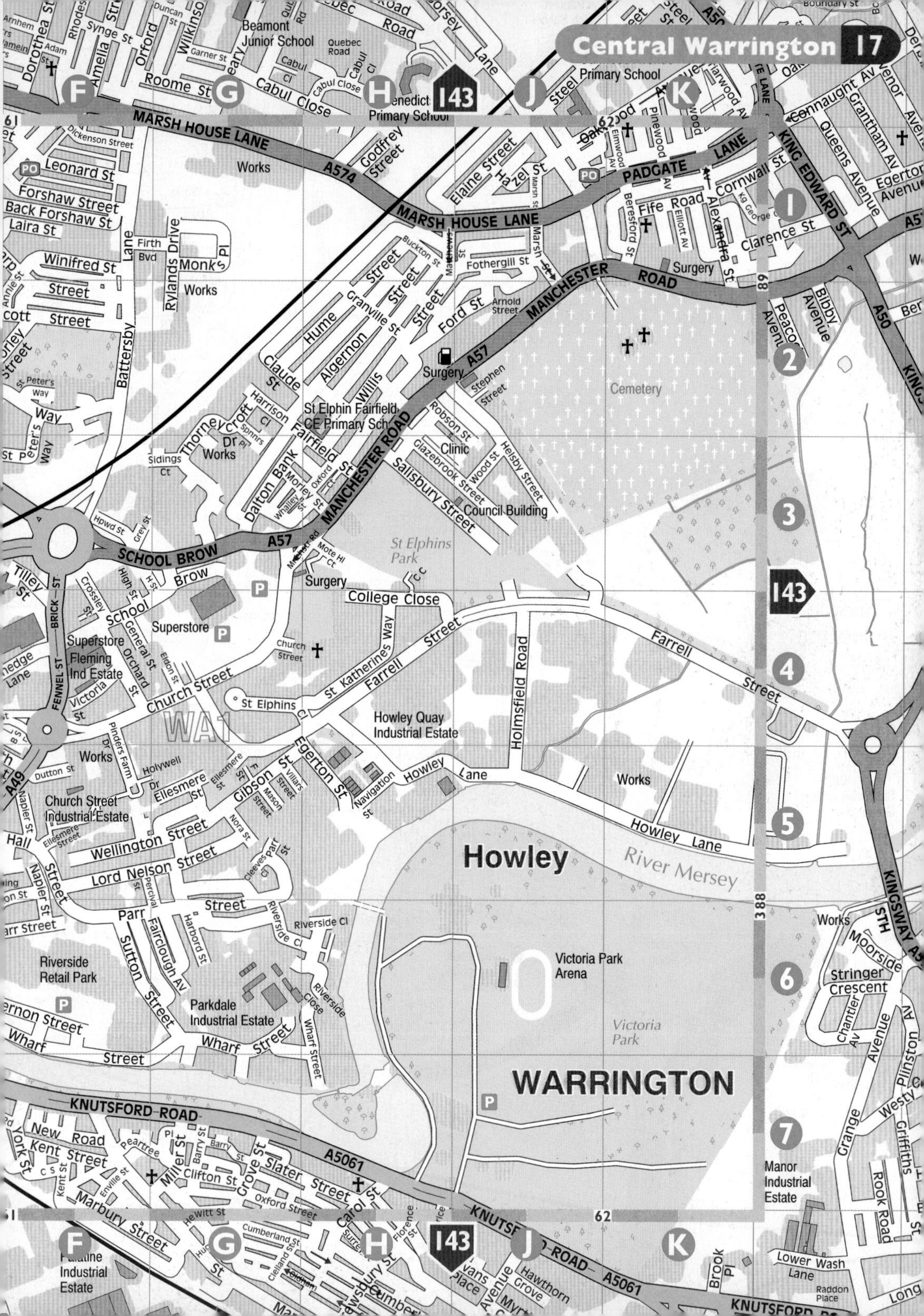
MARSH HOUSE LANE
A574
MANCHESTER ROAD
A57
SCHOOL BROW
PADGATE LANE
KING EDWARD ST
A50
KINGSWAY STH
KNUTSFORD ROAD
A5061
A49
Howley
WARRINGTON
WA1
River Mersey
Cemetery
St Elphins Park
Victoria Park
Victoria Park Arena
Howley Quay Industrial Estate
Church Street Industrial Estate
Fleming Ind Estate
Riverside Retail Park
Parkdale Industrial Estate
Manor Industrial Estate
Palatine Industrial Estate
St Elphin Fairfield CE Primary Sch
Beamont Junior School
Benedict's Primary School
Primary School
Council Building
Superstore
Surgery
Clinic
Works
Farrell Street
Howley Lane
Holmsfield Road
Church Street
Parr Street
Wellington Street
Lord Nelson Street
Wharf Street
Sutton Street
Salisbury Street
College Close
Fennel St
Brick St
Battersby Lane
Orford
Quebec Road
Cabul Close
Roome St
Dickenson Street
Leonard St
Forshaw Street
Back Forshaw St
Laira St
Winifred St
Rylands Drive
Thorneycroft Dr
Dalton Bank
Fairfield St
Claude St
Hume Street
Algernon Street
Willis Street
Granville St
Ford St
Fothergill St
Fife Road
Clarence St
Cornwall St
Queens Avenue
Grantham Av
Egerton Avenue
Connaught Av
Bibby Avenue
Peacock Avenue
Moorside
Stringer Crescent
Chantler Av
Grange Avenue
Rook Road
Lower Wash Lane
Raddon Place
Slater Street
Marbury Street
Kent Street
New Road
Clifton St
Oxford Street
Carol St
Hewitt St
Egerton St
Gibson St
Ellesmere St
Napier St
143
F G H J K
F G H J K
2 3 4 5 6 7
62
89
388

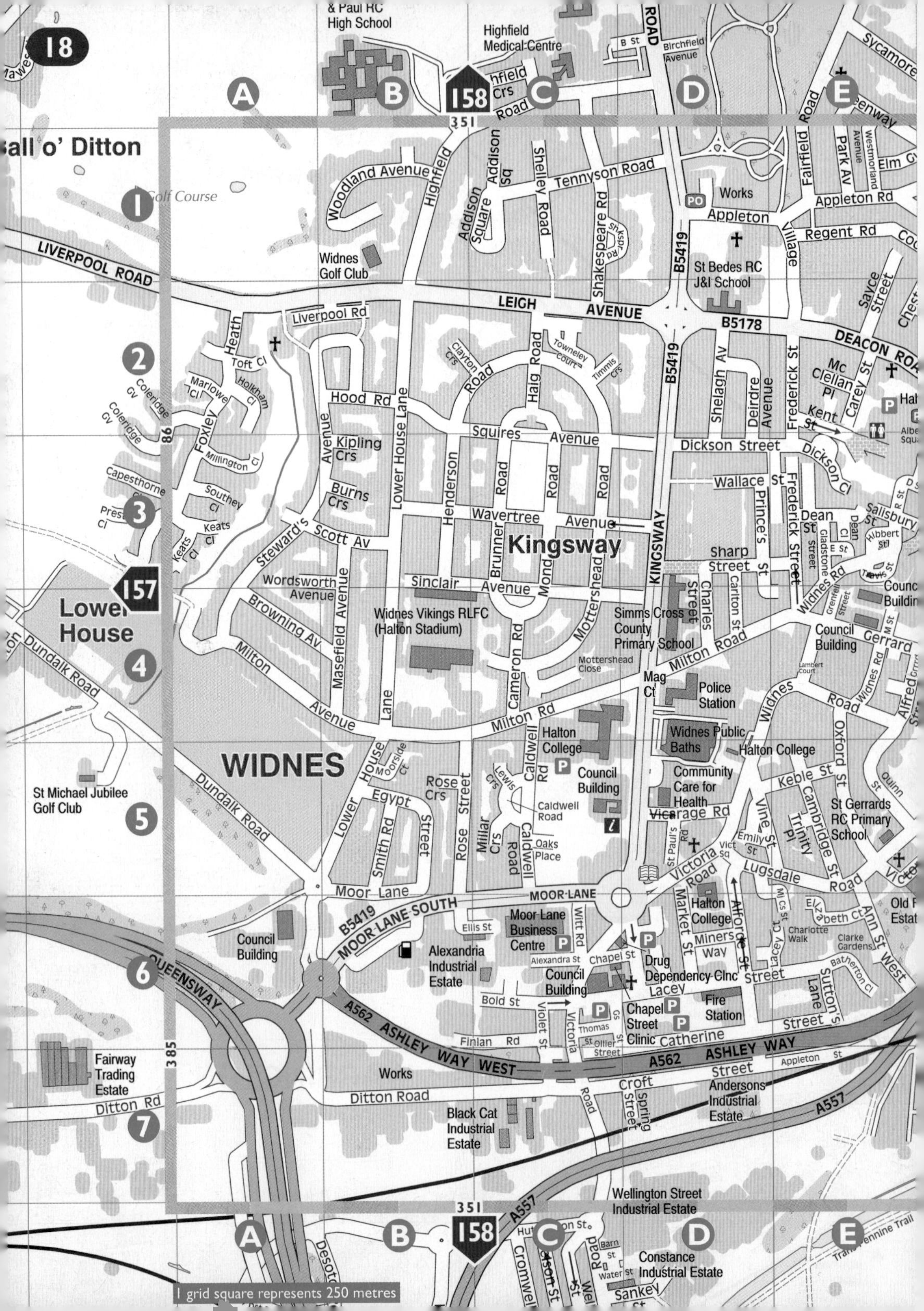
Hall o' Ditton
Golf Course
Liverpool Road
Widnes Golf Club
Leigh Avenue
Deacon Road
Kingsway
Lower House
Widnes Vikings RLFC (Halton Stadium)
WIDNES
St Michael Jubilee Golf Club
Dundalk Road
Milton Avenue
Milton Road
Queensway
Moor Lane
Moor Lane South
Ashley Way West
Ashley Way
Ditton Road
Fairway Trading Estate
Black Cat Industrial Estate
Alexandria Industrial Estate
Moor Lane Business Centre
Andersons Industrial Estate
Wellington Street Industrial Estate
Constance Industrial Estate
St Bedes RC J&I School
Simms Cross County Primary School
Police Station
Widnes Public Baths
Halton College
Community Care for Health
Council Building
Drug Dependency Clnc
Chapel Street Clinic
Fire Station
St Gerrards RC Primary School
Highfield Medical Centre
Works
Appleton
Victoria Road
Widnes Road
Trans Pennine Trail
1 grid square represents 250 metres

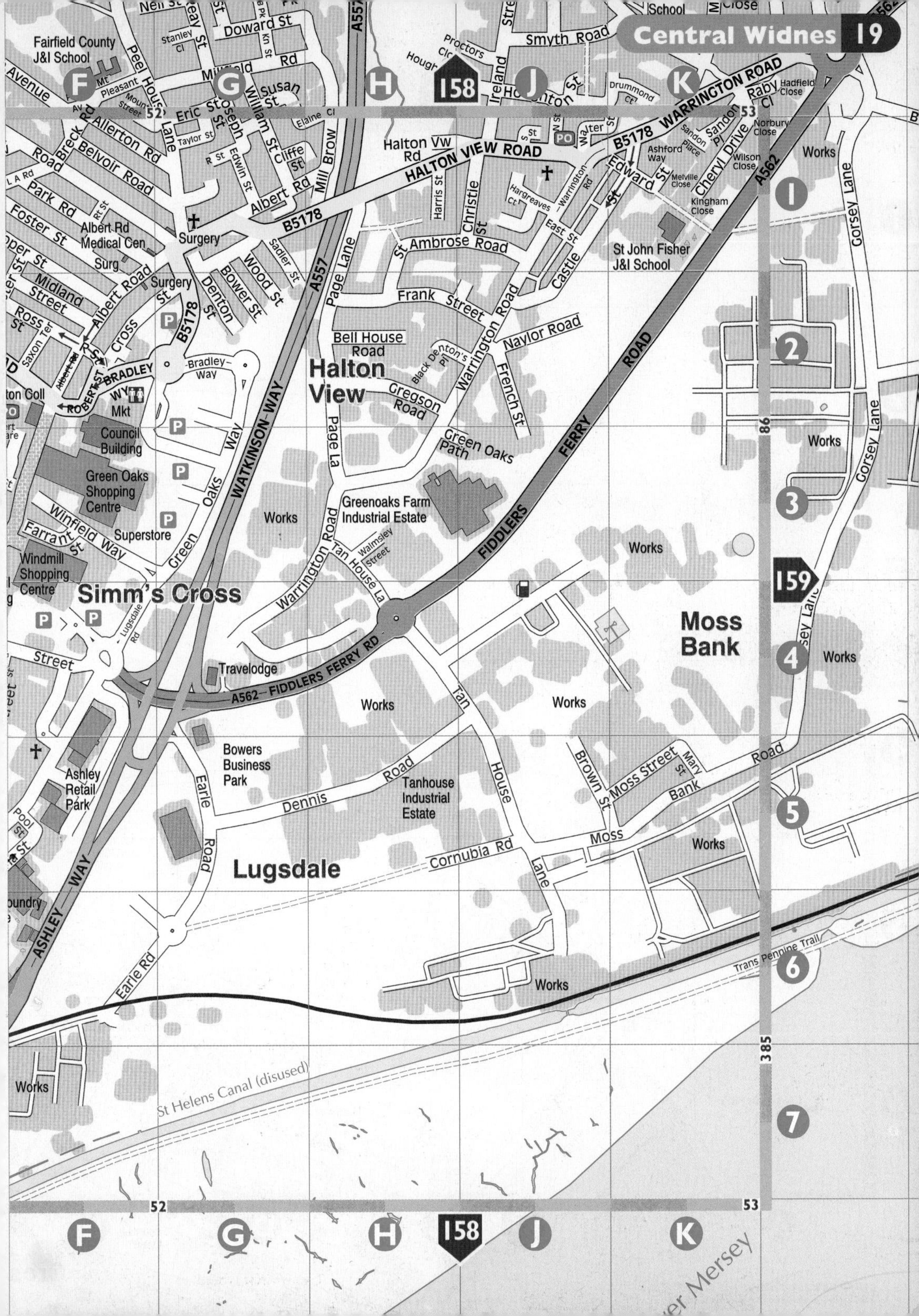
Fairfield County
J&I School
Halton View
Simm's Cross
Moss
Bank
Lugsdale
Green Oaks
Shopping
Centre
Windmill
Shopping
Centre
Council
Building
Greenoaks Farm
Industrial Estate
Bowers
Business
Park
Tanhouse
Industrial
Estate
Ashley
Retail
Park
St John Fisher
J&I School
Albert Rd
Medical Cen
Travelodge
Superstore
HALTON VIEW ROAD
B5178 WARRINGTON ROAD
FIDDLERS FERRY ROAD
A562 FIDDLERS FERRY RD
WATKINSON WAY
ASHLEY WAY
St Helens Canal (disused)
Trans Pennine Trail
Works
158
159
385
86
52
53

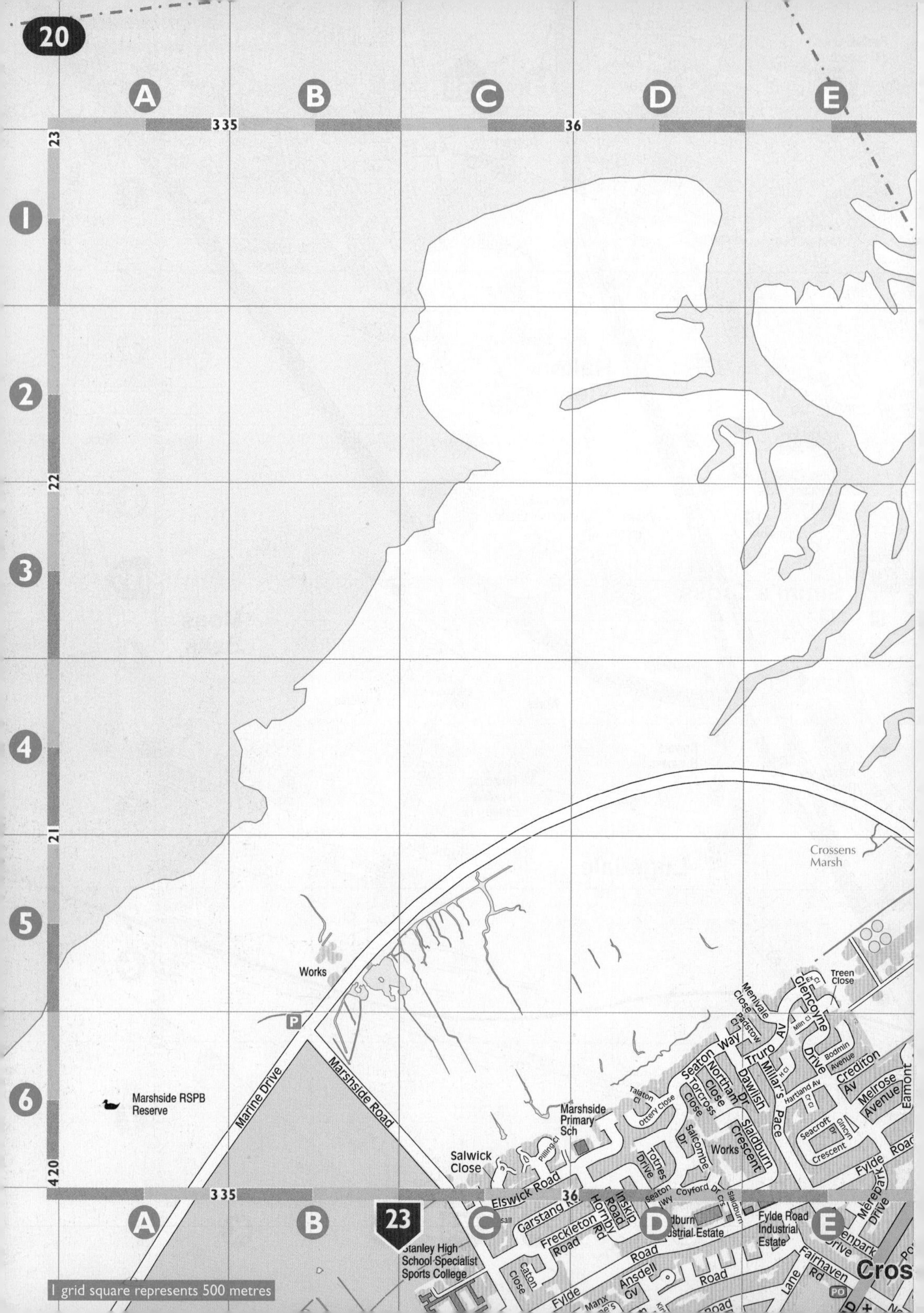
A
B
C
D
E
335
36
23
22
21
420
1
2
3
4
5
6
Crossens Marsh
Works
Marshside RSPB Reserve
Marine Drive
Marshside Road
Marshside Primary Sch
Salwick Close
Elswick Road
Garstang Rd
Freckleton Road
Hornby Rd
Inskip Road
Caton Close
Fylde Road
Ansdell Gv
Stanley High School Specialist Sports College
Fylde Road Industrial Estate
Fairhaven Rd
Lane
Road
Seaton Way
Northam Close
Torcross Close
Totnes Drive
Salcombe Dr
Dawlish Dr
Slaidburn Crescent
Truro Av
Millar's Pace
Menivale Close
Padstow Cl
Talaton Cl
Ottery Close
Coyford Dr
Glencoyne Drive
Treen Close
Bodmin Avenue
Hartland Av
Crediton Av
Melrose Avenue
Seacroft Crescent
Eamont
Merepark Drive
Fylde Road
Works
Cros
23
1 grid square represents 500 metres

Banks Marsh
Old Hollow Farm
Marsh Rd
Marsh Road
Lancashire County
Sefton
High Brow
George's Lane
Charnley's Lane
Goose Dub Farm
Bond's Lane
Vicarage Lane
Glebe Lane
Church Road
Chapel
Long
Fiddler's Ferry
Banks Road
Ralph's Wife's Lane
Fleetwood Drive
Fleetwood Crescent
Hesketh Av
Todd's Lane
Hoole Lane
Banks
Banks Health Centre
Schwartzman Drive
Caunce Av
Aveling Drive
Aveling
The Sluice
Station Road
Crossens Way
Marine Drive
Harrogate Way
Skipton Avenue
Ilkley Av
Whitby Av
Fellview
Primrose Cl
Kingston Crs
Norbury Cl
Ferry Side Lane
Avenue
Meadow Brow
Bartons Cl
WATER LANE
A565
Works
St Johns CE Primary Sch
Turnberry
Woodlea Close
Tarvin Cl
The Causeway
Pool Street
Ridge Cl
Brook Street
Land Lane
Works
Drewitt Crs
Douglas Road
Brade Street
Holmdale Av
Ribble Avenue
Roseland
Asland
Chorley Cl
Rufford Dr
The Avenue
Lancaster Gate
Lancaster Drive
Abrams Fold
Abrams Green
Guinea Hall Lane
Eversham Cl
Levens Cl
Abington Dr
Abington Drive
Fareham Cl
Guinea Hl Cl
Woodvale Ct
St Stephens CE Primary Sch
North Meols Community
Gravel Lane
Greaves Hall
The Close
Westerdale
Hollywood Farm
SOUTHPORT
A565
F G H J K
37 38 39
1 2 3 4 5 6
20 21 22 23
24

A
B
C
D
E
332
33
34
20
19
18
417
1
2
3
4
5
6
Marshside Sands
Golf Course
Fairway
Marine Drive
Southport Municipal Golf Club
Marine Lake
Promenade
Leyland Road
Lathom Road
Albany Road
Park Road West
Avondale Road N
Hesketh Centre (Hospital)
Knowsley Road
Best Western Stutelea Hotel
Irving St
Saunders St
Gordon Avenue
Southport Pier
14
15
Southport Sailing Club
West Lancs Yacht Club
Leicester St
A565
Alexandra Road
Police Station & Mag Courts
Premier Travel Inn
Marine Parade
Theatre & Floral Hall
Lower Promenade
Seabank Road
Avondale Road
Bank Sq
Bold St
Booth St
Fire Station
PH
Queens Road
Sandringham Court
Kenworthys Flats
Bold Hotel
B5245
YMCA
Hawkshead Street
Bradley Street
Thistleton Mews
York Terrace
SOUTHPORT
Marine Drive
Funland
Albert Pl
Back Bath St
Bath Street
Stanley St
Nevill St
Union St
Castle St
Hill St
Southport & Formby Hosp Health Cinc
Primary School
Trinity Mews
Marlborough Road
Pleasureland
Model Village
Promenade
Bus Station
Register Office
Cable St
Street
Lord St
Superstore
Houghton St
Mornington Rd
Little Thtr
Southport Coll of FE
Church St
Hope St
Best Western Royal Clifton Hotel
Scarisbrick Avenue
Hotel
Cambridge Arcade
Cambridge Walks
Atkinson Art Gal
Southport Business Cen
Arden Coll
Ashley Rd
Sussex Rd
Esplanade
Southport Swimming Baths
Victoria Way
Coronation Wk
Lord
Hulme St
Marble Place Shopping Cen
Southport Stn
London St
Scarisbrick Street
Vulcan St
YMCA
Hawesside Street
Derby Rd
Works
Kensington Industrial Estate
Southport Flower Show Site
Superstore
Kingsway
ABC Cinema
Market St
Mkt Hall
Metropole Hotel
Works
Duke
Carrick Pde
West St
Eastbank St
A57
Tulketh St
27
Southport New Synagogue
King Street
Princes St
Portland St
Yellowhouse La
Bridge St
Victoria Bridge Rd
Mill St
Hargreaves St
Virginia St
Back Virginia Street
Virginia
Arbour St
Works
Kensington Ind E
Marine Drive
Esplanade
Row
Beechfield Gdns
Priory Mews
Lord St
West
Sunnymede School
Talbot Drive
1 grid square represents 500 metres

Marshside RSPB Reserve
Marshside Primary
Marshside
Stanley High School Specialist Sports College
Slaidburn Industrial Estate
Fylde Road Industrial Estate
Crossens
Presfield Special Sch
Peterhouse School
Larkfield Primary Sch
Golf Course
Hesketh Golf Club
St Patricks RC Primary School
Churchtown Medical Centre
Churchtown Primary School
Botanic Gardens Museum
Argyle Lawn Tennis Club
Cambridge House Hotel
Churchtown
Meol's Hall
North Meols Lawn Tennis Club
Southport Old Links Golf Club
High Park
Holy Family Catholic Prim Sch
Norwood Primary School
Bishop David Sheppard CE Primary School
Meols Cop Stn
Rosehill Business Park
AK Business Park
Old Hall Farm Business Park
Canning Road Industrial Estate
Blowick
20
24
28

24
21
23
29
A
B
C
D
E
1
2
3
4
5
6
337
38
39
20
19
18
417
WATER LANE
A565
Crossens
Pool Street
Ridge Cl
Brook Street
Land Lane
Works
Drewitt Crs
St Johns CE Primary Sch
Causeway
Tarvin Cl
Turnberry
Woodlea
Bartons Cl
Lancaster
Drive
Abrams Fold
Gravel Lane
St Stephens CE Primary Sch
Hall Lane
Eaves Hall
The Close
Hollywood Farm
Fylde Road
Merepark Drive
Poolside Walk
Holmdale Av
Douglas Road
Brade Street
PO
Ribble Avenue
Roselea Drive
Asland Gardens
North Road
Drive
RUFFORD ROAD
The Crescent
Three Pools
Crossens CC
New Lane
PR9
The Mallards
Merlewood Av
BANKFIELD LANE
Blundell Lane
Three Pools Waterway
Cabin Lane
Gravel Lane
Bobbiners Lane
Mere Lane
The Sluice
Dolly's Lane
Long Meanygate
Winacre Farm
Moss Lane
Straight Up La
Wyke Hey Farm
Wyke Wood Lane
Wyke Lane
House Lane
Wyke Farm
1 grid square represents 500 metres

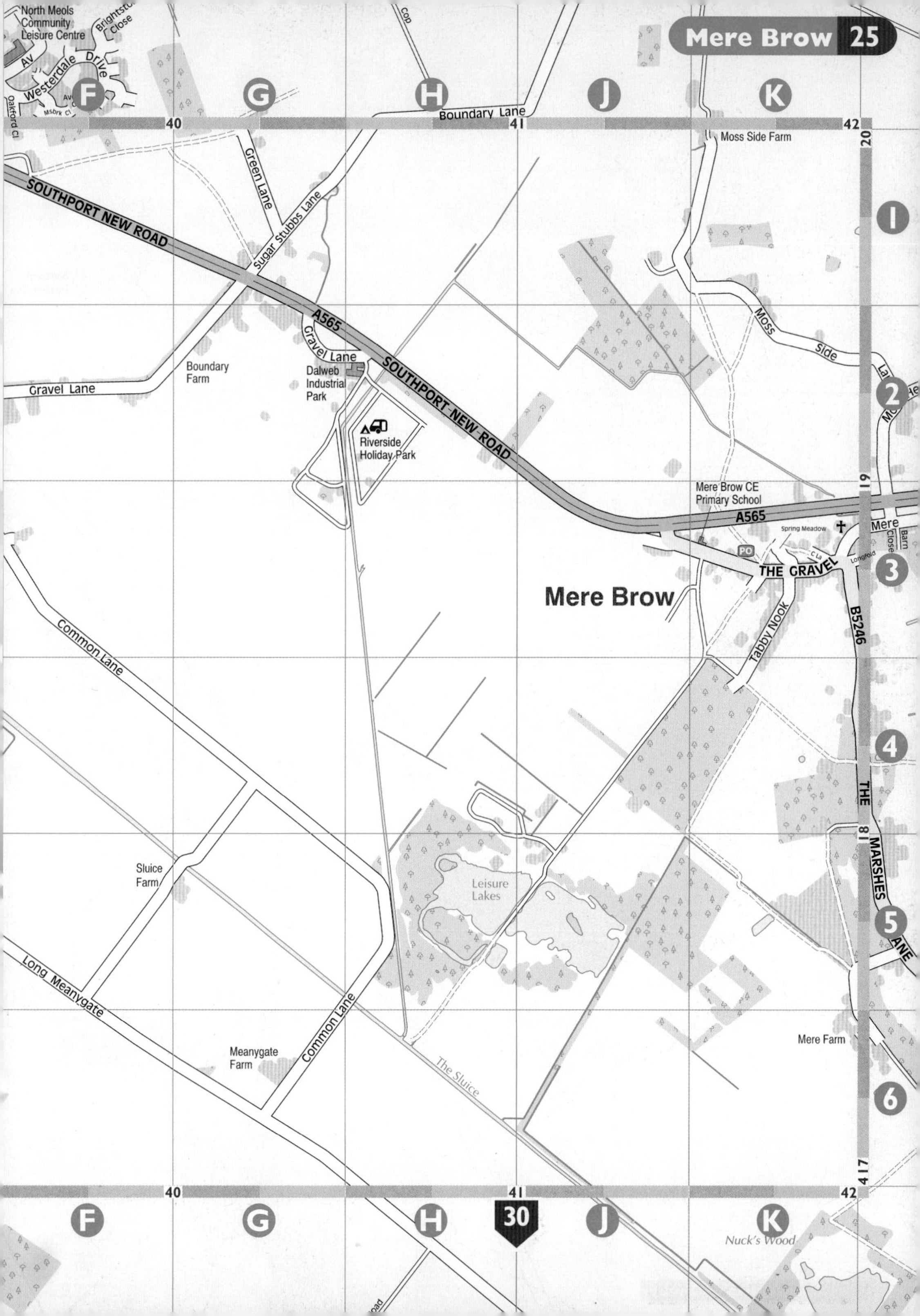
North Meols Community Leisure Centre
Brightstone Close
Westerdale Drive
Oakford Cl
Boundary Lane
Moss Side Farm
Green Lane
Sugar Stubbs Lane
SOUTHPORT NEW ROAD
A565
Gravel Lane
Boundary Farm
Gravel Lane
Dalweb Industrial Park
Riverside Holiday Park
Moss Side
Mere Brow CE Primary School
A565
Spring Meadow
Mere Close
THE GRAVEL
Mere Brow
Tabby Nook
B5246
Common Lane
THE MARSHES LANE
Leisure Lakes
Sluice Farm
Long Meanygate
Common Lane
Meanygate Farm
The Sluice
Mere Farm
Nuck's Wood
F
G
H
J
K
40
41
42
30

A
B
C
D
E
330
31
17
16
15
414
1
2
3
4
5
6
Southport
Landing Area
Birkdale Sands
Westbourne
Granville Road
Selworthy
Road
Coastal Road
Coastal Road
Hi
The Royal
Birkdale
Golf Club
Golf Course
33
1 grid square represents 500 metres

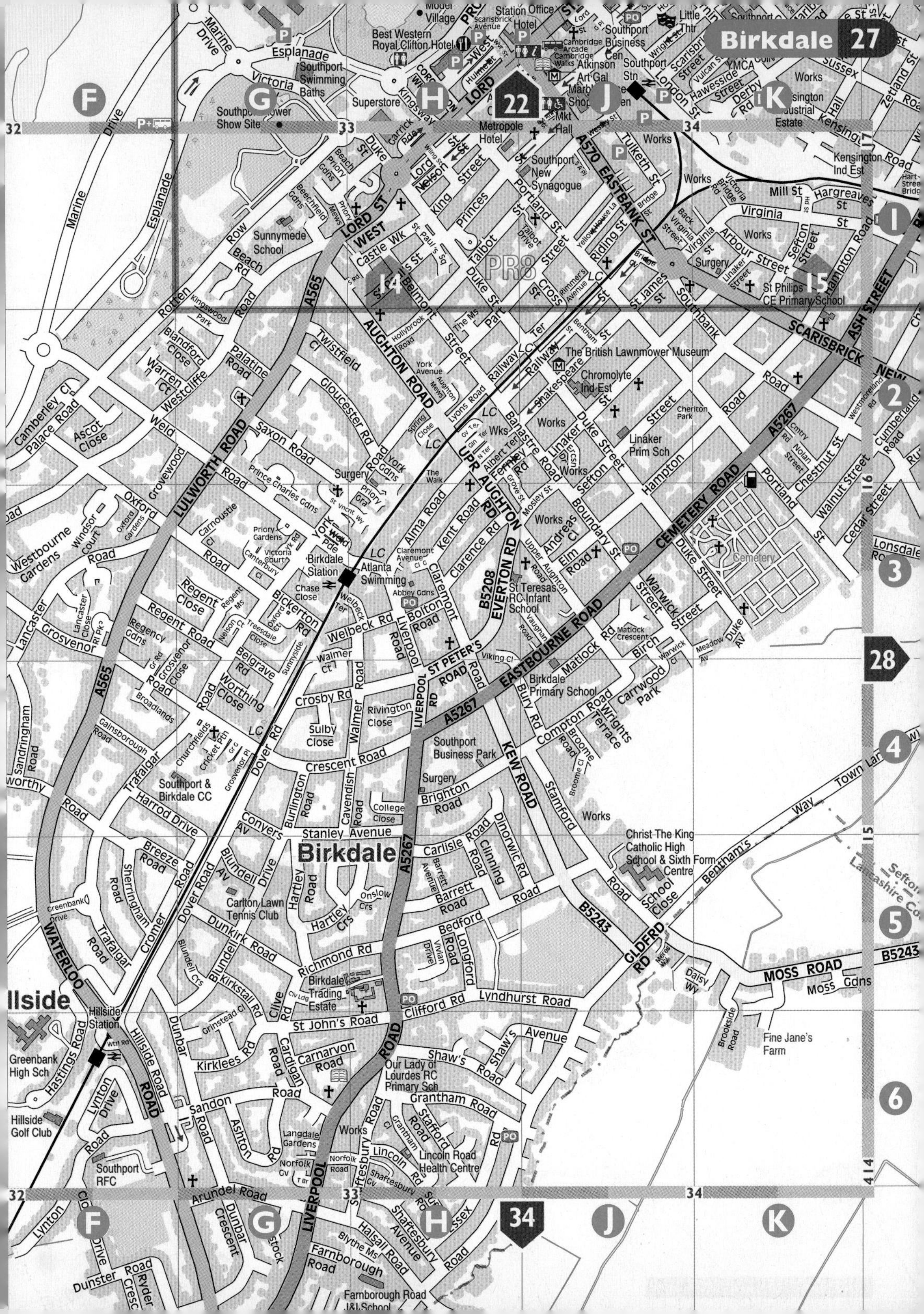

Birkdale
27
28
22
14
15
34
PR8
F
G
H
J
K
1
2
3
4
5
6
32
33
34
Marine Drive
Esplanade
Victoria
Southport Swimming Baths
Southport Flower Show Site
Superstore
Best Western Royal Clifton Hotel
Station Office Hotel
Model Village
Scarisbrick Avenue
Cambridge Arcade
Cambridge Walks
Atkinson Art Gal
Southport Business Cen
Little Thtr
Southport Stn
Mkt Hall
Metropole Hotel
Kingsway
Garrick Pde
Lord St
West
Duke St
Nelson St
King Street
Princes St
Portland St
Talbot St
Southport New Synagogue
A570 Eastbank St
Tulketh St
Works
London St
Hawesside Street
Derby Rd
YMCA
Kensington Industrial Estate
Kensington Road
Kensington Ind Est
Sussex
Hall
Zetland St
Mill St
Hargreaves St
Virginia St
Victoria Bridge Rd
Arbour Street
Sefton Street
Hampton Road
Surgery
Linaker Street
St Philips CE Primary School
Scarisbrick New Road
Ash Street
Sunnymede School
Beach Rd
Beach Priory Gdns
Beechfield Gdns
Rotten Row
Kingswood Park
Blandford Close
Warren Ct
Palatine Road
Westcliffe
Camberley Cl
Palace Road
Ascot Close
Weld Road
A565
Lulworth Road
Twistfield Cl
Gloucester Rd
Saxon Road
Aughton Road
Hollybrook Road
Belmont Street
Duke St
Cross St
Rimmer's Avenue
St James St
Southbank
Railway Ter
The British Lawnmower Museum
Shakespeare St
Chromolyte Ind Est
Linaker Street
Duke Street
Hampton Road
Cheriton Park
Linaker Prim Sch
A5267
Cemetery Road
Portland Street
Chestnut St
Walnut Street
Cedar Street
Cumberland Road
Westmoreland Rd
Nolan Street
Lonsdale Rd
Cemetery
Grovewood
Oxford Road
Oxford Gardens
Windsor Court
Westbourne Gardens
Carnoustie Cl
Prince Charles Gdns
Priory Gardens
Victoria Court
Canterbury Cl
York Road
York Gdns
The Walk
Upr Aughton Rd
Alma Road
Kent Road
Clarence Rd
Claremont Avenue
Claremont Road
B5208 Everton Rd
Upper Aughton Road
St Teresas RC Infant School
Andreas Cl
Elm Road
Boundary St
Mosley St
Birkdale Station
Atlanta Swimming
Chase Close
Abbey Gdns
Bolton Road
Welbeck Rd
Liverpool Road
St Peter's Road
Viking Cl
Eastbourne Road
Matlock Rd
Matlock Crescent
Birch Street
Warwick Street
Meadow Av
Duke Av
Birkdale Primary School
Carrwood Park
Compton Road
Wrights Terrace
Broome Road
Broome Cl
Lancaster Close
Regent Close
Regent Road
Regency Gdns
Grosvenor Road
Grosvenor Close
Bickerton Rd
Belgrave Rd
Worthing Close
Sunnyside
Walmer Road
Crosby Rd
Rivington Close
Sulby Close
Southport Business Park
Kew Road
Bury Rd
Stamford Road
Sandringham Road
Gainsborough Road
Broadlands
Churchfields
Cricket Pth
Grosvenor Pl
Dover Rd
Trafalgar Road
Southport & Birkdale CC
Harrod Drive
Crescent Road
Burlington Road
Cavendish Road
College Close
Brighton Road
Surgery
Conyers Av
Stanley Avenue
Breeze Road
Sherringham Road
Blundell Drive
Blundell Av
Dover Road
Carlton Lawn Tennis Club
Hartley Road
Hartley Crs
Onslow Crs
Carlisle Road
Barrett Avenue
Barrett Road
Clinning Road
Dinorwic Rd
Christ The King Catholic High School & Sixth Form Centre
School Close
Bentham's Way
Town Lane
Greenbank Drive
Waterloo Road
Cromer Road
Dunkirk Road
Richmond Rd
Bedford Road
Vivian Drive
Longford Road
B5243
Gldfrd Rd
Moss Road
Moss Gdns
Daisy Wy
Kirkstall Rd
Blundell Crs
Clive Rd
Birkdale Trading Estate
Clifford Rd
Lyndhurst Road
St John's Road
Hillside
Hillside Station
Hillside Road
Greenbank High Sch
Hastings Road
Grinstead Cl
Kirklees Rd
Cardigan Road
Carnarvon Road
Shaw's Road
Shaw's Avenue
Brookside Road
Fine Jane's Farm
Our Lady of Lourdes RC Primary Sch
Grantham Road
Stafford Road
Lynton Drive
Dunbar Road
Sandon Road
Ashton Rd
Langdale Gardens
Norfolk Gv
Lincoln Rd
Lincoln Road Health Centre
Shaftesbury Gv
Hillside Golf Club
Southport RFC
Arundel Road
Liverpool Road
Dunbar Crescent
Halsall Road
Shaftesbury Avenue
Farnborough Road
Blythe Ms
Farnborough Road J&I School
Dunster Road
Ryder Cresc
Lynton
Sefton
Lancashire

28
23
27
35
15
Blowick
Pool Hey
Brown Edge
Norwood Primary School
Rosehill Business Park
Kensington Ind Est
Surgery
Works
Southport Girls FC
Southport General Infirmary
Southport FC
King George V College
Meols Cop High School
Sphynx Tennis Club
Southbank Tennis Club
Southport & Formby District General Hospital
A&E
Queenscourt Hospice
Meols Cop Retail Park
Kew Retail Park
Superstore
Primary School
Kew Medical Centre
AK Business Park
Old Hall Farm Business Park
Canning Road Industrial Estate
Crowland Street Industrial Est
Blowick Business Centre
Old Hall Fm Business Park
Southport Crematorium
Moss Farm
Winston Crescent
Sefton
Lancashire County
SCARISBRICK NEW ROAD
A570
MEOLS COP ROAD
B5276
SCARISBRICK NEW RD
SOUTHPORT ROAD
BIRKDALE
COP
HEATHEY LANE
JACKSMERE
B5243
ASH STREET
ROSE HILL
ST LUKE'S RD
A5267
Town Lane
Town Lane (Kew)
Wight Moss Way
Foul Lane
Pool Hey Lane
Tinsley's Lane
Turning Lane
Crowland Street
Byrom Street
Hawkshead Street
Tithebarn Road
Sussex Road
Hart Street
Forest Road
Dodworth Av
Haig Avenue
Everard Road
Lonsdale Road
Jane's Brook Road
Poulton Road
Bispham Road
Newton Street
Milton Street
Scott St
Russell Road
Canning Road
Salisbury Street
Cobden Road
Wennington Road
Palmerston Road
Clifton Road
Peel St
Mellors Cl
Bowling Green Close
Butts Lane
Argameols Close
New Foul Lane
Folkestone Road
Ruddington Road
Sangness Dr
Ovington Drive
Cheltenham Way
Kempton Park Fold
Pine
Moss Gdns
ROAD
1 grid square represents 500 metres

F
G
H
24
J
K
37
38
39
17
1
2
3
30
4
5
6
Wyke House Farm
Wyke Lane
Perch Pool Lane
The Avenue
Midge Hall Farms
Wyke Thorn Farm
Wyke Wood
Pool Hey Lane
LC
Shaw's Farm
Wyke Cop Road
Woodmoss Lane
Wyke Road Farm
Perch Pool Lane
Pinewood Close
Greenfield Road
New Hall Drive
Hares Lane
Snape Green
Rimmer Green
Cat Tall Lane
Snape Gn
A570
SOUTHPORT ROAD
Carr Cross
PO
36

Farm
The Sluice
25
A
B
C
D
E
3 40
41
17
1
2
3
4
5
6
16
15
4 14
Nuck's Wood
Caunce's Road
Mere Hall
Long Meanygate
Whams Farm
Midge Hall Farms
Wyke Wood Lane
29
Wholesome Lane
Greenings Lane
Greenings
Midge Hall Lane
Perch Pool Lane
Bescar Lane
Bescar Lane Station
LC
PO
Drummersdale Lane
White House Lane
Small Lane
Copelands
37
1 grid square represents 500 metres

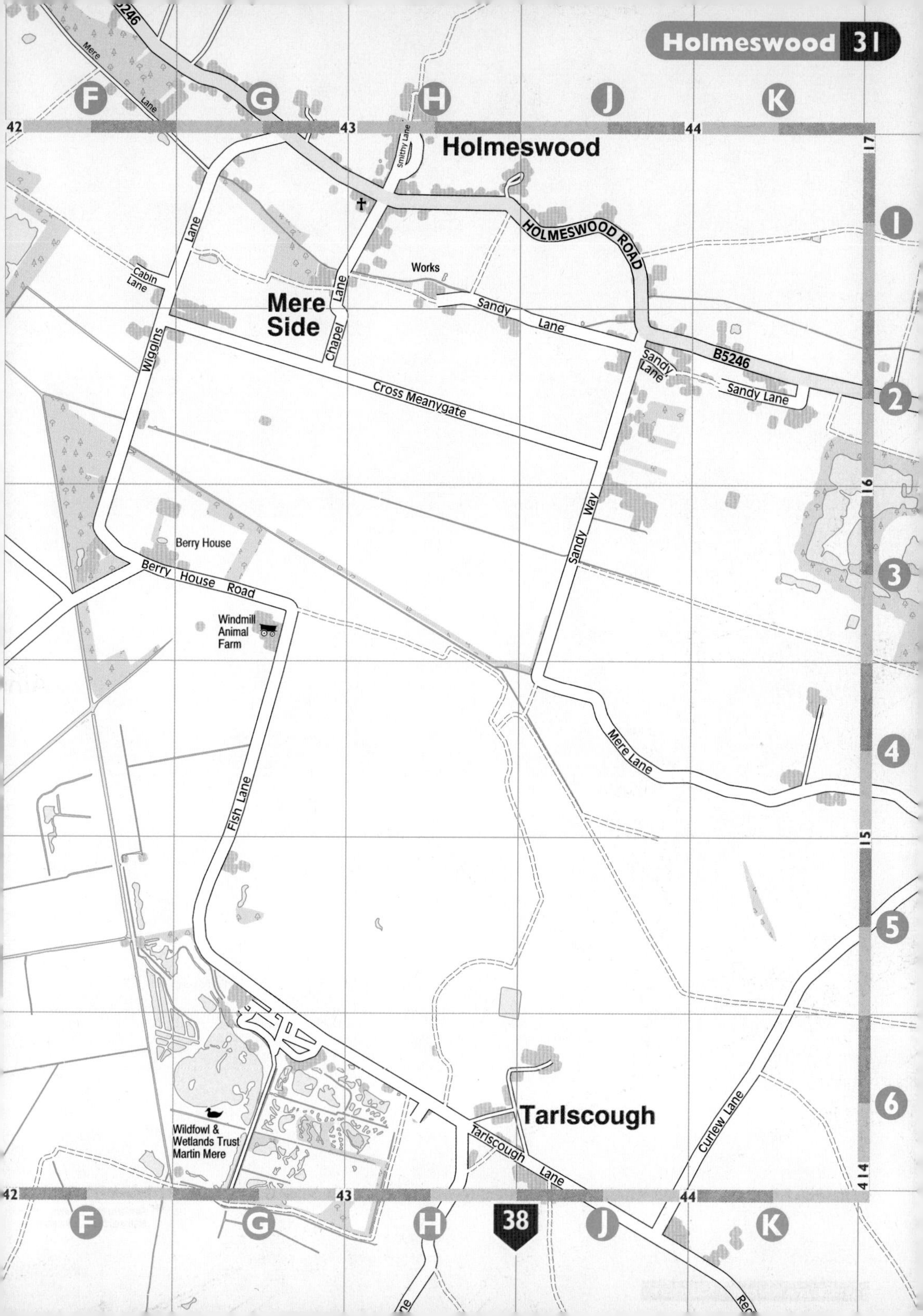

Holmeswood
Mere Side
Tarlscough
B5246
Mere Lane
Smithy Lane
HOLMESWOOD ROAD
Works
Lane
Cabin Lane
Chapel Lane
Sandy Lane
Sandy Lane
Sandy Lane
Wiggins
Cross Meanygate
Sandy Way
Berry House
Berry House Road
Windmill Animal Farm
Mere Lane
Fish Lane
Wildfowl & Wetlands Trust Martin Mere
Tarlscough Lane
Curlew Lane
F
G
H
J
K
42
43
44
17
16
15
414
1
2
3
4
5
6

38

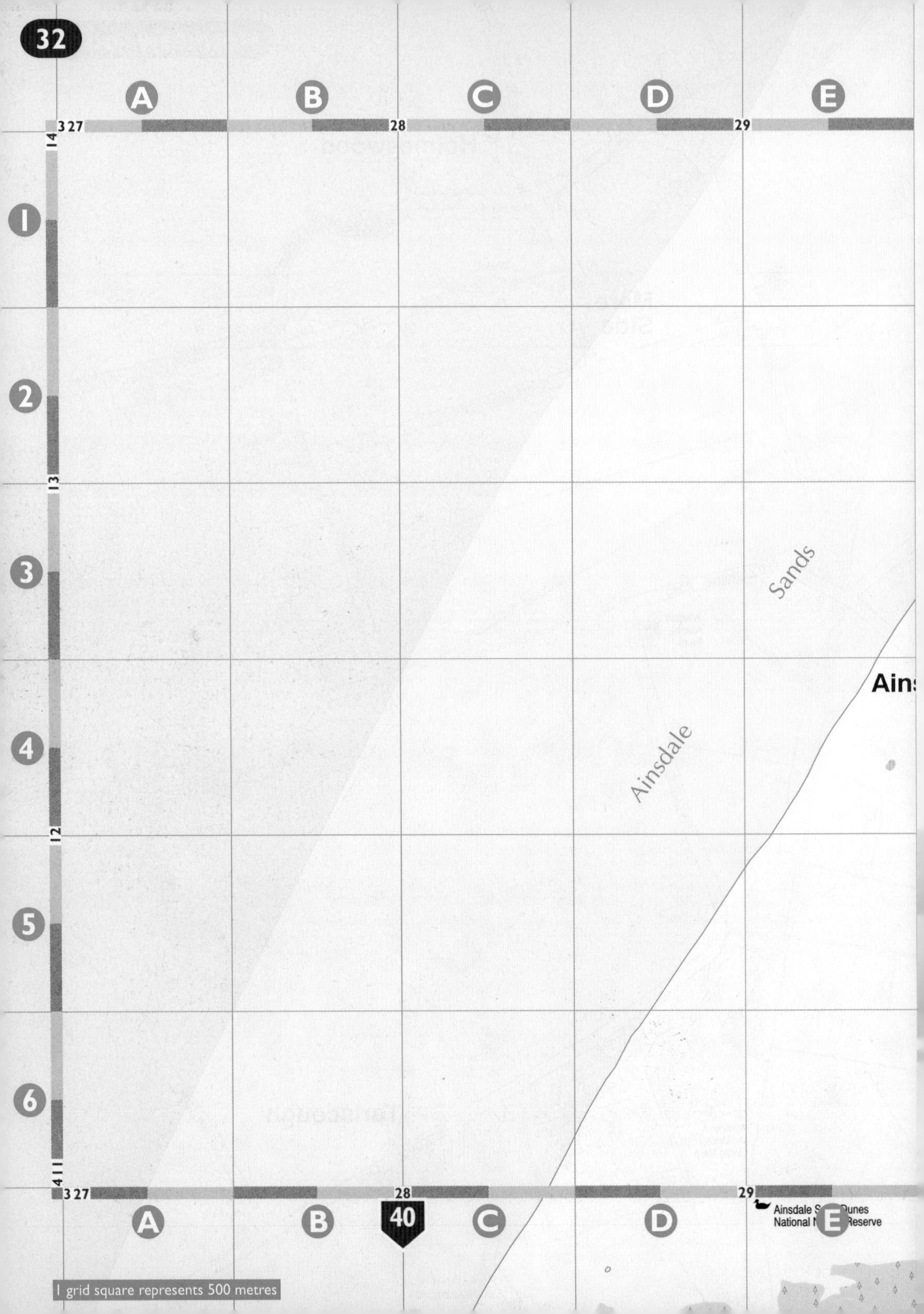
A
B
C
D
E
3 27
28
29
14
13
12
4 11
1
2
3
4
5
6
Sands
Ainsdale
Ains
40
Ainsdale S Dunes
National N Reserve
1 grid square represents 500 metres

Ainsdale
Ainsdale-on-Sea
Woodvale
Coastal Road
Shore Road
Promenade
Chatsworth Road
Liverpool Road
Ainsdale Station
Ainsdale Hope CE High School
Southport & Ainsdale Golf Club
Shoreside Primary School
Merefield Special School
Ainsdale CE Primary School
Ainsdale Clinic
The Brkdle Kings Meadow Primary School
St John Stone Catholic Primary
Hill House Farm
Willowbank Holiday Home & Touring Park
Hillside Golf Club
Greenbank High Sch
Kenilworth Road
Station Rd
Burnley Road
Sandringham Road
Pinfold Lane
Sandbrook Road
Meadow Lane
Woodvale Road
A565
26
34
41
30
31
32

34
27
33
42
A
B
C
D
E
1
2
3
4
5
6
332
33
34
Liverpool Road
A565
Carr Lane
Windy Harbour Road
Birkdale High School
Birkdale Cemetery
Birkdale RC Cemetery
Golf Course
Hillside Golf Club
Southport RFC
Arundel Road
Farnborough Road
Farnborough Road J&I School
Central Av
Guildford
New Cut Lane
PR8
Leybourne Av
Ranelagh Dr
Nixon's Lane
Philip Drive
Elizabeth Av
Heathfield Road
George Drive
Oakwood Drive
Elm Park Dr
Welwyn Avenue
Dunster Road
Ryder Crescent
Lynton Drive
Clovelly Drive
Dunbar Crescent
Woodstock Drive
Halsall Road
Shaftesbury Avenue
Suffolk Road
Essex Road
Grantham Road
Our Lady of Lourdes RC Primary Sch
Health Centre
Carr Moss Lane
White Otter Farm
Headbolt Lane
Segar's Lane
Spencers Lane
East Crantum Farm
Heather Farm
Hill House Farm
Sandbrook Road
CE School
Meadow La
1 grid square represents 500 metres

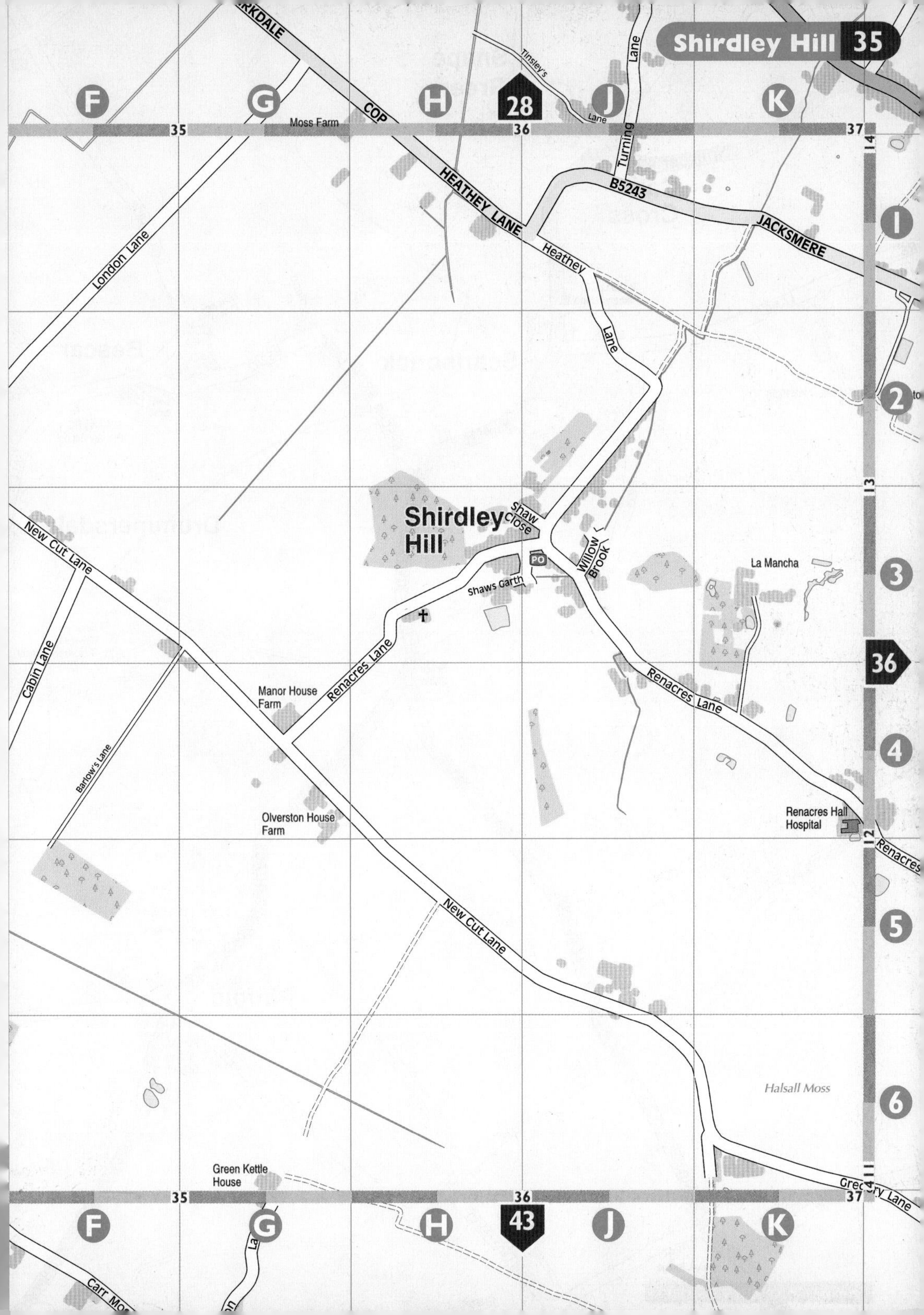
F
G
H
28
J
K
35
36
37
Moss Farm
COP
HEATHEY LANE
Tinsley's
Lane
Turning
Lane
B5243
JACKSMERE
Heathey
Lane
London Lane
Shirdley Hill
Shaw close
PO
Shaws Garth
Willow Brook
La Mancha
New Cut Lane
Cabin Lane
Renacres Lane
Manor House Farm
Renacres Lane
36
Barlow's Lane
Olverston House Farm
Renacres Hall Hospital
Renacres
New Cut Lane
Halsall Moss
Green Kettle House
Gregory Lane
43
14
13
12
11
1
2
3
4
5
6

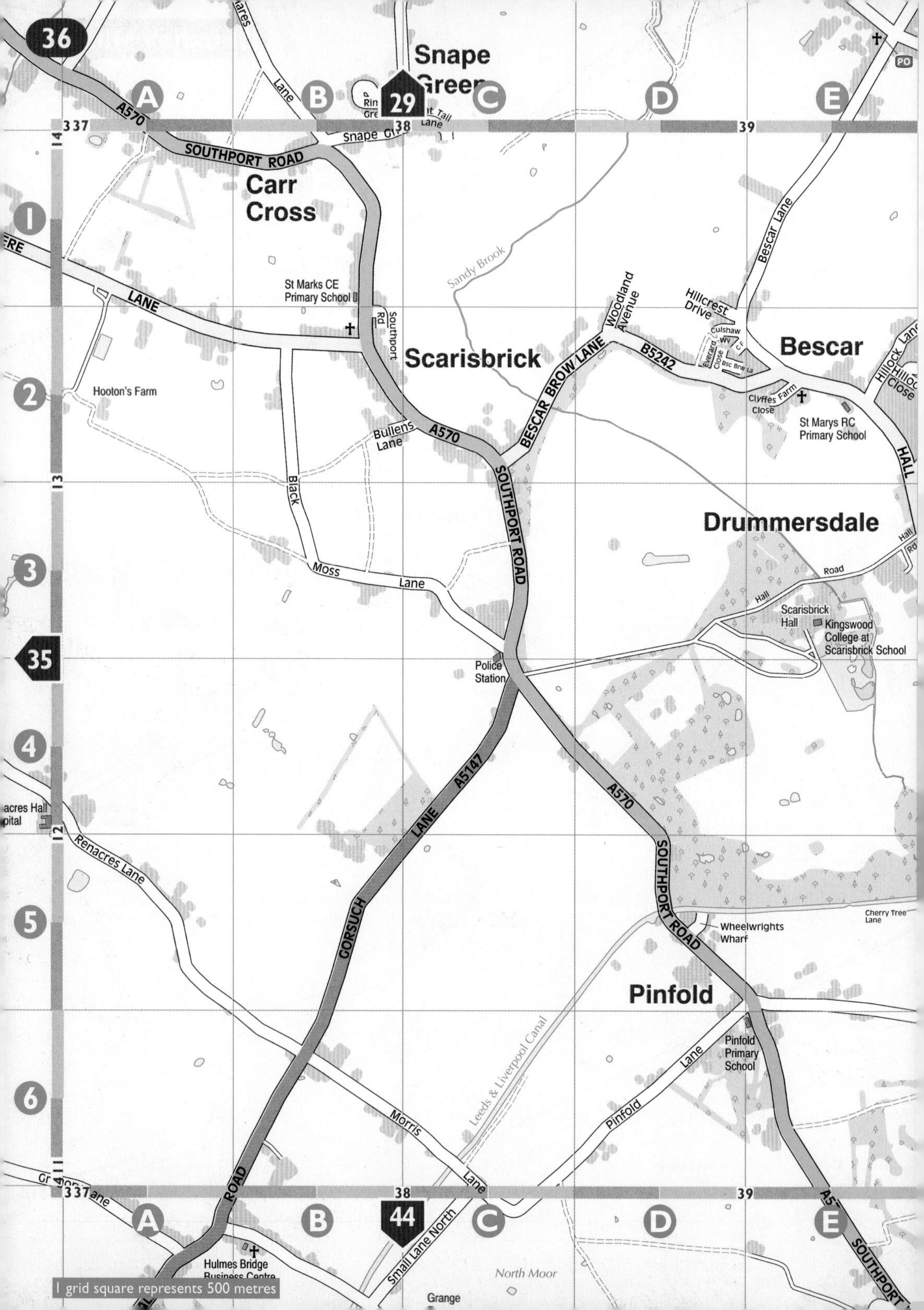

36
Snape Green
29
Carr Cross
St Marks CE Primary School
Scarisbrick
Bescar
Drummersdale
Hooton's Farm
Sandy Brook
Woodland Avenue
Hillcrest Drive
Bescar Lane
SOUTHPORT ROAD
A570
LANE
BESCAR BROW LANE
B5242
Bullens Lane
Black
Moss Lane
Hall Road
Scarisbrick Hall
Kingswood College at Scarisbrick School
St Marys RC Primary School
Clyffes Farm Close
Police Station
35
A5147
GORSUCH LANE
Renacres Lane
Wheelwrights Wharf
Cherry Tree Lane
Pinfold
Pinfold Primary School
Pinfold Lane
Leeds & Liverpool Canal
Morris Lane
ROAD
44
Small Lane North
Hulmes Bridge Business Centre
North Moor
Grange
1 grid square represents 500 metres

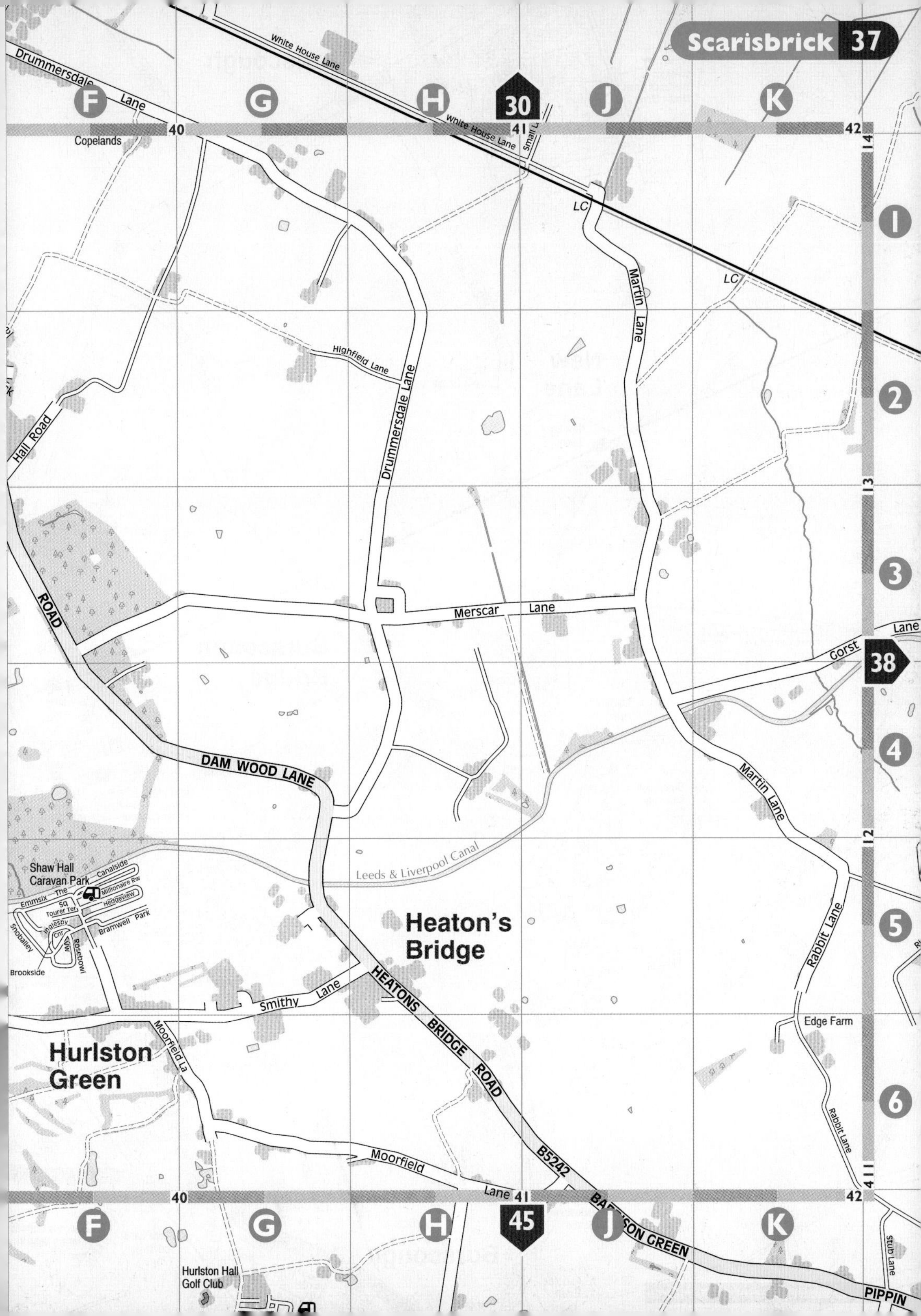
Drummersdale Lane
White House Lane
Small La
30
F
G
H
J
K
40
41
42
Copelands
LC
Martin Lane
Highfield Lane
Drummersdale Lane
Hall Road
ROAD
Merscar Lane
Gorst Lane
38
DAM WOOD LANE
Leeds & Liverpool Canal
Shaw Hall Caravan Park
Canalside
The
Millionaire Rw
Emmsix
Sq
Tourer Ter
Hedgeview
Inglesby
Bramwell Park
Snoballey
Rosebowl
Brookside
Heaton's Bridge
HEATONS BRIDGE ROAD
Smithy Lane
Moorfield La
Hurlston Green
Rabbit Lane
Edge Farm
Moorfield Lane
B5242
BARTON GREEN
45
Hurlston Hall Golf Club
PIPPIN
Stub Lane
1
2
3
4
5
6
14
13
12
11

1 grid square represents 500 metres

F
G
H
J
K
45
46
47
Low Meadows
Burscough Moss
Prescott Bridge
Meadow Lane
MOSS LANE
A59
Back Moss Lane
Leeds & Liverpool Canal (Rufford Branch)
LC
Eller Brook
Meadow Lane
Laburnum Grove
Rowan Cl
MOSS LANE
Warper's Moss
Warper's Moss Lane
Trent Close
Weaver Avenue
Lane
New Sutch House Farm
St Johns CE Primary School
Surg
Burscough Primary Sch
School Lane
Colburne Close
Burscough CC
Sutch Lane
Bleak Lane
Hoscar
Mill Lane
Delph Dr
Hawthorn Av
Daisy Lane
Meadow Lane
Moss Road
Hoscar Station
Green La
Boundary La
Willow End
Broom Cl
Gower Gdns
Rees Park
Field Cl
Abbey Dale
Croft Av
Carvel Wy
Delph Dr
Wheat Lane
Carr Lane
The Woodlands
Hoscar
Frog Lane
Council Building
Ellerbrook Dr
BRIARS LANE
A5209
Brooklands Grove
Flaxfields
Leeds & Liverpool Canal
Briars Brook
Hollowford Lane
A5209
Ring O'Bell Lane
47
Ring o' Bells
Flax Lane
Bridge Lane
Back Lane
Wanes
Lane
I
2
3
4
5
6
14
13
12
11

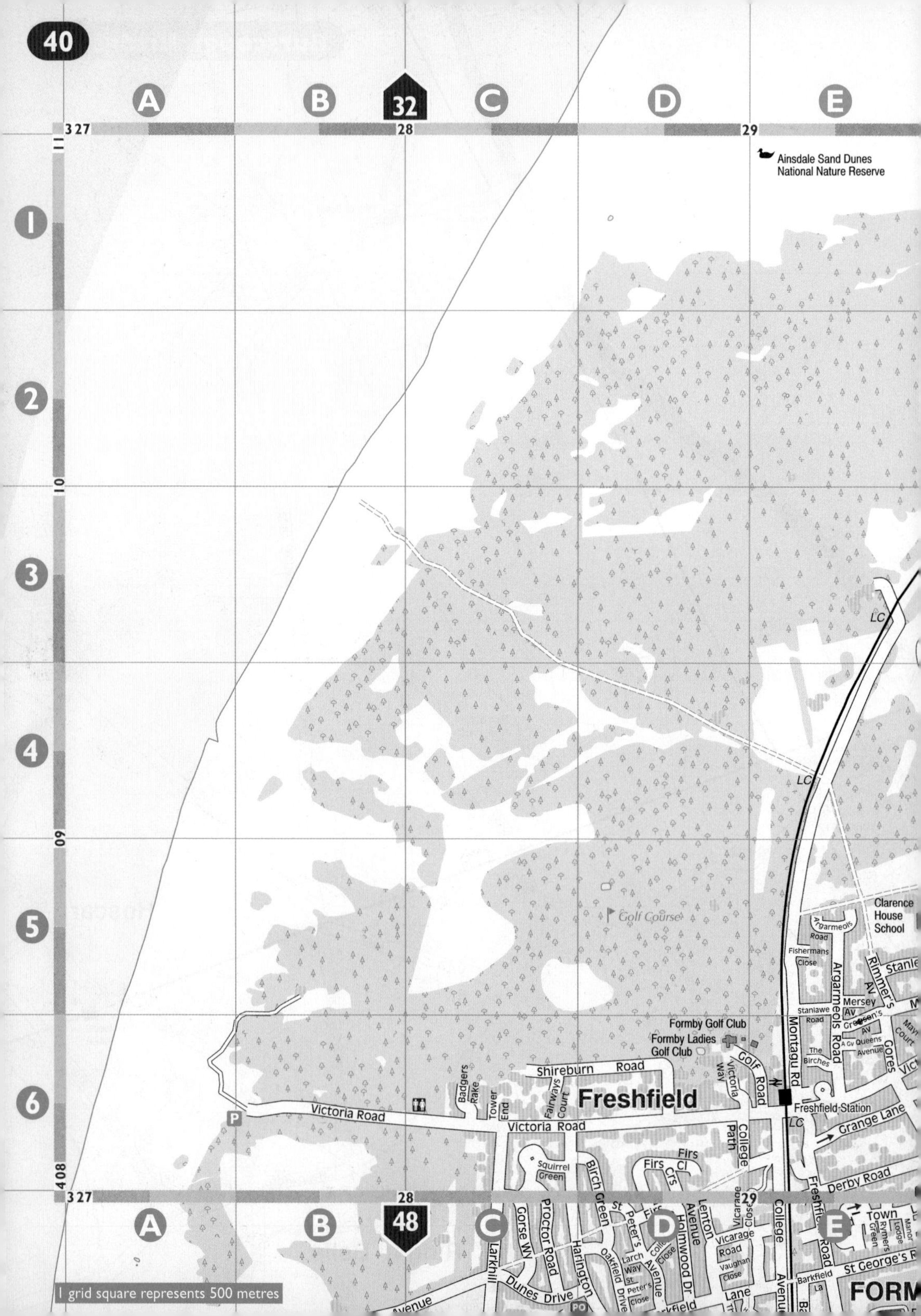

32
A
B
C
D
E
3 27
28
29
Ainsdale Sand Dunes
National Nature Reserve
1
2
3
4
5
6
11
10
09
408
LC
Golf Course
Clarence
House
School
Argarmeols
Road
Fishermans
Close
Argarmeols
Road
Rimmer's
Av
Stanley
Mersey
Av
Stanlawe
Road
Greenson's
Av
Queens
Avenue
Gores
The
Birches
Montagu Rd
Formby Golf Club
Formby Ladies
Golf Club
Shireburn
Road
Victoria
Way
Golf
Road
Freshfield
Freshfield Station
Grange Lane
Badgers
Rake
Tower
End
Fairways
Court
Victoria Road
Victoria Road
College
Path
Squirrel
Green
Birch Green
Firs
Crs
Firs
Cl
Derby Road
Freshfield
Road
48
Gorse Wy
Proctor Road
Harington
Larkhill
St
Peter's
Avenue
Larch
Way
St
Peter's
Close
Oakfield Drive
Holmwood Dr
Lenton
Avenue
Vicarage
Road
Vaughan
Close
Vicarage
Close
College
Avenue
Lane
Dunes Drive
Avenue
PO
P
Town
Rymers
Green
Manor
Lodge
St George's R
Barkfield
La
FORM
1 grid square represents 500 metres

Woodvale
33
42
49
F
G
H
J
K
30
31
32
1
2
3
4
5
6
10
09
408
11
Newby Cl
Coastal Road
Pinfold Lane
Pinfold Lane
Furness Cl
Thirlmere Drive
Penrith Av
Windermere
Keswick Close
Bowness
Kings Meadow Primary School
Sandbrook Road
Meadow Lane
Meadow
St John Stone Catholic Primary School
Somerset Dr
Dorset Avenue
Avenue Way
Cornwall
A565
LIVERPOOL ROAD
Rose Crs
Heather Cl
Cherry Road
Lilac Av
Woodvale Road
Woodvale Road
Vale Crescent
Moor Close
Moor Lane
Willowbank Holiday Home & Touring Park
Dunlop Avenue
Liverpool Old Road
Plex Moss Lane
FORMBY BY-PASS A565
Southport Old Rd
Golf Course
Woodvale Airfield
Formby Hall Golf & Country Club
Broad Lane
Broad Lane
North Moss Lane
FORMBY BY-PASS
Eight Acre Lane
Southport Old Road
A565
Sefton
Lancashire County
Downholland Brook
Moss
Downholland
Brewery La
Brewery Lane
Old La
Kenton Cl
West Lane
St Anne's Cl
St Anne's Road
St Anne's Path
York Cl
The Rydinge
Brackenway
Heatherways
Gorsefield
Deansgate Lane North
Longton Dr
Hawksworth Dr
Hawksworth Close
Hawksworth Drive
Turnacre
Lingdales
Canterbury Cl
Spymers Croft
Heathfield Cl
Hthfld Cl
The Spinney
Paradise Lane
Green Lane
Wrigleys Lane
Wrigleys Cl
St Peters CE Primary School
SOUTHPORT ROAD B5424
Primrose Close
Heather Close
Longfield
Timms Lane
Timms Close
Cricket Path
The Paddock
Formby CC
Formby Junior Sports Club
Deansgate Lane
Mount House Road
Mount House Close
Mount House
Formby Lawn Tennis Club
Deans Court
RYEGROUND LA
Clifton Rd
New Road
Piercefield Road
Surgery
Freshfield Primary School
Side
Willow Grove
Old Mill Lane
Cable Street
Dobbs Drive
Smithy Cl
Smt Gn
Formby Gdns
BY

42
34
41
50
A
B
C
D
E
1
2
3
4
5
6
332
33
34
11
10
09
408
Meadow Lane
Spencers Lane
Carr Moss Lane
Heather Farm
Road
Plex Moss
Lancashire County
Sefton
Gettern Farm
Plex Moss Lane
Plex Moss Lane
Heathy Lane
Alder Lane
Lane
Gorsey
Cheshire Lines Path
Moss Lane
Sefton
Lancashire County
Moss Lane
Old Moss Lane
Downholland Moss
1 grid square represents 500 metres

F
G
H
35
J
K
Green Kettle House
Carr Moss Lane
Plumpton Lane
The Runnel
Cross Lane
A5147
NEW STREET
Halsall Hall Drive
Halsall Manor Court
Halsall St Cuthberts CE Primary School
Carr Moss Lane
Linaker Drive
Park House Farm
Plex Moss Lane
44
Lane
SOUTHPORT ROAD A5147
Station Road
Plex Lane
Barton
Smithy Lane
WANISHAR LANE
Leeds & Liverpool Canal
Rosemary Lane
Haskayne
Jackson Close
Queens Green
Riding Lane
Park Crs
51
DELF
35
36
37
408
409
410
411
2
3
4
5
6
1

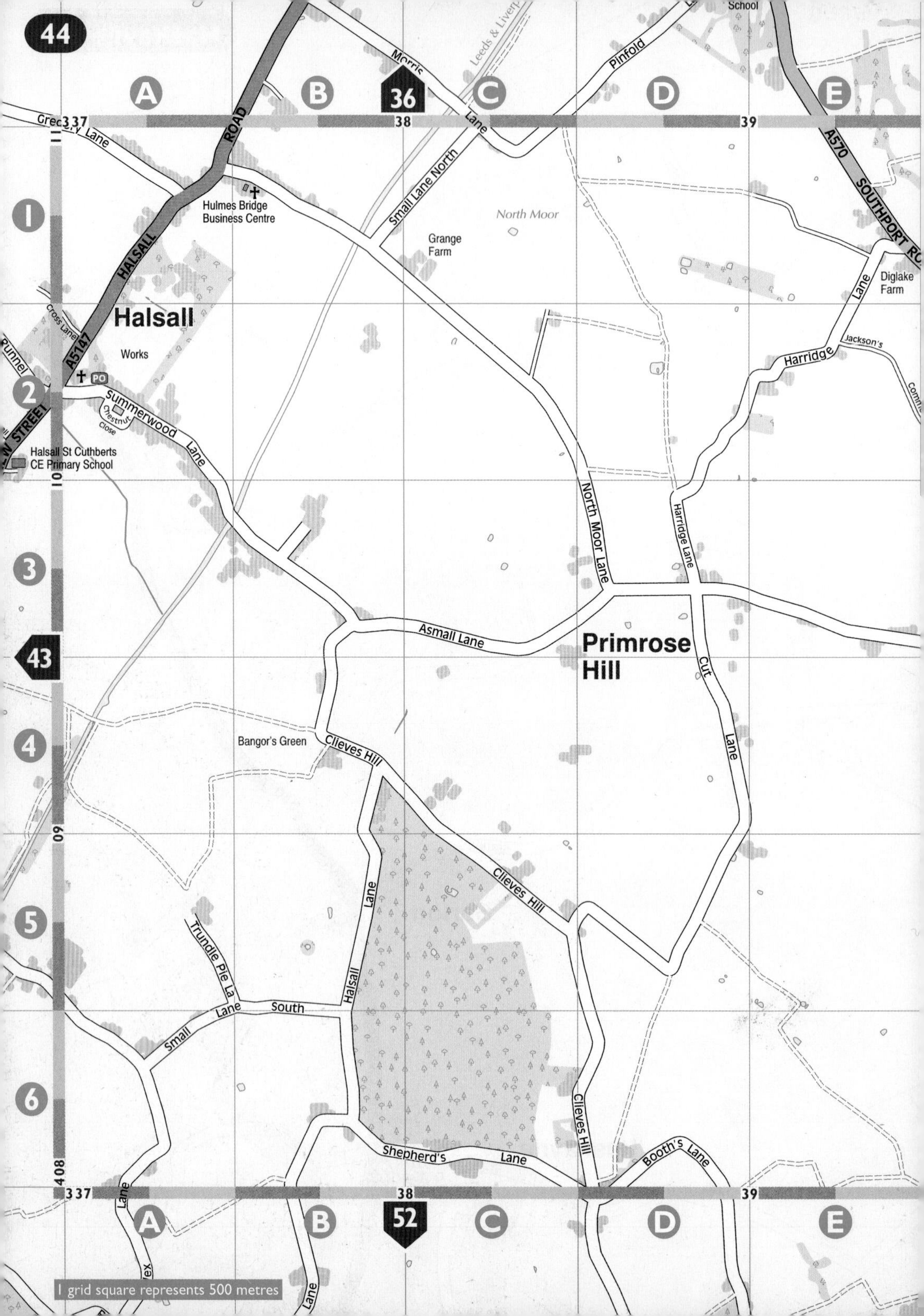

School
Morris Lane
Leeds & Liverp
Pinfold
36
A B C D E
337 38 39
Gregory Lane
HALSALL ROAD
A570 SOUTHPORT RO
Small Lane North
Hulmes Bridge
Business Centre
North Moor
Grange
Farm
Diglake
Farm
Lane
Halsall
Cross Lane
Runnel
A5147
Works
PO
Jackson's
Harridge
Summerwood
Chestnut
Close
Lane
Halsall St Cuthberts
CE Primary School
STREET
North Moor Lane
Harridge Lane
Asmall Lane
Primrose
Hill
Cut
Lane
43
Bangor's Green
Clieves Hill
Halsall Lane
Clieves Hill
Trundle Pie La
Small Lane South
Clieves Hill
Shepherd's Lane
Booth's Lane
1 2 3 4 5 6
11 10 09 408
Lane
52
1 grid square represents 500 metres

Green
ORMSKIRK
Hurlston Hall Golf Club
Hurlston Hall Country Caravan Park
Spout House Farm
Heskin Hall
Asmall House
Asmall Primary School
West End Primary School
Ormskirk RUFC
Ormskirk College
Civic Hall
Ormskirk Station
Register Office
Ormskirk Business Park
Ormskirk CE Primary School
Council Buildings
Park Pool
Superstore
Kingsbury School
St Annes RC
Ormskirk & District General Hospital
St Bedes Catholic High School
A570
SOUTHPORT ROAD
COUNTY ROAD
A59
BURSCOUGH STREET
B5319
BURSCOUGH ROAD
BARRISON GREEN
B5242
PIPPIN
WIGAN
AUGHTON ST
PARK ROAD
ST HELENS ROAD
KNOWSLEY RD
DERBY ST WEST
CHURCH ST
Narrow Moss Lane
Blackacre Lane
Blindman's Lane
Asmall Lane
Hurlston Lane
Moorfield Lane
37
46
53
40
41
42
F
G
H
J
K
1
2
3
4
5
6

38
45
54
A
B
C
D
E
1
2
3
4
5
6
Burscough
Westhead
PIPPIN STREET
B5242
LIVERPOOL ROAD
A59
SOUTH
SQUARE LANE
HIGH LANE
WIGAN ROAD
A577
CROSSHALL BROW
Ringtail Industrial Estate
Guys Industrial Estate
Abbey Lane Industrial Estate
Platts Lane Industrial Estate
St Johns Catholic Primary School
Surgery
Merridale Farm
Blythe Hall
Abbey Farm Caravan Park
Bath Farm
Works
Ormskirk Golf Club
Golf Course
Ormskirk CE Primary School
Cross Hall High School Adult Education Centre
Ormskirk School
Ormskirk & District General Hospital
Register Office
Tollgate Crescent
Tollgate Road
Lordsgate Lane
Abbey Lane
Mill Dam Lane
Mill Dam Close
Manor Avenue
Manor Gardens
Platts La
Chapel Lane
Springfield Close
Meadowbrook
The Poplars
Rivington Drive
Elm Road
Blythe Lane
Lady Alice's Drive
Dark Lane
Sandy Lane
Lathom Lane
Cranes Lane
Castle Lane
Lady's Walk
Nursery Avenue
Pendle Dr
Hill
Charlesbye Av
Greetby
Thompson
Edgley Drive
Taylor Avenue
Latham Avenue
Field Walk
Derby Hill Road
Derby Street
Sunnyfields
Tower Hill
Bath Springs
Waterworks Road
Sephton Drive
Pine Avenue
Old Boundary Way
Brooklands
Hall Brow Close
Crosshall Brow
Halton Chase
Greenacre
Meadow Close
Ormond Av
Weldon Drive
Milton
Blairgowrie Gdns
1 grid square represents 500 metres

Ring o' Bells
Council Building
Croft Av
Ellerbrook Dr
Delph Dr
The Woodlands
BRIARS LANE
A5209
Brooklands Grove
Flaxfields
Briars Brook
Leeds & Liverpool Canal
Three Oaks Close
Ring O'Bells Lane
Hollowford Lane
Moss Bridge Lane
Back Lane
Flax Lane
Hobcross Lane
B5240
LOWRY HILL LANE
HALL LANE
COURSE
Lathom Park CE Primary School
Cranes Lane
Halsall's Lodge Farm
Spa Fold
Dick's Lane
Spa Lane
Spa Farm
Cock Farm
39
55
45
46
47
F
G
H
J
K
1
2
3
4
5
6
11
10
09
408

Freshfield
Freshfield Station
Victoria Road
Grange Lane
Derby Road
College Avenue
College Path
Freshfield Road
FORMBY
Blundell Avenue
Larkhill Lane
Gorse Wy
Proctor Road
Harington Road
Dunes Drive
Oakfield Drive
Holmwood Avenue
Lenton Avenue
Vicarage Road
Vaughan Close
Barkfield Lane
Barkfield Avenue
St George's Road
Wicks Green
Warren Road
Beech Dr
Holmwood Close
Harington Gn
Wicks Lane
Wicks Crs
Ince Crs
Coppice Leys
Woodlands Primary School
Woodlands Road
Ennerdale
Tarn Road
Rydal Av
Langdale Av
Eskdale Dr
Greenloon's Drive
Greenloon's Walk
Foxhill Cl
Spruce Way
Edenhurst Dr
Edenhurst Cl
Kirklake Bank
Kirklake Road
Coniston Road
Grasmere Rd
Formby Station
Formby Bridge
Council Building
CAB
Duke St
Kings Road
Raven
Formby St
St Luke's Church Road
St Luke's Drive
Church Gn
Church Way
Bushby's Park
Bushby's Lane
Brooks Way
Brooks Road
Ward Av
Chindit Cl
Sefton Rd
Queen's Rd
Foster Rd
Sealand Av
Pinewood Close
Trap Hill
Lime Tree Way
Maple Close
St Lukes CE Primary School
Elm Drive
Pinewood Avenue
Elson Road
Carr's Crescent
Andrews Close
Rostron Cr's
Lifeboat Road
Shorrocks Hill Country Club
Beechwood Way
Aspen Gv
Cedar Drive
Sycamore Grove
Chestnut Drive
Cambridge Rd
Jubilee Road
Funchal Av
Crescent Av
Mayfield Av
Heydon Close
Hadstock Avenue
Burwell Avenue
Tadlow Close
Meldreth Close
Elsworth Cl
Stapleton Road
Barton Heys Road
Freshlea Private Clinic
Kew Road
Sutton Road
Park Road
Hampton Rd
Balmoral D
Lancaster
Osborne Road
Range High School
Alexandra Road
Albert Road
Formby Point & Squirrel Nature Reserve
A
B
C
D
E
1
2
3
4
5
6
40
58
1 grid square represents 500 metres

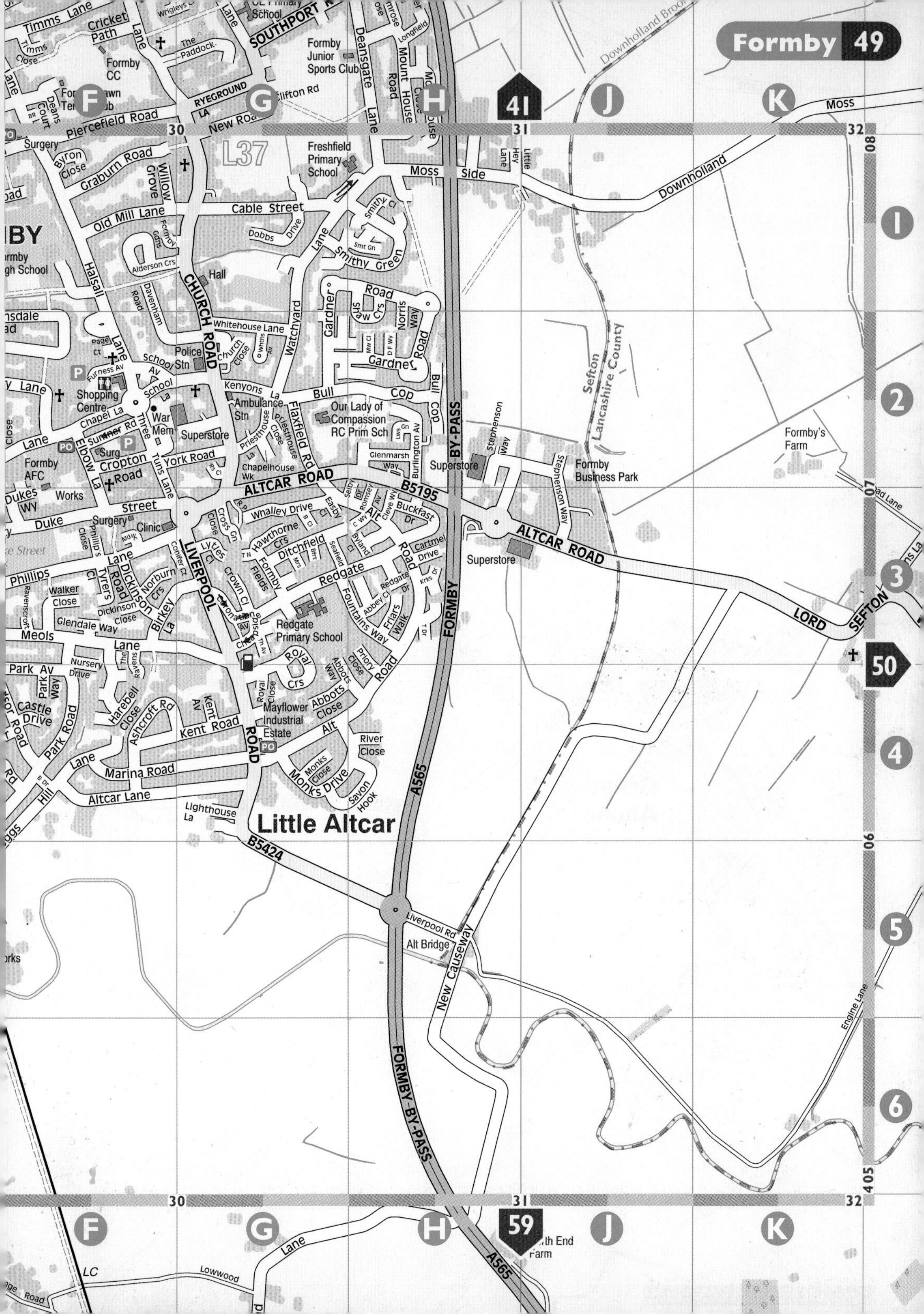
Formby
49
41
50
59
F
G
H
J
K
30
31
32
08
07
06
405
1
2
3
4
5
6
L37
Timms Lane
Cricket Path
Formby CC
The Paddock
Southport
Formby Junior Sports Club
Deansgate Lane
Mount House Road
Longfield
Downholland Brook
Ryeground La
Clifton Rd
Piercefield Road
New Road
Moss
Surgery
Byron Close
Graburn Road
Willow Grove
Freshfield Primary School
Moss Side
Little Hey Lane
Downholland
Old Mill Lane
Cable Street
Dobbs Drive
Smithy Cl
Smt Gn
Smithy Green
Lane
Formby High School
Halsall
Alderson Crs
Hall
Church Road
Davenham Road
Whitehouse Lane
Watchyard
Gardner Road
Shaw Crs
Norris Way
Gardner Road
Bull Cop
Page Ct
Police Stn
Church Close
School Av
Furness Av
Shopping Centre
School La
Kenyons La
Ambulance Stn
Flaxfield Rd
Our Lady of Compassion RC Prim Sch
Glenmarsh Way
Burlington Av
Sefton
Lancashire County
Stephenson Way
Formby's Farm
Chapel La
War Mem
Superstore
Priesthouse Close
Priesthouse La
Formby Business Park
Elbow La
Sumner Rd
Surg
Three Tuns Lane
Formby AFC
Cropton Road
York Road
Chapelhouse Wk
Altcar Road
B5195
Formby By-Pass
Dukes Wy
Works
Duke Street
Surgery
Clinic
Whalley Drive
Easby Cl
Buckfast Dr
Cartmel Drive
Altcar Road
Phillip's Close
Phillips Lane
Tyrers Cl
Dickinson Road
Norburn Crs
Liverpool Road
Crown Cl
Hawthorne Crs
Formby Fields
Ditchfield
Seafield
Redgate
Fountains Way
Abbey Cl
Redgate Dr
Friars Walk
Superstore
Lord Sefton
Walker Close
Ravenscroft
Dickinson Close
Glendale Way
Birkey La
Meols Lane
Redgate Primary School
Priory Close
Road
Park Av
Park Way
Nursery Drive
The Ravens
Harebell Close
Ashcroft Rd
Kent Av
Kent Road
Royal Crs
Royal Close
Abbots Way
Abbots Close
Mayflower Industrial Estate
River Close
Castle Drive
Park Road
Lane
Marina Road
PO
Alt
Monks Close
Monks Drive
Savon Hook
Altcar Lane
Lighthouse La
Little Altcar
A565
B5424
Liverpool Rd
Alt Bridge
New Causeway
Engine Lane
Formby-By-Pass
A565
North End Farm
Lane
Lowwood
LC
Road

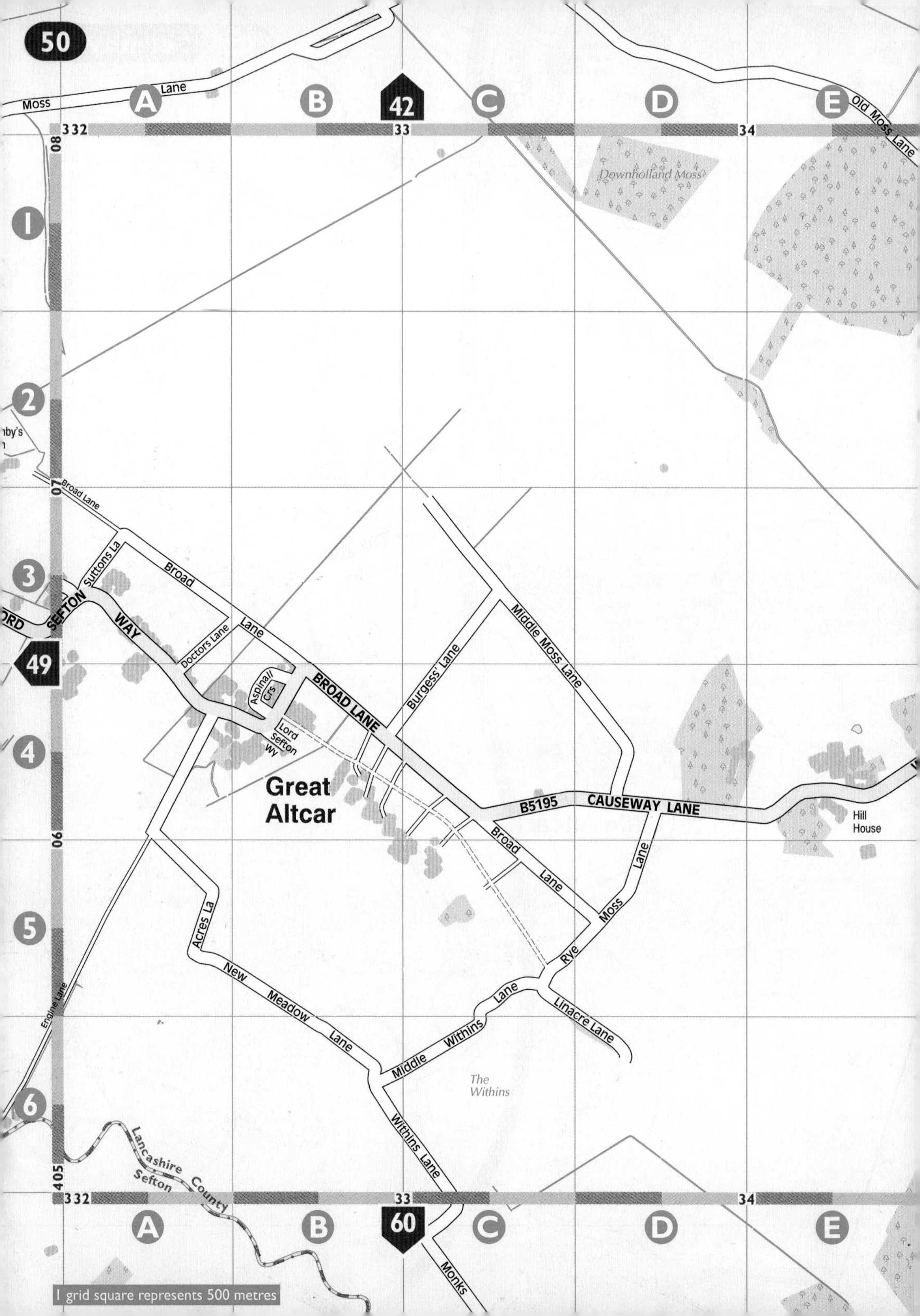
Moss Lane
A
B
42
C
D
E
Old Moss Lane
332
33
34
08
Downholland Moss
1
2
3
07
Broad Lane
Suttons La
Broad Lane
SEFTON WAY
Doctors Lane
49
BROAD LANE
Aspinall Crs
Lord Sefton Wy
Burgess' Lane
Middle Moss Lane
4
Great Altcar
B5195
CAUSEWAY LANE
Hill House
06
Broad Lane
Moss Lane
5
Acres La
Rye
New Meadow Lane
Lane
Linacre Lane
Middle Withins
Engine Lane
The Withins
6
Withins Lane
Lancashire County
Sefton
405
60
Monks
1 grid square represents 500 metres

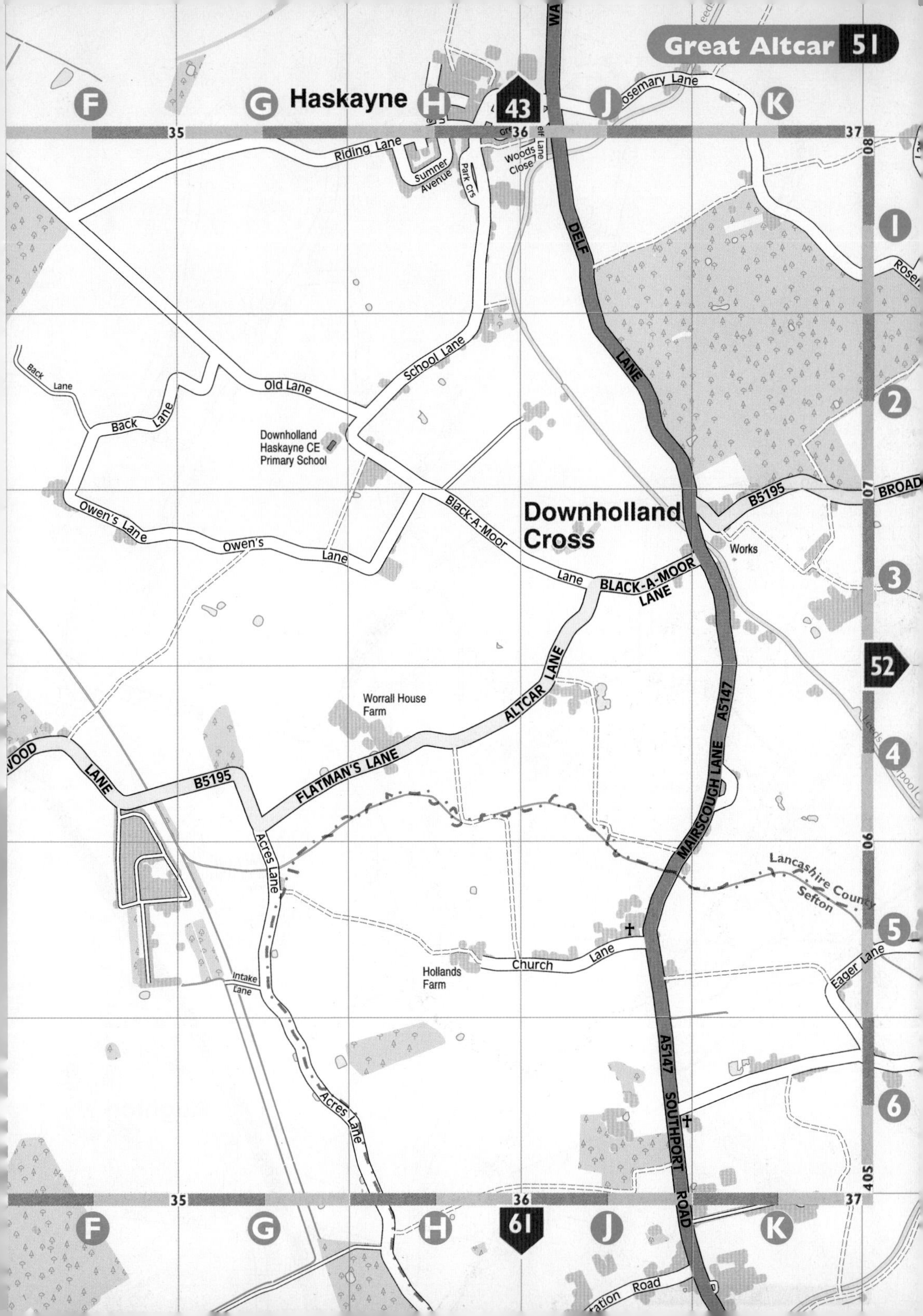
Haskayne
Downholland Cross
Riding Lane
Sumner Avenue
Park Crs
Woods Close
Delf Lane
Rosemary Lane
DELF LANE
School Lane
Old Lane
Back Lane
Downholland Haskayne CE Primary School
Owen's Lane
Black-A-Moor Lane
BLACK-A-MOOR LANE
B5195
BROAD
Works
ALTCAR LANE
Worrall House Farm
FLATMAN'S LANE
WOOD LANE
Acres Lane
MAIRSCOUGH LANE
A5147
Lancashire County
Sefton
Church Lane
Hollands Farm
Intake Lane
Eager Lane
SOUTHPORT ROAD
Station Road
43
52
61
F
G
H
J
K
1
2
3
4
5
6
35
36
37
08
07
06
405

44
A
B
C
D
E
337
38
39
1
2
3
4
5
6
08
07
06
405
51
62
Rosemary Lane
Plex Lane
Dicconson's Lane
Bye Lane
BROAD LANE
Cleeves Hill
Cleeves Hills Lane
Firs Lane
Hills Lane
Cleeves
BIRCH'S BROW
B5195
Small Lane
Gaw's
Holly House
Fir Tree Farm
Fir Tree Lane
Turnpike Road
Hill Rise
View
Bracknel
Close
A59
Green's Lane
Leeds & Liverpool Canal
Walsh Hall
Mill Lane
West Tower Country House Hotel
Back Lane
Eager Lane
Hall Lane
Canal Bank
Pygons Hill
Pygon's Hill
Hollin House Farm
Lane
Michael St
Church Road
Church Vw
St Michaels Park
Church Lane
Aughton
Old Rectory Green
Holt Coppice
The Rowans
NORTHWAY
Police Station
Smithy Lane
Swan Lane
Beech Road
Elmsfield Park
Road
1 grid square represents 500 metres

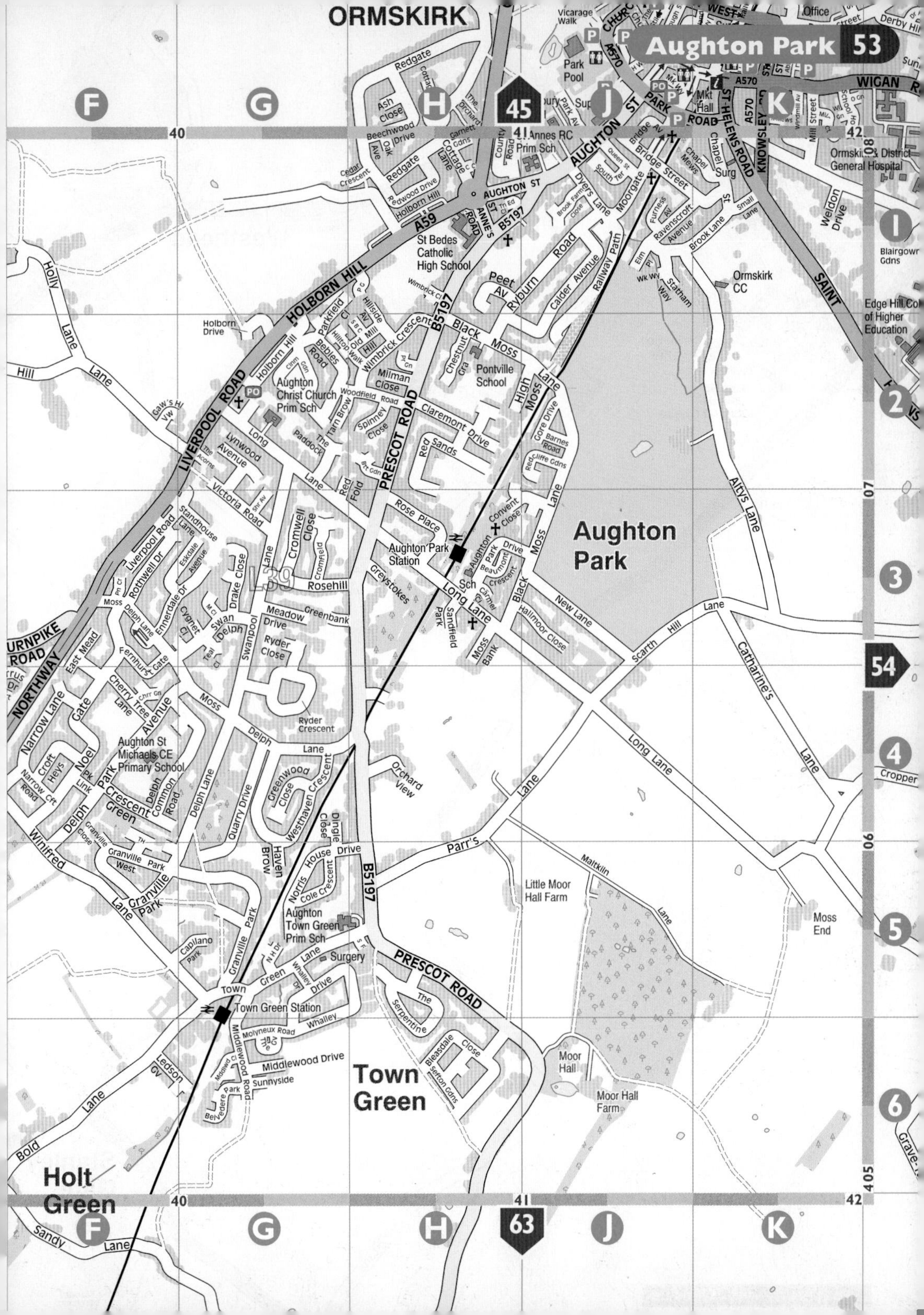
ORMSKIRK
Aughton Park
Town Green
Holt Green
45
54
63
F
G
H
J
K
40
41
42
2
3
4
5
6
07
06
405
LIVERPOOL ROAD
HOLBORN HILL
A59
PRESCOT ROAD
B5197
AUGHTON ST
NORTHWAY
TURNPIKE ROAD
Long Lane
Hill Lane
Holly Lane
Bold Lane
Sandy Lane
Winifred Lane
Parr's Lane
Scarth Hill Lane
Catharine's Lane
Altys Lane
New Lane
Black Moss Lane
High Moss Lane
Maltkiln Lane
Moss Delph Lane
Delph Lane
Swanpool Lane
Granville Park
Narrow Lane
Redgate
Beechwood Drive
Cottage Lane
Holborn Hill
Wimbrick Crescent
Peet Av
Ryburn Road
Calder Avenue
Railway Path
Dyers Lane
Moorgate
Bridge Street
Chapel Mews
ST HELENS ROAD
KNOWSLEY RD
WIGAN RD
Brook Lane
Ravenscroft Avenue
Statham Way
Claremont Drive
Red Sands
Rose Place
Cromwell Close
Rosehill
Greystokes
Meadow Drive
Ryder Close
Ryder Crescent
Greenwood Close
Westhaven Crescent
Quarry Drive
Haven Brow
Orchard View
Norris House Drive
Cole Crescent
Green Lane
Whalley Drive
Molyneux Road
Middlewood Drive
Middlewood Road
Sunnyside
Belvedere Park
Ledson Gv
Capilano Park
The Serpentine
Bleasdale Close
Sefton Gdns
Hallmoor Close
Sandfield Park
Moss Bank
Victoria Road
Lynwood Avenue
Standhouse Lane
Rothwell Dr
Ennerdale Dr
Drake Close
Cherry Tree Lane
Avenue
Noel Gate
Croft Heys
Crescent Green
Common Road
Moss End
Moor Hall
Moor Hall Farm
Little Moor Hall Farm
Aughton Park Station
Town Green Station
Aughton Christ Church Prim Sch
Aughton St Michaels CE Primary School
Aughton Town Green Prim Sch
St Bedes Catholic High School
Pontville School
St Annes RC Prim Sch
Ormskirk & District General Hospital
Edge Hill College of Higher Education
Ormskirk CC
Park Pool
Mkt Hall
Surgery
Surg
Blairgowrie Gdns
Cropper
Vicarage Walk
Office
Derby Hill
L39

54
46
53
64
A
B
C
D
E
1
2
3
4
5
6
342
43
44
408
407
406
405
Derby Street
Derby Hill Road
Sunnyfields
Wigan Road
Tower
Edgley Drive
Taylor Avenue
Latham Avenue
Avenue
Cross Hall High School Adult Education Centre
Lady's Walk
School House
Mill Street
Ormskirk & District General Hospital
Hall Brow Close
A577 CROSSHALL BROW
Crosshall Brow
Westhead
Ruff Lane
Milton Drive
Normanhurst
Beech Meadow
Blairgowrie Gdns
Woodlands Close
Edge Hill Coll of Higher Education
The Sporting Edge Track
Childrens Centre
Edge Hill University (Ormskirk Campus)
Ruff Farm
Vicarage Close
Ruff La
St James Close
Bewcastle Dr
Varlian Close
Wellfield Lane
Vicarage Lane
School Lane
Ormond Av
Halton Chase
Greenacre
Meadow Close
Holly Close
St James CE Primary School
A577 WIGAN
SAINT HELENS ROAD
A570
Slack House Farm
Scarth Hill Lane
Whiteley's Lane
Scarth Hill
Cropper's Lane
Poppy Lane
ORMSKIRK ROAD
Clock House
High Lane
Long Lane
Grave-Yard Lane
Heyescroft
Stanley Gate
Stockley Crescent
1 grid square represents 500 metres

Pennylands
Chapel House
Blaguegate
Spa Lane
Dick's Lane
Plough Lane
B5240
Road
Holland Business Park
Spa Farm
Cock Farm
Statham Road
Firswood Road
Slate Lane
Old Engine Lane
Dicket's Lane
A577 Blaguegate Lane
Ormskirk Road
Holland's Lane
Garden Centre
Lyelake Lane
Lyelake Farm
Lathom Road
Skelmersdale Road B5312
White Moss Road
Liverpool Rd
Railway Rd
A577 Neverstitch Road
Black Moss School
Brookfield Community Prim Sch
St Richards Catholic Primary Sch
Sandy Lane Health Cen
Council Building
Skelmersdale United FC
Orm Works
Works
Stanley Farm
Ormskirk Rd Old
A570
Rainford Road
M58
Bromilow Road
Kerfoot's Lane
Derby Rd
Swift's Fd
Old Town Wy
Village Cl
Witham Road
Sandy Lane
Clayton Street
Marchbank Road
Turnberry
Sherrat Street
Westgate
Oxford Rd
Laburnum Dr
Ash Grove
Olive Grove
Tintagel
Statham Road
Selby Place
Stanley Place
Seaton
Welbourne
Smith St
Birch Street
Ashwall Street
Wallcroft Street
Gladden
Waverley
School
High
F G H J K
45 46 47
47 56 65
1 2 3 4 5 6
08 07 06 405

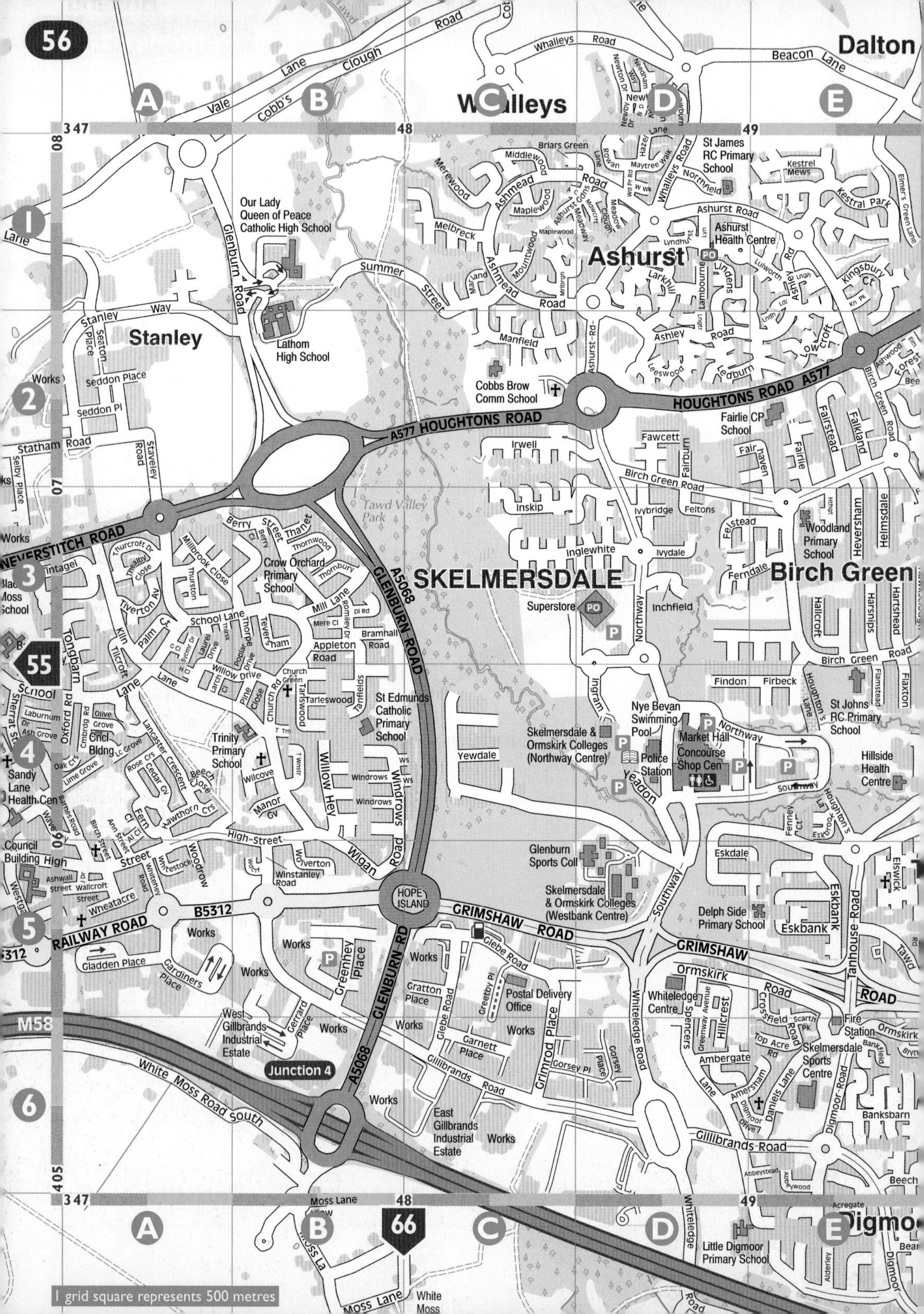

Dalton
Whalleys
Ashurst
Stanley
SKELMERSDALE
Birch Green
Digmoor
A577 HOUGHTONS ROAD
HOUGHTONS ROAD A577
A5068 GLENBURN ROAD
NEVERSTITCH ROAD
GRIMSHAW ROAD
B5312 RAILWAY ROAD
M58
Junction 4
Our Lady Queen of Peace Catholic High School
Lathom High School
Cobbs Brow Comm School
St James RC Primary School
Ashurst Health Centre
Fairlie CP School
Woodland Primary School
Crow Orchard Primary School
St Edmunds Catholic Primary School
Trinity Primary School
Superstore
Nye Bevan Swimming Pool
Skelmersdale & Ormskirk Colleges (Northway Centre)
Police Station
Market Hall Concourse Shop Cen
St Johns RC Primary School
Hillside Health Centre
Glenburn Sports Coll
Skelmersdale & Ormskirk Colleges (Westbank Centre)
Delph Side Primary School
Postal Delivery Office
Whiteledge Centre
Fire Station
Skelmersdale Sports Centre
West Gillbrands Industrial Estate
East Gillbrands Industrial Estate
Little Digmoor Primary School
Tawd Valley Park
HOPE ISLAND
Sandy Lane Health Cen
Council Building
1 grid square represents 500 metres

55
66

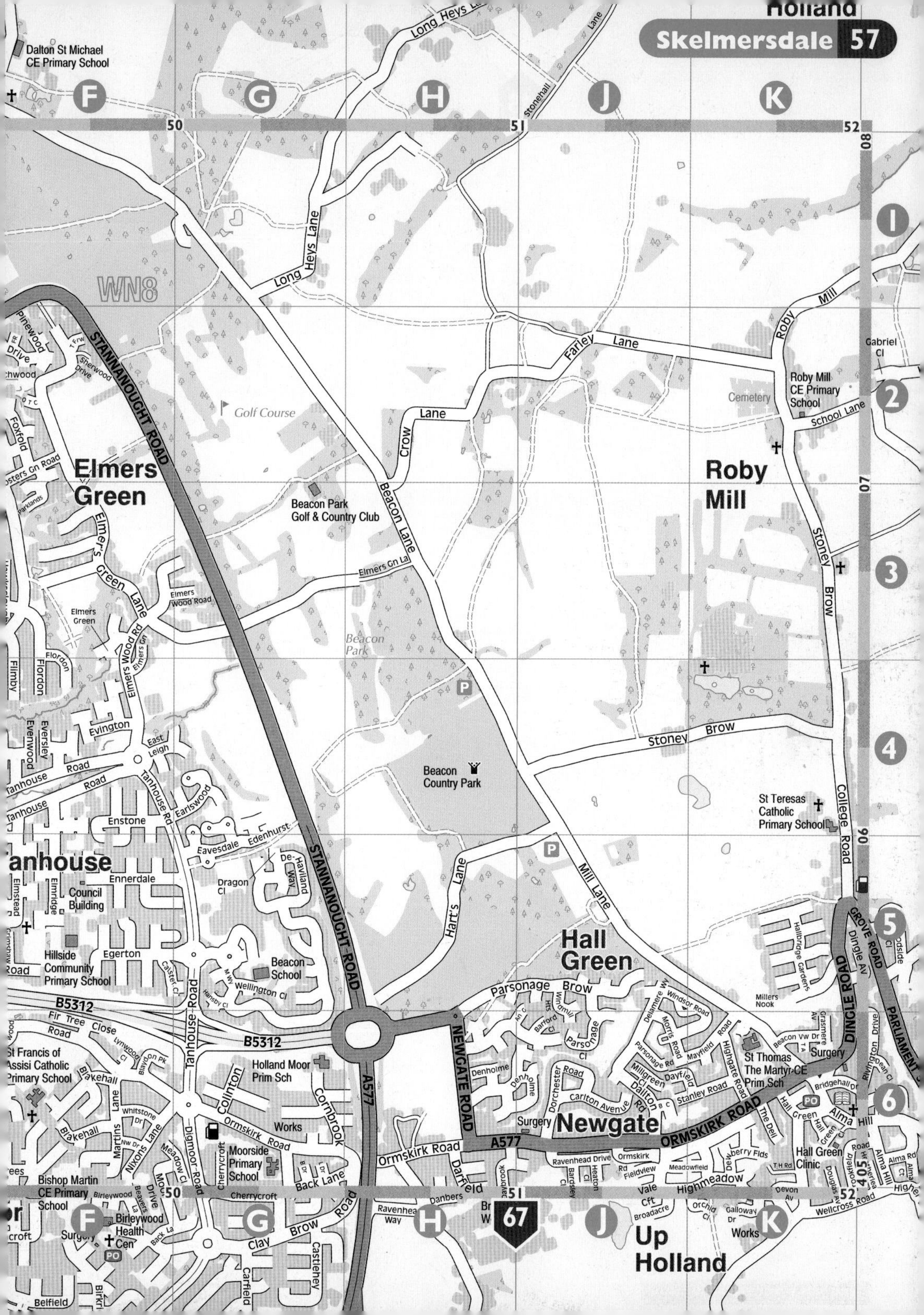
Holland
Dalton St Michael CE Primary School
Long Heys Lane
Stonehall Lane
WN8
Stannanought Road
Pinewood Drive
Sherwood Drive
Foxfold
Elmers Green
Golf Course
Crow Lane
Farley Lane
Roby Mill
Gabriel Cl
Roby Mill CE Primary School
Cemetery
School Lane
Roby Mill
Beacon Park Golf & Country Club
Beacon Lane
Elmers Gn La
Elmers Green Lane
Elmers Wood Road
Stoney Brow
Beacon Park
Flimby
Flordon
Evington
East Leigh
Tanhouse Road
Tanhouse Rd
Earlswood
Beacon Country Park
St Teresas Catholic Primary School
College Road
Enstone
Eavesdale
Edenhurst
Tanhouse
Ennerdale
Dragon Cl
De-Havilland Way
Hart's Lane
Mill Lane
Council Building
Hillside Community Primary School
Egerton
Beacon School
Wellington Cl
Hall Green
Parsonage Brow
Grove Road
Dingle Road
Parliament
B5312
Fir Tree Close
Tanhouse Road
Windsor Road
Morris Road
Highgate Road
Millers Nook
St Thomas The Martyr CE Prim Sch
Surgery
St Francis of Assisi Catholic Primary School
Blakehall
Holland Moor Prim Sch
Colinton
Cornbrook
Newgate Road
A577
Denholme
Dorchester Road
Carlton Avenue
Stanley Road
Ormskirk Road
Works
Moorside Primary School
Digmoor Road
Nixons Lane
Martins
Surgery
Newgate
Ormskirk Road
Hall Green Clinic
Alma Hill
Bishop Martin CE Primary School
Back Lane
Darfield
Highmeadow
Dewberry Flds
Birleywood Health Cen
Clay Brow Road
Ravenhead Way
Wellcross Road
Up Holland
Castlehey
Carfield
Belfield
F G H J K
50 51 52
08 07 06
1 2 3 4 5 6
405
67

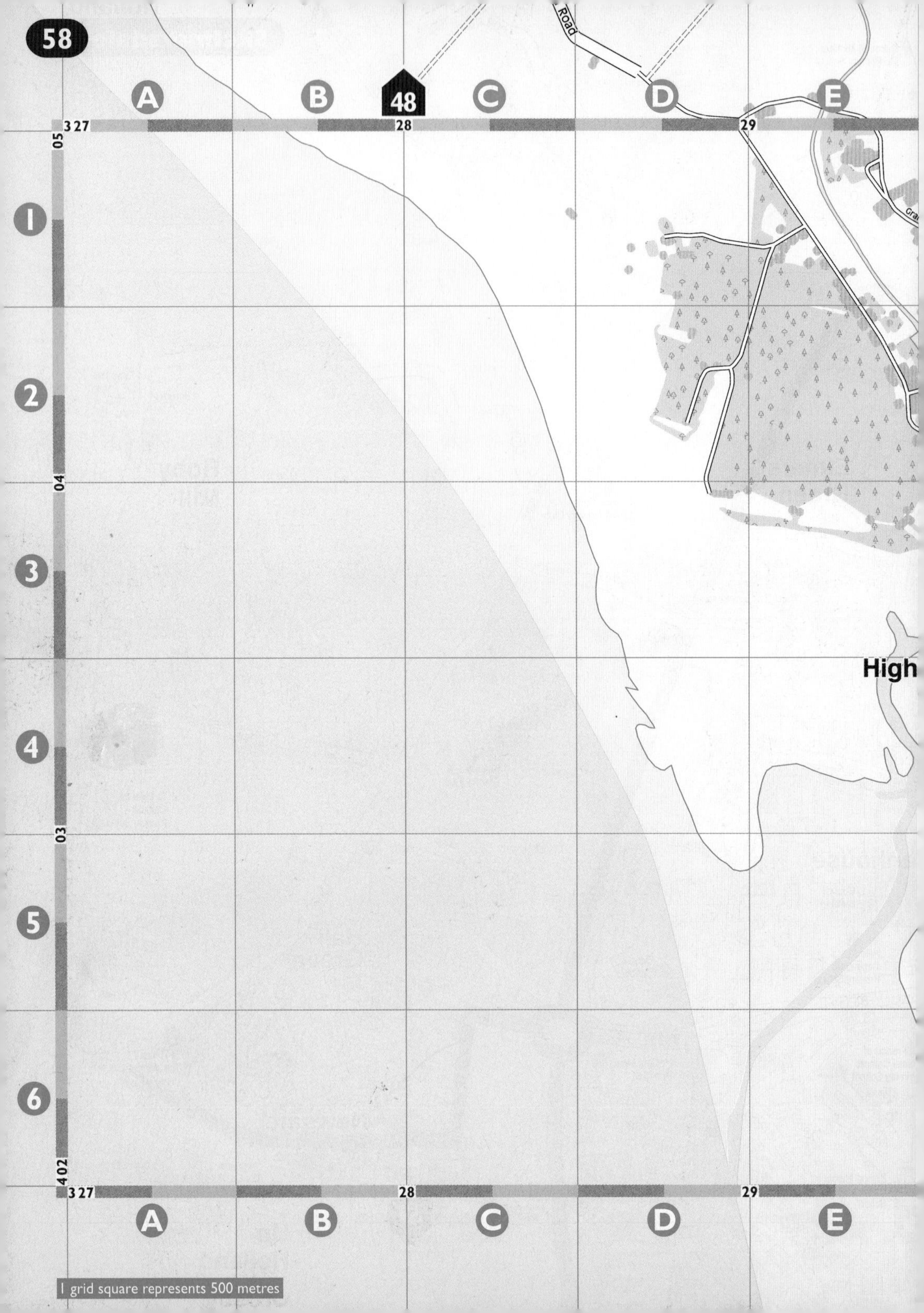
48
A
B
C
D
E
3 27
28
29
05
04
03
4 02
1
2
3
4
5
6
Road
High
1 grid square represents 500 metres

49
60
68
F
G
H
J
K
30
31
32
05
04
03
402
1
2
3
4
5
6
North End Farm
A565
SCAFFOLD LANE
Scaffold Lane
Lowwood
Lane
North End Road
Floodgates Rd
St George's Road
Whitedge Farm
Moss Lane
Marsh Lane
Lady Green Lane
Garden Centre
ORRELL HILL LANE
L38
Mark Road
Hester Cl
St Stephen's Road
Kerslake Way
LC
Hightown Station
Emerson Cl
Surgery
Windermere Road
Thirlmere Road
Lower Alt Road
Alt Road
Alt Rd
PO
North Dunes
R Rd
School Road
Riverside
Westway
Village Way
Sndlnds Gv
Blundell Av
Bankside
The Roundway
Sandy Lane
Elmcroft Lane
Sandhills
Wg M
Old Acre
Grove
Larkhill
Moorhouses
Thornbeck
Briary Cft
Blundell Crove
Withins Fld
Thornbeck Av
Avenue
Alton Close
Blundell Road
Elvington Road
Moor Farm
B5193
Moss Farm
Gorsey Lane
MOSS LANE
Brentwood Close
Whf Cl
Langley Cl
Oakfield Rd
Marston Crs
Richmond Close
Mayfair Cl
Nature Reserve
The Cr
Moor La
The Close
Delph Road
Ackers La
Little Crosby
St Marys
own

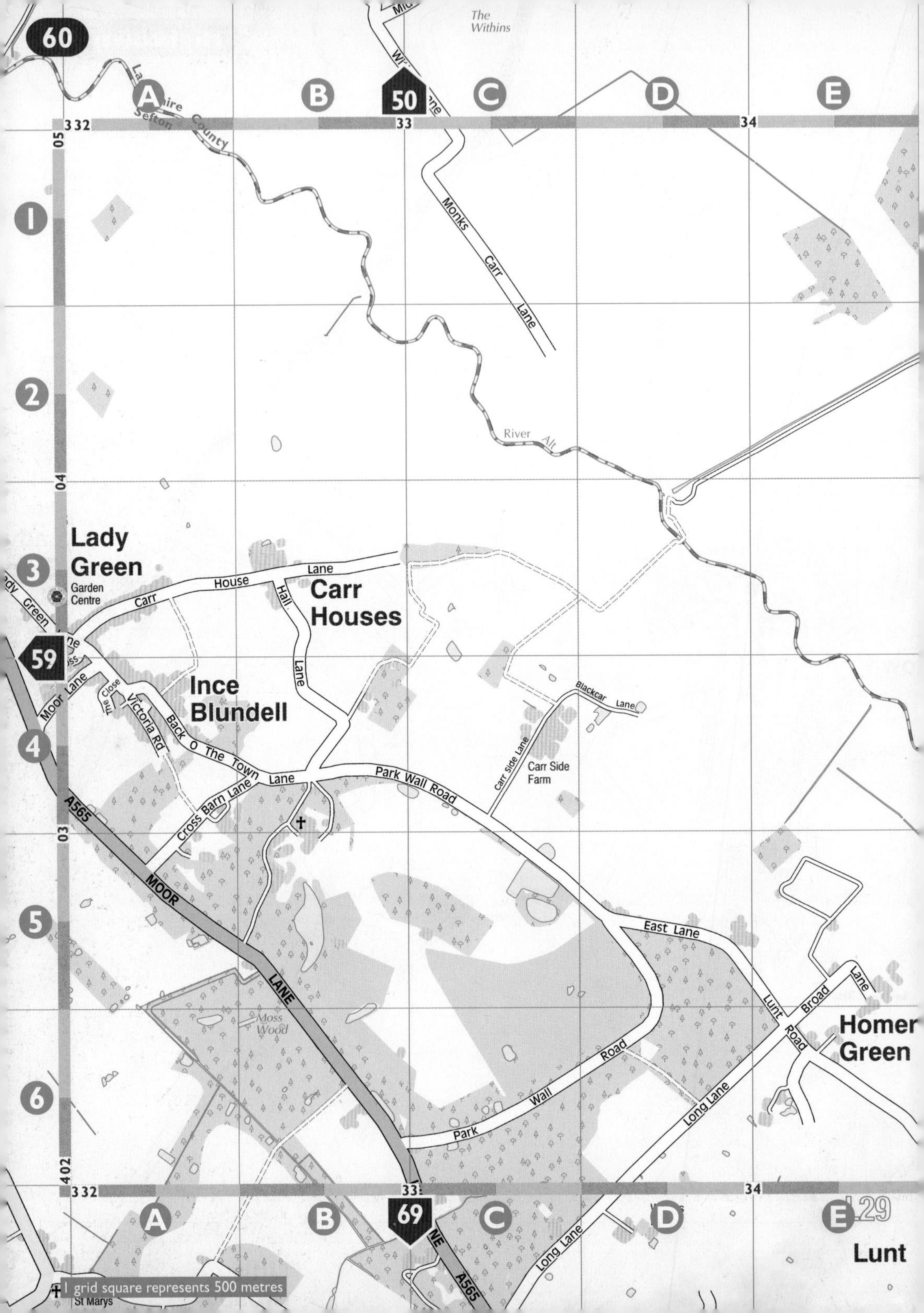

60
The Withins
50
A
B
C
D
E
332
33
34
05
1
2
04
3
4
03
5
6
402
Lancashire
Sefton
County
Monks Carr Lane
River Alt
Lady Green
Garden Centre
Carr House Lane
Hall Lane
Carr Houses
59
Moor Lane
The Close
Victoria Rd
Ince Blundell
Back O The Town Lane
Cross Barn Lane
Park Wall Road
Blackcar Lane
Carr Side Lane
Carr Side Farm
A565
MOOR LANE
East Lane
Lunt Road
Broad Lane
Homer Green
Moss Wood
Park Wall Road
Long Lane
69
A565
Lunt
1 grid square represents 500 metres
St Marys

Acres Lane
Station Road
Gore House Farm
Punnell's Lane
Carr Lane
Lydiate Station Road
Lydiate
Charlesworth Close
Sandhurst Way
Birchfield Way
Silver Birch Way
Manion Avenue
Manion Close
Avelon Cl
Pilling Lane
SOUTHPORT ROAD
A5147
Cadwell Rd
Silverstone Grove
Mallory Av
Woodleigh Close
Roseland Cl
Nursery
The Fieldings
The Moorings
Cabin Lane
Altcar Lane
Crisp's Farm
Seafore Close
Bell's Close
Bell's Lane
Upper Gore Farm
High Banks
The Conifers
Turnbridge Road
Stonebarn
Mosshill Close
Rigby Road
Crawford Av
Green Park Primary School
Green Lane
Green Link
North Meade
St John Bosco RC Primary School
The Round
West Meade
Meade
Milton Way
Empress Close
South Meade
Glebe Cl
Green Park Drive
Hinchley Green
B5422
River Alt
Lancashire County
Sefton
Moor Lane
Wingfield Close
Lane
Sefton Lane Industrial Estate
Sefton Drive
SEFTON LANE
Old Road
Claremont Avenue
Claremont Medical Centre
LIVERPOOL
F
G
H
J
K
35
36
37
51
62
70
2
3
4
5
6

Hall Lane
Canal Bank
Pygons Hill
Hollin House Farm
52
Aughton
St Michaels Park
St Michaels
Old Rectory Green
Holt Coppice
The Rowans
A
B
C
D
E
337
38
39
05
Police Station
Pygon's
Sudell
Hill
Lane
Back
Swan
Lane
Smithy Lane
Beech Road
Road
Elmsfield Park
Brookfield House
Rose Hill Farm
Back Lane
Springfield
Sandy
Silver Birch Way
Moss Lane
Aughton Chase
Nell's Lane
Butchers Lane
Brookfield
1
2
3
4
5
6
04
Clarendon
Kingsley
Blackhurst Road
Tyrer's Avenue
Nursery Road
St Gregorys Catholic Primary School
Roseland Cl
ROAD B5407
Old Lane
NORTHWAY A59
Lambshear
Lane
Lydiate Primary School
SOUTHPORT ROAD
Marshall's Close
Haigh Crs
Liverpool Road
St Thomas CE Primary School
Coppull Road
Knutsford Walk
Oakhill Dr
LIVERPOOL
Heskin Close
Kenyons
Seafore
61
Barnes Drive
Alexander Drive
Virginia Avenue
Park Av
Lane
High Banks
Nedens Gv
Nedens Lane
Saville Road
Sunnymede Dr
Ridgeway Dr
The Conifers
PO
Coronation
Halton Rd
Byron
Seymour Dr
The Cleves
Aragon
The Boleyn
Greenbank Avenue
Turnbridge Road
Hickson Avenue
Clent Gardens
Merrilox Av
Withens Road
Highgate Road
Fawcett Road
Northway
Northway Community Primary School
Lathom Drive
Croxteth
Scarisbrick Cl
Millbank
Lane
Moss Side
Rigby Road
Stonebarn
Mosshill Close
Crawford
Gordon Av
Clent Road
Clent Avenue
Wynnstay Av
Oakhill Rd
Park Lane
03
Lane
Upton Barn
North Meade
Granville Avenue
Wills Av
Surgery
Dodd's Lane
Moss Lane
Ribble Avenue
Wasdale Av
Lowther Av
Gilpin Avenue
Wenning Av
Derwent Cl
Kelkbeck
Watton
Parkbourn Drive
Parkbourn Nth
Ashworth Hospital
The Round
Windle Ash
Kidl Cl
Dale Cl
East Meade
Liverpool Road North
Roedean Cl
Sandford Dr
Leighton Av
Towers Av
Eastway
Kendal
Ennerdale Av
Hawkshead Close
Keswick Close
Eskdale Drive
Langdale Drive
Troutbeck Av
Lune Av
Calder Drive
Yarrow Av
Beck Cl
Douglas Drive
Trent Avenue
Sudell Avenue
Avenue
Surgery
Meade
Swaledate
Ambleside Rd
Ravenglass Av
Coniston Rd
Penrith
Crescent
Hindburn Av
Duddon Av
Hodder Av
L31
Dawson Gdns
Grasmere Road
Cartmel Av
Patterdale Crs
Tebay Close
Mersey
Milton Way
WESTWAY
B5422 GREEN LANE
Police Station
Ulverston Cl
Windermere Dr
Moss La
Bridge Farm Dr
School Lane
School
Meade
Glebe Cl
Westover Rd
Maghull Health Cen
Red Lion Shopping Centre
Deyes
Lane
Moss View
Green Heys Dr
Hesketh Dr
Deyes La
Shop Lane
Manor House Close
Council Building
Parkfield Grove
Holmefield
Hillary Crescent
Hunt Road
Scott Close
Tensing Road
Buttermere Cl
Eastway
Beechfield
Longfold
Birch Close
Highfield
Highfield Pk
South Meade
Greenville Drive
Grove
LIVERPOOL ROAD NORTH
A5147
Deyes High School
Deyes Lane
Bluestone
Haymans Green
Penfold
Meadow La
Grove Mead
Stansfield Av
LIVERPOOL ROAD SOUTH
Alexander Whf
DAMFIELD LA
St Andrews Maghull CE Prim Sch
Chilton Cl
Chilton Mews
Ridley Lane
Deyes End
Flatfield Way
Broadoak Road
Farmdale Drive
Twig La
Ripley Close
Croft Field
Briars Lane
Delifield La
Hillcrest
402
Saltpit Lane
Waltho Avenue
Newlyn Avenue
Aldykes
B5422
Damfield
71
Lane
Road
Foxhouse
Claremont Medical Centre
MAGHULL
Avondale Av
Brook
Maricourt Catholic High School
Orch Hey
Brooklands Drive
Spring Garden
Poverty
1 grid square represents 500 metres

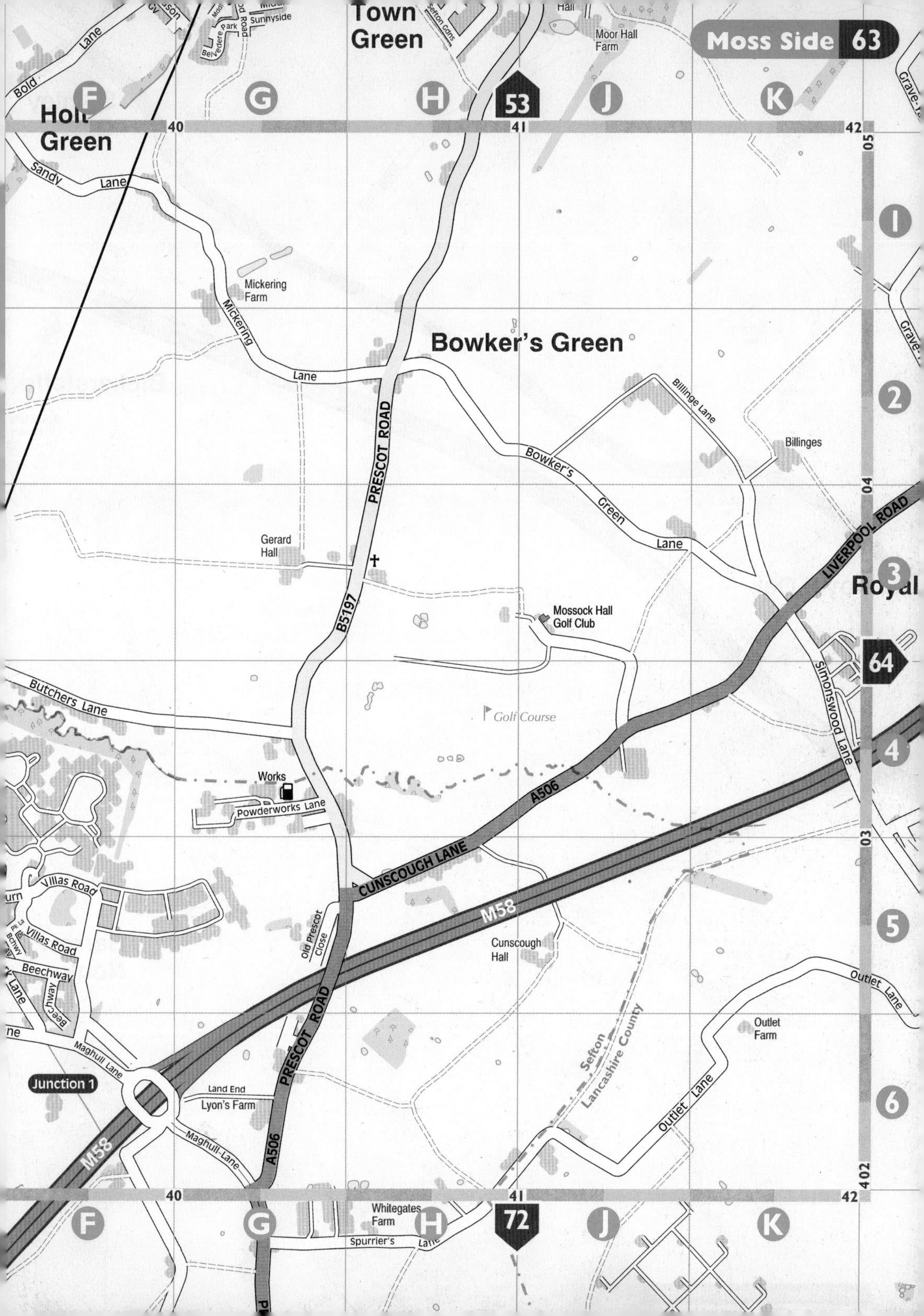
Town Green
Holt Green
Bold Lane
Sunnyside
Sefton Gdns
Moor Hall Farm
Sandy Lane
Mickering Farm
Mickering Lane
Bowker's Green
PRESCOT ROAD
B5197
Billinge Lane
Billinges
Bowker's Green Lane
Gerard Hall
Mossock Hall Golf Club
LIVERPOOL ROAD
Royal
Simonswood Lane
Butchers Lane
Golf Course
Works
Powderworks Lane
A506
CUNSCOUGH LANE
Villas Road
Old Prescot Close
M58
Cunscough Hall
Beechway
Maghull Lane
Outlet Lane
Outlet Farm
Junction 1
Land End
Lyon's Farm
Sefton
Lancashire County
Maghull-Lane
Whitegates Farm
Spurrier's Lane
53
64
72
F
G
H
J
K
1
2
3
4
5
6
40
41
42
05
04
03
402

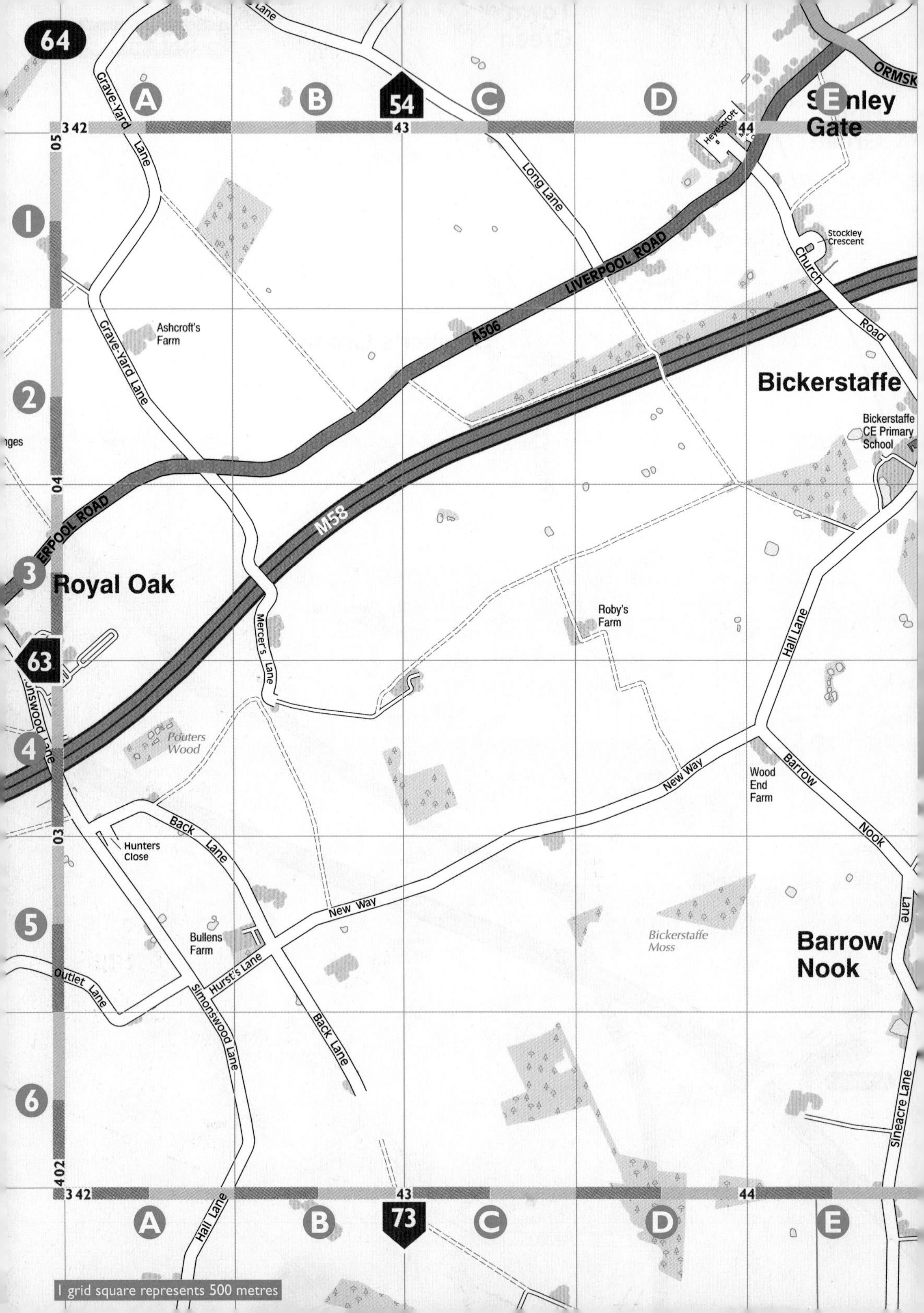

Lane
54
A
B
C
D
Stanley Gate
ORMSK
3 42
43
44
05
Heyescroft
Grave-Yard Lane
Long Lane
LIVERPOOL ROAD
Stockley Crescent
Church Road
A506
Ashcroft's Farm
Grave-Yard Lane
Bickerstaffe
Bickerstaffe CE Primary School
M58
04
LIVERPOOL ROAD
Royal Oak
Roby's Farm
Mercer's Lane
63
Hall Lane
Pouters Wood
New Way
Wood End Farm
Barrow Nook
Back Lane
03
Hunters Close
New Way
Lane
Bullens Farm
Bickerstaffe Moss
Barrow Nook
Outlet Lane
Hurst's Lane
Simonswood Lane
Back Lane
Sineacre Lane
402
3 42
43
44
Hall Lane
73
A
B
C
D
E
1
2
3
4
5
6
1 grid square represents 500 metres

SKELMERSDALE ROAD
Stanley Farm
55
45
46
47
RAINFORD ROAD
M58
Junction 3
Rainford Road
A570
Intake Lane
RAINFORD ROAD
Coal Pit Lane
Holly
66
Holly Fold Farm
Ben Lane Farm
Ben Lane Court
Ben Lane
Intake Lane
Moss Lane
Coach Road
Lodge Lane
Ormskirk
Park Hill
Bushey
Ormskirk Road
Red Delph Lane
RAINFORD BY-PASS
Works
Siding Lane
74
A570
05
04
03
402
F
G
H
J
K
1
2
3
4
5
6

Junction 4
White Moss Road South
Works
Gillibrands Road
East Gillibrands Industrial Estate
Works
Gillibrands Road
Banksbarn
Centre
Digmoor
Little Digmoor Primary School
Whiteledge Road
M58
Moss Lane View
Moss La
Moss Lane
White Moss Farm
Pennine Pl
Works
Pikelaw Place
Penketh Place
Pilling Place
Works
Pimbo Road
Works
Pit Hey Place
Paddock Road
Works
Paxton Place
Holland Moss
Nipe Lane
Works
Ferny Knoll
Ferny Knoll Road
Lancashire County
St. Helens
Holland Moss
Duke's Wd La
Holly Lane
Holly Fold Lane
Nipe Lane
Rainford Junction
News Lane
Windermere Drive
Buttermere Crs
Kendal Close
Kendal Drive
Rail Close
Rainford Station
Spring Field
Bushey Lane
Maggots Nook Road
Nook Road
News Lane
Maggots
Langwood
Henderson
Brow
Reeds
A570
1 grid square represents 500 metres

56
65
75

Assisi Catholic Primary School
Holland Moor Prim Sch
A577
Newgate
Surgery
Denholme
Dorchester Road
Carlton Avenue
Dalton
Millgreen
The Martyr CE
Ormskirk Road
Colinton
Cornbrook
Works
Brakehall
Whitstone Dr
Martins Lane
Nixons Lane
Meadow Moor Drive
Digmoor Road
Moor Primary School
Cherrycroft
Back Lane
Darfield
Danbers
Ravenhead Way
Brick Works
Bishop Martin CE Primary School
Birleywood
Birleywood Health Cen
Surgery
PO
Clay Brow Road
Castlehey
Carfield
Birkrig
Belfield
Brierfield
Hall Green Clinic
Alma Hill
Highmeadow
Vale Cft
Broadacre
Orchid Cl
Galloway Dr
Devon Av
Wellcross
Up Holland
Chequer Lane
Tower Hill Road
Tower Nook
Pimbo Road
Peel Rd
Peel Road
Potter Place
M58
Junction 5
Stannanought Road
Prospect Place
Chequer Cl
Quality Hotel
Industrial Estate
Priorswood Place
Prescot Road
Up Holland Station
Pinfold Place
Penrose Pl
Pendle Pl
Pendle Ct
LC
Pimbo Lane
Higher Pimbo
Long Lane
Crawford Village Primary School
Manor House Dr
Duke's Wood Lane
Millets
Bispham Business
Crawford
Crawford Road
Oakleigh
Holland Court
Lancashire County
St. Helens
Maddocks
Lane
Brownlo
F
G
H
J
K
57
76
50
51
52
05
04
03
402
1
2
3
4
5
6

59
80
A
B
C
D
E
330
31
02
01
400
399
1
2
3
4
5
6
Little Crosby
Golf Course
Delph Road
Ackers La
Ackers Lane
Dibb Lane
Sefton Coastal Footpath
West Lancashire Golf Club
Hall Road Station
Hall Road West
Hall Road East
Spinney Crs
Paddock Close
Saint Andrew's Drive
Sunningdale Drive
Prestwick Drive
Roehampton Drive
Manor Road
St Michaels Church of England High School
St Michael's Road
Boundary Drive
Kaigh Avenue
Ilford Avenue
Manor Avenue
Miller Avenue
Primary School
Valewood Primary School
Surgery
Far Moss Road
Briarwood
Dowhills Road
Dowhills Dr
Dowhills Pk
Ward Road
Richard Road
Burbo Bank Road North
Margaret Rd
Ingle Green
Warren Road
Waterloo FC
College Road North
Cambridge Road
Ennismore Road
Sherwood Road
Berwick Dr
Bonnington Av
Berkeley Rd
Cambridge Dr
Ince Av
Cambridge Av
Crescent Road
Merrilocks Road
Linville Avenue
Osbert Road
Holyrood
Park Drive
The Serpentine
St Anthony's Road
Eshe Road North
Linden Avenue
Elton Av
Victoria Av
Victoria Rd W
Kings Rd
Vermont Av
Vermont Rd
Kinyard Rd
Streatham House School
Alexandra Road
York Av
Princes Av
Merchant Taylors School for Girls
Ashbourne Av
Byron Road
Blundellsands & Crosby Station
Blundellsands
Bronte Cl
Nicholas Rd
Burbo Cl
Devon Cl
Channel Rd
Cheyne Cl
Bank Road
Ramleh Pk
The Mount-St Marys Prep Sch
Ursuline RC Prim Sch
Blundellsands Rd W
St Nicholas CE Prim School
Surgery
The Knowle
Agnes Road
Weld Rd
Abbotsford
Kenilworth Rd
Ivanhoe Rd
Waverley Rd
Eshe Rd
College Rd
Atherton House School
Regent Rd
Coronation Road
Coronation Drive
Kingswood
Woodville Av
Brookfield Av
Lancaster Av
Myers Ro
Mersey Road
Rossett Road
Marine FC
Jubilee Road
Sunnyside Road
Crosender Rd
Abbotsford Gardens
Brompton Av
Warwick Av
Harlech Rd
Cavendish Rd
Bridge Rd
Brighton le Sands
Riverslea Rd
Devonshire Rd
Somerset Rd
Pinehurst Avenue
Rosebery Av
Mersey View
Winchester Av
Canterbury Av
Lichfield Av
Shrewsbury Av
Brooke Road East
Park View
Waterloo
Warren House Rd
Holden Road
Leopold Road
Sudbury Rd
Hastings Rd
Green La
Ensleigh Road
Road West
Crosby Baths
Sefton
1 grid square represents 500 metres

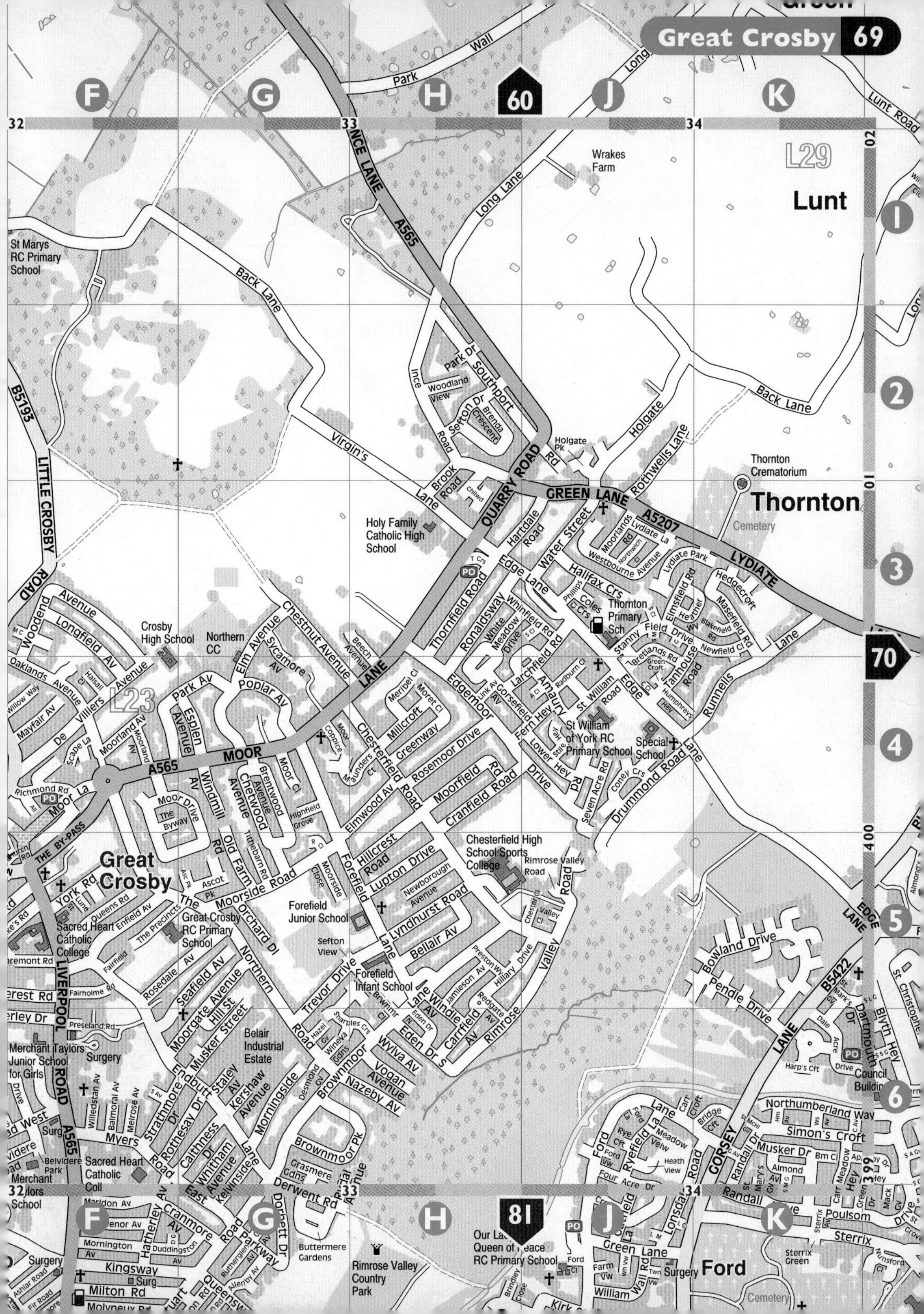
Great Crosby
Lunt
Thornton
Ford
L29
L23
Wrakes Farm
St Marys RC Primary School
Thornton Crematorium
Cemetery
Holy Family Catholic High School
Crosby High School
Northern CC
Thornton Primary Sch
St William of York RC Primary School
Special School
Chesterfield High School Sports College
Forefield Junior School
Forefield Infant School
Great Crosby RC Primary School
Sacred Heart Catholic College
Merchant Taylors Junior School for Girls
Belair Industrial Estate
Sacred Heart Catholic Coll
Merchant Taylors School
Rimrose Valley Country Park
Our Lady Queen of Peace RC Primary School
Buttermere Gardens
Council Building
Sterrix Green
Surgery
Park Wall
Long Lane
Lunt Road
Ince Lane
A565
Back Lane
Virgin's Lane
Southport Rd
Quarry Road
Green Lane
A5207
Lydiate Lane
Holgate
Rothwells Lane
Water Street
Edge Lane
Moor Lane
Little Crosby Road
B5193
The By-Pass
Liverpool Road
Moorside Road
Chesterfield Road
Rimrose Valley Road
Northern Rd
Gorsey Lane
B5422
Bowland Drive
Pendle Drive
Northumberland Way
Simon's Croft
Musker Dr
Sterrix Lane
Kingsway
Milton Rd
60
70
81
F
G
H
J
K
32
33
34
1
2
3
4
5
6
02
01
400
399

70
61
69
82
A
B
C
D
E
335
36
Sefton
Netherton
Buckley Hill
BRIDGES LANE
BRICKWALL LANE
SEFTON LANE
NORTHERN PERIMETER ROAD
DUNNINGS BR RD
Lunt Road
Sefton Lane Industrial Estate
St Ambrose Barlow Catholic Coll
St Benedicts RC Primary Sch
Grange Primary Sch
Bootle High School
Netherton Moss Primary School
Holy Spirit RC Primary School
St Oswalds CE Primary School
Odeon Cinema
Megabowl
Wakefield Industrial Estate
Bechers Business Centre
Premier Travel Inn
Council Building
Surgery
Trans Pennine Trail
Our Lady of Walsingham RC Junior Sch
Our Lady of Walsingham RC Infant Sch
L30
1 grid square represents 500 metres

MAGHULL
Melling
Waddicar
Aintree
M58
M57
A59
NORTHWAY
A5147
DAMFIELD LA
LIVERPOOL ROAD SOUTH
Deyes High School
St Andrews Maghull CE Prim Sch
Maricourt Catholic High School
Town Hall
Council Building
Maghull High School
St Georges RC Primary School
Summerhill Primary School
Maghull Station
Hudson Primary School
Wood Hall Farm
Junction 7
Superstore
Holy Rosary RC Junior School
Holy Rosary RC Primary School
Aintree Davenhill Primary School
Racecourse Retail Park
Moorfield House
Hall Lane
Station Road
Poverty Lane
Melling Lane
Leatherbarrows Lane
Weavers Lane
Rock Lane
Tithebarn Lane
Sandy Lane
Brewery Lane
Spencer's Lane
Moss Nook Lane
Waddicar La
Liddell Av
Station Rd
Moorhey Road
Dover Road
Church Road
Grosvenor Road
Bradfield Avenue
Sedbergh Avenue
Altway
Winchester Av
Harrow Drive
Sandhurst Dr
Works

62
72
83

72
Junction 1
63
71
84
Melling Mount
Tower Hill
Westvale
Sefton
Knowsley
PRESCOT ROAD
BANK LANE
COUNTY ROAD
A506
A5208
Whitegates Farm
Lyon's Farm
Moorfield House
Melling House
Saints Peter & Paul Catholic Sch
Tower Hill Health Centre
Ravenscroft Primary School
Eastcroft Park CP School
Knowsley Northern Prim Support Cen
Overdale Primary School
Melling Primary School
Millbrook Primary School
Kirkby CE Prim Sch
Ruffwood School
Simonswood Primary School
Kirkby Station
Council Building
Police Station
1 grid square represents 500 metres

64
74
85
Hall Lane
Grayson's Farm
Stopgate Lane
Simonswood Industrial Park
Pingwood Lane
Headbolt Lane
Dale Lane
Spencer's House
Urban Farm
North Perimeter Road
Works
Depot Road
North Mersey Business Centre
Woodward Road
Moss End Way
L33
Knowsley Industrial Park
Bradman Road
Hammond Road
Marl Road
Ashcroft Road
Woodlands Works
Courtyard Works
Lodge Works
Perimeter Road
Boundary Lane
Lancashire County
Knowsley
Northwood
Moss Lane
Quarryside Drive
Simonswood Lane
Roughwood Drive
Lapford Crescent
Pentland Road
Shacklady Road
Warrenhouse Road
Trecastle Rd
Jarrett Road
Kenbury Road
Glisecroft Avenue
Watts Close
Changford
Wingate Medical Centre
Quernmore Road
St Marie RC Prim Sch
Bigdale Medical Cen
Birbeck Road
Clorain Road
Darmond Road
Sanderling Road
Hardeston Road
Colwall Road
Mintor Road
Wyllin Road
Ormonde Crescent
Lees Road
Birchill Road
Stockpit
Draw Well Road
Kirkby Bank
Frecketon Dr
Dorchester Dr
Crofters La
Carr's Way
Brompton Av
Anders
Sinead

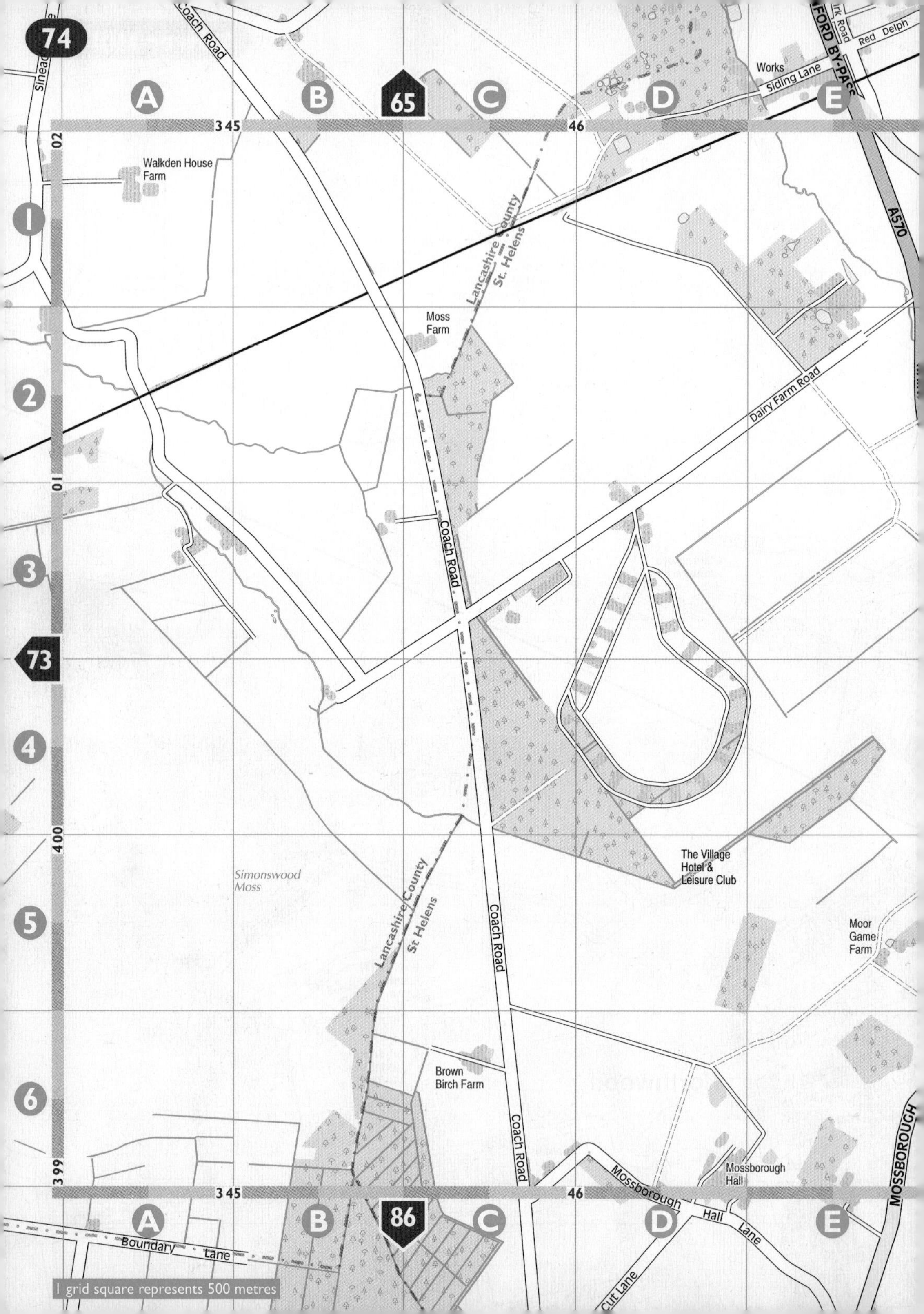

65
A
B
C
D
E
3 45
46
02
01
400
399
1
2
3
4
5
6
73
86
Walkden House Farm
Coach Road
Moss Farm
Lancashire County
St. Helens
Dairy Farm Road
Works
Siding Lane
Red Delph
FORD BY-PASS
A570
The Village Hotel & Leisure Club
Simonswood Moss
Lancashire County
St Helens
Moor Game Farm
Brown Birch Farm
Mossborough Hall
Mossborough Hall Lane
MOSSBOROUGH
Boundary Lane
Cut Lane
1 grid square represents 500 metres

RAINFORD
ORMSKIRK ROAD
RAINFORD BY-PASS
CROSS PIT LANE
CHURCH ROAD
MOSSBOROUGH ROAD
HIGHER LANE
B5203
B5205
A570
Old Lane
Higher Lane
Reeds Brow
Hyde's Brow
Henderson Drive
News Lane
Knowsley View
Junction Road
Randle Avenue
Dairy Farm Rd
Tudor Close
Randle Brook Court
Lords Fold
Works
Beech Gardens
Eden Avenue
Stanley Avenue
Harrison Drive
Helen Bank Dr
Graysons Road
Brook Lodge Primary School
Rainford High Technology College
Rufford Road
Witton Way
Scarisbrick Road
Lathom Drive
Duxbury Close
Standish Drive
Garswood Av
Parklands
Corpus Christi Catholic Prim Sch
Pine Dale
Fern Bank
Victoria St
Arnian Road
Arnian Way
Croxteth Drive
The Spinney
Muncaster Drive
Old Hall Gdns
Heyes Avenue
Heyes Grove
Sandon Grove
Rainford Health Centre
Rainford CE Prim Sch
Brookside Avenue
Central Dr
Beech Gardens
Ash Grove
Lime Gv
The Avenue
Leyland Road
Pilkington Street
Lakeside Gdns
Lakeside Court
Massam Cl
Eagle Crescent
Rookery Drive
Finch Av
Heron Gv
Council Building
Medical Centre
Parson's Brow
Moss Nook Lane
Inglenook Farm
Southern's Lane
Holly Crs
Derby Drive
Church Lane
All Saints Ct
Thickwood Moss Lane
Festival Road
Walmesley Drive
Carter Avenue
Green Lane
Rookery Lane
Rose Place
Rose Drive
Hopwood Crescent
Wellfield
Church Rd
Diamond Business Park
Hazel Business Park
Sandwash Close
Mill Lane
Fire Clay Farm
Holiday Moss
Pasture Lane
Rainford Industrial Estate
Millbrook Business Centre
Reed's Farm
Reed's Lane
Reed's Moss
WA11
Hill Top House
Berrington's
Langwood
66
76
87
F G H J K
47 48 49
1 2 3 4 5 6
02 01 400 399

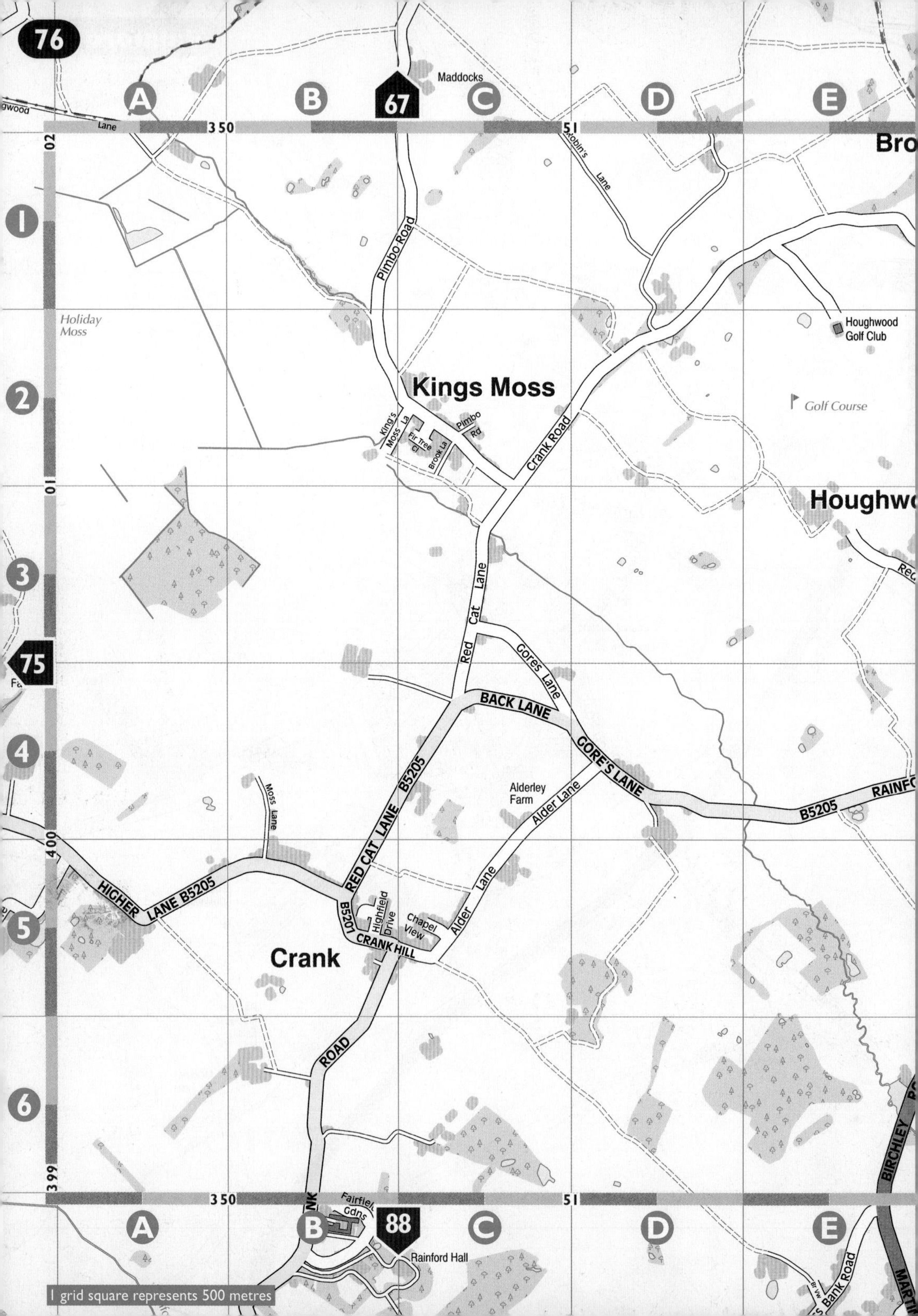
76
67
75
88
Maddocks
A
B
C
D
E
350
51
02
01
400
399
1
2
3
4
5
6
Lane
Robin's Lane
Bro
Holiday Moss
Pimbo Road
Kings Moss
King's Moss La
Fir Tree Cl
Brook La
Pimbo Rd
Crank Road
Houghwood Golf Club
Golf Course
Houghwo
Red Cat Lane
Gores Lane
BACK LANE
GORE'S LANE
B5205
RAINFO
Alderley Farm
Alder Lane
Moss Lane
RED CAT LANE B5205
HIGHER LANE B5205
B5201
Highfield Drive
Chapel View
CRANK HILL
Crank
ROAD
BIRCHLEY
Fairfield Gdns
Rainford Hall
Bank Road
1 grid square represents 500 metres

BILLINGE
Chadwick Green
Simm's La
End
wnlow
ood
WIGAN ROAD
MAIN STREET
NEWTON ROAD
BIRCHLEY ROAD
A571
B5207
B5206
Park Road
Beacon Road
Oakley Av
Coultshead Av
St Aidan's Cl
Garswood Road
Carr Mill Road
Barn Road
Roby Well Wy
Hillside Cl
Holt Crs
Holt Avenue
Delph Meadow Gdns
St Mary's Avenue
Birchley St Marys RC Prim School
Trent Road
Avon Road
Severn Close
Abbotts Way
Clifton Road
Ellis Road
Greenfield View
Nugent House School
Billinge Chapel End Primary School
Billinge Clinic
Council Building
St Aidans CE Prim Sch
Health Cen
Maddox Farm
Blackley Hurst Hall
Greenfield House
Works
Arch Lane
Lime Vale Road
Linden Grove
Ribble Crs
Douglas Avenue
Powell Drive
Brown Heath Avenue
Dean Close
Startham Avenue
Wigan
St. Helens
Ash Gv
Stuart Crs
Maple Cl
Larch Close
Elm Drive
Gorsey Brow
Sefton Fold Dr
Rainford Rd
Ashfield Crs
Standish Av
Lostock Cl
Cerrard Rd
Mitchell Rd
Goyt Hey Av
Brookside Cl
Danesbury Close
Blackleyhurst Av
Windsor Road
Royden Road
Conway Crs
Conway Dr
Claremont Rd
London Flds
Pingot Rd
School Brow
School Dr
Andrew Av
Greenhill Crs
Garswood Crescent
Coronation Walk
Lilac Grove
Longshaw Common
Hunters Cha
Paignton Cl
Longshaw Avenue
Cob Moor Rd
Wordsworth Av
Milton Gv
Trevelyan Dr
Brownlow La
Birchley Avenue
F G H J K
52 53 54
I 2 3 4 5 6
02 01 400 399
78
89

A
B
C
D
E
355
56
Premier Travel Inn
Cranberry Ley Farm
M6
Ashton Road
Works
Brocstedes Road
Drummer's Lane
Junction 25
Winstanley Road
Brocstedes Farm
Our Lady Immaculate Catholic Primary School
DOWNALL GREEN ROAD
Bryn
Booth's Brow Rd
Brocstedes Av
Coronation St
Leyland Green Road
Rectory CE Primary School
Garswood United FC
Downall Green
BILLINGE ROAD
Simm's Lane End
B5207
WN4
Stirling Drive
Thornhill Road
Smock Lane
Garswood Road
Spindle Hillock
Gordon Avenue
Austin Avenue
Low Bank Road
Victoria Road
Hamilton
Garswood Prim Sch
Hillbeck Crescent
Abinger Road
Station Rd
Old Colliery Yard
Surgery
Strange Road
Camp Road
Garswood Station
Gibbon's Road
Garswood
Park Industrial Estate
Junction 24
Tatton Drive
Sefton Road
Clifton Rd
Grange Road
Richmond Rd
Clough Grove
Chantry Wk
Sougher's Lane
Dryden Avenue
Chimes Rd
A49
Works
A58
1 grid square represents 500 metres

77
90

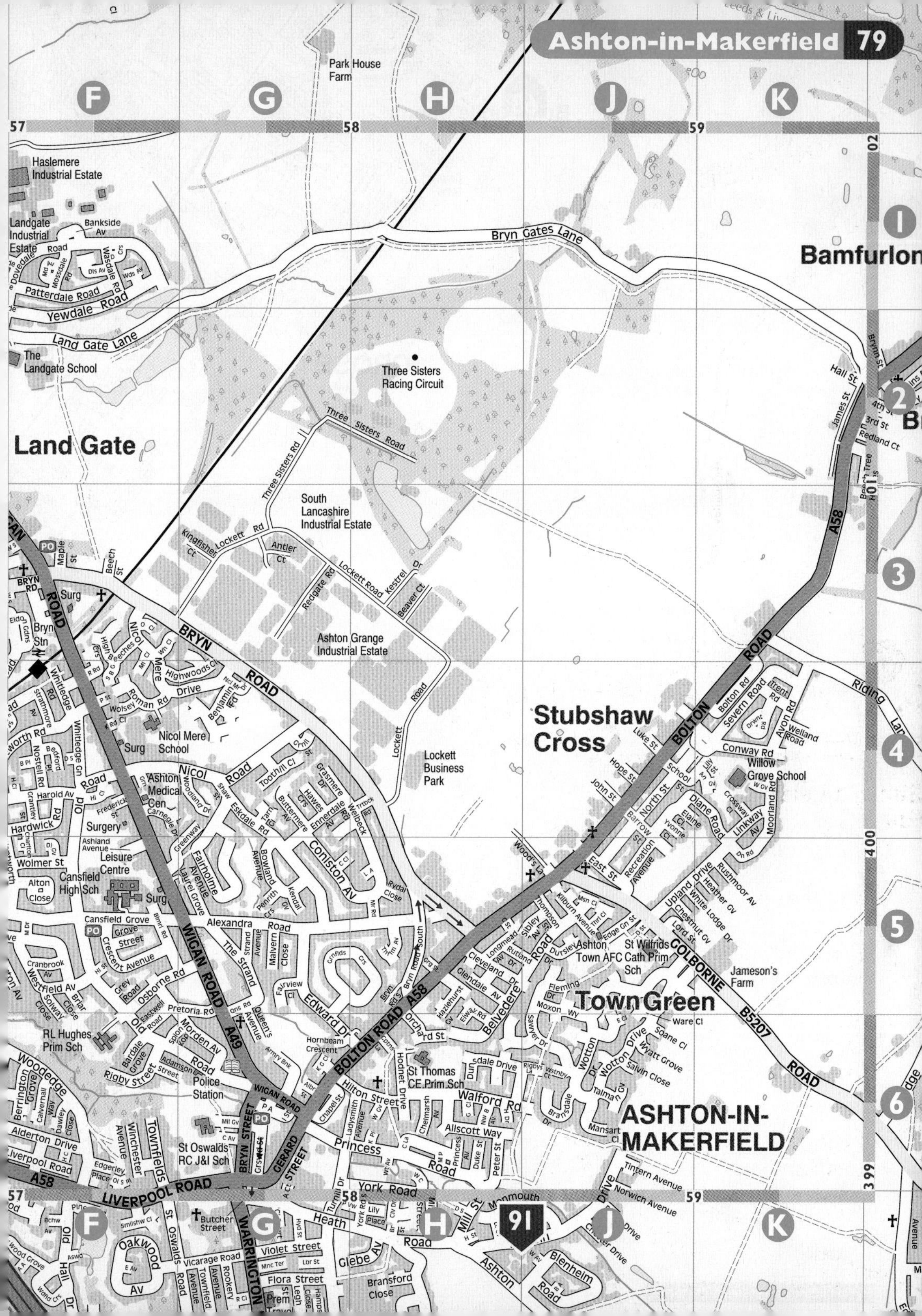

Park House Farm
Haslemere Industrial Estate
Landgate Industrial Estate
Bankside Av
Bryn Gates Lane
Bamfurlong
Patterdale Road
Yewdale Road
Land Gate Lane
The Landgate School
Three Sisters Racing Circuit
Three Sisters Road
Three Sisters Rd
Land Gate
South Lancashire Industrial Estate
Lockett Rd
Kingfisher Ct
Antler Ct
Lockett Road
Kestrel Dr
Beaver Ct
Redgate Rd
Ashton Grange Industrial Estate
Lockett Road
Lockett Business Park
BRYN ROAD
WIGAN ROAD
Bryn Stn
Nicol Mere School
Nicol Road
Stubshaw Cross
BOLTON ROAD
A58
Riding Lane
Willow Grove School
Conway Rd
Severn Road
Bolton Rd
Trent Rd
Avon Rd
Welland Road
Ashton Medical Cen
Surgery
Leisure Centre
Cansfield High Sch
Coniston Av
Alexandra Road
The Strand
Edward Dr
Bryn Road South
COLBORNE ROAD
B5207
Jameson's Farm
St Wilfrids Cath Prim Sch
Ashton Town AFC
Town Green
ASHTON-IN-MAKERFIELD
RL Hughes Prim Sch
Police Station
St Thomas CE Prim Sch
St Oswalds RC J&I Sch
LIVERPOOL ROAD
GERARD STREET
BRYN STREET
WARRINGTON
Princess Road
York Road
Heath Road
Tintern Avenue
Norwich Avenue
Oakwood Av
Butcher Street
Violet Street
Vicarage Road
Flora Street
Glebe Av
Bransford Close
Blenheim Road
Ashton
91
F G H J K
57 58 59

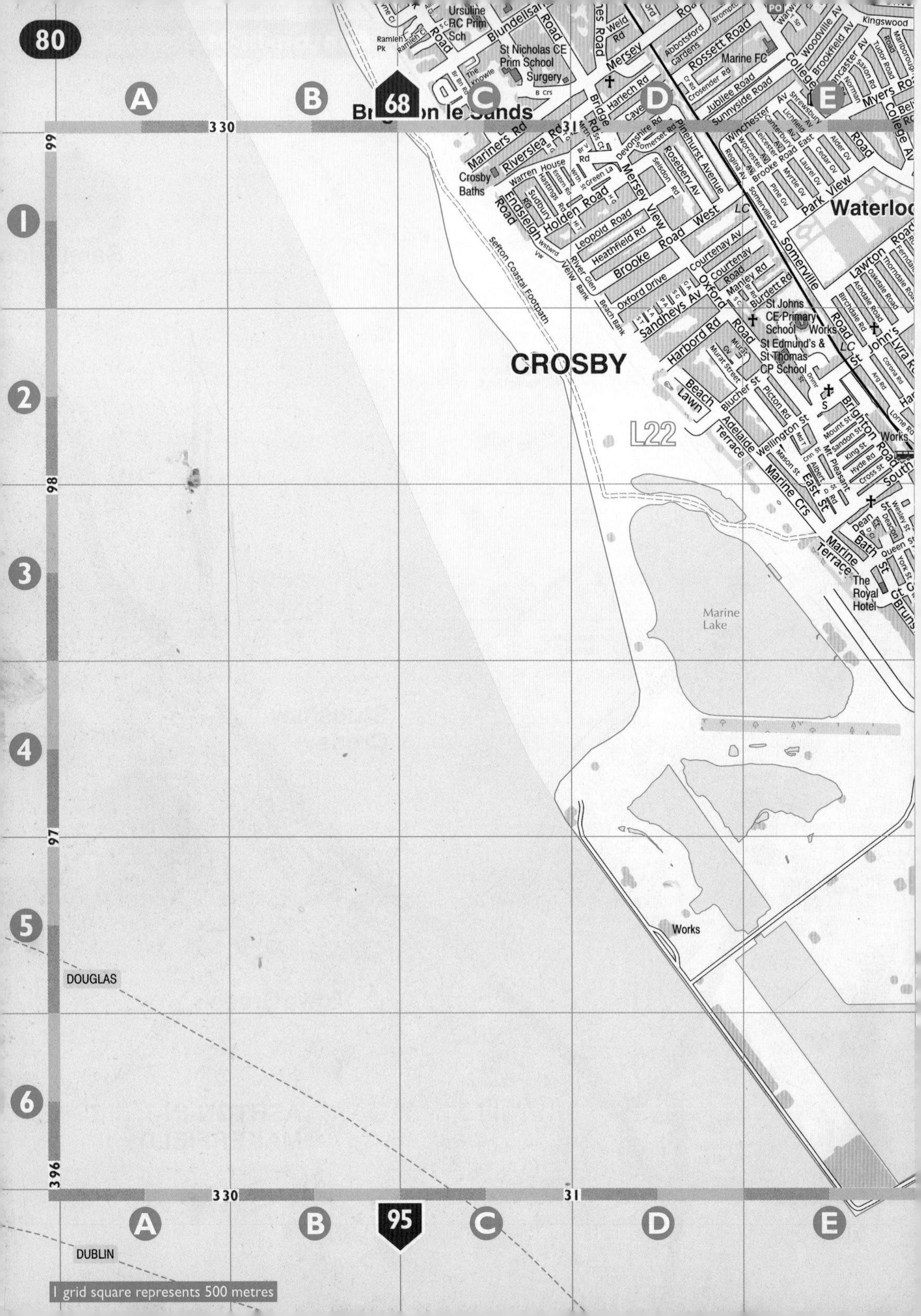
68
A
B
C
D
E
330
31
99
98
97
396
1
2
3
4
5
6
Ursuline RC Prim Sch
Ramleh Pk
St Nicholas CE Prim School
Surgery
Blundellsands Road
Mersey Road
Weld Rd
Abbotsford Gardens
Rossett Road
Marine FC
Jubilee Road
Sunnyside Road
College Road
Woodville Av
Brookfield Av
Kingswood
Myers Road
Harlech Rd
Bridge Rd
Mariners Rd
Riverslea Rd
Crosby Baths
Warren House
Devonshire Rd
Somerset Rd
Pinehurst Avenue
Rosebery Av
Winchester Av
Worcester Av
Leicester Av
Canterbury Av
Brooke Road East
Park View
Waterloo
Endsleigh Road
Sudbury Rd
Hastings Rd
Holden Road
Mersey View
Leopold Road
Heathfield Rd
Brooke Road West
Courtenay Av
Courtenay Road
Somerville Road
Sefton Coastal Footpath
River Glen
View Bank
Oxford Drive
Oxford Road
Manley Rd
Burdett Rd
Sandheys Av
Beach Bank
St Johns CE Primary School
Works
St Edmund's & St Thomas CP School
St John's Road
Lyra Rd
Harbord Rd
Murat Street
CROSBY
Beach Lawn
Blucher St
Picton Rd
L22
Adelaide Terrace
Wellington St
Mason St
Albert Rd
Mt Pleasant
Brighton Road
Marine Crs
East St
Works
Dean Ct
Bath St
Marine Terrace
The Royal Hotel
Marine Lake
Works
DOUGLAS
95
DUBLIN
1 grid square represents 500 metres

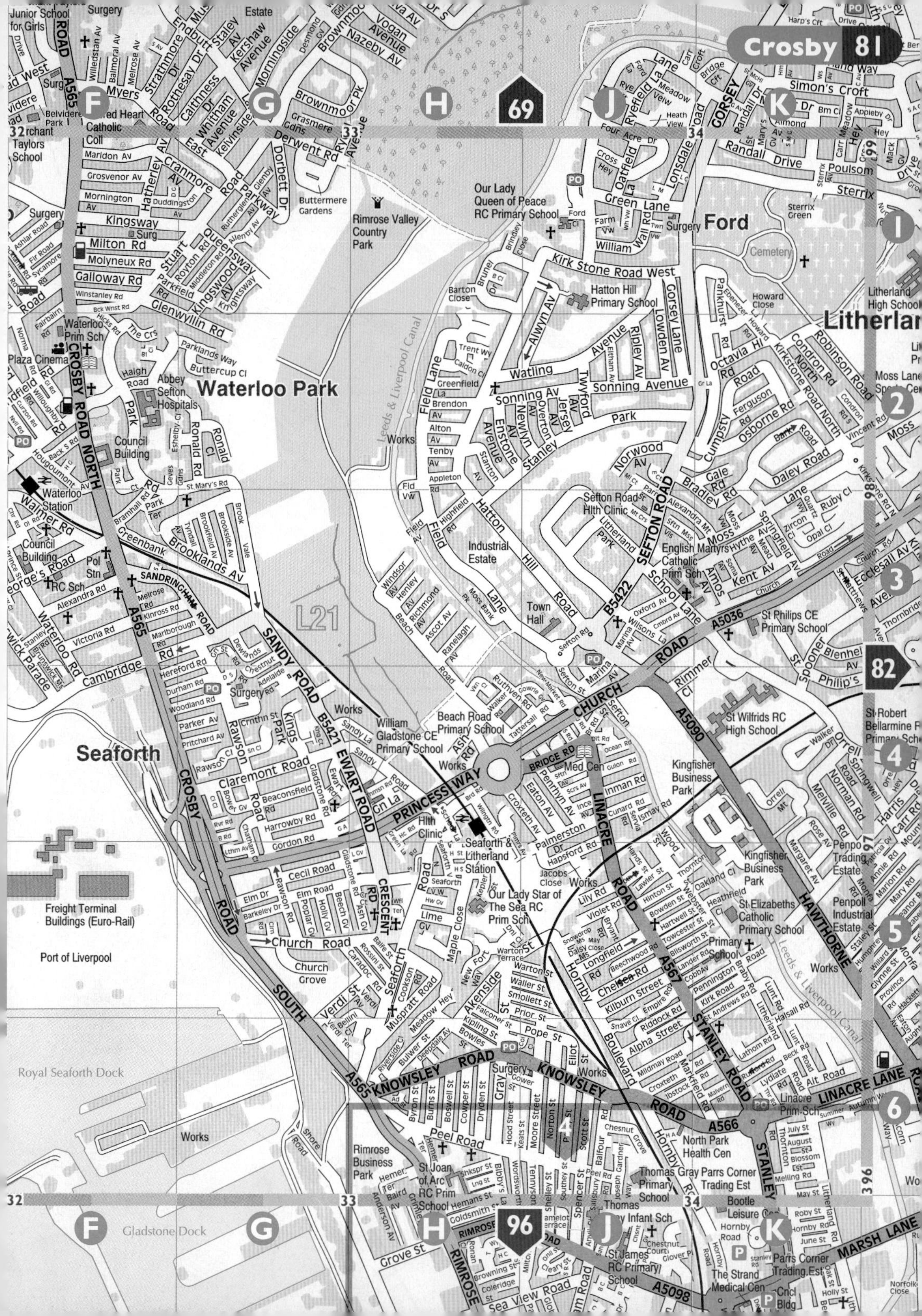
69
82
96
F
G
H
J
K
I
2
3
4
5
6
32
33
34
396
397
398
399
Junior School for Girls
Surgery
Estate
Sacred Heart Catholic Coll
Merchant Taylors School
Marldon Av
Grosvenor Av
Mornington Av
Kingsway
Milton Rd
Molyneux Rd
Galloway Rd
Winstanley Rd
Glenwyllin Rd
Waterloo Prim Sch
Plaza Cinema
CROSBY ROAD NORTH
A565
Myers Rd
Strathmore Dr
Rothesay Dr
Caithness Dr
Whitham Avenue
Kelvinside
Morningside
Kershaw Avenue
Staley Av
Endbutt La
Brownmoor Pk
Brownmoor La
Nazeby Av
Vogan Avenue
Grasmere Gdns
Derwent Rd
Rydal Avenue
Dorbett Dr
Buttermere Gardens
Hatherley Av
Cranmore Av
Duddingston Av
Road
Parkway
Queensway
Stuart Rd
Royton Rd
Middleton Rd
Kingswood Av
Knightsway
Parkfield Rd
The Crs
Parklands Way
Buttercup Cl
Haigh Road
Abbey Sefton Hospitals
Waterloo Park
Rimrose Valley Country Park
Council Building
Ronald Rd
Ronald Cl
St Mary's Rd
Park Ter
Waterloo Station
Walmer Rd
Council Building
Pol Stn
RC Sch
Alexandra Rd
Victoria Rd
Waterloo Rd
Brunswick Parade
Greenbank
Brooklands Av
Brookfield Av
Brookside Av
Tyndal Av
Brook Vale
SANDRINGHAM ROAD
Melrose Rd
Kinross Rd
Marlborough Rd
Cambridge Rd
Hereford Rd
Durham Rd
Woodland Rd
Parker Av
Pritchard Av
Surgery
Seaforth
CROSBY ROAD SOUTH
Rawson Rd
Rawson Cl
Claremont Road
Beaconsfield Rd
Harrowby Rd
Gordon Rd
Kings Park
SANDY ROAD
B5421 EWART ROAD
Gladstone Rd
Works
William Gladstone CE Primary School
L21
Cecil Road
Elm Dr
Elm Road
Barkeley Dr
Poplar Gv
Holly Gv
Beech Gv
Ash Gv
Church Road
Church Grove
CRESCENT RD
Seaforth Road
Lime Gv
Maple Close
Caradoc Rd
Rossini St
Verdi St
Verdi Av
Bellini Cl
Verdi Ter
Cookson Rd
Muspratt Road
Meadow Hey
Freight Terminal Buildings (Euro-Rail)
Port of Liverpool
Royal Seaforth Dock
Gladstone Dock
Works
Shore Road
Leeds & Liverpool Canal
Our Lady Queen of Peace RC Primary School
Ford
Green Lane
William Wall Rd
Surgery
Cemetery
Sterrix Green
Sterrix Lane
Poulsom Dr
Randall Drive
Simon's Croft
Harp's Cft
Four Acre Dr
Ryefield La
Meadow View
Heath View
Lonsdale Road
Oatfield La
Cross Hey
Corsey Road
Kirk Stone Road West
Hatton Hill Primary School
Barton Close
Brunel Dr
Brindley Close
Alwyn Av
Trent Wy
Caldon Cl
Field Lane
Greenfield La
Brendon Av
Alton Av
Tenby Av
Appleton Rd
Fld Vw
Field Av
Highfield Rd
Watling Avenue
Sonning Av
Sonning Avenue
Newlyn Av
Jersey Av
Overton Av
Twyford Av
Ripley Av
Lowden Av
Corsey Lane
Enstone Avenue
Stanton Av
Stanley Park
Works
Industrial Estate
Hatton Hill Road
Town Hall
Windsor Av
Henley Av
Richmond Av
Ascot Av
Ranelagh Av
Beach Road
Moss Bank Pk
Lane
Sefton Road Hlth Clinic
SEFTON ROAD
B5422
Litherland Park
English Martyrs Catholic Prim Sch
Norwood Av
Gale Rd
Bradley Rd
Alexandra Mt
Moss Lane
Springfield Av
Kent Av
Amos Av
School Lane
Oxford Av
Wilsons La
Marina Av
Sefton Rd
Sefton St
Howard Close
Litherland High School
Litherland
Pankhurst Rd
Octavia Hl
Cumpsty Road
Ferguson Rd
Osborne Rd
Condron Rd North
Kirkstone Road North
Robinson Road
Moss Lane
Daley Road
Barkbeth Road
Ruby Cl
Zircon Cl
Opal Cl
Ecclesall Av
St Philips CE Primary School
A5036
CHURCH ROAD
Rimmer Cl
Spooner Av
Blennel Av
Philip's
St Robert Bellarmine Primary Sch
St Wilfrids RC High School
A5090
HAWTHORNE
Orrell Hey
Springwell
Norman Rd
Melville Rd
Rose Av
Margaret Av
Penpol Trading Estate
Penpol Industrial Estate
Harris
Carr Rd
Annie Rd
Marion Rd
Mary Rd
Staley St
Humphrey
Glynne St
Province
Kingfisher Business Park
Ruthven Rd
Walker Rd
Tattersall Rd
Beach Road Primary School
Ash Rd
Works
PRINCESS WAY
BRIDGE RD
Med Cen
Ocean Rd
Gulon Rd
Inman Rd
Cunard Rd
Ismay Rd
Penrhyn Av
Eaton Av
Croxteth Av
Palmerston Dr
Hapsford Rd
LINACRE ROAD
A567
Hlth Clinic
Seaforth & Litherland Station
Our Lady Star of The Sea RC Prim Sch
Jacobs Close
Works
Lily Rd
Violet Rd
Longfield Rd
Beechwood Rd
Chelsea Rd
Kilburn Street
Empire Rd
Riddock Rd
Alpha Street
Mildmay Road
Croxteth
Ibstock
Markfield Rd
Hornby Boulevard
Hinton St
Bowden St
Hartwell St
Towcester St
Ellsworth St
Lander Rd
Pennington Rd
Kirk Road
St Andrews Rd
Lathom Rd
Lunt Rd
Halsall Rd
Beck Rd
Lydiate Rd
Ait Road
Oakland Cl
Heathfield Cl
St Elizabeths Catholic Primary School
Primary School
Works
Warton Terrace
Warton St
Waller St
Smollett St
Prior St
Pope St
Eliot St
Akenside St
Falconer St
Kipling St
Bowles St
Surgery
Works
KNOWSLEY ROAD
A565
A566
Byron St
Burns St
Boswell St
Cowper St
Dryden St
Hood Street
Keats St
Moore Street
Norton St
Scott St
Peel Road
Rimrose Business Park
St Joan of Arc RC Prim School
Hemans St
Goldsmith St
Bibby's La
Wordsworth
Tennyson
Shelley St
Southey St
Spencer St
Balfour Rd
Chesnut Grove
Joseph Gardner
Thomas Gray Primary School
Thomas Gray Infant Sch
Parrs Corner Trading Est
North Park Health Cen
Hornby Rd
Linacre Prim Sch
LINACRE LANE
STANLEY ROAD
Bootle Leisure Cen
Hornby Road
July St
August St
Blossom St
Melling Rd
May St
Roby St
Hornby Rd
June St
MARSH LANE
Parrs Corner Trading Est
Holly St
Norfolk Close
The Strand Medical Cen
Cncl Bldg
St James RC Primary School
A5098
Chestnut Court
Glover Pl
Sea View Road
RIMROSE ROAD
Grove St
Anderson Av
Browning St
Coleridge St
Ronan

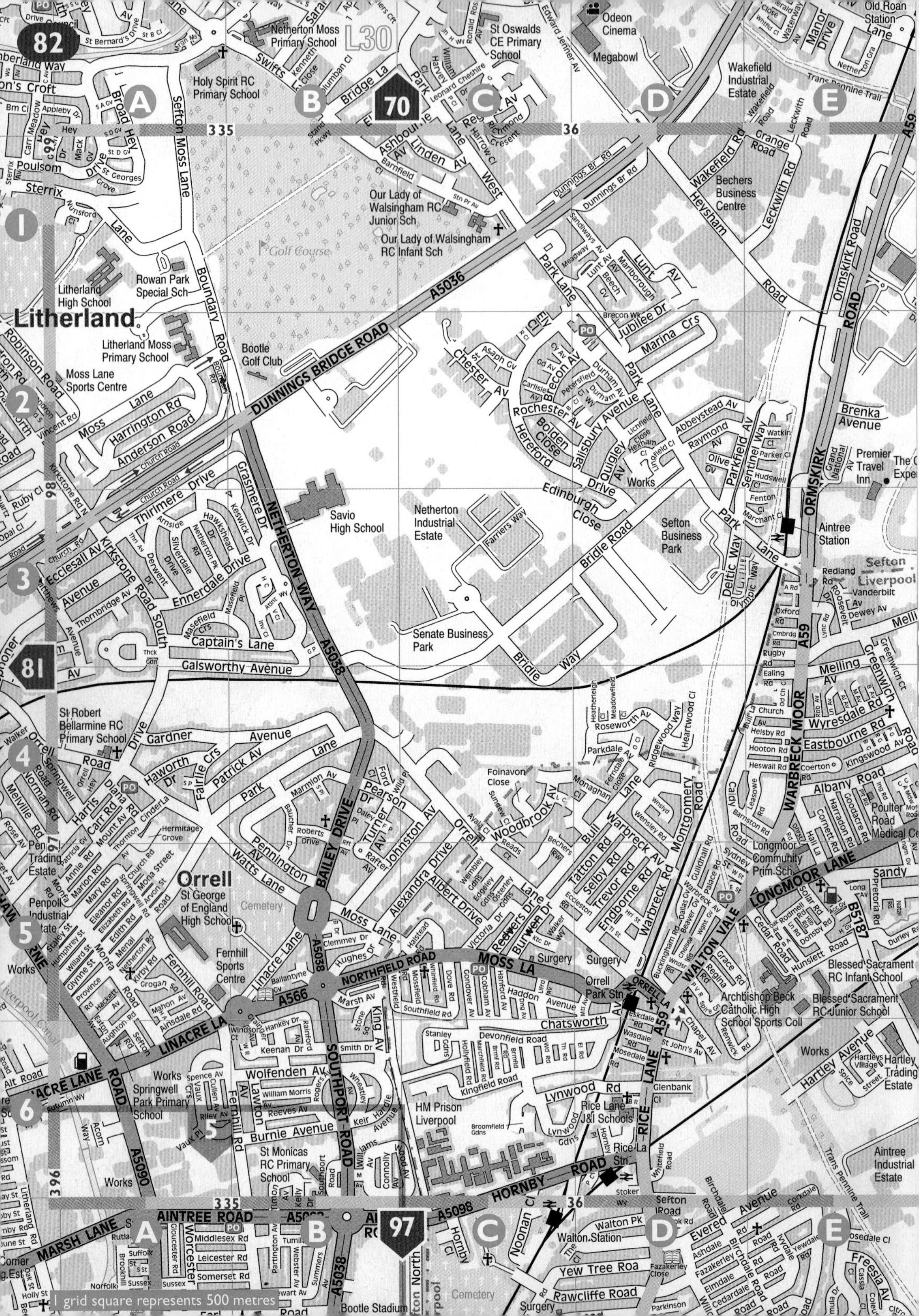

82
70
81
97
L30
A
B
C
D
E
1
2
3
4
5
6
335
36
98
97
396
Litherland
Orrell
Netherton Moss Primary School
Holy Spirit RC Primary School
St Oswalds CE Primary School
Odeon Cinema
Megabowl
Old Roan Station
Wakefield Industrial Estate
Becbers Business Centre
Our Lady of Walsingham RC Junior Sch
Our Lady of Walsingham RC Infant Sch
Golf Course
Litherland High School
Rowan Park Special Sch
Litherland Moss Primary School
Bootle Golf Club
Moss Lane Sports Centre
Savio High School
Netherton Industrial Estate
Sefton Business Park
Senate Business Park
Aintree Station
Premier Travel Inn
Sefton
Liverpool
St Robert Bellarmine RC Primary School
St George of England High School
Cemetery
Fernhill Sports Centre
Penpoll Industrial Estate
Works
Springwell Park Primary School
HM Prison Liverpool
St Monicas RC Primary School
Rice Lane J&I Schools
Longmoor Community Prim Sch
Archbishop Beck Catholic High School Sports Coll
Blessed Sacrament RC Infant School
Blessed Sacrament RC Junior School
Hartley Trading Estate
Aintree Industrial Estate
Orrell Park Stn
Rice La Stn
Walton Station
Bootle Stadium
Surgery
Trans Pennine Trail
Liverpool Canal
DUNNINGS BRIDGE ROAD
A5036
NETHERTON WAY
A5038
BAILEY DRIVE
SOUTHPORT ROAD
NORTHFIELD ROAD
MOSS LA
LINACRE LA
A566
LINACRE LANE
A5090
HORNBY ROAD
A5098
AINTREE ROAD
MARSH LANE
RICE LANE
A59
WALTON VALE
LONGMOOR LANE
B5187
WARBRECK MOOR
ORMSKIRK ROAD
Sefton Moss Lane
Boundary Road
Park Lane
Bridle Road
Bridle Way
Galsworthy Avenue
Captain's Lane
Moss Lane
Gardner Avenue
Watts Lane
Warbreck Av
Montgomery Road
Chatsworth Avenue
Hartley Avenue
Evered Avenue
Yew Tree Road
Rawcliffe Road
1 grid square represents 500 metres

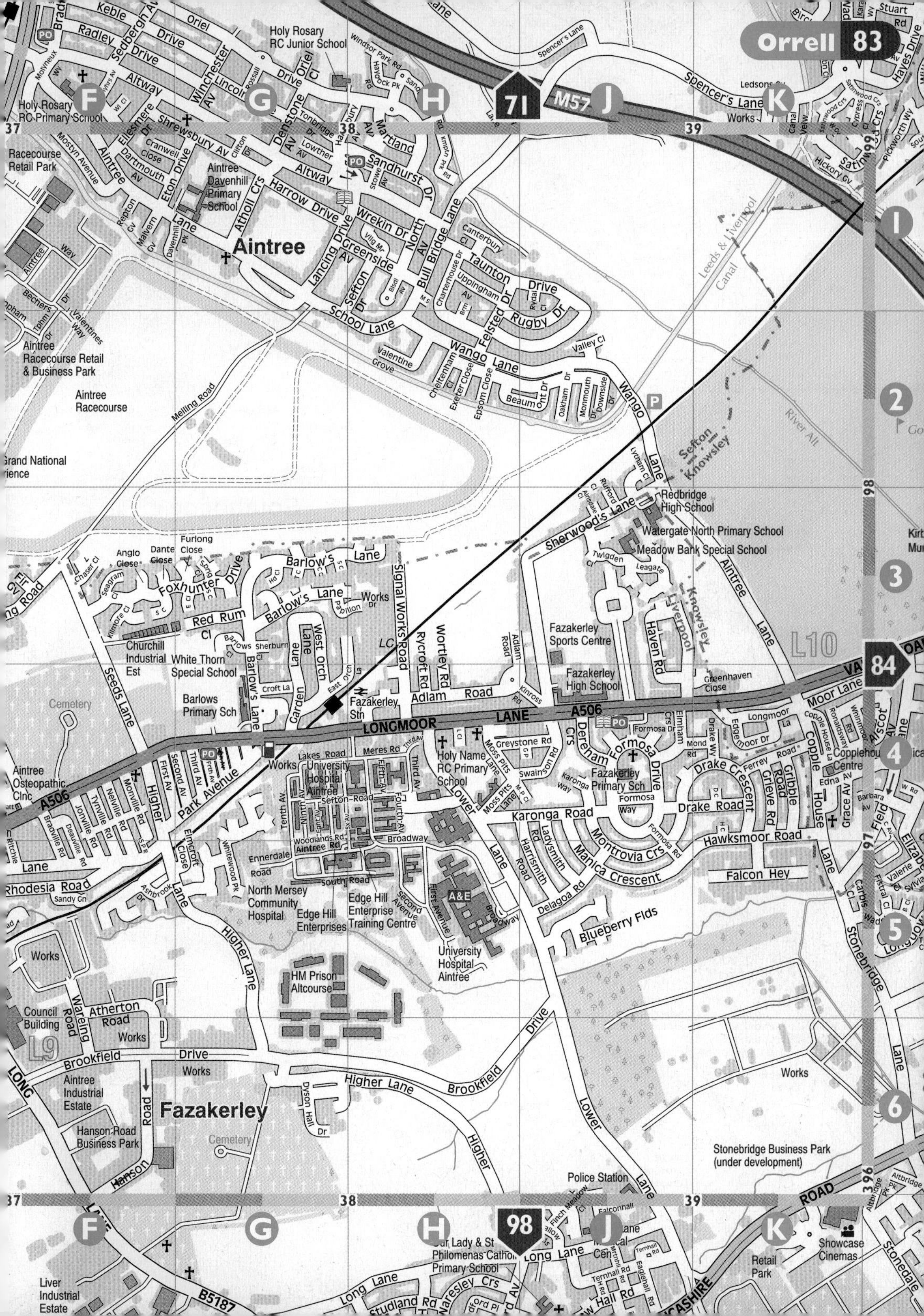

Orrell 83
71
84
98
Aintree
Fazakerley
L9
L10
Aintree Racecourse
Aintree Racecourse Retail & Business Park
Racecourse Retail Park
Grand National
Holy Rosary RC Junior School
Holy Rosary RC Primary School
Aintree Davenhill Primary School
Redbridge High School
Watergate North Primary School
Meadow Bank Special School
Fazakerley Sports Centre
Fazakerley High School
Churchill Industrial Est
White Thorn Special School
Barlows Primary Sch
Fazakerley Stn
Holy Name RC Primary School
Fazakerley Primary Sch
University Hospital Aintree
North Mersey Community Hospital
Edge Hill Enterprises
Edge Hill Enterprise Training Centre
HM Prison Altcourse
Aintree Osteopathic Clnc
Council Building
Aintree Industrial Estate
Hanson Road Business Park
Cemetery
Police Station
Stonebridge Business Park (under development)
Our Lady & St Philomenas Catholic Primary School
Showcase Cinemas
Retail Park
Liver Industrial Estate
Copplehouse Centre
Works
M57
A506
B5187
LONGMOOR LANE
Leeds & Liverpool Canal
River Alt
Sefton
Knowsley
Melling Road
Seeds Lane
Higher Lane
Lower Lane
Longmoor Lane
Aintree Lane
Wango Lane
School Lane
Bull Bridge Lane
Sherwood's Lane
Signal Works Road
Brookfield Drive
Stonebridge Lane
Hawksmoor Road
Falcon Hey
Blueberry Flds
Park Avenue
Rhodesia Road
Spencer's Lane
37
38
39
F
G
H
J
K
2
3
4
5
6
97
98
99
396

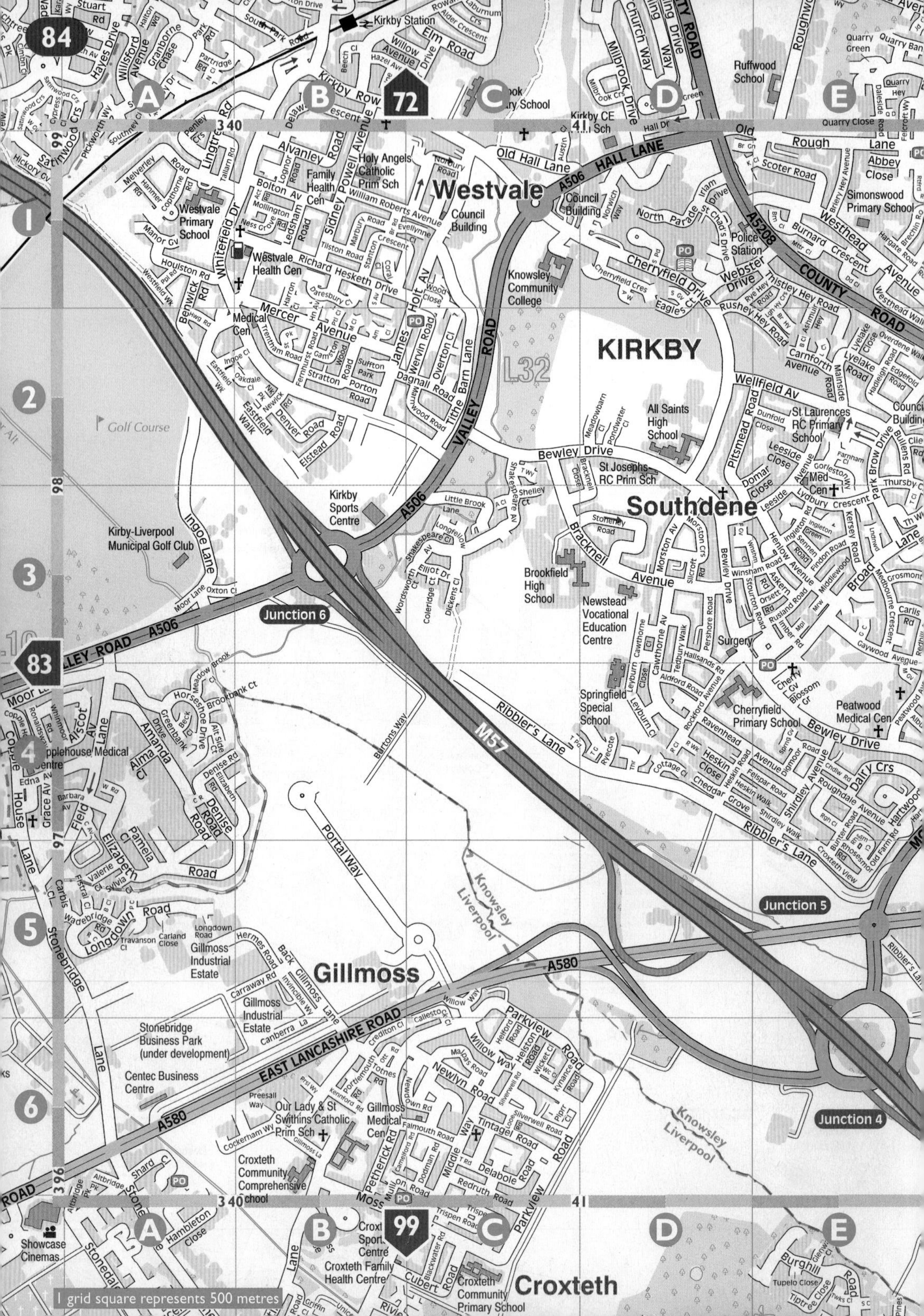
84
72
83
99
A
B
C
D
E
1
2
3
4
5
6
340
41
396
97
98
99
Kirkby Station
Westvale
KIRKBY
Southdene
Gillmoss
Croxteth
L32
Westvale Primary School
Westvale Health Cen
Holy Angels Catholic Prim Sch
Family Health Cen
Council Building
Knowsley Community College
Kirkby CE Sch
Ruffwood School
Simonswood Primary School
Police Station
All Saints High School
St Josephs RC Prim Sch
St Laurences RC Primary School
Brookfield High School
Newstead Vocational Education Centre
Springfield Special School
Cherryfield Primary School
Peatwood Medical Cen
Kirkby Sports Centre
Kirby-Liverpool Municipal Golf Club
Golf Course
Medical Cen
Surgery
Junction 6
Junction 5
Junction 4
M57
A506
A580
A5208
VALLEY ROAD
HALL LANE
COUNTY ROAD
EAST LANCASHIRE ROAD
Bewley Drive
Ribbler's Lane
Portal Way
Knowsley
Liverpool
Gillmoss Industrial Estate
Stonebridge Business Park (under development)
Centec Business Centre
Our Lady & St Swithins Catholic Prim Sch
Gillmoss Medical Cen
Croxteth Community Comprehensive School
Croxteth Sports Centre
Croxteth Family Health Centre
Croxteth Community Primary School
Showcase Cinemas
Applehouse Medical Centre
Parkview Road
Willow Way
Newlyn Road
Stonebridge Lane
Longdown Road
Denise Road
Elizabeth Road
Amanda Cl
Ingoe Lane
Whitefield Dr
Mercer Avenue
Richard Hesketh Drive
Sidney Powell Avenue
Cherryfield Drive
Bracknell Avenue
Westhead Avenue
Broad Lane
1 grid square represents 500 metres

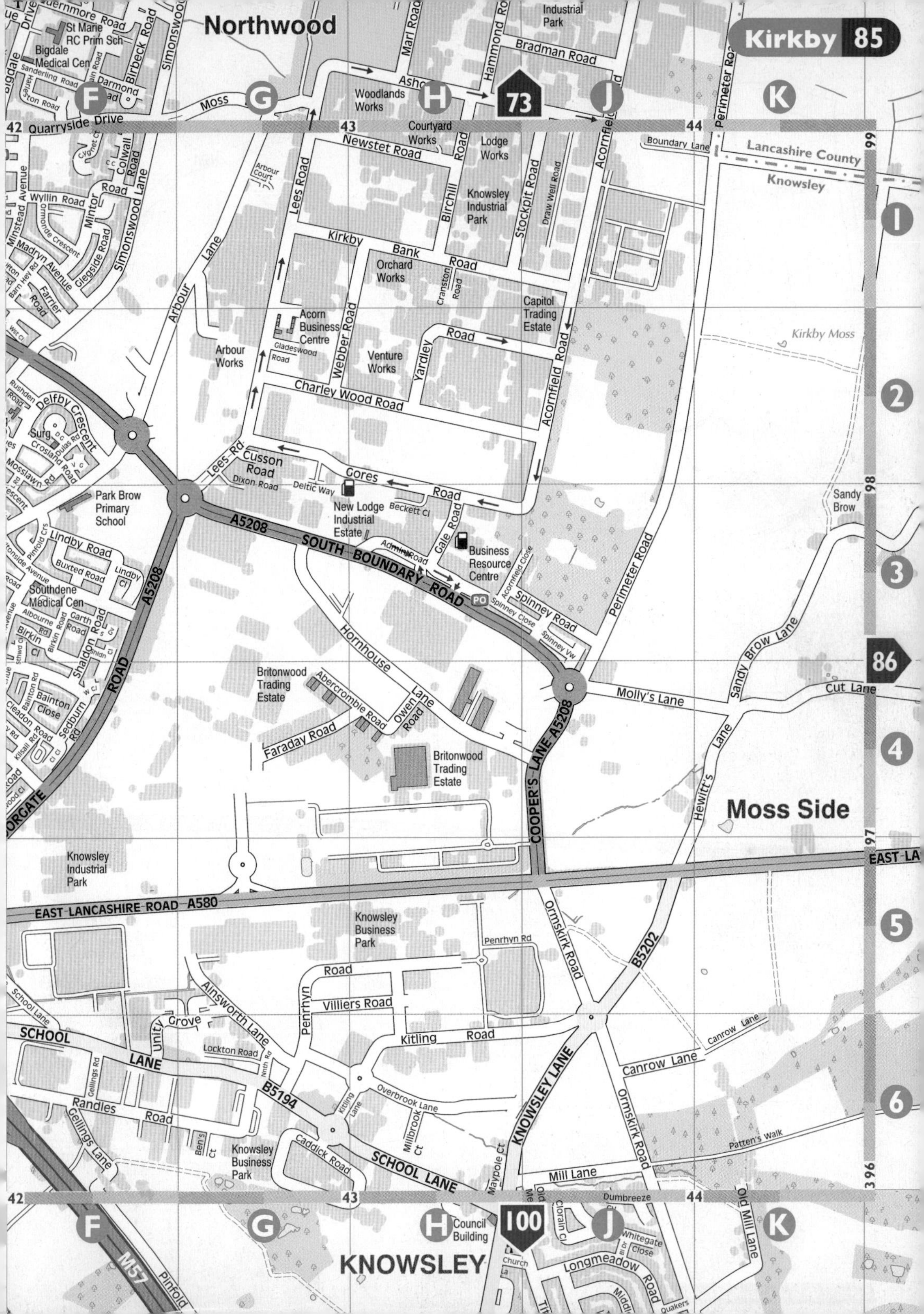
Northwood
Industrial Park
Bradman Road
Hammond Road
Marl Road
Woodlands Works
Courtyard Works
Lodge Works
Newstet Road
Lees Road
Birchill Road
Stockpit Road
Draw Well Road
Acornfield Road
Perimeter Road
Boundary Lane
Lancashire County
Knowsley
Knowsley Industrial Park
Kirkby Bank Road
Orchard Works
Cranston Road
Capitol Trading Estate
Acorn Business Centre
Gladeswood Road
Webber Road
Yardley Road
Venture Works
Arbour Works
Arbour Lane
Arbour Court
Charley Wood Road
Kirkby Moss
Cusson Road
Lees Rd
Dixon Road
Deltic Way
Gores Road
Beckett Cl
New Lodge Industrial Estate
Gale Road
Admin Road
Business Resource Centre
Acornfield Close
A5208
SOUTH BOUNDARY ROAD
Spinney Close
Spinney Road
Spinney Vw
Park Brow Primary School
Sandy Brow
Sandy Brow Lane
Cut Lane
Molly's Lane
Hornhouse Lane
Britonwood Trading Estate
Abercrombie Road
Owen Road
Faraday Road
COOPER'S LANE A5208
Hewitt's Lane
Moss Side
EAST LANCASHIRE ROAD A580
Knowsley Industrial Park
Knowsley Business Park
Penrhyn Rd
Penrhyn Road
Villiers Road
Kitling Road
Ainsworth Lane
Unity Grove
Lockton Road
SCHOOL LANE
B5194
B5202
Ormskirk Road
KNOWSLEY LANE
Canrow Lane
Overbrook Lane
Millbrook Ct
Kitling Lane
Caddick Road
Ben's Ct
Randles Road
Gellings Rd
Gellings Lane
School Lane
Patten's Walk
Mill Lane
Maypole Ct
Dumbreeze
Old Mill Lane
Council Building
Clorain Cl
Whitegate Close
Longmeadow Road
Church
KNOWSLEY
M57
Pinfold
Quarryside Drive
Moss
St Marie RC Prim Sch
Bigdale Medical Cen
Birbeck Road
Simonswood Lane
Darmond Road
Sanderling Road
Colwall Road
Mintor Road
Wyllin Road
Minstead Avenue
Ormonde Crescent
Madryn Avenue
Glegside Road
Farrier Road
Delfby Crescent
Surg
Crosland Road
Mosslawn Rd
Lindby Road
Buxted Road
Lindby Cl
Southdene Medical Cen
Albourne Rd
Birkin Cl
Garth Road
Shaldon Road
Bainton Close
Cleadon Road
Sedburn Rd
A5208
ROAD
Lancashire County
F G H J K
73
100
86
I 2 3 4 5 6
42 43 44
99 98 97 396
EAST LA

Brown
Birch Farm
74
A
B
C
D
E
3 45
46
Coach Road
Mossborough
Hall
Mossborough Hall Lane
MOSSBOROUGH
99
1
Boundary Lane
New Cut Lane
Coach Road
kby Moss
2
B5203
Blind
Foot Farm
98
Sandy
Brow
Red Cut Lane
3
Woodside
Farm
ROAD
FOOT
BLIND
85
Cut Lane
New Cut Lane
Cut Lane
Road
4
Coach
97
EAST LANCASHIRE ROAD A580
5
6
Patten's Walk
3 96
3 45
46
A
B
C
D
E
101
1 grid square represents 500 metres

Reed's Farm
Lane
Millbrook
RAINFORD BY-PASS
WA11
F
G
H
75
J
K
47
48
49
99
I
Reed's Moss
Lane
Hill Top House
St Helens Road
Hilltop Road
Berrington's Lane
2
Inglemoss Drive
Longwood Close
Inglewood Road
98
St Helens Rd
3
St Helens Road
RAINFORD ROAD A570
Moss Lane
Moss Lane
Liverpool St Helens RUFC
88
CRANK
Sadler's Lane
A580
EAST LANCASHIRE ROAD
4
A580
EAST LANCASHIRE ROAD
Houghton's Lane
B H Cl
Crantock Grove
Windle Farm
St Helens Crematorium
97
The Nook
Padstow Drive
Portreath Way
BLEAK HILL ROAD
Windle Grove
RAINFORD ROAD
Malt House Court
Way
Stuart Road
Lynton
Pentire Av
Fistral Drive
Calderhurst Drive
St Mawes Way
Windlebrook Crescent
Rutherford Road
Lawrence Road
Sackville Road
Dartmouth Dr
5
B5203
Catchdale Moss
B5201
Hamilton Road
Bleak Hill Primary School
Sidmouth Cl
Pr Andrew's Grove
Queens Drive
St George's Avenue
Eccleston
Ecclesfield Road
Carmelite Crescent
Nicholl Road
Sandfield Road
Oaktree Road
Eccleston Medical Centre
PO
Selkirk Drive
Melrose Av
Gunning Close
Fair Way
The Grove
Coronation Road
Regal Drive
Harrington Road
Rosebery
Dvns Rd
Kiln Lane
Green Lane
CATCHDALE MOSS LANE
Road
Walmesley
Osborne Road
Barrowfield Road
Gunning Avenue
Sidmouth Close
Brookside Avenue
Beaconsfield Rd
Fairfield Rd
Moorfield Road
6
Green Lane
Pike House Road
Lester Drive
Broadway
Davy Close
Ansdell Drive
MILLBROOK LANE
Kiln Lane
Smithy Heritage Centre
Villiers Crs
The Close
Springfield Lane
Daresbury Road
Crockett's Wk
Cranston Cl
Kenfield Way
Lynn Cl
396
Percival Way
47
48
Brookland Grove
Pike Pl
49
Washbrook Cl
F
G
H
102
J
K
WA10
Villiers Crs
Richmond Close
Road
Clarke's Cr
Avenue
Hey
Lane
Laurel Drive
St Julie RC Primary School
Sp Cl
T Cst
De La Salle School
Oleander Dr
Alpine Cl
Ellison
Fairclough Rd
Kelsey
Marsden
Beaumont
CHAPEL LANE
Long Meadow
Fiveways
Mosslands
Pikes Br

76
87
103
A
B
C
D
E
1
2
3
4
5
6
350
51
99
98
97
396
Fairfield Hospital
Fairfield Gdns
Rainford Hall
Rainford Brook
CRANK ROAD
B5201
Berrington's Lane
Sandy La
Sandy Lane
Cherry Tree Lane
Manor House Close
Moss Bank Road
Club Street
Clinkham Wood
Moss Bank
Broad Lane
Troutbeck Grove
Lingmell Av
Crossdale Way
Mosedale Av
Daiston Drive
Ingleton Drive
Rosthwaite Gv
Crag Grove
Bampton Av
Ghyll Grove
Loughrigg Avenue
Yewdale Av
Hillbrae Avenue
Devoke Av
Fell Grove
Lorton Avenue
Kingsway
Victoria Avenue
Bassenthwaite Av
Queensway
Africander Road
Woodside Avenue
Birch Tree Avenue
Ennerdale Avenue
Mardale Av
Bowness Avenue
Wasdale
Windermere
Eskdale Av
Grizedale Av
Thirlmere Avenue
Tarn Grove
Ullswater Av
Stainton Cl
Windle Hall
A580
EAST LANCASHIRE ROAD
Scafell Road
Rydal Grove
Coniston Grove
Folds Lane
Grasmere Avenue
Clover Hey
Derwent Rd
Shirebourne Av
A571 GREEN LEACH LANE
Dearham Avenue
Skelton Cl
The Brooks
Green Leach Avenue
Washway Lane
City Road
Haresfinch
Buckingham Drive
Kingfisher Drive
HARESFINCH VIEW
Teal Close
Mallard Way
Fulmar Close
Lincoln Crs
Ewart Road
Hamblett Crescent
Andrews Grove
St Helens Crematorium
Borough Cemetery
Furness Av
Windle Hall Drive
Cartmel Av
Wyresdale Av
Whalley Av
Priory Gardens
Abbey Road
Hard Lane
Seddon St
Friar St
PO
Birch Av
City Gardens
Birch Gdns
RAINFORD ROAD
Malt House Court
St Thomas of Canterbury Catholic Primary School
Gamble Av
Windlehurst Community Primary Sch
Princess Avenue
Martin Av
Windle City
Works
Eaton Road
Kingsley Road
Walton Road
Cowley Language College
Chaucer Road
Hammill Avenue
Huyton Av
Hillside Avenue
Windlehurst Av
Rivington Av
Pine Av
Bishop Road
A570
Speakman Road
King Edward Rd
Rivington Prim Sch
Rosebery Road
Harrington Road
Kiln Lane
St George's Avenue
Moorfield Road
Swinburne Road
Fairfield Rd
DENTONS GREEN LANE
GREENFIELD ROAD
Windleshaw Road
Carr St
Tennis St N
Elderflower Rd
St Helens CC
Moray Cl
Balker Dr
Rutland St
Oldfield St
North Road
Albert Street
Works
Denton's Green
Wynne Road
Briars Gn
Cowley Hill Lane
Windle Street
Queen St
Cowley St
Lord St
Peel Place
Fox Place
Hill Street
COLLEGE STREET
A571
Works
Smithy Heritage Centre
Ruskin Drive
Coleridge Avenue
Rivington Road
Keswick
Cooper St
DENTONS GREEN
Queens Park CE/URC Prim Sch
Harris Street
LINGHOLME ROAD
DUKE STREET
Surgery
Crab
Central Clinic
Police Stn
YMCA
Birchley St
Hardshaw
Standish St
Hospital St
Parish CE Prim Sch
Waterside
Marsden Av
Horace
Leisure Centre
St Teresas
Ellison
Fairclough Rd
Kelsey
Avenue
BIRCHLEY
1 grid square represents 500 metres

Greenfield House
Arch Lane
Works
Carr Mill Primary School
Carr Mill Dam
Old Garswood Hall Farm
Garswood Old Road
Council Building
Premier Travel Inn
A580
EAST LANCASHIRE ROAD
CARR MILL ROAD
A571
Laffak
Ashurst Prim Sch
Blackbrook St Marys Catholic Primary School
St Catherines Centre for Girls
Council Building
Richard Evans Comm Prim Sch
Legh Vale Primary School
Cemetery
STANLEY BANK WAY
BLACKBROOK ROAD
VICARAGE ROAD
St Helens Canal
Collins Industrial Estate
St Augustine of Canterbury RC High School
Blackbrook
Business Development Centre
Merton Bank Primary School
PARK ROAD
Broad Oak

Garswood
Garswood Station
Garswood Road
School Lane
Surgery
A
B
C
D
E
78
355
56
Park Industrial Estate
Junction 24
Gibbon's Road
Tithebarn Road
A58
LIVERPOOL ROAD
Ashton-In-Makerfield Golf Club
Garswood Park
Golf Course
Millfield Lane
Hall Wood Avenue
Liverpool Road
Winchester Road
Andover Road
Salisbury Road
Marlborough Way
Haydock Lane
Haydock Lane Industrial Estate
Yew Tree Trading Estate
Bahama Close
Bahama Rd
North Florida Road
N Florida Rd
Kilbuck
Fishwicks Industrial Estate
Withins Road
Kenyons Lane North
1
2
3
4
5
6
99
98
97
96
89
A580
EAST
Calday Grove
Slag Lane
Gt Delph
Travelodge
Wycliffe Road
Manor Road
Jubilee Crs
Beech Av
Piele Road
Elizabeth Road
Pimblett Rd
Alfred Road
Cook Avenue
James Road
Harold Road
Arrowsmith Rd
Avery Road
Avery Sq
Chistedon Cl
Compton Cl
Ashbury Drive
Haydock CC
Haydock English Martyrs Catholic Primary School
Willow Road
Birch Rd
Hall Rd
Sherlock Avenue
Oak Av
Woodside
Westminster Dr
Beilby Rd
Brookside Way
Brookside View
Vicarage Rd
Clipsley Crs
Myrtle Av
Maple Av
Avondale Road
Richmond Av
Grosvenor Rd
Regent Av
Teesdale Road
Wyedale Road
Darent Road
Haydock Cl
Zara Ct
Woolston Road
Askett Cl
A599
CLIPSLEY LANE
HAYDOCK
CHURCH ROAD
Chapel St
Taylor
Aster Road
Close
Shaftway
New Boston
Cumberland Crs
White House Cl
Gardiner Av
O'Connell Close
Poplar Road
Mercer Road
Lowes Water Crescent
Windermere Road
Central Drive
Leyland Grove
Haydock High Sch
Cooper Lane
Ireland Road
Greenwell Road
Haydock Medical Centre
Branch Way
Chapel Street
Lyme Street
Shaw Street
St James Primary School
Rose Avenue
Moore Drive
Tulip Road
Lupin Drive
Hyacinth Cl
Nathan Dr
Finney Grove
Wrigley Road
Hunt Road
Wharmby Road
Works
Legh Vale Primary School
Wagon Lane
Fairclough Crescent
Station Road
Quayle Close
Oakthorn Grove
The Ridings
Whiteside Road
Grange Valley
Gray Avenue
Canon Wilson Cl
Heyes Av
Ledger Rd
Wedgewood Av
Carnoustie Grove
Tobermory Close
Grange Valley Prim School
Grange Road
105
Swan Road
Lyme Street
Lancaster Close
Lyme Community Primary School
Clarence St
Brunswick Rd
Troutbeck Avenue
Birch Crs
1 grid square represents 500 metres

ASHTON-IN-MAKERFIELD
Haydock Park Racecourse
Haydock Park
Old Boston Trading Estate
Thistle Hotel
Junction 23
Haydock Park Farm
Old Boston
Woodlands Industrial Estate
NEWTON-LE-WILLOWS
Newton-le-Willows High School
Newton-le-Willows Community High School
Newton-le-Willows Sports Club
Borron Road Industrial Est
Health Clinic
Newton Bank Preparatory School
Surgery
St Edmund Arrowsmith Catholic High School
Byrchall High School
St Oswalds RC J&I Sch
St Thomas CE Prim Sch
Police Station
Premier Travel Inn
LIVERPOOL ROAD
WARRINGTON ROAD A49
LODGE LANE
EAST LANCASHIRE ROAD
A580
M6
A49 LODGE LANE
ASHTON ROAD
VISTA ROAD
B5209
CROW LANE WEST
CROW LANE EAST
A572
HIGH STREET
Billington Avenue
Heath Road
Ashton Heath
Wigan St Helens
WA12
Works
79
92
106

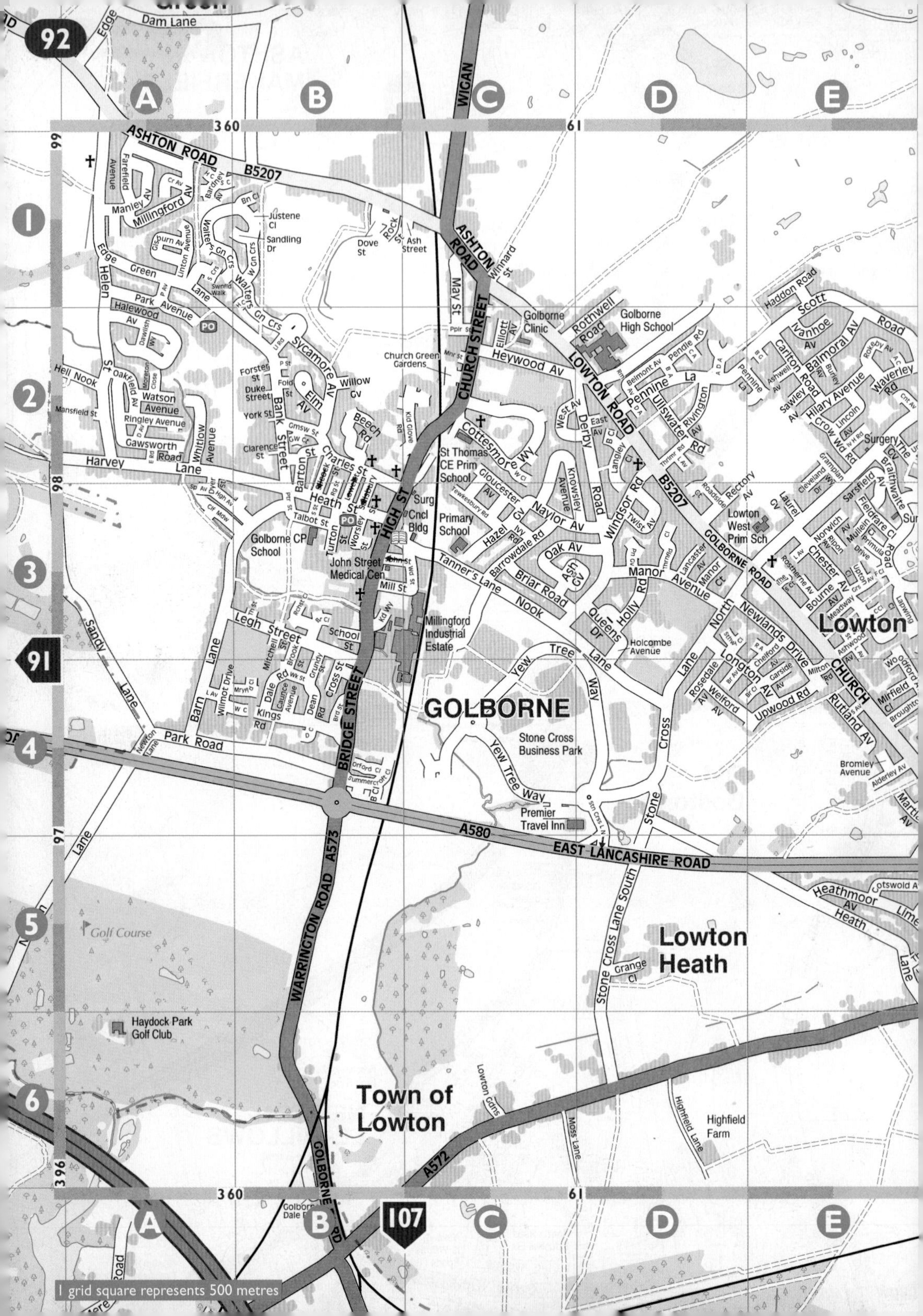
92
91
107
A
B
C
D
E
1
2
3
4
5
6
360
61
99
98
97
396
Dam Lane
Edge
WIGAN
ASHTON ROAD
B5207
Farefield Avenue
Manley Av
Millingford Av
Justene Cl
Sandling Dr
Dove St
Rock St
Ash Street
ASHTON ROAD
Winnard St
May St
CHURCH STREET
Helen
Edge Green Lane
Park Avenue
Halewood Av
Walters Gn Crs
Sycamore Av
Willow Gv
Elm Av
Church Green Gardens
Heywood Av
Elliott Av
Golborne Clinic
Rothwell Road
Golborne High School
LOWTON ROAD
Pennine La
Ullswater Rd
Rivington Av
Haddon Road
Scott Road
Ivanhoe Av
Carlton Road
Balmoral Av
Waverley Rd
Hilary Avenue
Crow Wd Rd
Surgery
Hell Nook
Oakfield Av
Mansfield St
Watson Avenue
Ringley Avenue
Gawsworth Road
Whitlow Avenue
Forster St
Duke Street
York St
Bank Street
Clarence St
Beech Rd
Kid Glove Rd
Cottesmore Wy
St Thomas CE Prim School
West Av
Derby Road
Knowsley Avenue
Harvey Lane
Barton St
Charles St
Heath St
Talbot St
Turton St
Worsley St
HIGH ST
Surg
Cncl Bldg
Gloucester Av
Primary School
Hazel Gv
Naylor Av
Windsor Rd
B5207
Rectory Av
Lowton West Prim Sch
GOLBORNE ROAD
Chester Av
Norwich Av
Golborne CP School
John Street Medical Cen
John St
Mill St
Tanner's Lane
Barrowdale Rd
Oak Av
Briar Road
Ash Gv
Manor Avenue
Holly Rd
Queens Dr
Holcombe Avenue
Newlands Drive
North Lane
Lowton
Sandy Lane
Legh Street
School St
Millingford Industrial Estate
Nook Lane
Yew Tree Way
Barn Lane
Wilmot Drive
Mitchell St
Dale Rd
Kings Rd
Cross St
BRIDGE STREET
GOLBORNE
Stone Cross Business Park
Stone Cross Lane
Rosedale Av
Welford Av
Longton Av
Upwood Rd
CHURCH
Rutland Av
Newton Lane
Park Road
Bromley Avenue
Premier Travel Inn
A580
EAST LANCASHIRE ROAD
A573
WARRINGTON ROAD
Heathmoor Av
Heath Lane
Golf Course
Stone Cross Lane South
Grange Cl
Lowton Heath
Haydock Park Golf Club
Town of Lowton
Lowton Gdns
Moss Lane
Highfield Lane
Highfield Farm
A572
GOLBORNE RD
1 grid square represents 500 metres

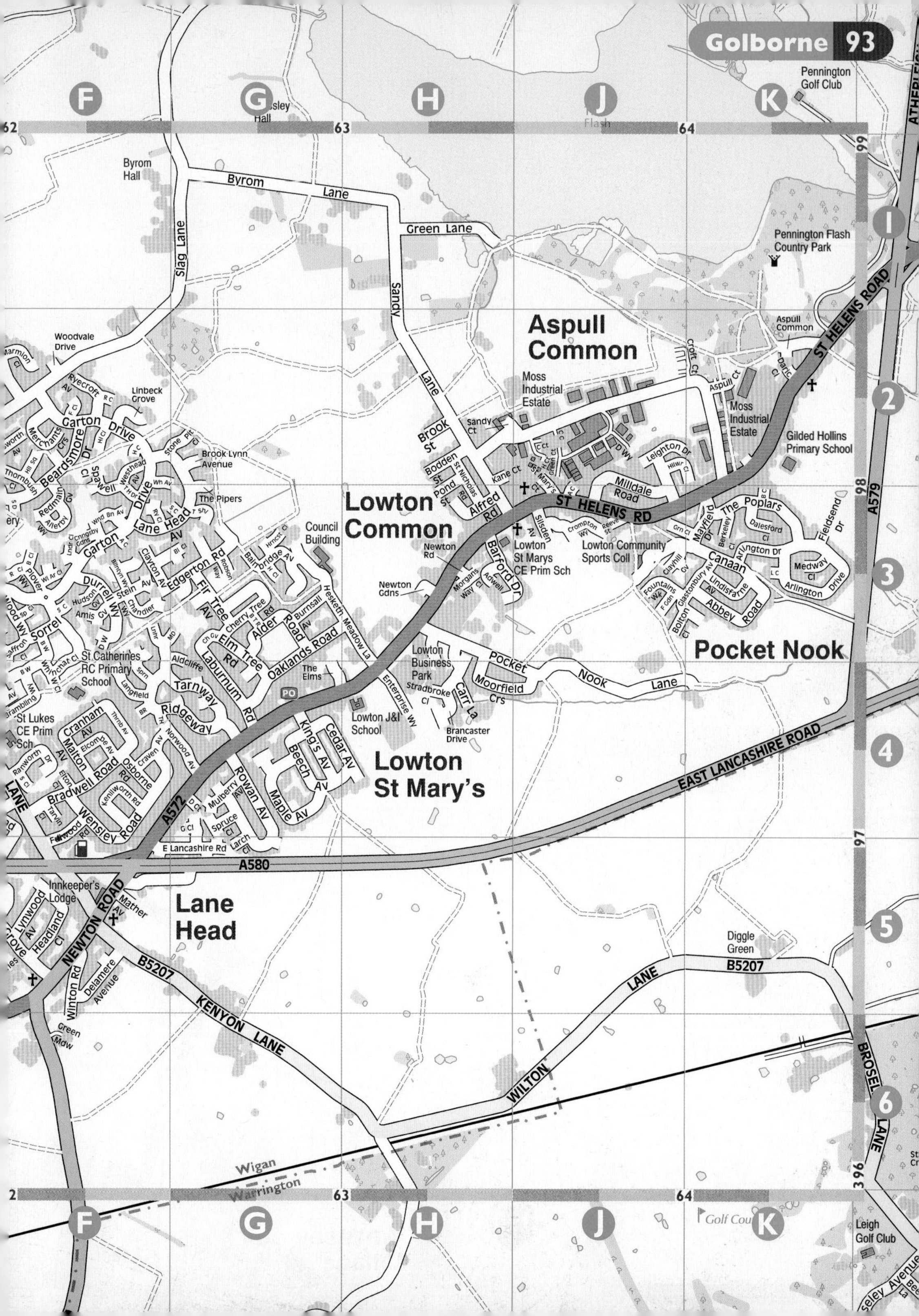
Aspull Common
Lowton Common
Pocket Nook
Lowton St Mary's
Lane Head
Pennington Flash Country Park
Pennington Golf Club
Moss Industrial Estate
Gilded Hollins Primary School
Lowton St Marys CE Prim Sch
Lowton Community Sports Coll
Council Building
Lowton Business Park
Lowton J&I School
St Catherines RC Primary School
St Lukes CE Prim Sch
Innkeeper's Lodge
Leigh Golf Club
Diggle Green
Byrom Hall
ST HELENS ROAD
EAST LANCASHIRE ROAD
A580
A572
A579
B5207
KENYON LANE
WILTON LANE
NEWTON ROAD
BROSELEY LANE
Wigan
Warrington

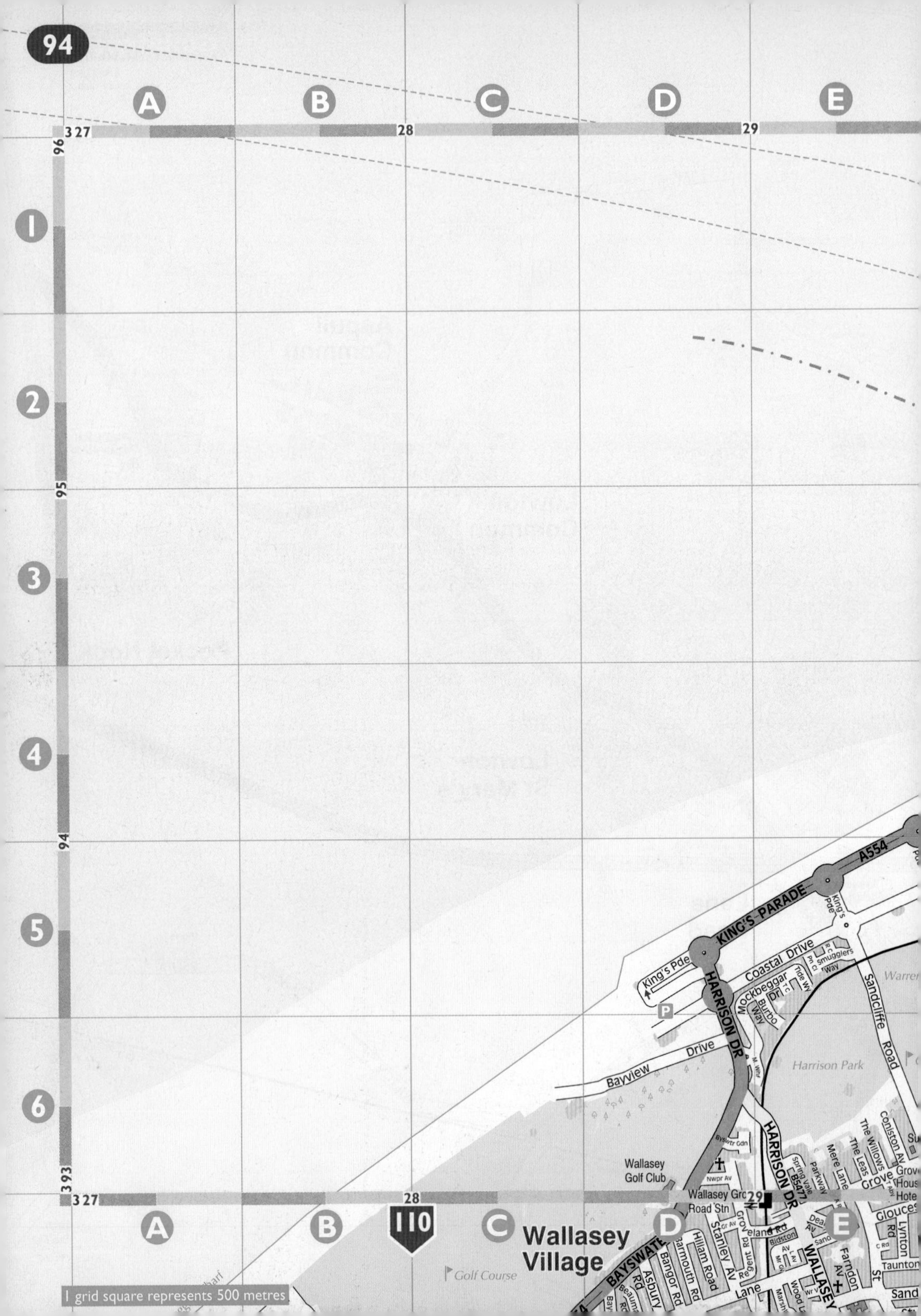
A
B
C
D
E
1
2
3
4
5
6
KING'S PARADE
A554
King's Pde
Coastal Drive
Smugglers Way
Tide Wy
Mockbeggar Dr
Burbo Way
HARRISON DR
Sandcliffe Road
Harrison Park
Bayview Drive
Wallasey Golf Club
HARRISON DR
B5427
Spring Vale
Parkway
Mere Lane
The Leas
The Willows
Coniston Av
Grove
Wallasey Grove Road Stn
110
Wallasey Village
Golf Course
BAYSWATER
Asbury Rd
Bangor Rd
Barmouth Rd
Hillam Road
Stanley Av
Regent Rd
Groveland Rd
Bidston
Lane
Farndon Av
WALLASEY
Gloucester Rd
Lynton
Taunton
Sand
1 grid square represents 500 metres

F
G
H
80
J
K
DUBLIN
DUBLIN
BELFAST
Sefton
Wirral
DOUGLAS
DUBLIN
96
Perch Rock
Marine Lake
King's Parade
A554 KING'S PARADE
Marine
Riverside Bowl
Floral Pavilion Theatre
Promenade
Virginia Rd
Coastal Drive
Alexandra Road
Wellington Road
Portland St
Atherton St
ROWSON STREET
Victoria Rd
Tollemache St
Tower Prom
Faith House Yoga & Natural Hlth Cen
Egerton Street
New Brighton Stn
Winton Cl
Montpellier Crs
Links View
Works
Albion Street
Prescot St
Dudley Road
Salisbury St
St James Rd
Pickering Rd
New Brighton
St Peter & Paul RC Primary School
St George's Mt
St George's Pk
ROWSON ST
Duke St
Grosvenor Rd
Seymour St
Lakeside Ct
New Tower Ct
Gregson Ct
Ross Tower Ct
Molyneux Drive
Rakersfield Rd
Dalmorton Road
Kirkland Rd
Vaughan Road
New Brighton Prim Sch
Ennerdale Rd
Warren Drive
Sea Road
Links Close
Linksway
Mount Primary School
Gorsehill Road
Sudworth Road
St Georges Medical Centre
A554
Onslow Rd
Ormiston Rd
Manville Rd
Vale Dr
Magazine Lane
Magazines Promenade
Sandymount Dr
Stoneby Drive
The Coppice
The Orch
Elleray Park School
Warren Golf Club
Danehurst Road
Grove Rd
Hose Side Rd
Elleray Park Rd
Glen Park Road
Mount Pleasant Road
Kirkway
Seabank Medical Cen
Cambridge Road
SEABANK
Osborne Av
Dalton Rd
Holland Road
Beach Gv
Brow
Beresford Road
Rolleston Dr
Lyndhurst
Evesham Road
School
The Oval
Queensway
Hamlet Road
Apsley Avenue
Grange Avenue
Cemetery
Zig Zag
Penkett Rd
Hale Road
Hertford Drive
Radnor Drive
Elgin Drive
Lincoln Drive
Westbourne
LAKE
LANE
111
30
31
32
93
94
95
96
393
1
2
3
4
5
6
F
G
H
J
K

96
Royal Seaforth Dock
Works
Gladstone Dock
Alexandra Dock
Langton Dock
Brocklebank Dock
Canada Dock
Huskisson Dock
BOOTLE
Sandhills
Sefton
Liverpool
81
95
112
A
B
C
D
E
1
2
3
4
5
6
332
33
34
393
94
95
96
Knowsley Road
A566
Linacre Prim Sch
North Park Health Cen
Thomas Gray Primary School
Parrs Corner Trading Est
Bootle Leisure Cen
Thomas Gray Infant Sch
St James RC Primary School
Rimrose Road
Grove St
Sea View Road
A5098
The Strand Medical Cen
Pol Stn
Bootle New Strand Stn
Strand Shopping Centre
Rimrose Business Park
Liverpool Intermodal Freeport Terminal
Strand Road
Church Gdns
Merton Road
Magistrates Court
Regent Road
Derby Road
A565
Bootle Oriel Rd Stn
Oriel Rd
South Sefton Business Centre
Everton Velw Business Centre
Canal Street
Trinity Rd
Town Hall
Balliol Road
Hugh Baird Coll of Technology
Council Building
Miller's Bridge
Stanley Road
Brasenose Road
Bedford Rd
Viola Street
Bianca St
Orlando St
B5318
Bank Hall Station
Bankhall Street
A5056
Bankfield Street
A5036
Juniper St
Studholme Street
Foster Street
Birchall Street
Belltower Rd
A5055
Sandhills Lane
Sandhills Station
Sandhills Business Park
Sandon Industrial Estate
Errington Street
Grundy Street
Boundary St
Luton
Wellington
A5038
1 grid square represents 500 metres

Walton
Kirkdale
Anfield
Stanley Park
Anfield Cemetery
Walton Hospital
HM Prison Liverpool
Everton FC (Goodison Park)
Liverpool FC (Anfield)
Liverpool FC Museum
Kirkdale Station
Walton Station
Rice La Stn
Aintree Industrial Estate
Bootle Stadium Sports Centre
Walton Sports Centre
Anfield Crematorium
Vernon Sangster Sports Centre
Hillside High School
Alsop High School
Anfield Community Comprehensive School
Westminster Road Swimming Pool
Notre Dame Catholic Coll
Hope Valley Community Primary School
Liverpool Community College
Langham Street Industrial Est
Queens Drive Family Health Clinic
Walton Hall Village Medical Cen
Anfield Medical Centre
Bousfield Health Cen
Temple of Praise
All Saints Catholic Primary School
Gwladys Street Community Primary School
Christ Church CE Primary School
Bootle CC
Dunnys Sports Club
Hebrew Cemetery
AINTREE ROAD A5098
SOUTHPORT ROAD A5038
RICE LANE A59
QUEENS DRIVE
COUNTY ROAD
WALTON ROAD
WALTON BRECK ROAD A5089
HALE ROAD
BREEZE HILL
BALLIOL ROAD EAST A5058
HAWTHORNE ROAD
MELROSE ROAD A5038
STANLEY RD A567
PRIORY ROAD
WALTON LANE A580
82
98
113

98
83
97
114
A
B
C
D
E
1
2
3
4
5
6
337
38
39
96
95
94
393
Fazakerley
Norris Green
Clubmoor
Aintree Industrial Estate
Hanson Road Business Park
Liver Industrial Estate
Cemetery
Works
Higher Lane
Brookfield
Police Station
Stonebridge Business Park (under development)
Long Lane Medical Cen
Our Lady & St Philomenas Catholic Primary School
Long Lane
Sparrow Hall Rd
Retail Park
Showcase Cinemas
Stopgate Medical Cen
STOPGATE LANE
Tilston Road
Charnock Road
B5187
EAST LANCASHIRE ROAD
A580
WALTON HALL AVENUE
TOWNSEND AVENUE
PARTHENON DR
STRAWBERRY RD
Leamington Community School
Wellesbourne Primary School
St Teresa of Lisieux Catholic Infant School
Utting Avenue East
Florence Melly Community Primary School
Superstore
Abingdon Medical Centre
Norris Green Family Hlth Clinic
Trans Pennine Trail
Broad Lane
Langbank Medical Cen
Broad Lane Precinct
Medical Centre
Broad Square Community Primary School
Hornspit Medical Centre
WALTON DRIVE
QUEENS DRIVE
A5058
St Matthews Catholic Primary Sch
The Stables Business Centre
Roscoe Junior Sch
Pinehurst Prim Sch Junior Dept
Pinehurst Prim Sch Infant Dept
TOWNSEND LANE
MUIRHEAD AVENUE
WEST DERBY
All Saints Catholic Primary School
Holly Lodge Girls College
1 grid square represents 500 metres

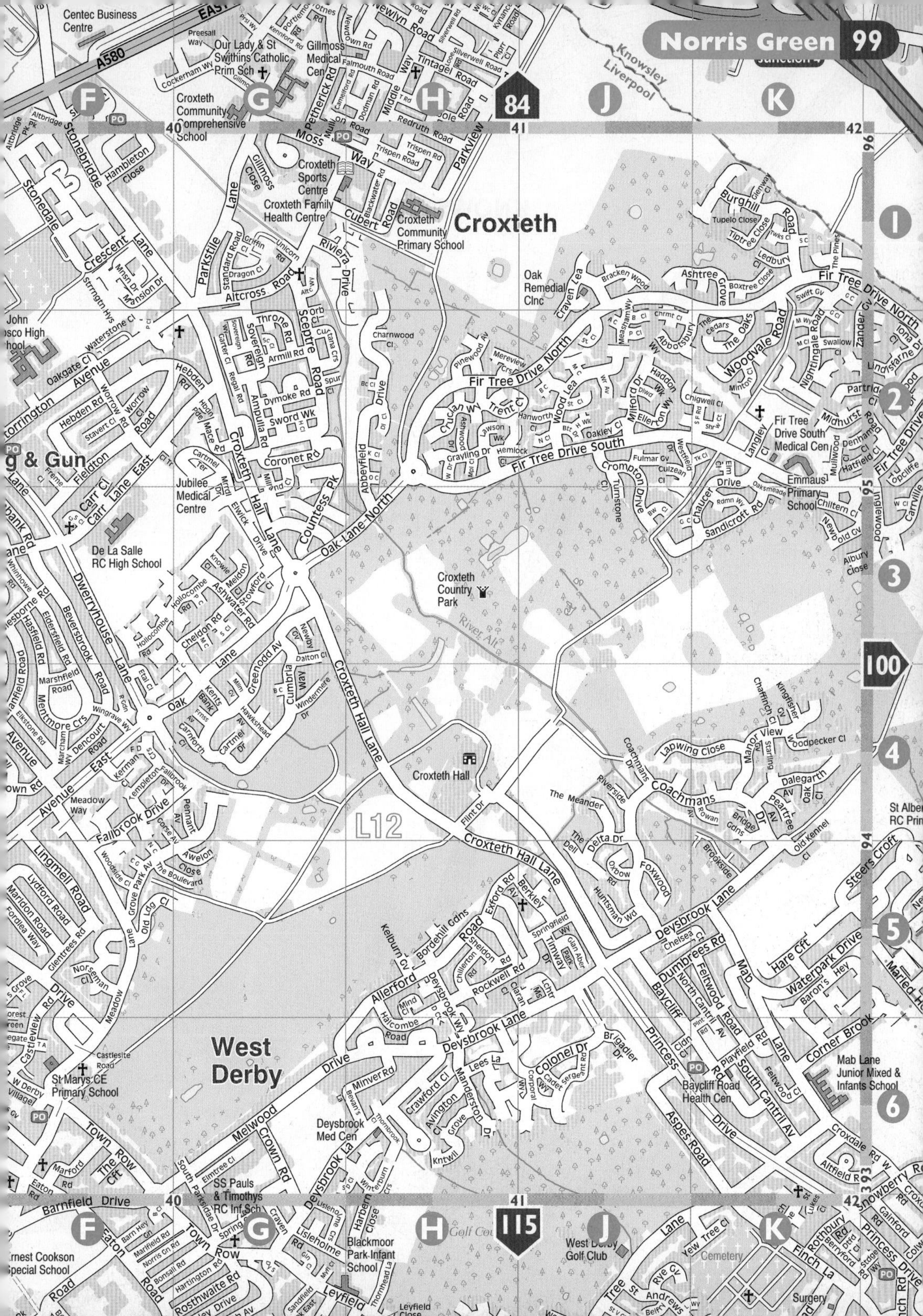

Norris Green 99
84
100
115
Croxteth
West Derby
Croxteth Country Park
Croxteth Hall
River Alt
L12
Knowsley
Liverpool
Centec Business Centre
A580
Our Lady & St Swithins Catholic Prim Sch
Gillmoss Medical Cen
Croxteth Community Comprehensive School
Croxteth Sports Centre
Croxteth Family Health Centre
Croxteth Community Primary School
Oak Remedial Clnc
Jubilee Medical Centre
De La Salle RC High School
Fir Tree Drive South Medical Cen
Emmaus Primary School
Mab Lane Junior Mixed & Infants School
Baycliff Road Health Cen
Deysbrook Med Cen
St Marys CE Primary School
SS Pauls & Timothys RC Inf Sch
Blackmoor Park Infant School
West Derby Golf Club
Cemetery
Surgery
Moss Way
Parkview
Petherick Rd
Stonebridge Lane
Stonedale Crescent
Crescent Lane
Hambleton Close
Parkstile Lane
Gillmoss Close
Altcross Road
Sceptre Road
Sovereign Rd
Throne Rd
Dymoke Rd
Sword Wk
Ampulla Rd
Coronet Rd
Croxteth Hall Lane
Countess Pk
Abbeyfield Drive
Charnwood Cl
Oak Lane North
Riviera Drive
Cubert Road
Fir Tree Drive North
Fir Tree Drive South
Compton Drive
Turnstone
Woodvale Road
Burghill Road
Ashtree Grove
Bracken Wood
Craven Lea
Wood Lea
Milford Dr
Chaucer Drive
Sandicroft Rd
Nightingale Road
Midhurst Road
Langley Cl
Torrington Avenue
Worrow Road
Hebden Rd
Fieldton
Carr Lane East
Dwerryhouse Lane
Beversbrook Road
Marshfield Road
Mentmore Crs
Oak Lane
Cumbria Way
Greenodd Av
Ashwater Rd
Cheldon Rd
Hollocombe
Avenue East
Fallbrook Drive
Meadow Way
Pennant Av
Awelon Close
The Boulevard
Grove Park Av
Lingmell Road
Lydford Road
Maridon Road
Fordlea Way
Glentrees Rd
Norseman Cl
Meadow Lane
Castleview Rd
Town Row
Melwood Drive
Crown Rd
Deysbrook Lane
Deysbrook La
Deysbrook Wy
Allerford Road
Manderston Dr
Colonel Dr
Brigadier Dr
Princess Drive
Aspes Road
Dumbrees Rd
Feltwood Road
South Cantril Av
Mab Lane
Corner Brook
Waterpark Drive
Hare Cft
Steers Croft
Coachmans Dr
Lapwing Close
Manor View
Woodpecker Cl
The Meander
Delta Dr
Foxwood
Old Kennel Cl
Barnfield Drive
Eaton Road
Harbern Close
Leyfield
Finch La

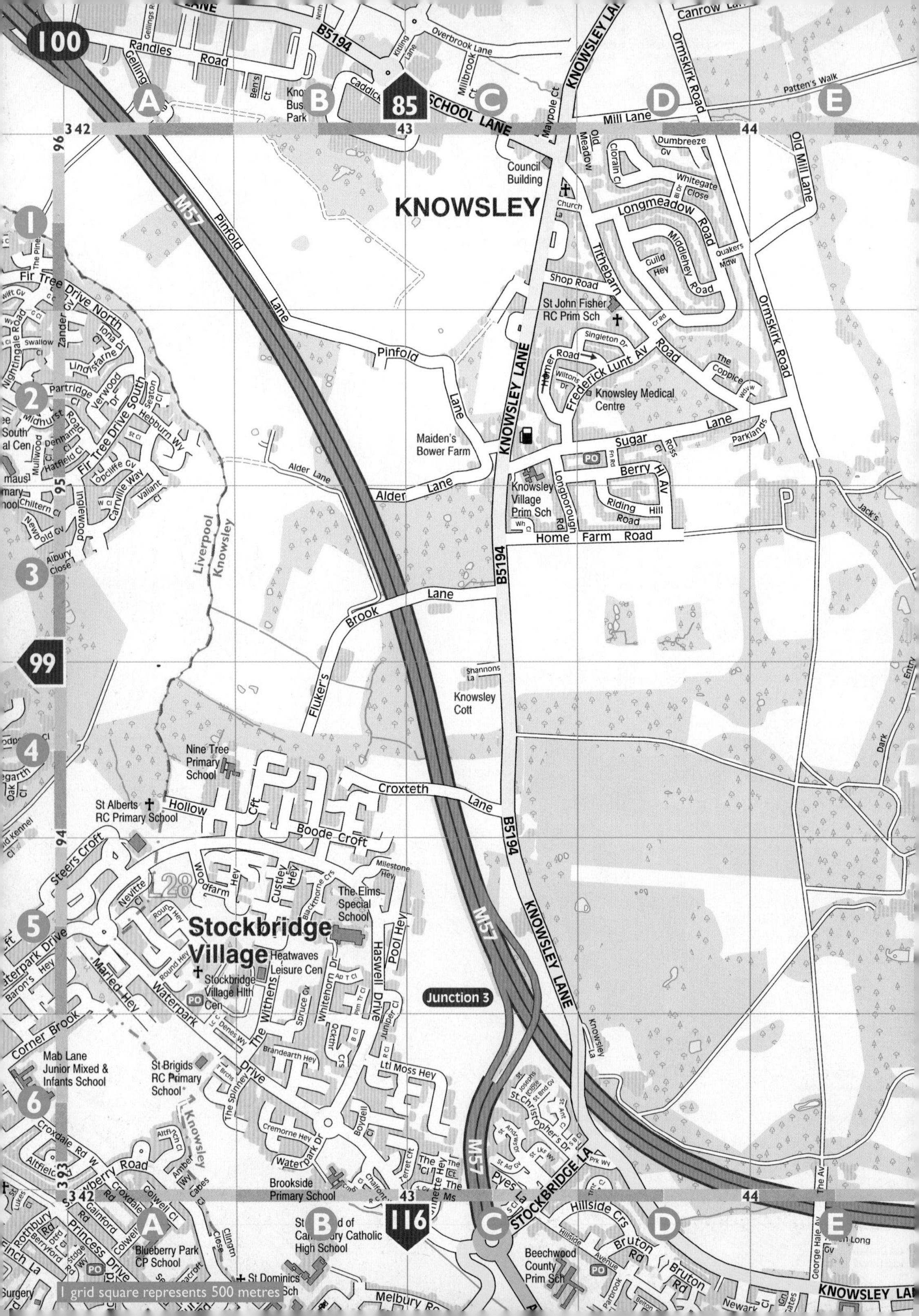

100
85
99
116
A
B
C
D
E
1
2
3
4
5
6
3 42
43
44
96
95
94
93
KNOWSLEY
Stockbridge Village
M57
B5194
KNOWSLEY LANE
SCHOOL LANE
Mill Lane
Ormskirk Road
Old Mill Lane
Pinfold Lane
Alder Lane
Brook Lane
Fluker's Lane
Croxteth Lane
Sugar Lane
Home Farm Road
Longmeadow Road
Middlehey Road
Tithebarn Road
Frederick Lunt Av
Shop Road
Berry Hl Av
Riding Hill Road
Longborough Rd
Council Building
Church
St John Fisher RC Prim Sch
Knowsley Medical Centre
Maiden's Bower Farm
Knowsley Village Prim Sch
Knowsley Cott
Nine Tree Primary School
St Alberts RC Primary School
The Elms Special School
Heatwaves Leisure Cen
Stockbridge Village Hlth Cen
St Brigids RC Primary School
Mab Lane Junior Mixed & Infants School
Brookside Primary School
Blueberry Park CP School
Beechwood County Prim Sch
Junction 3
Fir Tree Drive North
Fir Tree Drive South
Waterpark Drive
Corner Brook
Marled Hey
Haswell Drive
Pool Hey
Boode Croft
Hollow Cft
Steers Croft
The Withens
Ltl Moss Hey
Cremorne Hey
St Christopher's Dr
STOCKBRIDGE LA
Pyes La
Hillside Crs
Bruton Rd
Princess Drive
Croxdale Rd W
Knowsley Rd
Liverpool Knowsley
Randles Road
Canrow La
Patten's Walk
George Hale Av
The Av
Dark Entry
Jack's
Melbury Rd
Finch La
1 grid square represents 500 metres

Patten's Walk
F
G
H
86
J
K
45
46
47
96
1
2
95
3
102
4
94
5
6
93
Clay Lane
St Helens
Knowsley
Knowsley Park
White Man's Dam
Knowsley Safari Park
L34
No. 4 Reservoir
No. 3
nowsley all
Works
A58
Prescot School
Our Ladys RC Primary School
Knowsley
The Spinney
Park Road
Prescot AFC
Halsall St
Evans St
Ward St
Eaton St
Moss St
ST HELENS ROAD
Rowson St
Grosvenor Rd
Harvard Gv
Marlborough
Surgery
WARRINGTON ROAD
Columbia Rd
Albany Rd
Park Lane
Gn Rd
Stanley Crs
Police
Junction 2
M57
117
PRESCOT
Prescot Mus
Natural Hlth Clinic
Prescot Medical Cen
HIGH
B5200
LIVERPOOL ROAD A57
WEST STREET
Eccleston St
Park Ho Med Cen
Aspinall St
Cyprus St
Houghton St
Ashley
Oliver
Liverpool Rd
Driffield
Pratt
Wood
Vcrg Pl
B5194
E

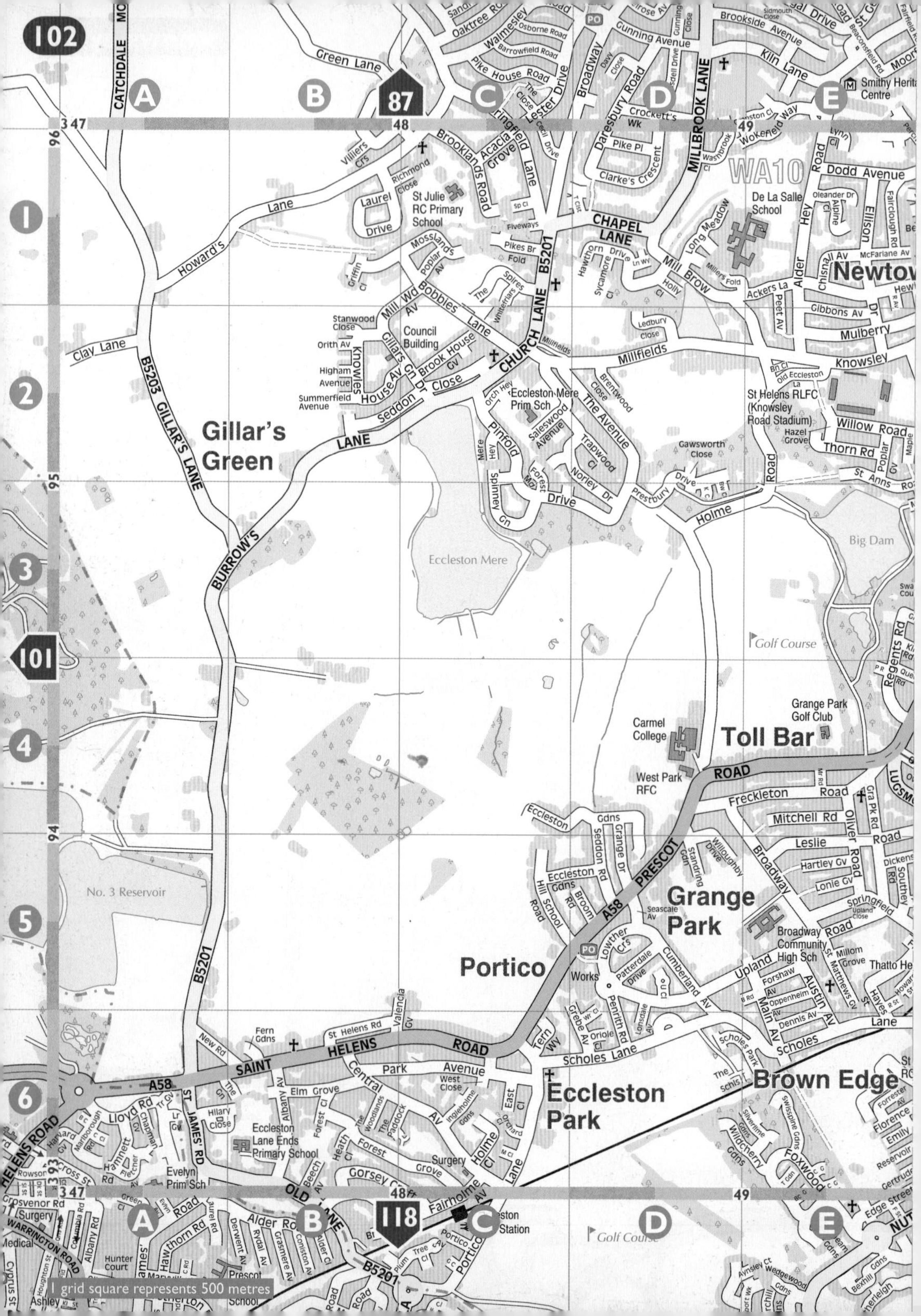

Gillar's Green
Eccleston Mere
Toll Bar
Grange Park
Portico
Eccleston Park
Brown Edge
Newtown
WA10
Big Dam
No. 3 Reservoir
Golf Course
Grange Park Golf Club
Carmel College
West Park RFC
St Helens RLFC (Knowsley Road Stadium)
De La Salle School
St Julie RC Primary School
Council Building
Eccleston Mere Prim Sch
Broadway Community High Sch
Eccleston Lane Ends Primary School
Evelyn Prim Sch
Smithy Heritage Centre
B5203 GILLAR'S LANE
BURROW'S LANE
CHURCH LANE
CHAPEL LANE
MILLBROOK LANE
A58 PRESCOT ROAD
SAINT HELENS ROAD
ST JAMES' RD
OLD LANE
B5201
87
101
118
1 grid square represents 500 metres

Newtown 103
88
104
119
12
13
Denton's Green
St Helens CC
Wynne Road
Keswick Rd
Dentons Green Lane
Lingholme Road
Duke Street
Kirkland Street
Queens Park CE/URC Prim Sch
Marsden Av
St Teresas Catholic Prim Sch
Leisure Centre
Kitchener St
Cambridge Rd
Boundary Road
Rivington Road
Ruskin Drive
Eccleston St
Westfield St
Croppers Hill
Borough Rd
Prescot Road
Superstore
Works
St Helens College
Cineworld
Sandfield Medical Centre
Linkway West
King St
Corporation St
Town Hall
Thtr Royal
Register Office
Central Clinic
Police Stn
Cncl Bldg
Mag & Co Cts
YMCA
Parish CE Prim Sch
Holy Cross RC Prim Sch
Hall Street
Trading Estate
Shop Cen
Market
St Helens Central Station
Parr Street
Linkway East
St Helens Retail Park
World of Glass
Chalon Way Industrial Estate
Warrington Old Rd
ST HELENS
West Park
Ravenhead
Alexandra Drive
Ravenhead Road
Burtonhead Rd
Ravenhead Retail Park
Milverny Way
Sutton Heath Road
Ravenhead Nature Park
Sherdley Road
Linkway
Scorecross
Saint Helens
The Caravan Pk
Sherdley Park Golf Club
Sherdley Park
Golf Course
The Score
Thatto Heath
Thatto Heath Road
Elm Road
Council Building
Police Stn
Thatto Heath Community Prim Sch
The Bowry Health Cen
Elephant Lane
Mayfield Avenue
Heathfield Av
Canberra Avenue
Queensland Av
Nutgrove Methodist Prim Sch
Sutton Heath
Marshalls Cross Road
Eaves Lane
Eaves Prim Sch
Sutton Community Leisure Centre Track
Sutton High Sports College
A58
A570
A571
A569
B5413
B5204
50
51
52
95
94
96
F
G
H
J
K
I
2
3
4
5
6

104
89
103
120
Collins Industrial Estate
Business Development Centre
Merton Bank Primary School
PARK ROAD
PARR STREET
PARR STOCKS ROAD
CHANCERY LANE
BROAD OAK ROAD
Broad Oak
Moorfoot Road Industrial Estate
Cemetery
Blackbrook
Parr Swimming Baths
Lansbury Bridge School
Maternity & Child Welfare Clinic
Broad Oak Prim Sch
Holy Spirit Prim Sch
Derbyshire Hill
Parr
Fleet Lane Industrial Estate
Parr Industrial Estate
Allanson Street CP School
Eastside Industrial Est
Westside Ind Est
Peasley Cross
St Helens Hospital
Moss Nook
St Cuthberts Catholic High Sch
Fishwicks Industrial Est
Robins Lane Community Primary School
Sutton Oak CE Primary Sch
Irwin Road Health Centre
Rainbow Medical Cen
St Helens Junction Station
St Helens AFC
St Annes RC Primary Sch
Sutton
Eaves Prim Sch
Reginald Road Industrial Park
MARSHALLS CROSS ROAD
REGINALD ROAD
BOLD ROAD
WA9
1 grid square represents 500 metres

Grange Valley Prim School
Grange
F
G
H
90
J
K
55
56
57
96
Road
Swan Road
Lyme Street
Lancaster Close
Lyme Community Primary School
Clarence St
Troutbeck Avenue
Birch Crs
Acacia St
Newton Common
COMMON ROAD
Siddeley Drive
Dene Av
Sturgess St
Sefton
Marian Av
Earlestown
Barnett Av
Lloyd
Tully Av
Watkins Avenue
Crs
Short Close
Short St
Common Street
Earle Cl
Head St
Bank St
Brick St
Viaduct St
Regent
Pavilion Ct
Earle St
Hillside Avenue
Dingle Av
Canal St
95
Deacon Trading Estate
Wharf Road
Penkford School
Havannah Lane
Winter Grove
TON ROAD
Pleasant Avenue
Luther Gv
Avenue
PENNINGTON LANE
A572
Reynolds Avenue
Waring
Neville Av
Winston Av
Sexton Avenue
Inman Av
Fleet Lane
PENKFORD LANE
106
Collins Green
PENNY LANE
Winwick View
Collins Green Lane
94
Broad Lane
Forshaw's Lane
Lumber Lane
Green Lane
Burtonwood Community Primary School
The Brambles
Bold Business Centre
Samphire Gdns
Orchid Wy
Columbine Wy
Peony Gdns
Celandine Wy
ERS' ENTRY
B5204
BOLD LANE
Back Lane
Phipps' La
Ollerton Pk
Winsford Dr
Rushton Cl
Melrose Avenue
Eastwood Rd
Bakewell Road
Sunningdale Drive
Aldridge Drive
St Paul of the Cross Catholic Primary School
Burtonwood Industrial Centre
Pinewood Rd
393
Cambourne Rd
Colne Road
Karen Close
Brookvale Cl
Arndil Cl
Kinnock Pk
121
Bold
Bold Industrial Park
Wheatacre Farm
Mercer St
Fairclough Street
Jackson Street
Milnthorpe Road
Chapel Lane
Cemetery
Hawkshead
Kilshaw Road

NEWTON-LE-WILLOWS
Wargrave
Vulcan Village
Newton-le-Willows High School
Newton-le-Willows Community High School
Borron Road Industrial Est
Newton-le-Willows Sports Club
Health Clinic
St Helens Community College
St Marys Catholic Sch
St Marys Catholic Jun Sch
St Aelreds RC Technology College
St Peter's CE Prim School
Newton Bank Preparatory School
Kirkfield Hotel
Newton-le-Willows Station
Newton-le-Willows Primary School
The District CE Prim Sch
Council Building
Superstore
Surgery
Med Cen
Earlestown Station
Deacon Trading Estate
Sankey Valley Industrial Estate
Wargrave Prim Sch
Newton Community Hospital
Wargrave House School
Vulcan Industrial Estate
Newton-le-Willows Cemetery
Bradleigh Old Hall
Boarded Barn Farm
Red House Farm
Alder Root Golf Club
Golf Course
Sankey Brook
St Helens
Warrington
CROW LANE WEST
CROW LANE EAST
HIGH STREET
CHURCH ST
MILL LANE
WINWICK ROAD
VISTA ROAD
Hall Lane
Alder Lane
Bradley Lane
Alder Root Lane
Wargrave Road
Victoria Road
Bradlegh Road
Market Street
Earle Street
1 grid square represents 500 metres

91
105
122

Town of Lowton
Newton Park
Hermitage Green
Winwick
Junction 22
M6
A572
A573
A49
NEWTON ROAD
GOLBORNE ROAD
PARKSIDE ROAD
LINK ROAD
WINWICK
SOUTHWORTH ROAD
Mere Road
Rosemary Dr
Holford Way
Newton Park Drive
Barrow Lane
Highfield Lane
Hermitage Green Lane
Red Bank Avenue
Red Bank
Cop Holt Farm
Parkside Farm
Wood Head
Oven Back Farm
Highfield Farm
Kenyon Hall
Wigan
St. Helens
Warrington
Waterworks Lane
Southworth Lane
Green Lane
Old School House Lane
Hollins Lane
Myddle
Maple Rd
Winwick CE Primary School
Winwick Parish Leisure Centre
Premier Travel Inn
Golborne Dale Rd
Lowton Gdns
Golborne Rd
Gerosa Av
Spires Gdns
The Priory
Hornby La
Church Walk
Ballantyne Pl
Marryat Cl
Austen Dr
Fleming
Rectory La
Hollins Dr
Linkside Av
Ash
Arbury
Sandy
Cem
PO
92
123
F
G
H
J
K
1
2
3
4
5
6
60
61
62
96
95
94
393

A
B
C
D
E
3 22
23
24
93
92
91
3 90
1
2
3
4
5
6
Parkfield House
Park
Lane
Parkfields
Dove
Point
Great
Meols
Meols
Parade
Newlyn Road
Bennet's Lane
Dovepoint
Road
Great Meols
Prim Sch
Cuffitt's Rake
Cuffitts
Cl
Centurion
Drive
Road
Flowermead Cl
Ashley
Lyndhurst
Park
Av
Celtic Rd
Cranborne
Beachcroft Rd
Mumfords
School Lane
Forest
Forest
Close
The
Gld
Roman Road
Meols Pde
Woodland
Sandfield Av
Edgewood Rd
Firshaw
Rd
Garden Hey
Road
Ashford
Rd
Shaws
Drive
BIRKENHEAD ROAD
Egbert
Road
King's
Road
Foxfield
Road
Gorse
Avenue
Leighton Av
Frankby
Rd
North Mannington Cl
Queen's
Derwent Rd
Meols
Station
Meols Parade
Great Meols Queen Elizabeth II Coronation Park
Hoylake
Hospital
LC
Carr Lane
A553
127
128
1 grid square represents 500 metres

F
G
H
J
K
25
26
27
Leasowe Golf Club
Leasowe Castle Hotel
North Wirral Coastal Park
New Brighton RUFC
Lingham Lane
Lingham Farm
Ditton Lane
Blackheath Dr
Wakefield Drive
Murrayfield Dr
Reeds Lane
Cheltenham Crs
Surgery
Goodwood Dr
Epsom Rd
Birket Avenue
Reeds Av
Farmside
A551
PASTURE ROAD
Tarran Way North
Tarran Way West
Tarran Way E
Tarran Way S
Works
Moreton Station
Leasowe Station
Station Approach
Pasture Avenue
CH46
Sunfield Road
Kingsmead Road
Saxon Road
Yew Tree
Danger Lane
East Way
Eastway Prim Sch
West Way
Ivy Lane
Pasture Crescent
Oundle Rd
Blundells Dr
Daneswell Drive
Avondale Av
Sacred Heart RC Primary Sch
Moreton
Fairmead Road
HOYLAKE ROAD
Stuart Av
Orchard
Knutsford Rd
Pasture Road Health Centre
Witley Av
Lyons Rd
Maryland Lane
Barnston Lane
Lingham Primary School
Meadow Lane
Harvest Lane
Flaxhill
Heathmoor Road
Felicity Grove
Berrylands Road
Meadfoot Rd
Bramble Way
Glasier Rd
Eleanor Rd
Bradman Road
Curlew Way
Curlew Court
Wastdale Dr
Mallard Wy
Tern Way
Millhouse Lane
Oakham Drive
Bermuda Road
Hardie Av
Town Meadow Lane
Linear Park
Belfry
Austell
Foxton Cl
Bradgate Cl
Desford
Digg Lane
Carr Lane
Huxley Cl
Kimmerton Cl
Rosewood Dr
Millhouse Dr
Alnwick
Rothbury Cl
Wooler Close
Kestrel Road
Macdonald Road
Edgehill Road
Joan Avenue
Douglas Drive
Doreen Av
Neva Av
Fairfield Crs
Foxfield School
Surgery
Holt Av
Police Stn
Winston Gv
Dawpool Dr
Moreton Medical Centre
Sandbrook
Carnsdale Road
Lomond Grove
Pine Tree Grove
Burnley Road
Gabriel Close
Wimbrick Hey
Stavordale Road
Sandbrook Primary Sch
Orrets Meadow School
Spencer Av
Castleway
129
110
93
92
91
90
1
2
3
4
5
6

94
Wallasey Village
Golf Course
Mockbeggar Wharf
Green Lane
BAYSWATER RD
A554
HARRISON DR
WALLASEY VILLAGE
Wallasey Grove Road Stn
Wallasey Village Station
Greenleas School
St Marys Catholic College
Surgery
Leasowe
LEASOWE ROAD
A551
Our Lady of Lourdes RC Primary School
New Solar School
Wallasey RFC
Ashville FC
Works
Mosslands School
Castleway Primary School
Leasowe Primary School
Leasowe Millennium Centre
Leasowe Recreation Centre
Wallasey School
109
A5139
Junction 1
Superstore
Junction 1 Retail Park
Bidston Golf Club
Bidston Moss
Bidston Industrial Estate
The Birket
Peninsula Business Park
M53
Bidston Station
LC
Wirral Tennis & Sports Centre
Claremount School
St Oswald's CE Primary School
Vyner Primary School
FENDER LANE
A553
HOYLAKE ROAD
Holy Cross RC Prim School
Bidston
Bidston Hill
Sandbrook Primary Sch
129
130
1 grid square represents 500 metres

Liscard 111
F
G
H
J
K
95
112
131
30
31
32
93
92
91
390
1
2
3
4
5
6
CH45
CH44
Liscard
Egremont
Poulton
Seacombe
Warren Golf Club
Elleray Park School
The Coppice
Special School
The Oval
Cemetery
Apsley Avenue
Surgery
Seabank Medical Cen
Westbourne School
Liscard Primary School
Quarry Bank
Oldershaw School
St Georges Primary School
Greenfield Way
School
Med Cen
Egremont Prim Sch
Weatherhead High School, Media Arts College
Victoria Central Hospital
Park Primary School
Central Park
Raymond Road
Walsingham Court
Primary School
Works
South Wallasey Neighbourhood College
Kingsway Primary School
Gallagher Industrial Est
Uveco Business Centre
Council Building
Wirral Business Centre
SMM Business Park
New Way Business Centre
Wheatland Business Park
Falcongate Industrial Est
Birkenhead North Station
Concrete Mixing Works
West Float
East Float
Historic Warships
Mirian Health Cen
Bertha Gardens
Pol Stn
Portland Primary School
Our Lady & St Edwards RC Prim Sch
Toll
KINGSWAY (TUNNEL)
SEABANK ROAD
KING STREET
MANOR ROAD
B5142
B5143
RAKE LANE
Zig Zag Road
WALLASEY ROAD
A551
LISCARD ROAD
LISCARD CRS
ST ALBAN'S ROAD
MILL LA
MILL LANE
A5088
WOODSTOCK ROAD
OXTON ROAD
A5027
POULTON ROAD
BRECK ROAD
B5145
WALLASEY BRIDGE ROAD
A5139
DOCK ROAD
GORSEY LA
DUKE STREET
BEAUFORT ROAD A5030
CORPORATION ROAD
A5030
LAIRD ST
STANLEY RD
WHEATLAND LANE
BOROUGH ROAD
MAINWARING RD
KELVIN ROAD
Promenade
Egremont Promenade
Magazines Promenade
Holland Road
Hale Road
Denton Drive
Hertford Drive
Radnor Drive
Elgin Drive
Lincoln Drive
Caithness Drive
Penkett Road
Withens La
Broadway Avenue
Belvidere Road
Prospect Vale
Vyner Road
Grove Rd
Mount Road
Pleasant St
Rice Lane
Church Street
Falkland Road
Clarendon Road
Littledale Road
Buchanan Road
Bell Road
Rappart Road
Brougham Rd
Albemarle Rd
Parkside
Hawarden Avenue
Manor Lane
Stringhey Road
Trafalgar Road
Charlotte Rd
Belgrave St
Park St
Grosvenor Street
St Mary's St
Annesley Road
Deveraux Dr
Rullerton Rd
Marlowe Road
Station Road
Cliff Road
Dawlish Road
Pennine Rd
Knaresborough Road
Gorsedale Road
Vernon Av
Oakdale Rd
Lucerne Rd
Geneva Rd
Westfield Road
Kelvinside
The Street
Sumner
Lansdowne Rd
Patten Street
Price Street
Cavendish St
Old Bidston Rd
Milner St
Ilchester Rd
Lincoln Street

WALLASEY
LIVERPOOL
Vauxhall
Huskisson Dock
Nelson Dock
Stanley Dock
Trafalgar Dock
Princes Dock
George's Dock
Albert Dock
Sandon Industrial Estate
Wellington Employment Park (under development)
Sandhills Station
Sandhills Business Park
Town Hall
Council Offices
Guinea Gap Baths & Recreation Centre
Riverside Primary School
Seacombe Ferry Terminal
Twelve Quays Ferry Terminal
Isle of Man Ferry Terminal
Liverpool Wirral
KINGSWAY (TUNNEL)
DOUGLAS
DUBLIN
BELFAST
DUBLIN
REGENT ROAD
GREAT HOWARD STREET
BRIGHTON STREET
BOROUGH ROAD
BIRKENHEAD ROAD
KELVIN ROAD
A5054 BOUNDARY STREET
A5055 SANDHILLS
A5053 LEEDS
Love Lane
King Edward Industrial Estate
Royal Liver Bldg
Cunard Building
Mersey Ferries
Titanic Memorial
Museum of Liverpool (due to open 2010)
Port of Liverpool Building
Merseyside Maritime Museum & International Slavery Museum
Fingerprints of Elvis
Tate Gallery
Albert Dock Village
Crowne Plaza Hotel
Elaine Norris Sports Cen
The Trinity RC Prim Sch
Cabinet War Rooms
Town Hall
Queen Elizabeth II Law Courts
James Street Stn
Moorfields Station
LJMU
Granada TV
Merseyside Police HQ
1 grid square represents 500 metres

Everton
Kensington
Edge
Anfield
97
114
133
SCOTLAND ROAD
KIRKDALE ROAD
NETHERFIELD ROAD NORTH
ST DOMINGO ROAD
HEYWORTH STREET
EVERTON ROAD
BRECK ROAD
WEST DERBY ROAD
PRESCOT STREET
LONDON ROAD
PEMBROKE PLACE
KENSINGTON
EDGE LANE
WAVERTREE ROAD
BELMONT ROAD
Lime Street Station
St George's Hall
Liverpool John Moores University
University of Liverpool
Royal Liverpool University Hospital
Metropolitan Cathedral of Christ the King
Campion Catholic High School
Breckfield Community Comprehensive Sch
Kingsway Industrial Park

114
Clubmoor
98
A
B
C
D
E
38
39
337
93
92
91
390
1
2
3
4
5
6
113
133
134
Townsend Lane
A580
All Saints Catholic Primary School
Works
Yelverton Rd
Westcombe Rd
Vallance Rd
Pinehurst Prim Sch Infant Dept
Junior Dept
The Stables Business Centre
Worcester Drive
Glastonbury Cl
Cumberland Cl
Adshead Road
Roscoe Junior Sch
Allison Rd
Halsey Crs
Culme Road
Clinton Place
Three Butt Lane
Tollerton Rd
Muirhead Avenue
A5049
West Derby Rd
Mill Bank
Derby
Holly Lodge Girls College
Liverpool Community Coll
Premier Travel Inn
West Derby Comprehensive School
A5058
Peter Lloyd Leisure Centre
Tuebrook
Green Lane Medical Cen
Cemetery
St Cecilias RC J&I School
Rockbank Road
Richland Road
Russian Drive
Moscow Drive
Kremlin Drive
Quarry Road
Lower Breck
Breckside Park
September Road
August Road
July Road
October Dr
St Margarets Anfield CE Prim Sch
The Priory Medical Centre
Belmont Gv
Sunlight St
Rocky Lane
Belmont Drive
Newsham Drive
Radnor Medical Cen
Police Station
Orphan Drive
Windsor Road
Marlborough Road
Ellerslie Road
Victoria Road
Osborne Road
Buckingham Road
Dorset Road
Gloucester Rd
Chester Rd
Clifton Rd
Alton Rd
Surgery
Silverdale Avenue
Snaefell Av
B5189
Sutton St
Brainerd Street
Balmoral Court
Lister Drive Infant School
Lister Drive Junior Sch
Carnegie Rd
Lister Drive
Green Lane
Tynwald Hill
Woburn Hill
Guernsey Road
Portelet Rd
Derwent Rd
Highfield Rd
Albany Rd
Cheadle Av
L13
Newsham Park
The Academy of St Francis of Assisi
Gardner's Drive
B5188 Sheil Road
Denman Dr
Council Building
Fairfield Medical Cen
Huntly Road
Radstock Road
Swiss Road
Balmoral Road
Rufford Road
Prospect Vale
Fairfield Crs
Prescot Drive
Council Building
Newton Road
Prescot Road
A57
Fairfield
University
Laurel Business Cen
Phoenix Primary School
St Sebastians Primary School
Holly Road
Lockerby Road
Lilley Road
Beech Street
Deane Road
Hebrew Cem
Holt Road
Med Cen
St Cuthberts RC Primary School
Council Building
Church Road
Etna St
Works
St Annes CE Primary Sch
Derby Lane Medical Cen
Old Swan
Liverpool Community Coll
St Oswald's Street
St Oswalds C Infant School
Health Centre
St Oswalds Catholic Jun Sch
Surgery
Homoeopathic Medical Cen
Edge Lane
Edge Lane Retail Park
A5047
Edge La Drive
Cineworld Liverpool
Edge Lane Retail Park
Binns Road
Binns Road Industrial Estate
Virgin Cinemas
Hollywood Superbowl
B5179
Rathbone Road
Works
Thistlewood Road
Dryden Road
Botanic Estate
Wavertree Technology Park
Pighue Lane
Tapton Way
Faraday Rd
Rutherford Cl
Wavertree Avenue
Durning Road
Botanic Road
Health Cen
Crosfield Rd
Wavertree Park
Wavertree Boulevard
Wavertree Bvd S
Enterprise Wy
Stephenson Way
B5178
Wavertree Retail Park
Police Stn
Harbord St
Chandos St
A5089
Combermere Street
Ventnor Rd
Edge Hill Station
Works
Alexandra
Cadogan St
Cecil St
Kempton Rd
Picton
Comm Prim Sch
Stevenson St
Wave CC
Victoria Ct
North
Surgery
Olive Grove
Pollard Road
Charlton Rd
Works
Stoneycroft
1 grid square represents 500 metres

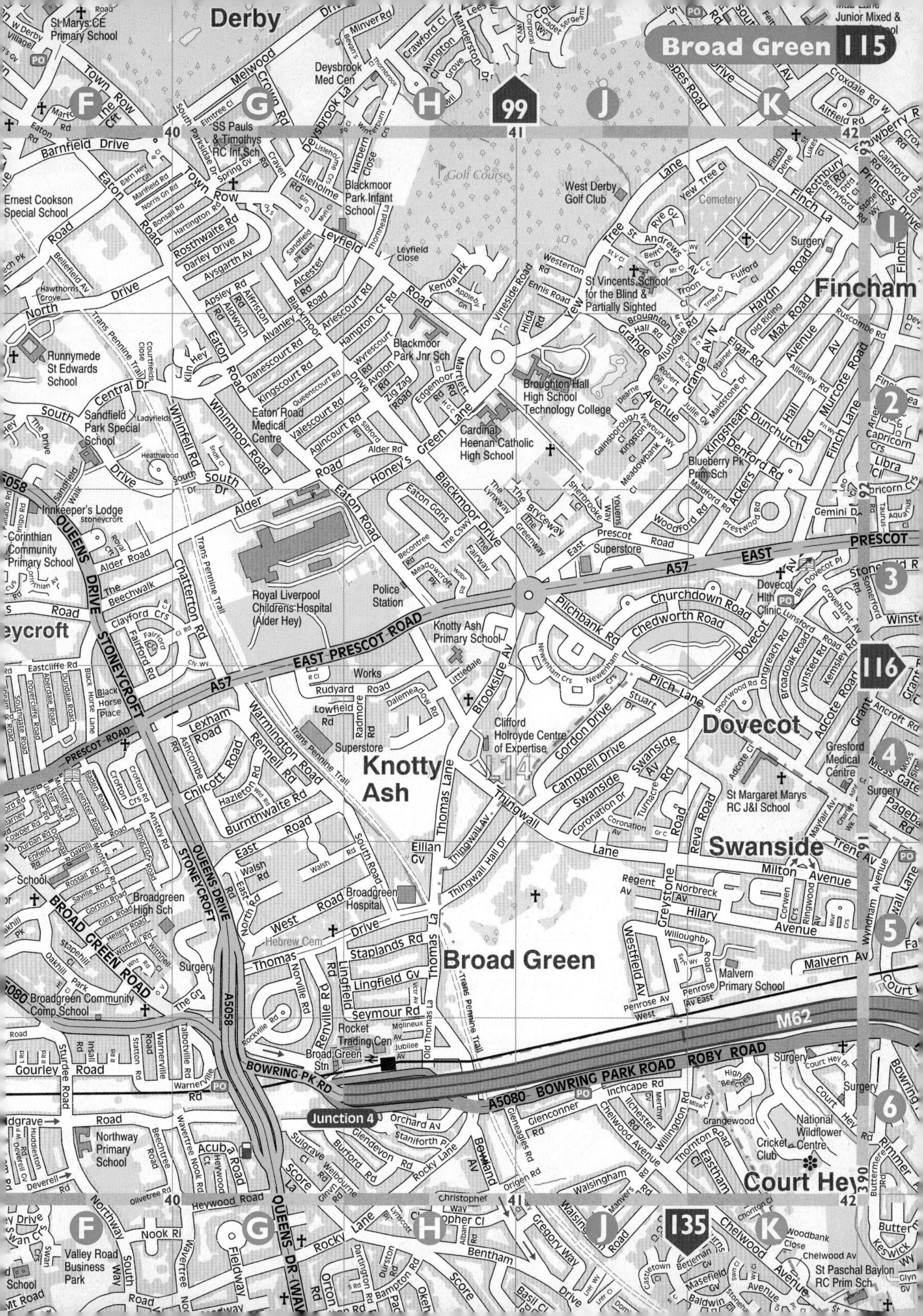
Derby
St Marys CE Primary School
Deysbrook Med Cen
99
Town Row
Melwood
Barnfield Drive
SS Pauls & Timothys RC Inf Sch
Golf Course
Blackmoor Park Infant School
West Derby Golf Club
Cemetery
Ernest Cookson Special School
Leyfield
Leyfield Close
St Vincents School for the Blind & Partially Sighted
Fincham
North Drive
Runnymede St Edwards School
Trans Pennine Trail
Blackmoor Park Jnr Sch
Broughton Hall High School Technology College
Sandfield Park Special School
Eaton Road Medical Centre
Cardinal Heenan Catholic High School
Blueberry Pk Prim Sch
Honey's Green Lane
Blackmoor Drive
Eaton Road
Alder Road
Innkeeper's Lodge
Corinthian Community Primary School
Queens Drive Stoneycroft
Royal Liverpool Childrens Hospital (Alder Hey)
Police Station
Superstore
East Prescot Road
A57
Knotty Ash Primary School
Churchdown Road
Chedworth Road
Pilchbank Rd
Dovecot Hlth Clinic
116
Stoneycroft
Works
Clifford Holroyde Centre of Expertise
Dovecot
L14
Knotty Ash
Superstore
Gresford Medical Centre
St Margaret Marys RC J&I School
Thingwall Lane
Swanside
Broadgreen High Sch
Broadgreen Hospital
Hebrew Cem
Broad Green Road
Broad Green
Malvern Primary School
Broadgreen Community Comp School
A5058
A5080
M62
Rocket Trading Cen
Broad Green Stn
Bowring Park Road
Roby Road
Junction 4
Gourley Road
Northway Primary School
Cricket Club
National Wildflower Centre
Court Hey
135
Valley Road Business Park
St Paschal Baylon RC Prim Sch
Heywood Road
Queens Dr (Wavertree)

116
100
115
135
136
A
B
C
D
E
1
2
3
4
5
6
42
43
44
390
91
92
93
St Brigids RC Primary School
Brookside Primary School
St Edmund of Canterbury Catholic High School
Blueberry Park CP School
St Dominics RC J&I Sch
Medical Cen
Fincham
Beechwood County Prim Sch
Longview Community Primary Sch
St Columbas RC Prim Sch
Cornerways Medical Centre
Council Building
Woolfall Heath
Page Moss
Dovecot JMI Sch
Roby Park Prim Sch
Bowring Community Sports Coll
Dinas Lane Medical Centre
Park View Primary School
St Aloysius RC Primary School
Twig Lane Clnc
HUYTON-WITH-ROBY
L36
Huyton with Roby CE Prim Sch
Knowsley Community College (Roby Campus)
Lathom Road Health Cen
Knowsley Comm Coll
Police Stn
Roby Medical Cen
Surgery
Roby
Roby Station
Huyton Station
Premier Travel Inn
Bowring Park Golf Club
Golf Course
Huyton Park
Huyton Leisure Centre
Blacklow Brow Prim Sch
St Annes RC Prim Sch
Oak Cottage Medical Cen
National Wildflower Centre
Junction 5
Bowring Park
St Paschal Baylon RC Prim Sch
M57
M62
A526
SETH POWELL WAY
STOCKBRIDGE LANE
B5198 STOCKBRIDGE LANE
KNOWSLEY LANE
A57
LIVERPOOL ROAD
PRESCOT ROAD
ROBY ROAD
A5080
TARBOCK ROAD
B5199 ARCHWAY ROAD
Princess Drive
Southdean Road
Wimborne Rd
St Davids Road
Melbury Road
Huyton House Road
Woolfall Crs
Lincombe Rd
Dinas Lane
Aldwark Road
Page Moss Lane
Western Avenue
Rupert Road
Church Road
Bridge Rd
Ashbourne Crs
Jeffereys Crescent
Merton Crescent
Fairfield Avenue
Court Hey Avenue
Bowring Park Avenue
Acacia Avenue
Oak Road
Kingsway
Gentwood Rd
Coral Av
Alamein Road
Cassino Road
Blue Bell Lane
Woolfall Heath Avenue
Hillside Road
Wastle Bridge Rd
Brookwood Road
Bakers Green Road
Larch Road
Blacklow Brow
Twickenham Drive
Lawton Rd
Carr Lane
1 grid square represents 500 metres

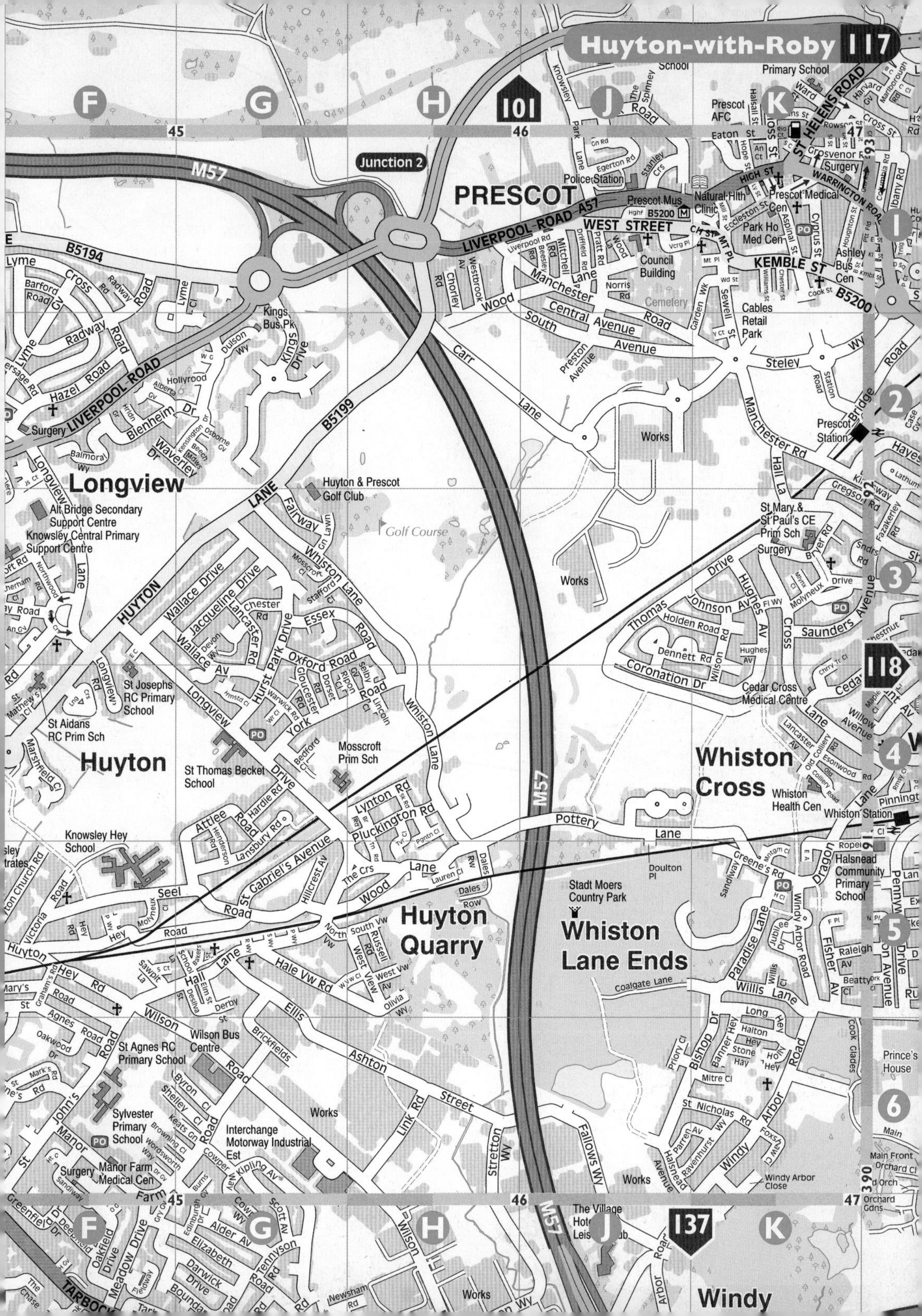
PRESCOT
Longview
Huyton
Whiston Cross
Huyton Quarry
Whiston Lane Ends
Windy
Junction 2
M57
LIVERPOOL ROAD A57
HUYTON LANE
B5199
B5194
B5200
Huyton & Prescot Golf Club
Golf Course
Stadt Moers Country Park
Prescot Station
Whiston Station
Kings Bus Pk
Cables Retail Park
Council Building
Cemetery
Police Station
Prescot Mus
Prescot AFC
Alt Bridge Secondary Support Centre
Knowsley Central Primary Support Centre
St Josephs RC Primary School
St Aidans RC Prim Sch
St Thomas Becket School
Mosscroft Prim Sch
Knowsley Hey School
St Agnes RC Primary School
Sylvester Primary School
Wilson Bus Centre
Interchange Motorway Industrial Est
Manor Farm Medical Cen
St Mary & St Paul's CE Prim Sch
Cedar Cross Medical Centre
Whiston Health Cen
Halsnead Community Primary School
Prince's House
The Village Hotel Leisure Club
Works
101
118
137
F
G
H
J
K
45
46
47
2
3
4
5
6

118
117
102
137
138
A
B
C
D
E
1
2
3
4
5
6
48
49
3 47
Eccleston Park
Brown Edge
Holt
Whiston
Nut Gro
Saint Avenue
Park Avenue
Central Av
Scholes La
Elm Grove
West Close
Albany Av
Lloyd Rd
Hilary Close
St James' Rd
Eccleston Lane Ends Primary Sch
Evelyn Prim Sch
Surgery
Gorsey Croft
Old Lane
Fairholme Av
Eccleston Park Station
Golf Course
Alder Road
Hawthorn Rd
Maryville Rd
Prescot Primary School
Hunter Court
Bretherton Rd
Scotchbarn Lane
B5200
B5201
B5204
B5413
Portico La
Portico Lane
Mcvinnie Rd
Honeybourne Dr
Litchborough Grove
Watling Way
Eccleston Park Golf Club
Wedgewood Gdns
Churchill Gdns
Rainhill Road
Martlew Day Hospital
Two Butt Lane
Prescot Leisure Centre
BICC Athletic Club
St Edmund Arrowsmith Catholic High School
A57 Warrington Road
Warrington Rd
Prescot Station
Bridge Road
Sinclair Av
Gilbert Road
Edward Rd
Delph Lane
Fire Station Road
Sandstone
Blundell Rd
Myers Av
Foster Road
Longview
Holt Lane
Council
Longton Lane
Amanda Road
Croston Av
Tarlton Cl
Longton Lane Community Primary School
Sandhurst Road
Stapleton Road
Nottingham Cl
Ellerslie Avenue
Brookfield Av
Field Wy
Gardeners Wy
Elderswood Rd
Hayes Avenue
Lathum Cl
Ash Grove
Poplar Gv
Maple Gv
Rufford Ct
Windsor Rd
Cable Rd
Brook St
Cook St
Beechwood
Kingsway
Fazakerley Rd
Shaw Lane
Brookside Av
St Lukes RC Primary School
Whiston Hospital
A&E
PO
Ruth Evans Court
Chatsworth Road
Honiston Av
Horwood
Norcliffe Rd
Batey Av
Millom Av
Ivy Farm Rd
Second Av
First Av
Vincent Rd
Stapleton Av
Ellaby Rd
Ansdell Villas
St Ann Pl
Roby Cl
Warburton Hey
Ritherup La
Saunders Avenue
Birch Cl
Hazel Av
Dragon Lane
Oak Road
Stoney Lane
Amb Stn
Works
Hulton Av
The Crs
Keats Av
Scott Av
Cartmel Dr
Arnside Av
Kendal Drive
Warrington Rd
Longton Med Cen
Rainhill Station
Station Rd
Victoria Terrace
Victoria Pl
Victoria Tr Estate
Surgery
Commercial Business Cen
Chestnut Cl
Cedar Cl
Lunt Av
Willow Avenue
Milton Cl
Byron Av
Whiston Willis Primary School
Higher Side Community Comprehensive School
Cumber Lane
Weyman Av
Walpole Av
Pinnington Rd
Harptree
Whiston Station
Hemmingsway
Kendricks Fold
Dee Road
Trent Cl
Trent Road
Severn Rd
Derwent
Weaver Av
St Anns CE Prim School
Calder Drive
Rainhill Clinic
The Priory
Ribble Av
Swale Av
Lowther Drive
Craven Rd
James Road
The Mdw
Owen Road
Halsnead Community Primary School
Driveway
Haslemere
Lyneham
Selborne
Kingsnorth
Dursley
Martock
Manorwood Drive
Copperwood Dr
Langbar
Exeley
Skeffington
Domville
Rudgate
Pennywood Drive
Nelson Avenue
Raleigh Av
Beatty Cl
St Leos RC Prim Sch
Southmead Comm Prim Sch
Lickers Lane
Old Lane
Eden Cl
Marian Dr
Heyes Mt
View
Saint
Ashton
Manor Av
Mill Lane
Oak Prim
Sandstone
Blundell's Lane
Cemetery
Cronton La
Blundells Hill Golf Club
L35
Prince's House
Cook Glades
Golf Course
Fox's Bank Lane
Hall Lane
Main
N Front
Lake Vw
East Front
Main Front
Orchard Cl
Old Orch
S Front
Cronton Lane
390
1 grid square represents 500 metres

Rainhill 119
Sutton Heath
Lea Green
Marshall's Cross
Rainhill
Rainhill Stoops
Sutton Manor
103
120
139
Sherdley Park Golf Club
Sherdley
Sutton Community Leisure Centre Track
Sutton High Sports College
Lea Green Station
Lowfield Industrial Estate
Lea Green Business Park
Premier Travel Inn
Micklehead Farm
Works
Rainhill High School
St Bartholomews RC Primary School
Sutton Manor Community Primary School
St John Vianney RC Prim Sch
Nutgrove Methodist Prim Sch
Eaves Prim Sch
Four Acre Lane Shop Cen
Tower College
Union Bank Farm
Junction 7
ELTON HEAD ROAD
B5204
A570
LINKWAY
SAINT HELENS
WARRINGTON ROAD
A57
CHESTER LANE
B5419
MARSHALLS CROSS
A569
M62
Lea Green Road
Lowfield Lane
Chapel Lane
School Lane
Bell Lane
Eurolink
The Score
Union Bank

120
104
119
139
140
Sutton
Sutton Leach
Clock Face
St Helens Junction Station
St Helens AFC
Penlake Industrial Estate
Reginald Road Industrial Park
Abbotsfield Road Industrial Park
Abbotsfield Farm
Willow Tree Primary School
Lyon Industrial Estate
Clock Face Country Park
Home Farm
Crow's Nest Farm
Union Bank Farm
Sutton CC
Eaves Prim Sch
Sherdley Prim Sch
St Theresas Prim.Sch
Four Acre Lane Shop Cen
REGINALD ROAD
BOLD ROAD
CLOCK FACE ROAD
MILL LANE
CHESTER LANE
MARSHALLS CROSS
Gorsey Lane
Finger House Lane
Tibbs Cross Lane
Hall Lane
Joy Lane
Leach Lane
A569
M62
352
53
54
1 grid square represents 500 metres

Bold Business Centre
B5204
Orchid Wy
Columbine Wy
Celandine Wy
ERS' ENTRY
Lane
Phipps' La
Ollerton Pk
Winsford Dr
Rushton Cl
Aldridge Drive
Eastwood
Tree
Pinewood Rd
Cambourne Rd
Fir
105
F
G
H
J
K
55
56
57
93
St Paul of the Cross Catholic Primary School
Burtonwood Industrial Centre
Kinnock Pk
Sunning
Weymouth Road
Colne Road
Arndil Cl
Karen Close
Brookvale Cl
Bold
Bold Industrial Park
Road
Neills
Wheatacre Farm
Clay Lane
PO
Mercer St
Fairclough Street
Jackson Street
Milnthorpe Road
Chapel
Lane
Cemetery
Webb Dr
Kilshaw Road
Perrins Road
Knight Rd
Green Jones Brow
Hawkshead Rd
Acton Rd
Gorsey Lane
Gorsey Lane
Douglas Avenue
Rosehill Av
Haley Road North
Haley Road South
Mitchell Av
Clay Lane
Almond Drive
Spurling Road
Burtonwood
I
2
3
Joy Lane
St Helens
Warrington
92
Tan
House
Clay Lane
Joy Lane Farm
Joy Lane
Burton
122
Wright's Lane
Limekiln Lane
Junction 8
4
M62
91
5
6
Orion Boulevard
Omega Bvd
Omega Bvd
390
Whittle Avenue
Tenbury
Tunbridge Cl
Leamington Cl
Malvern Cl
55
56
57
F
G
H
J
K
141
Lingley Mere
Lingley Mere Business Park
Avenue
Lingley
Green
Av

122
106
121
141
142
A
B
C
D
E
1
2
3
4
5
6
Alder Root Golf Club
Hall Lane
Red House Farm
Root Lane
Alder Lane
Hollins
Watery Lane
Mill Lane
Farmer's Lane
Brook Head Farm
Tan House Lane
M62
Burtonwood Service Area
Gemini
IKEA
Taurus Park
Superstore
Europa Boulevard
Charon Way
Kingswood
Burtonwood Road
International Business Centre
CROMWELL AVENUE
A574
Callands
Callands Road
Westbrook Way
Westbrook
St Philip Westbrook CE Prim Sch
Westbrook Medical Cen
Gulliver's World Theme Park
Sankey Valley Country Park
Bewsey
Westbrook Old Hall Primary
WA5
1 grid square represents 500 metres

Winwick Quay
Hulme
Longford
Orford
Dallam
WA2
M62
Junction 9
Winwick Parish Leisure Centre
Winwick CE Primary School
Warrington Community Health Care
Alban Retail Park
Warrington Collegiate
William Beamont Community High School & Specialist Sports College
Warrington Business Park
Winstanley Industrial Estate
Long Lane County Primary School
St Margarets CE Prim Sch
St Stephens Catholic Prim Sch
St Andrews CE Primary School
Fordton Leisure Centre
Quay Business Cen
Gemini Business Park
Dallam Community Prim Sch
Hawthorne Business Park
Kerfoot Business Park
St Anns CE Primary School
Peel Hall
Arbury
107
124
143

124
123
143
144
A
B
C
D
E
1
2
3
4
5
6
362
63
64
93
92
91
390
Junction 10/21a
M6
M62
Houghton Green
Cinnamon Brow
Locking Stumps
Blackbrook
Fearnhead
Padgate
Longbarn
Springfield Farm
Midhops Farm
Golf Course
Poulton Park Golf Club
Delph Lane
Millhouse Lane
Spring Lane
Smithy Lane
Dam Lane
New Lane
Eaves Brow
Browmere
Gosling Rd
Wadeson Way
Churchfields
Mill Lane
Ballater Drive
Enfield Park Road
Cinnamon Lane
Blackbrook Avenue
Dig Lane
Crab Lane
Locking Stumps
Fearnhead Lane
Cinnamon Brow CE Prim Sch
St Bridgets Catholic Primary School
Council Building
Fearnhead Cross Medical Cen
Padgate Community High School
Brook Acre Primary School
Christ Church CE Primary School
Longbarn County Primary School
Greyfriars
Templeton Drive
Ronald Dr
Barnes Av
Meadow Lane
Winfrith Rd
Insall Rd
Harrier Rd
Viscount Rd
Avery Cl
Capesthorne
Greenwood
Meteor Crs
Grasmere
Harding Av
Martin Av
Boyle Av
Poplars Av
Hilden
Bawtry Court
Rudloe Ct
Valley Court
Gosport
Waddington Cl
Handley Road
Westland Dr
Harpers Road
Pasture La
Duckworth Gv
Mullion Gr
Mayberry Gv
Grosvenor Grange
Kingsland
Aston Court
Works
BIRCHWOOD WAY
A574
B5210
WOOLSTON
Anderson Cl
Sorrel Cl
Burnet Cl
Saffron Cl
Fallowfield Gv
Carpenter Gv
Station Rd N
Orchard St
Kings Road
Parkfields La
Vallent Cl
Arran Cl
Mere Road
Capenhurst Av
Chapel Cross Rd
Windscale Rd
Dounrey Cl
Med Cen
Padgate Stn
Blackbrook Av
Station Road S
Whitchurch Cl
Ludlow Cl
Colemere Cl
Shawbury Gv
Paddington
Elizabeth Drive
Regent Avenue
Padgate Business Centre
Green Lane Special School
Green Lane
Springfield Avenue
Brownhill Drive
Delery
Lawn Av
Jubilee
Devonshire
Mead Rd
Poulton Crescent
Woolston CE Primary Sch
Norden Close
Lords La
Hawkshaw Cl
Topping Ct
Glover
Sandicroft Cl
Trefoil Cl
Strawberry Cl
Stonecrop
Carrington Cl
Picton Cl
Elton Close
Hapsford Close
Ledsham Close
Kelsall Cl
St Andrews Cl
Solway Cl
Kinross Cl
Dundee Cl
Cairloch Cl
Kilsyth Cl
Montrose Cl
Perth Cl
Gables Cl
Delafield Close
Welsby Cl
Mill Farm Close
Osprey Av
Teal Close
Merrick Crs
Tyne Cl
Orange Gv
Rowland Cl
Jervis Cl
Aspinall Cl
Aviemore Dr
Stirrup Cl
Cottam Dr
Stonehaven Dr
Oban Gv
Isherwood Cl
Wasley Cl
Bromley Cl
Appletree Gv
1 grid square represents 500 metres

Risley
Birchwood
Oakwood
Gorse Covert
M62
M6
Junction 11
Warrington Road
Birchwood Way
Birchwood Park
A574
Daten Avenue
Ordnance Avenue
Admirals Road
Dewhurst Road
Woolston Grange Avenue
Grange Avenue
Leacroft Road
Cross Lane
Silver Lane
Hey Farm
Birchwood Golf Club
Trident Industrial Est
Industrial Estate
Risley Moss Nature Park
Birchwood CE Prim Sch
Fox Wood Sch
Birchwood Community High School
Birchwood Medical Cen
Birchwood One Business Park
Birchwood Station
Gorse Covert Prim Sch
Woolston Moss
Marshall's Farm
Works
Killingworth Lane
Moss Gate
Moss Lane
Nicol Av
Hollyhurst Lane
Long Barn Lane
Hardwick Grange
Kingsland Gra
Kelvin Street
Cavendish Avenue
Cavendish Place
Maxwell St
Faraday Street
Griffith Av
Reynolds Av
Ravenhurst Ct
Adlington Ct
Heaton Court
Risley Rd
Clayton Ct
Raglan Ct
Melbury Ct
Bridgewater Pl
Garrett Fld
Powell Av
Delenty Dr
Armstrong Cl
Fern Cl
Heather Close
Havisham Av
Redshank La
Keyes Cl
Daniel Cl
Mansfield Cl
Jay Cl
McCarthy Cl
Palliser Cl
Pennant Close
Ashmore Cl
Halliday Rd
Burrough Cl
Lyster Cl
Mallard La
Curlew Gv
Pipit La
Whinchat Dr
Linnet Gv
Dunnock Gv
Chatfield Dr
Noble Cl
Brock Rd
Benson Road
Ainscough Rd
Birchwood Blvd
Woodhouse Close
Fisherfield Drive
Bramshill Cl
Gorse Covert Rd
Ashdown La
Gilderdale Cl
Langwell Cl
Dalby Close
Ringwood Cl
Rockingham Cl
Hazelborough Close
Woolmer Cl
Falstone Cl
Oakwood Ga
Warrington Rd
Dalton Rd
Walton Rd
Chadwick Pl
Wilson Lane
Trinity Ct
Dewar St
Stokes Av
Davy Av
Kingfisher Cl
Partridge Cl
Pheasant Cl
Woodpecker Cl
Dove Cl
Chaffinch Cl
Teal Gv
Miles Cl
Rawlings Cl
Talbot Cl
Layton Cl
Harcourt Cl
Leatham
Forbes Cl
Benson Rd
F G H J K
1 2 3 4 5 6
65 66 67
93 92 91 390
145

A
B
C
D
E
319
20
90
89
88
3 87
1
2
3
4
5
6
Red Rocks
Barton Close
Beach Road
The Royal
Crntn Rd
Hilbre Island
Little Hilbre Island
WEST KIRBY
1 grid square represents 500 metres

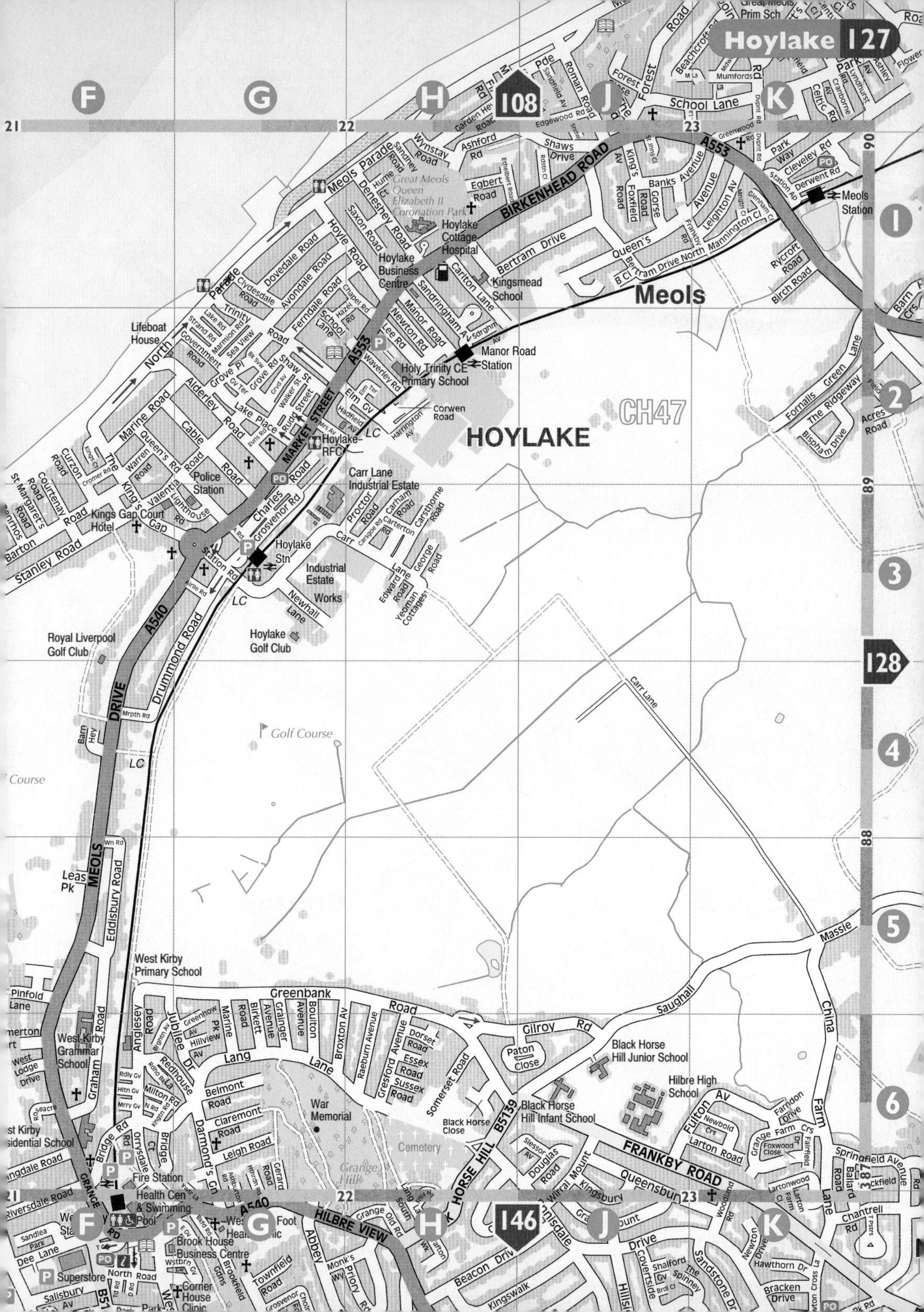

HOYLAKE
Meols
CH47
Meols Station
Manor Road Station
Hoylake Stn
Hoylake Cottage Hospital
Hoylake Business Centre
Kingsmead School
Holy Trinity CE Primary School
Carr Lane Industrial Estate
Industrial Estate
Works
Royal Liverpool Golf Club
Hoylake Golf Club
Golf Course
Lifeboat House
Police Station
Kings Gap Court Hotel
Great Meols Queen Elizabeth II Coronation Park
West Kirby Primary School
West Kirby Grammar School
Black Horse Hill Junior School
Black Horse Hill Infant School
Hilbre High School
War Memorial
Cemetery
Grange Hill
Fire Station
Health Cen & Swimming Pool
Brook House Business Centre
Corner House Clinic
Superstore
BIRKENHEAD ROAD
MARKET STREET
MEOLS DRIVE
FRANKBY ROAD
HILBRE VIEW
Greenbank Road
Saughall Massie

108 128 146

128
108
127
147
A
B
C
D
E
1
2
3
4
5
6
3 24
25
90
89
88
387
Meols Station
Works
BIRKENHEAD ROAD
A553
HOYLAKE ROAD
A553
Carr Farm
Heron Road
Saughall Massie
Barnacre Lane
Saughall Massie Road
W Kirby Rd
Oldfield Manor Farm
Oldfield Lane
Three Lanes End
Road
Pump Lane
Greasby Brook
Greasby
FRANKBY ROAD
B5139
Greasby Health Cen
Larton
China Lane
Frankby Stile
Newton
Frankby
The Nook
Carr Lane
Millhouse Lane
Town Meadow Lane
Bermuda Road
Lingham Primary Sch
Kestrel Road
Edgehill Road
Douglas Drive
Foxfield School
Surgery
Cobham Road
Meadowbrook Road
Borrowdale
Carr Gate
Carr House La
Saughall Road
Acton Lane
Garden Hey Road
Westbrook Road
Kingfisher Way
Birch Avenue
Elm Avenue
Beech Avenue
Oak Avenue
Woodpecker Close
Girtrell Road
Long Acres
Wood Lane
Hazelwood
Summertrees Av
Leaway
Bromsgrove Rd
Greasby Rd
Circular Drive
Lloyd Drive
Ferguson Avenue
Harvey Av
Dodd Av
Hall Dr
Greasby Infant School
Our Lady of Pity Primary School
Barn Hey Crs
Sherwood Road
Fieldway
Acres Road
Bispham Drive
Springfield Avenue
Chantrell Rd
Abingdon Rd
Stanmore Park
Ashdale Park
Locker Pk
Frankby Cl
Greasby Dr
Hillcrest Dr
Langstone
Miles Lane
Lombardy Avenue
Whitebeam Walk
1 grid square represents 500 metres

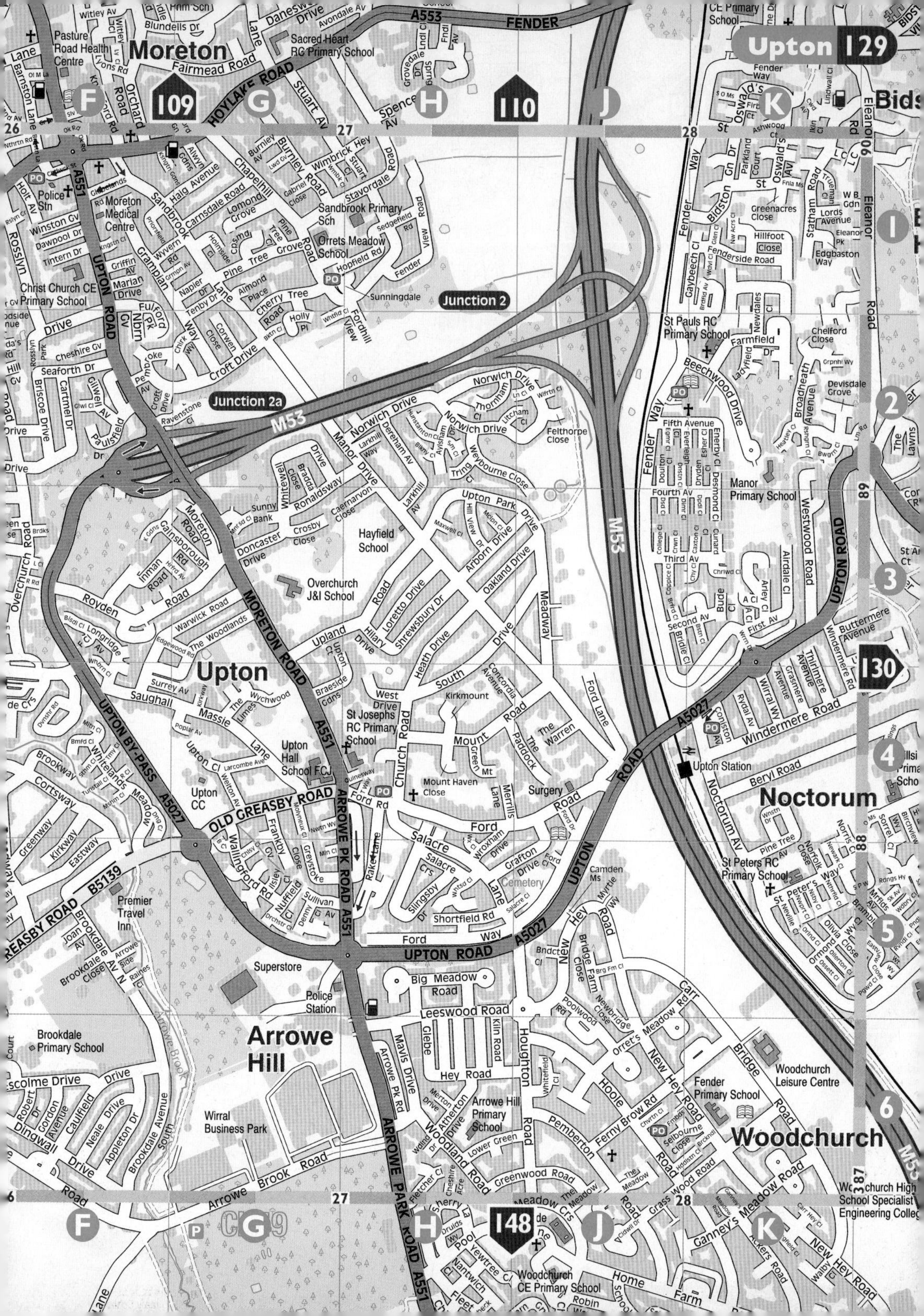

Upton 129
Moreton
109
110
130
148
F
G
H
J
K
Fairmead Road
Hoylake Road
Fender
A553
M53
Junction 2
Junction 2a
Sacred Heart RC Primary School
Pasture Road Health Centre
Police Stn
Moreton Medical Centre
Christ Church CE Primary School
Sandbrook Primary Sch
Orrets Meadow School
Sunningdale
St Pauls RC Primary School
Manor Primary School
Hayfield School
Overchurch J&I School
Upton
St Josephs RC Primary School
Upton Hall School FCJ
Upton CC
Mount Haven Close
Surgery
Cemetery
Upton Station
Noctorum
St Peters RC Primary School
Premier Travel Inn
Superstore
Police Station
Arrowe Hill
Brookdale Primary School
Wirral Business Park
Arrowe Hill Primary School
Fender Primary School
Woodchurch Leisure Centre
Woodchurch
Woodchurch High School Specialist Engineering College
Woodchurch CE Primary School
Upton Road
Moreton Road
Upton By-Pass
Old Greasby Road
Arrowe Park Road
Greasby Road
Ford Way
Woodland Road
Brook Road
Arrowe Road
Windermere Road
Beechwood Drive
Noctorum Av
Eleanor Road
Bidston Gn Dr
New Hey Road
Ganney's Meadow Road
A551
A5027
B5139
26
27
28
2
3
4
5
6
87
88
89
90

130
110
129
149
Bidston Hill
Claughton
Oxton
BIRKENH
Birkenhead Park
Birkenhead North Station
West Float
HOYLAKE ROAD
LAIRD STREET
PARK ROAD NORTH A5027
UPTON ROAD
BIDSTON ROAD
CORPORATION RD
BEAUFORT ROAD A5030
Wirral Ladies Golf Club
Golf Course
CH43
M53
1 grid square represents 500 metres

Birkenhead 131
LIVERPOOL
Historic Warships
Works
Merseyside International
QUEENSWAY (MERSEY TUNNEL)
CORPORATION ROAD
DUKE ST
DUKE STREET
A5027
TOWER ROAD
Tower Wharf
Morpeth Wharf
Morpeth Dock
Egerton Dock
Egerton Whf
TOWER RD
Wirral Metropolitan College
CANNING STREET
Transport Museum
Woodside Business Park
Pacific Rd
Hamilton Square Stn
Woodside Ferry Landing Stage
Pump Ho Mus
Cncl Bldg
Woodside Ferry Approach
Town Hall & Registry Office
Wirral Mus
Pol Stn
Wirral Borough Magistrates Court
Priory Wht
Council Building
Pilgrim St
Birkenhead Co Ct
CHESTER ST
Priory St
Church Street
Monks Ferry
St Mary's
Birkenhead Museum
Abbey St
132
CLEVELAND STREET
CH41
Cleveland Business Park
Price Street Business Centre
Vittoria Medical Centre
The Priory CE Primary School
Rosebank
Prim Sch
HAMILTON SQ
ARGYLE ST
Conway Pk Stn
Pool
Vue
Wirral Metropolitan College
CONWAY ST
NORTH ROAD
A553
A5029 WATSON STREET
EXMOUTH STREET
Cncl Bldg
Bus Cen
Fire Stn
Amb Stn
Claughton Rd
Conway Education Cen
Argyle Health Ctr
Market Hall
Pyramids Shopping Ctr
The Grange Shopping Precinct
Cole Street Primary School
Cloughton Rd
Little Theatre
Charing Cross
BOROUGH ROAD
BOROUGH RD
A5227
A41
Whetstone Lane Health Cen
WHETSTONE LANE
Council Building
Woodlands Primary School
Birkenhead Central Station
Rock Retail Park
Mollington Link
Unicorn Way
St Werburghs RC Primary Sch
Raffles Road
A552
Willmer Rd
Primary School
B5148
B5147
PEARSON RD
Hinderton Road
Holt Hill
Green Lane Station
Green Lane
Campbeltown Road
Lairdside Technology Park
Victoria Fields
Chesnut Grove
Maybank Rd
Elmswood Road
Harrowby Road
Whitford Road
Fountain Street
St Catherine's Hospital
BOROUGH ROAD
CHURCH RD
Thompson St
Holt Road
Sidney Road
B5149
NEW CHESTER ROAD
Tranmere
Mersey Park Prim Sch
Downham Road
Expressway Business Park
Oil Terminal
Ferries Industrial Estate
SINGLETON AVENUE
Westbank Road
Greenbank Road
Willowbank Road
Prenton Rd East
South Rd
Rock Ferry Medical
St Paul's Rd
Devonshire Park Primary School
Temple
Well Lane
150
Tranmere Rovers FC (Prenton Park)
BEBINGTON RD
Rock Ferry Primary Sch
Fairfield RFC
Bedford Rd
Rock Ferry
F
G
H
J
K
1
2
3
4
5
6
31
32
33
90
89
88
387

132
112
131
151
A
B
C
D
E
1
2
3
4
5
6
90
89
88
387
334
35
Titanic Memorial
Cunard Building
Mersey Ferries
SAE Institute
Museum of Liverpool (due to open 2010)
HM Customs & Excise Nat Museum
Merseyside Maritime Museum & International Slavery Museum
Fingerprints of Elvis
Tate Gallery
Albert Dock Village
The Beatles Story
Albert Dock
Premier Travel Inn
Wapping Basin
National Discovery Park
Fire Stn
Granada TV
Merseyside Police HQ
Hotel Ibis
Cavern Club
Beacon Radio City
Shopping Centre
Police Station
Central Stn
Shop Centre
BBC Radio
Lord St
James Street Stn
Brownlow Hill
LJMU
Primary School
Metropolitan Cathedral of Christ the King
Mount Pleasant
Oxford
Clinic
Health Cen
Liverpool John Moores University
Liverpool Community College
Philharmonic Hall
Community Cen
Natural Hlth Cen
Health Cen
Toxteth Community College
Canning St
Huskisson Street
Egerton Street
Liverpool Anglican Cathedral
Lady Chapel Close
St James Rd
Dean Dillistone Court
Gambier Terrace
Chinese Arch
Community College
Duke St
Henry
Lydia
Seel St
Parr St
Fleet St
Bold St
Wood St
Hanover St
Renshaw
Berry St
A5038 GT GEORGE ST
ST JAMES ST
A561
PARK LANE
WAPPING A562
STRAND
CANNING
LIVER ST PARADISE ST
Kings Dock
Kings Dock St
Waterfront Business Area
Parliament St N Waterfront Bus Area
Queens Wharf
Campanile Hotel
Queens Dock Business Centre
Queens Dock
VAT House & HM Customs & Excise
Kings Parade
Mariners Wharf
Liverpool Marina
Hill Street Business Centre
Coburg Wharf
South Ferry Quay
Quebec Quay
Navigation Wharf
CHALONER
Jamaica Street
Flint St
Brick St
Jordan St
New Bird St
Greenland St
Great George Square
PARLIAMENT ST A562
UPPER PARLIAMENT
PRINCES
Bus Area
Brewery
Hill Street Bus Cen
Ambulance Station
Council Building
Hill Street
Warwick Street
Grafton St
Mann St
Beaufort St
Gore St
Mill St
Hyslop St
Park Place A561
Primary School
Prim Sch
Toxteth Sports Centre
Upr Warwick St
Pickwick Street
Dombey Street
Dorrit Street
Northumberland
Toxteth
Primary School
SEFTON STREET
A5036
Small Business Centre
Travelodge
Brunswick Wy
Tower Street
Summers Road
Atlantic Way
Park St
Caryl Street
Grafton Street
Harlow St
Grain Industrial Estate
Park Rd Sports Cen
Beaufort Park County Prim Sch
Brunswick Business Park
Brunswick Station
Harrison Wy
Sefton Street
Harrington Rd
Atlantic Way
Royden Wy
Columbus Quay
Riverside Drive
Ellerman Road
Cockburn Street
Primary School
Glendale Cl
Liverpool
Wirral
The Sloyne
Works
Bedford Rd East
Rock Ferry
1 grid square represents 500 metres

Edge Hill
Edge Hill Station
Wavertree Park
Wavertree Retail Park
Wavertree Road
Tunnel Road
Picton Road
Smithdown Road
Lodge Lane
Princes Park
Princes Avenue
Sefton Park Road
Croxteth Road
Ullet Road
Aigburth Road
Aigburth Drive
Sefton Park
Mossley Hill
Dingle
St Michael's Hamlet
St Michael's Stn
Cemetery
Sefton Park Medical Centre
St Hildas CE High School
Bellerive High School
The Belvedere School
Liverpool Womens Hospital
Liverpool Community College
Princes Park Health Cen
Alicia Hotel
Auckland College
Shorefields Technology College
Liverpool College
Mossley Hill Hospital
Festival Gardens
Trans Pennine Trail
Allerton Remedial Clinic
Newstead Abbey
Charles Wooton Cen of FE
Elimu Academy
Community School
Princes Special School
Abercromby Health Centre
Comprehensive School
Sandringham Medical Cen
St Michael-In The Hamlet Primary Sch
St Charles RC Primary School
Sefton CC
Council Building
Greenbank Lane
Ibbotson's Lane
Park Avenue
Aigburth Vale
Ashfield Road
Victoria Road
Belvidere Road
Devonshire Rd
Riverside Drive
Grove St
Crown St
Falkner St
Selborne Street
Granby St
Kingsley Road
Wellington Road
Gainsborough Road
Arundel Avenue
Hartington Road
Croxteth Grove
Croxteth Drive
Mossley Hill Drive
Livingston Drive
Dingle Vale
A5089
A562
A561
A5058
B5178
B5179
B5174
F
G
H
J
K
113
114
134
152
1
2
3
4
5
6
36
37
38
387
88
89
90
L17

134
114
133
153
Junction 4
A
B
C
D
E
1
2
3
4
5
6
339
40
90
89
88
387
Wavertree
L15
L18
Mossley
Calderstones
Pighue Lane
Avenue
Railbrook Hey
Crawford Drive
Waldgrave
Road
Northway Primary School
Orchard AV
Glendevon Rd
Stephenson
Way
Ventnor Rd
Sandown
Long
Lane
Deverell
Heywood Road
Olive Lane
Crossley Drive
Swan Crs
Nook Ri
Fieldway
Rocky
Lane
Christopher Cl
Bentham
Rathbone Road
Wavertree CC
Victoria Ct
Valley Road Business Park
Millstead Special School
Olive Mt Road
Northway
South
Way
Wavertree Nook Rd
Meadway
Queens Dr (Wavertree)
Orton
Rudston Rd
Dartington Rd
Paignton Rd
Padstow Road
Okehampton
Rudston J&I Sch
Score
Molton Rd
Bampton Rd
North
Surgery
South Drive
Prim Sch
Millstead Road
Thingwall
Abbeystead Road
Westway
Charnley Dr
Childwall School
Wellington Road
High Street
Wavertree Town Hall
Chestnut Gv
Edgewell Dr
Davenham Court
Childwall Road
B5178
A5058
Rudston Road
Pearson St
Wavertree CE Prim Sch
Hunter's La
Wavertree Athletics Centre
Royal School for the Blind
Lance Lane Medical Centre
Abbeystead Medical Centre
The King David High Sch
King David Primary School
Childwall Crs
Kenilworth
Rose Bank
Yew Bank
Childwall Priory Rd
Hilltop Road
Corbridge Road
Surgery
Fir Lane
Prince Alfred Road
Church Road North
Tulip Road
Mimosa Rd
Daffodil Road
Woodsorrel Road
Moss Pits Lane
Banstead Gv
Epping Grove
Dorking
Beauclair Drive
Dunbabin Road
Highville Rd
The Blue Coat School
Wavertree Hlth Clinic
Barnhill Rd
Victoria Terrace
Wootton
Mosspits J&I School
Loreburn Rd
Lichfield Rd
Beverley Rd
Bristol Rd
Hereford Rd
Norwich Rd
Truro Rd
Charles Berrington Rd
Sinclair Drive
Dudlow Lane
Queens Dr (Wavertree)
A5058 Queens Dr
Hattons Lane
Eldred Road
Irene Road
Towers Road
Green Lane North
Oulton Road
Terence Road
Taggart Avenue
Stand Park
Liverpool Hope University College
Education Deanery
Liverpool Institute of HE
Works
Grant Avenue
Earlsfield Road
Fallowfield Road
A562
Rutherford Medical Centre
Montclair Dr
Heathfield
Rutherford Rd
Allerton Health Cen
Hallville Rd
Plattsville Rd
Allerton Road
Mayville Rd
Queens Dr Mossley Hl
A5058
Dudlow Nook Rd
Dairylands
Childwall CE Prim Sch
Mossley Prim Sch
Crawford Avenue
Russell Road
Ramilies Road
Dudley Road
Stalbridge
Karslake Rd
Alverstone Rd
Greenbank Road
Menlove Gardens W
Menlove Gdns South
Dudlow Lane
Friarsgate Cl
Cinder La
Woolton Road
Our Ladys Bishop Eton RC Primary School
Surgery
Lane
Oakdale
Dovedale Junior School
Barndale Rd
Ashdale Rd
Elm Hall Dr
Menlove Av
Allerton Road
Hillside Rd
Courtland Rd
Addingham Rd
Wembley Rd
Menlove Gdns N
Green La
Primrose Road
Gwydrin Rd
Surg
Calderfield Rd
Troutbeck
Hornby
Ingledene
Eton Ct
Streatham Av
Croydon Av
Norbury Av
Penny
Dovedale Road
Infant Sch
Limedale Rd
Mapledale Rd
Rosedale Rd
Meredale Rd
Beechenhurst School
Beech Lane
Beechfield
Lourdes Hospital
Herondale
Ivydale Rd
Briardale
A5058
Heydale Rd
Hallam Dr
Bleasdale Rd
Garthdale Road
Odeon Cinema
Green Lane
Harthill Av
Cldrstns Rd
Calderstones
Greenhill Av
Calder Dr
Calderstones Road
Druids Cross Rd
Mossley
Molyneux Road
St Anthony of Padua RC Primary School
Liverpool College
Mossley Hill
Queens Drive
Beechdale Rd
Boxdale Rd
Gorsedale Road
Heatherdale Rd
Dovedale Road
Reedale Rd
Edale Rd
Drive
Rose La
Police Stn
Tanat Dr
Allerton Dr
Garth Drive
Calderstones School
A562
Council Building
Mossley Hill Hospital
Elmsley Road
Drewell Rd
Lyndhurst
Park Avenue
Pennyford Dr
Carleton House Preparatory School
Palmerston Road
Palmerston Close
Millersdale Rd
Ribbledale Rd
Rose Lane
Rose Brae
Pitville Rd
Pitville Gv
B5180
Mather Avenue
Allerton Road
Greenhill
Harthill
Allerton Beeches
Road
Mossley Hill Station
Works
Pitville Avenue
Rose Lane
Avonmore Av
Glenmore
Ballantrae Road
Burnham Road
The Gln
The Calders
Yewtree
Storrsdale Medical Cen
Abbotts Close
Wyndale Close
Storrsdale
Asbury
Fawley
Glenathol Rd
Allerton Road
Brodie Avenue
Mayville
Mossville Rd
Pitville Close
Farmdale Close
Marion Gv
Greenhill Road
1 grid square represents 500 metres

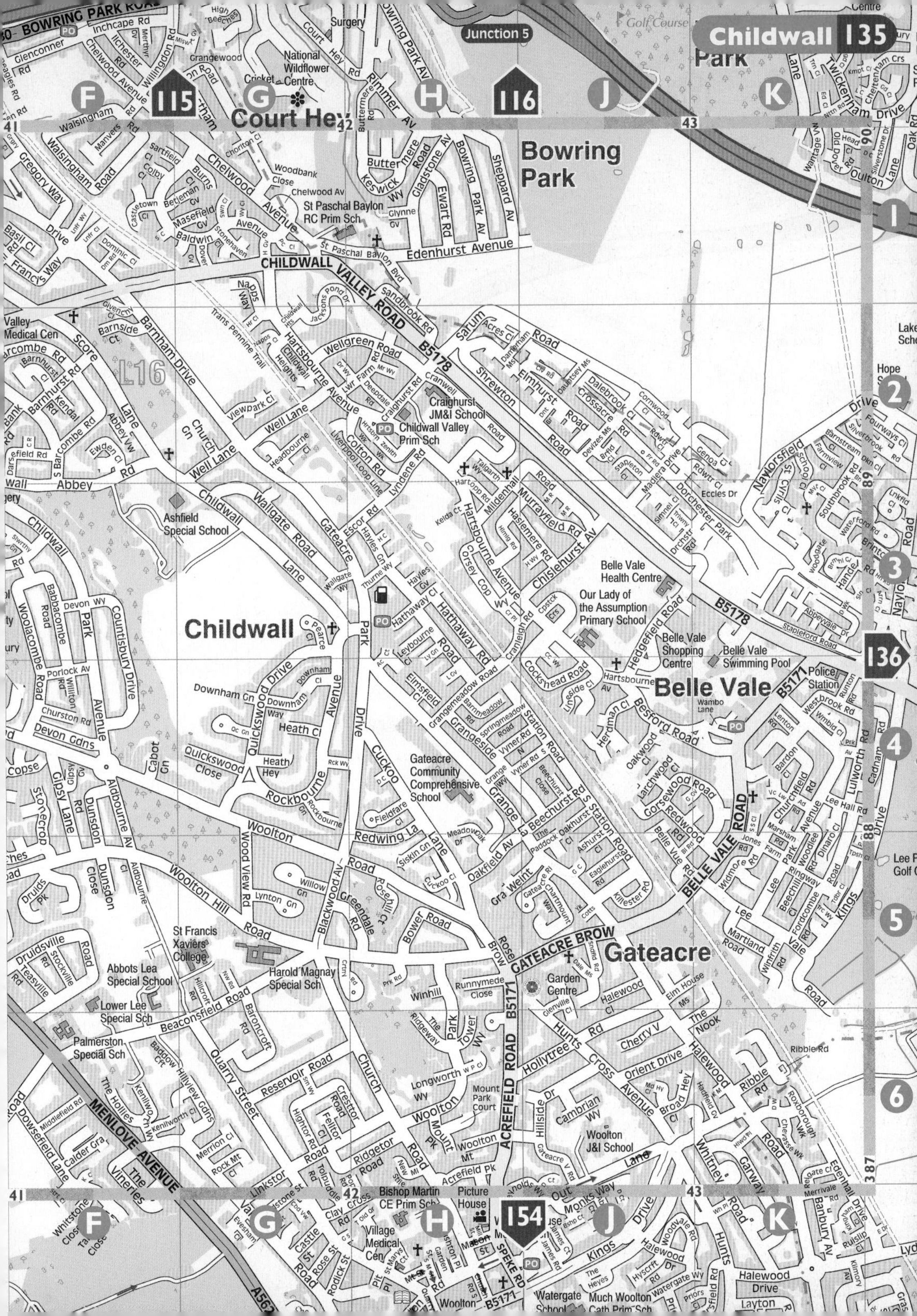
Court Hey
Bowring Park
Childwall
Belle Vale
Gateacre
Junction 5
115
116
136
154
F
G
H
J
K
1
2
3
4
5
6
41
42
43
387
88
89
90
L16
National Wildflower Centre
St Paschal Baylon RC Prim Sch
Craighurst JM&I School
Childwall Valley Prim Sch
Ashfield Special School
Belle Vale Health Centre
Our Lady of the Assumption Primary School
Belle Vale Shopping Centre
Belle Vale Swimming Pool
Police Station
Gateacre Community Comprehensive School
St Francis Xaviers College
Abbots Lea Special School
Harold Magnay Special Sch
Lower Lee Special Sch
Palmerston Special Sch
Garden Centre
Mount Park Court
Woolton J&I School
Bishop Martin CE Prim Sch
Village Medical Cen
Picture House
Much Woolton Cath Prim Sch
Valley Medical Cen
Trans Pennine Trail
Liverpool Loop Line
CHILDWALL VALLEY ROAD
B5178
B5171
BOWRING PARK ROAD
MENLOVE AVENUE
A562
ACREFIELD ROAD
GATEACRE BROW
BELLE VALE ROAD
SPEKE RD
Edenhurst Avenue
Childwall Lane
Woolton Road
Woolton Hill Road
Childwall Park Avenue
Countisbury Drive
Quickswood Drive
Cuckoo Lane
Hartsbourne Avenue
Hathaway Rd
Gateacre Park Drive
Grange La
Station Road
Naylorsfield Drive
Lee Vale Road
Kings Drive
Halewood Road
Hunts Cross Avenue
Quarry Street
Beaconsfield Road
Church Road
Well Lane
Wallgate Road
Barnham Drive
Score Lane
Abbey Rd
Besford Road
Hedgefield Road
Chiselhurst Av
Murrayfield Rd
Shrewton Road
Dorchester Park
Madeira Drive
Lee Park Golf Course
Woolton

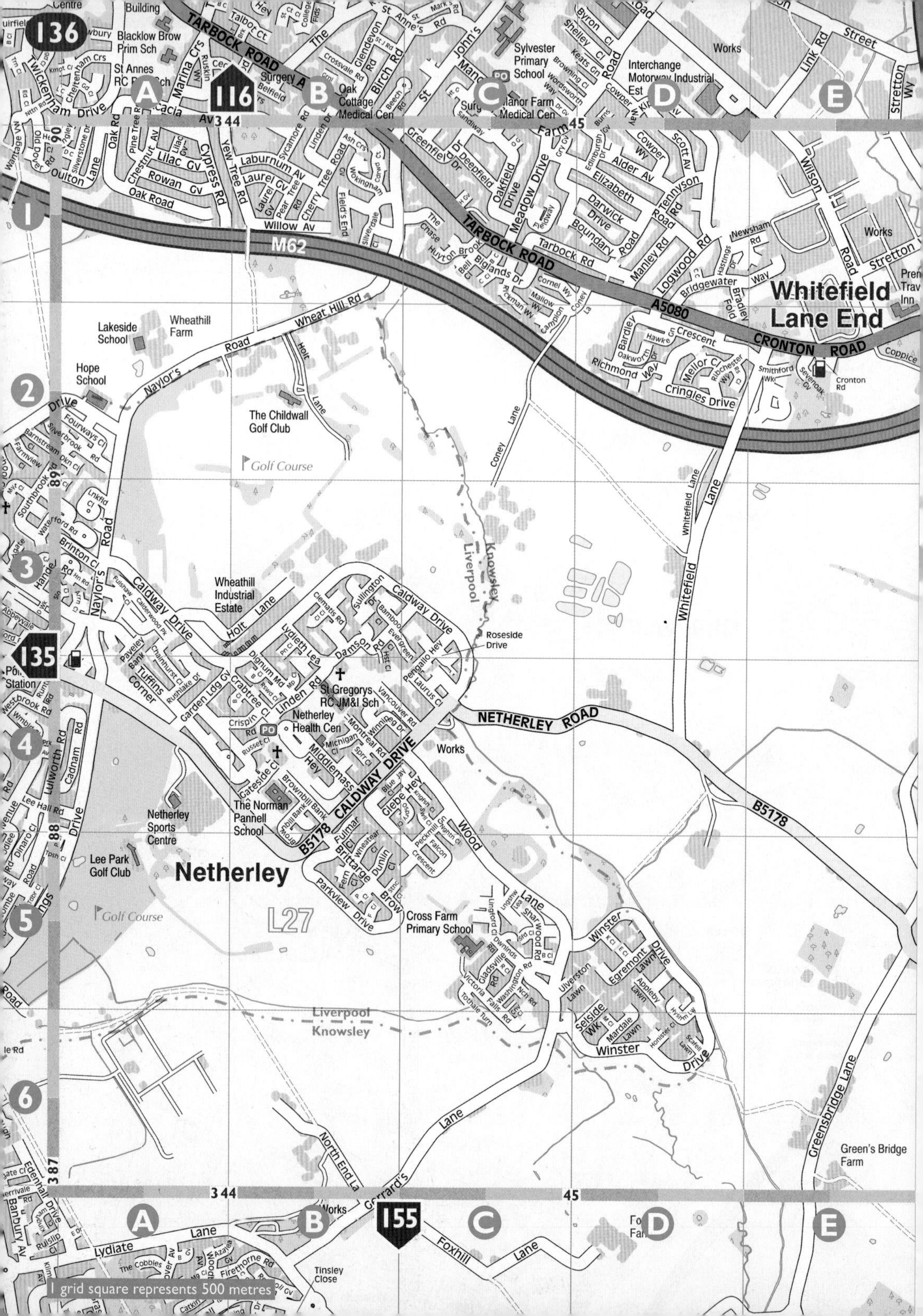

136
116
135
155
A
B
C
D
E
1
2
3
4
5
6
344
45
90
89
88
387
Blacklow Brow Prim Sch
St Annes RC Prim Sch
Surgery
Oak Cottage Medical Cen
Sylvester Primary School
Manor Farm Medical Cen
Interchange Motorway Industrial Est
Works
TARBOCK ROAD
Twickenham Drive
Cheltenham Crs
Marina Crs
Talbot Ct
St Anne's Rd
Glendevon Rd
Birch Rd
St John's Rd
Byron Cl
Shelley Cl
Keats Gn
Cowper Wy
Scott Av
Link Rd
Stretton Wy
Wilson Road
Stretton
Oulton Lane
Oak Rd
Pine Tree Rd
Chestnut Av
Lilac Gv
Rowan Gv
Oak Road
Cypress Rd
Yew Tree Rd
Laburnum Av
Laurel Gv
Sycamore Rd
Linden Dr
Cherry Tree Road
Willow Av
Field's End
Silverdale Cl
Greenfield Dr
Deepfield Dr
Oakfield Drive
Meadow Drive
Alder Av
Elizabeth Rd
Darwick Drive
Boundary Rd
Tennyson Road
Tarbock Rd
Manley Rd
Logwood Rd
Newsham Rd
Hastings Rd
Bridgewater Way
Bradley Fold
The Chase
Huyton Brook
Biglands Dr
Mallow Wy
Campion Wy
Coney La
M62
A5080
CRONTON ROAD
Whitefield Lane End
Crescent
Richmond Way
Mellor Cl
Cringles Drive
Smithford Wk
Cronton Rd
Coppice
Lakeside School
Wheathill Farm
Wheat Hill Rd
Naylor's Road
Hope School
Holt Lane
The Childwall Golf Club
Golf Course
Coney Lane
Whitefield Lane
Drive
Fourways Cl
Silverbrook Rd
Southbrook Rd
Brinton Cl
Naylor's Road
Wheathill Industrial Estate
Holt Lane
Caldway Drive
Knowsley
Liverpool
Roseside Drive
Sullington Dr
Bamboo Cl
Evergreen Cl
Clematis Rd
Lydieth Lea
Damson Rd
Pengallo Hey
Laurus Cl
Paveley Bank
Tuffins Corner
Chainhurst Cl
Rushlake Dr
Garden Ldg Gv
Dignum Md
Crabtree Cl
Linden Rd
St Gregorys RC JM&I Sch
Vancouver Rd
Netherley Health Cen
Crispin Rd
Russet Cl
Michigan Cl
Montreal Rd
Winnipeg Dr
Middlemass Hey
Gateside Cl
Brownbill Bank
CALDWAY DRIVE
B5178
NETHERLEY ROAD
Works
The Norman Pannell School
Netherley Sports Centre
Lee Park Golf Club
Netherley
Golf Course
L27
Fulmar Cl
Brittarge Brow
Glebe Hey
Blue Jay Cl
Peckmill Gn
Falcon Crescent
Dunlin Cl
Fern Cl
Parkview Drive
Wood Lane
Cross Farm Primary School
Lingford Cl
Downinds Rd
Gladsville Rd
Victoria Falls Rd
Washington Rd
Tothale Turn
Sharwood Rd
Winster Drive
Egremont Lawn
Ulverston Lawn
Appleby Lawn
Selside Wk
Mardale Lawn
Winster Drive
Scafell Lawn
Liverpool
Knowsley
Greensbridge Lane
Green's Bridge Farm
Lulworth Rd
Cadham Rd
Lee Hall Rd
Drive
Dinaro Cl
Road
Edenhall Drive
Banbury Av
Ruislip Cl
Lydiate Lane
The Cobbles
Firethorne Rd
North End La
Gerrard's Lane
Works
Foxhill Lane
Tinsley Close
1 grid square represents 500 metres

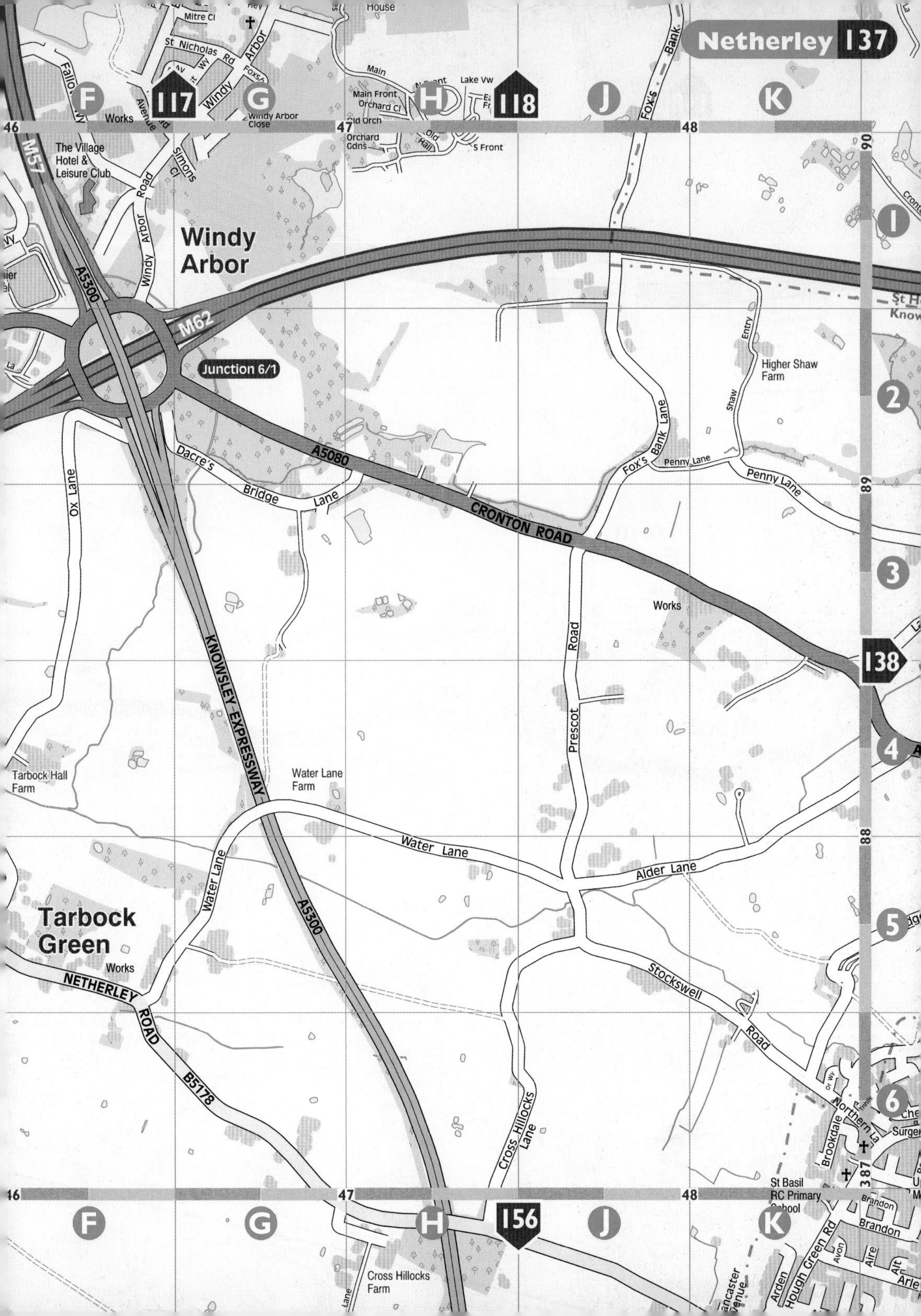
117
118
138
156
F
G
H
J
K
46
47
48
90
89
88
87
1
2
3
4
5
6
Windy Arbor
Tarbock Green
The Village Hotel & Leisure Club
Works
Junction 6/1
M57
M62
A5300
A5080
CRONTON ROAD
KNOWSLEY EXPRESSWAY
NETHERLEY ROAD
B5178
Mitre Cl
St Nicholas Rd
Windy Arbor Close
Windy Arbor Road
Simons Cl
Avenue
Main Front
Orchard Cl
Old Orch
Orchard Gdns
Lake Vw
S Front
Fox's Bank
Fox's Bank Lane
Higher Shaw Farm
Shaw Entry
Penny Lane
Dacre's Bridge Lane
Ox Lane
Prescot Road
Water Lane Farm
Water Lane
Alder Lane
Tarbock Hall Farm
Stockswell Road
Cross Hillocks Lane
Cross Hillocks Farm
St Basil RC Primary School
Northern La
Brookdale
Hough Green Rd
Brandon
Avon
Aire
Arden
Surgery
House

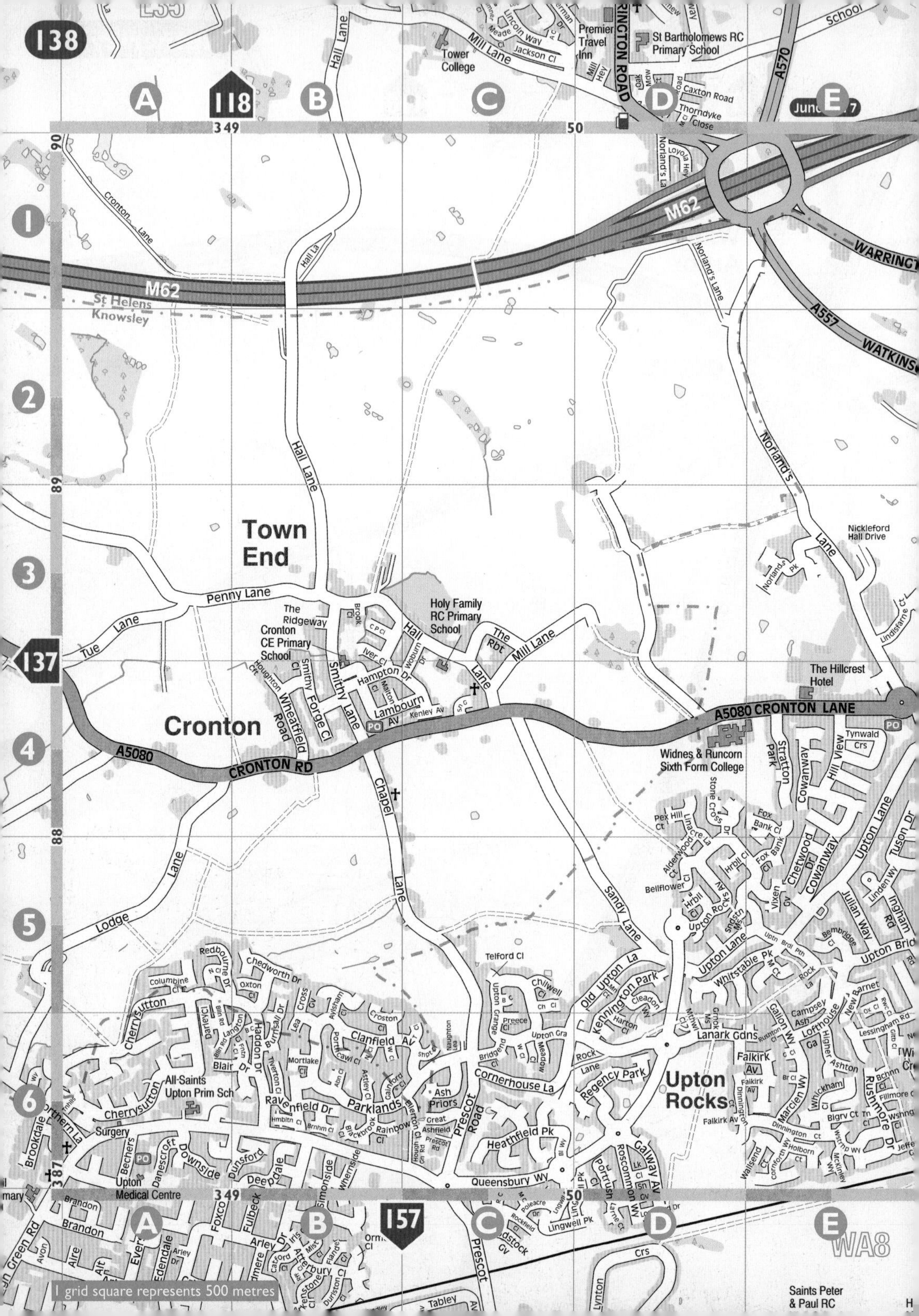

138
118
137
157
Town End
Cronton
Upton Rocks
M62
A5080 CRONTON LANE
A5080
CRONTON RD
A557
A570
WARRINGT
WATKINS
St Helens
Knowsley
Hall Lane
Penny Lane
Tue Lane
Mill Lane
Lodge Lane
Chapel Lane
Prescot Road
Sandy Lane
Norland's Lane
Cronton Lane
Smithy Lane
Wheatfield Road
Tower College
Premier Travel Inn
St Bartholomews RC Primary School
Holy Family RC Primary School
Cronton CE Primary School
The Hillcrest Hotel
Widnes & Runcorn Sixth Form College
Nickleford Hall Drive
All-Saints Upton Prim Sch
Upton Medical Centre
Surgery
Saints Peter & Paul RC
Upton Lane
Cornerhouse La
Queensbury Wy
Heathfield Pk
Regency Park
Kennington Park
Parklands
Ravenfield Dr
Cherrysutton
Falkirk Av
Lanark Gdns
WA8
1 grid square represents 500 metres

M62
Finger House Lane
Union Bank Lane
Union Bank Farm
Tibbs Cross Lane
A569
F
G
H
J
K
119
120
51
52
53
90
1
B5419
JUBITS LANE
Old Brook Hall
A57
Wilmere House
WARRINGTON ROAD
Bold Heath
CLOCK FACE RD
School La
2
Halton
St Helens
Bridge Farm
Ferndale Close
WILMERE LANE
A557
WATKINSON WAY
Twyford Lane
Mill Lane
89
3
140
Cranshaw Lane
LUNTS HEATH ROAD
Mill Green Farm
Mill Green Lane
4
Lunts Heath
Baileys Cl
Hartland
Monica Dr
Farndale Dr
Gleneagles
Churchfields
Birkdale Road
Minton Wy
Wenger Rd
Bold Industrial Est
Coroner's Lane
Glebe Lane
Lunts Heath Primary School
Tuscan Cl
Garrigill Cl
Finsbury Pk
Eastbury Cl
Wilcote Cl
Mill La
South Lane
88
Buckingham Av
Wedgwood Dr
Ryder Rd
Canton Cl
Trent Cl
DERBY ROAD A5080
Farnworth CE Primary School
Clarence Avenue
Holyrood Av
Grosvenor Cl
Claremont Dr
Derby Road
Hampton Ct Wy
Hmptn Ct Wy
Islington Gn
Cedardale Pk
Barrow's Green
5
BIRCHFIELD ROAD
Path
Pit Lane
Marsh Hall Road
Beaconsfield Crs
Beaconsfield Road
Farnworth Street
Moorfield Road
Brmndsy Gv
Greenwich Av
Windsor Rd
Balmoral Road
Mason Av
Widnes CC
Windermere St
Works
Works
A557
Daffodil Cl
Snowberry Cl
Farnworth
Wellfield
Factory La
Dykin Close
Weates Cl
Eltham Cl
Ribble Close
Crossgates
Humber Cl
Borough Cemetery
Derby Road
Gloucester Rd
Cornwall Rd
Whalley Gv
School Wy
Moorfield Primary School
Nursery Cl
Dykin Road
Green Lane
Ramsey Cl
Rathlin
6
Lancaster Road
Alder Rd
Birch
Acacia Av
Avenue
Peel House Lane
Fairfield High School
Bishops Way
Chorley's La
Hilary Cl
Barrow's Green
Guernsey Rd
Skye Cl
Orkney Cl
Severn Cl
Calder Cl
Widnes Station
Victoria Av
Lockett Road
Cypress Av
Cedar Av
Shell Green
387
F
G
H
158
J
K
Wade Deacon High School
Rose View Av
BIRCHFIELD ROAD
Elm Av
Chestnut Av
Lilac Av
Lytham Rd
St Anne's Rd
Fairhaven Rd
Kirkham Rd
Ansdell Road
Fir St
Brookfields Pk
Nell St
WAY
Crow Wood
Bancroft Rd
Rossall Rd
Moorfield Road
Romney
Belmont Rd
Fieldway
Brookfields School
Weates Cl
DANS ROAD A562
Appleton

120
A
B
C
D
E
354
55
90
89
88
387
1
2
3
4
5
6
Lingley Mere
Bold Heath
Mersey Valley Golf & Country Club
Golf Course
Whittle Brook
Wyevale Garden Centre
A57
A569
CLOCK FACE RD
Dawson House
Lingley Green
Lingley Green Avenue
Bembridge Cl
Foreland Cl
Shorwell Cl
Park Road
Lingley Green Av
Shanklin Cl
Pyecroft Rd
Pyecroft Cl
Muriel Cl
Audre Cl
Hilary Cl
Paul Cl
Fraser Road
Mayfair Cl
Kintore
Liverpool Road
Edward Road
Henderson Cl
Friends Lane
South Lane Entry
Sandy Lane
Laburnum Lane
Sandy Lane Farm
139
South Lane Farm
St Helens
Warrington
SOUTH LANE
A5080
FARNWORTH ROAD
Penketh
Penketh Community Primary School
Stocks Lane
Haslemere Drive
Farnworth Rd
WIDNES
Doe Green
Cuerdley Road
Beech Av
The Park
Newlyn Gdns
Penrose Gdns
Rothay Dr
Tannery Lane
WIDNES ROAD
A562
Mowcroft Lane
Back Lane
Cuerdley Cross
Cuerdley Green
Shell Green
Snowberry Cl
Ribble Cl
Crossgates
Close
Humber Cl
Coulton Rd
Severn Cl
Douglas Cl
Calder Cl
Skye Cl
WIDNES ROAD
Wrights Lane
159
1 grid square represents 500 metres

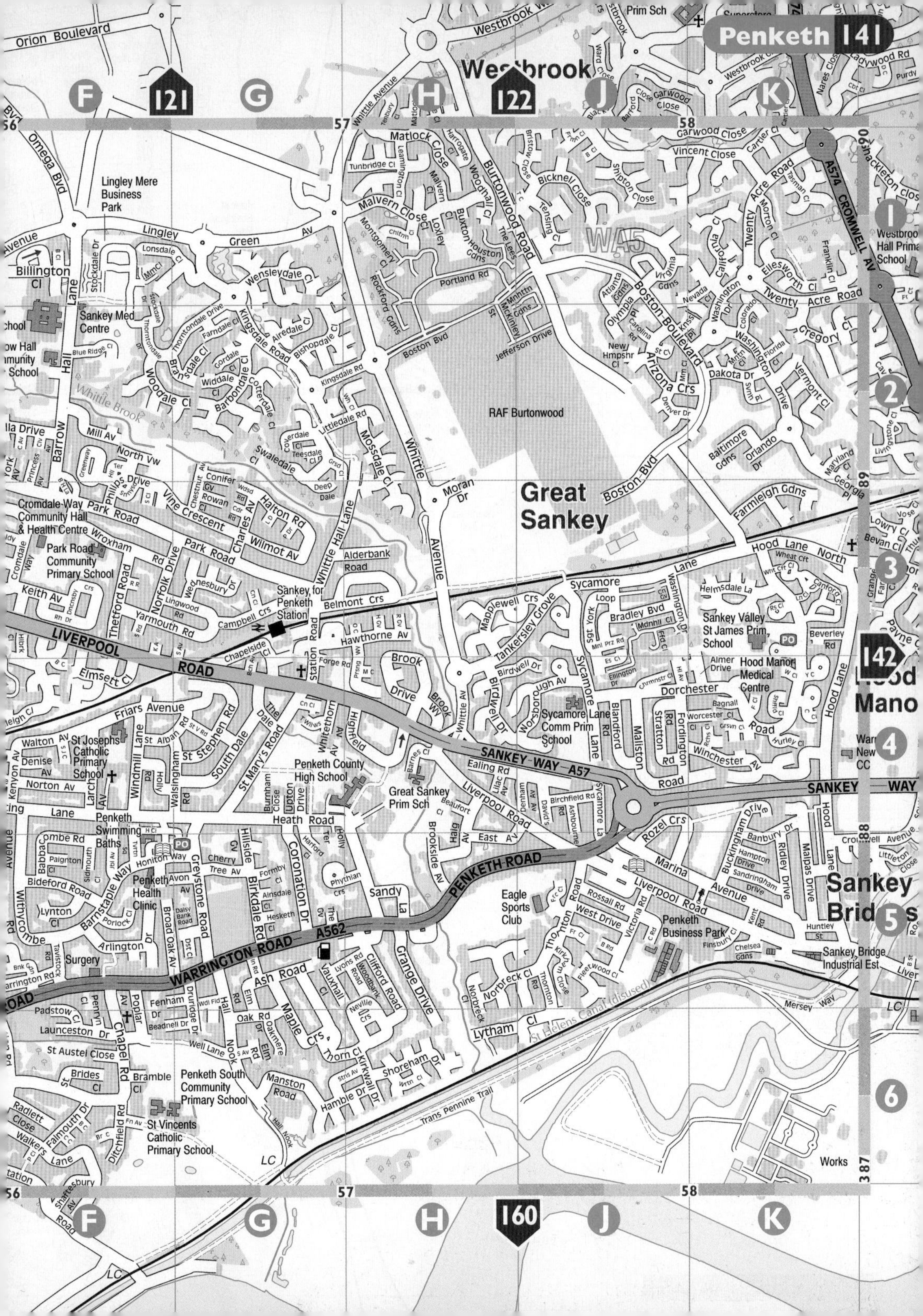

Penketh 141
121
122
142
160
Westbrook
Great Sankey
Sankey Bridges
Hood Manor
WA5
F
G
H
J
K
1
2
3
4
5
6
56
57
58
390
389
388
387
Orion Boulevard
Westbrook Way
Omega Bvd
Lingley Mere Business Park
Lingley Green Av
Billington Cl
Barrow Hall Lane
Sankey Med Centre
Whittle Brook
Wensleydale Cl
Kingsdale Road
Bishopdale Cl
Thorntondale Drive
Farndale Cl
Airedale Cl
Bransdale Cl
Woodale Cl
Barbondale Cl
Cotterdale Cl
Littledale Rd
Mosdale Cl
Swaledale Cl
Deep Dale
Mill Av
North Vw
Philips Drive
Conifer Gv
Rowan Cl
Halton Rd
Wilmot Av
Charles Av
Vine Crescent
Park Road
Cromdale Way Community Hall & Health Centre
Park Road Community Primary School
Wroxham Rd
Thetford Road
Norfolk Drive
Keith Av
Yarmouth Rd
Lingwood Rd
Campbell Crs
Sankey for Penketh Station
Whittle Hall Lane
Alderbank Road
Belmont Crs
Station Road
Hawthorne Av
Forge Rd
Chapelside Cl
Elmsert Cl
LIVERPOOL ROAD
Friars Avenue
St Josephs Catholic Primary School
Walton Av
Denise Av
Norton Av
Windmill Lane
St Alban Rd
St Stephen Rd
South Dale
The Dale
St Mary's Road
Walsingham Rd
Holly Rd
Larch Av
Lane
Penketh Swimming Baths
PO
Babbacombe Rd
Paignton Cl
Honiton Way
Bideford Road
Lynton Cl
Withycombe
Barnstaple Way
Penketh Health Clinic
Porlock Cl
Arlington Dr
Surgery
Greystone Road
Cherry Tree Av
Hillside Gv
Birkdale Rd
Broad Oak Av
Formby Cl
Ainsdale Cl
Hesketh Cl
Coronation Dr
Heath Road
Burnham Close
Upton Drive
Penketh County High School
Great Sankey Prim Sch
Whitethorn Av
Highfield
Brook Drive
Brook Wy
Barnes Cl
Phythian Crs
Sandy La
Grange Drive
Clifford Road
Woodbank Road
Vauxhall Cl
Lyons Rd
Neville Crs
Maple Crs
Thorn Cl
Kirkwall Dr
Hamble Dr
Shoreham Dr
Manston Road
Ash Road
Oak Rd
Oakmere Dr
Elm Dr
Hall Nook
Well Lane
WARRINGTON ROAD A562
PENKETH ROAD
Padstow Cl
Penryn Cl
Poplar Av
Chapel Rd
Fenham Dr
Beadnell Dr
Launceston Dr
St Austel Close
St Brides Cl
Bramble Cl
Penketh South Community Primary School
St Vincents Catholic Primary School
Radlett Close
Falmouth Dr
Walkers Lane
Ditchfield Rd
Shaftesbury Av
Trans Pennine Trail
St Helens Canal (disused)
LC
Matlock Close
Tunbridge Cl
Leamington Cl
Malvern Cl
Harrogate Cl
Woodhall Cl
Malvern Close
Loxley Cl
Montgomery Cl
Buxton Houston Gdns
Rockford Gdns
Portland Rd
Burtonwood Road
The Lees
Boston Bvd
McKinley St
Jefferson Drive
RAF Burtonwood
Whittle Avenue
Moran Dr
Bicknell Close
Bristow Close
Tensing Cl
Shipton Close
Vincent Close
Garwood Close
Twenty Acre Road
Morton Cl
California Cl
Virginia Gdns
Atlanta Gdns
Olympia Pl
Boston Boulevard
Carolina Rd
New Hmpshr Cl
Arizona Crs
Nevada Pl
Washington Dr
Colorado Cl
Washington Drive
Florida Cl
Dakota Dr
Vermont Cl
Denver Dr
Baltimore Gdns
Orlando Dr
Maryland Cl
Georgia Pl
Ellesworth Cl
Franklin Cl
Gregory Cl
Farmleigh Gdns
A574 CROMWELL AV
Shackleton Close
Westbrook Hall Primary School
Livingstone Cl
Lowry Cl
Bevan Cl
Hood Lane North
Wheat Cft
Helmsdale La
Canford Cl
Sycamore Lane
Mapplewell Crs
Tankersley Grove
Bradley Bvd
Loop
Sgt York
Washington Dr
Sankey Valley St James Prim. School
Beverley Rd
Almer Drive
Hood Manor Medical Centre
Birdwell Dr
Worsborough Av
Sycamore Lane Comm Prim School
Blandford Lane
Mallston Road
Stratton Rd
Fordington Rd
Dorchester Road
Bagnall Cl
Worcester Cl
Winchester Av
Hurley Cl
Hood Lane
Warrington New CC
SANKEY WAY A57
SANKEY WAY
Ealing Rd
Lilac Av
Birchfield Rd
Ashbourne
Beaufort Cl
Liverpool Road
Haig Av
East Av
Brookside Av
Rozel Crs
Marina Avenue
Buckingham Drive
Banbury Dr
Hampton Drive
Sandringham Drive
Ridley Drive
Malpas Drive
Cromwell Avenue
Littleton Cl
Eagle Sports Club
Thornton Road
Rossall Rd
West Drive
Victoria Rd
Penketh Business Park
Finsbury Cl
Chelsea Gdns
Huntley St
Kent Rd
Sankey Bridge Industrial Est
Mersey Way
Norbreck Cl
Fleetwood Cl
Kirkham Close
Thornton Cl
Lytham Cl
Works

142
122
141
161
16
Bewsey
Hood Manor
Sankey Bridges
Dallam
1 grid square represents 500 metres

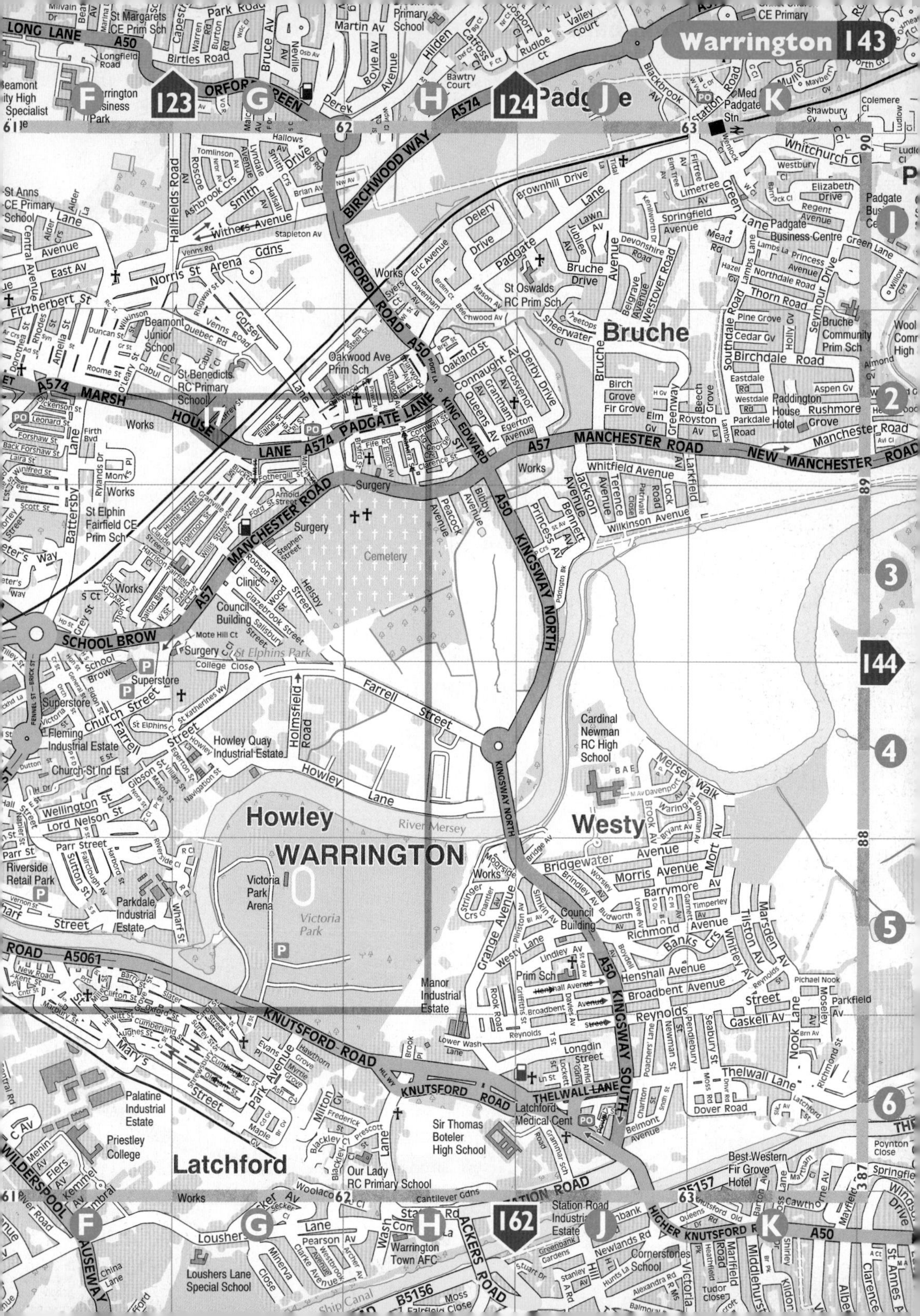

Warrington 143
123
124
144
162
17
F
G
H
J
K
1
2
3
4
5
6
61
62
63
87
88
89
90
Padgate
Bruche
Howley
WARRINGTON
Westy
Latchford
Long Lane
A50
Birtles Road
Orford Green
Park Road
Martin Av
Primary School
Padgate Stn
Med
Whitchurch Cl
Birchwood Way
A574
Orford Road
Hallows
Tomlinson
Lyndale Avenue
Smith Drive
Ashbrook Crs
Withers Avenue
Stapleton Av
Hallfields Road
Brownhill Drive
Limetree Av
Springfield Avenue
Green Lane
Padgate Business Centre
Elizabeth Drive
Regent Avenue
Princess Avenue
Northdale Road
Thorn Road
Pine Grove
Cedar Gv
Birchdale Road
Bruche Community Prim Sch
Paddington House Hotel
Rushmore Grove
Manchester Road
New Manchester Road
A57
Delery Drive
Padgate Lane
St Oswalds RC Prim Sch
Devonshire Road
Westover Road
Bruche Drive
Sheerwater Cl
Oakland St
Connaught Av
Grantham Av
Grosvenor
Derby Drive
Queens Av
Egerton Avenue
King Edward St
Birch Grove
Fir Grove
Royston Av
Parkdale Road
Whitfield Avenue
Wilkinson Avenue
Jackson Avenue
Bennett Av
Princess Av
Kingsway North
St Anns CE Primary School
Central Avenue
East Av
Fitzherbert St
Norris St
Arena Gdns
Venns Road
Beamont Junior School
Quebec Rd
Duncan St
Roome St
Cabul Cl
St Benedicts RC Primary School
Marsh House Lane
Oakwood Ave Prim Sch
Works
Firth Bvd
Battersby Lane
St Elphin Fairfield CE Prim Sch
Surgery
Cemetery
Peacock Avenue
Bibby Avenue
Manchester Road
Robson St
Clinic
Council Building
Helsby Street
Clazebrook Street
Salisbury Street
School Brow
Mote Hill Ct
St Elphins Park
College Close
Superstore
Church Street
Farrell Street
Fleming Industrial Estate
Church St Ind Est
Howley Quay Industrial Estate
Holmsfield Road
Howley Lane
River Mersey
Cardinal Newman RC High School
Mersey Walk
Bridgewater Avenue
Morris Avenue
Barrymore Av
Richmond Avenue
Banks Crs
Tilston Av
Marsden Av
Whitley Av
Mort Av
Wellington St
Lord Nelson St
Parr Street
Riverside Retail Park
Sutton St
Parkdale Industrial Estate
Wharf St
Victoria Park Arena
Victoria Park
Grange Avenue
Westy Lane
Council Building
Prim Sch
Henshall Avenue
Broadbent Avenue
Reynolds Street
Gaskell Av
Nook Lane
Parkfield Av
Rook Road
Longdin Street
Manor Industrial Estate
Lower Wash Lane
A5061
Knutsford Road
Kingsway South
Thelwall Lane
Thelwall Lane
Dover Road
Latchford Medical Cent
Sir Thomas Boteler High School
Palatine Industrial Estate
Priestley College
Park Avenue
Wilderspool Causeway
Our Lady RC Primary School
Frederick St
Milton Gv
Belmont Avenue
Best Western Fir Grove Hotel
Station Road
B5157
Higher Knutsford Road
Station Road Industrial Estate
Loushers Lane
Loushers Lane Special School
Pearson Av
Warrington Town AFC
Ackers Road
Newlands Rd
Cornerstones School
Victoria
Middlehurst
B5156
Ship Canal
Poynton Close

144
124
143
163
Longbarn
Paddington
Woolston
Martinscroft
Thelwall
WA1
River Mersey
The Eyes
Manchester Ship Canal
Works
M6
A57
A56
A50
B5210
B5157 LYMM ROAD
WOOLSTON GRANGE AVENUE
MANCHESTER ROAD
STOCKPORT ROAD
KNUTSFORD ROAD
THELWALL NEW ROAD
BELL LANE
Padgate Business Centre
Green Lane Special School
Woolston Community High Sch
Clinic & Welfare Centre
Surgery
Bruche Community Prim Sch
Woolston CE Primary School
St Peters RC Primary School
Woolston Primary School
Council Offices
Council Buildings
Premier Travel Inn
Thelwall New Road Industrial Est
Chaigley School
Laskey House
Thelwall Community Jun Sch
Thelwall Infant School
Grappenhall Clinic
Bradshaw Community Primary School
Thelwall Heys
Massey Hall School
1 grid square represents 500 metres

Marshall's Farm
125
Green Alley Farm
Holly Bush La
Brook Lane
Juniper Lane
A57
MANCHESTER ROAD
Brookside Farm
M6
Junction 21
River Mersey
Rixton Old Hall
Bollin Point
Golf Course
Lymm Golf Club
Thelwall Viaduct
Statham Lane
Pool Lane
Brookside Av
Statham
Whitbarrow Road
Warrington Road
Star Lane
Whitesands Rd
Albany Road
Statham Primary School
Statham Avenue
The Lymm Hotel
Lymmhay Lane
Yew Tree Close
Brooklyn Dr
Danebank Road
Surgery
Maltmans Rd
Brookfield Cl
Lymmington Av
CAMSLEY LANE A56
BOOTH'S HILL ROAD
EAGLE BROW A6144
THE CROSS
NEW ROAD
Cross Clinic
The Dingle
Dingle Bank Cl
Rectory Lane
LYMM
CHURCH RD
Wychwood Av
Massey Brook Lane
Works
Hardy Road
Heyes
164
ELM TREE RD
Cherry Tree Primary School
Bayclife
Mayfield View
Greenwood Road
The Hachings
Weaste Lane
Reddish Lane
The Peppers

127
WEST KIRBY
West Kirby Residential School
West Kirby Station
Health Cen & Swimming Pool
Fire Station
West Kirby Foot Health Clinic
Brook House Business Centre
Corner House Clinic
Park Med Cen
Superstore
War Memorial
Black Horse Hill Infant School
Black Horse Close
St Bridgets CE Primary School
Calday Grange Grammar School
Avalon School
Sailing Club
Tell's Tower
Marine Lake
Tanskey Rocks
Wirral Country Pk
CH48
Caldy
Riversdale Road
Lingdale Road
Dee Lane
Salisbury Av
Groveside
Victoria Drive
Shrewsbury Rd
Alexandra Rd
Albert Rd
South Parade
BANKS ROAD
Church Road
Eaton Rd
South Rd
Victoria Rd
Mostyn Avenue
Hydro Avenue
Hilbre Rd
Hilbre Ct
South Pde
SANDY LANE
B5140
Westbourne Road
Ashton Drive
Dunraven Rd
North Road
Carpenter's Lane
Wirral Way
Rectory Road
St Bridgets Lane
Ludlow Drive
Kale Cl
Macdona Drive
Riverside
Headland Cl
Beach Walk
Shelley Way
York Avenue
Ramsey Cl
CALDY ROAD
Mount Road
Warwick Drive
Kirby Mount
Surrey Dr
Kirby Park
Kirby Close
Devonshire Road
Holm Hill
Village
Lane
Wetstone Lane
The Kirklands
The Oatlands
Abbey Road
Priory Rd
Monk's Wy
HILBRE VIEW
A540
Townfield Road
Grosvenor Av
Egerton Dr
Princes Avenue
Chomondeley Rd
Melloncroft Dr
Carlsbrooke Cl
Croft Drive West
Shore Road
Barton Hey
Thorsway
King's Drive
Caldy Wood
The Green
Caldy Chase Dr
Croft Drive
Mill Hey Rd
Hey Drive
Westward Ho
Badger's Set
The Steeple
Mereworth
Meadow Gate
Fleck Lane
Boundary Rd
COLUMN
Grammar School Lane
Beacon Drive
Kingswalk
Croome Drive
Burlingham Avenue
Gourley's La
Bramhall Cl
Hillside Road
Coertside Avenue
Grange Mount
Kingsbury
Queensbury
FRANKBY
Wirral Mount
Enniscale
Gleggside
Douglas Road
BLACK HORSE HILL
B5139
Grange Old Rd
Belmont Road
Claremont Road
Leigh Rd
Darmond's Gn
Brookfield Gdns
Grange Rd
Orrysdale Rd
Sussex Road
Somerset Rd
Lodge Drive
321
22
87
86
85
384
1
2
3
4
5
6
A
B
C
D
E
166
1 grid square represents 500 metres

Frankby
Newton
Thurstaston
Larton
Greasby
Cemetery
Royden Park
Hillbark Hotel
Thurstaston Common
Irby Hill
Dawpool
Dawpool CE Primary School
Caldy Golf Club
Golf Course
Greasby Infant School
Greasby Junior School
B5139
B5140
A540
HILLBARK ROAD
MONTGOMERY HILL
TELEGRAPH ROAD
Hillbark Road
Mill Hill Road
Mill Lane
Sandy Lane
Sandy La North
School Lane
Thurstaston Road
Church Lane
Pikes Hey Road
Birch Heys
Irbyside Road
Ferndale Avenue
Frankby Stiles
Baytree Road
The Nook
Grange Cross Lane
Gorse Lane
Long Hey Rd
East Drive
Links Hey Road
Thorstone Dr
Hillview Road
Heathbank
Far Meadow Lane
Loomsway
Martin Close
Lyndhurst Road
Greenheys Rd
South Drive
Dawlish Road
Newton Drive
Hawthorn Dr
Bracken Drive
Sandstone Dr
Springfield Avenue
Frankby Road
Lombardy Avenue
Miles Lane
Danefield Rd
Allangate Close
Thorns Drive
Station Road
Wirral Way
128
148
167
F
G
H
J
K
2
3
4
5
6
23
24
25

148
129
147
167
168
Wirral Business Park
CH49
CH61
Arrowe Country Park
Arrowe Park Hospital
A&E
Landican Cemetery
Greasby Infant School
Our Lady of Pity Primary School
Greasby Junior School
Irby CC
Irby
Irby Primary School
Thingwall Primary School
Stanley School
Thingwall Recreation Centre
Pensby Recreation Centre
Arrowe Hill Primary School
Meadowside School
Woodchurch CE Primary School
Thingwall
Pensby
ARROWE PARK ROAD A551
Arrowe Brook Road
Arrowe Brook Lane
Thingwall Road
Thingwall Rd E
PENSBY ROAD B5138
Mill Hill Road
Irby Road
Barnston Road
Landican Lane
1 grid square represents 500 metres

Woodchurch
Woodchurch Leisure Centre
Fender Primary School
Woodchurch High School Specialist Engineering College
St Michael & All Angels RC Primary School
Townfield Primary Sch
Junction 3
WOODCHURCH ROAD
A552
M53
Landican
Landican Lane
North Cheshire Trading Estate
Wirral Stroke & Head Injury Clinic
Prenton J&I Schools
Prenton
Villa Medical Centre
Old Rockerrians RFC
Shopping Centre
Roman Road
Station Road
Murrayfield Hospital
Works
Ley Farm
A551
Lwr Thingwall La
Holmwood Avenue
Ltl Storeton Lane
Landican Lane
130
150
169
F G H J K
28 29 30
87 86 85 384
1 2 3 4 5 6

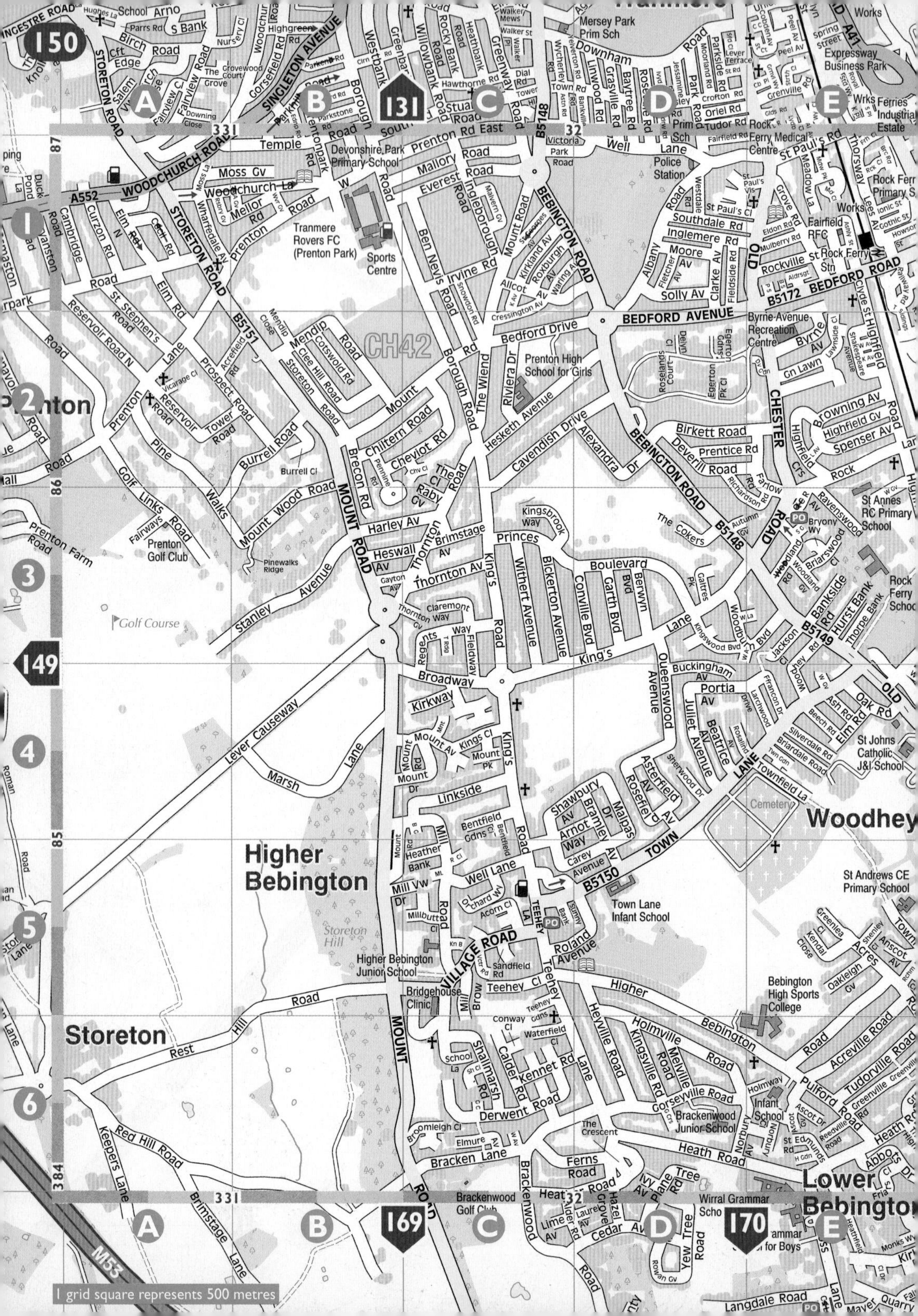
150
131
149
169
170
A
B
C
D
E
1
2
3
4
5
6
87
86
85
384
331
32
CH42
Higher Bebington
Storeton
Woodhey
Lower Bebington
Prenton
WOODCHURCH ROAD
A552
STORETON ROAD
SINGLETON AVENUE
BEBINGTON ROAD
BEDFORD AVENUE
B5172 BEDFORD ROAD
B5148
B5151
B5149
B5150
MOUNT ROAD
VILLAGE ROAD
TEEHEY LA
CHESTER ROAD
TOWN LANE
Prenton Rd East
Temple Road
Mallory Road
Everest Road
Ingleborough Road
Borough Road
The Wiend
Cavendish Drive
Hesketh Avenue
Kings Road
Withert Avenue
Bickerton Avenue
Conville Bvd
Garth Bvd
Queensway
Queenswood Avenue
Princes Boulevard
Kings Lane
Broadway
Kirkway
Lever Causeway
Marsh Lane
Stanley Avenue
Mount Wood Road
Golf Links Road
Prenton Farm Road
Rest Hill Road
Red Hill Road
Keepers Lane
Brimstage Lane
Higher Bebington Road
Heath Road
Heyville Road
Kingsville Road
Melville Road
Derwent Road
Bracken Lane
Brackenwood
Devonshire Park Primary School
Tranmere Rovers FC (Prenton Park)
Sports Centre
Prenton High School for Girls
Byrne Avenue Recreation Centre
Rock Ferry Medical Centre
Police Station
St Annes RC Primary School
St Johns Catholic J&I School
Cemetery
St Andrews CE Primary School
Town Lane Infant School
Higher Bebington Junior School
Bridgehouse Clinic
Bebington High Sports College
Brackenwood Junior School
Brackenwood Golf Club
Wirral Grammar School
Prenton Golf Club
Golf Course
Storeton Hill
Pinewalks Ridge
Mersey Park Prim Sch
Expressway Business Park
Ferries Industrial Estate
Fairfield RFC
Rock Ferry Stn
M53
1 grid square represents 500 metres

The Sloyne
Liverpool
Wirral
132
F
G
H
J
K
33
34
35
87
86
85
384
1
2
3
4
5
6
152
171
Rock Ferry
New Ferry
BEBINGTON
Bromborough Pool
Port Sunlight
River Mersey
ROCK FERRY BY-PASS
NEW FERRY BY-PASS
NEW CHESTER ROAD
NEW CHESTER ROAD
BEBINGTON ROAD
CHESTER ROAD
CHURCH ROAD
THE VILLAGE
A41
B5136
Cammell Laird's Sports Club
The Dell Primary School
Parkfield Medical Centre
Grove Street Primary School
The Oval Sports Cen
Blessington Catholic Technology College
Bebington Station
Lady Lever Art Gallery
Church Drive Primary School
Superstore
Police Station
Port Sunlight Stn
Bromborough Pool Primary School
The Village Hotel & Leisure Club
Church Road Medical Centre
Works
Dock Rd North
Woodhead Road
Shore Drive
Bolton Rd East
Old Ct House Road
South View
York Street
Dock Rd South
Stanley Road
Sefton Road
Thorburn Road
Knowsley Road
Harrogate Road
Greendale Road
Bromborough Road
Wood Street
Bath Street
Thermal
Port
Dock
Central Road
Westgate
Main
Alvega Close
Shorefields
Mersey Bank Rd
Cornwall Cl
Mersey Road
Bedford Rd
Victoria Drive

152
133
151
171
Dingle
St Michael's Hamlet
Otterspool
Festival Gardens
Riverside Drive
Aigburth Road
Aigburth Drive
Mersey
Devil's Bank
Works
Garston Channel
Liverpool
Wirral
St Michael's Stn
Shorefields Technology College
Matthew Arnold Prim Sch
St Michael In The Ham Primary School
St Charles RC Primary School
Council Building
Surgery
Bempton Road
Otterspool Road
Jericho Lane
Larkfield Road
Fulwood Road
Ashbourne Road
Ampthill Road
Annesley Rd
Promenade Gdns
Dingle Vale
Dingle Rd
Glendale Cl
Livingston Drive
Normanton Av
Mossley
L17
A
B
C
D
E
1
2
3
4
5
6
336
37
384
85
86
87
1 grid square represents 500 metres

Aigburth 153
L18
134
154
172
L19
F
G
H
J
K
38
39
40
87
86
85
84
1
2
3
4
5
6
Aigburth
Grassendale
Mossley Hill Station
Works
Storrsdale Medical Cen
Sudley House
Sudley Infant School
Sudley Junior School
Margarets High School
Mersey View Special Sch
Liverpool John Moores University
Booker Avenue J&I School
West Allerton Station
Aigburth Station
Innkeeper's Lodge
Liverpool CC
Surgery
St Austins RC Prim School
Gilmour Infant School
Junior School
Greenways Special School
Cressington Station
Garston Sports Centre
St Francis of Assisi RC Prim Sch
Sir Alfred Jones Meml Hosp
Garston Leis Cen
Garston Industrial Estate
Holy Tri Primary
Banks Prim
Aigburth Road
A561
St Mary's Road
Garston Way
Aigburth Vale
Victoria Road
A5058
Carnatic Road
Briarwood Rd
Fernwood Rd
Gladeville Rd
Elmswood Road
Mossley Hill
Mentmore Road
Rose Lane
Avonmore Av
Pitville Avenue
Brodie Avenue
Cooper Avenue North
Rangemore Road
Tullimore Road
Martin Rd
Brockholme Rd
Holmefield Road
Aigburth Hall Avenue
Aigburth Hall Road
Booker Avenue
Greenhill Road
Mather Avenue
B5180
Caithness Rd
Stroma Rd
Melbreck Road
Stairhaven Road
Mossley Hill
Allangate Road
Endfield Park
Ryegate Road
Garston Old Rd
Eastcote Rd
Shirley Rd
Brodie Av
Alexandria Rd
Long Lane
Heath Road
Wheatcroft Road
Moorcroft Road
Cleveley Rd
Forthlin Rd
Canterbury Pk
Hardinge Road
Clarendon Road
Island Road
Chapel Road
Wellington St
Church Rd
Railway St
Dale St
Byron Street
Window Lane
Canterbury Street
King St
Vulcan St
Chesterton Street
York Street
Durham St
Lincoln
Sinclair St
Dock Road
Cressington Esp
Grassendale Esp
North Road
South Road
Knowsley
Eaton Road
Salisbury
Beechwood Road
Beechwood Rd
Chaloner Grove
Wirral View
Eastern Dr
Western Drive
Grassendale Rd
Riversdale Road
The Spinnakers
Mersey Road
Desford Rd
Hailsham Road
Stratford Road
Mersey Av
Lucan Rd
Woodlands Road
Sudley Road
Lugard Rd
Wingate Road
Dundonald Road
Rosemount Road
Hillview
St Anne's Rd
The Barkhill
Chequers Gdns
Cheyne Gdns
Oakland Rd
The Serpentine
Ranelagh Dr N
Ranelagh Dr South
Fairacre Road
Darby Road
Bowden Road
Lumley Street
Whitehedge Road
Ranfurly Road
Kintore Rd
Duncombe Rd N
Bathurst Road
Swansea Cl
Barry Dr
Cardiff Wy
Moss St
Clifton St
Bennett St
Heald St
Russell Road
Woolton Rd
Queen Street
Speke Road

154
Calderstones
135
153
172
173
A
B
C
D
E
1
2
3
4
5
6
341
342
384
385
386
387
Allerton
Woolton
Garston
Hunt's Cross
L25
MENLOVE AVENUE
A562
HILLFOOT ROAD
SPEKE HALL ROAD
WOOLTON ROAD
B5171
B5180
MATHER AVENUE
ALLERTON RD
WOOLTON HIGH ST
A561
SPEKE
Allerton Park Golf Club
Golf Course
New Heys Comprehensive School
Springwood Crematorium
Allerton Cemetery
Springwood Avenue
Brunt Lane
Allerton Station
Garston Station
Garston CE Prim Sch
St Benedicts College
Sir Alfred Jones Meml Hosp
Garston Leis Cen
Garston Sports Centre
Springwood Heath Prim Sch
Bishop Martin CE Prim Sch
Village Medical Cen
Picture House
Woolton House Medical Cen
Woolton Swimming Pool
Watergate School
Much Woolton Cath Prim Sch
St Julies Catholic High School
Woolton Golf Club
Camp Hill
Hunts Cross Shop Park
Triumph Trading Park
Works
Edwards La Industrial Estate
Bridge Industrial Estate
New Mersey Retail Park
Holy Trinity RC Primary School
Banks Rd Prim Sch
Estuary Business Park
Liverpool Marriott Hotel
Vitesse Road
Spitfire Road
Triumph Way
Renown Way
Mayflower Av
Dolomite Av
Herald Av
Stag Rd
North Av
Goodlass Road
Windward Drive
Estuary Boulevard
Heath Road
Springwood Avenue
Hillfoot Rd
Kings Drive
Speke Road
School Lane
Camp Rd
Allerton Road
Vineyard St
Horrocks Av
Clarendon Road
Surgery
1 grid square represents 500 metres

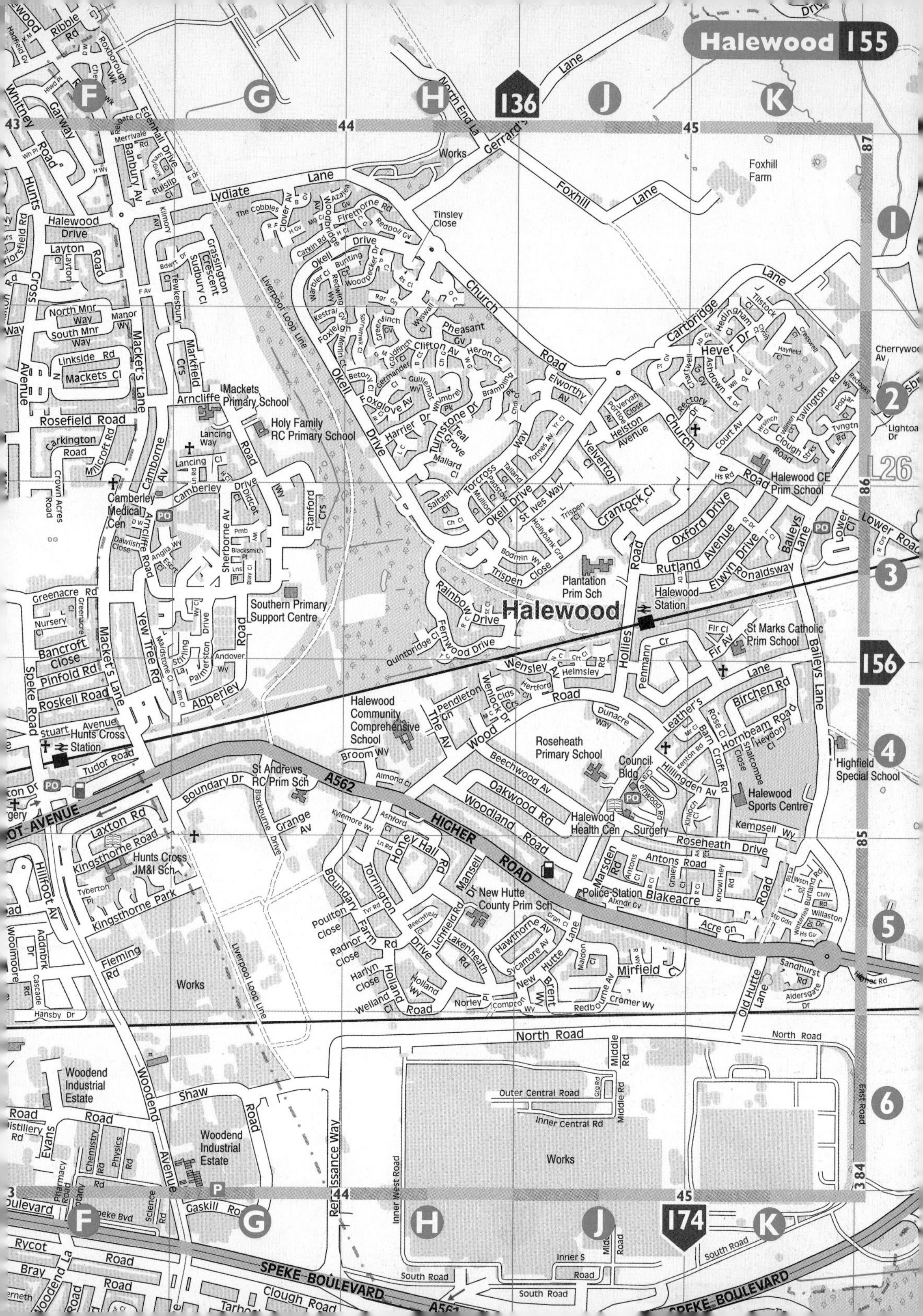

Halewood
Lydiate Lane
Gerrard's Lane
Foxhill Lane
Foxhill Farm
Church Road
Okell Drive
Liverpool Loop Line
Mackets Primary School
Holy Family RC Primary School
Southern Primary Support Centre
Camberley Medical Cen
Hunts Cross Station
Plantation Prim Sch
Halewood Station
St Marks Catholic Prim School
Halewood CE Prim School
Halewood Community Comprehensive School
Roseheath Primary School
Council Bldg
Halewood Health Cen
Surgery
Halewood Sports Centre
Highfield Special School
St Andrews RC Prim Sch
Hunts Cross JM&I Sch
New Hutte County Prim Sch
Police Station
A562 HIGHER ROAD
HILLFOOT AVENUE
Woodend Industrial Estate
Works
North Road
Outer Central Road
Inner Central Rd
Renaissance Way
Inner West Road
South Road
SPEKE BOULEVARD
A561
Wood Road
Hollies Road
Baileys Lane
Lower Road
Leather's Lane
Mackets Lane
Speke Road
Woodend Avenue
136
156
174
L26

Green's Bridge Farm
Greensbridge Lane
B5178
137
Cross Hillocks Lane
A
B
C
D
E
3 46
47
87
1
2
3
4
5
6
Cross Hillocks Farm
Lane
Garnetts
Cherrywood Av
Greensbridge La
Redoaks Wy
Tvngtn Rd
Lightoaks Dr
Springfield Farm
L26
ood CE
chool
86
Lower Cl
Lower Road
R Crs
PO
Lane
A5300
Ash Lane
Our
Perp
RC
Ditton Brook
155
Lane
Highfield Special School
Finch
Lane
Lower Road
Brook House Farm
SPEK
A562
Newstead Road
Wheldon Rd
Newst
85
Finch Farm
Works
Knowsley
Halton
Burland Rd
Civly Rd
Wstn Gr
Winterlea Hs
dhurst Rd
dersgate Dr
Higher Rd
A562
Higher Road
Old Higher Rd
Hale Bank Road
Manor Farm
n Road
Higher Road
East Road
Carr Lane
Burnt Mill
Potters La
384
174
175
1 grid square represents 500 metres

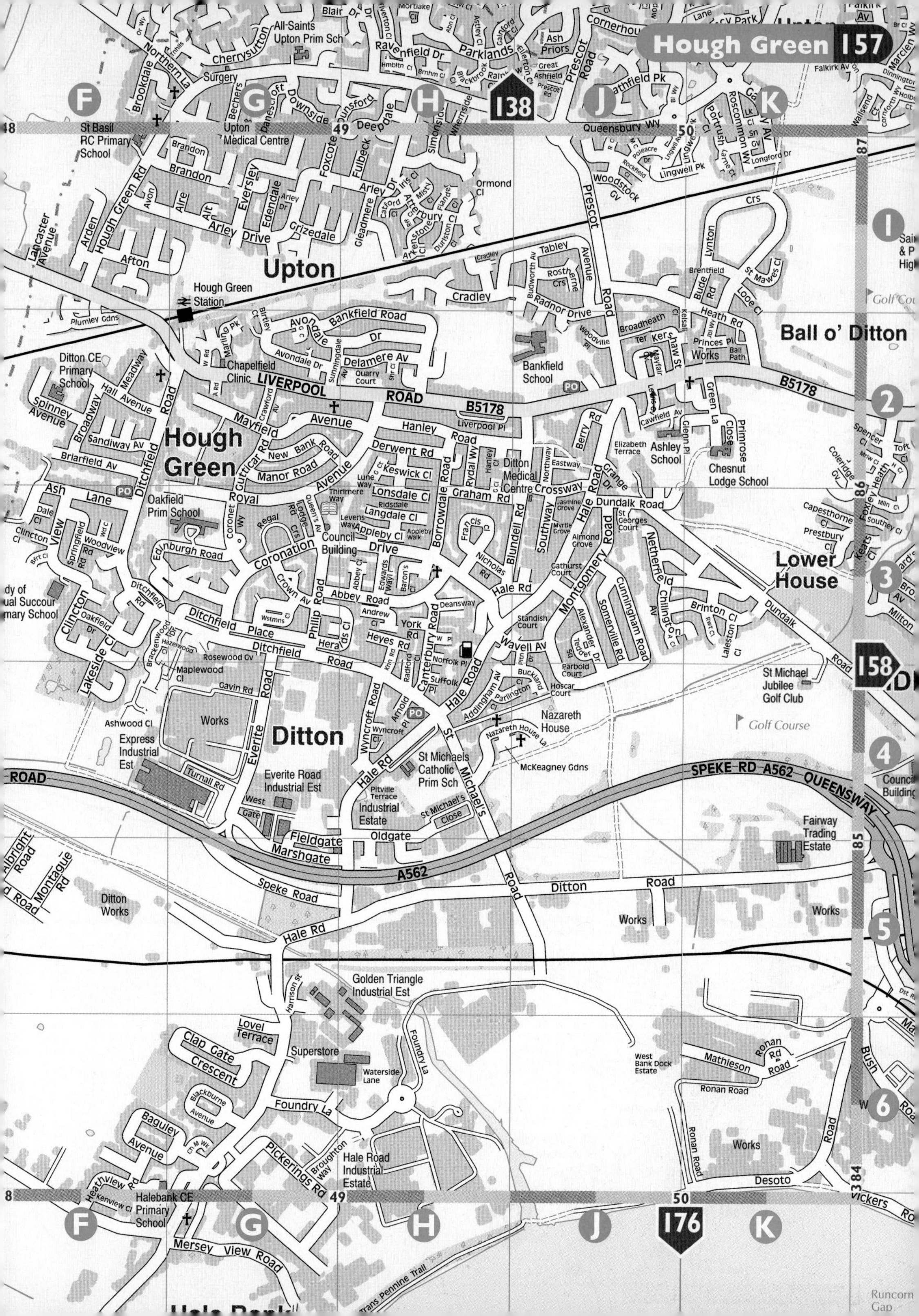
138
158
176
F
G
H
J
K
48
49
50
87
86
85
84
1
2
3
4
5
6
Upton
Hough Green
Ditton
Ball o' Ditton
Lower House
All-Saints Upton Prim Sch
St Basil RC Primary School
Upton Medical Centre
Surgery
Hough Green Station
Ditton CE Primary School
Chapelfield Clinic
Oakfield Prim School
Council Building
Bankfield School
Ditton Medical Centre
Ashley School
Chesnut Lodge School
Elizabeth Terrace
St Michael Jubilee Golf Club
Golf Course
Nazareth House
St Michaels Catholic Prim Sch
Express Industrial Est
Everite Road Industrial Est
Industrial Estate
Fairway Trading Estate
Ditton Works
Works
Golden Triangle Industrial Est
Superstore
West Bank Dock Estate
Hale Road Industrial Estate
Halebank CE Primary School
LIVERPOOL ROAD
B5178
SPEKE RD A562 QUEENSWAY
A562
Speke Road
Ditton Road
Hale Rd
Hale Road
St Michael's Road
Dundalk Road
Prescot Road
Queensbury Wy
Hough Green Rd
Ditchfield Road
Ditchfield Place
Coronation Drive
Royal Avenue
Mayfield Avenue
Bankfield Road
Avondale Dr
Delamere Av
Cradley
Radnor Drive
Tabley Avenue
Heath Rd
Broadheath
Kershaw St
Montgomery Road
Cunningham Road
Somerville Rd
Wavell Av
Crossway
Graham Rd
Borrowdale Road
Canterbury Road
Abbey Road
Philip Road
Everite Road
Turnall Rd
Fieldgate
Marshgate
Oldgate
St Michael's Close
Foundry La
Clap Gate Crescent
Lovel Terrace
Baguley Avenue
Blackburne Avenue
Pickerings Rd
Mersey View Road
Mathieson Road
Ronan Road
Desoto
Vickers Road
Trans Pennine Trail
Runcorn Gap

158
139
157
176
177
WA8
Appleton
Crow Wood
Kingsway
WIDNES
Halton View
Simm's Cross
Moss Bank
Lugsdale
West Bank
Hall o' Ditton
Spike Island
Widnes Station
Wade Deacon High School
Saints Peter & Paul RC High School
Highfield Medical Centre
Widnes Golf Club
Fairfield High Sc
Fairfield J&I School
Brookfields School
St Bedes RC J&I Sch
Simms Cross Prim Sch
Widnes Vikings RLFC (Halton Stadium)
Halton College
Council Buildings
Windmill Shopping Centre
Green Oaks Shop Cen
Greenoaks Farm Industrial Est
St John Fisher RC Prim Sch
Ashley Retail Park
Old Foundry Estate
St Gerrards RC P Sch
Widnes Public Baths
Alexandria Industrial Estate
Fairway Trading Estate
Black Cat Industrial Estate
Andersons Ind Est
Wellington Street Industrial Estate
Constance Industrial Estate
Queensway Business Cen
West Bank Medical Cen
Catalyst Science Discovery Centre
West Bank Prim Sch
Bowers Business Park
Travelodge
St Helens Canal (disused)
Trans Pennine Trail
BIRCHFIELD ROAD
KINGSWAY
LEIGH AVENUE
DEACON ROAD
HALTON VIEW RD
WARRINGTON RD
FIDDLERS FERRY ROAD
WATKINSON WAY
QUEENSWAY
ASHLEY WAY
ASHLEY WAY WEST
MOOR LANE SOUTH
MOOR LA
B5178
B5419
A557
A533
1 grid square represents 500 metres

Shell Green
Cuerdley Cross
WIDNES ROAD
A562
DANS ROAD A562
Works
Bennett's Lane
Warrington
Halton
Johnson's Lane
Gorsey Lane
Marsh Lane
Mowcroft Lane
Wrights Lane
Cuerdley Green
Back La
Fiddler's
River Mersey
Hempstones Point
Wigg Island
Sewage Works
Warrington Road
Stuart
Manor Park Av
Manor
Sarus Ct
Weates Cl
Kilsby Drive
Barrow's
Orkney Cl
Skye
Rathlin
Ramsey
Hilary Cl
Fieldway
Romney
Hadfield Close
Severn Cl
Calder Cl
Douglas Cl
Barnston Rd
Coulton Rd
Avebury Cl
Mithril
Tannery
140
160
178
F G H J K
1 2 3 4 5 6
53 54 55
87 86 85 84

160
141
159
178
Fiddler's Ferry
Moore
Penketh South Community Primary School
St Vincents
Manston Road
Hamble Dr
Trans Pennine Trail
St Helens Canal (disused)
Riverside Trading Estate
River Mersey
Moss Side
Lapwing Lane
Moss Side Lane
Norton Marsh
Moss Lane
Moore RUFC
Halton Moss
Manchester Ship Canal
Moore Prim Sch
Six Acre Lane
Six Acre Gdns
Gigg Lane
Hollybank
Beechmoore
Runcorn Road
Eastgate Road
Blackheath Lane
Warrington Road
Eastgate Wy
Chancellor Rd
Rokeby Court
Manor Park Av
Calmington La
Sunnyside Lane
Radlett Close
Falmouth Dr
Ditchfield Rd
Walkers Lane
Rothay Dr
Penrose Gdns
The Pk
Tannery Lane
Station Road
Shaftesbury Av
Brides Cl
Bramble Cl
A
B
C
D
E
1
2
3
4
5
6
356
57
87
86
85
384
1 grid square represents 500 metres

Higher Walton
Lower Walton
Birch Wood
Grange Green Farm
Works
Mill Lane
Bellhouse Lane
Runcorn Road
Hollyhedge Farm
Cheshire Ring Canal Walk
Holly Hedge Lane
Thomasons Br La
Underbridge La
A56 CHESTER NEW ROAD
A56 CHESTER ROAD
Warrington Road
Walton Lea Rd
Old Chester Road
Walton Lea Crematorium
Warrington Sports Club
Walton Hall Golf Club
Walton Hall
Golf Course
Hough's Lane
Park Lane
Appleton Reservoir
Rowswood Ctyd
Canal Side
Hobb Lane
Norton House
Eastford Road
Baronet Ms
Taylor St
Morley Rd
Pool La
B5156
A5060
CHESTER ROAD
Forrest Way
River Mersey
Firecrest Ct
Slutchers
Mandarin Ct
Meadow Av
Rydal Av
Derwent Rd
Elgin Av
Walton Lea Road
Hill Cliffe Road
Brookwood Cl
Runcorn Road
Halton Warrington
Row's Wood
142
162
179

162
143
161
Wilderspool
Stockton Heath
Cobbs
Hillcliffe
Appleton Park
Dudlows Green
Latchford
Palatine Industrial Estate
Priestley College
Causeway Medical Centre
St Weburgh CE Primary School
Loushers Lane Special School
Sir Thomas Boteler High School
Our Lady RC Primary School
Warrington Town AFC
Station Road Industrial Estate
Cornerstone School
Superstore
Medical Centre
The Forge Shopping Centre
Police Station
St Thomas CE Prim Sch
Primary School
Grappenhall Sports Club
Mountain Farm
The Cobbs Infant School
Council Building
Broomfield County Junior School
St Monica's RC Prim School
Bridgewater Upper School
Bridgewater High School
Warrington Sports Club
Hillfoot Farm
Witherwin Farm
Bellfield Farm
Golf Course
Warrington Golf Club
High Warren
Manchester Ship Canal
River Mersey
WILDERSPOOL CAUSEWAY
FAIRFIELD ROAD B5156
ELLESMERE ROAD B5156
GRAPPENHALL ROAD A56
WALTON NEW ROAD A56
WALTON ROAD
LONDON ROAD A49
KNUTSFORD ROAD
THELWALL LANE
STATION ROAD
ACKERS ROAD
WA4
1 grid square represents 500 metres

Stockton Heath
163
144
164
Grappenhall
Wright's Green
Appleton Thorn
Thelwall Lane
Dover Road
Thelwall
Pelham
Thelwall Infant School
Surgery
Poynton Close
Best-Western Fir Grove Hotel
Springfield Avenue
Bradshaw Lane
Knightsbridge Av
Westminster Cl
Bradshaw Community Primary School
Coronation Av
Ascot Cl
Knutsford Rd
A50
Knutsford Road
Windsor Drive
Mayfield Rd
Cross Lane
Barton Av
Marlfield Road
Middlehurst Road
Kildonan Road
Victoria Av
Albert Road
Clarence Road
St Annes Avenue
Euclid Avenue
East Vw
A56
Tudor Close
York Drive
York Road
Harwood Gdns
Shadewood Crs
Portola Cl
Gilwell Cl
Lindi Av
Glebe Av
St Wilfrid's Dr
Barnswood Cl
Laurel Bank
Sharon Pk Cl
Bellhouse Lane
St Wilfrids CE Aided Primary School
Stockton Lane
Church Lane
Canal Side
Australia Lane
Parrs Wd View
Grappenhall Hall School
Grappenhall CC
Thelwall Heys
Bridgewater Canal
Weaste Lane
Cuerdon Dr
Marie Drive
Cliff Lane
Stoneleigh Gardens
Knutsford Road
Knutsford Rd
Pickering Crs
Woodlands
Stockport Road
Tresham Dr
Tresham Drive
Bourchier Wy
Broad Lane
Hall Lane
Whitehouse Farm
Yew Tree Farm
Grappenhall Heys
Dashwood Cl
Lichfield Av
Chichester Cl
Curzon Drive
Witherwin Avenue
Strickland Cl
Croft Gdns
Curzon Dr
Bretland Dr
Stansfield Dr
Keeper's Rd
Boddington Dr
Grappenhall Heys School
Reddish Hall
Clifflane Farm
Cartridge Lane
Grappenhall Lane
B5356
Dodds Lane
Lumb Brook Road
New Lane
Ashberry Drive
Thorntree Green
Yew Tree La
Crofton Close
Green Lane
Greenlane Farm
Parkland Cl
HM Young Offenders Institute
Appleton Thorn Trading Estate
Booth's Farm
Barleycastle Lane
Lyncastle Way
Barleycastle Trading Estate
Barleycastle Farm
Blackcap Road
F
G
H
J
K
1
2
3
4
5
6
63
64
65
387
86
85
384

Thelwall
164
145
163
Lymmington Av
CAMSLEY LANE A56
BOOTH'S HILL ROAD
Brookfield Cl
Thornley Rd
John Rd
David Rd
Booth's Hill
Yeald Brow
Wychwood Av
Egerton Rd
Old Smithy La
Heyes Dr
Highfield
ELM TREE RD
Surgery
Massey Brook Lane
Massey Av
Works
Hardy Road
Cherry Tree Primary School
Hilltop Rd
Road
Highfield Dr
Lakeside Road
Lady Acre Cl
Hunts Field Cl
Cherrylane Farm
Massey Hall School
Weaste Lane
Booth's Lane
Cinder Lane
Thelwall Grange
Massey Brook
Higherhouse Farm
The Avenue
CHERRY
LANE
Cherry Hall Farm
M6
Oxheys Farm
A50 CLIFF LANE
Howshoots
Bradley Brook
B5158
Cherry Corner
Old Chrr La
Junction 20
Travelodge
Lymm Service Area
Bradley Hall
Brook House Farm
Wither's Lane
Wither's La
Broadheys La
Primrose Hill
A50
Junction 9/20a
M56
Fanner's Lane
Heath Lane
Barleycastle Farm
Crowsnest Farm
Moss Brow La
Swineyard Lane
Vineyard Lane
366
67
384
85
86
87
1 grid square represents 500 metres

WA13
LYMM
Deansgreen
High Legh
Sworton Heath
Ravenbank Community Primary School
Lymm High School
Lymm RFC
Crouchley Hall Farm
Yewtree Farm
Granthams
Great Oak Farm
Works
Crab Tree Farm
Crossroads Farm
Limetree Farm
High Legh CP School
Warrington
Cheshire County
Crouchley Lane
Mag Lane
Crabtree Lane
Mowpen Brow
Beechtree La
Beechtree Farm Close
West Lane
WEST LANE
HIGH LEGH ROAD
BURFORD LANE
HIGHER LANE
Kay Lane
Woodside Lane
Foxley Cl
Higher La
Whiteleggs Lane
Oughtrington Lane
Woodland Avenue
Longbutt Lane
Grammar School Road
Greenwood Road
Manor Road
Manor Rd
Tower Lane
CHURCH ROAD
Pepper Street
The Peppers
Rectory Lane
Swineyard Lane
Park Road
Chapel Walks
The Drive
Peacock Lane
Wrenshot Lane
Egerton
Gleyve
Surridge
Robert Moffat
Pheasant Walk
Arley End
Venables Wy
Kinderton Cl
Somerville Cl
Repton Cl
Holgrave Cl
Chollerton Cl
Ulviet Ca
Woodlands Crs
A56
A50
M56
B5159
A6144
THE CROSS
68
69
70
87
86
85
84
F
G
H
J
K
1
2
3
4
5
6

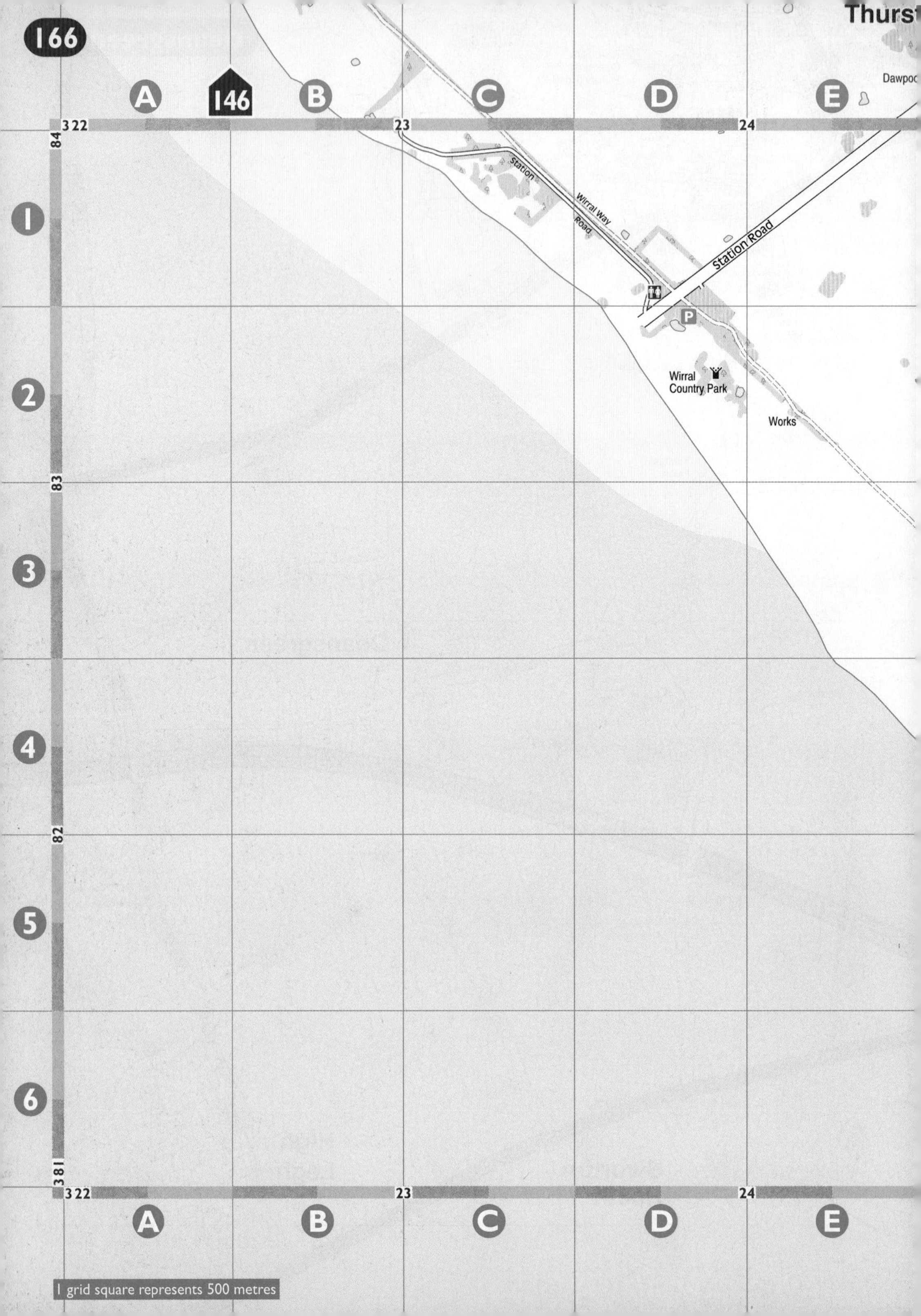
Thurst
Dawpoo
146
A
B
C
D
E
3 22
23
24
84
83
82
3 81
1
2
3
4
5
6
Station Road
Wirral Way
Station Road
Wirral Country Park
Works
P
1 grid square represents 500 metres

Pensby
Poll Hill
HESWALL
TELEGRAPH ROAD
A540
PENSBY ROAD
Oldfield
The Dungeon
The Dales
Pensby Park Primary Sch
Pensby High School for Boys
Cemetery
Heswall Preparatory School
Ladymount RC Prim Sch
Pensby Infant School
Pensby Junior School
Heswall Health Centre
Silverdale Medical Cen
Surgery
St Peters CE Primary School
Church Farm Court
The Beacons
Wirral Way
Piper's Lane
Oldfield Drive
Oldfield Road
Broad Lane
Target Road
Banks Road
The Moorings
Mostyn Av
Wittering Lane
Davenport Road
Park West
Rectory Lane
Station Road
Thurstaston Road
Quarry Road East
Tower Road North
Mere Lane
Birchmere
Fishers Lane
Bridgenorth Road
Kylemore Drive
Nelson Drive
Kentmere Drive
Rosemead Avenue
Ashlea Road
Greenbank
Hillfield Drive
Grange Rd
Florence Av
Poll Hill Road
Farr Hall Drive
Farr Hall Rd
School Hill
Dawstone Rise
Dawstone
Wallrake
Village Road
The Lydiate
Delavor Road
Dee View Rd
Beacon Lane
Rocky Lane
Manners Lane
Seabank Road
Riverbank
Westway
Hinderton Drive
Gayton Avenue
Victoria
Chantry Walk
Telegraph Road
Woodlands Road
Townshend Av
Irby Ro
Backford Rd
Penrhyd Road
Kenilworth Drive
Ridgewood
Haddon Drive
Ridgefield Rd
Woodend
Somerset Road
Woodfield Road
Dorset Dr
Devon
Sussex Cl
Nicholls Drive
Holmesway
Derwent Dr
Langdale
Rusland Avenue
Gleneagles Cl
Columbus Drive
Grenville Drive
Kylemore Close
Meadow Walk
Alexander Drive
Larchwood Close
Fairview Way
Pensby Hall Lane
Pensall Drive
Ashcroft Drive
Richmond Way
Elmwood Drive
Hillingdon Avenue
Berwyn Dr
Belldene Grove
Quarry Close
Pine Way
Strathallan Close
The Ridge
Greenfield Lane
The Akbar
Broomfield Close
Redstone Drive
Ferns Close
Oldfield Gardens
Dale Gdns
Laurelbanks Way
Quarry Rd West
Quaker Lane
Circular Drive
Warren Way
Hatton Close
The Pipers
Piper's End
Piper's Close
Sandfield Pk
Crossley Dr
Croftsway
Bush Way
Dalesway
Phillips Way
Queens Dr
Broomlands
Teals Way
Gulls Way
Hawks Way
Rooks Wy
Linnets Wy
Church Meadow Lane
Brow Lane
Castle Dr
Feather La
The Mt
Heath Dr
Grove Avenue
Radnor Avenue
Grange Mt
Dale Av
Tower Rd S
Woodcot La
Dee Side
F G H J K
25 26 27
147 148 168 180
1 2 3 4 5 6
84 83 82 81
CH61
CH60

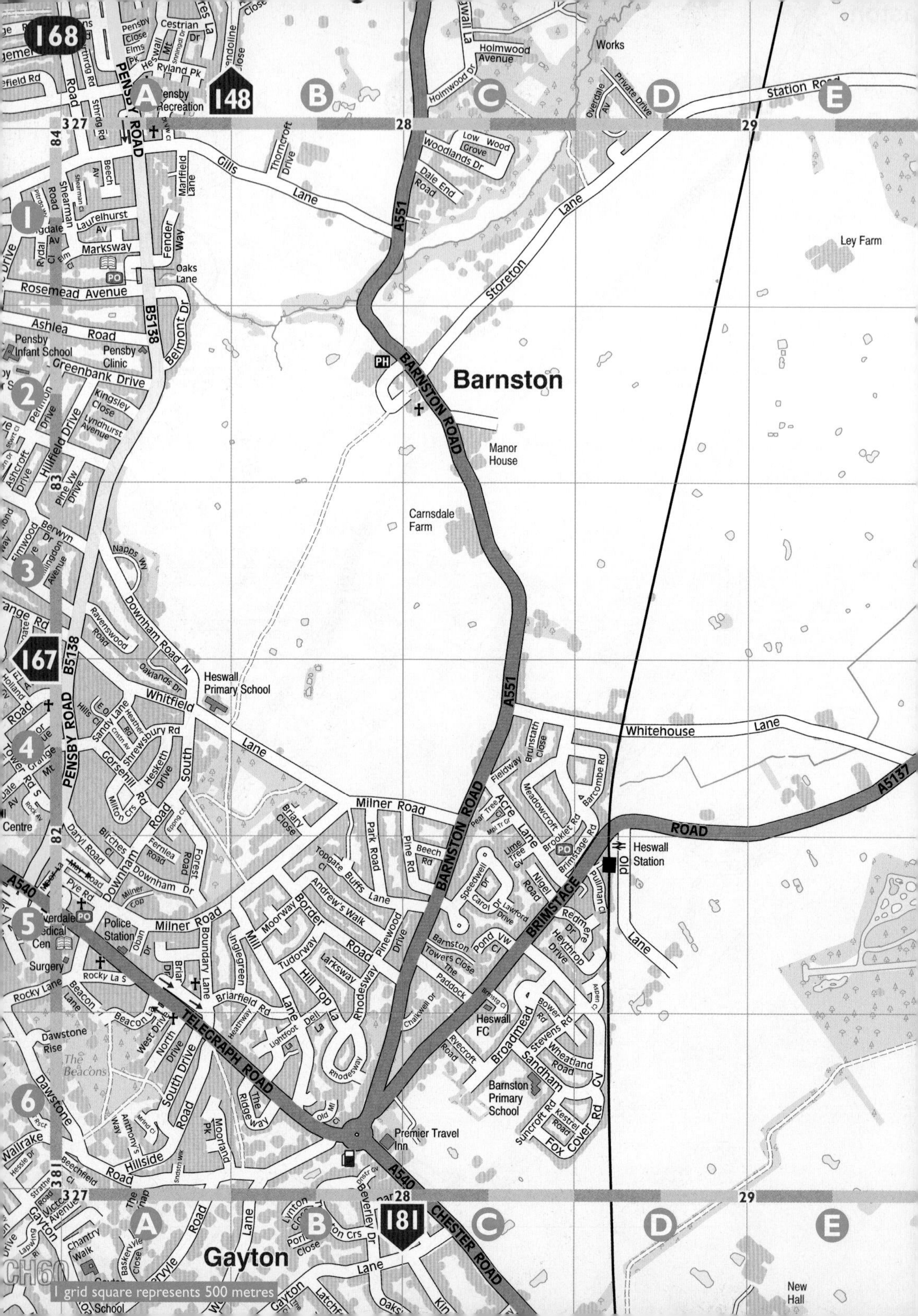

168
148
167
181
Barnston
Gayton
Works
Holmwood Avenue
Station Road
Private Drive
Overdale Av
Gills Lane
Thorncroft Drive
Woodlands Dr
Low Wood Grove
Dale End Road
Storeton Lane
Ley Farm
Pensby Recreation
Cestrian Dr
Pensby Close
Ryland Pk
PENSBY ROAD
Shearman Road
Laurelhurst Av
Marksway
Fender Way
Marlfield Lane
Oaks Lane
Rosemead Avenue
Ashlea Road
B5138
Belmont Dr
Pensby Infant School
Pensby Clinic
Greenbank Drive
Kingsley Close
Lyndhurst Avenue
Hillfield Drive
Ashcroft Drive
Pine Vw Drive
Berwyn Dr
Elmwood
Napps Wy
Downham Road N
Ravenswood Road
Oaklands Dr
Heswall Primary School
Whitfield Lane
Sandy Lane
Shrewsbury Rd
Gorsehill Rd
Hesketh Drive
South
Milton Crs
Birches Cl
Daryl Road
Downham Road
Fernlea Road
Forest Road
Downham Dr
Milner Road
Briary Close
Park Road
Pine Rd
Beech Rd
Topgate Cl
Buffs Lane
Andrew's Walk
Border Road
Pinewood Drive
Moorway
Mill
Inglegreen
Boundary Lane
Tudorway
Larksway
Hill Top Lane
Rhodesway
Briarfield Rd
Police Station
Oban Dr
Surgery
Rocky La S
Rocky Lane
Beacon Lane
Dawstone Rise
The Beacons
Dawstone Road
West Drive
North Drive
South Drive
Anthony's Way
Hillside Road
Moorland Pk
The Ridgeway
TELEGRAPH ROAD
A540
CHESTER ROAD
Premier Travel Inn
BARNSTON ROAD
A551
Manor House
Carnsdale Farm
Whitehouse Lane
A5137
ROAD
Fieldway
Brunstath Close
Barcombe Rd
Acre Lane
Meadowcroft
Brooklet Rd
Brimstage Rd
Lime Tree Gv
Nigel Road
Speedwell Dr
Carol Dr
Lawford Drive
Pond Vw Cl
Barnston Towers Close
The Paddock
BRIMSTAGE
Heswall Station
Old Lane
Pullman Cl
Redmere Dr
Heythrop Drive
Heswall FC
Ryecroft Road
Broadmead
Bower Rd
Stevens Rd
Wheatland Road
Sandham Gv
Barnston Primary School
Suncroft Rd
Kestrel Road
Fox Cover Rd
Beverley Dr
Lynton Close
Porlock Close
Lane
Chantry Walk
Gayton Avenue
New Hall
School
A B C D E
1 2 3 4 5 6
CH60
1 grid square represents 500 metres

Station Road
149
150
F
G
H
J
K
30
31
32
Red Hill Road
Keepers Lane
Brimstage Lane
M53
Brackenwood Golf Club
Brackenwood
Broomleigh Cl
Elmure
Bracken
Ferns Road
Heath Road
The Crescent
Lime Av
Alder Rd
Laurel Av
Grove
Hazel
Cedar
ROAD
B5151
Golf Course
MOUNT ROAD
2
3
4
5
6
83
82
381
Green Bank
Brimstage
A5137
BRIMSTAGE ROAD
CH63
170
Mount Rd
Clatterbridge Hospital
Wirral Hospital
Fairfield
Talbot Avenue
Manor Road
Thornton Manor
New Rocklands
Rocklands Lane
CLATTERBRIDGE ROAD
B5151
ROAD
B5136
THORNTON COMMON
Grange Dr
Works
Thornton Hough Primary School
Thornton Hough
Smithy Hill
St Grgs Wy
B5136
PO
Church Road
The Folds
Raby Road
Oxford Drive
ROAD
182
WILLASTON
Raby Vale
Thornton Farm

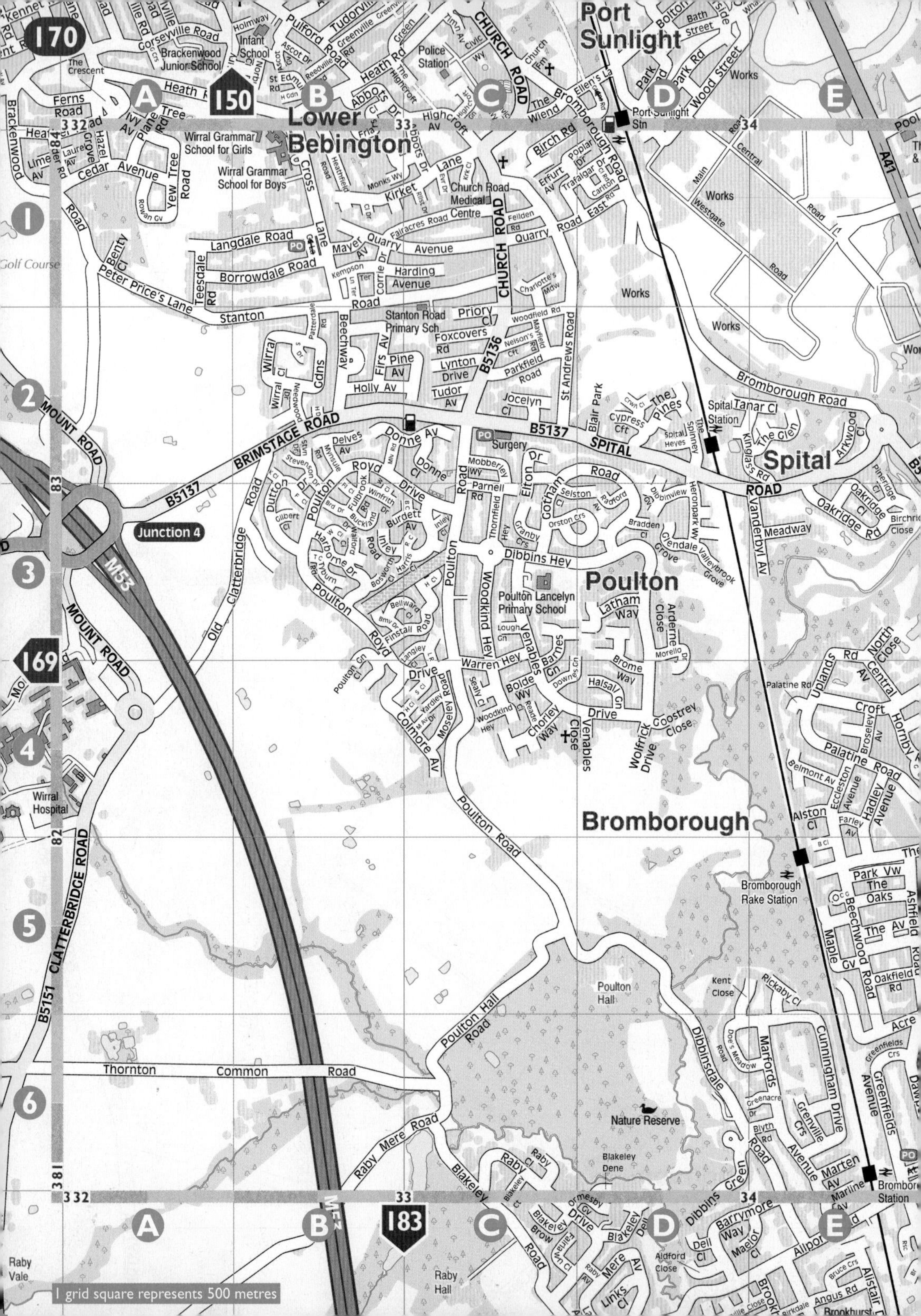

170
150
169
183
Port Sunlight
Lower Bebington
Spital
Poulton
Bromborough
A
B
C
D
E
1
2
3
4
5
6
332
33
34
381
82
83
84
Gorseyville Road
Brackenwood Junior School
Infant School
The Crescent
Heath Rd
Ferns Road
Brackenwood
Hazel Grove
Ivy Av
Plane Rd
Tree Rd
Cedar Avenue
Yew Tree Road
Lime Av
Laurel Av
Rowan Gv
Wirral Grammar School for Girls
Wirral Grammar School for Boys
Pulford Road
Tudorville
Greenville Road
Reedville
Heath Rd
Abbots Dr
The Highcroft
Highcroft Av
Police Station
Civic Wy
CHURCH ROAD
The Wiend
Bromborough Road
Ellen's La
Port Sunlight Stn
Bolton
Bath Street
Park Rd
Wood Street
Works
Birch Rd
Poplar Dr
Erfurt Av
Trafalgar Dr
Carlton
Quarry Road East
Central Road
Main
Westgate
Road
A41
Cross Lane
Heathfield
Monks Wy
Kirket Lane
Church Road Medical Centre
Fellden Rd
Fairacres Road
Quarry Avenue
Quarry Road
Mayer Av
Langdale Road
Borrowdale Road
Teesdale Rd
Benty Cl
Golf Course
Peter Price's Lane
Stanton Road
Kempson
Corrie Dr
Harding Avenue
Stanton Road Primary Sch
Priory Cl
Charlotte's Mdw
Woodfield Rd
Mayfield
Nelson's Cft
St Andrews Road
Foxcovers Rd
Lynton Drive
B5136
Parkfield Road
Jocelyn Cl
Tudor Av
Pine Av
Firs Av
Holly Av
Beechway
Patterdale Rd
Wirral Gdns
Wirral Cl
MOUNT ROAD
BRIMSTAGE ROAD
B5137
SPITAL ROAD
Blair Park
Cypress Cft
The Pines
Spital Heyes
The Spinney
Spital Station
Tanar Cl
Kinglass Rd
The Glen
Arkwood Cl
Bromborough Road
Surgery
Delves Av
Donne Av
Donne Cl
Royd Drive
Mobberley Wy
Parnell Rd
Elton Dr
Gotham Road
Selston Cl
Radford Av
Binview
Heronpark Wy
Vanderbyl Av
Meadway
Oakridge Cl
Oakridge Rd
Pineridge
Birchridge Close
Stevenson Dr
Dutton Dr
Gilbert Cl
Poulton Dr
Fullbrook Rd
Winfrith
Burdett Av
Buckland Rd
Harborne Dr
Tyburn Rd
Inley Rd
Inley Cl
Thornfield Hey
Granby Crs
Orston Crs
Bradden Cl
Glendale Grove
Valleybrook Grove
Junction 4
M53
Old Clatterbridge Road
Dibbins Hey
Poulton Lancelyn Primary School
Poulton Road
Woodkind Hey
Bellward Cl
Finstall Road
Latham Way
Ardeme Close
Morello Cl
Lough Gn
Venables Dr
Barnes Gn
Warren Hey
Brome Way
Halsal Gn
Poulton Royd Drive
Poulton Gn Cl
Langley Cl
Yardley Dr
Moseley Road
Colmore Av
Sealy Cl
Woodkind Hey
Bolde Wy
Chorley Way
Venables Close
Drive
Wolfrick Drive
Goostrey Close
Palatine Rd
Uplands Rd
North Close
Central Av
Croft Av
Hornby
Broseley Av
Palatine Road
Belmont Av
Eccleston Avenue
Hadley Avenue
Alston Cl
Farley Av
Wirral Hospital
CLATTERBRIDGE ROAD
B5151
Poulton Road
Bromborough Rake Station
Park Vw
The Oaks
Ashfield
Beechwood Road
The Av
Maple Gv
Oakfield Rd
Kent Close
Rickaby Cl
Poulton Hall
Poulton Hall Road
Dibbinsdale Road
Doe's Meadow
Marfords Av
Cunningham Drive
Grenville Crs
Greenacre Dr
Acre
Greenfields Crs
Greenfields Avenue
Thornton Common Road
Nature Reserve
Blyth Rd
Avenue
Marten Av
Marline Av
Bromborough Station
Raby Mere Road
Blakeley Road
Raby Cl
Blakeley Dene
Dibbins Green
Blakeley Brow
Ormesby Gv
Blakeley Drive
Blakeley Dell
Barrymore Way
Maelor Cl
Dell Cl
Aldford Close
Allport Rd
Bruce Crs
Angus Rd
Alistair
Brookhurst
Mere Av
Links Cl
Raby Vale
Raby Hall
1 grid square represents 500 metres

151
152
184
Eastham Ferry
Eastham Country Park
Wirral Metropolitan College
Eastham Lodge Golf Club
Eastham Locks
Job's Ferry
Wirral International Business Park
Plantation Business Park
Croft Business Park
Multibowl
Odeon Cinema
Woodslee Primary School
Mendell Primary School
Christ The King RC Primary School
Premier Travel Inn
The Cross
CH62
Cemetery
Golf Course
Old Hall Road
Commercial Road
Plantation Road
Riverwood Road
Power Road
Ferry Road
Stadium Road
Thermal Road
Causeway
Riverbank Road
Dock Road
Port
Old Ct House Road
Terminus Road
Magazine Road
Caldbeck Road
Bassendale Road
Thursby Road
Martindale Rd
Hardknott Road
Wrynose Rd
Tebay Road
Neville Road
NEW CHESTER ROAD
SPITAL ROAD
A41
Bromborough Village
Allport Road
Woodyear Road
Westminster Dr
Manor Road
Princes Avenue
Kilburn Avenue
Raeburn Av
Dearnford
Meadowside Road
Cambridge Rd
Harrow Gv
June Av
Mark Rake
Athelstan Close
Ludlow Gv
Heather Dene
Fairway North
Fairway South
Welton Road
Welton Rd
Georgia Av
Magazine La
Stanhope Dr
Churchwood Close
Croft Lane
Hornby
Forwood Rd
Mainwaring Rd
Dale Avenue
Valley Rd
Oteley Avenue
Mossley Av
Ambleside Close
Brancote Gdns
The Allports
Caldicott Av
Morland Av
Limehurst Gv
Bridle Cl
Mayfield Dr
Manchester S
Works

172
153
Dock
Works
Railway St
Church Rd
Dale St
Bank's
Byron Street
Holy Trinity Primary School
Matchwood Cl
Logfield Dr
Vineyard St
Almond Ct
Burnsall Street
SPEKE
ROAD
Bank's Road
Speke Rd
New
Park
Hughes St
Sinclair St
King St
Campania St
Saunby St
Vulcan St
Window Lane
Stanley St
Hardy St
Canterbury Street
Lincoln
Chesterton Street
York Street
Lyon Street
Durham St
Brunswick Street
Priory St
Banks Rd Prim Sch
Vesuvian Dr
Logfield Dr
Masters Wy
Vesta Road
Liverpool Marriott Hotel
Windwa
Estuary Boulevard
Es
Garston Industrial Estate
Windfield Road
Bank's La
Monkfield Wy
Blackburne Street
Garston Rocks
Works
Weaver Industrial Estate
Brunswick St
York Way
Windfield Cl
Dakota Drive
Mersey Way
Bank's Lane
Speke Hall (NT)
Liverpool
Cheshire County
340
41
84
83
82
381
A
B
C
D
E
1
2
3
4
5
6
1 grid square represents 500 metres

Woodend Industrial Estate
Evans Road
Old Distillery Rd
Shaw
Woodend
Road
154
155
F
G
H
J
K
Woodend Industrial Estate
A561
Speke Boulevard
Pharmacy Road
Botany Rd
Physics Rd
Speke Bvd
Science Rd
Gaskill Road
Renaissance Way
Inner West Road
Estuary Business Park
Leeward Drive
Petworth Cl
Barnham Cl
Rycot Road
Tonbridge Cl
Dymchurch Road
Lydd Cl
Bray Road
Woodend La
Bexhill Cl
Appledore Close
Gerneth Cl
Sandgate Cl
Speke Town La
Farm Road
Hall Road
Ramsbrook Rd
Works
Speke Hall Av
Banks
School Way
Gerneth Rd
Speke Church Rd
Greyhound
Blacklock
Blackrod Av
Stockton Wd Rd
Stockton Wood Community Primary School
Goldfinch Farm Road
Western Avenue
Linner Road
Speke Hall Avenue
Spindus Road
Speke Hall Industrial Estate
Stirling Rd
Blenheim Wy
Hale Road
All Saints Road
Sutton Wood Rd
Tewit Hall Rd
Tewit Hall Cl
Bailey's Lane
Skypark Industrial Park
Owen Dr
Dunlop Road
Oglet La
The Walk
Liverpool John Lennon International Airport
SPEKE BOULEVARD
A561
South Road
Clough Road
Tarbock Road
St Christophers Catholic Primary School
Speke
Stapleton Avenue
Lovel Wy
Lovel Road
Harefield Road
Conleach Road
Parklands High School
Austin Rawlinson Sports Centre
Police Stn
North Parade
South Parade
Central Avenue
Speke Family Health Clinic
Ganworth Road
Ganworth Rd
Holland
Heath Road
Little
Alder
Millwood
All Hallows Dr
Middlefield Primary School
Oldbridge
Dam Wood Road
Dam Wood Rd
Hale Road
L24
174
Oglet
Oglet Lane
Mersey Way
42
43
44
84
83
82
381
1
2
3
4
5
6
River Mersey

174
Central Road
Inner Central Rd
Middle Rd
East Road
Works
155
156
Higher Road
South Road
Inner S
Middle Road
Road
SPEKE BOULEVARD
Clough Road
Surgery
Millwood Road
East Millwood
Ramsfield Road
The Margaret Thompson Medical Centre
Maintree Crs
Sandham Rd
Heaton Close
All Hallows Dr
Harland Gn
Cassley Rd
West Mains
E Mains
Oak Vw
Elloway Rd
Miners Wy
Alder Wd Av
Croyde Rd
Leveret Rd
Alder Wood Avenue
Middlefield Primary School
Oldbridge Rd
Ardwick Rd
Withington Rd
Catford Gn
Greenway Rd
Alderfield Dr
Family Health
Central Way
Critchley Road
Heathgate Av
Church Way
Burnage Cl
Alwain Gn
Eastern Avenue
St Ambrose RC Primary School
Dam Wood Road
East Dam Wood Rd
Hale Drive
Hale Road
Ramsbrook Lane
Brook Farm
Hale
Morcott Lane
Carlow Cl
Arklow Drive
Wexford Av
Kildare Cl
Malin Cl
Aran Cl
Langford
Pheasant Fld
Ladypool
Police Station
Cocklade Lane
Holly Cl
Pepper St
Town La
High Street
Carriage Cl
PO
Carr Lane
Church End
Liverpool
Halton
173
Bailey's Lane
Dungeon Lane
Mersey Way
1 grid square represents 500 metres

Hale Bank
River Mersey
Manchester Ship Canal
Trans Pennine Trail
Pickerings Pasture
Halegate Farm
Hale Gate Road
Town Lane
Carr Lane
Mersey View Road
Garnetts Lane
Pickerings Rd
Foundry La
Waterside Lane
Blackburne Avenue
Broughton Way
Hale Road Industrial Estate
Halebank CE Primary School
Heathview Rd
Kenview Cl
Potters La
Within Way
Church Road
Vicarage Close
Hoghton Rd
Hesketh Road
Curlender Wy
Ellwood Cl
Ireland Road
Hale CE Prim Sch
Lighthouse Road
Mersey Way
Hale Head
Salt Works Wharf
Weston Point Dock
Post Office La
Canal Side
157
176
F G H J K
47 48 49
84 83 82 81
1 2 3 4 5 6

157
158
175
186
10
A
B
C
D
E
1
2
3
4
5
6
West Bank
Business Cen
Dock St
West Bank Medical Cen
Catalyst Sci Discovery
Ronan Road
Works
West Bank Dock
Desoto
Vickers Road
West Bank Prim Sch
Runcorn Gap
Runcorn-Widnes Bridge
A533
QUEENSWAY
Manchester Ship Canal
All Saints CE Prim Sch
Mersey Road
Mersey St
Church Street
Mkt
HIGH ST
BRIDGE ST
B5755
Surg
Arts Cen
Bridgewater Canal
DARESBURY EXPRESSWAY
Campanile Hotel
Runcorn Station
Old Coach Rd
Algernon Street
Percival Lane
Percival
WESTON POINT EXPRESSWAY
A557
Pimlico Rd
Farm Road
Westfield Prim Sch
Crofton Road
Victoria Road Prim Sch
Victoria Rd
Cemetery
RUNCORN SPUR ROAD
B5155
Ivy Street
Higher Runcorn
War Mem
St Clements RC Prim Sch
Runcorn Hill Nature Reserve
Lawson Ho Htl & Conf Cen
Moughland Lane
Heath Road
Heath Road Medical Cen
Weston Point
Salt Works Wharf
Weston Point Dock
Picow Farm Rd
Russell Rd
Weston Point Primary School
Weston Road
Weston
Heath
Highlands Road
Runcorn Golf Club
Pewithall Primary School
The Heath Specialist Tech College
Clifton Road
South Parade
Sandy Lane
Canal Side
Works
Prospect Row
Golf Course
WA7
RUN
1 grid square represents 500 metres

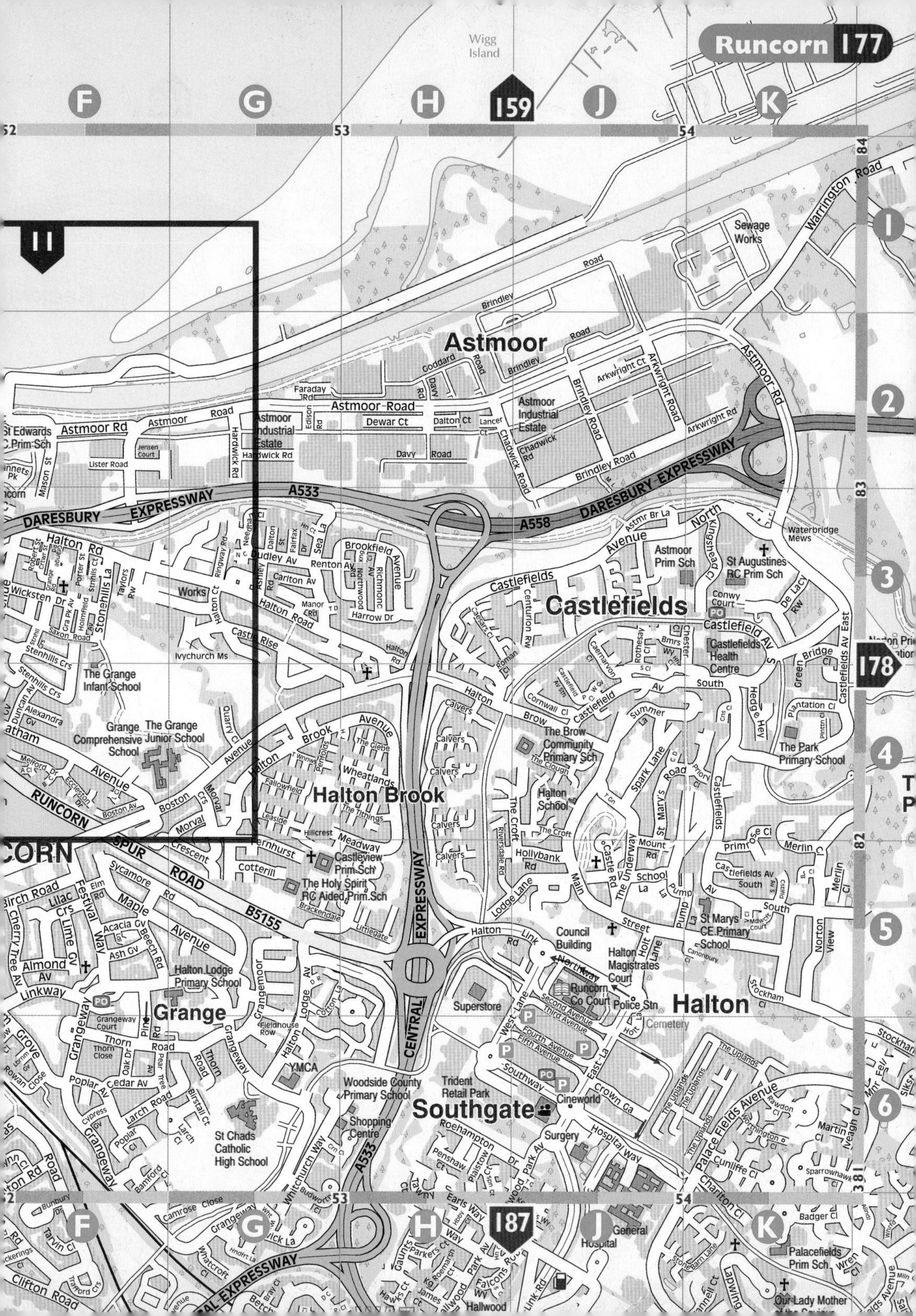
Wigg Island
159
F
G
H
J
K
52
53
54
84
83
82
381
I
2
3
4
5
6
11
178
187
Astmoor
Castlefields
Halton Brook
Grange
Halton
Southgate
DARESBURY EXPRESSWAY
A533
A558
CENTRAL EXPRESSWAY
RUNCORN SPUR ROAD
B5155
Warrington Road
Sewage Works
Astmoor Road
Astmoor Industrial Estate
Brindley Road
Arkwright Road
Astmoor Prim Sch
St Augustines RC Prim Sch
Castlefields Health Centre
The Park Primary School
The Brow Community Primary Sch
Halton School
Castleview Prim Sch
The Holy Spirit RC Aided Prim Sch
The Grange Infant School
The Grange Junior School
Grange Comprehensive School
Halton Lodge Primary School
St Chads Catholic High School
Woodside County Primary School
YMCA
Shopping Centre
Trident Retail Park
Superstore
Runcorn Co Court
Police Stn
Council Building
Halton Magistrates Court
St Marys CE Primary School
Cemetery
Cineworld
Surgery
General Hospital
Palacefields Prim Sch
St Edwards RC Prim Sch

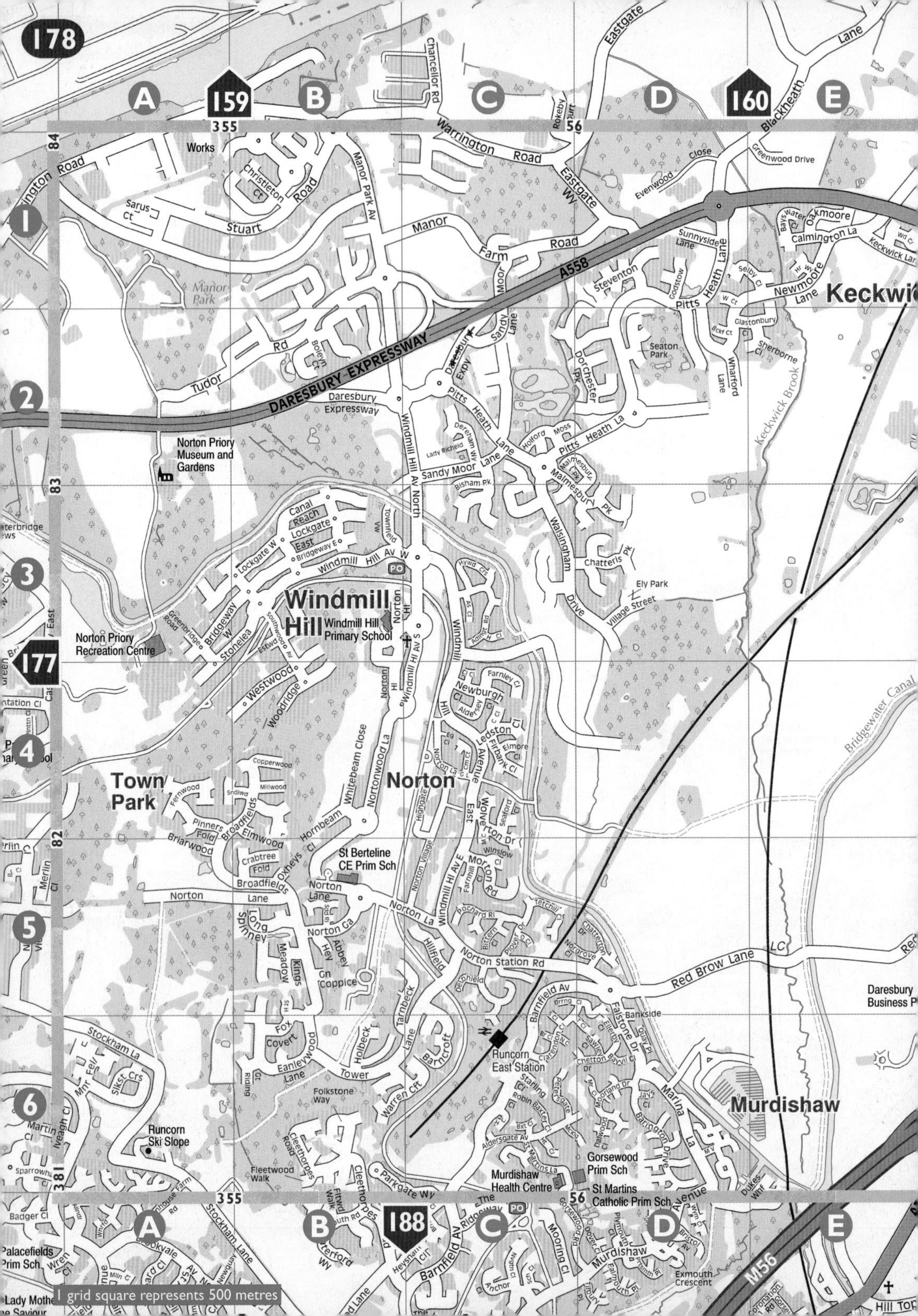

178
159
160
177
188
A
B
C
D
E
1
2
3
4
5
6
84
83
82
81
355
56
Works
Warrington Road
Manor Park Av
Christleton Ct
Sarus Ct
Stuart Road
Manor Farm Road
Eastgate
Eastgate Wy
Chancellor Rd
Rokeby Court
Blackheath Lane
Greenwood Drive
Evenwood Close
A558
DARESBURY EXPRESSWAY
Daresbury Expressway
Manor Park
Tudor Rd
Boleyn Ct
Sandy Lane
Moor Lane
Pitts Heath Lane
Sunnyside Lane
Steventon
Godstow
Oakmoore
Calmington La
Keckwick Lane
Newmoore Lane
Keckwick
Selby Cl
Glastonbury Cl
Sherborne Cl
Wharford Lane
Seaton Park
Dorchester Pk
Keckwick Brook
Norton Priory Museum and Gardens
Windmill Hill Av North
Dereham Wy
Lady Richeld Cl
Sandy Moor Lane
Holford Moss
Pitts Heath La
Malmesbury Pk
Bisham Pk
Walsingham Drive
Chatteris Pk
Ely Park
Village Street
Canal Reach
Lockgate East
Lockgate W
Bridgeway E
Windmill Hill Av W
Townfield Vw
PO
Windmill Hill
Windmill Hill Primary School
Norton Hl
Windmill Hl Av S
Hywd Crs
Windmill Hill
Norton Priory Recreation Centre
Greenbridge Road
Bridgeway W
Stonelea
Southwood Av
Westwood
Woodridge
Newburgh Cl
Farnley Cl
Ledston Cl
Firbank Cl
Elmore Cl
Norton Avenue
Whitebeam Close
Nortonwood La
Norton
Highgate
Norton Village
Wolverton Dr
Seaford
Winslow Cl
Town Park
Copperwood
Fernwood
Millwood
Broadfields
Elmwood
Pinners Fold
Briarwood
Crabtree Fold
Hornbeam Cl
Oxheys Cl
St Berteline CE Prim Sch
Windmill Hl Av E
Morton Rd
Norton Lane
Norton La
Norton Ga
Long Spinney
Meadow
Kings
Abbey Hey
Gn Coppice
Hillfield
Norton Station Rd
Red Brow Lane
LC
Daresbury Business P
Bittern Cl
Plover Dr
Tetchill Cl
Chatterton Dr
Norgrove Cl
Barnfield Av
Falstone Dr
Bankside
Runcorn East Station
Stockham La
Fox Covert
Eanleywood Lane
Holbeck
Tarnbeck
Barncroft
Tower Lane
Warren Cft
Folkstone Way
Starling Cl
Robin Bank
Petersgate
Moorland Dr
Barrington Drive
Marina La
Murdishaw
Aldersgate Av
St Martins La
Gorsewood Prim Sch
Murdishaw Health Centre
St Martins Catholic Prim Sch
Runcorn Ski Slope
Iveagh Cl
Martin Cl
Cleethorpes Road
Fleetwood Walk
Parkgate Wy
The Ridgeway
Barnfield Av
Mooring Cl
Avenue
Dukes Whf
M56
Badger Cl
Palacefields Prim Sch
Wren
Stockham Lane
Brookvale
Heysham Cl
Anchor
Plymouth
Bristol Av
Exmouth Crescent
Falmouth Pl
Hill Top
Lady Mother Saviour
Bridgewater Canal
Merlin Cl
1 grid square represents 500 metres

Acre Lane
Six Acre Gdns
Hollybank
Beechmoore
Hobb Lane
161
Runcorn Road
F
G
H
J
K
57
58
59
84
Norton House
Halton
Warrington
CHESTER ROAD
Row's Wood
A558 DARESBURY EXPRESSWAY
Keckwick Lane
Delph Lane
Warrington Road
Hall Lane
Chester Road
Commonside Farm
83
A56
B5356
Hall-lane Farm
DARESBURY LANE
B5356
Daresbury Primary School
Daresbury Firs
Daresbury
Crow's Nest
Delph Lane
The Brackens
Chester Road
CHESTER ROAD
82
Bank
Newton Lane
Brow Lane
De Vere Daresbury Park
Newtonbank Farm
Newton
M56
Junction 11
Little Manor Farm
Summer Lane
Windmill La
381
189
Hallamhall Farm
Morphany Hall
New Manor Road
Preston on
1
2
3
4
5
6

A
B
167
C
D
E
325
26
81
80
79
378
1
2
3
4
5
6
Lane
Church Meadow Lane
Church Farm Court
St Peter's Cl
PO
Park West
Davenport Road
Rectory Lane
Rectory Close
Raby Cl
The Lydiate
Wallrake
Hessle Dr
Dawstone
Marine Drive
Manners Lane
Seafield Av
Hilbre Av
Seabank Road
Station Road
Westway
Meadway
Riverbank Cl
Riverbank Road
Hinderton Drive
Gayton
Strathearn Road
Lapwing Rl
CH60
Long Meadow
P
Lillyfield
Lane
Cottage Drive West
Cottage
Gayton Cott
Cottage Drive East
Wirral
Cheshire County
190
1 grid square represents 500 metres

Gayton
Parkgate
Gayton Primary School
Heswall Golf Club
Golf Course
Barnston Primary School
Premier Travel Inn
Backwood Hall
Leighton Hall Farm
New Hall
Ashfield Hall
Parkgate Primary School
Brooklands Gardens
Mostyn House School
Neston CC
Neston Station
Westwood Court
CHESTER ROAD
BOATHOUSE LANE
B5135
THE PARADE
North Parade
Wirral Way
Leighton Road
Wood Lane
The Runnell
Parkgate Lane
Brook La
Baskervyle Road
Well Lane
Gayton Lane
Dee Park Road
Latchford Road
Oaksway
Kingsway
Birchway
Parkway
Cedarway
Queensway
The Spinney
Gayton Farm Rd
Chantry Walk
Brooklands Road
Bevyl Road
Hawthorn Road
Moorfield Drive
Springcroft
Grenfell Pk
Mostyn Square
Leighton Chase
Pinehey
The Priory
Newhey
Millfield
Water Tower Rd
Long Acres Road
Buildwas Road
Ringway
Clayhill
LIVERPOOL
B5136
Mayfield Gdns
Shakespeare Rd
Drake Road
Hawkins Road
Raleigh Rd
Raby
Breezehill
Blackeys Lane
Highfield Rd
Albert Drive
PARKGATE RD
F
G
H
J
K
1
2
3
4
5
6
27
28
29
79
80
81
168
182
191

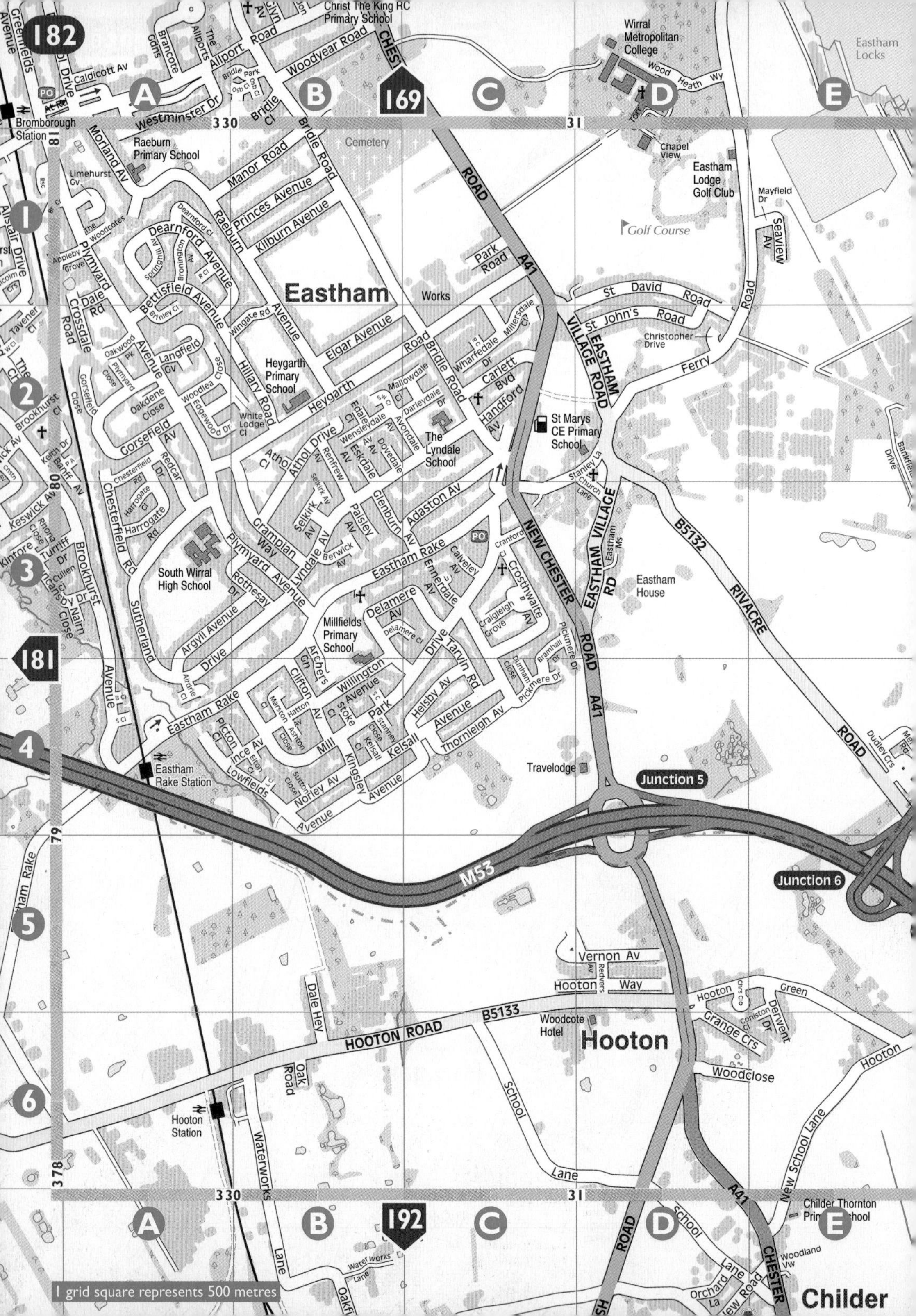
Eastham
Hooton
Childer
Eastham Locks
Wirral Metropolitan College
Christ The King RC Primary School
Raeburn Primary School
Bromborough Station
Cemetery
Eastham Lodge Golf Club
Golf Course
Works
Heygarth Primary School
The Lyndale School
St Marys CE Primary School
South Wirral High School
Millfields Primary School
Eastham House
Travelodge
Junction 5
Junction 6
M53
Eastham Rake Station
Hooton Station
Woodcote Hotel
Childer Thornton Primary School
NEW CHESTER ROAD
A41
B5132
RIVACRE ROAD
B5133
HOOTON ROAD
EASTHAM VILLAGE ROAD
Eastham Rake
Ferry Road
Hooton Green
Hooton Way
Vernon Av
Woodclose
School Lane
New School Lane
Waterworks Lane
Dale Hey
Oak Road
Plymyard Avenue
Heygarth Road
Bridle Road
Allport Road
Woodyear Road
Westminster Dr
Manor Road
Princes Avenue
Kilburn Avenue
Elgar Avenue
Raeburn Avenue
Dearnford Avenue
Bettisfield Avenue
Hillary Road
Crossdale Road
Sutherland Avenue
Argyll Avenue
Rothesay Dr
Grampian Way
Lyndale Av
Atholl Drive
Adaston Av
Glenburn Av
Delamere Av
Tarvin Rd
Thornleigh Av
Kelsall Avenue
Kingsley Avenue
Norley Av
Lowfields Avenue
Ince Av
Picton Cl
Willington Avenue
Stoke Park Cl
Helsby Av
Crosthwaite Av
Pickmere Dr
Gorsefield Av
Oakdene Close
Langfield Gv
Chesterfield Rd
Harrogate Rd
Redcar Dr
Brookhurst Av
St David Road
St John's Road
Christopher Drive
Seaview Av
Mayfield Dr
Park Road
Carlett Bvd
Handford Av
Wharfedale Dr
Stanley La
Church Lane
Wood Heath Wy
Chapel View
Grange Crs
Derwent Dr
Woodland Vw
Orchard La
1 grid square represents 500 metres

F
G
H
170
J
K
33
34
81
80
79
378
1
2
3
4
5
6
184
Manchester Ship Canal
Wirral
Cheshire County
Bankfields Drive
Eric Fountain Rd
North Road
River Mersey
Manchester Ship Canal
Booston Wood
Works
Rivacre Road
B5132
Lane
Motor Vehicle Works
M53
Junction 7
North Road
B5132
Poole Hall Industrial Estate
193
Poole Hall
Rivacre Valley Country Park
Hillside Drive
Poole Hall Lane
Gowy Court
Stapleford Court
Woodacre Grove
Plemston Court
Croughton Rd
Huxley Court
Gateacre
Poole Hall Industrial Estate

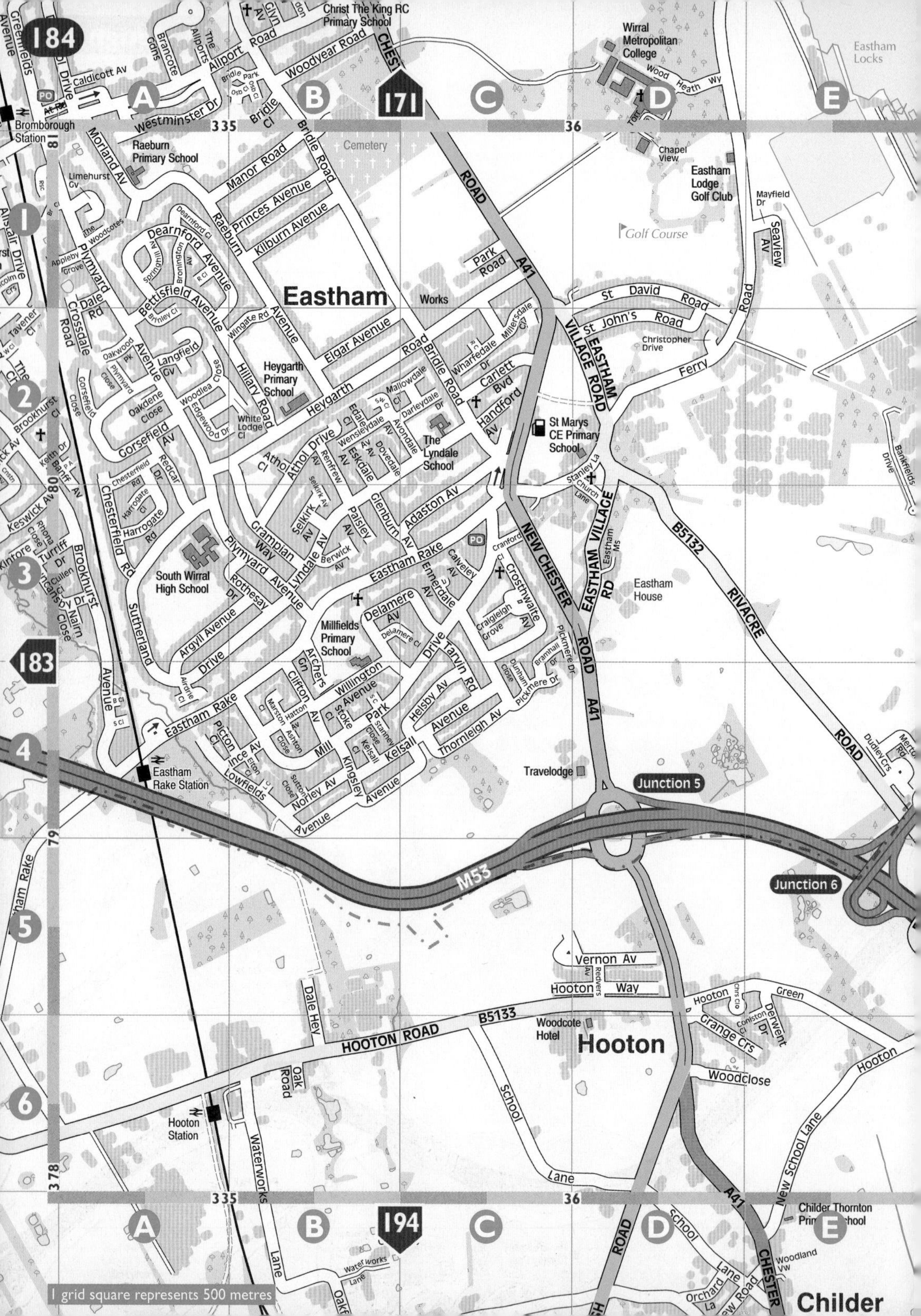

184
171
183
194
A
B
C
D
E
1
2
3
4
5
6
335
36
81
80
79
378
Greenfields Avenue
Caldicott Av
Braincote Gdns
The Allports
Allport Road
Glyn Av
Christ The King RC Primary School
Woodyear Road
Chester Road
Wirral Metropolitan College
Wood Heath Wy
Eastham Locks
Westminster Dr
Bridle Park
Bridle Cl
Bridle Road
Bromborough Station
PO
Morland Av
Raeburn Primary School
Cemetery
Chapel View
Eastham Lodge Golf Club
Mayfield Dr
Seaview Av
Limehurst Gv
Manor Road
Princes Avenue
Kilburn Avenue
Raeburn Avenue
Dearnford Avenue
Dearnford Cl
The Woodcotes
Appleby Grove
Plymyard Avenue
Springhill Av
Bronington Av
Golf Course
Park Road
A41
Eastham
Works
St David Road
St John's Road
Christopher Drive
Ferry Road
Bettisfield Avenue
Brynley Cl
Wingate Rd
Dale Rd
Crossdale Road
Tavener Cl
Oakwood Pk
Langfield Gv
Elgar Avenue
Heygarth Road
Bridle Road
Wharfedale Dr
Millersdale Cl
Village Road
Eastham Village Road
Plymyard Close
Gorsefield Close
Woodlea Close
Hillary Road
Heygarth Primary School
Mallowdale Cl
Carlett Bvd
Oakdene Close
Edgewood Dr
White Lodge Cl
Edale Cl
Darleydale Dr
Handford Av
Brookhurst Cl
Gorsefield Av
Athol Drive
Athol Cl
Wensleydale Av
Avondale Av
Dovedale Av
Eskdale Av
The Lyndale School
St Marys CE Primary School
Stanley La
Church Lane
Bankfields Drive
Keith Dr
Banff Av
Chesterfield Cl
Redcar Dr
Renfrew Av
Harrogate Cl
Harrogate Rd
Chesterfield Rd
Keswick Av
Selkirk Av
Glenburn Av
Adaston Av
Paisley Av
Grampian Way
Lyndale Av
Berwick Av
New Chester Road
Eastham Ms
B5132
Kintore Close
Rhona Close
Turriff Dr
Brookhurst Avenue
Cullen Cl
Duncansby Dr
Nairn Close
South Wirral High School
Rothesay Dr
Plymyard Avenue
Eastham Rake
Ennerdale Av
Calveley Av
Cranford Cl
Crosthwaite Av
Eastham Village Rd
Eastham House
Rivacre Road
Sutherland Avenue
Argyll Avenue
Millfields Primary School
Delamere Av
Delamere Cl
Craigleigh Grove
Drive
Tarvin Rd
Pickmere Dr
Bramhall Dr
Dunham Close
Airdrie Cl
Archers Gn
Clifton Av
Willington Avenue
Marston Cl
Hatton Av
Stoke Cl
Park Avenue
Helsby Av
Pickmere Dr
Ashton Close
Stanney Close
Kelsall Close
Kelsall Avenue
Thornleigh Av
Picton Cl
Ince Av
Elton Cl
Mill
Kingsley
Norley Av
Sutton Close
Lowfields Cl
Eastham Rake Station
Travelodge
Junction 5
Merton Rd
Dudley Crs
Avenue
M53
Junction 6
Eastham Rake
Vernon Av
Redvers Av
Hooton Way
Hooton Green
Grange Crs
Coniston Dr
Derwent
Dale Hey
B5133
Hooton Road
Woodcote Hotel
Hooton
School Lane
Woodclose
Oak Road
Hooton Station
Waterworks Lane
New School Lane
Childer Thornton Primary School
Chester Road
School Lane
Woodland Vw
Water Works Lane
Orchard
New Road
Childer
1 grid square represents 500 metres

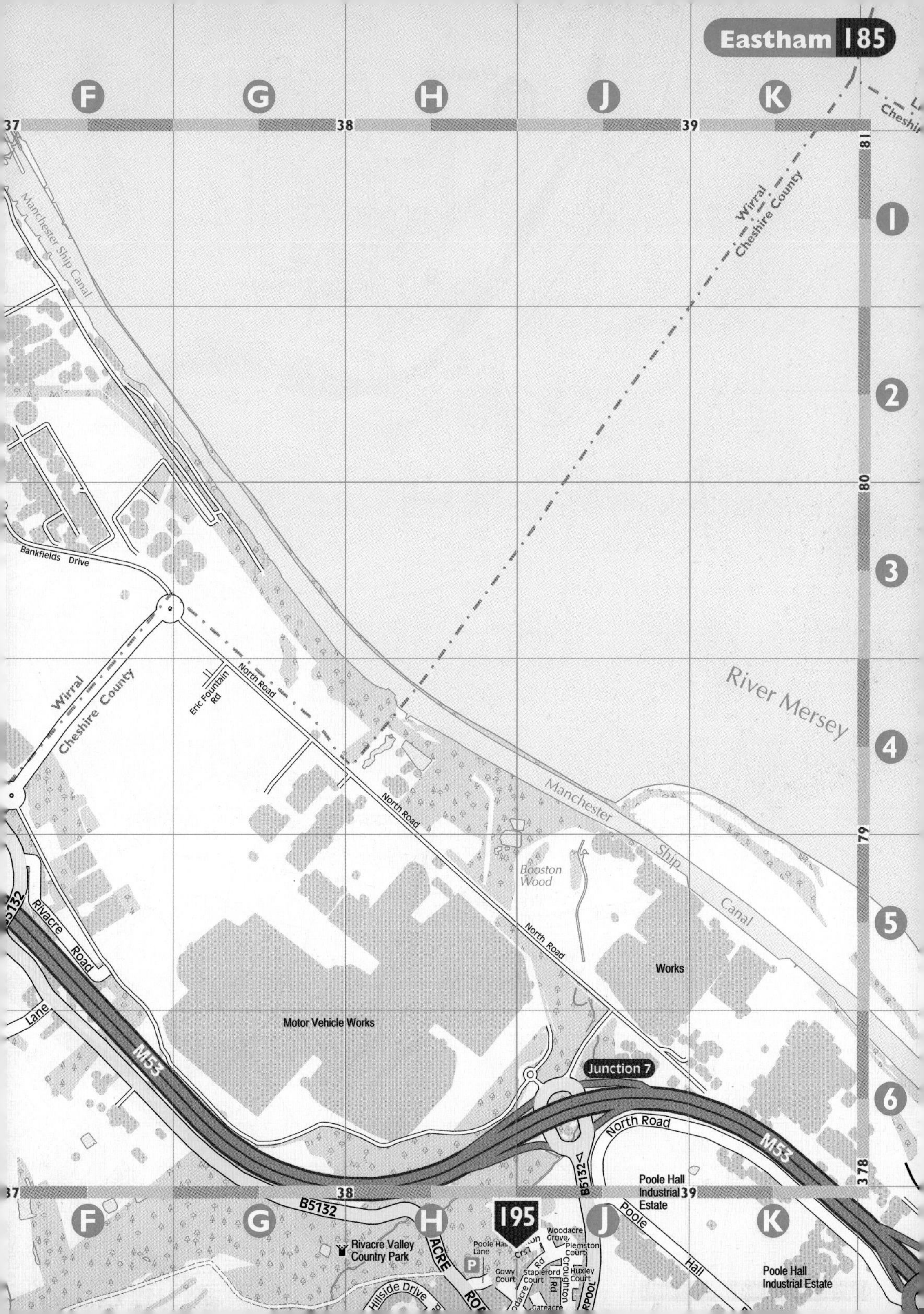
F
G
H
J
K
37
38
39
81
80
79
378
1
2
3
4
5
6
Wirral
Cheshire County
Manchester Ship Canal
Bankfields Drive
Wirral
Cheshire County
Eric Fountain Rd
North Road
North Road
North Road
River Mersey
Manchester Ship Canal
Booston Wood
Works
B5132
Rivacre Road
Lane
Motor Vehicle Works
M53
Junction 7
North Road
M53
B5132
Poole Hall Industrial Estate
B5132
195
Rivacre Valley Country Park
Poole Hall Lane
Woodacre Grove
Plemston Court
Gowy Court
Stapleford Court
Huxley Court
Croughton
Rd
Poole Hall
Poole Hall Industrial Estate
Hillside Drive
Gateacre

Weston
176
200
Works
Weston Road
Weston Primary School
Golf Course
Runcorn Golf Club
The Heath Specialist Tech College
Clifton Road
WESTON POINT EXPRESSWAY
A557
Cavendish Farm Rd
Cow Hey Lane
Frodsham Marsh Farm
Alder Lane
Brook Furlong
Frodsham Marsh
Weaver Lane
Moorditch Lane
Tadgers Lane
M56
Marsh Lane
MAIN STREET
CHURCH STREET
Frodsham Station
Frodsham Science & Technology College
Surgery
1 grid square represents 500 metres

Southgate
177
Palacefields
Beechwood
Clifton
Rocksavage
Newtown
Halton
Cheshire County
Junction 12
CENTRAL EXPRESSWAY
ROCKSAVAGE EXPRESSWAY
WHITEHOUSE EXPRESSWAY
M56
A533
A557
A56
CLIFTON ROAD A557
SUTTON CAUSEWAY
BRIDGE LANE
CHESTER ROAD
Wood Lane
Halton Station Rd
Clifton Lane
Mill Lane
The Quay
Weaver Road
Francis Rd
Ashton Drive
Palace Fields Avenue
Beechwood Avenue
Ashbrook Avenue
Halton General Hospital
Hallwood Park Prim Sch
Palacefields Prim Sch
Our Lady Mother of the Saviour Catholic Primary School
Beechwood Primary Sch
Hillview Primary School
Runcorn Rowing Club
Sutton Hall Golf Club
Golf Course
Marshgate Farm
Weaver Park Industrial Est
Weaver Vale Primary School
The Manor House Primary School
St Lukes RC Primary School
The Willows
St Chads Catholic High
Woodside County Primary School
Trident Retail Park
Shopping Centre
Cineworld
Surgery
YMCA
188
Weaver Navigation
F G H J K
1 2 3 4 5 6
53 54
201

188
178
187
Murdishaw
Brookvale
Preston
Brook
Sutton
Weaver
Aston
Heath
Aston
Runcorn Ski Slope
Palacefields Prim Sch
Gorsewood Prim Sch
Murdishaw Health Centre
St Martins Catholic Prim Sch
Brookvale Recreation Centre
Halton High School
Brookvale Primary School
Premier Travel Inn
Council Building
Sutton Fields Farm
Aston By Sutton Primary School
Aston Lodge
Beckett's Wood
Parkside Farm
Aston Grange
M56
A533
A56
CHESTER ROAD
NORTHWICH RD
Aston Lane
Aston Lane South
Aston Fields Road
Rivington Road
Stockham Lane
Wood Lane
Palace Fields Avenue
Brookvale Av North
Exmouth Crescent
Hill Top
Waterfront
Canal Side
355
56
1 grid square represents 500 metres

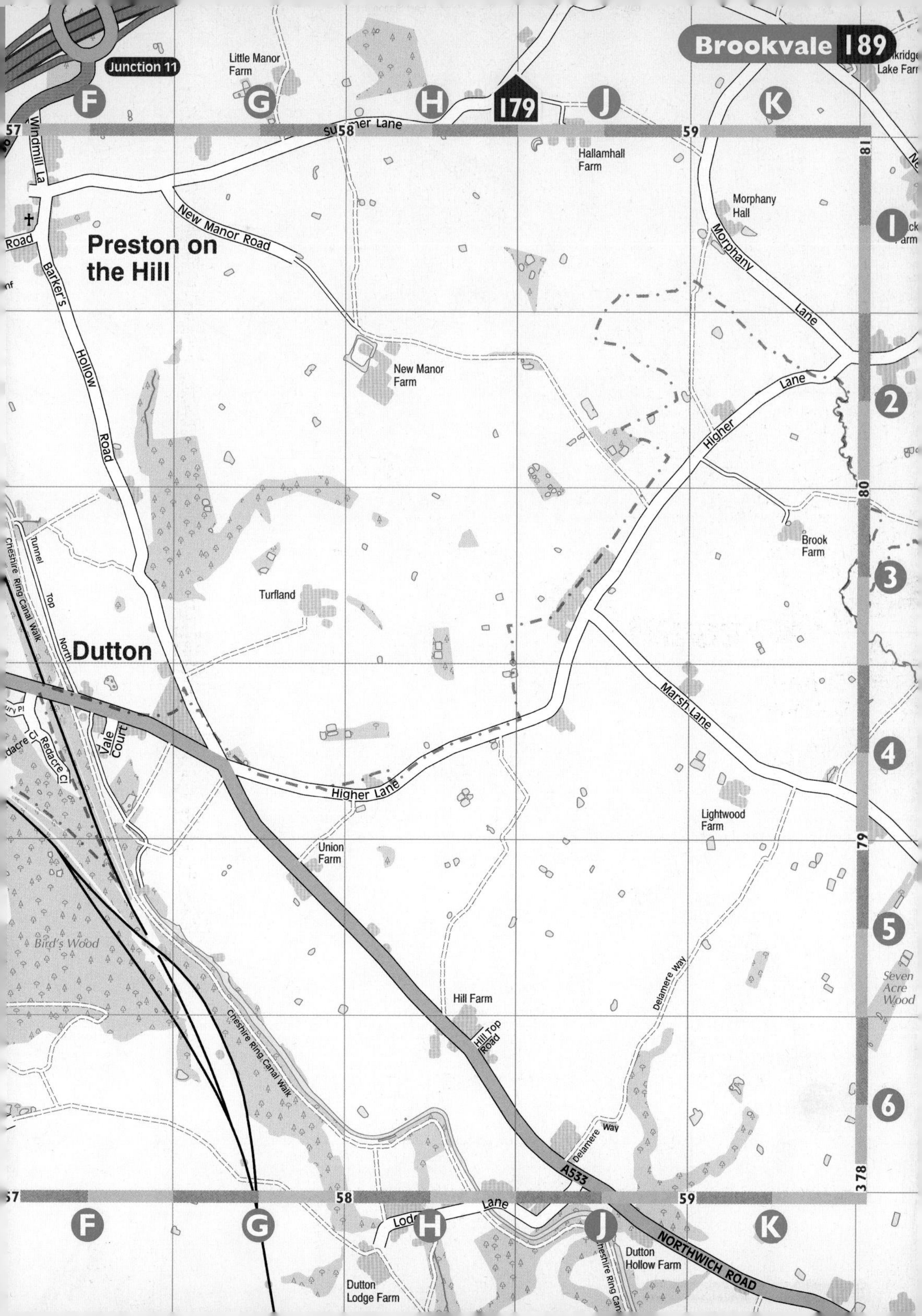

Junction 11
Little Manor Farm
179
Summer Lane
Windmill La
Hallamhall Farm
Morphany Hall
Morphany Lane
Preston on the Hill
New Manor Road
Barker's Hollow Road
New Manor Farm
Higher Lane
Brook Farm
Turfland
Tunnel Top North
Dutton
Cheshire Ring Canal Walk
Marsh Lane
Vale Court
Redacre Cl
Lightwood Farm
Union Farm
Bird's Wood
Seven Acre Wood
Delamere Way
Hill Farm
Hill Top Road
A533
NORTHWICH ROAD
Lodge Lane
Dutton Hollow Farm
Dutton Lodge Farm

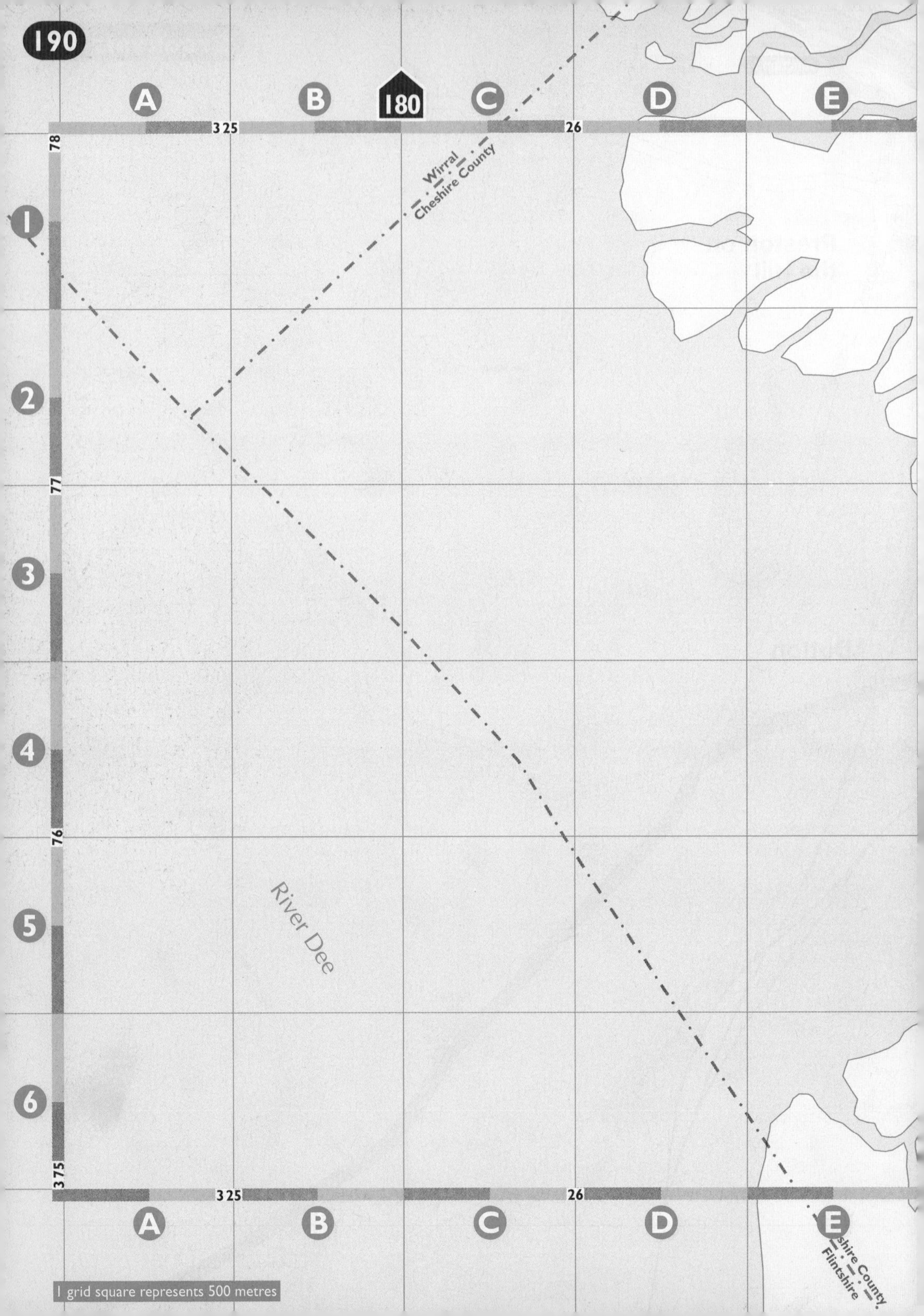
180
A
B
C
D
E
325
26
78
77
76
375
1
2
3
4
5
6
Wirral
Cheshire County
River Dee
shire County
Flintshire
1 grid square represents 500 metres

Parkgate
Moorside
NESTON
Little Neston
Nessh
Mostyn House School
Neston CC
Neston Station
Neston Medical Centre
Neston Primary School
Brooklands Gardens
Mostyn Square
PARKGATE RD
STATION RD
B5135
B5136
B5134
HIGH ST
CHESTER RD
Old Quay Lane
Marshlands Road
Greenfields Drive
Quayside
Riverside Walk
Burton Road
West Vale
Allans Meadow
181
192
F
G
H
J
K
28
29

192
182
191
Hinderton
Neston High School
Windle Hill
Ness
Nessholt
Burton
CH64
Weatherstone Business Centre
Leahurst
Hanns Hall Farm
The Lydiate
Hyfield
Haddon Hall Farm
Denhall House Farm
Liverpool University Botanic Gardens (Ness Gardens)
Woodfall Primary School
Woodfall Infant School
St Winefrides RC Prim Sch
Surgery
Cemetery
HINDERTON ROAD
B5134
B5133
HANNS HALL ROAD
CHESTER HIGH ROAD
Quarry Road
Cherry Close
Lees Lane
Wirral Way
Cuckoo Lane
Woodfall Lane
Mill Lane
Haddon Lane
Neston Road
Wood Lane
Burton Road
Bull Hill
Well Lane
School Lane
Station Road
Mellock Lane
Bendee Road
Waterford Drive
Sandy Lane
Gorstons La
Raymond Way
The Quillet
Bushell Road
Breezehill Rd
Badger Bait
Talbot Av
Romney Way
Raeburn Av
Rose Gardens
Victoria Rd
Rock Farm Dr
Rocklee Gdns
Dawn Close
Cumbers Dr
Holt Hey
Furrocks La
Riverview Rd
Cliffe Rd
Greenfields Drive
Flashes La
Hill Ct
Palace Hey
Shones Cft
1 grid square represents 500 metres

Willaston
Mill Lane
BIRKENHEAD ROAD
B5151
Lydiate Lane
Meadow Lane
Whitegates Crs
Meadow Cft
Willaston Primary School
Surgery
NESTON ROAD
Elm Road
The Chestnuts
The Ctyd
Broadlake
Briardale Road
Overdale Road
Delamore's Acre
The Knowe
B5133
Change Lane
Park Rd
Crosby Grove
Barford Gra
Heath Lane
HOOTON ROAD
Beech Hey
Hawthorne Lane
Old Vicarage Rd
Pemberton Cl
Moss Cl
Bennet Cl
Buckley La
Smithy Lane
Ash Fr Ct
Hadlow Lane
Ashtree Cft
Wallcroft
Wirral Way
Adfalent Lane
Wirral Country Park
New Hey Lane
HADLOW ROAD
Leaswood Farm
A540
A540 CHESTER HIGH ROAD
Dunstan Lane
Wood End La
Heath Farm
Garden Centre
Badgers Rake House
Hallwood Farm
Hallwood Drive
Mudhouse Lane
PARKCATE
183
194
F G H J K
1 2 3 4 5 6
32 33 34
78 77 76 375

194
184
193
Hooton Station
Oak Road
Waterworks Lane
School Lane
Woodclose
New School Lane
Childer Thornton Primary School
A41 CHESTER ROAD
A550 WELSH ROAD
The Oaklands
Waterworks Lane
Oakfield Road
School Lane
Orchard La
New Road
Woodland Vw
Childer Thornton
Cemetery
Garden Centre
Premier Travel Inn
Blackboards Lane
Heath Lane
Childer Crs
St Pauls Gdns
Meadway
Granville Dr
Beverley Way
Heath Grove
Heathlands Road
The Grange
Heath Lane
Margaret's Lane
Barnwood
Glade Drive
Meadowbank Dr
Berwick Road
Little Sutton CE Primary School
Quality Hotel
Snowdon Close
Stephens Gdns
Berwick Gdns
Ben Nevis Dr
Ledsham Park Dr
Clwyd Way
Sidlaw Cl
Chevoit Close
Hillcrest Road
Hillcrest Drive
Sutton Hall Gdns
Sutton Hall Dr
Wicklow Cl
Berwyn Cl
Orchil Cl
Cleveland Dr
Lochinvar Av
Ullapool Cl
Roxburgh Rd
Jedburgh Av
Coldstream Dr
B5463
ROAD
LEDSHAM ROAD
Little Sutton
Oaks Farm
Starbeck Dr
Askrigg Av
Dunmore
Dudleston Road
Sutton Prim S
Scotton Av
Wether
Penistone
Rudstone Cl
Collingham Gn
Sutton New Hall
CH66
Badgersrake Lane
Hallwood Farm
Hallwood Drive
Badgersrake Lane
Ledsham
WELSH ROAD
Sutt
Works
335
36
78
77
76
375
A
B
C
D
E
1
2
3
4
5
6
1 grid square represents 500 metres

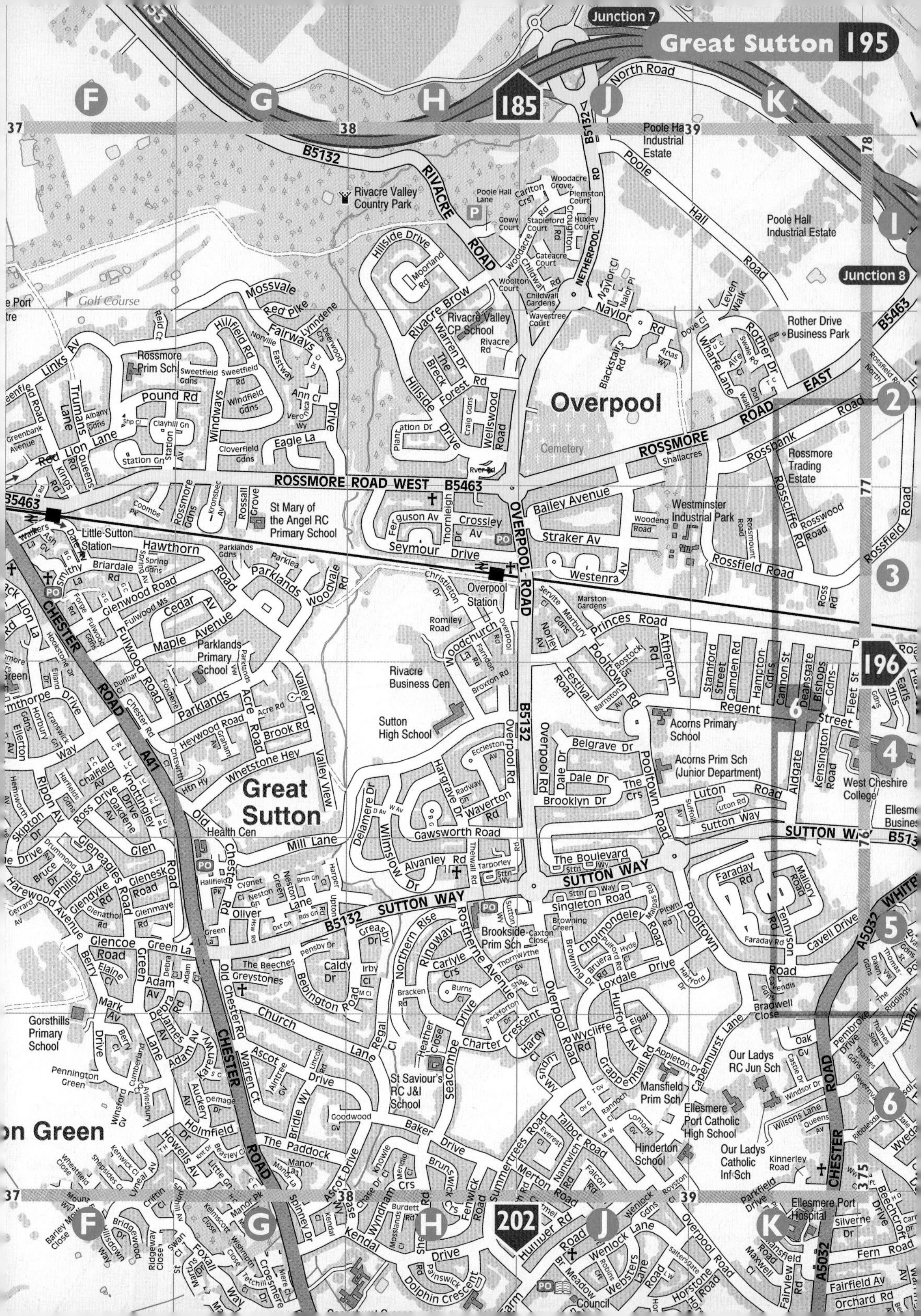
Junction 7
185
196
202
Junction 8
Overpool
Great Sutton
Rivacre Valley Country Park
Poole Hall Industrial Estate
Rother Drive Business Park
Rossmore Trading Estate
Westminster Industrial Park
Rivacre Business Cen
Sutton High School
Acorns Primary School
West Cheshire College
Little Sutton Station
Overpool Station
Rossmore Road West
Rossmore Road East
Overpool Road
Chester Road
Sutton Way
Ellesmere Port Hospital

ELLESMERE PORT
Wolverham
Whitby
Junction 8
Junction 9
Manchester Ship Canal
Canalside Industrial Estate
Boat Museum
Westminster Retail Park
Meadow Lane Ind Park
Works
Ellesmere Port Station
West Cheshire College
Ellesmere Port Business Cen
Civic Hall
Council Building
Port Arcades
Market Hall
Wolverham Primary School
Epic Leisure Centre
Whitby Heath Prim Sch
St Bernards RC Prim Sch
The Oaks Community Prim Sch
Ellesmere Port Stadium
Mill Lane Industrial Estate
Stanney Mill Industrial Park
Cheshire Oaks Outlet Village
Christ Church CE Primary Sch
Stanlaw Abbey Prim Sch
Cheshire Oaks High School
Westminster Primary School
William Stockton Primary School
Ellesmere Port Clinic
Ellesmere Port Hospital
M53
A5032
B5132
B5463
195
203
7
6
1 grid square represents 500 metres

F
G
H
J
K
42
43
44
78
77
76
3 75
1
2
3
4
5
6
198
Stanlow
Point
Manchester Ship Canal
CH65
Corridor Road
Oil Sites Road
Garth Rd
Stanlow
Stanlow & Thornton
Station
Oil Refinery
Shellway Road
A5117
Poole Lane

Ince
Banks
A
B
C
D
E
3 45
46
78
77
76
3 75
1
2
3
4
5
6
197
Holme
Farm
Marsh Lane
Ince
Kinsey's
Lane
Pool
Lane
Station
Road
Marsh Lane
Perimeter Road
Ince &
Elton Stn
Ince Orchards
Cherry
Tree
Cl
Mt
Pleasant
PO
Highfield
Orchard
Park
Lane
Orchard Pk
Od Pk
Hapsford Lane
Elton
Ince Lane
Laurels
Farm Ct
Anvil Cl
Coppice Green
Dove Cl
Mimosa Cl
Redwood Dr
Dairy
Bank
Elton Primary
School
The
Paddock
Farmdale Dr
Ryecroft
Whitefields
Anvil
Close
Holm Dr
Marsh Lane
Holm
Drive
Osler
Holm Drive
Ash
Road
Deansfield
Way
Ferndale
Av
Meadow View
Brackendale
Greenfield
Gdns
Hallfield
Dr
Lane
Pinewood
Cl
Firbank
Mulberry Cl
Lime Grove
Poplar
Gv
School
Parkland
Lawnswood
Grove
Hall
Alvanley
View
Manley
View
Ince Lane
Parkland
Drive
Drive
Willow
Grove
Old
Pool
Lane
A5117
Chester Service Area
Premier
Travel
Inn
A5117
Lane
Cryers Lane
ERS LANE
Elton
1 grid square represents 500 metres
Junction 14

F
G
H
J
K
47
48
49
78
1
2
77
3
200
4
76
5
6
375
Manchester Ship Canal
Cross Lane
Lordship Lane
Elton Lordship Lane
Ince Marshes
Rake Lane
Hill View Farm
Hornsmill Brook
Helsby Marsh
M56
Hoolpool Lane
Elton Lane
Smithy Lane
Holly Ct
Plovers Lane
Hillside Primary School
Bank House La
Hallastone Rd
Grove Ter
High View
Cambridge
Lower Rake Lane
Vale Gdns
Vicarage Lane
Hale View Road
Conery Cl
Helsby Station
The Beeches
Rake La
Old Chester Road
Red Stone Hl
Lodge Hollow
Station Av
Coppins Cl
Sandringham Av
HELSBY
PO
Crescent Drive
Mountain View
Kings Dr
Queens Drive
Longster Trail
Sherwood Grove
Parkfield Dr
Springfield Av
Lower Robin Hood Lane
Lwr Robin Hood La
Helsby Health Centre
Old Chester Road
Hill Rd South
Hill
Freshmeadow Lane
The Orchard
Alvanley
Hood Lane
The Paddock
Alvanley Dr
Road
Blue
Bridge

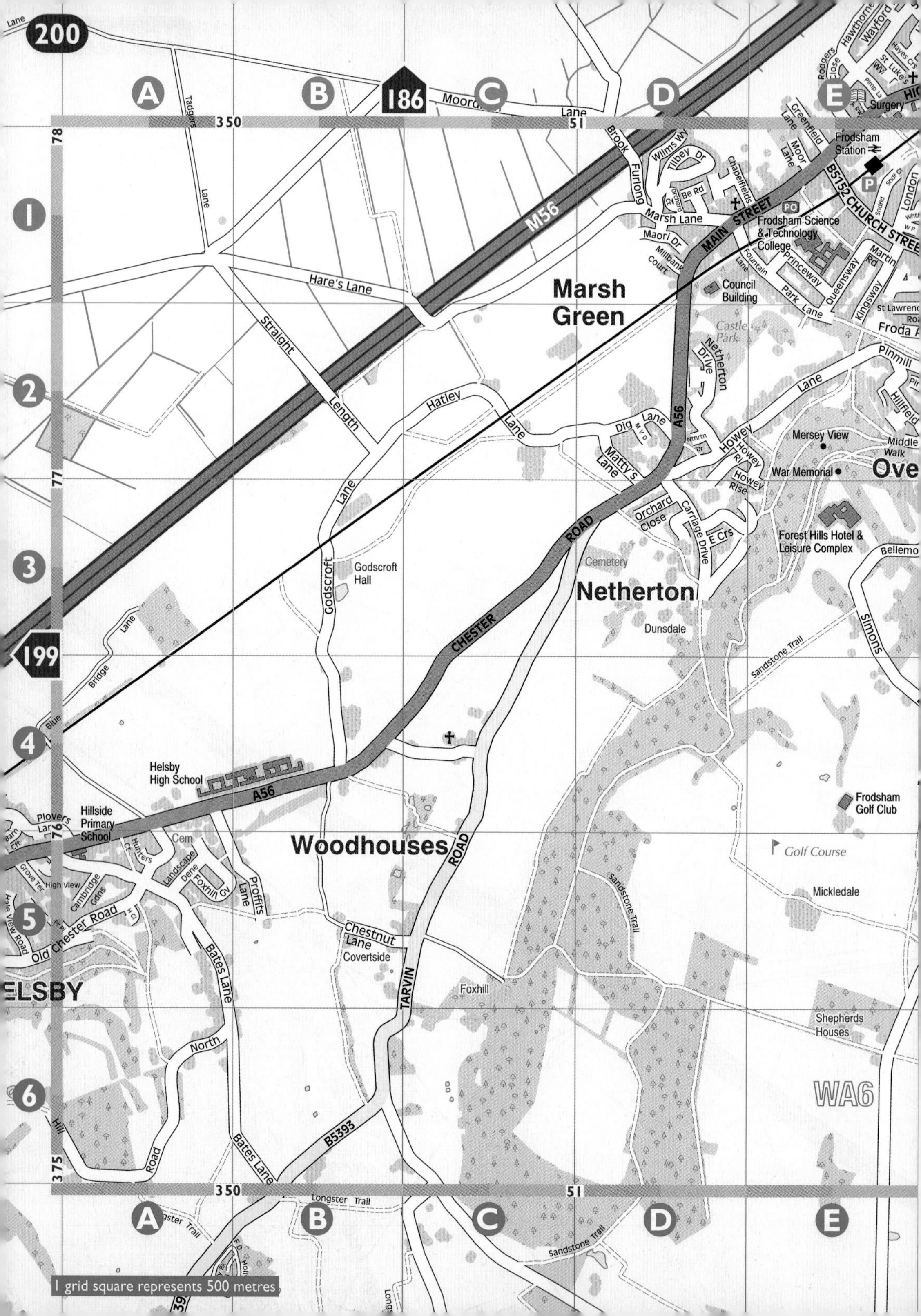

200
186
199
A
B
C
D
E
1
2
3
4
5
6
350
51
375
78
77
76
M56
Marsh Green
Netherton
Woodhouses
ELSBY
Hare's Lane
Straight Length
Hatley Lane
Godscroft Lane
Godscroft Hall
CHESTER ROAD
A56
MAIN STREET
B5152 CHURCH STREET
Frodsham Station
Frodsham Science & Technology College
Council Building
Castle Park
Netherton Drive
Dig Lane
Matty's Lane
Howey Lane
Howey Rise
Orchard Close
Carriage Drive
Cemetery
Dunsdale
Mersey View
War Memorial
Forest Hills Hotel & Leisure Complex
Pinmill Lane
Simons
Sandstone Trail
Frodsham Golf Club
Golf Course
Mickledale
Shepherds Houses
WA6
Helsby High School
Hillside Primary School
Old Chester Road
Bates Lane
North Road
Hill
Proffits Lane
Chestnut Lane
Covertside
Foxhill
TARVIN ROAD
B5393
Longster Trail
Marsh Lane
Maori Dr
Brook Furlong
Princeway
Queensway
Park Lane
Kingsway
Fountain Lane
Chapelfields
Greenfield Lane
Moor Lane
Surgery
Blue Bridge Lane
Tadgers Lane
Moorditch Lane
Landscape Dene
Cambridge Gdns
High View
1 grid square represents 500 metres

Newtown
187
F
G
H
J
K
52
53
54
78
77
76
75
1
2
3
4
5
6
FRODSHAM
Bradley
Fivecrosses
Newton
The Manor House Primary School
St Lukes RC Primary School
Frodsham CE Primary School
The Willows
Bradley Orchard
Hatley Farm
Belleair
Newton Hall
Lady Heyes Farm
Pike Noo
Weaver Navigation
Eddisbury Way
Bradley Lane
Watery Lane
Kingsley Road
B5152
Vicarage Lane
Red Lane
Bridge Lane
A56
Church Road
Hillside Road
Arran Drive
Manley Rd
Manley Road
Penkmans Lane
Hazlehurst Road
Top Road
Dobers Lane
Hillfoot Lane
Pike Lane
Hollow Lane
Meeting
Delamere Way
Townfield Lane
Fairways
Doric Avenue
Oakdale Avenue
Lansdowne
Royleen Drive
Springbourne
Ennerdale Drive
Coniston Drive
Keswick Drive
Grasmere Road
Foxglove Court
Langdale
Penrith Close
Thirlmere Close
Francis Rd
Ashton Drive
Crescent
Ellis La
Blue Hatch
Fluin Lane
Ashlands
Newlands Cl
Eversley
Marling
Warren Ct
Greenacres
Silverdale Close
Borrowdale Close
Greenside Av
Clover Av
Bickerton Av
Hillsboro Avenue
Ranulph Court
Lime Av
Beech Av
Kingsley Community Primary School

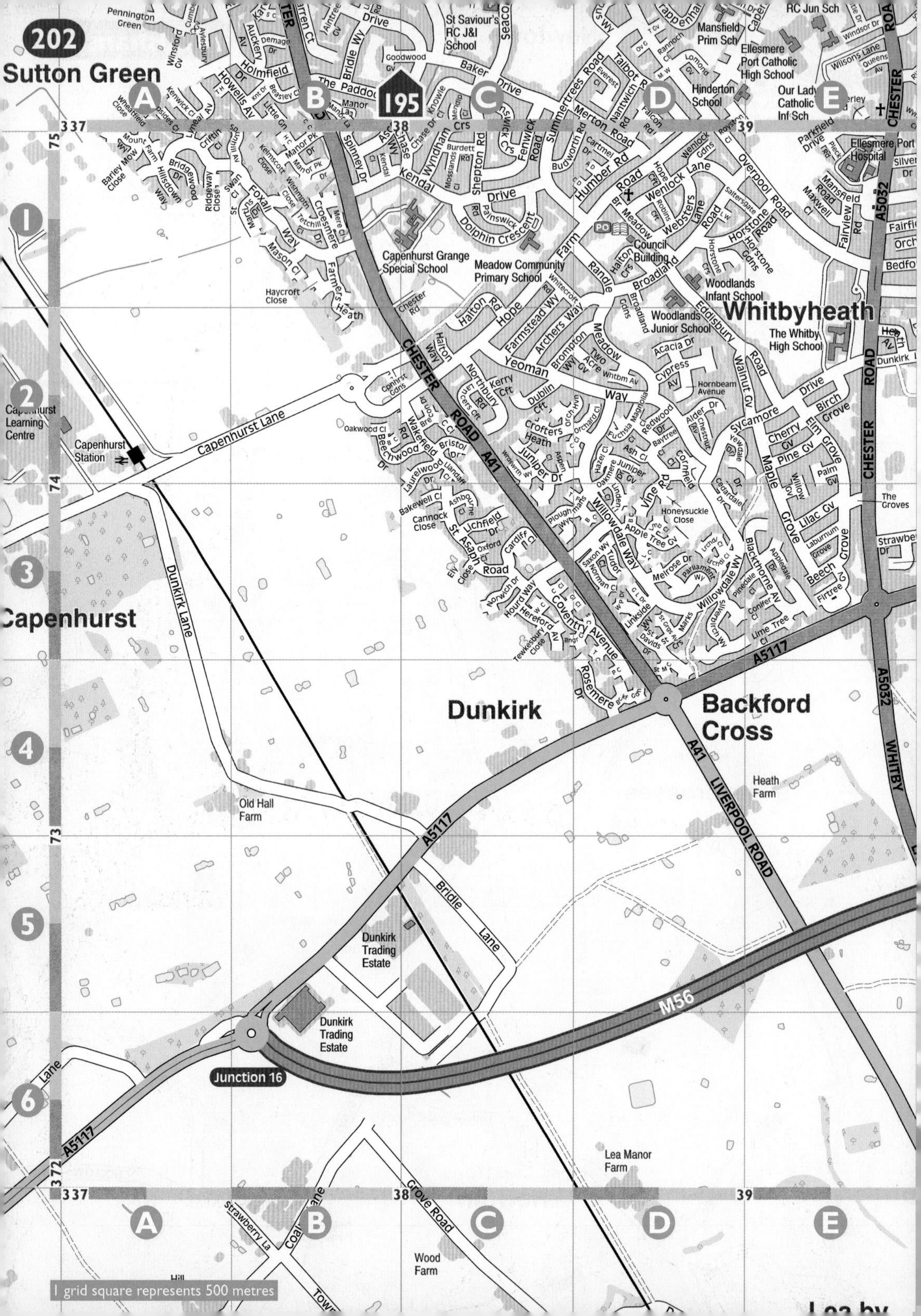
Sutton Green
195
Whitbyheath
Capenhurst
Dunkirk
Backford Cross
Capenhurst Lane
Capenhurst Station
Capenhurst Learning Centre
Dunkirk Lane
Old Hall Farm
Bridle Lane
Dunkirk Trading Estate
Junction 16
M56
A5117
A41
CHESTER ROAD
LIVERPOOL ROAD
A5032
WHITBY
Heath Farm
Lea Manor Farm
Wood Farm
Grove Road
Strawberry La
Capenhurst Grange Special School
Meadow Community Primary School
Council Building
Woodlands Infant School
Woodlands Junior School
The Whitby High School
Mansfield Prim Sch
Ellesmere Port Catholic High School
Hinderton School
Our Lady Catholic Inf Sch
Ellesmere Port Hospital
St Saviour's RC J&I School
RC Jun Sch
The Groves
337
38
39
372
73
74
75
A
B
C
D
E
1
2
3
4
5
6
1 grid square represents 500 metres

Whitby Heath Prim Sch
St Bernards RC Prim Sch
Ellesmere Port Stadium
Industrial Estate
Stanney Mill Industrial Park
196
Community Prim Sch
Christ Church CE Primary Sch
Cheshire Oaks High School
Stanlaw Abbey Prim Sch
Cheshire Oaks Outlet Village
Mill Lane Industrial Estate
Stanney Ten Industrial Estate
Stanney Mill Industrial Est
Vue Cinema
Blue Planet Aquarium
Stanney Woods Country Park
Junction 10
Little Stanney
Stoak Grange
Rake Hall
Heath Farm
Poplarhall
Stoak
M56
M53
A5117
B5132
KINSEY RD
STANNEY LANE
Junction 11/15
Mount Farm
The Grove
Croughton Cottage
Backford
Council Building
Chorlton Hall
Rake Lane
Little Rake Lane
Heath Lane
Little Stanney Lane
Poplar Hall Lane
Gordon Lane
Church Lane
Croughton Road
Wervin Road
Shropshire Union Canal
F
G
H
J
K
1
2
3
4
5
6
40
41
42
75
74
73
372

Aigburth 153 G2
Ainsdale 33 J4
Ainsdale-on-Sea 32 E4
Aintree 83 G1
Allerton 154 B2
Anfield 97 J6
Appleton 158 C1
Appleton Park 162 B6
Arrowe Hill 129 G6
Ashton-in-Makerfield 79 J6
Ashurst 56 D1
Aspull Common 93 J2
Astmoor 177 H2
Aston 188 C6
Aston Heath 188 C5
Aughton 52 D6
Aughton Park 53 J3
Backford Cross 202 D4
Ball o' Ditton 157 K2
Bamfurlong 79 K1
Banks 21 J5
Barnston 168 C2
Barrow Nook 64 E5
Barrow's Green 139 K5
Barton 43 H5
Bebington 151 H4
Beechwood 187 H2
Belle Vale 135 J4
Bescar 36 E2
Bewsey 142 B1
Bickerstaffe 64 E2
Bidston 110 D6
Bidston Hill 130 A1
Billinge 77 J4
Birch Green 56 E3
Birchwood 125 G3
Birkdale 27 G5
Birkenhead 2 A4
Blackbrook 124 A5
Blackbrook 89 K6
Blaguegate 55 H4
Blowick 28 B1
Blundellsands 68 B5
Bold Heath 139 K2
Bootle 4 A5
Bowker's Green 63 H2
Bowring Park 135 J1
Bradley 201 H2
Brighton le Sands 68 B6
Brimstage 169 H3
Broad Green 115 H5
Broad Oak 104 D1
Bromborough 170 D4
Bromborough Pool 151 J6
Brookhurst 183 J2
Brookvale 188 A2
Brown Edge 28 D5
Brown Edge 102 E6
Brownlow 76 E1
Bruche 143 J2
Bryn 78 E3
Buckley Hill 70 A5
Burscough 46 C1
Burscough Bridge 38 D3
Burtonwood 121 K1
Calderstones 134 D6
Caldy 146 E4
Callands 122 D5
Carr Cross 36 B1
Carr Houses 60 B3
Castlefields 177 J3
Chadwick Green 77 H5
Chapel House 55 K3
Childer Thornton 194 E1
Childwall 135 G3
Churchtown 23 K4
Cinnamon Brow 124 C3
Claughton 130 B4
Clifton 187 G3
Clinkham Wood 88 D2
Clock Face 120 B4
Clubmoor 98 A6
Cobbs 162 C3
Collins Green 105 H4
Court Hey 115 K6
Crank 76 B5
Crawford 66 E5
Cronton 138 A4
Crosby 80 C2
Crossens 23 K1
Crow Wood 158 E1
Croxteth 99 H1
Cuerdley Cross 140 B6
Dallam 123 F6
Daresbury 179 G4
Deansgreen 165 J3
Denton's Green 12 C1
Derbyshire Hill 104 D3
Digmoor 66 E1
Dingle 133 F6
Ditton 157 G4
Doe Green 140 D6
Dog & Gun 98 E2
Dovecot 115 K4
Downall Green 78 B4
Downholland Cross 51 J3
Drummersdale 36 D3
Dudlows Green 162 D6
Dunkirk 202 C4
Dutton 189 F3
Earlestown 105 K2
Eastham 184 B1
Eastham Ferry 171 J5
Eccleston 87 H5
Eccleston Park 102 C6
Edge Hill 133 G1
Egremont 111 J3
Ellesmere Port 6 B3
Elmers Green 57 F2
Elton 198 B5
Everton 113 H2
Fairfield 114 B4
Farnworth 139 F6
Fazakerley 83 F6
Fearnhead 124 C5
Fiddler's Ferry 21 G5
Fiddler's Ferry 159 K2
Fincham 115 K1
Fivecrosses 201 F4
Ford 81 K1
Formby 48 E1
Frankby 147 H1
Freshfield 40 C6
Frodsham 201 G2
Garston 154 A6
Garswood 78 A6
Gateacre 135 J5
Gayton 181 F1
Gemini 122 D4
Gillar's Green 102 A2
Gillmoss 84 B5
Golborne 92 C4
Gorse Covert 125 K1
Grange 146 E2
Grange 177 F6
Grange Park 102 D5
Grappenhall 163 G1
Grassendale 153 G4
Greasby 128 D5
Great Altcar 50 B4
Great Crosby 69 F5
Great Meols 108 D5
Great Sankey 141 J3
Great Sutton 195 G4
Hale 174 E3
Hale Bank 175 J1
Halewood 155 H3
Hall Green 57 J5
Halsall 44 A2
Halton 177 J5
Halton Brook 177 G4
Halton View 19 H2
Haresfinch 88 D4
Haskayne 43 G6
Haydock 90 C5
Heath 176 D6
Heaton's Bridge 37 H5
Helsby 199 K5
Hermitage Green 107 H5
Heswall 167 J5
Higher Bebington 150 B5
Higher Runcorn 10 D7
Higher Walton 161 H4
High Legh 165 J6
High Park 23 H5
Hightown 58 E4
Hillcliffe 162 B4
Hillside 26 E5
Hinderton 182 B6
Holmeswood 31 H1
Holt 118 C2
Holt Green 53 F6
Homer Green 60 E6
Hood Manor 141 K4
Hooton 184 D6
Hoscar 39 K5
Hough Green 157 F2
Houghton Green 124 A2
Houghwood 76 E3
Howley 17 H5
Hoylake 127 H2
Hulme 123 H4
Hunt's Cross 154 E5
Hurlston Green 37 F6
Huyton 117 F4
Huyton Park 116 C6
Huyton Quarry 117 H5
Huyton-With-Roby 116 C4
Ince 198 B3
Ince Blundell 60 A4
Irby 148 A5
Keckwick 178 E1
Kensington 113 J5
Kings Moss 76 C2
Kingsway 18 C3
Kingswood 122 A5
Kirkby 84 D2
Kirkdale 97 F5
Knotty Ash 115 H4
Knowsley 100 B1
Lady Green 60 A3
Laffak 89 H4
Land Gate 79 F2
Landican 149 F3
Lane Head 93 G5
Latchford 143 F6
Lea Green 119 H2
Leasowe 110 A3
Lingley Green 140 D2
Lingley Mere 140 E1
Liscard 111 H2
Litherland 81 K2
Little Altcar 49 G4
Little Crosby 68 D1
Little Neston 191 J3
Little Stanney 203 J2
Little Sutton 194 D4
Liverpool 8 A4
Locking Stumps 124 D3
Longbarn 124 E6
Longford 123 H6
Longview 117 F3
Lower Bebington 150 E6
Lower House 157 K3
Lower Walton 161 K3
Lowton 92 E3
Lowton Common 93 H3
Lowton Heath 92 D5
Lowton St Mary's 93 H4
Lugsdale 19 G5
Lunt 69 K1
Lunts Heath 139 F4
Lydiate 61 J2
Lymm 145 K6
Maghull 71 G1
Marshall's Cross 119 K2
Marsh Green 200 C1
Marshside 23 G2
Martinscroft 144 C2
Melling 71 J4
Melling Mount 72 C2
Meols 127 J1
Mere Brow 25 J3
Mere Side 31 G2
Moore 160 D5
Moorside 191 H2
Moreton 109 J6
Moss Bank 88 C2
Moss Bank 19 K4
Mossley Hill 133 K5
Moss Nook 104 D4
Moss Side 62 E4
Moss Side 85 K4
Murdishaw 178 D6
Ness 192 C4
Nessholt 191 K5
Neston 191 J2
Netherley 136 A5
Netherton 200 C3
Netherton 70 C4
New Boston 90 E5
New Brighton 95 G5
New Ferry 151 H3
Newgate 57 J6
New Lane 38 B2
Newton 147 G1
Newton-Le-Willows 91 J6
Newton Park 107 F3
Newtown 102 E1
Newtown 187 G6
Noctorum 129 K4
Norris Green 98 D4
Northwood 73 G6
Norton 178 B4
Nut Grove 118 E1
Oakwood 125 G4
Oglet 173 J5
Old Boston 91 G4
Old Swan 114 D4
Orford 123 K6
Ormskirk 45 G6
Orrell 82 A5
Otterspool 152 E2
Overpool 195 J2
Overton 200 E2
Oxton 130 C6
Paddington 144 A1
Padgate 124 B6
Page Moss 116 B4
Palacefields 187 J2
Parkgate 181 H6
Park Hill 65 K5
Parr 104 C3
Peasley Cross 104 A4
Penketh 140 E5
Pennylands 55 J5
Pensby 167 K1
Pinfold 36 D5
Pocket Nook 93 K3
Poll Hill 167 K4
Pool Hey 28 E4
Portico 102 C5
Port Sunlight 151 G6
Poulton 170 D3
Poulton 111 G5
Prenton 149 K2
Prescot 117 H1
Preston Brook 188 E2
Preston on the Hill 189 F1
Primrose Hill 44 D3
Princes Park 133 G3
Raby 182 D3
Rainford 75 H2
Rainford Junction 66 B5
Rainhill 119 F4
Rainhill Stoops 119 G5
Ravenhead 103 G4
Ring o' Bells 47 H1
Risley 125 G1
Roby 116 B5
Roby Mill 57 K2
Rock Ferry 151 F1
Rocksavage 186 E2
Royal Oak 63 K3
Runcorn 11 G7
St Helens 13 H2
St Michael's Hamlet 152 C1
Sandhills 96 E5
Sankey Bridges 141 K5
Saughall Massie 128 C3
Scarisbrick 36 C2
Scarth Hill 54 C3
Seacombe 111 K6
Seaforth 81 F4
Sefton 70 C2
Sefton Park 133 J5
Shell Green 159 F1
Shirdley Hill 35 H3
Simm's Cross 19 F4
Simm's Lane End 77 K4
Skelmersdale 56 C3
Snape Green 29 H6
Southdene 84 D3
Southgate 177 H6
Southport 14 A2
Speke 173 K1
Spital 170 E2
Stanley 56 A2
Stanley Gate 54 E6
Stanlow 197 G4
Statham 145 J5
Stoak 203 K4
Stockbridge Village 100 A5
Stockton Heath 162 C2
Stoneycroft 114 E3
Storeton 150 A6
Stubshaw Cross 79 J4
Sutton 104 C6
Sutton Green 194 E6
Sutton Heath 103 G6
Sutton Leach 120 C2
Sutton Manor 119 J5
Sutton Weaver 188 A4
Swanside 115 K5
Sworton Heath 165 G6
Tanhouse 56 E5
Tarbock Green 137 F5
Tarlscough 31 J6
Thatto Heath 103 F5
Thelwall 144 D6
Thingwall 148 E6
Thornton 69 K3
Thornton Hough 182 B1
Thurstaston 147 H6
Toll Bar 102 D4
Tower Hill 72 E4
Town End 138 B3
Town Green 53 H6
Town Green 79 J5
Town of Lowton 92 B6
Town Park 178 A4
Toxteth 132 D4
Tranmere 131 H6
Tuebrook 114 D2
Up Holland 67 J1
Upton 157 G1
Upton 129 G4
Upton Rocks 138 D6
Vauxhall 112 D3
Vulcan Village 106 C5
Waddicar 71 K5
Wallasey 112 A3
Wallasey Village 110 C1
Walton 97 K3
Wargrave 106 C4
Warrington 17 J7
Waterloo 80 E1
Waterloo Park 81 G2
Wavertree 134 A2
West Bank 158 A6
Westbrook 122 A6
West Derby 99 G6
Westhead 54 D1
West Kirby 146 A1
Weston 176 C6
Weston Point 176 A5
West Park 12 A7
Westvale 84 C1
Westy 143 J4
Whiston 118 A4
Whiston Cross 117 K4
Whiston Lane Ends 117 J5
Whitby 6 C7
Whitbyheath 202 D2
Whitefield Lane End 136 E1
Widnes 18 A5
Wilderspool 162 B1
Willaston 193 J1
Windle Hill 192 D2
Windmill Hill 178 B3
Windy Arbor 137 G1
Winwick 107 H6
Winwick Quay 123 H3
Wolverham 6 E7
Woodchurch 129 K6
Woodhey 150 E4
Woodhouses 200 B5
Woodvale 33 H6
Woolfall Heath 116 C2
Woolston 144 B2
Woolton 154 D2
Wright's Green 163 F6

USING THE STREET INDEX

Street names are listed alphabetically. Each street name is followed by its postal town or area locality, the Postcode District, the page number, and the reference to the square in which the name is found.

Standard index entries are shown as follows:

3rd St *WGNE/HIN* WN2 **79** K2

Street names and selected addresses not shown on the map due to scale restrictions are shown in the index with an asterisk:

Abbott Dr *BTL* L20 * **82** B6

GENERAL ABBREVIATIONS

ACC ACCESS
ALY ALLEY
AP APPROACH
AR ARCADE
ASS ASSOCIATION
AV AVENUE
BCH BEACH
BLDS BUILDINGS
BND BEND
BNK BANK
BR BRIDGE
BRK BROOK
BTM BOTTOM
BUS BUSINESS
BVD BOULEVARD
BY BYPASS
CATH CATHEDRAL
CEM CEMETERY
CEN CENTRE
CFT CROFT
CH CHURCH
CHA CHASE
CHYD CHURCHYARD
CIR CIRCLE
CIRC CIRCUS
CL CLOSE
CLFS CLIFFS
CMP CAMP
CNR CORNER
CO COUNTY
COLL COLLEGE
COM COMMON
COMM COMMISSION
CON CONVENT
COT COTTAGE
COTS COTTAGES
CP CAPE
CPS COPSE
CR CREEK
CREM CREMATORIUM
CRS CRESCENT
CSWY CAUSEWAY
CT COURT
CTRL CENTRAL
CTS COURTS
CTYD COURTYARD
CUTT CUTTINGS
CV COVE
CYN CANYON
DEPT DEPARTMENT
DL DALE
DM DAM
DR DRIVE
DRO DROVE
DRY DRIVEWAY
DWGS DWELLINGS
E EAST
EMB EMBANKMENT
EMBY EMBASSY
ESP ESPLANADE
EST ESTATE
EX EXCHANGE
EXPY EXPRESSWAY
EXT EXTENSION
F/O FLYOVER

FC FOOTBALL CLUB
FK FORK
FLD FIELD
FLDS FIELDS
FLS FALLS
FM FARM
FT FORT
FTS FLATS
FWY FREEWAY
FY FERRY
GA GATE
GAL GALLERY
GDN GARDEN
GDNS GARDENS
GLD GLADE
GLN GLEN
GN GREEN
GND GROUND
GRA GRANGE
GRG GARAGE
GT GREAT
GTWY GATEWAY
GV GROVE
HGR HIGHER
HL HILL
HLS HILLS
HO HOUSE
HOL HOLLOW
HOSP HOSPITAL
HRB HARBOUR
HTH HEATH
HTS HEIGHTS
HVN HAVEN
HWY HIGHWAY
IMP IMPERIAL
IN INLET
IND EST INDUSTRIAL ESTATE
INF INFIRMARY
INFO INFORMATION
INT INTERCHANGE
IS ISLAND
JCT JUNCTION
JTY JETTY
KG KING
KNL KNOLL
L LAKE
LA LANE
LDG LODGE
LGT LIGHT
LK LOCK
LKS LAKES
LNDG LANDING
LTL LITTLE
LWR LOWER
MAG MAGISTRATE
MAN MANSIONS
MD MEAD
MDW MEADOWS
MEM MEMORIAL
MI MILL
MKT MARKET
MKTS MARKETS
ML MALL
MNR MANOR
MS MEWS
MSN MISSION
MT MOUNT
MTN MOUNTAIN
MTS MOUNTAINS
MUS MUSEUM
MWY MOTORWAY
N NORTH
NE NORTH EAST
NW NORTH WEST
O/P OVERPASS
OFF OFFICE
ORCH ORCHARD
OV OVAL
PAL PALACE
PAS PASSAGE
PAV PAVILION
PDE PARADE
PH PUBLIC HOUSE
PK PARK
PKWY PARKWAY
PL PLACE
PLN PLAIN
PLNS PLAINS
PLZ PLAZA
POL POLICE STATION
PR PRINCE
PREC PRECINCT
PREP PREPARATORY
PRIM PRIMARY
PROM PROMENADE
PRS PRINCESS
PRT PORT
PT POINT
PTH PATH
PZ PIAZZA
QD QUADRANT
QU QUEEN
QY QUAY
R RIVER
RBT ROUNDABOUT
RD ROAD
RDG RIDGE
REP REPUBLIC
RES RESERVOIR
RFC RUGBY FOOTBALL CLUB
RI RISE
RP RAMP
RW ROW
S SOUTH
SCH SCHOOL
SE SOUTH EAST
SER SERVICE AREA
SH SHORE
SHOP SHOPPING
SKWY SKYWAY
SMT SUMMIT
SOC SOCIETY
SP SPUR
SPR SPRING
SQ SQUARE
ST STREET
STN STATION
STR STREAM
STRD STRAND
SW SOUTH WEST
TDG TRADING
TER TERRACE
THWY THROUGHWAY
TNL TUNNEL
TOLL TOLLWAY
TPK TURNPIKE
TR TRACK
TRL TRAIL
TWR TOWER
U/P UNDERPASS
UNI UNIVERSITY
UPR UPPER
V VALE
VA VALLEY
VIAD VIADUCT
VIL VILLA
VIS VISTA
VLG VILLAGE
VLS VILLAS
VW VIEW
W WEST
WD WOOD
WHF WHARF
WK WALK
WKS WALKS
WLS WELLS
WY WAY
YD YARD
YHA YOUTH HOSTEL

POSTCODE TOWNS AND AREA ABBREVIATIONS

AIG/SPK Aigburth/Sefton Park
AIMK Ashton-in-Makerfield
AIN/FAZ Aintree/Fazakerley
ALL/GAR Allerton/Garston
ANF/KKDL Anfield/Kirkdale
BEB Bebington
BIRK Birkenhead
BRSC Burscough
BTL Bootle
CALD/MH Calderstones/Mossley Hill
CH/BCN Chester/Blacon
CHLDW Childwall
CHNE Chester northeast
CHTN/BK Churchtown/Banks
CL/PREN Claughton/Prenton
CLB/OSW/ST Clubmoor/Old Swan/Stoneycroft
CLVP Central Liverpool
CLVPS Central Liverpool south
CSBY/BLUN Crosby/Blundellsands
CSBY/WL Crosby/Waterloo
DV/KA/FCH Dovecot/Knotty Ash/Fincham
ECCL Eccleston
EHL/KEN Edge Hill/Kensington
EP Ellesmere Port
EV Everton
FLINT Flint
FMBY Formby
FROD/HEL Frodsham/Helsby
GOL/RIS/CUL Golborne/Risley/Culcheth
GR/UP/WCH Greasby/Upton/Woodchurch
GTS/LS Great Sutton/Little Sutton
HES Heswall
HLWD Halewood
HOY Hoylake
HTWN Hightown
HUY Huyton
KIRK/FR/WAR Kirkham/Freckleton/Warton
KKBY Kirkby
KNUT Knutsford
LEIGH Leigh
LITH Litherland
LYMM Lymm
MGHL Maghull
MOR/LEA Moreton/Leasowe
NEWLW Newton-le-Willows
NG/CROX Norris Green/Croxteth
NPK/KEN Newsham Park/Kensington
NSTN Neston
NTHLY Netherley
NTHTN Netherton
NWD/KWIPK Northwood/Knowsley Industrial Park
ORM Ormskirk
PEN/TH Pensby/Thingwall
PR/KW Prescot/Knowsley
PS/BROM Port Sunlight/Bromborough
RAIN/WH Rainhill/Whiston
RF/TRAN Rock Ferry/Tranmere
RNFD/HAY Rainford/Haydock
RUNC Runcorn
SFTN Sefton
SKEL Skelmersdale
SPK/HALE Speke/Hale
STBRV Stockbridge Village
STHEL St Helens
STHP Southport
TOX Toxteth
VAUX/LVPD Vauxhall/Liverpool Docks
WAL/EG Wallasey/Egremont
WAL/NB Wallasey/New Brighton
WARR Warrington
WARRN/WOL Warrington north/Woolston
WARRS Warrington south
WARRW/BUR Warrington west/Burtonwood
WAV Wavertree
WD/CROXPK West Derby/Croxteth Park
WDN Widnes
WGNE/HIN Wigan east/Hindley
WGNS/IIMK Wigan south/Ince-in-Makerfield
WGNW/BIL/OR Wigan west/Billinge/Orrell
WKBY West Kirby
WLT/FAZ Walton/Fazakerley
WLTN Woolton

3

3rd St *WGNE/HIN* WN2 79 K2

A

Abacus Rd *CLB/OSW/ST* L13 114 E3
Abberley Cl *ECCL* WA10 12 E5
Abberley Rd *WLTN* L25 155 G4
Abberton Pk *NTHTN* L30 70 D4
Abbey Cl *BIRK* CH41 3 H6
FMBY L37 49 H3
NWD/KWIPK L33 84 E1
WDN WA8 157 H3
Abbey Ct *WLTN* L25 154 E1
Abbey Dl *BRSC* L40 39 F6
Abbeyfield Dr *WD/CROXPK* L12 99 H3
Abbey Fold *BRSC* L40 38 D4
Abbey Gdns *STHP* PR8 27 H3
Abbey Hey *RUNC* WA7 178 B5
Abbey La *BRSC* L40 46 C2
Abbey Rd *ECCL* WA10 88 B4
GOL/RIS/CUL WA3 93 K3
RNFD/HAY WA11 90 D4
WDN WA8 157 G3
WKBY CH48 146 C1
Abbeystead *SKEL* WN8 56 D6
Abbeystead Av *NTHTN* L30 82 D2
Abbeystead Rd *WAV* L15 134 C1
Abbey St *BIRK* CH41 3 H6
Abbeyvale Dr *WLTN* L25 135 K3
Abbey Vw *CHLDW* L16 135 F2
Abbeyway North
RNFD/HAY WA11 91 F4
Abbeyway South
RNFD/HAY WA11 91 F5
Abbeywood *SKEL* WN8 56 E6
Abbeywood Gv *RAIN/WH* L35 118 B5
Abbot Cl *CL/PREN* CH43 129 K3
Abbotsbury Wy
WD/CROXPK L12 99 J2
Abbots Cl *FMBY* L37 49 G4
Abbots Dr *BEB* CH63 150 E6
Abbotsfield Cl *WARRS* WA4 162 D5
Abbotsfield Rd *STHEL* WA9 120 C2
Abbotsford *ORM* L39 45 K6
Abbotsford Cl
GOL/RIS/CUL WA3 92 E2
Abbotsford Gdns
CSBY/BLUN L23 68 D6
Abbotsford Rd *CSBY/BLUN* L23 68 D6
NG/CROX L11 98 C3
Abbotsford St *WAL/EG* CH44 112 A5
Abbots Hall Av *STHEL* WA9 120 B4
Abbots Ms *EP* CH65 6 C2
Abbots Pk *RUNC* WA7 188 D2
Abbots Wy *FMBY* L37 49 G3
NSTN CH64 181 J6
Abbott Dr *BTL* L20 * 82 B6
Abbotts Cl *CALD/MH* L18 134 C6
RUNC WA7 176 D5
Abbottshey Av *CALD/MH* L18 134 C6
Abbotts Wy
WGNW/BIL/OR WN5 77 G6
Abdale Rd *NG/CROX* L11 98 D2
Abercrombie Rd
NWD/KWIPK L33 85 G4
Abercromby Sq *EHL/KEN* L7 9 K5
Aberdale Rd *CLB/OSW/ST* L13 115 F4
Aberdare Cl *WARRW/BUR* WA5 122 E6
Aberdeen St *BIRK* CH41 2 C3
Aberford Av *WAL/NB* CH45 110 E2
Abergele Rd *CLB/OSW/ST* L13 114 D5
Aber St *NPK/KEN* L6 113 J4
Abingdon Av *WARR* WA1 144 D2
Abingdon Gv *ANF/KKDL* L4 98 A3
HLWD L26 155 K2
Abingdon Rd *ANF/KKDL* L4 98 A3
GR/UP/WCH CH49 128 C6
Abinger Rd *AIMK* WN4 78 C5
Abington Dr *CHTN/BK* PR9 21 K6
Abney Cl *EHL/KEN* L7 133 G1
Aboyne Cl *WLT/FAZ* L9 97 J1
Abrams Fold *CHTN/BK* PR9 21 J6
Abrams Gn *CHTN/BK* PR9 21 J6
Abram St *EV* L5 113 G2
Abratio St *BIRK* CH41 2 D5
Abstone Cl *WARR* WA1 144 B2
Abyssinia Cl *WAV* L15 * 133 K2
Acacia Av *HUY* L36 116 D6
WARR WA1 144 C1
WDN WA8 139 G6
Acacia Cl *CHNE* CH2 198 D6
GR/UP/WCH CH49 147 K1
Acacia Dr *GTS/LS* CH66 202 D2
Acacia Gv *ECCL* WA10 102 C1
RUNC WA7 177 F5
WAL/EG CH44 112 A5
WKBY CH48 146 B1
WLT/FAZ L9 82 E5
Acacia St *NEWLW* WA12 105 K1
Academy St *WARR* WA1 16 E5
Academy Wy *WARR* WA1 16 D5
Acanthus Rd *CLB/OSW/ST* L13 114 E3
Access Rd *WD/CROXPK* L12 * 99 H6
Acer Leigh *AIG/SPK* L17 152 E2
Acheson Rd *CLB/OSW/ST* L13 114 C1
Achilles Av *WARRN/WOL* WA2 123 H5
Ackerley Cl *WARRN/WOL* WA2 124 B4
Ackers Hall Av *DV/KA/FCH* L14 115 K3
Ackers La *CSBY/BLUN* L23 68 D2
ECCL WA10 102 E1
WARRS WA4 162 D2
Ackers Rd *GR/UP/WCH* CH49 149 F1
WARRS WA4 162 D1
Acland Rd *WAL/EG* CH44 * 111 H3
Aconbury Cl *NG/CROX* L11 98 D2
Aconbury Pl *NG/CROX* L11 98 D2
Acorn Cl *BEB* CH63 150 C5
STHEL WA9 * 120 A3
Acorn Ct *TOX* L8 132 E3
Acorn Dr *EP* CH65 203 F2
Acornfield Cl *NWD/KWIPK* L33 85 H3
Acornfield Rd *NWD/KWIPK* L33 85 J2
The Acorns *ORM* L39 53 G2
Acorn St *NEWLW* WA12 106 C2
Acorn Wy *BTL* L20 5 G1
Acrefield Pk *WLTN* L25 135 H6
Acrefield Rd *RF/TRAN* CH42 150 A2
WDN WA8 157 G2
WLTN L25 135 H6
Acregate *SKEL* WN8 66 E1
Acre Gn *HLWD* L26 155 K5
Acre La *HES* CH60 168 C4
PS/BROM CH62 170 E6
Acre Rd *GTS/LS* CH66 195 G4
Acres Cl *WLTN* L25 135 H2
Acresfield *CLB/OSW/ST* L13 * 115 F5
Acresgate Ct *WLTN* L25 135 H4
Acres La *FMBY* L37 50 A5
MGHL L31 51 G6
Acres Rd *BEB* CH63 150 E5
HOY CH47 127 K2
Acreville Rd *BEB* CH63 150 E6
Acton Cl *RNFD/HAY* WA11 90 B5
Acton Gv *NPK/KEN* L6 114 A1
Acton La *MOR/LEA* CH46 128 D2
Acton Rd *KKBY* L32 84 B1
RF/TRAN CH42 151 F2
WARRW/BUR WA5 121 J1
Acton Wy *EHL/KEN* L7 133 H1
Acuba Gv *RF/TRAN* CH42 * 131 H5
Acuba Rd *WAV* L15 115 G6
Adair Pl *CLB/OSW/ST* L13 98 C6
Adair Rd *CLB/OSW/ST* L13 98 C6
Adam Av *GTS/LS* CH66 195 F5
Adam Cl *ALL/GAR* L19 153 K6
GTS/LS CH66 195 G5
Adams Cl *NEWLW* WA12 106 D3
Adamson Ct *WARRS* WA4 163 G1
Adamson St *AIMK* WN4 79 F6
EHL/KEN L7 114 B5
WARRS WA4 142 E6
Adam St *EV* L5 113 H1
WARRN/WOL WA2 143 F2
Adaston Av *PS/BROM* CH62 184 C3
Ada St *STHEL* WA9 104 A4
Adcote Cl *DV/KA/FCH* L14 115 K4
Adcote Rd *DV/KA/FCH* L14 115 K4
Addenbrook Cl *CL/PREN* CH43 129 K3
Addenbrooke Dr
SPK/HALE L24 155 F5
Adderley Cl *RUNC* WA7 11 H7
Adderley St *EHL/KEN* L7 113 K5
Addingham Av *WDN* WA8 157 H4
Addingham Rd *CALD/MH* L18 134 C4
Addington St *WAL/EG* CH44 111 K4
Addison Cl *KKBY* L32 84 C3
Addison Sq *WDN* WA8 18 B1
Addison St *BTL* L20 81 H6
VAUX/LVPD L3 8 E1
Addison Wy *VAUX/LVPD* L3 8 E1
Adelaide Av *STHEL* WA9 103 G6
Adelaide Ct *WDN* WA8 * 18 D6
Adelaide Pl *EV* L5 113 G3
Adelaide Rd *EHL/KEN* L7 113 K5
LITH L21 81 G4
RF/TRAN CH42 131 F5
Adelaide St *WAL/EG* CH44 111 H5
Adelaide Ter *CSBY/WL* L22 80 D2
Adela Rd *RUNC* WA7 10 B5
Adele Thompson Dr *TOX* L8 133 F2
Adelphi St *BIRK* CH41 3 F4
Adfalent La *NSTN* CH64 193 H2
Adkins St *EV* L5 * 113 J1
Adlam Crs *WLT/FAZ* L9 * 83 H4
Adlam Rd *AIN/FAZ* L10 83 H3
Adlington Ct
GOL/RIS/CUL WA3 125 H1
Adlington Rd *RUNC* WA7 178 C3
Adlington St *VAUX/LVPD* L3 8 E1
Admin Rd *NWD/KWIPK* L33 85 H3
Admiral Gv *TOX* L8 133 F4
Admirals Rd *GOL/RIS/CUL* WA3 125 G4
Admiral St *TOX* L8 132 E4
Admiralty Cl *BRSC* L40 * 46 C1
Adrian's Wy *KKBY* L32 84 D1
Adshead Rd *CLB/OSW/ST* L13 98 C6
Adstone Rd *WLTN* L25 135 K4
Adswood Rd *HUY* L36 116 E4
Adwell Cl *GOL/RIS/CUL* WA3 93 H3
Africander Rd *RNFD/HAY* WA11 88 D3
Afton *WDN* WA8 157 F1
Agar Rd *NG/CROX* L11 98 D6
Agate St *EV* L5 113 J2
Agincourt Rd *WD/CROXPK* L12 115 G2
Agnes Gv *WAL/EG* CH44 111 J2
Agnes Rd *CSBY/BLUN* L23 68 D6
RF/TRAN CH42 131 H6
Agnes St *STHEL* WA9 120 A4
Agnes Wy *EHL/KEN* L7 113 K6
Aiden Long Gv *PR/KW* L34 116 E1
Aigburth Dr *AIG/SPK* L17 133 H4
Aigburth Hall Av *ALL/GAR* L19 153 H3
Aigburth Hall Rd *ALL/GAR* L19 153 H3
Aigburth Rd *AIG/SPK* L17 133 G6
ALL/GAR L19 153 G3
Aigburth St *EHL/KEN* L7 133 G1
Aigburth V *AIG/SPK* L17 133 K6
Ailsa Rd *WAL/NB* CH45 111 G2
Ainley Cl *RUNC* WA7 187 K2
Ainscough Rd
GOL/RIS/CUL WA3 125 G4
Ainsdale Cl *AIN/FAZ* L10 83 J3
BEB CH63 183 K2
PEN/TH CH61 148 D6
WARRW/BUR WA5 141 G5
Ainsdale Rd *BTL* L20 82 A6
Ainsworth Av *MOR/LEA* CH46 128 D3
Ainsworth La *PR/KW* L34 85 G5
Ainsworth Rd *ECCL* WA10 12 B2
Ainsworth St *VAUX/LVPD* L3 9 H4
Aintree Cl *MOR/LEA* CH46 109 K4
Aintree Crs *STHP* PR8 28 C4
Aintree Gv *GTS/LS* CH66 195 G6
Aintree La *AIN/FAZ* L10 83 F1
Aintree Rd *BTL* L20 5 H2
WLT/FAZ L9 83 G5
Aintree Wy *WLT/FAZ* L9 83 F1
Airdale Cl *CL/PREN* CH43 129 K3
Airdale Rd *WAV* L15 134 A3
Airdrie Cl *PS/BROM* CH62 184 A4
Aire *WDN* WA8 157 G1
Aire Cl *EP* CH65 195 K2
Airedale Cl *WARRW/BUR* WA5 141 G2
Airegate *MGHL* L31 61 K5
Airlie Gv *CLB/OSW/ST* L13 114 B1
Airlie Rd *HOY* CH47 127 G3
Aisthorpe Gv *MGHL* L31 71 G2
Ajax Av *WARRN/WOL* WA2 123 H5
The Akbar *HES* CH60 167 G3
Akenside Ct *BTL* L20 * 81 H5
Akenside St *BTL* L20 81 H5
Alabama Wy *BIRK* CH41 3 J5
Alamein Crs
WARRN/WOL WA2 * 142 E2
Alamein Rd *HUY* L36 116 D3
Alastair Crs *CL/PREN* CH43 149 J2
Alban Rd *CHLDW* L16 134 E1
Albany Av *PR/KW* L34 102 B6
Albany Crs *LYMM* WA13 * 145 J5
Albany Gdns *GTS/LS* CH66 195 F2
Albany Gv *LYMM* WA13 145 H5
Albany Rd *CHTN/BK* PR9 22 D4
CLB/OSW/ST L13 114 E3
EHL/KEN L7 113 J5
LYMM WA13 145 H6
PR/KW L34 118 A1
RF/TRAN CH42 150 D1
WLT/FAZ L9 82 E4
Albany Ter *RUNC* WA7 10 D5
The Albany *VAUX/LVPD* L3 * 8 C3
Albemarle Rd *WAL/EG* CH44 111 K4
Alberta Gv *PR/KW* L34 117 F2
Albert Dr *NSTN* CH64 191 J1
WARRW/BUR WA5 140 E3
WLT/FAZ L9 82 C5
Albert Edward Rd *EHL/KEN* L7 113 J5
Albert Gv *CSBY/BLUN* L23 * 68 E5
WAV L15 134 B1

Albert Pk AIG/SPK L17 133 G4
Albert Pl CHTN/BK PR9 14 E3
Albert Rd CHTN/BK PR9 15 H2
CLB/OSW/ST L13 114 B1
CSBY/WL L22 80 E2
FMBY L37 48 B5
HOY CH47 127 G3
RF/TRAN CH42 131 F5
WARRS WA4 163 F1
WDN WA8 19 F2
WKBY CH48 146 B2
Albert Rw FROD/HEL WA6 186 E6
Albert Schweitzer Av
NTHTN L30 70 C6
Albert Sq WDN WA8 18 E3
Albert St AIMK WN4 79 G6
ECCL WA10 13 G1
EHL/KEN L7 113 J6
RUNC WA7 10 D5
Albert Ter STHP PR8 27 H2
Albion Pl WAL/NB CH45 95 H5
Albion St BIRK CH41 3 H4
ECCL WA10 12 C5
EV L5 113 G1
WAL/NB CH45 95 G5
Albourne Rd KKBY L32 85 F3
Albright Rd WDN WA8 157 F5
Albury Cl RNFD/HAY WA11 90 B4
WD/CROXPK L12 99 K3
Albury Rd KKBY L32 84 E4
Alcester Rd WD/CROXPK L12 115 G1
Alcock St RUNC WA7 10 E3
Alcott Pl WARRN/WOL WA2 123 G1
Aldams Gv ANF/KKDL L4 97 G4
Aldbourne Av WLTN L25 135 F4
Aldbourne Cl WLTN L25 135 F5
Aldcliffe GOL/RIS/CUL WA3 93 G4
Alder Av AIMK WN4 78 E4
HUY L36 136 D1
WDN WA8 139 F6
WGNW/BIL/OR WN5 * 77 G4
Alderbank Rd
WARRW/BUR WA5 141 H3
Alder Cl PR/KW L34 118 B1
Alder Crs KKBY L32 72 C6
WARRN/WOL WA2 143 F1
Alderdale Av STHP PR8 33 G4
Alder Dr GTS/LS CH66 202 D2
Alderfield Dr SPK/HALE L24 174 B3
Alder Gv CSBY/WL L22 80 E1
Alder Hey Rd ECCL WA10 102 E1
Alder La FMBY L37 42 A3
FROD/HEL WA6 186 A4
PR/KW L34 100 B2
RNFD/HAY WA11 76 C4
WARRN/WOL WA2 142 E1
WARRW/BUR WA5 106 A6
WDN WA8 137 J5
Alderley SKEL WN8 66 E1
Alderley Av BIRK CH41 130 C2
GOL/RIS/CUL WA3 92 E4
Alderley Rd HOY CH47 127 G2
WAL/EG CH44 111 H4
WARRS WA4 144 C5
Alderney Cl EP CH65 203 G2
Alderney Rd EV L5 113 F2
Alder Rd BEB CH63 169 K1
GOL/RIS/CUL WA3 93 G3
PR/KW L34 118 B1
WARR WA1 144 C2
WD/CROXPK L12 115 H2
Alder Root La
WARRN/WOL WA2 106 D6
Aldersey Cl RUNC WA7 178 C4
Aldersey St VAUX/LVPD L3 113 F4
Aldersgate RF/TRAN CH42 150 E1
Aldersgate Av RUNC WA7 178 C6
Aldersgate Dr HLWD L26 155 K5
Alderson Crs FMBY L37 49 F1
Alderson Rd WAV L15 133 J2
Alder St NEWLW WA12 106 C2
Alderton Dr AIMK WN4 79 F6
Alderville Rd ANF/KKDL L4 98 A3
Alder Wood Av SPK/HALE L24 173 K2
Alderwood Ct WDN WA8 138 D5
Aldewood Cl
GOL/RIS/CUL WA3 125 J1
Aldford Cl BEB CH63 183 J1
CL/PREN CH43 149 H1
Aldford Rd KKBY L32 84 D4
Aldgate EP CH65 6 A5
Aldridge Cl WD/CROXPK L12 99 J2
Aldridge Dr WARRW/BUR WA5 105 K6
Aldrins La NTHTN L30 70 C5
Aldwark Rd DV/KA/FCH L14 116 A3
Aldwych Rd WD/CROXPK L12 115 G1
Aldykes MGHL L31 71 H1
Alexander Cl BRSC L40 39 F6
Alexander Dr MGHL L31 62 B4
PEN/TH CH61 167 J2
WDN WA8 157 J3
Alexander Fleming Av
NTHTN L30 70 C5
Alexander Gv RUNC WA7 11 H6
Alexander Wk ANF/KKDL L4 97 H5
Alexander Whf MGHL L31 62 A6
Alexandra Cl NPK/KEN L6 113 K4
SKEL WN8 56 A5
Alexandra Dr AIG/SPK L17 133 G5
BTL L20 82 B5
ECCL WA10 103 F4
RF/TRAN CH42 150 D2
Alexandra Gn AIG/SPK L17 133 G5
Alexandra Gv HLWD L26 155 J5
Alexandra Ms CHTN/BK PR9 15 H2
ORM L39 45 J5
Alexandra Mt LITH L21 81 J3
Alexandra Pk AIG/SPK L17 133 G6
Alexandra Rd AIMK WN4 79 G5
BRSC L40 38 D5
CHTN/BK PR9 15 G1
CL/PREN CH43 2 B6
CLB/OSW/ST L13 114 E6
CSBY/BLUN L23 68 E5
CSBY/WL L22 81 F3
EHL/KEN L7 133 H1
FMBY L37 48 B5
WAL/NB CH45 95 G5
WARRS WA4 162 C2
WKBY CH48 146 B2
Alexandra St ECCL WA10 103 F4
EP CH65 * 6 D1
WARR WA1 17 K1
WDN WA8 18 C6
Alexandra Ter TOX L8 * 132 E2
Alexandria Rd ALL/GAR L19 153 K4
Alex Cl TOX L8 132 E3
Alfonso Rd ANF/KKDL L4 97 F5
Alford Av STHEL WA9 119 K3
Alforde St WDN WA8 18 D6
Alford St EHL/KEN L7 114 C5
Alfred Ms CLVPS L1 132 D2
Alfred Rd CL/PREN CH43 2 B6
GOL/RIS/CUL WA3 93 H3
RNFD/HAY WA11 90 D4
WAL/EG CH44 112 A6
Alfred St ECCL WA10 13 J3
NEWLW WA12 106 E2
RNFD/HAY WA11 75 G2
WAV L15 133 J1
WDN WA8 18 E4
Alfriston Rd WD/CROXPK L12 115 G1
Algernon St RUNC WA7 10 B3
WARR WA1 17 H2
WARRS WA4 162 B2
Alice Ct WDN WA8 176 D1
Alice St STHEL WA9 104 C5
Alison Av RF/TRAN CH42 131 J6
Alison Pl CLB/OSW/ST L13 98 C6
Alison Rd CLB/OSW/ST L13 98 C6
Alistair Dr BEB CH63 183 K1
Allangate Cl
GR/UP/WCH CH49 147 K1
Allangate Rd ALL/GAR L19 153 J3
Allan Rd RNFD/HAY WA11 89 F4
Allans Cl NSTN CH64 191 K3
Allans Mdw NSTN CH64 191 K3
Allanson St STHEL WA9 104 B3
Allcot Av RF/TRAN CH42 150 C1
Allenby Av CSBY/WL L22 81 G1
Allenby Sq CLB/OSW/ST L13 114 D5
Allendale RUNC WA7 188 A1
Allendale Av RAIN/WH L35 119 F4
WLT/FAZ L9 82 E4
Allengate CSBY/BLUN L23 69 F4
Allen Rd RUNC WA7 176 A6
Allen St WARRN/WOL WA2 16 C3
Allerby Wy GOL/RIS/CUL WA3 93 F3
Allerford Rd WD/CROXPK L12 99 H5
Allerton Beeches
CALD/MH L18 134 D6
Allerton Dr CALD/MH L18 134 C5
Allerton Gv RF/TRAN CH42 131 G6
Allerton Rd CHTN/BK PR9 23 G4
WAL/NB CH45 111 G1
WAV L15 134 B4
WDN WA8 19 F1
WLTN L25 154 C2
Allesley Rd DV/KA/FCH L14 115 K2
Alleyne Rd ANF/KKDL L4 98 B5
All Hallows Dr SPK/HALE L24 174 A2
Allington St AIG/SPK L17 133 G6
Allonby Cl CL/PREN CH43 130 B5
Allport La PS/BROM CH62 171 F4
Allport Rd BEB CH63 183 K1
PS/BROM CH62 170 E6
The Allports PS/BROM CH62 171 F6
All Saints Cl NTHTN L30 70 B6
All Saints Ct RNFD/HAY WA11 75 H4
All Saints Dr WARRS WA4 144 D6
All Saints Rd SPK/HALE L24 173 H2
Allscott Wy AIMK WN4 79 H6
Alma Cl AIN/FAZ L10 84 A4
Almacs Cl CSBY/BLUN L23 68 C6
Alma Hl SKEL WN8 57 K6
Alma Pl STHEL WA9 104 A3
Alma Rd AIG/SPK L17 153 F3
STHP PR8 27 H3
Alma St BIRK CH41 3 G5
NEWLW WA12 * 106 B2
PS/BROM CH62 * 151 F4
STHEL WA9 104 A3
Alma Vale Ter BTL L20 * 4 D5
Almeda Rd SPK/HALE L24 174 B3
Almer Dr WARRW/BUR WA5 141 K4
Almond Av BRSC L40 38 E3
NTHTN L30 69 K6
RUNC WA7 177 F5
Almond Cl HLWD L26 155 K4
RNFD/HAY WA11 89 J6
Almond Ct ALL/GAR L19 154 B6
Almond Dr WARRW/BUR WA5 121 H4
Almond Gv WARR WA1 144 A2
WDN WA8 157 J3
Almond Pl MOR/LEA CH46 129 G1
Almond's Gn WD/CROXPK L12 98 E5
Almond's Gv WD/CROXPK L12 98 E6
Almonds Pk WD/CROXPK L12 98 E5
Almond's Turn NTHTN L30 70 A5
Almond Wy
GR/UP/WCH CH49 * 147 K1
Alness Dr RAIN/WH L35 119 F5
Alnwick Dr EP CH65 203 H1
MOR/LEA CH46 128 D1
Aloeswood Cl NPK/KEN L6 113 K2
Alpass Rd AIG/SPK L17 * 133 G6
Alpha Dr RF/TRAN CH42 150 C1
Alpha St LITH L21 81 J6
Alpine Cl ECCL WA10 102 E1
Alpine St NEWLW WA12 106 A2
Alresford Rd ALL/GAR L19 153 G3
Alroy Rd ANF/KKDL L4 97 J6
Alscot Av AIN/FAZ L10 84 A4
Alscot Cl MGHL L31 71 G1
Alston Cl PS/BROM CH62 170 E4
Alstonfield Rd DV/KA/FCH L14 116 A3
Alston Rd AIG/SPK L17 153 F3
Alt WDN WA8 157 G1
Alt Av MGHL L31 71 F2
Altbridge Pk NG/CROX L11 84 A6
Alt Bridge Rd HUY L36 116 D3
Altcar Av EHL/KEN L7 133 J2
Altcar Dr MOR/LEA CH46 128 E2
Altcar La FMBY L37 49 F4
MGHL L31 61 J3
ORM L39 51 H4
Altcar Rd FMBY L37 49 G3
Altcross Rd NG/CROX L11 99 G1
Altcross Wy NG/CROX L11 99 G1
Altfield Rd DV/KA/FCH L14 99 K6
Altfinch Cl DV/KA/FCH L14 100 A6
Altham Rd NG/CROX L11 98 D6
STHP PR8 28 B5
Althorpe Dr STHP PR8 28 B4
Althorp St TOX L8 132 E5
Altmoor Rd HUY L36 116 D1
Alton Av LITH L21 81 H2
Alton Cl AIMK WN4 79 F5
HTWN L38 59 F5
Alton Rd CL/PREN CH43 130 D4
NPK/KEN L6 114 B2
Alt Rd BTL L20 81 K6
FMBY L37 49 G4
HTWN L38 59 F3
HUY L36 116 E4
Alt Side Ct AIN/FAZ L10 84 A4
Alt St TOX L8 133 G2
Altway AIN/FAZ L10 71 F6
Altys La ORM L39 53 K2
Alundale Rd WD/CROXPK L12 115 J2
Alvanley Pl CL/PREN CH43 2 B5
Alvanley Rd GTS/LS CH66 195 H5
KKBY L32 84 B1
WD/CROXPK L12 115 G2
Alvanley Vw CHNE CH2 198 C6
Alva Rd RAIN/WH L35 119 F5
Alvega Cl PS/BROM CH62 151 H4
Alverstone Av BIRK CH41 130 C2
Alverstone Cl
WARRW/BUR WA5 140 D2
Alverstone Rd CALD/MH L18 134 A4
WAL/EG CH44 111 K4
Alverton Cl WDN WA8 157 J3
Alvina La ANF/KKDL L4 97 G6
NWD/KWIPK L33 73 F4
Alwain Gn SPK/HALE L24 174 A3
Alwen St BIRK CH41 111 F6
Alwyn Av LITH L21 81 J2
Alwyn Gdns MOR/LEA CH46 129 G1
Alwyn St AIG/SPK L17 133 G6
Amanda Rd AIN/FAZ L10 84 A4
RAIN/WH L35 118 D2
Amanda Wy MGHL L31 * 72 A5
Amaury Cl CSBY/BLUN L23 69 J4
Amaury Rd CSBY/BLUN L23 69 J4
Ambassador Dr HLWD L26 155 K2
Ambergate SKEL WN8 56 D6
Ambergate Cl STHEL WA9 * 104 B6
Ambergate Rd ALL/GAR L19 153 J3
Amberley Av MOR/LEA CH46 128 D2
Amberley Cl MOR/LEA CH46 128 D2
NPK/KEN L6 98 B6
Amber Wy DV/KA/FCH L14 100 A6
Ambleside Av MOR/LEA CH46 128 E1
Ambleside Cl PEN/TH CH61 148 D5
PS/BROM CH62 171 G6
Ambleside Crs
WARRN/WOL WA2 123 J4
Ambleside Dr NWD/KWIPK L33 72 C5
Ambleside Rd CALD/MH L18 154 A2
EP CH65 203 G1
MGHL L31 62 B5
Amelia Cl NPK/KEN L6 9 K1
WDN WA8 139 G5
Amelia St WARRN/WOL WA2 143 F2
Amersham SKEL WN8 56 D6
Amersham Rd ANF/KKDL L4 98 A3
Amery Gv RF/TRAN CH42 150 B1
Amethyst Cl NPK/KEN L6 113 K3
Amherst Rd AIG/SPK L17 152 D1
Amis Gv GOL/RIS/CUL WA3 93 F3
Amity St TOX L8 132 E4
Amos Av LITH L21 81 K3
Ampleforth Cl KKBY L32 84 B2
Ampthill Rd AIG/SPK L17 152 D1
Ampulla Rd NG/CROX L11 99 G2
Ancaster Rd AIG/SPK L17 152 E1
Ancholme Cl RAIN/WH L35 118 C1
Anchorage La CALD/MH L18 133 K6
The Anchorage LYMM WA13 145 J6
NSTN CH64 191 H2
VAUX/LVPD L3 132 C3
Anchor Cl RUNC WA7 188 C1
Anchor St CHTN/BK PR9 15 F4
Ancient Mdw WLT/FAZ L9 82 E4
Ancroft Rd DV/KA/FCH L14 116 A4
Ancrum Rd NWD/KWIPK L33 72 C3
Anders Dr NWD/KWIPK L33 73 F4
Anderson Av BTL L20 4 A2
Anderson Cl PEN/TH CH61 148 D5
RAIN/WH L35 119 F6
WARRN/WOL WA2 124 D5
Anderson Rd LITH L21 82 A2
Anderson St EV L5 113 G1
Anderton Ter HUY L36 116 C5
Andover Cl WARRN/WOL WA2 124 A6
Andover Rd RNFD/HAY WA11 90 D3
Andover Wy WLTN L25 155 G4
Andreas Cl STHP PR8 27 J3
Andrew Av MGHL L31 71 F1
WGNW/BIL/OR WN5 77 H4
Andrew Cl WDN WA8 157 H3
Andrews Cl FMBY L37 48 E4
Andrews La FMBY L37 48 E4
Andrew St ANF/KKDL L4 97 H4
Andrew's Wk HES CH60 168 B5
Andrews Yort FMBY L37 48 E4
Andromeda Wy STHEL WA9 104 E6
Anemone Wy STHEL WA9 104 E6
Anfield Rd ANF/KKDL L4 97 H6
Angela St EHL/KEN L7 133 G1
Angers La MGHL L31 72 A3
Anglesea Rd WLT/FAZ L9 97 H2
Anglesea Wy TOX L8 132 E5
Anglesey Cl EP CH65 203 G2
Anglesey Rd WAL/EG CH44 111 H2
WKBY CH48 127 F6
Anglezark Cl EHL/KEN L7 113 K5
Anglia Wy WLTN L25 155 F3
Anglican Ct TOX L8 132 D2
Anglo Cl WLT/FAZ L9 83 F3
Angus Rd BEB CH63 183 K1
NG/CROX L11 98 D5
Annandale Cl NWD/KWIPK L33 72 C3
Annandale Gdns SKEL WN8 57 J6
Annan Gv AIMK WN4 79 G5
Ann Cl GTS/LS CH66 195 G2
Anne Av STHP PR8 34 A3
Anne Gv STHEL WA9 104 A6
Annerley St EHL/KEN L7 * 133 H1
Annesley Rd AIG/SPK L17 152 D1
WAL/EG CH44 111 H4
Anne St STHEL WA9 120 B4
Annette Av NEWLW WA12 91 F6
Annie Rd BTL L20 82 A5
Annie St WARRN/WOL WA2 16 E2
Ann St RUNC WA7 11 F3
SKEL WN8 56 A4
Ann St West WDN WA8 18 E6
Anscot Av BEB CH63 150 E5
Ansdell Dr ECCL WA10 87 J6
Ansdell Gv CHTN/BK PR9 23 J1
Ansdell Rd WDN WA8 158 C1
Ansdell Villas' Rd
RAIN/WH L35 118 E3
Anson Pl VAUX/LVPD L3 9 J2
Anson St VAUX/LVPD L3 9 J3
Anstey Cl MOR/LEA CH46 109 F6
Anstey Rd CLB/OSW/ST L13 115 F4
Ansty Cl RNFD/HAY WA11 89 G6
Anthony's Wy HES CH60 168 A6
Anthorn Cl CL/PREN CH43 130 A5
Antler Ct AIMK WN4 79 G3
Antonio St BTL L20 97 F4
Antons Cl HLWD L26 155 J5
Antons Ct HLWD L26 155 K5
Antons Rd HLWD L26 155 J5
PEN/TH CH61 148 C6
Antony Rd WARRS WA4 162 A1
Antrim Cl RNFD/HAY WA11 90 B5
Antrim Dr GTS/LS CH66 202 D1
Antrim Rd WARRN/WOL WA2 123 G5
Antrim St CLB/OSW/ST L13 98 C6
Anvil Cl BTL L20 4 C2
CHNE CH2 198 C5
The Anzacs PS/BROM CH62 151 H5
Anzio Rd HUY L36 116 D3
Apex Ct PS/BROM CH62 * 171 G4
Apollo Crs NWD/KWIPK L33 72 D5
Apollo Wy NPK/KEN L6 * 113 K2
NTHTN L30 70 C5
Apostles Wy NWD/KWIPK L33 72 C4
Appin Rd BIRK CH41 3 F7
Appleby Cl WDN WA8 157 H3
Appleby Dr NTHTN L30 69 K6
Appleby Gn WD/CROXPK L12 115 H1
Appleby Gv PS/BROM CH62 183 K1
Appleby Lawn NTHLY L27 136 D5
Appleby Rd NWD/KWIPK L33 72 D5
WARRN/WOL WA2 123 J4
Appleby Wk WDN WA8 157 H3
Applecorn Cl STHEL WA9 120 B1
Apple Ct NPK/KEN L6 113 K4
Applecross Cl
GOL/RIS/CUL WA3 125 J1
Appledale Dr GTS/LS CH66 202 E3
Apple Dell Av GOL/RIS/CUL WA3 92 D2
Appledore Cl SPK/HALE L24 173 G1
Appledore Gv STHEL WA9 120 A3
Appleford Cl WARRS WA4 162 D4
Applegarth MOR/LEA CH46 128 D3
Appleton Dr EP CH65 195 J6
GR/UP/WCH CH49 129 F6
Appleton Rd ANF/KKDL L4 97 J4
KKBY L32 72 D5
LITH L21 81 H2
SKEL WN8 56 B3
STHEL WA9 104 A3
WDN WA8 18 E1
Appleton St WDN WA8 18 E7
Appleton Village WDN WA8 18 D1
Appletree Cl CALD/MH L18 153 K2
Apple Tree Cl STBRV L28 100 B5
Apple Tree Gv GTS/LS CH66 202 D3
Appletree Gv
WARRN/WOL WA2 124 B5
April Gv NPK/KEN L6 114 B2
April Ri NTHTN L30 70 B6
Apsley Av WAL/NB CH45 111 H1
Apsley Brow MGHL L31 61 K6
Apsley Gv BEB CH63 151 F5
Apsley Rd PS/BROM CH62 151 G3
WD/CROXPK L12 115 G1
Aquarius Cl DV/KA/FCH L14 116 A3
Aragon Cl MGHL L31 62 C4
Aran Cl SPK/HALE L24 174 E3
Arborn Dr GR/UP/WCH CH49 129 H3
Arbour Ct NWD/KWIPK L33 85 G1
Arbour La NWD/KWIPK L33 85 F2
Arbour St STHP PR8 15 G7
Arbury Av RNFD/HAY WA11 89 G5
Arbury La WARRN/WOL WA2 123 J1
Arcadia Av MGHL L31 62 B4
Archbishop Worlock Ct
VAUX/LVPD L3 112 E3
Archer Av WARRS WA4 162 D1
Archer Cl ANF/KKDL L4 97 G6
Archerfield Rd CALD/MH L18 153 J2
Archer Gv STHEL WA9 104 C1
Archers Cft PS/BROM CH62 * 171 F4
Archers Fold MGHL L31 72 A5
Archers Gn PS/BROM CH62 184 B3
Archers Green Rd
WARRW/BUR WA5 122 A4
Archer St ANF/KKDL L4 * 97 G6
Archers Wy
GR/UP/WCH CH49 * 148 D1
GTS/LS CH66 202 C2
The Arches PR/KW L34 * 117 K1
Arch La AIMK WN4 77 K6
Arch View Crs CLVPS L1 9 G7
Archway Rd HUY L36 116 E5
Arctic Rd BTL L20 4 B4
Arden WDN WA8 157 F1
Arden Cl GOL/RIS/CUL WA3 125 K1
STHP PR8 33 G3
Arden Dr NSTN CH64 191 K3
Ardennes Rd HUY L36 116 E4
Arderne Cl BEB CH63 170 D3
Ardleigh Av STHP PR8 28 B4
Ardleigh Cl CLB/OSW/ST L13 114 D5
Ardleigh Gv CLB/OSW/ST L13 114 D5
Ardleigh Pl CLB/OSW/ST L13 114 D5
Ardleigh Rd CLB/OSW/ST L13 114 C5
Ardmore Rd CALD/MH L18 153 H1
Ardrossan Rd ANF/KKDL L4 98 A5
Ardville Rd NG/CROX L11 98 B2
Ardwick Rd SPK/HALE L24 174 A2
Ardwick St STHEL WA9 13 K5
Arena Gdns WARRN/WOL WA2 143 G1
Argameols Cl STHP PR8 28 C2
Argarmeols Gv FMBY L37 40 E6
Argarmeols Rd FMBY L37 40 E5
Argo Rd CSBY/WL L22 80 E2
Argos Pl BTL L20 97 F4
Argos Rd BTL L20 97 F4
Argyle Rd ALL/GAR L19 153 K5
ANF/KKDL L4 113 K1
CHTN/BK PR9 23 F4
Argyle St BIRK CH41 3 G4
CLVPS L1 8 E6
ECCL WA10 13 F1
Argyle St South BIRK CH41 2 E7
Argyll Av PS/BROM CH62 184 A3
Argyll Cl AIMK WN4 78 B5
Aries Cl DV/KA/FCH L14 116 A2
Ariss Gv RAIN/WH L35 * 118 C2
Arizona Crs WARRW/BUR WA5 141 J2
Arkenstone Cl WDN WA8 157 H1
Arkle Rd CL/PREN CH43 130 C1
Arkles La ANF/KKDL L4 97 K6
Arkles Rd ANF/KKDL L4 113 J1
Arklow Dr SPK/HALE L24 174 E3
Ark Royal Wy BIRK CH41 131 J5
Arkwood Cl PS/BROM CH62 170 E2
Arkwright Ct RUNC WA7 177 J2
Arkwright Rd RUNC WA7 177 J2
Arkwright St EV L5 113 G2
Arlescourt Rd
WD/CROXPK L12 115 G2
Arley Av WARRS WA4 162 C2
Arley Cl CL/PREN CH43 129 K3
Arley Dr WDN WA8 157 G1
Arley St VAUX/LVPD L3 112 E3
Arlington Av CALD/MH L18 134 A4
Arlington Cl STHP PR8 33 G4
Arlington Dr LEIGH WN7 93 K3
WARRW/BUR WA5 141 F5
Arlington Rd WAL/NB CH45 110 E1
Armill Rd NG/CROX L11 99 G2
Armitage Gdns CALD/MH L18 153 J2
Armley Rd ANF/KKDL L4 97 K6
Armour Av WARRN/WOL WA2 123 H5
Armoury Bank AIMK WN4 79 G6
The Armoury WD/CROXPK L12 99 F6
Armscot Cl WLTN L25 154 E4
Armscot Pl WLTN L25 154 E4
Armstrong Cl
GOL/RIS/CUL WA3 125 F3
Armstrong Quay
VAUX/LVPD L3 132 E6
Armthorpe Dr GTS/LS CH66 194 E4
Arncliffe Dr WARRW/BUR WA5 121 K1
Arncliffe Rd WLTN L25 155 F3
Arndale RUNC WA7 187 H2
Arnhem Crs WARRN/WOL WA2 143 F2
Arnhem Rd HUY L36 116 D3
Arnian Rd RNFD/HAY WA11 75 G2
Arnian Wy RNFD/HAY WA11 75 G2
Arnold Av ECCL WA10 12 B2
Arnold Cl STHEL WA9 104 A4
TOX L8 133 F3
Arnold Crs TOX L8 133 F3
Arnold Gv WAV L15 134 B1
Arnold Pl WDN WA8 157 H4
Arnold St WAL/NB CH45 * 111 H2
WARR WA1 17 J2
Arno Rd CL/PREN CH43 130 E6
Arnot Cl ECCL WA10 13 F2
Arnot St ANF/KKDL L4 97 H4
Arnot Wy BEB CH63 150 C5
Arnside LITH L21 82 A3
Arnside Av RAIN/WH L35 118 C3
RNFD/HAY WA11 89 K5
Arnside Gv WARRS WA4 162 A1
Arnside Rd CHTN/BK PR9 15 G4
CL/PREN CH43 130 D5
EHL/KEN L7 114 A6
HUY L36 116 B5
WAL/NB CH45 111 H2
Arnside Ter CHTN/BK PR9 15 H4
Aron Ct PR/KW L34 117 K1
Arpley Rd WARR WA1 16 D7
Arpley St WARR WA1 16 B5
Arrad St EHL/KEN L7 9 J6
Arran Av EP CH65 203 G2
Arran Cl RNFD/HAY WA11 89 H5
WARRN/WOL WA2 124 C5
Arran Dr FROD/HEL WA6 201 F2
Arranmore Rd CALD/MH L18 153 H1
Arrowe Av MOR/LEA CH46 128 E2
Arrowe Brook La
GR/UP/WCH CH49 148 B2
Arrowe Brook Rd
GR/UP/WCH CH49 148 C1
Arrowe Park Rd
GR/UP/WCH CH49 129 G4
Arrowe Rd GR/UP/WCH CH49 128 E6
Arrowe Side
GR/UP/WCH CH49 129 F5
Arrowe Vw
GR/UP/WCH CH49 * 129 H4
Arrowsmith Rd
RNFD/HAY WA11 90 E4
Arthur Av EP CH65 6 E5
Arthur St ALL/GAR L19 * 154 A6
BIRK CH41 2 B1
RUNC WA7 10 C5
WARRN/WOL WA2 16 B3
WLT/FAZ L9 97 H2
Arundel Av AIG/SPK L17 133 H3
WAL/NB CH45 111 F1
Arundel Cl PEN/TH CH61 148 B6
TOX L8 133 F5
Arundel Ct EP CH65 196 D6
Arundell Cl WARRW/BUR WA5 121 K1
Arundel Rd STHP PR8 34 B1
Arundel St ANF/KKDL L4 97 G4
Arvon St BTL L20 82 A5
Asbridge St TOX L8 133 G3
Asbury Cl CALD/MH L18 134 E6
Asbury Rd WAL/NB CH45 110 D1
Ascot Av LITH L21 81 H3
RUNC WA7 186 E1
Ascot Cl STHP PR8 27 F2
WARR WA1 144 D2
WARRS WA4 163 H1
Ascot Dr BEB CH63 150 E6
GTS/LS CH66 202 B1
NWD/KWIPK L33 72 D4

Ascot Gv BEB CH63 150 E6
Ascot Pk CSBY/BLUN L23 69 G5
Ascroft Rd WLT/FAZ L9 82 E3
Ash Av NEWLW WA12 106 C3
Ashbank Rd NG/CROX L11 98 E3
Ashberry Dr WARRS WA4 163 G6
Ashbourne Av CSBY/BLUN L23 68 D5
NTHTN L30 82 B1
RUNC WA7 186 E1
Ashbourne Cl GTS/LS CH66 202 C3
Ashbourne Crs HUY L36 116 B5
Ashbourne Rd AIG/SPK L17 152 D1
WARRW/BUR WA5 141 J4
Ashbrook Av RUNC WA7 187 H3
Ashbrook Crs
WARRN/WOL WA2 143 G1
Ashbrook Dr WLT/FAZ L9 83 F5
Ashburn Av NWD/KWIPK L33 72 D5
Ashburton Av CL/PREN CH43 130 C3
Ashburton Rd CL/PREN CH43 130 B3
WKBY CH48 127 G6
Ashbury Cl RUNC WA7 178 C3
Ashbury Dr RNFD/HAY WA11 90 C4
Ashbury Rd DV/KA/FCH L14 116 B1
Ashby Cl MOR/LEA CH46 109 F6
Ash Cl GTS/LS CH66 202 D2
ORM L39 45 H6
WAV L15 133 K1
Ashcombe Rd
DV/KA/FCH L14 115 G4
Ash Crs HUY L36 136 B1
Ashcroft Av ORM L39 45 K5
Ashcroft Dr PEN/TH CH61 167 K3
Ashcroft Rd FMBY L37 49 F4
NWD/KWIPK L33 73 H6
Ashcroft St BTL L20 4 D5
STHEL WA9 104 A2
Ashdale HUY L36 116 D5
Ashdale Cl FMBY L37 48 C3
Ashdale Pk GR/UP/WCH CH49 128 C6
Ashdale Rd CALD/MH L18 134 B4
CSBY/WL L22 80 E1
WLT/FAZ L9 97 J1
Ashdown Cl STHP PR8 28 A3
Ashdown Crs STHEL WA9 120 A3
Ashdown Dr
GR/UP/WCH CH49 147 K1
Ashdown Gv HLWD L26 155 K2
Ashdown La
GOL/RIS/CUL WA3 125 J2
Ashfarm Ct DV/KA/FCH L14 115 K4
Ashfield RAIN/WH L35 119 F4
WAV L15 133 J1
Ashfield Crs PS/BROM CH62 171 F5
WGNW/BIL/OR WN5 77 H4
Ashfield Gdns WARRS WA4 143 J6
Ashfield Rd AIG/SPK L17 152 E1
PS/BROM CH62 170 E5
Ashfield Rd North EP CH65 6 D4
Ashfield St EV L5 112 E2
Ashford Cl HLWD L26 155 H4
Ashford Rd BIRK CH41 131 F5
HOY CH47 127 H1
Ashford Wy WDN WA8 19 K1
Ash Gv FMBY L37 48 C4
GOL/RIS/CUL WA3 92 C3
GTS/LS CH66 195 F3
LITH L21 81 H5
RAIN/WH L35 118 A3
RNFD/HAY WA11 75 G3
RUNC WA7 177 F5
SKEL WN8 55 K4
STHEL WA9 120 A3
WAL/NB CH45 95 J6
WARRS WA4 143 G6
WAV L15 133 J1
Ash Grove Crs
WGNW/BIL/OR WN5 77 G3
Ashland Av AIMK WN4 79 F5
Ashlands FROD/HEL WA6 201 F1
Ash La WARRS WA4 162 D3
WDN WA8 156 E3
Ashlar Gv AIG/SPK L17 153 F1
Ashlar Rd AIG/SPK L17 153 F1
CSBY/WL L22 81 F1
Ashlea Rd PEN/TH CH61 167 K2
Ashleigh Rd MGHL L31 71 J2
Ashley Av HOY CH47 108 D6
Ashley Cl NWD/KWIPK L33 72 D4
RAIN/WH L35 119 F5
WARRS WA4 144 B6
Ashley Rd CHTN/BK PR9 15 H5
RUNC WA7 177 G3
RUNC WA7 11 K5
SKEL WN8 56 D2
Ashley St RF/TRAN CH42 150 E1
Ashley Wy WDN WA8 18 D7
Ashley Wy West WDN WA8 18 B6
Ashmead Rd SKEL WN8 56 C1
Ashmore Cl GOL/RIS/CUL WA3 125 J4
WKBY CH48 146 D5
Ashmuir Hey KKBY L32 84 E2
Ashover Av DV/KA/FCH L14 116 A3
Ash Priors WDN WA8 138 C6
Ashridge St RUNC WA7 10 C3
Ash Rd BEB CH63 150 E4
CHNE CH2 198 D6
LITH L21 81 H4
LYMM WA13 145 H6
RF/TRAN CH42 * 131 G5
RNFD/HAY WA11 90 D4
WARRN/WOL WA2 123 H1
WARRW/BUR WA5 141 G5
Ash St BTL L20 5 F3
GOL/RIS/CUL WA3 92 C1
STHP PR8 27 K2
Ashton Av RAIN/WH L35 118 E5
Ashton Cl FROD/HEL WA6 187 F6
PS/BROM CH62 184 B4
RUNC WA7 186 C1
Ashton Dr FROD/HEL WA6 187 F5
WKBY CH48 146 B2
WLTN L25 154 E4
Ashton Heath AIMK WN4 91 H1
Ashton Rd GOL/RIS/CUL WA3 92 A1
NEWLW WA12 91 H5
STHP PR8 27 G6
WGNW/BIL/OR WN5 78 A1
Ashtons Green Dr STHEL WA9 104 D3
Ashton St CLB/OSW/ST L13 114 E4
Ashton St VAUX/LVPD L3 9 K3
WARRN/WOL WA2 16 D3
Ashtree Cl NSTN CH64 192 B2
Ashtree Cft NSTN CH64 193 H2
Ashtree Dr NSTN CH64 192 B3
Ashtree Farm Ct NSTN CH64 193 H1
Ashtree Gv WD/CROXPK L12 99 J1
Ashurst Cl RNFD/HAY WA11 89 H5
SKEL WN8 56 C1
WLTN L25 135 J5
Ashurst Ct FMBY L37 48 E3
Ashurst Dr RNFD/HAY WA11 89 G5
Ashurst Gdns SKEL WN8 56 C1
Ashurst Rd SKEL WN8 56 D2
Ash V WAV L15 133 K1
Ash Vls WAL/EG CH44 * 111 K5
Ashville Rd BIRK CH41 2 A3
CL/PREN CH43 130 E2
WAL/EG CH44 111 J5
Ashville Wy RUNC WA7 187 H4
Ashwall St SKEL WN8 55 K5
Ashwater Rd WD/CROXPK L12 99 G3
Ash Wy HES CH60 181 G2
Ashwell Av GOL/RIS/CUL WA3 92 E2
Ashwell St TOX L8 132 D2
Ashwood SKEL WN8 56 E2
Ashwood Av AIMK WN4 91 F1
GOL/RIS/CUL WA3 92 E3
WARR WA1 143 H2
Ashwood Cl GTS/LS CH66 * 202 B2
NWD/KWIPK L33 72 D4
WDN WA8 157 F4
Ashwood Ct CL/PREN CH43 110 C6
Ashwood Dr WD/CROXPK L12 99 H2
Askern Rd KKBY L32 84 E3
Askett Cl RNFD/HAY WA11 90 B4
Askew Cl WAL/EG CH44 111 K3
Askew St ANF/KKDL L4 97 H4
Askham Cl TOX L8 133 G2
Askrigg Av GTS/LS CH66 194 E4
Asland Gdns CHTN/BK PR9 24 A1
Asmall Cl ORM L39 45 H5
Asmall La ORM L39 44 C3
Aspen Cl GTS/LS CH66 202 C2
HES CH60 168 D5
NWD/KWIPK L33 72 E3
Aspendale Rd RF/TRAN CH42 131 G5
Aspen Gv FMBY L37 48 C4
TOX L8 133 H3
WARR WA1 143 K2
Aspenwood AIMK WN4 91 F1
Aspes Rd WD/CROXPK L12 99 J6
Aspinall Cl WARRN/WOL WA2 124 C4
Aspinall Crs FMBY L37 50 B4
Aspinall St BIRK CH41 2 B2
Aspinal St PR/KW L34 117 K1
Aspull Cl GOL/RIS/CUL WA3 124 E3
Aspull Common LEIGH WN7 93 K2
Aspull Ct LEIGH WN7 93 K2
Asquith Av BIRK CH41 2 A2
Asser Rd NG/CROX L11 98 C5
Assheton Cl NEWLW WA12 106 A1
Assheton Wk SPK/HALE L24 175 F3
Assissian Crs NTHTN L30 70 B5
Astbury Cl GOL/RIS/CUL WA3 93 J3
Aster Crs RUNC WA7 * 187 J3
Aster Dr NWD/KWIPK L33 72 C4
Asterfield Av BEB CH63 150 D4
Aster Rd RNFD/HAY WA11 90 E5
Astley Cl RNFD/HAY WA11 75 G2
WARRS WA4 142 E6
WDN WA8 138 B6
Astley Rd HUY L36 116 E1
Astmoor Bridge La RUNC WA7 177 J3
Astmoor Rd RUNC WA7 11 H3
Aston Av GOL/RIS/CUL WA3 125 H3
Aston Cl CL/PREN CH43 130 C6
Aston Ct WARR WA1 124 E6
Aston Fields Rd RUNC WA7 188 C3
Aston Forge RUNC WA7 188 E2
Aston Gn RUNC WA7 * 188 D1
Aston La RUNC WA7 188 A4
Aston La North RUNC WA7 188 D3
Aston La South RUNC WA7 188 D6
Aston St ALL/GAR L19 172 C1
Astonwood Rd RF/TRAN CH42 131 G6
Astor Dr WARRS WA4 162 E3
Astor St ANF/KKDL L4 97 H3
Atheldene Rd ANF/KKDL L4 98 A3
Athelstan Cl PS/BROM CH62 171 F4
Atherton Cl EV L5 113 H2
Atherton Dr
GR/UP/WCH CH49 129 H6
Atherton Rd EP CH65 195 J3
WLT/FAZ L9 83 F5
Atherton St ECCL WA10 12 E2
PR/KW L34 * 117 K1
WAL/NB CH45 95 G4
Athlone Rd WARRN/WOL WA2 123 G6
Athol Cl NEWLW WA12 105 K1
PS/BROM CH62 184 B2
Athol Dr PS/BROM CH62 184 B2
Athole Gv CHTN/BK PR9 23 H6
Atholl Crs AIN/FAZ L10 83 G1
Athol St BIRK CH41 3 G3
EV L5 112 D2
Atkinson Gv HUY L36 117 F3
Atlanta Ct NWD/KWIPK L33 72 C3
Atlanta Gdns
WARRW/BUR WA5 141 J1
Atlantic Point Village
VAUX/LVPD L3 113 F4
Atlantic Rd BTL L20 4 C4
Atlantic Wy NTHTN L30 82 B3
VAUX/LVPD L3 132 C5
Atlas Rd BTL L20 4 B4
Atlas St STHEL WA9 13 K4
Atlas Wy GTS/LS CH66 195 J2
Atterbury Cl WDN WA8 157 H1
Atterbury St TOX L8 132 D4
Attlee Rd HUY L36 117 G4
Attwood St ANF/KKDL L4 97 H6
Atwell St NPK/KEN L6 113 J3
Aubourn Cl WDN WA8 138 B6
Aubrey Ct NPK/KEN L6 113 J3
Auburn Rd CLB/OSW/ST L13 114 C2
WAL/NB CH45 95 G6
The Aubynes WAL/NB CH45 94 E6
Auckery Av GTS/LS CH66 195 G6
Audlem Av CL/PREN CH43 130 C6
Audlem Cl RUNC WA7 187 J3
Audley St VAUX/LVPD L3 9 H2
Audre Cl WARRW/BUR WA5 140 E3
Aughton Cl
WGNW/BIL/OR WN5 77 H5
Aughton Ms STHP PR8 27 H2
Aughton Park Dr ORM L39 53 H3
Aughton Rd BTL L20 82 A6
STHP PR8 27 H2
Aughton St ORM L39 53 H1
Augusta Cl CLB/OSW/ST L13 114 E5
August Rd NPK/KEN L6 114 A2
August St BTL L20 5 F1
Aukland Gv STHEL WA9 103 F6
Aukland Rd WAV L15 134 B4
Aurorean Cl NTHLY L27 136 A3
Austell Cl RNFD/HAY WA11 89 G4
Austen Dr WARRN/WOL WA2 123 F1
Austin Av AIMK WN4 78 D5
ECCL WA10 102 E5
Austin Cl KKBY L32 84 C1
Austin St WAL/EG CH44 * 111 G5
Austral Av WARR WA1 144 A2
Australia La WARRS WA4 163 H2
Autumn Gv RF/TRAN CH42 150 D3
Autumn Wy BTL L20 5 F1
Avalon Ter BTL L20 4 B2
Avebury Cl GOL/RIS/CUL WA3 93 F3
WDN WA8 139 K6
Aveley Cl WARR WA1 144 A2
Aveling Dr CHTN/BK PR9 21 K5
Avelon Cl CL/PREN CH43 130 A4
MGHL L31 61 K2
The Avenue ALL/GAR L19 154 B6
CHTN/BK PR9 29 J2
CHTN/BK PR9 21 J6
ECCL WA10 102 D2
HLWD L26 155 H4
HUY L36 116 E4
KNUT WA16 165 K6
LYMM WA13 164 D2
NEWLW WA12 106 C1
ORM L39 45 H5
PR/KW L34 100 E6
PS/BROM CH62 170 E5
RNFD/HAY WA11 75 G3
Averham Cl AIMK WN4 91 G2
Avery Cl WARRN/WOL WA2 124 A5
Avery Crs RNFD/HAY WA11 90 B4
Avery Rd RNFD/HAY WA11 90 B4
Avery Sq RNFD/HAY WA11 90 B4
Aviary Ct WLT/FAZ L9 * 82 C5
Aviemore Cl AIMK WN4 78 C5
Aviemore Dr
WARRN/WOL WA2 124 C4
Aviemore Rd CLB/OSW/ST L13 114 D4
Avington Cl WD/CROXPK L12 99 H6
Avocet Cl NEWLW WA12 106 C1
WARRN/WOL WA2 123 K4
Avolon Rd WD/CROXPK L12 115 H2
Avon WDN WA8 157 F1
Avon Av WARRW/BUR WA5 141 F5
Avon Cl ANF/KKDL L4 97 G5
NSTN CH64 191 K3
NWD/KWIPK L33 72 E3
Avondale EP CH65 196 A6
Avondale Av MGHL L31 71 F1
MOR/LEA CH46 109 K6
PS/BROM CH62 184 B2
Avondale Dr WDN WA8 157 G2
Avondale Rd CHTN/BK PR9 15 F2
HOY CH47 127 G2
RNFD/HAY WA11 90 B4
WAV L15 133 K3
Avondale Rd North
CHTN/BK PR9 15 G1
Avonmore Av CALD/MH L18 134 B6
Avon Rd AIMK WN4 79 K4
WGNW/BIL/OR WN5 77 G6
Avon St BIRK CH41 111 F6
NPK/KEN L6 * 113 K2
Awelon Cl WD/CROXPK L12 99 G5
Axbridge Av STHEL WA9 120 B2
Axholme Cl PEN/TH CH61 148 E6
Axholme Rd PEN/TH CH61 148 D6
Ayala Cl BTL L20 82 C4
Aycliffe Rd STHEL WA9 * 119 F1
Aylesbury Av CL/PREN CH43 149 H1
Aylesbury Cl GTS/LS CH66 195 F6
Aylesbury Rd WAL/NB CH45 95 J6
Aylesford Rd CLB/OSW/ST L13 114 E4
Aylsham Cl WDN WA8 138 B6
Aylsham Dr GR/UP/WCH CH49 129 H2
Aylton Rd HUY L36 116 B3
Aylward Pl BTL L20 * 4 D2
Aynsley Ct STHEL WA9 118 D1
Ayr Cl STHP PR8 28 C3
Ayres Ct STHEL WA9 103 G6
Ayrshire Gdns ECCL WA10 12 D7
Ayrshire Rd ANF/KKDL L4 98 A5
Aysgarth Av WD/CROXPK L12 115 G1
Aysgarth Rd WAL/NB CH45 111 F1
Azalea Gv HLWD L26 155 G1
RUNC WA7 187 J3

B

Babbacombe Rd CHLDW L16 135 F3
WARRW/BUR WA5 141 F5
Back Bath St CHTN/BK PR9 14 E3
Back Beau St VAUX/LVPD L3 * 113 G3
Back Bedford St EHL/KEN L7 9 K6
Back Belmont Rd NPK/KEN L6 113 K1
Back Berry St CLVPS L1 9 G6
Back Blackfield Ter EV L5 97 F6
Back Bold St CLVPS L1 9 F5
Back Boundary St EV L5 113 F1
Back Bridge St NEWLW WA12 106 B2
Back Bridport St VAUX/LVPD L3 9 G3
Back Canning St CLVPS L1 9 J7
Back Catharine St TOX L8 * 9 J7
Back Chadwick Mt EV L5 97 G6
Back Chatham Pl EHL/KEN L7 113 K6
Back Colquitt St CLVPS L1 9 G6
Back Commutation Rw
VAUX/LVPD L3 9 G3
Back Cross La NEWLW WA12 106 B1
Back Dovecot Pl
DV/KA/FCH L14 115 K3
Back Eastford Rd WARRS WA4 161 K2
Back Egerton St North
TOX L8 * 132 E2
Back Falkner St South
TOX L8 133 F1
TOX L8 9 K7
Backford Cl CL/PREN CH43 130 B6
RUNC WA7 188 B2
Backford Gdns CH/BCN CH1 202 D4
Backford Rd PEN/TH CH61 148 A6
Backford Wy CL/PREN CH43 130 B6
Back Forest Rd STHP PR8 15 J7
Back Forshaw St
WARRN/WOL WA2 16 E1
Back Gillmoss La NG/CROX L11 84 B5
Back Granton Rd EV L5 113 J1
Back Guilford St NPK/KEN L6 113 H3
Back High St RUNC WA7 10 D4
Back Holland Pl EHL/KEN L7 113 K6
Back Hope Pl CLVPS L1 9 J6
Back Huskisson St TOX L8 * 132 E2
Back Kelvin Gv TOX L8 133 F3
Back Knight St CLVPS L1 9 G7
Back La BRSC L40 38 E3
CSBY/BLUN L23 69 G1
ORM L39 64 A4
ORM L39 52 C5
ORM L39 51 F2
RNFD/HAY WA11 76 C4
SKEL WN8 67 G1
WARRW/BUR WA5 159 H1
WARRW/BUR WA5 105 H6
Back Leeds St VAUX/LVPD L3 8 B1
Back Legh St NEWLW WA12 106 A2
Back Lime St CLVPS L1 9 F4
Back Little Canning St
TOX L8 * 132 E2
Back Luton Gv ANF/KKDL L4 97 G5
Back Market St NEWLW WA12 106 A1
Back Maryland St CLVPS L1 * 9 H6
Back Menai St BIRK CH41 2 C5
Back Moss La BRSC L40 39 F2
Back Mount St CSBY/WL L22 * 80 E2
Back Mount Vernon Gn
EHL/KEN L7 * 113 J6
Back Mulberry St EHL/KEN L7 9 K7
Back Oliver St BIRK CH41 3 G5
Back Orford St WAV L15 134 A1
Back O The Town La HTWN L38 60 A4
Back Percy St CLVPS L1 132 E2
Back Pickop St VAUX/LVPD L3 8 D2
Back Renshaw St CLVPS L1 9 H6
Back Rockfield Rd
ANF/KKDL L4 97 H6
Back St Bride St EHL/KEN L7 9 K7
Back Sandon St TOX L8 132 E2
Back Sandown La WAV L15 134 A1
Back Sandstone Rd
CLB/OSW/ST L13 114 D3
Back School La SKEL WN8 55 K4
Back Seaview HOY CH47 127 G2
Back Seel St CLVPS L1 9 F6
Back Sir Howard St EHL/KEN L7 9 K7
Back South Rd CSBY/WL L22 81 F2
Back Stanley Rd BTL L20 5 F4
Back Towerlands St
EHL/KEN L7 113 K6
Back Virginia St STHP PR8 15 F7
Back Wellesley Rd TOX L8 133 F5
Back Windsor Vw TOX L8 * 133 G2
Back Winstanley Rd
CSBY/WL L22 81 F1
Back York Ter EV L5 * 113 G1
Badbury Cl RNFD/HAY WA11 90 C4
Badby Wd NWD/KWIPK L33 72 E5
Baddow Cft WLTN L25 135 F6
Baden Rd CLB/OSW/ST L13 115 F4
Bader Cl PEN/TH CH61 167 J2
Badger Bait NSTN CH64 192 A3
Badger Cl RUNC WA7 187 K1
Badgers Cl GTS/LS CH66 202 D3
Badgers Pk NSTN CH64 192 A3
Badgers Rake FMBY L37 40 C6
Badgersrake La GTS/LS CH66 194 A5
Badger's Set WKBY CH48 146 E5
Badger Wy CL/PREN CH43 149 H3
Badminton St TOX L8 132 E6
Baffin Cl MOR/LEA CH46 110 A3
Bagnall Cl WARRW/BUR WA5 141 K4
Bagnall St ANF/KKDL L4 97 J6
Bagot Av WARRW/BUR WA5 142 C1
Bagot St WAV L15 133 J2
Baguley Av WDN WA8 157 F6
Bahama Cl RNFD/HAY WA11 90 C3
Bahama Rd RNFD/HAY WA11 90 C3
Bailey Av EP CH65 195 J3
Bailey Dr BTL L20 82 B5
Baileys Cl WDN WA8 139 F4
Baileys La HLWD L26 155 K3
SPK/HALE L24 173 F2
Bailey St CLVPS L1 9 G7
Bailey Wy MGHL L31 71 F2
Bainbridge Av
GOL/RIS/CUL WA3 93 G3
Bainton Cl KKBY L32 85 F4
Bainton Rd KKBY L32 85 F4
Baird Av BTL L20 4 A2
Baker Dr GTS/LS CH66 195 H6
Baker Rd RUNC WA7 176 A6
Bakers Green Rd HUY L36 116 E3
Baker's La CHTN/BK PR9 23 H2
Bakers St HUY L36 117 G5
Baker St NPK/KEN L6 113 J4
STHEL WA9 104 A2
Baker Wy NPK/KEN L6 113 J4
Bakewell Cl GTS/LS CH66 202 C3
Bakewell Gv WLT/FAZ L9 82 E4
Bakewell Rd
WARRW/BUR WA5 106 A6
Bala Cl WARRW/BUR WA5 * 122 E5
Bala Gv WAL/EG CH44 * 111 G4
Bala St ANF/KKDL L4 113 K1
Balcarres Av CALD/MH L18 134 A4
Baldock Cl WARRS WA4 144 B6
Baldwin Av CHLDW L16 135 G1
Baldwin St ECCL WA10 13 G4
The Bales NTHTN L30 70 D5
Balfe St LITH L21 81 H5
Balfour Av BTL L20 * 4 D1
Balfour Rd BTL L20 4 C1
CL/PREN CH43 2 A7
Balfour Rd STHP PR8 28 B2
WAL/EG CH44 111 G5
Balfour St ANF/KKDL L4 97 H6
ECCL WA10 12 A6
RUNC WA7 10 C6
Balham Cl WDN WA8 139 F5
Balharry Av RNFD/HAY WA11 90 E4
Balker Dr ECCL WA10 12 E1
Ballantrae Rd CALD/MH L18 134 D6
Ballantyne Dr CL/PREN CH43 110 C6
Ballantyne Gv BTL L20 82 B5
CLB/OSW/ST L13 98 C6
Ballantyne Pl CLB/OSW/ST L13 98 C6
WARRN/WOL WA2 123 G1
Ballantyne Rd
CLB/OSW/ST L13 114 C1
Ballantyne Wy
GOL/RIS/CUL WA3 93 F3
Ballard Rd WKBY CH48 127 K6
Ballater Dr WARRN/WOL WA2 124 A3
Ball Av WAL/NB CH45 95 G5
Balliol Cl CL/PREN CH43 110 C6
Balliol Gv CSBY/BLUN L23 80 C1
Balliol Rd BTL L20 5 F7
Balliol Rd East BTL L20 5 H6
Balliol Wy AIMK WN4 78 E5
Ball Pth WDN WA8 157 K2
Ball's Rd CL/PREN CH43 2 B7
Ball's Rd East BIRK CH41 2 B7
Balmer St STHEL WA9 103 F5
Balmoral Av CSBY/BLUN L23 69 F6
GOL/RIS/CUL WA3 92 E2
STHEL WA9 104 A6
Balmoral Cl CHTN/BK PR9 23 K2
NWD/KWIPK L33 72 D4
Balmoral Ct CLB/OSW/ST L13 114 C2
Balmoral Dr CHTN/BK PR9 23 K2
FMBY L37 48 E4
FROD/HEL WA6 199 J5
Balmoral Gdns
CL/PREN CH43 * 149 J2
EP CH65 203 H1
Balmoral Gv CL/PREN CH43 130 A6
Balmoral Rd AIMK WN4 79 F5
MGHL L31 62 A6
NPK/KEN L6 114 A4
WAL/NB CH45 95 H4
WARRS WA4 162 E1
WDN WA8 139 F5
WLT/FAZ L9 * 82 D5
Balmoral Wy PR/KW L34 117 F2
Balm St EHL/KEN L7 113 K5
Balniel St STHEL WA9 120 B4
Balsham Cl WLTN L25 155 G4
Baltic Rd BTL L20 4 C4
Baltic St ANF/KKDL L4 97 J6
Baltimore Gdns
WARRW/BUR WA5 141 K2
Baltimore St CLVPS L1 9 H6
Bamber Gdns CHTN/BK PR9 23 J5
Bamboo Cl NTHLY L27 136 B3
Bamburgh Ct EP CH65 196 D6
Bamburgh Pl AIMK WN4 79 F4
Bamford Cl RUNC WA7 177 F6
Bampton Av RNFD/HAY WA11 88 E2
Bampton Rd CHLDW L16 134 E1
Banastre Dr NEWLW WA12 107 F2
Banastre Rd STHP PR8 27 H2
Banbury Av WLTN L25 155 F1
Banbury Dr WARRW/BUR WA5 141 K5
Banbury Wy CL/PREN CH43 149 H1
Bancroft Cl WLTN L25 155 F4
Bancroft Rd WDN WA8 158 E1
Bandon Cl SPK/HALE L24 174 E3
Banff Av BEB CH63 183 K2
Bangor Cl GTS/LS CH66 202 C3
Bangor Rd WAL/NB CH45 110 D1
Bangor St EV L5 112 E2
Bankburn Rd CLB/OSW/ST L13 114 C1
Bank Cl NSTN CH64 192 B3
Bank Dene RF/TRAN CH42 151 F3
Bankes' La RUNC WA7 186 B1
Bankfield SKEL WN8 56 E6
Bankfield Ct CLB/OSW/ST L13 114 D2
Bankfield La CHTN/BK PR9 23 K3
Bankfield Rd CLB/OSW/ST L13 114 D2
WDN WA8 157 G2
Bankfields Dr EP CH65 185 F3
PS/BROM CH62 184 E2
Bankfield St BTL L20 96 D5
Bank Gdns WARRW/BUR WA5 141 F5
Bankhall La BTL L20 96 E6
Bankhall St BTL L20 96 E5
Bankhey NSTN CH64 192 A4
Bank House La
FROD/HEL WA6 199 K5
Bankland Rd CLB/OSW/ST L13 114 D2
Bank La MGHL L31 72 B3
Bank Ms FROD/HEL WA6 * 199 K5
Bank Nook CHTN/BK PR9 * 23 H2
Bank Pas GOL/RIS/CUL WA3 * 92 B2
Bank Rd BTL L20 4 D4
Banks Av HOY CH47 127 J1
Banksbarn SKEL WN8 56 E6
Banks Crs WARRS WA4 143 J5
Bankside HTWN L38 59 F4
RUNC WA7 178 D6
WARR WA1 16 A4
Bankside Av AIMK WN4 79 F1
Bankside Rd RF/TRAN CH42 150 E3
Bank's La ALL/GAR L19 172 C1
Bank Sq CHTN/BK PR9 14 E2
Bank's Rd ALL/GAR L19 153 K6
CHTN/BK PR9 21 G5
HES CH60 167 G5
WKBY CH48 146 B2
The Banks WAL/NB CH45 * 94 E6
Bank St BIRK CH41 3 G5
ECCL WA10 12 C6
GOL/RIS/CUL WA3 92 B2
NEWLW WA12 105 K2
WARR WA1 16 D5
WDN WA8 176 D1
Bank's Wy ALL/GAR L19 172 C1
Bankville Rd RF/TRAN CH42 131 H6
Banner Hey RAIN/WH L35 117 K6
Bannerman St EHL/KEN L7 133 J1

Banner St ECCL WA10 12 D6
WAV L15 133 K2
Banner Wk ECCL WA10 12 D6
Banning Cl BIRK CH41 2 D3
Banstead Gv WAV L15 134 C2
Barbara Av AIN/FAZ L10 83 K4
Barbara St STHEL WA9 120 C4
Barbauld St WARR WA1 16 D5
Barberry Cl MOR/LEA CH46 128 C1
Barberry Crs NTHTN L30 70 D5
Barber St STHEL WA9 13 K4
Barbondale Cl
WARRW/BUR WA5 141 G2
Barbour Dr BTL L20 82 B5
Barbrook Wy WLT/FAZ L9 97 K2
Barchester Dr AIG/SPK L17 152 D2
Barclay St TOX L8 * 132 E5
Barcombe Rd HES CH60 168 D4
Bardale Gv AIMK WN4 79 F6
Bardley Crs RAIN/WH L35 136 D2
Bardney Av GOL/RIS/CUL WA3 92 A1
Bardon Cl WLTN L25 135 K4
Bardsay Rd ANF/KKDL L4 97 H4
Bardsey Cl EP CH65 203 G2
Bardsley Av WARRW/BUR WA5 123 F5
Bardsley Cl SKEL WN8 57 J6
Barford Cl CL/PREN CH43 129 J3
SKEL WN8 57 J6
STHP PR8 33 G3
WARRW/BUR WA5 122 B6
Barford Dr GOL/RIS/CUL WA3 93 H3
Barford Gra NSTN CH64 193 J1
Barford Rd HUY L36 117 F1
WLTN L25 154 E5
Barham Ct GOL/RIS/CUL WA3 125 F3
Barholm CL/PREN CH43 * 130 B5
Barington Dr RUNC WA7 178 D6
Barkbeth Rd HUY L36 116 C2
Barkeley Dr LITH L21 81 G5
Barker Cl HUY L36 136 C1
Barker La GR/UP/WCH CH49 147 K1
Barker Rd PEN/TH CH61 148 C5
Barker's Hollow Rd
WARRS WA4 189 F1
Barkerville Cl CLB/OSW/ST L13 98 B6
Barker Wy NPK/KEN L6 113 K2
Barkfield Av FMBY L37 48 E1
Barkfield La FMBY L37 48 D1
Barkhill Ct AIG/SPK L17 * 153 G2
Barkhill Rd AIG/SPK L17 153 G2
Barkiss Cl TOX L8 132 E4
Bark Rd LITH L21 81 K2
Barleycastle La WARRS WA4 163 J6
Barleyfield PEN/TH CH61 167 J1
Barley Mow Cl GTS/LS CH66 202 A1
Barley Rd WARRS WA4 144 B6
Barlow Av BEB CH63 151 F4
Barlow Gv STHEL WA9 104 E3
Barlow La ANF/KKDL L4 97 G5
Barlows Cl WLT/FAZ L9 83 G3
Barlow's La ORM L39 35 F4
WLT/FAZ L9 83 G3
Barlow St ANF/KKDL L4 97 G5
Barmouth Cl
WARRW/BUR WA5 122 E5
Barmouth Rd WAL/NB CH45 110 D1
Barmouth Wy EV L5 112 E2
Barnack Cl WARR WA1 143 K1
Barnacre Dr NSTN CH64 181 G5
Barnacre La WKBY CH48 128 C3
Barnard Rd CL/PREN CH43 2 A7
Barnard St WARRW/BUR WA5 142 A6
Barn Cl NTHTN L30 70 D5
Barn Cft FROD/HEL WA6 199 K5
Barncroft RUNC WA7 178 C6
Barn Croft Rd HLWD L26 155 K4
The Barncroft
GR/UP/WCH CH49 * 128 E5
Barndale Rd CALD/MH L18 134 A5
Barnes Av WARRN/WOL WA2 124 D5
Barnes Cl NWD/KWIPK L33 72 D3
WARRW/BUR WA5 141 H4
WDN WA8 * 158 E1
Barnes Dr MGHL L31 62 A3
Barnes Gn BEB CH63 170 C4
Barnes Rd ORM L39 53 J2
SKEL WN8 55 K4
WDN WA8 158 D1
Barnes St NPK/KEN L6 113 J2
Barneston Rd WDN WA8 139 K6
Barnet Cl EHL/KEN L7 133 H1
Barnett Av NEWLW WA12 105 J2
Barnfield Av RUNC WA7 188 C1
Barnfield Cl GTS/LS CH66 * 202 A1
HOY CH47 108 C6
NTHTN L30 82 B1
WD/CROXPK L12 115 F1
Barnfield Dr SKEL WN8 57 G6
WD/CROXPK L12 115 F1
Barnfield Rd WARR WA1 144 B2
Barnham Cl GOL/RIS/CUL WA3 92 B3
SPK/HALE L24 173 G1
Barnham Dr CHLDW L16 135 F2
Barn Hey HOY CH47 127 F4
Barn Hey Crs HOY CH47 128 A1
Barn Hey Gn WD/CROXPK L12 115 F1
Barn Hey Rd NWD/KWIPK L33 85 F1
Barnhill Rd WAV L15 134 B3
Barnhurst Cl CHLDW L16 135 F2
Barnhurst Rd CHLDW L16 135 F2
Barn La GOL/RIS/CUL WA3 92 A4
Barnmeadow Rd WLTN L25 135 H4
Barnsbury Rd ANF/KKDL L4 97 K3
Barnsdale Av PEN/TH CH61 148 E6
Barnside Ct CHLDW L16 135 F2
Barnstaple Wy
WARRW/BUR WA5 141 F5
Barnston Av EP CH65 195 J4
Barnston La MOR/LEA CH46 109 J6
Barnston Rd HES CH60 168 C5
PEN/TH CH61 148 E4
WLT/FAZ L9 82 D4
Barnston Towers Cl HES CH60 168 C5
Barnstream Cl NTHLY L27 135 K2
Barn St WDN WA8 158 B5
Barnswood Cl WARRS WA4 163 H1
Barnton Cl GOL/RIS/CUL WA3 92 E4
Barn Wy NEWLW WA12 106 B2
Barnwell Av WAL/EG CH44 111 H2
Barnwood GTS/LS CH66 194 C2
Barnwood Rd HUY L36 116 B3
Baron Cl WARR WA1 144 C2
Baroncroft Rd WLTN L25 135 G5
Baronet Ms WARRS WA4 161 K2
Baron's Cl WDN WA8 157 H3
Baron's Hey STBRV L28 99 K5
Barren Gv CL/PREN CH43 130 E5
Barrett Av STHP PR8 27 H5
Barrett Rd STHP PR8 27 H5
Barrington Dr STHP PR8 33 H4
Barrington Rd WAL/EG CH44 111 J4
WAV L15 133 K3
Barrison Gn BRSC L40 45 J1
Barrow Av WARRN/WOL WA2 124 A5
Barrow Cl WD/CROXPK L12 99 G4
Barrowdale Rd
GOL/RIS/CUL WA3 92 C3
Barrowfield Rd ECCL WA10 87 H6
Barrow Hall La
WARRW/BUR WA5 141 F2
Barrow La WARRN/WOL WA2 107 J3
Barrow Nook La ORM L39 64 E4
Barrow's Green La WDN WA8 139 K5
Barrow's Rw WDN WA8 139 G5
Barrow St AIMK WN4 79 J4
ECCL WA10 13 G5
Barrule Cl WARRS WA4 162 C4
Barry Cl EP CH65 203 G3
Barry Dr ALL/GAR L19 153 J5
Barrymore Av WARRS WA4 143 J5
Barrymore Rd
CLB/OSW/ST L13 114 D4
RUNC WA7 176 E6
WARRS WA4 163 F2
Barrymore Wy BEB CH63 183 J1
Barry St WARRS WA4 17 G7
Barsbank Cl LYMM WA13 145 H6
Barsbank La LYMM WA13 145 H6
Bartholomew Cl RAIN/WH L35 119 G6
Bartlegate RUNC WA7 188 A2
Bartlett St WAV L15 133 K2
Barton Av WARRS WA4 143 K6
Barton Cl ECCL WA10 12 E4
HOY CH47 126 E3
LITH L21 81 H1
RUNC WA7 178 C6
Barton Clough
WGNW/BIL/OR WN5 77 H4
Barton Hey Dr WKBY CH48 146 D5
Barton Heys Rd FMBY L37 48 D4
Barton Rd HOY CH47 127 F3
WLT/FAZ L9 97 H1
Bartons Cl CHTN/BK PR9 21 G6
Barton St BIRK CH41 2 C5
GOL/RIS/CUL WA3 92 B3
Barwell Av RNFD/HAY WA11 89 F5
Barwell Cl GOL/RIS/CUL WA3 92 D2
Basil Cl CHLDW L16 135 F1
Basildon Cl STHEL WA9 119 G1
Basil Rd CHLDW L16 134 E1
Basing St ALL/GAR L19 153 K5
Baskervyle Cl HES CH60 181 F1
Baskervyle Rd HES CH60 181 F1
Basnett St CLVPS L1 8 E4
Bassendale Rd
PS/BROM CH62 171 G3
Bassenthwaite Av
CL/PREN CH43 130 A4
NWD/KWIPK L33 72 C5
RNFD/HAY WA11 88 D3
Bates Crs ECCL WA10 103 F5
Bates La FROD/HEL WA6 200 A6
Batey Av RAIN/WH L35 118 D3
Batherton Cl WDN WA8 18 E6
Bathgate Wy NWD/KWIPK L33 72 C3
Bath Springs ORM L39 45 K6
Bath St CHTN/BK PR9 14 E3
CSBY/WL L22 80 E3
ECCL WA10 12 E6
PS/BROM CH62 151 G6
VAUX/LVPD L3 8 A2
WARR WA1 16 C4
Bath St North CHTN/BK PR9 15 F2
Bathurst Rd ALL/GAR L19 153 J4
Bathwood Dr NSTN CH64 191 K4
Batley St CLB/OSW/ST L13 114 E4
Battenberg St EHL/KEN L7 113 J5
Battersby La WARRN/WOL WA2 17 F2
Battersea Ct WDN WA8 * 138 E6
Battery Cl AIG/SPK L17 152 D1
Battery La WARR WA1 144 E3
Battle Wy FMBY L37 * 49 H3
Baucher Dr BTL L20 82 B4
Baumville Dr BEB CH63 170 B3
Bawtry Ct WARRN/WOL WA2 124 A6
Baxter Cl RUNC WA7 178 C6
Baxters La STHEL WA9 104 B5
Baxter St WARRW/BUR WA5 142 B4
Baycliffe LYMM WA13 164 E1
Baycliffe Cl RUNC WA7 187 G2
Baycliff Rd WD/CROXPK L12 99 J5
Bayfield Rd ALL/GAR L19 153 H4
Bayhorse La VAUX/LVPD L3 9 J2
Baysdale Cl TOX L8 133 F5
Bayswater Cl RUNC WA7 178 E1
Bayswater Gdns WAL/NB CH45 94 D6
Bayswater Rd WAL/NB CH45 110 D1
Baythorne Rd ANF/KKDL L4 98 A3
Baytree Cl CHTN/BK PR9 21 G6
GTS/LS CH66 202 D2
Baytree Gv MGHL L31 71 K6
Bay Tree Gv STHEL WA9 104 A5
Baytree Rd RF/TRAN CH42 131 H6
WKBY CH48 147 G1
Bayview Dr WAL/NB CH45 94 D6
Bayvil Cl RUNC WA7 178 D6
Beacham Rd STHP PR8 23 G6
Beach Bank CSBY/WL L22 80 D1
Beachcroft Rd HOY CH47 108 B6
Beach Gv WAL/NB CH45 95 J6
Beach Lawn CSBY/WL L22 80 D2
Beach Priory Gdns STHP PR8 14 B6
Beach Rd HOY CH47 126 E3
LITH L21 81 H3
STHP PR8 14 A7
Beach Wk WKBY CH48 146 C3
Beacon Dr WKBY CH48 146 D1
Beacon Gv RNFD/HAY WA11 89 G5
Beacon Hl
WGNW/BIL/OR WN5 * 77 G2
Beacon Hill Vw RUNC WA7 176 A6
Beacon La EV L5 113 H1
HES CH60 168 A5
Beacon Rd
WGNW/BIL/OR WN5 77 G3
Beaconsfield Cl
RF/TRAN CH42 131 J6
Beaconsfield Crs WDN WA8 139 F5
Beaconsfield Gv WDN WA8 139 G5
Beaconsfield Rd CHTN/BK PR9 28 C1
ECCL WA10 87 K6
LITH L21 81 G4
PS/BROM CH62 151 G4
RUNC WA7 176 B5
WDN WA8 139 G6
WLTN L25 135 F6
Beaconsfield St TOX L8 133 F3
Beaconsfield Ter
ALL/GAR L19 * 153 J5
Beacon St EV L5 112 D1
Beacon View Dr SKEL WN8 57 K6
Beadnell Dr
WARRW/BUR WA5 141 F6
Beames Cl EHL/KEN L7 114 A6
Beamont St WDN WA8 176 D1
Beardsmore Dr
GOL/RIS/CUL WA3 93 F2
Bearncroft SKEL WN8 66 E1
Beasley Cl GTS/LS CH66 195 G6
Beatrice Av BEB CH63 150 D4
Beatrice St BTL L20 97 F4
WARRS WA4 143 G6
Beattock Cl NWD/KWIPK L33 72 C3
Beatty Av WARRN/WOL WA2 123 J6
Beatty Cl RAIN/WH L35 117 K5
WKBY CH48 * 146 D5
Beatty Rd CLB/OSW/ST L13 114 E5
STHP PR8 28 B2
Beauclair Dr WAV L15 134 C3
Beaufort FMBY L37 49 G3
Beaufort Cl ORM L39 52 E4
RUNC WA7 176 E6
WARRW/BUR WA5 141 H4
WDN WA8 157 F3
Beaufort Dr WAL/EG CH44 110 E3
Beaufort Rd BIRK CH41 111 G6
Beaufort St STHEL WA9 104 A4
TOX L8 132 D3
WARRW/BUR WA5 142 B5
Beaumaris Dr EP CH65 203 H1
PEN/TH CH61 148 E5
Beaumaris Rd WAL/NB CH45 110 D1
Beaumaris St BTL L20 96 D5
Beaumaris Wy RUNC WA7 177 J3
Beaumont Av ECCL WA10 102 E1
Beaumont Crs ORM L39 53 H3
Beaumont Dr AIN/FAZ L10 83 H2
Beaumont St TOX L8 133 G2
Beau St VAUX/LVPD L3 113 G4
Beauworth Av
GR/UP/WCH CH49 * 128 D6
Beaver Ct AIMK WN4 79 H3
Beaver Gv WLT/FAZ L9 82 D5
Beavers La SKEL WN8 67 F1
Bebington Rd GTS/LS CH66 195 G5
PS/BROM CH62 151 F5
RF/TRAN CH42 150 C1
Bebles Rd ORM L39 53 G2
Bechers WDN WA8 138 A6
Bechers Dr WLT/FAZ L9 83 F1
Bechers Rw WLT/FAZ L9 82 C4
Beck Cl AIN/FAZ L10 84 A4
Beckenham Av CALD/MH L18 134 A4
Beckenham Rd WAL/NB CH45 95 H4
Becket St ANF/KKDL L4 97 F6
Beckett Cl NWD/KWIPK L33 85 H3
Beckett Dr WARRN/WOL WA2 123 G2
Beckett Gv BEB CH63 150 C4
Beck Gv RNFD/HAY WA11 88 E3
Beck Rd BTL L20 81 K6
Beckwith St BIRK CH41 2 A1
CLVPS L1 8 E7
Beckwith St East BIRK CH41 2 E3
Becky St NPK/KEN L6 113 K2
Becontree Rd
WD/CROXPK L12 115 H3
Bective St EHL/KEN L7 * 133 H1
Bedburn Dr HUY L36 116 A4
Bedford Av EP CH65 202 E1
MGHL L31 71 H3
RF/TRAN CH42 150 D2
Bedford Av East EP CH65 203 F1
Bedford Cl EHL/KEN L7 9 K7
HUY L36 117 G4
Bedford Dr RF/TRAN CH42 150 C2
Bedford Gdns
RF/TRAN CH42 * 151 F1
Bedford Pl AIMK WN4 79 F4
BTL L20 96 D4
LITH L21 * 81 G4
RF/TRAN CH42 151 F1
Bedford Rd ANF/KKDL L4 5 K7
BTL L20 96 E4
RF/TRAN CH42 150 E1
STHP PR8 27 H5
WAL/NB CH45 111 H1
Bedford Rd East
RF/TRAN CH42 151 F1
Bedford St STHEL WA9 104 B3
WARRS WA4 162 B3
Bedford St North EHL/KEN L7 9 K5
Bedford St South
EHL/KEN L7 9 K7
Bedford Wk EHL/KEN L7 9 K7
Beecham Cl HUY L36 116 D6
Beech Av AIG/SPK L17 152 C1
CSBY/BLUN L23 69 H3
FROD/HEL WA6 201 F1
GOL/RIS/CUL WA3 93 G4
GR/UP/WCH CH49 128 E3
MGHL L31 72 A6
PEN/TH CH61 168 A1
PR/KW L34 118 B1
RNFD/HAY WA11 90 E4
STHEL WA9 120 A3
WARRS WA4 144 C6
WARRW/BUR WA5 140 D6
Beechbank Rd CALD/MH L18 133 K4
Beechburn Crs HUY L36 116 B4
Beechburn Rd HUY L36 116 A4
Beech Cl KKBY L32 72 B6
NEWLW WA12 106 C3
SKEL WN8 56 A4
WD/CROXPK L12 99 H2
Beech Ct CALD/MH L18 153 K1
RF/TRAN CH42 131 G5
Beechcroft Dr EP CH65 196 A6
Beechcroft Rd WAL/EG CH44 111 J5
Beechdale Rd CALD/MH L18 134 B5
Beechdene Rd ANF/KKDL L4 97 K6
Beech Dr FMBY L37 48 D1
The Beeches CALD/MH L18 134 E4
FROD/HEL WA6 199 K5
GTS/LS CH66 195 G5
MOR/LEA CH46 109 J4
RF/TRAN CH42 * 151 F2
STHEL WA9 120 B2
Beechfield MGHL L31 62 C6
Beechfield Cl HES CH60 167 K6
HLWD L26 155 H5
Beechfield Gdns STHP PR8 14 B6
Beechfield Rd CALD/MH L18 134 E5
EP CH65 6 C4
WARRS WA4 163 F2
Beech Gdns RNFD/HAY WA11 75 F2
Beech Gn WD/CROXPK L12 98 E5
Beech Gv CHTN/BK PR9 23 G6
GTS/LS CH66 202 E3
LITH L21 81 G5
LYMM WA13 164 C1
NTHTN L30 82 D1
WARR WA1 143 K2
WLT/FAZ L9 * 82 E5
Beech Hey La NSTN CH64 183 J6
Beechill Cl WLTN L25 135 K5
Beech La CALD/MH L18 134 D4
Beech Lawn ALL/GAR L19 153 G4
Beech Meadow ORM L39 54 A1
Beech Mdw PR/KW L34 117 G2
Beechmoore WARRS WA4 160 E6
Beech Pk WD/CROXPK L12 114 E1
Beech Rd ANF/KKDL L4 97 J4
BEB CH63 150 E4
GOL/RIS/CUL WA3 92 B2
HES CH60 168 C5
HUY L36 116 E6
ORM L39 62 E1
RF/TRAN CH42 131 F5
RUNC WA7 177 F5
WARRS WA4 162 B3
Beech St AIMK WN4 79 F3
BTL L20 5 F2
ECCL WA10 * 103 F5
EHL/KEN L7 114 A5
Beech Ter EHL/KEN L7 * 114 A5
Beechtree Farm Cl
KNUT WA16 165 K4
Beech Tree Houses
WGNE/HIN WN2 79 K3
Beechtree La KNUT WA16 165 K4
Beechtree Rd WAV L15 115 F6
Beechtrees SKEL WN8 56 E6
Beechurst Cl WLTN L25 135 J4
Beechurst Rd WLTN L25 135 J4
The Beechwalk
CLB/OSW/ST L13 115 F3
Beechway BEB CH63 170 B2
MGHL L31 63 F5
Beechway Av MGHL L31 62 E5
Beechways WARRS WA4 162 C6
Beechways Dr NSTN CH64 191 J1
Beechwood SKEL WN8 56 E2
Beechwood Av AIMK WN4 91 F1
HLWD L26 155 H4
NEWLW WA12 106 D1
RUNC WA7 187 F1
WAL/NB CH45 110 E2
WARR WA1 143 H1
WARRW/BUR WA5 141 G4
Beechwood Cl ALL/GAR L19 153 H4
RAIN/WH L35 118 A3
Beechwood Dr
CL/PREN CH43 129 J2
FMBY L37 48 C4
GTS/LS CH66 202 B2
ORM L39 53 H1
Beechwood Gdns
ALL/GAR L19 153 G4
Beechwood Rd ALL/GAR L19 153 G4
LITH L21 81 J5
PS/BROM CH62 170 E5
Beecroft Cl WARRW/BUR WA5 122 D6
Beesands Cl NTHLY L27 136 C5
Beesley Rd PR/KW L34 117 J1
Beeston Cl CL/PREN CH43 129 K3
GOL/RIS/CUL WA3 125 F3
Beeston Ct RUNC WA7 * 178 B1
Beeston Dr NTHTN L30 70 E4
PEN/TH CH61 167 J1
Beeston Gn GTS/LS CH66 195 H4
Beeston Gv ALL/GAR L19 153 H4
Beeston St ANF/KKDL L4 97 G5
Beetham Wy NWD/KWIPK L33 72 E6
Begonia Gdns STHEL WA9 104 E6
Beilby Rd RNFD/HAY WA11 90 E4
Beldale Pk KKBY L32 72 B5
Beldon Crs HUY L36 116 B4
Belem Cl AIG/SPK L17 133 H4
Belfast Rd CLB/OSW/ST L13 115 F4
Belfield SKEL WN8 67 F1
Belfield Crs HUY L36 116 E6
Belfield Dr CL/PREN CH43 130 E6
Belford Dr MOR/LEA CH46 128 C1
Belfort Rd WLTN L25 135 J5
Belfry Cl MOR/LEA CH46 109 F6
WD/CROXPK L12 115 J1
Belgrave Av WAL/EG CH44 111 J3
WARR WA1 143 J2
Belgrave Cl LEIGH WN7 93 K3
WDN WA8 139 K6
Belgrave Dr EP CH65 195 J4
Belgrave Rd AIG/SPK L17 133 G6
LITH L21 81 G4
STHP PR8 27 G3
Belgrave St WAL/EG CH44 111 J2
Belgravia Ct WDN WA8 138 E6
Belhaven Rd CALD/MH L18 134 A4
Bellair Av CSBY/BLUN L23 69 H5
Bellairs Rd NG/CROX L11 98 C5
Bellamy Rd ANF/KKDL L4 5 K7
Bellcast Cl WARRS WA4 162 B5
Bell Cl HUY L36 136 C1
Belldene Gv HES CH60 167 K3
Bellefield Av WD/CROXPK L12 115 F1
Bellemonte Rd
FROD/HEL WA6 200 E3
Belle Vale Rd WLTN L25 135 J5
Belle Vue Rd WAL/EG CH44 112 A5
WLTN L25 135 J4
Bellew Rd NG/CROX L11 98 D6
Bellfield Crs WAL/NB CH45 95 G5
Bellflower Cl WDN WA8 138 D5
Bellgreen Rd NG/CROX L11 98 E3
Bellhouse La WARRS WA4 163 H2
WARRS WA4 161 G4
Bell House Rd WDN WA8 19 H2
Bellingham Dr RUNC WA7 176 D5
Bellini Cl LITH L21 81 G6
Bellis Av CHTN/BK PR9 23 G3
Bellis Gv NWD/KWIPK L33 * 72 C4
Bell La RAIN/WH L35 119 J5
WARRS WA4 144 D5
Bellmore St ALL/GAR L19 153 K4
Bell Rd WAL/EG CH44 111 K4
Bell's Cl MGHL L31 61 K3
Bell's La MGHL L31 61 J4
Bell St CLB/OSW/ST L13 114 E4
Belltower Rd BTL L20 96 D6
Bellward Cl BEB CH63 170 B3
Belmont BIRK CH41 2 B7
Belmont Av GOL/RIS/CUL WA3 92 D2
PS/BROM CH62 170 E4
WARRS WA4 143 J6
Belmont Cl BRSC L40 38 E6
Belmont Crs
WARRW/BUR WA5 141 G3
Belmont Dr NPK/KEN L6 114 A2
PEN/TH CH61 168 A2
Belmont Gv CL/PREN CH43 2 B7
NPK/KEN L6 114 A2
Belmont Rd NPK/KEN L6 113 K2
WAL/NB CH45 95 H4
WDN WA8 158 E1
WKBY CH48 127 G6
Belmont St ECCL WA10 12 A6
STHP PR8 14 C7
Beloe St TOX L8 132 E5
Belper St ALL/GAR L19 153 J5
Belsford Wy SPK/HALE L24 173 G1
Belston Rd CHLDW L16 134 E2
Belton Cl GOL/RIS/CUL WA3 92 B4
Belton Rd HUY L36 116 D1
Belvedere Av STHEL WA9 120 B1
Belvedere Cl FROD/HEL WA6 187 F6
PR/KW L34 102 A6
Belvedere Dr FMBY L37 49 F4
Belvedere Pk ORM L39 53 G6
Belvedere Rd AIMK WN4 79 H6
NEWLW WA12 106 B1
STHP PR8 33 J4
Belvidere Pk CSBY/BLUN L23 69 F6
Belvidere Rd CSBY/BLUN L23 68 E6
TOX L8 133 F4
WAL/NB CH45 111 F1
Belvoir Rd CALD/MH L18 153 K3
WARRS WA4 162 A3
WDN WA8 19 F1
Bembridge Cl
WARRW/BUR WA5 140 D2
WDN WA8 138 E5
Bempton Rd AIG/SPK L17 152 C1
Benbow Cl BIRK CH41 130 C1
Benbow St BTL L20 4 C7
Bendee Av NSTN CH64 192 B2
Bendee Rd NSTN CH64 192 A2
Benedict Cl GR/UP/WCH CH49 129 J5
Benedict Ct BTL L20 96 E4
Benedict St BTL L20 97 F4
Bengarth Rd CHTN/BK PR9 23 H5
Bengel St EHL/KEN L7 113 J5
Benjamin Fold AIMK WN4 79 G4
Ben La ORM L39 65 G5
Ben Lane Ct ORM L39 65 H5
Benledi St EV L5 113 F2
Benmore Rd CALD/MH L18 153 H1
Bennet Cl NSTN CH64 193 H1
Bennet's La HOY CH47 108 C5
Bennett Av WARR WA1 143 J3
Bennetts Hl CL/PREN CH43 130 E5
Bennett's La WDN WA8 159 F1
Bennett St ALL/GAR L19 153 K5
WARR WA1 16 E5
Ben Nevis Dr GTS/LS CH66 194 C3
Ben Nevis Rd RF/TRAN CH42 150 C1
Bennison Dr ALL/GAR L19 * 153 H4
Ben's Ct PR/KW L34 85 G6
Benson Cl
GR/UP/WCH CH49 129 G5
Benson Rd
GOL/RIS/CUL WA3 125 F5
Benson St CLVPS L1 9 G5
Bentfield AIG/SPK L17 153 G3
Bentfield Cl BEB CH63 150 C4
Bentfield Gdns BEB CH63 150 C4
Bentham Av
WARRN/WOL WA2 123 J4
Bentham Cl CL/PREN CH43 130 B6
Bentham Dr CHLDW L16 134 E1
Bentham St STHP PR8 27 J2
Bentham's Wy STHP PR8 27 K5
Bentinck Cl BIRK CH41 2 C4
Bentinck Pl BIRK CH41 2 C5
Bentinck St BIRK CH41 2 C5
EV L5 112 D2
RUNC WA7 10 B3
STHEL WA9 104 B4
Bentley Rd CL/PREN CH43 130 E5
PEN/TH CH61 148 C6
TOX L8 133 G3
Bentley St STHEL WA9 120 A3
Benton Cl EV L5 113 F1
Benty Cl BEB CH63 170 A1
Benty Farm Gv PEN/TH CH61 148 D6
Benty Heath La NSTN CH64 183 H4
Benwick Rd KKBY L32 84 A2
Berbice Rd WAV L15 134 B3
Beresford Av BEB CH63 151 F5
Beresford Cl CL/PREN CH43 130 D4
Beresford Dr CHTN/BK PR9 23 H4
Beresford Gdns CHTN/BK PR9 23 H3

Beresford Rd CL/PREN CH43 130 D4
TOX L8 132 E5
WAL/NB CH45 95 F6
Beresford St BTL L20 96 D4
EV L5 113 G3
STHEL WA9 103 G6
Beresford St WARR WA1 17 K1
Bergen Cl BTL L20 5 J6
Berkeley Av CL/PREN CH43 149 H2
Berkeley Cl LEIGH WN7 93 K3
Berkeley Ct NEWLW WA12 105 K1
Berkeley Dr WAL/NB CH45 95 J6
Berkeley Rd CSBY/BLUN L23 68 D4
Berkeswell Rd NG/CROX L11 98 E4
Berkley Av WD/CROXPK L12 99 H5
Berkley St TOX L8 132 E2
Berkshire Dr WARR WA1 144 C2
Berkshire Gdns ECCL WA10 103 H3
Bermondsey Gv WDN WA8 139 J5
Bermuda Rd MOR/LEA CH46 109 G6
Bernard Av WAL/NB CH45 * 95 J6
WARRS WA4 162 C3
Berner's Rd ALL/GAR L19 153 J4
Berner St BIRK CH41 2 D1
Berrington Av WLTN L25 154 D1
Berrington Gv AIMK WN4 79 F6
Berrington's La
RNFD/HAY WA11 87 K1
Berry Cl GTS/LS CH66 195 F6
SKEL WN8 56 B3
Berry Dr GTS/LS CH66 195 F5
Berryford Rd DV/KA/FCH L14 115 K1
Berry Hill Av PR/KW L34 100 D2
Berry House Rd BRSC L40 31 F3
Berrylands Cl MOR/LEA CH46 109 H6
Berrylands Rd MOR/LEA CH46 109 H5
Berry Rd WDN WA8 157 J2
Berrys La STHEL WA9 104 D4
Berry St BTL L20 4 D5
CLVPS L1 9 G7
SKEL WN8 56 A3
Berrywood Dr RAIN/WH L35 118 B5
Bertha Gdns BIRK CH41 130 C1
Bertha St BIRK CH41 130 C1
Bertram Cl HOY CH47 127 J1
Bertram Dr HOY CH47 127 H1
Bertram Dr North HOY CH47 127 J1
Bertram Rd AIG/SPK L17 133 H5
Bertram St NEWLW WA12 106 A2
Berwick Av PS/BROM CH62 184 B3
STHP PR8 33 J3
Berwick Cl CL/PREN CH43 * 129 K3
MOR/LEA CH46 128 C1
NPK/KEN L6 113 K3
WARR WA1 144 D3
Berwick Dr CSBY/BLUN L23 68 D4
Berwick Gdns GTS/LS CH66 194 E3
Berwick Gv GTS/LS CH66 194 E3
Berwick Rd GTS/LS CH66 194 C3
Berwick St NPK/KEN L6 113 K3
Berwyn Av HOY CH47 * 127 H2
PEN/TH CH61 * 148 D5
Berwyn Bvd BEB CH63 150 D3
Berwyn Cl GTS/LS CH66 194 D3
Berwyn Dr PEN/TH CH61 167 K3
Berwyn Gv STHEL WA9 104 D2
Berwyn Rd ANF/KKDL L4 98 A5
WAL/EG CH44 111 J2
Beryl Rd CL/PREN CH43 129 K4
Beryl St CLB/OSW/ST L13 114 E6
Bescar Brow La BRSC L40 36 C2
Bescar La BRSC L40 36 E1
Besford Rd WLTN L25 135 J4
Bessborough Rd
CL/PREN CH43 130 E5
Bessbrook Rd AIG/SPK L17 152 E1
Bessemer St TOX L8 132 E5
Beta Cl PS/BROM CH62 151 F4
Betchworth Crs RUNC WA7 187 G1
Bethany Cl RNFD/HAY WA11 89 K4
Bethel Gv AIG/SPK L17 133 J3
Betjeman Cl WARRS WA4 143 J5
Betjeman Gv CHLDW L16 135 F1
Betony Cl HLWD L26 155 H2
Bettisfield Av PS/BROM CH62 184 A2
Betula Cl WLT/FAZ L9 98 A1
Beulah Av WGNW/BIL/OR WN5 77 G5
Bevan Cl STHEL WA9 119 F1
WARRW/BUR WA5 142 A3
Bevan's La WD/CROXPK L12 99 H6
Beverley Av WARRS WA4 162 C3
Beverley Cl CHTN/BK PR9 21 F6
Beverley Dr HES CH60 168 B6
Beverley Gdns PEN/TH CH61 148 E5
Beverley Rd PS/BROM CH62 151 G3
WAL/NB CH45 111 F1
WARRW/BUR WA5 141 K3
WAV L15 134 B3
Beverley Wy GTS/LS CH66 194 E2
Beversbrook Rd NG/CROX L11 99 F3
Bevington Bush
VAUX/LVPD L3 113 F4
Bevington St AIMK WN4 78 E4
VAUX/LVPD L3 113 F3
Bevyl Rd NSTN CH64 181 G5
Bewcastle Dr BRSC L40 54 B2
Bewey Cl TOX L8 132 D5
Bewley Dr KKBY L32 84 C2
Bewsey Farm Cl
WARRW/BUR WA5 142 A1
Bewsey Park Cl
WARRW/BUR WA5 142 C2
Bewsey Rd WARRW/BUR WA5 142 C2
Bewsey St ECCL WA10 103 F4
WARRN/WOL WA2 16 C3
Bexhill Av WARRN/WOL WA2 123 H3
Bexhill Cl SPK/HALE L24 173 G1
Bexhill Gdns STHEL WA9 118 E1
Bianca St BTL L20 96 E4
Bibby Av WARR WA1 143 H3
Bibby Rd CHTN/BK PR9 23 J4
Bibby's La BTL L20 4 B1
Bibby St CLB/OSW/ST L13 114 D4
Bickerstaffe St ECCL WA10 13 H5
VAUX/LVPD L3 113 G4
Bickerton Av BEB CH63 150 C3
FROD/HEL WA6 201 G2
Bickerton Cl
GOL/RIS/CUL WA3 125 F3
Bickerton Rd STHP PR8 27 G3
Bickerton St AIG/SPK L17 133 H6
Bickley Cl RUNC WA7 11 H7
WARRN/WOL WA2 124 B4
Bicknell Cl WARRW/BUR WA5 141 J1
Bidder St VAUX/LVPD L3 9 H1
Bideford Av STHEL WA9 120 A2
Bideford Rd
WARRW/BUR WA5 141 F5
Bidston Av BIRK CH41 130 C2
RNFD/HAY WA11 89 G6
WAL/NB CH45 110 E1
Bidston Gn GTS/LS CH66 195 G5
Bidston Green Ct
CL/PREN CH43 * 129 K1
Bidston Green Dr
CL/PREN CH43 129 K1
Bidston Moss WAL/EG CH44 110 D4
Bidston Rd ANF/KKDL L4 97 K5
CL/PREN CH43 130 C3
Bidston Station Ap
CL/PREN CH43 110 C5
Bidston Village Rd
CL/PREN CH43 110 C6
Bidston Wy RNFD/HAY WA11 89 G6
Bigdale Dr NWD/KWIPK L33 73 F6
Biggin Ct WARRN/WOL WA2 124 A6
Bigham Rd NPK/KEN L6 114 A4
Biglands Dr HUY L36 136 C1
Big Meadow Rd
GR/UP/WCH CH49 129 H5
Billinge Crs RNFD/HAY WA11 89 G5
Billinge La ORM L39 63 J2
Billinge Rd AIMK WN4 78 A4
Billingham Rd STHEL WA9 103 F6
Billings Cl EV L5 112 E1
Billington Av NEWLW WA12 91 G5
Billington Cl
WARRW/BUR WA5 141 F1
Billington Rd WDN WA8 138 A5
Bilston Rd AIG/SPK L17 153 F3
Bilton Cl WDN WA8 159 F1
Bingley Rd ANF/KKDL L4 97 K6
Binns Rd EHL/KEN L7 114 C5
Binns Wy CLB/OSW/ST L13 114 D6
Binsey Cl GR/UP/WCH CH49 128 E4
Birbeck Rd NWD/KWIPK L33 73 F6
Birchall St BTL L20 96 E6
Birch Av BRSC L40 38 E5
ECCL WA10 88 C5
GR/UP/WCH CH49 128 E3
WARRN/WOL WA2 123 G3
WLT/FAZ L9 82 E5
Birchcliffe Rd RF/TRAN CH42 150 E1
Birch Cl CL/PREN CH43 130 E6
MGHL L31 62 D6
RAIN/WH L35 118 A3
Birch Crs NEWLW WA12 105 K1
Birchdale Cl
GR/UP/WCH CH49 128 E4
Birchdale Ct WARRS WA4 162 B3
Birchdale Crs WARRS WA4 162 B3
Birchdale Rd CSBY/WL L22 80 E1
WARR WA1 143 K2
WARRS WA4 162 B4
WLT/FAZ L9 82 D6
Birchen Rd HLWD L26 155 K4
Birches Cl HES CH60 168 A4
The Birches FMBY L37 40 E6
STBRV L28 100 A6
WAL/EG CH44 112 A5
Birchfield MOR/LEA CH46 128 D2
Birchfield Av WDN WA8 158 B1
Birchfield Cl EHL/KEN L7 114 C5
MOR/LEA CH46 128 D3
Birchfield Rd ANF/KKDL L4 97 J4
EHL/KEN L7 114 C5
WARRW/BUR WA5 141 J4
WDN WA8 139 F6
Birchfield St STHEL WA9 103 F6
VAUX/LVPD L3 9 H1
Birchfield Wy MGHL L31 61 K2
Birch Gdns ECCL WA10 88 C5
Birch Gn FMBY L37 40 D6
Birch Green Rd SKEL WN8 56 D2
Birch Gv AIMK WN4 78 B4
GTS/LS CH66 202 E2
HUY L36 116 D5
RAIN/WH L35 118 A3
WAL/NB CH45 95 J6
WARR WA1 143 J2
WARRS WA4 143 G6
WAV L15 114 E6
Birch Heys WKBY CH48 147 H2
Birchill Rd NWD/KWIPK L33 85 H1
Birchley Av
WGNW/BIL/OR WN5 77 F6
Birchley Rd RNFD/HAY WA11 76 E6
WGNW/BIL/OR WN5 77 F6
Birchley St ECCL WA10 13 H3
Birchley Vw RNFD/HAY WA11 88 E1
Birchmere HES CH60 167 J3
Birchmuir Hey KKBY L32 84 E2
Birchridge Cl PS/BROM CH62 170 E3
Birch Rd BEB CH63 170 C1
CL/PREN CH43 130 E6
HOY CH47 127 K1
HUY L36 116 E6
RNFD/HAY WA11 90 D4
RUNC WA7 177 F5
WDN WA8 139 F6
Birch's Brow ORM L39 52 C3
Birch St EV L5 112 D2
SKEL WN8 56 A4
STHP PR8 27 J4
Birch Tree Av
RNFD/HAY WA11 88 C3
Birch Tree Ct WD/CROXPK L12 114 E1
Birchtree Dr MGHL L31 71 K6
Birchtree Rd AIG/SPK L17 133 K6
Birch Tree Rd
GOL/RIS/CUL WA3 93 C3
Birchview Wy CL/PREN CH43 130 A4
Birchway HES CH60 181 H1
Birchways WARRS WA4 162 D6
Birchwood Av BIRK CH41 2 E3
Birchwood Bvd
GOL/RIS/CUL WA3 125 F5
Birchwood Cl BIRK CH41 2 E3
CHNE CH2 198 D5
GTS/LS CH66 202 B2
Birchwood Park Av
GOL/RIS/CUL WA3 125 F2
Birchwood Wy
GOL/RIS/CUL WA3 125 H3
NWD/KWIPK L33 73 F4
WARRN/WOL WA2 124 C6
Bird St EHL/KEN L7 133 H2
Birdwell Dr WARRW/BUR WA5 141 H4
Birdwood Rd NG/CROX L11 98 D5
Birkdale Av BEB CH63 183 K1
Birkdale Cl HUY L36 116 C6
NPK/KEN L6 114 B1
Birkdale Cop STHP PR8 28 B6
Birkdale Rd WARRW/BUR WA5 141 G5
WDN WA8 139 G4
Birkenhead Rd HOY CH47 127 H1
NSTN CH64 183 F6
WAL/EG CH44 112 A6
Birkenshaw Av CSBY/BLUN L23 68 C5
Birket Av MOR/LEA CH46 109 K4
Birket Cl MOR/LEA CH46 110 A4
Birket Sq MOR/LEA CH46 109 K4
Birkett Av EP CH65 203 G1
Birkett Rd RF/TRAN CH42 150 D2
WKBY CH48 127 G5
Birkett St VAUX/LVPD L3 9 G1
Birkey La FMBY L37 49 F3
Birkin Cl KKBY L32 85 F3
Birkin Rd KKBY L32 85 F3
Birkrig SKEL WN8 67 F1
Birley St NEWLW WA12 106 D1
Birleywood SKEL WN8 67 F1
Birnam Dr RAIN/WH L35 119 F5
Birnam Rd WAL/EG CH44 111 K4
Birstall Av RNFD/HAY WA11 89 F6
Birstall Ct RUNC WA7 177 G6
Birstall Rd NPK/KEN L6 113 K4
Birt Cl TOX L8 133 G2
Birtles Rd WARRN/WOL WA2 123 J6
Bisham Pk RUNC WA7 178 C3
Bishopdale Cl
WARRW/BUR WA5 141 G2
Bishopdale Dr RAIN/WH L35 119 F5
Bishop Dr RAIN/WH L35 117 K6
Bishopgate St WAV L15 133 K2
Bishop Reeves Rd
RNFD/HAY WA11 90 D4
Bishop Rd ECCL WA10 12 D2
NPK/KEN L6 98 A6
WAL/EG CH44 111 H5
Bishops Ct WARRN/WOL WA2 123 F3
WLTN L25 154 E1
Bishops Gdns EP CH65 6 A4
Bishop Sheppard Ct
VAUX/LVPD L3 112 E3
Bishops Wy WDN WA8 139 J6
Bisley St WAL/NB CH45 111 H2
WAV L15 133 K2
Bispham Dr AIMK WN4 78 E4
HOY CH47 127 K2
Bispham Rd CHTN/BK PR9 23 H6
WARRW/BUR WA5 141 J5
Bittern Cl RUNC WA7 178 C5
WARRN/WOL WA2 123 K4
Bixteth St VAUX/LVPD L3 8 C2
Blackacre La BRSC L40 45 K2
Black-a-Moor La ORM L39 51 H3
Blackberry Gv HLWD L26 155 G1
Blackboards La GTS/LS CH66 194 D2
Blackbrook Av
WARRN/WOL WA2 124 A4
Blackbrook Cl WDN WA8 138 B6
WLT/FAZ L9 97 J2
Blackbrook Rd
RNFD/HAY WA11 89 H6
Blackburn Cl GOL/RIS/CUL WA3 93 G3
Blackburne Av WDN WA8 157 G6
Blackburne Cl
WARRN/WOL WA2 124 E5
Blackburne Dr NEWLW WA12 106 A1
WLTN L25 155 G4
Blackburne Pl TOX L8 9 J7
Blackburne St ALL/GAR L19 172 C2
Blackburne Ter TOX L8 9 J7
Blackburn Ter TOX L8 132 E2
Blackcar La SFTN L29 60 C4
Black Denton's Pl WDN WA8 19 H2
Blackdown Cl GTS/LS CH66 194 D4
Blackdown Gv STHEL WA9 104 D3
Blackeys La NSTN CH64 191 K1
Blackfield St EV L5 113 F1
Blackheath Dr MOR/LEA CH46 109 K4
Blackheath La RUNC WA7 178 E1
Black Horse Cl WKBY CH48 127 H6
Black Horse Hl WKBY CH48 146 D1
Black Horse La
CLB/OSW/ST L13 115 F4
Black Horse Pl
CLB/OSW/ST L13 115 F4
Blackhorse St STHEL WA9 104 A1
Blackhurst Rd MGHL L31 62 A2
Blackhurst St WARR WA1 16 E5
Blackledge Cl
WARRN/WOL WA2 124 C4
Blackley Cl WARRS WA4 143 G6
Blackley Gv NWD/KWIPK L33 * 73 F3
Blackleyhurst Av
WGNW/BIL/OR WN5 77 H4
Black Lion La GTS/LS CH66 194 E3
Blacklock Hall Rd
SPK/HALE L24 173 H2
Blacklow Brow HUY L36 116 D5
Blackmoor Dr
WD/CROXPK L12 115 G1
Black Moss La BRSC L40 36 B2
Blackpool St BIRK CH41 3 G6
Blackrod Av SPK/HALE L24 173 H2
Blackshaw Dr
WARRW/BUR WA5 122 B6
Blacksmith Pl WLTN L25 155 G3
Blackstairs Rd GTS/LS CH66 195 J2
Blackstock St VAUX/LVPD L3 112 E4
Blackstone Av RNFD/HAY WA11 89 G6
Blackstone St EV L5 112 D2
Blackthorn Cl MOR/LEA CH46 129 G2
Blackthorne Av GTS/LS CH66 202 E3
Blackthorne Crs STBRV L28 100 B5
Blackthorne Rd WLT/FAZ L9 98 A2
Blackwater Rd NG/CROX L11 99 H1
Blackwood Av WLTN L25 135 G5
Blaguegate La SKEL WN8 55 H3
Blair Dr WDN WA8 138 A6
Blairgowrie Gdns ORM L39 54 A1
Blair Gv CHTN/BK PR9 23 H6
Blair Pk BEB CH63 170 D2
Blair St TOX L8 132 D2
Blaisdon Cl NG/CROX L11 98 E4
Blakeacre Cl HLWD L26 155 J5
Blakeacre Rd HLWD L26 155 J5
Blakefield Rd CSBY/BLUN L23 69 K3
Blakehall SKEL WN8 57 F6
Blakeley Brow BEB CH63 183 H1
Blakeley Ct BEB CH63 183 H1
Blakeley Dell BEB CH63 183 J1
Blakeley Dene BEB CH63 170 D6
Blakeley Rd BEB CH63 170 C6
Blakemere Ct EP CH65 6 D1
Blakeney Cl GR/UP/WCH CH49 129 H2
Blakenhall Wy
GR/UP/WCH CH49 128 E3
Blaking Dr PR/KW L34 100 D1
Blandford Cl STHP PR8 27 F2
Blandford Rd
WARRW/BUR WA5 141 J4
Blantyre Rd WAV L15 133 K3
Blantyre St RUNC WA7 10 B2
Blay Cl WLTN L25 155 G3
Blaydon Cl NTHTN L30 82 C2
Blaydon Gv STHEL WA9 103 F6
Blaydon Pk SKEL WN8 57 F6
Blaydon Wk CL/PREN CH43 130 B3
Bleak Hill Cl ECCL WA10 87 K4
Bleak Hill Rd ECCL WA10 87 J5
Bleak La BRSC L40 39 K4
Bleasdale Av AIN/FAZ L10 83 H1
Bleasdale Cl
GR/UP/WCH CH49 129 F3
ORM L39 53 H6
Bleasdale Rd CALD/MH L18 134 C5
NEWLW WA12 106 B1
Blenheim Av LITH L21 81 K3
Blenheim Cl WARRN/WOL WA2 124 A5
Blenheim Dr PR/KW L34 117 F2
Blenheim Rd AIMK WN4 91 J1
CALD/MH L18 * 134 A4
STHP PR8 33 H3
WAL/EG CH44 111 K2
Blenheim St EV L5 112 E3
Blenheim Wy RNFD/HAY WA11 88 E5
SPK/HALE L24 173 G2
Blessington Rd ANF/KKDL L4 97 H6
Bletchley Av WAL/EG CH44 111 F3
Bligh St WAV L15 133 K2
Blind Foot Rd RNFD/HAY WA11 86 E3
Blindman's La ORM L39 45 G4
Blisworth St LITH L21 81 J5
Blomfield Rd ALL/GAR L19 154 A3
Bloomsbury Wy WDN WA8 138 C6
Blossom Gv KKBY L32 84 E4
Blossom St BTL L20 5 F1
Birtley Ct WDN WA8 157 G1
Blucher St CSBY/WL L22 80 D2
Bluebell Av BIRK CH41 130 C1
RNFD/HAY WA11 90 D4
Bluebell Cl CSBY/WL L22 81 F2
KKBY L32 72 D5
Bluebell Ct RUNC WA7 187 J3
Blue Bell La HUY L36 116 E3
Blueberry Flds AIN/FAZ L10 83 J5
Blue Bridge La FROD/HEL WA6 199 K4
Bluecoat St WARRN/WOL WA2 16 D1
Bluefields St TOX L8 132 E2
Blue Hatch FROD/HEL WA6 201 F1
Blue Jay Cl NTHLY L27 136 B4
Blue Ridge Cl
WARRW/BUR WA5 141 F2
Bluestone La MGHL L31 62 C6
Bluewood Dr BIRK CH41 110 D6
Blundell Av FMBY L37 48 B1
HTWN L38 59 F4
STHP PR8 27 G5
Blundell Crs STHP PR8 27 G5
Blundell Dr STHP PR8 27 G5
Blundell Gv HTWN L38 59 F4
Blundell La CHTN/BK PR9 24 A3
Blundell Rd HTWN L38 59 F5
RAIN/WH L35 118 B2
WDN WA8 157 J3
Blundellsands Rd East
CSBY/BLUN L23 68 D5
Blundellsands Rd West
CSBY/BLUN L23 68 C6
Blundells Dr MOR/LEA CH46 109 J6
Blundell's La RAIN/WH L35 118 C6
Blundell St CLVPS L1 132 C2
Blyth Cl RUNC WA7 188 C2
Blythe Av WDN WA8 139 G5
Blythe La BRSC L40 46 E2
Blythe Ms STHP PR8 34 B1
Blythewood SKEL WN8 56 E6
Blyth Hey NTHTN L30 70 A6
Blyth Rd BEB CH63 170 E6
Blythswood St AIG/SPK L17 133 G6
Boaler St NPK/KEN L6 113 K4
Boardmans La
RNFD/HAY WA11 104 C1
Boathouse La NSTN CH64 181 G5
Boat Stage LYMM WA13 145 K6
Bobbies La ECCL WA10 102 C1
Bobbiners La CHTN/BK PR9 24 E2
Bobby Langton Wy BRSC L40 38 E4
Bodden St GOL/RIS/CUL WA3 93 H2
STHEL WA9 120 B3
Boddington Dr WARRS WA4 163 F5
Bodiam Ct EP CH65 203 J1
Bodley St ANF/KKDL L4 * 97 H6
Bodmin Av CHTN/BK PR9 20 E6
Bodmin Cl RUNC WA7 188 A1
Bodmin Gv RNFD/HAY WA11 89 G4
Bodmin Rd ANF/KKDL L4 97 H4
Bodmin Wy HLWD L26 155 H3
Bognor Cl SPK/HALE L24 173 G1
Bolan St CLB/OSW/ST L13 114 E4
Bolden Cl NTHTN L30 82 C2
Bolde Wy BEB CH63 170 C4
Bold La ORM L39 53 F6
WARRW/BUR WA5 105 G6
Bold Pl CLVPS L1 9 G6
Bold Rd STHEL WA9 104 D6
Bold St CHTN/BK PR9 14 E3
CLVPS L1 9 F5
ECCL WA10 12 E6
RUNC WA7 11 F3
WARR WA1 16 C5
WDN WA8 18 C6
Boleyn Ct RUNC WA7 178 B2
The Boleyn MGHL L31 62 C4
Bollington Cl CL/PREN CH43 130 C6
Bolton Av KKBY L32 84 B1
WARRS WA4 143 J5
Bolton Cl FMBY L37 49 G3
GOL/RIS/CUL WA3 93 J3
Bolton Rd AIMK WN4 79 G6
PS/BROM CH62 151 H5
STHP PR8 27 H3
Bolton Rd East
PS/BROM CH62 151 H5
Bolton St AIMK WN4 78 C4
STHEL WA9 104 A1
VAUX/LVPD L3 9 G4
Bonchurch Dr WAV L15 114 D6
Bond Cl WARRW/BUR WA5 142 A5
Bond's La CHTN/BK PR9 21 K4
Bond St PR/KW L34 117 K1
VAUX/LVPD L3 113 F3
Bonnington Av
CSBY/BLUN L23 68 D4
Bonnington Cl ECCL WA10 102 E2
Bonsall Rd WD/CROXPK L12 115 F1
Boode Cft STBRV L28 100 B4
Booker Av CALD/MH L18 153 J2
Booth's Brow Rd AIMK WN4 78 C3
Booths Hill Cl LYMM WA13 145 J6
Booth's Hill La LYMM WA13 145 H6
Booth's Hill Rd LYMM WA13 145 H6
Booth's La LYMM WA13 164 C1
ORM L39 44 D6
Booth St CHTN/BK PR9 14 E3
CLB/OSW/ST L13 114 E4
STHEL WA9 103 F6
WARRW/BUR WA5 142 B5
Boothwood Cl EHL/KEN L7 * 113 K6
Borax St CLB/OSW/ST L13 114 E5
Bordehill Gdns
WD/CROXPK L12 99 H5
Border Rd HES CH60 168 B5
Border Wy EV L5 113 G1
Borella Rd CLB/OSW/ST L13 114 D1
Borough Pl BIRK CH41 * 3 G5
Borough Rd BIRK CH41 2 D6
ECCL WA10 12 C7
RF/TRAN CH42 2 C7
WAL/EG CH44 111 K4
Borough Rd East BIRK CH41 3 G5
WAL/EG CH44 * 112 A5
Borough Wy WAL/EG CH44 112 A5
Borron Rd NEWLW WA12 91 G6
Borrowdale FMBY L37 41 F6
Borrowdale Av
WARRN/WOL WA2 123 H4
Borrowdale Cl
FROD/HEL WA6 201 G1
Borrowdale Rd BEB CH63 170 A1
ECCL WA10 102 D5
MOR/LEA CH46 128 E1
WAV L15 133 K3
WDN WA8 157 H3
Boscow Crs STHEL WA9 104 B6
Bosnia St TOX L8 133 F6
Bostock Gn EP CH65 195 J4
Bostock St EV L5 113 F2
WARRW/BUR WA5 142 B3
Boston Bvd WARRW/BUR WA5 141 H2
Boswell Av WARRS WA4 162 A1
Boswell Rd CL/PREN CH43 149 J2
Boswell St BTL L20 4 B1
TOX L8 133 H2
Bosworth Cl BEB CH63 170 B3
Bosworth Dr STHP PR8 33 H5
Bosworth Rd RNFD/HAY WA11 89 F5
Botanic Gv EHL/KEN L7 114 A5
Botanic Pl EHL/KEN L7 114 A5
Botanic Rd CHTN/BK PR9 23 J4
EHL/KEN L7 114 A6
Botany Rd SPK/HALE L24 155 F6
Boteler Av WARRW/BUR WA5 142 C2
Botley Cl GR/UP/WCH CH49 * 128 E4
The Boulevard EP CH65 195 J5
WD/CROXPK L12 99 F5
Boulting Av WARRW/BUR WA5 123 F5
Boulton Av PS/BROM CH62 151 G3
WKBY CH48 127 G5
Boundary Dr CSBY/BLUN L23 68 D3
WLTN L25 155 G4
Boundary Farm Rd HLWD L26 155 G5
Boundary La BRSC L40 39 F6
HES CH60 168 A5
NPK/KEN L6 113 K3
NWD/KWIPK L33 86 A1
Boundary Pk NSTN CH64 191 J1
Boundary Rd CL/PREN CH43 130 A1
ECCL WA10 12 C6
HUY L36 136 C1
LITH L21 82 A1
PS/BROM CH62 151 G4
WKBY CH48 146 E3
Boundary St EV L5 112 D1
STHP PR8 27 J3
Boundary St East EV L5 113 F1
Bourchier Wy WARRS WA4 163 F3
Bourne Av GOL/RIS/CUL WA3 92 E3
Bourne Gdns STHEL WA9 103 K4
Bournemouth Cl RUNC WA7 188 C1
Bourton Rd WLTN L25 154 E5
Bousfield St ANF/KKDL L4 * 97 G6
Bowden Cl ECCL WA10 102 D2
WD/CROXPK L12 99 J3
Bowden Rd ALL/GAR L19 153 J5
Bowden St LITH L21 81 J5
Bowdon Cl WARR WA1 * 143 J1
Bowdon Rd WAL/NB CH45 111 G1
Bowen Cl WDN WA8 138 C5
Bower Gv LITH L21 81 G4
Bower Rd HES CH60 168 C5
HUY L36 116 E3
WLTN L25 135 H5
Bower St WDN WA8 19 G1
Bowfell Cl PS/BROM CH62 184 A4
Bowfield Rd ALL/GAR L19 153 J4

Bowgreen Cl CL/PREN CH43 ... 129 K2
Bowker's Green La ORM L39 ... 63 J2
Bowland Av AIMK WN4 ... 79 G5
CHLDW L16 ... 115 H6
GOL/RIS/CUL WA3 ... 92 D2
STHEL WA9 ... 119 J4
Bowland Cl GOL/RIS/CUL WA3 ... 125 K2
PS/BROM CH62 ... 171 F4
RUNC WA7 ... 187 H2
Bowland Dr LITH L21 ... 69 K5
Bowles St BTL L20 ... 81 H6
Bowley Rd CLB/OSW/ST L13 ... 114 D2
Bowling Green Cl STHP PR8 ... 28 C2
Bowman Av WARRS WA4 ... 143 K4
Bowness Av BEB CH63 ... 183 K2
CL/PREN CH43 ... 149 K1
RNFD/HAY WA11 ... 88 E3
STHP PR8 ... 33 J6
WARRN/WOL WA2 ... 123 J5
Bowood Ct WARRN/WOL WA2 ... 123 G3
Bowood St TOX L8 ... 132 E6
Bowring Cl TOX L8 * ... 133 F5
Bowring Dr NSTN CH64 ... 181 G6
Bowring Park Av CHLDW L16 ... 116 A6
Bowring Park Rd DV/KA/FCH L14 ... 115 G6
Bowring St TOX L8 * ... 133 F5
Bowscale Cl GR/UP/WCH CH49 * ... 129 F4
Bowscale Rd NG/CROX L11 ... 98 E4
Boxdale Rd CALD/MH L18 ... 134 B5
Boxgrove Cl WDN WA8 ... 139 G6
Boxmoor Rd CALD/MH L18 ... 153 H1
Boxtree Cl WD/CROXPK L12 ... 99 K1
Boxwood Cl HUY L36 ... 116 C5
Boycott St EV L5 ... 113 J1
Boyd Cl MOR/LEA CH46 ... 110 B4
Boydell Av WARRS WA4 ... 143 J5
Boydell Cl STBRV L28 ... 100 B6
Boyer Av MGHL L31 ... 71 G2
Boyes Brow NWD/KWIPK L33 ... 72 C5
Boyle Av WARRN/WOL WA2 ... 124 A6
Boyton Ct EHL/KEN L7 ... 133 H1
Brabant Rd AIG/SPK L17 ... 153 F2
Braby Rd LITH L21 ... 81 K5
Bracebridge Dr STHP PR8 ... 28 C5
Bracewell Cl STHEL WA9 ... 120 A1
Bracken Cl GOL/RIS/CUL WA3 ... 124 E2
Bracken Ct STHEL WA9 ... 120 A3
Brackendale CHNE CH2 ... 198 C6
GR/UP/WCH CH49 ... 129 K6
RUNC WA7 ... 177 G5
WLT/FAZ L9 * ... 82 E4
Brackendale Av WLT/FAZ L9 ... 82 E4
Bracken Dr WKBY CH48 ... 147 F1
Brackenhurst Dr WAL/NB CH45 ... 95 J6
Brackenhurst Gn NWD/KWIPK L33 ... 84 D1
Bracken La BEB CH63 ... 150 C6
Bracken Rd GTS/LS CH66 ... 195 H5
Brackenside HES CH60 * ... 167 K3
The Brackens WARRS WA4 ... 179 F4
Brackenway FMBY L37 ... 41 G5
Bracken Wy FROD/HEL WA6 ... 201 F3
Bracken Wd WD/CROXPK L12 ... 99 J1
Brackenwood Dr WDN WA8 ... 157 F4
Brackenwood Gv RAIN/WH L35 ... 118 B4
Brackenwood Rd BEB CH63 ... 150 C6
Brackley Cl WAL/EG CH44 ... 111 G4
Brackley St RUNC WA7 ... 10 B3
WARRS WA4 ... 162 B2
Bracknell Av KKBY L32 ... 84 C3
Bracknell Cl KKBY L32 ... 84 C2
Bracknel Wy ORM L39 ... 52 E4
Bradbourne Cl WD/CROXPK L12 ... 99 J2
Bradda Cl GR/UP/WCH CH49 ... 129 G2
Braddan Av CLB/OSW/ST L13 * ... 114 C2
Bradden Cl BEB CH63 ... 170 D3
Brade St CHTN/BK PR9 ... 24 A1
Bradewell Cl ANF/KKDL L4 ... 97 G5
Bradewell St ANF/KKDL L4 ... 97 G5
Bradfield Av AIN/FAZ L10 ... 71 F6
Bradfield St EHL/KEN L7 ... 114 A5
Bradgate Cl MOR/LEA CH46 ... 109 F6
Bradlegh Rd NEWLW WA12 ... 106 C3
Bradley Bvd WARRW/BUR WA5 ... 141 J3
Bradley Fold HUY L36 ... 136 D1
Bradley La FROD/HEL WA6 ... 201 G3
WARRW/BUR WA5 ... 106 A5
Bradley Rd LITH L21 ... 81 J2
Bradley St CHTN/BK PR9 ... 15 H3
Bradley Wy WDN WA8 ... 19 F2
Bradman Rd MOR/LEA CH46 ... 109 G6
NWD/KWIPK L33 ... 73 H6
Bradmoor Rd PS/BROM CH62 ... 171 F5
Bradshaw Cl ECCL WA10 ... 12 A3
Bradshaw La WARRS WA4 ... 144 A6
Bradshaw's La STHP PR8 ... 33 K3
Bradshaw St WDN WA8 ... 158 B1
Bradstone Cl AIN/FAZ L10 ... 84 A5
Bradville Rd WLT/FAZ L9 ... 83 F4
Bradwell Cl EP CH65 ... 195 K5
WKBY CH48 ... 146 E1
Bradwell Rd GOL/RIS/CUL WA3 ... 93 F4
Braehaven Rd WAL/NB CH45 ... 95 J6
Braemar Av CHTN/BK PR9 ... 23 G3
Braemar Cl RAIN/WH L35 ... 118 B4
WARRN/WOL WA2 ... 124 C4
Braemar Ct EP CH65 ... 196 D6
Braemar St BTL L20 * ... 97 F4
Braemore Rd WAL/EG CH44 ... 111 F3
Braeside Cl GTS/LS CH66 ... 195 F4
Braeside Crs WGNW/BIL/OR WN5 ... 77 G4
Braeside Gdns GR/UP/WCH CH49 ... 129 G4
Brae St EHL/KEN L7 ... 113 K5
Brahms Cl TOX L8 ... 133 G3
Braid St BIRK CH41 ... 2 D1
Brainerd St CLB/OSW/ST L13 ... 114 C2
Braithwaite Cl RAIN/WH L35 ... 118 E4
RUNC WA7 ... 187 G2
Braithwaite Rd GOL/RIS/CUL WA3 ... 92 E2
Brakenwood Ms WARRS WA4 * ... 163 H2
Bramberton Pl ANF/KKDL L4 ... 98 A4
Bramberton Rd ANF/KKDL L4 ... 98 A4
Bramble Av BIRK CH41 ... 130 C1
Bramble Cl WARRW/BUR WA5 ... 141 F6
The Brambles AIMK WN4 ... 78 C4
NWD/KWIPK L33 * ... 85 G2
WARRW/BUR WA5 ... 105 K6
Bramble Wy BRSC L40 ... 39 F5
MOR/LEA CH46 ... 109 H5
RUNC WA7 ... 187 H3
Bramblewood Cl CL/PREN CH43 ... 129 K5
NTHLY L27 ... 136 B4
Brambling Cl RUNC WA7 ... 187 H2
Brambling Pk HLWD L26 ... 155 H2
Brambling Wy GOL/RIS/CUL WA3 ... 93 F3
Bramcote Av RNFD/HAY WA11 ... 89 G5
Bramcote Cl NWD/KWIPK L33 ... 73 F5
Bramcote Rd NWD/KWIPK L33 ... 72 E5
Bramcote Wk NWD/KWIPK L33 ... 72 E5
Bramerton Ct WKBY CH48 ... 126 E6
Bramford Cl GR/UP/WCH CH49 ... 129 F4
Bramhall Cl SPK/HALE L24 ... 173 K3
WKBY CH48 ... 146 E2
Bramhall Dr PS/BROM CH62 ... 184 C4
Bramhall Rd CSBY/WL L22 ... 81 F3
SKEL WN8 ... 56 B3
Bramhall St WARRW/BUR WA5 ... 142 B4
Bramley Av BEB CH63 ... 150 D4
Bramley Cl GTS/LS CH66 ... 202 D3
NTHLY L27 ... 136 B4
Bramley Ms WARRS WA4 ... 162 B3
The Bramleys MGHL L31 ... 71 F2
Brampton Cl KKBY L32 ... 72 D5
Brampton Ct STHEL WA9 ... 105 F2
Brampton Dr TOX L8 ... 133 F1
Bramshill Cl GOL/RIS/CUL WA3 ... 125 J1
Bramwell Av CL/PREN CH43 ... 149 K2
Bramwell Pk BRSC L40 ... 37 F5
Bramwell St STHEL WA9 ... 104 C1
Brancaster Dr GOL/RIS/CUL WA3 ... 93 H4
Brancepeth Ct EP CH65 ... 196 C6
Branch Wy RNFD/HAY WA11 ... 90 C5
Brancker Av RAIN/WH L35 ... 118 D3
Brancote Gdns PS/BROM CH62 ... 171 F6
Brancote Mt CL/PREN CH43 * ... 130 C3
Brancote Rd CL/PREN CH43 ... 130 C3
Brandearth Hey STBRV L28 ... 100 B6
Brandon WDN WA8 ... 157 F1
Brandon Cl SKEL WN8 ... 57 J6
Brandon St BIRK CH41 ... 3 H4
Brandreth Cl RAIN/WH L35 ... 118 E4
Brandwood Av WARRN/WOL WA2 ... 123 H5
Branfield Cl WD/CROXPK L12 ... 99 J2
Bransdale Cl WARRW/BUR WA5 ... 141 F2
Bransdale Dr AIMK WN4 ... 79 J6
Bransford Cl AIMK WN4 ... 91 H1
Branson Cl GOL/RIS/CUL WA3 ... 92 B1
Branstree Av NG/CROX L11 ... 98 D3
Brantfield Ct WARRN/WOL WA2 ... 124 A5
Branthwaite Cl NG/CROX L11 ... 98 E4
Branthwaite Crs NG/CROX L11 ... 98 E4
Branthwaite Gv NG/CROX L11 ... 98 E4
Brasenose Rd BTL L20 ... 96 D4
Brassey St BIRK CH41 ... 130 E1
Brathay Cl WARRN/WOL WA2 ... 123 J4
Brattan Rd BIRK CH41 ... 131 F5
Braunton Rd AIG/SPK L17 ... 153 F3
WAL/NB CH45 ... 111 G1
Braybrooke Rd NG/CROX L11 ... 98 E2
Bray Cl RUNC WA7 ... 187 G1
Braydon Cl WLTN L25 * ... 155 F5
Brayfield Rd ANF/KKDL L4 ... 98 B4
Bray Rd SPK/HALE L24 ... 173 H1
Bray St BIRK CH41 ... 130 E1
Brechin Rd NWD/KWIPK L33 ... 84 E1
Breckfield Pl EV L5 * ... 113 H2
Breckfield Rd North EV L5 ... 113 H1
Breckfield Rd South EV L5 ... 113 J2
Breck Pl WAL/EG CH44 ... 111 G4
Breck Rd NPK/KEN L6 ... 113 J2
WAL/EG CH44 ... 111 F2
WDN WA8 ... 19 F1
Breckside Av WAL/EG CH44 ... 110 E3
Breckside Pk NPK/KEN L6 ... 114 A1
The Breck GTS/LS CH66 ... 195 H2
Brecon Av NTHTN L30 ... 82 C2
Brecon Dr GTS/LS CH66 ... 202 C2
Brecon Rd RF/TRAN CH42 ... 150 B2
Brecon Wk NTHTN L30 ... 82 D2
Bredon Cl GTS/LS CH66 ... 194 D3
Breeze Hl ANF/KKDL L4 ... 97 H3
BTL L20 ... 5 K6
Breezehill Cl NSTN CH64 ... 191 K1
Breezehill Pk NSTN CH64 ... 192 A1
Breezehill Rd NSTN CH64 ... 192 A1
Breeze La WLT/FAZ L9 ... 97 H2
Breeze Rd STHP PR8 ... 27 F5
Brelade Rd CLB/OSW/ST L13 ... 114 D3
Bremhill Rd NG/CROX L11 ... 98 D2
Bremner Cl EHL/KEN L7 ... 114 A6
Brenda Crs CSBY/BLUN L23 ... 69 H2
Brendale Av MGHL L31 ... 71 F1
Brendon Av LITH L21 ... 81 H2
WARRN/WOL WA2 ... 123 G4
Brendon Gv STHEL WA9 * ... 104 E1
Brendor Rd WLTN L25 ... 154 E2
Brenig St BIRK CH41 ... 111 F6
Brenka Av WLT/FAZ L9 ... 82 E2
Brentfield WDN WA8 ... 157 K1
Brentnall Cl WARRW/BUR WA5 * ... 141 K4
Brent Wy HLWD L26 ... 155 J5
Brentwood Av AIG/SPK L17 ... 133 H6
CSBY/BLUN L23 ... 69 G4
Brentwood Cl ECCL WA10 ... 102 D2
HTWN L38 ... 59 F5
Brentwood Ct CHTN/BK PR9 ... 15 K1
Brentwood St WAL/EG CH44 ... 111 J5
Brereton Av BEB CH63 ... 151 F5
WAV L15 ... 134 B2
Brereton Cl RUNC WA7 ... 177 K5
Bretherton Pl RAIN/WH L35 ... 118 E3
Bretherton Rd PR/KW L34 ... 118 A1
Bretland Dr WARRS WA4 ... 163 F4
Bretlands Rd CSBY/BLUN L23 ... 69 J4
Bretton Fold STHP PR8 ... 28 C2
Brett St BIRK CH41 ... 130 E1
Brewery La FMBY L37 ... 41 F5
MGHL L31 ... 71 H5
Brewster St ANF/KKDL L4 ... 97 G4
Breydon Gdns STHEL WA9 ... 119 G1
Brian Av PEN/TH CH61 ... 148 C5
WARRN/WOL WA2 ... 143 G1
WARRS WA4 ... 162 D2
Briar Cl AIMK WN4 ... 79 F5
Briardale Gdns GTS/LS CH66 ... 195 F3
Briardale Rd BEB CH63 ... 150 E4
CALD/MH L18 ... 134 A5
GTS/LS CH66 ... 195 F3
NSTN CH64 ... 193 H1
RF/TRAN CH42 ... 131 F5
WAL/EG CH44 ... 112 A5
Briar Dr HES CH60 ... 168 A5
HUY L36 ... 116 D5
Briarfield Av WDN WA8 ... 157 F2
Briarfield Rd EP CH65 ... 6 C4
HES CH60 ... 168 A5
Briar Rd GOL/RIS/CUL WA3 ... 92 C3
STHP PR8 ... 33 K5
Briars Brook BRSC L40 ... 39 G6
Briars Cl RAIN/WH L35 ... 119 F6
Briars Gn ECCL WA10 ... 12 E2
SKEL WN8 ... 56 C1
Briars La BRSC L40 ... 39 G6
MGHL L31 ... 62 C6
The Briars STHP PR8 ... 27 G6
Briar St ANF/KKDL L4 ... 97 F6
Briarswood Cl RAIN/WH L35 ... 118 B4
RF/TRAN CH42 ... 150 E3
Briarwood CSBY/BLUN L23 ... 68 C3
RUNC WA7 ... 178 A4
Briarwood Av WARR WA1 ... 143 H2
Briarwood Rd AIG/SPK L17 ... 133 K6
Briary Cl HES CH60 ... 168 B4
Briary Cft HTWN L38 ... 59 F4
Brickfields HUY L36 ... 117 G6
Brickhurst Wy WARR WA1 ... 144 A1
Brick St CLVPS L1 ... 132 C2
NEWLW WA12 ... 105 K2
WARR WA1 ... 17 F4
Brickwall Gn SFTN L29 ... 70 C2
Brickwall La SFTN L29 ... 70 B3
Bride St ANF/KKDL L4 ... 97 H3
Bridge Av ORM L39 ... 53 J1
WARRS WA4 ... 143 J5
Bridge Av East WARRS WA4 ... 143 J4
Bridge Ct NSTN CH64 ... 191 K2
STHEL WA9 * ... 120 B4
WKBY CH48 ... 127 F6
Bridge Cft LITH L21 ... 69 K6
Bridgecroft Rd WAL/NB CH45 ... 111 H1
Bridge Farm Cl GR/UP/WCH CH49 ... 129 J5
Bridge Farm Dr MGHL L31 ... 62 D5
Bridgefield Cl WLTN L25 ... 135 J2
Bridgeford Av WD/CROXPK L12 ... 98 E6
Bridge Gdns WD/CROXPK L12 ... 99 K4
Bridge Gv STHP PR8 ... 15 F7
Bridgehall Dr SKEL WN8 ... 57 K6
Bridge La FROD/HEL WA6 ... 187 F6
NTHTN L30 ... 70 B6
WARR WA1 ... 144 B3
WARRS WA4 ... 162 D4
Bridgeman St ECCL WA10 ... 12 B6
WARRW/BUR WA5 ... 142 A5
Bridge Meadow GTS/LS CH66 ... 202 D1
Bridgend Cl WDN WA8 ... 138 C6
Bridgend Dr STHP PR8 ... 33 H5
Bridgenorth Rd PEN/TH CH61 ... 167 J1
Bridge Rd CALD/MH L18 ... 134 B6
CSBY/BLUN L23 ... 68 D6
EHL/KEN L7 ... 133 J1
HUY L36 ... 116 C5
LITH L21 ... 81 H4
MGHL L31 ... 71 G2
PR/KW L34 ... 117 K2
STHEL WA9 ... 120 B5
WARR WA1 ... 144 B2
WKBY CH48 ... 127 F6
Bridges La SFTN L29 ... 70 C2
Bridges Rd EP CH65 ... 7 K5
Bridge St BIRK CH41 ... 3 F2
BTL L20 ... 4 D7
ECCL WA10 ... 13 F6
GOL/RIS/CUL WA3 ... 92 B4
NEWLW WA12 ... 106 B2
NSTN CH64 ... 191 K2
ORM L39 ... 53 J1
RUNC WA7 ... 11 F4
STHP PR8 ... 15 F6
WARR WA1 ... 16 D5
Bridge View Cl WDN WA8 ... 176 D1
Bridgeview Dr NWD/KWIPK L33 ... 72 E5
Bridge Wk RUNC WA7 * ... 177 J6
Bridgewater Av WARRS WA4 ... 143 J5
Bridgewater Cl FROD/HEL WA6 ... 187 F6
LITH L21 ... 81 H1
Bridgewater Gra RUNC WA7 ... 188 E1
Bridgewater Ms WARRS WA4 ... 162 B3
Bridgewater Pl GOL/RIS/CUL WA3 ... 125 G2
Bridgewater St CLVPS L1 ... 132 C2
LYMM WA13 ... 145 K6
RUNC WA7 ... 10 D3
Bridgewater Wy HUY L36 ... 136 D1
Bridgeway NG/CROX L11 ... 98 C4
Bridgeway East RUNC WA7 ... 178 B3
Bridgeway West RUNC WA7 ... 178 A3
Bridge Wills La CHTN/BK PR9 ... 21 F6
Bridgewood Dr GTS/LS CH66 ... 202 A1
Bridle Av WAL/EG CH44 ... 112 A5
Bridle Cl CL/PREN CH43 ... 129 J3
PS/BROM CH62 ... 171 G6
Bridle Ct STHEL WA9 ... 104 A5
Bridle La CH/BCN CH1 ... 202 C5
Bridlemere Ct WARR WA1 ... 143 H1
Bridle Pk PS/BROM CH62 ... 171 F6
Bridle Rd NTHTN L30 ... 82 D3
PS/BROM CH62 ... 171 G6
WAL/EG CH44 ... 112 A5
Bridle Wy GTS/LS CH66 ... 195 G6
NTHTN L30 ... 82 C3
NWD/KWIPK L33 ... 72 C3
Bridport St VAUX/LVPD L3 ... 9 G3
Briedden Wy GTS/LS CH66 ... 194 D3
Brierfield SKEL WN8 ... 67 F2
Brierfield Rd WAV L15 ... 134 A3
Brierley Cl NTHTN L30 ... 70 E5
Brierley St WARRW/BUR WA5 * ... 16 A3
Briers Cl WARRN/WOL WA2 ... 124 B4
Briery Hey Av NWD/KWIPK L33 ... 84 E1
Brigadier Dr WD/CROXPK L12 ... 99 J6
Brighouse Cl ORM L39 ... 45 H5
Brightgate Cl EHL/KEN L7 * ... 133 G1
Brighton Rd CSBY/WL L22 ... 80 E2
HUY L36 ... 117 H4
STHP PR8 ... 27 H4
Brighton St WAL/EG CH44 ... 112 A4
WARRW/BUR WA5 ... 142 B3
Brighton V CSBY/WL L22 ... 80 D1
Bright St BIRK CH41 ... 2 C5
CHTN/BK PR9 ... 23 H6
NPK/KEN L6 ... 113 J4
Brightwell Cl GR/UP/WCH CH49 * ... 129 G5
WARRW/BUR WA5 ... 141 F4
Brignall Gv GOL/RIS/CUL WA3 ... 92 E2
Brill St BIRK CH41 ... 130 E1
Brimelow Crs WARRW/BUR WA5 ... 141 F6
Brimstage Av BEB CH63 ... 150 C3
Brimstage Cl HES CH60 ... 168 C5
Brimstage Gn HES CH60 * ... 168 D5
Brimstage La BEB CH63 ... 169 H1
Brimstage Rd ANF/KKDL L4 ... 5 K6
BEB CH63 ... 169 J3
HES CH60 ... 168 C5
Brimstage St BIRK CH41 ... 131 F5
Brindley Av WARRS WA4 ... 143 J5
Brindley Cl LITH L21 ... 81 H1
Brindley Rd KKBY L32 ... 84 B1
RUNC WA7 ... 177 H1
STHEL WA9 ... 120 C1
Brindley St RUNC WA7 ... 10 C3
TOX L8 ... 132 C3
Brindley Whf WARRS WA4 ... 188 E1
Brinklow Cl STHP PR8 ... 33 G4
Brinley Cl PS/BROM CH62 ... 184 A2
Brinton Cl NTHLY L27 ... 135 K3
WDN WA8 ... 157 K3
Brisbane Av WAL/NB CH45 ... 95 G5
Brisbane St STHEL WA9 ... 103 F6
Briscoe Dr MOR/LEA CH46 ... 129 F2
Bristol Av RUNC WA7 ... 188 D1
WAL/EG CH44 ... 111 J3
Bristol Dr GTS/LS CH66 ... 202 C2
Bristol Rd WAV L15 ... 134 B3
Bristow Cl WARRW/BUR WA5 ... 141 J1
Britannia Av WAV L15 ... 133 J2
Britannia Crs TOX L8 ... 132 E6
Britannia Rd WAL/NB CH45 ... 111 G3
Britannic Buildings WAL/EG CH44 * ... 111 G3
Britonside Av KKBY L32 ... 84 E3
Brittarge Brow NTHLY L27 ... 136 B5
Britten Cl TOX L8 ... 133 G3
Broadacre SKEL WN8 ... 67 J1
Broadbelt St ANF/KKDL L4 ... 97 H3
Broadbent Av WARRS WA4 ... 143 J5
Broadfield Av CL/PREN CH43 ... 129 K1
Broadfield Cl CL/PREN CH43 * ... 129 J2
Broadfields RUNC WA7 ... 178 A5
Broadgate Av STHEL WA9 ... 103 K4
Broad Green Rd CLB/OSW/ST L13 ... 115 F5
Broadheath Av CL/PREN CH43 ... 129 K2
Broadheath Ter WDN WA8 ... 157 J2
Broad Hey NTHTN L30 ... 70 A6
Broad Hey Cl WLTN L25 ... 135 J6
Broadheys La KNUT WA16 ... 164 E5
Broadhurst Av WARRW/BUR WA5 ... 142 A5
Broadhurst St AIG/SPK L17 ... 133 H6
Broadlake NSTN CH64 ... 193 G1
Broadland Gdns GTS/LS CH66 ... 202 D1
Broadland Rd GTS/LS CH66 ... 202 D1
Broadlands RAIN/WH L35 ... 118 A2
STHP PR8 ... 27 F4
Broad La ANF/KKDL L4 ... 98 B4
FMBY L37 ... 49 K2
HES CH60 ... 167 G4
KKBY L32 ... 84 E3
NG/CROX L11 ... 98 C4
ORM L39 ... 52 A3
RNFD/HAY WA11 ... 88 E1
SFTN L29 ... 60 E6
WARRS WA4 ... 163 G3
WARRW/BUR WA5 ... 105 H5
Broad Lane Prec NG/CROX L11 ... 98 C4
Broadley Av GOL/RIS/CUL WA3 ... 92 D4
Broadmead ALL/GAR L19 ... 154 B4
HES CH60 ... 168 C6
Broad Oak Av RNFD/HAY WA11 ... 89 K5
WARRW/BUR WA5 ... 141 F5
Broadoak Rd DV/KA/FCH L14 ... 115 K4
MGHL L31 ... 62 C6
Broad Oak Rd STHEL WA9 ... 104 C2
Broadoaks GR/UP/WCH CH49 ... 129 F3
Broad Pl NG/CROX L11 ... 98 D5
Broad Sq NG/CROX L11 ... 98 D5
Broadstone Dr BEB CH63 ... 170 B3
Broad Vw NG/CROX L11 ... 98 D5
Broadway BEB CH63 ... 150 C4
ECCL WA10 ... 87 J6
GR/UP/WCH CH49 ... 128 E4
NG/CROX L11 ... 98 C4
WAL/NB CH45 ... 111 F2
WDN WA8 ... 157 F2
WLT/FAZ L9 ... 83 H5
Broadway Av WAL/NB CH45 ... 111 F2
Broadway Cl STHP PR8 ... 33 H4
Broadwood Av MGHL L31 ... 71 F2
Broadwood St WAV L15 ... 133 K2
Brockenhurst Rd WLT/FAZ L9 ... 82 D6
Brockhall Cl RAIN/WH L35 ... 118 C1
Brock Hall Cl STHEL WA9 ... 120 A3
Brockholme Rd ALL/GAR L19 ... 153 H2
Brocklebank La ALL/GAR L19 ... 154 A3
Brocklebank Rd CHTN/BK PR9 ... 23 G4
Brock Rd GOL/RIS/CUL WA3 ... 125 F4
Brockstedes Av AIMK WN4 ... 78 D3
Brock St ANF/KKDL L4 ... 97 G5
Brocstedes Rd AIMK WN4 ... 78 C2
Brodie Av CALD/MH L18 ... 134 B6
Bromborough Rd BEB CH63 ... 151 F6
Bromborough Village Rd PS/BROM CH62 ... 171 F4
Brome Wy BEB CH63 ... 170 D3
Bromilow Rd SKEL WN8 ... 55 J4
STHEL WA9 ... 104 D3
Bromley Av CALD/MH L18 ... 134 A4
GOL/RIS/CUL WA3 ... 92 E4
Bromley Cl HES CH60 ... 167 J6
WARRN/WOL WA2 ... 124 B4
Bromley Rd WAL/NB CH45 ... 95 G6
Brompton Av AIG/SPK L17 ... 133 H4
CSBY/BLUN L23 ... 68 D6
NWD/KWIPK L33 ... 73 F4
WAL/EG CH44 ... 111 J3
Brompton Gdns WARRW/BUR WA5 ... 142 B2
Brompton Rd STHP PR8 ... 23 G6
Brompton Wy GTS/LS CH66 ... 202 C2
Bromsgrove Rd GR/UP/WCH CH49 ... 128 D5
Bromyard Cl BTL L20 ... 4 C3
Bronington Av PS/BROM CH62 ... 184 A1
Bronte Cl CSBY/BLUN L23 ... 68 C5
WARRN/WOL WA2 ... 123 G1
Bronte St ECCL WA10 ... 12 B4
VAUX/LVPD L3 ... 9 H3
Brook Av MGHL L31 ... 62 C5
WARRS WA4 ... 143 J4
Brookbank Ct AIN/FAZ L10 ... 84 A4
Brookbridge Rd CLB/OSW/ST L13 ... 114 C1
Brook Cl WAL/EG CH44 ... 111 J2
WDN WA8 ... 138 B3
Brookdale WDN WA8 ... 137 K6
Brookdale Av North GR/UP/WCH CH49 ... 129 F5
Brookdale Av South GR/UP/WCH CH49 ... 129 F6
Brookdale Cl GR/UP/WCH CH49 ... 129 F5
Brookdale Rd WAV L15 ... 133 K3
The Brookdale STHP PR8 ... 33 K6
Brook Dr WARRW/BUR WA5 ... 141 H4
Brooke Cl CHTN/BK PR9 ... 23 K6
Brook End STHEL WA9 ... 104 E4
Brooke Rd East CSBY/WL L22 ... 80 E1
Brooke Rd West CSBY/WL L22 ... 80 D1
Brook Farm Cl ORM L39 ... 53 J1
Brookfield Av CSBY/BLUN L23 ... 68 E6
CSBY/WL L22 ... 81 G3
RAIN/WH L35 ... 118 E2
RUNC WA7 ... 177 H3
Brookfield Cl LYMM WA13 ... 145 J6
Brookfield Dr WLT/FAZ L9 ... 83 F6
Brookfield Gdns WKBY CH48 ... 146 C1
Brookfield La ORM L39 ... 62 E2
Brookfield Pk WARRS WA4 ... 163 F1
Brookfield Rd LYMM WA13 ... 145 J6
SKEL WN8 ... 57 K6
WKBY CH48 ... 146 C1
Brookfield St NEWLW WA12 ... 106 B2
Brook Furlong FROD/HEL WA6 ... 186 B5
Brook Hey NSTN CH64 ... 181 G5
Brook Hey Dr NWD/KWIPK L33 ... 72 E5
Brookhill Cl BTL L20 ... 5 G4
Brookhill Rd BTL L20 ... 5 G2
Brook House Ct LYMM WA13 * ... 145 K6
Brook House Gv ECCL WA10 ... 102 C2
Brookhouse Rd ORM L39 ... 45 H5
Brookhurst Av BEB CH63 ... 183 K1
Brookhurst Cl BEB CH63 ... 183 K2
Brookhurst Rd BEB CH63 ... 183 K1
Brookland La STHEL WA9 ... 104 E3
Brookland Rd BIRK CH41 ... 2 E6
Brookland Rd East CLB/OSW/ST L13 ... 114 E4
Brookland Rd West CLB/OSW/ST L13 ... 114 E4
Brooklands BIRK CH41 ... 2 E2
ORM L39 ... 45 K5
Brooklands Av AIMK WN4 ... 91 J1
CSBY/WL L22 ... 81 F3
Brooklands Dr MGHL L31 ... 71 G1
Brooklands Gdns NSTN CH64 ... 181 H6
Brooklands Gv BRSC L40 ... 39 F6
Brooklands Pk WDN WA8 ... 158 D1
Brooklands Rd ECCL WA10 ... 102 C1
NSTN CH64 ... 181 H6
The Brooklands HUY L36 ... 116 E6
Brookland St WARR WA1 ... 143 H2
Brook La GOL/RIS/CUL WA3 ... 145 F1
NSTN CH64 ... 181 H5
ORM L39 ... 45 J1
RNFD/HAY WA11 ... 76 C2
Brooklet Rd HES CH60 ... 168 C5
Brooklyn Dr EP CH65 ... 195 J4
LYMM WA13 ... 145 K5
Brook Lynn Av GOL/RIS/CUL WA3 ... 93 G2
Brook Meadow PEN/TH CH61 ... 148 B4
Brook Pk MGHL L31 ... 71 F2
Brook Pl WARRS WA4 ... 143 H6
Brook Rd BTL L20 ... 4 C4
CSBY/BLUN L23 ... 69 H3
GTS/LS CH66 ... 195 G4
LYMM WA13 ... 145 J5
MGHL L31 ... 71 H1
WLT/FAZ L9 ... 97 J1
Brooks Aly CLVPS L1 ... 9 F5
Brookside BRSC L40 ... 37 F5
WD/CROXPK L12 ... 99 K5
Brookside Av AIMK WN4 ... 78 E1
CSBY/WL L22 ... 81 G3
DV/KA/FCH L14 ... 115 H4
ECCL WA10 ... 87 J6
LYMM WA13 ... 145 H5
RNFD/HAY WA11 ... 75 F2
WARRS WA4 ... 162 C2
WARRW/BUR WA5 ... 141 H4

Brookside Cl RAIN/WH L35 118 A3
WGNW/BIL/OR WN5 77 H5
Brookside Crs
GR/UP/WCH CH49 128 E4
Brookside Dr
GR/UP/WCH CH49 * 129 F4
Brookside Rd FROD/HEL WA6 200 D1
RAIN/WH L35 118 A3
STHP PR8 27 K6
Brookside Vw RNFD/HAY WA11 90 A4
Brookside Wy RNFD/HAY WA11 90 A4
Brooks Rd FMBY L37 48 D3
The Brooks RNFD/HAY WA11 88 D4
Brook St AIMK WN4 91 H1
BIRK CH41 2 C1
CHTN/BK PR9 24 A1
ECCL WA10 13 F5
GOL/RIS/CUL WA3 93 H2
GOL/RIS/CUL WA3 92 B4
NSTN CH64 191 K1
PS/BROM CH62 151 F5
RAIN/WH L35 118 B2
RUNC WA7 10 D4
VAUX/LVPD L3 8 B2
Brook St East BIRK CH41 3 F3
Brooks Wy FMBY L37 48 D3
Brookthorpe Cl WAL/NB CH45 111 H2
Brook V CSBY/WL L22 81 G3
Brookvale Av North
RUNC WA7 188 A1
Brookvale Av South
RUNC WA7 188 A1
Brookvale Cl
WARRW/BUR WA5 121 K1
Brook Wk PEN/TH CH61 148 A4
Brookway CL/PREN CH43 149 H2
GR/UP/WCH CH49 129 F4
WAL/NB CH45 111 G2
Brook Wy WARRW/BUR WA5 141 H4
Brookway La STHEL WA9 104 D4
Brook Well NSTN CH64 191 K4
Brookwood Cl WARRS WA4 162 A3
Brookwood Rd HUY L36 116 E3
Broom Av WARRS WA4 162 D5
Broom Cl BRSC L40 39 F5
PR/KW L34 118 B1
Broome Cl STHP PR8 27 J4
Broome Ct RUNC WA7 188 A2
Broome Rd STHP PR8 27 J4
Broomfield Cl HES CH60 167 G4
Broomfield Gdns WLT/FAZ L9 82 C6
Broomfield Rd WLT/FAZ L9 82 C6
Broomfields Rd WARRS WA4 162 C4
Broom Hl CL/PREN CH43 130 C2
Broomhill Cl NTHLY L27 135 K3
Broomlands HES CH60 167 J5
Broomleigh Cl BEB CH63 150 C6
Broom Rd ECCL WA10 102 D5
Broomsgrove AIN/FAZ L10 83 H2
Broom Wy HLWD L26 155 G4
Broseley Av PS/BROM CH62 170 E4
Broster Av MOR/LEA CH46 128 D1
Broster Cl MOR/LEA CH46 128 D1
Brosters La HOY CH47 108 B6
Brotherhood Dr STHEL WA9 104 B6
Brotherton Cl PS/BROM CH62 170 E5
Brotherton Wy NEWLW WA12 106 B1
Brougham Av BIRK CH41 131 H5
Brougham Rd WAL/EG CH44 111 K4
Brougham Ter NPK/KEN L6 113 J4
Broughton Av
GOL/RIS/CUL WA3 92 E4
STHP PR8 28 A3
WKBY CH48 127 F6
Broughton Cl WARRS WA4 162 E3
Broughton Dr ALL/GAR L19 153 H4
Broughton Hall Rd
WD/CROXPK L12 115 J2
Broughton Rd WAL/EG CH44 111 H4
Broughton Wy WDN WA8 157 G6
Brow La HES CH60 167 K6
Brownbill Bank NTHLY L27 136 B4
Brown Edge Cl STHP PR8 28 D5
Brown Heath Av
WGNW/BIL/OR WN5 77 G6
Brownhill Dr WARR WA1 143 J1
Browning Av RF/TRAN CH42 150 E2
WDN WA8 18 A4
Browning Cl HUY L36 117 F6
Browning Dr EP CH65 195 J5
WARRN/WOL WA2 123 F2
Browning Gn GTS/LS CH66 195 J5
Browning Rd CSBY/WL L22 80 E1
WAL/NB CH45 * 110 D2
Browning St BTL L20 4 B2
Brownlow Ar ECCL WA10 * 13 H6
Brownlow Hl VAUX/LVPD L3 9 G4
Brownlow Rd PS/BROM CH62 151 G4
Brownlow St VAUX/LVPD L3 9 J4
Brownmoor Cl CSBY/BLUN L23 69 H5
Brownmoor La CSBY/BLUN L23 69 G6
Brownmoor Pk CSBY/BLUN L23 69 G6
Brown's La NTHTN L30 70 C6
Brown St WDN WA8 19 J5
Brownville Rd
CLB/OSW/ST L13 * 114 B1
Brow Rd CL/PREN CH43 110 D6
Brows Cl FMBY L37 48 E2
Brow Side NPK/KEN L6 113 H3
Brows La FMBY L37 48 E2
Broxholme Wy MGHL L31 71 G2
Broxton Av CL/PREN CH43 149 J1
WKBY CH48 127 G6
Broxton Cl WDN WA8 138 B6
Broxton Rd GTS/LS CH66 195 H4
Broxton St WAV L15 133 K1
Bruce Av WARRN/WOL WA2 123 K6
Bruce Crs BEB CH63 183 K1
Bruce Dr GTS/LS CH66 195 F5
Bruce St ECCL WA10 12 D5
TOX L8 133 F5
Bruche Av WARR WA1 143 J2
Bruche Dr WARR WA1 143 J1
Bruera Rd EP CH65 195 J5
Brunel Dr LITH L21 81 H1
Brunel Rd PS/BROM CH62 171 G4
Brunner Rd WDN WA8 18 C3
Brunsborough Cl
PS/BROM CH62 183 K1
Brunsfield Cl MOR/LEA CH46 128 D2
Brunstath Cl HES CH60 168 C4
Brunswick Cl ANF/KKDL L4 * 97 G5
Brunswick Ct BIRK CH41 3 F3
Brunswick Crs GTS/LS CH66 195 H6
Brunswick Ms BIRK CH41 3 G3
CSBY/WL L22 81 F3
Brunswick Pde CSBY/WL L22 80 E3
Brunswick Pl BTL L20 96 D5
Brunswick Rd NEWLW WA12 105 K1
NPK/KEN L6 9 K1
Brunswick St ALL/GAR L19 172 B2
Brunswick St CLVP L2 8 C4
STHEL WA9 104 E2
Brunswick Wy VAUX/LVPD L3 132 C4
Brunt La ALL/GAR L19 154 B4
Bruntleigh Av WARRS WA4 143 K6
Bruton Rd HUY L36 116 D1
Bryanston Rd AIG/SPK L17 133 G6
RF/TRAN CH42 149 K1
Bryant Av WARRS WA4 143 J5
Bryant Rd LITH L21 81 J5
The Bryceway
WD/CROXPK L12 115 H3
Brydges St EHL/KEN L7 * 113 J6
Bryer Rd RAIN/WH L35 117 K3
Bryn Bank WAL/EG CH44 111 J3
Bryn Gates La WGNE/HIN WN2 79 H1
Brynmor Rd CALD/MH L18 153 H2
Brynmoss Av WAL/EG CH44 111 F3
Brynn St ECCL WA10 13 H3
Bryn Rd AIMK WN4 79 F3
Bryn Rd South AIMK WN4 79 H5
Bryn St AIMK WN4 79 G6
Bryony Wy RF/TRAN CH42 150 E3
Brythen St CLVPS L1 9 F4
Buchanan Cl WDN WA8 138 E6
Buchanan Rd WAL/EG CH44 111 K4
WLT/FAZ L9 97 H2
Buchan Cl WARRW/BUR WA5 141 J1
Buckfast Av RNFD/HAY WA11 90 E4
Buckfast Cl NTHTN L30 70 C5
WARRW/BUR WA5 141 F6
Buckfast Ct RUNC WA7 178 D2
Buckfast Dr FMBY L37 49 H3
Buckingham Av AIG/SPK L17 133 J4
BEB CH63 150 D4
CL/PREN CH43 130 C2
WDN WA8 139 F5
Buckingham Cl ECCL WA10 12 D7
NTHTN L30 69 K6
Buckingham Ct
NWD/KWIPK L33 72 E6
Buckingham Dr
RNFD/HAY WA11 88 D4
WARRW/BUR WA5 141 K5
Buckingham Gdns EP CH65 203 H1
Buckingham Gv FMBY L37 48 E3
Buckingham Rd
CLB/OSW/ST L13 114 B1
MGHL L31 71 H1
WAL/EG CH44 111 F3
WLT/FAZ L9 82 D5
Buckingham St EV L5 113 G2
Buckland Cl WDN WA8 157 J4
Buckland Dr BEB CH63 170 B3
Buckland St AIG/SPK L17 133 J6
Buckley Hill La NTHTN L30 70 A4
Buckley La NSTN CH64 193 G1
Buckley St WARRN/WOL WA2 16 C2
Buckthorn Cl STBRV L28 100 B6
Buckthorn Gdns STHEL WA9 118 E1
Buckton St WARR WA1 17 H1
Bude Cl CL/PREN CH43 129 K3
Bude Rd WDN WA8 157 K1
Budworth Av STHEL WA9 119 K4
WARRS WA4 143 J5
WDN WA8 157 J1
Budworth Cl CL/PREN CH43 130 B5
RUNC WA7 177 G6
Budworth Dr WLTN L25 155 F1
Budworth Rd CL/PREN CH43 130 B5
GTS/LS CH66 202 C1
Buerton Cl CL/PREN CH43 130 A5
Buffs La HES CH60 168 B5
Buggen La NSTN CH64 191 J1
Buildwas Rd NSTN CH64 181 K5
Bulford Rd WLT/FAZ L9 98 C1
Bulkeley Rd WAL/EG CH44 111 K4
Bull Bridge La AIN/FAZ L10 83 H1
Bull Cop FMBY L37 49 G2
Bullens La BRSC L40 36 B2
Bullens Rd ANF/KKDL L4 97 H5
KKBY L32 84 E2
Bullfinch Ct HLWD L26 155 H2
Bull Hl NSTN CH64 192 A3
Bull La WLT/FAZ L9 82 E4
Bullrush Dr MOR/LEA CH46 110 A5
The Bulrushes AIG/SPK L17 132 E6
Bulwer St BTL L20 81 H6
EV L5 * 113 J2
RF/TRAN CH42 150 E1
Bunbury Dr RUNC WA7 187 F1
Bunbury Gn EP CH65 203 H1
Bundoran Rd AIG/SPK L17 153 F1
Bungalow Rd NEWLW WA12 106 E4
The Bungalows Red Bank
NEWLW WA12 * 106 E4
Bunter Rd KKBY L32 84 E5
Bunting Cl GOL/RIS/CUL WA3 93 F3
Bunting Ct HLWD L26 155 G1
Buntingford Rd WARRS WA4 144 B6
Burbo Bank Rd CSBY/BLUN L23 68 B5
Burbo Bank Rd North
CSBY/BLUN L23 68 A4
Burbo Bank Rd South
CSBY/BLUN L23 68 C6
Burbo Crs CSBY/BLUN L23 68 C6
Burbo Man CSBY/BLUN L23 * 68 C6
Burbo Wy WAL/NB CH45 94 E5
Burden Rd MOR/LEA CH46 128 D1
Burdett Av BEB CH63 170 B3
Burdett Cl BEB CH63 170 C3
Burdett Rd CSBY/WL L22 80 E2
GTS/LS CH66 202 C1
WAL/NB CH45 110 D2
Burdett St AIG/SPK L17 133 H6
Burfield Dr WARRS WA4 162 B5
Burford Av WAL/EG CH44 111 F4
Burford La LYMM WA13 165 K2
Burford Rd CHLDW L16 115 G6
Burgess Av WARRS WA4 142 E6
Burgess Gdns MGHL L31 62 A5
Burgess' La FMBY L37 50 C4
Burgess St VAUX/LVPD L3 9 H2
Burghill Rd WD/CROXPK L12 99 K1
Burgundy Cl AIG/SPK L17 152 D1
Burkhardt Dr NEWLW WA12 106 E2
Burland Cl RUNC WA7 10 C6
Burland Rd HLWD L26 155 K5
Burleigh Ms EV L5 113 H1
Burleigh Rd North EV L5 97 H6
Burleigh Rd South EV L5 113 H1
Burley Av GOL/RIS/CUL WA3 92 E2
Burley Cl KKBY L32 84 E2
Burlingham Av WKBY CH48 146 D2
Burlington Av FMBY L37 49 H2
Burlington Rd STHP PR8 27 G4
WAL/NB CH45 95 H4
Burlington St BIRK CH41 3 F4
VAUX/LVPD L3 112 E3
Burman Crs ALL/GAR L19 153 K4
Burman Rd ALL/GAR L19 154 A4
Burnage Av STHEL WA9 120 A3
Burnage Cl SPK/HALE L24 174 A3
Burnand St ANF/KKDL L4 97 H6
Burnard Cl NWD/KWIPK L33 84 E1
Burnard Crs NWD/KWIPK L33 84 E1
Burnard Wk NWD/KWIPK L33 * 84 E1
Burnell Cl ECCL WA10 12 E4
Burnell Rd EP CH65 7 H7
Burnet Cl WARRN/WOL WA2 124 E5
Burnfell GOL/RIS/CUL WA3 93 F4
Burnham Cl WARRW/BUR WA5 141 G4
WDN WA8 138 B6
Burnham Rd CALD/MH L18 134 D6
Burnie Av BTL L20 5 J1
Burnley Av MOR/LEA CH46 129 G1
Burnley Cl NPK/KEN L6 113 J3
Burnley Rd MOR/LEA CH46 129 G1
STHP PR8 33 J4
Burnsall Av GOL/RIS/CUL WA3 93 G3
Burnsall Dr WDN WA8 138 B6
Burnsall St ALL/GAR L19 154 B6
Burns Av WAL/NB CH45 111 G2
Burns Cl AIMK WN4 78 E3
CHLDW L16 135 G1
GTS/LS CH66 195 H5
RAIN/WH L35 118 A4
Burns Crs WDN WA8 18 B3
Burns Gv HUY L36 117 G6
WARRN/WOL WA2 123 J5
Burnside Av WAL/EG CH44 111 H5
WARRS WA4 162 C2
Burnside Rd WAL/EG CH44 111 H5
Burns Rd STHEL WA9 119 J4
Burns St BTL L20 4 A1
Burnt Ash Cl ALL/GAR L19 153 G4
Burnthwaite Rd
DV/KA/FCH L14 115 G4
Burrell Cl RF/TRAN CH42 150 B2
Burrell Dr MOR/LEA CH46 128 E2
Burrell Rd RF/TRAN CH42 150 B2
Burrell St ANF/KKDL L4 97 H5
Burrough Cl GOL/RIS/CUL WA3 125 H4
Burroughs Gdns
VAUX/LVPD L3 * 113 F3
Burrows Av RNFD/HAY WA11 89 J6
Burrows Ct VAUX/LVPD L3 112 E3
Burrow's La ECCL WA10 102 A3
Burrows St RNFD/HAY WA11 89 K5
Bursar Cl NEWLW WA12 106 D1
Burscough Rd ORM L39 45 K4
Burscough St ORM L39 45 J6
Burton Av RAIN/WH L35 118 C3
WAL/NB CH45 110 E2
Burton Cl CLVPS L1 8 E7
RAIN/WH L35 118 C3
WDN WA8 138 E6
Burton Gn GTS/LS CH66 195 G5
Burtonhead Rd STHEL WA9 103 H3
Burton Rd NSTN CH64 191 K3
WARRN/WOL WA2 123 K6
Burton St EV L5 112 E1
Burtons Wy AIN/FAZ L10 84 B4
Burtonwood Cottages
STHEL WA9 * 105 G2
Burtonwood Rd
WARRW/BUR WA5 121 K3
Burtree Rd DV/KA/FCH L14 116 A1
Burwell Av FMBY L37 48 D4
Burwen Dr WLT/FAZ L9 82 C5
Bury Rd STHP PR8 27 H4
Busby's Cottages
WAL/NB CH45 95 H5
Bushby's La FMBY L37 48 C3
Bushby's Pk FMBY L37 48 C3
Bushell Cl NSTN CH64 192 A2
Bushell Rd NSTN CH64 192 A1
Bushel's Dr STHEL WA9 120 B5
Bushey La RNFD/HAY WA11 66 A5
Bushey Rd ANF/KKDL L4 98 A3
Bushley Cl BTL L20 4 D3
Bush Rd WDN WA8 158 A6
Bush Wy HES CH60 167 J5
Butchers La ORM L39 62 D2
Butcher St AIMK WN4 91 G1
Bute St VAUX/LVPD L3 113 G4
Butleigh Rd HUY L36 116 D2
Butler Crs NPK/KEN L6 113 K4
Butler St NPK/KEN L6 113 K3
Buttercup Cl CSBY/WL L22 81 G2
MOR/LEA CH46 110 A5
WARRW/BUR WA5 142 B6
Buttercup Wy WLT/FAZ L9 97 K1
Butterfield Gdns ORM L39 53 H2
Butterfield St ANF/KKDL L4 97 H6
Buttermarket St WARR WA1 16 E4
Buttermere Av AIMK WN4 79 G4
CL/PREN CH43 129 K3
EP CH65 196 B6
RNFD/HAY WA11 88 D3
WARRN/WOL WA2 123 J4
Buttermere Cl FMBY L37 48 D2
FROD/HEL WA6 201 G1
MGHL L31 62 B6
NWD/KWIPK L33 72 C5
Buttermere Crs
RNFD/HAY WA11 66 B5
Buttermere Gdns
CSBY/BLUN L23 81 G1
Buttermere Gv RUNC WA7 187 G1
Buttermere Rd CHLDW L16 116 A6
Buttermere St TOX L8 133 G2
Butterton Av
GR/UP/WCH CH49 128 E3
Butterwick Dr
WD/CROXPK L12 99 J2
Button St CLVP L2 8 E4
Butts Gn WARRW/BUR WA5 122 A4
Butts La STHP PR8 28 C2
Buxted Rd KKBY L32 85 F3
Buxton Cl WARRW/BUR WA5 141 H1
Buxton Rd RF/TRAN CH42 151 F1
Bye La ORM L39 52 A2
Byerley St WAL/EG CH44 112 A4
Byland Cl FMBY L37 49 H3
WDN WA8 139 H4
Byles St TOX L8 133 F5
Byng Pl ANF/KKDL L4 98 B5
Byng Rd ANF/KKDL L4 98 B5
Byng St BTL L20 4 C7
The By-Pass CSBY/BLUN L23 69 F5
Byrne Av RF/TRAN CH42 150 E2
Byrom La GOL/RIS/CUL WA3 93 G1
Byrom St CHTN/BK PR9 28 C1
CLVP L2 9 F2
Byrom Wy VAUX/LVPD L3 9 F1
Byron Av RAIN/WH L35 118 B4
Byron Cl CL/PREN CH43 149 J3
ECCL WA10 13 G2
FMBY L37 49 F1
HUY L36 117 F6
Byron Ct WARRN/WOL WA2 123 J5
Byron Rd CSBY/BLUN L23 68 C5
MGHL L31 62 B4
Byron St ALL/GAR L19 153 K6
BTL L20 4 A1
RUNC WA7 10 C6
The Byway CSBY/BLUN L23 69 F4

C

Cabes Cl DV/KA/FCH L14 116 A1
Cabin La BRSC L40 31 F1
CHTN/BK PR9 24 C2
MGHL L31 61 H3
ORM L39 35 F4
Cable Rd HOY CH47 127 G2
RAIN/WH L35 118 B2
Cable St CHTN/BK PR9 14 E4
CLVP L2 8 D5
FMBY L37 49 G1
Cabot Cl WARRW/BUR WA5 122 C6
Cabot Gn WLTN L25 135 F4
Cabul Cl WARRN/WOL WA2 143 F2
Caddick Rd PR/KW L34 85 G6
Cadet Wy WD/CROXPK L12 99 J6
Cadnam Rd WLTN L25 136 A4
Cadogan St EHL/KEN L7 133 J1
Cadshaw Cl GOL/RIS/CUL WA3 124 E2
Cadwell Rd MGHL L31 61 K2
Caernarvon Cl
GR/UP/WCH CH49 129 G3
RUNC WA7 177 J3
Caernarvon Ct EP CH65 203 H1
Caerwys Gv RF/TRAN CH42 131 H5
Caesars Cl RUNC WA7 177 H3
Caird St NPK/KEN L6 113 J4
Cairn Brae NEWLW WA12 106 C1
Cairn Ct STHEL WA9 103 F6
Cairnmore Rd CALD/MH L18 153 H1
Cairns St TOX L8 133 F3
Cairo St ANF/KKDL L4 97 G4
ECCL WA10 103 F4
WARR WA1 16 C5
Caister Cl SKEL WN8 57 F5
Caithness Ct RUNC WA7 10 E4
Caithness Dr CSBY/BLUN L23 69 G6
WAL/NB CH45 111 J1
Caithness Gdns
CL/PREN CH43 * 149 J2
Caithness Rd CALD/MH L18 153 J2
Calday Grange Cl WKBY CH48 146 E2
Calday Gv RNFD/HAY WA11 89 K3
Caldbeck Av
WARRN/WOL WA2 123 K5
Caldbeck Cl AIMK WN4 79 G5
Caldbeck Gv RNFD/HAY WA11 89 F2
Caldbeck Rd PS/BROM CH62 171 G3
Calder Av CL/PREN CH43 149 K1
ORM L39 53 J1
Calder Cl NWD/KWIPK L33 72 E3
WDN WA8 140 A6
Calder Dr CALD/MH L18 134 D4
MGHL L31 62 D5
RAIN/WH L35 118 D4
Calderfield Cl WARRS WA4 162 A3
Calderfield Rd CALD/MH L18 134 E4
Calder Gra CALD/MH L18 135 F6
Calderhurst Dr ECCL WA10 87 J5
Calder Rd BEB CH63 150 C6
EV L5 113 H1
The Calders CALD/MH L18 134 D6
Calderstones Av CALD/MH L18 134 D4
Calderstones Rd
CALD/MH L18 134 C5
Calder Wy GTS/LS CH66 195 F4
Calderwood Pk NTHLY L27 136 A3
Caldicott Av PS/BROM CH62 171 F6
Caldon Cl LITH L21 81 H2
Caldway Dr NTHLY L27 136 A3
Caldwell Av WARRW/BUR WA5 123 F5
Caldwell Cl NWD/KWIPK L33 * 72 E5
Caldwell Dr GR/UP/WCH CH49 148 E1
Caldwell Rd ALL/GAR L19 154 A3
WDN WA8 18 C5
Caldwell St STHEL WA9 104 B2
Caldy Chase Dr WKBY CH48 146 E4
Caldy Dr GTS/LS CH66 195 G5
Caldy Gv RNFD/HAY WA11 89 G6
Caldy Rd WAL/NB CH45 111 H2
WKBY CH48 146 D3
WLT/FAZ L9 82 D4
Caldy Wd WKBY CH48 146 E4
Caldywood Dr RAIN/WH L35 118 A4
Caledonia St CLVPS L1 9 J6
Calgarth Rd HUY L36 116 C2
California Cl
WARRW/BUR WA5 141 K1
California Rd CLB/OSW/ST L13 98 B6
Callaghan Cl EV L5 113 F2
Callander Rd NPK/KEN L6 114 B4
Callands Rd WARRW/BUR WA5 122 D5
Callestock Cl NG/CROX L11 84 C6
Callington Cl DV/KA/FCH L14 116 A1
Callon Av RNFD/HAY WA11 89 H6
Callow Rd WAV L15 133 J2
Calmet Cl EV L5 113 G1
Calmington La RUNC WA7 178 E1
Calne Cl PEN/TH CH61 148 A4
Calstock Cl WARRW/BUR WA5 141 F6
Calthorpe St ALL/GAR L19 153 J5
Calthorpe Wy CL/PREN CH43 130 A3
Calton Av CALD/MH L18 * 134 B4
Calvados Cl AIG/SPK L17 152 D2
Calveley Av PS/BROM CH62 184 C3
Calveley Cl CL/PREN CH43 130 B6
Calveley Rd HLWD L26 155 K5
Calverhall Wy AIMK WN4 79 F6
Calverly Cl RUNC WA7 188 B2
Calver Rd WARRN/WOL WA2 123 F3
Calvers RUNC WA7 177 H4
Camarthen Crs TOX L8 132 C3
Camberley Cl STHP PR8 27 F2
Camberley Dr WLTN L25 155 G3
Camberwell Park Rd
WDN WA8 139 J5
Camborne Av WLTN L25 155 F3
Camborne Cl RUNC WA7 188 B1
Cambourne Av
RNFD/HAY WA11 89 G4
Cambourne Rd
WARRW/BUR WA5 121 K1
Cambrai Av WARRS WA4 162 B1
Cambrian Cl GTS/LS CH66 194 D3
MOR/LEA CH46 * 128 C2
Cambrian Rd MOR/LEA CH46 128 D2
Cambrian Wy WLTN L25 135 J6
Cambria St NPK/KEN L6 113 K4
Cambridge Ar STHP PR8 14 E5
Cambridge Av CHTN/BK PR9 23 H3
CSBY/BLUN L23 68 E5
LITH L21 81 J3
Cambridge Cl WARRS WA4 162 A3
Cambridge Dr CSBY/BLUN L23 68 D4
HLWD L26 155 J3
Cambridge Gdns CHTN/BK PR9 23 H3
FROD/HEL WA6 200 A5
WARRS WA4 162 B5
Cambridge Rd BTL L20 5 H6
CHTN/BK PR9 23 G4
CSBY/BLUN L23 68 D4
CSBY/WL L22 81 F4
ECCL WA10 12 C3
EP CH65 6 E5
FMBY L37 48 D4
PS/BROM CH62 171 F5
RF/TRAN CH42 149 K1
SKEL WN8 56 A4
WAL/NB CH45 95 H6
WLT/FAZ L9 82 E3
Cambridge St EHL/KEN L7 133 F1
PR/KW L34 * 117 K1
RUNC WA7 11 H4
WAV L15 133 J1
WDN WA8 18 E5
Cambridge Wks STHP PR8 14 E5
Camdale Cl STBRV L28 100 B6
Camden Ct RUNC WA7 178 C4
Camden Ms GR/UP/WCH CH49 129 J5
Camden Pl BIRK CH41 3 F4
Camden Rd EP CH65 195 K4
Camden St VAUX/LVPD L3 9 G2
Camelford Rd NG/CROX L11 84 B6
Camelia Ct AIG/SPK L17 152 B1
Camellia Gdns STHEL WA9 105 F6
Camelot Cl NEWLW WA12 105 K1
Camelot Ter BTL L20 4 C2
Cameo Cl NPK/KEN L6 113 K3
Cameron Av RUNC WA7 176 B5
Cameron Ct WARRN/WOL WA2 123 G3
Cameron Rd MOR/LEA CH46 110 B4
WDN WA8 18 C4
Cameron St EHL/KEN L7 114 A5
Campania St ALL/GAR L19 172 B1
Campbell Av RUNC WA7 176 D5
Campbell Crs NWD/KWIPK L33 72 C3
WARRW/BUR WA5 141 G3
Campbell Dr DV/KA/FCH L14 115 J4
Campbell St BTL L20 4 B5
CLVPS L1 8 E6
ECCL WA10 12 D4
Camperdown St BIRK CH41 3 H4
Camphill Rd WLTN L25 154 D4
Campion Cl
GOL/RIS/CUL WA3 124 E3
RNFD/HAY WA11 88 E4
Campion Gv AIMK WN4 78 E5
Campion Wy HUY L36 136 C2
Camp Rd AIMK WN4 78 D6
WLTN L25 154 E2
Campsey Ash WDN WA8 138 E6
Camrose Cl RUNC WA7 187 F1
Camsley La LYMM WA13 145 G6
Cam St WLTN L25 * 154 D2
Canaan GOL/RIS/CUL WA3 93 K3
Canada Bvd VAUX/LVPD L3 8 B4
Canada Cl WARRN/WOL WA2 124 C5
Canal Bank BRSC L40 * 38 B3
Canal Bank Pygons Hl
MGHL L31 52 A6
Canal Reach RUNC WA7 178 B3
Canalside BRSC L40 37 F5
EP CH65 7 G2
Canal Side RUNC WA7 188 E2
RUNC WA7 176 A6
WARRS WA4 163 H2
WARRS WA4 161 F6
Canalside Gv EV L5 112 E2
Canal St BTL L20 4 D6
ECCL WA10 13 F7
NEWLW WA12 105 K3
RUNC WA7 11 G4
Canal Vw LYMM WA13 * 145 H6
MGHL L31 83 K1
Canberra Av STHEL WA9 103 G6
Canberra La NG/CROX L11 84 B6

Canberra Sq
WARRN/WOL WA2 123 K5
Candleston Cl
WARRW/BUR WA5 122 E6
Canford Cl WARRW/BUR WA5 141 K3
Cannell Ct RUNC WA7 187 K1
Cannell St WARRW/BUR WA5 142 A5
Canning Pl CLVPS L1 8 D6
Canning Rd CHTN/BK PR9 23 J6
Canning St BIRK CH41 3 G2
CSBY/WL L22 80 E2
TOX L8 9 J7
Canniswood Rd
RNFD/HAY WA11 89 K6
Cann La North WARRS WA4 162 D5
Cannock Cl GTS/LS CH66 202 C3
Cannock Gn MGHL L31 61 K6
Cannon Hl CL/PREN CH43 130 E3
Cannon St EP CH65 6 A4
STHEL WA9 120 A4
Canonbury Cl RUNC WA7 177 K5
Canon Rd NPK/KEN L6 98 A6
Canons Rd
WARRW/BUR WA5 142 A3
Canon St RUNC WA7 10 C3
Canon Wilson Cl
RNFD/HAY WA11 90 C5
Canova Cl NTHLY L27 136 C6
Canrow La PR/KW L34 85 J6
Cansfield Gv AIMK WN4 79 F5
Cansfield St ECCL WA10 13 H4
Canterbury Av CSBY/WL L22 68 E6
GOL/RIS/CUL WA3 92 E2
Canterbury Cl AIN/FAZ L10 83 H1
FMBY L37 41 F6
GTS/LS CH66 202 C3
PR/KW L34 102 A6
STHP PR8 27 G3
Canterbury Pk CALD/MH L18 153 K3
Canterbury Rd RF/TRAN CH42 151 F2
WAL/EG CH44 111 J4
WDN WA8 157 H4
Canterbury St ALL/GAR L19 172 B1
ECCL WA10 12 D2
VAUX/LVPD L3 9 H1
WARRS WA4 17 F7
Canterbury Wy NTHTN L30 70 C5
VAUX/LVPD L3 * 9 J1
Canter Cl WLT/FAZ L9 83 G3
Cantilever Gdns WARRS WA4 162 D1
Cantley Cl RUNC WA7 187 G1
Cantlow Fold STHP PR8 33 G5
Cantsfield St EHL/KEN L7 133 H2
Canvey Cl WAV L15 134 C2
Capenhurst Av
WARRN/WOL WA2 124 C5
Capenhurst Gdns
GTS/LS CH66 202 B2
Capenhurst La EP CH65 195 K6
Cape Rd WLT/FAZ L9 * 83 F5
Capesthorne Cl WDN WA8 157 K3
Capesthorne Rd
WARRN/WOL WA2 123 K6
Capilano Pk ORM L39 53 G5
Caplin Cl NWD/KWIPK L33 72 D3
Capper Gv HUY L36 116 E4
Capricorn Crs DV/KA/FCH L14 115 K2
Capricorn Wy BTL L20 4 D3
Capstick Crs WLTN L25 135 J3
Captain's La AIMK WN4 79 H6
NTHTN L30 82 A3
Caradoc Rd LITH L21 81 G5
The Caravan Pk STHEL WA9 103 J5
Caraway Cl CSBY/BLUN L23 69 J4
Caraway Gv ECCL WA10 12 A3
Carbis Cl AIN/FAZ L10 83 K5
Carden Cl ANF/KKDL L4 97 G6
GOL/RIS/CUL WA3 124 E3
Cardeston Cl RUNC WA7 187 J4
Cardiff Cl GTS/LS CH66 202 C3
Cardiff St SKEL WN8 55 K4
Cardiff Wy ALL/GAR L19 153 J5
Cardigan Av BIRK CH41 2 E4
Cardigan Cl ECCL WA10 12 E7
WARRW/BUR WA5 122 D5
Cardigan Rd STHP PR8 27 G6
WAL/NB CH45 95 H6
Cardigan St WAV L15 133 J1
Cardigan Wy NPK/KEN L6 113 K3
NTHTN L30 * 70 E5
Cardus Cl MOR/LEA CH46 128 C1
Cardwell St EHL/KEN L7 133 F1
Carey Av BEB CH63 150 C5
Carey St WDN WA8 18 E2
Carfax Rd NWD/KWIPK L33 73 F5
Carfield SKEL WN8 67 G1
Cargill Gv RF/TRAN CH42 151 G3
Carham Rd HOY CH47 127 H3
Carina Pk WARRW/BUR WA5 122 B5
Carisbrooke Cl WKBY CH48 146 D3
Carisbrooke Dr
CHTN/BK PR9 23 H4
Carisbrooke Pl ANF/KKDL L4 * 97 H4
Carisbrooke Rd ANF/KKDL L4 97 G4
BTL L20 5 J7
Carkington Rd WLTN L25 155 F2
Carland Cl AIN/FAZ L10 84 A5
Carlaw Rd RF/TRAN CH42 149 K1
Carleen Cl AIG/SPK L17 152 C1
Carlett Bvd PS/BROM CH62 184 C2
Carlile Wy NWD/KWIPK L33 72 E3
Carlingford Cl TOX L8 133 F2
Carlingford Rd WARRS WA4 162 A3
Carlisle Av NTHTN L30 82 C2
Carlisle Cl ANF/KKDL L4 98 B5
Carlisle Ms CL/PREN CH43 2 C6
Carlisle Rd STHP PR8 27 H5
Carlisle St WARRS WA4 162 B3
Carlis Rd KKBY L32 84 E3
Carlow Cl SPK/HALE L24 174 D3
Carlow St ECCL WA10 103 F4
Carlsruhe Ct TOX L8 * 133 F4
Carl's Wy NWD/KWIPK L33 73 F3
Carlton Av RUNC WA7 177 G3
SKEL WN8 57 J6
Carlton Cl NSTN CH64 181 H5
Carlton Crs GTS/LS CH66 195 H1
Carlton La CLB/OSW/ST L13 114 E3
HOY CH47 127 H1
Carlton Mt RF/TRAN CH42 131 H6
Carlton Rd BEB CH63 170 D1
GOL/RIS/CUL WA3 92 E2
RF/TRAN CH42 131 F5
STHP PR8 33 J3
WAL/NB CH45 95 H5
Carlton St ECCL WA10 12 D6
PR/KW L34 101 K6
VAUX/LVPD L3 112 D3
WARRS WA4 162 B3
WDN WA8 18 D3
Carlton Ter CSBY/BLUN L23 * 68 E5
Carlyle Crs GTS/LS CH66 195 H5
Carlyon Wy HLWD L26 * 155 H3
Carmarthen Cl
WARRW/BUR WA5 122 D5
Carmel Cl ORM L39 53 H3
Carmel Ct WDN WA8 139 G5
Carmelite Crs ECCL WA10 87 H6
Carmichael Av
GR/UP/WCH CH49 148 A1
Carnaby Cl HUY L36 136 D1
Carnarvon Rd STHP PR8 27 G6
WLT/FAZ L9 97 H2
Carnarvon St STHEL WA9 103 F6
Carnatic Rd AIG/SPK L17 133 K6
Carnation Rd WLT/FAZ L9 97 K1
Carnegie Av CSBY/BLUN L23 68 E6
Carnegie Crs STHEL WA9 104 C5
Carnegie Dr AIMK WN4 79 F4
Carnegie Rd CLB/OSW/ST L13 114 D3
Carnforth Av KKBY L32 84 E2
Carnforth Cl BIRK CH41 2 C7
WD/CROXPK L12 99 G4
Carnforth Rd CALD/MH L18 153 K1
Carno St WAV L15 * 133 K1
Carnoustie Cl MOR/LEA CH46 109 F6
STHP PR8 27 G3
WD/CROXPK L12 115 K1
Carnoustie Gv
RNFD/HAY WA11 89 K6
Carnsdale Rd MOR/LEA CH46 129 G1
Carol Dr HES CH60 168 C5
Carole Cl STHEL WA9 120 C1
Carolina Rd WARRW/BUR WA5 141 J2
Carolina St BTL L20 4 E4
Caroline Pl CL/PREN CH43 130 E4
Caroline St WDN WA8 * 18 E6
Carol St WARRS WA4 143 G6
Caronia St ALL/GAR L19 * 172 B1
Carpathia St ALL/GAR L19 172 B1
Carpenter Gv
WARRN/WOL WA2 124 C6
Carpenter's La WKBY CH48 146 C1
Carpenters Rw CLVPS L1 8 D7
Carraway Rd NG/CROX L11 84 A5
Carr Bridge Rd
GR/UP/WCH CH49 129 J5
Carr Cl NG/CROX L11 99 F3
Carr Cft LITH L21 69 J6
Carrfield Av CSBY/BLUN L23 69 H6
Carr Ga MOR/LEA CH46 128 C2
Carr Hey MOR/LEA CH46 128 C1
Carr Hey Cl GR/UP/WCH CH49 149 F1
Carr House La HTWN L38 60 A3
MOR/LEA CH46 128 C1
Carriage Cl SPK/HALE L24 174 E4
Carriage Dr FROD/HEL WA6 200 D3
Carrick Dr EP CH65 203 F1
Carrickmore Av CALD/MH L18 153 H1
Carrington Cl
GOL/RIS/CUL WA3 124 E3
Carrington Rd WAL/NB CH45 111 H1
Carrington St BIRK CH41 130 D1
Carr La BRSC L40 39 H6
GOL/RIS/CUL WA3 93 H4
HOY CH47 127 G3
HUY L36 116 C6
MGHL L31 61 H2
MOR/LEA CH46 128 C1
NG/CROX L11 98 D3
PR/KW L34 117 H2
SPK/HALE L24 174 E3
STHP PR8 34 B2
Carr La East NG/CROX L11 99 F3
Carr Meadow Hey NTHTN L30 81 K1
Carr Mill Crs
WGNW/BIL/OR WN5 77 H5
Carr Mill Rd RNFD/HAY WA11 89 F3
WGNW/BIL/OR WN5 77 H5
Carr Moss La STHP PR8 34 A5
Carrock Rd PS/BROM CH62 171 G3
Carroll Crs ORM L39 45 K4
Carrow Cl MOR/LEA CH46 128 C2
Carr Rd BTL L20 82 A4
Carr's Crs FMBY L37 48 D4
Carr's Crs West FMBY L37 48 D4
Carr Side La SFTN L29 60 C4
Carr St ECCL WA10 12 B1
Carruthers St VAUX/LVPD L3 112 E4
Carrville Wy WD/CROXPK L12 100 A3
Carrwood Cl RNFD/HAY WA11 89 K5
Carrwood Pk STHP PR8 27 J4
Carsdale Rd CALD/MH L18 134 B4
Carsgoe Rd HOY CH47 127 H3
Carsington Rd NG/CROX L11 98 E3
Carstairs Rd NPK/KEN L6 114 A3
Carsthorne Rd HOY CH47 127 H3
Cartbridge La HLWD L26 155 J2
Carter Av RNFD/HAY WA11 75 H4
The Carters GR/UP/WCH CH49 128 D5
NTHTN L30 70 D5
Carter St TOX L8 132 E2
Carterton Rd HOY CH47 127 H3
Cartier Cl WARRW/BUR WA5 122 C6
Cartmel Av ECCL WA10 88 B4
MGHL L31 62 C5
WARRN/WOL WA2 123 J4
Cartmel Cl BIRK CH41 * 2 C7
HUY L36 116 D3
STHP PR8 28 C4
WARRW/BUR WA5 122 E5
Cartmel Dr FMBY L37 49 H3
GTS/LS CH66 202 D1
MOR/LEA CH46 129 F2
RAIN/WH L35 118 C3
WD/CROXPK L12 99 G4
Cartmell Cl RUNC WA7 186 E1
Cartmel Rd HUY L36 116 C3
Cartmel Ter NG/CROX L11 99 F2
Cartmel Wy HUY L36 116 C3
Cartridge La WARRS WA4 163 J5
Cartwright St RUNC WA7 11 H5
WARRW/BUR WA5 142 B3
Carvel Wy BRSC L40 39 F6
Carver St VAUX/LVPD L3 9 J1
Caryl Gv TOX L8 132 D5
Caryl St TOX L8 132 C3
Cascade Rd SPK/HALE L24 155 F5
Cascades SKEL WN8 * 56 E6
Case Gv RAIN/WH L35 118 A2
Case Rd RNFD/HAY WA11 90 C5
Cashel Rd BIRK CH41 111 H5
Caspian Pl BTL L20 5 F4
Caspian Rd ANF/KKDL L4 98 A3
Cassia Cl WLT/FAZ L9 97 K1
Cassino Rd HUY L36 116 D4
Cassio St BTL L20 * 5 J7
Cassley Rd SPK/HALE L24 174 B2
Cassville Rd WAV L15 134 B3
Castell Gv ECCL WA10 12 E5
Casterton St EHL/KEN L7 * 133 H1
Castle Av STHEL WA9 104 C2
Castle Cl MOR/LEA CH46 110 A4
Castle Dr EP CH65 195 K6
FMBY L37 49 F4
HES CH60 167 K5
Castlefield Av South
RUNC WA7 177 J4
Castlefield Cl WD/CROXPK L12 98 E5
Castlefield Rd WD/CROXPK L12 98 E6
Castlefields Av East
RUNC WA7 177 K3
Castlefields Av North
RUNC WA7 177 H3
Castlefields Av South
RUNC WA7 177 J4
Castle Fields Est
MOR/LEA CH46 109 K3
Castleford Ri MOR/LEA CH46 109 J4
Castleford St WAV L15 134 B2
Castlegate Gv WD/CROXPK L12 98 E6
Castlegrange Cl
MOR/LEA CH46 109 J3
Castle Gn WARRW/BUR WA5 122 B5
Castleheath Cl MOR/LEA CH46 109 J4
Castlehey SKEL WN8 67 G1
Castle Hl CLVP L2 * 8 C4
NEWLW WA12 106 E1
Castle La BRSC L40 46 D5
Castle Mt HES CH60 * 167 K5
Castle Ri RUNC WA7 11 K5
Castle Rd RUNC WA7 177 J5
WAL/NB CH45 111 G1
Castlesite Rd WD/CROXPK L12 99 F6
Castle St BIRK CH41 3 H4
CHTN/BK PR9 15 F4
CLVP L2 8 C4
WDN WA8 19 J2
WLTN L25 154 C1
Castleton Dr NTHTN L30 70 E5
Castletown Cl CHLDW L16 135 F1
Castleview Rd WD/CROXPK L12 99 F6
Castle Wk STHP PR8 14 C7
Castleway North
MOR/LEA CH46 110 A3
Castleway South
MOR/LEA CH46 110 A4
Castlewood Rd NPK/KEN L6 113 K2
Castner Av RUNC WA7 176 B6
Castor St NPK/KEN L6 113 K2
Catchdale Moss La ECCL WA10 87 F6
Catford Cl WDN WA8 157 H1
Catford Gn SPK/HALE L24 174 A2
Catfoss Cl WARRN/WOL WA2 124 A6
Catharine's La ORM L39 53 K3
Catharine St TOX L8 132 E2
Cathcart St BIRK CH41 2 D3
Cathedral Cl CLVPS L1 132 D2
Cathedral Ga CLVPS L1 9 H7
Cathedral Rd NPK/KEN L6 114 A1
Cathedral Wk VAUX/LVPD L3 9 H5
Catherine St BIRK CH41 2 D5
LITH L21 81 J5
WARRW/BUR WA5 16 A1
WDN WA8 18 D7
Catherine Wy NEWLW WA12 106 B3
RNFD/HAY WA11 * 89 J5
Catkin Rd HLWD L26 155 G1
Caton Cl CHTN/BK PR9 23 H1
Catonfield Rd CALD/MH L18 134 E4
Cat Tail La STHP PR8 29 H6
Catterall Av STHEL WA9 120 B1
WARRN/WOL WA2 123 K5
Catterick Cl HLWD L26 155 J3
Catterick Fold STHP PR8 28 C4
Caulfield Dr GR/UP/WCH CH49 129 F6
Caunce Av CHTN/BK PR9 21 K5
GOL/RIS/CUL WA3 92 B4
RNFD/HAY WA11 90 A5
Caunce's Rd CHTN/BK PR9 30 B2
Causeway Av WARRS WA4 143 F6
Causeway Cl PS/BROM CH62 151 G6
Causeway La FMBY L37 50 D4
The Causeway CHTN/BK PR9 21 F6
PS/BROM CH62 151 G6
WD/CROXPK L12 115 H3
Cavalier Dr ALL/GAR L19 154 B6
Cavan Dr RNFD/HAY WA11 90 C4
Cavan Rd NG/CROX L11 98 C5
Cavell Cl WLTN L25 154 D2
Cavell Dr EP CH65 6 A7
Cavendish Av
GOL/RIS/CUL WA3 125 G2
Cavendish Cl
WARRW/BUR WA5 142 A2
Cavendish Dr RF/TRAN CH42 150 C2
WLT/FAZ L9 97 J2
Cavendish Farm Rd
RUNC WA7 186 C2
Cavendish Gdns EP CH65 6 A7
TOX L8 * 133 F4
Cavendish Pl
GOL/RIS/CUL WA3 125 H2
Cavendish Rd BIRK CH41 130 E2
CSBY/BLUN L23 68 D6
STHP PR8 27 G4
WAL/NB CH45 95 H4
Cavendish St BIRK CH41 2 A1
RUNC WA7 10 C5
Cavendish Whf BIRK CH41 * 111 J6
Cavern Ct NPK/KEN L6 113 K4
Caversham Cl WARRS WA4 162 C4
Cawdor St RUNC WA7 10 B3
TOX L8 133 F3
WARRS WA4 162 B3
Cawfield Av WDN WA8 157 J2
Cawley St RUNC WA7 10 D7
Cawood Cl GTS/LS CH66 194 E4
Cawthorne Av KKBY L32 84 D4
WARRS WA4 163 F1
Cawthorne Cl KKBY L32 84 D3
Cawthorne Wk KKBY L32 * 84 D3
Caxton Cl CL/PREN CH43 129 K3
GTS/LS CH66 195 J5
WDN WA8 * 138 B6
Caxton Rd RAIN/WH L35 119 G6
Cazneau St VAUX/LVPD L3 113 F4
C Ct AIMK WN4 91 G1
Cearns Rd CL/PREN CH43 130 D4
Cecil Dr ECCL WA10 87 H6
Cecil Rd LITH L21 81 G5
PS/BROM CH62 151 G3
RF/TRAN CH42 150 A1
WAL/NB CH45 111 G3
Cecil St STHEL WA9 104 D6
WAV L15 133 J1
Cedab Rd EP CH65 6 E3
Cedar Av BEB CH63 170 A1
GOL/RIS/CUL WA3 93 G4
GTS/LS CH66 195 F3
RUNC WA7 177 F6
WDN WA8 139 G6
Cedar Cl CALD/MH L18 134 E6
RAIN/WH L35 118 A3
Cedar Crs HUY L36 116 D6
NEWLW WA12 106 D3
ORM L39 53 G1
Cedardale Dr GTS/LS CH66 202 D2
Cedardale Pk WDN WA8 139 K5
Cedardale Rd WLT/FAZ L9 97 J1
Cedar Dr FMBY L37 48 C4
Cedar Gv AIMK WN4 78 C4
CSBY/WL L22 80 E1
MGHL L31 71 G3
NSTN CH64 192 A1
RNFD/HAY WA11 90 D4
SKEL WN8 56 A4
TOX L8 133 H3
WARR WA1 143 K2
WARRS WA4 143 G6
Cedar Rd RAIN/WH L35 117 K4
WARRW/BUR WA5 141 G3
WLT/FAZ L9 82 E5
The Cedars MOR/LEA CH46 128 D2
WD/CROXPK L12 99 K2
Cedar St BIRK CH41 2 D6
BTL L20 5 F3
ECCL WA10 12 A7
NEWLW WA12 * 106 C3
STHP PR8 27 K3
Cedar Ter TOX L8 133 G3
Cedarway HES CH60 181 G2
Cedarways WARRS WA4 162 C6
Cedarwood Cl
GR/UP/WCH CH49 128 C5
Cedarwood Ct HUY L36 136 B1
Celandine Wy STHEL WA9 105 F6
Celebration Dr NPK/KEN L6 114 A2
Celedine Cl WAV L15 133 K1
Celia St BTL L20 97 F4
Celtic Rd HOY CH47 108 C6
Celtic St TOX L8 133 F3
Celt St NPK/KEN L6 * 114 A3
Cemeas Cl EV L5 112 E2
Cemetery Rd STHP PR8 27 J3
Centenary Cl ANF/KKDL L4 98 A5
Central Av EP CH65 6 D6
PR/KW L34 117 J1
PS/BROM CH62 170 E4
SPK/HALE L24 173 J2
STHP PR8 34 B1
WARRN/WOL WA2 143 F1
WARRS WA4 142 E6
Central Dr RNFD/HAY WA11 90 A5
RNFD/HAY WA11 75 G2
WD/CROXPK L12 114 E2
Central Expy RUNC WA7 187 G1
Central Park Av WAL/EG CH44 111 J3
Central Rd PS/BROM CH62 151 G4
WARRS WA4 142 E6
Central Sq MGHL L31 62 B5
Central St ECCL WA10 13 G3
Central Wy NEWLW WA12 106 E3
SPK/HALE L24 173 K3
WARRN/WOL WA2 16 D3
Centre Ct LEIGH WN7 93 J2
Centre Pk WARR WA1 142 D6
Centre Park Sq WARR WA1 16 C7
Centreville Rd CALD/MH L18 134 B3
Centre Wy HUY L36 116 E5
Centurion Cl
GOL/RIS/CUL WA3 125 F3
HOY CH47 108 C6
Centurion Dr HOY CH47 108 C6
Centurion Rw RUNC WA7 177 J3
Ceres St BTL L20 96 E4
Cestrian Dr PEN/TH CH61 148 D6
Chadlow Rd KKBY L32 84 E4
Chadwell Rd NWD/KWIPK L33 72 E5
Chadwick Av WARRS WA4 162 D2
Chadwick Pl
GOL/RIS/CUL WA3 125 G2
Chadwick Rd RNFD/HAY WA11 89 F4
RUNC WA7 177 H2
Chadwick St MOR/LEA CH46 129 F1
VAUX/LVPD L3 112 D4
Chadwick Wy NWD/KWIPK L33 72 D3
Chaffinch Cl GOL/RIS/CUL WA3 125 H4
WD/CROXPK L12 99 K4
Chaffinch Gld HLWD L26 155 H2
Chainhurst Cl NTHLY L27 136 A3
Chain La RNFD/HAY WA11 89 G5
Chalfield Av GTS/LS CH66 195 F4
Chalfield Cl GTS/LS CH66 195 F4
Chalfont Cl WARRS WA4 162 D5
Chalfont Rd CALD/MH L18 154 A2
Chalfont Wy STBRV L28 100 B6
Chalgrave Cl WDN WA8 139 K6
Chalkwell Dr HES CH60 168 C6
Challis St BIRK CH41 110 E6
Challoner Cl HUY L36 136 C1
Chaloner Gv ALL/GAR L19 153 G4
Chaloner St CLVPS L1 132 C2
Chalon Wy East ECCL WA10 13 H6
Chalon Wy West ECCL WA10 13 F6
Chamberlain Dr
NWD/KWIPK L33 72 E4
Chamberlain St BIRK CH41 * 131 H5
ECCL WA10 12 A6
WAL/EG CH44 111 G5
Chambres Rd STHP PR8 28 A2
Chambres Rd North STHP PR8 15 K7
Chancellor Ct TOX L8 133 F1
Chancellor Rd RUNC WA7 160 A6
Chancel St ANF/KKDL L4 97 G6
Chancery La STHEL WA9 104 C2
Chandlers Ct RUNC WA7 10 A6
Chandlers Wy STHEL WA9 119 K4
Chandler Wy GOL/RIS/CUL WA3 93 F3
Chandley Cl STHP PR8 33 G4
Chandos St EHL/KEN L7 113 K6
Change La NSTN CH64 193 J1
Changford Rd NWD/KWIPK L33 73 F6
Channell Rd NPK/KEN L6 114 A4
Channel Rd CSBY/BLUN L23 68 C6
The Channel WAL/NB CH45 * 94 E5
Chantler Av WARRS WA4 143 H5
Chantrell Rd WKBY CH48 147 F1
Chantry Cl CL/PREN CH43 129 K3
Chantry Wk AIMK WN4 78 E4
HES CH60 181 F1
Chapel Av WLT/FAZ L9 82 D6
Chapel Cl EP CH65 6 D1
Chapel Cross Rd
WARRN/WOL WA2 124 C5
Chapelfields FROD/HEL WA6 200 D1
Chapel Gdns EV L5 113 F2
Chapelhill Rd MOR/LEA CH46 129 G1
Chapelhouse Wk FMBY L37 49 G2
Chapel La BRSC L40 46 E1
BRSC L40 31 G2
ECCL WA10 102 D1
FMBY L37 49 F2
MGHL L31 71 K5
NTHTN L30 70 D4
RAIN/WH L35 119 H5
WARRS WA4 162 B3
WARRW/BUR WA5 121 K1
WDN WA8 138 B4
Chapel Ms EP CH65 6 B6
ORM L39 53 J1
Chapel Pl AIMK WN4 * 79 G6
ALL/GAR L19 153 K5
Chapel Rd ALL/GAR L19 153 K5
HOY CH47 127 G1
NPK/KEN L6 114 A1
WARRW/BUR WA5 141 F6
Chapelside Cl
WARRW/BUR WA5 141 G3
Chapel St AIMK WN4 79 G6
CLVP L2 8 B4
ECCL WA10 13 F1
NEWLW WA12 106 B2
ORM L39 45 K6
PR/KW L34 * 117 K1
RNFD/HAY WA11 90 C5
RUNC WA7 10 D4
STHP PR8 14 E5
WDN WA8 18 C6
Chapel Ter BTL L20 4 C6
Chapel Vw PS/BROM CH62 184 D1
RNFD/HAY WA11 76 C5
Chapel Wks LYMM WA13 165 K2
Chapel Yd WARRN/WOL WA2 16 C3
WAV L15 134 B2
Chapman Cl TOX L8 * 132 D4
WDN WA8 138 C5
Chapman Gv PR/KW L34 102 A6
Chardstock Dr WLTN L25 * 135 K5
Charing Cross BIRK CH41 2 D5
Charlecombe St
RF/TRAN CH42 131 G5
Charlecote St TOX L8 132 E6
Charles Av STHP PR8 34 A3
WARRW/BUR WA5 141 G3
Charles Berrington Rd
WAV L15 134 B3
Charlesbye Av ORM L39 46 A5
Charles Price Gdns EP CH65 6 D3
Charles Rd HOY CH47 127 G3
Charles St BIRK CH41 2 D2
ECCL WA10 13 H4
GOL/RIS/CUL WA3 92 B2
WDN WA8 18 D3
Charleston Cl GTS/LS CH66 195 G6
Charleston Gv
WARRW/BUR WA5 141 J3
Charleston Rd TOX L8 132 E5
Charlesville Cl CL/PREN CH43 130 E4
Charles Wk DV/KA/FCH L14 115 K4
Charlesworth Cl MGHL L31 61 K2
Charley Wood Rd
NWD/KWIPK L33 85 G2
Charlock Cl NTHTN L30 70 D5
Charlotte Rd WAL/EG CH44 111 K2
Charlotte's Mdw BEB CH63 170 C1
Charlotte Wk WDN WA8 18 E6
Charlton Cl AIMK WN4 79 F4
RUNC WA7 177 K6
Charlton Ct CL/PREN CH43 130 C3
Charlton Pl CLB/OSW/ST L13 114 E6
Charlton Rd CLB/OSW/ST L13 114 E6
Charlton St WARRS WA4 143 J6
Charlwood Av HUY L36 116 E6
Charlwood Cl CL/PREN CH43 129 K3
Charminster Cl
WARRW/BUR WA5 141 J4
Charmouth Cl NEWLW WA12 106 B1
WD/CROXPK L12 99 J2
Charnley Dr WAV L15 134 D1
Charnley's La CHTN/BK PR9 21 H3
Charnock Av NEWLW WA12 105 K2
Charnock Rd WLT/FAZ L9 98 A2
Charnwood Cl
GOL/RIS/CUL WA3 125 K2
WD/CROXPK L12 99 H2
Charnwood Rd HUY L36 116 B4
Charnwood St STHEL WA9 104 C1
Charon Wy WARRW/BUR WA5 122 A4
Charter Av WARRW/BUR WA5 142 D1

Charter Crs GTS/LS CH66 195 H6
Charterhouse Cl EP CH65 7 J4
Charterhouse Dr AIN/FAZ L10 83 H1
Charterhouse Rd WLTN L25 154 E2
Chartmount Wy WLTN L25 135 J5
Chartwell Gv HLWD L26 155 K2
Chartwell Rd STHP PR8 33 H3
Chase Cl STHP PR8 27 G3
Chase Dr GTS/LS CH66 202 C1
Chase Heys CHTN/BK PR9 23 H4
Chaser Cl WLT/FAZ L9 83 F3
The Chase BEB CH63 183 K2
HUY L36 136 C1
Chase Wy EV L5 113 G3
GTS/LS CH66 202 B1
Chatburn Av GOL/RIS/CUL WA3 92 D2
Chatburn Wk TOX L8 * 132 E5
Chater Cl RAIN/WH L35 118 B2
Chatfield Dr GOL/RIS/CUL WA3 125 G4
Chatham Cl LITH L21 81 G4
Chatham Pl EHL/KEN L7 113 K6
Chatham Rd RF/TRAN CH42 151 F1
Chatham St EHL/KEN L7 9 K7
Chatsworth Av WAL/EG CH44 111 J3
WLT/FAZ L9 82 C6
Chatsworth Cl AIMK WN4 78 E5
GTS/LS CH66 195 F4
Chatsworth Dr EHL/KEN L7 133 G1
WDN WA8 * 138 B6
Chatsworth Rd PEN/TH CH61 148 C6
RAIN/WH L35 118 D3
RF/TRAN CH42 151 F1
STHP PR8 33 G3
Chatteris Pk RUNC WA7 178 D3
Chatterton Dr RUNC WA7 178 D5
Chatterton Rd DV/KA/FCH L14 115 G3
Chatwell Gdns WARRS WA4 162 E6
Chaucer Dr WD/CROXPK L12 99 K3
Chaucer Pl WARRS WA4 143 J5
Chaucer Rd ECCL WA10 88 A5
Chaucer St BTL L20 4 B2
RUNC WA7 10 D6
VAUX/LVPD L3 113 F4
Cheadle Av CLB/OSW/ST L13 114 D4
Cheapside CLVP L2 8 D2
FMBY L37 49 G3
Cheapside Aly CLVP L2 * 8 D3
Cheddar Cl WLTN L25 154 C1
Cheddar Gv KKBY L32 84 D4
WARRW/BUR WA5 105 K6
Cheddon Wy PEN/TH CH61 167 J1
Chedworth Dr WDN WA8 138 B5
Chedworth Rd
DV/KA/FCH L14 115 J3
Cheldon Rd WD/CROXPK L12 99 G3
Chelford Av GOL/RIS/CUL WA3 92 E4
Chelford Cl CL/PREN CH43 129 K2
WARRS WA4 162 B3
Chellowdene CSBY/BLUN L23 69 H3
Chelmarsh Av AIMK WN4 79 H6
Chelmsford Cl EV L5 97 F6
Chelsea Ct WD/CROXPK L12 99 J5
Chelsea Gdns
WARRW/BUR WA5 141 K5
Chelsea Rd LITH L21 81 J5
WLT/FAZ L9 82 D5
Cheltenham Av AIG/SPK L17 133 J3
Cheltenham Cl AIN/FAZ L10 83 H2
WARRW/BUR WA5 141 H1
Cheltenham Crs HUY L36 116 D6
MOR/LEA CH46 109 J4
RUNC WA7 186 E1
Cheltenham Dr NEWLW WA12 91 H6
Cheltenham Rd EP CH65 196 C6
WAL/NB CH45 110 E1
Cheltenham Wy STHP PR8 28 C3
Chelwood Av CHLDW L16 115 J6
Chelwood Pk AIMK WN4 91 G2
Chemical St NEWLW WA12 106 B2
Chemistry Rd SPK/HALE L24 155 F6
Chenotrie Gdns
CL/PREN CH43 130 A4
Chepstow Av WAL/EG CH44 111 J3
Chepstow Cl
WARRW/BUR WA5 122 E4
Chepstow St ANF/KKDL L4 97 G4
Chequer Cl SKEL WN8 67 H2
Chequer La SKEL WN8 67 H1
Chequers Gdns ALL/GAR L19 153 G3
Cheriton Av WKBY CH48 146 E1
Cheriton Cl HLWD L26 155 H3
Cheriton Pk STHP PR8 27 J2
Chermside Rd AIG/SPK L17 153 F2
Cherry Av ANF/KKDL L4 97 K4
Cherrybank WAL/EG CH44 111 H5
Cherry Blossom Rd
RUNC WA7 187 J2
Cherry Cl ANF/KKDL L4 97 K4
NEWLW WA12 105 K1
NSTN CH64 192 D1
Cherry Cnr LYMM WA13 164 B5
Cherrycroft SKEL WN8 67 G1
Cherrydale Rd CALD/MH L18 134 B5
Cherryfield Crs KKBY L32 84 D1
Cherryfield Dr KKBY L32 84 D1
Cherry Gn ORM L39 53 F4
Cherry Gv BRSC L40 38 E3
GTS/LS CH66 202 E2
KKBY L32 84 E4
Cherry La ANF/KKDL L4 97 K4
LYMM WA13 164 C3
Cherry Rd STHP PR8 41 K1
Cherrysutton WDN WA8 138 A6
Cherrysutton Ms WDN WA8 * 138 A5
Cherry Tree Av LYMM WA13 164 E1
RUNC WA7 177 F5
WARRW/BUR WA5 141 G5
Cherry Tree Cl CHNE CH2 198 C5
RAIN/WH L35 117 K3
RNFD/HAY WA11 * 89 K6
Cherry Tree Dr STHEL WA9 104 E3
Cherry Tree La BRSC L40 36 E5
ORM L39 53 F4
RNFD/HAY WA11 88 D1
Cherry Tree Rd
GOL/RIS/CUL WA3 93 G3
HUY L36 136 B1
MOR/LEA CH46 129 G2
Cherry V WLTN L25 135 J6
Cherry Vw NWD/KWIPK L33 72 E4
Cherrywood Av HLWD L26 156 A2
Cherwell Cl WARRN/WOL WA2 123 K5
Cheryl Dr WDN WA8 19 K1
Chesford Gra WARR WA1 144 D2
Chesham Ct EP CH65 7 F7
Cheshire Acre
GR/UP/WCH CH49 148 D1
Cheshire Av AIN/FAZ L10 84 A4
Cheshire Cl NEWLW WA12 106 E2
Cheshire Gdns ECCL WA10 12 D7
Cheshire Gv MOR/LEA CH46 129 F2
Cheshire Lines Pth ORM L39 42 B5
Cheshire Oaks Wy EP CH65 203 J2
Cheshire Ring Canal Wk
WARRS WA4 189 F3
WARRS WA4 161 F5
Cheshyre Dr RUNC WA7 177 J4
Cheshyres La RUNC WA7 176 B6
Chesnell Gv NWD/KWIPK L33 72 E4
Chesney Cl TOX L8 132 D3
Chesnut Gv BTL L20 4 D1
RF/TRAN CH42 131 G5
Chessington Cl WARRS WA4 162 D4
Chester Av CHTN/BK PR9 23 H5
GOL/RIS/CUL WA3 92 E3
NTHTN L30 82 C2
Chester Cl CSBY/BLUN L23 69 J5
RUNC WA7 177 J3
Chester Dr AIMK WN4 91 J1
Chesterfield Cl STHP PR8 33 H5
Chesterfield Dr
NWD/KWIPK L33 72 D4
Chesterfield Rd
CSBY/BLUN L23 69 H4
PS/BROM CH62 184 A3
STHP PR8 33 H5
Chesterfield St TOX L8 132 D2
Chester High Rd NSTN CH64 181 K3
Chester La STHEL WA9 119 K3
Chester New Rd WARRS WA4 161 J4
Chester Rd CHTN/BK PR9 23 H5
EP CH65 195 K6
FROD/HEL WA6 200 C3
GTS/LS CH66 195 G6
HES CH60 181 H1
HUY L36 117 G3
NPK/KEN L6 114 B1
NSTN CH64 191 K2
RUNC WA7 187 K4
WARRS WA4 179 G4
WARRS WA4 161 K1
Chester St BIRK CH41 3 H4
PR/KW L34 117 K1
TOX L8 132 D2
WAL/EG CH44 * 111 G4
WDN WA8 18 E2
Chesterton Dr
WARRN/WOL WA2 123 G2
Chesterton St ALL/GAR L19 172 B1
Chestnut Av CSBY/BLUN L23 69 G3
GTS/LS CH66 202 D2
HUY L36 136 A1
RNFD/HAY WA11 89 J6
WARRW/BUR WA5 141 G2
WDN WA8 158 C1
Chestnut Cl GR/UP/WCH CH49 147 K1
ORM L39 44 A2
RAIN/WH L35 118 A3
Chestnut Ct BTL L20 4 D2
ORM L39 45 K5
Chestnut Gra ORM L39 53 H2
Chestnut Gv AIMK WN4 79 J5
GOL/RIS/CUL WA3 93 G3
PS/BROM CH62 170 E5
RNFD/HAY WA11 89 G4
WAV L15 134 A1
Chestnut La FROD/HEL WA6 200 B5
Chestnut Rd LITH L21 81 G4
WLT/FAZ L9 97 K2
The Chestnuts NSTN CH64 193 G1
Chestnut St EHL/KEN L7 9 K5
STHP PR8 27 K3
Chestnut Wk MGHL L31 71 K5
Chestnut Wy FMBY L37 48 C4
Cheswood Cl RAIN/WH L35 118 A5
Chetham Ct WARRN/WOL WA2 123 G4
Chetton Dr RUNC WA7 178 D6
Chetwode Av AIMK WN4 91 G1
Chetwood Av CSBY/BLUN L23 69 G4
Chetwood Dr WDN WA8 138 E5
Chetwynd Cl CL/PREN CH43 130 C5
Chetwynd Rd CL/PREN CH43 * 130 D4
Chetwynd St AIG/SPK L17 133 G6
Chevasse Wk WLTN L25 135 K6
Cheverton Cl
GR/UP/WCH CH49 129 J6
Cheviot Av STHEL WA9 104 D2
WARRN/WOL WA2 123 G4
Cheviot Cl RF/TRAN CH42 150 C2
Cheviot Rd EHL/KEN L7 114 C5
RF/TRAN CH42 150 B2
Cheviot Wy NWD/KWIPK L33 72 E3
Chevoit Cl GTS/LS CH66 194 D3
Cheyne Cl CSBY/BLUN L23 68 B6
Cheyne Gdns ALL/GAR L19 153 G3
Cheyne Wk STHEL WA9 119 H1
Chichester Cl RUNC WA7 188 C1
WARRS WA4 163 F4
WAV L15 133 J1
Chidden Cl GR/UP/WCH CH49 128 D6
Chidlow Cl WDN WA8 158 B6
Chigwell Cl WD/CROXPK L12 99 J2
Chilcott Rd CLB/OSW/ST L13 115 G4
Childer Crs GTS/LS CH66 194 E2
Childer Gdns GTS/LS CH66 194 E2
Childers St CLB/OSW/ST L13 114 E4
Childwall Abbey Rd
CHLDW L16 134 E3
Childwall Av EHL/KEN L7 133 J2
MOR/LEA CH46 128 E2
Childwall Bank Rd CHLDW L16 134 E2
Childwall Cl GR/UP/WCH CH49 128 E2
Childwall Crs CHLDW L16 134 E2
Childwall Gdns GTS/LS CH66 195 J1
Childwall Gn
GR/UP/WCH CH49 148 D1
Childwall Hts WLTN L25 135 G2
Childwall La WLTN L25 135 G3
Childwall Mount Rd
CHLDW L16 134 E2
Childwall Park Av CHLDW L16 135 F3
Childwall Priory Rd
CHLDW L16 134 E2
Childwall Rd GTS/LS CH66 195 J1
WAV L15 134 B2
Childwall Valley Rd
CHLDW L16 135 G1
Chilhem Cl TOX L8 132 E5
Chilington Av WDN WA8 157 J3
Chillerton Rd WD/CROXPK L12 99 H5
Chillingham St TOX L8 133 F5
Chiltern Av WARRN/WOL WA2 123 G4
Chiltern Cl AIMK WN4 91 G1
WD/CROXPK L12 99 K3
Chiltern Crs WARRN/WOL WA2 123 G4
Chiltern Dr KKBY L32 72 B5
Chiltern Rd RF/TRAN CH42 150 B2
STHEL WA9 104 E2
STHP PR8 33 G3
WARRN/WOL WA2 123 G4
Chilton Cl MGHL L31 62 B6
Chilton Dr GTS/LS CH66 202 C1
Chilton Ms MGHL L31 62 B6
Chilwell Cl WDN WA8 138 C5
Chimes Rd AIMK WN4 78 E3
China Farm La WKBY CH48 127 K5
China La WARRS WA4 162 B1
Chindit Cl FMBY L37 48 D3
Chippenham Av
GR/UP/WCH CH49 128 D5
Chipping Av STHP PR8 33 G4
Chippingdall Cl
WARRW/BUR WA5 141 K4
Chirkdale St ANF/KKDL L4 97 G4
Chirk Gdns EP CH65 196 C6
Chirk Wy MOR/LEA CH46 129 G2
Chirton Cl RNFD/HAY WA11 90 C4
Chisenhale St VAUX/LVPD L3 112 E4
Chisledon Cl RNFD/HAY WA11 90 C4
Chislehurst Av WLTN L25 135 J3
Chislett Cl BRSC L40 * 38 D5
Chisnall Av ECCL WA10 102 E1
Chiswell St EHL/KEN L7 114 A5
Chiswick Cl RUNC WA7 * 178 C6
Chiswick Gdns WARRS WA4 162 E5
Cholmley Dr NEWLW WA12 106 E3
Cholmondeley Rd EP CH65 195 J5
RUNC WA7 187 G2
WKBY CH48 146 C1
Cholmondeley St WDN WA8 176 D1
Cholsey Cl GR/UP/WCH CH49 129 G5
Chorley Cl CHTN/BK PR9 21 H6
Chorley Rd PR/KW L34 117 H1
Chorley's La WDN WA8 139 J6
Chorley St ECCL WA10 12 E3
WARRN/WOL WA2 16 E2
Chorley Wy BEB CH63 170 C4
Chorlton Cl CHLDW L16 135 G1
RUNC WA7 178 C4
Chorlton Gv WAL/NB CH45 110 D2
Christchurch Rd
CL/PREN CH43 130 E5
Christian St VAUX/LVPD L3 9 F1
Christie Cl GTS/LS CH66 184 D5
Christie St WDN WA8 19 J1
Christines Crs BRSC L40 38 D5
Christleton Cl CL/PREN CH43 149 G1
Christleton Ct RUNC WA7 178 B1
Christleton Dr GTS/LS CH66 195 H3
Christmas St BTL L20 97 F4
Christopher Cl CHLDW L16 134 E1
RAIN/WH L35 118 D5
Christopher Dr
PS/BROM CH62 184 D2
Christophers Cl
PEN/TH CH61 * 168 A1
Christopher St ANF/KKDL L4 97 H5
Christopher Wy CHLDW L16 134 E1
Chris Ward Cl EHL/KEN L7 114 A6
Chudleigh Cl HLWD L26 155 H2
Chudleigh Rd
CLB/OSW/ST L13 114 D4
Church Av WLT/FAZ L9 82 E4
Church Cl CHTN/BK PR9 23 J5
FMBY L37 49 G2
WAL/EG CH44 111 K3
Church Close Ct FMBY L37 * 49 G2
Church Crs WAL/EG CH44 112 A5
Churchdown Cv
DV/KA/FCH L14 * 115 J3
Churchdown Rd
DV/KA/FCH L14 115 J3
Church Dr NEWLW WA12 106 C4
PS/BROM CH62 151 G5
WARRN/WOL WA2 124 C6
Church End SPK/HALE L24 174 E4
Church End Ms
SPK/HALE L24 174 E4
Church Farm BEB CH63 151 F6
Church Farm Ct HES CH60 167 K6
Churchfield Rd
FROD/HEL WA6 201 F2
WLTN L25 135 K4
Church Flds ORM L39 45 J6
BRSC L40 36 D2
Churchfields FROD/HEL WA6 199 K5
STHEL WA9 120 A3
STHP PR8 27 G4
WDN WA8 139 G4
Church Gdns BTL L20 4 C5
WAL/EG CH44 111 K3
Churchgate CHTN/BK PR9 23 H4
Churchgate Ms
CHTN/BK PR9 23 J4
Church Gn CHLDW L16 135 G2
FMBY L37 48 C3
KKBY L32 72 D6
SKEL WN8 56 B4
Church Green Gdns
GOL/RIS/CUL WA3 92 B2
Church Gv LITH L21 81 G5
Church Hl WAL/NB CH45 111 F2
Churchhill Av BIRK CH41 2 A2
Church Hill Rd ORM L39 45 H5
Churchill Av CHTN/BK PR9 23 H3
Churchill Gdns STHEL WA9 118 E1
Churchill Gv
WAL/EG CH44 * 111 J2
Churchill Wy NSTN CH64 191 K1
VAUX/LVPD L3 8 E2
Church La AIG/SPK L17 153 F2
ANF/KKDL L4 97 H3
ECCL WA10 102 C2
GOL/RIS/CUL WA3 92 E4
GR/UP/WCH CH49 148 E1
GTS/LS CH66 195 G5
MGHL L31 51 H5
NSTN CH64 191 K2
ORM L39 52 E6
PEN/TH CH61 147 J6
PR/KW L34 100 C1
PS/BROM CH62 171 F4
WAL/EG CH44 111 K3
WARRS WA4 163 G2
Churchmeadow Cl
WAL/EG CH44 111 K3
Church Meadow La HES CH60 167 J6
Church Meadow Wk
WDN WA8 157 G6
Church Ms RF/TRAN CH42 151 F2
Church Mt EHL/KEN L7 113 K6
Church Pde EP CH65 6 E2
Church Rd ALL/GAR L19 153 K6
ANF/KKDL L4 97 J3
BEB CH63 182 C1
BEB CH63 151 F6
BTL L20 82 A5
CHTN/BK PR9 21 K5
CLB/OSW/ST L13 114 D4
CSBY/WL L22 81 F3
FMBY L37 49 G1
FROD/HEL WA6 201 F2
GR/UP/WCH CH49 129 H4
HLWD L26 155 H1
HUY L36 116 C4
LITH L21 81 G5
LYMM WA13 164 E1
MGHL L31 71 G2
ORM L39 64 E1
RF/TRAN CH42 131 G5
RNFD/HAY WA11 90 D5
RNFD/HAY WA11 75 H5
SKEL WN8 56 B4
SPK/HALE L24 175 F5
WAL/EG CH44 112 A5
WAV L15 134 B3
WKBY CH48 146 B2
WLTN L25 135 H6
Church Rd North WAV L15 134 B2
Church Rd South WLTN L25 154 D1
Church Rd West ANF/KKDL L4 97 H3
Church Sq ECCL WA10 13 G5
Church St BIRK CH41 3 J4
BTL L20 4 B5
CHTN/BK PR9 15 G4
CLVPS L1 8 E4
ECCL WA10 13 H6
EP CH65 6 D3
FROD/HEL WA6 200 E1
GOL/RIS/CUL WA3 92 C2
NEWLW WA12 106 E1
ORM L39 45 J6
PR/KW L34 117 J1
RUNC WA7 10 D3
WAL/EG CH44 111 K3
WARR WA1 17 F4
WDN WA8 158 B6
Church Ter RF/TRAN CH42 131 G6
Church Vw BTL L20 4 D5
ORM L39 52 E6
Churchview Rd BIRK CH41 2 A1
Church Wk BTL L20 4 C5
WARRN/WOL WA2 123 G1
Church Wy FMBY L37 48 C3
KKBY L32 72 D6
Churchway Rd
SPK/HALE L24 174 B3
Churchwood Cl
PS/BROM CH62 171 F4
Churnet St ANF/KKDL L4 97 G5
Churn Wy GR/UP/WCH CH49 128 E5
Churston Rd CHLDW L16 135 F4
Churton Av CL/PREN CH43 130 C6
Churton Ct NPK/KEN L6 * 113 J4
Ciaran Cl WD/CROXPK L12 99 H5
Cicely St EHL/KEN L7 113 K6
Cinder La BTL L20 82 A4
CALD/MH L18 134 D4
KIRK/FR/WAR PR4 25 K3
WARRS WA4 164 A3
Cinnamon La
WARRN/WOL WA2 124 B4
Cinnamon La North
WARRN/WOL WA2 124 B3
Cinnamon Pk
WARRN/WOL WA2 * 124 E5
Circular Dr GR/UP/WCH CH49 128 E6
HES CH60 167 J4
PS/BROM CH62 151 G4
Circular Rd BIRK CH41 2 E6
Circular Rd East NG/CROX L11 98 D5
Circular Rd West
NG/CROX L11 98 D4
Cirencester Av
GR/UP/WCH CH49 128 D5
Cirrus Dr ORM L39 52 E4
Citrine Rd WAL/EG CH44 111 K5
Citron Cl WLT/FAZ L9 97 K1
City Gdns ECCL WA10 88 C5
City Rd ANF/KKDL L4 97 H4
ECCL WA10 88 C5
Civic Wy BEB CH63 151 F6
EP CH65 6 C6
HUY L36 116 E5
Clairville Cl BTL L20 4 E5
Clairville Wy CLB/OSW/ST L13 114 C2
Clamley Ct SPK/HALE L24 174 B2
Clandon Rd CALD/MH L18 154 A2
Clanfield Av WDN WA8 138 B6
Clanfield Rd NG/CROX L11 99 F4
Clap Gate Crs WDN WA8 157 G6
Clap Gates Rd
WARRW/BUR WA5 142 B2
Clapham Rd ANF/KKDL L4 113 K1
Clare Cl STHEL WA9 103 G6
Clare Crs WAL/EG CH44 110 E3
Clare Dr EP CH65 203 F2
Claremont Av MGHL L31 70 E1
STHP PR8 27 H3
WDN WA8 139 G5
Claremont Cl LITH L21 81 G4
Claremont Dr ORM L39 53 H2
WDN WA8 139 G5
Claremont Gdns STHP PR8 27 H3
Claremont Rd CSBY/BLUN L23 68 E5
LITH L21 81 G4
RUNC WA7 11 G5
STHP PR8 27 H3
WAV L15 133 K3
WGNW/BIL/OR WN5 77 H4
WKBY CH48 127 G6
Claremont Ter
CSBY/BLUN L23 * 68 E4
Claremont Wy BEB CH63 150 C3
Claremount Dr BEB CH63 170 B1
Claremount Rd
WAL/NB CH45 111 F1
Clarence Av
WARRW/BUR WA5 140 E3
WDN WA8 139 F5
Clarence Cl STHEL WA9 * 104 A3
Clarence Rd RF/TRAN CH42 131 F6
STHP PR8 27 H3
WAL/EG CH44 111 K5
WARRS WA4 163 G1
Clarence St AIMK WN4 78 E5
GOL/RIS/CUL WA3 92 B2
NEWLW WA12 105 K1
RUNC WA7 10 C3
VAUX/LVPD L3 9 H4
WARR WA1 17 K1
Clarence Ter RUNC WA7 10 D3
Clarendon Cl CL/PREN CH43 2 B6
RUNC WA7 178 C6
Clarendon Ct
WARRN/WOL WA2 123 F3
Clarendon Gv MGHL L31 62 A2
Clarendon Rd ALL/GAR L19 153 K5
LITH L21 81 G5
NPK/KEN L6 114 A1
WAL/EG CH44 111 K4
Clare Rd BTL L20 5 H7
Clares Farm Cl WARR WA1 144 E2
Claret Cl AIG/SPK L17 152 D2
Clare Wy WAL/NB CH45 111 F2
Claribel St TOX L8 133 F3
Clarke Av RF/TRAN CH42 150 D1
WARRS WA4 162 C1
Clarke Gdns WDN WA8 18 E6
Clarke's Crs ECCL WA10 102 D1
Clarkes Ter RUNC WA7 176 A6
Clarkfield Cl BRSC L40 39 F6
Classic Rd CLB/OSW/ST L13 114 E2
Clatterbridge Rd BEB CH63 169 K5
Claude Rd NPK/KEN L6 114 A1
Claude St WARR WA1 17 G2
Claughton Cl EHL/KEN L7 114 A6
Claughton Dr WAL/EG CH44 111 H4
Claughton Firs CL/PREN CH43 130 E5
Claughton Gn CL/PREN CH43 130 E4
Claughton Pl BIRK CH41 2 C5
Claughton Rd BIRK CH41 2 E5
Claughton St ECCL WA10 13 G4
Clavell Rd ALL/GAR L19 154 A3
Claverton Cl RUNC WA7 186 E1
Clay Brow Rd SKEL WN8 67 G1
Clay Cross Rd WLTN L25 154 C1
Claydon Ct HLWD L26 155 K2
Clayfield Cl BTL L20 5 H5
Clayford Crs DV/KA/FCH L14 115 F3
Clayford Pl DV/KA/FCH L14 115 F3
Clayford Rd DV/KA/FCH L14 115 G3
Clayford Wy DV/KA/FCH L14 115 G3
Clayhill NSTN CH64 182 A5
Clayhill Gn GTS/LS CH66 195 F2
Clayhill Gv GOL/RIS/CUL WA3 93 J3
Clay La ECCL WA10 102 A2
WARRW/BUR WA5 121 J1
Claypole Cl EHL/KEN L7 133 H1
Clay St VAUX/LVPD L3 112 D3
Clayton Av GOL/RIS/CUL WA3 93 F3
Clayton Crs RUNC WA7 10 B6
WDN WA8 18 B2
Clayton Gdns BRSC L40 38 E5
Clayton La WAL/EG CH44 111 G5
Clayton Ms SKEL WN8 55 K4
Clayton Pl BIRK CH41 2 C6
Clayton Rd GOL/RIS/CUL WA3 125 H1
Clayton St CL/PREN CH43 2 C6
SKEL WN8 55 K4
Cleadon Cl KKBY L32 85 F4
Cleadon Rd KKBY L32 84 E4
Cleadon Wy WDN WA8 138 D5
Clearwater Cl EHL/KEN L7 113 K5
Cleary St BTL L20 4 C2
Clee Hill Rd RF/TRAN CH42 150 B2
Cleethorpes Rd RUNC WA7 178 B6
Cleeves Cl WARR WA1 17 G5
Clegge St WARRN/WOL WA2 16 E1
Clegg St EV L5 113 G3
SKEL WN8 55 K4
Clelland St WARRS WA4 143 F6
Clematis Rd NTHLY L27 136 B3
Clement Gdns VAUX/LVPD L3 112 E3
Clementina Rd
CSBY/BLUN L23 68 C5
Clements Wy NWD/KWIPK L33 72 C4
Clemmey Dr BTL L20 82 B5
Clengers Brow CHTN/BK PR9 23 J2
Clent Av MGHL L31 62 A4
Clent Gdns MGHL L31 62 B4
Clent Rd MGHL L31 62 A5
Cleopas St TOX L8 132 E5
Clevedon St TOX L8 133 F5
Cleveland Cl KKBY L32 72 B5
Cleveland Dr AIMK WN4 79 H5
GOL/RIS/CUL WA3 92 E3
GTS/LS CH66 194 D3
Cleveland Rd
WARRN/WOL WA2 123 H4
Cleveland Sq CLVPS L1 8 E6
Cleveland St STHEL WA9 104 A4
Cleveley Pk CALD/MH L18 154 A2
Cleveley Rd CALD/MH L18 154 A2
HOY CH47 127 K1
Cleveleys Av CHTN/BK PR9 23 J1
WDN WA8 139 J6
Cleveleys Rd CHTN/BK PR9 23 J2
WARRW/BUR WA5 141 J5
The Cleves MGHL L31 62 C4

Cleve Wy *FMBY* L37 ... **49** H3
Clieves Hl *ORM* L39 ... **44** B4
Clieves Hills La *ORM* L39 ... **52** B3
Clieves Rd *KKBY* L32 ... **84** E2
Cliff Dr *WAL/EG* CH44 ... **111** K2
Cliffe Rd *NSTN* CH64 ... **192** A4
Cliffe St *WDN* WA8 ... **19** G1
Cliff La *LYMM* WA13 ... **164** C5
WARRS WA4 ... **163** J1
Clifford Rd *STHP* PR8 ... **27** H6
WAL/EG CH44 ... **111** H4
WARRW/BUR WA5 ... **141** H5
Clifford St *BIRK* CH41 ... **130** D1
VAUX/LVPD L3 ... **9** H2
Cliff Rd *CHTN/BK* PR9 ... **23** F3
WAL/EG CH44 ... **111** G4
Cliff St *EHL/KEN* L7 ... **114** A5
Clifton Av *HLWD* L26 ... **155** H2
PS/BROM CH62 ... **184** B4
Clifton Cl *WARR* WA1 ... **144** B2
Clifton Ct *RUNC* WA7 ... **10** A6
Clifton Crs *BIRK* CH41 ... **3** F5
FROD/HEL WA6 ... **187** F6
Clifton Dr *AIN/FAZ* L10 ... **83** G1
Clifton Gdns *EP* CH65 ... **196** B6
Clifton Gv *EV* L5 * ... **113** G3
WAL/EG CH44 ... **111** K3
Clifton La *RUNC* WA7 ... **187** H4
Cliftonmill Mdw
GOL/RIS/CUL WA3 ... **92** A3
Clifton Rd *AIMK* WN4 ... **78** E3
BIRK CH41 ... **2** E7
FMBY L37 ... **41** G6
NPK/KEN L6 ... **114** B2
RUNC WA7 ... **187** H4
STHP PR8 ... **28** C1
WGNW/BIL/OR WN5 ... **77** G5
Clifton Rd East *NPK/KEN* L6 ... **114** B2
Clifton St *ALL/GAR* L19 ... **153** K5
ECCL WA10 ... **13** H3
WARRS WA4 ... **17** G7
Clifton Vls *CH/BCN* CH1 * ... **202** E3
Cliftonville Rd *PR/KW* L34 ... **118** A1
WARR WA1 ... **144** B3
Clincton Cl *WDN* WA8 ... **157** F3
Clincton Vw *WDN* WA8 ... **157** F3
Clinning Rd *STHP* PR8 ... **27** H5
Clinton Pl *WD/CROXPK* L12 ... **98** D6
Clinton Rd *WD/CROXPK* L12 ... **98** D6
Clint Rd *EHL/KEN* L7 ... **114** A6
Clint Wy *EHL/KEN* L7 ... **114** A6
Clipper Vw *PS/BROM* CH62 ... **151** G3
Clipsley Brook Vw
RNFD/HAY WA11 ... **89** J5
Clipsley Crs *RNFD/HAY* WA11 ... **90** A4
Clipsley La *RNFD/HAY* WA11 ... **90** A5
Clive Av *WARRN/WOL* WA2 ... **123** J6
Clive Ldg *STHP* PR8 ... **27** G5
Clive Rd *CL/PREN* CH43 ... **131** F5
STHP PR8 ... **27** G6
Clock Face Rd *STHEL* WA9 ... **120** A3
Clock Tower Dr *WLT/FAZ* L9 ... **97** H2
Clocktower St *ECCL* WA10 ... **13** F5
The Cloisters *CSBY/BLUN* L23 ... **68** E6
ECCL WA10 ... **102** D1
FMBY L37 * ... **49** F2
Cloister Wy *EP* CH65 ... **7** J5
Clorain Cl *PR/KW* L34 ... **100** D1
Clorain Rd *NWD/KWIPK* L33 ... **73** F6
Closeburn Av *HES* CH60 * ... **180** D1
Close St *STHEL* WA9 ... **103** G6
The Close *BEB* CH63 ... **150** C2
CHTN/BK PR9 ... **21** K6
CSBY/BLUN L23 ... **68** E6
ECCL WA10 ... **87** H6
GR/UP/WCH CH49 ... **148** A1
HTWN L38 ... **60** A4
NEWLW WA12 ... **106** E3
PEN/TH CH61 ... **148** A5
RNFD/HAY WA11 ... **89** J6
STBRV L28 ... **100** C6
WLT/FAZ L9 ... **97** H1
Cloudberry Cl *NTHLY* L27 ... **136** B3
Clough Av *BRSC* L40 ... **39** F5
WARRN/WOL WA2 ... **123** H5
Clough Gv *AIMK* WN4 ... **78** E4
Clough Rd *HLWD* L26 ... **155** K2
SPK/HALE L24 ... **173** J1
The Clough *AIMK* WN4 ... **78** C5
RUNC WA7 ... **177** J4
Cloughton Rd *BIRK* CH41 ... **2** C5
Clovelly Av *STHEL* WA9 ... **120** B1
WARRW/BUR WA5 ... **141** F2
Clovelly Dr *STHP* PR8 ... **34** A1
Clovelly Gv *RUNC* WA7 ... **188** A2
Clovelly Rd *ANF/KKDL* L4 ... **113** K1
Clover Av *FROD/HEL* WA6 ... **201** G2
HLWD L26 ... **155** G1
Clover Ct *RUNC* WA7 ... **188** A2
Cloverdale Dr *AIMK* WN4 ... **91** H1
Cloverdale Rd *WLTN* L25 ... **135** J2
Clover Dr *BIRK* CH41 ... **110** E6
Cloverfield *RUNC* WA7 * ... **178** B6
Cloverfield Gdns *GTS/LS* CH66 ... **195** G2
Clover Hey *RNFD/HAY* WA11 ... **88** E4
Club St *RNFD/HAY* WA11 ... **88** D2
Clucas Gdns *ORM* L39 ... **45** J5
Clwyd Gv *WD/CROXPK* L12 ... **99** F5
Clwyd St *BIRK* CH41 ... **2** E4
WAL/NB CH45 ... **95** G6
Clwyd Wy *GTS/LS* CH66 ... **194** D3
Clyde Rd *EHL/KEN* L7 ... **114** C5
Clydesdale *EP* CH65 ... **196** A6
Clydesdale Rd *HOY* CH47 ... **127** G1
WAL/EG CH44 ... **111** K2
WARRS WA4 ... **162** C3
Clyde St *BTL* L20 ... **96** E5
RF/TRAN CH42 ... **150** E1
Clyffes Farm Cl *BRSC* L40 ... **36** E2
Coach House Ct *BRSC* L40 ... **38** E6
Coachmans Dr
WD/CROXPK L12 ... **99** J4
Coach Rd *ORM* L39 ... **65** F6
PR/KW L34 ... **86** C4
Coalbrookdale Rd *NSTN* CH64 ... **182** A5
Coalgate La *RAIN/WH* L35 ... **117** J5
Coalpit La *CH/BCN* CH1 * ... **202** C6
Coal Pit La *ORM* L39 ... **65** J3
Coalport Wk *STHEL* WA9 ... **118** E1
Coal St *CLVPS* L1 ... **9** G3
Coalville Rd *RNFD/HAY* WA11 ... **89** G5
Coastal Dr *WAL/NB* CH45 ... **94** D5
Coastal Rd *STHP* PR8 ... **33** G3
Coastgaurd La *NSTN* CH64 ... **181** G6
Coastline Ms *CHTN/BK* PR9 ... **23** J1
Cobb Av *LITH* L21 ... **81** J5
The Cobbles *HLWD* L26 ... **155** G1
Cobblestone Cnr *ALL/GAR* L19 ... **153** H4
Cobbs La *WARRS* WA4 ... **162** D3
Cobden Av *RF/TRAN* CH42 ... **131** J6
Cobden Ct *RF/TRAN* CH42 ... **131** J6
Cobden Pl *RF/TRAN* CH42 ... **131** J6
Cobden Rd *CHTN/BK* PR9 ... **28** C1
Cobden St *NEWLW* WA12 ... **106** D1
NPK/KEN L6 ... **113** H4
WARRN/WOL WA2 ... **16** E1
WLTN L25 ... **154** C1
Cobden Vw *WLTN* L25 ... **154** C1
Cobham Av *WLT/FAZ* L9 ... **82** C5
Cobham Rd *MOR/LEA* CH46 ... **128** E1
Coburg Whf *VAUX/LVPD* L3 ... **132** B3
Cochrane St *EV* L5 ... **113** H2
Cockburn St *TOX* L8 ... **132** E5
Cockerell Cl *ANF/KKDL* L4 * ... **97** H6
Cockerham Wy *NG/CROX* L11 ... **84** A6
Cockhedge La *WARR* WA1 ... **16** E4
Cockhedge Wy *WARR* WA1 ... **16** D4
Cocklade La *SPK/HALE* L24 ... **174** E4
Cock Lane Ends *WDN* WA8 * ... **157** G6
Cockle Dick's La *CHTN/BK* PR9 ... **23** G3
Cockshead Rd *WLTN* L25 ... **135** J4
Cockshead Wy *WLTN* L25 ... **135** J3
Cockspur St *VAUX/LVPD* L3 ... **8** D2
Cockspur St West
VAUX/LVPD L3 * ... **8** C2
Coerton Rd *WLT/FAZ* L9 ... **82** E4
The Cokers *RF/TRAN* CH42 ... **150** D3
Colbern Cl *MGHL* L31 ... **71** H1
Colbrooke Rd *AIG/SPK* L17 ... **133** G6
Colburne Cl *BRSC* L40 ... **39** F4
Colby Cl *CHLDW* L16 ... **135** F1
Colchester Rd *STHP* PR8 ... **28** C5
Colden Cl *WD/CROXPK* L12 ... **99** J6
Coldstone Dr *AIMK* WN4 ... **78** C5
Coldstream Cl
WARRN/WOL WA2 ... **124** A3
Coldstream Dr *GTS/LS* CH66 ... **194** C3
Cole Av *NEWLW* WA12 ... **106** C1
Colebrook Cl
GOL/RIS/CUL WA3 ... **125** J3
Cole Crs *ORM* L39 ... **53** G5
Coleman Dr *GR/UP/WCH* CH49 ... **128** C6
Colemere Cl *WARR* WA1 ... **124** C6
Colemere Ct *EP* CH65 ... **6** C1
Colemere Dr *PEN/TH* CH61 ... **148** E5
Coleridge Av *ECCL* WA10 ... **12** B3
Coleridge Ct *KKBY* L32 ... **84** C3
Coleridge Dr *PS/BROM* CH62 ... **151** F4
Coleridge Gv *WDN* WA8 ... **157** K2
Coleridge St *BTL* L20 ... **4** B3
NPK/KEN L6 ... **113** K4
Colesborne Rd *NG/CROX* L11 ... **98** E3
Coles Crs *CSBY/BLUN* L23 ... **69** J3
Coleshill Rd *NG/CROX* L11 ... **98** C2
Cole St *CL/PREN* CH43 ... **2** C5
Colette Rd *AIN/FAZ* L10 ... **84** A4
Coleus Cl *WLT/FAZ* L9 ... **97** K1
Colin Cl *HUY* L36 ... **116** C6
Colindale Rd *CHLDW* L16 ... **135** F2
Colin Dr *VAUX/LVPD* L3 ... **112** E2
Colinmander Gdns *ORM* L39 ... **53** G2
Colinton *SKEL* WN8 ... **57** G6
Colinton St *WAV* L15 ... **133** K1
Coliseum Wy *EP* CH65 ... **203** H1
College Av *CSBY/BLUN* L23 ... **68** E6
FMBY L37 ... **48** E1
College Cl *CL/PREN* CH43 ... **129** J3
FMBY L37 ... **48** D1
STHP PR8 ... **27** H4
WAL/NB CH45 ... **110** E1
WARR WA1 ... **17** H3
WARRN/WOL WA2 ... **124** D5
College Ct *WD/CROXPK* L12 ... **114** E2
College Dr *BEB* CH63 ... **151** F4
College Flds *HUY* L36 ... **116** E6
College La *CLVPS* L1 ... **8** E5
College Pth *FMBY* L37 ... **40** D6
College Rd *CSBY/BLUN* L23 ... **68** D5
SKEL WN8 ... **57** K4
College Rd North
CSBY/BLUN L23 ... **68** D4
College St *ECCL* WA10 ... **13** G3
College St North *NPK/KEN* L6 ... **9** J1
College St South *NPK/KEN* L6 ... **9** K1
College Vw *BTL* L20 ... **4** E7
Collier's Rw *RUNC* WA7 ... **176** B6
Collier St *RUNC* WA7 ... **10** B2
Colliery Green Cl *NSTN* CH64 ... **191** K4
Colliery Green Ct *NSTN* CH64 ... **191** K4
Colliery Green Dr *NSTN* CH64 ... **191** K4
Collingham Gn *GTS/LS* CH66 ... **194** E4
Collingwood Cl *ANF/KKDL* L4 ... **97** F5
Collingwood Rd *BEB* CH63 ... **170** D1
NEWLW WA12 ... **106** B2
Collin Rd *CL/PREN* CH43 ... **130** B1
Collins Cl *BTL* L20 ... **81** J6
Collins Green La
WARRW/BUR WA5 ... **105** J4
Collin St *WARRW/BUR* WA5 ... **142** B4
Colmore Av *BEB* CH63 ... **170** B4
Colmore Rd *NG/CROX* L11 ... **98** C3
Colne Dr *STHEL* WA9 ... **104** B6
Colne Rd *WARRW/BUR* WA5 ... **121** K1
Colonel Dr *WD/CROXPK* L12 ... **99** J6
Colorado Cl
WARRW/BUR WA5 ... **141** K2
Colquitt St *CLVPS* L1 ... **9** G6
Coltart Rd *TOX* L8 ... **133** G3
Colton Rd *WLTN* L25 ... **135** G2
Columban Cl *NTHTN* L30 ... **70** B6
Columbia La *CL/PREN* CH43 ... **130** E5
Columbia Rd *ANF/KKDL* L4 ... **97** J3
PR/KW L34 ... **118** A1
Columbine Cl *MGHL* L31 ... **71** K6
WDN WA8 ... **138** A5
Columbine Wy *STHEL* WA9 ... **105** F6
Columbus Dr *PEN/TH* CH61 ... **167** J2
Columbus Quay
VAUX/LVPD L3 ... **132** D6
Columbus Wy *LITH* L21 * ... **81** J4
Column Rd *WKBY* CH48 ... **146** E2
Colville Ct *WARRN/WOL* WA2 ... **123** G4
Colville Rd *WAL/EG* CH44 ... **111** G3
Colville St *WAV* L15 ... **133** K1
Colwall Cl *NWD/KWIPK* L33 ... **85** F1
Colwall Rd *NWD/KWIPK* L33 ... **85** F1
Colwell Cl *DV/KA/FCH* L14 ... **100** A6
Colwell Rd
DV/KA/FCH L14 ... **116** A1
Colworth Rd *SPK/HALE* L24 ... **173** G1
Colwyn Cl *EP* CH65 ... **196** C6
WARRW/BUR WA5 ... **122** E5
Colwyn Rd
CLB/OSW/ST L13 ... **114** D5
Colwyn St *BIRK* CH41 ... **130** D1
Colyton Av *STHEL* WA9 ... **120** B2
Combermere St *TOX* L8 * ... **132** E3
Comely Av *WAL/EG* CH44 ... **111** J3
Comely Bank Rd
WAL/EG CH44 ... **111** K3
Comer Gdns *MGHL* L31 ... **62** A4
Comfrey Gv *HLWD* L26 ... **155** H1
Commerce Wy *TOX* L8 ... **133** G2
Commercial Rd *EV* L5 ... **112** E1
PS/BROM CH62 ... **171** G2
Common Field Rd
GR/UP/WCH CH49 ... **148** E2
Common La *CHTN/BK* PR9 ... **25** F3
WARRS WA4 ... **162** D1
Common Rd
NEWLW WA12 ... **105** J2
Common St *NEWLW* WA12 ... **105** J2
STHEL WA9 * ... **103** F6
Commutation Rw
VAUX/LVPD L3 ... **9** G3
Company's Cl *RUNC* WA7 ... **186** C1
Compass Cl *RUNC* WA7 ... **188** C2
Compton Cl
RNFD/HAY WA11 ... **90** B4
Compton Pl *EP* CH65 ... **6** C4
Compton Rd *BIRK* CH41 ... **110** D6
NPK/KEN L6 ... **113** J3
STHP PR8 ... **27** J4
Compton Wk *BTL* L20 ... **4** D3
Compton Wy *HLWD* L26 ... **155** H5
Comus St *VAUX/LVPD* L3 ... **113** F4
Concert St *CLVPS* L1 ... **9** F6
Concorde Pl
WARRN/WOL WA2 ... **123** K5
Concordia Av
GR/UP/WCH CH49 ... **129** H4
The Concourse *WKBY* CH48 * ... **127** F6
Concourse Wy *STHEL* WA9 ... **104** D3
Condor Cl *ALL/GAR* L19 ... **154** A5
Condron Rd North *LITH* L21 ... **81** K2
Condron Rd South *LITH* L21 ... **81** K2
Conery Cl *FROD/HEL* WA6 ... **199** K5
Coney Crs *CSBY/BLUN* L23 ... **69** J4
Coney Gv *RUNC* WA7 ... **188** A2
Coney La *HUY* L36 ... **136** C2
Coney Wk *GR/UP/WCH* CH49 ... **128** E3
Conifer Cl *GTS/LS* CH66 ... **202** E3
NWD/KWIPK L33 ... **72** D4
WLT/FAZ L9 ... **97** K2
Conifer Ct *FMBY* L37 ... **49** F3
Conifer Gv *WARRW/BUR* WA5 ... **141** G2
The Conifers *MGHL* L31 ... **62** A4
Coningsby Dr *WAL/EG* CH44 ... **111** G3
Coningsby Gdns
GOL/RIS/CUL WA3 ... **93** F3
Coningsby Rd *ANF/KKDL* L4 ... **97** J6
Coniston Av *AIMK* WN4 ... **79** G5
BEB CH63 ... **183** K2
CL/PREN CH43 ... **129** K4
PR/KW L34 ... **118** B1
WAL/NB CH45 ... **94** E6
WARRW/BUR WA5 ... **140** E5
Coniston Cl *GTS/LS* CH66 ... **184** D6
NWD/KWIPK L33 ... **72** C5
RUNC WA7 ... **187** G1
WLT/FAZ L9 ... **82** E4
Coniston Dr *FROD/HEL* WA6 ... **201** F1
Coniston Gv *RNFD/HAY* WA11 ... **88** D4
Coniston Rd *FMBY* L37 ... **48** D3
MGHL L31 ... **62** C5
NSTN CH64 ... **191** K3
PEN/TH CH61 ... **148** A5
Coniston St *EV* L5 ... **113** J1
Coniston Wy *RNFD/HAY* WA11 ... **66** B5
Conleach Rd *SPK/HALE* L24 ... **173** K2
Connaught Av *WARR* WA1 ... **143** K2
Connaught Dr *NEWLW* WA12 ... **106** C3
Connaught Rd *EHL/KEN* L7 ... **113** K5
Connaught Wy *BIRK* CH41 ... **130** D1
Connolly Av *BTL* L20 ... **5** K2
Conroy Wy *NEWLW* WA12 ... **106** C4
Consett Rd *STHEL* WA9 ... **119** F1
Constables Cl *RUNC* WA7 ... **177** K4
Constance St *ECCL* WA10 ... **12** A7
VAUX/LVPD L3 ... **9** J2
Constance Wy *WDN* WA8 ... **158** B6
Constantine Av *HES* CH60 ... **168** A4
Convent Cl *ALL/GAR* L19 ... **153** H4
ORM L39 ... **53** H3
RF/TRAN CH42 ... **131** G5
Conville Bvd *BEB* CH63 ... **150** D3
Conway Av *WARRW/BUR* WA5 ... **123** F5
Conway Cl *BEB* CH63 ... **150** C6
NWD/KWIPK L33 ... **72** C4
WARRW/BUR WA5 ... **141** G3
Conway Crs
WGNW/BIL/OR WN5 ... **77** H3
Conway Dr *BIRK* CH41 ... **2** D4
NEWLW WA12 ... **106** E2
WGNW/BIL/OR WN5 ... **77** J4
Conway Rd *AIMK* WN4 ... **79** K4
Conway St *BIRK* CH41 ... **2** C3
EV L5 ... **113** G2
Conwy Ct *RUNC* WA7 ... **177** K3
Conwy Dr *NPK/KEN* L6 ... **113** K2
Conyers Av *STHP* PR8 ... **27** G4
Coogee Av *WARRW/BUR* WA5 ... **141** F2
Cook Av *RNFD/HAY* WA11 ... **90** D4
Cookes Cl *NSTN* CH64 ... **181** K6
Cooke St *AIMK* WN4 ... **78** E3
Cook Glades *RAIN/WH* L35 ... **117** K6
Cook Rd *MOR/LEA* CH46 ... **110** B3
Cooks Ct *CSBY/BLUN* L23 * ... **68** D4
Cookson Rd *LITH* L21 ... **81** H5
Cookson St *CLVPS* L1 ... **132** D2
Cook St *BIRK* CH41 ... **2** D6
CLVP L2 ... **8** D4
EP CH65 ... **6** E3
PR/KW L34 ... **117** K1
RAIN/WH L35 ... **118** B2
Coombe Dr *RUNC* WA7 ... **176** C5
Coombe Pk *GTS/LS* CH66 ... **195** F3
Coombe Rd *PEN/TH* CH61 ... **148** B4
Cooperage Cl *TOX* L8 ... **132** D5
Cooper Av *NEWLW* WA12 ... **105** K2
WARRN/WOL WA2 ... **123** H5
Cooper Av North
CALD/MH L18 ... **153** H2
Cooper Av South
ALL/GAR L19 ... **153** H2
Cooper Cl *ALL/GAR* L19 ... **153** H3
Cooper La *RNFD/HAY* WA11 ... **90** B5
Cooper's La *NWD/KWIPK* L33 ... **85** J5
Coopers Pl *WARRS* WA4 ... **162** B2
Cooper St *ECCL* WA10 ... **12** E3
RUNC WA7 ... **10** D3
WDN WA8 ... **18** E1
Copeland Cl *PEN/TH* CH61 ... **167** J1
Copeland Gv *RUNC* WA7 ... **187** H2
Copeland Rd *WARRS* WA4 ... **162** A1
Copperas Hl *VAUX/LVPD* L3 ... **9** G4
Copperas St *ECCL* WA10 ... **13** F6
Copperfield Cl
GOL/RIS/CUL WA3 ... **124** E2
TOX L8 ... **132** E4
Copperwood *RUNC* WA7 ... **178** B4
Copperwood Dr
RAIN/WH L35 ... **118** A5
Coppice Cl *CL/PREN* CH43 ... **129** J3
Coppice Crs *HUY* L36 ... **117** F3
Coppice Gra
MOR/LEA CH46 ... **128** D2
Coppice Gn *CHNE* CH2 ... **198** D5
WARRW/BUR WA5 ... **122** A6
Coppice Gv
GR/UP/WCH CH49 * ... **147** K1
Coppice La *HUY* L36 ... **136** E2
Coppice Leys *FMBY* L37 ... **48** E2
The Coppice *NPK/KEN* L6 ... **114** A1
PR/KW L34 ... **100** D2
WAL/NB CH45 ... **95** G6
Coppins Cl *FROD/HEL* WA6 ... **199** J5
The Coppins
WARRN/WOL WA2 ... **123** J5
Copple House La *AIN/FAZ* L10 ... **83** K4
Coppull Rd *MGHL* L31 ... **62** A3
Copse Gv *PEN/TH* CH61 ... **148** B4
The Copse *CALD/MH* L18 ... **134** E4
NEWLW WA12 ... **106** A1
RUNC WA7 ... **187** K1
Copsmead *MOR/LEA* CH46 ... **129** G1
Copthorne Rd *KKBY* L32 ... **84** A1
Copy La *NTHTN* L30 ... **70** D5
Copy Wy *NTHTN* L30 ... **70** C4
Coral Av *HUY* L36 ... **116** D4
STHEL WA9 ... **103** H6
Coral Cl *KKBY* L32 ... **84** B1
Coral Dr *BTL* L20 ... **5** F4
Coralin Wy *AIMK* WN4 ... **78** E2
Coral Rdg *CL/PREN* CH43 ... **130** A3
Coral St *CLB/OSW/ST* L13 ... **114** E6
Corbet Av *WARRN/WOL* WA2 ... **142** E1
Corbet St *WARRN/WOL* WA2 * ... **142** E1
Corbridge Rd *CHLDW* L16 ... **134** D3
Corbyn St *WAL/EG* CH44 ... **112** A6
Corfu St *BIRK* CH41 * ... **2** C5
Corinthian Av
CLB/OSW/ST L13 ... **114** E3
Corinthian St *LITH* L21 ... **81** G4
RF/TRAN CH42 * ... **150** E1
Corinto St *TOX* L8 ... **132** E2
Corkdale Rd *WLT/FAZ* L9 ... **97** K1
Cormorant Dr *RUNC* WA7 ... **10** A5
Cornbrook *SKEL* WN8 ... **57** G6
Corncroft Rd *PR/KW* L34 ... **100** D2
Corndale Rd *CALD/MH* L18 ... **134** B5
Cornelian Gv *AIMK* WN4 ... **78** E4
Cornelius Dr *PEN/TH* CH61 ... **148** C6
Cornel Wy *HUY* L36 ... **136** C1
Corner Brook *STBRV* L28 ... **99** K6
Cornerhouse La *WDN* WA8 ... **138** C6
Cornett Rd
WLT/FAZ L9 ... **82** E4
Corney St *EHL/KEN* L7 ... **133** H2
Cornfield Cl *GTS/LS* CH66 ... **202** D2
Cornfields Cl *ALL/GAR* L19 ... **153** J5
Cornflower Wy
MOR/LEA CH46 ... **110** A5
Cornforth Wy *WDN* WA8 ... **138** E6
Cornhill *CLVPS* L1 ... **8** E7
Cornice Rd *CLB/OSW/ST* L13 ... **114** E3
Corniche Rd *PS/BROM* CH62 ... **151** G5
Corn St *TOX* L8 ... **132** D4
Cornubia Rd *WDN* WA8 ... **19** H5
Cornwall Av *RUNC* WA7 ... **10** D5
Cornwall Cl *PS/BROM* CH62 ... **151** G3
RUNC WA7 ... **177** J4
Cornwall Dr
CL/PREN CH43 ... **149** K2
Cornwallis St *CLVPS* L1 ... **9** G7
Cornwall Rd *WDN* WA8 ... **139** G6
Cornwall St *STHEL* WA9 ... **104** B3
WARR WA1 ... **17** K1
Cornwall Wy *STHP* PR8 ... **41** H1
Cornwood Cl *WLTN* L25 ... **135** J2
Corona Av *MGHL* L31 ... **62** A2
Corona Rd *CLB/OSW/ST* L13 ... **114** E3
CSBY/WL L22 ... **80** E2
PS/BROM CH62 ... **151** H5
Coronation Av
DV/KA/FCH L14 ... **115** J4
FMBY L37 ... **49** G3
WAL/NB CH45 ... **95** H6
WARRS WA4 ... **163** G1
Coronation Buildings
WAL/NB CH45 * ... **111** H2
Coronation Dr *CSBY/BLUN* L23 ... **68** E6
DV/KA/FCH L14 ... **115** J4
FROD/HEL WA6 ... **187** G6
NEWLW WA12 ... **106** E4
PS/BROM CH62 ... **171** F2
RAIN/WH L35 ... **117** J4
RNFD/HAY WA11 ... **91** F4
WARRW/BUR WA5 ... **141** G5
WDN WA8 ... **157** G3
Coronation Rd
CSBY/BLUN L23 ... **68** E6
ECCL WA10 ... **87** K5
EP CH65 ... **6** C6
HOY CH47 ... **126** E3
MGHL L31 ... **62** B4
RUNC WA7 ... **11** F6
Coronation St *AIMK* WN4 ... **78** C3
Coronation Vls
WD/CROXPK L12 * ... **99** H6
Coronation Wk *STHP* PR8 ... **14** C5
WGNW/BIL/OR WN5 ... **77** G5
Coroner's La *WDN* WA8 ... **139** F4
Coronet Rd *NG/CROX* L11 ... **99** G2
Coronet Wy *WDN* WA8 ... **157** G3
Corporal Wy *WD/CROXPK* L12 ... **99** J6
Corporation Rd *BIRK* CH41 ... **130** D1
Corporation St *ECCL* WA10 ... **13** G4
Corridor Rd *EP* CH65 ... **197** G4
Corrie Dr *BEB* CH63 ... **170** B1
Corsewall St *EHL/KEN* L7 ... **133** J1
Corsican Gdns *STHEL* WA9 ... **118** E1
Cortsway *GR/UP/WCH* CH49 ... **129** F4
Cortsway West
GR/UP/WCH CH49 ... **128** E4
Corwen Cl *CL/PREN* CH43 ... **129** J3
MOR/LEA CH46 ... **129** G2
WARRW/BUR WA5 ... **122** E6
Corwen Crs *DV/KA/FCH* L14 ... **115** K5
Corwen Dr *NTHTN* L30 ... **70** D5
Corwen Rd *ANF/KKDL* L4 ... **98** A5
HOY CH47 ... **127** H2
Cosgrove Cl *NPK/KEN* L6 ... **98** B6
Cossack Av *WARRN/WOL* WA2 ... **123** H6
Costain St *BTL* L20 ... **96** E5
Cote Lea Ct *RUNC* WA7 * ... **187** J1
Cotham St *ECCL* WA10 ... **13** G5
Cotsford Cl *HUY* L36 ... **116** C3
Cotsford Pl *HUY* L36 ... **116** C3
Cotsford Rd *HUY* L36 ... **116** C3
Cotsford Wy *HUY* L36 ... **116** C3
Cotswold Av *GOL/RIS/CUL* WA3 ... **92** E5
Cotswold Gv *STHEL* WA9 ... **104** E2
Cotswold Rd *RF/TRAN* CH42 ... **150** B2
WARRN/WOL WA2 ... **123** H4
Cotswolds Crs *HLWD* L26 ... **155** H4
Cotswold St *EHL/KEN* L7 ... **113** K5
Cottage Cl *BEB* CH63 ... **183** K2
KKBY L32 ... **84** D4
NSTN CH64 ... **191** K2
ORM L39 ... **53** H1
Cottage Dr East *HES* CH60 ... **180** E2
Cottage Dr West *HES* CH60 ... **180** E2
Cottage La *HES* CH60 ... **180** E2
ORM L39 ... **53** H1
Cottage Ms *ORM* L39 ... **45** H6
Cottage Pl *STHEL* WA9 * ... **120** A3
Cottage St *BIRK* CH41 ... **2** D2
Cottam Dr *WARRN/WOL* WA2 ... **124** C4
Cottenham St *NPK/KEN* L6 ... **113** K4
Cotterdale Cl *STHEL* WA9 ... **120** A1
WARRW/BUR WA5 ... **141** G2
Cotterill *RUNC* WA7 ... **177** G5
Cotterill Dr *WARR* WA1 ... **144** B2
Cottesbrook Cl *NG/CROX* L11 ... **98** E2
Cottesbrook Pl *NG/CROX* L11 ... **98** E2
Cottesbrook Rd *NG/CROX* L11 ... **98** E2
Cottesmore Dr *HES* CH60 * ... **168** D5
Cottesmore Wy
GOL/RIS/CUL WA3 ... **92** C2
Cotton Dr *ORM* L39 ... **45** H5
Cotton La *RUNC* WA7 ... **177** G5
Cotton St *VAUX/LVPD* L3 ... **112** D3
Cotton Ter *STHEL* WA9 ... **104** D5
Cottonwood *AIG/SPK* L17 ... **132** E6
Cottrell Cl *ALL/GAR* L19 ... **172** B1
Cottys Brow *CHTN/BK* PR9 ... **23** H2
Coudray Rd *CHTN/BK* PR9 ... **23** G4
Coulport Cl *DV/KA/FCH* L14 ... **116** A3
Coulsdon Pl *TOX* L8 ... **133** F5
Coulthard Rd *RF/TRAN* CH42 ... **151** F3
Coulton Rd *WDN* WA8 ... **139** K6
Coultshead Av
WGNW/BIL/OR WN5 ... **77** H3
Council Av *AIMK* WN4 ... **79** G6
Council St *RAIN/WH* L35 ... **118** C2
Countess Pk *NG/CROX* L11 ... **99** G3
Countisbury Dr *CHLDW* L16 ... **135** F3
County Dr *ECCL* WA10 ... **12** D7
County Rd *ANF/KKDL* L4 ... **97** H3
KKBY L32 ... **72** D5
ORM L39 ... **53** H1
Court Av *HLWD* L26 ... **155** K2
Courtenay Av *CSBY/WL* L22 ... **80** D1
WAL/EG CH44 ... **111** G4
Courtenay Rd *CSBY/WL* L22 ... **80** D1
HOY CH47 ... **127** F2
WLTN L25 ... **135** G5
Courtfield *ORM* L39 ... **45** H4
Courtfields Cl
WD/CROXPK L12 ... **115** F2
Courtgreen *ORM* L39 ... **45** H4
Court Hey Av *DV/KA/FCH* L14 ... **116** A5
Court Hey Dr *CHLDW* L16 ... **115** K6
Court Hey Rd *CHLDW* L16 ... **115** K6
Courthope Rd *ANF/KKDL* L4 ... **97** K4
Courtland Rd *CALD/MH* L18 ... **134** C4
Court Ms *CHTN/BK* PR9 * ... **23** J4
Courtney Av *WAL/EG* CH44 ... **111** G4
Courtney Rd *RF/TRAN* CH42 ... **151** F3
Court Rd *CHTN/BK* PR9 ... **15** G3
The Court *BEB* CH63 * ... **170** C1
NSTN CH64 ... **192** A3
STBRV L28 ... **100** C6
The Courtyard *CHNE* CH2 ... **198** C5
NSTN CH64 ... **193** G1
Covent Gdn *CLVP* L2 ... **8** C4
Coventry Av *GTS/LS* CH66 ... **202** C3
NTHTN L30 ... **82** C2
Coventry Rd *WAV* L15 ... **134** B3
Coventry St *BIRK* CH41 ... **2** D5
Coverdale Av *RAIN/WH* L35 ... **119** F5
Coverdale Cl
WARRW/BUR WA5 ... **141** G2
Covertside *WKBY* CH48 ... **146** E1
Covertside Rd *STHP* PR8 ... **28** D5
Cowan Dr *NPK/KEN* L6 ... **113** J3
Cowanway *WDN* WA8 ... **138** E4
Cowdell St *WARRN/WOL* WA2 ... **142** E2
Cowdrey Av *CL/PREN* CH43 ... **110** C6

Cow Hey La RUNC WA7 186 D2
Cowley Cl GR/UP/WCH CH49 * 128 E4
Cowley Ct ECCL WA10 * 12 E3
Cowley Hill La ECCL WA10 12 D1
Cowley Rd ANF/KKDL L4 97 H4
Cowley St ECCL WA10 13 G2
Cowper Rd CLB/OSW/ST L13 115 F5
Cowper St BTL L20 4 B1
STHEL WA9 * 104 A4
Cowper Wy HUY L36 117 G6
Coyford Dr CHTN/BK PR9 23 J1
Coylton Av RAIN/WH L35 119 F5
Crab La WARRN/WOL WA2 124 C4
Crab St ECCL WA10 13 F3
Crabtree Cl BRSC L40 38 D5
NEWLW WA12 106 E2
NTHLY L27 136 A4
Crabtree Fold RUNC WA7 178 B5
Crabtree La BRSC L40 38 C4
KNUT WA16 165 H6
Cradley WDN WA8 157 H1
Crag Gv RNFD/HAY WA11 88 E2
Craigburn Rd
CLB/OSW/ST L13 114 C1
Craig Gdns GTS/LS CH66 195 H2
Craighurst Rd WLTN L25 135 H2
Craigleigh Gv PS/BROM CH62 184 C3
Craigmore Rd CALD/MH L18 153 H2
Craigside Av WD/CROXPK L12 98 E6
Craigs Rd CLB/OSW/ST L13 114 C1
Craigwood Wy HUY L36 116 B4
Craine Cl ANF/KKDL L4 97 K5
Cramond Av CALD/MH L18 134 B4
Cranage Cl RUNC WA7 177 G6
Cranberry Cl ECCL WA10 12 E2
Cranborne Av HOY CH47 108 C6
WARRS WA4 162 A2
Cranborne Rd WAV L15 133 J2
Cranbourne Av BIRK CH41 130 C2
MOR/LEA CH46 128 E2
Cranbrook Av AIMK WN4 79 F5
Crane Av STHEL WA9 120 B1
Cranehurst Rd ANF/KKDL L4 97 K3
Cranes La BRSC L40 46 D4
Cranfield Rd CSBY/BLUN L23 69 H4
Cranford Cl PS/BROM CH62 184 C3
Cranford Ct WARR WA1 * 144 D1
Cranford Rd ALL/GAR L19 153 J3
Cranford St WAL/EG CH44 111 G4
Cranham Av GOL/RIS/CUL WA3 93 F4
Crank Hl RNFD/HAY WA11 76 B5
Crank Rd RNFD/HAY WA11 87 K4
RNFD/HAY WA11 76 C2
Cranleigh Cl WARRS WA4 162 A4
Cranleigh Pl WLTN L25 135 H3
Cranleigh Rd WLTN L25 135 H4
Cranmer St EV L5 112 E2
Cranmore Av CSBY/BLUN L23 81 F1
Cranshaw Av STHEL WA9 120 B4
Cranshaw La WDN WA8 139 G4
Cranston Cl ECCL WA10 87 K5
Cranston Rd NWD/KWIPK L33 85 H1
Cranswick Gn GTS/LS CH66 195 F4
Crantock Cl HLWD L26 155 J3
NG/CROX L11 * 99 G1
Crantock Gv ECCL WA10 87 K5
Cranwell Cl AIN/FAZ L10 83 F1
Cranwell Rd
GR/UP/WCH CH49 128 C6
WLTN L25 135 H2
Craven Av GOL/RIS/CUL WA3 93 F4
Craven Cl BIRK CH41 2 D4
Craven Ct WARRN/WOL WA2 123 F3
Craven Lea WD/CROXPK L12 99 J2
Craven Rd RAIN/WH L35 118 E4
WD/CROXPK L12 115 G1
Craven St BIRK CH41 2 C5
VAUX/LVPD L3 9 H2
Cravenwood Rd HLWD L26 155 J4
Crawford Av CALD/MH L18 134 A4
MGHL L31 61 K4
WDN WA8 157 G2
Crawford Cl STHEL WA9 120 B3
WD/CROXPK L12 99 H6
Crawford Dr WAV L15 114 E6
Crawford Pk CALD/MH L18 134 A6
Crawford Pl RUNC WA7 186 E1
Crawford Rd SKEL WN8 67 F5
Crawford St STHEL WA9 120 C3
Crawford Wy EHL/KEN L7 114 C5
Crawley Av
WARRN/WOL WA2 * 123 G4
Crediton Av CHTN/BK PR9 20 E6
Crediton Cl NG/CROX L11 84 B6
The Creek WAL/NB CH45 94 E5
Cremorne Hey STBRV L28 100 B6
Crescent Av AIMK WN4 79 F5
FMBY L37 48 E4
Crescent Ct LITH L21 81 H5
Crescent Dr FROD/HEL WA6 199 J6
Crescent Gn ORM L39 53 F4
Crescent Rd CSBY/BLUN L23 68 C4
EP CH65 7 F3
LITH L21 81 H5
STHP PR8 27 G4
WAL/EG CH44 111 J3
WLT/FAZ L9 97 K1
The Crescents RAIN/WH L35 118 C3
The Crescent BEB CH63 150 D6
CHTN/BK PR9 24 A2
CSBY/BLUN L23 69 H3
CSBY/WL L22 81 F2
EP CH65 195 J4
GR/UP/WCH CH49 128 E6
HES CH60 181 G1
HUY L36 117 G5
LYMM WA13 165 G1
MGHL L31 71 F2
PEN/TH CH61 148 C5
RAIN/WH L35 118 B3
WKBY CH48 146 B1
Cressbrook Rd WARRS WA4 162 B3
Cressingham Rd WAL/NB CH45 95 H5
Cressington Av RF/TRAN CH42 150 C2
Cressington Esp ALL/GAR L19 153 G5
Cressington Gdns EP CH65 6 D2
Cresswell Cl HLWD L26 155 K2
WARRW/BUR WA5 122 D5
Cresswell St NPK/KEN L6 113 H3
Cresta Dr RUNC WA7 186 C1
Cresttor Rd WLTN L25 135 G6
Creswell St ECCL WA10 12 C5
Cretan Rd WAV L15 133 J2
Crewe Gn GR/UP/WCH CH49 148 D1
Criccieth Ct EP CH65 203 H1
Cricket Pth FMBY L37 41 F6
STHP PR8 27 G4
Cricklade Cl BTL L20 4 C3
Criftin Cl GTS/LS CH66 202 A1
Cringles Dr RAIN/WH L35 136 D2
Crispin Rd NTHLY L27 136 A4
Crispin St ECCL WA10 12 D6
Critchley Rd SPK/HALE L24 174 B3
Critchley Wy NWD/KWIPK L33 72 E4
Croasdale Dr RUNC WA7 187 H2
Crockett's Wk ECCL WA10 87 J6
Crockleford Av STHP PR8 28 B4
Crocus Av BIRK CH41 130 C1
Crocus Gdns STHEL WA9 104 E6
Crocus St EV L5 97 F6
Croesmere Dr GTS/LS CH66 202 B1
Croft Av BRSC L40 39 F6
GOL/RIS/CUL WA3 92 A1
PS/BROM CH62 170 E4
Croft Av East PS/BROM CH62 171 F3
Croft Cl CL/PREN CH43 130 B5
Croft Ct EP CH65 196 D6
LEIGH WN7 93 K2
Croft Dr MOR/LEA CH46 129 F2
WKBY CH48 146 D5
Croft Dr East WKBY CH48 147 F4
Croft Dr West WKBY CH48 146 D4
Croft Edge CL/PREN CH43 130 E6
Croft End STHEL WA9 104 D4
Croften Dr NSTN CH64 191 K4
Crofters Cl GTS/LS CH66 202 C2
Crofters Heath GTS/LS CH66 202 C2
Crofters La NWD/KWIPK L33 73 F4
The Crofters
GR/UP/WCH CH49 128 E5
Croft Fld MGHL L31 62 C6
Croft Gdns WARRS WA4 163 F4
Croft Gn PS/BROM CH62 171 F2
Croft Heys ORM L39 53 F4
Croft La PS/BROM CH62 171 F4
WLT/FAZ L9 83 G4
Crofton Cl WARRS WA4 163 H6
Crofton Crs CLB/OSW/ST L13 115 F4
Crofton Rd CLB/OSW/ST L13 115 F4
RF/TRAN CH42 131 H6
RUNC WA7 176 B4
Croftside WARR WA1 144 E2
Croftson Av ORM L39 45 K4
Croft St GOL/RIS/CUL WA3 * 92 B3
WDN WA8 18 C7
Croftsway HES CH60 167 H5
The Croft GR/UP/WCH CH49 148 A1
MGHL L31 61 K2
RUNC WA7 177 H4
STBRV L28 * 100 A5
WD/CROXPK L12 99 F6
Croftwood Gv RAIN/WH L35 118 A5
Cromarty Rd CLB/OSW/ST L13 114 D1
WAL/EG CH44 111 F3
Cromdale Gv STHEL WA9 104 C3
Cromdale Wy
WARRW/BUR WA5 141 F3
Cromer Dr WAL/NB CH45 111 G2
Cromer Rd AIG/SPK L17 153 F2
HOY CH47 127 F3
STHP PR8 27 F5
Cromer Wy HLWD L26 155 J5
Cromfield ORM L39 53 G3
Cromford Rd HUY L36 116 E2
Crompton Dr
WARRN/WOL WA2 123 G1
WD/CROXPK L12 99 J2
Cromptons La CALD/MH L18 134 E4
Crompton St EV L5 113 F2
Crompton Wy
GOL/RIS/CUL WA3 93 J3
Cromwell Av
WARRW/BUR WA5 122 C5
Cromwell Av South
WARRW/BUR WA5 141 K5
Cromwell Cl NEWLW WA12 106 A1
ORM L39 53 G3
Cromwell Ct WARR WA1 16 B5
Cromwell Rd ANF/KKDL L4 97 H3
EP CH65 6 E4
Cromwell St WDN WA8 158 B5
Crondall Gv WAV L15 134 C2
Cronton Av MOR/LEA CH46 109 J4
Cronton La RAIN/WH L35 118 D6
WDN WA8 138 E4
Cronton Park Cl WDN WA8 138 B3
Cronton Rd RAIN/WH L35 136 E2
WAV L15 134 B4
Cronulla Dr WARRW/BUR WA5 140 E2
Crookall St AIMK WN4 79 H5
Crookhurst Av
WGNW/BIL/OR WN5 77 G3
Croome Dr WKBY CH48 146 D1
Croppers Hl ECCL WA10 12 D6
Cropper's La ORM L39 54 A4
Croppers Rd
WARRN/WOL WA2 124 B4
Cropper St CLVPS L1 9 G5
Cropton Rd FMBY L37 49 F2
Crosby Av WARRW/BUR WA5 142 D1
Crosby Cl GR/UP/WCH CH49 129 G3
Crosby Gn WD/CROXPK L12 98 E6
Crosby Gv ECCL WA10 103 F4
NSTN CH64 183 J6
Crosby Rd STHP PR8 27 G4
Crosby Rd North CSBY/WL L22 81 F2
Crosby Rd South LITH L21 81 G4
Crosender Rd CSBY/BLUN L23 68 D6
Crosfield Cl EHL/KEN L7 114 A6
Crosfield Rd EHL/KEN L7 114 A6
RAIN/WH L35 118 B3
WAL/EG CH44 111 J4
Crosfield St WARR WA1 16 B4
Crosfield Wk EHL/KEN L7 114 A6
Crosgrove Rd ANF/KKDL L4 98 A4
Crosland Rd KKBY L32 85 F2
Crossacre Rd WLTN L25 135 J2
Cross Barn La HTWN L38 60 A5
Crossdale Rd CSBY/BLUN L23 68 D6
PS/BROM CH62 184 A1
Crossdale Wy RNFD/HAY WA11 88 E2
Crossens Wy CHTN/BK PR9 21 F5
Cross Farm Rd STHEL WA9 104 A4
Crossfield Rd SKEL WN8 56 E5
Crossford Rd DV/KA/FCH L14 116 A1
Crossgates WDN WA8 140 A6
Cross Green Cl FMBY L37 49 G3
Crosshall Brow BRSC L40 54 C1
Crosshall St CLVPS L1 8 E3
Cross Hey LITH L21 81 J1
MGHL L31 * 71 H2
Cross Hey Av CL/PREN CH43 130 A4
Cross Hillocks La RAIN/WH L35 137 H6
The Crossings NEWLW WA12 106 C2
Crossland Ms LYMM WA13 145 H5
Cross La BEB CH63 170 B1
FROD/HEL WA6 199 J1
NEWLW WA12 106 B2
NSTN CH64 191 K4
ORM L39 43 K2
RAIN/WH L35 117 K3
WAL/NB CH45 110 D2
WARRS WA4 163 F1
Cross La South
GOL/RIS/CUL WA3 125 F1
Crossley Av GTS/LS CH66 195 H3
Crossley Dr HES CH60 167 H5
WAV L15 134 B1
Crossley Rd ECCL WA10 103 F5
Crossley St WARR WA1 17 F3
Cross Meanygate BRSC L40 31 H2
Cross Pit La RNFD/HAY WA11 75 G3
Cross St BIRK CH41 3 H4
CSBY/WL L22 80 E3
ECCL WA10 13 F5
GOL/RIS/CUL WA3 92 B4
NSTN CH64 191 K1
PR/KW L34 101 K6
PS/BROM CH62 * 151 G6
RUNC WA7 * 10 D3
STHP PR8 14 E7
WARRN/WOL WA2 142 E2
WDN WA8 19 F2
The Cross HTWN L38 59 K4
LYMM WA13 145 K6
MOR/LEA CH46 * 129 F1
PS/BROM CH62 171 F4
Crossvale Rd HUY L36 116 E6
Crossway CL/PREN CH43 130 B1
WDN WA8 157 J3
Crossway Cl AIMK WN4 79 K4
Crossways PS/BROM CH62 171 F2
The Crossway BEB CH63 182 C3
Crosswood Crs HUY L36 116 C4
Crosthwaite Av
PS/BROM CH62 184 C3
Croston Av RAIN/WH L35 118 D2
Croston Cl WDN WA8 138 B5
Croston's Brow CHTN/BK PR9 23 H2
Crouchley Hall Ms
LYMM WA13 * 165 G2
Crouchley La LYMM WA13 165 G2
Crouch St EV L5 113 J1
STHEL WA9 * 104 B5
Croughton Rd CHNE CH2 203 K5
GTS/LS CH66 195 J1
Crowe Av WARRN/WOL WA2 123 H4
Crowland Cl CHTN/BK PR9 28 D1
Crowland St CHTN/BK PR9 28 D1
Crowland Wy FMBY L37 49 H3
Crow La SKEL WN8 57 H2
Crow La East NEWLW WA12 106 C1
Crow La West NEWLW WA12 106 A1
Crowmarsh Cl
GR/UP/WCH CH49 * 129 G5
Crown Acres Rd WLTN L25 155 F2
Crown Av WDN WA8 157 G3
Crown Cl FMBY L37 49 G3
Crown Fields Cl NEWLW WA12 91 G6
Crown Gdns NEWLW WA12 106 B1
Crown Ga RUNC WA7 177 J6
Crown Park Dr NEWLW WA12 91 G6
Crown Rd WD/CROXPK L12 99 G6
Crown Station Pl EHL/KEN L7 133 F1
Crown St EHL/KEN L7 133 F1
NEWLW WA12 106 A2
STHEL WA9 103 F6
TOX L8 133 F2
WARR WA1 16 D3
Crownway HUY L36 116 D3
Crow St TOX L8 132 C3
Crowther St ECCL WA10 12 B6
Crow Wood La WDN WA8 158 E1
Crow Wood Pl WDN WA8 * 139 J6
Crow Wood Rd
GOL/RIS/CUL WA3 92 E2
Croxdale Rd DV/KA/FCH L14 100 A6
Croxdale Rd West
DV/KA/FCH L14 99 K6
Croxteth Av LITH L21 81 H4
WAL/EG CH44 111 H3
Croxteth Cl MGHL L31 62 C4
Croxteth Dr AIG/SPK L17 133 H4
RNFD/HAY WA11 75 G2
Croxteth Gv TOX L8 133 G3
Croxteth Hall La
WD/CROXPK L12 99 G3
Croxteth La STBRV L28 100 B4
Croxteth Rd BTL L20 81 J6
TOX L8 133 G4
Croxteth Vw KKBY L32 84 E5
Croyde Cl CHTN/BK PR9 20 E6
Croyde Pl STHEL WA9 120 A3
Croyde Rd SPK/HALE L24 174 B2
Croydon Av CALD/MH L18 134 A4
Croylands St ANF/KKDL L4 97 G5
Crucian Wy WD/CROXPK L12 99 H2
Crump St CLVPS L1 132 D2
Crutchley Av BIRK CH41 130 E1
Crystal Cl CLB/OSW/ST L13 114 E5
Cubbin Crs EV L5 113 F1
Cubert Rd NG/CROX L11 99 G1
Cuckoo Cl WLTN L25 135 H5
Cuckoo La NSTN CH64 192 C2
WLTN L25 135 H4
Cuerden St VAUX/LVPD L3 9 F2
Cuerdley Gn
WARRW/BUR WA5 159 H1
Cuerdley Rd
WARRW/BUR WA5 140 D6
Cuerdon Dr WARRS WA4 163 J2
Culbin Cl GOL/RIS/CUL WA3 125 J1
Culford Cl RUNC WA7 178 C4
Cullen Av BTL L20 82 A6
Cullen Cl BEB CH63 183 K3
Cullen Rd RUNC WA7 176 A6
Cullen St TOX L8 133 H2
Culme Rd WD/CROXPK L12 98 D6
Culshaw Wy BRSC L40 36 D2
Culzean Cl WD/CROXPK L12 99 J2
Cumberland Av AIG/SPK L17 133 J3
CL/PREN CH43 149 K1
ECCL WA10 102 D5
NTHTN L30 69 K6
Cumberland Cl NPK/KEN L6 114 B1
Cumberland Crs
RNFD/HAY WA11 89 K5
Cumberland Ga NTHTN L30 70 D5
Cumberland Gv GTS/LS CH66 195 F6
Cumberland Rd STHP PR8 28 A2
WAL/NB CH45 95 J6
Cumberland St CLVP L2 * 8 D3
WARRS WA4 143 F6
Cumber La RAIN/WH L35 118 B4
Cumbers Dr NSTN CH64 192 B4
Cumbers La NSTN CH64 192 B4
Cumbrae Dr EP CH65 203 G2
Cumbria Cl GTS/LS CH66 202 C2
Cumbria Wy
WD/CROXPK L12 99 G4
Cummings St CLVPS L1 9 G7
Cumpsty Rd LITH L21 81 K2
Cunard Av WAL/EG CH44 111 K2
Cunard Cl CL/PREN CH43 129 K3
Cunard Rd LITH L21 81 J4
Cunliffe Av NEWLW WA12 91 G6
Cunliffe Cl RUNC WA7 177 K6
Cunliffe St CLVP L2 8 D2
Cunningham Cl
WARRW/BUR WA5 141 G4
WKBY CH48 * 146 D5
Cunningham Dr BEB CH63 170 E6
RUNC WA7 10 A7
Cunningham Rd
CLB/OSW/ST L13 114 E5
WDN WA8 157 J3
Cunscough La MGHL L31 63 H5
Cuper Crs HUY L36 116 D3
Curate Rd NPK/KEN L6 98 A6
Curlender Cl BIRK CH41 110 E6
Curlender Wy SPK/HALE L24 175 F3
Curlew Av GR/UP/WCH CH49 128 E3
Curlew Cl GOL/RIS/CUL WA3 92 E3
GR/UP/WCH CH49 128 E3
Curlew Ct MOR/LEA CH46 109 G6
Curlew Gv GOL/RIS/CUL WA3 125 G4
Curlew La BRSC L40 31 K6
Curlew Wy MOR/LEA CH46 109 G6
Currans Rd WARRN/WOL WA2 123 G5
Curran Wy NWD/KWIPK L33 72 C3
Curtana Crs NG/CROX L11 99 G2
Curtis Rd ANF/KKDL L4 98 A4
Curwell Cl BEB CH63 170 D2
Curzon Av BIRK CH41 2 A2
WAL/NB CH45 95 H5
Curzon Dr WARRS WA4 163 F4
Curzon Rd CSBY/WL L22 81 F2
HOY CH47 127 F2
RF/TRAN CH42 150 A1
STHP PR8 28 B2
Curzon St RUNC WA7 10 C6
Cusson Rd NWD/KWIPK L33 85 G2
Custley Hey STBRV L28 100 B5
Custom House La CLVPS L1 * 8 D5
Cut La BRSC L40 44 D3
NWD/KWIPK L33 85 K4
Cygnet Cl GTS/LS CH66 195 G5
ORM L39 53 G3
Cygnet Ct NWD/KWIPK L33 85 F1
WARR WA1 142 D6
Cynthia Av WARR WA1 144 A2
Cynthia Rd RUNC WA7 10 B6
Cypress Av GTS/LS CH66 202 D2
WDN WA8 139 G6
Cypress Cl MGHL L31 71 K6
WARR WA1 144 D2
Cypress Cft BEB CH63 170 D2
Cypress Gdns STHEL WA9 102 E6
Cypress Gv RUNC WA7 177 F6
Cypress Rd HUY L36 136 A1
STHP PR8 28 B1
Cyprus Gv TOX L8 133 F5
Cyprus St PR/KW L34 117 K1
Cyprus Ter WAL/NB CH45 * 95 H6
Cyril Gv AIG/SPK L17 153 F1
Cyril St WARRN/WOL WA2 16 E1

D

Dacre's Bridge La
RAIN/WH L35 137 G2
Dacre St BIRK CH41 3 F4
BTL L20 96 D4
Dacy Rd EV L5 113 J2
Daffodil Cl WDN WA8 139 K5
Daffodil Gdns STHEL WA9 104 E6
Daffodil Rd BIRK CH41 130 C2
WAV L15 134 C3
Dagnall Av WARRW/BUR WA5 123 F5
Dagnall Rd KKBY L32 84 B2
Dahlia Cl STHEL WA9 104 E6
WLT/FAZ L9 97 K1
Dailton Rd SKEL WN8 57 J6
Dairy Bank CHNE CH2 198 C5
Dairy Farm Rd
RNFD/HAY WA11 74 E2
Dairylands Cl CHLDW L16 134 D3
Daisy Av NEWLW WA12 106 C3
Daisy Bank Rd LYMM WA13 145 H6
WARRW/BUR WA5 141 G5
Daisy La BRSC L40 39 H5
Daisy Ms LITH L21 81 J5
Daisy Mt MGHL L31 71 H1
Daisy St EV L5 97 F6
Daisy Wy STHP PR8 27 J5
Dakota Dr ALL/GAR L19 172 D2
WARRW/BUR WA5 141 K2
Dalby Cl GOL/RIS/CUL WA3 125 K2
RNFD/HAY WA11 89 F6
Dale Acre Dr NTHTN L30 69 K6
Dale Av GTS/LS CH66 195 F3
HES CH60 167 K4
PS/BROM CH62 171 F5
Dalebrook Cl WLTN L25 135 J2
Dale Cl MGHL L31 62 A5
WARRW/BUR WA5 142 A5
WDN WA8 157 F3
Dale Crs STHEL WA9 120 B1
Dale Dr EP CH65 195 J4
Dale End Rd PEN/TH CH61 168 C1
Dale Gdns HES CH60 167 H4
Dalegarth Av WD/CROXPK L12 99 K4
Dalehead Pl RNFD/HAY WA11 88 E2
Dale Hey GTS/LS CH66 184 B5
WAL/EG CH44 111 H4
Dalehurst Cl WAL/EG CH44 111 K3
Dale La NWD/KWIPK L33 73 F5
WARRS WA4 162 D3
Dalemeadow Rd
DV/KA/FCH L14 115 H4
Dale Ms WLTN L25 135 J5
Dale Rd GOL/RIS/CUL WA3 92 B4
PS/BROM CH62 184 A2
Dalesford Cl LEIGH WN7 93 K3
Daleside Av AIMK WN4 79 F1
Daleside Cl PEN/TH CH61 148 C5
Daleside Rd NWD/KWIPK L33 72 E6
Dales Rw HUY L36 117 H5
Dale St ALL/GAR L19 153 K6
CLVP L2 8 D3
RUNC WA7 10 D7
Dalesway HES CH60 167 J5
The Dale NSTN CH64 191 J3
WARRW/BUR WA5 141 G4
Dale Vw NEWLW WA12 106 E1
Dale View Cl PEN/TH CH61 148 D6
Dalewood WD/CROXPK L12 99 J2
Dalewood Cl WARRN/WOL WA2 16 A3
Dalewood Crs CHNE CH2 198 B6
Dalewood Gdns RAIN/WH L35 118 B5
Daley Pl BTL L20 82 B4
Daley Rd LITH L21 81 K2
Dallam Ct WARRN/WOL WA2 * 16 C1
Dallam La WARRW/BUR WA5 16 C1
Dallas Gv WLT/FAZ L9 82 D5
Dalmeny St AIG/SPK L17 133 G6
Dalmorton Rd WAL/NB CH45 95 J5
Dalry Crs KKBY L32 84 E4
Dalrymple St EV L5 113 F2
Dalston Dr RNFD/HAY WA11 88 E2
Dalton Av WARRW/BUR WA5 142 C2
Dalton Bank WARR WA1 17 G3
Dalton Cl WD/CROXPK L12 99 G3
Dalton Ct RUNC WA7 177 H2
Dalton Gv AIMK WN4 79 F5
Dalton Rd WAL/NB CH45 95 J6
Dalton St GOL/RIS/CUL WA3 125 G2
RUNC WA7 177 G3
Daltry Cl WD/CROXPK L12 98 E6
Dalwood Cl RUNC WA7 178 D6
Damerham Ms WLTN L25 135 H2
Damfield La MGHL L31 62 A6
Damhead La NSTN CH64 193 F2
Damian Dr NEWLW WA12 91 F6
Dam La WARR WA1 144 C2
Damson Rd NTHLY L27 136 B4
Dam Wood La BRSC L40 37 F4
Dam Wood Rd SPK/HALE L24 173 J3
Danbers SKEL WN8 67 H1
Danby Cl EV L5 113 H2
RUNC WA7 187 G1
WARRW/BUR WA5 142 B2
Danby Fold RAIN/WH L35 118 D4
Danebank Rd LYMM WA13 145 K5
Danebank Rd East
LYMM WA13 145 K5
Dane Cl PEN/TH CH61 148 C5
Danefield Pl ALL/GAR L19 154 A3
Danefield Rd ALL/GAR L19 154 A3
GR/UP/WCH CH49 147 K1
Danehurst Rd WAL/NB CH45 95 F6
WLT/FAZ L9 82 E4
Danesbury Cl
WGNW/BIL/OR WN5 77 H5
Danescourt Rd BIRK CH41 130 D1
WD/CROXPK L12 115 G2
Danescroft WDN WA8 138 A6
Dane St ANF/KKDL L4 97 H4
Daneswell Dr MOR/LEA CH46 109 K6
Daneswell Rd SPK/HALE L24 174 B3
Daneville Rd ANF/KKDL L4 98 B3
Daneway STHP PR8 33 H3
Danger La MOR/LEA CH46 109 K5
Daniel Cl BTL L20 81 H5
GOL/RIS/CUL WA3 125 J3
Daniel Davies Dr TOX L8 133 F2
Daniels La SKEL WN8 56 E6
Dannette Hey STBRV L28 116 C1
Dansie St VAUX/LVPD L3 9 J4
Dans Rd WDN WA8 159 F1
Dante Cl WLT/FAZ L9 83 F3
Danube St TOX L8 * 133 H2
Darby Cl NSTN CH64 191 K5
Darby Gv ALL/GAR L19 153 J5
Darby Rd ALL/GAR L19 153 H3
Darent Rd RNFD/HAY WA11 90 A5
Daresbury Av STHP PR8 33 G4
Daresbury Cl KKBY L32 84 B1
Daresbury Expy RUNC WA7 10 C4
Daresbury La WARRS WA4 179 J3
Daresbury Rd ECCL WA10 102 D1
WAL/EG CH44 111 G3
Darfield SKEL WN8 57 H6
Daric Cl LEIGH WN7 93 K2
Dark Entry PR/KW L34 100 E4
Dark La BRSC L40 46 B5
MGHL L31 62 B6
Darley Av WARRN/WOL WA2 124 A4
Darley Cl WDN WA8 138 A6
Darleydale Dr PS/BROM CH62 184 C2
Darley Dr WD/CROXPK L12 115 G1
Darlington Cl WAL/EG CH44 111 K3
Darlington St WAL/EG CH44 111 K3
Darmond Rd NWD/KWIPK L33 73 F6
Darmond's Gn WKBY CH48 127 G6
Darmonds Green Av
NPK/KEN L6 114 B1

Darnaway Cl
GOL/RIS/CUL WA3 125 K1
Darnley St TOX L8 132 D4
Darrel Dr EHL/KEN L7 133 H2
Darsefield Rd CHLDW L16 135 F2
Dartford Cl DV/KA/FCH L14 115 K1
Dartington Rd CHLDW L16 134 E1
Dartmouth Av AIN/FAZ L10 83 F1
Dartmouth Dr ECCL WA10 87 K5
NTHTN L30 69 K5
Darvel Av AIMK WN4 78 B5
Darwall Rd ALL/GAR L19 154 A3
Darwen St EV L5 * 112 E2
Darwick Dr HUY L36 136 D1
Darwin Gv STHEL WA9 103 G6
Daryl Rd HES CH60 168 A4
Dashwood Cl WARRS WA4 163 F4
Daten Av GOL/RIS/CUL WA3 125 G1
Daulby St VAUX/LVPD L3 9 K3
Dauntsey Brow WLTN L25 135 J2
Dauntsey Ms WLTN L25 135 J2
Davenham Av CL/PREN CH43 130 C6
WARR WA1 143 H1
Davenham Cl CL/PREN CH43 149 J1
Davenham Ct WAV L15 134 C2
Davenham Rd FMBY L37 49 F1
Davenhill Pk AIN/FAZ L10 83 F1
Davenport Av WARRS WA4 143 J4
Davenport Cl WKBY CH48 146 D5
Davenport Gv NWD/KWIPK L33 72 D5
Davenport Rd HES CH60 167 J6
Davenport Rw RUNC WA7 177 G5
Daventree Rd WAL/NB CH45 111 H2
Daventry Rd AIG/SPK L17 153 F1
David Rd LYMM WA13 145 H6
David's Av WARRW/BUR WA5 141 J4
Davidson Rd CLB/OSW/ST L13 114 D4
David St TOX L8 132 E5
Davids Wk WLTN L25 135 K6
Davies Av NEWLW WA12 106 C1
WARRS WA4 143 J5
Davies Cl WDN WA8 176 D1
Davies St BTL L20 5 G3
CLVP L2 * 8 D3
STHEL WA9 104 A1
Davies Wy LYMM WA13 145 J6
Davis Rd MOR/LEA CH46 110 B4
Davy Av GOL/RIS/CUL WA3 125 G2
Davy Cl ECCL WA10 87 J6
Davy Rd RUNC WA7 177 H2
Davy St EV L5 113 J1
Dawber Cl NPK/KEN L6 113 J3
Dawber St AIMK WN4 79 J5
Dawley Cl AIMK WN4 79 F6
Dawlish Cl WLTN L25 155 F3
Dawlish Dr CHTN/BK PR9 20 D6
Dawlish Rd PEN/TH CH61 147 K6
WAL/EG CH44 111 F3
Dawlish Wy GOL/RIS/CUL WA3 92 A2
Dawn Cl NSTN CH64 192 A4
STHEL WA9 103 G6
Dawn Gdns EP CH65 6 B7
Dawpool Dr MOR/LEA CH46 129 F1
PS/BROM CH62 170 E6
Dawson Av BIRK CH41 130 E1
CHTN/BK PR9 21 F6
STHEL WA9 104 B6
Dawson Gdns MGHL L31 62 A5
Dawson Rd ORM L39 45 K4
Dawson St CLVPS L1 8 E4
Dawstone Ri HES CH60 167 K6
Dawstone Rd HES CH60 167 K6
Daybrook SKEL WN8 67 H1
Dayfield SKEL WN8 57 J6
Days Meadow
GR/UP/WCH CH49 128 D6
Day St CLB/OSW/ST L13 114 E4
Deacon Cl CSBY/WL L22 80 E3
Deacon Ct CSBY/WL L22 80 E3
WLTN L25 154 E1
Deacon Rd WDN WA8 18 E2
Deakin St BIRK CH41 130 C1
Dean Av WAL/NB CH45 110 E1
Dean Cl WDN WA8 18 E3
WGNW/BIL/OR WN5 77 G6
Dean Ct GOL/RIS/CUL WA3 92 B4
Dean Crs WARRN/WOL WA2 123 H5
Dean Dillistone Ct CLVPS L1 132 D2
Deane Rd EHL/KEN L7 114 A5
Dean Meadow NEWLW WA12 106 C1
Dean Rd GOL/RIS/CUL WA3 92 B4
Deansburn Rd
CLB/OSW/ST L13 114 C1
Deanscales Rd NG/CROX L11 98 D3
Deans Ct FMBY L37 41 F6
Deansfield Wy CHNE CH2 198 B6
Deansgate EP CH65 6 A4
Deansgate La FMBY L37 41 H6
Deansgate La North FMBY L37 41 G5
Deans La WARRS WA4 144 E6
Deans Rd EP CH65 196 E6
Dean St CSBY/WL L22 80 E3
WDN WA8 18 E3
Deans Wy BIRK CH41 130 C1
Deansway WDN WA8 157 H3
Deanwater Cl
GOL/RIS/CUL WA3 125 F3
Dean Wood Cl RAIN/WH L35 118 B5
Dearham Av RNFD/HAY WA11 88 D4
Dearne Cl WD/CROXPK L12 115 J2
Dearnford Av PS/BROM CH62 184 A1
Dearnford Cl PS/BROM CH62 184 A1
Dearnley Av RNFD/HAY WA11 89 H6
Deauville Rd WLT/FAZ L9 83 F4
Debra Cl GTS/LS CH66 195 F5
MGHL L31 72 A5
Debra Rd GTS/LS CH66 195 F6
Dee Cl NWD/KWIPK L33 72 E3
Dee La WKBY CH48 146 B1
Deeley Cl EHL/KEN L7 114 A6
Dee Park Cl HES CH60 181 G1
Dee Park Rd HES CH60 181 G1
Deep Dl WARRW/BUR WA5 141 G3
Deepdale WDN WA8 138 B6
Deepdale Av BTL L20 81 H6
RNFD/HAY WA11 * 89 F2
Deepdale Cl CL/PREN CH43 129 K3
Deepdale Dr RAIN/WH L35 119 F4
Deepdale Rd WLTN L25 135 H2
Deepfield Dr HUY L36 136 C1
Deepfield Rd WAV L15 134 A3
Deepwood Gv RAIN/WH L35 118 A5
Deerbarn Dr NTHTN L30 70 E6
Deerbolt Cl KKBY L32 72 B6
Deerbolt Crs KKBY L32 72 B6
Deerbolt Wy KKBY L32 72 B6
Dee Rd RAIN/WH L35 118 D4
Deer Park Ct RUNC WA7 187 J1
Deerwood Cl GTS/LS CH66 195 G2
Deerwood Crs GTS/LS CH66 195 G2
Deeside EP CH65 196 A6
Dee Side HES CH60 167 G5
Deeside Cl CL/PREN CH43 129 J3
EP CH65 203 F1
Dee View Rd HES CH60 167 K5
De Grouchy St WKBY CH48 * 127 G6
De-Haviland Wy SKEL WN8 57 G5
Deirdre Av WDN WA8 18 D2
Dekker Rd NWD/KWIPK L33 72 D3
Delabole Rd NG/CROX L11 84 C6
De Lacy Rw RUNC WA7 177 K3
Delafield Cl WARRN/WOL WA2 124 B4
Delagoa Rd AIN/FAZ L10 83 J5
Delamain Rd
CLB/OSW/ST L13 114 C1
Delamere Av
GOL/RIS/CUL WA3 93 F5
GTS/LS CH66 195 H4
PS/BROM CH62 184 B3
STHEL WA9 119 J4
WDN WA8 157 H2
Delamere Cl CL/PREN CH43 129 J3
PS/BROM CH62 184 B3
WD/CROXPK L12 99 H2
Delamere Dr GTS/LS CH66 195 H5
Delamere Gv WAL/EG CH44 * 112 A5
Delamere Rd SKEL WN8 56 B3
STHP PR8 33 H4
Delamere St
WARRW/BUR WA5 142 B4
Delamere Wy SKEL WN8 57 J6
WARRS WA4 189 J5
Delamore Pl ANF/KKDL L4 * 97 G4
Delamore's Acre NSTN CH64 193 H1
Delamore St ANF/KKDL L4 97 G4
Delavor Cl HES CH60 167 J5
Delavor Rd HES CH60 167 J5
Delaware Crs KKBY L32 72 B6
Delaware Rd BTL L20 4 E3
Delenty Dr GOL/RIS/CUL WA3 125 F3
Delery Dr WARR WA1 143 H1
Delfby Crs KKBY L32 85 F2
Delf La ANF/KKDL L4 97 J3
ORM L39 43 J6
SPK/HALE L24 154 E6
Dell Cl BEB CH63 183 J1
Dell Dr WARRN/WOL WA2 124 C5
Dellfield La MGHL L31 62 C6
Dell Gv RF/TRAN CH42 151 F3
Dell La HES CH60 168 B6
Dellside Cl AIMK WN4 78 C3
Dellside Gv STHEL WA9 104 A5
Dell St EHL/KEN L7 114 A5
The Dell RF/TRAN CH42 151 G2
SKEL WN8 57 K6
WD/CROXPK L12 99 J4
Delph Common Rd ORM L39 53 F4
Delph Dr BRSC L40 39 F5
Delphfields Rd WARRS WA4 162 B4
Delph Hollow Wy STHEL WA9 103 K5
Delphield RUNC WA7 178 C5
Delph La FMBY L37 48 C2
ORM L39 53 F5
RAIN/WH L35 118 B3
WARRN/WOL WA2 123 F3
WARRS WA4 179 F2
Delph Meadow Gdns
WGNW/BIL/OR WN5 77 F5
Delph Park Av ORM L39 53 F4
Delph Rd CSBY/BLUN L23 68 E1
Delph Top ORM L39 46 A5
Delphwood Dr STHEL WA9 103 K4
Delta Crs WARRW/BUR WA5 122 C5
Delta Dr WD/CROXPK L12 99 J5
Delta Rd LITH L21 81 J4
STHEL WA9 104 D1
Delta Rd East RF/TRAN CH42 151 G2
Delta Rd West
RF/TRAN CH42 * 151 G2
Deltic Wy NTHTN L30 82 D3
NWD/KWIPK L33 85 G3
Delves Av BEB CH63 170 B2
WARRW/BUR WA5 142 C2
Delyn Cl RF/TRAN CH42 150 D2
Demage Dr GTS/LS CH66 195 G6
Demesne St WAL/EG CH44 112 A4
Denbigh Av CHTN/BK PR9 23 H2
STHEL WA9 104 A6
Denbigh Ct EP CH65 196 C6
Denbigh Gdns EP CH65 196 B6
Denbigh Rd WLT/FAZ L9 97 H2
Denbigh St EV L5 112 D2
Denbury Av WARRS WA4 162 E1
Dencourt Rd NG/CROX L11 99 F4
Dene Av NEWLW WA12 105 K1
Denebank Rd ANF/KKDL L4 97 K6
Denehurst Cl
WARRW/BUR WA5 141 G5
Deneshey Rd HOY CH47 127 H1
Denes Wy STBRV L28 100 A6
Denford Rd DV/KA/FCH L14 115 K2
Denham Av WARRW/BUR WA5 141 J4
Denham Cl WD/CROXPK L12 99 K2
Denholme SKEL WN8 57 H6
Denise Av WARRW/BUR WA5 141 F4
Denise Rd AIN/FAZ L10 84 A4
Denison Gv STHEL WA9 * 103 G6
Denman Dr NPK/KEN L6 114 A3
Denman Gv WAL/EG CH44 * 112 A4
Denman St NPK/KEN L6 113 K4
Denman Wy NPK/KEN L6 114 A3
Denmark Rd CHTN/BK PR9 23 J3
Denmark St CSBY/WL L22 80 E2
Dennett Cl MGHL L31 71 G2
WARR WA1 144 D3
Dennett Rd RAIN/WH L35 117 J3
Denning Dr PEN/TH CH61 148 A4
Dennis Av ECCL WA10 102 E6
Dennis Rd WDN WA8 19 G5
Denny Cl GR/UP/WCH CH49 129 G5
Densham Av
WARRN/WOL WA2 123 H5
Denston Cl CL/PREN CH43 129 J2
Denstone Av AIN/FAZ L10 83 G1
Denstone Cl WLTN L25 154 E3
Dentdale Dr EV L5 113 G3
Denton Dr WAL/NB CH45 111 J1
Denton Gv NPK/KEN L6 114 A2
Dentons Green La ECCL WA10 12 B2
Denton St TOX L8 132 E5
WDN WA8 19 G2
Dentwood St TOX L8 133 F5
Denver Dr WARRW/BUR WA5 141 J2
Denver Rd KKBY L32 84 B2
WARRS WA4 143 K6
Depot Rd NWD/KWIPK L33 73 H5
Derby Cl NEWLW WA12 106 B2
Derby Dr RNFD/HAY WA11 75 H4
WARR WA1 143 J2
Derby Gv MGHL L31 71 G3
Derby Hill Crs ORM L39 46 A6
Derby Hill Rd ORM L39 46 A6
Derby La CLB/OSW/ST L13 114 E3
Derby Rd BTL L20 4 C6
CHTN/BK PR9 15 G5
EV L5 112 D1
FMBY L37 48 E1
GOL/RIS/CUL WA3 92 D2
HUY L36 116 E5
RF/TRAN CH42 131 G5
SKEL WN8 55 J5
WAL/NB CH45 111 G1
WARRS WA4 162 B3
WDN WA8 139 G6
Derby Rw NEWLW WA12 106 C5
Derbyshire Hill Rd STHEL WA9 104 E2
Derby Sq CLVP L2 8 D5
PR/KW L34 118 A1
Derby St CLB/OSW/ST L13 * 114 D4
HUY L36 117 G5
NEWLW WA12 106 B2
ORM L39 45 K6
Derby St West ORM L39 45 J6
Dereham Av
GR/UP/WCH CH49 129 H2
Dereham Crs AIN/FAZ L10 83 J4
Dereham Wy RUNC WA7 178 C2
Derek Av WARRN/WOL WA2 123 K6
Derna Rd HUY L36 116 D4
Derringstone Cl ECCL WA10 103 F4
Derwent Av CHTN/BK PR9 23 H4
FMBY L37 48 D3
GOL/RIS/CUL WA3 92 E2
PR/KW L34 118 B1
Derwent Cl BEB CH63 * 150 C6
MGHL L31 62 D5
NWD/KWIPK L33 72 C5
RAIN/WH L35 118 D4
Derwent Dr GTS/LS CH66 184 E5
LITH L21 82 A3
PEN/TH CH61 167 K1
WAL/NB CH45 111 G1
Derwent Rd AIMK WN4 79 K4
BEB CH63 150 C6
CL/PREN CH43 130 E5
CSBY/BLUN L23 81 G1
HOY CH47 127 K1
RNFD/HAY WA11 88 E4
WARRS WA4 161 K1
WDN WA8 157 H2
Derwent Rd East
CLB/OSW/ST L13 114 E3
Derwent Rd West
CLB/OSW/ST L13 114 D3
Derwent Sq CLB/OSW/ST L13 114 E3
Derwent Wy LEIGH WN7 93 J2
NSTN CH64 192 A3
Desborough Crs
WD/CROXPK L12 98 E6
Desford Av RNFD/HAY WA11 89 G5
Desford Cl MOR/LEA CH46 109 F6
Desford Rd AIG/SPK L17 153 F3
Desilva St HUY L36 117 G5
Desmond Cl CL/PREN CH43 129 K2
Desmond Gv CSBY/BLUN L23 69 G6
Desoto Rd WDN WA8 157 K6
Desoto Rd East WDN WA8 158 A5
Desoto Rd West WDN WA8 158 A5
Deva Cl NWD/KWIPK L33 72 D2
Deva Rd WKBY CH48 146 B1
Deveraux Dr WAL/EG CH44 111 H4
Deverell Gv WAV L15 115 F6
Deverell Rd WAV L15 115 F6
Deverill Rd RF/TRAN CH42 150 D2
Devilla Cl DV/KA/FCH L14 116 A2
De Villiers Av
CSBY/BLUN L23 69 F4
Devisdale Gv CL/PREN CH43 129 K2
Devizes Dr PEN/TH CH61 148 A4
Devizes Ms WLTN L25 135 J2
Devoke Av RNFD/HAY WA11 88 D2
Devon Av SKEL WN8 67 K1
WAL/NB CH45 111 J2
Devon Cl CSBY/BLUN L23 68 B5
Devon Ct EV L5 113 J2
Devondale Rd CALD/MH L18 134 B4
Devon Dr PEN/TH CH61 167 J1
Devon Farm Wy FMBY L37 49 H2
Devonfield Rd WLT/FAZ L9 82 C6
Devon Gdns CHLDW L16 135 F4
RF/TRAN CH42 150 E2
Devon Pl WDN WA8 139 F6
Devonport St TOX L8 132 E4
Devonshire Cl NWD/KWIPK L33 72 D5
Devonshire Gdns
NEWLW WA12 106 C3
Devonshire Pl CL/PREN CH43 130 D4
EV L5 113 G1
RUNC WA7 10 D4
Devonshire Rd CHTN/BK PR9 23 J6
CL/PREN CH43 130 E4
CSBY/WL L22 80 D1
ECCL WA10 12 A1
GR/UP/WCH CH49 129 F4
PEN/TH CH61 167 J1
TOX L8 132 F4
WAL/EG CH44 111 H3
WARR WA1 143 J1
WKBY CH48 146 D2
Devonshire Rd West TOX L8 133 F4
Devon St ECCL WA10 12 B4
VAUX/LVPD L3 9 J2
Devonwall Gdns TOX L8 133 G4
Devon Wy CHLDW L16 135 F3
HUY L36 117 G3
Dewar Ct RUNC WA7 177 H2
Dewar St GOL/RIS/CUL WA3 125 G2
Dewberry Cl RF/TRAN CH42 131 G5
Dewberry Flds SKEL WN8 57 K6
Dewey Av WLT/FAZ L9 82 E3
Dewhurst Rd
GOL/RIS/CUL WA3 125 F4
Dewlands Rd LITH L21 81 G3
Dewsbury Rd ANF/KKDL L4 113 K1
Dexter St TOX L8 132 D3
Deycroft Av NWD/KWIPK L33 73 F5
Deyes End MGHL L31 62 C6
Deyes La MGHL L31 62 B6
Deysbrook La
WD/CROXPK L12 115 G1
Deysbrook Side
WD/CROXPK L12 115 G1
Deysbrook Wy
WD/CROXPK L12 99 H5
Dial Rd RF/TRAN CH42 131 G6
Dial St EHL/KEN L7 114 A5
WARR WA1 16 E4
Diamond St EV L5 113 F3
Diana Rd BTL L20 82 A4
Diana St ANF/KKDL L4 97 H5
Diane Rd AIMK WN4 79 J4
Dibbinsdale Rd BEB CH63 170 D6
Dibbins Gn BEB CH63 183 J1
Dibbins Hey BEB CH63 170 C3
Dibbinview Gv BEB CH63 170 D3
Dibb La CSBY/BLUN L23 68 D2
Dicconson's La ORM L39 52 A2
Dicconson St ECCL WA10 * 13 G3
Dicconson Wy ORM L39 * 54 A1
Dickens Av CL/PREN CH43 149 J2
Dickens Cl CL/PREN CH43 149 J2
KKBY L32 84 C3
Dickenson St CLVPS L1 * 8 E7
Dickens Rd ECCL WA10 102 E5
Dickens St TOX L8 * 132 E3
Dicket's La SKEL WN8 55 G3
Dickinson Cl FMBY L37 49 F3
RNFD/HAY WA11 89 K5
Dickinson Rd FMBY L37 49 F3
Dick's La BRSC L40 55 F1
Dickson Cl WDN WA8 18 E3
Dickson St VAUX/LVPD L3 112 D3
WDN WA8 18 D3
Didcot Cl WLTN L25 155 G3
Didsbury Cl NWD/KWIPK L33 84 E1
Digg La MOR/LEA CH46 109 H6
Dig La FROD/HEL WA6 200 D2
WARRN/WOL WA2 124 C3
Digmoor Dr SKEL WN8 56 D6
Digmoor Rd KKBY L32 84 E4
SKEL WN8 56 E6
Dignum Md NTHLY L27 136 B3
Dilloway St ECCL WA10 12 C3
Dinaro Cl WLTN L25 135 K5
Dinas La HUY L36 116 A3
Dinesen Rd ALL/GAR L19 153 K4
Dingle Av NEWLW WA12 105 K3
SKEL WN8 57 K5
Dingle Bank Cl LYMM WA13 145 K6
Dingle Brow TOX L8 133 F6
Dingle Cl ORM L39 53 G4
Dingle Gv TOX L8 133 F5
Dingle La TOX L8 133 F6
WARRS WA4 162 E5
Dingle Mt TOX L8 133 F6
Dingle Rd RF/TRAN CH42 131 F5
SKEL WN8 57 K6
TOX L8 132 E6
The Dingle LYMM WA13 145 K6
Dingle V TOX L8 133 F6
Dingleway WARRS WA4 162 C3
Dingley Av WLT/FAZ L9 82 C5
Dingwall Dr GR/UP/WCH CH49 129 F6
Dinmore Rd WAL/EG CH44 111 H3
Dinnington Ct WDN WA8 138 D6
Dinorwic Rd ANF/KKDL L4 113 J1
STHP PR8 27 H4
Dinsdale Rd PS/BROM CH62 171 G3
Ditchfield FMBY L37 49 G3
Ditchfield Pl WDN WA8 157 G3
Ditchfield Rd
WARRW/BUR WA5 141 F6
WDN WA8 157 F3
Ditton La MOR/LEA CH46 109 J4
Ditton Rd WDN WA8 18 B7
Dixon Av NEWLW WA12 91 H6
Dixon Cl RNFD/HAY WA11 91 F3
Dixon Rd NWD/KWIPK L33 85 G2
Dixon St WARR WA1 16 B5
Dobbs Dr FMBY L37 49 G1
Dobers La FROD/HEL WA6 201 F6
Dobson St NPK/KEN L6 113 J3
Dock Rd ALL/GAR L19 153 J6
BIRK CH41 111 G5
WDN WA8 158 A6
Dock Rd North
PS/BROM CH62 151 H5
Dock Rd South
PS/BROM CH62 171 F1
Dock St EP CH65 6 E1
WDN WA8 158 B6
Dock Yard Rd EP CH65 7 G3
Doctors La FMBY L37 50 A4
Dodd Av ECCL WA10 102 E1
GR/UP/WCH CH49 128 E6
Doddridge Rd TOX L8 132 D4
Dodd's La MGHL L31 62 B5
WARRS WA4 163 F6
Dodleston Cl CL/PREN CH43 130 A5
Dodman Rd NG/CROX L11 84 C6
Dodworth Av STHP PR8 28 B2
Doe Park Ctyd WLTN L25 * 154 E3
Doe's Meadow Rd BEB CH63 170 D6
Dolly's La CHTN/BK PR9 24 B5
Dolomite Av SPK/HALE L24 154 C5
Dolphin Crs GTS/LS CH66 202 C1
Domar Cl KKBY L32 84 D3
Dombey St TOX L8 132 E3
Domingo Dr NWD/KWIPK L33 72 C4
Dominic Cl CHLDW L16 135 F1
Dominic Rd CHLDW L16 135 F1
Dominion St NPK/KEN L6 * 114 A2
Domville RAIN/WH L35 118 A5
Domville Cl LYMM WA13 145 K6
Domville Rd CLB/OSW/ST L13 114 E6
Donaldson St EV L5 113 J1
Donalds Wy AIG/SPK L17 153 F2
Doncaster Dr
GR/UP/WCH CH49 129 G3
Donegal Rd CLB/OSW/ST L13 115 F4
Donne Av BEB CH63 170 B2
Donne Cl BEB CH63 170 C2
Donnington Cl HUY L36 136 A1
Donsby Rd WLT/FAZ L9 82 E5
Don Wk EP CH65 195 K2
Dooley Dr NTHTN L30 70 E5
Doon Cl ANF/KKDL L4 97 G5
Dorbett Dr CSBY/BLUN L23 81 G1
Dorchester Cl
GR/UP/WCH CH49 129 G5
Dorchester Dr
NWD/KWIPK L33 73 F4
Dorchester Pk CL/PREN CH43 130 A6
RUNC WA7 178 C2
WLTN L25 135 J3
Dorchester Rd SKEL WN8 57 J6
WARRW/BUR WA5 141 J4
WLTN L25 135 J3
Dorchester Wy
WARRW/BUR WA5 121 K1
Doreen Av MOR/LEA CH46 128 E1
Dorgan Cl RAIN/WH L35 118 D3
Doric Av FROD/HEL WA6 201 F2
Doric Rd CLB/OSW/ST L13 114 E3
Doric St LITH L21 81 G4
RF/TRAN CH42 * 150 E1
Dorien Rd CLB/OSW/ST L13 114 D5
Dorking Gv WAV L15 134 C2
Dorney Cl WARRS WA4 162 D5
Dorney Ct WD/CROXPK L12 99 H5
Dorothea St
WARRN/WOL WA2 143 F2
Dorothy St EHL/KEN L7 113 K6
STHEL WA9 103 G6
Dorrington Cl RUNC WA7 178 C5
Dorrit St TOX L8 132 E3
Dorset Av EHL/KEN L7 133 J2
STHP PR8 41 J1
Dorset Cl BTL L20 5 H4
Dorset Dr PEN/TH CH61 167 J1
Dorset Rd ECCL WA10 103 F4
HUY L36 117 G4
NPK/KEN L6 114 B1
WAL/NB CH45 95 G6
WKBY CH48 127 H6
Dorset Wy WARR WA1 144 A1
Douglas Av SKEL WN8 57 K6
STHEL WA9 121 F1
WGNW/BIL/OR WN5 77 G6
Douglas Cl CLB/OSW/ST L13 114 D3
WDN WA8 140 A6
Douglas Dr MGHL L31 62 D5
MOR/LEA CH46 128 D1
ORM L39 45 H4
Douglas Pl BTL L20 4 D7
Douglas Rd ANF/KKDL L4 113 K1
CHTN/BK PR9 24 A1
WKBY CH48 127 J6
Douglas St BIRK CH41 3 G4
ECCL WA10 12 B5
Douglas Wy NWD/KWIPK L33 72 E3
Doulton Cl CL/PREN CH43 129 J2
Doulton Pl RAIN/WH L35 117 J5
Doulton St ECCL WA10 12 A6
Doune Ct EP CH65 196 C6
Dounrey Cl WARRN/WOL WA2 124 C5
Douro Pl CLB/OSW/ST L13 114 D5
Douro St VAUX/LVPD L3 113 G3
Dove Cl CHNE CH2 198 D5
FROD/HEL WA6 199 K4
GOL/RIS/CUL WA3 125 H3
GTS/LS CH66 195 J2
Dovecot Av DV/KA/FCH L14 115 K3
Dovecote Dr RNFD/HAY WA11 90 B4
Dovecote Gn
WARRW/BUR WA5 122 A6
Dove Ct WLTN L25 154 E1
Dovedale Av MGHL L31 62 A5
PS/BROM CH62 184 B2
Dovedale Cl CL/PREN CH43 149 J1
WARRN/WOL WA2 124 A4
Dovedale Crs AIMK WN4 79 F1
Dovedale Rd AIMK WN4 79 F1
CALD/MH L18 134 A4
HOY CH47 127 G1
WAL/NB CH45 95 G6
Dovepoint Rd HOY CH47 108 C6
Dovercliffe Rd
CLB/OSW/ST L13 115 F4
Dover Cl BIRK CH41 2 D3
RUNC WA7 188 D1
Dover Ct EP CH65 203 H1
Dover Dr EP CH65 203 H1
Dover Gv CHLDW L16 135 G1
Dove Rd WLT/FAZ L9 82 C5
Dover Rd MGHL L31 71 F3
STHP PR8 27 G5
WARRS WA4 143 K6
Dover St RUNC WA7 11 F3
VAUX/LVPD L3 9 J4
Dovesmead Rd HES CH60 * 168 C6
Dovestone Cl EHL/KEN L7 133 G1
Dove St GOL/RIS/CUL WA3 92 B1
TOX L8 133 G2
Dovey St TOX L8 132 E4
Doward St WDN WA8 158 D1
Dowhills Dr CSBY/BLUN L23 68 C4
Dowhills Pk CSBY/BLUN L23 68 C3
Dowhills Rd CSBY/BLUN L23 68 C4
Downall Green Rd AIMK WN4 78 C3
Downes Gn BEB CH63 170 C4
Downham Cl WLTN L25 135 G4
Downham Dr HES CH60 168 A5
Downham Gn WLTN L25 135 G4
Downham Rd RF/TRAN CH42 131 H6
Downham Rd North
PEN/TH CH61 168 A3
Downham Rd South
HES CH60 168 A5
Downham Wy WLTN L25 135 G4

Downholland Moss La
  FMBY L37 49 J1
Downing Cl CL/PREN CH43 130 E6
Downing Rd BTL L20 5 H7
Downing St EV L5 113 J2
Downlands Rd NTHLY L27 136 C5
Downland Wy STHEL WA9 104 D4
Downside WDN WA8 138 A6
Downside Cl NTHTN L30 70 B5
Downside Dr AIN/FAZ L10 83 J2
Downs Rd ECCL WA10 12 B6
  RUNC WA7 10 E7
Downway La STHEL WA9 104 E4
Dowsefield La CALD/MH L18 135 F6
Dragon Cl NG/CROX L11 99 G1
  SKEL WN8 57 G5
Dragon Crs RAIN/WH L35 118 B3
Dragon La RAIN/WH L35 118 A3
Dragon Yd WDN WA8 139 G5
Drake Cl AIN/FAZ L10 83 K4
  ORM L39 53 G3
  RAIN/WH L35 118 A5
  WARRW/BUR WA5 122 D6
Drake Crs AIN/FAZ L10 83 K4
Drakefield Rd NG/CROX L11 98 C2
Drake Gdns STHEL WA9 119 G1
Drake Pl AIN/FAZ L10 * 83 J4
Drake Rd AIN/FAZ L10 83 J4
  MOR/LEA CH46 110 B3
  NSTN CH64 181 K6
Drake St BTL L20 96 D4
  ECCL WA10 12 B4
Drake Wy AIN/FAZ L10 83 K4
Drapers Ct GOL/RIS/CUL WA3 93 G4
Draw Well Rd NWD/KWIPK L33 85 J1
Draycott St TOX L8 132 E6
Drayton Cl PEN/TH CH61 148 A6
  RUNC WA7 10 B6
Drayton Crs RNFD/HAY WA11 89 G5
Drayton Rd ANF/KKDL L4 * 97 J3
  WAL/EG CH44 111 K4
Drennan Rd ALL/GAR L19 154 B3
Drewell Rd CALD/MH L18 134 A6
Drewitt Crs CHTN/BK PR9 24 A1
Driffield Rd PR/KW L34 117 J1
Drinkwater Gdns
  VAUX/LVPD L3 113 G4
The Drive WD/CROXPK L12 115 F2
Driveway RAIN/WH L35 118 B4
Droitwich Av
  GR/UP/WCH CH49 128 D5
Dromore Av CALD/MH L18 134 B6
Dronfield Wy WLTN L25 135 G2
Druids Cross Gdns
  CALD/MH L18 134 E5
Druids Cross Rd
  CALD/MH L18 134 E5
Druids Pk CALD/MH L18 135 F5
Druid St AIMK WN4 91 H1
Druidsville Rd CALD/MH L18 135 F5
Druids Wy GR/UP/WCH CH49 148 D1
Drum Cl DV/KA/FCH L14 116 A2
Drummersdale La BRSC L40 30 A6
Drummer's La AIMK WN4 78 D2
Drummond Av GTS/LS CH66 195 F5
Drummond Ct WDN WA8 158 E1
Drummond Rd ANF/KKDL L4 98 A4
  CSBY/BLUN L23 69 J4
  HOY CH47 127 F4
Druridge Dr WARRW/BUR WA5 141 G5
Drury La CLVP L2 8 C4
Dryburgh Wy ANF/KKDL L4 97 G5
Dryden Av AIMK WN4 78 E2
Dryden Cl CL/PREN CH43 129 K2
  RAIN/WH L35 118 A4
Dryden Gv HUY L36 117 F6
Dryden Pl WARRN/WOL WA2 123 J5
Dryden Rd EHL/KEN L7 114 C6
Dryden St BTL L20 4 B1
  EV L5 113 F3
Dryebeck Gv STHEL WA9 120 B1
Dryfield Cl
  GR/UP/WCH CH49 * 128 E5
Drysdale Wk TOX L8 133 F5
Dublin Cft GTS/LS CH66 202 C2
Dublin St VAUX/LVPD L3 112 D3
Ducie St TOX L8 133 G3
Duckinfield St VAUX/LVPD L3 9 J4
Duck Pond La RF/TRAN CH42 149 K1
Duckworth Gv
  WARRN/WOL WA2 124 C6
Duddingston Av
  CALD/MH L18 * 134 B4
  CSBY/BLUN L23 81 F1
Duddon Av MGHL L31 62 D5
Duddon Cl CL/PREN CH43 130 C5
Dudleston Rd GTS/LS CH66 194 E3
Dudley Cl CL/PREN CH43 130 E5
Dudley Crs EP CH65 184 E4
Dudley Gv CSBY/BLUN L23 81 F1
Dudley Pl STHEL WA9 104 B2
Dudley Rd CALD/MH L18 134 A4
  EP CH65 6 C5
  WAL/NB CH45 95 G5
Dudley St AIMK WN4 79 F4
  WARRN/WOL WA2 142 E2
Dudlow Dr CALD/MH L18 134 D4
Dudlow Gdns CALD/MH L18 134 D3
Dudlow Green Rd
  WARRS WA4 162 C6
Dudlow La CALD/MH L18 134 C3
Dudlow Nook Rd
  CALD/MH L18 134 D3
Dugdale Cl ALL/GAR L19 153 H4
Duke Av STHP PR8 27 K3
Duke Cl RUNC WA7 10 B4
Dukes Rd EV L5 113 G1
Duke St AIMK WN4 79 H6
  ALL/GAR L19 153 K5
  BIRK CH41 2 A2
  CLVPS L1 9 F6
  CSBY/WL L22 80 E3
  ECCL WA10 12 E3
  FMBY L37 48 E3
  GOL/RIS/CUL WA3 92 B2
  NEWLW WA12 106 B2
  PR/KW L34 101 K6
  STHP PR8 14 C6
  WAL/NB CH45 95 H5
Duke Street La CLVPS L1 * 8 E6
Dukes Wy FMBY L37 49 F3
Dukes Whf RUNC WA7 188 D1
Duke's Wood La SKEL WN8 66 E3
Dulas Gn KKBY L32 85 F2
Dulas Rd KKBY L32 85 F2
  WAV L15 134 C3
Dulson Wy PR/KW L34 117 G2
Dulverton Rd AIG/SPK L17 153 F3
Dumbarton St ANF/KKDL L4 97 G4
Dumbrees Rd WD/CROXPK L12 99 J5
Dumbreeze Gv PR/KW L34 100 D1
Dumfries Wy NWD/KWIPK L33 72 C3
Dunacre Wy HLWD L26 155 J4
Dunbabin Rd CHLDW L16 134 D3
Dunbar Cl GTS/LS CH66 195 F4
Dunbar Crs STHP PR8 34 B1
Dunbar Rd STHP PR8 27 F6
Dunbar St ANF/KKDL L4 97 H3
Dunbeath Av RAIN/WH L35 119 F6
Dunbeath Cl RAIN/WH L35 119 F6
Dunblane Cl AIMK WN4 78 B5
Duncan Av NEWLW WA12 91 H6
  RUNC WA7 11 H6
Duncan Cl ECCL WA10 12 D7
Duncan Dr GR/UP/WCH CH49 128 E5
Duncansby Crs
  WARRW/BUR WA5 141 F3
Duncansby Dr BEB CH63 183 K3
Duncan St BIRK CH41 3 H4
  CLVPS L1 132 D2
  ECCL WA10 12 D6
  WARRN/WOL WA2 143 F2
Dunchurch Rd DV/KA/FCH L14 115 K2
Duncombe Rd North
  ALL/GAR L19 153 J4
Duncombe Rd South
  ALL/GAR L19 153 J4
Duncote Cl CL/PREN CH43 130 D5
  RAIN/WH L35 118 C2
Dundale Rd CLB/OSW/ST L13 115 F4
Dundalk Rd WDN WA8 157 J3
Dundas St BTL L20 96 D4
Dundee Cl WARRN/WOL WA2 124 A3
Dundee Ct EP CH65 196 D6
Dundee Gv WAL/EG CH44 111 G4
Dundonald Av WARRS WA4 162 B2
Dundonald Rd AIG/SPK L17 153 F2
Dundonald St BIRK CH41 130 D1
Dunedin St STHEL WA9 103 G6
Dunes Dr FMBY L37 48 C1
Dunes Wy EV L5 112 E1
Dunfold Cl KKBY L32 84 E2
Dungeon La SPK/HALE L24 174 A4
Dunham Av GOL/RIS/CUL WA3 92 A2
Dunham Cl PS/BROM CH62 184 C3
Dunham Rd WAV L15 114 E6
Dunkeld Cl NPK/KEN L6 113 J4
Dunkeld St NPK/KEN L6 * 113 J4
Dunkerron Cl NTHLY L27 135 K2
Dunkirk Dr EP CH65 202 E2
Dunkirk La CH/BCN CH1 202 A3
  GTS/LS CH66 202 E2
Dunkirk Rd STHP PR8 27 G5
Dunley Cl GOL/RIS/CUL WA3 125 J1
Dunlin Av NEWLW WA12 106 C1
Dunlin Cl NTHLY L27 136 B5
  RUNC WA7 187 J2
  WARRN/WOL WA2 124 A4
Dunlop Av STHP PR8 41 J1
Dunlop Dr MGHL L31 72 A5
Dunlop Rd SPK/HALE L24 173 G3
Dunlop St WARRS WA4 142 E6
Dunluce St ANF/KKDL L4 97 G4
Dunmail Av RNFD/HAY WA11 89 F2
Dunmail Gv RUNC WA7 187 G3
Dunmore Crs GTS/LS CH66 194 E3
Dunmore Rd CLB/OSW/ST L13 114 C4
  GTS/LS CH66 194 E3
Dunmow Rd WARRS WA4 144 B6
Dunmow Wy WLTN L25 155 F3
Dunnerdale Rd NG/CROX L11 98 E3
Dunnett St BTL L20 96 D4
Dunning Cl GR/UP/WCH CH49 129 F4
Dunnings Bridge Rd LITH L21 82 B2
Dunnock Cl WARRN/WOL WA2 124 A4
  WLTN L25 135 H4
Dunnock Gv
  GOL/RIS/CUL WA3 125 G3
Dunraven Rd NSTN CH64 192 B2
  WKBY CH48 146 B1
Dunriding La ECCL WA10 12 A6
Dunscar Cl GOL/RIS/CUL WA3 125 F2
Dunscroft STHEL WA9 104 B6
Dunsdale Dr AIMK WN4 79 H6
Dunsdon Cl CALD/MH L18 135 F5
Dunsdon Rd WLTN L25 135 F4
Dunsford WDN WA8 138 B6
Dunsmore Cl RNFD/HAY WA11 90 B4
Dunsop Av STHEL WA9 120 B3
Dunstall Cl MOR/LEA CH46 109 J4
Dunstan La EHL/KEN L7 133 H1
  NSTN CH64 193 F5
Dunstan St WAV L15 133 K1
Dunster Gv HES CH60 168 B6
  STHEL WA9 120 B3
Dunster Rd STHP PR8 34 A1
Durban Rd CLB/OSW/ST L13 115 F5
  WAL/NB CH45 111 H1
Durden St EHL/KEN L7 133 H2
Durham Av NTHTN L30 82 D2
Durham Cl WARR WA1 144 D2
Durham Ms East NTHTN L30 * 82 D2
Durham Ms West NTHTN L30 * 82 D2
Durham Rd LITH L21 81 F4
  WDN WA8 * 139 G6
Durham St ALL/GAR L19 172 C1
  SKEL WN8 55 K3
Durham Wy NTHTN L30 82 D2
Durley Dr CL/PREN CH43 149 H2
Durley Park Cl CL/PREN CH43 149 H3
Durley Rd WLT/FAZ L9 82 E5
Durliston Cl WDN WA8 157 H1
Durning Rd EHL/KEN L7 114 A6
Durrant Rd NG/CROX L11 98 C5
Durrell Wy GOL/RIS/CUL WA3 93 F3
Dursley RAIN/WH L35 118 B5
Dursley Dr AIMK WN4 79 J5
Durston Rd CHLDW L16 134 E1
Durweston Wk WLTN L25 135 K3
Dutton Dr BEB CH63 170 B3
Dutton Gn CHNE CH2 196 E6
Dutton St WARR WA1 17 F5
Duxbury Cl MGHL L31 62 C4
  RNFD/HAY WA11 75 G2
Duxford Ct WARRN/WOL WA2 124 A6
Dwerryhouse La NG/CROX L11 99 F3
Dwerryhouse St TOX L8 132 C3
Dyers La ORM L39 53 J1
Dyer St GOL/RIS/CUL WA3 92 A3
Dyke St NPK/KEN L6 113 J3
Dykin Cl WDN WA8 139 K6
Dykin Rd WDN WA8 139 J6
Dymchurch Rd SPK/HALE L24 173 G1
Dymoke Rd NG/CROX L11 99 G2
Dyson Hall Dr WLT/FAZ L9 83 G6
Dyson St ANF/KKDL L4 97 H4

E

Eager La MGHL L31 51 K5
Eagle Brow LYMM WA13 145 J6
Eagle Crs RNFD/HAY WA11 75 H3
Eaglehall Rd WLT/FAZ L9 98 D1
Eaglehurst Rd WLTN L25 135 J5
Eagle La GTS/LS CH66 195 G2
Eagle Park Dr
  WARRN/WOL WA2 123 G6
Eagles Ct KKBY L32 84 D1
Eaglesfield Cl STHEL WA9 * 104 A6
Eagles Wy RUNC WA7 187 H1
Ealing Cl RUNC WA7 178 C4
Ealing Rd WARRW/BUR WA5 141 H4
  WLT/FAZ L9 82 E4
Eamont Av CHTN/BK PR9 20 E6
Eanleywood La RUNC WA7 178 B6
Eardisley Rd WAV L15 134 B3
Earle Cl NEWLW WA12 105 K2
Earle Crs NSTN CH64 181 J6
Earle Dr NSTN CH64 191 J1
Earle Rd EHL/KEN L7 133 H1
  WDN WA8 19 F6
Earle St NEWLW WA12 105 K3
  VAUX/LVPD L3 8 B2
Earl Rd BTL L20 5 H3
Earl's Cl CSBY/BLUN L23 68 E6
Earlsfield Rd WAV L15 134 A3
Earls Gdns EP CH65 6 B4
Earlston Rd WAL/NB CH45 111 G1
Earl St PS/BROM CH62 151 G4
  STHEL WA9 104 A1
  WARRN/WOL WA2 142 E2
Earls Wy RUNC WA7 187 H1
Earlswood SKEL WN8 57 G4
Earlswood Cl MOR/LEA CH46 128 C1
Earlwood Gdns RAIN/WH L35 118 A5
Earp St ALL/GAR L19 153 K5
Easby Cl FMBY L37 49 G3
  RUNC WA7 11 H5
Easby Rd ANF/KKDL L4 97 F6
Easby Wk ANF/KKDL L4 97 F6
Easedale Dr STHP PR8 33 H5
Easedale Wk NWD/KWIPK L33 72 C4
Easenhall Cl WDN WA8 139 G5
Easington Rd STHEL WA9 119 F1
East Albert Rd AIG/SPK L17 133 G5
East Av GOL/RIS/CUL WA3 92 D2
  WARRN/WOL WA2 143 F1
  WARRS WA4 162 C2
  WARRW/BUR WA5 141 H5
Eastbank St STHP PR8 14 E5
Eastbourne Rd BIRK CH41 2 C5
  CSBY/WL L22 80 C1
  STHP PR8 27 H4
  WLT/FAZ L9 82 E4
Eastbourne Wy NPK/KEN L6 113 H4
Eastbury Cl WDN WA8 139 H4
Eastcliffe Rd CLB/OSW/ST L13 115 F4
East Cl PR/KW L34 102 C6
Eastcote Rd ALL/GAR L19 153 K3
Eastcott Cl GR/UP/WCH CH49 128 D6
Eastcroft NWD/KWIPK L33 72 E4
Eastcroft Rd WAL/EG CH44 111 J4
Eastdale Rd WARR WA1 143 K2
  WAV L15 134 A1
East Dam Wood Rd
  SPK/HALE L24 174 A3
Easter Ct WARRW/BUR WA5 122 B5
Eastern Av PS/BROM CH62 171 F1
  SPK/HALE L24 174 A3
Eastern Dr ALL/GAR L19 153 H4
Eastfield Dr AIG/SPK L17 133 H6
Eastfield Wk KKBY L32 84 A2
East Float BIRK CH41 * 111 K6
Eastford Rd WARRS WA4 161 K2
East Front RAIN/WH L35 118 A6
Eastgate Rd RUNC WA7 160 B6
Eastgate Wy RUNC WA7 178 C1
Eastham Cl CHLDW L16 115 K6
Eastham Crs STHEL WA9 120 A3
Eastham Ms PS/BROM CH62 184 D3
Eastham Rake NSTN CH64 183 K5
Eastham Village Rd
  PS/BROM CH62 184 D2
Eastlake Av EV L5 113 H2
East Lancashire Rd ECCL WA10 88 C4
  GOL/RIS/CUL WA3 92 C5
  NG/CROX L11 98 D1
  PR/KW L34 85 F5
East La RUNC WA7 177 J6
  SFTN L29 60 D5
East Leigh SKEL WN8 57 F4
Eastleigh Dr PEN/TH CH61 148 A4
East Mains SPK/HALE L24 174 B2
Eastman Rd CLB/OSW/ST L13 98 C6
East Md ORM L39 53 F4
East Meade MGHL L31 62 A5
East Millwood Rd
  SPK/HALE L24 174 B1
East O' Hills Cl HES CH60 168 A4
Easton Rd HUY L36 116 A4
  PS/BROM CH62 151 G3
East Orchard La WLT/FAZ L9 83 G4
East Park Ct WAL/EG CH44 112 A4
East Prescot Rd
  DV/KA/FCH L14 115 J3
East Rd CLB/OSW/ST L13 115 G5
  HLWD L26 156 A6
East Side STHEL WA9 104 A3
East St AIMK WN4 79 J5
  CHTN/BK PR9 15 J4
  CSBY/WL L22 80 E2
  PR/KW L34 118 A1
  VAUX/LVPD L3 8 C2
  WAL/EG CH44 112 A5
  WDN WA8 19 J1
East Vw WARRS WA4 163 G1
Eastview Cl CL/PREN CH43 130 A5
Eastway GR/UP/WCH CH49 129 F5
  GTS/LS CH66 195 G2
  MGHL L31 62 B5
East Wy MOR/LEA CH46 109 J6
Eastway WDN WA8 157 J2
Eastwell Rd AIMK WN4 79 F6
Eastwood AIG/SPK L17 133 F6
  RUNC WA7 178 B3
Eastwood Av NEWLW WA12 107 F2
Eastwood Rd
  WARRW/BUR WA5 105 K6
Eaton Av LITH L21 81 J4
  WAL/EG CH44 111 J3
Eaton Cl HUY L36 116 C5
  WD/CROXPK L12 98 E6
Eaton Gdns WD/CROXPK L12 115 H2
Eaton Pl PR/KW L34 * 117 K1
Eaton Rd ALL/GAR L19 153 H5
  CL/PREN CH43 2 A6
  ECCL WA10 88 A5
  MGHL L31 71 G3
  WD/CROXPK L12 99 F6
  WKBY CH48 146 B2
Eaton Rd North
  WD/CROXPK L12 98 E6
Eaton St PR/KW L34 117 K1
  RUNC WA7 10 D5
  VAUX/LVPD L3 8 C1
  WAL/EG CH44 111 H3
Eavesdale SKEL WN8 57 G5
Eaves La STHEL WA9 119 K1
Ebenezer Howard Rd LITH L21 81 K1
Ebenezer St RF/TRAN CH42 151 F1
  RNFD/HAY WA11 89 J5
Eberle St CLVP L2 8 D3
Ebony Cl MOR/LEA CH46 * 128 C1
Ebony Wy NWD/KWIPK L33 72 D4
Ebor La EV L5 113 G3
Ebrington St ALL/GAR L19 153 K5
Eccleshall Av LITH L21 81 K3
Eccles Dr WLTN L25 135 K3
Ecclesfield Rd ECCL WA10 87 H6
Eccles Gv STHEL WA9 120 C4
Eccleshall Rd PS/BROM CH62 151 H5
Eccleshill Rd CLB/OSW/ST L13 114 E2
Eccles Rd FMBY L37 48 D4
Eccleston Av GTS/LS CH66 195 H4
  PS/BROM CH62 170 E4
Eccleston Cl CL/PREN CH43 130 C6
  GOL/RIS/CUL WA3 124 E3
Eccleston Dr RUNC WA7 11 H7
Eccleston Gdns ECCL WA10 102 C4
Eccleston Rd WLT/FAZ L9 82 C5
Eccleston St ECCL WA10 12 C5
  PR/KW L34 117 K1
Edale Cl PS/BROM CH62 184 B2
Edale Rd CALD/MH L18 134 B5
Eddisbury Rd GTS/LS CH66 202 D1
  WAL/EG CH44 111 J2
  WKBY CH48 127 F5
Eddisbury Wy FROD/HEL WA6 201 H6
  WD/CROXPK L12 98 E6
Eddleston St AIMK WN4 79 G6
Edelsten St WARRW/BUR WA5 142 C4
Eden Av CHTN/BK PR9 23 H2
  RNFD/HAY WA11 75 F2
Eden Cl GTS/LS CH66 195 F4
  NWD/KWIPK L33 72 E3
  RAIN/WH L35 118 D5
Edendale WDN WA8 157 G1
Eden Dr North CSBY/BLUN L23 69 H6
Eden Dr South CSBY/BLUN L23 69 H6
Edenfield Cl STHP PR8 28 B4
Edenfield Crs HUY L36 117 F3
Edenfield Rd WAV L15 134 A3
Edenhall Dr WLTN L25 135 K6
Edenhurst SKEL WN8 57 G5
Edenhurst Av CHLDW L16 135 H1
  WAL/EG CH44 111 J2
Edenhurst Cl FMBY L37 48 C3
Edenhurst Ct HUY L36 * 116 B3
Edenhurst Dr FMBY L37 48 C3
Edenpark Rd RF/TRAN CH42 131 F6
Eden V NTHTN L30 70 B5
Edgar Ct BIRK CH41 2 D3
  LITH L21 81 J2
Edgars Dr WARRN/WOL WA2 124 C5
Edgar St VAUX/LVPD L3 113 F4
Edgbaston Cl HUY L36 116 C6
Edgbaston Wy CL/PREN CH43 129 K1
Edgefield Cl CL/PREN CH43 130 A5
Edgefold Rd KKBY L32 84 E2
Edge Green La
  GOL/RIS/CUL WA3 92 A1
Edge Green St AIMK WN4 79 J5
Edge Gv EHL/KEN L7 114 C5
Edgehill Rd MOR/LEA CH46 128 D1
Edge La CLB/OSW/ST L13 114 C5
  CSBY/BLUN L23 69 K5
  EHL/KEN L7 113 K6
Edge Lane Dr
  CLB/OSW/ST L13 114 E5
Edgeley Gdns WLT/FAZ L9 82 C5
Edgemoor Cl CL/PREN CH43 129 J2
  WD/CROXPK L12 115 H2
Edgemoor Dr AIN/FAZ L10 83 K4
  CSBY/BLUN L23 69 H4
  PEN/TH CH61 147 K4
Edgemoor Rd
  WD/CROXPK L12 115 H2
Edgerley Pl AIMK WN4 79 F6
Edgerton Rd
  GOL/RIS/CUL WA3 93 F3
Edge St STHEL WA9 118 E1
Edgewell Dr WAV L15 134 B1
Edgewood Dr PS/BROM CH62 184 A2
Edgewood Rd
  GR/UP/WCH CH49 129 F3
  HOY CH47 108 B6
Edgeworth Cl STHEL WA9 104 C5
Edgeworth Rd
  GOL/RIS/CUL WA3 92 A2
Edgeworth St STHEL WA9 104 C6
Edgley Dr ORM L39 46 A6
Edgworth Rd ANF/KKDL L4 113 K1
Edgworth St
  WARRN/WOL WA2 16 C4
Edinburgh Cl NTHTN L30 82 C3
Edinburgh Ct EP CH65 196 C6
Edinburgh Dr CL/PREN CH43 149 K2
  HUY L36 136 D1
Edinburgh Rd EHL/KEN L7 113 J5
  FMBY L37 48 E4
  WAL/NB CH45 * 111 H2
  WDN WA8 157 F3
Edington St WAV L15 133 K1
Edison Rd RUNC WA7 177 G2
Edith Rd ANF/KKDL L4 113 J1
  BTL L20 82 A5
  WAL/EG CH44 112 A4
Edith St RUNC WA7 10 C3
  STHEL WA9 * 104 D6
Edith Vls BTL L20 * 5 J2
Edmondson St STHEL WA9 * 104 D2
Edmonton Cl EV L5 113 F1
Edmund St VAUX/LVPD L3 8 C3
Edna Av AIN/FAZ L10 83 K4
Edrich Av CL/PREN CH43 * 129 K1
Edward Dr AIMK WN4 79 G5
Edward Gdns WARR WA1 144 E3
Edward Jenner Av NTHTN L30 70 C6
Edward Rd HOY CH47 127 H3
  RAIN/WH L35 118 B2
  WARRW/BUR WA5 140 E3
Edward's La SPK/HALE L24 154 E5
Edward St EP CH65 * 6 D1
  RNFD/HAY WA11 89 K5
  STHEL WA9 104 B4
  VAUX/LVPD L3 9 H4
  WDN WA8 19 J1
Edwards Wy WDN WA8 157 H3
Edwin St WDN WA8 19 G1
Effingham St BTL L20 96 D4
Egan Rd BIRK CH41 130 B1
Egbert Rd HOY CH47 127 H1
Egdon Cl WDN WA8 159 F1
Egerton KNUT WA16 165 K6
  SKEL WN8 57 F5
Egerton Av WARR WA1 143 H2
Egerton Dr WKBY CH48 146 C1
Egerton Gdns RF/TRAN CH42 150 D2
Egerton Gv WAL/NB CH45 111 H2
Egerton Park Cl
  RF/TRAN CH42 150 D2
Egerton Rd CL/PREN CH43 130 D3
  LYMM WA13 164 D1
  PR/KW L34 117 J1
  PS/BROM CH62 151 G4
  WAV L15 133 J2
Egerton St EP CH65 6 D2
  RUNC WA7 10 C3
  STHEL WA9 104 B4
  TOX L8 132 E2
  WAL/NB CH45 95 H5
  WARR WA1 17 G4
  WARRS WA4 162 B2
Egerton Whf BIRK CH41 3 G2
Eglington Av RAIN/WH L35 117 K5
Egremont Cl NTHLY L27 136 D5
Egremont Lawn NTHLY L27 136 D5
Egremont Prom
  WAL/NB CH45 111 K1
Egypt St WARR WA1 16 C5
  WDN WA8 18 B5
Eight Acre La FMBY L37 41 H5
Eighth Av WLT/FAZ L9 83 G4
Eilian Gv DV/KA/FCH L14 115 H5
Eisenhower Cl
  WARRW/BUR WA5 141 J4
Elaine Cl AIMK WN4 79 J4
  GTS/LS CH66 195 F5
  WDN WA8 19 G1
Elaine St TOX L8 132 E3
  WARR WA1 17 H1
Elbow La FMBY L37 49 F2
Elcombe Av
  GOL/RIS/CUL WA3 93 F4
Elderdale Rd ANF/KKDL L4 97 K6
Elderflower Rd ECCL WA10 120 C1
Elder Gdns ALL/GAR L19 153 J3
Elder Gv WKBY CH48 146 C1
Eldersfield Rd NG/CROX L11 99 F3
Elderswood Rd RAIN/WH L35 118 E3
Elderwood Rd
  RF/TRAN CH42 131 H6
Eldon Cl ECCL WA10 12 C7
Eldon Gdns AIMK WN4 79 F3
Eldonian Wy VAUX/LVPD L3 112 E3
Eldon Pl VAUX/LVPD L3 112 E3
Eldon Rd RF/TRAN CH42 150 E1
  WAL/EG CH44 111 H3
Eldons Cft STHP PR8 33 K4
Eldon St ECCL WA10 12 C7
  VAUX/LVPD L3 112 E3
  WARR WA1 17 F4
Eldon Ter NSTN CH64 191 K2
Eldred Rd CHLDW L16 134 D3
Eleanor Pk
  CL/PREN CH43 129 K1
Eleanor Rd BTL L20 82 A5
  CL/PREN CH43 110 C6
  MOR/LEA CH46 109 G6
Eleanor St BTL L20 96 D4
  EP CH65 6 E2
  WDN WA8 * 18 D6
Elephant La STHEL WA9 103 F6
Elfet St BIRK CH41 130 C1
Elgar Av PS/BROM CH62 184 B2
Elgar Cl EP CH65 195 J6
Elgar Rd DV/KA/FCH L14 115 K2
Elgin Av AIMK WN4 78 C5
  WARRS WA4 161 K1
Elgin Ct RAIN/WH L35 * 119 F5
Elgin Dr WAL/NB CH45 111 J1
Elgin Wy BIRK CH41 3 G3
Eliot Cl PS/BROM CH62 151 F4
Eliot St BTL L20 81 J6
Elizabeth Av STHP PR8 34 A3
Elizabeth Ct WDN WA8 18 E6
Elizabeth Dr WARR WA1 143 K1

Elizabeth Rd AIN/FAZ L10 84 A4
BTL L20 82 A5
HUY L36 136 D1
RNFD/HAY WA11 90 D4
Elizabeth St STHEL WA9 120 B4
VAUX/LVPD L3 * 9 K3
Elizabeth Ter WDN WA8 157 J2
Eliza St STHEL WA9 104 D6
Elkan Cl WDN WA8 139 K6
Elkan Rd WDN WA8 139 J6
Elkstone Rd NG/CROX L11 99 F4
Ellaby Rd RAIN/WH L35 118 E3
Ellamsbridge Rd STHEL WA9 104 C6
Elland Dr GTS/LS CH66 195 F4
Ellel Gv NPK/KEN L6 114 A2
Ellen Gdn STHEL WA9 104 C6
Ellen's Cl NPK/KEN L6 113 J5
Ellen's La BEB CH63 151 F6
Ellen St STHEL WA9 104 C6
WARRW/BUR WA5 16 A1
Elleray Dr TOX L8 132 E5
Elleray Park Rd
WAL/NB CH45 95 G6
Ellerbrook Dr BRSC L40 39 F6
Ellerbrook Wy ORM L39 45 J5
Ellerby Cl RUNC WA7 178 D6
Ellergreen Rd NG/CROX L11 98 D3
Ellerman Rd VAUX/LVPD L3 132 E6
Ellerslie Av RAIN/WH L35 118 E2
Ellerslie Rd CLB/OSW/ST L13 114 B1
Ellerton Av GTS/LS CH66 195 F4
Ellerton Cl WDN WA8 138 C6
Ellerton Wy WD/CROXPK L12 99 J2
Ellesmere Dr AIN/FAZ L10 83 F1
Ellesmere Gv WAL/NB CH45 111 H1
Ellesmere Rd AIMK WN4 78 E4
WARRS WA4 162 A2
Ellesmere St RUNC WA7 11 F4
WARR WA1 17 F5
Ellesworth Cl
WARRW/BUR WA5 141 K1
Ellington Dr
WARRW/BUR WA5 141 J4
Elliot Dr KKBY L32 84 C3
Elliot St CLVPS L1 9 F4
ECCL WA10 12 C5
WDN WA8 18 E3
Elliott Av GOL/RIS/CUL WA3 92 C2
WARR WA1 17 K1
Ellis Ashton St HUY L36 117 G5
Ellis La FROD/HEL WA6 187 G6
Ellison Dr ECCL WA10 102 E1
Ellison Gv HUY L36 116 D5
Ellison St CLB/OSW/ST L13 114 D3
WARRS WA4 162 C2
Ellis Pl TOX L8 132 E4
Ellis Rd WGNW/BIL/OR WN5 77 G5
Ellis St WDN WA8 18 B6
Ellon Av RAIN/WH L35 119 F5
Elloway Rd SPK/HALE L24 174 B2
Ellwood Cl SPK/HALE L24 175 F3
Elmar Rd AIG/SPK L17 153 F1
Elm Av AIMK WN4 78 C4
CSBY/BLUN L23 69 G4
GOL/RIS/CUL WA3 92 B2
GR/UP/WCH CH49 128 E3
WDN WA8 158 C1
Elm Bank ANF/KKDL L4 97 H6
Elmbank Rd CALD/MH L18 133 K4
PS/BROM CH62 151 G5
Elmbank St WAL/EG CH44 * 111 J4
Elm Cl PEN/TH CH61 167 K1
WD/CROXPK L12 99 K2
Elmcroft Cl WLT/FAZ L9 83 G4
Elmcroft La HTWN L38 59 G4
Elmdale Cl FMBY L37 48 D3
Elmdale Rd WLT/FAZ L9 97 J1
Elmdene Ct
GR/UP/WCH CH49 * 147 K1
Elm Dr FMBY L37 48 D4
GR/UP/WCH CH49 128 D6
LITH L21 81 G5
WGNW/BIL/OR WN5 77 G4
Elmers Gn SKEL WN8 57 F3
Elmer's Green La SKEL WN8 56 E1
Elmers Wood Rd SKEL WN8 57 F3
Elmfield Cl STHEL WA9 103 G5
Elmfield Rd WLT/FAZ L9 82 D6
Elm Gdns LITH L21 * 81 H5
RNFD/HAY WA11 75 G3
Elm Gv EHL/KEN L7 113 J6
GTS/LS CH66 202 E2
HOY CH47 127 G2
PR/KW L34 102 B6
RF/TRAN CH42 131 G5
SKEL WN8 * 56 A4
WARR WA1 143 J2
WDN WA8 18 E1
Elm Hall Dr CALD/MH L18 134 B4
Elmham Crs AIN/FAZ L10 83 J4
Elm House Ms WLTN L25 135 J5
Elmhurst Rd WLTN L25 135 H2
Elmore Cl EV L5 113 H2
RUNC WA7 178 C4
Elm Park Dr STHP PR8 34 A4
Elm Park Rd WAL/NB CH45 95 G6
Elm Pl ORM L39 53 J1
Elmridge SKEL WN8 57 F5
Elm Ri FROD/HEL WA6 201 F2
Elm Rd ANF/KKDL L4 97 J4
BEB CH63 150 E4
BRSC L40 38 E6
ECCL WA10 103 F5
KKBY L32 72 C6
LITH L21 81 G5
NSTN CH64 193 G1
PEN/TH CH61 148 C5
RF/TRAN CH42 131 G6
RNFD/HAY WA11 * 90 D4
RUNC WA7 177 F5
STHP PR8 27 J3
WARRN/WOL WA2 123 H3
WARRW/BUR WA5 141 G5
Elm Rd North RF/TRAN CH42 150 A1
Elmsbury St AIMK WN4 78 E4
Elmsdale Rd CALD/MH L18 134 B4
Elmsett Cl WARRW/BUR WA5 141 F4
Elmsfield Cl WLTN L25 135 H4
Elmsfield Pk ORM L39 62 E1
Elmsfield Rd CSBY/BLUN L23 69 J3
Elms House Rd
CLB/OSW/ST L13 114 D4
Elmsley Rd CALD/MH L18 134 A5
Elms Pk PEN/TH CH61 148 D6
Elms Rd MGHL L31 71 F3
Elm St EP CH65 196 B2
Elmstead SKEL WN8 57 F5
The Elms GOL/RIS/CUL WA3 93 G4
MGHL L31 62 B4
RUNC WA7 10 C7
TOX L8 133 F5
Elm St BIRK CH41 2 E4
HUY L36 117 G5
Elmswood Av RAIN/WH L35 119 F5
Elmswood Ct CALD/MH L18 * 134 A6
Elmswood Gv HUY L36 116 B4
Elmswood Rd AIG/SPK L17 153 F1
RF/TRAN CH42 131 F5
WAL/EG CH44 111 K3
Elm Ter EHL/KEN L7 * 114 A5
HOY CH47 127 H2
Elm Tree Av LYMM WA13 164 E1
WARR WA1 143 J1
Elmtree Cl WD/CROXPK L12 99 G6
Elmtree Gv CL/PREN CH43 130 B1
Elm Tree Rd GOL/RIS/CUL WA3 93 G3
LYMM WA13 164 E1
Elmure Av BEB CH63 150 C6
Elm V NPK/KEN L6 114 B4
Elmway Cl CLB/OSW/ST L13 114 D6
Elmwood RUNC WA7 178 B4
SKEL WN8 56 E2
Elmwood Av AIMK WN4 91 F1
CSBY/BLUN L23 69 G5
Elmwood Dr PEN/TH CH61 167 K3
Elphin Gv ANF/KKDL L4 97 J4
Elsbeck Gv STHEL WA9 120 B1
Elsie Rd ANF/KKDL L4 113 K1
Elsmere Av AIG/SPK L17 133 H6
Elson Rd FMBY L37 48 D4
Elstead Gv AIMK WN4 78 C5
Elstead Rd KKBY L32 84 B2
WLT/FAZ L9 98 C1
Elston Av NEWLW WA12 91 G6
Elstow St EV L5 97 F6
Elstree Rd NPK/KEN L6 114 B4
Elswick SKEL WN8 56 E5
Elswick Rd CHTN/BK PR9 23 H1
Elswick St TOX L8 132 E6
Elsworth Cl FMBY L37 48 C5
Eltham Av LITH L21 81 J2
Eltham Cl AIMK WN4 79 J6
GR/UP/WCH CH49 148 E1
WDN WA8 139 K6
Eltham Gn GR/UP/WCH CH49 148 D1
Eltham St EHL/KEN L7 114 B5
Elton Av CSBY/BLUN L23 68 D5
NTHTN L30 70 B6
Elton Cl GOL/RIS/CUL WA3 124 E3
GOL/RIS/CUL WA3 93 F4
PS/BROM CH62 184 B4
Elton Dr BEB CH63 170 C3
Elton Head Rd STHEL WA9 119 F2
Elton La CHNE CH2 199 F5
Elton Lordship La
FROD/HEL WA6 199 H2
Elton St ANF/KKDL L4 97 H3
Elvington Cl RUNC WA7 187 J4
Elvington Rd HTWN L38 59 G5
Elway Rd AIMK WN4 79 H6
Elwick Dr NG/CROX L11 99 G3
Elwood Cl NWD/KWIPK L33 72 D3
Elworth Av WDN WA8 139 F4
Elworthy Av HLWD L26 155 J2
Elwyn Dr HLWD L26 155 K3
Elwyn Rd HOY CH47 108 C6
Elwy St TOX L8 133 F6
Ely Av MOR/LEA CH46 128 D1
Ely Cl GTS/LS CH66 202 C3
NTHTN L30 82 C2
Ely Ms CHTN/BK PR9 23 J3
Ely Pk RUNC WA7 178 D3
Ember Crs NPK/KEN L6 113 H3
Embleton Ct RUNC WA7 187 G2
Emerald Cl NTHTN L30 70 E6
Emerald St TOX L8 132 E6
Emerson Cl HTWN L38 59 G3
Emerson St TOX L8 132 E2
Emery St ANF/KKDL L4 97 H4
Emily St STHEL WA9 102 E6
WDN WA8 18 D5
Emlyn St STHEL WA9 104 B4
Emmanuel Rd CHTN/BK PR9 23 H3
Emmett St STHEL WA9 104 A4
Emmsix BRSC L40 37 F5
Empire Rd LITH L21 81 J5
Empress Cl MGHL L31 61 K6
Empress Rd EHL/KEN L7 113 K5
NPK/KEN L6 114 A1
WAL/EG CH44 111 J3
Emslie Ct NSTN CH64 191 H1
Endborne Rd WLT/FAZ L9 82 D5
Endbutt La CSBY/BLUN L23 69 F6
Enderby Av RNFD/HAY WA11 89 F5
Endfield Pk ALL/GAR L19 153 J3
Endmoor Rd HUY L36 116 C2
Endsleigh Rd CLB/OSW/ST L13 114 C4
CSBY/WL L22 80 C1
Enerby Cl CL/PREN CH43 129 K2
Enfield Av CSBY/BLUN L23 69 F5
Enfield Park Rd
WARRN/WOL WA2 124 A3
Enfield Rd CLB/OSW/ST L13 115 F5
EP CH65 6 C4
Enfield St ECCL WA10 12 C7
Enfield Ter CL/PREN CH43 2 A7
Enford Dr STHEL WA9 104 B6
Engine La FMBY L37 49 K6
Enid St TOX L8 132 E3
Ennerdale SKEL WN8 57 F5
Ennerdale Av AIMK WN4 79 G4
MGHL L31 62 C5
PS/BROM CH62 184 C3
RNFD/HAY WA11 88 E3
WARRN/WOL WA2 123 H4
Ennerdale Cl FMBY L37 48 D2
NWD/KWIPK L33 72 C4
Ennerdale Dr FROD/HEL WA6 201 F1
LITH L21 82 A3
ORM L39 53 F3
Ennerdale Rd CL/PREN CH43 149 H2
FMBY L37 48 D2
WAL/NB CH45 95 F5
WLT/FAZ L9 83 G5
Ennerdale St VAUX/LVPD L3 113 F3
Ennisdale Dr WKBY CH48 146 E1
Ennismore Rd
CLB/OSW/ST L13 114 D4
CSBY/BLUN L23 68 D4
Ennis Rd WD/CROXPK L12 115 J1
Ensor St BTL L20 96 D4
Enstone SKEL WN8 57 F4
Enstone Av LITH L21 81 H2
Enstone Rd WLTN L25 154 E5
Ensworth Rd CALD/MH L18 134 C4
Enterprise Wy
CLB/OSW/ST L13 114 C6
GOL/RIS/CUL WA3 93 H4
Enville St WARRS WA4 17 F7
Epping Av STHEL WA9 119 K4
Epping Cl RAIN/WH L35 119 F5
Epping Ct HES CH60 168 A4
Epping Dr WARR WA1 144 C1
Epping Gv WAV L15 134 C3
Epsom Cl AIN/FAZ L10 83 H2
Epsom Gdns WARRS WA4 162 D4
Epsom Gv NWD/KWIPK L33 73 F3
Epsom Rd MOR/LEA CH46 109 K4
Epsom St STHEL WA9 104 C1
Epsom Wy EV L5 113 F2
Epstein Ct NPK/KEN L6 113 K4
Epworth Cl CL/PREN CH43 130 D3
Epworth Gra CL/PREN CH43 * 130 D3
Epworth St NPK/KEN L6 9 K2
Eremon Cl WLT/FAZ L9 83 G3
Erfurt Av BEB CH63 170 C1
Erica Ct HES CH60 167 J3
Eric Av WARR WA1 143 H1
Eric Fountain Rd EP CH65 185 G4
Eric Gv WAL/EG CH44 111 G3
Eric Rd WAL/EG CH44 111 G3
Ericson Dr STHP PR8 27 J2
Eric St WDN WA8 19 G1
Eridge St TOX L8 133 F5
Erin Cl TOX L8 132 D3
Erindale Crs FROD/HEL WA6 200 D3
Erl St WLT/FAZ L9 82 D5
Ermine Crs EV L5 113 H2
Errington Av EP CH65 6 D2
Errington Ct AIG/SPK L17 153 F3
Errington St EV L5 112 D1
Errol St AIG/SPK L17 133 G6
Erskine Cl RNFD/HAY WA11 89 F5
Erskine Rd WAL/EG CH44 111 J4
Erskine St NPK/KEN L6 9 K2
Erwood St WARRN/WOL WA2 16 C2
Erylmore Rd CALD/MH L18 153 H2
Escolme Dr GR/UP/WCH CH49 129 F6
Escor Rd WLTN L25 135 G3
Escort Cl WLTN L25 155 F3
Eshelby Cl CSBY/WL L22 81 F2
Esher Cl CL/PREN CH43 129 K2
Eshe Rd CSBY/BLUN L23 68 D5
Eshe Rd North CSBY/BLUN L23 68 D5
Esher Rd NPK/KEN L6 114 A4
PS/BROM CH62 151 G3
Eskbank SKEL WN8 56 E5
Eskbrook SKEL WN8 56 E4
Eskburn Rd CLB/OSW/ST L13 114 C1
Eskdale EP CH65 196 A6
SKEL WN8 56 D5
Eskdale Av ORM L39 53 G3
PS/BROM CH62 184 B2
RNFD/HAY WA11 88 E3
Eskdale Cl FMBY L37 48 D3
RUNC WA7 187 G2
Eskdale Dr FMBY L37 48 D3
MGHL L31 62 B5
Eskdale Rd AIMK WN4 79 G4
WLT/FAZ L9 82 D5
Esk St BTL L20 96 D5
Eslington St ALL/GAR L19 153 H4
Esmond St NPK/KEN L6 113 K2
Esonwood Rd RAIN/WH L35 117 K4
Espin St ANF/KKDL L4 97 H4
Esplanade STHP PR8 27 F1
Esplen Av CSBY/BLUN L23 69 G4
Essex Rd HUY L36 117 G3
STHP PR8 34 C1
WKBY CH48 127 H6
Essex St TOX L8 132 E4
Essex Wy BTL L20 5 G3
Esthwaite Av RNFD/HAY WA11 89 F3
Estuary Banks SPK/HALE L24 172 E1
Estuary Bvd SPK/HALE L24 172 E1
Etal Cl NG/CROX L11 99 F4
Ethelbert Rd HOY CH47 127 H1
Ethel Rd WAL/EG CH44 111 K4
Etna St CLB/OSW/ST L13 114 D4
Eton Ct CALD/MH L18 134 E4
Eton Dr AIN/FAZ L10 83 F1
BEB CH63 182 A1
Eton Hall Dr STHEL WA9 104 A6
Eton Rd EP CH65 7 F7
Eton St ANF/KKDL L4 97 H4
Etruria St ALL/GAR L19 172 B1
Etruscan Rd CLB/OSW/ST L13 114 E3
Ettington Dr STHP PR8 33 G4
Ettington Rd ANF/KKDL L4 97 K6
Ettrick Cl NWD/KWIPK L33 72 C3
Euclid Av WARRS WA4 163 G1
Eurolink STHEL WA9 119 H3
Europa Bvd BIRK CH41 3 F3
WARRW/BUR WA5 122 C4
Europa Wy EP CH65 6 E3
Eustace St WARRN/WOL WA2 16 A3
Euston Gv CL/PREN CH43 2 B7
Euston St ANF/KKDL L4 97 H3
Evans Cl RNFD/HAY WA11 90 E4
Evans Pl WARRS WA4 143 G6
Evans Rd HOY CH47 127 G2
SPK/HALE L24 154 E6
Evans St PR/KW L34 101 K6
Evellynne Cl KKBY L32 84 B1
Evelyn Av PR/KW L34 118 A1
STHEL WA9 104 C2
Evelyn Rd WAL/EG CH44 111 J4
Evelyn St EV L5 113 F1
WARRW/BUR WA5 142 A5
Evenson Wy CLB/OSW/ST L13 114 E4
Evenwood SKEL WN8 57 F4
STHEL WA9 120 A1
Evenwood Cl RUNC WA7 178 D1
Evenwood Ct SKEL WN8 * 56 E4
Everard Cl BRSC L40 36 D2
Everard Rd STHP PR8 28 A3
Everdon Wd NWD/KWIPK L33 72 D6
Evered Av WLT/FAZ L9 97 J1
Everest Cl GTS/LS CH66 195 J6
Everest Rd CSBY/BLUN L23 68 E5
RF/TRAN CH42 150 C1
Evergreen Cl
GR/UP/WCH CH49 128 E3
NTHLY L27 136 B3
Evergreen Rd STHEL WA9 104 E6
The Evergreens FMBY L37 48 D1
Everite Rd WDN WA8 157 G4
Everleigh Cl CL/PREN CH43 129 J2
Eversham Cl CHTN/BK PR9 21 K6
Eversleigh Dr BEB CH63 170 C1
Eversley SKEL WN8 57 F4
WDN WA8 157 G1
Eversley Cl FROD/HEL WA6 201 F3
WARRS WA4 162 E6
Eversley Pk CL/PREN CH43 * 130 E6
Eversley St TOX L8 133 F3
Everton Brow VAUX/LVPD L3 113 G4
Everton Gv
RNFD/HAY WA11 89 G6
Everton Rd NPK/KEN L6 113 H3
STHP PR8 27 H3
Everton St AIMK WN4 78 C4
Everton Ter EV L5 113 H3
Everton Va EV L5 97 G6
Everton Vw BTL L20 4 C6
Every St NPK/KEN L6 113 K3
Evesham Cl WARRS WA4 162 B3
WLTN L25 154 C1
Evesham Rd ANF/KKDL L4 98 B4
WAL/NB CH45 111 F1
Evington SKEL WN8 57 F4
Ewanville HUY L36 116 E6
Ewart Rd CHLDW L16 135 H1
LITH L21 81 G4
RNFD/HAY WA11 88 E5
Ewden Cl CHLDW L16 135 F2
Ewloe Ct EP CH65 203 H1
Exchange Pas West CLVP L2 * 8 C3
Exchange Pl RAIN/WH L35 118 E4
Exchange St ECCL WA10 13 G6
Exchange St East CLVP L2 8 C3
Exchange St West CLVP L2 8 C3
Exeley RAIN/WH L35 118 A5
Exeter Cl AIN/FAZ L10 83 H2
Exeter Rd BTL L20 4 E7
EP CH65 6 D4
WAL/EG CH44 111 J2
Exeter St ECCL WA10 12 B5
Exford Rd WD/CROXPK L12 99 H5
Exmoor Cl CHTN/BK PR9 20 E5
PEN/TH CH61 148 C6
Exmouth Cl BIRK CH41 2 D4
Exmouth Crs RUNC WA7 188 D1
Exmouth Gdns BIRK CH41 2 D4
Exmouth St BIRK CH41 2 D4
Exmouth Wy BIRK CH41 2 D4
WARRW/BUR WA5 121 K1
Extension Vw STHEL WA9 104 B5

F

Factory La WARR WA1 16 A5
WDN WA8 139 G6
Factory Rw ECCL WA10 103 G4
Fairacre Rd ALL/GAR L19 153 H4
Fairacres Rd BEB CH63 170 B1
Fairbairn Rd CSBY/WL L22 81 F2
Fairbank St WAV L15 133 K2
Fairbeech Ms
CL/PREN CH43 * 129 K2
Fairbourne Cl
WARRW/BUR WA5 122 E4
Fairbrook Dr BIRK CH41 110 D6
Fairbrother Crs
WARRN/WOL WA2 123 K5
Fairburn SKEL WN8 56 D2
Fairburn Cl WDN WA8 139 K6
Fairburn Rd
CLB/OSW/ST L13 114 C1
Fairclough Av WARR WA1 17 F6
Fairclough Crs
RNFD/HAY WA11 89 K5
Fairclough La CL/PREN CH43 130 E5
Fairclough Rd ECCL WA10 102 E1
HUY L36 116 C1
RAIN/WH L35 118 D4
Fairclough St CLVPS L1 9 F5
WARRW/BUR WA5 121 J1
Fairfax Dr RUNC WA7 177 G3
Fairfax Pl NG/CROX L11 98 B3
Fairfax Rd NG/CROX L11 98 C3
RF/TRAN CH42 131 H5
Fairfield CSBY/BLUN L23 69 F5
Fairfield Av EP CH65 202 E1
HUY L36 116 A5
Fairfield Cl HUY L36 116 A5
ORM L39 45 J4
Fairfield Crs HUY L36 116 A5
MOR/LEA CH46 128 E1
NPK/KEN L6 114 B4
Fairfield Dr ORM L39 45 J4
WKBY CH48 127 K6
Fairfield Gdns
RNFD/HAY WA11 88 B1
WARRS WA4 162 D1
Fairfield Rd ECCL WA10 87 K6
RF/TRAN CH42 150 D1
STHP PR8 33 J3
WARRS WA4 162 C1
WDN WA8 18 E1
Fairfield St EHL/KEN L7 114 C4
WARR WA1 17 G2
Fairford Cl WARRW/BUR WA5 141 J3
Fairford Crs DV/KA/FCH L14 115 F3
Fairford Rd DV/KA/FCH L14 115 F3
Fairhaven NWD/KWIPK L33 72 D4
SKEL WN8 56 D2
Fairhaven Cl RF/TRAN CH42 150 E1
WARRW/BUR WA5 141 J5
Fairhaven Dr BEB CH63 183 K2
Fairhaven Rd CHTN/BK PR9 23 K1
WDN WA8 158 D1
Fairholme Av AIMK WN4 79 G5
NSTN CH64 181 J6
PR/KW L34 118 C1
Fairholme Cl WD/CROXPK L12 98 E5
Fairholme Rd CSBY/BLUN L23 69 F5
Fairhurst Ter PR/KW L34 * 118 A1
Fair Isle Cl EP CH65 203 G2
Fairlawn Cl BEB CH63 183 H1
Fairlawne Cl NWD/KWIPK L33 72 D4
Fairlie SKEL WN8 56 E2
Fairlie Crs BTL L20 82 A4
Fairlie Dr RAIN/WH L35 119 F5
Fairmead Rd MOR/LEA CH46 109 J6
NG/CROX L11 98 C3
Fairoak Cl RUNC WA7 188 E4
Fairoak La RUNC WA7 188 E4
Fairoak Ms CL/PREN CH43 * 129 K2
Fairstead SKEL WN8 56 E2
Fairview BIRK CH41 131 H5
Fair Vw WGNW/BIL/OR WN5 77 G4
Fairview Av WAL/NB CH45 111 G2
Fair View Av
WGNW/BIL/OR WN5 77 G4
Fairview Cl AIMK WN4 79 G5
CL/PREN CH43 130 E6
Fair View Pl TOX L8 * 133 F5
Fairview Rd CL/PREN CH43 130 E6
GTS/LS CH66 202 E1
Fairview Wy PEN/TH CH61 167 K2
Fair Wy ECCL WA10 87 K6
Fairway CHTN/BK PR9 22 E3
HUY L36 117 G3
Fairway Crs PS/BROM CH62 171 F1
Fairway North
PS/BROM CH62 171 F1
Fairways CSBY/BLUN L23 68 E4
FROD/HEL WA6 201 G2
RF/TRAN CH42 150 A3
WARRS WA4 162 C6
Fairways Cl WLTN L25 154 E3
Fairways Ct FMBY L37 40 C6
Fairways Dr GTS/LS CH66 195 G2
Fairway South
PS/BROM CH62 171 F2
The Fairways AIMK WN4 90 C1
SKEL WN8 57 F2
WKBY CH48 146 E5
The Fairway WD/CROXPK L12 115 H3
Falcon Crs NTHLY L27 136 C5
Falcon Cresent NTHLY L27 136 C5
Falcondale Rd
WARRN/WOL WA2 123 H1
Falconers Gn
WARRW/BUR WA5 122 B5
Falconer St BTL L20 81 H5
Falconhall Rd WLT/FAZ L9 98 D1
Falcon Hey AIN/FAZ L10 83 K5
Falcon Rd GTS/LS CH66 195 J6
RF/TRAN CH42 131 F5
Falcons Wy RUNC WA7 187 H1
Falkirk Av WDN WA8 138 D6
Falkland SKEL WN8 56 E2
Falkland Dr AIMK WN4 78 B5
Falkland Rd STHP PR8 28 A2
WAL/EG CH44 111 K3
Falklands Ap NG/CROX L11 98 C3
Falkland St BIRK CH41 130 D1
VAUX/LVPD L3 9 J2
Falkner Sq TOX L8 133 F1
Falkner St TOX L8 9 J7
Fallbrook Dr WD/CROXPK L12 99 F4
Fallow Cl STHEL WA9 120 A3
Fallowfield NWD/KWIPK L33 72 D4
RUNC WA7 177 G4
Fallowfield Gv
WARRN/WOL WA2 124 D6
Fallowfield Rd WAV L15 134 A3
Fallows Wy HUY L36 117 J6
Falmouth Dr
WARRW/BUR WA5 141 F6
Falmouth Pl RUNC WA7 188 D1
Falmouth Rd NG/CROX L11 84 B6
Falstaff St BTL L20 96 E5
Falstone Cl GOL/RIS/CUL WA3 125 K1
Falstone Dr RUNC WA7 178 D5
Fanner's La KNUT WA16 164 D6
Faraday Rd CLB/OSW/ST L13 114 C6
EP CH65 195 K5
NWD/KWIPK L33 85 G4
RUNC WA7 177 G2
Faraday St EV L5 113 J2
GOL/RIS/CUL WA3 125 G2
Farefield Av GOL/RIS/CUL WA3 92 A1
Fareham Cl GR/UP/WCH CH49 128 E3
Fareham Dr CHTN/BK PR9 21 K6
Fareham Rd EHL/KEN L7 114 B5
Faringdon Cl WLTN L25 * 154 E5
Faringdon Rd
WARRN/WOL WA2 123 H1
Farley Av PS/BROM CH62 170 E4
Farley La SKEL WN8 57 J2
Farlow Rd RF/TRAN CH42 150 E2
Farmbrook Rd WLTN L25 135 J2
Farm Cl CHTN/BK PR9 23 J5
GR/UP/WCH CH49 128 D5
Farmdale Cl CALD/MH L18 153 J1
Farmdale Dr CHNE CH2 198 B6
MGHL L31 62 C6
Far Meadow La PEN/TH CH61 147 K5
Farmer Pl BTL L20 82 B4
Farmers Heath GTS/LS CH66 202 B1
Farmer's La WARRW/BUR WA5 122 A1
Farmfield Dr CL/PREN CH43 129 K2
Farm La WARRS WA4 162 D3
Farmleigh Gdns
WARRW/BUR WA5 141 K3
Far Moss Rd CSBY/BLUN L23 68 C3
Farm Rd STHEL WA9 120 B4
Farmside MOR/LEA CH46 109 K4
Farmside Cl WARRW/BUR WA5 142 B2
Farmstead Wy GTS/LS CH66 202 C2
Farm Vw LITH L21 81 J1
Farmview Cl NTHLY L27 135 K2
Farm Wy NEWLW WA12 106 E4
Farmworth St NPK/KEN L6 113 K4

Farnborough Gv HLWD L26 155 J2
Farnborough Rd STHP PR8 34 B1
Farndale WDN WA8 139 F4
Farndale Cl
WARRW/BUR WA5 141 G2
Farndale Gv AIMK WN4 91 H1
Farndon Av STHEL WA9 119 K3
WAL/NB CH45 110 E1
Farndon Dr WKBY CH48 127 K6
Farndon Rd GTS/LS CH66 195 H3
Farndon Wy CL/PREN CH43 130 C5
Farne Cl EP CH65 203 G3
Farnham Cl KKBY L32 84 E2
WARRS WA4 162 D4
Farnhill Cl RUNC WA7 178 C5
Farnley Cl RUNC WA7 178 C4
Farnworth Av
MOR/LEA CH46 109 J4
Farnworth Cl WDN WA8 139 G5
Farnworth Gv
NWD/KWIPK L33 72 D4
Farnworth Rd
WARRW/BUR WA5 140 D6
Farnworth St STHEL WA9 104 A1
WDN WA8 139 G5
Farrant St WDN WA8 19 F3
Farrar St CLB/OSW/ST L13 98 B6
Farrell Cl MGHL L31 72 A5
Farrell Rd WARRS WA4 162 B3
Farrell St WARR WA1 17 G5
Farr Hall Dr HES CH60 167 J6
Farr Hall Rd HES CH60 167 J5
Farrier Rd NWD/KWIPK L33 85 F1
Farriers Wy NTHTN L30 82 C3
WKBY CH48 147 J1
Farrier Wk STHEL WA9 120 A3
Farringdon Cl STHEL WA9 119 H2
Farringdon Rd
WARRN/WOL WA2 123 H1
Farrington Dr ORM L39 45 J5
Farthing Cl WLTN L25 154 D4
The Farthings LYMM WA13 145 J6
Farthingstone Cl
RAIN/WH L35 118 C1
Fatherside Dr NTHTN L30 * 69 K6
Faulkner Cl STHP PR8 33 J4
Faulkner Gdns STHP PR8 33 J3
Faversham Rd NG/CROX L11 98 C2
Fawcett SKEL WN8 56 D2
Fawcett Rd MGHL L31 62 B4
Fawley Rd CALD/MH L18 153 K1
RAIN/WH L35 119 G6
Fazakerley Cl WLT/FAZ L9 97 J1
Fazakerley Rd RAIN/WH L35 118 A3
WLT/FAZ L9 97 J1
Fazakerley St VAUX/LVPD L3 8 C3
Fearnhead Cross
WARRN/WOL WA2 * 124 A6
Fearnhead La
WARRN/WOL WA2 124 C5
Fearnley Rd BIRK CH41 2 E6
Fearnside St EHL/KEN L7 133 H1
Feather La HES CH60 167 K5
Feeny St STHEL WA9 * 119 K5
Feilden Rd BEB CH63 170 C1
Felcroft Wy NWD/KWIPK L33 84 E1
Felicity Gv MOR/LEA CH46 109 H6
Fell Gv RNFD/HAY WA11 88 D3
Fell St EHL/KEN L7 113 K5
WAL/EG CH44 112 A5
Felltor Cl WLTN L25 135 G6
Fellview CHTN/BK PR9 21 G5
Fellwood Gv RAIN/WH L35 118 A5
Felmersham Av NG/CROX L11 98 D2
Felspar Rd KKBY L32 84 D4
Felstead SKEL WN8 56 D3
Felsted Av WLTN L25 155 F1
Felsted Dr AIN/FAZ L10 83 H2
Felthorpe Cl
GR/UP/WCH CH49 129 J2
Felton Gv CLB/OSW/ST L13 114 D3
Feltons SKEL WN8 56 D3
Feltwell Rd ANF/KKDL L4 113 K1
Feltwood Cl WD/CROXPK L12 99 K6
Feltwood Rd WD/CROXPK L12 99 K5
Fendale Av MOR/LEA CH46 110 A6
Fender La MOR/LEA CH46 110 A6
Fenderside Rd CL/PREN CH43 129 K1
Fender View Rd
MOR/LEA CH46 129 H1
Fender Wy CL/PREN CH43 129 J2
PEN/TH CH61 168 A1
Fenham Dr WARRW/BUR WA5 141 F5
Fennel St WARR WA1 17 F4
Fenney Ct SKEL WN8 56 E4
Fenton Cl ECCL WA10 12 E3
NTHTN L30 82 E3
SPK/HALE L24 173 J2
WDN WA8 138 B6
Fenton Gn SPK/HALE L24 173 J3
Fenwick La RUNC WA7 187 G1
Fenwick Rd GTS/LS CH66 202 C1
Fenwick St CLVP L2 8 C4
Ferguson Av
GR/UP/WCH CH49 128 D6
GTS/LS CH66 195 H3
Ferguson Dr
WARRN/WOL WA2 123 K6
Ferguson Rd LITH L21 81 K2
NG/CROX L11 98 C5
Fern Av NEWLW WA12 106 D3
Fern Bank RNFD/HAY WA11 75 F2
Fernbank Av HUY L36 116 D5
Fernbank Cl GOL/RIS/CUL WA3 125 G3
Fernbank Dr NTHTN L30 70 D5
Fern Cl GOL/RIS/CUL WA3 125 F3
KKBY L32 72 D5
NTHLY L27 136 B5
SKEL WN8 56 A4
Ferndale SKEL WN8 56 D3
Ferndale Av CHNE CH2 198 B6
WAL/EG CH44 111 J3
WKBY CH48 147 J2
Ferndale Cl WARR WA1 144 B2
WDN WA8 139 K2
WLT/FAZ L9 82 D4
Ferndale Rd CSBY/WL L22 80 E1
HOY CH47 127 G2
WAV L15 133 K3
Fern Gdns PR/KW L34 102 B6
Fern Gv BTL L20 5 F3
CL/PREN CH43 130 A4
TOX L8 133 H3
Fern Hey CSBY/BLUN L23 69 H4
Fern Hl WAL/NB CH45 95 H5
Fernhill Av BTL L20 5 J4
Fernhill Cl BTL L20 5 J5
Fernhill Dr TOX L8 133 F3
Fernhill Gdns BTL L20 5 J5
Fernhill Ms East BTL L20 5 J5
Fernhill Ms West BTL L20 * 5 J5
Fernhill Rd BTL L20 5 J1
Fernhill Wy BTL L20 5 J5
Fernhurst RUNC WA7 177 G5
Fernhurst Ga ORM L39 53 F3
Fernhurst Rd KKBY L32 84 B2
Fernlea Av STHEL WA9 103 F6
Fernlea Gv AIMK WN4 78 C4
Fernlea Ms CL/PREN CH43 129 K1
Fernlea Rd HES CH60 168 A5
Fernleigh Rd
CLB/OSW/ST L13 * 115 F4
Fernley Rd STHP PR8 27 H2
Fern Rd EP CH65 202 E1
Ferns Cl HES CH60 167 G4
Ferns Rd BEB CH63 150 C6
Fern Vls WAL/EG CH44 * 112 A5
Fernwood RUNC WA7 178 A4
Fernwood Dr HLWD L26 155 H3
Fernwood Rd AIG/SPK L17 153 F1
Ferny Brow Rd
GR/UP/WCH CH49 129 J6
Ferny Knoll Rd
RNFD/HAY WA11 66 B3
Ferrer St AIMK WN4 78 E3
Ferrey Rd AIN/FAZ L10 83 K4
Ferries Cl RF/TRAN CH42 * 151 F3
Ferry La WARRS WA4 144 D5
Ferry Rd PS/BROM CH62 171 J5
Ferryside WAL/EG CH44 112 A5
Ferry Side La CHTN/BK PR9 21 F6
Ferry View Rd WAL/EG CH44 112 A5
Festival Av WARRN/WOL WA2 123 K5
Festival Ct NG/CROX L11 * 99 F2
Festival Crs WARRN/WOL WA2 123 K5
Festival Rd EP CH65 195 J4
RNFD/HAY WA11 75 H4
Festival Wy RUNC WA7 177 F5
Ffrancon Dr BEB CH63 150 E4
Fiddlers Ferry Rd WDN WA8 19 J3
Fidler St ECCL WA10 103 F4
Field Av LITH L21 81 H3
Field Cl BRSC L40 39 F6
PS/BROM CH62 151 G3
Fieldfare Cl GOL/RIS/CUL WA3 125 H3
GOL/RIS/CUL WA3 92 E3
WLTN L25 135 H4
Fieldgate WDN WA8 157 G5
Field Hey La NSTN CH64 183 J6
Fieldhouse Rw RUNC WA7 177 G6
The Fieldings MGHL L31 61 K3
Fielding St NPK/KEN L6 * 113 J4
Fieldlands STHP PR8 28 D5
Field La AIN/FAZ L10 84 A4
LITH L21 81 H2
WARRS WA4 162 B5
Field Rd STHEL WA9 120 B4
WAL/NB CH45 95 H6
Field's End HUY L36 136 B1
Fieldsend Cl NTHLY L27 136 B5
Fieldsend Dr LEIGH WN7 93 K3
Fieldside Rd RF/TRAN CH42 150 D1
Field St VAUX/LVPD L3 113 G4
Fieldsway RUNC WA7 186 D1
Fieldton Rd NG/CROX L11 99 F2
Field Vw LITH L21 81 H2
Fieldview SKEL WN8 57 J6
Fieldview Dr
WARRN/WOL WA2 123 J6
Field Wk ORM L39 46 B6
Field Wy RAIN/WH L35 118 E2
Fieldway BEB CH63 150 C3
FROD/HEL WA6 201 F2
GTS/LS CH66 194 E2
HES CH60 168 C4
HOY CH47 128 A2
HUY L36 136 C1
MGHL L31 71 H2
WAL/NB CH45 111 G2
WAV L15 134 D1
WDN WA8 159 F1
Fieldway Ct BIRK CH41 2 B1
Fife Rd WARR WA1 17 K1
Fifth Av CL/PREN CH43 129 J2
RUNC WA7 177 J6
WLT/FAZ L9 83 G4
Filbert Cl NWD/KWIPK L33 72 E3
Fildes Cl WARRW/BUR WA5 141 K4
Fillmore Gv WDN WA8 138 E6
Filton Rd DV/KA/FCH L14 116 B2
Finborough Rd ANF/KKDL L4 98 A3
Fincham Cl DV/KA/FCH L14 116 B2
Fincham Gn DV/KA/FCH L14 116 B2
Fincham Rd DV/KA/FCH L14 116 A2
Fincham Sq DV/KA/FCH L14 116 A2
Finch Av RNFD/HAY WA11 75 H4
Finch Cl DV/KA/FCH L14 * 115 K1
STHEL WA9 120 B4
Finch Ct BIRK CH41 2 D2
Finchdale Gdns
GOL/RIS/CUL WA3 93 J3
Finchdean Cl
GR/UP/WCH CH49 128 D5
Finch Dene DV/KA/FCH L14 115 K1
Finch La DV/KA/FCH L14 115 K1
HLWD L26 156 A5
Finch Lea Dr DV/KA/FCH L14 116 A2
Finchley Dr RNFD/HAY WA11 89 F4
Finchley Rd ANF/KKDL L4 97 K6
Finch Meadow Cl WLT/FAZ L9 98 D1
Finch Pl VAUX/LVPD L3 9 J2
Finch Rd DV/KA/FCH L14 116 A1
Finch Wy DV/KA/FCH L14 115 K2
Findlay Cl NEWLW WA12 106 B3
Findley Dr MOR/LEA CH46 109 K4
Findon SKEL WN8 56 D4
Findon Rd KKBY L32 84 E3
Fine Jane's Wy CHTN/BK PR9 23 K5
Fingall Rd WAV L15 134 C3
Finger House La WDN WA8 120 B6
Fingland Rd WAV L15 133 K2
Finlan Rd WDN WA8 18 B6
Finlay Av WARRW/BUR WA5 141 F6
Finlay St NPK/KEN L6 114 A4
Finney Gv RNFD/HAY WA11 90 D5
The Finney WKBY CH48 * 146 E5
Finningley Ct
WARRN/WOL WA2 124 A6
Finsbury Cl
WARRW/BUR WA5 141 K5
Finsbury Pk WDN WA8 139 H4
Finstall Rd BEB CH63 170 B3
Finvoy Rd CLB/OSW/ST L13 98 C6
Fir Avenue HLWD L26 155 K3
Firbank CHNE CH2 198 D6
Firbank Cl RUNC WA7 178 C4
Firbeck SKEL WN8 56 E4
Firbrook Ct CL/PREN CH43 110 C6
Fir Cl HLWD L26 155 K3
Firdale Rd WLT/FAZ L9 97 J1
Firdene Crs CL/PREN CH43 130 B5
Firecrest Ct WARR WA1 142 D6
Fire Station Rd
RAIN/WH L35 118 B2
Firethorne Rd HLWD L26 155 G1
Fir Gv WARR WA1 143 J2
WLT/FAZ L9 83 F3
Fir La WAV L15 134 B2
Firman Cl WARRW/BUR WA5 141 J1
Fir Rd CSBY/WL L22 81 F1
Firs Av BEB CH63 170 B2
Firs Cl FMBY L37 40 D6
Firs Crs FMBY L37 40 D6
Firshaw Rd HOY CH47 108 A6
Firs La ORM L39 52 C2
WARRS WA4 162 A5
Firs Link FMBY L37 48 D1
First Av CL/PREN CH43 129 K3
CSBY/BLUN L23 * 68 E5
RAIN/WH L35 118 D3
WLT/FAZ L9 83 F4
Firstone Gv KKBY L32 84 D3
Fir St ECCL WA10 102 E5
STHP PR8 28 C1
WDN WA8 158 D1
Firswood Rd SKEL WN8 55 J1
Firth Bvd WARRN/WOL WA2 17 F1
Firthland Wy STHEL WA9 104 D3
Fir Tree Av GOL/RIS/CUL WA3 93 G3
Firtree Av WARR WA1 143 K1
Fir Tree Cl RNFD/HAY WA11 76 C2
SKEL WN8 57 F6
Fir Tree Dr North
WD/CROXPK L12 99 H2
Fir Tree Dr South
WD/CROXPK L12 99 H2
Firtree Gv GTS/LS CH66 202 E3
Fir Tree La ORM L39 52 E3
WARRW/BUR WA5 106 A6
Fir Wy HES CH60 181 G2
Firwood SKEL WN8 57 F2
Firwood Gv AIMK WN4 90 E1
Fisher Av RAIN/WH L35 117 K5
WARRN/WOL WA2 123 H6
Fisher Dr CHTN/BK PR9 23 H6
Fisherfield Dr
GOL/RIS/CUL WA3 125 J1
Fishermans Cl FMBY L37 40 E5
Fisher Pl RAIN/WH L35 117 K5
Fishers La PEN/TH CH61 167 J1
Fisher St RUNC WA7 11 G3
STHEL WA9 104 C6
TOX L8 132 C3
Fish La BRSC L40 31 G4
Fistral Cl AIN/FAZ L10 84 A5
Fistral Dr ECCL WA10 87 J5
Fitzclarence Wy
NPK/KEN L6 113 H3
Fitzgerald Rd
CLB/OSW/ST L13 114 E4
Fitzherbert St
WARRN/WOL WA2 143 F2
Fitzpatrick Ct VAUX/LVPD L3 112 E3
Fitzroy Wy NPK/KEN L6 113 J4
Fitzwalter Rd WARR WA1 144 C2
Fiveways ECCL WA10 102 C1
Flag La NSTN CH64 192 A2
Flail Cl GR/UP/WCH CH49 128 D5
Flambards GR/UP/WCH CH49 129 J6
Flamstead SKEL WN8 56 E4
Flander Cl WDN WA8 157 H1
Flashes La NSTN CH64 192 C4
Flatfield Wy MGHL L31 62 C6
Flatman's La ORM L39 51 G4
Flatt La CL/PREN CH43 130 C6
EP CH65 6 B4
Flawn Rd NG/CROX L11 98 C5
Flaxfield Rd FMBY L37 49 G2
Flaxfields BRSC L40 39 F6
Flaxhill MOR/LEA CH46 109 H6
Flax La BRSC L40 47 F1
Flaxley Cl GOL/RIS/CUL WA3 125 J2
Flaxman St EHL/KEN L7 * 114 A5
Flaxton SKEL WN8 56 E4
Flaybrick Cl CL/PREN CH43 130 B1
Fleck La WKBY CH48 146 E2
Fleet Croft Rd
GR/UP/WCH CH49 148 D1
Fleet La STHEL WA9 104 C3
Fleet St CLVPS L1 9 F5
EP CH65 6 A4
Fleetwood Cl CHTN/BK PR9 23 H2
WARRW/BUR WA5 141 J5
Fleetwood Crs CHTN/BK PR9 21 K5
Fleetwood Dr CHTN/BK PR9 21 K5
NEWLW WA12 106 B1
Fleetwood Gdns
NWD/KWIPK L33 72 E4
Fleetwood Rd CHTN/BK PR9 22 E4
Fleetwood's La NTHTN L30 70 A5
Fleetwood Wk RUNC WA7 178 B6
Fleming Ct VAUX/LVPD L3 112 E3
Fleming Dr AIMK WN4 79 J5
WARRN/WOL WA2 123 F1
Fleming Rd SPK/HALE L24 155 F5
Fleming St EP CH65 6 E2
Flemington Av ANF/KKDL L4 98 B4
Flers Av WARRS WA4 143 F6
Fletcher Av PR/KW L34 102 A6
RF/TRAN CH42 150 D1
Fletcher Cl GR/UP/WCH CH49 148 D1
Fletcher Dr ALL/GAR L19 153 H4
Fletcher's Dr BRSC L40 38 E5
Fletcher St WARRS WA4 142 E6
Flimby SKEL WN8 57 F4
Flint Cl NSTN CH64 191 J3
Flint Ct EP CH65 203 H1
Flint Dr NSTN CH64 191 K2
WD/CROXPK L12 99 H4
Flint Meadow NSTN CH64 191 K2
Flintshire Gdns ECCL WA10 12 E7
Flint St CLVPS L1 132 C2
Floodgates Rd HTWN L38 59 F2
Floral Wd AIG/SPK L17 152 A1
Flora St AIMK WN4 91 G1
Flordon SKEL WN8 57 F4
Florence Av HES CH60 167 K4
Florence Cl WLT/FAZ L9 97 H2
Florence Nightingale Cl
NTHTN L30 70 C5
Florence Rd WAL/EG CH44 112 A4
Florence St ANF/KKDL L4 97 H5
BIRK CH41 2 E4
STHEL WA9 102 E6
WARRS WA4 143 G6
Florentine Rd
CLB/OSW/ST L13 114 E3
Florida Cl WARRW/BUR WA5 141 K2
Florida Ct ALL/GAR L19 153 J3
Florida Wy RAIN/WH L35 117 K3
Flowermead Cl HOY CH47 108 D6
Fluin La FROD/HEL WA6 201 F1
Fluker's Brook La PR/KW L34 100 B3
Fog Cottages STHEL WA9 * 119 J2
Foinavon Cl WLT/FAZ L9 82 C4
Folds La RNFD/HAY WA11 88 D4
Folds Rd RNFD/HAY WA11 89 J5
The Folds BEB CH63 182 B1
Fold St GOL/RIS/CUL WA3 92 B2
Foley St ANF/KKDL L4 97 G6
Folkestone Rd STHP PR8 28 B4
Folkestone Wy RUNC WA7 178 B6
Folly La WAL/EG CH44 110 E2
WARRW/BUR WA5 142 C2
Fontenoy St CLVP L2 8 E2
Fonthill Cl ANF/KKDL L4 97 F6
Fonthill Rd ANF/KKDL L4 97 F5
Forbes Cl GOL/RIS/CUL WA3 125 G3
Ford Av NWD/KWIPK L33 72 D3
Ford Cl BTL L20 82 B4
GR/UP/WCH CH49 129 J5
LITH L21 81 J1
Fordcombe Rd WLTN L25 135 K5
Ford Dr GR/UP/WCH CH49 129 J4
Fordham Cl STHP PR8 28 B4
Fordham St ANF/KKDL L4 97 G5
Fordhill Vw MOR/LEA CH46 129 H1
Fordington Rd
WARRW/BUR WA5 141 J4
Fordland Cl GOL/RIS/CUL WA3 93 F2
Ford La GR/UP/WCH CH49 129 J4
LITH L21 69 J6
Fordlea Rd WD/CROXPK L12 98 E5
Fordlea Wy WD/CROXPK L12 99 F5
Ford Rd GR/UP/WCH CH49 129 H4
RAIN/WH L35 118 B1
Ford St VAUX/LVPD L3 112 E4
WARR WA1 17 H2
Ford Vw LITH L21 69 J6
Ford Wy GR/UP/WCH CH49 129 H5
Forefield La CSBY/BLUN L23 69 G5
Foreland Cl WARRW/BUR WA5 140 D2
Forest Cl HOY CH47 108 B6
PR/KW L34 102 B6
Forest Ct CL/PREN CH43 130 C3
Forest Dr HUY L36 116 C4
SKEL WN8 56 E2
Forest Gn WD/CROXPK L12 99 F5
Forest Gv PR/KW L34 102 B6
Forest Lawn WD/CROXPK L12 99 F5
Forest Md ECCL WA10 102 C2
Forest Rd CL/PREN CH43 130 D2
GTS/LS CH66 195 H2
HES CH60 168 A5
HOY CH47 108 B6
STHEL WA9 119 J4
STHP PR8 15 J7
Forest Wk RUNC WA7 * 177 J6
Forfar Rd CLB/OSW/ST L13 114 B1
Forge Cl BRSC L40 54 E1
WDN WA8 138 B4
Forge Cottages AIG/SPK L17 * 133 H5
Forge Rd GTS/LS CH66 195 F3
WARRW/BUR WA5 141 G4
Forge St BTL L20 96 E5
Formby Br FMBY L37 48 E3
Formby By-Pass FMBY L37 49 H3
Formby Cl WARRW/BUR WA5 141 G5
Formby Flds FMBY L37 49 G3
Formby Gdns FMBY L37 49 F1
Formby Rd ECCL WA10 103 F4
Formby St FMBY L37 48 E3
Formosa Dr AIN/FAZ L10 83 J4
Formosa Rd AIN/FAZ L10 83 J4
Formosa Wy AIN/FAZ L10 83 J4
Fornalls Green La HOY CH47 127 K2
Forres Gv AIMK WN4 78 B5
Forrester Av STHEL WA9 102 E6
Forrest St CLVPS L1 8 E6
Forrest Wy WARRW/BUR WA5 142 A6
Forshaw Av ECCL WA10 102 E5
Forshaw's La
WARRW/BUR WA5 105 J5
Forshaw St WARRN/WOL WA2 17 F1
Forster St GOL/RIS/CUL WA3 92 B2
WARRN/WOL WA2 16 D1
Forsythia Cl WLT/FAZ L9 * 98 A2
Forthlin Rd CALD/MH L18 153 K2
Forth St BTL L20 96 E4
Forton Lodge Flats
CSBY/BLUN L23 * 68 D5
Fort St WAL/NB CH45 95 J6
Forwood Rd PS/BROM CH62 171 F5
Foscote Rd NWD/KWIPK L33 73 F5
Foster Cl RAIN/WH L35 118 C2
Foster Rd FMBY L37 48 D3
Fosters Cl CHTN/BK PR9 23 K5
Fosters Green Rd SKEL WN8 56 E3
Fosters Gv RNFD/HAY WA11 89 J5
Fosters Rd RNFD/HAY WA11 89 J5
Foster St BTL L20 96 E6
WDN WA8 19 F1
Fothergill St WARR WA1 17 H1
Fotheringay Ct EP CH65 203 H1
Foul La STHP PR8 28 D3
Foundry La WDN WA8 157 G6
Foundry St ECCL WA10 13 G6
NEWLW WA12 106 B2
WARRN/WOL WA2 16 D3
Fountain Ct CSBY/BLUN L23 68 B4
Fountain La FROD/HEL WA6 200 D1
Fountain Rd PR/KW L34 100 D2
WAL/NB CH45 95 H6
Fountains Av RNFD/HAY WA11 90 E4
Fountains Cl ANF/KKDL L4 97 H6
RUNC WA7 188 B2
Fountains Ct EV L5 97 F6
Fountains Rd ANF/KKDL L4 97 F6
Fountain St RF/TRAN CH42 131 F6
STHEL WA9 118 E1
Fountains Wk
GOL/RIS/CUL WA3 93 J3
Fountains Wy FMBY L37 49 G3
Four Acre Dr LITH L21 69 J6
Four Acre La STHEL WA9 120 A3
Fouracres MGHL L31 70 E2
Fourth Av CL/PREN CH43 129 J3
RUNC WA7 177 J6
WLT/FAZ L9 83 G4
Fourways Cl NTHLY L27 136 A2
Fowell Rd WAL/NB CH45 95 H5
Fowler Cl EHL/KEN L7 114 A6
Foxall Wy GTS/LS CH66 202 B1
Fox Bank Cl WDN WA8 138 E4
Foxcote WDN WA8 157 G1
Fox Cover Rd HES CH60 168 C6
Foxcovers Rd BEB CH63 170 C2
Fox Covert RUNC WA7 178 B6
Foxdale Cl CL/PREN CH43 130 D4
STHP PR8 28 B4
Foxdale Rd WAV L15 134 A3
Foxdell Cl CLB/OSW/ST L13 114 E5
Foxdene GTS/LS CH66 195 F4
The Foxes PEN/TH CH61 148 D5
Foxfield Cl WARRN/WOL WA2 124 A4
Foxfield Rd HOY CH47 127 J1
Foxfold SKEL WN8 57 F2
Fox Gdns LYMM WA13 145 H5
Foxglove Av HLWD L26 155 H2
Foxglove Cl GOL/RIS/CUL WA3 92 E3
WLT/FAZ L9 98 D1
Foxglove Ct FROD/HEL WA6 201 F1
Foxglove Rd BIRK CH41 * 130 C2
Foxglove Wy NSTN CH64 191 K4
Fox Hey Rd WAL/EG CH44 111 F4
Foxhill Cl FMBY L37 48 C2
TOX L8 133 F4
Foxhill Gv FROD/HEL WA6 200 A5
Foxhill La HLWD L26 155 J1
Foxhouse La MGHL L31 71 H1
Foxhunter Dr WLT/FAZ L9 83 F3
Foxleigh HLWD L26 155 G2
Foxley Cl LYMM WA13 165 H1
Foxley Hall Ms LYMM WA13 * 165 H2
Foxley Heath WDN WA8 18 A3
Fox Pl ECCL WA10 13 G2
Fox's Bank La RAIN/WH L35 118 B6
Foxshaw Cl RAIN/WH L35 117 K6
Fox St BIRK CH41 2 C4
RUNC WA7 10 D6
VAUX/LVPD L3 113 G3
WARRW/BUR WA5 142 B4
Foxton Cl MOR/LEA CH46 109 F6
RNFD/HAY WA11 * 89 G6
Foxwood STHEL WA9 102 E6
WD/CROXPK L12 99 J5
Foxwood Cl WKBY CH48 127 K6
Foy St AIMK WN4 * 79 G6
Frailey Cl STHP PR8 33 J5
Frampton Rd ANF/KKDL L4 98 B3
Franceys St VAUX/LVPD L3 * 9 H4
Francine Cl VAUX/LVPD L3 112 E2
Francis Av CL/PREN CH43 2 A5
MOR/LEA CH46 128 E1
Francis Cl RAIN/WH L35 118 E3
WDN WA8 157 H3
Francis Rd FROD/HEL WA6 187 F6
WARRS WA4 162 A2
Francis St STHEL WA9 104 D6
Francis Wy CHLDW L16 135 F1
Frankby Av WAL/EG CH44 111 G3
Frankby Cl GR/UP/WCH CH49 128 C6
Frankby Gv GR/UP/WCH CH49 129 G4
Frankby Rd ANF/KKDL L4 97 K5
GR/UP/WCH CH49 128 D6
WKBY CH48 127 J6
Frankby Stiles WKBY CH48 128 A6
Franklin Cl WARRW/BUR WA5 141 K1
Franklin Gv NWD/KWIPK L33 72 D3
Franklin Pl NPK/KEN L6 * 113 K2
Franklin Rd MOR/LEA CH46 110 A3
Frank St TOX L8 132 D4
WDN WA8 19 H2
Fraser Rd WARRW/BUR WA5 140 E3
Fraser St VAUX/LVPD L3 9 G2
Frawley Av NEWLW WA12 91 G6
Freckleton Cl
WARRW/BUR WA5 141 J5
Freckleton Dr NWD/KWIPK L33 73 F4
Freckleton Rd CHTN/BK PR9 23 H1
ECCL WA10 102 D4
Freda Av STHEL WA9 * 120 A1
Frederick Banting Cl
NTHTN L30 70 C5
Frederick Gv WAV L15 134 B1
Frederick Lunt Av PR/KW L34 100 C2
Frederick St AIMK WN4 79 F4
STHEL WA9 104 D6
WARRS WA4 143 G6
WDN WA8 18 E2
Fredric Pl RUNC WA7 11 F3
Freedom Cl EHL/KEN L7 133 F1
Freehold St EHL/KEN L7 114 B4
Freeland St ANF/KKDL L4 * 97 G6
Freeman St BIRK CH41 3 F2
EHL/KEN L7 133 H1
Freemantle Av STHEL WA9 103 H6
Freemasons Rw VAUX/LVPD L3 8 D1
Freemont Rd WD/CROXPK L12 98 E6
Freeport Gv WLT/FAZ L9 82 E4

Freesia Av WLT/FAZ L9 97 K1
Freme Cl NG/CROX L11 99 F2
French St ECCL WA10 103 F4
WDN WA8 19 J2
Frensham Cl BEB CH63 170 B3
Freshfield Cl HUY L36 116 C4
Freshfield Rd FMBY L37 40 E6
WAV L15 134 A3
Freshfields Dr
WARRN/WOL WA2 124 D6
Freshford STHEL WA9 120 B1
Freshwater WARRW/BUR WA5 140 E2
Freshwater Cl
WARRW/BUR WA5 140 E2
Friars Av WARRW/BUR WA5 141 F4
Friars Cl BEB CH63 170 B1
Friars Ga WARR WA1 16 D6
Friarsgate Cl CALD/MH L18 134 D4
Friars La WARR WA1 16 D6
Friar St ECCL WA10 88 C4
EV L5 * 113 J2
Friars Wk FMBY L37 49 H3
Friends La WARRW/BUR WA5 140 E3
Frinsted Rd NG/CROX L11 98 E4
Frobisher Ct
WARRW/BUR WA5 142 A1
Frobisher Rd MOR/LEA CH46 110 A3
NSTN CH64 191 K1
Froda Av FROD/HEL WA6 200 E2
Frodsham Dr RNFD/HAY WA11 89 G6
Frodsham St ANF/KKDL L4 97 H4
BIRK CH41 131 H5
Froghall La WARRW/BUR WA5 142 C4
Frog La BRSC L40 39 K6
Frogmore Rd
CLB/OSW/ST L13 114 C4
Frome Cl PEN/TH CH61 148 A4
Frome Ct EP CH65 196 A2
Frome Wy WLTN L25 155 G3
Frost Dr PEN/TH CH61 147 K4
Frosts Ms EP CH65 6 C2
Frost St EHL/KEN L7 114 A5
Fryer St RUNC WA7 10 D3
Fry St STHEL WA9 104 C2
Fuchsia Cl GTS/LS CH66 202 D2
Fuchsia Wk GR/UP/WCH CH49 147 K1
Fulbeck WDN WA8 157 H1
Fulbrook Cl BEB CH63 170 B3
Fulbrook Rd BEB CH63 170 B3
Fulford Cl WD/CROXPK L12 115 K1
Fulford Pk MOR/LEA CH46 129 F2
Fullerton Gv HUY L36 116 E3
Fulmar Cl NTHLY L27 136 B5
RNFD/HAY WA11 88 E5
Fulmar Gv WD/CROXPK L12 99 J2
Fulshaw Cl NTHLY L27 136 A3
Fulton Av WKBY CH48 127 J6
Fulton St EV L5 112 D1
Fulwood Av STHP PR8 28 A3
Fulwood Cl AIG/SPK L17 152 E1
Fulwood Dr AIG/SPK L17 152 D1
Fulwood Gdns GTS/LS CH66 195 F3
Fulwood Ms GTS/LS CH66 195 F3
Fulwood Pk AIG/SPK L17 152 D2
Fulwood Rd AIG/SPK L17 152 D1
GOL/RIS/CUL WA3 93 F5
GTS/LS CH66 195 F3
Funchal Av FMBY L37 48 D4
Furlong Cl WLT/FAZ L9 83 G3
Furness Av ECCL WA10 88 B4
FMBY L37 49 F2
ORM L39 53 J1
WD/CROXPK L12 99 G4
Furness Cl GR/UP/WCH CH49 129 F3
STHP PR8 33 H6
Furness St ANF/KKDL L4 97 G6
Furnival Dr BRSC L40 38 D5
Furrocks Cl NSTN CH64 192 A4
Furrocks La NSTN CH64 192 A4
Furrocks Wy NSTN CH64 192 A4
The Furrows GTS/LS CH66 202 C3
Fylde Rd CHTN/BK PR9 23 H1

G

Gable Ct NG/CROX L11 * 98 C2
Gables Cl WARRN/WOL WA2 124 B4
The Gables MGHL L31 * 71 H2
Gable St NEWLW WA12 106 A2
Gable Vw NG/CROX L11 * 98 C2
Gabriel Cl MOR/LEA CH46 129 G1
Gainford Cl WDN WA8 138 B6
Gainford Rd DV/KA/FCH L14 116 A1
Gainsborough Av MGHL L31 70 E1
Gainsborough Cl
DV/KA/FCH L14 115 J2
Gainsborough Ct WDN WA8 157 G2
Gainsborough Rd
GR/UP/WCH CH49 129 F3
STHP PR8 27 F4
WAL/NB CH45 110 E2
WARRS WA4 162 A1
WAV L15 133 K3
Gairloch Cl WARRN/WOL WA2 124 B3
Gaisgill Ct WDN WA8 157 H2
Galbraith Cl AIG/SPK L17 152 D1
Gale Av WARRW/BUR WA5 123 F6
Galemeade NG/CROX L11 * 99 F2
Gale Rd LITH L21 81 K2
NWD/KWIPK L33 85 H3
Galion Wy WDN WA8 138 E5
Galloway Dr SKEL WN8 67 K1
Galloway Rd CSBY/WL L22 81 F1
Galloway St EHL/KEN L7 133 J1
Galston Av RAIN/WH L35 119 F5
Galston Cl NWD/KWIPK L33 72 C3
Galsworthy Av NTHTN L30 82 A4
Galsworthy Pl NTHTN L30 82 B3
Galton St VAUX/LVPD L3 8 A1
Galtres Pk BEB CH63 150 D3
Galway Av WDN WA8 138 D6
Gambier Ter CLVPS L1 132 D2
Gamble Av ECCL WA10 88 B5
Gamlin St BIRK CH41 130 C1
Gamston Wd KKBY L32 84 B2
Ganney's Meadow Rd
GR/UP/WCH CH49 129 K6
Gannock St EHL/KEN L7 114 A5
Ganton Cl STHP PR8 28 B3
WDN WA8 139 G5
Ganworth Cl SPK/HALE L24 173 K3
Ganworth Rd SPK/HALE L24 173 K2
Garage Rd HLWD L26 155 J6
Gardeners Vw NWD/KWIPK L33 72 E3
Gardeners Wy RAIN/WH L35 118 E2
Garden Hey Rd HOY CH47 127 H1
Gardenia Gv AIG/SPK L17 152 B1
Garden La EV L5 * 113 H3
MOR/LEA CH46 109 J6
WLT/FAZ L9 83 G4
Garden Lodge Gv NTHLY L27 136 A4
Garden Pl BTL L20 * 5 F4
Gardenside MOR/LEA CH46 110 B3
Gardenside St NPK/KEN L6 113 H4
Gardens Rd BEB CH63 151 G6
Garden St WLTN L25 154 D1
Garden Wk PR/KW L34 117 K1
Gardiner Av RNFD/HAY WA11 90 B5
Gardiners Pl SKEL WN8 56 A5
Gardner Av BTL L20 82 A4
Gardner Rd CLB/OSW/ST L13 114 C2
FMBY L37 49 G2
Gardner's Dr NPK/KEN L6 114 A3
Gareth Av RNFD/HAY WA11 88 E5
Garfield Ter
GR/UP/WCH CH49 * 129 H4
Garfourth Cl ALL/GAR L19 154 A4
Garfourth Rd ALL/GAR L19 154 A4
Garmoyle Cl WAV L15 133 K2
Garmoyle Rd WAV L15 133 K3
Garner St WARRN/WOL WA2 143 F2
Garnet St CLB/OSW/ST L13 114 D6
STHEL WA9 104 B6
Garnett Av ANF/KKDL L4 97 F5
WARRS WA4 143 J5
Garnett Gdns ORM L39 53 H1
Garnett Pl SKEL WN8 56 C6
Garnetts La RAIN/WH L35 156 C2
WDN WA8 175 H1
Garrett Fld GOL/RIS/CUL WA3 125 F2
Garrick Av MOR/LEA CH46 128 D1
Garrick Pde STHP PR8 14 C6
Garrick Rd CL/PREN CH43 149 J3
Garrick St EHL/KEN L7 133 H2
Garrigill Cl WDN WA8 139 G4
Garrison Cl TOX L8 133 G3
Garrowby Dr HUY L36 116 C4
Garsdale Av RAIN/WH L35 119 F5
Garsdale Cl WARRW/BUR WA5 141 G2
Garsfield Rd ANF/KKDL L4 98 B4
Garside Av GOL/RIS/CUL WA3 92 E4
Garstang Rd CHTN/BK PR9 23 H1
Garston Old Rd ALL/GAR L19 153 J4
Garston Wy ALL/GAR L19 153 K6
Garswood Av RNFD/HAY WA11 75 H2
Garswood Cl MGHL L31 62 C4
MOR/LEA CH46 109 J3
Garswood Crs
WGNW/BIL/OR WN5 77 G5
Garswood Old Rd AIMK WN4 89 J2
Garswood Rd
WGNW/BIL/OR WN5 77 H5
Garswood St AIMK WN4 79 G6
ECCL WA10 13 G3
TOX L8 132 E6
Garter Cl NG/CROX L11 99 G2
Garth Bvd BEB CH63 150 D3
Garthdale Rd CALD/MH L18 134 B5
Garth Dr CALD/MH L18 134 C5
Garthowen Rd EHL/KEN L7 114 B5
Garth Rd EP CH65 196 E4
KKBY L32 85 F3
The Garth HUY L36 116 E4
Garton Dr GOL/RIS/CUL WA3 93 F2
Gartons La STHEL WA9 120 A4
Garven Pl WARR WA1 16 C5
Garway WLTN L25 135 K6
Garwood Cl WARRW/BUR WA5 122 B6
Gascoyne St VAUX/LVPD L3 8 C1
Gaskell Av WARRS WA4 143 K6
Gaskell St STHEL WA9 104 B4
WARRS WA4 162 B2
Gaskill Rd SPK/HALE L24 173 J1
Gatclif Rd CLB/OSW/ST L13 98 C5
Gateacre Brow WLTN L25 135 H5
Gateacre Ct GTS/LS CH66 195 J1
Gateacre Park Dr WLTN L25 135 G3
Gateacre Ri WLTN L25 135 J5
Gateacre Vale Rd WLTN L25 135 J6
Gateley Cl WARRS WA4 144 D6
Gateside Cl NTHLY L27 136 B4
Gate Warth St
WARRW/BUR WA5 * 142 A6
Gathurst Ct WDN WA8 157 J3
Gatley Dr MGHL L31 71 H1
Gaunts Wy RUNC WA7 187 H1
Gautby Rd BIRK CH41 110 E6
Gavin Rd WDN WA8 157 G4
Gaw's Hill La ORM L39 52 E2
Gaw's Hill Vw ORM L39 53 F2
Gawsworth Cl CL/PREN CH43 130 C6
ECCL WA10 102 D2
Gawsworth Ct
GOL/RIS/CUL WA3 * 125 H1
Gawsworth Rd
GOL/RIS/CUL WA3 92 A2
GTS/LS CH66 195 H5
Gaybeech Cl CL/PREN CH43 129 K1
Gayhurst Av
WARRN/WOL WA2 124 B5
Gayhurst Crs NG/CROX L11 98 E3
Gaynor Av RNFD/HAY WA11 90 E4
Gayton Av BEB CH63 150 B3
WAL/NB CH45 95 H5
Gayton Farm Rd HES CH60 181 F2
Gayton La HES CH60 181 G1
Gayton Mill Cl HES CH60 * 168 B6
Gayton Pkwy HES CH60 181 G2
Gayton Rd HES CH60 180 E1
Gaywood Av KKBY L32 84 E3
Gaywood Cl CL/PREN CH43 * 129 K2
KKBY L32 84 E3
Gellings La PR/KW L34 85 F6
Gellings Rd PR/KW L34 85 F6
Gelling St TOX L8 132 E4
Gemini Cl BTL L20 4 D3
Gemini Dr DV/KA/FCH L14 115 K3
General St WARR WA1 17 F4
Geneva Rd NPK/KEN L6 114 A4
WAL/EG CH44 111 K5
Genista Cl WLT/FAZ L9 97 J2
Genoa Cl WLTN L25 135 K2
Gentwood Rd HUY L36 116 C3
George Dr STHP PR8 34 A4
George Hale Av PR/KW L34 116 E1
George Harrison Cl
NPK/KEN L6 113 K4
George Moore Ct
CSBY/BLUN L23 * 69 K3
George Rd HOY CH47 127 H3
WARRW/BUR WA5 141 K5
Georges Crs WARRS WA4 163 G1
George's Dock Gates
VAUX/LVPD L3 8 B3
Georges Dockway
VAUX/LVPD L3 8 B5
George's La CHTN/BK PR9 21 J3
Georges Pierhead
VAUX/LVPD L3 8 B5
Georges Rd NPK/KEN L6 114 A2
George St AIMK WN4 79 H5
BIRK CH41 3 G2
CLVP L2 8 C3
ECCL WA10 13 H5
EP CH65 6 D1
NEWLW WA12 * 106 A1
Georgia Av NWD/KWIPK L33 72 C3
PS/BROM CH62 171 G2
Georgia Cl BTL L20 4 E5
Georgian Cl HLWD L26 155 J5
RAIN/WH L35 118 C1
Georgian Pl FMBY L37 48 E4
Georgia Pl WARRW/BUR WA5 141 K3
Geraint St TOX L8 132 E3
Gerald Rd CL/PREN CH43 130 D5
Gerard Av WAL/NB CH45 95 G6
Gerard Rd WAL/NB CH45 111 G1
WKBY CH48 127 G6
Gerards Ct RNFD/HAY WA11 * 89 F3
Gerards La STHEL WA9 104 B6
Gerard St AIMK WN4 79 G6
VAUX/LVPD L3 9 F2
Germander Cl HLWD L26 155 H2
Gerneth Cl SPK/HALE L24 173 H1
Gerneth Rd SPK/HALE L24 173 G2
Gerosa Av WARRN/WOL WA2 107 H5
Gerrard Av GTS/LS CH66 195 F5
WARRW/BUR WA5 142 C2
Gerrard Pl SKEL WN8 56 B6
Gerrard Rd
WGNW/BIL/OR WN5 77 H4
Gerrard's La HLWD L26 155 H1
Gerrard St WDN WA8 18 E4
Gertrude Rd ANF/KKDL L4 113 J1
Gertrude St BIRK CH41 3 H4
STHEL WA9 118 E1
Geves Gdns CSBY/WL L22 81 F2
Ghyll Gv RNFD/HAY WA11 88 E2
Gibbons Av ECCL WA10 102 E2
Gibbon's Rd AIMK WN4 90 C1
Gibraltar Rw VAUX/LVPD L3 8 B2
Gibson Cl NWD/KWIPK L33 72 C4
PEN/TH CH61 167 K2
Gibson Ct EP CH65 * 196 A1
Gibson Rd TOX L8 132 E2
Gibson St TOX L8 132 E2
WARR WA1 17 G5
Giddygate La MGHL L31 72 A2
Gidlow Rd CLB/OSW/ST L13 114 D4
Gidlow Rd South
CLB/OSW/ST L13 114 D4
Gigg La WARRS WA4 160 E6
WARRS WA4 144 D5
Gig La WARR WA1 144 C1
Gilbert Cl BEB CH63 170 B3
Gilbert Pl BRSC L40 38 B5
Gilbert Rd RAIN/WH L35 118 B2
Gilbert St CLVPS L1 8 E6
Gilbrook Sq BIRK CH41 130 C1
Gildarts Gdns VAUX/LVPD L3 * 113 F3
Gildart St VAUX/LVPD L3 9 J2
Gilderdale Cl
GOL/RIS/CUL WA3 125 K2
Gilead St EHL/KEN L7 113 K5
Gillan Cl RUNC WA7 188 B2
Gillars Green Dr ECCL WA10 102 B2
Gillar's La ECCL WA10 102 A2
Gilleney Gv RAIN/WH L35 118 C2
Gillibrands Rd SKEL WN8 56 C6
Gillmoss Cl NG/CROX L11 99 G1
Gillmoss La NG/CROX L11 84 B6
Gills La PEN/TH CH61 168 A1
Gill St VAUX/LVPD L3 9 J3
Gilman St ANF/KKDL L4 97 J6
Gilmartin Gv NPK/KEN L6 113 J5
Gilmour Mt CL/PREN CH43 130 E5
Gilpin Av MGHL L31 62 C5
Gilroy Rd NPK/KEN L6 113 K4
WKBY CH48 127 J6
Gilsecroft Av NWD/KWIPK L33 73 F6
Giltbrook Cl WDN WA8 138 E6
Gilwell Av MOR/LEA CH46 129 F2
Gilwell Cl MOR/LEA CH46 129 F2
WARRS WA4 163 H1
The Ginnel PS/BROM CH62 151 G6
Gipsy Gv CALD/MH L18 135 F4
Gipsy La CALD/MH L18 135 F4
Girton Av AIMK WN4 78 E5
BTL L20 5 J6
Girton Cl EP CH65 7 F6
Girton Rd EP CH65 7 F6
Girtrell Cl GR/UP/WCH CH49 128 E4
Girtrell Rd GR/UP/WCH CH49 128 E4
Girvan Crs AIMK WN4 78 B5
Girvin Dr NSTN CH64 191 K3
Gisburn Av GOL/RIS/CUL WA3 92 A1
Givenchy Cl CHLDW L16 135 F1
Gladden Pl SKEL WN8 56 A5
Glade Dr GTS/LS CH66 194 C2
Glade Rd HUY L36 116 E3
Gladeswood Rd
NWD/KWIPK L33 85 G2
The Glade HOY CH47 108 B6
Gladeville Rd AIG/SPK L17 153 F1
Gladstone Av CHLDW L16 135 H1
LITH L21 81 G4
Gladstone Cl BIRK CH41 2 C4
Gladstone Hall Rd
PS/BROM CH62 * 170 D1
Gladstone Rd ALL/GAR L19 153 K5
CHTN/BK PR9 28 C1
EHL/KEN L7 113 K6
LITH L21 81 G4
NSTN CH64 191 K1
RF/TRAN CH42 131 J6
WAL/EG CH44 111 K4
WLT/FAZ L9 97 H2
Gladstone St BIRK CH41 * 2 C4
ECCL WA10 12 A6
VAUX/LVPD L3 8 D1
WARRN/WOL WA2 16 B3
WDN WA8 18 E3
WLTN L25 154 C1
Gladstone Wy NEWLW WA12 106 B1
Gladsville Rd NTHLY L27 136 C5
Glaisdale Cl AIMK WN4 79 H6
Glaisdale Dr STHP PR8 28 C4
Glaisher St EV L5 113 J1
Glamis Cl CL/PREN CH43 130 A6
Glamis Dr CHTN/BK PR9 23 K2
Glamis Gv STHEL WA9 104 A6
Glamis Rd CLB/OSW/ST L13 114 B1
Glamorgan Cl ECCL WA10 12 E7
Glan Aber Pk WD/CROXPK L12 99 J5
Glasier Rd MOR/LEA CH46 109 G6
Glaslyn Wy WLT/FAZ L9 97 J2
Glassonby Crs NG/CROX L11 98 E4
Glassonby Wy NG/CROX L11 98 E4
Glastonbury Av
GOL/RIS/CUL WA3 93 J3
Glastonbury Cl NPK/KEN L6 98 B6
RUNC WA7 178 D2
Glasven Rd NWD/KWIPK L33 72 E6
Glazebrook St WARR WA1 17 H3
Gleadmere WDN WA8 157 H1
Gleaston Cl PS/BROM CH62 170 E4
Gleave Crs NPK/KEN L6 113 H3
Gleave Rd WARRW/BUR WA5 121 K1
Gleave St ECCL WA10 13 H3
Glebe Av AIMK WN4 91 G1
WARRS WA4 163 H2
Glebe Cl MGHL L31 61 K6
Glebecroft Av CHNE CH2 198 B6
Glebe End SFTN L29 70 B2
Glebe Hey NTHLY L27 136 B4
Glebe Hey Rd
GR/UP/WCH CH49 129 H6
Glebelands Rd MOR/LEA CH46 129 F1
Glebe La CHTN/BK PR9 21 K4
WDN WA8 139 F4
Glebe Pl STHP PR8 14 E4
Glebe Rd SKEL WN8 56 C6
WAL/NB CH45 111 G1
The Glebe RUNC WA7 177 H4
Glebeway Rd EP CH65 7 K5
Gleggside WKBY CH48 146 D1
Glegg St VAUX/LVPD L3 112 D3
Glegside Rd NWD/KWIPK L33 85 F1
Glenacres WLTN L25 * 135 H6
Glenalmond Rd
WAL/EG CH44 * 111 K3
Glenathol Rd CALD/MH L18 153 K1
GTS/LS CH66 195 F5
Glenavon Rd CHLDW L16 134 D1
CL/PREN CH43 149 K2
Glen Bank CSBY/WL L22 80 D1
Glenbank Cl WLT/FAZ L9 82 D6
Glenburn Av PS/BROM CH62 184 B3
Glenburn Rd SKEL WN8 56 A1
WAL/EG CH44 111 K4
Glenby Av CSBY/BLUN L23 81 G1
Glencairn Rd CLB/OSW/ST L13 114 D5
Glencoe Rd GTS/LS CH66 195 F5
WAL/NB CH45 111 H1
Glenconner Rd CHLDW L16 115 J6
Glencourse Rd WDN WA8 139 F4
Glencoyne Dr CHTN/BK PR9 20 E6
Glencroft Cl HUY L36 116 C2
Glendale Av AIMK WN4 79 H5
CHNE CH2 198 B6
Glendale Cl TOX L8 132 E6
Glendale Gv BEB CH63 170 D3
Glendale Wy FMBY L37 49 F3
Glendevon Rd CHLDW L16 115 H6
HUY L36 116 E6
Glendower Rd CSBY/WL L22 81 F2
Glendower St BTL L20 96 E5
Glendyke Rd CALD/MH L18 153 K1
GTS/LS CH66 195 F5
Gleneagles Cl
GOL/RIS/CUL WA3 93 G4
NWD/KWIPK L33 72 C3
PEN/TH CH61 167 K1
Gleneagles Dr RNFD/HAY WA11 89 K6
STHP PR8 33 H6
WDN WA8 139 F4
Gleneagles Rd CHLDW L16 115 J6
GTS/LS CH66 195 F5
Glenesk Rd GTS/LS CH66 195 F5
Glenfield Cl CL/PREN CH43 129 K1
MOR/LEA CH46 109 F6
Glenfield Rd WAV L15 134 B3
Glengariff St CLB/OSW/ST L13 98 C6
Glenham Cl HOY CH47 127 K1
Glenhead Rd ALL/GAR L19 153 J3
Glenholm Rd MGHL L31 * 71 F2
Glenluce Rd ALL/GAR L19 153 J3
Glenmarsh Cl BEB CH63 150 C6
WD/CROXPK L12 115 G1
Glenmarsh Wy FMBY L37 49 H2
Glenmaye Cl WD/CROXPK L12 99 J3
Glenmaye Rd GTS/LS CH66 195 F5
Glenmore Av CALD/MH L18 134 A6
Glenmore Rd CL/PREN CH43 130 D5
Glenn Pl WDN WA8 157 J2
Glenpark Dr CHTN/BK PR9 23 K1
Glen Park Rd WAL/NB CH45 95 G6
Glen Rd CLB/OSW/ST L13 115 F5
GTS/LS CH66 195 F5
Glen Ronald Dr
GR/UP/WCH CH49 128 E4
Glenrose Ter STHP PR8 27 H2
Glenroyd Dr BRSC L40 38 E5
Glenside CALD/MH L18 153 K1
The Glen BEB CH63 170 E2
CALD/MH L18 134 D6
RUNC WA7 187 J1
Glenton Pk NSTN CH64 192 A3
Glentrees Cl
GR/UP/WCH CH49 128 E4
Glentrees Rd WD/CROXPK L12 99 F5
Glentworth Cl MGHL L31 71 G1
Glenville Cl RUNC WA7 186 E1
WLTN L25 135 J6
Glen Vine Cl CHLDW L16 * 135 G1
Glenway NWD/KWIPK L33 72 E3
Glenway Cl WD/CROXPK L12 99 K1
Glenwood Cl GTS/LS CH66 195 F3
RAIN/WH L35 118 B5
Glenwood Dr PEN/TH CH61 148 B4
Glenwood Gdns GTS/LS CH66 195 F3
Glenwood Rd GTS/LS CH66 195 F3
Glenwyllin Rd CSBY/WL L22 81 F1
Gleyve KNUT WA16 165 K6
Globe Rd BTL L20 4 C3
Globe St ANF/KKDL L4 97 G6
Gloucester Av
GOL/RIS/CUL WA3 92 C2
Gloucester Cl GTS/LS CH66 202 C3
WARR WA1 144 C2
Gloucester Ct NPK/KEN L6 113 J4
Gloucester Pl NPK/KEN L6 113 J4
Gloucester Rd BTL L20 5 H3
HUY L36 117 G4
NPK/KEN L6 114 B2
STHP PR8 27 G2
WAL/NB CH45 110 E1
WDN WA8 139 G6
Gloucester Rd North
NPK/KEN L6 114 B1
Gloucester St STHEL WA9 104 B2
Gloucestor Ct NPK/KEN L6 113 J4
Glover Pl BTL L20 4 D2
Glover Rd GOL/RIS/CUL WA3 124 E2
Glover's Brow KKBY L32 72 B5
Glover's La NTHTN L30 70 B5
Glover St ECCL WA10 12 E6
NEWLW WA12 106 C2
RF/TRAN CH42 131 F5
Glyn Av PS/BROM CH62 171 G6
Glynne Gv CHLDW L16 135 H1
Glynne St BTL L20 82 A5
Glynn St WAV L15 134 A2
Glyn Rd WAL/EG CH44 111 H2
Goddard Rd RUNC WA7 177 H2
Godetia Cl WLT/FAZ L9 * 98 D1
Godfrey St WARRN/WOL WA2 17 H1
Godscroft La FROD/HEL WA6 200 B3
Godshill Cl WARRW/BUR WA5 140 E2
Godstow RUNC WA7 178 D1
Golborne Dale Rd
NEWLW WA12 92 B6
Golborne Rd AIMK WN4 79 J5
GOL/RIS/CUL WA3 92 D3
WARRN/WOL WA2 107 G6
Golborne St NEWLW WA12 106 E1
WARR WA1 16 C4
Goldcliffe Cl
WARRW/BUR WA5 122 D5
Goldcrest Cl RUNC WA7 187 J2
WD/CROXPK L12 99 K1
Goldcrest Ms HLWD L26 155 H2
Golden Gv ANF/KKDL L4 97 J4
Goldfinch Cl HLWD L26 155 H2
Goldfinch Farm Rd
SPK/HALE L24 173 H2
Goldfinch La
GOL/RIS/CUL WA3 125 G3
Goldie St ANF/KKDL L4 97 H6
Goldsmith Rd CL/PREN CH43 149 J2
Goldsmith St BTL L20 4 B2
NPK/KEN L6 * 113 K4
Goldsmith Wy
CL/PREN CH43 * 149 J2
Goldsworth Fold
RAIN/WH L35 118 D4
Golf Links Rd RF/TRAN CH42 150 A2
Golf Rd FMBY L37 40 D6
Gondover Av WLT/FAZ L9 82 C5
Gonville Rd BTL L20 5 H7
Gooch Dr NEWLW WA12 106 D3
Goodacre Rd WLT/FAZ L9 82 E4
Goodaker's Mdw
GR/UP/WCH CH49 * 148 D1
Goodall Pl ANF/KKDL L4 97 G4
Goodall St ANF/KKDL L4 97 G5
Goodban St STHEL WA9 104 C5
Goodison Av ANF/KKDL L4 97 H5
Goodison Pl ANF/KKDL L4 97 H4
Goodison Rd ANF/KKDL L4 97 H4
Goodlass Rd SPK/HALE L24 154 D6
Goodleigh Pl STHEL WA9 120 A2
Good Shepherd Cl
NG/CROX L11 99 F3
Goodwood Cl HUY L36 116 D6
Goodwood Ct STHEL WA9 119 F1
Goodwood Dr MOR/LEA CH46 109 J4
Goodwood Gv GTS/LS CH66 195 G6
Goodwood St EV L5 113 F2
Gooseberry La RUNC WA7 178 C4
Goostrey Cl BEB CH63 170 D4
Gordale Cl TOX L8 * 133 F5
WARRW/BUR WA5 141 G2
Gordon Av AIMK WN4 78 D5
CHTN/BK PR9 15 G1
CSBY/WL L22 80 D1
GR/UP/WCH CH49 129 F6
MGHL L31 62 A4
PS/BROM CH62 171 G6
RNFD/HAY WA11 90 E4
WARR WA1 144 A2
Gordon Ct GR/UP/WCH CH49 129 F6
Gordon Dr ALL/GAR L19 153 H4
DV/KA/FCH L14 115 J4
Gordon La CHNE CH2 203 F6
Gordon Rd LITH L21 81 G5
WAL/NB CH45 95 H6
Gordon St BIRK CH41 2 C5
CHTN/BK PR9 15 G2
WAV L15 133 K2
Gore Dr ORM L39 53 J2
Gores La FMBY L37 40 E6
RNFD/HAY WA11 76 C3
Gores Rd NWD/KWIPK L33 85 G2
Gore St TOX L8 132 D3
Gorleston Wy KKBY L32 84 E2
Gorran Hvn RUNC WA7 188 B1

Gorse Av WD/CROXPK L12 99 F4
Gorsebank Rd CALD/MH L18 * 133 K4
Gorsebank St WAL/EG CH44 111 J4
Gorseburn Rd
CLB/OSW/ST L13 114 C1
Gorse Covert Rd
GOL/RIS/CUL WA3 125 J2
Gorse Crs WAL/EG CH44 111 J5
Gorsedale Pk WAL/EG CH44 * 111 K5
Gorsedale Rd CALD/MH L18 134 B5
WAL/EG CH44 111 J5
Gorsefield FMBY L37 41 G5
STHEL WA9 103 F6
Gorsefield Av CSBY/BLUN L23 69 H4
PS/BROM CH62 184 A2
Gorsefield Cl PS/BROM CH62 184 A1
Gorsefield Rd RF/TRAN CH42 131 F6
Gorse Hey Ct CLB/OSW/ST L13 114 E2
Gorsehill Rd HES CH60 168 A4
WAL/NB CH45 95 G6
Gorse La WKBY CH48 147 F2
Gorse Rd HOY CH47 127 J1
Gorse Wy FMBY L37 47 C1
Gorsewood Gv WLTN L25 135 J4
Gorsewood Rd RUNC WA7 188 C1
WLTN L25 135 J4
Gorsey Av NTHTN L30 69 K6
Gorsey Brow
WGNW/BIL/OR WN5 77 G4
Gorsey Brow Cl
WGNW/BIL/OR WN5 77 G4
Gorsey Cop Wy WLTN L25 135 H3
Gorsey Cft PR/KW L34 102 B6
Gorsey La HTWN L38 59 G6
LITH L21 81 J1
ORM L39 42 E4
STHEL WA9 120 D3
WAL/EG CH44 111 J5
WARRN/WOL WA2 143 G2
WDN WA8 159 F3
Gorsey Pl SKEL WN8 56 C6
Gorseyville Crs BEB CH63 150 D6
Gorseyville Rd BEB CH63 150 D6
Gorseywell La RUNC WA7 188 E1
Gorst La BRSC L40 37 K3
Gorstons La NSTN CH64 192 B3
Gorst St ANF/KKDL L4 97 H6
Gorsuch La BRSC L40 36 B5
Gorton Rd CLB/OSW/ST L13 115 F5
Gort Rd HUY L36 116 E4
Goschen St CLB/OSW/ST L13 114 D4
EV L5 97 H6
Gosford St TOX L8 132 E5
Gosforth Rd CHTN/BK PR9 23 H5
Gosport Cl WARRN/WOL WA2 124 A6
Goswell St WAV L15 133 K2
Gotham Rd BEB CH63 170 C3
Gothic St RF/TRAN CH42 150 E1
Gough Av WARRN/WOL WA2 123 H5
Gough Rd CLB/OSW/ST L13 98 C6
Goulden St WARRW/BUR WA5 142 B3
Goulders Ct RUNC WA7 188 A2
Gourley Rd CLB/OSW/ST L13 115 F6
Gourley's La WKBY CH48 146 E2
Government Rd HOY CH47 127 G2
Govett Rd STHEL WA9 102 E6
Gower Gdns BRSC L40 39 F6
Gower St BTL L20 81 H6
STHEL WA9 104 B4
VAUX/LVPD L3 8 C7
Gowrie Gv LITH L21 81 H4
Gowy Ct GTS/LS CH66 195 H1
Goyt Hey Av
WGNW/BIL/OR WN5 77 H5
Graburn Rd FMBY L37 49 F1
Grace Av AIN/FAZ L10 83 K4
WARRN/WOL WA2 142 E1
Grace Cl WAL/NB CH45 111 H2
Grace Rd EP CH65 6 D2
WLT/FAZ L9 82 D5
Grace St STHEL WA9 104 A5
TOX L8 132 E5
Gradwell St CLVPS L1 8 E5
Grafton Crs TOX L8 132 D3
Grafton Dr GR/UP/WCH CH49 129 H5
STHP PR8 33 G4
Grafton Gv TOX L8 132 D5
Grafton Rd EP CH65 6 D1
WAL/NB CH45 95 H6
Grafton St CL/PREN CH43 2 A6
ECCL WA10 12 B5
NEWLW WA12 106 B2
TOX L8 132 D4
WARRW/BUR WA5 142 B3
Grafton Wk WKBY CH48 146 D1
Graham Av GTS/LS CH66 195 G4
Graham Cl WDN WA8 157 H3
Graham Dr HLWD L26 155 K3
Graham Rd WDN WA8 157 H3
WKBY CH48 127 F6
Graham's Rd HUY L36 117 F5
Graham St STHEL WA9 104 A1
Grainger Av BTL L20 82 B5
CL/PREN CH43 149 J1
WKBY CH48 127 G5
Graley Cl HLWD L26 155 J5
Grammar School Ct
WARRS WA4 * 143 J6
Grammar School La
WKBY CH48 146 E2
Grammar School Rd
LYMM WA13 165 G1
WARRS WA4 143 J6
Grampian Av MOR/LEA CH46 129 F1
Grampian Rd EHL/KEN L7 114 C5
Grampian Wy
GOL/RIS/CUL WA3 92 E2
MOR/LEA CH46 129 F1
NSTN CH64 191 K4
PS/BROM CH62 184 B3
Granams Cft NTHTN L30 70 A5
Granard Rd WAV L15 134 B3
Granary Wy VAUX/LVPD L3 132 C3
Granborne Cha KKBY L32 72 A6
Granby Cl CHTN/BK PR9 23 H2
RUNC WA7 * 188 B2
Granby Crs BEB CH63 170 C3
Granby Rd WARRS WA4 162 A3
Granby St TOX L8 133 F2
Grandison Rd ANF/KKDL L4 98 A4
Grand National Av WLT/FAZ L9 82 E2
Grange Av CHTN/BK PR9 23 G5
WAL/NB CH45 111 H1
WARRS WA4 143 H5
WD/CROXPK L12 115 J2
WLTN L25 155 G4
Grange Av North
WD/CROXPK L12 115 K2
Grange Cl GOL/RIS/CUL WA3 92 D5
Grange Crs GTS/LS CH66 184 D6
Grange Cross Cl WKBY CH48 147 F2
Grange Cross Hey
WKBY CH48 147 F2
Grange Cross La WKBY CH48 147 F2
Grange Dr BEB CH63 169 G6
ECCL WA10 102 D4
HES CH60 167 K4
WARRW/BUR WA5 141 H5
WDN WA8 157 J2
Grange Farm Cl
WARRW/BUR WA5 142 A3
Grange Farm Crs WKBY CH48 127 K6
Grange Green Mnr
WARRS WA4 * 161 H4
Grangehurst Ct WLTN L25 135 J5
Grange La FMBY L37 40 E6
WLTN L25 135 H4
Grangemeadow Rd WLTN L25 135 H4
Grange Ms WLTN L25 * 135 J5
Grangemoor RUNC WA7 177 G6
Grange Mt CL/PREN CH43 2 B6
HES CH60 167 K4
WKBY CH48 146 E1
Grange Old Rd WKBY CH48 146 D1
Grange Pk MGHL L31 71 H2
Grange Park Av RUNC WA7 11 H5
Grange Park Rd ECCL WA10 102 E4
RUNC WA7 11 H5
Grange Pl BIRK CH41 2 C5
Grange Rd AIMK WN4 78 E3
BIRK CH41 2 D5
CHTN/BK PR9 23 G6
EP CH65 6 D5
HES CH60 167 K3
HTWN L38 58 E1
NTHTN L30 82 E1
RNFD/HAY WA11 90 C6
RUNC WA7 11 H5
WKBY CH48 127 F6
Grange Rd North RUNC WA7 11 H4
Grange Rd West CL/PREN CH43 2 B5
Grangeside WLTN L25 135 H4
Grange St NPK/KEN L6 114 B2
Grange Ter WAV L15 134 A2
The Grange CHTN/BK PR9 24 A2
WAL/EG CH44 111 J3
Grange V RF/TRAN CH42 151 F2
Grange Va RNFD/HAY WA11 90 C5
Grange Vw CL/PREN CH43 2 B6
Grange Wk WKBY CH48 146 E2
Grangeway RUNC WA7 177 F6
Grange Wy WLTN L25 135 H4
Grangeway Ct RUNC WA7 177 F6
Grange Weint WLTN L25 135 H5
Grangewood CHLDW L16 115 K6
Grange Wd WKBY CH48 146 E2
Granston Cl WARRW/BUR WA5 122 E5
Grant Av WAV L15 134 A3
Grant Cl DV/KA/FCH L14 116 A4
ECCL WA10 12 D4
WARRW/BUR WA5 122 D6
Grantham Av WARR WA1 143 H2
WARRS WA4 162 A3
Grantham Cl PEN/TH CH61 167 J1
STHP PR8 27 H6
Grantham Crs RNFD/HAY WA11 89 F6
Grantham Rd NWD/KWIPK L33 72 D4
STHP PR8 27 H6
Grantham St NPK/KEN L6 113 K4
Grantham Wy NTHTN L30 70 D5
Grantley Rd WAV L15 134 B3
Grantley St AIMK WN4 79 F4
Granton Cl FMBY L37 48 E2
Granton Rd EV L5 113 H1
Grant Rd DV/KA/FCH L14 115 K4
MOR/LEA CH46 110 B3
Grantwood AIMK WN4 79 F4
Granville Av MGHL L31 62 A5
Granville Cl ORM L39 53 F4
WAL/NB CH45 110 E1
Granville Dr GTS/LS CH66 194 E2
Granville Pk ORM L39 53 F5
Granville Pk West ORM L39 53 F5
Granville Rd ALL/GAR L19 * 153 K5
STHP PR8 26 E4
WAV L15 133 J2
Granville St RUNC WA7 10 E3
STHEL WA9 104 B2
WARR WA1 17 H2
Grappenhall La WARRS WA4 163 H6
Grappenhall Rd EP CH65 195 J6
WARRS WA4 162 C2
Grappenhall Wy
CL/PREN CH43 129 K2
Grasmere Av CL/PREN CH43 129 K4
PR/KW L34 118 B1
RNFD/HAY WA11 88 E4
SKEL WN8 57 K5
WARRN/WOL WA2 123 K4
Grasmere Cl NWD/KWIPK L33 72 C5
RNFD/HAY WA11 * 88 E4
Grasmere Ct RNFD/HAY WA11 88 D4
Grasmere Dr AIMK WN4 79 G4
LITH L21 82 B2
RUNC WA7 187 G2
WAL/NB CH45 111 G2
Grasmere Fold
RNFD/HAY WA11 88 E4
Grasmere Gdns CSBY/BLUN L23 69 G6
Grasmere Rd EP CH65 203 G1
FMBY L37 48 D2
FROD/HEL WA6 201 F1
MGHL L31 62 B5
NSTN CH64 191 K3
Grasmere St EV L5 113 J1
Grassendale Esp ALL/GAR L19 153 G5
Grassendale La ALL/GAR L19 153 H4
Grassendale Rd ALL/GAR L19 153 H4
Grassington Crs WLTN L25 155 G1
Grassmoor Cl PS/BROM CH62 171 G5
Grass Wood Rd
GR/UP/WCH CH49 148 E1
Grasville Rd RF/TRAN CH42 131 H6
Gratrix Rd PS/BROM CH62 171 F5
Gratton Pl SKEL WN8 56 C5
Gravel La CHTN/BK PR9 24 E1
The Gravel KIRK/FR/WAR PR4 25 K3
Grave-yard La ORM L39 54 A6
Gray Av RNFD/HAY WA11 90 C5
Gray Gv HUY L36 136 C1
Graylag Cl RUNC WA7 187 J2
Graylands Pl ANF/KKDL L4 98 A4
Graylands Rd ANF/KKDL L4 98 A4
PS/BROM CH62 151 H5
Grayling Dr WD/CROXPK L12 99 H2
Grays Av RAIN/WH L35 118 B1
Graysons Rd RNFD/HAY WA11 75 G1
Grayson St CLVPS L1 8 D7
Grayston Av STHEL WA9 120 B1
Gray St BTL L20 81 H6
Greasby Dr GTS/LS CH66 195 H5
Greasby Rd GR/UP/WCH CH49 128 D6
WAL/EG CH44 111 G3
Great Ashfield WDN WA8 138 C6
Great Charlotte St CLVPS L1 * 9 F4
Great Crosshall St VAUX/LVPD L3 8 E2
Great Delph RNFD/HAY WA11 90 C4
Great George Pl CLVPS L1 132 D2
Great George Sq CLVPS L1 132 D2
Great George's Rd
CSBY/WL L22 80 E3
Great George St CLVPS L1 9 G7
Great Hey NTHTN L30 70 A4
Great Homer St EV L5 113 G2
Great Howard St EV L5 112 D2
VAUX/LVPD L3 8 B1
Great Mersey St EV L5 113 F1
Great Newton St VAUX/LVPD L3 9 J3
Great Orford St VAUX/LVPD L3 9 J5
Great Richmond St
VAUX/LVPD L3 113 G4
Great Riding RUNC WA7 178 B6
Greaves Cl CHTN/BK PR9 21 K6
Greaves Hall Av CHTN/BK PR9 21 K6
Greaves St TOX L8 * 132 E4
Grebe Av ECCL WA10 102 C5
Grecian St LITH L21 81 G3
Grecian Ter EV L5 113 H1
Gredington St TOX L8 133 F6
Greeba Av WARRS WA4 142 E6
Greek St RUNC WA7 10 C3
VAUX/LVPD L3 9 H3
Greenacre BRSC L40 54 E1
Greenacre Cl WLTN L25 155 F3
Greenacre Dr BEB CH63 170 D6
Greenacre Rd WLTN L25 155 F3
Greenacres FROD/HEL WA6 201 F3
Greenacres Cl CL/PREN CH43 129 K1
LEIGH WN7 93 J3
Greenall Av WARRW/BUR WA5 140 E5
Greenall's Av WARRS WA4 162 B2
Greenall St AIMK WN4 79 G4
ECCL WA10 12 B3
Green Bank BEB CH63 169 G3
Greenbank CSBY/WL L22 81 F3
ORM L39 53 G3
Greenbank Av GTS/LS CH66 195 F2
MGHL L31 62 A4
WAL/NB CH45 95 H6
Greenbank Ct AIG/SPK L17 133 K4
Greenbank Crs ECCL WA10 12 E6
Greenbank Dr AIG/SPK L17 133 K4
AIN/FAZ L10 84 A4
PEN/TH CH61 167 K2
STHP PR8 27 F5
Greenbank Gdns WARRS WA4 162 E1
Greenbank La AIG/SPK L17 133 K5
Greenbank Rd CALD/MH L18 134 A4
RF/TRAN CH42 131 F6
WARRS WA4 162 E1
WKBY CH48 127 G5
Greenbank St WARRS WA4 162 B1
Green Bridge Cl RUNC WA7 177 K3
Greenbridge Rd RUNC WA7 178 A3
Greenburn Av RNFD/HAY WA11 89 F2
Green Coppice RUNC WA7 178 B5
Green Ct GOL/RIS/CUL WA3 93 J2
Green Cft CSBY/BLUN L23 69 J4
Greencroft Rd WAL/EG CH44 111 J4
Greendale Rd PS/BROM CH62 151 F5
WLTN L25 135 G5
Green End La STHEL WA9 103 K5
Green End Pk WD/CROXPK L12 98 E6
Greene's Rd RAIN/WH L35 117 K5
Greenfield Dr HUY L36 136 C1
Greenfield Gdns CHNE CH2 198 C6
Greenfield Gv HUY L36 * 136 C1
Greenfield La FROD/HEL WA6 186 E6
HES CH60 167 G3
LITH L21 81 H2
Greenfield Rd
CLB/OSW/ST L13 114 E4
ECCL WA10 12 B1
GTS/LS CH66 194 E2
STHP PR8 29 F6
Greenfields Av
PS/BROM CH62 170 E6
WARRS WA4 162 C3
Greenfields Cl NEWLW WA12 106 C1
NSTN CH64 192 A4
WARR WA1 144 B2
Greenfields Crs AIMK WN4 79 G5
PS/BROM CH62 170 E6
Greenfields Cft NSTN CH64 191 K4
Greenfields Dr NSTN CH64 191 K5
Greenfield Vw
WGNW/BIL/OR WN5 77 G5
Greenfield Wy CALD/MH L18 153 K2
WAL/EG CH44 111 H3
Greenfinch Cl WD/CROXPK L12 99 K2
Greenfinch Gv HLWD L26 155 H2
Greenford Rd STHP PR8 33 J5
Greengables Cl TOX L8 133 F4
Green Gates HUY L36 116 E1
Greengates Crs NSTN CH64 191 K4
Greenham Av NWD/KWIPK L33 72 E3
Greenhaven Cl AIN/FAZ L10 83 K4
Greenheath Wy
MOR/LEA CH46 109 K4
Green Hey Dr NTHTN L30 81 K1
Greenhey Pl SKEL WN8 56 B5
Green Heys Dr MGHL L31 62 D5
Greenheys Gdns TOX L8 * 133 G3
Greenheys Rd PEN/TH CH61 147 K6
TOX L8 133 G3
WAL/EG CH44 111 H3
Greenhill Av CALD/MH L18 134 D4
Greenhill Cl CALD/MH L18 153 J1
Greenhill Crs
WGNW/BIL/OR WN5 77 J4
Greenhill Pl HUY L36 116 E6
Greenhill Rd CALD/MH L18 134 C6
WGNW/BIL/OR WN5 77 H4
Greenholme Cl NG/CROX L11 98 E2
Greenhouse Farm Rd
RUNC WA7 188 A1
Greenhow Av WKBY CH48 127 G6
Greenings La CHTN/BK PR9 30 B4
Green Jones Brow
WARRW/BUR WA5 121 K1
Greenlake Rd CALD/MH L18 153 J1
Greenlands HUY L36 116 E6
Greenland St TOX L8 132 C2
Green La BEB CH63 150 E6
BIRK CH41 131 H5
BRSC L40 39 F5
CALD/MH L18 134 C5
CHTN/BK PR9 25 G1
CLB/OSW/ST L13 114 D3
CSBY/BLUN L23 69 J3
CSBY/WL L22 80 D1
ECCL WA10 87 F5
EP CH65 6 D7
FMBY L37 41 F5
GOL/RIS/CUL WA3 93 H1
GTS/LS CH66 195 F5
LITH L21 81 H4
MGHL L31 61 J5
MOR/LEA CH46 110 B2
ORM L39 45 J5
RNFD/HAY WA11 75 H4
VAUX/LVPD L3 9 H5
WAL/NB CH45 110 D1
WARR WA1 143 K1
WARRN/WOL WA2 107 G6
WARRS WA4 162 E6
WARRW/BUR WA5 105 J6
WDN WA8 157 K2
Green Lane Av ORM L39 * 45 J5
Green Lane Cl
WARRN/WOL WA2 107 G6
Green La North CHLDW L16 134 D3
Green Lawn HUY L36 117 G3
RF/TRAN CH42 150 E2
Green Lawn Gv
RF/TRAN CH42 * 150 E2
Green Lawns Dr GTS/LS CH66 202 D3
Green Leach Av
RNFD/HAY WA11 88 E4
Green Leach Ct
RNFD/HAY WA11 89 F4
Green Leach La
RNFD/HAY WA11 88 E4
Greenlea Cl BEB CH63 150 E5
EP CH65 203 F1
Greenleaf St TOX L8 133 H2
Greenleas Cl WAL/NB CH45 110 D1
Greenleas Rd WAL/NB CH45 110 D1
Greenleigh Rd CALD/MH L18 153 J1
Green Link MGHL L31 61 K5
Greenloon's Dr FMBY L37 48 C2
Greenloon's Wk FMBY L37 48 C3
Green Mdw GOL/RIS/CUL WA3 93 F6
Green Mt GR/UP/WCH CH49 129 H4
Green Oaks Pth WDN WA8 19 H3
Green Oaks Wy WDN WA8 19 G3
Greenock Ms WDN WA8 138 D5
Greenock St VAUX/LVPD L3 8 A1
Greenodd Av WD/CROXPK L12 99 G4
Greenore Dr SPK/HALE L24 174 E3
Greenough Av RAIN/WH L35 118 E2
Greenough St WLTN L25 154 C1
Green Pk NTHTN L30 70 C4
Green Park Dr MGHL L31 61 K6
Green Rd PR/KW L34 117 J1
Greensbridge La HLWD L26 156 A2
Greenshank Cl NEWLW WA12 106 C1
Greenside NPK/KEN L6 9 K1
Greenside Av AIN/FAZ L10 83 G1
FROD/HEL WA6 201 G2
WAV L15 134 B2
Greenside Cl NWD/KWIPK L33 73 F3
Green's La MGHL L31 52 A4
Green St EV L5 112 E3
WARRW/BUR WA5 142 C4
The Green BEB CH63 182 D3
CLB/OSW/ST L13 115 G5
EP CH65 203 F1
NSTN CH64 191 J1
PR/KW L34 102 A6
PS/BROM CH62 151 K6
RUNC WA7 177 J4
WKBY CH48 146 E4
Greenville Cl BEB CH63 150 E6
Greenville Dr MGHL L31 62 A6
Greenville Rd BEB CH63 150 E6
NSTN CH64 182 A6
Green Wk STHP PR8 33 K4
Green Wy HUY L36 116 B3
Greenway AIMK WN4 79 F5
CSBY/BLUN L23 69 H4
GR/UP/WCH CH49 129 F5
NSTN CH64 181 G5
PEN/TH CH61 167 J1
PS/BROM CH62 171 F2
WARR WA1 143 J2
WARRS WA4 162 C4
WARRW/BUR WA5 141 F2
Greenway Av SKEL WN8 56 D6
Greenway Cl FROD/HEL WA6 199 J6
Green Way Cl HUY L36 116 B3
Greenway Cl SKEL WN8 56 A3
Greenway Rd RF/TRAN CH42 131 G6
RUNC WA7 10 C7
SPK/HALE L24 174 B2
WDN WA8 158 C1
The Greenway
WD/CROXPK L12 115 J3
Greenwell Rd
RNFD/HAY WA11 90 B5
Greenwich Av WDN WA8 139 J5
Greenwich Ct WLT/FAZ L9 82 E3
Greenwich Rd WLT/FAZ L9 82 E3
Greenwood Cl ORM L39 53 G4
PR/KW L34 118 A1
Greenwood Ct STHEL WA9 120 A3
Greenwood Crs
WARRN/WOL WA2 123 K5
Greenwood Dr NEWLW WA12 106 D3
RUNC WA7 178 E1
Greenwood La WAL/EG CH44 111 J2
Greenwood Rd CALD/MH L18 153 J2
GR/UP/WCH CH49 129 H6
HOY CH47 127 K1
LYMM WA13 165 F1
Greetby Hl ORM L39 46 A6
Greetby Pl SKEL WN8 56 C5
Greetham St CLVPS L1 8 E7
Gregory Cl CHLDW L16 134 E1
WARRW/BUR WA5 141 K2
Gregory La ORM L39 35 K6
Gregory Wy CHLDW L16 135 F1
Gregson Ct WAL/NB CH45 95 J5
Gregson Rd RAIN/WH L35 117 K2
WDN WA8 19 H2
Gregson's Av FMBY L37 40 E6
Gregson St NPK/KEN L6 113 H4
Grenfell Cl NSTN CH64 181 H6
Grenfell Pk NSTN CH64 181 H6
Grenfell Rd CLB/OSW/ST L13 98 C5
Grenfell St WDN WA8 18 E4
Grennan Ct WAL/NB CH45 * 95 H5
The Grennan WAL/NB CH45 * 95 H5
Grenville Crs BEB CH63 170 E6
Grenville Dr PEN/TH CH61 167 J2
Grenville Rd RF/TRAN CH42 131 J6
Grenville St South CLVPS L1 9 F7
Grenville Wy RF/TRAN CH42 131 J6
Gresford Av AIG/SPK L17 133 J3
CL/PREN CH43 149 K1
WKBY CH48 127 H6
Gresford Cl RAIN/WH L35 118 B4
WARRW/BUR WA5 122 D5
Gresham St EHL/KEN L7 114 B5
Gresley Cl EHL/KEN L7 * 114 A6
Gressingham Rd
CALD/MH L18 134 D6
Gretton Rd DV/KA/FCH L14 116 B2
Greyfriars AIMK WN4 78 E6
Greyfriars Cl
WARRN/WOL WA2 124 D4
Greyfriars Rd STHP PR8 33 H3
Greyhound Farm Rd
SPK/HALE L24 173 H1
Greymist Av WARR WA1 144 B2
Grey Rd AIMK WN4 79 F5
WLT/FAZ L9 97 H1
Greys Ct WARR WA1 * 124 E6
Greystoke Cl
GR/UP/WCH CH49 129 G5
Greystokes ORM L39 53 H3
Greystone Crs DV/KA/FCH L14 115 J4
Greystone Pl AIN/FAZ L10 83 J4
Greystone Rd AIN/FAZ L10 83 H4
DV/KA/FCH L14 115 J5
WARRW/BUR WA5 141 G5
Greystones GTS/LS CH66 195 G5
Grey St TOX L8 132 E3
WARR WA1 17 F3
Gribble Rd AIN/FAZ L10 83 K4
Grice St WARRS WA4 162 B2
Grierson St TOX L8 133 G2
Grieve Rd AIN/FAZ L10 83 K4
Griffin Av MOR/LEA CH46 129 F1
Griffin Cl ECCL WA10 102 B1
NG/CROX L11 99 G1
WARRW/BUR WA5 121 J1
Griffin Ms WDN WA8 139 G6
Griffin St STHEL WA9 104 C6
Griffith Av GOL/RIS/CUL WA3 125 G2
Griffiths Cl GR/UP/WCH CH49 128 D6
Griffiths Dr CHTN/BK PR9 23 H5
Griffith's Rd HUY L36 116 E5
Griffiths St CLVPS L1 * 9 G7
WARRS WA4 143 J5
Grimley Av BTL L20 4 A2
Grimrod Pl SKEL WN8 56 C6
Grimshaw Ct GOL/RIS/CUL WA3 92 B2
Grimshaw La ORM L39 45 J5
Grimshaw Rd SKEL WN8 56 D5
Grimshaw St BTL L20 4 C6
GOL/RIS/CUL WA3 92 B2
STHEL WA9 120 A1
Grindley Gdns EP CH65 203 G1
Grinfield St EHL/KEN L7 113 J6
Grinshill Cl TOX L8 133 F3
Grinstead Cl STHP PR8 27 G6
Grinton Crs HUY L36 116 D5
Grisedale Av
WARRN/WOL WA2 123 H4
Grisedale Cl FMBY L37 48 E2
RUNC WA7 187 H2
Grisedale Rd PS/BROM CH62 171 G5
Grizedale WDN WA8 157 G1
Grizedale Av
RNFD/HAY WA11 88 E3
Grizedale Rd EV L5 113 H1
Groarke Dr
WARRW/BUR WA5 140 E4
Groes Rd ALL/GAR L19 153 J4
Grogan Sq BTL L20 82 A5
Gronow Pl BTL L20 * 82 B5
Grosmont Rd KKBY L32 84 E3
Grosvenor Av
CSBY/BLUN L23 81 F1
GOL/RIS/CUL WA3 92 E3
WARR WA1 143 H2
WKBY CH48 146 C1
Grosvenor Cl NTHTN L30 70 C6
STHP PR8 27 F4
WARRW/BUR WA5 141 K4
Grosvenor Ct CL/PREN CH43 130 E4
WAV L15 * 134 D2
Grosvenor Dr WAL/NB CH45 95 H5
Grosvenor Gdns
NEWLW WA12 106 B3
STHP PR8 27 G4
Grosvenor Gra WARR WA1 124 D6
Grosvenor Pl CL/PREN CH43 130 D4
STHP PR8 27 G4

Grosvenor Rd ALL/GAR L19 153 H5
CL/PREN CH43 130 D3
ECCL WA10 102 E3
HOY CH47 127 G3
MGHL L31 71 F3
PR/KW L34 117 K1
RNFD/HAY WA11 90 A5
STHP PR8 27 F3
WAL/NB CH45 95 H5
WAV L15 133 J2
WDN WA8 139 G5
Grosvenor St RUNC WA7 11 G3
WAL/EG CH44 111 H2
Grosvenor Ter TOX L8 133 F5
Grounds St WARRN/WOL WA2 16 E1
Grove Av HES CH60 167 K4
LYMM WA13 145 H6
Grovedale Dr MOR/LEA CH46 110 A6
Grovedale Rd CALD/MH L18 134 A4
Grovehurst Av DV/KA/FCH L14 115 K3
Groveland Av HOY CH47 127 G2
WAL/NB CH45 110 D1
Groveland Rd WAL/NB CH45 110 D1
Grovelands EHL/KEN L7 * 133 F1
Grove Md MGHL L31 62 D6
Grove Pk CHTN/BK PR9 23 H4
ORM L39 45 K4
TOX L8 133 H3
Grove Park Av WD/CROXPK L12 99 F5
Grove Pl ANF/KKDL L4 97 G6
HOY CH47 127 G2
Grove Ri LYMM WA13 145 K6
Grove Rd CH/BCN CH1 202 C6
HOY CH47 127 G2
NPK/KEN L6 114 B4
RF/TRAN CH42 150 E1
SKEL WN8 57 K5
WAL/NB CH45 110 E1
Grove Side EHL/KEN L7 133 F1
Groveside WKBY CH48 146 B1
Grove Sq PS/BROM CH62 151 F4
The Groves EHL/KEN L7 * 133 F1
GTS/LS CH66 202 E3
KKBY L32 84 D4
Grove St AIMK WN4 79 F5
BTL L20 4 A2
ECCL WA10 13 F6
EHL/KEN L7 133 F1
PS/BROM CH62 151 G4
RUNC WA7 10 C3
STHP PR8 27 H2
TOX L8 133 F2
WARRS WA4 17 G7
WAV L15 134 A1
Grove Ter FROD/HEL WA6 199 K5
HOY CH47 127 G2
STHP PR8 27 H2
The Grove BEB CH63 151 F6
CL/PREN CH43 130 E6
CLB/OSW/ST L13 * 114 D2
ECCL WA10 87 K6
GOL/RIS/CUL WA3 92 E2
LYMM WA13 145 K6
ORM L39 53 G6
STBRV L28 116 C1
WAL/EG CH44 111 J4
WARRW/BUR WA5 141 G5
Grove Wy EHL/KEN L7 133 F1
Grovewood STHP PR8 27 F3
Grovewood Ct CL/PREN CH43 130 E6
Grovewood Gdns
RAIN/WH L35 118 A4
Grundy Cl STHP PR8 28 B2
WDN WA8 138 E6
Grundy St EV L5 112 D1
GOL/RIS/CUL WA3 92 B4
Guardian St
WARRW/BUR WA5 142 B3
Guelph St EHL/KEN L7 113 J5
Guernsey Cl WARRS WA4 162 C3
Guernsey Dr EP CH65 203 G1
Guernsey Rd CLB/OSW/ST L13 114 D3
WDN WA8 139 K6
Guest St WDN WA8 18 C6
Guffitts Cl HOY CH47 108 C6
Guffitt's Rake HOY CH47 108 C6
Guildford Av NTHTN L30 82 C2
Guildford Cl WARRN/WOL WA2 124 C6
Guildford Rd STHP PR8 34 C1
Guildford St WAL/EG CH44 111 K3
Guildhall Rd WLT/FAZ L9 82 D5
Guild Hey PR/KW L34 100 D1
Guillemot Wy HLWD L26 155 H2
Guilsted Rd NG/CROX L11 98 E3
Guinea Hall Cl CHTN/BK PR9 21 K6
Guinea Hall La CHTN/BK PR9 21 K6
Guion Rd LITH L21 81 J4
Guion St NPK/KEN L6 113 K3
Gulls Wy HES CH60 167 H5
Gunn Gv NSTN CH64 192 A1
Gunning Av ECCL WA10 87 J6
Gunning Cl ECCL WA10 87 J6
Gurnall St ANF/KKDL L4 97 H6
Gutticar Rd WDN WA8 157 G3
Guy Cl BIRK CH41 131 H5
Gwendoline Cl PEN/TH CH61 148 D6
Gwendoline St TOX L8 132 E3
Gwenfron Rd NPK/KEN L6 113 K4
Gwent Cl NPK/KEN L6 113 K2
Gwent St TOX L8 133 F3
Gwladys St ANF/KKDL L4 97 H4
Gwydir St TOX L8 133 F4
Gwydrin Rd CALD/MH L18 134 D4

H

The Hachings LYMM WA13 165 F1
Hackett Av BTL L20 82 A5
Hackins Hey CLVP L2 8 C3
Hackthorpe St EV L5 97 G6
Hadassah Gv AIG/SPK L17 133 H5
Hadden Cl RAIN/WH L35 * 118 C3
Haddock St BTL L20 96 D4
Haddon Av WLT/FAZ L9 82 C5
Haddon Dr PEN/TH CH61 167 K1
WDN WA8 138 B6
Haddon La NSTN CH64 192 C5
Haddon Rd GOL/RIS/CUL WA3 92 E1
RF/TRAN CH42 151 F1
Haddon Wk WD/CROXPK L12 99 J2
Hadfield Av HOY CH47 127 G2
Hadfield Cl WDN WA8 159 F1
Hadfield Gv WLTN L25 135 K6
Hadleigh Cl WARRW/BUR WA5 140 E4
Hadleigh Rd KKBY L32 84 E2
Hadley Av PS/BROM CH62 170 E4
Hadlow Gdns RF/TRAN CH42 131 H6
Hadlow La NSTN CH64 193 G2
Hadlow Rd NSTN CH64 193 G3
Hadstock Av FMBY L37 48 D4
Haggerston Rd ANF/KKDL L4 97 J3
Hague Bush Cl
GOL/RIS/CUL WA3 * 93 F2
Hahnemann Rd ANF/KKDL L4 5 K7
Haig Av MOR/LEA CH46 129 F1
STHP PR8 28 B2
WARRW/BUR WA5 141 H5
Haigh Crs MGHL L31 62 A3
Haigh Rd CSBY/WL L22 81 F2
Haigh St VAUX/LVPD L3 113 H4
Haig Rd WDN WA8 18 C2
Haileybury Av AIN/FAZ L10 83 G1
Haileybury Rd WLTN L25 154 E3
Hailsham Rd ALL/GAR L19 153 F3
Halby Rd WLT/FAZ L9 82 E5
Halcombe Rd
WD/CROXPK L12 99 H5
Halcyon Rd BIRK CH41 131 F5
Haldane Av BIRK CH41 130 C2
Haldane Rd ANF/KKDL L4 97 J3
Hale Bank Rd WDN WA8 156 D6
Hale Dr SPK/HALE L24 174 A3
Halefield St ECCL WA10 12 E3
Hale Gate Rd WDN WA8 175 G2
Hale Gv AIMK WN4 78 E4
WARRW/BUR WA5 141 H3
Hale Rd ANF/KKDL L4 97 G4
SPK/HALE L24 173 H2
WAL/NB CH45 111 J1
WDN WA8 157 G5
Hale St CLVP L2 8 D3
WARRN/WOL WA2 16 D1
Hale Vw RUNC WA7 176 B5
Hale View Rd FROD/HEL WA6 199 K5
HUY L36 117 G5
Halewood Av
GOL/RIS/CUL WA3 92 A2
Halewood Cl WLTN L25 135 J5
Halewood Dr WLTN L25 154 E1
Halewood Pl WLTN L25 135 K6
Halewood Rd WLTN L25 135 J6
Halewood Wy WLTN L25 155 F1
Haley Rd North
WARRW/BUR WA5 121 J1
Haley Rd South
WARRW/BUR WA5 121 J1
Halfacre La WARRS WA4 144 D6
Half Crown St EV L5 112 E1
Halfpenny Cl ALL/GAR L19 153 J4
Halidon Ct BTL L20 4 B2
Halifax Cl WARRN/WOL WA2 123 K5
Halifax Crs CSBY/BLUN L23 69 J3
Halifax Rd STHP PR8 33 J4
Halkirk Rd CALD/MH L18 153 K3
Halkyn Av AIG/SPK L17 133 J3
Halkyn Dr EV L5 113 J2
Hallam Wk EHL/KEN L7 114 A6
Hallastone Rd FROD/HEL WA6 199 J5
Hall Av WDN WA8 157 F2
Halla-way WARRS WA4 143 H6
Hallbridge Gdns SKEL WN8 57 K5
Hall Brow Cl ORM L39 54 B1
Hallcroft SKEL WN8 56 E3
Hallcroft Pl WARRS WA4 163 F1
Hall Dr GR/UP/WCH CH49 128 D6
KKBY L32 84 D1
WARRS WA4 162 C5
Hallfield Dr CHNE CH2 198 C6
Hallfield Pk GTS/LS CH66 195 G5
Hallfields Rd
WARRN/WOL WA2 143 G1
Hall Gn SKEL WN8 57 K6
Hall Green Cl SKEL WN8 57 K6
Halliday Cl GOL/RIS/CUL WA3 125 H4
Hall La BRSC L40 47 G4
EHL/KEN L7 113 J5
HTWN L38 60 B3
HUY L36 117 G5
KKBY L32 84 D1
MGHL L31 71 G1
MGHL L31 52 A6
NWD/KWIPK L33 72 E2
ORM L39 64 E3
PR/KW L34 117 K2
RAIN/WH L35 118 E6
STHEL WA9 120 D4
WARRS WA4 179 J3
WARRS WA4 163 G3
WARRW/BUR WA5 106 B5
WDN WA8 138 B2
WLT/FAZ L9 82 E4
Hallmoor Cl ORM L39 53 H3
Hall Nook WARRW/BUR WA5 141 G5
Hallows Av WARRN/WOL WA2 143 G1
Hall Rd BRSC L40 36 E3
RNFD/HAY WA11 90 D4
WARR WA1 144 B2
Hall Rd East CSBY/BLUN L23 68 C3
Hall Rd West CSBY/BLUN L23 68 B3
Hallsands Rd KKBY L32 84 D3
Hallside Cl ALL/GAR L19 153 H3
Hall St CHTN/BK PR9 15 H5
ECCL WA10 13 H5
STHEL WA9 120 C4
WARR WA1 16 E5
WGNE/HIN WN2 79 K2
Hall Ter WARRW/BUR WA5 141 F2
Halltine Cl CSBY/BLUN L23 68 B4
Hallville Rd CALD/MH L18 134 B4
Hall Wood Av RNFD/HAY WA11 90 E3
Hallwood Cl RUNC WA7 186 E1
Hallwood Dr GTS/LS CH66 193 K5
Hallwood Link Rd RUNC WA7 187 H1
Hallwood Park Av RUNC WA7 187 H1
Hallworthy Cl LEIGH WN7 93 J2
Halsall Av WARRN/WOL WA2 143 G1
Halsall Buildings CHTN/BK PR9 15 H3
Halsall Cl CSBY/BLUN L23 69 F4
RUNC WA7 188 B2
Halsall Gn BEB CH63 170 D4
Halsall Hall Dr ORM L39 43 K2
Halsall La FMBY L37 49 F1
ORM L39 44 B5
Halsall Manor Ct ORM L39 43 K2
Halsall Rd BTL L20 81 K6
ORM L39 44 A1
STHP PR8 34 C1
Halsalls Cottages WDN WA8 * 156 D6
Halsall St PR/KW L34 101 K6
Halsbury Rd NPK/KEN L6 114 A4
WAL/NB CH45 111 H1
Halsey Av WD/CROXPK L12 98 D6
Halsey Crs WD/CROXPK L12 98 D6
Halsnead Av RAIN/WH L35 117 J6
Halstead Rd WAL/EG CH44 111 J4
WLT/FAZ L9 82 C5
Halton Brook Av RUNC WA7 11 K6
Halton Brow RUNC WA7 177 H4
Halton Cha BRSC L40 54 E1
Halton Ct RUNC WA7 11 K5
Halton Crs GR/UP/WCH CH49 128 C6
GTS/LS CH66 202 D1
Halton Hey RAIN/WH L35 117 K6
Halton Link Rd RUNC WA7 177 H5
Halton Lodge Av RUNC WA7 177 G5
Halton Rd GTS/LS CH66 202 C2
MGHL L31 62 B4
RUNC WA7 11 G4
WAL/NB CH45 111 G1
WARRW/BUR WA5 141 G3
Halton Station Rd RUNC WA7 187 J4
Halton St RNFD/HAY WA11 * 90 D5
Halton View Rd WDN WA8 19 H1
Halton Wy GTS/LS CH66 202 C2
Halton Wd KKBY L32 72 A6
Halville Rd WAL/EG CH44 111 J4
Hambledon Cl GTS/LS CH66 194 D3
Hambledon Dr
GR/UP/WCH CH49 128 D5
Hamble Dr WARRW/BUR WA5 141 G6
Hambleton Cl NG/CROX L11 99 F1
WDN WA8 138 B6
Hamblett Crs RNFD/HAY WA11 88 E5
Hamer St ECCL WA10 13 F4
Hamil Cl HOY CH47 108 C6
Hamilton Cl NSTN CH64 181 G5
Hamilton La BIRK CH41 3 G3
Hamilton Rd AIMK WN4 78 B5
ECCL WA10 87 J5
EV L5 113 H2
WAL/NB CH45 95 G5
Hamilton Sq BIRK CH41 3 G3
Hamilton St BIRK CH41 3 G5
Hamlet Rd WAL/NB CH45 111 F1
Hamlin Cl RUNC WA7 186 D1
Hammersley Av STHEL WA9 120 A4
Hammersley St STHEL WA9 * 120 A4
Hammill Av ECCL WA10 88 B5
Hammill St ECCL WA10 12 B1
Hammond Rd NWD/KWIPK L33 73 H6
Hammond St STHEL WA9 104 B3
Hamnett Ct GOL/RIS/CUL WA3 125 G4
Hamnett Rd PR/KW L34 102 A6
Hampden Gv RF/TRAN CH42 131 H5
Hampden Rd RF/TRAN CH42 * 131 G5
Hampden St ANF/KKDL L4 97 H3
Hampshire Av NTHTN L30 69 K6
Hampshire Gdns ECCL WA10 103 H3
Hampson Cl AIMK WN4 91 G1
Hampson St NPK/KEN L6 114 A2
Hampstead Rd NPK/KEN L6 114 B3
WAL/EG CH44 111 J4
Hampton Cha CL/PREN CH43 130 A6
Hampton Cl NSTN CH64 191 K3
WDN WA8 139 K6
Hampton Court Rd
WD/CROXPK L12 115 G2
Hampton Court Wy WDN WA8 139 J5
Hampton Crs NSTN CH64 191 K4
Hampton Dr
WARRW/BUR WA5 141 K5
WDN WA8 138 B4
Hampton Gdns EP CH65 195 K4
Hampton Pl RNFD/HAY WA11 88 E5
Hampton Rd FMBY L37 48 E4
STHP PR8 27 J3
Hampton St TOX L8 132 E2
Hamsterley Cl
GOL/RIS/CUL WA3 125 K1
Hanbury Rd ANF/KKDL L4 98 B5
Handa Dr EP CH65 203 G3
Handel Ct TOX L8 * 133 G3
Handel Rd NTHLY L27 135 K3
Handfield Pl EV L5 113 J2
Handfield Rd CSBY/WL L22 80 E2
Handfield St EV L5 113 J2
Handford Av PS/BROM CH62 184 C2
Handforth Cl WARRS WA4 144 B5
Handforth La RUNC WA7 187 G1
Handley Ct ALL/GAR L19 153 G3
Handley Dr WARRN/WOL WA2 124 A5
Hands St LITH L21 81 J5
Hanford Av WLT/FAZ L9 82 C5
Hankey Dr BTL L20 82 B6
Hankey St RUNC WA7 10 C4
Hankin St EV L5 113 F2
Hanley Cl WDN WA8 157 H2
Hanley Rd WDN WA8 157 H2
Hanlon Av BTL L20 82 A5
Hanmer Rd KKBY L32 84 A1
Hannah Cl PEN/TH CH61 167 J2
Hannan Rd NPK/KEN L6 114 A4
Hanns Hall Rd NSTN CH64 192 D1
Hanover Cl CL/PREN CH43 130 C3
Hanover St CLVPS L1 8 E5
WARR WA1 16 B6
Hansard Ct STHEL WA9 103 F6
Hansby Cl SKEL WN8 57 G5
Hansby Dr SPK/HALE L24 155 F6
Hanson Pk CL/PREN CH43 130 B4
Hanson Rd WLT/FAZ L9 83 F6
Hans Rd ANF/KKDL L4 97 J4
Hants La ORM L39 45 J5
Hanwell St NPK/KEN L6 113 K1
Hanworth Cl WD/CROXPK L12 99 H2
Hapsford Cl GOL/RIS/CUL WA3 124 E3
Hapsford La CHNE CH2 198 E5
Hapsford Rd LITH L21 81 J5
Hapton St EV L5 113 G1
Harbern Cl WD/CROXPK L12 115 H1
Harbord Rd CSBY/WL L22 80 D2
Harbord St EHL/KEN L7 113 K6
WARR WA1 17 G6
Harborne Dr BEB CH63 170 B3
Harbury Av STHP PR8 33 G5
Harcourt Av WAL/EG CH44 112 A4
Harcourt Cl
GOL/RIS/CUL WA3 125 G4
Harcourt St ANF/KKDL L4 97 F6
BIRK CH41 2 B2
Hardacre St ORM L39 45 K5
Hardie Av MOR/LEA CH46 109 G6
Hardie Cl STHEL WA9 119 J4
Hardie Rd HUY L36 117 G4
Harding Av BEB CH63 170 B1
WARRN/WOL WA2 123 K6
Harding Cl EV L5 113 J2
Hardinge Rd ALL/GAR L19 153 K3
Harding Rd BRSC L40 38 D5
Harding St TOX L8 133 G1
Hardknott Rd PS/BROM CH62 171 G4
Hard La ECCL WA10 88 A5
Hardman St CLVPS L1 9 H6
Hardshaw St ECCL WA10 13 G5
Hardwick Gra WARR WA1 125 F6
Hardwick Rd AIMK WN4 79 F4
RUNC WA7 11 K3
Hardy Cl GTS/LS CH66 195 J6
Hardy Rd LYMM WA13 164 D1
Hardy St ALL/GAR L19 172 C1
CLVPS L1 132 C2
WARRN/WOL WA2 16 E2
Harebell Cl FMBY L37 49 F4
WDN WA8 138 D5
Harebell St EV L5 97 F6
Hare Cft STBRV L28 99 K5
Harefield Gn SPK/HALE L24 173 J2
Harefield Rd SPK/HALE L24 173 J2
Haresfinch Cl HLWD L26 155 K2
Haresfinch Rd
RNFD/HAY WA11 13 J1
Haresfinch Vw
RNFD/HAY WA11 88 E5
Hare's La FROD/HEL WA6 200 B1
STHP PR8 29 G6
Harewell Rd NG/CROX L11 98 E4
Harewood Av GTS/LS CH66 195 F5
STHP PR8 33 J3
Harewood Cl HUY L36 116 E4
Harewood Rd WAL/NB CH45 95 G6
Harewood St NPK/KEN L6 * 113 J3
Harfield Gdns GTS/LS CH66 195 F4
Harford Cl WARRW/BUR WA5 141 G5
Hargate Rd NWD/KWIPK L33 84 E1
Hargrave Av CL/PREN CH43 130 B6
Hargrave Cl CL/PREN CH43 130 B6
Hargrave Dr GTS/LS CH66 195 H4
Hargrave La BEB CH63 183 G2
Hargreaves Ct WDN WA8 19 J1
Hargreaves Rd AIG/SPK L17 133 H6
Hargreaves St STHEL WA9 104 C1
STHP PR8 15 H6
Harington Cl FMBY L37 48 D2
Harington Gn FMBY L37 48 D2
Harington Rd FMBY L37 48 C1
Harker St VAUX/LVPD L3 9 G1
Harke St EHL/KEN L7 133 G1
Harland Dr AIMK WN4 79 H6
Harland Gn SPK/HALE L24 174 A2
Harland Rd RF/TRAN CH42 131 G5
Harlech Cl RUNC WA7 177 J3
WARRW/BUR WA5 122 E5
Harlech Rd CSBY/BLUN L23 68 D6
Harlech St AIMK WN4 78 E4
ANF/KKDL L4 97 G4
WAL/EG CH44 112 A6
Harlech Wy EP CH65 196 C6
Harleston Rd NWD/KWIPK L33 73 F6
Harley Av BEB CH63 150 B3
Harley St WLT/FAZ L9 82 D5
Harlian Av MOR/LEA CH46 128 E2
Harlow Cl STHEL WA9 103 H6
WARRS WA4 144 B6
Harlow St TOX L8 132 D5
Harlyn Cl HLWD L26 155 H5
Harlyn Gdns
WARRW/BUR WA5 140 E6
Harmony Wy
CLB/OSW/ST L13 114 E6
The Harn GTS/LS CH66 195 F6
Harold Av AIMK WN4 79 F4
Haroldene Gv PR/KW L34 117 F2
Harold Rd RNFD/HAY WA11 90 E4
Harper Cl GTS/LS CH66 195 G5
Harper Rd WLT/FAZ L9 97 J1
Harpers Pond La WAV L15 134 B1
Harpers Rd WARRN/WOL WA2 124 C6
Harp's Cft NTHTN L30 69 K6
Harptree Cl RAIN/WH L35 118 A4
Harradon Rd WLT/FAZ L9 82 E4
Harridge La ORM L39 44 D3
Harrier Dr HLWD L26 155 H2
Harrier Rd WARRN/WOL WA2 124 B5
Harringay Av CALD/MH L18 134 A4
Harrington Av HOY CH47 127 H2
Harrington Rd CSBY/BLUN L23 68 E5
LITH L21 82 A2
VAUX/LVPD L3 132 D5
Harrington St CLVP L2 8 D4
Harris Cl BEB CH63 170 B3
Harris Dr BTL L20 82 A4
Harris Gdns STHEL WA9 103 K4
Harrismith Rd AIN/FAZ L10 83 J4
Harrison Cl WARR WA1 17 G2
Harrison Dr BTL L20 5 J4
RNFD/HAY WA11 89 K5
RNFD/HAY WA11 75 G2
WAL/NB CH45 94 D5
Harrison Hey HUY L36 116 D6
Harrison St WDN WA8 157 G5
Harrisons Yd
PS/BROM CH62 * 184 C1
Harrison Wy NEWLW WA12 106 C1
VAUX/LVPD L3 132 D5
Harris St ECCL WA10 12 C3
WDN WA8 19 H1
Harrocks Cl NTHTN L30 70 A4
Harrock Wood Cl
PEN/TH CH61 148 B5
Harrod Dr STHP PR8 27 F4
Harrogate Cl PS/BROM CH62 184 A3
WARRW/BUR WA5 122 A6
Harrogate Dr EV L5 113 H2
Harrogate Rd PS/BROM CH62 184 A3
RF/TRAN CH42 151 F3
Harrogate Wy CHTN/BK PR9 21 F5
Harron Cl KKBY L32 84 B1
Harrop Rd RUNC WA7 11 F7
Harrops Cft NTHTN L30 70 B4
Harrowby Cl TOX L8 133 F2
Harrowby Rd LITH L21 81 G4
RF/TRAN CH42 131 F5
WAL/EG CH44 112 A3
Harrowby Rd South
RF/TRAN CH42 131 F5
Harrowby St TOX L8 * 133 F2
Harrow Cl NTHTN L30 70 C6
WAL/EG CH44 111 F2
WARRS WA4 162 D5
Harrow Dr AIN/FAZ L10 83 G1
RUNC WA7 177 H3
Harrow Gv PS/BROM CH62 171 G5
Harrow Rd ANF/KKDL L4 113 K1
EP CH65 7 F7
WAL/EG CH44 111 F2
Harsnips SKEL WN8 56 E3
Hartdale Rd CALD/MH L18 134 B5
CSBY/BLUN L23 69 H3
Hartford Cl CL/PREN CH43 130 C6
Hartford Dr EP CH65 195 J5
Harthill Av CALD/MH L18 134 C5
Harthill Rd CALD/MH L18 134 D6
Hartington Av BIRK CH41 2 A2
Hartington Rd ALL/GAR L19 153 K5
ECCL WA10 87 K6
TOX L8 133 H3
WAL/EG CH44 111 H3
WD/CROXPK L12 115 G1
Hartismere Rd WAL/EG CH44 111 K4
Hartland Av CHTN/BK PR9 20 E6
Hartland Cl WDN WA8 139 F4
Hartland Gdns STHEL WA9 119 F1
Hartland Rd NG/CROX L11 98 C3
Hartley Av WLT/FAZ L9 82 E6
Hartley Cl ANF/KKDL L4 97 H6
Hartley Crs STHP PR8 27 G5
Hartley Gv ECCL WA10 102 E5
Hartley Quay VAUX/LVPD L3 8 B6
Hartley Rd STHP PR8 27 G5
Hartleys Village WLT/FAZ L9 82 E6
Hartnup St EV L5 113 J1
Harton Cl WDN WA8 138 D6
Hartopp Rd WLTN L25 135 H3
Hartsbourne Av WLTN L25 135 G2
Hartsbourne Cl WLTN L25 135 G2
Hartsbourne Wk WLTN L25 135 H2
Hartshead SKEL WN8 56 E3
Hart's La SKEL WN8 57 H5
Hart St STHP PR8 15 K6
VAUX/LVPD L3 9 H3
Hart Street Br STHP PR8 15 K6
Hartswell Cl GOL/RIS/CUL WA3 92 B2
Hartwell St LITH L21 81 J5
Hartwood Cl KKBY L32 84 E4
Hartwood Rd CHTN/BK PR9 15 K3
KKBY L32 84 E4
Hartwood Sq KKBY L32 * 84 E4
Harty Rd RNFD/HAY WA11 89 K6
Harvard Cl RUNC WA7 178 C3
Harvard Ct WARRN/WOL WA2 123 G4
Harvard Gv PR/KW L34 101 K6
Harvester Wy
GR/UP/WCH CH49 * 128 D5
NTHTN L30 70 D5
Harvest La MOR/LEA CH46 109 H6
Harvest Wy STHEL WA9 120 A3
Harvey Av GR/UP/WCH CH49 128 E6
NEWLW WA12 105 K2
Harvey Ct LEIGH WN7 93 J2
WARRN/WOL WA2 123 H4
Harvey La GOL/RIS/CUL WA3 92 A2
Harvey Rd WAL/NB CH45 111 G1
Harvington Dr STHP PR8 33 G4
Harwich Gv CHLDW L16 135 G1
Harwood Gdns WARRS WA4 163 F1
Harwood Rd ALL/GAR L19 154 A5
Haryngton Av
WARRW/BUR WA5 142 C2
Haselbeech Cl NG/CROX L11 98 D2
Haselbeech Crs NG/CROX L11 98 D2
Haseldine St AIMK WN4 78 E3
Hasfield Rd NG/CROX L11 99 F3
Haslam Dr ORM L39 45 H4
Haslemere RAIN/WH L35 118 B4
Haslemere Dr
WARRW/BUR WA5 140 E5
Haslemere Rd WLTN L25 135 H3
Haslemere Wy WLTN L25 135 J3
Haslingden Cl
CLB/OSW/ST L13 115 F5
Haslington Gv HLWD L26 155 K5
Hassal Rd RF/TRAN CH42 151 F3
Hastie Cl NTHLY L27 136 B3
Hastings Av WARRN/WOL WA2 123 H3
Hastings Dr HUY L36 136 D1
Hastings Rd CSBY/WL L22 80 C1
STHP PR8 27 F6
Haswell Dr STBRV L28 100 B5
Hatchmere Cl CL/PREN CH43 130 C6
WARRW/BUR WA5 142 B4
Hatfield Cl STHEL WA9 103 H6
WD/CROXPK L12 99 K2
Hatfield Gdns HUY L36 117 F6
Hatfield Rd BTL L20 5 J5
STHP PR8 33 J3
Hathaway MGHL L31 70 E2
Hathaway Cl WLTN L25 135 H3
Hathaway Rd WLTN L25 135 H3
Hatherley Av CSBY/BLUN L23 81 F1
Hatherley Cl TOX L8 133 F2
Hatherley St TOX L8 133 F3
WAL/EG CH44 112 A5
Hathersage Rd HUY L36 116 E2
Hatley La FROD/HEL WA6 200 C2
Hatters Rw WARR WA1 * 16 D4
Hatton Av PS/BROM CH62 184 B4
Hatton Cl HES CH60 167 H4

Hatton Gdn VAUX/LVPD L3 8 D2
Hatton Hill Rd LITH L21 81 H3
Hattons La CHLDW L16 134 D3
Hatton Station Rd RUNC WA7 187 J3
Hauxwell Gv RNFD/HAY WA11 89 F5
Havannah La STHEL WA9 105 F2
Havelock Cl ECCL WA10 12 D5
Haven Brow ORM L39 53 G5
Haven Rd AIN/FAZ L10 83 J3
Havergal St RUNC WA7 10 C6
Haverstock Rd NPK/KEN L6 114 B4
Haverton Wk WD/CROXPK L12 99 J2
Havisham Cl
GOL/RIS/CUL WA3 125 F2
Hawarde Cl NEWLW WA12 106 A1
Hawarden Av AIG/SPK L17 133 J3
CL/PREN CH43 2 B5
WAL/EG CH44 111 J3
Hawarden Gdns EP CH65 196 C6
Hawarden Gv LITH L21 81 H5
Hawdon Ct EHL/KEN L7 133 H1
Hawes Av RNFD/HAY WA11 89 F3
Hawes Crs AIMK WN4 79 G4
Hawesside St CHTN/BK PR9 15 F5
Haweswater Av
RNFD/HAY WA11 89 K5
Haweswater Cl
NWD/KWIPK L33 72 C4
RUNC WA7 187 K2
Haweswater Gv MGHL L31 62 D5
Hawgreen Rd KKBY L32 84 A2
Hawick Cl GTS/LS CH66 194 D4
NWD/KWIPK L33 72 C3
Hawke Gn RAIN/WH L35 136 D2
Hawke St VAUX/LVPD L3 9 G4
Hawkesworth St
ANF/KKDL L4 113 J1
Hawkhurst Cl TOX L8 132 E5
Hawkins Rd NSTN CH64 182 A6
Hawkins St NPK/KEN L6 113 K4
Hawksclough SKEL WN8 56 E3
Hawks Ct RUNC WA7 187 H1
Hawkshaw Cl
GOL/RIS/CUL WA3 124 E3
Hawkshead Av
WD/CROXPK L12 99 G4
Hawkshead Cl MGHL L31 62 C5
RUNC WA7 * 187 K2
Hawkshead Dr LITH L21 82 A3
Hawkshead Rd
PS/BROM CH62 171 G4
WARRW/BUR WA5 121 J1
Hawkshead St CHTN/BK PR9 15 H3
Hawksmoor Cl AIN/FAZ L10 83 K4
Hawksmoor Rd AIN/FAZ L10 83 K5
Hawksmore Cl
GR/UP/WCH CH49 128 E3
Hawkstone Gv
FROD/HEL WA6 199 K5
Hawkstone St TOX L8 133 F4
Hawkstone Wk TOX L8 * 133 F5
Hawks Wy HES CH60 167 J5
Hawksworth Cl FMBY L37 41 G5
Hawksworth Dr FMBY L37 41 G5
Hawley's La WARRN/WOL WA2 123 G6
Haworth Dr BTL L20 82 A4
Hawthorn Av AIMK WN4 78 B4
BRSC L40 39 F5
NEWLW WA12 106 C2
RUNC WA7 10 E6
WDN WA8 * 158 C1
Hawthorn Cl
WGNW/BIL/OR WN5 77 G4
Hawthorn Crs SKEL WN8 56 A4
Hawthorn Dr ECCL WA10 102 D1
PEN/TH CH61 167 K3
WKBY CH48 147 F1
Hawthorne Av HLWD L26 155 H5
WARR WA1 144 A2
WARRW/BUR WA5 141 G3
Hawthorne Cl RNFD/HAY WA11 89 K6
Hawthorne Crs FMBY L37 49 G3
Hawthorne Dr NSTN CH64 183 J6
Hawthorne Gv CHTN/BK PR9 23 H6
EHL/KEN L7 113 K6
WAL/EG CH44 112 A5
WARR WA1 143 J2
Hawthorne Rd BTL L20 81 K5
BTL L20 5 H2
FROD/HEL WA6 186 E6
RF/TRAN CH42 131 G6
STHEL WA9 120 B1
WARRS WA4 162 B3
The Hawthornes NTHLY L27 * 135 K3
Hawthorne St
WARRW/BUR WA5 142 D1
Hawthorn Gv EHL/KEN L7 113 K6
WARRS WA4 143 G6
Hawthorn La PS/BROM CH62 171 F5
Hawthorn Rd GTS/LS CH66 195 F3
HUY L36 116 C5
LYMM WA13 145 J6
NSTN CH64 181 G5
PR/KW L34 118 A1
Hawthorns Gv
WD/CROXPK L12 115 F1
Haxted Gdns ALL/GAR L19 154 A5
Haycroft Cl GTS/LS CH66 202 B1
Haydn Rd DV/KA/FCH L14 115 K2
Haydock La RNFD/HAY WA11 90 B5
Haydock Park Gdns
NEWLW WA12 91 G2
Haydock Park Rd AIN/FAZ L10 71 H6
Haydock Rd WAL/NB CH45 95 J6
Haydock St AIMK WN4 91 G1
ECCL WA10 13 H5
NEWLW WA12 106 A1
WARRN/WOL WA2 16 D3
Hayes Av RAIN/WH L35 118 A2
Hayes Crs FROD/HEL WA6 186 E6
Hayes Dr MGHL L31 72 A6
Hayes St ECCL WA10 102 E5
Hayfield Rd ORM L39 45 J4
WARR WA1 144 B1
Hayfield St ANF/KKDL L4 * 97 H6
Hayfield Cl HLWD L26 155 K2
Hayles Cl WLTN L25 135 H3
Hayles Gn WLTN L25 135 H3
Hayles Gv WLTN L25 135 H3
Haylock Cl TOX L8 132 E5
Hayman's Cl WD/CROXPK L12 * 98 E6
Haymans Gn MGHL L31 62 C6
WD/CROXPK L12 98 E6
Hayman's Gv WD/CROXPK L12 98 E6
Hayscastle Cl
WARRW/BUR WA5 122 E6
Haywood Cl GOL/RIS/CUL WA3 93 F2
Haywood Crs RUNC WA7 178 C3
Haywood Gdns ECCL WA10 12 A7
Hazel Av KKBY L32 72 B6
RAIN/WH L35 118 A3
RUNC WA7 176 B5
Hazelbank Gdns FMBY L37 * 40 E6
Hazelborough Cl
GOL/RIS/CUL WA3 125 K1
Hazel Cl GTS/LS CH66 202 D2
Hazeldale Rd WLT/FAZ L9 97 J1
Hazeldene Av
PEN/TH CH61 148 D5
WAL/NB CH45 111 G2
Hazeldene Wy
PEN/TH CH61 148 E5
Hazel Dr LYMM WA13 165 G1
Hazelfield Ct STHEL WA9 * 120 A3
Hazel Gv BEB CH63 170 A1
CSBY/BLUN L23 69 G6
ECCL WA10 102 E2
GOL/RIS/CUL WA3 92 C3
PEN/TH CH61 148 A4
STHP PR8 23 G6
WARR WA1 143 K1
WLT/FAZ L9 82 E5
Hazelhurst Rd ANF/KKDL L4 97 K6
Hazel La SKEL WN8 56 D1
Hazel Ms MGHL L31 * 72 A6
Hazel Rd BIRK CH41 2 D6
HOY CH47 127 G2
HUY L36 117 F2
Hazelslack Rd NG/CROX L11 98 E3
Hazel St WARR WA1 17 J1
Hazelwood GR/UP/WCH CH49 128 E5
Hazelwood Av BRSC L40 38 E5
Hazelwood Cl STHEL WA9 119 K4
WDN WA8 157 F3
Hazelwood Gv HLWD L26 155 G1
Hazelwood Ms WARRS WA4 163 H2
Hazlehurst Cl FMBY L37 48 C3
Hazlehurst Gv AIMK WN4 79 H6
Hazlehurst Rd
FROD/HEL WA6 201 F4
Hazleton Rd DV/KA/FCH L14 115 G4
Headbolt La NWD/KWIPK L33 72 D5
ORM L39 34 C5
Headbourne Cl WLTN L25 135 G2
Headingley Cl HUY L36 135 K1
STHEL WA9 120 A1
Headingly Av SKEL WN8 55 J3
Headington Rd
GR/UP/WCH CH49 128 E4
Headland Cl GOL/RIS/CUL WA3 93 F5
WKBY CH48 146 C3
Headley Cl ECCL WA10 12 D4
Head St TOX L8 132 D3
Heald St ALL/GAR L19 153 K5
NEWLW WA12 105 K2
Heanor Dr STHP PR8 28 C4
Hearne Rd ECCL WA10 102 E1
Heartwood Cl WLT/FAZ L9 82 D4
Heath Av GTS/LS CH66 202 E2
Heathbank Av PEN/TH CH61 147 K4
WAL/EG CH44 111 G4
Heathbank Rd RF/TRAN CH42 131 G6
Heath Cl PR/KW L34 102 B6
WKBY CH48 146 C3
WLTN L25 135 G4
Heathcote Cl EHL/KEN L7 * 133 H1
Heathcote Gdns BEB CH63 150 E6
Heathcote Rd ANF/KKDL L4 97 H3
Heath Dl BEB CH63 170 B2
Heath Dr GR/UP/WCH CH49 129 H4
HES CH60 167 K4
RUNC WA7 176 D6
Heather Bank BEB CH63 150 C5
Heather Brae NEWLW WA12 106 A1
Heather Brow CL/PREN CH43 130 C3
Heather Cl ANF/KKDL L4 * 97 H5
BRSC L40 38 E5
FMBY L37 41 H6
GOL/RIS/CUL WA3 125 F2
GTS/LS CH66 195 H6
RUNC WA7 187 H3
STHP PR8 41 K1
Heatherdale Cl CL/PREN CH43 130 E6
Heatherdale Rd CALD/MH L18 134 B5
Heather Dene PS/BROM CH62 171 F2
Heatherdene Rd WKBY CH48 127 G6
Heathergreen Cl ANF/KKDL L4 97 K4
Heather Gv AIMK WN4 79 K5
Heatherlea Cl SKEL WN8 57 K6
Heatherleigh STHEL WA9 118 E1
WKBY CH48 146 E5
Heatherleigh Cl WLT/FAZ L9 82 D4
Heather Rd BEB CH63 169 K1
HES CH60 168 A4
Heathers Cft NTHTN L30 70 B6
Heather Wy CSBY/BLUN L23 69 J3
Heatherways FMBY L37 41 G5
Heathey La STHP PR8 35 H1
Heathfield Av STHEL WA9 103 G5
Heathfield Cl FMBY L37 41 G5
LITH L21 81 K5
Heathfield Dr NWD/KWIPK L33 72 D4
Heathfield Pk WARRS WA4 163 F1
WDN WA8 138 C6
Heathfield Rd BEB CH63 170 B1
CL/PREN CH43 131 F5
CSBY/WL L22 80 D1
EP CH65 6 C4
MGHL L31 71 J2
STHP PR8 34 A4
WAV L15 134 B3
Heathfield St CLVPS L1 9 G5
Heathgate SKEL WN8 56 E3
Heathgate Av SPK/HALE L24 174 B3
Heath Gv GTS/LS CH66 194 E2
Heath Hey WLTN L25 135 G4
Heathland Rd STHEL WA9 120 A3
Heathlands Rd GTS/LS CH66 194 E2
The Heathlands
MOR/LEA CH46 109 J3
Heath La CHNE CH2 203 J4
GOL/RIS/CUL WA3 92 E5
GTS/LS CH66 194 A2
NSTN CH64 193 K1
Heathmoor Av
GOL/RIS/CUL WA3 92 E5
Heathmoor Rd
MOR/LEA CH46 109 H6
Heath Park Gv RUNC WA7 176 C5
Heath Rd AIMK WN4 91 G1
ALL/GAR L19 153 K3
BEB CH63 150 D6
HUY L36 116 B2
RUNC WA7 176 E5
WARRW/BUR WA5 141 G4
WDN WA8 157 K2
Heath Road Crs RUNC WA7 11 F7
Heathside HES CH60 167 G4
Heath St AIMK WN4 91 H1
GOL/RIS/CUL WA3 92 B3
STHEL WA9 103 F6
WARRS WA4 162 B3
The Heath RUNC WA7 * 176 D6
Heath Vw LITH L21 69 J6
Heathview Rd WDN WA8 175 H1
Heathwaite Crs NG/CROX L11 98 E4
Heathway HES CH60 168 B6
Heathwood WD/CROXPK L12 115 F2
Heathwood Gv WARR WA1 144 A2
Heathy La ORM L39 42 C3
Heatley Cl CL/PREN CH43 129 K2
Heaton Cl BRSC L40 38 D5
SKEL WN8 57 J6
SPK/HALE L24 174 A2
Heaton Ct GOL/RIS/CUL WA3 125 H1
Heatons Bridge Rd BRSC L40 37 H5
Hebburn Wy WD/CROXPK L12 100 A2
Hebden Pde NG/CROX L11 99 G2
Hebden Rd NG/CROX L11 99 F2
Hebdon Cl AIMK WN4 79 F4
Hector Pl BTL L20 97 F4
Hedgebank Cl WLT/FAZ L9 83 G3
Hedgecroft CSBY/BLUN L23 69 K3
Hedgefield Rd WLTN L25 135 J4
Hedge Hey RUNC WA7 177 K4
The Hedgerows
RNFD/HAY WA11 90 E4
Hedges Crs CLB/OSW/ST L13 98 C6
Hedgeview BRSC L40 37 F5
Hedingham Cl HLWD L26 155 K2
Hedworth Gdns STHEL WA9 119 F1
Heigham Gdns STHEL WA9 119 G1
The Heights FROD/HEL WA6 199 K5
Helena Rd STHEL WA9 104 D6
Helena St BIRK CH41 3 F6
EHL/KEN L7 113 K6
WLT/FAZ L9 97 H2
Helen Bank Dr RNFD/HAY WA11 75 G1
Helen St AIMK WN4 79 F5
GOL/RIS/CUL WA3 92 A1
Helford Cl RAIN/WH L35 118 C1
Helford Rd NG/CROX L11 84 C6
Heliers Rd CLB/OSW/ST L13 115 F5
Hell Nook GOL/RIS/CUL WA3 91 K2
Helmdon Cl NG/CROX L11 98 E4
Helmingham Gv BIRK CH41 131 H5
Helmsdale SKEL WN8 56 E3
Helmsdale La
WARRW/BUR WA5 141 K3
Helmsley Cl WARRW/BUR WA5 142 B2
Helmsley Rd HLWD L26 155 J4
Helsby Av PS/BROM CH62 184 C4
Helsby Rd WLT/FAZ L9 82 E4
Helsby St EHL/KEN L7 113 J6
STHEL WA9 104 B4
WARR WA1 17 J3
Helston Av HLWD L26 155 J2
RNFD/HAY WA11 89 G4
Helston Cl CHTN/BK PR9 20 E6
RUNC WA7 188 A2
WARRW/BUR WA5 141 F4
Helston Rd NG/CROX L11 84 C6
Helton Cl CL/PREN CH43 130 B6
Hemans St BTL L20 4 B2
Hemer Ter BTL L20 4 A1
Hemingford Cl GTS/LS CH66 202 B1
Hemingford St BIRK CH41 2 E4
Hemlock Cl WD/CROXPK L12 99 H2
Hemmingsway RAIN/WH L35 118 C4
Hempstead Cl STHEL WA9 103 H6
Hemsworth Av GTS/LS CH66 195 F5
Henbury Pl RUNC WA7 186 E1
Henderson Cl
GR/UP/WCH CH49 128 E3
WARRW/BUR WA5 140 E3
Henderson Dr RNFD/HAY WA11 75 H1
Henderson Rd HUY L36 117 G4
WDN WA8 18 B3
Hendon Rd NPK/KEN L6 114 B3
Hendon Wk GR/UP/WCH CH49 128 D6
Henglers Cl NPK/KEN L6 * 113 J4
Henley Av LITH L21 81 H3
Henley Cl BEB CH63 170 C3
NSTN CH64 191 K3
WARRS WA4 162 D5
Henley Ct ECCL WA10 103 F4
RUNC WA7 177 G3
Henley Dr CHTN/BK PR9 23 G4
Henley Rd CALD/MH L18 134 C4
NSTN CH64 191 K3
Henllan Gdns STHEL WA9 104 D6
Henlow Av KKBY L32 84 E3
Hennawood Cl NPK/KEN L6 113 K2
Henry Edward St
VAUX/LVPD L3 * 8 E1
Henry Hickman Cl NTHTN L30 70 C5
Henry St BIRK CH41 3 G4
CLB/OSW/ST L13 114 D5
CLVPS L1 8 E6
ECCL WA10 13 F4
LYMM WA13 145 K6
WARR WA1 16 B5
WDN WA8 * 19 H1
Henshall Av WARRS WA4 143 J5
Henthorne Rd PS/BROM CH62 151 G3
Henthorne St CL/PREN CH43 2 B5
Hepherd St WARRW/BUR WA5 142 A5
Hepworth Cl GOL/RIS/CUL WA3 92 A1
Herald Av SPK/HALE L24 154 C5
Herald Cl NG/CROX L11 99 G2
Heralds Cl WDN WA8 157 G3
Heralds Gn WARRW/BUR WA5 122 A5
Herbarth Cl WLT/FAZ L9 97 H2
Herbert St STHEL WA9 104 D6
WARRW/BUR WA5 * 121 J1
Herbert Taylor Cl NPK/KEN L6 114 A1
Herculaneum Ct TOX L8 132 E6
Herculaneum Rd TOX L8 132 D5
Herdman Cl WLTN L25 135 J4
Hereford Av
GOL/RIS/CUL WA3 * 92 C3
GR/UP/WCH CH49 129 F3
GTS/LS CH66 202 C3
Hereford Cl AIMK WN4 91 H1
WARR WA1 144 C2
Hereford Dr NTHTN L30 82 C2
Hereford Gv SKEL WN8 67 K1
Hereford Rd CHTN/BK PR9 23 H6
LITH L21 81 F4
WAV L15 134 B3
Heriot St EV L5 113 F1
Heriot Wk EV L5 113 F1
Hermes Cl NTHTN L30 82 B3
Hermes Rd NG/CROX L11 84 B5
Hermitage Green La
WARRN/WOL WA2 107 G5
Hermitage Gv BTL L20 82 A4
Herm Rd EV L5 112 E2
Heron Cl RUNC WA7 * 178 C5
Heron Ct HLWD L26 155 H2
NSTN CH64 191 H2
Herondale Rd CALD/MH L18 134 A5
Heron Gv RNFD/HAY WA11 75 J4
Heronhall Rd WLT/FAZ L9 98 D1
Heronpark Wy BEB CH63 170 D2
Heron Rd HOY CH47 128 B3
Herons Wy RUNC WA7 178 E1
Hero St BTL L20 5 H7
Herrick St CLB/OSW/ST L13 114 D4
Herschell St EV L5 113 H1
Hertford Cl HLWD L26 155 J4
WARR WA1 144 D2
Hertford Dr WAL/NB CH45 111 J1
Hertford Rd BTL L20 4 E7
Hertford St STHEL WA9 104 B3
Hesketh Av CHTN/BK PR9 21 K5
RF/TRAN CH42 150 C2
Hesketh Cl
WARRW/BUR WA5 141 G5
Hesketh Dr CHTN/BK PR9 23 G3
HES CH60 168 A4
MGHL L31 62 D5
Hesketh Meadow La
GOL/RIS/CUL WA3 93 G3
Hesketh Rd BRSC L40 38 D5
CHTN/BK PR9 23 F2
SPK/HALE L24 175 F3
Hesketh St North
WARRW/BUR WA5 142 A5
Hesketh St AIG/SPK L17 * 133 H5
WARRW/BUR WA5 142 A5
Heskin Cl KKBY L32 84 D4
MGHL L31 62 B3
RAIN/WH L35 118 D4
Heskin La ORM L39 45 H3
Heskin Rd KKBY L32 84 D4
Heskin Wk KKBY L32 84 D4
Hessle Dr HES CH60 167 K6
Hester Cl HTWN L38 59 F3
Heswall Av BEB CH63 150 B3
STHEL WA9 119 K3
Heswall Mt PEN/TH CH61 148 D6
Heswall Rd GTS/LS CH66 195 G5
WLT/FAZ L9 82 E4
Hever Dr HLWD L26 155 K2
Heversham SKEL WN8 56 E3
Heward Av STHEL WA9 * 120 A1
Hewitson Av CLB/OSW/ST L13 114 D1
Hewitson Rd CLB/OSW/ST L13 114 D1
Hewitt Av ECCL WA10 102 E1
Hewitt's La PR/KW L34 85 K4
Hewitts Pl CLVP L2 * 8 D3
Hewitt St WARRS WA4 143 F6
Hexham Cl NTHTN L30 82 D2
STHEL WA9 103 F6
Heyburn Rd CLB/OSW/ST L13 114 C1
Heydale Rd CALD/MH L18 134 B5
Heydean Rd CALD/MH L18 153 K2
Heydon Av KKBY L32 84 B2
Heydon Cl FMBY L37 48 D4
HLWD L26 155 K4
Heyes Av RNFD/HAY WA11 90 C6
RNFD/HAY WA11 75 H5
Heyescroft ORM L39 64 D1
Heyes Dr LYMM WA13 164 D1
WAL/NB CH45 110 C3
Heyes Gv RNFD/HAY WA11 75 H3
Heyes La WARRS WA4 162 D3
Heyesmere Ct AIG/SPK L17 153 G4
Heyes Mt RAIN/WH L35 118 E5
Heyes Rd WDN WA8 157 H3
Heyes St EV L5 113 J2
The Heyes WLTN L25 154 E1
Heyfield Park Rd GTS/LS CH66 194 E2
Heygarth Dr
GR/UP/WCH CH49 128 E5
Heygarth Rd PS/BROM CH62 184 B2
Hey Green Rd WAV L15 133 K1
Hey Lock Cl NEWLW WA12 * 106 C5
Hey Rd HUY L36 117 F5
Heys Av PS/BROM CH62 171 F5
Heyscroft Rd WLTN L25 154 E1
Heysham Cl RUNC WA7 188 B1
Heysham Lawn NTHLY L27 136 D5
Heysham Rd CHTN/BK PR9 23 H6
NTHTN L30 82 D1
Heysmoor Hts TOX L8 133 G4
The Heys RUNC WA7 177 H4
Heythrop Dr HES CH60 168 C5
Heyville Rd BEB CH63 150 D5
Heywood Av GOL/RIS/CUL WA3 92 C2
Heywood Bvd PEN/TH CH61 148 D5
Hey Wood Cl NEWLW WA12 * 106 C5
Heywood Cl FMBY L37 48 D2
PEN/TH CH61 148 D5
Heywood Ct WAV L15 115 G6
Heywood Gdns RAIN/WH L35 118 A5
Heywood Rd GTS/LS CH66 195 G4
WAV L15 134 D1
Heyworth St NPK/KEN L6 113 H3
Hibbert St WDN WA8 18 E3
Hickling Gdns STHEL WA9 119 G1
Hickmans Rd BIRK CH41 111 H6
Hickory Cl WARR WA1 144 D2
Hickory Gv MGHL L31 83 K1
Hickson Av MGHL L31 62 A4
Hicks Rd CSBY/WL L22 81 F2
Higgin's La BRSC L40 38 C5
Highacre Rd WAL/NB CH45 * 95 G6
Higham Av ECCL WA10 102 B2
WARRW/BUR WA5 123 F6
Higham Sq EV L5 113 G3
High Bank Cl CL/PREN CH43 * 130 A4
Highbank Dr ALL/GAR L19 154 A5
High Banks MGHL L31 62 A4
High Beeches CHLDW L16 115 K6
High Beeches Crs AIMK WN4 79 F3
High Carrs HUY L36 116 B5
High Clere Crs HUY L36 116 E2
Highcroft Av BEB CH63 151 F6
Highcroft Gn BEB CH63 151 F6
The Highcroft BEB CH63 150 E6
Higher Ashton WDN WA8 138 E6
Higher Bebington Rd
BEB CH63 150 D5
Higher End Pk NTHTN L30 70 A4
Higher Knutsford Rd
WARRS WA4 162 E1
Higher La LYMM WA13 165 H2
RNFD/HAY WA11 76 A5
WARRS WA4 189 G4
WLT/FAZ L9 83 F4
Higher Parr St STHEL WA9 104 A2
Higher Rd HLWD L26 155 H4
Highfield CHNE CH2 198 C5
NWD/KWIPK L33 72 E3
Highfield Av GOL/RIS/CUL WA3 92 A3
WARRW/BUR WA5 141 G4
Highfield Cl NSTN CH64 191 K1
WAL/EG CH44 111 G4
Highfield Crs RF/TRAN CH42 150 E2
WDN WA8 158 B1
Highfield Dr
GR/UP/WCH CH49 128 E5
LYMM WA13 164 D1
RNFD/HAY WA11 76 B5
Highfield Gv CSBY/BLUN L23 69 G4
RF/TRAN CH42 150 E2
Highfield La BRSC L40 37 G2
GOL/RIS/CUL WA3 92 D6
WARRN/WOL WA2 107 J5
Highfield Pk MGHL L31 62 D6
Highfield Pl PR/KW L34 * 117 K1
Highfield Rd CHTN/BK PR9 23 K2
CLB/OSW/ST L13 114 E3
GTS/LS CH66 194 E3
LITH L21 81 H3
LYMM WA13 164 D1
NSTN CH64 191 K1
ORM L39 45 J5
RF/TRAN CH42 150 E2
WDN WA8 18 B1
WLT/FAZ L9 97 H1
Highfield Rd North EP CH65 6 D4
Highfields HES CH60 167 K4
PR/KW L34 117 J1
Highfield South
RF/TRAN CH42 150 E2
Highfield St STHEL WA9 104 B5
VAUX/LVPD L3 8 C1
Highfield Vw CLB/OSW/ST L13 114 D3
Highgate Cl HES CH60 167 K4
RUNC WA7 178 C4
Highgate Ct EHL/KEN L7 113 J6
Highgate Rd MGHL L31 62 B4
SKEL WN8 57 K6
High Gates Cl
WARRW/BUR WA5 142 B2
Highgate St EHL/KEN L7 113 J6
Highgreen Rd RF/TRAN CH42 131 F6
Highgrove Pk ALL/GAR L19 153 H3
Highlands Rd RUNC WA7 176 C5
High La BRSC L40 46 A3
ORM L39 54 C5
High Legh Rd LYMM WA13 165 K3
Highmarsh Crs NEWLW WA12 91 G6
Highmeadow SKEL WN8 67 J1
High Moss ORM L39 53 J2
Highoaks Rd WLTN L25 154 E2
High Park Pl CHTN/BK PR9 23 J5
High Park Rd CHTN/BK PR9 23 J5
Highpark Rd RF/TRAN CH42 * 131 F6
High Park St TOX L8 132 E4
Highsted Gv NWD/KWIPK L33 72 D4
High St CLVP L2 8 C3
FROD/HEL WA6 186 E6
GOL/RIS/CUL WA3 92 B3
NEWLW WA12 106 D1
NSTN CH64 191 K2
PR/KW L34 117 K1
PS/BROM CH62 * 171 G4
RUNC WA7 10 C4
SKEL WN8 55 K5
SPK/HALE L24 174 E4
WARR WA1 17 F3
WAV L15 134 A2
WLTN L25 154 D1
Hightor Rd WLTN L25 135 G6
High Vw FROD/HEL WA6 199 K5
Highville Rd CHLDW L16 134 E3
High Warren Cl WARRS WA4 162 A6
Highwood Ct KKBY L32 72 D5
Highwood Rd WARRS WA4 162 B4
Highwoods Cl AIMK WN4 79 F4
Highett Av STHEL WA9 104 E3
Hilary Av DV/KA/FCH L14 115 J5
GOL/RIS/CUL WA3 92 E2
Hilary Cl ANF/KKDL L4 98 A5
PR/KW L34 102 A6
WARRW/BUR WA5 140 E3
WDN WA8 139 K6
Hilary Dr GR/UP/WCH CH49 129 H3
Hilary Rd ANF/KKDL L4 98 A5
Hilberry Av CLB/OSW/ST L13 114 C2
Hilbre Av HES CH60 180 D1
WAL/EG CH44 111 G3
Hilbre Cl CHTN/BK PR9 23 G4
Hilbre Ct WKBY CH48 146 B2
Hilbre Dr EP CH65 203 G2
Hilbre Rd WKBY CH48 146 C2

Hilbre St BIRK CH41 2 D1
VAUX/LVPD L3 9 G4
Hilbre Vw WKBY CH48 146 C1
Hilcrest Rd ANF/KKDL L4 98 B4
Hilda Rd WD/CROXPK L12 115 J2
Hildebrand Rd ANF/KKDL L4 98 A5
Hilden Rd WARRN/WOL WA2 124 A6
Hillaby Cl TOX L8 * 133 F3
Hillam Rd WAL/NB CH45 110 D1
Hillary Crs MGHL L31 62 B6
Hillary Dr CSBY/BLUN L23 69 H5
Hillary Rd PS/BROM CH62 184 B2
Hillary Wk CSBY/BLUN L23 * 69 H5
Hillbark Rd WKBY CH48 147 H1
Hillbeck Crs AIMK WN4 78 C5
Hillberry Crs WARRS WA4 142 E6
Hillbrae Av RNFD/HAY WA11 88 D3
Hillburn Dr BIRK CH41 110 E6
Hill Cliffe Rd WARRS WA4 161 K2
Hill Cl NSTN CH64 192 B4
Hill Ct NSTN CH64 192 C4
Hill Crest BTL L20 5 K6
Hillcrest MGHL L31 71 J1
RUNC WA7 177 G4
SKEL WN8 56 D6
Hillcrest Av HUY L36 117 G5
Hillcrest Dr BRSC L40 36 D1
GR/UP/WCH CH49 128 D6
GTS/LS CH66 194 D3
Hillcrest Rd CSBY/BLUN L23 69 H5
GTS/LS CH66 194 E3
ORM L39 45 J5
Hillcroft Rd WAL/EG CH44 111 J5
WLTN L25 135 G5
Hillerton Cl
WD/CROXPK L12 * 99 G3
Hillfield FROD/HEL WA6 200 E2
RUNC WA7 178 C5
Hillfield Dr PEN/TH CH61 167 K2
Hillfield Rd GTS/LS CH66 195 G2
Hillfoot Av WLTN L25 154 E5
Hillfoot Cl CL/PREN CH43 129 K1
Hillfoot Crs WARRS WA4 162 A4
Hillfoot Gn WLTN L25 154 D4
Hillfoot La FROD/HEL WA6 201 H6
Hillfoot Rd WLTN L25 154 D2
Hill Gv MOR/LEA CH46 129 F2
Hillhead Rd BTL L20 5 J6
Hillingden Av HLWD L26 155 J4
Hillingdon Av PEN/TH CH61 167 K3
Hillingdon Rd WAV L15 134 C3
Hillock Cl BRSC L40 36 E2
Hillock La BRSC L40 36 E2
WARR WA1 144 B1
Hill Rdg CL/PREN CH43 130 A4
Hill Rise Vw ORM L39 52 E4
Hill Rd CL/PREN CH43 130 B2
Hill Rd North FROD/HEL WA6 199 K6
Hill Rd South FROD/HEL WA6 199 K6
Hillsboro Av FROD/HEL WA6 201 F2
Hill School Rd ECCL WA10 102 C5
Hillsdown Wy GTS/LS CH66 202 A1
Hillside Av AIMK WN4 78 E1
ECCL WA10 88 B5
HUY L36 116 C1
NEWLW WA12 105 K3
ORM L39 53 H1
RUNC WA7 176 B5
Hillside Cl BIRK CH41 131 H5
BTL L20 5 J6
FROD/HEL WA6 200 A5
WGNW/BIL/OR WN5 77 G4
Hillside Ct BIRK CH41 131 H5
Hillside Crs HUY L36 116 C1
Hillside Dr GTS/LS CH66 195 H1
WLTN L25 135 J6
Hillside Gv WARRW/BUR WA5 141 G4
Hillside Rd CALD/MH L18 134 C4
CL/PREN CH43 130 A1
FROD/HEL WA6 201 F2
HES CH60 168 A6
HUY L36 116 E2
RF/TRAN CH42 131 H5
STHP PR8 27 F6
WAL/EG CH44 110 E3
WKBY CH48 146 E1
Hillside St NPK/KEN L6 113 H4
Hillside Vw CL/PREN CH43 130 D6
Hills Moss Rd STHEL WA9 104 D6
Hills Pl WAV L15 * 134 B2
Hill St CHTN/BK PR9 15 F3
CSBY/BLUN L23 69 G6
ECCL WA10 13 G2
RUNC WA7 10 E5
VAUX/LVPD L3 132 C3
WARR WA1 16 D4
Hillsview Rd STHP PR8 33 J5
Hill Top La HES CH60 168 B5
NSTN CH64 192 C4
Hilltop Rd CHLDW L16 134 E2
LYMM WA13 164 D1
RNFD/HAY WA11 87 J1
Hill Top Rd WARR WA1 144 B1
WARRS WA4 188 E1
WARRS WA4 162 E1
Hilltop Wk ORM L39 53 G2
Hillview AIG/SPK L17 153 F1
Hill Vw WDN WA8 138 E4
Hillview Av WKBY CH48 127 G6
Hillview Cl FROD/HEL WA6 201 F2
Hill View Dr GR/UP/WCH CH49 129 H3
Hillview Gdns WLTN L25 135 F6
Hillview Rd PEN/TH CH61 147 K5
Hillwood Cl BEB CH63 170 C4
Hilton Av WARRW/BUR WA5 141 J4
Hilton Cl BIRK CH41 2 C4
Hilton Gv WKBY CH48 127 F6
Hilton St AIMK WN4 79 G6
Hinchley Gn MGHL L31 61 K6
Hinckley Rd RNFD/HAY WA11 89 F5
Hindburn Av MGHL L31 62 D5
Hinderton Cl BIRK CH41 131 H5
Hinderton Dr HES CH60 180 E1
WKBY CH48 147 F2
Hinderton Gn NSTN CH64 192 A1
Hinderton La NSTN CH64 182 B6
Hinderton Rd BIRK CH41 3 F7
NSTN CH64 192 A2
Hindle Av WARRW/BUR WA5 123 F6
Hindley Beech MGHL L31 62 A5
Hindlip St TOX L8 133 F6
Hind St BIRK CH41 3 G6
Hinson St BIRK CH41 3 G4
Hinton Crs WARRS WA4 162 D3
Hinton Rd RUNC WA7 10 E7
Hinton St LITH L21 81 J5
NPK/KEN L6 114 A4
Hitchen's Cl RUNC WA7 178 C6
Hobart Dr NWD/KWIPK L33 72 D3
Hobart St EV L5 113 G1
STHEL WA9 103 F5
Hobb La WARRS WA4 161 F6
Hobby Ct RUNC WA7 187 H1
Hobcross La BRSC L40 47 G2
Hobhouse Ct CL/PREN CH43 * 2 A5
Hoblyn Rd CL/PREN CH43 130 B1
Hockenhall Aly CLVP L2 8 D3
Hockenhull Cl BEB CH63 * 170 C3
Hodder Av MGHL L31 62 D5
Hodder Cl RNFD/HAY WA11 88 E4
Hodder Pl EV L5 113 H1
Hodder Rd EV L5 113 H1
Hodder St EV L5 113 H1
Hodge St STHP PR8 14 E5
Hodgkinson Av
WARRW/BUR WA5 123 F6
Hodnet Dr AIMK WN4 79 H6
Hodson Pl NPK/KEN L6 113 H3
Hodson St STHP PR8 15 H6
Hogarth Dr CL/PREN CH43 130 A6
Hogarth St LITH L21 81 H5
Hogarth Wk ANF/KKDL L4 97 F5
Hoggs Hill La FMBY L37 48 E5
Hoghton Cl STHEL WA9 104 D5
Hoghton Gv CHTN/BK PR9 15 G3
Hoghton Rd SPK/HALE L24 175 F4
STHEL WA9 104 C5
Hoghton St CHTN/BK PR9 15 F4
Holbeck RUNC WA7 178 B6
Holbeck St ANF/KKDL L4 113 K1
Holborn Ct WDN WA8 138 E6
Holborn Dr ORM L39 53 G2
Holborn Hl BIRK CH41 131 H5
ORM L39 53 G2
Holborn Sq BIRK CH41 131 H5
Holbrook Cl STHEL WA9 120 A1
WARRW/BUR WA5 141 F3
Holcombe Av
GOL/RIS/CUL WA3 92 D3
Holcombe Cl
GR/UP/WCH CH49 * 128 E5
Holden Gv CSBY/WL L22 80 D1
Holden Rd CSBY/WL L22 80 C1
RAIN/WH L35 117 J3
Holden Rd East CSBY/WL L22 * 80 D1
Holden Ter CSBY/WL L22 80 D1
Holdsworth St EHL/KEN L7 113 K5
Holes La WARR WA1 144 A1
Holford Av WARRW/BUR WA5 142 C1
Holford Moss RUNC WA7 178 C2
Holford Wy NEWLW WA12 107 F2
Holgate CSBY/BLUN L23 69 J2
Holgate Pk CSBY/BLUN L23 69 J2
Holkham Cl WDN WA8 18 A2
Holland Ct SKEL WN8 67 F5
Holland Gv HES CH60 167 K4
Holland Moss SKEL WN8 66 C2
Holland Pl EHL/KEN L7 113 K6
Holland Rd HLWD L26 155 H5
SPK/HALE L24 173 K3
WAL/NB CH45 95 J6
Holland's La SKEL WN8 55 G3
Holland St EHL/KEN L7 114 B4
Holland Wy HLWD L26 155 H5
Hollies Rd HLWD L26 155 J4
The Hollies RUNC WA7 * 177 G5
WLTN L25 135 F6
Hollingbourne Pl NG/CROX L11 98 E2
Hollingbourne Rd
NG/CROX L11 98 E2
Hollinghurst Rd
NWD/KWIPK L33 72 E4
Hollingwood Cl AIMK WN4 79 F6
Hollingworth Cl WLT/FAZ L9 97 K2
Hollinhey Cl NTHTN L30 70 D4
Hollin Hey Cl
WGNW/BIL/OR WN5 77 G6
Hollins Cl AIMK WN4 78 C5
WAV L15 134 B1
Hollins Dr WARRN/WOL WA2 123 G1
Hollins La WARRN/WOL WA2 122 E1
Hollocombe Rd
WD/CROXPK L12 99 F3
Holloway RUNC WA7 10 C6
Hollow Cft STBRV L28 100 A4
Hollow Dr WARRS WA4 162 D2
Hollowford La BRSC L40 39 J6
Hollow La FROD/HEL WA6 201 K6
Holly Av BEB CH63 170 B2
NEWLW WA12 106 D2
Holly Bank LYMM WA13 * 164 E1
Hollybank WARRS WA4 160 D6
Hollybank Ct WDN WA8 * 18 B1
Hollybank Gra HLWD L26 155 J3
Hollybank Rd BIRK CH41 2 D6
CALD/MH L18 133 K4
RUNC WA7 177 J5
Holly Bank St STHEL WA9 104 A1
Hollybrook Rd STHP PR8 27 H2
Hollybush Sq GOL/RIS/CUL WA3 93 F2
Holly Cl BRSC L40 54 E1
ECCL WA10 102 D1
SKEL WN8 56 A4
SPK/HALE L24 174 E4
Holly Ct FROD/HEL WA6 199 K4
Holly Crs RNFD/HAY WA11 75 H4
Hollydale Rd CALD/MH L18 134 B4
Holly Farm Rd ALL/GAR L19 154 A5
Hollyfield Rd EP CH65 6 C4
WLT/FAZ L9 82 C6
Holly Fold La ORM L39 66 A4
Holly Gv HUY L36 116 B5
LITH L21 81 G5
RF/TRAN CH42 131 H5
WARR WA1 143 K2
Holly Hedge La WARRS WA4 161 G5
Holly Hey RAIN/WH L35 117 K6
Holly La ORM L39 65 K3
ORM L39 53 F1
Holly Mt WD/CROXPK L12 114 E1
Holly Pl MOR/LEA CH46 129 G2
Holly Rd EHL/KEN L7 114 B5
EP CH65 6 E4
GOL/RIS/CUL WA3 92 D3
RNFD/HAY WA11 89 J6
WARRW/BUR WA5 141 F4
Hollyrood PR/KW L34 117 F2
Holly St BTL L20 5 F3
Holly Ter WARRW/BUR WA5 141 G4
Hollytree Rd WLTN L25 135 J6
Hollywood Rd AIG/SPK L17 133 K6
Holman Rd ALL/GAR L19 154 A5
Holmdale Av CHTN/BK PR9 24 A1
Holm Dr CHNE CH2 198 C6
Holme Cl PR/KW L34 102 C6
Holmefield Av ALL/GAR L19 153 H3
Holmefield Gv MGHL L31 62 A6
Holmefield Rd ALL/GAR L19 153 G2
Holme Rd ECCL WA10 102 D3
Holmes Ct GOL/RIS/CUL WA3 124 E3
Holmes La LITH L21 * 81 H4
Holmes St TOX L8 133 H2
Holme St EV L5 112 E1
Holmesway PEN/TH CH61 167 K1
Holmeswood Rd BRSC L40 31 J1
Holmfield CL/PREN CH43 * 149 K1
Holmfield Av RUNC WA7 11 H5
Holmfield Dr GTS/LS CH66 195 G6
Holmfield Gv HUY L36 136 C1
Holmfield Pk FMBY L37 48 D1
Holm Hey Rd CL/PREN CH43 149 J1
Holm Hl WKBY CH48 146 D2
Holmlands Crs
CL/PREN CH43 * 149 H1
Holmlands Dr CL/PREN CH43 149 H1
Holmlands Wy
CL/PREN CH43 149 H1
Holm La CL/PREN CH43 149 J1
Holmleigh Rd WLTN L25 135 H3
Holmrook Rd NG/CROX L11 98 E3
Holmsfield Rd WARR WA1 17 J5
Holmside Cl MOR/LEA CH46 129 G1
Holmside La CL/PREN CH43 149 J1
Holm View Cl CL/PREN CH43 130 D6
Holmville Rd BEB CH63 150 D6
Holmway BEB CH63 150 E6
Holmwood Av PEN/TH CH61 149 F6
Holmwood Cl AIMK WN4 79 F4
FMBY L37 48 D2
Holmwood Dr EP CH65 203 F1
FMBY L37 48 D1
PEN/TH CH61 149 F6
Holmwood Gdns FMBY L37 48 D1
Holt Av MOR/LEA CH46 129 F1
WGNW/BIL/OR WN5 77 G5
Holt Coppice ORM L39 52 E6
Holt Crs WGNW/BIL/OR WN5 77 G5
Holt Hey NSTN CH64 192 B4
Holt Hl BIRK CH41 131 H5
Holt Hill Ter RF/TRAN CH42 3 F7
Holt La HUY L36 136 B2
NTHLY L27 136 A3
RAIN/WH L35 118 C3
RUNC WA7 177 J5
Holt Rd BIRK CH41 131 H5
EHL/KEN L7 114 A5
Holtswell Cl GOL/RIS/CUL WA3 93 F3
Holycross Cl VAUX/LVPD L3 8 E1
Holyhead Cl
WARRW/BUR WA5 122 D4
Holyrood CSBY/BLUN L23 68 B5
Holyrood Av WDN WA8 139 F5
Holywell Cl NSTN CH64 181 G6
STHEL WA9 120 B1
Holywell Dr WARR WA1 17 F5
Homecrofts NSTN CH64 191 K4
Home Farm Cl
GR/UP/WCH CH49 149 F1
Home Farm Rd
GR/UP/WCH CH49 148 E1
PR/KW L34 100 C3
Homer Rd PR/KW L34 100 C2
Homerton Rd NPK/KEN L6 114 B4
Homestall Rd NG/CROX L11 98 E3
Homestead Av NTHTN L30 70 E6
RNFD/HAY WA11 * 90 D4
Homestead Cl HUY L36 117 G4
Homestead Ms WKBY CH48 * 146 C1
Honeybourne Dr
RAIN/WH L35 118 C1
Honey Hall Rd HLWD L26 155 H5
Honeys Green Cl
WD/CROXPK L12 115 H2
Honey's Green La
WD/CROXPK L12 115 H2
Honey St STHEL WA9 * 102 E6
Honeysuckle Cl GTS/LS CH66 202 D3
HLWD L26 155 G1
WDN WA8 139 G5
Honeysuckle Dr WLT/FAZ L9 97 K2
Honister Av RNFD/HAY WA11 89 F3
WARRN/WOL WA2 123 J5
Honister Cl NTHLY L27 136 D6
Honister Gv RUNC WA7 187 H2
Honiston Av RAIN/WH L35 118 D3
Honiton Rd AIG/SPK L17 153 F3
Honiton Wy
WARRW/BUR WA5 141 F5
Hood La WARRW/BUR WA5 141 K4
Hood La North
WARRW/BUR WA5 141 K3
Hood Rd WDN WA8 18 B2
Hood St BTL L20 4 B1
CLVPS L1 8 E3
WAL/EG CH44 111 K4
Hookstone Dr GTS/LS CH66 195 F3
Hoole La CHTN/BK PR9 21 K5
Hoole Rd GR/UP/WCH CH49 129 J5
Hoolpool La FROD/HEL WA6 199 G4
Hooton Gn GTS/LS CH66 184 D5
Hooton Hey GTS/LS CH66 195 G4
Hooton La GTS/LS CH66 184 E4
Hooton Rd GTS/LS CH66 184 B6
NSTN CH64 183 J6
WLT/FAZ L9 82 E4
Hooton Wy GTS/LS CH66 184 C5
Hope Cl ECCL WA10 12 D4
Hope Cft GTS/LS CH66 202 D1
Hope Farm Rd GTS/LS CH66 202 C2
Hope Island SKEL WN8 56 B5
Hope Pk CHLDW L16 134 E4
Hope Pl CLVPS L1 * 9 H6
Hope Sq CHTN/BK PR9 15 H4
Hope St AIMK WN4 79 J4
BIRK CH41 2 D3
CHTN/BK PR9 15 H4
CLVPS L1 9 J7
NEWLW WA12 106 B2
PR/KW L34 117 K1
WAL/NB CH45 95 H5
Hope Wy TOX L8 9 J7
Hopfield Rd MOR/LEA CH46 129 G1
Hopkins Cl ECCL WA10 12 A4
Hopwood Cl GOL/RIS/CUL WA3 93 G3
Hopwood Crs RNFD/HAY WA11 75 H4
Hopwood St EV L5 112 E2
WARR WA1 17 F3
Horace Black Gdns EP CH65 6 D3
Horace St ECCL WA10 12 B3
Horbury Gdns GTS/LS CH66 195 F4
Hornbeam Av GTS/LS CH66 202 D2
Hornbeam Cl MOR/LEA CH46 * 128 C1
RNFD/HAY WA11 89 J6
RUNC WA7 178 B5
Hornbeam Crs AIMK WN4 79 G6
Hornbeam Rd HLWD L26 155 K4
WLT/FAZ L9 98 A2
Hornby Av BTL L20 4 D1
PS/BROM CH62 171 F4
Hornby Bvd LITH L21 81 J5
Hornby Cha MGHL L31 71 G2
Hornby Cl WLT/FAZ L9 97 H1
Hornby Crs STHEL WA9 120 B3
Hornby Flats LITH L21 * 81 J5
Hornby La CALD/MH L18 134 E4
WARRN/WOL WA2 123 G1
Hornby Pk CALD/MH L18 134 E4
Hornby Pl WLT/FAZ L9 82 D6
Hornby Rd BTL L20 4 D1
CHTN/BK PR9 23 J1
PS/BROM CH62 170 E4
WLT/FAZ L9 97 H1
Hornby St BIRK CH41 3 H4
CSBY/BLUN L23 * 69 F5
Hornby Wk EV L5 112 E3
Horncastle Cl
GOL/RIS/CUL WA3 93 G3
Horne St NPK/KEN L6 113 K3
Hornet Cl NPK/KEN L6 113 J3
Hornhouse La NWD/KWIPK L33 85 G3
Hornsey Rd ANF/KKDL L4 113 K1
Hornspit La WD/CROXPK L12 98 E5
Horridge Av NEWLW WA12 91 H6
Horringford Rd ALL/GAR L19 153 G3
Horrocks Av ALL/GAR L19 154 A5
Horrocks Cl HUY L36 116 D3
Horrocks La WARR WA1 16 D5
Horrocks Rd HUY L36 116 D4
Horseman Pl WAL/EG CH44 112 A5
Horseshoe Crs
WARRN/WOL WA2 124 A4
Horseshoe Dr AIN/FAZ L10 84 A4
Horseymere Gdns STHEL WA9 119 G1
Horsfall Gv TOX L8 132 D5
Horsfall St TOX L8 132 D5
Horstone Crs GTS/LS CH66 202 D1
Horstone Gdns GTS/LS CH66 202 D1
Horstone Rd GTS/LS CH66 202 D1
Horton Cl NWD/KWIPK L33 72 D3
Horwood Av RAIN/WH L35 118 D3
Horwood Cl WD/CROXPK L12 * 99 G3
Hoscar Ct WDN WA8 157 J4
Hoscar Moss Rd BRSC L40 39 J6
Hoscote Pk WKBY CH48 146 B1
Hose Side Rd WAL/NB CH45 95 G6
Hospital St ECCL WA10 13 H3
Hospital Wy RUNC WA7 177 J6
Hosta Cl NWD/KWIPK L33 72 C4
Hostock Cl RAIN/WH L35 117 K5
Hotel St NEWLW WA12 106 B2
Hotham St VAUX/LVPD L3 9 G3
Hothfield Rd WAL/EG CH44 * 111 K4
Hotspur St BTL L20 96 E5
Hough Green Rd WDN WA8 138 C6
Hough's La WARRS WA4 161 K5
Houghton Cl NEWLW WA12 * 106 B2
WDN WA8 158 D1
Houghton Cft WDN WA8 138 B4
Houghton La CLVPS L1 * 9 F4
Houghton Rd
GR/UP/WCH CH49 129 J6
Houghton's La ECCL WA10 87 G4
SKEL WN8 56 E4
Houghtons Rd SKEL WN8 56 C2
Houghton St CLVPS L1 9 F4
NEWLW WA12 106 B2
PR/KW L34 117 K1
RAIN/WH L35 * 118 E4
WARRN/WOL WA2 16 D2
WDN WA8 158 E1
Houghwood Gra AIMK WN4 78 E6
Hougoumont Av
CSBY/WL L22 81 F2
Hougoumont Gv
CSBY/WL L22 81 F2
Houlding St ANF/KKDL L4 * 113 J1
Houlgrave Rd EV L5 112 E2
Houlston Rd KKBY L32 84 A1
Houlton St EHL/KEN L7 114 A5
Hourd Wy GTS/LS CH66 202 C3
Houston Gdns
WARRW/BUR WA5 141 H1
The Hove RUNC WA7 188 C1
Howard Av PS/BROM CH62 171 F5
Howard Cl LITH L21 81 K1
MGHL L31 62 D6
Howard Dr ALL/GAR L19 153 H4
Howard Florey Av
NTHTN L30 70 C5
Howard's La ECCL WA10 102 A1
Howards Rd PEN/TH CH61 148 E5
Howard St ECCL WA10 102 E5
Howards Wy NSTN CH64 192 B3
Howarth Ct RUNC WA7 11 F4
Howbeck Cl CL/PREN CH43 130 C3
Howbeck Dr CL/PREN CH43 130 C3
Howbeck Rd CL/PREN CH43 130 C3
Howden Dr HUY L36 116 A5
Howell Dr GR/UP/WCH CH49 148 A1
Howell Rd PS/BROM CH62 151 F4
Howells Av GTS/LS CH66 195 F6
Howells Cl MGHL L31 62 B5
Howe St BTL L20 96 D4
Howey La FROD/HEL WA6 200 D2
Howey Ri FROD/HEL WA6 200 D2
Howley La WARR WA1 17 H5
Howley Quay WARR WA1 * 17 H5
Howson Rd WARRN/WOL WA2 123 J5
Howson St RF/TRAN CH42 150 E1
Hoylake Cl RUNC WA7 188 B1
Hoylake Gv STHEL WA9 120 A3
Hoylake Rd MOR/LEA CH46 109 K6
Hoyle Rd HOY CH47 127 G1
Hoyle St WARRW/BUR WA5 16 A1
Huddleston Cl
GR/UP/WCH CH49 129 J6
Huddleston Rd WAV L15 115 F6
Hudson Cl WARRW/BUR WA5 142 A1
Hudson Gv GOL/RIS/CUL WA3 93 F3
Hudson Rd MGHL L31 71 G2
MOR/LEA CH46 110 A3
Hudswell Cl NTHTN L30 82 E2
Hughenden Rd
CLB/OSW/ST L13 114 D2
Hughes Av RAIN/WH L35 117 K3
WARRN/WOL WA2 123 K5
Hughes Cl EHL/KEN L7 114 A6
Hughes Dr BTL L20 82 B5
Hughes La CL/PREN CH43 130 E6
Hughes Pl WARRN/WOL WA2 123 K5
Hughes St ALL/GAR L19 153 K6
NPK/KEN L6 113 J3
STHEL WA9 104 B5
WARRS WA4 143 F6
Hughestead Gv ALL/GAR L19 153 J5
Hughson St TOX L8 132 D4
Hulme St STHP PR8 14 D5
Hulmewood BEB CH63 151 F4
Hulton Av RAIN/WH L35 118 B3
Humber Cl ANF/KKDL L4 97 G5
WDN WA8 140 A6
Humber Crs STHEL WA9 120 A2
Humber Rd GTS/LS CH66 202 D1
WARRN/WOL WA2 124 A5
Hume Ct HOY CH47 127 H1
Hume St WARR WA1 17 G2
Humphrey's Cl RUNC WA7 178 C6
Humphreys Hey
CSBY/BLUN L23 69 J4
Humphrey St BTL L20 81 K5
Huncote Av RNFD/HAY WA11 89 G5
Hunslett Rd WLT/FAZ L9 82 E5
Hunstanton Cl
GR/UP/WCH CH49 129 H2
Hunt Cl WARRW/BUR WA5 * 141 J1
Hunter Av WARRN/WOL WA2 123 H5
Hunter Ct PR/KW L34 118 A1
Hunters Cl ORM L39 64 A5
Hunters Ct FROD/HEL WA6 200 A5
RUNC WA7 187 H1
Hunter's La WAV L15 134 B2
Hunter St STHEL WA9 * 104 A3
VAUX/LVPD L3 9 F2
Hunters Wy NSTN CH64 191 H1
Huntingdon Cl
MOR/LEA CH46 128 C1
Huntingdon Ct CHTN/BK PR9 * 23 J3
Huntingdon Gv MGHL L31 62 A3
Huntley Gv STHEL WA9 104 A6
Huntley St WARRW/BUR WA5 141 K5
Huntly Rd NPK/KEN L6 114 A4
Hunt Rd MGHL L31 62 B6
RNFD/HAY WA11 90 D5
Hunts Cross Av WLTN L25 135 J6
Hunts Field Cl LYMM WA13 164 E1
Hunts La WARRS WA4 162 E1
Huntsman Cl WLTN L25 155 G2
Huntsman Wd WD/CROXPK L12 99 J5
Hurford Av EP CH65 195 J5
Hurley Cl WARRW/BUR WA5 141 K4
Hurlingham Rd ANF/KKDL L4 98 A3
Hurlston Av SKEL WN8 * 56 E5
Hurlston Dr ORM L39 45 J4
Hurlston La BRSC L40 45 F2
Hurrell Rd BIRK CH41 110 D6
Hursley Rd WLT/FAZ L9 98 C1
Hurst Bank RF/TRAN CH42 150 E3
Hurstlyn Rd CALD/MH L18 153 K2
Hurst Park Cl HUY L36 * 117 G3
Hurst Park Dr HUY L36 117 G4
Hurst Rd MGHL L31 71 H2
Hurst's La ORM L39 64 A5
Hurst St CLVPS L1 8 D7
WDN WA8 10 D1
Huskisson St TOX L8 132 E2
Huskisson Wy NEWLW WA12 106 B1
Hutchinson St NPK/KEN L6 113 J4
WDN WA8 158 B5
Hutchinson Wk NPK/KEN L6 113 J4
Huttfield Rd SPK/HALE L24 174 B1
Hutton Ct SKEL WN8 55 K4
Hutton Rd SKEL WN8 55 K4
Hutton Wy ORM L39 45 J6
Huxley Cl MOR/LEA CH46 128 C1
Huxley Ct GTS/LS CH66 195 J1
Huxley St CLB/OSW/ST L13 98 B6
Huyton Av ECCL WA10 88 B5
Huyton Brook HUY L36 136 C1
Huyton Church Rd HUY L36 116 E5
Huyton Hall Crs HUY L36 * 116 E5
Huyton Hey Rd HUY L36 117 F5
Huyton House Cl HUY L36 116 B3
Huyton House Rd HUY L36 116 B3
Huyton La HUY L36 117 F3
Hyacinth Cl RNFD/HAY WA11 90 E5
Hyacinth Gv MOR/LEA CH46 110 A5
Hyde Cl EP CH65 195 J5
RUNC WA7 * 187 G1
Hyde Rd CSBY/WL L22 80 E2
Hyde's Brow
RNFD/HAY WA11 75 H1
Hydro Av WKBY CH48 146 C2
Hygeia St NPK/KEN L6 113 J3
Hylton Av WAL/EG CH44 111 G3
Hylton Ct EP CH65 203 J1
Hylton Rd ALL/GAR L19 154 A3
Hyslop St TOX L8 132 D3
Hythe Av LITH L21 81 K3
Hythe Cl STHP PR8 28 B4
Hythedale Cl AIG/SPK L17 152 D1

I

Ibbotson's La AIG/SPK L17 133 K5
Iberis Gdns STHEL WA9 104 E6
Ibis Ct WARR WA1 142 D6
Ibstock Rd BTL L20 81 J6
Iffley Cl GR/UP/WCH CH49 128 E4
Ikin Cl CL/PREN CH43 110 C6
Ilchester Rd BIRK CH41 111 F6
CHLDW L16 115 J6
Ilex Av WARRN/WOL WA2 123 H1
Ilford Av CSBY/BLUN L23 68 E4
WAL/EG CH44 111 H4
Ilford St VAUX/LVPD L3 9 J2
Ilfracombe Rd STHEL WA9 120 A2
Iliad St EV L5 113 G3
Ilkley Av CHTN/BK PR9 21 F5
Ilsley Cl GR/UP/WCH CH49 129 G5
Imber Rd KKBY L32 84 E3
Imison St WLT/FAZ L9 97 H2
Imison Wy BTL L20 5 K5
Imperial Av WAL/NB CH45 111 J1
Imperial Ms EP CH65 6 C2
Imrie St ANF/KKDL L4 97 H3
Ince Av ANF/KKDL L4 97 K5
CSBY/BLUN L23 68 D4
LITH L21 81 J4
PS/BROM CH62 184 B4
Ince Cl CL/PREN CH43 * 130 C5
Ince Crs FMBY L37 48 D2
Ince Gv CL/PREN CH43 130 C6
Ince La SFTN L29 60 B6
Incemore Rd CALD/MH L18 153 J2
Ince Orchards CHNE CH2 198 C5
Ince Rd CSBY/BLUN L23 69 H2
Inchcape Rd CHLDW L16 115 J6
WAL/NB CH45 * 110 D2
Inchfield SKEL WN8 56 D3
Index St ANF/KKDL L4 97 H4
Indigo Rd EP CH65 196 E4
Ingestre Rd CL/PREN CH43 130 D6
Ingham Rd WDN WA8 138 E5
Ingleborough Rd
RF/TRAN CH42 150 C1
Ingleby Rd PS/BROM CH62 151 G3
WAL/EG CH44 111 G4
Ingledene Rd CALD/MH L18 134 E4
Ingle Gn CSBY/BLUN L23 68 B4
Inglegreen HES CH60 168 A5
Ingleholme Gdns PR/KW L34 102 C6
Ingleholme Rd ALL/GAR L19 153 H2
Inglemere Rd RF/TRAN CH42 150 D1
Inglemoss Dr
RNFD/HAY WA11 87 J2
Inglenook Rd
WARRW/BUR WA5 141 G5
Inglesby Cnr BRSC L40 37 F5
Ingleton Cl
GR/UP/WCH CH49 * 128 E5
NEWLW WA12 * 106 B1
Ingleton Dr RNFD/HAY WA11 88 E2
Ingleton Gn KKBY L32 84 E3
Ingleton Gv RUNC WA7 187 G2
Ingleton Rd CALD/MH L18 134 A4
KKBY L32 84 E3
STHP PR8 28 B4
Inglewhite SKEL WN8 56 C3
Inglewood WD/CROXPK L12 100 A3
Inglewood Av
MOR/LEA CH46 128 E2
Inglewood Cl
GOL/RIS/CUL WA3 125 K1
Inglewood Rd RNFD/HAY WA11 87 K2
Inglis Rd WLT/FAZ L9 82 E4
Ingoe Cl KKBY L32 84 A2
Ingoe La KKBY L32 84 A3
Ingram SKEL WN8 56 D4
Ingrave Rd ANF/KKDL L4 98 A3
Ingrow Rd NPK/KEN L6 113 K4
Inigo Rd CLB/OSW/ST L13 115 F3
Inley Cl BEB CH63 170 C3
Inley Rd BEB CH63 170 B3
Inman Av STHEL WA9 105 F3
Inman Rd GR/UP/WCH CH49 129 F3
LITH L21 81 J4
Inner Central Rd
SPK/HALE L24 155 J6
Inner Forum NG/CROX L11 98 C2
Inner South Rd SPK/HALE L24 174 A1
Inner West Rd SPK/HALE L24 173 K1
Innisfree Cl GTS/LS CH66 195 F4
Insall Rd CLB/OSW/ST L13 115 F6
WARRN/WOL WA2 124 B5
Inskip SKEL WN8 56 C3
Inskip Rd CHTN/BK PR9 23 J1
Intake Cl NSTN CH64 193 H2
Intake La ORM L39 65 G3
ORM L39 51 G5
Inveresk Ct CL/PREN CH43 130 B3
Invincible Cl NTHTN L30 82 B3
Invincible Wy NG/CROX L11 84 B5
Inward Wy EP CH65 196 A2
Inwood Rd ALL/GAR L19 153 K4
Iona Cl WD/CROXPK L12 100 A2
Iona Gdns STHEL WA9 104 B6
Ionic Rd CLB/OSW/ST L13 114 E3
Ionic St LITH L21 * 81 G4
RF/TRAN CH42 150 E1
Irby Av WAL/EG CH44 111 G3
Irby Cl GTS/LS CH66 195 H5
Irby Rd ANF/KKDL L4 97 K5
PEN/TH CH61 148 A6
Irbyside Rd WKBY CH48 147 J2
Ireland Rd RNFD/HAY WA11 90 B5
SPK/HALE L24 175 F4
Ireland St WARRN/WOL WA2 142 E1
WDN WA8 158 E1
Irene Av RNFD/HAY WA11 89 F4
Irene Rd CHLDW L16 134 D3
Ireton St ANF/KKDL L4 97 H3
Iris Av BIRK CH41 130 C1
Iris Cl WDN WA8 157 H1
Iris Park Wk MGHL L31 71 K6
Irlam Av KKBY L32 84 D1
Irlam Pl BTL L20 4 C3
Irlam Rd BTL L20 4 C3
Ironbridge Vw TOX L8 132 D5
Ironside Rd HUY L36 116 D3
Irton Rd CHTN/BK PR9 23 G5
Irvin Av CHTN/BK PR9 21 F6
Irvine Rd RF/TRAN CH42 150 C1
Irvine St EHL/KEN L7 113 J6
Irving St CHTN/BK PR9 15 F1
Irwell SKEL WN8 56 C2
Irwell Cl AIG/SPK L17 133 K6
Irwell La AIG/SPK L17 133 K6
RUNC WA7 11 G3
Irwell Rd WARRS WA4 162 A1
Irwell St WDN WA8 176 D1
Irwin Rd STHEL WA9 104 A6
Isaac St TOX L8 132 E3
Isabel Gv CLB/OSW/ST L13 98 C6
Isherwood Cl
WARRN/WOL WA2 124 B4
Island Pl ALL/GAR L19 * 153 K5
Island Rd ALL/GAR L19 153 K5
Island Rd South ALL/GAR L19 154 A5
Islands Brow
RNFD/HAY WA11 88 E5
Islay Cl EP CH65 203 G3
Isleham Cl CALD/MH L18 153 K3
Islington CSBY/BLUN L23 68 E5
VAUX/LVPD L3 9 G2
Islington Gn WDN WA8 139 J5
Islip Cl PEN/TH CH61 148 A4
Ismay Dr WAL/EG CH44 111 K2
Ismay Rd LITH L21 81 J4
Ismay St ANF/KKDL L4 97 H4
Ivanhoe Av GOL/RIS/CUL WA3 92 E2
Ivanhoe Rd AIG/SPK L17 133 H5
CSBY/BLUN L23 68 D6
Ivatt Wy EHL/KEN L7 114 A6
Iveagh Cl RUNC WA7 177 K6
Iver Cl WDN WA8 138 B3
Ivernia Rd ANF/KKDL L4 97 K3
Ivor Rd WAL/EG CH44 111 J2
Ivory Dr NWD/KWIPK L33 72 D4
Ivy Av ALL/GAR L19 153 H4
BEB CH63 150 D6
NEWLW WA12 106 C3
RAIN/WH L35 118 C3
Ivybridge SKEL WN8 56 D3
Ivychurch Ms RUNC WA7 11 K5
Ivy Cl BRSC L40 39 G6
Ivy Ct STHEL WA9 * 104 A2
Ivydale SKEL WN8 56 D3
Ivydale Rd CALD/MH L18 134 A5
RF/TRAN CH42 131 H6
WLT/FAZ L9 97 K1
Ivy Farm Ct SPK/HALE L24 * 174 E4
Ivy Farm Dr NSTN CH64 192 A3
Ivy Farm Rd RAIN/WH L35 118 D3
Ivy House Rd
GOL/RIS/CUL WA3 92 E2
Ivyhurst Cl ALL/GAR L19 153 G3
Ivy La MOR/LEA CH46 109 J6
Ivy Leigh CLB/OSW/ST L13 114 C2
Ivy Rd GOL/RIS/CUL WA3 92 C3
WARR WA1 144 D2
Ivy St AIMK WN4 79 G6
BIRK CH41 3 H5
RUNC WA7 10 E6
STHP PR8 15 K7

J

Jack McBain Ct
VAUX/LVPD L3 * 112 E3
Jack's Brow PR/KW L34 100 E3
Jacksfield Wy ALL/GAR L19 153 G4
Jacksmere La BRSC L40 35 K1
Jackson Av WARR WA1 143 J2
Jackson Cl BEB CH63 150 E3
ORM L39 43 H6
RAIN/WH L35 119 F6
Jackson's Common La
BRSC L40 44 E2
Jacksons Pond Dr WLTN L25 135 G2
Jackson St ALL/GAR L19 153 K5
BIRK CH41 3 G5
RNFD/HAY WA11 * 89 K4
STHEL WA9 104 A2
WARRW/BUR WA5 121 J1
Jacobs Cl LITH L21 81 J5
Jacob St TOX L8 132 E5
Jacqueline Dr HUY L36 117 G3
Jade Cl NWD/KWIPK L33 72 E6
Jade Rd NPK/KEN L6 113 K3
Jamaica St CLVPS L1 132 C2
James Av GTS/LS CH66 195 F6
Jamesbrook Cl BIRK CH41 130 D1
James Clarke St EV L5 112 E3
James Cl WDN WA8 176 D1
James Ct WLTN L25 154 E1
James Dunne Av EV L5 112 E2
James Gv ECCL WA10 12 C7
James Holt Av KKBY L32 84 B2
James Hopkins Wy
ANF/KKDL L4 97 F6
James Larkin Wy
ANF/KKDL L4 97 F6
James Rd RNFD/HAY WA11 90 E4
WLTN L25 154 E1
James St ALL/GAR L19 153 K6
CL/PREN CH43 2 B7
CLVP L2 8 C5
STHEL WA9 120 B4
WAL/EG CH44 112 A5
WARR WA1 16 E4
WGNE/HIN WN2 79 K2
Jamieson Av CSBY/BLUN L23 69 H5
Jamieson Rd WAV L15 133 K3
Jane's Brook Rd STHP PR8 28 A3
Jane St STHEL WA9 104 D6
Janet St EHL/KEN L7 113 K6
Japonica Gdns STHEL WA9 104 E6
Jarrett Rd NWD/KWIPK L33 73 F5
Jarrow Cl CL/PREN CH43 130 E5
Jasmine Cl EV L5 113 H3
GR/UP/WCH CH49 128 E2
Jasmine Ct HUY L36 117 F2
Jasmine Gdns STHEL WA9 104 E6
Jasmine Gv WDN WA8 157 J3
Jasmine Ms AIG/SPK L17 133 F6
Jason St EV L5 113 G1
Jason Wk EV L5 113 G1
Java Rd ANF/KKDL L4 98 B3
Jay Cl GOL/RIS/CUL WA3 125 J3
Jays Cl RUNC WA7 178 D6
Jedburgh Av GTS/LS CH66 194 D3
Jedburgh Dr NWD/KWIPK L33 72 C3
Jeffereys Crs HUY L36 116 B5
Jeffereys Dr HUY L36 116 A4
Jefferson Dr
WARRW/BUR WA5 141 H2
Jefferson Gdns WDN WA8 138 E6
Jeffreys Dr GR/UP/WCH CH49 128 E4
Jellicoe Cl WKBY CH48 * 146 E5
Jenkinson St VAUX/LVPD L3 113 G4
Jennet Hey AIMK WN4 78 E3
Jensen Ct RUNC WA7 11 K3
Jericho Cl AIG/SPK L17 152 E1
Jericho Ct AIG/SPK L17 * 152 E1
Jericho Farm Cl AIG/SPK L17 152 E2
Jericho La AIG/SPK L17 152 E2
Jermyn St TOX L8 133 F3
Jerningham Rd NG/CROX L11 98 B2
Jersey Av EP CH65 203 G2
LITH L21 81 J2
Jersey Cl BTL L20 4 E4
Jersey St BTL L20 4 E4
STHEL WA9 120 A4
Jervis Cl WARRN/WOL WA2 124 C4
Jesmond St WAV L15 133 J1
Jessamine Rd RF/TRAN CH42 131 H6
Jet Cl NPK/KEN L6 113 K3
Jeudwine Cl WLTN L25 154 E3
Joan Av GR/UP/WCH CH49 129 F5
MOR/LEA CH46 128 E1
Jocelyn Cl BEB CH63 170 C2
Jockey St WARRN/WOL WA2 142 E2
John Bagot Cl EV L5 113 G2
John F Kennedy Hts
VAUX/LVPD L3 113 G3
John Hunter Wy NTHTN L30 70 C6
John Lennon Dr NPK/KEN L6 113 K4
John Moores Cl EHL/KEN L7 * 133 F1
John Nicholas Crs EP CH65 6 D3
John Rd LYMM WA13 145 H6
Johns Av RUNC WA7 10 C7
Johnson Av NEWLW WA12 91 G6
RAIN/WH L35 117 J3
Johnson Gv WD/CROXPK L12 115 J2
Johnson Rd CL/PREN CH43 149 J2
Johnson's La WDN WA8 159 F3
Johnson St STHEL WA9 104 A1
VAUX/LVPD L3 8 E2
Johnson Wk EHL/KEN L7 114 A6
Johnston Av BTL L20 82 B5
John St AIMK WN4 79 J4
BIRK CH41 3 H3
ECCL WA10 * 13 G4
EP CH65 6 C2
GOL/RIS/CUL WA3 92 B3
VAUX/LVPD L3 113 G4
WARRN/WOL WA2 16 D3
Jones Farm Rd WLTN L25 135 K5
Jones St VAUX/LVPD L3 9 H4
Jonson Rd NSTN CH64 181 K6
Jonville Rd WLT/FAZ L9 83 F4
Jordan St CLVPS L1 132 C2
Joseph Gardner Wy BTL L20 4 D2
Joseph Groome Towers
EP CH65 6 D3
Joseph Lister Cl NTHTN L30 70 C6
Joseph St STHEL WA9 104 C6
WDN WA8 158 D1
Joshua Cl EV L5 113 G1
Joy La STHEL WA9 121 G2
WDN WA8 120 C5
Jubilee Av DV/KA/FCH L14 115 H6
ORM L39 45 K5
WARR WA1 143 J1
WARRW/BUR WA5 141 F5
Jubilee Crs PS/BROM CH62 151 G6
RNFD/HAY WA11 90 E4
Jubilee Dr EHL/KEN L7 113 K5
NTHTN L30 82 D2
RAIN/WH L35 117 K5
SKEL WN8 56 A5
WKBY CH48 127 F5
Jubilee Gn EP CH65 6 E7
Jubilee Gv LYMM WA13 145 H5
Jubilee Rd CSBY/BLUN L23 68 D6
FMBY L37 48 D4
LITH L21 81 J4
Jubilee Wy WDN WA8 157 K2
Jubits La WDN WA8 139 F1
Juddfield St RNFD/HAY WA11 89 K5
Judges Dr NPK/KEN L6 114 A3
Judges Wy NPK/KEN L6 114 A3
Julian Wy WDN WA8 138 E5
Julie Gv WD/CROXPK L12 115 J2
Juliet Av BEB CH63 150 D4
Juliet Gdns BEB CH63 * 150 D4
July Rd NPK/KEN L6 114 B2
July St BTL L20 5 F1
Junction La BRSC L40 38 E5
NEWLW WA12 106 B2
STHEL WA9 104 C6
Junction Rd RNFD/HAY WA11 75 F1
June Av PS/BROM CH62 171 G5
June Rd NPK/KEN L6 114 B2
June St BTL L20 5 F2
Juniper Cl ECCL WA10 12 A3
GR/UP/WCH CH49 147 K1
STBRV L28 100 B6
Juniper Dr GTS/LS CH66 202 C2
Juniper Gdns CSBY/BLUN L23 69 J3
Juniper Gv GTS/LS CH66 202 D2
Juniper La GOL/RIS/CUL WA3 145 F1
Juniper St BTL L20 96 E6
Jurby Ct WARRN/WOL WA2 124 A6
Justene Cl GOL/RIS/CUL WA3 92 B1
Justin Wy RAIN/WH L35 118 D2
Juvenal Pl VAUX/LVPD L3 113 G3
Juvenal St VAUX/LVPD L3 113 F4

K

Kaigh Av CSBY/BLUN L23 68 E4
Kale Cl WKBY CH48 146 C2
Kale Gv NWD/KWIPK L33 73 F4
Kane Ct GOL/RIS/CUL WA3 93 H2
Kansas Pl WARRW/BUR WA5 141 J2
Kara Cl BTL L20 5 F4
Karan Wy MGHL L31 71 K6
Karen Cl WARRW/BUR WA5 121 K1
Karen Wy GTS/LS CH66 195 G6
Karonga Rd AIN/FAZ L10 83 H4
Karonga Wy AIN/FAZ L10 83 J4
Karslake Rd CALD/MH L18 134 A4
WAL/EG CH44 111 K5
Kay La LYMM WA13 165 K3
Kearsley Cl ANF/KKDL L4 * 97 G6
Kearsley St ANF/KKDL L4 97 G6
Keates St STHEL WA9 104 D5
Keats Av RAIN/WH L35 118 B4
Keats Cl GTS/LS CH66 * 202 C3
WDN WA8 18 A3
Keats Gn HUY L36 117 F6
Keats Gv WARRN/WOL WA2 123 J5
Keats St BTL L20 4 C1
Keats Ter STHP PR8 28 C1
Keble Dr AIN/FAZ L10 71 F6
WAL/NB CH45 110 D1
Keble Rd BTL L20 96 E4
Keble St EHL/KEN L7 113 J4
WDN WA8 18 E5
Keckwick La RUNC WA7 178 E1
Kedleston St TOX L8 133 F5
Keegan Dr WAL/EG CH44 112 A5
Keele Cl CL/PREN CH43 110 C6
Keel Hey NSTN CH64 183 J6
Keenan Dr BTL L20 82 B6
Keepers La BEB CH63 150 A6
Keeper's Rd WARRS WA4 163 F4
Keighley Av WAL/NB CH45 110 E2
Keightley St BIRK CH41 2 D3
Keir Hardie Av BTL L20 5 K1
Keith Av ANF/KKDL L4 97 H4
WARRW/BUR WA5 141 F3
Keith Dr BEB CH63 183 K2
Kelbey Cl TOX L8 133 F5
Kelbrook Cl STHEL WA9 120 B1
Kelburn Ct
GOL/RIS/CUL WA3 125 H1
Kelburn Gv WD/CROXPK L12 99 H5
Kelby Cl TOX L8 * 133 F5
Kelda Ct WLTN L25 135 H3
Kelday Cl NWD/KWIPK L33 84 D1
Kelkbeck Cl MGHL L31 62 D5
Kellet's Pl RF/TRAN CH42 131 J6
Kellett Rd MOR/LEA CH46 110 B4
Kellitt Rd WAV L15 133 K2
Kelly Dr BTL L20 5 J2
Kelly St PR/KW L34 118 A1
Kelmscott Cl GTS/LS CH66 202 B1
Kelmscott Dr WAL/EG CH44 110 E3
Kelsall Av PS/BROM CH62 184 B4
STHEL WA9 119 K3
Kelsall Cl CL/PREN CH43 130 D6
GOL/RIS/CUL WA3 124 E4
PS/BROM CH62 184 B4
WDN WA8 157 J1
Kelsey Cl ECCL WA10 12 A3
Kelso Cl NWD/KWIPK L33 72 C3
Kelso Rd NPK/KEN L6 114 A4
Kelton Gv AIG/SPK L17 153 F1
Kelvin Cl AIMK WN4 * 78 C5
GOL/RIS/CUL WA3 125 F1
Kelvin Gv TOX L8 133 F3
Kelvin Pk BIRK CH41 112 A6
Kelvin Rd BIRK CH41 131 H5
WAL/EG CH44 112 A6
Kelvinside CSBY/BLUN L23 81 G1
WAL/EG CH44 111 K6
Kelvin St GOL/RIS/CUL WA3 125 G1
Kemberton Dr WDN WA8 139 F4
Kemble St EHL/KEN L7 * 113 K5
PR/KW L34 117 K1
Kemlyn Rd ANF/KKDL L4 113 J1
Kemmel Av WARRS WA4 162 B1
Kempsell Wy HLWD L26 155 K4
Kempsey Gv STHEL WA9 103 G6
Kempson Ter BEB CH63 170 B1
Kempston St VAUX/LVPD L3 9 H2
Kempton Cl HUY L36 116 C6
NEWLW WA12 91 J6
RUNC WA7 187 F1
Kempton Park Fold STHP PR8 28 C4
Kempton Park Rd AIN/FAZ L10 83 H1
Kempton Rd PS/BROM CH62 151 G3
WAV L15 133 J1
Kemsley Rd DV/KA/FCH L14 115 K4
Kenbury Cl NWD/KWIPK L33 73 F5
Kenbury Rd NWD/KWIPK L33 73 F5
Kendal Av WARRN/WOL WA2 123 J5
Kendal Cl BEB CH63 150 E5
GTS/LS CH66 202 B1
RNFD/HAY WA11 66 B5
Kendal Dr GTS/LS CH66 202 B1
MGHL L31 62 B5
RAIN/WH L35 118 C4
RNFD/HAY WA11 89 F3
RNFD/HAY WA11 66 B6
Kendal Gv AIMK WN4 79 G5
Kendal Pk WD/CROXPK L12 115 H1
Kendal Ri RUNC WA7 187 G2
Kendal Rd CHLDW L16 135 F2
NWD/KWIPK L33 72 C5
WAL/EG CH44 111 G5
WDN WA8 * 157 H2
Kendal St BIRK CH41 * 3 F5
Kendal Wy STHP PR8 33 H6
Kendricks Fold RAIN/WH L35 118 D4
Kendrick St WARR WA1 16 B4
Kenilworth Av RUNC WA7 176 D5
Kenilworth Cl WLTN L25 135 F6
Kenilworth Ct EP CH65 203 J1
Kenilworth Dr PEN/TH CH61 148 B6
WARR WA1 143 J1
Kenilworth Gdns
GR/UP/WCH CH49 129 F3
NEWLW WA12 106 C3
Kenilworth Rd CHLDW L16 134 E2
CSBY/BLUN L23 68 D6
GOL/RIS/CUL WA3 93 F4
NSTN CH64 191 K3
STHP PR8 33 J5
WAL/EG CH44 111 K4
Kenilworth St BTL L20 4 D4
Kenilworth Wy WLTN L25 135 F6
Kenley Av WDN WA8 138 C4
Kenley Pde NPK/KEN L6 114 A3
Kenmare Rd WAV L15 133 K3
Kenmore Cottages LITH L21 * 69 K6
Kenmore Gv AIMK WN4 78 C5
Kenmore Rd CL/PREN CH43 149 H2
Kennelwood Av
NWD/KWIPK L33 72 E6
Kennessee Cl MGHL L31 71 H1
Kenneth Cl NTHTN L30 70 B6
Kenneth Rd WDN WA8 157 H4
Kennet Rd BEB CH63 150 C6
RNFD/HAY WA11 90 B5
Kennford Rd NG/CROX L11 84 B6
Kennington Pk WDN WA8 138 D6
Kensington EHL/KEN L7 113 K5
Kensington Av STHEL WA9 104 A6
WARRS WA4 163 H1
Kensington Cl WDN WA8 139 J5
Kensington Dr PR/KW L34 117 G2
Kensington Gdns
MOR/LEA CH46 129 F1
Kensington Rd CHTN/BK PR9 15 H5
EP CH65 6 A5
FMBY L37 48 E4
Kensington St NPK/KEN L6 113 J4
Kent Av FMBY L37 49 G4
LITH L21 81 K3
Kent Cl BEB CH63 170 D5
BTL L20 5 G3
Kent Gv RUNC WA7 11 G6
Kentmere Av RNFD/HAY WA11 89 F2
Kentmere Dr PEN/TH CH61 167 K2
Kentmere Pl
WARRN/WOL WA2 123 G4
Kenton Cl FMBY L37 41 F5
Kenton Rd HLWD L26 155 J4
Kentridge Dr GTS/LS CH66 195 G6
Kent Rd FMBY L37 49 G4
STHEL WA9 104 A5
STHP PR8 27 H3
WAL/EG CH44 111 G4
WARRW/BUR WA5 141 K5
Kents Bank WD/CROXPK L12 99 G4
Kent St CLVPS L1 9 F7
WARRS WA4 17 F7
WDN WA8 18 E2
Kentwell Gv WD/CROXPK L12 99 H6
Kenview Cl WDN WA8 175 H1
Kenway RNFD/HAY WA11 75 H3
Kenwick Cl GTS/LS CH66 195 F6
Kenworthys Flats
CHTN/BK PR9 14 E3
Kenwright Crs STHEL WA9 104 A5
Kenwyn Rd WAL/NB CH45 111 H2
Kenyon Av WARRW/BUR WA5 141 F4
Kenyon Cl NWD/KWIPK L33 72 E3
Kenyon Rd WAV L15 134 B4
Kenyons La FMBY L37 49 G2
MGHL L31 62 B3
Kenyons La North
RNFD/HAY WA11 90 E3
Kenyon's La South
RNFD/HAY WA11 90 E3
Kepler St LITH L21 81 H5
Keppel St BTL L20 96 D4
Kerfoot's La SKEL WN8 55 J5
Kerfoot St WARRN/WOL WA2 142 D2
Kerman Cl WD/CROXPK L12 99 F4
Kerr Cl NWD/KWIPK L33 72 D3
Kerr Gv STHEL WA9 104 C2
Kerris Cl AIG/SPK L17 152 D1
Kerry Cft GTS/LS CH66 202 C2
Kerrysdale Cl STHEL WA9 104 B6
Kersey Rd KKBY L32 84 E3
Kershaw Av CSBY/BLUN L23 69 G6
Kershaw St WDN WA8 157 J2
Kershaw Wy NEWLW WA12 91 H6
Kerslake Wy HTWN L38 59 F3
Kerswell Cl STHEL WA9 120 B1
Kerton Rw STHP PR8 * 27 G3
Kestral Gv HLWD L26 155 G2
Kestral Pk SKEL WN8 56 E1
Kestrel Av GR/UP/WCH CH49 128 E3
Kestrel Cl GR/UP/WCH CH49 128 E3
RNFD/HAY WA11 88 E5
Kestrel Ct CHTN/BK PR9 15 J4
Kestrel Dr AIMK WN4 79 H3
Kestrel La GOL/RIS/CUL WA3 125 G3
Kestrel Ms SKEL WN8 56 E1
Kestrel Rd HES CH60 168 C6
MOR/LEA CH46 128 D1
Kestrels Wy RUNC WA7 187 J1
Keswick Av BEB CH63 183 K2
WARRN/WOL WA2 123 J5
Keswick Cl MGHL L31 62 C5
STHP PR8 33 J6
WDN WA8 157 H2
Keswick Crs WARRN/WOL WA2 123 J5
Keswick Dr FROD/HEL WA6 201 G1
LITH L21 82 B3
Keswick Pl CL/PREN CH43 110 D6
Keswick Rd CALD/MH L18 153 K1
ECCL WA10 12 D2
WAL/NB CH45 94 E6
Keswick Vls CHLDW L16 * 135 H1
Keswick Wy CHLDW L16 135 H1
RNFD/HAY WA11 66 B5
Kettering Rd STHP PR8 33 H4
Kevelioc Cl BEB CH63 170 B2
Kew House Dr STHP PR8 28 D5
Kew Rd FMBY L37 48 D4
STHP PR8 27 H4
Kew St EV L5 113 F2
Keybank Rd WD/CROXPK L12 98 E5
Keyes Cl GOL/RIS/CUL WA3 125 H3
Keyes Gdns GOL/RIS/CUL WA3 125 H3
Kiddman St WLT/FAZ L9 97 H2
Kid Glove Rd GOL/RIS/CUL WA3 92 B2
Kidstone Cl STHEL WA9 104 B6
Kielder Cl AIMK WN4 78 E2
Kilbuck La RNFD/HAY WA11 90 E3
Kilburn Av AIMK WN4 79 J5
PS/BROM CH62 184 B1
Kilburn Gv STHEL WA9 103 G6
Kilburn St LITH L21 81 J5
Kildale Cl MGHL L31 62 A5
Kildare Cl SPK/HALE L24 174 E3
Kildonan Rd AIG/SPK L17 152 E1
WARRS WA4 163 F1

Kilford Cl WARRW/BUR WA5 122 E5
Kilgraston Gdns AIG/SPK L17 153 G2
Killarney Gv WAL/EG CH44 * 111 G4
Killarney Rd CLB/OSW/ST L13 114 E4
Killester Rd WLTN L25 135 J5
Killingbeck Cl BRSC L40 38 D5
Killington Wy ANF/KKDL L4 97 G5
Killingworth La
GOL/RIS/CUL WA3 125 K2
Kilmalcolm Cl CL/PREN CH43 130 C5
Kilmore Cl WLT/FAZ L9 83 F3
Kilmory Av WLTN L25 155 F1
Kilncroft RUNC WA7 * 188 A2
Kiln Hey WD/CROXPK L12 115 G2
Kiln La ECCL WA10 87 K6
SKEL WN8 56 A3
Kiln Rd GR/UP/WCH CH49 129 H6
Kilnyard Rd CSBY/BLUN L23 68 E5
Kilrea Cl NG/CROX L11 98 D5
Kilrea Rd NG/CROX L11 98 C5
Kilsail Rd KKBY L32 85 F4
Kilsby Dr WDN WA8 159 F1
Kilshaw Rd WARRW/BUR WA5 121 K1
Kilshaw St NPK/KEN L6 113 J3
Kilsyth Cl WARRN/WOL WA2 124 B3
Kimberley Av
CSBY/BLUN L23 * 68 E6
STHEL WA9 103 H6
Kimberley Cl TOX L8 133 F2
Kimberley Dr CSBY/BLUN L23 68 E6
WARRS WA4 162 B2
Kimberley Pl AIMK WN4 79 H6
Kimberley Rd WAL/NB CH45 111 H1
Kimberley St
WARRW/BUR WA5 142 B4
Kindale Rd CL/PREN CH43 149 H2
Kinder Gv AIMK WN4 78 E3
Kinder St NPK/KEN L6 9 K1
King Av BTL L20 82 B5
King Edward Rd ECCL WA10 88 A5
RAIN/WH L35 118 D3
King Edward's Dr
PS/BROM CH62 151 G5
King Edward St VAUX/LVPD L3 8 B2
WARR WA1 143 H2
Kingfield Rd WLT/FAZ L9 82 C6
Kingfisher Cl
GOL/RIS/CUL WA3 125 G3
NTHLY L27 136 C4
NWD/KWIPK L33 72 D3
RUNC WA7 187 J2
Kingfisher Ct AIMK WN4 79 G3
CHTN/BK PR9 15 K3
Kingfisher Dr RNFD/HAY WA11 88 E5
Kingfisher Gv WD/CROXPK L12 99 K4
Kingfisher Pk SKEL WN8 56 E1
Kingfisher Wy
GR/UP/WCH CH49 128 E3
King George Cl AIMK WN4 79 G6
King George Crs WARR WA1 17 K1
King George Dr WAL/EG CH44 111 J2
King George Rd
RNFD/HAY WA11 91 F4
King George's Dr
PS/BROM CH62 151 G5
Kingham Cl WDN WA8 19 K1
WLTN L25 155 F1
King James Ct RUNC WA7 187 H1
Kinglake Rd WAL/EG CH44 111 K3
Kinglake St EHL/KEN L7 113 K6
Kinglass Rd BEB CH63 170 D2
King's Av GOL/RIS/CUL WA3 93 G4
HOY CH47 127 J1
Kingsbrook Wy BEB CH63 150 C3
King's Brow BEB CH63 150 C5
Kingsbury WKBY CH48 127 J6
Kingsbury Cl STHP PR8 33 G5
Kingsbury Ct SKEL WN8 56 E1
Kings Cl AIG/SPK L17 152 D1
BEB CH63 150 C4
FMBY L37 48 E3
Kings Ct HOY CH47 127 F2
LITH L21 81 G4
RUNC WA7 * 178 C1
Kingscourt Rd
WD/CROXPK L12 115 G2
Kingsdale Av RAIN/WH L35 119 F4
RF/TRAN CH42 150 C1
Kingsdale Rd CALD/MH L18 134 B4
WARRW/BUR WA5 141 G2
Kings Dock St CLVPS L1 132 C2
Kingsdown Rd NG/CROX L11 98 E4
Kingsdown St BIRK CH41 131 H5
Kings Dr FROD/HEL WA6 199 J6
PEN/TH CH61 148 C5
PR/KW L34 117 G2
WKBY CH48 146 E3
WLTN L25 135 K5
Kingsfield Rd MGHL L31 71 F2
The King's Gap HOY CH47 127 F2
Kingshead Cl RUNC WA7 177 K3
Kingsheath Av DV/KA/FCH L14 115 K2
Kings Hey Dr CHTN/BK PR9 23 H4
Kingsland Crs NG/CROX L11 98 C2
Kingsland Gra WARR WA1 125 F6
Kingsland Rd NG/CROX L11 98 B2
RF/TRAN CH42 131 F5
King's La BEB CH63 150 D4
Kingsley Av PS/BROM CH62 184 B4
Kingsley Cl MGHL L31 62 A2
PEN/TH CH61 168 A2
Kingsley Crs RUNC WA7 10 E7
Kingsley Dr WARRS WA4 162 B4
Kingsley Rd ECCL WA10 88 A5
EP CH65 6 E4
FROD/HEL WA6 201 G3
RUNC WA7 10 E6
TOX L8 133 G2
WAL/EG CH44 111 H4
Kingsley St BIRK CH41 130 D1
Kingsmead Dr WLTN L25 154 E4
Kingsmead Gv CL/PREN CH43 130 C4
Kings Meadow RUNC WA7 178 B5
STHP PR8 33 K6
Kingsmead Rd CL/PREN CH43 130 C4
MOR/LEA CH46 109 K5
Kingsmead Rd North
CL/PREN CH43 130 C4
Kingsmead Rd South
CL/PREN CH43 130 C4
Kings Ms WARRS WA4 * 162 B3
King's Moss La
RNFD/HAY WA11 76 B2
Kings Mt CL/PREN CH43 130 E5
Kingsnorth RAIN/WH L35 118 B5
Kings Pde VAUX/LVPD L3 132 B2
WAL/NB CH45 94 D5
Kings Pk LITH L21 81 G4
King's Rd AIMK WN4 79 F4
BEB CH63 150 C3
CSBY/BLUN L23 68 E5
ECCL WA10 102 E3
FMBY L37 48 E3
GOL/RIS/CUL WA3 92 B4
GTS/LS CH66 195 F2
WARRN/WOL WA2 124 C5
King's Sq BIRK CH41 3 H5
Kings Ter BTL L20 4 E7
Kingsthorne Pk WLTN L25 155 F5
Kingsthorne Rd WLTN L25 155 F5
Kingston Av
WARRW/BUR WA5 141 F3
Kingston Cl DV/KA/FCH L14 115 J2
MOR/LEA CH46 129 F1
RUNC WA7 177 H3
Kingston Crs CHTN/BK PR9 21 F6
King St ALL/GAR L19 172 B1
CSBY/WL L22 80 E2
ECCL WA10 12 E5
EP CH65 6 E2
NEWLW WA12 106 B2
RF/TRAN CH42 151 F2
RUNC WA7 10 E3
STHP PR8 14 D6
WAL/EG CH44 111 K2
Kings Vw HOY CH47 * 126 E3
Kingsville Rd BEB CH63 150 D6
Kingswalk WKBY CH48 146 D1
Kingsway CSBY/WL L22 81 F1
FROD/HEL WA6 200 E2
HES CH60 181 H1
HUY L36 116 D3
NEWLW WA12 106 C3
RAIN/WH L35 117 K2
RNFD/HAY WA11 88 D3
STHP PR8 14 C5
WAL/NB CH45 111 G1
WDN WA8 18 D3
Kingsway Ct VAUX/LVPD L3 113 F3
Kingsway North WARR WA1 143 H4
Kingsway Pk VAUX/LVPD L3 * 113 F3
Kingsway South WARRS WA4 143 J5
Kingsway (Tunnel)
VAUX/LVPD L3 112 C4
WAL/EG CH44 111 J5
Kingswell Cl EHL/KEN L7 133 G1
Kings Whf BIRK CH41 112 A6
Kingswood HUY L36 116 D3
Kingswood Av CSBY/WL L22 81 G2
WLT/FAZ L9 82 E4
Kingswood Bvd BEB CH63 150 D3
Kingswood Ct NWD/KWIPK L33 72 E5
Kingswood Dr CSBY/BLUN L23 68 E6
Kingswood Pk STHP PR8 14 A7
Kingswood Rd WAL/EG CH44 111 J2
WARRW/BUR WA5 122 B5
Kington Rd WKBY CH48 127 F6
Kinley Gdns BTL L20 * 82 B6
Kinloch Cl HLWD L26 155 K4
Kinloch Wy ORM L39 45 H6
Kinloss Rd GR/UP/WCH CH49 128 D6
Kinmel Cl ANF/KKDL L4 98 B5
BIRK CH41 2 E3
Kinmel St STHEL WA9 104 A5
TOX L8 133 F4
Kinnaird Rd WAL/NB CH45 111 G1
Kinnaird St TOX L8 133 F6
Kinnerley Rd EP CH65 195 K6
Kinnerton Cl MOR/LEA CH46 128 C1
Kinnington Wy CH/BCN CH1 * 202 D4
Kinnock Pk WARRW/BUR WA5 121 J1
Kinross Av AIMK WN4 78 B5
Kinross Cl WARRN/WOL WA2 124 B3
Kinross Rd AIN/FAZ L10 83 H4
CSBY/WL L22 81 F3
WAL/NB CH45 110 D1
Kinsale Dr GOL/RIS/CUL WA3 124 E3
Kinsey Rd EP CH65 203 J2
Kinsey's La CHNE CH2 198 A3
Kintore Cl BEB CH63 183 K3
Kintore Dr WARRW/BUR WA5 140 E3
Kintore Rd ALL/GAR L19 153 J4
Kintyre Cl EP CH65 203 G2
Kipling Av HUY L36 117 G6
RF/TRAN CH42 150 E2
WARRN/WOL WA2 123 J6
Kipling Crs WDN WA8 18 B3
Kipling Gv STHEL WA9 119 J4
Kipling St BTL L20 81 H6
Kirby Cl WKBY CH48 146 C2
Kirby Mt WKBY CH48 146 D3
Kirby Pk WKBY CH48 146 C2
Kirby Park Man WKBY CH48 * 146 C2
Kirby Rd BTL L20 82 A5
Kirkacre Av NEWLW WA12 106 C5
Kirkbride Cl NTHLY L27 136 D5
Kirkburn Cl TOX L8 132 E5
Kirkby Bank Rd
NWD/KWIPK L33 85 G1
Kirkby Rw KKBY L32 72 B6
Kirkcaldy Av
WARRW/BUR WA5 140 E3
Kirkdale Gdns SKEL WN8 * 57 H6
Kirkdale Rd EV L5 113 F1
Kirkdale V ANF/KKDL L4 97 G6
Kirket Cl BEB CH63 170 C1
Kirket La BEB CH63 170 B1
Kirkfield Gv RF/TRAN CH42 151 F2
Kirkham Av GOL/RIS/CUL WA3 * 93 F5
Kirkham Cl WARRW/BUR WA5 141 J5
Kirkham Rd CHTN/BK PR9 23 J1
WDN WA8 158 D1
Kirklake Bank FMBY L37 48 C3
Kirklake Rd FMBY L37 48 C3
Kirkland Av RF/TRAN CH42 150 C1
Kirkland Cl WLT/FAZ L9 * 82 C4
Kirkland Rd WAL/NB CH45 95 J5
The Kirklands WKBY CH48 146 D1
Kirkland St ECCL WA10 12 D4
Kirklees Rd STHP PR8 27 G6
Kirkmaiden Rd ALL/GAR L19 153 J3
Kirkman Fold RAIN/WH L35 118 D4
Kirkmore Rd CALD/MH L18 153 H1
Kirkmount GR/UP/WCH CH49 129 H4
Kirk Rd LITH L21 81 K5
Kirkside Cl WD/CROXPK L12 99 H2
Kirkstall Dr FMBY L37 49 H3
Kirkstall Rd STHP PR8 27 G5
Kirkstead Wk MGHL L31 72 A6
Kirkstead Wy
GOL/RIS/CUL WA3 92 B3
Kirkstone Av RNFD/HAY WA11 89 F3
WARRN/WOL WA2 123 J4
Kirkstone Crs RUNC WA7 187 K3
Kirkstone Rd North LITH L21 81 K2
Kirkstone Rd South LITH L21 82 A3
Kirk Stone Rd West LITH L21 81 J1
Kirk St EV L5 113 G1
Kirkwall Dr WARRW/BUR WA5 141 G4
Kirkway BEB CH63 150 C4
GR/UP/WCH CH49 129 F5
WAL/NB CH45 95 H6
Kitchener Dr WLT/FAZ L9 82 C5
Kitchener St ECCL WA10 12 C4
Kitchen St CLVPS L1 132 C2
Kitling La PR/KW L34 85 G6
Kitling Rd PR/KW L34 85 H6
Kiverley Cl CALD/MH L18 135 F6
Kiveton Dr AIMK WN4 91 H1
The Knap HES CH60 181 F1
Knaresborough Rd
WAL/EG CH44 111 F3
Knighton Rd ANF/KKDL L4 98 A3
Knight Rd WARRW/BUR WA5 121 K1
Knightsbridge Av WARRS WA4 144 B6
Knightsbridge Cl WDN WA8 139 J5
Knightsbridge Ct
CL/PREN CH43 130 A5
WARR WA1 * 16 C5
Knightsbridge Wk
NWD/KWIPK L33 72 C3
Knights Gra STHEL WA9 104 A1
Knight St CLVPS L1 9 G7
Knightsway CSBY/WL L22 81 G1
Knob Hall Gdns CHTN/BK PR9 23 H2
Knob Hall La CHTN/BK PR9 23 H2
Knoclaid Rd CLB/OSW/ST L13 98 C6
The Knoll CL/PREN CH43 130 D6
Knottingley Dr GTS/LS CH66 195 F4
Knotty Ms WLTN L25 135 K6
The Knowe NSTN CH64 193 H1
Knowle Av STHP PR8 33 J3
Knowle Cl GTS/LS CH66 195 H6
WD/CROXPK L12 99 G3
Knowles House Av ECCL WA10 102 B2
Knowles St BIRK CH41 2 C3
WDN WA8 158 D1
The Knowle CSBY/BLUN L23 68 C6
Knowl Hey Rd HLWD L26 155 K5
Knowsley Av GOL/RIS/CUL WA3 92 C2
Knowsley Cl RF/TRAN CH42 151 F2
Knowsley Expy RAIN/WH L35 137 G3
Knowsley La PR/KW L34 100 D6
Knowsley Ms ORM L39 45 K6
Knowsley Park La PR/KW L34 101 J6
Knowsley Rd ALL/GAR L19 153 H5
BTL L20 81 H6
CHTN/BK PR9 23 G6
ECCL WA10 102 E2
ORM L39 45 K6
RAIN/WH L35 119 F5
RF/TRAN CH42 151 F2
WAL/NB CH45 111 G1
Knowsley St ANF/KKDL L4 97 H3
Knowsley Vw RNFD/HAY WA11 75 F1
Knox Cl PS/BROM CH62 151 G5
Knox St BIRK CH41 3 H5
Knutsford Cl ECCL WA10 102 D3
Knutsford Gn MOR/LEA CH46 109 J6
Knutsford Old Rd WARRS WA4 163 F1
Knutsford Rd MOR/LEA CH46 109 J6
WARRS WA4 163 K3
WARRS WA4 17 F7
Knutsford Wk MGHL L31 62 B3
Kremlin Dr CLB/OSW/ST L13 114 D2
Kronsbec Av GTS/LS CH66 195 G3
Kylemore Av CALD/MH L18 134 A6
Kylemore Cl PEN/TH CH61 167 J2
Kylemore Dr PEN/TH CH61 167 J2
Kylemore Rd CL/PREN CH43 130 D5
Kylemore Wy HLWD L26 155 G4
PEN/TH CH61 167 J2
Kynance Rd NG/CROX L11 84 C6

L

Laburnum Av HUY L36 136 B1
RNFD/HAY WA11 89 G4
WARR WA1 144 B2
Laburnum Crs KKBY L32 72 C6
Laburnum Dr SKEL WN8 55 K4
Laburnum Farm Cl NSTN CH64 192 B4
Laburnum Gv BRSC L40 39 F3
GTS/LS CH66 202 E3
MGHL L31 62 D6
PEN/TH CH61 148 A5
RUNC WA7 176 E5
STHP PR8 23 H6
Laburnum La
WARRW/BUR WA5 140 D3
Laburnum Pl BTL L20 5 G4
Laburnum Rd CL/PREN CH43 131 F5
EHL/KEN L7 114 B4
GOL/RIS/CUL WA3 93 G3
WAL/NB CH45 95 H6
Laburnum St AIMK WN4 91 G1
Laburnum Ter ALL/GAR L19 * 153 K5
Lace St VAUX/LVPD L3 8 E2
Lacey Ct WDN WA8 18 E6
Lacey Rd PR/KW L34 118 A2
Lacey St ECCL WA10 103 F5
WDN WA8 18 D6
Lad La VAUX/LVPD L3 * 8 B2
Lady Acre Cl LYMM WA13 164 E1
Lady Alice's Dr BRSC L40 46 E3
Ladybarn Av
GOL/RIS/CUL WA3 92 A4
Ladybower Cl EHL/KEN L7 133 G1
GR/UP/WCH CH49 129 F3
Lady Chapel Cl CLVPS L1 132 D2
Ladycroft Cl WARR WA1 144 D2
Ladyewood Rd WAL/EG CH44 111 J4
Ladyfield CL/PREN CH43 129 K2
Ladyfields WD/CROXPK L12 115 F2
Lady Green Cl HTWN L38 * 60 A4
Lady Green La HTWN L38 59 K3
Ladypool SPK/HALE L24 174 D4
Lady Richeld Cl RUNC WA7 178 C2
Ladysmith Av AIMK WN4 79 H6
Ladysmith Rd AIN/FAZ L10 83 J4
Lady's Wk BRSC L40 46 B6
Ladywood Rd
WARRW/BUR WA5 122 C6
Laffak Rd RNFD/HAY WA11 89 G3
Laggan St EHL/KEN L7 * 113 K5
Lagrange Ar ECCL WA10 * 13 G5
Laira Ct WARRN/WOL WA2 * 17 F1
Laira St WARRN/WOL WA2 16 E1
Laird Cl BIRK CH41 130 C1
Lairds Pl VAUX/LVPD L3 113 F3
Laird St BIRK CH41 130 D1
CL/PREN CH43 130 C1
Laithwaite Cl STHEL WA9 119 K4
Lakeland Av AIMK WN4 79 H5
Lakeland Cl CLVPS L1 8 E6
Lakemoor Cl STHEL WA9 104 B6
Lakenheath Rd HLWD L26 155 H5
Lake Pl HOY CH47 127 G2
Lake Rd HOY CH47 127 G2
WAV L15 134 B2
Lakeside Cl WDN WA8 157 F4
Lakeside Ct RNFD/HAY WA11 75 H3
STHP PR8 * 14 E3
WAL/NB CH45 95 J5
Lakeside Dr WARR WA1 142 D6
Lakeside Gdns RNFD/HAY WA11 75 H3
Lakeside Rd LYMM WA13 164 E2
Lakeside Vw CSBY/WL L22 * 80 E3
Lakes Rd WLT/FAZ L9 83 G4
Lake St ANF/KKDL L4 97 J6
Lake Vw RAIN/WH L35 118 A6
Laleston Cl WDN WA8 157 K3
Lambert Ct WDN WA8 18 E4
Lambert St VAUX/LVPD L3 9 H2
Lambert Wy VAUX/LVPD L3 9 H2
Lambeth Rd EV L5 97 F6
Lambeth Wk ANF/KKDL L4 97 F6
Lambourn Av WDN WA8 138 B4
Lambourne SKEL WN8 56 D1
Lambourne Cl GTS/LS CH66 202 D3
Lambourne Gv STHEL WA9 104 E2
Lambourne Rd ANF/KKDL L4 98 B4
Lambshear La MGHL L31 62 A3
Lambsickle Cl RUNC WA7 186 C1
Lambsickle La RUNC WA7 186 C1
Lambs La WARR WA1 143 K1
Lambton Rd AIG/SPK L17 133 G6
Lamburth Dr AIG/SPK L17 133 H5
Lamerton Cl
WARRW/BUR WA5 140 E5
Lammermoor Rd
CALD/MH L18 153 H1
Lampeter Cl
WARRW/BUR WA5 * 122 E5
Lampeter Rd NPK/KEN L6 114 A1
Lamport Cl WDN WA8 139 K6
Lamport St TOX L8 132 D3
Lanark Cl ECCL WA10 12 E7
Lanark Gdns WDN WA8 138 D6
Lancashire Gdns ECCL WA10 12 E7
Lancaster Av AIG/SPK L17 133 J3
CSBY/BLUN L23 68 E6
GOL/RIS/CUL WA3 92 D3
RAIN/WH L35 117 K4
RUNC WA7 176 B5
WAL/NB CH45 111 H2
WDN WA8 157 F1
Lancaster Cl EV L5 113 F1
MGHL L31 62 D6
NEWLW WA12 90 E6
PS/BROM CH62 151 G5
STHP PR8 27 F3
WARRN/WOL WA2 * 124 B5
Lancaster Ct WARRS WA4 * 162 D2
Lancaster Crs SKEL WN8 56 A4
Lancaster Dr CHTN/BK PR9 21 H6
Lancaster Gdns EP CH65 196 C6
Lancaster Ga CHTN/BK PR9 21 J6
Lancaster Rd FMBY L37 48 E4
HUY L36 117 G3
STHP PR8 27 F3
WDN WA8 139 F6
Lancaster St EV L5 113 F1
WARRW/BUR WA5 142 B4
WLT/FAZ L9 97 H2
Lancaster Ter PR/KW L34 * 118 A1
Lancaster Wk EV L5 113 F1
Lance Cl EV L5 113 H3
Lancefield Rd WLT/FAZ L9 * 82 C6
Lance Gv WAV L15 134 B2
Lance La WAV L15 134 B2
Lancelyn Prec BEB CH63 * 170 C2
Lancelyn Dr BEB CH63 170 B1
Lancer Ct RUNC WA7 177 H2
Lancers Cft GTS/LS CH66 202 C2
Lancing Av WARRN/WOL WA2 123 G3
Lancing Cl WLTN L25 155 G2
Lancing Dr AIN/FAZ L10 83 G1
Lancing Rd EP CH65 7 F6
WLTN L25 155 G3
Lancing Wy WLTN L25 155 G2
Lancots La STHEL WA9 120 B4
Land Cut La GOL/RIS/CUL WA3 125 F4
Land End MGHL L31 63 G6
Lander Cl WARRW/BUR WA5 142 A2
Lander Rd LITH L21 81 J5
Landford Av WLT/FAZ L9 98 C1
Landford Pl WLT/FAZ L9 98 C1
Land Gate La AIMK WN4 79 F2
Landican La
GR/UP/WCH CH49 149 F2
Landican Rd PEN/TH CH61 148 E4
Land La CHTN/BK PR9 24 A1
Landor Cl EV L5 112 E2
GOL/RIS/CUL WA3 93 F3
Landscape Dene
FROD/HEL WA6 200 A5
Landseer Av NSTN CH64 192 A2
Landseer Rd EV L5 113 H2
Lane Head Av
GOL/RIS/CUL WA3 93 F3
Lanfranc Cl CHLDW L16 135 F1
Lanfranc Wy CHLDW L16 135 F1
Langbar RAIN/WH L35 118 A5
Langdale Av FMBY L37 48 D2
GOL/RIS/CUL WA3 92 D2
PEN/TH CH61 167 K1
Langdale Cl FMBY L37 48 D3
KKBY L32 84 E2
WARRN/WOL WA2 124 A5
WDN WA8 157 H3
Langdale Dr BRSC L40 38 E5
MGHL L31 62 C5
Langdale Gdns STHP PR8 27 G6
Langdale Gv
RNFD/HAY WA11 88 E4
Langdale Rd BEB CH63 170 A1
RUNC WA7 11 F6
WAL/NB CH45 95 G6
WAV L15 133 K3
Langdale St BTL L20 5 G5
Langdale Wy FROD/HEL WA6 187 F6
Langfield GOL/RIS/CUL WA3 93 F4
Langfield Gv PS/BROM CH62 184 A2
Langford SPK/HALE L24 174 D4
Langford Rd ALL/GAR L19 153 G3
Langham Av AIG/SPK L17 133 H6
Langham St ANF/KKDL L4 97 H5
Langholm Rd AIMK WN4 78 B5
Langland Cl ANF/KKDL L4 98 B5
WARRW/BUR WA5 122 E5
Lang La WKBY CH48 127 G6
Lang La South WKBY CH48 127 H6
Langley Cl BEB CH63 170 C4
GOL/RIS/CUL WA3 92 D2
HTWN L38 59 F5
WD/CROXPK L12 99 K2
Langley Ct EP CH65 196 D6
Langley Pl BRSC L40 38 B5
Langley Rd BEB CH63 170 C3
BRSC L40 38 B5
Langley St TOX L8 * 132 D3
Langrove St EV L5 113 G2
Langsdale St VAUX/LVPD L3 9 H1
Langshaw Lea NTHLY L27 136 C5
Langstone Av
GR/UP/WCH CH49 147 J1
Langton Cl NEWLW WA12 106 A1
WDN WA8 138 A6
Langton Gn WARR WA1 144 C2
Langton Rd NWD/KWIPK L33 72 E4
WAV L15 133 J2
Langtree SKEL WN8 56 D2
Langtree St STHEL WA9 104 A2
Langtry Cl ANF/KKDL L4 97 F5
Langtry Rd ANF/KKDL L4 97 F5
Langwell Cl GOL/RIS/CUL WA3 125 J2
Langwood La RNFD/HAY WA11 66 E6
Lansbrook Cl RUNC WA7 * 11 H5
Lansbury Av STHEL WA9 104 C3
Lansbury Rd HUY L36 117 G5
Lansdown WD/CROXPK L12 114 E1
Lansdowne FROD/HEL WA6 201 G3
Lansdowne Cl BIRK CH41 130 D1
Lansdowne Ct CL/PREN CH43 130 C1
Lansdowne Pl CL/PREN CH43 130 C1
EV L5 113 H1
Lansdowne Rd BIRK CH41 130 C1
STHP PR8 28 B1
WAL/NB CH45 95 F5
Lanville Rd ALL/GAR L19 153 J2
Lanyork Rd VAUX/LVPD L3 8 B1
Lapford Crs NWD/KWIPK L33 73 F5
Lapwing Cl GOL/RIS/CUL WA3 92 E3
WD/CROXPK L12 99 J4
Lapwing Ct HLWD L26 155 H2
Lapwing Gv RUNC WA7 187 K1
Lapwing La WARRS WA4 160 C4
Lapwing Ri HES CH60 180 E1
Lapworth Cl MOR/LEA CH46 128 C1
Lapworth St EV L5 113 F1
Larch Av NEWLW WA12 106 C3
WARRW/BUR WA5 141 F4
WDN WA8 158 C1
Larch Cl ALL/GAR L19 153 G4
GOL/RIS/CUL WA3 93 G5
RUNC WA7 177 G6
SKEL WN8 56 A4
WGNW/BIL/OR WN5 77 G4
Larchdale Cl GTS/LS CH66 202 D3
Larchdale Gv WLT/FAZ L9 97 K1
Larchfield Rd CSBY/BLUN L23 69 H4
Larch Gv CL/PREN CH43 130 B1
WAV L15 114 E6
Larch Lea NPK/KEN L6 113 K2
Larch Rd HUY L36 116 C5
RF/TRAN CH42 2 C7
RNFD/HAY WA11 * 90 D4
RUNC WA7 177 F6
Larch St STHP PR8 28 B2
Larchtree Ms
WD/CROXPK L12 99 J5
Larch Wy FMBY L37 48 D1
Larchways WARRS WA4 162 C6
Larchwood Av MGHL L31 71 F2
Larchwood Cl PEN/TH CH61 167 K2
WLTN L25 135 J4
Larchwood Dr BEB CH63 150 E4
Larcombe Av
GR/UP/WCH CH49 129 G4
Larkfield Av WARR WA1 143 J2
Larkfield Cl AIG/SPK L17 152 D1
Larkfield Gv AIG/SPK L17 152 D1
Larkfield La CHTN/BK PR9 23 J2
Larkfield Rd AIG/SPK L17 152 D1
Larkfield Vw WAV L15 133 K1
Larkhill SKEL WN8 56 D1
Larkhill Av GR/UP/WCH CH49 129 H3
Larkhill Cl CLB/OSW/ST L13 98 C6
Larkhill Gv HTWN L38 59 F4
Larkhill La CLB/OSW/ST L13 98 C6
FMBY L37 48 C1
Larkhill Pl CLB/OSW/ST L13 98 C6
Larkhill Vw CLB/OSW/ST L13 98 D6
Larkhill Wy GR/UP/WCH CH49 129 H2
Larkin Cl PS/BROM CH62 151 F4
Lark La AIG/SPK L17 133 H6

Larkspur Cl RUNC WA7 187 J3
STHP PR8 15 J7
WARRW/BUR WA5 142 A6
Larkstoke Cl WARRS WA4 162 D5
Larksway HES CH60 168 B5
Lark Wy AIG/SPK L17 133 G6
Larne Ct WDN WA8 157 K1
Larton Farm Cl WKBY CH48 127 K6
Larton Rd WKBY CH48 127 J6
Lartonwood WKBY CH48 147 F1
Lascelles Rd ALL/GAR L19 154 A4
Lascelles St STHEL WA9 104 A2
Lasky La WARRS WA4 144 E5
Latchford Rd HES CH60 181 G1
Latchford St WARRS WA4 143 K6
Late Moffatt Rd West
WLT/FAZ L9 * 82 E4
Latham Av NEWLW WA12 106 C1
ORM L39 46 A6
RUNC WA7 11 G6
Latham St EV L5 113 F1
Latham Wy BEB CH63 170 D3
Lathbury La AIG/SPK L17 133 K4
Lathom Av LITH L21 81 G5
WAL/EG CH44 111 H3
WARRN/WOL WA2 142 E1
Lathom Cl BRSC L40 38 E5
Lathom Dr MGHL L31 62 C4
RNFD/HAY WA11 75 G2
Lathom La BRSC L40 46 C4
Lathom Rd BTL L20 81 K6
CHTN/BK PR9 15 G1
HUY L36 116 E5
ORM L39 55 F6
Lathum Cl RAIN/WH L35 118 A2
Latimer St EV L5 113 F2
Latrigg Rd AIG/SPK L17 153 F1
Lauder Cl NWD/KWIPK L33 72 C3
Launceston Cl RUNC WA7 188 B1
Launceston Dr
WARRW/BUR WA5 141 F6
The Laund WAL/NB CH45 111 F2
Laurel Av BEB CH63 170 A1
BRSC L40 38 E3
HES CH60 167 K4
NEWLW WA12 106 D3
WARR WA1 * 144 C2
Laurel Bank WARRS WA4 163 H2
WDN WA8 139 F6
Laurelbanks HES CH60 167 J4
Laurel Ct RNFD/HAY WA11 88 E4
Laurel Dr ECCL WA10 102 B1
EP CH65 203 F1
NSTN CH64 183 J6
SKEL WN8 56 A3
Laurel Gv AIMK WN4 79 G5
CSBY/WL L22 80 E1
GOL/RIS/CUL WA3 92 E3
HUY L36 136 B1
STHP PR8 23 G6
TOX L8 133 H3
Laurelhurst Av PEN/TH CH61 168 A1
Laurel Rd ECCL WA10 12 A7
EHL/KEN L7 114 B5
PR/KW L34 118 A1
RF/TRAN CH42 131 G5
RNFD/HAY WA11 89 J6
Laurels Farm Ct CHNE CH2 198 C5
Laurel Wy ECCL WA10 * 103 F3
Laurelwood Dr GTS/LS CH66 202 C3
Laurence Deacon Ct
BIRK CH41 * 2 D2
Lauren Cl HUY L36 117 H5
Lauriston Rd ANF/KKDL L4 98 A4
Laurus Cl NTHLY L27 136 C4
Lavan Cl NPK/KEN L6 113 J4
Lavan St NPK/KEN L6 113 J4
Lavender Cl RUNC WA7 11 J7
Lavender Crs PR/KW L34 118 A1
Lavender Gdns STHEL WA9 104 E6
Lavender Wy WLT/FAZ L9 97 K2
Lavrock Bank TOX L8 132 D5
Lawford Dr HES CH60 168 C5
Lawler Gv PR/KW L34 102 A6
Lawler St LITH L21 81 J5
Lawn Av WARR WA1 143 J1
Lawnhurst Gv AIG/SPK L17 153 F3
Lawns Av BEB CH63 183 J1
Lawnside Cl RF/TRAN CH42 150 E2
The Lawns CHTN/BK PR9 23 H3
CL/PREN CH43 130 A2
Lawnswood Gv CHNE CH2 198 C6
Lawrence Cl ALL/GAR L19 153 H4
Lawrence Gv WAV L15 133 K2
Lawrence Rd ECCL WA10 87 K5
WAV L15 133 J2
Lawrenson St ECCL WA10 12 D6
Lawson Cl WARR WA1 144 D2
Lawson St CHTN/BK PR9 23 J6
Lawson Wk WD/CROXPK L12 99 H2
Lawton Av BTL L20 82 B6
Lawton Rd CSBY/WL L22 80 E1
HUY L36 116 C5
RAIN/WH L35 119 F5
Lawton St CLVPS L1 9 F5
Laxey Av WARR WA1 144 C3
Laxey St TOX L8 132 D3
Laxton Cl GTS/LS CH66 202 D3
Laxton Rd WLTN L25 155 F5
Layford Cl HUY L36 116 D1
Layford Rd HUY L36 116 D2
Layton Av CL/PREN CH43 149 J1
Layton Cl GOL/RIS/CUL WA3 125 G4
WLTN L25 155 F1
Layton Rd WLTN L25 155 F1
Lazenby Crs AIMK WN4 78 E6
Lazonby Cl CL/PREN CH43 129 K1
Leach Cft STBRV L28 100 A6
Leach La STHEL WA9 120 B1
Leach St ECCL WA10 13 F3
Leach Vw RNFD/HAY WA11 * 88 E4
Leach Wy PEN/TH CH61 147 K5
Lea Cl CL/PREN CH43 130 B5
Lea Crs ORM L39 45 J4
Leacroft AIMK WN4 78 D3
Leacroft Rd GOL/RIS/CUL WA3 125 J1
Lea Cross Gv WDN WA8 138 B5
Leadenhall Cl EV L5 113 H1
Leafield Cl PEN/TH CH61 148 C5
Leafield Rd WLTN L25 154 E5
Leagate AIN/FAZ L10 83 J3
Lea Green Rd STHEL WA9 119 J2
Leamington Av NEWLW WA12 106 C4
Leamington Cl NSTN CH64 191 K3
WARRW/BUR WA5 141 H1
Leamington Rd NG/CROX L11 98 B3
STHP PR8 33 J4
Leander Rd WAL/NB CH45 111 G2
Lea Rd WAL/EG CH44 111 J2
Leas Cl GTS/LS CH66 195 F4
Leaside RUNC WA7 11 K7
Leasowe Av WAL/NB CH45 110 E1
Leasowe Gdns
MOR/LEA CH46 109 J4
Leasowe Rd MOR/LEA CH46 110 A3
WLT/FAZ L9 82 E4
Leasoweside MOR/LEA CH46 110 A3
Leas Pk HOY CH47 127 F5
The Leas PEN/TH CH61 148 E5
WAL/NB CH45 94 E6
Leatham Cl
GOL/RIS/CUL WA3 125 G4
Leatherbarrows La
MGHL L31 71 K2
Leather La CLVP L2 8 D3
Leather's La HLWD L26 155 J4
Leathwood MGHL L31 * 71 H1
Leaway GR/UP/WCH CH49 128 E5
Leawood Gv MOR/LEA CH46 129 G1
Leckwith Rd NTHTN L30 70 E6
Ledburn SKEL WN8 56 D2
Ledbury Cl CL/PREN CH43 149 H1
ECCL WA10 102 D2
WD/CROXPK L12 99 K1
Ledger Rd RNFD/HAY WA11 89 K6
Ledmore Gv AIMK WN4 78 C6
Ledsham Cl CL/PREN CH43 130 B5
GOL/RIS/CUL WA3 124 E4
Ledsham La GTS/LS CH66 194 C6
Ledsham Park Dr
GTS/LS CH66 194 D3
Ledsham Rd GTS/LS CH66 194 D4
KKBY L32 84 B1
Ledson Gv ORM L39 53 F6
Ledsons Gv MGHL L31 71 K6
Ledston Cl RUNC WA7 178 C4
Ledyard Cl WARRW/BUR WA5 142 A2
Leece St CLVPS L1 9 G6
Lee Cl RAIN/WH L35 119 F6
Lee Ct WARRN/WOL WA2 123 J5
Leecourt Cl WD/CROXPK L12 115 H2
Leeds St VAUX/LVPD L3 8 C1
Lee Hall Rd WLTN L25 135 K4
Leeming Cl ALL/GAR L19 153 K6
Lee Park Av WLTN L25 135 K4
Lee Rd HOY CH47 127 H2
WARRW/BUR WA5 * 141 J3
Lees Av RF/TRAN CH42 150 E1
Leeside Av KKBY L32 84 E3
Leeside Cl KKBY L32 84 E2
Lees La EP CH65 7 G6
NSTN CH64 192 C1
WD/CROXPK L12 99 H6
Lees Rd NWD/KWIPK L33 85 G1
The Lees WARRW/BUR WA5 141 H1
Lee St STHEL WA9 104 C5
Leeswood SKEL WN8 56 D2
Leeswood Rd
GR/UP/WCH CH49 129 H6
Lee Vale Rd WLTN L25 135 K5
Leeward Dr SPK/HALE L24 173 F1
Legh Rd PS/BROM CH62 151 G4
RNFD/HAY WA11 89 K5
Legh St AIMK WN4 91 G1
GOL/RIS/CUL WA3 92 B3
LYMM WA13 145 K6
NEWLW WA12 106 A2
WARR WA1 16 C4
Legion La PS/BROM CH62 171 F4
Legion Rd ECCL WA10 103 F5
Leicester Av CSBY/WL L22 80 E1
Leicester Rd BTL L20 5 H2
Leicester St CHTN/BK PR9 15 F2
STHEL WA9 103 F5
WARRW/BUR WA5 142 B4
Leigh Av WDN WA8 18 C2
Leigh Pl CLVPS L1 * 9 F4
Leigh Rd WKBY CH48 127 G6
Leighs Hey Crs KKBY L32 84 E2
Leigh St CLVPS L1 9 F4
Leighton Av HOY CH47 127 K1
MGHL L31 62 B5
Leighton Cha NSTN CH64 181 J6
Leighton Ct NSTN CH64 191 J1
Leighton Dr LEIGH WN7 93 J2
Leighton Pk NSTN CH64 191 J1
Leighton Rd BIRK CH41 131 H5
NSTN CH64 181 H4
The Leightons NSTN CH64 191 J1
Leighton St ANF/KKDL L4 97 G4
Leinster Gdns RUNC WA7 10 B3
Leinster Rd CLB/OSW/ST L13 115 F4
Leinster St RUNC WA7 10 B3
Leiria Wy RUNC WA7 11 F4
Leison St ANF/KKDL L4 97 F6
Leiston Cl PEN/TH CH61 148 B4
Lemon Cl EHL/KEN L7 114 A6
Lemon Gv TOX L8 133 H3
Lemon St EV L5 113 F1
Lemon Tree Wk ECCL WA10 103 F4
Lendel Cl FMBY L37 48 E2
Lenfield Dr RNFD/HAY WA11 89 J5
Lenham Wy SPK/HALE L24 173 G1
Lennox Av WAL/NB CH45 * 95 H6
Lennox La CL/PREN CH43 110 C6
Lenthall St ANF/KKDL L4 97 H3
Lenton Av FMBY L37 48 D1
Lenton Rd WLTN L25 135 K4
Leo Cl DV/KA/FCH L14 115 K3
Leominster Rd WAL/EG CH44 111 H3
Leonard Cheshire Dr
NTHTN L30 70 C6
Leonards Cl HUY L36 116 D1
Leonard St RUNC WA7 176 A6
STHEL WA9 104 D6
WARRN/WOL WA2 17 F1
WARRS WA4 162 B2
Leon Cl WARRW/BUR WA5 * 140 E2
Leonora St TOX L8 * 133 F5
Leopold Gv STHEL WA9 120 A2
Leopold Rd CSBY/WL L22 80 D1
EHL/KEN L7 113 K5
Leopold St WAL/EG CH44 * 112 A4
Lesley Rd STHP PR8 23 G6
Leslie Av GR/UP/WCH CH49 128 E6
Leslie Rd ECCL WA10 102 E5
Lesseps Rd TOX L8 133 H2
Lessingham Rd WDN WA8 138 E6
Lester Cl ANF/KKDL L4 97 G6
Lester Dr ECCL WA10 87 H6
PEN/TH CH61 147 K4
Lester Gv HUY L36 * 117 F3
Lestock St TOX L8 132 D2
Leta St ANF/KKDL L4 97 H4
Letchworth St NPK/KEN L6 114 A2
Lethbridge Cl EV L5 112 E1
Lethbridge Rd STHP PR8 28 A2
Letitia St TOX L8 132 E4
Levens Cl CHTN/BK PR9 21 K6
WARRW/BUR WA5 16 A2
Levens Hey MOR/LEA CH46 128 E1
Leven St ANF/KKDL L4 97 G5
Levens Wy WDN WA8 157 H3
Leven Wk GTS/LS CH66 195 K1
Lever Av WAL/EG CH44 112 A5
Lever Cswy BEB CH63 150 A4
Leveret Rd SPK/HALE L24 174 B2
Lever St STHEL WA9 120 B3
Lever Ter RF/TRAN CH42 131 H6
Leveson Rd CLB/OSW/ST L13 115 F6
Levisham Gdns
WARRW/BUR WA5 142 B2
Lewis Av WARRW/BUR WA5 123 F5
Lewis Cl EP CH65 203 G3
Lewis Crs WDN WA8 18 C5
Lewis Gv WDN WA8 157 J2
Lewisham Rd NG/CROX L11 98 D3
PS/BROM CH62 151 H5
Lewis St ECCL WA10 12 D5
Lewis Wk NWD/KWIPK L33 72 D3
Lexden St WARRW/BUR WA5 142 B3
Lexham Rd DV/KA/FCH L14 115 G4
Lexington Wy NWD/KWIPK L33 72 C3
Lexton Dr CHTN/BK PR9 23 K2
Leybourne Av STHP PR8 34 B2
Leybourne Cl WLTN L25 135 H3
Leybourne Gn WLTN L25 135 H4
Leybourne Gv WLTN L25 135 H4
Leybourne Rd WLTN L25 135 H3
Leyburn Cl KKBY L32 84 D4
Leyburn Rd WAL/NB CH45 111 F2
Ley Cl STHEL WA9 120 A3
Leyfield Cl WD/CROXPK L12 115 H1
Leyfield Rd WD/CROXPK L12 115 G1
Leyland Cl CHTN/BK PR9 21 H6
Leyland Green Rd AIMK WN4 78 B4
Leyland Gv RNFD/HAY WA11 90 A5
Leyland Rd CHTN/BK PR9 15 H1
RNFD/HAY WA11 75 G3
Leyland St PR/KW L34 117 K1
Leyland Wy ORM L39 45 K6
Leyton Cl RUNC WA7 186 E1
Liberton Ct EV L5 113 H1
Liberty St WAV L15 133 K2
Libra Cl DV/KA/FCH L14 116 A2
Libson Cl WARRN/WOL WA2 124 C4
Lichfield Av CSBY/WL L22 68 E6
GOL/RIS/CUL WA3 92 E3
WARRS WA4 163 F4
Lichfield Cl NTHTN L30 82 D2
Lichfield Dr GTS/LS CH66 202 C3
Lichfield Gv AIMK WN4 91 H1
Lichfield Rd HLWD L26 155 H5
WAV L15 134 B3
Lichfield St WAL/NB CH45 95 J6
Lickers La RAIN/WH L35 118 A5
Liddell Av MGHL L31 71 K5
Liddell Rd WD/CROXPK L12 98 D6
Lidderdale Rd WAV L15 133 K3
Lidgate Cl NWD/KWIPK L33 72 D4
Lifeboat Rd FMBY L37 48 A4
Liffey St TOX L8 133 G2
Lifton Rd NWD/KWIPK L33 84 E1
Lightbody St EV L5 112 D2
Lightburn St RUNC WA7 10 C6
Lightfoot Cl HES CH60 * 168 B6
Lightfoot La HES CH60 168 B6
Lighthorne Dr STHP PR8 33 G5
Lighthouse La FMBY L37 49 G4
Lighthouse Rd HOY CH47 127 F3
SPK/HALE L24 175 F6
Lightoaks Dr HLWD L26 156 A2
Lightwood Dr EHL/KEN L7 133 H1
Lightwood St EHL/KEN L7 133 H1
Lilac Av AIMK WN4 78 C4
STHP PR8 41 K1
WARRW/BUR WA5 141 H4
WDN WA8 158 C1
Lilac Crs RUNC WA7 177 F5
Lilac Gv GTS/LS CH66 202 E3
HUY L36 136 A1
RNFD/HAY WA11 89 J6
SKEL WN8 56 A4
WARRS WA4 162 D2
WGNW/BIL/OR WN5 77 G5
Lilac Rd GOL/RIS/CUL WA3 92 B2
Lilford Av WARRW/BUR WA5 142 C1
WLT/FAZ L9 82 C5
Lilford Dr WARRW/BUR WA5 141 G3
Lilford St WARRW/BUR WA5 16 A1
Lilley Rd EHL/KEN L7 114 B4
Lillian Rd ANF/KKDL L4 113 K1
Lillie Cl CL/PREN CH43 129 K1
Lillyfield HES CH60 180 E1
Lilly Gn ANF/KKDL L4 97 K4
Lilly Gv ANF/KKDL L4 97 K4
Lilly V EHL/KEN L7 114 B4
Lily Av NEWLW WA12 106 C3
Lily Pl AIMK WN4 91 H1
Lily Rd LITH L21 81 J5
Lily St AIMK WN4 79 K4
Lime Av BEB CH63 169 K1
FROD/HEL WA6 201 F1
WDN WA8 * 158 C1
Lime Cl CLB/OSW/ST L13 114 E3
Limedale Rd CALD/MH L18 134 B4
Limefield Av LYMM WA13 165 G1
Limefield Dr SKEL WN8 57 G6
Lime Gv CHNE CH2 198 B6
GOL/RIS/CUL WA3 92 E5
LITH L21 81 H5
RNFD/HAY WA11 75 G3
RUNC WA7 177 F5
SKEL WN8 56 A4
TOX L8 133 H3
Limehurst Gv
PS/BROM CH62 184 A1
Limekiln Ct EV L5 113 F3
Limekiln La VAUX/LVPD L3 113 F3
WAL/EG CH44 111 G5
WARRW/BUR WA5 121 J4
Limerick Cl WDN WA8 138 D6
The Limes GOL/RIS/CUL WA3 92 E5
GR/UP/WCH CH49 129 G4
Lime St CLVPS L1 9 F3
EP CH65 6 D1
STHP PR8 28 B1
Limetree Av WARR WA1 143 J1
WARRS WA4 162 D2
Lime Tree Cl GTS/LS CH66 202 E3
WLT/FAZ L9 97 K2
Lime Tree Gv HES CH60 168 C5
Lime Tree Wy FMBY L37 48 C3
Lime Vale Rd
WGNW/BIL/OR WN5 77 F6
Limeways WARRS WA4 162 D6
Limont Rd STHP PR8 33 K4
Linacre La BTL L20 81 K6
FMBY L37 50 C5
WDN WA8 138 D4
Linacre Rd LITH L21 81 J4
Linaker Dr ORM L39 43 K3
Linaker St STHP PR8 27 J2
Linbeck Gv GOL/RIS/CUL WA3 93 F2
Lincoln Av GOL/RIS/CUL WA3 92 E2
Lincoln Cl HUY L36 117 H4
LEIGH WN7 93 K3
NPK/KEN L6 113 K3
RUNC WA7 187 F1
WARR WA1 144 D3
Lincoln Crs RNFD/HAY WA11 88 E5
Lincoln Dr AIMK WN4 91 H1
AIN/FAZ L10 71 G6
WAL/NB CH45 111 J1
Lincoln Gdns BIRK CH41 * 130 D1
Lincoln Gn MGHL L31 70 E1
Lincoln Rd ECCL WA10 103 F3
GTS/LS CH66 195 G6
STHP PR8 27 H6
Lincoln Sq WDN WA8 158 C1
Lincoln St ALL/GAR L19 172 B1
BIRK CH41 111 G6
Lincoln Wy RAIN/WH L35 119 F6
Lincombe Rd HUY L36 116 B3
Lindale Cl MOR/LEA CH46 110 A6
Lindale Dr STHEL WA9 120 A3
Lindale Rd EHL/KEN L7 114 C4
Lindby Cl KKBY L32 85 F3
Lindby Rd KKBY L32 85 F3
Linden Av AIMK WN4 78 E4
CSBY/BLUN L23 68 D5
NTHTN L30 82 C1
Linden Cl GTS/LS CH66 202 D3
WARR WA1 144 C2
Linden Ct WDN WA8 * 138 E5
Linden Dr CL/PREN CH43 149 H2
HUY L36 136 B1
Linden Gv WAL/NB CH45 95 H6
WGNW/BIL/OR WN5 77 F6
Linden Rd NTHLY L27 136 B4
Lindens SKEL WN8 56 D1
The Lindens CL/PREN CH43 2 B6
MGHL L31 71 F2
Linden Wy ECCL WA10 102 D1
WDN WA8 138 E5
Lindenwood KKBY L32 84 E3
Lindeth Av WAL/EG CH44 111 H5
Lindfield Cl TOX L8 132 D5
WARRS WA4 160 D6
Lindholme SKEL WN8 56 E2
Lindi Av WARRS WA4 163 G2
Lindisfarne Av EP CH65 203 G2
GOL/RIS/CUL WA3 93 K3
Lindisfarne Ct WDN WA8 138 E3
Lindisfarne Dr
WD/CROXPK L12 100 A2
Lindley Av WARRS WA4 143 J5
Lindley Cl EHL/KEN L7 133 H1
Lindley St EHL/KEN L7 133 H1
Lindrick Cl RAIN/WH L35 118 C3
Lindsay Rd ANF/KKDL L4 98 B5
Lindsay St STHEL WA9 120 C4
Lind St ANF/KKDL L4 97 H4
Lindsworth Cl
WARRW/BUR WA5 141 K3
Lindwall Cl CL/PREN CH43 110 C6
Linear Pk MOR/LEA CH46 109 G6
Linear Vw NEWLW WA12 106 C5
Lineside Cl WLTN L25 135 J4
Linford Gv RNFD/HAY WA11 89 F6
Lingdale Av CL/PREN CH43 130 C3
Lingdale Rd CL/PREN CH43 130 C2
WKBY CH48 127 F6
Lingdale Rd North BIRK CH41 130 C2
Lingdales FMBY L37 41 H5
Lingfield Cl HUY L36 116 C6
NTHTN L30 82 D2
Lingfield Gv DV/KA/FCH L14 115 H5
Lingfield Rd DV/KA/FCH L14 115 G5
RUNC WA7 176 B5
Lingford Cl NTHLY L27 136 C5
Lingham Cl MOR/LEA CH46 109 H6
Lingham La MOR/LEA CH46 109 G4
Lingholme Rd ECCL WA10 12 D3
Lingley Green Av
WARRW/BUR WA5 141 F1
Lingley Rd WARRW/BUR WA5 140 E3
Lingmell Av RNFD/HAY WA11 88 E2
Lingmell Rd WD/CROXPK L12 99 F5
Ling St EHL/KEN L7 113 K5
Lingtree Rd KKBY L32 84 A1
Lingwell Av WDN WA8 157 J1
Lingwell Pk WDN WA8 157 J1
Lingwood Rd
WARRW/BUR WA5 141 F3
Linhope Wy AIG/SPK L17 133 H6
Link Av CSBY/BLUN L23 69 H4
RNFD/HAY WA11 89 H6
Linkfield Cl NTHLY L27 136 A3
Link Rd HUY L36 117 H6
Links Av CHTN/BK PR9 23 G3
GTS/LS CH66 195 F2
Links Cl BEB CH63 183 J1
WAL/NB CH45 95 F5
Links Hey Rd WKBY CH48 147 F5
Linkside BEB CH63 150 C4
Linkside Av WARRN/WOL WA2 123 H1
Linkside Wy GTS/LS CH66 202 D3
Links Rd KKBY L32 85 F3
The Links GOL/RIS/CUL WA3 * 125 F1
Linkstor Rd WLTN L25 154 C1
Links Vw CL/PREN CH43 130 B4
WAL/NB CH45 95 F5
Linksway WAL/NB CH45 95 F6
Linkway ECCL WA10 87 J5
RUNC WA7 177 F5
Linkway Av AIMK WN4 79 K4
Linkway East ECCL WA10 13 J7
Linkway West ECCL WA10 13 F6
Linner Rd SPK/HALE L24 173 J2
Linnet Cl AIG/SPK L17 133 H4
NEWLW WA12 106 C2
WARRN/WOL WA2 123 K4
Linnet Gv GOL/RIS/CUL WA3 125 G4
Linnet La AIG/SPK L17 133 G4
Linnets Pk RUNC WA7 11 H3
Linnets Wy HES CH60 167 J5
Linnet Wy NWD/KWIPK L33 72 D2
Linslade Cl NWD/KWIPK L33 72 E5
Linslade Crs NWD/KWIPK L33 72 E5
Linton Av GOL/RIS/CUL WA3 92 A1
Linton St ANF/KKDL L4 97 H4
Linum Gdns STHEL WA9 105 F6
Linville Av CSBY/BLUN L23 68 C5
Linwood Cl RUNC WA7 188 B2
Linwood Gv RAIN/WH L35 118 A5
Linwood Rd RF/TRAN CH42 131 H6
Lionel St STHEL WA9 104 D6
Lipton Cl BTL L20 4 D7
Lisburn La CLB/OSW/ST L13 98 C6
Lisburn Rd AIG/SPK L17 153 F1
Liscard Crs WAL/NB CH45 111 H2
Liscard Gv WAL/EG CH44 111 G3
Liscard Rd WAL/EG CH44 111 J3
WAV L15 133 J2
Liscard Village WAL/NB CH45 111 H2
Liscard Wy WAL/NB CH45 111 H3
Liskeard Cl RUNC WA7 188 A1
Lisleholme Crs
WD/CROXPK L12 115 G1
Lisleholme Rd
WD/CROXPK L12 115 G1
Lismore Rd CALD/MH L18 153 H2
Lister Crs EHL/KEN L7 114 A5
Lister Dr CLB/OSW/ST L13 114 C3
Lister Rd EHL/KEN L7 114 A5
RUNC WA7 11 H3
Liston St ANF/KKDL L4 * 97 H3
Litcham Cl GR/UP/WCH CH49 129 H2
Litchborough Gv
RAIN/WH L35 118 C1
Litherland Av MOR/LEA CH46 109 H6
Litherland Crs RNFD/HAY WA11 89 F4
Litherland Pk LITH L21 81 J3
Litherland Rd BTL L20 81 K5
BTL L20 5 F1
Lithou Cl EV L5 113 F2
Little Acre MGHL L31 71 H1
Little Barn Hey NTHTN L30 70 A5
Little Brook La KKBY L32 84 C3
Little Canning St TOX L8 132 E2
Little Catharine St TOX L8 132 E2
Littlecote Cl STHEL WA9 120 A3
Littlecourt VAUX/LVPD L3 112 E3
Little Crosby Rd
CSBY/BLUN L23 69 F2
Little Dl DV/KA/FCH L14 * 115 H4
Littledale DV/KA/FCH L14 115 H4
Littledale Rd WAL/EG CH44 111 K4
WARRW/BUR WA5 141 G2
Little Delph RNFD/HAY WA11 90 B4
Littlegate RUNC WA7 177 H5
Little Gn GTS/LS CH66 195 G6
Little Hardman St CLVPS L1 * 9 H6
Little Heath Rd SPK/HALE L24 173 K2
Little Heyes St EV L5 113 J1
Little Hey La FMBY L37 49 H1
Little Howard St
VAUX/LVPD L3 112 D3
Little Huskisson St TOX L8 132 E2
Little La CHTN/BK PR9 23 K4
NSTN CH64 181 G6
Littlemore Cl
GR/UP/WCH CH49 128 E4
Little Moss Hey STBRV L28 100 B6
Little Parkfield Rd
AIG/SPK L17 133 G5
Little Rake La CHNE CH2 203 H6
Littler Rd RNFD/HAY WA11 89 K6
Little St Bride St TOX L8 9 J7
Little Stanney La CHNE CH2 203 J3
Littlestone Cl WDN WA8 139 F5
Little Storeton La BEB CH63 149 K5
Little St STHEL WA9 104 C4
Littleton Cl CL/PREN CH43 * 130 B5
WARRW/BUR WA5 142 A5
Little Wissage GTS/LS CH66 202 D1
Littlewood Cl RAIN/WH L35 118 A5
Little Woolton St
VAUX/LVPD L3 113 J6
Littondale Av RAIN/WH L35 * 119 F5
Liverpool Loop Line
HLWD L26 155 G1
WLTN L25 135 G2
Liverpool Old Rd FMBY L37 41 J2
Liverpool Pl WDN WA8 157 H2
Liverpool Rd AIMK WN4 78 E6
CH/BCN CH1 202 D4
CSBY/BLUN L23 69 F5
FMBY L37 49 G3
HUY L36 116 C3
MGHL L31 62 B3
NSTN CH64 181 K6
ORM L39 63 K3
ORM L39 53 F3
PR/KW L34 117 H1
RNFD/HAY WA11 89 K4
SKEL WN8 55 J5
STHP PR8 41 J1
STHP PR8 33 K4

WARRW/BUR WA5 16 A5
WDN WA8 18 A2
Liverpool Rd North BRSC L40 38 E4
MGHL L31 62 A5
Liverpool Rd South BRSC L40 46 C1
MGHL L31 71 F2
Liverpool Rw NEWLW WA12 106 D5
Liverpool St ECCL WA10 12 E6
Liversidge Rd RF/TRAN CH42 131 G5
Liver St CLVPS L1 8 D7
Livingston Av AIG/SPK L17 133 H5
Livingston Dr AIG/SPK L17 133 H6
Livingston Dr North
AIG/SPK L17 133 H6
Livingston Dr South
AIG/SPK L17 133 H6
Livingstone Cl
WARRW/BUR WA5 142 A2
Livingstone Gdns BIRK CH41 2 C2
Livingstone Rd EP CH65 6 D1
MOR/LEA CH46 110 A3
RF/TRAN CH42 131 J6
Livingstone St BIRK CH41 2 C2
Llandaff Cl GTS/LS CH66 202 C2
Llanrwst Cl TOX L8 132 D4
Lloyd Av BIRK CH41 2 A2
Lloyd Cl NPK/KEN L6 113 H3
Lloyd Crs NEWLW WA12 105 K2
Lloyd Dr EP CH65 203 G2
GR/UP/WCH CH49 128 E6
Lloyd Rd PR/KW L34 102 A6
Lloyd St RNFD/HAY WA11 89 J5
Lobelia Av WLT/FAZ L9 97 K1
Lobelia Gv RUNC WA7 187 J3
Lochinvar Av GTS/LS CH66 194 C3
Lochinvar St WLT/FAZ L9 97 H2
Lochmore Rd CALD/MH L18 153 H2
Lochryan Rd ALL/GAR L19 153 J3
Loch St RUNC WA7 10 D3
Locker Av WARRN/WOL WA2 123 H5
Lockerbie Cl
WARRN/WOL WA2 124 A3
Lockerby Rd EHL/KEN L7 114 B4
Locker Pk GR/UP/WCH CH49 128 D5
Locke St ALL/GAR L19 172 B1
Lockett Rd AIMK WN4 79 G3
WDN WA8 158 B1
Lockett St WARRS WA4 143 J6
Lockfields Vw VAUX/LVPD L3 112 E2
Lockgate East RUNC WA7 178 B3
Lockgate West RUNC WA7 178 B3
Locking Stumps La
WARRN/WOL WA2 124 D4
Lockington Cl TOX L8 133 F5
Lock Rd PS/BROM CH62 171 K6
WARR WA1 143 J2
Lock St STHEL WA9 89 F6
Lockton La WARRW/BUR WA5 142 B2
Lockton Rd PR/KW L34 85 G6
Lock Vls WARRS WA4 * 144 A6
Lockwood Vw RUNC WA7 188 E2
Loddon Cl GR/UP/WCH CH49 129 H2
Lodge Hollow FROD/HEL WA6 199 J6
Lodge La NEWLW WA12 91 G4
ORM L39 65 J6
PS/BROM CH62 151 G5
RUNC WA7 177 H5
TOX L8 133 G2
WARRW/BUR WA5 142 B2
Lodge Rd WDN WA8 157 G3
Lodwick St BTL L20 96 D4
Lofthouse Ga WDN WA8 138 E6
Logan Rd BIRK CH41 111 H6
Logfield Dr ALL/GAR L19 154 A6
Lognor Rd KKBY L32 84 B1
Logwood Rd HUY L36 136 D1
Lombard Rd MOR/LEA CH46 109 K5
Lombardy Av
GR/UP/WCH CH49 147 J1
Lomond Gv GTS/LS CH66 195 J6
MOR/LEA CH46 129 G1
Lomond Rd EHL/KEN L7 114 C5
Londonderry Rd
CLB/OSW/ST L13 98 B6
London Flds
WGNW/BIL/OR WN5 77 H4
London La STHP PR8 35 F1
London Rd FROD/HEL WA6 200 E1
VAUX/LVPD L3 9 G3
WARRS WA4 162 C3
London Rw NEWLW WA12 106 D5
London Sq STHP PR8 14 E4
London St STHP PR8 15 F5
Longacre CHTN/BK PR9 23 H2
Longacre Cl WAL/NB CH45 110 D2
Long Acres GR/UP/WCH CH49 128 E4
Long Acres Rd NSTN CH64 181 K5
Long Av WLT/FAZ L9 82 E5
Longbarn Bvd
WARRN/WOL WA2 124 E5
Long Barn La
WARRN/WOL WA2 124 D5
Longborough Rd PR/KW L34 100 C2
Longbutt La LYMM WA13 165 G1
Longcliffe Dr STHP PR8 33 H5
Longcroft Av ALL/GAR L19 154 A4
Longcroft Sq ALL/GAR L19 154 A4
Longdale La SFTN L29 70 A2
Longdin St WARRS WA4 143 J6
Longdown Rd AIN/FAZ L10 84 A5
Longfellow Cl KKBY L32 84 C3
Longfellow Dr PS/BROM CH62 151 F3
Longfellow St BTL L20 4 B1
TOX L8 133 H2
Longfield FMBY L37 41 H6
Longfield Av CSBY/BLUN L23 69 F3
Longfield Cl
GR/UP/WCH CH49 128 E5
Longfield Rd LITH L21 81 J5
WARRN/WOL WA2 123 J6
Longfold KIRK/FR/WAR PR4 25 K3
MGHL L31 62 C6
Longford Dr WDN WA8 157 K1
Longford Rd STHP PR8 27 H5
Longford St TOX L8 133 F6
WARRN/WOL WA2 142 E2
Long Hey RAIN/WH L35 117 K5
Longhey SKEL WN8 56 E1
Long Hey Rd WKBY CH48 147 F4
Long Heys La SKEL WN8 57 G1
Longland Rd WAL/NB CH45 111 H1
Long La ALL/GAR L19 153 K4
ORM L39 53 G2
SFTN L29 69 H1
SKEL WN8 67 G4
WARRN/WOL WA2 123 J6
WAV L15 134 A1
WLT/FAZ L9 98 B1
Longlooms Rd EP CH65 203 H2
Longmead Av AIMK WN4 79 H5
Long Meadow ECCL WA10 102 D1
HES CH60 180 E1
Longmeadow Rd PR/KW L34 100 D1
Long Meanygate CHTN/BK PR9 24 D5
Longmoor Cl AIN/FAZ L10 83 H4
Longmoor Gv WLT/FAZ L9 82 E4
Longmoor La WLT/FAZ L9 83 H4
Longreach Rd DV/KA/FCH L14 115 K4
Longridge Av
GR/UP/WCH CH49 129 F3
RNFD/HAY WA11 89 G6
Longridge Wk ANF/KKDL L4 97 G5
Longshaw St
WARRW/BUR WA5 123 F5
Long Spinney RUNC WA7 178 B5
Longstone Wk EHL/KEN L7 133 G1
Longton Av GOL/RIS/CUL WA3 92 D3
Longton Dr FMBY L37 41 G5
Longton La RAIN/WH L35 118 D2
Longview Av RAIN/WH L35 118 C3
WAL/NB CH45 111 G2
Longview Crs HUY L36 117 F4
Longview Dr HUY L36 117 G4
Longview La HUY L36 117 F2
Longview Rd HUY L36 117 F3
RAIN/WH L35 118 C2
Longville St TOX L8 132 D4
Longwood Cl RNFD/HAY WA11 87 J2
Longwood Rd WARRS WA4 162 D6
Longworth Wy WLTN L25 135 H6
Lonie Gv ECCL WA10 102 E5
Lonmore Cl CHTN/BK PR9 21 K6
Lonsboro Rd WAL/EG CH44 111 J4
Lonsdale Av ECCL WA10 102 D6
ORM L39 45 K4
WAL/NB CH45 111 G1
Lonsdale Cl LITH L21 81 J1
WARRW/BUR WA5 141 F1
WDN WA8 157 H3
Lonsdale Ms LITH L21 81 J1
Lonsdale Rd FMBY L37 48 E2
HLWD L26 155 H5
LITH L21 81 J1
STHP PR8 28 A3
Lonsdale Vls WAL/NB CH45 * 111 G1
Looe Cl WDN WA8 157 K1
Looe Rd NG/CROX L11 84 C6
The Looms NSTN CH64 181 G5
Loomsway PEN/TH CH61 147 K5
Loraine St EV L5 113 H2
Lordens Cl DV/KA/FCH L14 116 A2
Lordens Rd DV/KA/FCH L14 116 A2
Lord Nelson St CLVPS L1 9 G3
WARR WA1 17 F5
Lords Av CL/PREN CH43 129 K1
Lord Sefton Wy FMBY L37 49 K3
Lords Fold RNFD/HAY WA11 75 F2
Lordsgate Dr BRSC L40 38 E6
Lordsgate La BRSC L40 46 B1
Lordship La FROD/HEL WA6 199 G3
Lords La GOL/RIS/CUL WA3 124 E3
Lord St AIMK WN4 79 J5
ALL/GAR L19 172 B1
BIRK CH41 3 G3
BRSC L40 38 E4
CHTN/BK PR9 15 F3
CLVP L2 8 D4
ECCL WA10 13 F2
NEWLW WA12 106 A2
RUNC WA7 10 C3
STHP PR8 14 C6
WARRS WA4 16 E7
Lord St West STHP PR8 14 C7
Loreburn Rd WAV L15 134 B3
Lorenzo Dr NG/CROX L11 98 D4
Loretto Dr GR/UP/WCH CH49 129 H3
Loretto Rd WAL/EG CH44 111 F2
Lorn Ct BIRK CH41 * 3 G4
Lorne Ct CL/PREN CH43 * 130 E4
Lorne Rd CL/PREN CH43 130 D5
CSBY/WL L22 80 E2
Lorne St EHL/KEN L7 114 C4
Lorn St BIRK CH41 3 G4
Lorton Av RNFD/HAY WA11 88 D3
Lorton St TOX L8 133 G2
Lostock Av WARRW/BUR WA5 142 C1
Lostock Cl WGNW/BIL/OR WN5 77 H4
Lothair Rd ANF/KKDL L4 97 J6
Lothian St TOX L8 133 F3
Lotus Gdns STHEL WA9 104 E6
Loudon Gv TOX L8 133 F3
Lough Gn BEB CH63 170 C3
Loughlin Dr NWD/KWIPK L33 72 E4
Loughrigg Av RNFD/HAY WA11 88 E2
Louis Braille Cl NTHTN L30 70 C5
Louis Pasteur Av NTHTN L30 70 C5
Loushers La WARRS WA4 162 C1
Lovage Cl WARRN/WOL WA2 124 E5
Lovelace Rd ALL/GAR L19 153 J4
Love La VAUX/LVPD L3 112 E3
WAL/EG CH44 111 H4
Lovel Rd SPK/HALE L24 173 J3
Lovel Ter WDN WA8 157 G6
Lovel Wy SPK/HALE L24 173 J2
Lovely La WARRW/BUR WA5 142 B3
Lovett Dr RAIN/WH L35 118 A2
Low Bank Rd AIMK WN4 78 B3
Lowbridge Ct ALL/GAR L19 154 A6
Lowcroft SKEL WN8 56 E2
Lowden Av LITH L21 81 J1
Lowe Av WARRS WA4 143 J5
Lowell St ANF/KKDL L4 97 H4
Lower Alt Rd HTWN L38 59 F3
Lower Appleton Rd WDN WA8 19 F1
Lower Bank Vw BTL L20 96 D4
Lower Breck Rd NPK/KEN L6 114 A1
Lower Castle St CLVP L2 8 C4
Lower Church St WDN WA8 158 B6
Lower Cl HLWD L26 155 K3
Lower Farm Rd WLTN L25 135 G2
Lower Flaybrick Rd
CL/PREN CH43 130 B1
Lower Gn GR/UP/WCH CH49 129 H6
Lower Hey CSBY/BLUN L23 69 J4
Lower House La NG/CROX L11 98 E2
WDN WA8 18 B3
Lower La WLT/FAZ L9 83 H4
Lower Mersey St EP CH65 196 B2
Lower Mersey Vw BTL L20 96 D4
Lower Milk St VAUX/LVPD L3 8 D2
Lower Prom CHTN/BK PR9 14 E2
STHP PR8 14 C4
Lower Rake La
FROD/HEL WA6 199 J5
Lower Rd HLWD L26 156 A3
PS/BROM CH62 151 G5
Lower Robin Hood La
FROD/HEL WA6 199 H6
Lowerson Crs NG/CROX L11 98 C5
Lowerson Rd NG/CROX L11 98 C5
Lower Thingwall La
PEN/TH CH61 149 F5
Lower Wash La WARRS WA4 143 H6
Lowes Gn FMBY L37 49 H2
Lowestoft Dr ALL/GAR L19 153 J5
Lowe St ECCL WA10 12 E4
GOL/RIS/CUL WA3 92 B3
Lowe St South ECCL WA10 13 F5
Loweswater Cl
WARRN/WOL WA2 123 H4
Loweswater Crs
RNFD/HAY WA11 89 K5
Loweswater Wy
NWD/KWIPK L33 72 C5
Lowfield La STHEL WA9 119 H2
Lowfield Rd DV/KA/FCH L14 115 G4
Lowfields Av PS/BROM CH62 184 B3
Lowfields Cl PS/BROM CH62 184 B4
Lowlands Rd RUNC WA7 10 C4
Lowndes Rd NPK/KEN L6 114 B1
Lowry Bank WAL/EG CH44 112 A4
Lowry Cl NWD/KWIPK L33 72 D3
WARRW/BUR WA5 142 A3
Lowry Hill La BRSC L40 47 H1
Lowther Av AIN/FAZ L10 83 G1
MGHL L31 62 C5
Lowther Crs ECCL WA10 102 D5
Lowther Dr RAIN/WH L35 118 D4
Lowther St TOX L8 133 F2
Lowton Gdns
GOL/RIS/CUL WA3 92 C6
Lowton Rd GOL/RIS/CUL WA3 92 C2
Lowwood HTWN L38 59 F1
Lowwood Gv BIRK CH41 2 E6
Low Wood Gv PEN/TH CH61 168 C1
Lowwood Rd BIRK CH41 2 E6
Low Wood St NPK/KEN L6 113 J5
Loxdale Cl TOX L8 133 F6
Loxdale Dr EP CH65 195 J5
Loxley Cl WARRW/BUR WA5 141 H1
Loxley Rd STHP PR8 28 A3
Loyola Hey RAIN/WH L35 138 D1
Lucania St ALL/GAR L19 172 B1
Lucan Rd AIG/SPK L17 153 F1
Lucerne Rd WAL/EG CH44 111 K5
Lucerne St AIG/SPK L17 133 H6
Lucius Cl WLT/FAZ L9 82 C4
Lucknow St AIG/SPK L17 * 133 H5
Ludlow SKEL WN8 56 E1
Ludlow Cl WARR WA1 124 C6
Ludlow Crs RUNC WA7 176 E5
Ludlow Dr EP CH65 196 D6
ORM L39 45 H4
WKBY CH48 146 C2
Ludlow Gv PS/BROM CH62 171 F4
Ludlow St ANF/KKDL L4 97 H4
Ludwig Rd ANF/KKDL L4 113 K2
Lugard Rd AIG/SPK L17 153 F1
Lugsdale Rd WDN WA8 18 D5
Lugsmore La ECCL WA10 102 E4
Luke St AIMK WN4 79 J4
TOX L8 132 E3
WAL/EG CH44 112 A5
Lulworth SKEL WN8 56 E1
Lulworth Av CSBY/WL L22 80 D2
Lulworth Rd STHP PR8 27 G3
WLTN L25 135 K4
Lumb Brook Ms WARRS WA4 162 D2
Lumb Brook Rd WARRS WA4 162 D3
Lumber La WARRW/BUR WA5 105 J5
Lumley Rd WAL/EG CH44 111 K4
Lumley St ALL/GAR L19 153 J5
Lunar Dr NTHTN L30 70 C4
Lunar Rd WLT/FAZ L9 82 E5
Lunds Cl BRSC L40 54 E1
Lundy Dr EP CH65 203 G3
Lune Av MGHL L31 62 C5
Lunehurst GOL/RIS/CUL WA3 93 F3
Lunesdale Av WLT/FAZ L9 82 E4
Lune St CSBY/BLUN L23 69 F5
Lune Wy WDN WA8 157 H2
Lunsford Rd DV/KA/FCH L14 115 K3
Lunt Av NTHTN L30 82 D1
RAIN/WH L35 118 A4
Lunt Rd BTL L20 81 K5
SFTN L29 60 E5
Lunts Heath Rd WDN WA8 139 F4
Luntswood Gv NEWLW WA12 106 A1
Lupin Dr RNFD/HAY WA11 90 E5
Lupton Dr CSBY/BLUN L23 69 H5
Lupus Wy GTS/LS CH66 195 J6
Luscombe Cl HLWD L26 155 K3
Lusitania Rd ANF/KKDL L4 97 J3
Luther Gv STHEL WA9 105 F3
Luton Gv ANF/KKDL L4 97 H5
Luton Rd EP CH65 195 K4
Luton St EV L5 112 E1
WDN WA8 * 18 D6
Lutyens Cl ANF/KKDL L4 97 H6
Luxmore Rd ANF/KKDL L4 97 H4
Lycett Rd ANF/KKDL L4 98 A6
WAL/EG CH44 110 E2
Lychgate WARRS WA4 161 J4
Lycroft Cl RUNC WA7 186 E1
Lydbrook Cl RF/TRAN CH42 131 J6
Lydbury Cl WARRW/BUR WA5 122 D5
Lydbury Crs KKBY L32 84 E3
Lydd Cl SPK/HALE L24 173 G1
Lydden Rd EP CH65 6 C1
Lydford Rd WD/CROXPK L12 99 F5
Lydia Ann St CLVPS L1 9 F6
Lydiate La CSBY/BLUN L23 69 J3
NSTN CH64 193 F1
RUNC WA7 176 B6
WLTN L25 155 G1
Lydiate Pk CSBY/BLUN L23 69 J3
Lydiate Rd BTL L20 81 K6
Lydiate Station Rd MGHL L31 61 G2
The Lydiate HES CH60 167 K6
Lydieth Lea NTHLY L27 136 B3
Lydney Rd HUY L36 116 B3
Lydstep Ct
WARRW/BUR WA5 * 122 E5
Lyelake Cl KKBY L32 84 E2
Lyelake La BRSC L40 55 F4
Lyelake Rd KKBY L32 84 E2
Lyle St EV L5 113 F2
Lyme Cl HUY L36 117 G1
Lyme Cross Rd HUY L36 117 F1
Lyme Gv HUY L36 117 F2
LYMM WA13 164 D1
Lyme St NEWLW WA12 105 J1
RNFD/HAY WA11 90 D5
Lymington Gv NTHTN L30 70 C6
Lymington Rd WAL/EG CH44 111 F3
Lymmhay La LYMM WA13 145 K5
Lymmington Av
LYMM WA13 145 H6
Lymm Rd CL/PREN CH43 129 K2
WARRS WA4 144 E6
Lynas Gdns ALL/GAR L19 153 J3
Lynas St BIRK CH41 2 D1
Lyncot Rd WLT/FAZ L9 82 E3
Lyncroft Rd WAL/EG CH44 111 J5
Lyndale RUNC WA7 177 F5
SKEL WN8 56 D1
Lyndale Av PS/BROM CH62 184 B3
WARRN/WOL WA2 143 G1
Lyndene Rd WLTN L25 135 H2
Lyndhurst SKEL WN8 56 D1
Lyndhurst Av CALD/MH L18 134 A6
PEN/TH CH61 168 A2
Lyndhurst Cl PEN/TH CH61 148 D6
Lyndhurst Rd CALD/MH L18 134 A5
CSBY/BLUN L23 69 H5
HOY CH47 108 C6
PEN/TH CH61 147 K6
STHP PR8 27 H5
WAL/NB CH45 111 F1
Lyndhurst Wy HUY L36 116 E5
Lyndon Dr CALD/MH L18 134 C5
Lyndon Gv RUNC WA7 176 E5
Lyndor Cl WLTN L25 154 E2
Lyndor Rd WLTN L25 154 E2
Lyneal Av GTS/LS CH66 202 A1
Lyneham RAIN/WH L35 118 B5
Lynham Av
WARRW/BUR WA5 * 141 J4
Lynholme Rd ANF/KKDL L4 97 K6
Lynmouth Rd AIG/SPK L17 153 F3
Lynnbank CL/PREN CH43 130 E5
Lynnbank Rd CALD/MH L18 134 E4
Lynn Cl ECCL WA10 102 E1
RUNC WA7 177 F6
Lynndene GTS/LS CH66 195 G2
Lynscott Pl CHLDW L16 134 E1
Lynsted Rd DV/KA/FCH L14 115 K4
Lynton Cl ALL/GAR L19 153 J3
HES CH60 181 G1
WARRW/BUR WA5 141 F5
Lynton Crs WDN WA8 157 K1
Lynton Dr BEB CH63 170 C2
STHP PR8 27 F6
Lynton Gn WLTN L25 135 G5
Lynton Gv STHEL WA9 120 A2
Lynton Rd HUY L36 117 H4
STHP PR8 34 A1
WAL/NB CH45 110 E1
Lynton Wy ECCL WA10 87 J5
Lynwood Av GOL/RIS/CUL WA3 93 F5
ORM L39 53 G2
WAL/EG CH44 111 G4
WARRS WA4 162 B4
Lynwood Cl SKEL WN8 57 F6
Lynwood Dr PEN/TH CH61 148 B5
Lynwood End ORM L39 * 53 G2
Lynwood Gdns WLT/FAZ L9 82 C6
Lynwood Rd WLT/FAZ L9 82 C6
The Lynxway
WD/CROXPK L12 115 H2
Lyon Cl ECCL WA10 12 E5
Lyon Rd ANF/KKDL L4 113 K1
Lyons Cl MOR/LEA CH46 109 J6
Lyon's La WARRS WA4 162 C5
Lyons Pl WLTN L25 155 G3
Lyons Rd MOR/LEA CH46 109 J6
STHP PR8 27 H2
WARRW/BUR WA5 141 G5
Lyon St AIMK WN4 78 E2
ALL/GAR L19 172 B1
ECCL WA10 12 D5
WARRS WA4 143 J6
Lyra Rd CSBY/WL L22 80 E2
Lyster Cl GOL/RIS/CUL WA3 125 H4
Lyster Rd BTL L20 4 B4
Lytham Cl AIN/FAZ L10 83 J2
WARRW/BUR WA5 141 H6
Lytham Ct KKBY L32 72 B5
Lytham Rd AIMK WN4 78 E4
CHTN/BK PR9 23 J1
WDN WA8 158 C1
Lytham Wy WD/CROXPK L12 115 J1
Lythgoes La WARRN/WOL WA2 16 D2
Lytles Cl FMBY L37 49 G3
Lyttelton Rd AIG/SPK L17 153 F1
Lytton Av RF/TRAN CH42 150 E2
Lytton Gv LITH L21 81 H5
Lytton St NPK/KEN L6 113 H4

M

Mab La WD/CROXPK L12 99 K5
Macalpine Cl
GR/UP/WCH CH49 129 H3
Macarthur Rd
WARRW/BUR WA5 * 141 J3
Macbeth St BTL L20 96 E4
Macdermott Rd WDN WA8 158 A6
Macdona Dr WKBY CH48 146 C3
Macdonald Av
RNFD/HAY WA11 * 89 H6
Macdonald Dr
GR/UP/WCH CH49 128 E6
Macdonald Rd MOR/LEA CH46 128 D1
Macdonald St WAV L15 133 K1
Mace Rd NG/CROX L11 99 G2
Macfarren St CLB/OSW/ST L13 114 E4
Mackenzie Rd MOR/LEA CH46 110 B4
Mackenzie St NPK/KEN L6 113 J2
Mackets Cl WLTN L25 155 F2
Macket's La WLTN L25 155 F2
Mack Gv NTHTN L30 82 A1
Macqueen St CLB/OSW/ST L13 114 E5
Maddock Rd WAL/EG CH44 111 K2
Maddocks St CLB/OSW/ST L13 114 E5
Maddock St BIRK CH41 2 C1
Maddrell St VAUX/LVPD L3 112 D3
Madelaine St TOX L8 133 F3
Madeley Cl WKBY CH48 146 C2
Madeley Dr WKBY CH48 146 C2
Madeley St NPK/KEN L6 114 A3
Madeline McKenna Ct
WDN WA8 * 138 B6
Madiera Dr WLTN L25 135 J3
Madingley Ct CHTN/BK PR9 * 23 H3
Madryn Av NWD/KWIPK L33 85 F1
Madryn St TOX L8 133 F4
Maelor Cl BEB CH63 183 J1
Mafeking Cl WAV L15 134 A1
Mafeking Pl AIMK WN4 79 H6
Magazine Av WAL/NB CH45 95 H6
Magazine Brow WAL/NB CH45 95 J6
Magazine La PS/BROM CH62 171 G2
WAL/NB CH45 95 H6
Magazine Rd PS/BROM CH62 171 F2
Magazines Prom WAL/NB CH45 95 J6
Magazine Wk
PS/BROM CH62 * 171 F2
Magdala St TOX L8 133 H2
Magdalen Dr AIMK WN4 78 E5
Magdalene Sq NTHTN L30 * 70 C5
Maggots Nook Rd
RNFD/HAY WA11 66 C6
Maghull La MGHL L31 63 F6
Maghull St CLVPS L1 8 D7
Mag La LYMM WA13 165 G4
Magnolia Cl GTS/LS CH66 202 D2
HLWD L26 155 G1
RNFD/HAY WA11 89 J6
WARR WA1 144 D2
Magnolia Dr RUNC WA7 187 J3
Magnolia Wk
GR/UP/WCH CH49 147 K1
Magnus Cl CLB/OSW/ST L13 114 D2
Maguire Av BTL L20 5 K3
Mahon Av BTL L20 82 A5
Mahon Ct TOX L8 * 132 E2
Maiden Cl SKEL WN8 55 J3
Maiden Gdns EP CH65 196 C6
Maiden La CLB/OSW/ST L13 98 B6
Maidford Rd DV/KA/FCH L14 115 K2
Maidstone Cl WLTN L25 155 F3
Maidstone Dr
WD/CROXPK L12 115 K2
Main Av ECCL WA10 102 E5
Main Cl RNFD/HAY WA11 89 K5
Main Dr RAIN/WH L35 118 A6
Main Front RAIN/WH L35 118 A6
Main Rd BEB CH63 170 D1
Mainside Rd KKBY L32 84 E2
Main St FROD/HEL WA6 200 D1
RUNC WA7 177 J5
WGNW/BIL/OR WN5 77 H4
Maintree Crs SPK/HALE L24 174 B1
Mainwaring Rd
PS/BROM CH62 171 F5
WAL/EG CH44 111 K4
Mairesfield Av WARRS WA4 163 G1
Mairscough La ORM L39 51 J5
Maitland Cl TOX L8 133 G2
Maitland Rd WAL/NB CH45 95 J5
Maitland St TOX L8 * 133 G2
Major Cross St WDN WA8 18 E5
Major St EV L5 113 F1
Makerfield Dr NEWLW WA12 91 F6
Makin St ANF/KKDL L4 97 H3
Malcolm Av WARRN/WOL WA2 123 K6
Malcolm Crs BEB CH63 183 K1
Malcolm Gv BTL L20 97 F4
Malcolm Pl WAV L15 114 D6
Malcolm St RUNC WA7 11 G5
Malden Rd NPK/KEN L6 114 A4
Maldon Cl HLWD L26 155 J5
Maldwyn Rd WAL/EG CH44 111 H2
Maley Cl TOX L8 133 F5
Malham Cl STHP PR8 28 B4
WARRW/BUR WA5 141 F1
Malhamdale Av RAIN/WH L35 119 F5
Malika Pl AIMK WN4 * 78 D3
Malin Cl SPK/HALE L24 174 E3
Maliston Rd WARRW/BUR WA5 141 J4
Mallaby St BIRK CH41 130 D1
Mallard Cl HLWD L26 155 H2
ORM L39 53 G3
RUNC WA7 187 J2
WARRN/WOL WA2 123 K4
WD/CROXPK L12 99 K2
Mallard Gdns STHEL WA9 119 G1
Mallard La GOL/RIS/CUL WA3 125 H4
The Mallards CHTN/BK PR9 24 A2
Mallard Wy MOR/LEA CH46 109 G6
RNFD/HAY WA11 88 E5
Mallee Av CHTN/BK PR9 23 J2
Mallee Crs CHTN/BK PR9 23 J2
Malleson Rd CLB/OSW/ST L13 98 C6
Mallins Cl TOX L8 133 F5
Mallory Av MGHL L31 61 K3
Mallory Gv RNFD/HAY WA11 89 G5
Mallory Rd EP CH65 6 A6
RF/TRAN CH42 150 C1
Mallowdale Cl PS/BROM CH62 184 B2
Mallow Rd NPK/KEN L6 114 A4
Mallow Wy HUY L36 136 C1
The Mall EV L5 * 113 J2
Malmesbury Cl
GR/UP/WCH CH49 128 D5
Malmesbury Pk RUNC WA7 178 C2

Malmesbury Rd NG/CROX L11 98 C3
Malpas Av CL/PREN CH43 149 K1
Malpas Dr BEB CH63 150 D4
WARRW/BUR WA5 141 K5
Malpas Gv WAL/NB CH45 111 G1
Malpas Rd EP CH65 195 J5
NG/CROX L11 84 C6
RUNC WA7 176 E6
WAL/NB CH45 111 F1
Malpas Wy
WARRW/BUR WA5 * 141 K5
Malta Cl HUY L36 116 D4
Malta St TOX L8 132 E4
Malta Wk TOX L8 132 E4
Malt House Ct ECCL WA10 87 K5
Maltkiln La ORM L39 53 J5
Maltmans Rd LYMM WA13 145 J6
Malton Av GOL/RIS/CUL WA3 93 F4
Malton Cl WDN WA8 138 B4
Malton Rd WLTN L25 155 F2
Malt St EHL/KEN L7 133 G1
Malvern Av DV/KA/FCH L14 115 K5
EP CH65 196 B6
Malvern Cl AIMK WN4 79 G5
KKBY L32 72 B5
WARRW/BUR WA5 141 H1
Malvern Crs DV/KA/FCH L14 115 K5
Malvern Gv AIN/FAZ L10 83 F1
RF/TRAN CH42 150 C1
Malvern Rd BTL L20 81 K6
NPK/KEN L6 114 A4
STHEL WA9 104 D2
WAL/NB CH45 110 D2
The Malverns CL/PREN CH43 * 130 D6
Malwood St TOX L8 132 E6
Manchester Rd CHTN/BK PR9 15 G3
GOL/RIS/CUL WA3 145 F2
PR/KW L34 117 J1
WARR WA1 17 G3
Manchester Rw NEWLW WA12 106 D5
Mancroft Cl WARR WA1 144 D2
Mandarin Ct WARR WA1 142 D6
Manderston Dr
WD/CROXPK L12 99 H6
Mandeville Rd STHP PR8 33 H4
Mandeville St ANF/KKDL L4 97 H3
Manesty's La CLVPS L1 8 E5
Manfield SKEL WN8 56 C2
Manhattan Gdns
WARRW/BUR WA5 141 H2
Manica Crs AIN/FAZ L10 83 J5
Manion Av MGHL L31 61 K2
Manion Cl MGHL L31 61 K2
Manley Av GOL/RIS/CUL WA3 92 A1
Manley Cl CL/PREN CH43 130 C6
Manley Gdns
WARRW/BUR WA5 142 C4
Manley Pl STHEL WA9 103 G6
Manley Rd CSBY/WL L22 80 D1
FROD/HEL WA6 201 F5
HUY L36 136 D1
Manley Vw CHNE CH2 198 D6
Manna Dr CHNE CH2 198 D6
Mannering Rd AIG/SPK L17 133 G5
Manners La HES CH60 180 D1
Manningham Rd ANF/KKDL L4 113 K1
Manning Rd STHP PR8 28 B1
Manning St ECCL WA10 12 E6
Mannington Cl HOY CH47 127 K1
Mann Island VAUX/LVPD L3 8 B5
Mann St TOX L8 132 D3
Manor Av BRSC L40 46 D1
CSBY/BLUN L23 68 E4
GOL/RIS/CUL WA3 92 D3
NEWLW WA12 105 K1
RAIN/WH L35 118 E5
Manorbier Crs WLT/FAZ L9 97 J2
Manor Cl AIMK WN4 78 B6
BTL L20 5 K6
NSTN CH64 191 H2
WARR WA1 144 C2
Manor Ct GOL/RIS/CUL WA3 92 D3
Manor Crs BRSC L40 46 D1
WLTN L25 154 E2
Manor Dr BRSC L40 46 D1
CSBY/BLUN L23 68 E4
GR/UP/WCH CH49 129 G2
NTHTN L30 70 E6
Manor Farm Ct
FROD/HEL WA6 187 F6
Manor Farm Rd HUY L36 117 F6
RUNC WA7 178 C1
Manor Fell RUNC WA7 178 A6
Manor Gdns BRSC L40 46 D1
Manor Gv KKBY L32 84 A1
SKEL WN8 56 B4
Manor Hl CL/PREN CH43 130 D3
Manor House Cl MGHL L31 62 A6
RNFD/HAY WA11 88 D1
Manor House Dr SKEL WN8 67 G4
Manorial Rd NSTN CH64 191 H1
Manorial Rd South NSTN CH64 191 H1
Manor La GTS/LS CH66 195 G6
RF/TRAN CH42 151 F1
WAL/NB CH45 111 J2
Manor Ldg FMBY L37 48 E1
Manor Ms WAL/NB CH45 * 111 J2
Manor Park Av RUNC WA7 178 B1
Manor Park Cl PEN/TH CH61 148 D5
Manor Park Dr GTS/LS CH66 202 B1
Manor Pl PS/BROM CH62 151 J6
Manor Rd BEB CH63 169 F4
BRSC L40 46 D1
CHTN/BK PR9 23 J3
CSBY/BLUN L23 68 D3
FROD/HEL WA6 187 F6
HOY CH47 127 H1
LYMM WA13 165 F1
PEN/TH CH61 148 A5
PS/BROM CH62 184 B1
RNFD/HAY WA11 90 E4
RUNC WA7 177 G3
WAL/EG CH44 111 H2
WDN WA8 157 G2
WLTN L25 154 E2
Manorside Cl
GR/UP/WCH CH49 129 G3
Manor St GOL/RIS/CUL WA3 92 C2
STHEL WA9 104 A3
The Manor WARR WA1 144 E2
Manor Vw WD/CROXPK L12 99 K4
Manor Wy WLTN L25 154 E2
Manorwood Dr RAIN/WH L35 118 A5
Mansart Cl AIMK WN4 79 J6
Manse Gdns NEWLW WA12 106 D1
Mansell Cl WDN WA8 139 H4
Mansell Dr HLWD L26 155 H5
Mansell Rd NPK/KEN L6 113 K4
Mansfield Cl
GOL/RIS/CUL WA3 125 J3
Mansfield Rd EP CH65 202 E1
Mansfield St
GOL/RIS/CUL WA3 91 K2
VAUX/LVPD L3 9 G1
Mansion Dr NG/CROX L11 99 F1
Manston Rd
WARRW/BUR WA5 141 G6
Manton Rd NPK/KEN L6 114 A4
Manuel Perez Rd
WARRW/BUR WA5 141 J3
Manvers Rd CHLDW L16 115 J6
Manville Rd WAL/NB CH45 95 H6
Manville St STHEL WA9 104 A4
Manx Jane's La CHTN/BK PR9 23 J1
Manx Rd WARRS WA4 142 E6
Maori Dr FROD/HEL WA6 200 D1
Maple Av BRSC L40 38 E5
GOL/RIS/CUL WA3 93 G4
GTS/LS CH66 195 F3
NEWLW WA12 106 D3
RNFD/HAY WA11 90 A4
RUNC WA7 177 F5
WDN WA8 * 19 F1
Maple Cl FMBY L37 48 C4
LITH L21 81 H5
RAIN/WH L35 118 A4
WD/CROXPK L12 99 H2
WGNW/BIL/OR WN5 77 G4
Maple Crs HUY L36 116 D5
WARRW/BUR WA5 141 G5
Mapledale Rd CALD/MH L18 134 B4
Maple Gv ECCL WA10 102 E2
GTS/LS CH66 202 E2
PS/BROM CH62 170 E5
RAIN/WH L35 118 A2
TOX L8 133 H3
WARRS WA4 143 G6
Maple Rd WARR WA1 144 D2
WARRN/WOL WA2 123 H1
Maple St AIMK WN4 79 F3
BIRK CH41 2 D7
STHP PR8 15 K7
Mapleton Cl CL/PREN CH43 149 H2
Mapleton Dr RUNC WA7 187 J4
Maple Tree Gv HES CH60 168 C4
Maplewood KKBY L32 84 E3
SKEL WN8 56 C1
Maplewood Cl NTHLY L27 136 B4
WDN WA8 157 G4
Maplewood Gv CL/PREN CH43 130 B1
Mapplewell Crs
WARRW/BUR WA5 141 H3
Maranatha Bungalows
HES CH60 * 168 A4
Marathon Cl NPK/KEN L6 113 H3
Marble Cl BTL L20 4 E7
Marbury Gdns EP CH65 195 J3
Marbury Rd KKBY L32 84 B1
Marbury St WARRS WA4 17 F7
Marc Av MGHL L31 72 A5
Marcham Wy NG/CROX L11 99 F4
Marchant Cl NTHTN L30 82 D3
Marchbank Rd SKEL WN8 55 K4
Marchfield Rd WLT/FAZ L9 82 C6
March Rd NPK/KEN L6 114 B2
Marchwiel Rd EP CH65 7 G6
Marchwood Wy WLTN L25 135 H2
Marcien Wy WDN WA8 138 E6
Marcot Rd NPK/KEN L6 114 B3
Marcross Cl WARRW/BUR WA5 122 E6
Marcus St BIRK CH41 2 E1
Mardale Av RNFD/HAY WA11 88 E3
WARRN/WOL WA2 123 J4
Mardale Cl NTHLY L27 136 D6
STHP PR8 33 H5
Mardale Lawn NTHLY L27 136 D6
Mardale Rd HUY L36 116 C2
Mareth Cl CALD/MH L18 153 H1
Marford Rd WD/CROXPK L12 99 F6
Marfords Av BEB CH63 170 E6
Margaret Av BTL L20 81 K4
STHEL WA9 104 A6
WARR WA1 144 A2
Margaret Ct WDN WA8 * 18 E6
Margaret Rd ANF/KKDL L4 5 K7
CSBY/BLUN L23 68 B4
Margaret's La GTS/LS CH66 194 D2
Margaret St NPK/KEN L6 113 J3
STHEL WA9 * 120 C4
Margery Rd ECCL WA10 102 E4
Marian Av NEWLW WA12 105 J2
Marian Cl RAIN/WH L35 118 E5
The Marian Cl NTHTN L30 70 B5
Marian Dr MOR/LEA CH46 129 F1
RAIN/WH L35 118 D5
Marian Rd RNFD/HAY WA11 90 D4
Marians Dr ORM L39 45 H3
The Marian Sq NTHTN L30 70 B5
The Marian Wy NTHTN L30 70 B6
Maria Rd WLT/FAZ L9 97 H2
Marie Curie Av NTHTN L30 70 C5
Marie Dr WARRS WA4 163 J1
Marigold Pl WARRW/BUR WA5 142 A6
Marigold Wy STHEL WA9 104 E6
Marina Av LITH L21 81 J3
STHEL WA9 104 A6
WARRW/BUR WA5 141 J5
Marina Crs HUY L36 116 D6
NTHTN L30 82 D2
Marina Dr EP CH65 6 C5
WARRN/WOL WA2 123 J6
Marina Gv RUNC WA7 11 G5
Marina La RUNC WA7 178 D6
Marina Rd FMBY L37 49 F4
The Marina CSBY/WL L22 * 80 D1
Marina Village RUNC WA7 178 D6
Marine Crs CSBY/WL L22 80 E2
Marine Dr CHTN/BK PR9 22 D3
HES CH60 167 H6
STHP PR8 14 D1
Marine Gate Man
CHTN/BK PR9 * 15 F2
Marine House VAUX/LVPD L3 * 132 C3
Marine Pde STHP PR8 14 C2
Marine Pk WKBY CH48 127 G5
Marine Prom WAL/NB CH45 95 H4
Mariner Cl RUNC WA7 188 C1
Marine Rd HOY CH47 127 F2
Mariners Rd CSBY/BLUN L23 80 C1
WAL/NB CH45 95 J6
Mariners Whf VAUX/LVPD L3 132 B3
Marine Ter CSBY/WL L22 80 E3
Marion Dr RUNC WA7 186 C1
Marion Gv CALD/MH L18 153 K1
Marion Rd BTL L20 82 A5
Marion St BIRK CH41 3 F4
Maritime Cl NEWLW WA12 91 H6
Maritime Ct NTHTN L30 70 C4
Maritime Pk BIRK CH41 * 2 C6
Maritime Pl VAUX/LVPD L3 * 9 H1
Maritime Vw RF/TRAN CH42 131 G6
Mariton Cl CALD/MH L18 154 A1
Marius Cl ANF/KKDL L4 97 H5
Mark Av GTS/LS CH66 195 F5
Market Ap AIMK WN4 * 79 G6
Market Ga WARR WA1 16 D5
Market Pl BIRK CH41 3 G5
PR/KW L34 117 K1
Market St BIRK CH41 3 G4
ECCL WA10 13 G6
EP CH65 6 C6
HOY CH47 127 G2
NEWLW WA12 106 A1
STHP PR8 14 D5
WDN WA8 18 D5
Market Wy ORM L39 45 J6
Markfield Crs RNFD/HAY WA11 89 F6
WLTN L25 155 G2
Markfield Rd BTL L20 81 J6
Markham Dr STHP PR8 28 B5
Markham Gv CL/PREN CH43 130 C1
Mark Rake PS/BROM CH62 171 F4
Mark Rd HTWN L38 59 F3
Mark St EV L5 113 G1
Marksway PEN/TH CH61 168 A1
Marland SKEL WN8 56 C1
Marlborough SKEL WN8 56 C1
Marlborough Av MGHL L31 62 B4
NTHTN L30 82 D1
Marlborough Crs WARRS WA4 162 E1
WDN WA8 139 F4
Marlborough Gv
CL/PREN CH43 130 E5
Marlborough Pl VAUX/LVPD L3 * 8 D1
Marlborough Rd CHTN/BK PR9 15 H4
CLB/OSW/ST L13 114 B1
CSBY/BLUN L23 68 E6
CSBY/WL L22 81 F3
EP CH65 196 C6
PR/KW L34 102 A6
Marlborough St VAUX/LVPD L3 8 D1
Marlborough Wk EP CH65 196 B6
Marlborough Wy
RNFD/HAY WA11 90 D3
Marlbrook Rd WLTN L25 135 J3
Marlcroft Dr AIG/SPK L17 153 F4
Marldon Av CSBY/BLUN L23 81 F1
Marldon Rd WD/CROXPK L12 99 F5
Marled Hey STBRV L28 100 A5
Marley Cl RAIN/WH L35 119 G6
Marlfield La PEN/TH CH61 168 A1
Marlfield Rd WARRS WA4 163 F1
WD/CROXPK L12 115 F1
Marline Av BEB CH63 183 K1
Marling Cl FROD/HEL WA6 201 G3
Marling Pk WDN WA8 157 G2
Marlow Cl GOL/RIS/CUL WA3 124 E2
Marlowe Cl ALL/GAR L19 153 K6
WDN WA8 18 A2
Marlowe Dr WD/CROXPK L12 114 E1
Marlowe Rd NSTN CH64 191 K1
WAL/EG CH44 111 G3
Marl Rd NTHTN L30 70 E6
NWD/KWIPK L33 73 H6
Marlsford St NPK/KEN L6 114 A4
Marlston Av PEN/TH CH61 148 C5
Marlston Pl RUNC WA7 186 E1
Marlwood Av WAL/NB CH45 110 E2
Marmaduke St EHL/KEN L7 113 K6
Marmion Av BTL L20 82 B4
Marmion Cl GOL/RIS/CUL WA3 93 F2
Marmion Rd AIG/SPK L17 133 G5
HOY CH47 127 G2
Marmonde St ANF/KKDL L4 97 G5
Marnwood Rd KKBY L32 84 C2
Marple Cl CL/PREN CH43 130 B6
Marquis St BIRK CH41 131 H5
PS/BROM CH62 151 G4
VAUX/LVPD L3 9 H3
Marram Cl MOR/LEA CH46 110 A6
Marron Av WARRN/WOL WA2 123 H5
Marryat Cl WARRN/WOL WA2 123 G1
Marsden Av ECCL WA10 12 A3
WARRS WA4 143 K5
Marsden Cl WAL/EG CH44 111 K2
Marsden Ct WDN WA8 138 D5
Marsden Rd CHTN/BK PR9 23 G6
HLWD L26 155 J5
Marsden St NPK/KEN L6 113 J4
Marsden Wy NPK/KEN L6 * 113 J4
Marshall Av STHEL WA9 * 104 A5
WARRW/BUR WA5 123 F5
Marshall Pl VAUX/LVPD L3 * 112 E3
Marshall Rd WARR WA1 144 C2
Marshallsay FMBY L37 49 G3
Marshall's Cl MGHL L31 62 A3
Marshalls Cross Rd
STHEL WA9 103 K6
Marshall St BIRK CH41 2 C1
Marsham Cl
GR/UP/WCH CH49 * 129 H2
Marsham Rd WLTN L25 135 K4
Marsh Av BTL L20 82 B5
Marsh Brows FMBY L37 48 E3
Marshfield Cl HUY L36 117 F4
Marshfield Ct MOR/LEA CH46 109 J4
Marshfield Rd NG/CROX L11 99 F4
Marshgate WDN WA8 157 G5
Marshgate Pl FROD/HEL WA6 187 F5
Marsh Hall Rd WDN WA8 139 G5
Marsh House La
WARRN/WOL WA2 143 F2
Marshlands Rd NSTN CH64 191 K4
WAL/NB CH45 110 E1
Marsh La BEB CH63 150 B4
BTL L20 4 C2
CHNE CH2 198 C6
FROD/HEL WA6 200 D1
HTWN L38 59 K3
RUNC WA7 177 J2
WARRS WA4 189 J4
WARRW/BUR WA5 159 K1
Marsh Moss La BRSC L40 38 C1
Marsh Rd CHTN/BK PR9 21 K1
Marshside Cl TOX L8 132 E4
Marshside Rd CHTN/BK PR9 20 B6
Marsh St BTL L20 97 F4
STHEL WA9 104 A1
WARR WA1 17 J1
WDN WA8 158 B5
Marshway Dr NEWLW WA12 106 B1
Marsland Gv STHEL WA9 104 C5
Marson St WARRN/WOL WA2 16 C3
Marston Cl CL/PREN CH43 149 J1
PS/BROM CH62 184 B4
Marston Crs HTWN L38 59 G5
Marston Gdns EP CH65 195 J3
Marsworth Dr NPK/KEN L6 113 H3
Marten Av BEB CH63 170 E6
Martensen St EHL/KEN L7 113 K6
Martham Cl WARRS WA4 143 K6
Martham Gdns STHEL WA9 119 G1
Martin Av ECCL WA10 88 C5
NEWLW WA12 91 G6
WARRN/WOL WA2 123 K6
Martin Cl CALD/MH L18 153 H2
PEN/TH CH61 147 K5
RAIN/WH L35 118 C3
RUNC WA7 177 K6
Martindale Gv RUNC WA7 187 G2
Martindale Rd CHLDW L16 134 E4
PS/BROM CH62 171 G4
RNFD/HAY WA11 88 E1
Martine Cl MGHL L31 72 A5
Martin Gv RAIN/WH L35 118 A2
Martinhall Rd WLT/FAZ L9 98 D1
Martin La BRSC L40 37 J1
Martin Rd CALD/MH L18 153 H2
FROD/HEL WA6 200 E1
Martins La SKEL WN8 57 F6
WAL/EG CH44 111 J3
Martland Av AIN/FAZ L10 71 H6
GOL/RIS/CUL WA3 92 E4
Martland Rd WLTN L25 135 K5
Mart La BRSC L40 38 E4
Martlesham Crs
GR/UP/WCH CH49 128 C6
Martlett Rd WD/CROXPK L12 115 H2
Martock RAIN/WH L35 118 B5
Marton Cl SPK/HALE L24 173 J3
Marton Gn SPK/HALE L24 * 173 J3
Marton Rd HUY L36 116 E1
Marvin St EHL/KEN L7 113 J4
Mary Av STHP PR8 34 A3
Marybone VAUX/LVPD L3 8 E2
Maryfield Cl GOL/RIS/CUL WA3 92 B4
Maryhill Rd RUNC WA7 176 D5
Maryland Cl WARRW/BUR WA5 141 K2
Maryland La MOR/LEA CH46 109 H6
Maryland St CLVPS L1 9 H6
Marylebone Av STHEL WA9 119 H1
Maryport Cl EV L5 113 H1
Mary Rd BTL L20 82 A5
Mary Stockton Ct LITH L21 * 81 H5
Mary St STHEL WA9 120 C4
WDN WA8 19 K5
Maryton Gra CALD/MH L18 154 A1
Maryville Cl EP CH65 6 E1
Maryville Rd PR/KW L34 118 A1
Marywell Cl STHEL WA9 104 B6
Masefield Av WDN WA8 18 B4
Masefield Cl PS/BROM CH62 151 F4
Masefield Crs NTHTN L30 82 A3
Masefield Dr
WARRN/WOL WA2 123 G2
Masefield Gv CHLDW L16 135 G1
ECCL WA10 12 A1
Masefield Pl NTHTN L30 82 B3
Masefield Rd CSBY/BLUN L23 69 K3
Maskell Rd CLB/OSW/ST L13 114 D4
Mason Av WARR WA1 143 H1
WDN WA8 139 F5
Mason Cl AIMK WN4 79 J5
GTS/LS CH66 202 B1
Mason St CSBY/WL L22 80 E2
EHL/KEN L7 113 J6
RUNC WA7 11 H3
WAL/NB CH45 95 H5
WARR WA1 17 G5
WLTN L25 154 D1
Massam Cl RNFD/HAY WA11 75 H3
Massam's La FMBY L37 40 E5
Massey Av LYMM WA13 164 B1
WARRW/BUR WA5 123 F5
Massey Brook La LYMM WA13 164 C1
Masseyfield Rd RUNC WA7 187 K2
Massey Pk WAL/NB CH45 111 G2
Massey St BIRK CH41 2 D1
STHEL WA9 104 A5
Masters Wy ALL/GAR L19 172 C1
Matchwood Cl ALL/GAR L19 154 A6
Mather Av CALD/MH L18 134 C5
GOL/RIS/CUL WA3 93 F5
STHEL WA9 104 C2
Mather Rd CL/PREN CH43 130 E4
Mathers Cl WARRN/WOL WA2 124 C3
Mathew St CLVP L2 8 D4
Mathieson Rd WDN WA8 157 K6
Matlock Av WLT/FAZ L9 82 D5
Matlock Cl WARRW/BUR WA5 122 A6
Matlock Crs STHP PR8 27 J3
Matlock Rd STHP PR8 27 J4
Matterdale Cl FROD/HEL WA6 201 G2
Matthew Cl WAL/EG CH44 112 A5
Matthews St WARR WA1 17 H1
Matthew St WAL/EG CH44 112 A5
Matty's La FROD/HEL WA6 200 D2
Maud St TOX L8 133 F3
Maunders Ct CSBY/BLUN L23 69 G4
Mauretania Rd ANF/KKDL L4 97 J3
Mavis Dr GR/UP/WCH CH49 129 H6
Mawdsley Av WARR WA1 144 D2
Mawdsley Cl FMBY L37 49 H2
Mawdsley Ter ORM L39 45 K3
Mawson Cl WARRW/BUR WA5 142 A1
Max Rd DV/KA/FCH L14 115 K2
Maxton Rd NPK/KEN L6 114 A4
Maxwell Cl EP CH65 202 E1
GR/UP/WCH CH49 129 H3
Maxwell Pl CLB/OSW/ST L13 114 D1
Maxwell Rd CLB/OSW/ST L13 114 D1
Maxwell St ECCL WA10 12 D6
GOL/RIS/CUL WA3 125 G1
May Av WAL/EG CH44 111 K5
Maybank Cl CHTN/BK PR9 23 J4
Maybank Gv AIG/SPK L17 153 G2
Maybank Rd RF/TRAN CH42 131 G5
Mayberry Gv
WARRN/WOL WA2 124 C6
Maybury Wy AIG/SPK L17 152 D1
May Cl LITH L21 81 J5
Mayer Av BEB CH63 170 B1
Mayew Rd PEN/TH CH61 148 C5
Mayfair Av CSBY/BLUN L23 69 F4
DV/KA/FCH L14 115 K4
Mayfair Cl HTWN L38 59 F5
NPK/KEN L6 113 K3
WARRW/BUR WA5 140 E2
Mayfair Gv WDN WA8 157 J2
Mayfayre Av MGHL L31 61 K2
Mayfield ANF/KKDL L4 97 G5
Mayfield Av FMBY L37 48 C4
STHEL WA9 103 G5
WDN WA8 157 G2
Mayfield Cl WD/CROXPK L12 115 G1
Mayfield Ct FMBY L37 40 E6
Mayfield Dr LEIGH WN7 93 K3
PS/BROM CH62 184 E1
Mayfield Gdns ALL/GAR L19 153 H4
NSTN CH64 181 K6
Mayfield Rd ALL/GAR L19 153 H4
BEB CH63 170 C2
SKEL WN8 57 J6
WAL/NB CH45 110 E2
WARRS WA4 144 A6
Mayfields North
PS/BROM CH62 151 G4
Mayfields South
PS/BROM CH62 151 G4
Mayfield St AIMK WN4 * 79 F6
Mayfield Vw LYMM WA13 165 F1
Mayflower Av SPK/HALE L24 154 D5
May Pl VAUX/LVPD L3 9 H5
Maypole Ct NTHTN L30 70 A4
PR/KW L34 100 C1
May Rd HES CH60 168 A5
May St BTL L20 5 F2
GOL/RIS/CUL WA3 92 C1
VAUX/LVPD L3 9 H5
Maytree Cl NTHLY L27 135 K3
Maytree Wk SKEL WN8 56 D1
Mayville Rd CALD/MH L18 134 C4
Mazenod Ct VAUX/LVPD L3 8 E1
Mazzini Cl EV L5 113 G2
McBride St ALL/GAR L19 153 K5
McCarthy Cl GOL/RIS/CUL WA3 125 J4
Mc Clellan Pl WDN WA8 18 E2
McCormack Av STHEL WA9 104 C1
McCulloch St STHEL WA9 13 K5
McFarlane Av ECCL WA10 102 E1
McGarva Wy EP CH65 6 D7
McGough Cl STHEL WA9 119 J4
McKeagney Gdns WDN WA8 157 J4
McKee Av WARRN/WOL WA2 123 H5
McKeown Cl EV L5 113 F2
McKinley St WARRW/BUR WA5 141 H2
McKinley Wy WDN WA8 138 E6
McMinnis Av STHEL WA9 104 E3
McVinnie Rd RAIN/WH L35 118 B1
Mead Av LITH L21 81 K3
Meade Cl RAIN/WH L35 119 F6
Meade Rd CLB/OSW/ST L13 114 C1
Meadfoot Rd MOR/LEA CH46 109 H6
Meadow Av STHEL WA9 120 B4
STHP PR8 27 K3
WARRS WA4 161 K1
Meadow Bank MGHL L31 61 K5
ORM L39 * 45 K6
Meadowbank Cl
DV/KA/FCH L14 115 J2
Meadowbank Dr GTS/LS CH66 194 D3
Meadowbarn Cl KKBY L32 84 D2
Meadowbridge Cl BRSC L40 54 E1
Meadowbrook BRSC L40 46 D1
Meadow Brook Cl AIN/FAZ L10 84 A4
Meadowbrook Rd
MOR/LEA CH46 128 E2
Meadow Brow CHTN/BK PR9 21 G6
Meadow Cl BRSC L40 54 E1
NSTN CH64 193 G1
NSTN CH64 191 K3
SKEL WN8 57 F6
WDN WA8 138 C6
Meadow Clough SKEL WN8 56 D1
Meadow Crs
GR/UP/WCH CH49 148 E1
Meadowcroft AIMK WN4 78 E3
Meadow Cft NSTN CH64 193 F1
Meadowcroft FMBY L37 49 F3
HES CH60 168 C4
SKEL WN8 56 D1
STHEL WA9 120 A1
Meadowcroft Ct RUNC WA7 177 K5
Meadowcroft Pk
WD/CROXPK L12 115 H3
Meadowcroft Rd HOY CH47 108 C6
Meadow Dr HUY L36 136 C1
ORM L39 53 G3
Meadowfield SKEL WN8 57 J6
Meadowfield Cl
RF/TRAN CH42 150 E1
WLT/FAZ L9 82 D4
Meadow Ga WKBY CH48 146 E6
Meadow Hey BTL L20 81 H6
Meadow Hey Cl WLTN L25 135 J6
Meadow La BRSC L40 39 J6
EP CH65 7 F3
MGHL L31 62 C6
NSTN CH64 183 F6
RF/TRAN CH42 150 E1

STHEL WA9 .... **104** D4
STHP PR8 .... **33** J6
WARRN/WOL WA2 .... **124** C5
WD/CROXPK L12 .... **99** F6
Meadow Oak Dr *WLTN* L25 .... **135** H4
Meadow Pk *RF/TRAN* CH42 .... **150** E1
Meadow Rd *WKBY* CH48 .... **128** A6
Meadowside
MOR/LEA CH46 .... **110** B3
Meadowside Av *AIMK* WN4 .... **79** F1
Meadowside Dr
NWD/KWIPK L33 .... **72** E3
Meadowside Rd
PS/BROM CH62 .... **171** F6
The Meadows *MGHL* L31 .... **62** B6
NSTN CH64 .... **192** A3
RAIN/WH L35 .... **118** E5
STHP PR8 * **33** K5
Meadow St *WAL/NB* CH45 .... **95** G5
The Meadow
GR/UP/WCH CH49 .... **129** J6
Meadow Vw *CHNE* CH2 .... **198** B6
LITH L21 .... **69** J6
STHP PR8 .... **28** A3
Meadow View Dr
FROD/HEL WA6 .... **200** D2
Meadow Wk *PEN/TH* CH61 .... **167** J2
RUNC WA7 * **177** J6
Meadow Wy *NG/CROX* L11 .... **99** F4
Mead Rd *WARR* WA1 .... **143** K1
Meadway *GOL/RIS/CUL* WA3 .... **92** E3
GR/UP/WCH CH49 .... **129** J3
GTS/LS CH66 .... **194** E2
HES CH60 .... **180** E1
MGHL L31 .... **70** E2
NTHTN L30 .... **82** C1
PS/BROM CH62 .... **170** E3
RAIN/WH L35 .... **118** B3
RUNC WA7 .... **177** G4
SKEL WN8 .... **56** C1
WAL/NB CH45 .... **111** G2
WAV L15 .... **134** D1
WDN WA8 .... **157** F2
The Meander *WD/CROXPK* L12 .... **99** J4
Measham Cl *RNFD/HAY* WA11 .... **89** F6
Measham Wy *WD/CROXPK* L12 .... **99** J2
Medbourne Crs *KKBY* L32 .... **84** E3
Medea St *EV* L5 .... **113** G1
Medlar Wy *AIMK* WN4 .... **78** E4
Medlock St *ANF/KKDL* L4 .... **97** G5
Medway Cl *AIMK* WN4 * **78** E3
LEIGH WN7 .... **93** K3
WARRN/WOL WA2 .... **124** A5
Medway Ct *STHEL* WA9 .... **104** D2
Medway Rd *RF/TRAN* CH42 .... **151** F1
Meeting La *WARRW/BUR* WA5 .... **140** E4
Melbreck *SKEL* WN8 .... **56** C1
Melbreck Rd *CALD/MH* L18 .... **153** J2
Melbury Ct *GOL/RIS/CUL* WA3 .... **125** H1
Melbury Rd *DV/KA/FCH* L14 .... **116** B1
Melda Cl *NPK/KEN* L6 .... **9** K1
Meldon Cl *WD/CROXPK* L12 .... **99** G3
Meldreth Cl *FMBY* L37 .... **48** C4
Meldrum Rd *WAV* L15 .... **134** C3
Melford Ct *WARR* WA1 * **144** C1
Melford Dr *AIMK* WN4 .... **79** F5
CL/PREN CH43 .... **149** H2
RUNC WA7 .... **11** H7
Melford Gv *NPK/KEN* L6 .... **114** B1
Meliden Gdns *STHEL* WA9 .... **104** D6
Melksham Dr *PEN/TH* CH61 .... **148** A4
Melling Av *WLT/FAZ* L9 .... **82** E4
Melling Dr *KKBY* L32 .... **72** D6
Melling La *MGHL* L31 .... **71** H2
Melling Rd *BTL* L20 .... **5** F1
CHTN/BK PR9 .... **23** G5
WAL/NB CH45 .... **95** J6
WLT/FAZ L9 .... **82** E3
Melling Wy *KKBY* L32 .... **72** D6
Mellock Cl *NSTN* CH64 .... **192** A3
Mellock La *NSTN* CH64 .... **192** A2
Melloncroft Dr *WKBY* CH48 .... **146** C3
Melloncroft Dr West
WKBY CH48 .... **146** D4
Mellor Cl *RAIN/WH* L35 .... **136** D2
RUNC WA7 .... **178** C5
Mellor Rd *RF/TRAN* CH42 .... **150** B1
Mellors Cl *STHP* PR8 .... **28** C2
Melly Rd *AIG/SPK* L17 .... **133** G6
Melmerby Cl *AIMK* WN4 .... **78** E6
Melrose Av *CHTN/BK* PR9 .... **20** E6
CSBY/BLUN L23 .... **69** F6
ECCL WA10 .... **87** J6
HOY CH47 .... **127** G2
WARRS WA4 .... **162** C3
WARRW/BUR WA5 .... **105** K6
Melrose Crs *AIMK* WN4 .... **78** B6
Melrose Dr *GTS/LS* CH66 .... **202** D3
Melrose Gdns *CL/PREN* CH43 * **149** J2
Melrose Rd *ANF/KKDL* L4 .... **97** F5
CSBY/WL L22 .... **81** F3
NWD/KWIPK L33 .... **72** C3
Melton Av *WARRS* WA4 .... **162** A3
Melton Cl *GR/UP/WCH* CH49 .... **129** F4
Melton Rd *RUNC* WA7 .... **186** E1
Melverley Rd *KKBY* L32 .... **84** A1
Melville Av *RF/TRAN* CH42 .... **151** F2
Melville Cl *WARRN/WOL* WA2 .... **16** D1
WDN WA8 .... **19** K1
Melville Pl *EHL/KEN* L7 .... **133** F1
Melville Rd *BEB* CH63 .... **150** D6
BTL L20 .... **81** K4
Melville St *TOX* L8 .... **132** E4
Melwood Dr *WD/CROXPK* L12 .... **99** G6
Menai Ms *PR/KW* L34 * **118** A1
Menai Rd *BTL* L20 .... **82** A5
Menai St *BIRK* CH41 .... **2** C5
Mendell Cl *PS/BROM* CH62 .... **171** G5
Mendip Av *WARRN/WOL* WA2 .... **123** H4
Mendip Cl *GTS/LS* CH66 .... **195** H6
HLWD L26 .... **155** H4
RF/TRAN CH42 .... **150** B2
Mendip Gv *STHEL* WA9 .... **104** D2
Mendip Rd *RF/TRAN* CH42 .... **150** B2
WAV L15 .... **134** B3
Menin Av *WARRS* WA4 .... **143** F6
Menivale Cl *CHTN/BK* PR9 .... **20** D5
Menlo Av *PEN/TH* CH61 .... **148** C5
Menlo Cl *CL/PREN* CH43 .... **130** B5
Menlove Av *CALD/MH* L18 .... **134** B4
Menlove Gdns North
CALD/MH L18 .... **134** C4
Menlove Gdns South
CALD/MH L18 .... **134** C4
Menlove Gdns West
CALD/MH L18 .... **134** C4
Menlove Man *CALD/MH* L18 .... **134** D3
Menlow Cl *WARRS* WA4 .... **163** H2
Menstone Rd
CLB/OSW/ST L13 .... **114** D3
Mentmore Crs *NG/CROX* L11 .... **99** F4
Mentmore Gdns *WARRS* WA4 .... **162** E6
Mentmore Rd *CALD/MH* L18 .... **153** G2
Menzies St *TOX* L8 .... **133** F5
Meols Cl *FMBY* L37 .... **48** E3
GTS/LS CH66 .... **195** H5
Meols Cop Centre
CHTN/BK PR9 * **28** D3
Meols Cop Rd *STHP* PR8 .... **28** C2
Meols Dr *WKBY* CH48 .... **127** F5
Meols Pde *HOY* CH47 .... **127** G1
Mercer Av *KKBY* L32 .... **84** B2
Mercer Ct *WD/CROXPK* L12 .... **115** J2
Mercer Dr *ANF/KKDL* L4 .... **97** G5
Mercer Rd *CL/PREN* CH43 .... **130** B1
RNFD/HAY WA11 .... **90** B5
Mercer's La *ORM* L39 .... **64** B3
Mercer St *ALL/GAR* L19 * **153** K6
WARRW/BUR WA5 .... **121** J1
Mercer Wk *EP* CH65 .... **6** D5
Merchants Crs
GOL/RIS/CUL WA3 .... **93** F2
Mercury Wy *SKEL* WN8 .... **57** G5
Mere Av *BEB* CH63 .... **183** J1
BRSC L40 .... **38** E3
Merebank *CL/PREN* CH43 .... **130** B5
Merebrook Gv *NWD/KWIPK* L33 .... **72** E4
Mere Cl *GTS/LS* CH66 .... **202** B1
SKEL WN8 .... **56** B3
Merecroft Av *WAL/EG* CH44 .... **111** J5
Meredale Rd *CALD/MH* L18 .... **134** B5
Meredith Av *WARRS* WA4 .... **163** G1
Meredith St *ALL/GAR* L19 .... **154** B6
Mere Farm Gv *CL/PREN* CH43 .... **130** C5
Mere Farm Rd *CL/PREN* CH43 .... **130** B5
Mere Fld *CL/PREN* CH43 * **130** C5
Mere Gn *ANF/KKDL* L4 .... **97** J4
Mere Gv *RNFD/HAY* WA11 .... **88** E2
Mereheath *MOR/LEA* CH46 .... **109** J4
Mere Hey *ECCL* WA10 .... **102** C2
Mereland Wy *STHEL* WA9 .... **104** D3
Mere La *BRSC* L40 .... **31** J4
CHTN/BK PR9 .... **24** E2
EV L5 .... **113** H2
HES CH60 .... **167** J3
WAL/NB CH45 .... **94** E6
Merepark Dr *CHTN/BK* PR9 .... **23** K1
Mere Park Rd
GR/UP/WCH CH49 .... **128** D6
Mere Rd *AIMK* WN4 .... **79** H5
FMBY L37 .... **48** D3
NEWLW WA12 .... **107** F1
WARRN/WOL WA2 .... **124** C5
Meres Rd *WLT/FAZ* L9 .... **83** H4
Meres Wy *STHP* PR8 .... **27** J5
Merevale Cl *RUNC* WA7 .... **187** H1
Mereview Crs *WD/CROXPK* L12 .... **99** H2
Merewood *KKBY* L32 .... **84** E3
SKEL WN8 .... **56** C1
Merewood Cl
WARRN/WOL WA2 .... **123** K4
Mereworth *WKBY* CH48 .... **146** E5
Meribel Cl *CSBY/BLUN* L23 .... **69** H4
Meriden Av *BEB* CH63 .... **170** C4
Meriden Cl *RNFD/HAY* WA11 .... **89** G5
STHP PR8 .... **33** H4
Meriden Rd *WLTN* L25 .... **135** J3
Merlewood Av *CHTN/BK* PR9 .... **23** K2
Merlin Av *GR/UP/WCH* CH49 .... **128** E3
Merlin Cl *GR/UP/WCH* CH49 .... **128** D3
RNFD/HAY WA11 .... **88** E5
RUNC WA7 .... **177** K5
Merlin Ct *HLWD* L26 .... **155** G2
Merlin Rd *RF/TRAN* CH42 .... **131** F6
Merlin St *TOX* L8 .... **132** E3
Merrick Cl *WARRN/WOL* WA2 .... **124** A5
Merrills La *GR/UP/WCH* CH49 .... **129** H4
Merrilocks Rd *CSBY/BLUN* L23 .... **68** B4
Merrilox Av *MGHL* L31 .... **62** B5
Merrion Cl *WLTN* L25 .... **135** G6
Merritt Av *BIRK* CH41 .... **130** E1
Merrivale Rd *WLTN* L25 .... **155** F1
Merrydale Dr *NG/CROX* L11 .... **99** G2
Merryford Gn *ANF/KKDL* L4 .... **97** K4
Merscar La *BRSC* L40 .... **37** H3
Mersey Av *ALL/GAR* L19 .... **153** G3
FMBY L37 .... **40** E5
MGHL L31 .... **62** D5
Mersey Bank Rd
PS/BROM CH62 .... **151** G3
Mersey La South
RF/TRAN CH42 .... **151** F1
Mersey Rd *AIG/SPK* L17 .... **153** F3
CSBY/BLUN L23 .... **68** D6
RF/TRAN CH42 .... **131** K6
RUNC WA7 .... **10** C2
WDN WA8 .... **176** D1
Mersey St *STHEL* WA9 .... **104** E2
WAL/EG CH44 .... **112** A5
WARR WA1 .... **16** E6
Merseyton Rd *EP* CH65 .... **196** A1
Mersey Vw *ALL/GAR* L19 .... **153** K5
CSBY/WL L22 .... **80** D1
RUNC WA7 .... **176** A5
Mersey View Rd *WDN* WA8 .... **175** J1
Mersey View South Rd
RUNC WA7 .... **176** A6
Mersey Wk *WARRS* WA4 .... **143** J4
Mersey Wy *ALL/GAR* L19 .... **172** C3
WARRW/BUR WA5 .... **141** K5
Mersham Ct *WDN* WA8 .... **138** E5
Merstone Cl *HLWD* L26 .... **155** J4
Merthyr Gv *CHLDW* L16 .... **115** J6
Merton Bank Rd *STHEL* WA9 .... **89** F6
Merton Cl *NSTN* CH64 .... **191** K4
Merton Crs *HUY* L36 .... **116** B5
Merton Dr *GR/UP/WCH* CH49 .... **129** H6
HUY L36 .... **116** A5
Merton Gv *BTL* L20 .... **4** E5
CSBY/BLUN L23 .... **68** D6
Merton Pl *CL/PREN* CH43 .... **2** B5
Merton Rd *BTL* L20 .... **4** D5
EP CH65 .... **184** E4
GTS/LS CH66 .... **195** H6
WAL/NB CH45 .... **111** G2
Merton St *STHEL* WA9 .... **89** F6
Mertoun Rd *WARRS* WA4 .... **162** A2
Mesham Cl *GR/UP/WCH* CH49 .... **129** F4
Metcalf Cl *NWD/KWIPK* L33 .... **72** C3
Meteor Crs *WARRN/WOL* WA2 .... **123** K5
Methuen St *BIRK* CH41 .... **130** D1
WAV L15 .... **133** K2
Mevagissey Rd *RUNC* WA7 .... **188** B2
The Mews *AIG/SPK* L17 .... **153** G2
STBRV L28 .... **100** C6
STHP PR8 .... **27** H2
WARRW/BUR WA5 * **121** J1
Meyrick Rd *NG/CROX* L11 .... **98** C3
Miami Cl *WARRW/BUR* WA5 .... **141** J2
Micawber Cl *TOX* L8 .... **132** E4
Michael Dragonette Ct
VAUX/LVPD L3 .... **112** E3
Michaels Cl *FMBY* L37 .... **48** E2
Michigan Cl *NTHLY* L27 .... **136** B4
Mickering La *ORM* L39 .... **63** G1
Micklefield Rd *WAV* L15 * **134** A3
Micklegate *RUNC* WA7 .... **178** C6
Mickleton Dr *STHP* PR8 .... **33** G4
Middlefield Rd *CALD/MH* L18 .... **135** F6
Middleham Cl *KKBY* L32 .... **84** B2
Middlehey Rd *PR/KW* L34 .... **100** D1
Middlehurst Av *ECCL* WA10 .... **13** F3
Middlehurst Cl *PR/KW* L34 .... **102** C6
Middlehurst Rd *WARRS* WA4 .... **163** F1
Middlemass Hey *NTHLY* L27 .... **136** B4
Middle Moss La *FMBY* L37 .... **50** C3
Middle Rd *HLWD* L26 .... **155** J6
SPK/HALE L24 .... **174** A1
Middlesex Rd *BTL* L20 .... **5** H2
Middleton Rd *CSBY/WL* L22 .... **81** G1
EHL/KEN L7 .... **114** C5
Middle Wk *FROD/HEL* WA6 .... **200** E2
Middle Wy *NG/CROX* L11 .... **84** C6
Middle Withins La *FMBY* L37 .... **50** B6
Middlewood *GOL/RIS/CUL* WA3 .... **93** F3
KKBY L32 .... **84** E3
SKEL WN8 .... **56** C1
Middlewood Cl *ORM* L39 .... **53** G6
Middlewood Dr *ORM* L39 .... **53** G6
Middlewood Rd *ORM* L39 .... **53** G6
Midge Hall La *CHTN/BK* PR9 .... **30** B5
Midghall St *VAUX/LVPD* L3 .... **8** D1
Midhurst Dr *STHP* PR8 .... **33** H5
Midhurst Rd *WD/CROXPK* L12 .... **99** K2
Midland St *BIRK* CH41 * **2** C6
WDN WA8 .... **19** F2
Midland Ter *CSBY/WL* L22 .... **80** E2
Midland Wy *WARR* WA1 .... **16** B4
Midlothian Dr *CSBY/BLUN* L23 .... **68** D6
Midway Rd *HUY* L36 .... **116** E3
Midwood St *WDN* WA8 .... **18** E4
Milbrook Crs *KKBY* L32 .... **72** D6
Milbrook Dr *KKBY* L32 .... **72** D6
Mildenhall Cl
WARRW/BUR WA5 .... **141** J3
Mildenhall Rd *WLTN* L25 .... **135** H3
Mildmay Rd *BTL* L20 .... **81** J6
NG/CROX L11 * **98** C3
Mile End *EV* L5 .... **113** F3
Miles Cl *GOL/RIS/CUL* WA3 .... **125** H4
GR/UP/WCH CH49 .... **147** K1
Miles La *GR/UP/WCH* CH49 .... **147** K1
Miles St *TOX* L8 .... **133** F5
Milestone Hey *STBRV* L28 .... **100** B5
Milford Cl *FMBY* L37 .... **48** C4
Milford Dr *WD/CROXPK* L12 .... **99** J2
Milford St *EV* L5 .... **112** D1
Milland Cl *NG/CROX* L11 .... **99** G2
Millar Crs *WDN* WA8 .... **18** C5
Millar's Pace *CHTN/BK* PR9 .... **20** E6
Mill Av *WARRW/BUR* WA5 .... **141** F2
Mill Bank *NSTN* CH64 .... **192** B4
CLB/OSW/ST L13 .... **114** D1
Millbank *LYMM* WA13 .... **145** K6
Millbank Brow *BRSC* L40 .... **39** F6
Millbank Ct *FROD/HEL* WA6 .... **200** D1
Millbank La *MGHL* L31 .... **62** D4
Millbank Rd *WAL/EG* CH44 * **111** G4
Millbeck Cl *KKBY* L32 .... **72** D5
Millbeck Gv *RNFD/HAY* WA11 .... **88** E1
Millbrook Cl *SKEL* WN8 .... **56** A3
Millbrook Ct *PR/KW* L34 .... **85** H6
Millbrook La *ECCL* WA10 .... **102** D1
Millbrook Rd *BIRK* CH41 .... **111** H5
Mill Brow *BEB* CH63 .... **150** C5
ECCL WA10 .... **102** D1
STHEL WA9 .... **120** B2
WDN WA8 .... **19** H1
Mill Brow Cl *STHEL* WA9 .... **120** B2
Millbutt Cl *BEB* CH63 .... **150** C5
Mill Cl *CSBY/BLUN* L23 .... **69** F3
EP CH65 .... **203** G2
WARRN/WOL WA2 .... **124** A3
Mill Ct *NTHTN* L30 .... **70** A4
Millcroft *CSBY/BLUN* L23 .... **69** H4
NSTN CH64 .... **181** K6
Millcroft Pk *GR/UP/WCH* CH49 .... **128** C6
Millcroft Rd *WLTN* L25 .... **155** F2
Milldale Rd *LEIGH* WN7 .... **93** J2
Mill Dam Cl *BRSC* L40 .... **46** C1
Mill Dam La *BRSC* L40 .... **46** C1
Millenium Rd *TOX* L8 .... **133** F3
Millennium Rd *TOX* L8 .... **133** F3
Miller Av *CSBY/BLUN* L23 .... **68** E4
Miller Cl *TOX* L8 .... **132** E5
Miller's Br *BTL* L20 .... **4** C7
Millers Cl *MOR/LEA* CH46 .... **128** C2
Millers Ct *ORM* L39 .... **45** K6
Millerscroft *KKBY* L32 .... **72** B6
Millersdale *STHEL* WA9 .... **120** A3
Millersdale Av *WLT/FAZ* L9 .... **82** E4
Millersdale Cl *PS/BROM* CH62 .... **184** C2
Millersdale Gv *RUNC* WA7 .... **187** G2
Millersdale Rd *CALD/MH* L18 .... **134** B5
Millers Fold *ECCL* WA10 .... **102** D1
Millers Nook *SKEL* WN8 .... **57** K5
Miller St *WARRS* WA4 .... **17** G7
Millers Wy *MOR/LEA* CH46 * **128** D1
Mill Farm Cl *WARRN/WOL* WA2 .... **124** A4
Millfield *NSTN* CH64 .... **181** K6
Millfield Cl *CLB/OSW/ST* L13 .... **114** E1
Millfield La *AIMK* WN4 .... **90** D2
Millfield Rd *WDN* WA8 .... **158** D1
Millfields *ECCL* WA10 .... **102** C2
Mill Gn *NSTN* CH64 .... **193** G1
Millgreen Cl *SKEL* WN8 .... **57** J6
WD/CROXPK L12 .... **99** J2
Mill Green La *WDN* WA8 .... **139** J4
Mill Hey *RAIN/WH* L35 .... **119** G6
Mill Hey Rd *WKBY* CH48 .... **146** E5
Mill Hl *CL/PREN* CH43 .... **130** D6
Mill Hill Rd *PEN/TH* CH61 .... **147** K4
Millhouse Av *WARRS* WA4 .... **162** C2
Millhouse Cl *MOR/LEA* CH46 .... **109** F6
Millhouse La
GOL/RIS/CUL WA3 .... **124** C1
MOR/LEA CH46 .... **109** F6
Millingford Av
GOL/RIS/CUL WA3 .... **92** A1
Millingford Gv *AIMK* WN4 .... **79** G6
Millington Cl *CL/PREN* CH43 .... **149** H2
RUNC WA7 .... **187** J3
WDN WA8 .... **18** A3
Millionaire Rw *BRSC* L40 .... **37** F5
Mill La *BRSC* L40 .... **38** E4
BTL L20 .... **5** G4
CHTN/BK PR9 .... **23** J4
CLB/OSW/ST L13 .... **114** E5
FROD/HEL WA6 .... **187** H5
GR/UP/WCH CH49 .... **147** K2
GTS/LS CH66 .... **195** G5
HES CH60 .... **168** B5
KKBY L32 .... **72** B5
NEWLW WA12 .... **106** E2
NSTN CH64 .... **192** D4
ORM L39 .... **52** D4
PR/KW L34 .... **85** J6
RAIN/WH L35 .... **118** E6
RNFD/HAY WA11 .... **75** K5
SKEL WN8 .... **57** J5
SKEL WN8 .... **56** B3
STHEL WA9 .... **120** A2
VAUX/LVPD L3 .... **9** G2
WAL/EG CH44 .... **111** G4
WARRN/WOL WA2 .... **123** G4
WARRS WA4 .... **161** H4
WAV L15 .... **134** B1
WD/CROXPK L12 .... **114** E1
WDN WA8 .... **138** C4
Mill Meadow *NEWLW* WA12 .... **106** E2
Millom Av *RAIN/WH* L35 .... **118** D3
Millom Gv *ECCL* WA10 .... **102** E5
WD/CROXPK L12 .... **99** G4
Mill Park Dr *PS/BROM* CH62 .... **184** B4
Millport Cl *WARRN/WOL* WA2 .... **124** C5
Mill Rd *BEB* CH63 .... **150** C4
NPK/KEN L6 .... **113** J4
PEN/TH CH61 .... **148** D5
PS/BROM CH62 .... **171** F2
STHP PR8 .... **33** K4
Mill Sq *AIN/FAZ* L10 .... **83** H1
Millstead Rd *WAV* L15 .... **134** B1
Mill St *AIMK* WN4 .... **91** H1
ECCL WA10 .... **13** F3
GOL/RIS/CUL WA3 .... **92** B3
NSTN CH64 .... **191** K1
ORM L39 .... **53** K1
PR/KW L34 .... **117** K1
RF/TRAN CH42 .... **131** G5
STHP PR8 .... **15** H6
TOX L8 .... **132** D3
WLTN L25 .... **154** D1
Mill Ter *BEB* CH63 * **150** C6
Millthwaite Rd *WAL/EG* CH44 .... **111** F3
Millvale St *NPK/KEN* L6 .... **114** A4
Mill Vw *TOX* L8 .... **132** D4
Mill View Ct *ORM* L39 .... **64** D1
Mill View Dr *BEB* CH63 .... **150** B5
Millway Rd *SPK/HALE* L24 .... **174** B1
Millwood *BEB* CH63 .... **150** C5
RUNC WA7 .... **178** B4
Mill Wood Av *ECCL* WA10 .... **102** B2
Millwood Cl *AIMK* WN4 .... **79** F4
Millwood Ct *SPK/HALE* L24 * **174** B1
Millwood Gdns *RAIN/WH* L35 .... **118** B5
Millwood Rd *SPK/HALE* L24 .... **173** K2
Mill Yd *PEN/TH* CH61 .... **148** E5
Milman Cl *GR/UP/WCH* CH49 .... **129** G5
ORM L39 .... **53** H2
Milman Rd *ANF/KKDL* L4 .... **97** H4
Milner Cop *HES* CH60 .... **168** A5
Milne Rd *CLB/OSW/ST* L13 .... **98** C5
Milner Rd *AIG/SPK* L17 .... **153** F2
HES CH60 .... **168** B4
Milner St *BIRK* CH41 .... **130** D1
WARRW/BUR WA5 .... **16** A5
Milnthorpe Cl *ANF/KKDL* L4 .... **97** G5
Milnthorpe Rd
WARRW/BUR WA5 .... **121** J1
Milnthorpe St *ALL/GAR* L19 .... **153** K5
Milroy St *EHL/KEN* L7 .... **113** K6
Milton Av *DV/KA/FCH* L14 .... **115** K5
NEWLW WA12 .... **106** B2
RAIN/WH L35 .... **118** A4
WDN WA8 .... **18** A4
Milton Cl *EP* CH65 .... **7** F6
RAIN/WH L35 .... **118** A4
Milton Crs *HES* CH60 .... **168** A4
Milton Dr *ORM* L39 .... **54** A1
Milton Gn *PEN/TH* CH61 .... **148** E5
Milton Gv *WARRS* WA4 .... **143** G6
Milton Rd *ANF/KKDL* L4 .... **5** K6
CSBY/WL L22 .... **81** F1
EHL/KEN L7 .... **114** C5
EP CH65 .... **7** F6
GOL/RIS/CUL WA3 .... **92** E4
RF/TRAN CH42 .... **131** F5
WAL/EG CH44 .... **111** K5
WDN WA8 .... **18** C4
WKBY CH48 .... **127** F6
Milton Rd East *RF/TRAN* CH42 .... **131** G5
Milton St *BTL* L20 .... **4** C2
CHTN/BK PR9 .... **23** J6
STHEL WA9 .... **119** J5
WDN WA8 .... **158** B6
Milton Wy *MGHL* L31 .... **61** K6
Milvain Dr *WARRN/WOL* WA2 .... **123** J6
Milverny Wy *STHEL* WA9 .... **103** J3
Milverton St *NPK/KEN* L6 .... **114** A3
Mimosa Cl *CHNE* CH2 .... **198** D5
Mimosa Rd *WAV* L15 .... **134** C2
Minehead Gv *STHEL* WA9 .... **120** B2
Minehead Rd *AIG/SPK* L17 .... **153** F2
Miners Wy *SPK/HALE* L24 .... **174** B2
WDN WA8 .... **18** D6
Minerva Cl *WARRS* WA4 .... **162** C1
Mines Av *AIG/SPK* L17 .... **153** G3
PR/KW L34 .... **118** A1
Mine Wy *RNFD/HAY* WA11 * **90** E4
Minshull St *EHL/KEN* L7 .... **113** J6
Minstead Av *NWD/KWIPK* L33 .... **85** F1
Minster Ct *EHL/KEN* L7 .... **133** F1
RUNC WA7 .... **176** B5
Minto Cl *EHL/KEN* L7 .... **114** A5
Minton Cl *WD/CROXPK* L12 .... **99** K2
Minton Wy *WDN* WA8 .... **139** G4
Mintor Rd *NWD/KWIPK* L33 .... **85** F1
Minto St *EHL/KEN* L7 .... **113** K5
Minver Rd *WD/CROXPK* L12 .... **99** H6
Miranda Pl *BTL* L20 .... **97** F4
Miranda Rd *BTL* L20 .... **5** G7
Mirfield Cl *GOL/RIS/CUL* WA3 .... **92** E4
HLWD L26 .... **155** J5
Mirfield St *NPK/KEN* L6 .... **113** K4
Miriam Rd *ANF/KKDL* L4 .... **113** J1
Miskelly St *BTL* L20 .... **96** E5
Mission Wk *NPK/KEN* L6 .... **113** K4
Missouri Rd *CLB/OSW/ST* L13 .... **98** B6
Mistlethrush Wy
WD/CROXPK L12 .... **99** K2
Misty Cl *WDN* WA8 .... **157** H1
Mitchell Av
WARRW/BUR WA5 .... **121** J2
Mitchell Crs *LITH* L21 .... **81** J2
Mitchell Pl *CLVPS* L1 .... **9** G4
Mitchell Rd *ECCL* WA10 .... **102** E4
PR/KW L34 .... **117** J1
WGNW/BIL/OR WN5 .... **77** H4
Mitchell St *AIMK* WN4 .... **91** H1
GOL/RIS/CUL WA3 .... **92** B3
WARRS WA4 .... **162** B3
Mithril Cl *WDN* WA8 .... **139** K6
Mitre Cl *RAIN/WH* L35 .... **117** K6
Mitylene St *EV* L5 * **113** G1
Mobberley Cl *WARRS* WA4 .... **144** C6
Mobberley Wy *BEB* CH63 .... **170** C2
Mockbeggar Dr *WAL/NB* CH45 .... **94** D6
Mockbeggar Whf
WAL/NB CH45 .... **94** D6
Modred St *TOX* L8 .... **132** E4
Moel Famau Vw *AIG/SPK* L17 .... **152** C1
Moffatdale Rd *ANF/KKDL* L4 .... **98** A5
Moffat Rd *WLT/FAZ* L9 * **83** F4
Moffatt Rd *WLT/FAZ* L9 .... **82** E4
Molesworth Gv *CHLDW* L16 .... **115** K6
Molineux Av *DV/KA/FCH* L14 .... **115** H6
Molland Cl *WD/CROXPK* L12 .... **99** H5
Mollington Av *NG/CROX* L11 .... **98** D3
Mollington Link *BIRK* CH41 .... **3** G7
Mollington Rd *KKBY* L32 .... **84** B1
WAL/EG CH44 .... **111** J4
Mollington St *BIRK* CH41 .... **3** F6
Molly's La *NWD/KWIPK* L33 .... **85** J4
Molton Rd *WAV* L15 .... **134** D1
Molyneux Av
WARRW/BUR WA5 .... **142** C1
Molyneux Cl
GR/UP/WCH CH49 .... **129** G4
HUY L36 .... **117** F5
RAIN/WH L35 .... **117** K3
Molyneux Ct *NG/CROX* L11 * **99** F2
Molyneux Dr *RAIN/WH* L35 .... **117** K3
WAL/NB CH45 .... **95** H5
Molyneux Rd *CALD/MH* L18 .... **134** A5
CSBY/WL L22 .... **81** F1
MGHL L31 .... **71** J2
NPK/KEN L6 .... **113** K4
ORM L39 .... **53** G6
Molyneux Wy *AIN/FAZ* L10 .... **71** F6
Monaghan Cl *WLT/FAZ* L9 .... **82** C4
Monash Rd *NG/CROX* L11 .... **98** D5
Monastery La *STHEL* WA9 .... **104** B6
Monastery Rd *NPK/KEN* L6 .... **114** A1
STHEL WA9 .... **104** C6
Mona St *BIRK* CH41 .... **130** C2
BTL L20 .... **82** A5
ECCL WA10 .... **12** A6
Mond Rd *AIN/FAZ* L10 .... **83** J4
WDN WA8 .... **18** C4
Monfa Rd *BTL* L20 .... **81** K5
Monica Dr *WDN* WA8 .... **139** F4
Monica Rd *WLTN* L25 .... **154** E2
Monica Ter *AIMK* WN4 .... **91** G1
Monkfield Wy *ALL/GAR* L19 .... **172** C1
Monk Rd *WAL/EG* CH44 .... **111** H3
Monks Carr La *HTWN* L38 .... **60** C1
Monks Cl *FMBY* L37 .... **49** G4
Monksdown Rd *NG/CROX* L11 .... **98** E4
Monks Dr *FMBY* L37 .... **49** G4
Monks Ferry *BIRK* CH41 .... **3** J5
Monksferry Wk *ALL/GAR* L19 .... **153** G4
Monks Gv *EP* CH65 .... **6** C3
Monks Pl *WARRN/WOL* WA2 .... **17** G1
Monks St *WARRW/BUR* WA5 * **142** B3
Monk St *BIRK* CH41 .... **3** H5
EV L5 * **113** H1
Monks Wy *BEB* CH63 .... **170** B1
WKBY CH48 .... **146** C1
WLTN L25 .... **154** E1
Monkswell Dr *WAV* L15 .... **134** B1
Monkswell St *TOX* L8 .... **133** F6
Monkswood Cl
WARRW/BUR WA5 .... **122** E5
Monmouth Cl *WARR* WA1 .... **144** D2
Monmouth Crs *AIMK* WN4 .... **91** H1
Monmouth Dr *AIN/FAZ* L10 .... **83** J2
Monmouth Gv *STHEL* WA9 .... **104** B3
Monmouth Rd *WAL/EG* CH44 .... **111** F3
Monro Cl *TOX* L8 * **132** E5
Monroe Cl *WARR* WA1 .... **144** A2
Monro St *TOX* L8 .... **132** E5
Montague Rd
CLB/OSW/ST L13 .... **114** E5
WDN WA8 .... **157** F5
Montagu Rd *FMBY* L37 .... **40** E6
Montana Cl *WARRW/BUR* WA5 .... **141** K2
Montclair Dr *CALD/MH* L18 .... **134** C4
Montclare Crs *WARRS* WA4 .... **162** D2
Montcliffe Cl
GOL/RIS/CUL WA3 .... **124** E2

Monterey Rd CLB/OSW/ST L13 115 F5
Montfort Dr ALL/GAR L19 153 H4
Montgomery Av
CHTN/BK PR9 28 D1
Montgomery Cl RAIN/WH L35 117 K5
WARRW/BUR WA5 141 H1
Montgomery Hl WKBY CH48 147 H3
Montgomery Rd HUY L36 116 D3
WDN WA8 157 J3
WLT/FAZ L9 82 D4
Montgomery Wy NPK/KEN L6 113 K5
Montpelier Av RUNC WA7 186 C1
Montpelier Dr TOX L8 132 E5
Montpellier Crs WAL/NB CH45 95 G5
Montreal Rd NTHLY L27 136 B4
Montrey Crs AIMK WN4 78 B6
Montrose Av WAL/EG CH44 112 A6
Montrose Cl WARRN/WOL WA2 124 B3
Montrose Dr CHTN/BK PR9 23 H4
Montrose Rd CLB/OSW/ST L13 114 C1
Montrose Wy
CLB/OSW/ST L13 114 D5
Montrovia Crs AIN/FAZ L10 83 J4
Monville Rd WLT/FAZ L9 83 F4
Moorbridge Cl NTHTN L30 70 D5
Moor Cl CSBY/BLUN L23 69 G4
STHP PR8 41 J1
Moor Coppice CSBY/BLUN L23 69 G4
Moorcroft Rd CALD/MH L18 153 K2
HUY L36 116 E2
WAL/NB CH45 110 D2
Moor Dr CSBY/BLUN L23 69 F4
SKEL WN8 57 F6
Moore Av RF/TRAN CH42 150 D1
STHEL WA9 104 E2
WARRS WA4 144 C6
Moore Cl WDN WA8 158 E1
Moore Dr RNFD/HAY WA11 90 E5
Moore La WARRS WA4 160 E4
Moore St BTL L20 4 C1
Mooreway RAIN/WH L35 119 G6
Moorfield NWD/KWIPK L33 72 E4
Moorfield Crs
GOL/RIS/CUL WA3 93 H4
Moorfield Dr NSTN CH64 181 H5
Moorfield La BRSC L40 37 F6
Moorfield Rd CSBY/BLUN L23 69 H4
ECCL WA10 87 K6
WDN WA8 139 J5
Moorfields CLVP L2 8 D3
Moorfields Av CL/PREN CH43 130 A5
Moorfoot Rd STHEL WA9 104 D2
Moorfoot Wy NWD/KWIPK L33 72 C3
Moorgate ORM L39 53 J1
Moorgate Av CSBY/BLUN L23 69 F6
Moorgate Rd KKBY L32 84 E5
Moorgate St EHL/KEN L7 113 K6
Moorhey Rd MGHL L31 * 71 G2
Moorhouses HTWN L38 59 F4
Mooring Cl RUNC WA7 188 C1
Moorings Cl NSTN CH64 181 G6
The Moorings BIRK CH41 * 2 E6
HES CH60 167 G5
MGHL L31 61 K3
Moorland Av CSBY/BLUN L23 69 F4
Moorland Cl HES CH60 168 A6
Moorland Dr RUNC WA7 178 D6
Moorland Pk HES CH60 168 A6
Moorland Rd AIMK WN4 79 K4
GTS/LS CH66 195 H1
MGHL L31 71 F3
RF/TRAN CH42 131 H6
Moorlands Rd CSBY/BLUN L23 69 J3
Moor La AIN/FAZ L10 83 K4
ANF/KKDL L4 97 J3
CSBY/BLUN L23 69 F4
FROD/HEL WA6 200 E1
HES CH60 167 K5
HTWN L38 59 K4
KKBY L32 84 A3
SFTN L29 61 F6
STHP PR8 41 J1
WDN WA8 18 B6
Moor La South WDN WA8 18 B6
Moor Pl VAUX/LVPD L3 9 H3
Moorside WARRS WA4 143 H5
Moorside Av NSTN CH64 191 H1
Moorside Cl CSBY/BLUN L23 69 G5
Moorside Ct WDN WA8 18 B5
Moorside La NSTN CH64 191 H2
Moorside Rd CSBY/BLUN L23 69 G5
Moor St CLVP L2 8 C5
Moorway HES CH60 168 B5
Moorwood Crs STHEL WA9 120 A3
Moran Dr WARRW/BUR WA5 141 H3
Moray Cl ECCL WA10 12 D1
Morcott La SPK/HALE L24 174 E3
Morden Av AIMK WN4 79 G6
Morden St NPK/KEN L6 114 A4
Morecambe St NPK/KEN L6 * 114 A2
Morecroft Rd RF/TRAN CH42 151 F1
Morella Rd ANF/KKDL L4 98 A5
Morello Cl ECCL WA10 13 F2
Morello Dr BEB CH63 170 D3
Moresby Cl RUNC WA7 178 D6
Moret Cl CSBY/BLUN L23 69 H4
Moreton Av STHEL WA9 120 A3
Moreton Cl GOL/RIS/CUL WA3 92 A2
Moreton Gv WAL/NB CH45 110 E1
Moreton Rd
GR/UP/WCH CH49 129 G3
Morgan Av WARRN/WOL WA2 123 J5
Morgan Ms NTHTN L30 70 A6
Morgan St STHEL WA9 104 B3
Morgans Wy GOL/RIS/CUL WA3 93 H3
Morland Av NSTN CH64 192 A2
PS/BROM CH62 171 F6
Morley Av BIRK CH41 130 E2
Morley Rd CHTN/BK PR9 15 K1
RUNC WA7 10 D7
WAL/EG CH44 111 G4
WARRS WA4 161 K2
Morley St ANF/KKDL L4 * 97 G6
ECCL WA10 12 E1
WARR WA1 17 G3
Morley Wy ECCL WA10 12 E3
Morningside CSBY/BLUN L23 69 G6
Morningside Pl NG/CROX L11 98 D4
Morningside Rd NG/CROX L11 98 D5
Morningside Wy NG/CROX L11 98 D5
Mornington Av CSBY/BLUN L23 81 F1
EP CH65 6 E5
Mornington Rd CHTN/BK PR9 15 G4
WAL/NB CH45 111 H1
Mornington St TOX L8 132 D4
Morpeth Cl MOR/LEA CH46 128 C1
Morpeth Rd HOY CH47 127 F4
Morpeth St TOX L8 132 E2
Morpeth Whf BIRK CH41 3 G1
Morphany La WARRS WA4 189 K1
Morris Av WARRS WA4 143 J5
Morris Cl RNFD/HAY WA11 89 K6
Morris La ORM L39 36 B6
Morrison Cl
WARRW/BUR WA5 141 H4
Morris Rd SKEL WN8 57 J6
Morrissey Cl ECCL WA10 12 A3
Morris St STHEL WA9 104 C4
Morston Av KKBY L32 84 D3
Morston Crs KKBY L32 84 D3
Mort Av WARRS WA4 143 K5
Mortimer Av
WARRN/WOL WA2 142 E1
Mortimer St BIRK CH41 3 H4
Mortlake Cl WDN WA8 138 B6
Morton Cl WARRW/BUR WA5 141 K1
Morton Rd RUNC WA7 178 C5
Morton St TOX L8 132 E4
Morvah Cl WD/CROXPK L12 99 G3
Morval Crs ANF/KKDL L4 5 K6
RUNC WA7 11 J7
Morven Cl WARRN/WOL WA2 124 A4
Morven Gv STHP PR8 23 G6
Moscow Dr CLB/OSW/ST L13 114 D2
Mosedale Av RNFD/HAY WA11 88 E2
Mosedale Gv RUNC WA7 * 187 H2
Mosedale Rd PS/BROM CH62 171 G3
WLT/FAZ L9 82 D6
Moseley Av WAL/NB CH45 111 G3
WARRS WA4 143 K5
Moseley Rd BEB CH63 170 C4
Moses St TOX L8 132 E5
Mosley St STHP PR8 27 J3
Moss Bank ORM L39 53 H3
Moss Bank Pk LITH L21 81 H3
Moss Bank Rd RNFD/HAY WA11 88 D2
WDN WA8 19 J5
Mossborough Hall La
RNFD/HAY WA11 74 D6
Mossborough Rd
RNFD/HAY WA11 86 E1
Moss Bridge La BRSC L40 47 J1
Moss Brow RNFD/HAY WA11 75 F2
Mossbrow Rd HUY L36 116 E3
Moss Cl NSTN CH64 193 H1
WARRS WA4 162 D1
Mosscroft Cl HUY L36 117 G3
Mossdale Cl WARRW/BUR WA5 141 H2
Mossdale Dr RAIN/WH L35 119 F4
Mossdale Rd AIMK WN4 79 F1
NWD/KWIPK L33 72 E4
Moss Delph La ORM L39 53 F3
Mossdene Rd WAL/EG CH44 111 F3
Moss End Wy NWD/KWIPK L33 73 J6
Mossfield Rd WLT/FAZ L9 82 C5
Moss Gdns STHP PR8 27 K5
Moss Ga GOL/RIS/CUL WA3 125 J2
Moss Gate Gv DV/KA/FCH L14 116 A4
Moss Gate Rd DV/KA/FCH L14 116 A4
Mossgiel Av STHP PR8 33 H4
Moss Green Wy STHEL WA9 104 E4
Moss Gv RF/TRAN CH42 150 A1
TOX L8 133 H3
Mosshill Cl MGHL L31 62 A4
Mosslands ECCL WA10 102 C1
Mosslands Cl GTS/LS CH66 202 C1
Mosslands Dr WAL/NB CH45 110 E3
Moss La BRSC L40 39 F3
BTL L20 82 B5
CHTN/BK PR9 23 K5
CHTN/BK PR9 24 B5
GOL/RIS/CUL WA3 125 G6
GOL/RIS/CUL WA3 92 C6
HTWN L38 59 J5
LITH L21 81 K3
MGHL L31 62 B2
NWD/KWIPK L33 73 G6
ORM L39 65 F5
ORM L39 42 C6
RF/TRAN CH42 150 A1
RNFD/HAY WA11 87 H4
SKEL WN8 66 B1
STHEL WA9 104 E4
WARRS WA4 160 D5
WLT/FAZ L9 82 C5
Moss Lane Vw SKEL WN8 66 B1
Mosslawn Rd KKBY L32 84 E2
Mosslea Pk CALD/MH L18 134 A5
Mossley Av CALD/MH L18 134 A4
PS/BROM CH62 171 F5
Mossley Hill Dr AIG/SPK L17 133 J4
Mossley Hill Rd CALD/MH L18 153 G1
Mossley Rd RF/TRAN CH42 131 H6
Moss Nook BRSC L40 38 E3
ORM L39 * 53 G3
Moss Nook La MGHL L31 72 A1
RNFD/HAY WA11 75 F3
Moss Pits Cl AIN/FAZ L10 83 H4
Moss Pits La AIN/FAZ L10 83 H4
WAV L15 134 C2
Moss Rd STHP PR8 27 K5
WARRS WA4 143 K6
Moss Side DV/KA/FCH L14 116 A4
FMBY L37 49 H1
Moss Side La
KIRK/FR/WAR PR4 25 K2
WARRS WA4 160 B4
Moss St ALL/GAR L19 153 K5
NPK/KEN L6 9 J2
PR/KW L34 101 K6
WDN WA8 19 K5
Mossvale GTS/LS CH66 195 G1
Moss Vw LITH L21 81 K3
MGHL L31 62 D6
Mossville Cl CALD/MH L18 153 H1
Mossville Rd CALD/MH L18 153 J1
Moss Wy NG/CROX L11 99 G1
Mossy Bank Rd WAL/EG CH44 111 K3
Moston Gv LYMM WA13 145 J6
Moston Wy GTS/LS CH66 195 J6
Mostyn Av AIN/FAZ L10 83 F1
ALL/GAR L19 154 A3
HES CH60 167 G5
WKBY CH48 146 C2
Mostyn Cl ANF/KKDL L4 * 97 G6
Mostyn Sq NSTN CH64 181 G6
Mostyn St WAL/EG CH44 111 H4
Mote Hill Ct WARR WA1 17 H3
Motherwell Cl WDN WA8 138 D5
Motherwell Crs STHP PR8 28 C4
Mottershead Cl WDN WA8 18 C4
Mottershead Rd WDN WA8 18 C4
Mottram Cl NWD/KWIPK L33 84 E1
WARRS WA4 144 A6
Moughland La RUNC WA7 176 D5
Moulders La WARR WA1 16 E6
Mould St EV L5 113 F2
Moulton Cl RUNC WA7 187 J3
Mounsey Rd RF/TRAN CH42 2 D7
Mountain Vw
FROD/HEL WA6 199 J6
Mount Av BEB CH63 150 C4
BTL L20 82 A5
HES CH60 * 167 K5
Mount Cl KKBY L32 72 B5
Mount Ct HES CH60 * 167 K5
Mount Crs KKBY L32 72 B5
Mount Dr BEB CH63 150 B4
Mount Farm Wy GTS/LS CH66 202 A1
Mount Gv BIRK CH41 2 C7
Mount Grove Pl BIRK CH41 2 B7
Mount Haven Cl
GR/UP/WCH CH49 129 H4
Mount House Cl FMBY L37 41 H6
Mount House Rd FMBY L37 41 H6
Mount Ms HES CH60 * 167 K5
Mount Olive CL/PREN CH43 130 D6
Mount Pk BEB CH63 150 C4
WLTN L25 135 H6
Mount Park Ct WLTN L25 135 H6
Mount Pleasant CHNE CH2 198 B5
CL/PREN CH43 130 E6
CLVPS L1 9 H5
CSBY/WL L22 80 E2
EHL/KEN L7 9 K5
WDN WA8 158 C1
Mount Pleasant Av
STHEL WA9 104 E2
Mount Pleasant Cl
WAL/NB CH45 95 H6
Mount Pleasant Rd
WAL/NB CH45 95 G6
Mount Rd BEB CH63 169 K4
GR/UP/WCH CH49 129 H4
KKBY L32 72 A5
RF/TRAN CH42 150 B2
RUNC WA7 177 J5
WAL/NB CH45 95 G5
WKBY CH48 146 D2
Mount St CHTN/BK PR9 15 J4
CLVPS L1 9 H7
CSBY/WL L22 80 E2
WDN WA8 158 C1
WLTN L25 154 D1
Mount Ter CHTN/BK PR9 15 J4
The Mount HES CH60 167 K5
SKEL WN8 * 56 D5
WAL/EG CH44 111 J3
Mount Vernon EHL/KEN L7 113 J5
Mount Vernon St EHL/KEN L7 113 J5
Mount Vernon Vw
EHL/KEN L7 113 J5
Mountview Cl TOX L8 133 F4
Mountway BEB CH63 150 C4
Mountwood SKEL WN8 56 C1
Mount Wood Rd
RF/TRAN CH42 150 B3
Mourne Cl GTS/LS CH66 194 D3
Mowbray Av RNFD/HAY WA11 89 F6
Mowbray Gv CLB/OSW/ST L13 114 E6
Mowcroft La
WARRW/BUR WA5 140 C6
Mowpen Brow KNUT WA16 165 J5
Moxon Av WARRS WA4 143 J4
Moxon St ECCL WA10 12 A7
Moxon Wy AIMK WN4 79 J5
Moyles Cl WDN WA8 157 J1
Mozart Cl TOX L8 133 G3
Muirfield Cl WARRN/WOL WA2 124 C4
WD/CROXPK L12 115 J1
Muirfield Dr STHP PR8 33 J5
Muirfield Rd HUY L36 116 C6
Muirhead Av CLB/OSW/ST L13 114 C1
Muirhead Av East
NG/CROX L11 98 E5
Mulberry Av ECCL WA10 102 E2
GOL/RIS/CUL WA3 93 G4
Mulberry Cl CHNE CH2 198 D6
NWD/KWIPK L33 72 E3
WARR WA1 144 D2
Mulberry Ct WARRS WA4 * 162 C2
Mulberry Gv WAL/EG CH44 111 K4
Mulberry Pl EHL/KEN L7 * 9 K6
Mulberry Rd RF/TRAN CH42 150 E1
Mulberry St EHL/KEN L7 9 K5
Mulcrow Cl STHEL WA9 104 B1
Mulgrave St TOX L8 113 G6
Mullein Cl GOL/RIS/CUL WA3 92 E3
Mullen Cl WARRW/BUR WA5 * 142 C3
Mulliner St EHL/KEN L7 133 H2
Mullins Av NEWLW WA12 91 H6
Mullion Cl CHTN/BK PR9 20 E6
HLWD L26 155 H3
RUNC WA7 188 A1
Mullion Gv WARRN/WOL WA2 124 C6
Mullion Rd NG/CROX L11 99 G1
Mullion Wk NG/CROX L11 * 84 B6
Mullwood Cl WD/CROXPK L12 99 K2
Mulveton Rd BEB CH63 170 B2
Mumfords La HOY CH47 108 B6
Muncaster Cl PS/BROM CH62 171 F4
Muncaster Dr RNFD/HAY WA11 75 H2
Munster Rd CLB/OSW/ST L13 115 F4
Murat Gv CSBY/WL L22 80 D2
Murat St CSBY/WL L22 80 D2
Murcote Rd DV/KA/FCH L14 115 K2
Murdishaw Av RUNC WA7 188 B2
Muriel Cl WARRW/BUR WA5 140 E3
Muriel St ANF/KKDL L4 97 J4
Murphy Gv STHEL WA9 104 C1
Murrayfield Dr
MOR/LEA CH46 109 K3
Murrayfield Rd WLTN L25 135 H3
Murray Gv WKBY CH48 127 F6
Museum St WARR WA1 16 B6
Musker Dr NTHTN L30 69 K6
Musker St CSBY/BLUN L23 69 G6
Muspratt Rd LITH L21 81 H6
Myddleton La
WARRN/WOL WA2 123 H1
Myers Av RAIN/WH L35 118 C2
Myerscough Av BTL L20 5 K1
Myers Rd East CSBY/BLUN L23 69 F6
Myers Rd West
CSBY/BLUN L23 68 E6
Mynsule Rd BEB CH63 170 B2
Myrtle Av AIMK WN4 78 E3
NEWLW WA12 106 C3
RNFD/HAY WA11 90 A4
Myrtle Gv CSBY/WL L22 80 E1
STHP PR8 15 K6
WAL/EG CH44 111 K4
WARRS WA4 143 G6
WDN WA8 157 J3
WGNW/BIL/OR WN5 * 77 G5
Myrtle Pde EHL/KEN L7 9 K7
Myrtle St CLVPS L1 9 J6
EHL/KEN L7 133 F1
EP CH65 196 B2
Myrtle Wy GR/UP/WCH CH49 129 J5

N

Naburn Gv MOR/LEA CH46 129 F2
Nairn Cl BEB CH63 184 A3
WARRN/WOL WA2 124 C4
Nalor Pl GTS/LS CH66 195 J1
Nansen Cl WARRW/BUR WA5 142 A2
Nansen Gv ANF/KKDL L4 97 J4
Nant Park Ct WAL/NB CH45 95 J5
Nantwich Cl
GR/UP/WCH CH49 148 D1
Nantwich Rd GTS/LS CH66 195 J6
Napier Cl ECCL WA10 12 D5
Napier Dr MOR/LEA CH46 129 G1
Napier Rd PS/BROM CH62 151 G3
Napier St BTL L20 96 D4
ECCL WA10 12 D5
WARR WA1 17 F5
Napier Ter STHP PR8 27 H2
Naples Rd WAL/EG CH44 111 K4
Napps Cl WLTN L25 135 G2
Napps Wy PEN/TH CH61 168 A3
WLTN L25 135 G1
Nares Cl WARRW/BUR WA5 122 C6
Narrow Croft Rd ORM L39 53 F4
Narrow La ORM L39 53 F4
Narrow Moss La BRSC L40 45 H1
Naseby Cl CL/PREN CH43 129 K5
Naseby St ANF/KKDL L4 97 H3
Natal Rd WLT/FAZ L9 82 E5
Nathan Dr RNFD/HAY WA11 90 D5
Nathan Gv NWD/KWIPK L33 72 E5
Naughton Lea WDN WA8 138 C6
Navigation Cl NTHTN L30 70 D5
RUNC WA7 188 C1
Navigation St WARR WA1 17 H5
Navigation Whf
VAUX/LVPD L3 132 C3
Naylor Av GOL/RIS/CUL WA3 92 C3
Naylor Cl GTS/LS CH66 195 J1
Naylor Rd CL/PREN CH43 130 B1
GTS/LS CH66 195 J1
WDN WA8 19 J2
Naylorsfield Dr NTHLY L27 135 K3
Naylor's Rd NTHLY L27 136 A2
Naylor St VAUX/LVPD L3 8 D1
WARR WA1 16 E4
Nazareth House La WDN WA8 157 H4
Nazeby Av CSBY/BLUN L23 69 G6
Neale Dr GR/UP/WCH CH49 129 F6
Neales Fold CHTN/BK PR9 21 G6
Neasham Cl HLWD L26 155 J4
Nedens Gv MGHL L31 62 A4
Nedens La MGHL L31 62 A4
Needham Cl RUNC WA7 11 K4
Needham Rd EHL/KEN L7 114 A5
Needwood Dr BEB CH63 170 B2
Neills Rd STHEL WA9 121 F1
Neilson Rd AIG/SPK L17 133 G6
Neil St WDN WA8 158 C1
Nell's La ORM L39 62 D2
Nelson Av RAIN/WH L35 118 A5
Nelson Ct RF/TRAN CH42 151 F2
STHP PR8 27 G3
Nelson Dr PEN/TH CH61 167 J2
Nelson Pl RAIN/WH L35 118 A5
Nelson Rd EHL/KEN L7 113 K6
EP CH65 6 D1
GOL/RIS/CUL WA3 125 F3
LITH L21 * 81 J4
RF/TRAN CH42 151 F2
Nelson's Cft BEB CH63 170 C2
Nelson St BTL L20 4 C7
CLVPS L1 9 G7
NEWLW WA12 106 A2
STHP PR8 14 D6
WAL/NB CH45 95 J6
WAV L15 133 K2
WDN WA8 158 B5
Nelville Rd WLT/FAZ L9 83 F4
Neptune Cl RUNC WA7 178 C6
Neptune St BIRK CH41 2 E2
Ness Gv KKBY L32 84 B1
Neston Av STHEL WA9 119 K3
Neston Gdns BIRK CH41 2 A1
Neston Gn GTS/LS CH66 195 G5
Neston Rd NSTN CH64 192 A4
NSTN CH64 182 A2
Neston St ANF/KKDL L4 97 H4
Netherby St TOX L8 132 E6
Netherfield WDN WA8 157 J3
Netherfield Cl CL/PREN CH43 129 K5
Netherfield Rd North EV L5 113 G1
Netherfield Rd South EV L5 113 G3
Netherley Rd NTHLY L27 136 C4
RAIN/WH L35 137 F5
Netherpool Rd GTS/LS CH66 195 J1
Netherton Dr FROD/HEL WA6 200 D2
Netherton Gra NTHTN L30 70 E6
Netherton Gn NTHTN L30 70 C4
Netherton La NTHTN L30 70 B4
Netherton Park Rd LITH L21 82 A3
Netherton Rd ALL/GAR L19 153 H2
BTL L20 82 A5
MOR/LEA CH46 129 F1
Netherton Wy LITH L21 82 B3
Netherwood Rd NG/CROX L11 98 C3
Netley St ANF/KKDL L4 97 G5
Nettlestead Rd NG/CROX L11 98 E5
Neva Av MOR/LEA CH46 128 E1
Nevada Cl WARRW/BUR WA5 141 K1
Neverstitch Cl SKEL WN8 * 56 B3
Neverstitch Rd SKEL WN8 55 K3
Neville Av STHEL WA9 105 F3
WARRN/WOL WA2 123 K6
Neville Cl CL/PREN CH43 129 K5
Neville Crs WARRW/BUR WA5 141 H6
Neville Rd CSBY/WL L22 81 F2
PS/BROM CH62 171 G6
WAL/EG CH44 111 G3
Neville St NEWLW WA12 106 A2
Nevill St CHTN/BK PR9 14 E3
Nevin St NPK/KEN L6 113 J4
Nevison St EHL/KEN L7 113 K6
Nevitte Cl STBRV L28 100 A5
New Acres Cl CL/PREN CH43 129 K1
Newark Cl CL/PREN CH43 129 K5
HUY L36 116 D1
NTHTN L30 70 E4
Newark St ANF/KKDL L4 97 G4
New Bank Rd WDN WA8 157 G2
New Barn Av AIMK WN4 79 H6
New Barnet WDN WA8 138 E6
New Bird St CLVPS L1 132 C2
Newbold Crs WKBY CH48 127 K6
Newbold Gv WD/CROXPK L12 99 K3
Newborough Av
CALD/MH L18 134 A4
CSBY/BLUN L23 69 H5
Newborough Cl
WARRW/BUR WA5 122 D5
Newbridge Cl AIMK WN4 78 C6
GR/UP/WCH CH49 129 J5
RUNC WA7 188 B1
WARRW/BUR WA5 122 C5
Newbridge Rd CHNE CH2 196 E6
New Bridge Rd EP CH65 7 K7
Newburgh Cl RUNC WA7 178 C4
Newburns La CL/PREN CH43 130 E6
Newburn St ANF/KKDL L4 97 H4
Newbury Cl HUY L36 116 D6
WDN WA8 138 E6
Newbury Wy MOR/LEA CH46 109 J4
WD/CROXPK L12 115 J2
Newby Av RAIN/WH L35 118 C3
Newby Cl STHP PR8 33 H6
Newby Dr HUY L36 116 C4
Newby Gv WD/CROXPK L12 99 G3
Newby St ANF/KKDL L4 97 H5
Newcastle Rd WAV L15 134 B3
New Cswy FMBY L37 49 H5
New Chester Rd BIRK CH41 3 H6
RF/TRAN CH42 151 F2
Newchurch Rd NTHLY L27 136 C5
Newcombe Av
WARRN/WOL WA2 143 G1
Newcombe St NPK/KEN L6 113 K2
New Court Wy ORM L39 45 K5
Newcroft Rd WLTN L25 135 G5
New Cross St ECCL WA10 13 F4
PR/KW L34 * 101 K6
New Cut Cl STHP PR8 34 C1
New Cut La NWD/KWIPK L33 86 B3
STHP PR8 34 C1
WARR WA1 144 A2
Newdales Cl CL/PREN CH43 129 K2
Newdown Rd NG/CROX L11 84 C6
Newell Rd WAL/EG CH44 111 H3
Newenham Crs
DV/KA/FCH L14 115 J3
New Ferry By-Pass
PS/BROM CH62 151 G4
New Ferry Rd PS/BROM CH62 151 G3
Newfield Cl CSBY/BLUN L23 69 K3
Newfield Rd LYMM WA13 145 J6
Newfields ECCL WA10 102 E1
New Fort Wy BTL L20 81 H5
New Foul La CHTN/BK PR9 28 C3
Newgate Rd SKEL WN8 57 H6
New Glade Hl RNFD/HAY WA11 89 G5
New Grey Rock Cl
NPK/KEN L6 113 K3
New Grosvenor Rd EP CH65 6 C1
New Hall Dr STHP PR8 29 F6
Newhall La HOY CH47 127 G3
New Hall La NG/CROX L11 98 C4
Newhall St CLVPS L1 * 132 D2
New Hampshire Cl
WARRW/BUR WA5 141 J2
Newhaven Rd WAL/NB CH45 95 J6
WARRN/WOL WA2 123 H3
New Hedley Gv EV L5 112 E2
New Henderson St TOX L8 132 D3
New Hey CLB/OSW/ST L13 114 E2
Newheyes NSTN CH64 181 K6
New Hey La NSTN CH64 193 H2
New Hey Rd
GR/UP/WCH CH49 129 J5
New Heys Dr CALD/MH L18 154 A2
Newholme Cl
WD/CROXPK L12 99 J2
Newhope Rd BIRK CH41 2 B2
Newhouse Rd WAV L15 * 133 J2
New Hutte La HLWD L26 155 J5
Newick Pk KKBY L32 84 B2
Newick Rd KKBY L32 84 B2
Newington CLVPS L1 9 G5
New Islington
VAUX/LVPD L3 9 H2
Newland Cl WDN WA8 138 B6
Newland Ct AIG/SPK L17 133 H6
Newland Dr WAL/EG CH44 111 G3
Newlands Av BRSC L40 39 F5
Newlands Cl FROD/HEL WA6 201 F3
Newlands Dr
GOL/RIS/CUL WA3 92 D3

Newlands Rd BEB CH63 * 170 C1
RNFD/HAY WA11 89 F4
WARRS WA4 162 E1
New La BRSC L40 38 B3
CHTN/BK PR9 24 B1
ORM L39 53 J3
WARRS WA4 163 G6
Newling St BIRK CH41 2 B2
Newlyn Av LITH L21 81 H2
MGHL L31 62 C6
Newlyn Cl HOY CH47 108 C5
RUNC WA7 188 A1
Newlyn Dr AIMK WN4 91 G1
SKEL WN8 57 F6
Newlyn Gdns
WARRW/BUR WA5 140 E6
Newlyn Gv RNFD/HAY WA11 89 G4
Newlyn Rd HOY CH47 108 C6
NG/CROX L11 84 C6
Newlyn Wk NG/CROX L11 * 84 C6
New Manchester Rd
WARR WA1 143 K2
New Manor Rd
WARRS WA4 189 G1
Newman St ANF/KKDL L4 97 F5
WARRS WA4 143 J6
New Market Rd LITH L21 81 J4
New Meadow La FMBY L37 50 A5
New Mill Stile WLTN L25 135 H6
Newmoore La RUNC WA7 178 E1
Newmorn Ct AIG/SPK L17 152 D1
Newnham Dr EP CH65 6 E7
Newport Av WAL/NB CH45 94 D6
Newport Cl CL/PREN CH43 129 K5
Newport Ct EV L5 112 E2
New Quay VAUX/LVPD L3 8 B3
Newquay Cl RUNC WA7 188 A1
New Red Rock Cl NPK/KEN L6 113 K3
New Rd CLB/OSW/ST L13 114 C2
FMBY L37 41 G6
GTS/LS CH66 194 D1
LYMM WA13 145 K6
PR/KW L34 102 A6
WARRS WA4 16 E7
New School La GTS/LS CH66 184 E6
Newsham Cl WDN WA8 138 A5
Newsham Dr NPK/KEN L6 114 A2
Newsham Rd HUY L36 136 D1
Newsham St EV L5 113 F2
News La RNFD/HAY WA11 66 B5
Newstead Av CSBY/BLUN L23 68 C6
Newstead Rd HLWD L26 156 E5
TOX L8 * 133 H2
Newstet Rd NWD/KWIPK L33 85 G1
New St NSTN CH64 191 K4
ORM L39 43 K2
RUNC WA7 10 D5
STHEL WA9 120 A1
WAL/EG CH44 112 A5
Newton Av GOL/RIS/CUL WA3 125 G2
Newton Bank WARRS WA4 179 G6
Newton Cl WD/CROXPK L12 99 F5
Newton Ct CLB/OSW/ST L13 114 C6
Newton Cross La
WKBY CH48 147 F1
Newton Dr WKBY CH48 147 F1
Newton Gdns
GOL/RIS/CUL WA3 93 H3
Newton Gv WARRN/WOL WA2 124 B4
Newton La NEWLW WA12 91 K5
WARRS WA4 179 H5
Newton Park Dr
NEWLW WA12 107 F3
Newton Park Rd WKBY CH48 147 F1
Newton Rd CLB/OSW/ST L13 114 C3
EP CH65 6 E4
GOL/RIS/CUL WA3 93 F5
HOY CH47 127 H2
STHEL WA9 104 E2
WAL/EG CH44 111 G3
WARRN/WOL WA2 123 G4
WGNW/BIL/OR WN5 77 J3
Newton St BIRK CH41 2 C3
CHTN/BK PR9 23 J6
Newton Wk BTL L20 4 D3
Newton Wy GR/UP/WCH CH49 129 G4
VAUX/LVPD L3 9 J4
New Tower Ct WAL/NB CH45 95 J5
Newtown NSTN CH64 192 A3
Newway DV/KA/FCH L14 116 A2
New Wy ORM L39 64 B5
Nicander Rd CALD/MH L18 134 A4
Nicholas Rd CSBY/BLUN L23 68 C5
WDN WA8 157 H3
Nicholas St VAUX/LVPD L3 * 113 F4
Nicholl Rd ECCL WA10 87 H5
Nicholls Dr PEN/TH CH61 167 K1
Nicholls St WARRS WA4 163 G1
Nicholson St STHEL WA9 104 C1
WARR WA1 16 A4
Nickleby Cl TOX L8 132 E4
Nickleford Hall Dr WDN WA8 138 E3
Nicol Av GOL/RIS/CUL WA3 125 H6
Nicol Mere Dr AIMK WN4 79 F3
Nicol Rd AIMK WN4 79 F4
Nidderdale Av RAIN/WH L35 119 F4
Nigel Rd HES CH60 168 C5
Nightingale Cl
GOL/RIS/CUL WA3 125 H3
KKBY L32 72 A6
NTHLY L27 136 C4
RUNC WA7 187 H2
Nightingale Rd
WD/CROXPK L12 99 K2
Nimrod St ANF/KKDL L4 97 H4
Ninth Av WLT/FAZ L9 83 G4
Nipe La RNFD/HAY WA11 66 B3
Nithsdale Rd WAV L15 133 K3
Nixons La SKEL WN8 57 F6
STHP PR8 34 A2
Nixon St ANF/KKDL L4 97 H3
Noble Cl GOL/RIS/CUL WA3 125 G4
Noctorum Av CL/PREN CH43 129 K4
Noctorum Dell CL/PREN CH43 130 A5
Noctorum La CL/PREN CH43 130 B3
Noctorum Rd CL/PREN CH43 130 A4
Noctorum Wy CL/PREN CH43 130 A5
Noel Ga ORM L39 53 F4
Noel St TOX L8 133 G2
Nolan St STHP PR8 27 K2
Nook La GOL/RIS/CUL WA3 92 C3
STHEL WA9 104 D4
WARRN/WOL WA2 124 D5
WARRS WA4 143 K6
Nook Ri WAV L15 134 C1
The Nook CL/PREN CH43 2 A6
ECCL WA10 87 J5
WKBY CH48 147 J1
WLTN L25 135 J6
Noonan Cl WLT/FAZ L9 97 H1
Nora St WARR WA1 17 G5
Norbreck Av DV/KA/FCH L14 115 J5
Norbreck Cl
WARRW/BUR WA5 141 H5
Norbreck Crs
WARRW/BUR WA5 141 H5
Norburn Crs FMBY L37 49 F3
Norbury Av BEB CH63 150 D6
CALD/MH L18 134 A4
WARRN/WOL WA2 143 G1
WGNW/BIL/OR WN5 77 G3
Norbury Cl BEB CH63 150 E6
CHTN/BK PR9 21 F6
WDN WA8 19 K1
Norbury Fold RAIN/WH L35 119 G6
Norbury Rd KKBY L32 84 C1
Norcliffe Rd RAIN/WH L35 118 D3
Norcott Av WARRS WA4 162 C1
Norcott Dr WARRW/BUR WA5 121 K1
Norden Cl GOL/RIS/CUL WA3 124 E2
Norfolk Cl BTL L20 5 G3
CL/PREN CH43 129 K4
Norfolk Dr WARRW/BUR WA5 141 F3
WKBY CH48 146 D2
Norfolk Gv STHP PR8 27 G6
Norfolk Pl LITH L21 * 81 H4
WDN WA8 157 H3
Norfolk Rd ECCL WA10 103 F4
EP CH65 6 D5
MGHL L31 71 F2
STHP PR8 27 G6
Norfolk St CLVPS L1 132 C2
RUNC WA7 11 G3
Norgate St ANF/KKDL L4 97 H6
Norgrove Cl RUNC WA7 178 C5
Norland's La RAIN/WH L35 138 D1
Norlands Pk WDN WA8 138 E3
Norland St WDN WA8 19 J1
Norleane Crs RUNC WA7 176 E5
Norley Av GTS/LS CH66 195 J3
PS/BROM CH62 184 B4
Norley Cl WARRW/BUR WA5 142 B4
Norley Dr ECCL WA10 102 C2
Norley Pl HLWD L26 155 H5
Norman Av NEWLW WA12 106 E2
RNFD/HAY WA11 91 F4
Normanby Cl
WARRW/BUR WA5 142 B2
Norman Cl GTS/LS CH66 202 D3
Normandale Rd ANF/KKDL L4 98 B4
Normandy Rd HUY L36 116 D4
Normanhurst ORM L39 54 A1
Norman Rd BTL L20 81 K4
CSBY/BLUN L23 68 E6
RUNC WA7 10 D7
WAL/EG CH44 112 A5
Norman Salisbury
Ct ECCL WA10 13 F3
Normans Rd STHEL WA9 104 D6
Normanston Rd
CL/PREN CH43 130 E5
Norman St BIRK CH41 130 C1
WARRN/WOL WA2 16 E2
Normanton Av AIG/SPK L17 133 H6
Normanton Cl CL/PREN CH43 130 D5
Norma Rd CSBY/WL L22 81 F2
Norreys Av WARRW/BUR WA5 142 C1
Norric Ct SPK/HALE L24 * 154 E6
Norris Cl CL/PREN CH43 129 K5
Norris Green Crs NG/CROX L11 98 E4
Norris Green Rd
WD/CROXPK L12 115 F1
Norris Green Wy NG/CROX L11 98 E4
Norris House Dr ORM L39 53 G5
Norris Rd PR/KW L34 117 J1
Norris St WARRN/WOL WA2 143 F1
Norris Wy FMBY L37 49 H2
Norseman Cl WD/CROXPK L12 99 F5
Northam Cl CHTN/BK PR9 20 D6
North Av AIN/FAZ L10 83 H1
SPK/HALE L24 154 D5
WARRN/WOL WA2 142 E1
North Barcombe Rd
CHLDW L16 134 E2
Northbrook Cl TOX L8 133 F2
Northbrook Rd WAL/EG CH44 111 K4
Northbrook St TOX L8 133 F2
Northbury Rd GTS/LS CH66 202 C2
North Cantril Av
WD/CROXPK L12 99 J5
North Cl PS/BROM CH62 170 E3
Northcote Cl EV L5 113 H3
Northcote Rd WAL/NB CH45 110 D1
WLT/FAZ L9 * 97 H2
Northdale Rd WARR WA1 143 K1
WAV L15 134 A1
North Dingle ANF/KKDL L4 97 F5
North Dr HES CH60 168 A6
WAV L15 134 A1
WD/CROXPK L12 115 F2
North Dunes HTWN L38 59 F3
North End La HLWD L26 136 B6
HTWN L38 59 G2
Northern La WDN WA8 137 K6
Northern Perimeter Rd
NTHTN L30 70 B4
Northern Ri GTS/LS CH66 195 H5
The Northern Rd
CSBY/BLUN L23 69 F5
Northfield SKEL WN8 56 D1
Northfield Cl NWD/KWIPK L33 73 F5
STHEL WA9 120 B4
Northfield Rd BTL L20 82 B5
North Florida Rd
RNFD/HAY WA11 90 C3
North Front RAIN/WH L35 118 A6
Northgate Rd
CLB/OSW/ST L13 114 D2
North Gv CALD/MH L18 153 K2
North Hill St TOX L8 132 E4
North John St CLVP L2 8 D3
ECCL WA10 13 F4
North Leach Dr STHP PR8 33 G4
North Linkside Rd WLTN L25 155 F2
North Manor Wy WLTN L25 155 F2
North Meade MGHL L31 61 K5
Northmead Rd ALL/GAR L19 154 B4
North Moor La ORM L39 44 D3
North Moss La FMBY L37 41 K4
North Mossley Hill Rd
CALD/MH L18 134 A5
North Mount Rd KKBY L32 72 A5
Northolt Ct
WARRN/WOL WA2 124 A6
North Pde HOY CH47 127 F2
KKBY L32 84 D1
NSTN CH64 181 F5
SPK/HALE L24 173 K2
North Park Brook Rd
WARRW/BUR WA5 122 E6
North Park Ct WAL/EG CH44 112 A4
North Park Rd KKBY L32 72 B5
North Perimeter Rd
NWD/KWIPK L33 73 J5
Northridge Rd
PEN/TH CH61 148 D6
North Rd ALL/GAR L19 153 G5
CHTN/BK PR9 23 K1
DV/KA/FCH L14 115 G5
ECCL WA10 13 F1
EP CH65 185 G4
HLWD L26 155 J6
RF/TRAN CH42 131 F6
WKBY CH48 146 B1
North St AIMK WN4 79 J4
CHTN/BK PR9 15 G2
NEWLW WA12 105 K1
RNFD/HAY WA11 90 D5
VAUX/LVPD L3 8 E2
North Sudley Rd AIG/SPK L17 153 F1
Northumberland Gv TOX L8 132 C4
Northumberland St TOX L8 132 D4
Northumberland Ter EV L5 113 G1
Northumberland Wy
NTHTN L30 69 K6
North Vw EHL/KEN L7 113 J6
HUY L36 117 G5
WARRW/BUR WA5 141 F2
Northway HES CH60 * 168 D4
LYMM WA13 145 J5
MGHL L31 62 B5
ORM L39 62 D1
RUNC WA7 177 J5
SKEL WN8 56 D3
WARRN/WOL WA2 123 H5
WAV L15 134 C1
WDN WA8 157 J2
Northways PS/BROM CH62 171 F2
Northwich Cl CSBY/BLUN L23 69 J3
Northwich Rd RUNC WA7 188 B2
North William St
WAL/EG CH44 * 112 A5
Northwood Av NEWLW WA12 107 F1
Northwood Rd
CL/PREN CH43 149 J1
HUY L36 117 F3
RUNC WA7 177 H3
Norton Av WARRW/BUR WA5 141 F4
Norton Dr PEN/TH CH61 147 K4
Norton Ga RUNC WA7 178 B5
Norton Gv MGHL L31 71 F3
STHEL WA9 103 F6
Norton Hl RUNC WA7 178 B3
Norton La RUNC WA7 178 A5
Norton Rd WKBY CH48 127 F6
Norton Station Rd RUNC WA7 178 C5
Norton St BTL L20 4 C1
VAUX/LVPD L3 9 G2
Norton Vw RUNC WA7 177 K5
Norton Village RUNC WA7 178 C5
Nortonwood La RUNC WA7 178 B4
Norville GTS/LS CH66 195 G2
Norville Rd DV/KA/FCH L14 115 G5
Norwich Av AIMK WN4 91 J1
GOL/RIS/CUL WA3 92 E3
Norwich Dr GR/UP/WCH CH49 129 H2
GTS/LS CH66 202 C3
Norwich Rd WAV L15 134 B3
Norwich Wy KKBY L32 84 D1
Norwood Av AIMK WN4 78 E3
CHTN/BK PR9 23 G5
GOL/RIS/CUL WA3 93 F4
LITH L21 81 J2
Norwood Ct
GR/UP/WCH CH49 128 E6
Norwood Crs CHTN/BK PR9 23 G5
Norwood Gv NPK/KEN L6 113 K3
RNFD/HAY WA11 75 H3
Norwood Rd
GR/UP/WCH CH49 128 E5
STHP PR8 23 H6
WAL/EG CH44 111 H5
Norwyn Rd NG/CROX L11 98 C3
Nostell Rd AIMK WN4 79 F4
Nottingham Cl RAIN/WH L35 118 E2
WARR WA1 144 C3
Nottingham Rd HUY L36 116 C6
Nowshera Av PEN/TH CH61 148 C6
Nuffield Cl GR/UP/WCH CH49 129 G5
Nun Cl CL/PREN CH43 130 E5
Nunn St STHEL WA9 104 B2
Nunsford Cl LITH L21 82 A1
Nunthorpe Rd PR/KW L34 85 G6
The Nurseries FMBY L37 49 G3
Nurse Rd PEN/TH CH61 148 E5
Nursery Av ORM L39 46 A5
Nursery Cl CL/PREN CH43 130 E6
WDN WA8 139 J6
WLTN L25 155 F3
Nursery Dr FMBY L37 49 F3
Nursery La ALL/GAR L19 153 K4
Nursery Rd MGHL L31 62 A3
STHEL WA9 103 F6
Nutgrove Av STHEL WA9 * 103 F6
Nutgrove Hall Dr STHEL WA9 103 F6
Nutgrove Rd STHEL WA9 118 E1
Nuthall Rd STHP PR8 28 B4
Nut St STHEL WA9 103 F6
Nuttall Ct GOL/RIS/CUL WA3 124 E3
Nuttall St EHL/KEN L7 114 A6
Nyland Rd HUY L36 116 D2

O

Oak Av GOL/RIS/CUL WA3 92 C3
GR/UP/WCH CH49 128 E3
NEWLW WA12 106 C2
ORM L39 53 H1
RNFD/HAY WA11 90 D4
WLT/FAZ L9 82 E5
Oak Bank BIRK CH41 2 C6
Oakbank Rd CALD/MH L18 133 K4
Oakbank St WAL/EG CH44 111 J4
Oakbourne Cl AIG/SPK L17 152 D1
Oak Cl MOR/LEA CH46 128 E2
RAIN/WH L35 118 A4
WD/CROXPK L12 99 K4
Oak Crs SKEL WN8 55 K4
Oakdale Av FROD/HEL WA6 201 G3
WAL/EG CH44 111 K5
WARRS WA4 162 C2
Oakdale Cl KKBY L32 84 A2
Oakdale Dr
GR/UP/WCH CH49 147 K1
Oakdale Rd BIRK CH41 111 K6
CALD/MH L18 134 B4
CSBY/WL L22 80 E1
WAL/EG CH44 111 K5
Oakdene Av GTS/LS CH66 195 F4
WARR WA1 144 B2
Oakdene Cl PS/BROM CH62 184 A2
Oakdene Rd ANF/KKDL L4 97 K6
RF/TRAN CH42 131 F6
Oak Dr BRSC L40 39 F6
RUNC WA7 177 F6
Oakenden Cl AIMK WN4 79 F3
Oakenholt Rd
MOR/LEA CH46 109 J6
Oakes St VAUX/LVPD L3 9 J3
Oakfield ANF/KKDL L4 113 K1
Oakfield Av GOL/RIS/CUL WA3 92 A2
WLTN L25 135 H5
Oakfield Cl STHEL WA9 103 F6
Oakfield Dr FMBY L37 48 D1
HUY L36 136 C1
WDN WA8 157 F3
Oakfield Gv HUY L36 136 C1
Oakfield Rd ANF/KKDL L4 113 J1
GTS/LS CH66 194 B1
HTWN L38 59 F5
PS/BROM CH62 170 E5
Oakfields ORM L39 46 A6
Oakgate Cl NG/CROX L11 99 F2
Oak Gn ORM L39 45 K6
Oak Gv EP CH65 195 K6
Oakham Ct CHTN/BK PR9 * 15 H3
Oakham Dr AIN/FAZ L10 83 J2
MOR/LEA CH46 109 F6
Oakham St TOX L8 132 C3
Oakhill Cl MGHL L31 62 B5
WD/CROXPK L12 99 H2
Oakhill Cottage La MGHL L31 62 B3
Oakhill Dr MGHL L31 62 A3
Oakhill Pk CLB/OSW/ST L13 115 F5
Oakhill Rd CLB/OSW/ST L13 115 F5
MGHL L31 62 B5
Oakhurst Cl WLTN L25 135 J5
Oakland Cl LITH L21 81 K5
Oakland Dr GR/UP/WCH CH49 129 H3
Oakland Rd ALL/GAR L19 153 G3
Oaklands RAIN/WH L35 118 E5
Oaklands Av CSBY/BLUN L23 69 F4
Oaklands Ct STHEL WA9 120 A3
Oaklands Dr BEB CH63 151 F5
LYMM WA13 164 E1
PEN/TH CH61 168 A4
Oaklands Rd GOL/RIS/CUL WA3 93 G4
Oaklands Ter PEN/TH CH61 * 168 A3
Oakland St WARR WA1 143 H2
WDN WA8 176 D1
Oak La NG/CROX L11 99 F4
Oak La North NG/CROX L11 99 G3
Oakleaf Ms CL/PREN CH43 130 A4
Oaklea Rd PEN/TH CH61 148 C5
Oaklee Gv NWD/KWIPK L33 73 F5
Oak Leigh CLB/OSW/ST L13 114 C2
Oakleigh SKEL WN8 67 F5
Oakleigh Gv BEB CH63 150 E5
Oakley Av WGNW/BIL/OR WN5 77 G3
Oakley Cl WD/CROXPK L12 99 J2
Oakley Ct EP CH65 6 E7
Oak Meadows Ct
RAIN/WH L35 119 G6
Oakmere Cl MOR/LEA CH46 109 J3
WLT/FAZ L9 82 D4
Oakmere Dr
GR/UP/WCH CH49 128 D5
GTS/LS CH66 202 D3
WARRW/BUR WA5 141 G6
Oakmere St RUNC WA7 10 D5
Oakmoore RUNC WA7 178 E1
Oakridge Cl PS/BROM CH62 170 E3
Oakridge Rd PS/BROM CH62 170 E3
Oak Rd BEB CH63 150 E4
GTS/LS CH66 184 B6
HUY L36 136 A1
LYMM WA13 145 H6
RAIN/WH L35 118 A4
WARRW/BUR WA5 141 G6
Oaks Cl STHEL WA9 120 B4
Oaks La PEN/TH CH61 168 A1
Oaksmeade Cl
WD/CROXPK L12 99 K2
Oaks Pl WDN WA8 18 C5
The Oaks PS/BROM CH62 170 E5
STHEL WA9 * 120 B3
WD/CROXPK L12 99 K2
WKBY CH48 * 146 D2
Oakston Av RAIN/WH L35 119 F5
Oak St BTL L20 5 F2
EP CH65 196 B2
STHEL WA9 104 C5
STHP PR8 28 B1
Oakway HES CH60 181 G1
Oak Ter EHL/KEN L7 * 114 A5
Oakthorn Gv RNFD/HAY WA11 90 B5
Oak Tree Ct SKEL WN8 57 F2
Oaktree Pl RF/TRAN CH42 131 J6
Oaktree Rd ECCL WA10 87 H6
Oak V CLB/OSW/ST L13 115 F5
Oak Vw SPK/HALE L24 174 B2
Oakways WARRS WA4 162 C6
Oak Wharf Ms WARRS WA4 * 162 B3
Oakwood SKEL WN8 * 57 F2
Oakwood Av AIMK WN4 91 F1
STHP PR8 33 K3
WARR WA1 17 J1
Oakwood Cl GTS/LS CH66 202 B2
WLTN L25 135 J4
Oakwood Dr CL/PREN CH43 130 B1
HUY L36 117 F6
STHP PR8 34 A4
Oakwood Ga
GOL/RIS/CUL WA3 125 F3
Oakwood Pk PS/BROM CH62 184 A2
Oakwood Rd HLWD L26 155 H4
Oakworth Cl NWD/KWIPK L33 72 D5
Oakworth Dr PS/BROM CH62 151 H4
RAIN/WH L35 136 D2
Oarside Dr WAL/NB CH45 111 G1
Oatfield La LITH L21 81 J1
Oatlands Rd KKBY L32 * 84 B1
The Oatlands WKBY CH48 146 D2
Oban Dr AIMK WN4 78 B5
HES CH60 168 A5
Oban Gv WARRN/WOL WA2 124 C4
Oban Rd ANF/KKDL L4 113 K1
Oberon St BTL L20 96 E4
O'Brien Gv STHEL WA9 104 C1
Observatory Rd
CL/PREN CH43 130 A1
Oceanic Rd CLB/OSW/ST L13 114 D5
Ocean Rd LITH L21 81 J4
O'Connell Cl RNFD/HAY WA11 90 B5
O'Connell Rd VAUX/LVPD L3 113 F3
O'Connor Dr NWD/KWIPK L33 72 D3
Octavia Ct HUY L36 * 117 G6
Octavia Hill Rd LITH L21 81 K2
October Dr NPK/KEN L6 114 B1
Odsey St EHL/KEN L7 114 A5
Ogle Cl RAIN/WH L35 118 A2
Oglet La SPK/HALE L24 173 H3
Oil Sites Rd EP CH65 197 G4
EP CH65 7 F2
Oil St VAUX/LVPD L3 112 D3
O'Keeffe Rd STHEL WA9 104 A1
Okehampton Rd CHLDW L16 134 E1
Okell Dr HLWD L26 155 G1
Okell St RUNC WA7 10 D5
Old Acre HTWN L38 59 F4
Old Barn Rd ANF/KKDL L4 113 K1
WAL/EG CH44 111 G4
Old Bidston Rd BIRK CH41 2 A1
Old Boston RNFD/HAY WA11 91 F4
Old Boundary Wy ORM L39 45 K5
Oldbridge Rd SPK/HALE L24 174 A2
Old Cherry La LYMM WA13 164 B5
Old Chester Rd BEB CH63 150 E4
FROD/HEL WA6 199 J6
GTS/LS CH66 195 G5
RF/TRAN CH42 150 E1
WARRS WA4 161 J4
Old Church Cl EP CH65 * 6 E1
WLT/FAZ L9 82 E4
Old Church Yd CLVP L2 8 B4
Old Clatterbridge Rd
BEB CH63 170 A3
Old Coach Rd RUNC WA7 10 A3
Old College Pl EHL/KEN L7 114 A6
Old Colliery Rd RAIN/WH L35 117 K4
Old Colliery Yd AIMK WN4 78 B6
Old Court House Rd
PS/BROM CH62 151 J6
Old Distillery Rd
SPK/HALE L24 154 E6
Old Dover Rd HUY L36 135 K1
Old Eccleston La ECCL WA10 102 E2
Old Engine La SKEL WN8 55 J3
Old Farm Cl NSTN CH64 193 H1
Old Farm Rd CSBY/BLUN L23 69 G5
KKBY L32 84 E5
Oldfield Cl HES CH60 167 J3
Oldfield Dr HES CH60 167 G4
Oldfield Gdns HES CH60 167 H4
Oldfield La WKBY CH48 128 B4
Oldfield Rd ALL/GAR L19 153 H2
EP CH65 6 C5
HES CH60 167 H3
LYMM WA13 145 H5
Oldfield St ECCL WA10 13 F1
Oldfield Wy HES CH60 167 H3
Oldgate WDN WA8 157 H5
Old Gorsey La WAL/EG CH44 111 H5
Old Greasby Rd
GR/UP/WCH CH49 129 G4
Old Hall RAIN/WH L35 137 H1
Old Hall Cl MGHL L31 71 G2
WARRS WA4 161 K3
Old Hall Dr AIMK WN4 91 F1
EP CH65 6 C7
Old Hall Gdns RNFD/HAY WA11 75 H3
Old Hall La CHNE CH2 198 C6
KKBY L32 84 C1
Old Hall Rd MGHL L31 71 G2
PS/BROM CH62 171 G4
WARRW/BUR WA5 142 A1
Old Hall St VAUX/LVPD L3 8 B2
Oldham Pl CLVPS L1 9 G5
Oldham St CLVPS L1 9 G6
WARRS WA4 143 G6
Old Haymarket CLVPS L1 8 E3
Old Higher Rd WDN WA8 156 C6
Old Hutte La HLWD L26 155 K5
Old Kennel Cl WD/CROXPK L12 99 K5
Old La FMBY L37 41 F5
HES CH60 168 D5
MGHL L31 62 C3
ORM L39 51 G2
PR/KW L34 118 B1
RAIN/WH L35 118 D5
RNFD/HAY WA11 75 G2
Old Leeds St VAUX/LVPD L3 8 B2
Old Links Cl CHTN/BK PR9 23 K5
Old Liverpool Rd
WARRW/BUR WA5 142 B5
Old Lodge Cl WD/CROXPK L12 99 F5
Old Market Pl WARR WA1 16 C4

Old Maryland La
MOR/LEA CH46 109 J6
Old Meadow PR/KW L34 85 J6
Old Meadow Rd
PEN/TH CH61 167 J2
Old Mill Av STHEL WA9 120 B2
Old Mill Cl HES CH60 168 B6
Old Mill Hl ORM L39 53 H2
Old Mill La FMBY L37 49 F1
PR/KW L34 85 K6
WAV L15 134 B1
Old Moss La ORM L39 42 E6
Old Nook La RNFD/HAY WA11 89 H5
Old Orch RAIN/WH L35 118 A6
Old Park La CHTN/BK PR9 23 J5
Old Post Office Pl CLVPS L1 * 8 E5
Old Prescot Cl MGHL L31 63 G5
Old Pump La
GR/UP/WCH CH49 128 D6
The Old Quarry WLTN L25 154 D1
Old Quay Cl NSTN CH64 191 H2
Old Quay La NSTN CH64 191 J2
Old Quay St RUNC WA7 11 G3
Old Racecourse Rd MGHL L31 70 E1
Old Rectory Gn ORM L39 52 E6
SFTN L29 70 B2
Old Riding DV/KA/FCH L14 115 K2
Old Rd AIMK WN4 79 F6
WARRS WA4 16 E7
Old Ropery CLVP L2 * 8 C4
Old Rough La NWD/KWIPK L33 84 D1
Old School Cl NSTN CH64 192 A4
Old School House La
WARRN/WOL WA2 107 G6
Old School Pl AIMK WN4 79 F6
Old School Wy CL/PREN CH43 * 130 B2
Old Smithy La LYMM WA13 164 D1
The Old Tennis Club
RF/TRAN CH42 * 150 A1
Old Thomas La
DV/KA/FCH L14 115 H6
Old Town Cl SKEL WN8 55 K5
Old Town La FMBY L37 48 E1
Old Town Wy SKEL WN8 55 K5
Old Upton La WDN WA8 138 D5
Old Vicarage Rd NSTN CH64 193 H1
Old Wargrave Rd
NEWLW WA12 106 B2
Old Whint Rd RNFD/HAY WA11 89 K5
Old Wood Rd PEN/TH CH61 167 K1
Oleander Dr ECCL WA10 102 E1
O'Leary St WARRN/WOL WA2 143 F2
Olga Rd STHEL WA9 104 A6
Olinda St PS/BROM CH62 151 G4
Olive Cl MGHL L31 * 83 K1
Olive Crs BIRK CH41 131 H5
Olivedale Rd CALD/MH L18 134 A5
Olive Dr NSTN CH64 191 K1
Olive Gv HUY L36 116 D5
NTHTN L30 82 D2
SKEL WN8 56 A4
STHP PR8 23 G6
WAV L15 114 E6
Olive La WAV L15 114 E6
Olive Mt BIRK CH41 131 H5
Olive Mount Rd WAV L15 134 B1
Oliver La BIRK CH41 3 F5
GTS/LS CH66 195 G5
Oliver Lyme Rd PR/KW L34 118 A1
Olive Rd CSBY/WL L22 81 F3
NSTN CH64 191 K1
Oliver Rd ECCL WA10 102 E4
Oliver St BIRK CH41 2 D5
WARRN/WOL WA2 16 D2
Oliver St East BIRK CH41 3 F5
Olivetree Rd WAV L15 134 C1
Olive V WAV L15 134 A1
Olivia Cl CL/PREN CH43 129 K5
Olivia St BTL L20 97 F4
Olivia Wy HUY L36 117 H5
Ollerton Cl CL/PREN CH43 129 K5
WARRS WA4 144 A6
Ollerton Pk
WARRW/BUR WA5 105 J6
Ollery Gn NTHTN L30 70 E5
Ollier St WDN WA8 18 C6
Olney St ANF/KKDL L4 97 H3
Olton St WAV L15 133 K1
Olympia Pl WARRW/BUR WA5 141 J2
Olympia St NPK/KEN L6 113 J4
Olympic Wy NTHTN L30 82 D3
Omega Bvd
WARRW/BUR WA5 121 H6
O'Neill St BTL L20 4 C2
Onslow Crs STHP PR8 27 H5
Onslow Rd NPK/KEN L6 114 A4
PS/BROM CH62 151 G3
WAL/NB CH45 95 H5
Opal Cl LITH L21 81 K3
NPK/KEN L6 113 K3
Openfields Cl HLWD L26 155 H1
Oppenheim Av ECCL WA10 102 E5
Orange Gv TOX L8 133 H3
WARRN/WOL WA2 124 A5
Orange Tree Cl STBRV L28 * 100 B5
Oran Wy HUY L36 116 D4
Orb Cl NG/CROX L11 99 G2
Orchard Av DV/KA/FCH L14 115 H6
Orchard Cl FROD/HEL WA6 200 D3
GTS/LS CH66 202 D2
PR/KW L34 102 C6
RAIN/WH L35 118 A6
RNFD/HAY WA11 89 G4
Orchard Ct BIRK CH41 131 J6
FROD/HEL WA6 200 D1
Orchard Dl CSBY/BLUN L23 69 G5
Orchard Dr NSTN CH64 191 K4
Orchard Gdns RAIN/WH L35 137 H1
Orchard Gra MOR/LEA CH46 128 D2
Orchard Hvn GTS/LS CH66 202 C2
Orchard Hey ECCL WA10 102 C2
MGHL L31 71 H1
NTHTN L30 70 E6
Orchard La GTS/LS CH66 194 D1
STHP PR8 33 K5
Orchard Pk CHNE CH2 198 C5
Orchard Park La CHNE CH2 198 C5
Orchard Pl FROD/HEL WA6 199 K5
Orchard Rd EP CH65 202 E1
MOR/LEA CH46 109 J6
Orchard St AIMK WN4 79 H6
WARR WA1 17 F4
WARRN/WOL WA2 124 C5
WARRS WA4 162 B3
The Orchard AIG/SPK L17 153 G2
HUY L36 116 E6
ORM L39 45 H6
WAL/NB CH45 95 G6
Orchard Vw ORM L39 53 H4
Orchard Wk NSTN CH64 191 K1
RUNC WA7 * 177 J6
Orchard Wy BEB CH63 150 C5
WDN WA8 137 K6
Orchid Cl SKEL WN8 67 K1
Orchid Gv AIG/SPK L17 132 E6
Orchid Wy STHEL WA9 105 F6
Orchil Cl GTS/LS CH66 194 D3
Ordnance Av
GOL/RIS/CUL WA3 125 H3
O'Reilly Ct VAUX/LVPD L3 112 E3
Orford Cl GOL/RIS/CUL WA3 92 B4
Orford Gn WARRN/WOL WA2 123 K6
Orford La WARRN/WOL WA2 16 E1
Orford Rd WARRN/WOL WA2 143 G1
Orford St WARR WA1 16 E4
WAV L15 134 A1
Oriel Cl AIN/FAZ L10 71 G6
Oriel Crs BTL L20 96 E4
Oriel Dr AIN/FAZ L10 71 G6
Oriel Rd AIMK WN4 78 E5
BTL L20 4 D6
RF/TRAN CH42 131 H6
Oriel St VAUX/LVPD L3 112 E4
Orient Dr WLTN L25 135 J6
Origen Rd CHLDW L16 115 H6
Oriole Cl ECCL WA10 102 D6
Orion Bvd WARRW/BUR WA5 121 J6
Orith Av ECCL WA10 102 B2
Orkney Cl EP CH65 203 G2
RNFD/HAY WA11 89 G4
WDN WA8 139 K6
Orlando Cl CL/PREN CH43 129 K5
Orlando Dr WARRW/BUR WA5 141 K2
Orlando St BTL L20 96 E4
Orleans Rd CLB/OSW/ST L13 114 E4
Ormande St STHEL WA9 103 K4
Ormesby Gv BEB CH63 183 H1
Ormiston Rd WAL/NB CH45 95 H6
Ormond Av BRSC L40 54 D1
Ormond Cl WDN WA8 157 H1
Ormonde Av MGHL L31 71 F2
Ormonde Crs
NWD/KWIPK L33 85 F1
Ormonde Dr MGHL L31 71 F1
Ormond St VAUX/LVPD L3 8 C3
WAL/NB CH45 111 H2
Ormond Wy CL/PREN CH43 129 K5
Ormsby St WAV L15 133 K2
Ormside Gv STHEL WA9 104 B6
Ormskirk Old Rd ORM L39 55 F6
Ormskirk Rd ORM L39 54 C4
PR/KW L34 85 J5
RNFD/HAY WA11 65 K5
SKEL WN8 55 J4
WLT/FAZ L9 82 E3
Ormskirk St ECCL WA10 13 F4
Orms Wy FMBY L37 48 E2
Orphan Dr NPK/KEN L6 114 B2
Orphan St EHL/KEN L7 133 F1
Orrell Cl WARRW/BUR WA5 141 H3
Orrell Hey BTL L20 82 A4
Orrell Hill La HTWN L38 59 J3
Orrell La BRSC L40 38 D4
BTL L20 82 C4
Orrell Ms BRSC L40 * 38 E4
Orrell Mt BTL L20 81 K4
Orrell Rd BTL L20 81 K4
WAL/NB CH45 95 J6
Orrell St STHEL WA9 104 A2
Orret's Meadow Rd
GR/UP/WCH CH49 129 J6
Orrysdale Rd WKBY CH48 127 F6
Orry St EV L5 113 F2
Orsett Rd KKBY L32 84 E3
Orston Crs BEB CH63 170 C3
Ortega Cl PS/BROM CH62 151 H4
Orthes St VAUX/LVPD L3 9 J5
Orton Wy AIMK WN4 78 E6
Orville St STHEL WA9 104 D6
Orwell Cl FMBY L37 48 D4
STHEL WA9 119 J4
Orwell Rd ANF/KKDL L4 97 F5
Osbert Rd CSBY/BLUN L23 68 C5
Osborne Av WAL/NB CH45 95 H6
WARRN/WOL WA2 123 K6
Osborne Ct PS/BROM CH62 151 G4
Osborne Gv PR/KW L34 117 G2
WAL/NB CH45 111 H1
Osborne Rd AIMK WN4 79 F5
CL/PREN CH43 2 A6
CLB/OSW/ST L13 114 C1
ECCL WA10 87 H6
FMBY L37 48 E4
GOL/RIS/CUL WA3 93 F4
LITH L21 81 K2
STHP PR8 33 H3
WAL/NB CH45 95 J6
WARRS WA4 162 A2
Osborne Wd AIG/SPK L17 152 E2
Osbourne Cl PS/BROM CH62 171 G6
Osier Cl CHNE CH2 198 D6
Osmaston Rd RF/TRAN CH42 149 K1
Osprey Cl NTHLY L27 136 C4
RUNC WA7 187 J2
WARRN/WOL WA2 124 A4
Ossett Cl CL/PREN CH43 129 K5
RUNC WA7 178 C5
Osterley Gdns WLT/FAZ L9 82 C5
O'Sullivan Crs RNFD/HAY WA11 89 H6
Oteley Av PS/BROM CH62 171 F5
Othello Cl BTL L20 96 E4
Otterburn Cl MOR/LEA CH46 128 C1
Otterspool Dr AIG/SPK L17 152 E3
Otterspool Rd AIG/SPK L17 152 E2
Otterton Rd NG/CROX L11 84 B6
Ottery Cl CHTN/BK PR9 20 D6
Ottley St NPK/KEN L6 114 A4
Otway St ALL/GAR L19 153 K6
Oueenswood Av BEB CH63 150 D3
Oughtrington La LYMM WA13 165 H1
Oulton Cl CL/PREN CH43 130 B6
MGHL L31 61 K3
Oulton La HUY L36 135 K1
Oulton Rd CHLDW L16 134 E3
Oulton Wy CL/PREN CH43 149 H1
Oundle Dr AIN/FAZ L10 71 F6
Oundle Pl WLTN L25 154 E4
Oundle Rd MOR/LEA CH46 109 J6
Outer Central Rd HLWD L26 155 H6
Outer Forum NG/CROX L11 98 C3
Out La WLTN L25 154 E1
Outlet La MGHL L31 63 J6
The Oval EP CH65 196 B6
WAL/NB CH45 111 F1
Overbrook La PR/KW L34 85 H6
Overbury St EHL/KEN L7 113 K6
Overchurch Rd
GR/UP/WCH CH49 129 F3
Overdale Av PEN/TH CH61 149 G6
Overdale Rd NSTN CH64 183 H6
Overdene Wk KKBY L32 84 E2
Overgreen Gv
MOR/LEA CH46 109 H6
Overpool Gdns GTS/LS CH66 195 J6
Overpool Rd GTS/LS CH66 202 D1
Overton Av LITH L21 81 J2
Overton Cl CL/PREN CH43 130 C6
KKBY L32 84 C2
Overton Dr FROD/HEL WA6 201 F3
Overton Rd WAL/EG CH44 111 H3
Overton St EHL/KEN L7 113 K6
Overton Wy CL/PREN CH43 130 C6
Ovington Cl RUNC WA7 187 J3
Ovington Dr STHP PR8 28 B4
Ovolo Rd CLB/OSW/ST L13 114 E3
Owen Av ORM L39 45 K5
Owen Cl ECCL WA10 102 E4
Owen Dr SPK/HALE L24 173 G3
Owen Rd ANF/KKDL L4 97 F5
NWD/KWIPK L33 85 H4
RAIN/WH L35 118 E5
Owen's La ORM L39 51 F3
Owen St ECCL WA10 102 E4
WARRN/WOL WA2 142 D2
Owlsfield NEWLW WA12 106 E2
Oxborough Cl WDN WA8 138 E6
Oxbow Rd WD/CROXPK L12 99 J5
Oxendale Cl TOX L8 133 G2
Oxenham Rd
WARRN/WOL WA2 123 G4
Oxenholme Crs NG/CROX L11 98 E4
Oxford Av BTL L20 5 J5
LITH L21 81 J3
Oxford Cl AIG/SPK L17 152 D1
GTS/LS CH66 202 D2
Oxford Ct STHP PR8 27 G3
WARR WA1 17 G3
Oxford Dr BEB CH63 182 A1
CSBY/WL L22 80 D2
HLWD L26 155 J3
Oxford Gdns STHP PR8 27 F3
Oxford Rd BTL L20 5 H5
CSBY/WL L22 80 D1
HUY L36 117 G3
RUNC WA7 10 D7
SKEL WN8 56 A4
STHP PR8 27 F3
WAL/EG CH44 111 J3
WLT/FAZ L9 82 E3
Oxford St ECCL WA10 12 E2
NEWLW WA12 106 A2
WARRS WA4 17 G7
WDN WA8 18 E4
Oxheys RUNC WA7 178 B5
Ox La RAIN/WH L35 137 F3
Oxley Av MOR/LEA CH46 110 B4
Oxley St STHEL WA9 104 B6
Oxmead Cl WARRN/WOL WA2 124 D6
Oxmoor Cl RUNC WA7 187 K2
Oxton Cl AIG/SPK L17 152 D1
KKBY L32 84 A3
WDN WA8 138 B5
Oxton Gn GTS/LS CH66 195 G5
Oxton Rd BIRK CH41 2 C7
WAL/EG CH44 111 H4
Oxton St ANF/KKDL L4 97 H5

P

Pacific Rd BIRK CH41 3 H2
BTL L20 4 C3
Packenham Rd
CLB/OSW/ST L13 114 D1
Padbury St TOX L8 133 F4
Paddington EHL/KEN L7 113 J6
Paddington Bank WARR WA1 143 J3
Paddock Cl CSBY/BLUN L23 68 C3
Paddock Dr NSTN CH64 181 J5
Paddock Gv STHEL WA9 120 B4
Paddock Ri RUNC WA7 187 H3
Paddock Rd SKEL WN8 66 E2
The Paddock AIMK WN4 78 E3
CHNE CH2 198 B6
FMBY L37 41 G6
GR/UP/WCH CH49 129 J4
GTS/LS CH66 195 G6
HES CH60 168 C5
KKBY L32 84 C4
MOR/LEA CH46 128 D2
ORM L39 53 G2
PR/KW L34 102 B6
STHP PR8 33 H5
WLTN L25 135 J5
Padeswood Cl STHEL WA9 120 A1
Padgate La WARR WA1 143 H1
Padstow Cl CHTN/BK PR9 20 D6
HLWD L26 155 H2
WARRW/BUR WA5 141 F6
Padstow Dr ECCL WA10 87 J5
Padstow Rd CHLDW L16 134 E1
GR/UP/WCH CH49 147 K1
Pagebank Rd DV/KA/FCH L14 116 A4
Page Ct FMBY L37 49 F2
Pagefield Rd WAV L15 134 B3
Page La WDN WA8 19 H2
Page Moss Av HUY L36 116 B3
Page Moss La DV/KA/FCH L14 116 A4
Page Wk VAUX/LVPD L3 9 H1
Pagewood Cl
CL/PREN CH43 130 A5
Paignton Cl HUY L36 117 H5
WARRW/BUR WA5 141 F5
WGNW/BIL/OR WN5 77 H1
Paignton Rd CHLDW L16 134 E1
WAL/NB CH45 110 E1
Painswick Rd GTS/LS CH66 202 C1
Paisley Av PS/BROM CH62 184 B3
RNFD/HAY WA11 89 G4
Paisley St VAUX/LVPD L3 8 B1
Palace Ar AIMK WN4 79 G6
Palace Fields Av RUNC WA7 177 K6
Palace Hey NSTN CH64 192 B4
Palace Rd STHP PR8 27 F2
WLT/FAZ L9 82 D5
Palatine Ar ECCL WA10 * 13 G5
Palatine Rd PS/BROM CH62 170 E4
STHP PR8 27 G2
WAL/EG CH44 111 K5
Palermo Cl WAL/EG CH44 111 K5
Paley Cl ANF/KKDL L4 97 H6
Palin Dr WARRW/BUR WA5 141 G3
Palladio Rd CLB/OSW/ST L13 115 F3
Palliser Cl GOL/RIS/CUL WA3 125 J4
Pall Ml VAUX/LVPD L3 112 D4
Palm Av AIMK WN4 78 C4
Palm Cl WLT/FAZ L9 98 A2
Palm Ct SKEL WN8 56 A3
Palmer Cl CL/PREN CH43 130 A6
ECCL WA10 12 E4
Palmer Crs WARRW/BUR WA5 142 A1
Palmerston Av LITH L21 81 H4
Palmerston Cl CALD/MH L18 134 A6
Palmerston Crs ALL/GAR L19 153 K5
Palmerston Dr LITH L21 81 J5
WLTN L25 155 G3
Palmerston Rd CALD/MH L18 134 A6
CHTN/BK PR9 28 C1
WAL/EG CH44 111 F3
Palmerston St RF/TRAN CH42 150 E1
Palm Gv CL/PREN CH43 130 E4
GTS/LS CH66 202 E2
STHP PR8 15 K6
WLTN L25 154 E2
Palm Hl CL/PREN CH43 130 E5
Palmwood Av RAIN/WH L35 119 F5
Palmwood Cl CL/PREN CH43 149 H2
Palmyra Sq North WARR WA1 16 C5
Palmyra Sq South WARR WA1 16 C5
Paltridge Wy PEN/TH CH61 167 K1
Pamela Cl AIN/FAZ L10 84 A4
Pampas Gv WLT/FAZ L9 97 K1
Pangbourne Cl WARRS WA4 162 D5
Pankhurst Rd LITH L21 81 K1
Pansy St EV L5 97 F6
Papillon Dr WLT/FAZ L9 83 G3
Parade Crs SPK/HALE L24 173 K3
Parade St ECCL WA10 13 G4
The Parade NSTN CH64 181 G5
Paradise La FMBY L37 41 G6
RAIN/WH L35 117 K5
Paradise Rw WLTN L25 * 135 J5
Paradise St CLVPS L1 8 E4
Paragon Cl WDN WA8 139 G4
Parbold Av RNFD/HAY WA11 89 G6
Parbold Cl BRSC L40 38 E6
Parbold Ct WDN WA8 157 J4
Parbrook Cl HUY L36 116 D1
Parbrook Rd HUY L36 116 D2
The Parchments
NEWLW WA12 106 D1
Park Av CALD/MH L18 133 K6
CHTN/BK PR9 23 G4
CSBY/BLUN L23 69 F4
FMBY L37 49 F4
GOL/RIS/CUL WA3 92 A1
MGHL L31 62 B4
ORM L39 45 J6
PR/KW L34 102 B6
RAIN/WH L35 118 E3
RNFD/HAY WA11 89 K5
WAL/EG CH44 111 K4
WARRS WA4 143 G6
WDN WA8 18 E1
WLT/FAZ L9 83 G6
Park Av North NEWLW WA12 106 C3
Park Av South NEWLW WA12 106 C3
Park Bvd WARR WA1 16 C7
Parkbourn MGHL L31 62 E5
Parkbourn Dr MGHL L31 62 E5
Parkbourn North MGHL L31 62 E5
Parkbourn Sq MGHL L31 62 E5
Parkbridge Rd RF/TRAN CH42 131 F6
Park Brow Dr KKBY L32 84 E3
Parkbury Ct CL/PREN CH43 130 D6
Park Cl BIRK CH41 2 C4
FMBY L37 48 E5
KKBY L32 72 A6
Park Ct CSBY/WL L22 81 F2
RUNC WA7 176 D5
Park Crs CHTN/BK PR9 15 K1
ORM L39 51 H1
WARRS WA4 162 C5
Parkdale WKBY CH48 146 E5
Parkdale Av WLT/FAZ L9 82 D4
Parkdale Rd WARR WA1 143 K2
Park Dr BIRK CH41 130 D2
CL/PREN CH43 130 D2
CSBY/BLUN L23 69 H2
CSBY/BLUN L23 68 B5
EP CH65 196 A6
Parkend Rd RF/TRAN CH42 131 F6
Parker Av LITH L21 81 G4
Parker Cl NTHTN L30 82 E2
Parker Crs ORM L39 45 K4
Parkers Ct RUNC WA7 187 H1
Parker St CLVPS L1 9 F4
RUNC WA7 11 F3
WARR WA1 16 B6
Parkfield Av BIRK CH41 2 E4
NTHTN L30 82 D2
WARRS WA4 143 K5
Parkfield Cl ORM L39 53 G2
Parkfield Dr EP CH65 202 E1
FROD/HEL WA6 199 J6
WAL/EG CH44 111 H3
Parkfield Gv MGHL L31 62 A6
Parkfield Pl BIRK CH41 2 D4
Parkfield Rd AIG/SPK L17 133 G5
BEB CH63 170 C2
CSBY/WL L22 81 F1
Parkfields La
WARRN/WOL WA2 124 B5
Parkgate Cl AIG/SPK L17 153 F2
Parkgate La NSTN CH64 181 K2
Parkgate Rd NSTN CH64 191 H1
WARRS WA4 162 C2
Parkgate Wy RUNC WA7 178 B6
Park Gv BIRK CH41 2 D7
Parkhill Ct TOX L8 132 E5
Parkhill Rd RF/TRAN CH42 131 F6
Park Hill Rd TOX L8 132 E5
Parkhurst Rd NG/CROX L11 98 D4
RF/TRAN CH42 * 150 B1
Parkinson Rd WLT/FAZ L9 97 J1
Parkland Cl TOX L8 133 F4
Parkland Ct CL/PREN CH43 129 K1
Parkland Dr CHNE CH2 198 C6
Parklands CHTN/BK PR9 23 G5
GTS/LS CH66 195 G4
PR/KW L34 100 D2
RNFD/HAY WA11 75 G2
SKEL WN8 57 F3
WDN WA8 138 B6
Parklands Dr HES CH60 181 G1
Parklands Gdns GTS/LS CH66 195 G3
Parklands Vw GTS/LS CH66 195 G3
Parklands Wy CSBY/WL L22 81 G2
Park La BTL L20 82 B4
CLVPS L1 8 E6
FROD/HEL WA6 200 E1
HOY CH47 108 E5
MGHL L31 62 C4
NTHTN L30 82 C1
WARRS WA4 161 J6
Park Lane Dr MGHL L31 63 F5
Park La West NTHTN L30 70 C6
Parklea GTS/LS CH66 195 G3
Park Link ORM L39 53 F4
Park Pl BTL L20 5 F5
TOX L8 132 D3
Park Rd CHTN/BK PR9 15 J1
CSBY/WL L22 81 F2
EP CH65 6 D6
FMBY L37 48 E4
GOL/RIS/CUL WA3 92 A4
HES CH60 168 B4
HOY CH47 108 C6
KKBY L32 72 A6
NSTN CH64 193 J1
ORM L39 45 J6
PR/KW L34 101 J6
PS/BROM CH62 184 C1
PS/BROM CH62 151 G6
RF/TRAN CH42 131 H6
RUNC WA7 176 C5
STHEL WA9 104 A1
TOX L8 132 E4
WAL/EG CH44 111 J4
WARRN/WOL WA2 123 K6
WARRW/BUR WA5 140 D2
WDN WA8 19 F1
WKBY CH48 146 B1
Park Rd East BIRK CH41 2 C4
Park Rd North BIRK CH41 130 D2
NEWLW WA12 106 E2
Park Rd South CL/PREN CH43 2 B5
NEWLW WA12 106 D2
Park Rd West CHTN/BK PR9 22 E4
CL/PREN CH43 130 D2
Parkside WAL/EG CH44 111 J4
Parkside Av AIMK WN4 78 E1
SKEL WN8 55 K5
STHEL WA9 119 K4
Parkside Cl BEB CH63 151 F5
NSTN CH64 191 J1
NTHLY L27 136 B5
Parkside Dr WD/CROXPK L12 98 E5
Parkside Rd RF/TRAN CH42 131 H6
WARRN/WOL WA2 107 H4
Parkside St NPK/KEN L6 113 H4
The Parks NEWLW WA12 91 G2
Parkstile La NG/CROX L11 99 G1
Parkstone Rd RF/TRAN CH42 131 F6
Park St BIRK CH41 2 E3
BTL L20 5 H4
NSTN CH64 191 K1
RNFD/HAY WA11 89 J5
STHEL WA9 104 A1
TOX L8 132 D4
WAL/EG CH44 111 J3
Parksway WARR WA1 144 C2
Park Ter CSBY/WL L22 81 F3
The Park HUY L36 116 E6
WARRW/BUR WA5 140 E6
Parkvale Av CL/PREN CH43 149 H3
Park Vale Rd WLT/FAZ L9 82 D5
Park Vw AIMK WN4 91 G1
CSBY/WL L22 80 E1
HUY L36 116 C3
NPK/KEN L6 114 B2
PS/BROM CH62 170 E5
WARRN/WOL WA2 * 124 A4
Parkview Cl BIRK CH41 2 B2
Parkview Dr NTHLY L27 136 B5
Park View Flats LITH L21 * 81 H3
Parkview Rd NG/CROX L11 99 H1
Park Wall Rd HTWN L38 60 B4
Parkway NTHTN L30 70 C4
WAL/NB CH45 94 E6
CSBY/BLUN L23 81 G1
Park Wy FMBY L37 49 F4
HOY CH47 127 K1
HUY L36 100 D6
TOX L8 132 E2
Parkway Cl PEN/TH CH61 148 C4
Park Wy West KKBY L32 * 72 A6
Park West HES CH60 167 H6
Parkwood Cl LYMM WA13 164 E1
PS/BROM CH62 171 G4
Parkwood Rd RAIN/WH L35 118 A5
WLTN L25 135 H5
Park Works SPK/HALE L24 * 154 E5
Parlane St STHEL WA9 104 A1
Parliament Cl CLVPS L1 132 D2
Parliament Pl TOX L8 132 E2
Parliament St STHEL WA9 103 F6
TOX L8 132 C2

Parliament Wy GTS/LS CH66 202 D3
Parlington Cl WDN WA8 157 H4
Parlow Rd NG/CROX L11 98 C5
Parnell Rd BEB CH63 170 C3
Parren Av RAIN/WH L35 117 J6
Parr Gv GR/UP/WCH CH49 128 D5
RNFD/HAY WA11 89 K5
Parr Mount Ct STHEL WA9 104 A2
Parr Mount St STHEL WA9 104 A2
Parr's La ORM L39 53 H5
Parrs Rd CL/PREN CH43 130 E6
Parr Stocks Rd STHEL WA9 104 B2
Parr St CLVPS L1 9 F6
LITH L21 81 J2
STHEL WA9 13 J6
WARR WA1 16 E6
WDN WA8 * 19 G1
Parrs Wood View WARRS WA4 163 F2
Parry Dr WARRS WA4 144 D6
Parry St WAL/EG CH44 111 K5
Parsonage Brow SKEL WN8 57 H5
Parsonage Cl SKEL WN8 57 J6
Parsonage Rd SKEL WN8 57 J6
WDN WA8 176 D1
WDN WA8 10 D1
Parsonage Wy
WARRW/BUR WA5 141 H4
Parson's Brow
RNFD/HAY WA11 75 F3
Parthenon Dr NG/CROX L11 98 B2
Partington Av BTL L20 5 J2
Parton St NPK/KEN L6 114 A4
Partridge Cl GOL/RIS/CUL WA3 125 G3
WD/CROXPK L12 99 K2
Partridge Rd CSBY/BLUN L23 68 C5
KKBY L32 72 A6
Part St STHP PR8 27 H2
Pasture Av MOR/LEA CH46 109 J5
Pasture Cl AIMK WN4 78 D3
STHEL WA9 120 A3
WLTN L25 154 E2
Pasture Crs MOR/LEA CH46 109 J6
Pasture La RNFD/HAY WA11 75 H5
WARRN/WOL WA2 124 D6
Pasture Rd MOR/LEA CH46 109 H4
The Pastures CHTN/BK PR9 21 G6
STHEL WA9 104 E6
WKBY CH48 147 G1
Pateley Cl KKBY L32 84 B2
Paterson St BIRK CH41 2 C5
Patmos Cl EV L5 113 G1
Paton Cl WKBY CH48 127 H6
Patricia Av BIRK CH41 110 E6
Patricia Gv BTL L20 82 A5
Patrick Av BTL L20 82 A4
Patrivale Cl WARR WA1 143 J2
Patten La WARR WA1 * 16 D5
Patten's Cl NTHTN L30 70 A5
Patten St BIRK CH41 130 E1
Patten's Wk PR/KW L34 85 K6
Patterdale Av
WARRN/WOL WA2 123 J5
Patterdale Cl STHP PR8 33 H6
Patterdale Crs MGHL L31 62 C5
Patterdale Dr ECCL WA10 102 D5
Patterdale Rd AIMK WN4 79 F1
BEB CH63 170 B2
WAV L15 133 K3
Patterson Cl
GOL/RIS/CUL WA3 125 G4
Patterson St NEWLW WA12 106 B1
Paul Cl WARRW/BUR WA5 140 E3
Paul McCartney Wy
NPK/KEN L6 113 K4
Paul Orr Ct VAUX/LVPD L3 112 E3
Paulsfield Dr MOR/LEA CH46 129 F2
Paul's La CHTN/BK PR9 23 H2
Paul St VAUX/LVPD L3 112 E4
WARRN/WOL WA2 16 B3
Paulton Cl TOX L8 132 E5
Paveley Bank NTHLY L27 136 A4
Pavilion Cl TOX L8 133 G2
Pavilion Ct NEWLW WA12 106 A2
Paxton Pl SKEL WN8 66 E3
Paxton Rd HUY L36 116 E3
Payne Cl WARRW/BUR WA5 142 A3
Peace Dr WARRW/BUR WA5 142 A3
Peacehaven Cl CHLDW L16 135 G1
Peach Gv MGHL L31 72 A5
RNFD/HAY WA11 * 90 D4
Peach St EHL/KEN L7 9 K5
Peacock Av WARR WA1 143 H3
Peacock La KNUT WA16 165 K5
Pearce Cl WLTN L25 135 G3
Pear Gv NPK/KEN L6 113 K4
Pearson Av WARRS WA4 162 C1
Pearson Ct WAV L15 * 134 B3
Pearson Dr BTL L20 82 B4
Pearson Rd BIRK CH41 3 F7
Pearson St WAV L15 134 A2
Pear Tree Av RUNC WA7 177 F6
Peartree Av WD/CROXPK L12 99 K4
Peartree Cl FROD/HEL WA6 187 G6
Pear Tree Cl HES CH60 168 C4
Peartree Pl WARR WA1 142 D6
WARRS WA4 17 F7
Pear Tree Rd HUY L36 136 B1
Pear Tree Wy GTS/LS CH66 * 202 C2
Peasefield Rd DV/KA/FCH L14 116 A3
Peasley Cl WARRN/WOL WA2 124 D6
Peasley Cross La STHEL WA9 13 K6
Peatwood Av KKBY L32 84 E4
Peckers Hill Rd STHEL WA9 104 C6
Peckfield Cl RUNC WA7 187 K2
Peckforton Cl
CLB/OSW/ST L13 114 C1
Peckforton Dr GTS/LS CH66 195 H6
RUNC WA7 187 J3
Peckmill Gn NTHLY L27 136 C5
Pecksniff Cl TOX L8 132 E4
Peebles Av RNFD/HAY WA11 89 G5
Peebles Cl AIMK WN4 78 B5
GTS/LS CH66 * 194 C3
NWD/KWIPK L33 72 C3
Peel Av RF/TRAN CH42 131 J6
Peel Cl RAIN/WH L35 118 A4
WARR WA1 144 C3
Peel House La WDN WA8 139 G6
Peel Pl ECCL WA10 13 G2
TOX L8 132 E2
Peel Rd BTL L20 4 A1
SKEL WN8 67 F2
Peel St NEWLW WA12 106 A2
RUNC WA7 10 C3
STHP PR8 28 C1
TOX L8 133 F5
Peerswood Ct NSTN CH64 191 K4
Peet Av ECCL WA10 102 E1
ORM L39 53 H1
Peet's La CHTN/BK PR9 23 J4
Peet St EHL/KEN L7 113 K6
Pelham Gv AIG/SPK L17 133 H5
Pelham Rd WAL/EG CH44 111 G4
WARRS WA4 144 B6
Pemberton Cl NSTN CH64 193 H1
Pemberton Rd
CLB/OSW/ST L13 114 E4
GR/UP/WCH CH49 129 J6
Pembertons Ct PR/KW L34 118 A1
Pemberton St ECCL WA10 * 12 D6
Pembrey Wy WLTN L25 155 G3
Pembridge Gdns EP CH65 196 D6
Pembroke Av MOR/LEA CH46 129 F2
Pembroke Ct BIRK CH41 131 H5
Pembroke Dr EP CH65 195 K6
Pembroke Gdns VAUX/LVPD L3 9 J3
Pembroke Pl VAUX/LVPD L3 9 H3
Pembroke Rd BTL L20 4 E5
Pembroke St VAUX/LVPD L3 9 J3
Pembury Cl WD/CROXPK L12 99 J2
Penarth Cl EHL/KEN L7 133 G1
Pencombe Rd HUY L36 116 B3
Penda Dr NWD/KWIPK L33 72 D3
Pendennis Rd WAL/EG CH44 111 H4
Pendennis St ANF/KKDL L4 113 K2
Pendine Cl NPK/KEN L6 114 A3
WARRW/BUR WA5 122 C5
Pendle Av RNFD/HAY WA11 89 G6
Pendlebury St STHEL WA9 120 A3
WARRS WA4 143 J6
Pendle Cl GR/UP/WCH CH49 * 129 F3
Pendle Ct SKEL WN8 67 F4
Pendle Dr LITH L21 69 K5
ORM L39 46 A5
Pendle Pl SKEL WN8 67 F3
Pendle Rd GOL/RIS/CUL WA3 92 D2
Pendleton Gn HLWD L26 155 H4
Pendleton Rd ANF/KKDL L4 97 J3
Penfold MGHL L31 62 C6
Penfold Cl CALD/MH L18 134 E4
Penfolds RUNC WA7 177 G4
Pengallo Hey NTHLY L27 136 C4
Pengwern Gv WAV L15 133 J1
Pengwern St TOX L8 133 F4
Penhale Cl AIG/SPK L17 152 C1
Peninsula Cl WAL/NB CH45 94 E5
Penistone Dr GTS/LS CH66 194 E4
Penketh Av WARRW/BUR WA5 142 C1
Penketh Ct RUNC WA7 10 E4
Penketh Pl SKEL WN8 66 E2
Penketh Rd WARRW/BUR WA5 141 H5
Penkeths La RUNC WA7 10 E3
Penkett Gv WAL/NB CH45 111 J1
Penkett Rd WAL/NB CH45 111 H1
Penkford La
WARRW/BUR WA5 105 H4
Penkmans La FROD/HEL WA6 201 F3
Penlake La STHEL WA9 104 C6
Penley Crs KKBY L32 84 A1
Penlinken Dr NPK/KEN L6 * 113 K3
Penmann Cl HLWD L26 * 155 J4
Penmann Crs HLWD L26 155 J4
Penmark Cl WARRW/BUR WA5 122 C5
Penmon Dr PEN/TH CH61 167 K2
Pennant Av WD/CROXPK L12 99 G4
Pennant Cl GOL/RIS/CUL WA3 125 J4
Pennard Av HUY L36 116 D2
Penn Gdns EP CH65 6 C4
Pennine Cl STHEL WA9 104 C2
Pennine Dr STHEL WA9 104 D2
Pennine La GOL/RIS/CUL WA3 92 D2
Pennine Pl SKEL WN8 66 D1
Pennine Rd RF/TRAN CH42 150 B2
WAL/EG CH44 111 F3
WARRN/WOL WA2 124 A5
Pennine Wy KKBY L32 72 B5
Pennington Av BTL L20 82 B4
ORM L39 45 J5
Pennington Cl FROD/HEL WA6 187 F6
Pennington Dr NEWLW WA12 106 E2
Pennington Gn GTS/LS CH66 195 F6
Pennington La STHEL WA9 105 G2
Pennington Rd LITH L21 81 K5
Pennington St ANF/KKDL L4 97 H3
Pennington's Went
NSTN CH64 191 K2
Penn La RUNC WA7 10 B6
Pennsylvania Rd NPK/KEN L6 98 B6
Pennyford Dr CALD/MH L18 133 K6
Penny La CALD/MH L18 134 A4
RAIN/WH L35 137 J2
RNFD/HAY WA11 91 F4
WARRW/BUR WA5 105 H5
Pennystone Cl
GR/UP/WCH CH49 128 E3
Pennywood Dr RAIN/WH L35 118 A5
Penrhos Rd HOY CH47 126 E3
Penrhyd Rd PEN/TH CH61 148 A6
Penrhyn Av LITH L21 81 J4
PEN/TH CH61 148 D5
Penrhyn Crs RUNC WA7 176 D6
Penrhyn Rd PR/KW L34 85 G6
Penrhyn St EV L5 113 F2
Penrith Av STHP PR8 33 H6
WARRN/WOL WA2 123 J4
Penrith Cl FROD/HEL WA6 201 G1
Penrith Crs AIMK WN4 79 G5
MGHL L31 62 C5
Penrith Rd ECCL WA10 102 D5
Penrith St BIRK CH41 2 C7
Penrose Av East
DV/KA/FCH L14 115 J5
Penrose Av West
DV/KA/FCH L14 115 J5
Penrose Gdns
WARRW/BUR WA5 140 E6
Penrose Pl SKEL WN8 67 G3
Penrose St EV L5 113 H1
Penryn Av RNFD/HAY WA11 89 G4
Penryn Cl WARRW/BUR WA5 141 F5
Pensall Dr PEN/TH CH61 167 K3
Pensarn Gdns
WARRW/BUR WA5 * 122 D5
Pensarn Rd CLB/OSW/ST L13 114 D5
Pensby Cl PEN/TH CH61 148 D6
Pensby Dr GTS/LS CH66 195 G5
Pensby Hall La PEN/TH CH61 167 K3
Pensby Rd HES CH60 168 A4
PEN/TH CH61 148 D5
Penshaw Ct RUNC WA7 177 H6
Pentire Av ECCL WA10 87 J5
Pentire Cl AIN/FAZ L10 84 A5
Pentland Av ANF/KKDL L4 97 J4
STHEL WA9 104 D2
WARRN/WOL WA2 123 H4
Pentland Pl WARRN/WOL WA2 123 H4
Pentland Rd NWD/KWIPK L33 73 F5
Penuel Rd ANF/KKDL L4 97 H3
Penvalley Crs NPK/KEN L6 114 A3
Peony Gdns STHEL WA9 105 F6
Peover St VAUX/LVPD L3 113 F4
Peploe Rd ANF/KKDL L4 98 B3
Peplow Rd KKBY L32 84 A1
The Peppers LYMM WA13 145 K6
Pepper St LYMM WA13 145 K6
SPK/HALE L24 174 E4
Pera Cl NPK/KEN L6 113 J4
Perch Pool La CHTN/BK PR9 29 J3
Percival La RUNC WA7 176 B4
Percival Rd EP CH65 6 C3
Percival St WARR WA1 17 F5
Percival Wy ECCL WA10 87 K6
Percy Rd WAL/EG CH44 112 A5
Percy St BTL L20 4 C1
STHEL WA9 104 D6
TOX L8 132 E2
WARRW/BUR WA5 * 142 B4
Percy Vls WLT/FAZ L9 * 97 J1
Perimeter Rd CHNE CH2 198 D4
NWD/KWIPK L33 85 J3
Perrey St RUNC WA7 11 G4
Perriam Rd ALL/GAR L19 154 A3
Perrin Av RUNC WA7 176 B5
Perrin Rd WAL/EG CH44 110 E2
Perrins Rd WARRW/BUR WA5 121 K1
Perrygate Cl EHL/KEN L7 133 G1
Perry St TOX L8 132 C3
Pershore Gv STHP PR8 33 G5
Pershore Rd KKBY L32 84 D3
Perth Av STHEL WA9 103 G6
Perth Cl NWD/KWIPK L33 72 C3
WARRN/WOL WA2 124 B3
Perth St NPK/KEN L6 113 J4
Peterborough Cl GTS/LS CH66 202 D4
Peterborough Dr NTHTN L30 70 B5
Peterborough Rd WAV L15 134 B3
Peterlee Cl STHEL WA9 103 H6
Peter Mahon Wy BTL L20 4 C3
Peter Price's La BEB CH63 170 A1
Peter Rd ANF/KKDL L4 97 G4
Peters Av BRSC L40 38 E5
Petersfield Cl NTHTN L30 82 C2
Petersgate RUNC WA7 178 C6
Petersham Dr WARRS WA4 162 D6
Peter's La CLVPS L1 8 E5
Peterstone Cl
WARRW/BUR WA5 122 D5
Peter St AIMK WN4 79 H6
CLVPS L1 8 E3
ECCL WA10 12 D4
GOL/RIS/CUL WA3 92 B3
WAL/EG CH44 112 A5
Peterwood RF/TRAN CH42 151 F2
Petherick Rd NG/CROX L11 84 B6
Petton St EV L5 113 H1
Petunia Cl DV/KA/FCH L14 * 116 A3
STHEL WA9 104 E6
Petworth Av
WARRN/WOL WA2 123 H4
Petworth Cl SPK/HALE L24 173 G1
Petworth Rd STHP PR8 33 H3
Peveril Cl WARRS WA4 162 C4
Peveril St WLT/FAZ L9 97 H2
Pex Hill Ct WDN WA8 138 D4
Pharmacy Rd SPK/HALE L24 173 H1
Pheasant Cl GOL/RIS/CUL WA3 125 H3
Pheasant Fld SPK/HALE L24 174 D3
Pheasant Gv HLWD L26 155 H2
Pheasant Wk KNUT WA16 165 K6
Philbeach Rd ANF/KKDL L4 98 B3
Philip Dr STHP PR8 34 A3
Philip Gv STHEL WA9 104 A6
Philip Rd WDN WA8 157 G3
Philips Dr WARRW/BUR WA5 141 F3
Philips La GTS/LS CH66 195 F5
Phillimore Rd NPK/KEN L6 * 114 A4
Phillip Gv WD/CROXPK L12 115 K2
Phillips Cl CSBY/BLUN L23 69 J3
FMBY L37 49 F3
Phillips La FMBY L37 49 F3
Phillips St VAUX/LVPD L3 8 D1
Phillips Wy HES CH60 167 J5
Phipps' La WARRW/BUR WA5 105 J6
Phoenix Av WARRW/BUR WA5 123 F5
Phoenix Brow STHEL WA9 13 K5
Phoenix Dr DV/KA/FCH L14 116 A3
Physics Rd SPK/HALE L24 155 F6
Phythian Cl NPK/KEN L6 113 K4
Phythian Crs
WARRW/BUR WA5 141 G5
Phythian St NPK/KEN L6 113 J4
RNFD/HAY WA11 89 J5
Picadilly WGNW/BIL/OR WN5 77 H4
Pichael Nook WARRS WA4 143 K5
Pickerill Rd GR/UP/WCH CH49 128 E6
Pickering Crs WARRS WA4 144 C6
Pickering Rd WAL/NB CH45 95 H5
Pickerings Cl RUNC WA7 187 F1
Pickerings Rd WDN WA8 157 G6
Pickering St NPK/KEN L6 113 J2
Pickles Dr BRSC L40 38 D5
Pickmere Dr PS/BROM CH62 184 C3
RUNC WA7 188 B2
Pickmere St
WARRW/BUR WA5 142 B4
Pickop St VAUX/LVPD L3 8 D2
Pickwick St TOX L8 132 E3
Pickworth Wy MGHL L31 84 A1
Picow Farm Rd RUNC WA7 176 A5
Picow St RUNC WA7 10 C6
Picton Av RUNC WA7 11 G6
Picton Cl CL/PREN CH43 130 C6
GOL/RIS/CUL WA3 124 E3
PS/BROM CH62 184 A4
Picton Crs WAV L15 133 K1
Picton Gv WAV L15 133 J1
Picton Rd CSBY/WL L22 80 E2
WAV L15 133 K1
Piele Rd RNFD/HAY WA11 90 D4
Piercefield Rd FMBY L37 49 F1
Pier Head VAUX/LVPD L3 8 B5
Pierpoint St WARRW/BUR WA5 16 A1
Pighue La CLB/OSW/ST L13 114 C6
Pigot Pl WARRS WA4 143 J4
Pigot St ECCL WA10 12 D5
Pike House Rd ECCL WA10 87 H6
Pike La FROD/HEL WA6 201 K6
Pikelaw Pl SKEL WN8 66 E2
Pike Pl ECCL WA10 102 D1
Pikes Bridge Fold ECCL WA10 102 C1
Pikes Hey Rd WKBY CH48 147 G4
Pike St WARRS WA4 162 B2
Pilchbank Rd DV/KA/FCH L14 115 J3
Pilch La DV/KA/FCH L14 115 J4
Pilch La East HUY L36 116 A5
Pilgrim Cl WARRN/WOL WA2 123 G1
Pilgrim St BIRK CH41 3 H4
CLVPS L1 9 H7
Pilkington Rd STHP PR8 28 A2
Pilkington St RNFD/HAY WA11 75 G3
Pilling Cl CHTN/BK PR9 20 C6
Pilling La MGHL L31 61 J2
Pilling Pl SKEL WN8 66 E2
Pilot Gv WAV L15 133 J1
Pimblett Rd RNFD/HAY WA11 90 D4
Pimblett St GOL/RIS/CUL WA3 * 92 B4
Pimbley Gv East MGHL L31 71 F3
Pimbley Gv West MGHL L31 71 F3
Pimbo La SKEL WN8 67 H4
Pimbo Rd RNFD/HAY WA11 76 B1
Pimhill Cl TOX L8 133 F3
Pimlico Rd RUNC WA7 10 A5
Pincroft Wy ANF/KKDL L4 97 F6
Pinders Farm Dr WARR WA1 17 F4
Pine Av BEB CH63 170 B2
ECCL WA10 88 C5
NEWLW WA12 106 C3
ORM L39 45 K4
WDN WA8 158 C1
Pine Cl HUY L36 116 D3
KKBY L32 72 B6
RAIN/WH L35 118 A4
RNFD/HAY WA11 90 B5
SKEL WN8 56 B4
Pine Ct BIRK CH41 2 E4
Pine Crest ORM L39 53 F3
Pine Dl RNFD/HAY WA11 75 F2
Pinedale Cl CL/PREN CH43 130 A5
GTS/LS CH66 202 D3
Pine Dr ORM L39 45 K5
Pine Gv BTL L20 5 G3
CHTN/BK PR9 15 K6
CSBY/WL L22 80 E1
GOL/RIS/CUL WA3 92 D3
GTS/LS CH66 202 E2
ORM L39 45 K4
WARR WA1 143 K2
Pinehey NSTN CH64 181 J6
Pinehurst Av ANF/KKDL L4 97 K6
CSBY/WL L22 68 D6
Pinehurst Rd ANF/KKDL L4 97 K6
Pinellas RUNC WA7 11 G3
Pine Ms CLVPS L1 132 D2
Pinemore Rd CALD/MH L18 153 H1
Pineridge Cl PS/BROM CH62 170 E2
Pine Rd HES CH60 168 C4
RUNC WA7 177 F6
The Pines BEB CH63 170 D2
WD/CROXPK L12 99 K1
Pinetop Cl NPK/KEN L6 113 K3
Pine Tree Av CL/PREN CH43 129 K5
Pine Tree Cl MOR/LEA CH46 129 G1
Pinetree Cl NTHTN L30 70 C6
Pinetree Ct WAL/NB CH45 111 F2
Pinetree Dr WKBY CH48 146 E2
Pine Tree Gv MOR/LEA CH46 129 G1
Pine Tree Rd HUY L36 136 A1
Pine View Dr PEN/TH CH61 167 K3
Pine Wks RF/TRAN CH42 150 A2
Pinewalks Rdg RF/TRAN CH42 150 B3
Pine Wy HES CH60 167 J3
Pineways WARRS WA4 162 C6
Pinewood AIMK WN4 91 F1
SKEL WN8 57 F2
Pinewood Av FMBY L37 48 D4
WARR WA1 143 H2
WD/CROXPK L12 99 H2
Pinewood Cl CHNE CH2 198 D6
FMBY L37 48 D3
NTHLY L27 136 B3
STHP PR8 29 F6
Pinewood Dr HES CH60 168 B5
Pinewood Gdns
NWD/KWIPK L33 72 D4
Pinewood Rd
WARRW/BUR WA5 105 K6
Pinfold Cl NTHTN L30 70 A4
Pinfold Crs KKBY L32 85 F3
Pinfold Dr ECCL WA10 102 C2
Pinfold La BRSC L40 36 D6
PR/KW L34 100 B2
STHP PR8 33 G6
WKBY CH48 127 F5
Pinfold Pl SKEL WN8 67 F3
Pinfold Rd WLTN L25 155 F4
Pingot Rd WGNW/BIL/OR WN5 77 H4
Pingwood La NWD/KWIPK L33 73 F3
Pinmill Brow FROD/HEL WA6 200 E2
Pinmill Cl FROD/HEL WA6 200 E2
Pinners Brow
WARRN/WOL WA2 16 D2
Pinners Fold RUNC WA7 178 A4
Pinnington Pl HUY L36 116 D5
Pinnington Rd RAIN/WH L35 118 A4
Pintail Cl RNFD/HAY WA11 88 E5
Piper's Cl HES CH60 167 H5
Piper's End HES CH60 167 H5
Piper's La HES CH60 167 G3
The Pipers GOL/RIS/CUL WA3 93 G3
HES CH60 167 G4
Pipit Av NEWLW WA12 106 C2
Pipit Cl HLWD L26 155 H1
Pipit La GOL/RIS/CUL WA3 125 G4
Pippin St BRSC L40 46 A1
Pippits Rw RUNC WA7 187 H3
Pirrie Rd WLT/FAZ L9 98 B2
Pitch Cl GR/UP/WCH CH49 * 128 E5
Pit Hey Pl SKEL WN8 66 E2
Pit La WDN WA8 139 F5
Pit Pl WLTN L25 154 D1
Pitsmead Rd KKBY L32 84 D2
Pitts Heath La RUNC WA7 178 C2
Pitts House La CHTN/BK PR9 23 K5
Pitt St CHTN/BK PR9 28 C1
CLVPS L1 9 F7
STHEL WA9 104 A1
WARRW/BUR WA5 16 A2
WDN WA8 158 B6
Pitville Av CALD/MH L18 134 B6
Pitville Cl CALD/MH L18 153 H1
Pitville Gv CALD/MH L18 134 B6
Pitville Rd CALD/MH L18 134 B6
Pitville Ter WDN WA8 157 H4
Plaistow Ct RUNC WA7 177 H6
Plane Cl WLT/FAZ L9 98 A2
Plane Tree Gv
RNFD/HAY WA11 * 91 F4
Plane Tree Rd BEB CH63 170 A1
Planetree Rd WD/CROXPK L12 99 K6
Plantation Cl RUNC WA7 177 K4
Plantation Dr GTS/LS CH66 195 H2
Plantation Rd BRSC L40 38 B5
PS/BROM CH62 171 H4
The Planters
GR/UP/WCH CH49 128 D5
NTHTN L30 70 D5
Platt Gv RF/TRAN CH42 151 F3
Platts La BRSC L40 46 D1
Platts St RNFD/HAY WA11 89 K5
Plattsville Rd CALD/MH L18 134 B4
Playfield Rd WD/CROXPK L12 99 K6
Pleasance Wy NEWLW WA12 106 C1
Pleasant Hill St TOX L8 132 C3
Pleasant St BTL L20 4 C6
VAUX/LVPD L3 9 H5
WAL/NB CH45 95 H6
Pleasant Vw BTL L20 4 C6
Pleasington Cl CL/PREN CH43 130 B5
Pleasington Dr CL/PREN CH43 130 B5
Pleck Rd EP CH65 202 E1
Plemont Rd CLB/OSW/ST L13 114 E2
Plemston Ct GTS/LS CH66 195 J1
Plex La ORM L39 52 A1
Plex Moss La STHP PR8 41 K2
Plimsoll St EHL/KEN L7 113 K6
Plinston Av WARRS WA4 143 J5
Plough La BRSC L40 55 G2
Ploughmans Wy GTS/LS CH66 202 C3
Plover Cl NEWLW WA12 106 C2
Plover Dr RUNC WA7 178 C5
Plovers La FROD/HEL WA6 199 K4
Plover Wy GOL/RIS/CUL WA3 93 F3
Pluckington Rd HUY L36 117 H5
Plumbers Wy HUY L36 117 F5
Plumer St BIRK CH41 130 D1
WAV L15 133 K2
Plumley Gdns WDN WA8 157 F2
Plumpstons La
FROD/HEL WA6 186 E6
Plumpton La ORM L39 43 G1
Plumpton St NPK/KEN L6 113 H3
Plumtre Av WARRW/BUR WA5 142 C1
Plum Tree Cl RAIN/WH L35 118 B1
STBRV L28 100 B5
Plymouth Cl RUNC WA7 188 D1
Plymyard Av PS/BROM CH62 184 A1
Plymyard Cl PS/BROM CH62 184 A2
Poachers' La WARRS WA4 143 J6
Pochard Ri RUNC WA7 178 C5
Pocket Nook La
GOL/RIS/CUL WA3 93 H3
Pocket Nook St STHEL WA9 13 K4
Pocklington Ct
WARRN/WOL WA2 124 B6
Podium Rd CLB/OSW/ST L13 114 E3
Poets Cnr PS/BROM CH62 * 151 G6
Polden Cl GTS/LS CH66 194 D3
Poleacre Dr WDN WA8 157 J1
Pollard Rd WAV L15 114 E6
Poll Hill Rd HES CH60 167 K4
Pollitt Crs STHEL WA9 120 A4
Pollitt Sq PS/BROM CH62 151 H3
Polperro Cl NG/CROX L11 84 C6
WARRW/BUR WA5 141 F6
Pomfret St TOX L8 132 E3
Pomona St VAUX/LVPD L3 9 H5
Pond Cl NPK/KEN L6 114 A3
Pond Green Wy STHEL WA9 104 D4
Pond St GOL/RIS/CUL WA3 93 H3
Pond View Cl HES CH60 168 C5
Pond Wk STHEL WA9 104 E4
Pondwater Cl KKBY L32 84 D2
Ponsonby Rd WAL/NB CH45 110 E2
Ponsonby St TOX L8 133 F3
Pool Bank PS/BROM CH62 151 G4
Poolbank Rd PS/BROM CH62 151 G4
Poole Av WARRN/WOL WA2 123 H5
Poole Crs WARRN/WOL WA2 123 H5
Poole Hall La GTS/LS CH66 195 H1
Poole Hall Rd GTS/LS CH66 195 J1
Pool End STHEL WA9 104 D3
Poole Rd WAL/EG CH44 111 K2
Poole Wk TOX L8 133 F5
Pool Hey STBRV L28 100 B5
Pool Hey La STHP PR8 28 E4
Pool La CHNE CH2 198 A6
GR/UP/WCH CH49 148 D1
LYMM WA13 145 G5
PS/BROM CH62 170 E1
RUNC WA7 11 F3
WARRS WA4 161 K2
Poolside Rd RUNC WA7 11 F6
Poolside Wk CHTN/BK PR9 23 K1
Pool St BIRK CH41 2 E2
CHTN/BK PR9 24 A1
WDN WA8 19 F5
Pooltown Rd EP CH65 195 J5
Poolwood Rd
GR/UP/WCH CH49 129 J5
Pope St BTL L20 81 J6

Poplar Av *AIMK* WN4 **78** C4
CSBY/BLUN L23 **69** G4
ECCL WA10 **102** C1
GR/UP/WCH CH49 **129** G4
NEWLW WA12 **106** D2
RUNC WA7 **177** F6
WARRW/BUR WA5 **141** F5
Poplar Bank *HUY* L36 **116** E5
Poplar Cl *EP* CH65 **6** B7
HLWD L26 **155** K2
RUNC WA7 **177** F6
Poplar Dr *BEB* CH63 **170** C1
EV L5 **113** J2
KKBY L32 **72** C6
SKEL WN8 **56** B4
Poplar Farm Cl
MOR/LEA CH46 **128** D3
Poplar Gv *CHNE* CH2 **198** B6
ECCL WA10 **102** E2
LITH L21 **81** G5
RAIN/WH L35 **118** A2
RNFD/HAY WA11 **90** B5
Poplar Hall La *CHNE* CH2 **203** G5
Poplar Rd *CL/PREN* CH43 **130** E5
RNFD/HAY WA11 **90** B5
WLTN L25 **135** G6
Poplars Av *WARRN/WOL* WA2 **123** G3
The Poplars *BRSC* L40 **46** E1
LEIGH WN7 **93** K3
LYMM WA13 **145** J5
Poplar St *GOL/RIS/CUL* WA3 **92** C2
STHP PR8 **28** B1
Poplar Ter *WAL/NB* CH45 **95** H6
Poplar Vw *WARRS* WA4 * **160** D4
Poplar Wy *ANF/KKDL* L4 **97** F5
HUY L36 **117** G5
Poppleford Cl *WLTN* L25 **135** K5
Poppy Cl *MOR/LEA* CH46 **109** K5
Poppy La *ORM* L39 **54** B4
Porchester Rd *NG/CROX* L11 **98** D4
Porchfield Cl *NG/CROX* L11 **99** F2
Porlock Av *CHLDW* L16 **135** F4
STHEL WA9 **120** A2
Porlock Cl *HES* CH60 **181** G1
WARRW/BUR WA5 **141** F5
Portal Ms *PEN/TH* CH61 **167** K2
Portal Rd *PEN/TH* CH61 **167** K2
Portal Wy *AIN/FAZ* L10 **84** B4
Portbury Cl *PS/BROM* CH62 **151** G5
Portbury Wy *PS/BROM* CH62 **151** G5
Port Cswy *PS/BROM* CH62 **171** F1
Portelet Rd *CLB/OSW/ST* L13 **114** D3
Porter Av *NEWLW* WA12 **91** H6
Porter Cl *RAIN/WH* L35 **119** F6
Porter St *RUNC* WA7 **11** J4
VAUX/LVPD L3 **112** D3
Portgate Cl *WD/CROXPK* L12 **99** G3
Porthcawl Cl *WDN* WA8 **138** B6
Porthleven Rd *RUNC* WA7 **188** A2
Portia Av *BEB* CH63 **150** D4
Portia Gdns *BEB* CH63 * **150** D4
Portia St *BTL* L20 **96** E5
Portico Av *RAIN/WH* L35 **118** C1
Portico La *RAIN/WH* L35 **118** B2
Portland Av *CSBY/WL* L22 **80** D1
Portland Gdns *VAUX/LVPD* L3 **112** E3
Portland Pl *EV* L5 **113** G3
FROD/HEL WA6 **199** K5
Portland Rd
WARRW/BUR WA5 **141** H1
Portland St *BIRK* CH41 **130** D1
EV L5 **112** E3
NEWLW WA12 **105** K1
RUNC WA7 **10** B3
STHP PR8 **14** D6
WAL/NB CH45 **95** G4
Portland Wy *STHEL* WA9 **104** D4
Portlemouth Rd *NG/CROX* L11 **84** B6
Portloe Av *HLWD* L26 **155** J2
Portman Rd *WAV* L15 **133** J2
Porto Hey Rd *PEN/TH* CH61 **148** A6
Portola Cl *WARRS* WA4 **163** H1
Porton Rd *KKBY* L32 **84** B2
Portreath Wy *ECCL* WA10 **87** J5
Portree Av *BEB* CH63 **184** A2
Portree Cl *WLT/FAZ* L9 **82** D6
Portrush Cl *WDN* WA8 **138** D6
Portrush St *CLB/OSW/ST* L13 **114** C1
Portside North *EP* CH65 **196** A1
Portsmouth Pl *RUNC* WA7 **188** D1
Portwood Cl *EHL/KEN* L7 * **133** G1
Post Office Av *CHTN/BK* PR9 **15** F4
Post Office La *RUNC* WA7 **176** A6
Potter Pl *SKEL* WN8 **67** F2
Potters La *WDN* WA8 **175** G1
Pottery Flds *PR/KW* L34 **118** A1
Pottery La *RAIN/WH* L35 **117** J4
Poulsom Dr *NTHTN* L30 **81** K1
Poulter Rd *WLT/FAZ* L9 **82** E4
Poulton Cl *HLWD* L26 **155** G5
Poulton Crs *WARR* WA1 **144** B1
Poulton Dr *AIMK* WN4 * **78** E5
WDN WA8 **157** J3
Poulton Green Cl *BEB* CH63 **170** B4
Poulton Hall Rd *BEB* CH63 **170** C6
WAL/EG CH44 **111** G4
Poulton Rd *BEB* CH63 **170** C3
CHTN/BK PR9 **23** H6
WAL/EG CH44 **111** G4
Poulton Royd Dr *BEB* CH63 **170** B3
Pound Rd *GTS/LS* CH66 **195** F2
Poverty La *MGHL* L31 **71** J1
Povey Rd *WARRN/WOL* WA2 **123** J6
Powderworks La *MGHL* L31 **63** G4
Powell Av *GOL/RIS/CUL* WA3 **125** G3
Powell Dr *WGNW/BIL/OR* WN5 **77** G6
Powell St *STHEL* WA9 **104** C6
WARRS WA4 **143** J6
Power Rd *PS/BROM* CH62 **171** H4
RF/TRAN CH42 **151** F3
Powis St *TOX* L8 **133** F4
Pownall St *CLVPS* L1 **8** D6
Powys St *WARRW/BUR* WA5 **142** C4
Poynter St *STHEL* WA9 **103** G6
Poynton Cl *WARRS* WA4 **144** A6
Pratt Rd *PR/KW* L34 **117** J1
The Precincts *CSBY/BLUN* L23 **69** F4
Preece Cl *WDN* WA8 **138** C6
Preesall Cl *CHTN/BK* PR9 **23** H1
Preesall Wy *NG/CROX* L11 **84** B6
Premier St *EV* L5 **113** H2
Prentice Rd *RF/TRAN* CH42 **150** D2
Prenton Av *STHEL* WA9 **119** K3
Prenton Dell Av
CL/PREN CH43 **149** K3
Prenton Dell Rd
CL/PREN CH43 **149** H2
Prenton Farm Rd
CL/PREN CH43 **149** K3
Prenton Gn *SPK/HALE* L24 **173** K2
Prenton Hall Rd
CL/PREN CH43 **149** J2
Prenton La *RF/TRAN* CH42 **150** A2
Prentonpark Rd
RF/TRAN CH42 **131** F6
Prenton Rd East
RF/TRAN CH42 **150** C1
Prenton Rd West
RF/TRAN CH42 **150** B1
Prenton Village Rd
CL/PREN CH43 **149** J2
Prenton Wy *CL/PREN* CH43 **149** G2
Prescot Centre *PR/KW* L34 * **117** K1
Prescot Dr *EHL/KEN* L7 **114** B4
Prescot Gn *ORM* L39 **53** H2
Prescot Rd *CLB/OSW/ST* L13 **115** F4
ECCL WA10 **102** D5
KKBY L32 **72** B5
NPK/KEN L6 **114** C4
ORM L39 **63** H3
RAIN/WH L35 **118** B2
WDN WA8 **137** J4
Prescot St *EHL/KEN* L7 **9** K2
WAL/NB CH45 **95** G5
Prescott Av *GOL/RIS/CUL* WA3 **92** A1
Prescott Br *BRSC* L40 **39** J1
Prescott Rd *SKEL* WN8 **67** G3
Prescott St *GOL/RIS/CUL* WA3 **92** B2
WARRS WA4 **143** H6
Preseland Rd *CSBY/BLUN* L23 **69** F6
Prestbury Av *CL/PREN* CH43 **149** H1
STHP PR8 **33** H4
Prestbury Cl *CL/PREN* CH43 **149** H1
WDN WA8 **157** K3
Prestbury Dr *ECCL* WA10 **102** D3
WARRS WA4 **144** C6
Prestbury Rd *NG/CROX* L11 **98** D1
Preston Av *PR/KW* L34 **117** J2
Preston Gv *NPK/KEN* L6 **114** A2
Preston New Rd *CHTN/BK* PR9 **23** J2
Preston Rd *CHTN/BK* PR9 **23** G5
Preston St *CLVPS* L1 **8** E3
STHEL WA9 **119** K5
Preston Wy *CSBY/BLUN* L23 **69** H5
Prestwick Dr *CSBY/BLUN* L23 **68** D3
Prestwood Rd
DV/KA/FCH L14 **115** K3
Pretoria Rd *AIMK* WN4 **79** F5
WLT/FAZ L9 **82** E5
Price Gv *STHEL* WA9 **104** E3
Price's La *CL/PREN* CH43 **130** E5
Price St *BIRK* CH41 **130** E1
CLVPS L1 * **8** E6
Pride Cl *NEWLW* WA12 **106** E3
Priestfield Rd *EP* CH65 **6** C4
Priesthouse Cl *FMBY* L37 **49** G2
Priesthouse La *FMBY* L37 **49** G2
Primary Av *NTHTN* L30 **70** E5
Primrose Cl *CHTN/BK* PR9 **21** F5
FMBY L37 **41** H6
RUNC WA7 **177** K5
WARRN/WOL WA2 **123** J6
WDN WA8 **157** K2
Primrose Ct *HUY* L36 **116** E2
Primrose Dr *HUY* L36 **116** E2
Primrose Gv *RNFD/HAY* WA11 **90** D4
WAL/EG CH44 * **112** A5
Primrose Hl *PS/BROM* CH62 **151** G5
VAUX/LVPD L3 **8** E2
Primrose Rd *BIRK* CH41 **130** C2
CALD/MH L18 **134** D4
Primrose St *EV* L5 **97** F6
Primrose Vw *AIMK* WN4 **91** G1
Primula Cl *STHEL* WA9 **104** E6
Primula Dr *GOL/RIS/CUL* WA3 **92** E3
WLT/FAZ L9 **97** K1
Prince Albert Ct *STHEL* WA9 **104** D4
Prince Albert Ms *CLVPS* L1 **132** D2
Prince Alfred Rd *WAV* L15 **134** B2
Prince Andrew's Gv *ECCL* WA10 **87** K5
Prince Charles Gdns *STHP* PR8 **27** G2
Prince Edward St *BIRK* CH41 **2** C2
Prince Edwin St *EV* L5 **113** G3
Prince Henry Sq *WARR* WA1 **16** D4
Princes Av *CSBY/BLUN* L23 **68** E5
PS/BROM CH62 **184** B1
TOX L8 **132** E2
WKBY CH48 **146** C1
Princes Bvd *BEB* CH63 **150** C3
Princes Cl *RUNC* WA7 **177** J4
Princes Gdn *STHP* PR8 **28** B2
Princes Gdns *VAUX/LVPD* L3 **8** D2
Princes Ga West *TOX* L8 **133** G3
Princes Pde *VAUX/LVPD* L3 **8** A2
Princes Pl *WDN* WA8 **157** K2
Princes Rd *ECCL* WA10 **102** E4
EP CH65 **6** B3
TOX L8 **132** E2
Princess Av *ECCL* WA10 **88** B5
RNFD/HAY WA11 **91** F4
WARR WA1 **143** K1
WARRW/BUR WA5 **141** F3
Princess Crs *WARR* WA1 **143** J3
Princess Dr *WD/CROXPK* L12 **99** J6
Princess Rd *AIMK* WN4 **79** G6
LYMM WA13 **145** H6
WAL/NB CH45 **95** H6
Princess St *CLVP* L2 **8** D4
RUNC WA7 **10** D3
WARRW/BUR WA5 **142** A5
Princess Ter *CL/PREN* CH43 **2** B7
Princes St *BTL* L20 **96** D4
CLVP L2 **8** D3
NEWLW WA12 **106** B2
STHP PR8 **14** D6
WDN WA8 **18** D3
Princess Wy *LITH* L21 **81** H4
Prince St *AIMK* WN4 **79** F4
CSBY/WL L22 **80** E3
Princes Wy *RNFD/HAY* WA11 **88** D3
Princesway *WAL/NB* CH45 **111** G1
Princeway *FROD/HEL* WA6 **200** E1
Prince William St *TOX* L8 **132** D3
Prior Farm Cl *ALL/GAR* L19 **153** H4
Priors Cl *WLTN* L25 **154** E1
Priorsfield *MOR/LEA* CH46 **129** F1
Priorsfield Rd *WLTN* L25 **154** E1
Prior St *BTL* L20 **81** H5
Priorswood Pl *SKEL* WN8 **67** H3
Priory Cl *AIG/SPK* L17 **152** C1
BEB CH63 **170** C2
BRSC L40 **38** D4
FMBY L37 **49** H3
RAIN/WH L35 **117** J6
RUNC WA7 **177** K4
Priory Ct *HUY* L36 * **116** E5
RUNC WA7 * **188** D2
Priory Gdns *ECCL* WA10 **88** C4
STHP PR8 **27** G3
Priory Gra *STHP* PR8 **27** H3
Priory Gv *ORM* L39 **53** H1
Priory Ms *BIRK* CH41 **3** J5
STHP PR8 **14** B6
Priory Rd *AIMK* WN4 **78** E4
ANF/KKDL L4 **97** J5
RUNC WA7 * **178** B3
WAL/EG CH44 **112** A4
WKBY CH48 **146** C1
Priory St *ALL/GAR* L19 **172** C1
BIRK CH41 **3** J5
WARRS WA4 **142** E6
The Priory *NSTN* CH64 **181** J6
RAIN/WH L35 **118** E4
WARRN/WOL WA2 **107** G6
Priory Wy *WLTN* L25 **154** E1
Priory Whf *BIRK* CH41 **3** J4
Pritchard Av *LITH* L21 **81** G4
Pritt St *VAUX/LVPD* L3 **113** G4
Private Dr *PEN/TH* CH61 **149** G6
Prizett Rd *ALL/GAR* L19 **153** J4
Probyn Rd *WAL/NB* CH45 **110** E2
Procter Rd *RF/TRAN* CH42 **151** F2
Proctor Rd *FMBY* L37 **48** C1
HOY CH47 **127** H3
Proctors Cl *WDN* WA8 **158** D1
Proffits La *FROD/HEL* WA6 **200** B5
Progress La *CLVPS* L1 **8** D3
Promenade *CHTN/BK* PR9 **22** D4
STHP PR8 **14** C6
Promenade Gdns *AIG/SPK* L17 **133** F6
The Promenade
WARRS WA4 * **160** D4
Prospect Ct *NPK/KEN* L6 * **114** B4
Prospect Pl *SKEL* WN8 **67** H2
Prospect Rd *RF/TRAN* CH42 **150** A2
STHEL WA9 **104** B1
Prospect Rw *RUNC* WA7 **176** C6
Prospect V *NPK/KEN* L6 **114** B3
WAL/NB CH45 **111** F2
Prospect Wy *NTHTN* L30 **70** E6
Providence Crs *TOX* L8 **132** D3
Provident St *STHEL* WA9 **104** E2
Province Rd *BTL* L20 **82** A5
Prussia St *VAUX/LVPD* L3 **8** C2
Public Hall St *RUNC* WA7 **10** E3
Pudsey St *CLVPS* L1 **9** G3
Puffin Cl *EP* CH65 **203** G2
Pugin St *ANF/KKDL* L4 **97** G6
Pulford Av *CL/PREN* CH43 **149** K1
Pulford Cl *RUNC* WA7 **187** G1
Pulford Rd *BEB* CH63 **150** E6
EP CH65 **195** J5
Pulford St *ANF/KKDL* L4 **97** H6
Pullman Cl *HES* CH60 **168** D5
Pumpfields Rd *VAUX/LVPD* L3 **112** E4
Pump La *GR/UP/WCH* CH49 **128** C5
RUNC WA7 **177** J5
Punnell's La *MGHL* L31 **61** H2
Purbeck Dr *PEN/TH* CH61 **148** A4
Purdy Cl *WARRW/BUR* WA5 **122** D6
Purley Gv *CALD/MH* L18 **153** H1
Purley Rd *CSBY/WL* L22 * **80** D1
Purser Gv *WAV* L15 **133** J1
Putney Ct *RUNC* WA7 * **177** H6
Pye Cl *RNFD/HAY* WA11 **91** G3
Pyecroft Cl *WARRW/BUR* WA5 **140** E3
Pyecroft Rd
WARRW/BUR WA5 **140** E3
Pye Rd *HES* CH60 **168** A5
Pyes Gdns *RNFD/HAY* WA11 **88** E4
Pyes La *HUY* L36 **100** C6
Pye St *WAV* L15 **134** B2
Pygon's Hill La *MGHL* L31 **52** B6
Pym St *ANF/KKDL* L4 **97** H3
Pyrus Gv *FROD/HEL* WA6 * **199** K5

Q

The Quadrangle
CALD/MH L18 * **134** C5
Quadrant Cl *RUNC* WA7 **188** C1
Quail Cl *WARRN/WOL* WA2 **123** K4
Quaker La *HES* CH60 **167** J4
Quakers Meadow *PR/KW* L34 **100** D1
Quantock Cl *GTS/LS* CH66 **194** D3
Quarry Av *BEB* CH63 **170** B1
Quarry Bank *BIRK* CH41 **2** D6
NWD/KWIPK L33 **72** E6
WAL/NB CH45 **111** H1
Quarrybank St *BIRK* CH41 **2** C6
Quarry Cl *CLB/OSW/ST* L13 **114** D2
NWD/KWIPK L33 **72** E6
PEN/TH CH61 **167** K3
RUNC WA7 **11** K6
Quarry Ct *HES* CH60 * **167** J4
WDN WA8 **157** H2
Quarry Dl *NWD/KWIPK* L33 **72** E6
Quarry Dr *ORM* L39 **53** G4
Quarry Gn *NWD/KWIPK* L33 **72** E6
Quarry Hey *NWD/KWIPK* L33 **72** E6
Quarry La *PEN/TH* CH61 **148** D5
WARRS WA4 **162** C5
Quarry Mt *ORM* L39 **46** A5
Quarry Rd *BTL* L20 **5** H6
CLB/OSW/ST L13 **114** E2
CSBY/BLUN L23 **69** H3
NSTN CH64 **182** C6
Quarry Rd East *BEB* CH63 **170** C1
HES CH60 **167** J4
Quarry Rd West *HES* CH60 **167** J4
Quarryside Dr
NWD/KWIPK L33 **85** F1
Quarry St *WLTN* L25 **135** G6
Quarry St South *WLTN* L25 **154** D1
Quartz Wy *LITH* L21 **81** K3
Quay Fold *WARRW/BUR* WA5 **142** B5
Quayle Cl *RNFD/HAY* WA11 **90** B5
Quay Pl *RUNC* WA7 **178** D6
Quay Side *FROD/HEL* WA6 **187** G5
Quayside *NSTN* CH64 **191** J4
The Quay *FROD/HEL* WA6 **187** G5
Quebec Quay *VAUX/LVPD* L3 **132** B3
Quebec Rd *WARRN/WOL* WA2 **143** G2
Queen Anne St *STHP* PR8 **14** E5
VAUX/LVPD L3 **9** G1
Queen Av *CLVP* L2 * **8** D4
Queen Mary's Dr
PS/BROM CH62 **151** G5
Queen's Av *AIMK* WN4 **79** G5
EP CH65 **195** K6
FMBY L37 **40** E6
HOY CH47 **127** J1
WARR WA1 **143** H2
WDN WA8 **157** G3
Queensberry St *TOX* L8 **132** E4
Queensbury *WKBY* CH48 **127** J6
Queensbury Av
PS/BROM CH62 **171** G4
Queensbury Wy *WDN* WA8 **138** C6
Queen's Cl *RUNC* WA7 **10** C7
Queens Ct *NPK/KEN* L6 **113** J2
Queenscourt Rd
WD/CROXPK L12 **115** G2
Queens Crs *WARR* WA1 * **143** K1
Queens Cft *FMBY* L37 **48** D3
Queensdale Rd *CALD/MH* L18 **134** B4
Queens Dr *CL/PREN* CH43 **149** K2
ECCL WA10 **87** K5
FROD/HEL WA6 **199** J6
GOL/RIS/CUL WA3 **92** D3
HES CH60 **167** J5
NEWLW WA12 **91** H6
WARRS WA4 **162** E1
Queens Drive Mossley Hl
CALD/MH L18 **133** K5
Queens Drive Stoneycroft
CLB/OSW/ST L13 **115** F3
Queens Drive Walton
ANF/KKDL L4 **97** J3
Queens Drive (Wavertree)
WAV L15 **134** D1
Queens Drive West Derby
CLB/OSW/ST L13 **98** C5
Queens Gdns *EP* CH65 **6** B4
Queens Gn *ORM* L39 **43** H6
Queensland Av *STHEL* WA9 **103** G6
Queensland Pl *STHEL* WA9 **103** G6
Queensland St *EHL/KEN* L7 **113** K6
Queens Ms *NPK/KEN* L6 **113** J2
Queen Sq *CLVPS* L1 **9** F3
Queen's Rd *AIMK* WN4 **79** G6
BTL L20 **4** E7
CHTN/BK PR9 **15** H3
CSBY/BLUN L23 **69** F5
ECCL WA10 **102** E4
FMBY L37 **48** D3
GTS/LS CH66 **195** F2
HOY CH47 **127** F2
NPK/KEN L6 **113** J3
PR/KW L34 **118** A1
RF/TRAN CH42 **151** F2
RNFD/HAY WA11 **91** F4
RUNC WA7 **10** C6
WAL/EG CH44 **112** A4
Queen St *ALL/GAR* L19 **153** K6
BIRK CH41 **131** H5
CSBY/WL L22 **80** E3
ECCL WA10 **13** F2
EP CH65 **6** E1
GOL/RIS/CUL WA3 * **92** C3
NEWLW WA12 **106** B2
ORM L39 **53** J1
RUNC WA7 **10** D3
WAL/NB CH45 **111** H2
Queensway *CSBY/WL* L22 **81** G1
FROD/HEL WA6 **200** E2
HES CH60 **181** H1
RNFD/HAY WA11 **88** D3
RNFD/HAY WA11 **75** H4
RUNC WA7 **10** C3
WAL/NB CH45 **111** G1
WDN WA8 **157** K4
Queensway (Mersey Tunnel)
BIRK CH41 **3** F2
VAUX/LVPD L3 **8** B3
Queens Whf *VAUX/LVPD* L3 **132** B2
Quernmore Rd
NWD/KWIPK L33 **73** F6
Quernmore Wk
NWD/KWIPK L33 **73** F6
Quickswood Cl *WLTN* L25 **135** G4
Quickswood Dr *WLTN* L25 **135** G4
Quickswood Gn *WLTN* L25 **135** G4
Quickthorn Crs *STBRV* L28 **100** B6
Quigley Av *NTHTN* L30 **82** D2
Quigley St *BIRK* CH41 **131** H5
The Quillet *NSTN* CH64 **192** A2
Quinesway *GR/UP/WCH* CH49 **129** H4
Quinn St *WDN* WA8 **18** E5
Quintbridge Cl *HLWD* L26 **155** H3
Quinton Cl *STHP* PR8 **33** G5
Quorn St *EHL/KEN* L7 **113** K5

R

Rabbit La *BRSC* L40 **37** K6
Raby Av *BEB* CH63 **183** J1
Raby Cl *BEB* CH63 **170** C6
HES CH60 **167** K6
WDN WA8 **158** E1
Raby Dr *BEB* CH63 **170** C6
MOR/LEA CH46 **128** E2
Raby Gdns *NSTN* CH64 **191** K1
Raby Gv *BEB* CH63 **150** C3
Raby Hall Rd *BEB* CH63 **183** F2
Raby Mere Rd *BEB* CH63 **182** D2
Raby Park Cl *NSTN* CH64 **191** K1
Raby Park Rd *NSTN* CH64 **191** K1
Raby Rd *BEB* CH63 **182** C1
NSTN CH64 **182** C3
Rachel St *EV* L5 **113** F3
Radburn Cl *CSBY/BLUN* L23 **69** J4
Raddon Pl *WARRS* WA4 * **143** H6
Radford Av *BEB* CH63 **170** D3
Radford Cl *WDN* WA8 **157** H3
Radlett Cl *WARRW/BUR* WA5 **141** F6
Radley Dr *AIN/FAZ* L10 **71** F6
BEB CH63 **182** A1
Radley La *WARRN/WOL* WA2 **123** K4
Radley Rd *WAL/EG* CH44 **111** F2
Radleys Ct *TOX* L8 * **132** E3
Radley St *STHEL* WA9 **103** G6
Radmore Rd *DV/KA/FCH* L14 **115** H4
Radnor Av *HES* CH60 **167** K4
Radnor Cl *HLWD* L26 **155** G5
Radnor Dr *BTL* L20 **5** J3
CHTN/BK PR9 **23** H2
WAL/NB CH45 **111** J1
WDN WA8 **157** J1
Radnor Pl *CL/PREN* CH43 **2** B5
NPK/KEN L6 **114** B2
Radnor St *WARRW/BUR* WA5 **142** B3
Radstock Gv *STHEL* WA9 **120** B2
Radstock Rd *NPK/KEN* L6 **114** A4
WAL/EG CH44 **110** E2
Radway Gn *GTS/LS* CH66 **195** H4
Radway Rd *HUY* L36 **117** F1
Raeburn Av *NSTN* CH64 **192** A2
PS/BROM CH62 **184** A1
WKBY CH48 **127** H6
Raffles Rd *RF/TRAN* CH42 **2** D7
Raffles St *CLVPS* L1 **132** D2
Rafter Av *BTL* L20 **82** B5
Raglan Ct *GOL/RIS/CUL* WA3 **125** H1
Raglan St *ALL/GAR* L19 **153** K6
Railbrook Hey
CLB/OSW/ST L13 **114** D6
Rail Cl *RNFD/HAY* WA11 **66** B5
Railside Ct *EV* L5 * **112** E2
Railton Av *RAIN/WH* L35 **119** F5
Railton Cl *RAIN/WH* L35 **119** F6
Railton Rd *NG/CROX* L11 **98** C3
Railway Ap *ORM* L39 **45** K6
Railway Pth *ORM* L39 **53** J1
Railway Rd
GOL/RIS/CUL WA3 * **92** C3
RF/TRAN CH42 **150** E1
SKEL WN8 **55** K5
Railway St *ALL/GAR* L19 **153** K6
ECCL WA10 **13** J3
NEWLW WA12 **106** B2
STHP PR8 **27** J2
Railway Ter *STHP* PR8 **27** H2
Rainbow Cl *WDN* WA8 **138** B6
Rainbow Dr *HLWD* L26 **155** H3
MGHL L31 **72** A5
Raines Cl *GR/UP/WCH* CH49 **129** F5
Rainford Av *BTL* L20 **82** B6
Rainford By-Pass
RNFD/HAY WA11 **74** E2
Rainford Rd *ECCL* WA10 **87** K5
ORM L39 **65** J3
WGNW/BIL/OR WN5 **76** E4
Rainham Cl *CALD/MH* L18 **153** K3
Rainhill Rd *RAIN/WH* L35 **118** E2
Rake Hey *MOR/LEA* CH46 **128** C1
Rake Hey Cl *MOR/LEA* CH46 **128** D1
Rake La *CHNE* CH2 **203** H5
FROD/HEL WA6 **199** H3
GR/UP/WCH CH49 **129** H5
WAL/NB CH45 **111** H1
Rakersfield Ct *WAL/NB* CH45 **95** J5
Rakersfield Rd *WAL/NB* CH45 **95** J5
The Rake *PS/BROM* CH62 **171** G4
Raleigh Av *RAIN/WH* L35 **117** K5
Raleigh Cl *WARRW/BUR* WA5 **122** D6
Raleigh Rd *MOR/LEA* CH46 **110** B3
NSTN CH64 **181** K6
Raleigh St *BTL* L20 **96** D4
Ralph's Wife's La *CHTN/BK* PR9 **21** J5
Rame Cl *AIN/FAZ* L10 **84** A5
Ramford St *STHEL* WA9 **104** B3
Ramilies Rd *CALD/MH* L18 **134** A4
Ramleh Cl *CSBY/BLUN* L23 **68** C6
Ramleh Pk *CSBY/BLUN* L23 **68** B6
Rampit Cl *RNFD/HAY* WA11 **90** E4
Ramsay Cl *GOL/RIS/CUL* WA3 **125** G4
Ramsbrook Cl *SPK/HALE* L24 **173** H1
Ramsbrook La *SPK/HALE* L24 **174** D2
Ramsbrook Rd *SPK/HALE* L24 **173** H1
Ramsey Cl *AIMK* WN4 **91** G1
ALL/GAR L19 **154** A3
RAIN/WH L35 **118** A4
WDN WA8 **139** K6
Ramsey Ct *WKBY* CH48 **146** C2
Ramsey Rd *ALL/GAR* L19 **154** A3
EP CH65 **203** G2
Ramsfield Rd *SPK/HALE* L24 **174** B1
Ramsons Cl *HLWD* L26 **155** H2
Randall Dr *NTHTN* L30 **69** K6
Randle Av *RNFD/HAY* WA11 **75** F1
Randle Brook Ct
RNFD/HAY WA11 **75** F1
Randle Cl *BEB* CH63 **170** C3
Randle Meadow *GTS/LS* CH66 **202** D1
Randles Rd *PR/KW* L34 **85** F6
Randolph St *ANF/KKDL* L4 **97** H6
Randon Gv *ECCL* WA10 **12** E4
Ranelagh Av *LITH* L21 **81** H3
Ranelagh Dr *STHP* PR8 **34** B2
Ranelagh Dr North
ALL/GAR L19 **153** H3
Ranelagh Dr South
ALL/GAR L19 **153** H4
Ranelagh St *CLVPS* L1 **9** F5
Ranfurly Rd *ALL/GAR* L19 **153** J4
Rangemoor Cl
GOL/RIS/CUL WA3 **125** J1
Rangemore Rd *CALD/MH* L18 **153** H2
Rankin St *WAL/EG* CH44 **111** G5
Ranmore Av *AIMK* WN4 **78** C5
Rannoch Cl *GTS/LS* CH66 **195** J6
Ranulph Ct *FROD/HEL* WA6 **201** F2
Ranworth Cl *NG/CROX* L11 **98** C2

Ranworth Dr GOL/RIS/CUL WA3 93 F4
Ranworth Pl NG/CROX L11 98 D2
Ranworth Rd
WARRW/BUR WA5 141 F3
Ranworth Sq NG/CROX L11 98 D2
Ranworth Wy NG/CROX L11 98 D2
Rappart Rd WAL/EG CH44 111 K4
Ratcliff Pl RAIN/WH L35 118 D3
Rathbone Rd HTWN L38 59 F3
WAV L15 114 D6
Rathlin Cl WDN WA8 139 K6
Rathmore Av CALD/MH L18 134 B6
Rathmore Cl CL/PREN CH43 130 D6
Rathmore Crs CHTN/BK PR9 23 K2
Rathmore Dr CL/PREN CH43 130 D5
Rathmore Rd CL/PREN CH43 130 D5
Raven Cl NPK/KEN L6 * 113 J4
Ravendale Cl CL/PREN CH43 130 A5
Ravenfield Cl HLWD L26 155 H3
Ravenfield Dr WDN WA8 138 B6
Ravenglass Av MGHL L31 62 B5
Ravenhead Av KKBY L32 84 D4
Ravenhead Colliery Yd
STHEL WA9 * 103 J4
Ravenhead Dr SKEL WN8 57 J6
Ravenhead Rd ECCL WA10 103 G4
Ravenhead Rw ECCL WA10 * 103 G4
Ravenhead Wy SKEL WN8 67 H1
Ravenhill Crs MOR/LEA CH46 109 K4
Ravenhurst Ct
GOL/RIS/CUL WA3 125 H2
Ravenhurst Wy RAIN/WH L35 117 J6
Raven Meols La FMBY L37 48 E3
Ravenna Rd ALL/GAR L19 154 A3
Ravenscourt HLWD L26 * 155 J4
Ravenscroft FMBY L37 49 F3
Ravenscroft Av ORM L39 53 J1
Ravenscroft Rd CL/PREN CH43 2 B6
Ravensdale Cl
WARRN/WOL WA2 123 K4
The Ravens FMBY L37 49 F3
Ravensthorpe Gn NG/CROX L11 98 D2
Ravenstone Cl
GR/UP/WCH CH49 129 F2
Ravenstone Dr STHEL WA9 104 B6
Ravenstone Rd ALL/GAR L19 153 J3
Ravenswood Av
RF/TRAN CH42 150 E3
Ravenswood Rd
CLB/OSW/ST L13 114 E4
PEN/TH CH61 168 A3
Rawcliffe Cl WDN WA8 138 E5
Rawcliffe Rd RF/TRAN CH42 2 D7
WLT/FAZ L9 97 H1
Rawdon Cl RUNC WA7 177 K6
Rawlings Cl GOL/RIS/CUL WA3 125 H4
Rawlinson Ct CHTN/BK PR9 * 15 K2
Rawlinson Crs HLWD L26 156 A3
Rawlinson Gv CHTN/BK PR9 23 G4
Rawlinson Rd CHTN/BK PR9 23 G4
CLB/OSW/ST L13 114 D4
Rawlins St EHL/KEN L7 114 B4
Rawson Cl LITH L21 81 G4
Rawson Rd LITH L21 81 G4
Raydale Cl GOL/RIS/CUL WA3 93 F2
WLT/FAZ L9 97 J2
Raymond Av NTHTN L30 82 D2
WARRS WA4 162 C1
Raymond Pl EV L5 113 F3
Raymond Rd WAL/EG CH44 111 J4
Raymond Wy NSTN CH64 192 B2
Raynham Rd CLB/OSW/ST L13 114 D5
Reade Cl BEB CH63 170 C4
Reading Cl EV L5 97 F6
Reads Ct WLT/FAZ L9 82 C5
Reaper Cl WARRW/BUR WA5 142 A3
Reapers Wy NTHTN L30 70 D5
Reay St WDN WA8 158 D1
Rebecca Gdns STHEL WA9 104 A6
Recreation Av AIMK WN4 79 J5
Recreation Dr
WGNW/BIL/OR WN5 * 77 H4
Recreation St STHEL WA9 104 A2
Rector Rd NPK/KEN L6 98 A6
Rectory Av GOL/RIS/CUL WA3 92 D3
Rectory Cl HES CH60 167 K6
RF/TRAN CH42 131 G5
WARRN/WOL WA2 123 G1
Rectory Dr HLWD L26 155 J2
Rectory Gdns LYMM WA13 165 F1
STHEL WA9 120 A1
Rectory La HES CH60 167 J6
LYMM WA13 165 F1
WARRN/WOL WA2 123 G1
Rectory Rd AIMK WN4 78 C4
CHTN/BK PR9 23 H4
WKBY CH48 146 C2
Redacre Cl RUNC WA7 188 E4
WARRS WA4 189 F4
Red Bank Av NEWLW WA12 107 F4
Red Barnes FMBY L37 41 F5
Red Barn Rd
WGNW/BIL/OR WN5 76 E3
Redbourne Av HLWD L26 155 J5
Redbourne Dr WDN WA8 138 A5
Redbourn St NPK/KEN L6 114 A1
Redbrook Cl PS/BROM CH62 184 A1
Redbrook St NPK/KEN L6 114 A1
Red Brow La RUNC WA7 178 D5
Redbrow Wy NWD/KWIPK L33 72 D5
Redburn Cl TOX L8 133 F5
Redcap Cl WAL/NB CH45 94 E5
Redcar Cl STHP PR8 28 C4
Redcar Dr PS/BROM CH62 184 A2
Redcar Ms NPK/KEN L6 113 K1
Redcar Rd WAL/NB CH45 110 D1
Redcar St NPK/KEN L6 114 A1
Red Cat La BRSC L40 38 E1
RNFD/HAY WA11 76 B5
Redcliffe Gdns ORM L39 53 J2
Redcroft GR/UP/WCH CH49 * 128 D6
Red Cross St VAUX/LVPD L3 8 C5
Red Cut La NWD/KWIPK L33 86 A3
Red Delph La RNFD/HAY WA11 65 K6
Reddish La LYMM WA13 145 K5
Redditch Cl GR/UP/WCH CH49 128 D5
Redesdale Cl
WARRN/WOL WA2 124 A5
Redfern St BTL L20 96 E5
Redfield Cl WAL/EG CH44 111 K3
Red Fold ORM L39 53 G3
Redford Cl GR/UP/WCH CH49 128 D5
Redford St NPK/KEN L6 114 A2
Redgate FMBY L37 49 G3
ORM L39 45 H6
Redgate Av CSBY/BLUN L23 69 H5
Redgate Dr FMBY L37 49 H3
STHEL WA9 104 B2
Redgate Rd AIMK WN4 79 G3
Redgrave St EHL/KEN L7 114 A5
Redhill Av KKBY L32 84 E3
Redhill Ms EP CH65 6 C2
Red Hill Rd BEB CH63 150 A6
Redhills Dr STHP PR8 28 C4
Redhouse Bank WKBY CH48 127 F6
Redhouse La WKBY CH48 127 F6
Redington Rd ALL/GAR L19 154 A3
Redland Ct WGNE/HIN WN2 79 K2
Redland Rd WLT/FAZ L9 82 E3
Red La FROD/HEL WA6 201 F1
WARRS WA4 162 B4
Red Lion Cl MGHL L31 62 A6
Red Lion La GTS/LS CH66 195 F2
Red Lomes NTHTN L30 70 A4
Redmain Gv GOL/RIS/CUL WA3 93 F3
Redmain Wy WD/CROXPK L12 99 K3
Redmayne Cl NEWLW WA12 106 B1
Redmere Dr HES CH60 168 C5
Redmires Cl EHL/KEN L7 * 133 G1
Redmond St BIRK CH41 131 H5
Redmoor Crs NWD/KWIPK L33 72 D5
Redoaks Wy HLWD L26 155 K2
Red Pike GTS/LS CH66 195 G2
Redpoll Gv HLWD L26 155 H1
Redpoll La GOL/RIS/CUL WA3 125 G3
Red Rock Ct NPK/KEN L6 113 K3
Red Rum Cl WLT/FAZ L9 83 G3
Redruth Av RNFD/HAY WA11 89 G4
Redruth Cl RUNC WA7 188 B1
Redruth Rd NG/CROX L11 84 C6
Red Sands ORM L39 53 H2
Redshank Cl NEWLW WA12 106 C1
Redshank La
GOL/RIS/CUL WA3 125 H3
Redstart Cl GOL/RIS/CUL WA3 93 F3
Redstone Cl HOY CH47 127 J1
Redstone Dr HES CH60 167 G4
Red Stone Hl FROD/HEL WA6 199 J5
Redstone Pk WAL/NB CH45 * 95 G5
Redstone Ri CL/PREN CH43 130 A3
Redvales Ct GOL/RIS/CUL WA3 124 E3
Redvers Av GTS/LS CH66 184 D5
Redvers Dr WLT/FAZ L9 82 C5
Redwald Cl NWD/KWIPK L33 72 E3
Redwing La WLTN L25 135 H5
Redwing Wy HLWD L26 155 G1
Redwood Av MGHL L31 62 A4
Redwood Cl CL/PREN CH43 * 149 J1
WARR WA1 144 D3
Redwood Dr CHNE CH2 198 D5
GTS/LS CH66 202 D2
ORM L39 53 H1
RNFD/HAY WA11 89 J6
Redwood Gv BTL L20 * 5 F3
Redwood Rd WLTN L25 135 J4
Redwood Wy NWD/KWIPK L33 72 D3
Reedale Cl CALD/MH L18 134 B5
Reedale Rd CALD/MH L18 134 B5
Reeds Av East MOR/LEA CH46 109 K4
Reeds Av West
MOR/LEA CH46 109 K4
Reeds Brow RNFD/HAY WA11 75 J1
Reeds La MOR/LEA CH46 109 K4
RNFD/HAY WA11 75 G6
Reedsmere Cl WARRS WA4 162 D1
Reeds Rd HUY L36 116 E3
The Reeds ORM L39 45 H5
Reedville CL/PREN CH43 2 A7
Reedville Gv MOR/LEA CH46 109 K5
Reedville Rd BEB CH63 150 E6
Rees Pk BRSC L40 39 F6
Reeves Av BTL L20 5 J1
Reeves St STHEL WA9 104 C1
Reeve St GOL/RIS/CUL WA3 93 J3
Regal Cl GTS/LS CH66 195 H6
Regal Crs WDN WA8 157 G3
Regal Dr ECCL WA10 87 K6
Regal Rd NG/CROX L11 99 G2
Regal Wk ANF/KKDL L4 97 H6
Regency Gdns STHP PR8 27 F3
Regency Pk WDN WA8 138 D6
Regency Sq WARRW/BUR WA5 142 C2
Regent Av AIMK WN4 78 E4
DV/KA/FCH L14 115 J5
NTHTN L30 70 C6
RNFD/HAY WA11 90 A4
WARR WA1 143 K1
Regent Cl STHP PR8 27 G3
Regent Ms STHP PR8 27 G3
Regent Rd BTL L20 96 D4
CSBY/BLUN L23 68 E5
EV L5 112 D1
STHP PR8 27 F3
VAUX/LVPD L3 112 D2
WAL/NB CH45 110 D1
WDN WA8 18 E1
Regents Cl PEN/TH CH61 148 E5
Regents Fld FMBY L37 * 40 D6
Regents Rd ECCL WA10 102 E4
Regent St EP CH65 195 K4
EP CH65 6 A4
NEWLW WA12 106 A2
RUNC WA7 10 D3
VAUX/LVPD L3 112 D3
WARR WA1 16 C5
Regents Wy BEB CH63 150 C4
Regina Av CSBY/WL L22 80 D1
Reginald Rd STHEL WA9 120 C1
Regina Rd WLT/FAZ L9 82 D5
Reid Av WARRW/BUR WA5 142 C1
Reid Ct GTS/LS CH66 195 F2
Reigate Cl WLTN L25 155 F1
Reins Cft NSTN CH64 181 K6
Rembury Pl WARRS WA4 188 E4
Renacres La ORM L39 36 A5
Renaissance Wy
SPK/HALE L24 173 J1
Rendal Cl EV L5 113 J2
Rendcombe Gn NG/CROX L11 98 D2
Rendel Cl NEWLW WA12 106 D3
Rendelsham Cl
GR/UP/WCH CH49 129 F4
Rendel St BIRK CH41 2 E2
Rendlesham Cl
GOL/RIS/CUL WA3 125 K1
Renfrew Av PS/BROM CH62 184 B2
RNFD/HAY WA11 89 H4
Renfrew St EHL/KEN L7 113 J5
Renfrey Cl ORM L39 45 J3
Rennell Rd DV/KA/FCH L14 115 G4
Rennie Av ECCL WA10 102 E1
Renown Cl GOL/RIS/CUL WA3 125 F3
Renown Wy SPK/HALE L24 154 D5
Renshaw St CLVPS L1 9 G5
Rensherds Pl KNUT WA16 165 K6
Renton Av RUNC WA7 177 G3
Renville Rd DV/KA/FCH L14 115 G6
Renwick Av RAIN/WH L35 118 C3
Renwick Rd WLT/FAZ L9 82 D6
Renwick Sq AIMK WN4 78 E6
Repton Gv AIN/FAZ L10 83 F1
Repton Rd CHLDW L16 134 E1
EP CH65 7 G7
Reservoir Rd RF/TRAN CH42 150 A2
WLTN L25 135 G6
Reservoir Rd North
RF/TRAN CH42 150 A1
Reservoir St NPK/KEN L6 113 J3
STHEL WA9 102 E6
Rest Hill Rd BEB CH63 150 B5
Retford Rd NWD/KWIPK L33 84 E1
Reva Rd DV/KA/FCH L14 115 K4
Revesby Cl WDN WA8 157 J1
Rexmore Rd CALD/MH L18 153 H1
Rexmore Wy WAV L15 133 K2
Reynolds Av
GOL/RIS/CUL WA3 125 G2
STHEL WA9 105 F3
Reynolds Cl NPK/KEN L6 113 J3
Reynolds St WARRS WA4 143 H6
Reynolds Wy WLTN L25 154 D1
Rhiwlas St TOX L8 133 F4
Rhodesia Rd WLT/FAZ L9 82 E5
Rhodes St WARRN/WOL WA2 143 F2
Rhodesway HES CH60 168 B6
Rhona Cl BEB CH63 183 K3
Rhona Dr WARRW/BUR WA5 141 F3
Rhosesmor Cl KKBY L32 84 E5
Rhosesmor Rd KKBY L32 84 E5
Rhuddlan Cl CLB/OSW/ST L13 114 D5
Rhuddlan Ct EP CH65 203 H1
Rhum Cl EP CH65 203 G2
Rhyl St TOX L8 132 E4
WDN WA8 * 18 B6
Rialto Cl TOX L8 132 E2
Ribble Av CHTN/BK PR9 24 A1
MGHL L31 62 C5
RAIN/WH L35 118 E4
Ribble Cl WDN WA8 140 A6
Ribble Crs WGNW/BIL/OR WN5 77 F6
Ribbledale Rd CALD/MH L18 134 B5
Ribble Rd WLTN L25 135 K6
Ribbler's La KKBY L32 84 C4
Ribblesdale EP CH65 195 K6
Ribblesdale Av WLT/FAZ L9 82 E4
Ribblesdale Cl PS/BROM CH62 184 C2
Ribble St BIRK CH41 111 F6
Ribchester Wy RAIN/WH L35 136 D2
Rice Hey Rd WAL/EG CH44 111 J2
Rice La WAL/EG CH44 111 J2
WLT/FAZ L9 97 H2
Rice St CLVPS L1 9 H7
Richard Allen Wy EV L5 113 G3
Richard Chubb Dr
WAL/NB CH45 111 K1
Richard Gv WD/CROXPK L12 115 J2
Richard Hesketh Dr KKBY L32 84 B1
Richard Kelly Cl ANF/KKDL L4 * 98 B5
Richard Kelly Dr ANF/KKDL L4 98 B3
Richard Kelly Pl ANF/KKDL L4 * 98 B5
Richard Martin Rd LITH L21 * 81 K2
Richard Rd CSBY/BLUN L23 68 B3
Richards Gv STHEL WA9 104 C1
Richardson Rd RF/TRAN CH42 150 D2
Richardson St EHL/KEN L7 133 H2
WARRN/WOL WA2 143 F1
Richland Rd CLB/OSW/ST L13 114 D2
Richmond Av BRSC L40 38 E6
LITH L21 81 H3
RNFD/HAY WA11 90 A4
RUNC WA7 177 H3
WARRS WA4 143 J5
Richmond Cl BEB CH63 150 E5
ECCL WA10 102 B1
HTWN L38 59 F5
Richmond Ct EP CH65 196 C6
LITH L21 * 81 J4
Richmond Crs NTHTN L30 70 C6
Richmond Gdns NEWLW WA12 106 C3
Richmond Gv MGHL L31 62 C4
Richmond Ms BRSC L40 38 E6
Richmond Pk NPK/KEN L6 113 K1
Richmond Rd AIMK WN4 78 E4
BEB CH63 150 E5
CSBY/BLUN L23 69 F4
STHP PR8 27 G5
Richmond Rw VAUX/LVPD L3 113 G4
Richmond St CLVPS L1 * 8 E4
WAL/NB CH45 95 H4
WARRS WA4 143 K6
WDN WA8 19 G1
Richmond Ter NPK/KEN L6 113 J2
Richmond Wy PEN/TH CH61 * 148 D5
RAIN/WH L35 136 D2
Rich Vw CL/PREN CH43 130 E6
Rickaby Cl BEB CH63 170 E5
Rickman St ANF/KKDL L4 97 F5
Rickman Wy HUY L36 136 C1
Ridding La RUNC WA7 188 A2
The Riddings EP CH65 6 B7
Riddock Rd LITH L21 81 J6
Ridgeborne Cl
WARRW/BUR WA5 122 D5
Ridge Cl CHTN/BK PR9 21 F6
Ridgefield Rd PEN/TH CH61 148 C6
Ridgemere Rd PEN/TH CH61 148 C6
The Ridge HES CH60 167 H3
Ridgetor Rd WLTN L25 135 H6
Ridgeview Rd CL/PREN CH43 130 A4
Ridgeway GOL/RIS/CUL WA3 93 F4
Ridgeway Cl GTS/LS CH66 202 A1
Ridgeway Dr MGHL L31 62 B4
Ridgeway Gdns LYMM WA13 145 J6
The Ridgeway BEB CH63 150 C3
HES CH60 168 B6
HOY CH47 127 K2
RUNC WA7 188 C1
WDN WA8 138 B3
WLTN L25 135 H6
Ridgewell Av GOL/RIS/CUL WA3 92 E3
Ridgewood Dr PEN/TH CH61 167 K1
STHEL WA9 120 B1
Ridgewood Wy WLT/FAZ L9 82 D4
Ridgmont Av NG/CROX L11 98 D3
Ridgway St WARRN/WOL WA2 143 G1
Riding Cl STHEL WA9 * 120 A3
Riding Fold HLWD L26 155 G1
Riding Hill Rd PR/KW L34 100 D3
Riding La AIMK WN4 79 K4
ORM L39 51 G1
Ridings Hey CL/PREN CH43 130 A5
The Ridings CHTN/BK PR9 23 J2
CL/PREN CH43 130 A4
RNFD/HAY WA11 90 C5
Riding St STHP PR8 14 E7
VAUX/LVPD L3 9 J3
Ridley Dr WARRW/BUR WA5 141 K5
Ridley Gv WKBY CH48 127 F6
Ridley La MGHL L31 62 B6
Ridley Rd NPK/KEN L6 114 A4
Ridley St CL/PREN CH43 2 B6
Ridsdale WDN WA8 157 H3
Riesling Dr NWD/KWIPK L33 72 D4
Rigby Dr GR/UP/WCH CH49 148 A1
Rigby Rd MGHL L31 61 K4
Rigbys La AIMK WN4 79 J6
Rigby St AIMK WN4 79 F6
ECCL WA10 13 F4
GOL/RIS/CUL WA3 92 B3
VAUX/LVPD L3 8 B2
Riley Av BTL L20 5 H1
Riley Dr RUNC WA7 176 D5
Rimington Av
GOL/RIS/CUL WA3 92 D2
Rimmer Av CHLDW L16 116 A6
Rimmer Cl LITH L21 81 J4
Rimmer Gn STHP PR8 29 G6
Rimmer Gv STHEL WA9 104 C2
Rimmer's Av FMBY L37 40 E5
STHP PR8 14 E7
Rimmers Ct BIRK CH41 * 130 C2
Rimmer St VAUX/LVPD L3 9 H2
Rimmington Rd AIG/SPK L17 153 F1
Rimrose Rd BTL L20 4 B4
Rimrose Valley Rd
CSBY/BLUN L23 69 J5
Rimsdale Cl AIG/SPK L17 153 F4
Ringcroft Rd
CLB/OSW/ST L13 115 F4
Ringley Av GOL/RIS/CUL WA3 92 A2
Ring O'Bells La BRSC L40 47 H1
Ringo Starr Dr NPK/KEN L6 * 113 K4
Ringsfield Rd SPK/HALE L24 174 B2
Ringtail Ct BRSC L40 38 B5
Ringtail Pl BRSC L40 38 B6
Ringtail Rd BRSC L40 38 A5
Ringway GTS/LS CH66 195 H5
NSTN CH64 181 K6
Ringway Rd RUNC WA7 11 K5
WLTN L25 135 K5
Ringways PS/BROM CH62 171 F2
Ringwood CL/PREN CH43 130 D6
Ringwood Av DV/KA/FCH L14 115 K5
Ringwood Cl
GOL/RIS/CUL WA3 125 K2
Ringwood Ct CL/PREN CH43 * 130 D6
Rio Ct PR/KW L34 101 K6
Ripley Av LITH L21 81 J2
Ripley Cl MGHL L31 62 C6
Ripley St WARRW/BUR WA5 142 B2
Ripon Av GOL/RIS/CUL WA3 92 E3
GTS/LS CH66 195 F4
Ripon Cl HUY L36 117 G4
NEWLW WA12 106 C1
NTHTN L30 82 C2
STHP PR8 28 C4
Ripon Dr AIMK WN4 91 J1
Ripon Rd WAL/NB CH45 110 E1
Ripon St ANF/KKDL L4 97 H4
BIRK CH41 * 131 H5
Risbury Cl NG/CROX L11 98 D3
Rishton Cl EV L5 113 J2
Risley Rd GOL/RIS/CUL WA3 125 H1
Ritchie Av WLT/FAZ L9 83 F4
Ritherup La RAIN/WH L35 118 E3
Ritson St TOX L8 133 G3
Rivacre Brow GTS/LS CH66 195 H2
Rivacre Rd EP CH65 185 F5
PS/BROM CH62 184 D3
River Avon St TOX L8 * 133 H2
Riverbank Cl HES CH60 180 E1
Riverbank Rd ALL/GAR L19 153 H4
HES CH60 180 D1
PS/BROM CH62 171 G1
River Cl FMBY L37 49 H4
River Gv PS/BROM CH62 151 G3
Rivermeade STHP PR8 28 A3
River Rd WARRS WA4 142 E6
Riversdale FROD/HEL WA6 187 F6
WARR WA1 144 E2
Riversdale Cl NWD/KWIPK L33 72 D5
Riversdale Ct AIG/SPK L17 153 G3
Riversdale Ms ALL/GAR L19 153 G3
Riversdale Rd ALL/GAR L19 153 G4
LITH L21 81 G4
RUNC WA7 177 H4
WAL/EG CH44 111 K3
WKBY CH48 146 B1
Riverside HTWN L38 59 F3
PS/BROM CH62 151 G6
WD/CROXPK L12 99 J4
WKBY CH48 146 C3
Riverside Cl BTL L20 81 H6
WARR WA1 17 G5
Riverside Dr VAUX/LVPD L3 132 E6
Riverside Gv STHEL WA9 104 B6
Riverside Wk NSTN CH64 191 J4
Riverslea Rd CSBY/BLUN L23 80 C1
River St BIRK CH41 2 D5
River Vw CSBY/WL L22 80 C1
Riverview Rd NSTN CH64 192 A4
WAL/EG CH44 112 A4
Riverview Wk TOX L8 132 E5
River Wk RUNC WA7 * 177 J6
Riverwood Rd
PS/BROM CH62 171 H4
Riviera Dr NG/CROX L11 99 G1
RF/TRAN CH42 150 C2
Rivington Av CL/PREN CH43 130 B5
ECCL WA10 88 B5
GOL/RIS/CUL WA3 92 D2
Rivington Cl STHP PR8 27 H4
Rivington Ct WARR WA1 * 144 D1
Rivington Dr BRSC L40 38 E6
Rivington Rd ECCL WA10 12 B4
EP CH65 6 C5
RUNC WA7 188 E4
WAL/EG CH44 111 K4
Rivington St ECCL WA10 12 A7
Rixton Av WARRW/BUR WA5 142 C1
Roadside Ct
GOL/RIS/CUL WA3 92 D3
Roadwater Cl WLTN L25 135 K2
Robarts Rd ANF/KKDL L4 113 J1
Robeck Rd CLB/OSW/ST L13 115 F6
Robert Dr GR/UP/WCH CH49 129 F6
Robert Gv WD/CROXPK L12 115 J2
Robert Moffat KNUT WA16 165 K6
Roberts Av RNFD/HAY WA11 89 K6
Roberts Ct RUNC WA7 187 H1
Roberts Dr BTL L20 82 B4
Robertson St TOX L8 132 D4
Roberts St VAUX/LVPD L3 8 A1
Robert St BIRK CH41 2 E3
RUNC WA7 11 H4
WARRW/BUR WA5 142 C3
WDN WA8 19 F2
Robina Rd STHEL WA9 104 B5
Robin Cl RUNC WA7 178 C6
Robins Cft GTS/LS CH66 202 D1
Robin's La RNFD/HAY WA11 76 C1
STHEL WA9 104 A5
Robinson Ms BIRK CH41 * 3 H4
Robinson Pl STHEL WA9 104 B2
Robinson Rd LITH L21 81 K2
Robin Wy GR/UP/WCH CH49 148 E1
Rob La NEWLW WA12 106 E1
Robsart St EV L5 113 G2
Robson St CLB/OSW/ST L13 114 D6
EV L5 113 H1
WARR WA1 17 H2
Robson Wy GOL/RIS/CUL WA3 93 G3
Roby Cl RAIN/WH L35 118 E3
Roby Gv WARRW/BUR WA5 141 H3
Roby Ml SKEL WN8 57 K2
Roby Mount Av HUY L36 116 D5
Roby Rd HUY L36 116 A5
Roby St BTL L20 5 F2
ECCL WA10 103 F4
WAV L15 133 K2
Roby Well Wy
WGNW/BIL/OR WN5 77 G4
Rocastle Cl NPK/KEN L6 113 J4
Rochester Av NTHTN L30 82 C2
Rochester Cl GOL/RIS/CUL WA3 92 B3
WARRW/BUR WA5 141 K4
Rochester Dr EP CH65 196 C6
Rochester Gdns ECCL WA10 103 F4
Rochester Rd RF/TRAN CH42 151 F1
Rock Av HES CH60 167 K4
Rockbank Rd
CLB/OSW/ST L13 114 D2
Rockbourne Av WLTN L25 135 G4
Rockbourne Gn WLTN L25 135 G4
Rockbourne Wy WLTN L25 135 G4
Rock Cl RF/TRAN CH42 150 E1
Rock Dr FROD/HEL WA6 187 F6
Rock Farm Cl NSTN CH64 192 B3
Rock Farm Dr NSTN CH64 192 B3
Rock Farm Gv NSTN CH64 * 192 B3
Rock Ferry By-Pass
RF/TRAN CH42 151 F1
Rockfield Cl WDN WA8 157 J1
Rockfield Ms WARRS WA4 162 E1
Rockfield Rd ANF/KKDL L4 97 H6
Rockford Av KKBY L32 84 D4
Rockford Cl KKBY L32 84 D4
Rockford Gdns
WARRW/BUR WA5 141 H1
Rockford Wk KKBY L32 84 D4
Rock Gv CLB/OSW/ST L13 114 E4
Rockhill Rd WLTN L25 154 E2
Rockhouse St NPK/KEN L6 114 A2
Rockingham Cl
GOL/RIS/CUL WA3 125 K1
Rockingham Ct
NWD/KWIPK L33 * 72 E5
Rockland Rd CSBY/WL L22 80 E1
Rocklands Av BEB CH63 151 F4
Rocklands La BEB CH63 169 J6
Rock La MGHL L31 71 J3
WDN WA8 138 D6
Rock La East RF/TRAN CH42 151 F2
Rock La West RF/TRAN CH42 150 E2
Rocklee Gdns NSTN CH64 192 B3
Rockley St ANF/KKDL L4 97 G5
Rock Mount Cl WLTN L25 135 G6
Rockmount Rd AIG/SPK L17 153 G2
Rock Park Rd RF/TRAN CH42 151 G2
Rockpoint Av WAL/NB CH45 95 J6
Rocksavage Expy RUNC WA7 187 F2
Rockside Rd CALD/MH L18 153 H1
Rock St CLB/OSW/ST L13 114 E4
ECCL WA10 102 E5
GOL/RIS/CUL WA3 92 B1
Rock Vw EV L5 113 G1
MGHL L31 71 K5
Rockville Rd DV/KA/FCH L14 115 G6
Rockville St RF/TRAN CH42 150 E1
Rockwell Rd WD/CROXPK L12 99 H5
Rocky Bank Rd RF/TRAN CH42 131 G6
Rocky La CHLDW L16 134 D1
HES CH60 167 K5
NPK/KEN L6 114 A2
Rocky La South HES CH60 168 A5
Roderick Rd ANF/KKDL L4 97 J3
Roderick St VAUX/LVPD L3 * 9 H1
Rodgers Cl FROD/HEL WA6 186 E6
Rodick St WLTN L25 154 C1
Rodmell Rd WLT/FAZ L9 82 E5

Rodney St BIRK CH41 2 E7
CLVPS L1 9 H6
ECCL WA10 12 C5
WARRN/WOL WA2 16 D2
Rodwater Cl WLTN L25 135 J2
Roe Aly CLVPS L1 9 F5
Roeburn Wy
WARRW/BUR WA5 140 E6
Roedean Cl MGHL L31 62 B5
WLTN L25 154 E3
Roehampton Dr
CSBY/BLUN L23 68 D3
RUNC WA7 177 H6
Roe La CHTN/BK PR9 23 G5
Roemarsh Ct RUNC WA7 187 H1
Roe St CLVPS L1 9 F4
Rogers Av BTL L20 82 B6
BTL L20 5 K1
Rogerson's Gn HLWD L26 155 H1
Rokeby Av GOL/RIS/CUL WA3 92 E2
Rokeby Cl VAUX/LVPD L3 113 G4
Rokeby Ct RUNC WA7 160 A6
Rokeby St VAUX/LVPD L3 113 G4
Rokeden NEWLW WA12 106 D1
Roker Av WAL/EG CH44 111 G4
Rokesmith Av EHL/KEN L7 133 H1
Roland Av BEB CH63 150 C5
RNFD/HAY WA11 89 F4
RUNC WA7 10 B6
Roleton Cl NTHTN L30 70 E5
Rolleston Dr BEB CH63 170 C1
WAL/NB CH45 95 F6
Rolleston St WARRN/WOL WA2 16 B3
Rolling Mill La STHEL WA9 104 D5
Rollo St ANF/KKDL L4 97 F6
Roman Cl NEWLW WA12 106 C3
RUNC WA7 177 H4
Roman Ct NSTN CH64 192 A2
Roman Rd AIMK WN4 79 F4
BEB CH63 149 K4
CL/PREN CH43 149 K3
HOY CH47 108 B6
WARRS WA4 162 B2
Rome Cl HUY L36 116 D4
Romer Rd NPK/KEN L6 114 A4
Romford Wy HLWD L26 155 J5
Romiley Dr SKEL WN8 56 B3
Romiley Rd GTS/LS CH66 195 H3
Romilly St NPK/KEN L6 113 J4
Romley St ANF/KKDL L4 97 H4
Romney Cl WDN WA8 158 E1
Romney Wy NSTN CH64 192 A2
Romsey Av FMBY L37 49 H3
Romulus St EHL/KEN L7 114 B5
Rona Av EP CH65 203 G2
Ronald Cl CSBY/WL L22 81 G2
Ronald Dr WARRN/WOL WA2 124 D5
Ronald Rd CSBY/WL L22 81 G2
Ronald Ross Av NTHTN L30 70 C6
Ronaldshay WDN WA8 159 F1
Ronald St CLB/OSW/ST L13 114 D4
Ronaldsway AIN/FAZ L10 83 K4
CSBY/BLUN L23 69 H3
GR/UP/WCH CH49 129 G3
HES CH60 180 E1
HLWD L26 155 K3
Ronan Cl BTL L20 4 B2
Ronan Rd WDN WA8 157 K6
Rone Cl MOR/LEA CH46 128 E1
Roofers Wy HUY L36 117 G5
Rookery Av AIMK WN4 91 G1
Rookery Dr ALL/GAR L19 153 G3
RNFD/HAY WA11 75 H4
Rookery La RNFD/HAY WA11 75 H4
Rookery Rd CHTN/BK PR9 23 G4
The Rookery NEWLW WA12 106 D1
Rookley Cl NTHLY L27 136 C5
Rook Rd WARRS WA4 143 H5
Rooks Wy HES CH60 167 J5
The Rooley HUY L36 116 D6
Roome St WARRN/WOL WA2 143 F2
Roosevelt Dr WLT/FAZ L9 82 E3
Ropers Bridge Cl
RAIN/WH L35 117 K5
Roper St STHEL WA9 104 A1
TOX L8 132 E4
The Ropewalk NSTN CH64 191 H1
Rosalind Av BEB CH63 150 D4
Rosalind Wy BTL L20 97 F4
Rosam Ct RUNC WA7 187 H1
Rosclare Dr WAL/NB CH45 111 F1
Roscoe Av NEWLW WA12 106 E2
WARRN/WOL WA2 143 G1
Roscoe Cl RAIN/WH L35 136 D2
Roscoe Crs RUNC WA7 176 B6
Roscoe La CLVPS L1 9 G6
Roscoe Pl CLVPS L1 9 G6
Roscoe St CLVPS L1 9 H7
ECCL WA10 12 B6
Roscommon St EV L5 113 G3
Roscommon Wy WDN WA8 138 D6
Roscote Cl HES CH60 * 167 K6
The Roscote HES CH60 167 K6
Roseacre WKBY CH48 127 F6
Rose Av BTL L20 81 K4
RNFD/HAY WA11 90 D5
STHEL WA9 104 A6
Rose Bank LYMM WA13 145 K6
Rose Bank Rd CHLDW L16 134 E2
Rosebank Rd HUY L36 116 C1
Rosebank Wy HUY L36 116 C2
Rosebay Cl FMBY L37 49 G2
Roseberry Rd AIMK WN4 79 F4
Rosebery Av CSBY/WL L22 80 D1
WAL/EG CH44 111 J3
Rosebery Gv RF/TRAN CH42 150 A1
Rosebery Rd ECCL WA10 88 A5
Rosebery St CHTN/BK PR9 28 D1
TOX L8 133 F2
Rosebourne Cl AIG/SPK L17 152 D1
Rosebowl Vw BRSC L40 37 F5
Rose Brae CALD/MH L18 134 C5
Rose Brow WLTN L25 135 H5
Rose Cl HLWD L26 155 K4
RUNC WA7 188 C2
Rose Ct WAV L15 133 K2
Rose Crs SKEL WN8 56 A4
STHP PR8 41 J1
WDN WA8 18 B5
Rosecroft PS/BROM CH62 183 K1
Rosecroft Cl ORM L39 45 J5
Rosecroft Ct HOY CH47 * 127 F3
Rosedale Av CSBY/BLUN L23 69 F5
GOL/RIS/CUL WA3 92 D4
WARR WA1 144 B2
Rosedale Cl WLT/FAZ L9 97 K1
Rosedale Rd CALD/MH L18 134 B5
RF/TRAN CH42 131 H6
Rose Dr RNFD/HAY WA11 75 H4
Rosefield Av BEB CH63 150 D4
Rosefield Rd WLTN L25 155 F2
Rose Gdns NSTN CH64 192 A3
Roseheath Dr HLWD L26 155 J5
Rose Hl STHP PR8 15 J7
VAUX/LVPD L3 113 F4
Rosehill Av STHEL WA9 121 F2
Rosehill Ct WLTN L25 135 H5
Rosehill Dr ORM L39 53 G3
Rose Hill Vw AIMK WN4 78 E2
Roseland Cl MGHL L31 61 K3
Roselands Ct RF/TRAN CH42 150 D2
Rose La CALD/MH L18 134 A6
Rose Lea Cl WDN WA8 139 F5
Roselea Dr CHTN/BK PR9 24 A1
Rosemary Av RUNC WA7 187 J2
WARRS WA4 162 D1
Rosemary Cl CL/PREN CH43 130 B1
EHL/KEN L7 133 F1
WARRW/BUR WA5 141 K3
Rosemary Dr NEWLW WA12 107 F2
Rosemary La FMBY L37 48 E2
ORM L39 52 A1
Rosemead Av PEN/TH CH61 167 K1
Rosemere Dr CH/BCN CH1 202 D4
Rosemont Rd AIG/SPK L17 153 G1
Rosemoor Dr CSBY/BLUN L23 69 H4
Rosemoor Gdns WARRS WA4 162 E6
Rose Mt CL/PREN CH43 130 E6
CSBY/WL L22 * 80 D2
RUNC WA7 * 188 E1
Rose Mount Cl CL/PREN CH43 130 D6
Rose Mount Dr
WAL/NB CH45 111 G1
Rose Pth FMBY L37 49 G3
Rose Pl BIRK CH41 131 J6
ORM L39 53 H3
RF/TRAN CH42 131 G5
RNFD/HAY WA11 75 H4
VAUX/LVPD L3 113 F4
Roseside Dr NTHLY L27 136 C3
Rose St CLVPS L1 * 9 F3
WDN WA8 18 B5
WLTN L25 154 C1
Rose V EV L5 113 G2
Rose View Av WDN WA8 158 B1
Rose Vls WAV L15 134 A2
Rosewarne Cl AIG/SPK L17 152 C1
Rosewell Ct STBRV L28 116 B1
Rosewood Av FROD/HEL WA6 201 G2
WARR WA1 143 H2
Rosewood Cl NTHLY L27 136 B4
STBRV L28 100 B6
Rosewood Dr MOR/LEA CH46 128 C1
Rosewood Gdns
NG/CROX L11 99 F4
Rosewood Gv WDN WA8 157 G3
Roseworth Av WLT/FAZ L9 82 D4
Rosina Cl AIMK WN4 78 E3
Roskell Rd WLTN L25 155 F4
Roslin Rd CL/PREN CH43 130 E5
PEN/TH CH61 148 A5
Roslyn St BIRK CH41 131 J6
Rossall Av AIN/FAZ L10 71 G6
Rossall Ct MOR/LEA CH46 109 K5
Rossall Gv GTS/LS CH66 195 G3
Rossall Rd CLB/OSW/ST L13 115 F5
MOR/LEA CH46 109 K6
WARRW/BUR WA5 141 J5
WDN WA8 158 E1
Ross Av MOR/LEA CH46 110 C3
Rossbank Rd EP CH65 195 K2
Rosscliffe Rd EP CH65 195 K2
Ross Cl PR/KW L34 100 D2
WARRW/BUR WA5 142 A1
WGNW/BIL/OR WN5 77 H4
Ross Dr GTS/LS CH66 195 F4
Rossendale Cl CL/PREN CH43 130 A5
Rossendale Dr
GOL/RIS/CUL WA3 125 J1
Rossett Av AIG/SPK L17 133 J3
Rossett Cl WARRW/BUR WA5 122 E5
Rossett Rd CSBY/BLUN L23 68 D6
Rossett St NPK/KEN L6 114 A2
Rossfield Rd EP CH65 6 A3
Rossfield Rd North EP CH65 196 A2
Rossini St LITH L21 81 H5
Rosslyn Av MGHL L31 70 E1
Rosslyn Crs MOR/LEA CH46 129 F1
Rosslyn Dr MOR/LEA CH46 129 F1
Rosslyn Pk MOR/LEA CH46 129 F2
Rosslyn St AIG/SPK L17 133 G6
Rossmore Gdns ANF/KKDL L4 97 K6
GTS/LS CH66 195 G3
Rossmore Rd East EP CH65 195 J2
Rossmore Rd West
GTS/LS CH66 195 G2
Rossmount Rd EP CH65 195 K3
Ross Rd EP CH65 6 A3
Ross St STHEL WA9 104 A1
WDN WA8 19 F2
Ross Tower Ct WAL/NB CH45 95 J5
Rosswood Rd EP CH65 6 A2
Rostherne Av
GOL/RIS/CUL WA3 92 E3
GTS/LS CH66 195 H5
WAL/EG CH44 111 G4
Rostherne Cl
WARRW/BUR WA5 142 A5
Rostherne Crs WDN WA8 157 J1
Rosthwaite Gv
RNFD/HAY WA11 88 E2
Rosthwaite Rd
WD/CROXPK L12 115 G1
Rostron Crs FMBY L37 48 E4
Rosyth Cl WARRN/WOL WA2 124 B4
Rothay Dr WARRW/BUR WA5 140 E6
Rothbury Cl MOR/LEA CH46 128 D1
RUNC WA7 187 G1
Rothbury Ct STHEL WA9 119 K5
Rothbury Rd DV/KA/FCH L14 115 K1
Rother Dr EP CH65 195 K2
Rotherham Cl HUY L36 116 E3
Rotherwood Cl BEB CH63 150 C5
Rothesay Cl RUNC WA7 177 J3
Rothesay Dr CSBY/BLUN L23 69 F6
PS/BROM CH62 184 A3
Rothesay Gdns
CL/PREN CH43 * 149 J2
Rothley Av STHP PR8 33 G5
Rothsay Cl RNFD/HAY WA11 89 H4
Rothwell Cl ORM L39 45 H6
Rothwell Dr ORM L39 53 F3
STHP PR8 33 G4
Rothwell Rd GOL/RIS/CUL WA3 92 D2
Rothwells La CSBY/BLUN L23 69 J3
Rothwell St NPK/KEN L6 113 J3
Rotten Rw STHP PR8 27 F2
Rotunda St EV L5 113 F2
Roughdale Av KKBY L32 84 E4
STHEL WA9 * 119 K3
Roughdale Cl KKBY L32 84 E4
Roughley Av
WARRW/BUR WA5 142 A5
Roughwood Dr
NWD/KWIPK L33 72 E6
The Roundabout WDN WA8 138 C3
Round Hey STBRV L28 100 A5
The Round Meade MGHL L31 61 K5
The Roundway HTWN L38 59 F4
Roundwood Dr STHEL WA9 103 K4
Routledge St WDN WA8 19 F1
Rowan Av GOL/RIS/CUL WA3 93 G4
WD/CROXPK L12 99 J4
Rowan Cl BRSC L40 39 F3
RNFD/HAY WA11 89 G4
RUNC WA7 177 F6
WARRW/BUR WA5 141 G3
Rowan Ct AIG/SPK L17 153 F1
GR/UP/WCH CH49 147 J1
Rowan Dr KKBY L32 72 C6
Rowan Gv BEB CH63 170 A1
HUY L36 136 A1
Rowan La SKEL WN8 56 D1
The Rowans ORM L39 52 E6
Rowan Tree Cl
GR/UP/WCH CH49 128 C6
Rowena Cl CSBY/BLUN L23 69 G5
Rowland Cl WARRN/WOL WA2 124 C4
Rowlings Wy KKBY L32 * 84 E3
Rowsley Gv WLT/FAZ L9 82 E4
Rowson St PR/KW L34 101 K6
WAL/NB CH45 95 H4
Rowswood Ctyd WARRS WA4 161 H6
Rowthorn Cl WDN WA8 157 K3
Rowton Cl CL/PREN CH43 130 C6
Roxborough Cl
WARRW/BUR WA5 122 A1
Roxborough Wk WLTN L25 135 K6
Roxburgh Av AIG/SPK L17 133 H6
RF/TRAN CH42 150 C1
Roxburgh Rd GTS/LS CH66 194 C3
Roxburgh St ANF/KKDL L4 97 G4
BTL L20 5 J7
Royal Av WDN WA8 157 G3
Royal Cl FMBY L37 49 G4
Royal Crs FMBY L37 49 G3
Royal Cft WD/CROXPK L12 115 F3
Royal Gv ECCL WA10 103 F4
Royal Mail St VAUX/LVPD L3 9 G4
Royal Pk STHP PR8 27 F3
Royal Standard Wy
RF/TRAN CH42 131 J6
Royal St ANF/KKDL L4 97 G6
Royal Ter STHP PR8 14 D5
The Royal HOY CH47 126 E3
Royden Av RUNC WA7 176 C5
WAL/EG CH44 111 K2
Royden Crs
WGNW/BIL/OR WN5 77 H4
Royden Rd GR/UP/WCH CH49 129 F3
WGNW/BIL/OR WN5 77 H4
Royden Wy VAUX/LVPD L3 132 D6
Royhsay Cl EV L5 113 G3
Royleen Dr FROD/HEL WA6 201 G3
Roysten Gdns STHEL WA9 104 B3
Royston Av WAL/EG CH44 111 K3
WARR WA1 143 J2
Royston Cl GOL/RIS/CUL WA3 93 F3
GTS/LS CH66 202 D1
Royston St EHL/KEN L7 113 K6
Royton Rd CSBY/WL L22 81 G1
Rozel Crs WARRW/BUR WA5 141 J5
Rubbing Stone WKBY CH48 * 146 E5
Ruby Cl LITH L21 81 K3
Ruby St TOX L8 132 E6
Rudd Av STHEL WA9 104 E3
Ruddington Rd STHP PR8 28 B5
Rudd St HOY CH47 127 G2
Rudgate RAIN/WH L35 118 A5
Rudgrave Ms WAL/EG CH44 111 K2
Rudgrave Pl WAL/EG CH44 111 K2
Rudgrave Sq WAL/EG CH44 111 K2
Rudloe Ct WARRN/WOL WA2 124 B6
Rudstone Cl GTS/LS CH66 194 E4
Rudston Rd CHLDW L16 134 D1
Rudyard Cl DV/KA/FCH L14 115 G4
Rudyard Rd DV/KA/FCH L14 115 G4
Ruff La ORM L39 54 A1
Rufford Av MGHL L31 62 C4
Rufford Cl AIN/FAZ L10 83 J2
RAIN/WH L35 118 B2
WDN WA8 157 H1
Rufford Dr CHTN/BK PR9 21 J6
Rufford Rd BTL L20 81 K6
CHTN/BK PR9 21 F6
NPK/KEN L6 114 A4
RNFD/HAY WA11 75 G1
WAL/EG CH44 111 J4
Rugby Dr AIN/FAZ L10 83 H2
Rugby Rd EP CH65 196 B6
WAL/EG CH44 111 F2
WLT/FAZ L9 82 E3
Rugby Wk EP CH65 196 C6
Ruislip Cl WLTN L25 155 F1
Ruislip Ct WARRN/WOL WA2 124 B6
Rullerton Rd WAL/EG CH44 111 G3
Rumford Pl VAUX/LVPD L3 8 B3
Rumford St CLVP L2 8 C3
Rumney Pl ANF/KKDL L4 97 F5
Rumney Rd ANF/KKDL L4 97 G5
Rumney Rd West ANF/KKDL L4 97 F5
Runcorn Docks Rd RUNC WA7 10 A5
Runcorn Rd WARRS WA4 179 F1
Runcorn Spur Rd RUNC WA7 11 G6
Runcorn-Widnes Br WDN WA8 10 D1
Rundle Rd AIG/SPK L17 153 F1
Rundle St BIRK CH41 130 D1
Runic St CLB/OSW/ST L13 114 D5
Runnells La CSBY/BLUN L23 69 K4
The Runnell NSTN CH64 181 J3
The Runnel ORM L39 43 K1
Runnymede WARR WA1 144 B2
Runnymede Cl WLTN L25 135 H5
Runnymede Dr
RNFD/HAY WA11 * 89 K5
Runnymede Wk WDN WA8 * 158 D1
Runton Rd WLTN L25 135 K4
Rupert Dr NPK/KEN L6 113 J4
Rupert Rd HUY L36 116 C4
Ruscar Cl HLWD L26 155 H1
Ruscolm Cl WARRW/BUR WA5 140 E2
Ruscombe Rd DV/KA/FCH L14 115 K1
Rushden Rd KKBY L32 85 F2
Rushey Hey Rd KKBY L32 84 D2
Rushfield Crs RUNC WA7 188 A2
Rushgreen Cl CL/PREN CH43 129 K2
Rushlake Dr NTHLY L27 136 A4
Rushmere Rd NG/CROX L11 98 D3
Rushmoor Av AIMK WN4 79 K5
Rushmore Dr WDN WA8 138 E6
Rushmore Gv WARR WA1 143 K2
Rusholme Cl HLWD L26 155 K5
Rushton Av NEWLW WA12 106 B1
Rushton Cl
WARRW/BUR WA5 105 K6
WDN WA8 138 E6
Rushton Pl WLTN L25 154 D1
Rushy Vw NEWLW WA12 106 A1
Ruskin Av NEWLW WA12 106 C1
RF/TRAN CH42 * 150 E2
WAL/EG CH44 111 G4
WARRN/WOL WA2 123 J5
Ruskin Cl BTL L20 4 E5
Ruskin Dr ECCL WA10 12 B3
EP CH65 196 C6
Ruskin Wy CL/PREN CH43 130 A6
HUY L36 116 D6
Rusland Av PEN/TH CH61 167 K1
Rusland Rd KKBY L32 84 E3
Russell Av CHTN/BK PR9 23 J6
Russell Rd ALL/GAR L19 153 K5
CALD/MH L18 134 A4
CHTN/BK PR9 23 J6
HUY L36 117 H5
RF/TRAN CH42 131 J6
RUNC WA7 176 B5
WAL/EG CH44 110 E2
Russell St BIRK CH41 3 F3
VAUX/LVPD L3 9 H4
Russet Cl ECCL WA10 12 E2
NTHLY L27 136 B4
Russian Dr CLB/OSW/ST L13 114 D2
Rutherford Cl
CLB/OSW/ST L13 114 C6
Rutherford Rd CALD/MH L18 134 C3
ECCL WA10 87 K5
MGHL L31 71 H2
Rutherglen Av
CSBY/BLUN L23 81 G1
Ruth Evans Ct RAIN/WH L35 118 C3
Ruthin Cl WARRW/BUR WA5 * 122 E4
Ruthin Ct EP CH65 196 C6
Ruthven Rd CLB/OSW/ST L13 115 F6
LITH L21 81 H4
Rutland Av AIG/SPK L17 133 J3
GOL/RIS/CUL WA3 92 E4
HLWD L26 155 J3
WARRS WA4 162 A3
Rutland Cl EV L5 113 J2
Rutland Crs ORM L39 45 H4
Rutland Dr AIMK WN4 79 H5
Rutland Rd STHP PR8 28 A2
Rutland St BTL L20 5 G2
ECCL WA10 12 E2
RUNC WA7 10 C4
Rutter Av WARRW/BUR WA5 123 F5
Rutter St TOX L8 132 D4
Ryburn Rd ORM L39 53 H1
Rycot Rd SPK/HALE L24 173 H1
Rycroft Rd AIN/FAZ L10 83 H3
HOY CH47 127 K1
WAL/EG CH44 111 J5
Rydal Av CL/PREN CH43 129 K4
CSBY/BLUN L23 81 G1
FMBY L37 48 D3
PR/KW L34 118 B1
WARRS WA4 161 K1
Rydal Bank BEB CH63 151 F4
WAL/EG CH44 111 J3
Rydal Cl AIMK WN4 79 H5
AIN/FAZ L10 83 J1
EP CH65 203 G1
NSTN CH64 192 A3
NWD/KWIPK L33 72 C5
PEN/TH CH61 167 K1
Rydal Gv RNFD/HAY WA11 88 D4
RUNC WA7 176 E5
Rydal Rd HUY L36 116 E6
Rydal St EV L5 113 J1
NEWLW WA12 106 C2
Rydal Wy WDN WA8 157 H3
Ryder Cl ORM L39 53 G3
RAIN/WH L35 118 C3
Ryder Crs ORM L39 53 G4
STHP PR8 34 A1
Ryder Rd WARR WA1 144 B1
WDN WA8 139 G5
The Rydinge FMBY L37 41 G5
Rye Cl STHEL WA9 120 A3
Ryecote KKBY L32 84 D4
Ryecroft CHNE CH2 198 C6
Rye Cft LITH L21 69 J6
Ryecroft Av
GOL/RIS/CUL WA3 93 F2
Ryecroft Rd HES CH60 168 C6
Ryedale Cl TOX L8 133 G2
Ryefield La LITH L21 69 J6
Ryegate Rd ALL/GAR L19 153 J4
Ryeground La FMBY L37 41 G6
Rye Gv WD/CROXPK L12 115 J1
Rye Hey Rd KKBY L32 84 D1
Rye Moss La FMBY L37 50 C5
Ryland Pk PEN/TH CH61 148 D6
Rylands Dr WARRN/WOL WA2 17 G2
Rylands Hey
GR/UP/WCH CH49 128 E5
Rylands St WARR WA1 16 D5
WDN WA8 18 E3
Ryleys Gdns CLVP L2 8 D3
Rymer Gv ANF/KKDL L4 97 J4
Rymers Gn FMBY L37 48 E1

S

Sabre Cl RUNC WA7 * 178 C6
Sackville Rd ECCL WA10 87 K5
Saddle Cl WLT/FAZ L9 83 G3
Saddlers Ri RUNC WA7 178 B5
Saddlestone Gv TOX L8 132 D4
Sadler's La RNFD/HAY WA11 87 F4
Sadler St WDN WA8 19 G1
Saffron Cl GOL/RIS/CUL WA3 93 F3
WARRN/WOL WA2 124 D6
Saffron Gdns STHEL WA9 104 B3
Saffron Ms CSBY/BLUN L23 69 J3
Sagar Fold ORM L39 53 H5
Sage Cl WARRN/WOL WA2 124 E5
St Agnes Rd ANF/KKDL L4 97 F5
HUY L36 117 F5
St Aidan's Cl
WGNW/BIL/OR WN5 77 H3
St Aidans Ct CL/PREN CH43 130 C3
St Aidan's Gv HUY L36 100 C6
St Aidan's Ter CL/PREN CH43 130 C3
EV L5 113 F1
St Aidan's Wy NTHTN L30 70 B5
St Alban Rd WARRW/BUR WA5 141 F4
St Albans NPK/KEN L6 113 K2
St Albans Cl RNFD/HAY WA11 90 E4
St Albans Ct EV L5 112 E2
St Alban's Rd BTL L20 5 F5
CL/PREN CH43 130 D2
WAL/NB CH45 111 H3
St Alban's Sq BTL L20 5 F6
St Alexander Cl BTL L20 97 F4
St Ambrose Cft NTHTN L30 70 B5
St Ambrose Gv ANF/KKDL L4 113 K1
St Ambrose Rd WDN WA8 19 H1
St Ambrose Wy EV L5 113 G3
St Andrew Rd ANF/KKDL L4 113 K1
St Andrews Av
WD/CROXPK L12 115 J1
St Andrews Cl
WARRN/WOL WA2 124 C3
St Andrews Ct CL/PREN CH43 130 A3
St Andrew's Dr
CSBY/BLUN L23 68 C3
HUY L36 100 C6
St Andrew's Gv NTHTN L30 * 69 K6
RNFD/HAY WA11 88 E5
St Andrew's Pl STHP PR8 14 E6
St Andrews Rd BEB CH63 170 C2
CL/PREN CH43 130 E3
CSBY/BLUN L23 68 C2
EP CH65 196 C6
LITH L21 81 K6
St Andrew St VAUX/LVPD L3 9 H4
St Andrew's Vw
NWD/KWIPK L33 72 D4
St Annes Av WARRS WA4 163 G1
St Annes Av East WARRS WA4 163 G1
St Anne's Cl BIRK CH41 2 E3
FMBY L37 41 F5
St Annes Ct VAUX/LVPD L3 * 113 G4
St Anne's Gdns AIG/SPK L17 153 G2
St Anne's Gv AIG/SPK L17 153 F2
BIRK CH41 2 B1
St Anne's Pth FMBY L37 41 F5
St Anne's Pl BIRK CH41 2 B1
St Anne's Rd AIG/SPK L17 153 F2
CHTN/BK PR9 23 H1
FMBY L37 41 F5
HUY L36 116 E6
ORM L39 53 H1
WDN WA8 158 C1
St Annes Ter BIRK CH41 2 B2
St Anne St BIRK CH41 2 B1
VAUX/LVPD L3 113 G4
St Anne Wy BIRK CH41 2 E3
St Ann Pl RAIN/WH L35 118 E3
St Anns Rd ECCL WA10 102 E2
St Anthony Pl
WARRN/WOL WA2 123 H1
St Anthony's Cl HUY L36 100 C6
St Anthony's Gv NTHTN L30 70 A6
St Anthony's Rd
CSBY/BLUN L23 68 C5
St Asaph Dr WARRW/BUR WA5 122 D5
St Asaph Gv NTHTN L30 82 C2
St Asaph Rd GTS/LS CH66 202 C3
St Augustine's Av WARRS WA4 143 J5
St Augustine St EV L5 * 113 F2
St Augustine's Wy NTHTN L30 70 A5
St Austel Cl WARRW/BUR WA5 141 F6
St Austell Cl MOR/LEA CH46 109 F6
RUNC WA7 188 A1
St Austells Rd ANF/KKDL L4 5 K7
St Austins La WARR WA1 16 C6
St Barnabas Pl
WARRW/BUR WA5 142 B3
St Bedes Cl ORM L39 53 H2
St Benard's Cl TOX L8 133 G2
St Benedicts Cl
WARRN/WOL WA2 16 E1
St Benedict's Gv HUY L36 100 C6
St Benet's Wy NTHTN L30 70 B6
St Bernard's Cl NTHTN L30 70 A6
St Bernard's Dr NTHTN L30 70 A6
St Brendan's Cl HUY L36 100 C6
St Brides Cl WARRW/BUR WA5 141 F6
St Bride's Rd WAL/EG CH44 111 K2
St Bride St TOX L8 9 K7
St Bridget's Cl
WARRN/WOL WA2 124 B4
WDN WA8 158 B6
St Bridget's Gv NTHTN L30 * 70 A6
St Bridgets La WKBY CH48 146 C2

St Brigids Crs VAUX/LVPD L3 112 E2
St Catherine's RF/TRAN CH42 131 G5
St Catherines Cl HUY L36 116 E6
St Catherines Gdns
RF/TRAN CH42 131 G5
St Catherine's Rd BTL L20 4 E5
St Chad's Dr KKBY L32 84 D1
St Christopher's Av NTHTN L30 70 A5
St Christopher's Dr HUY L36 100 C6
St Clair Dr CHTN/BK PR9 23 J4
St Columba's Cl
WAL/EG CH44 * 111 K2
St Cuthbert's Cl
WD/CROXPK L12 * 99 J2
St Cuthbert's Rd CHTN/BK PR9 23 K3
St Cyrils Cl NTHLY L27 135 K2
St Damian's Cft NTHTN L30 70 B6
St David Rd CL/PREN CH43 130 D3
PS/BROM CH62 184 D1
St Davids Cl RAIN/WH L35 118 E3
St Davids Dr GTS/LS CH66 202 D3
WARRW/BUR WA5 122 E5
St Davids Gv NTHTN L30 82 A1
St Davids La CL/PREN CH43 130 A4
St David's Rd ANF/KKDL L4 113 K1
DV/KA/FCH L14 116 B2
St Domingo Gv EV L5 113 J1
St Domingo Rd EV L5 113 G1
St Domingo V EV L5 113 J1
St Dunstan's Gv NTHTN L30 82 A1
St Edmond's Rd BTL L20 4 E6
St Edmunds Rd BEB CH63 150 E6
St Edwards Cl BIRK CH41 2 A1
St Edwards Ms BIRK CH41 * 2 A1
St Elmo Rd WAL/EG CH44 111 K2
St Elphins Cl WARR WA1 17 G4
St Gabriel's Av HUY L36 117 G5
St George's Av ECCL WA10 87 K6
GTS/LS CH66 202 D3
RF/TRAN CH42 150 C1
St Georges Ct WDN WA8 157 J3
St Georges Gv NTHTN L30 82 A1
St George's Hl EV L5 113 H2
St George's Mt WAL/NB CH45 95 H5
St George's Pk WAL/NB CH45 95 H5
St George's Pl CHTN/BK PR9 14 E4
CLVPS L1 9 F3
St Georges Rd ECCL WA10 12 A7
FMBY L37 48 E1
HTWN L38 59 F2
HUY L36 116 E2
WAL/NB CH45 110 E1
St George's Wy BEB CH63 169 G6
St Gerard's Cl EV L5 113 F1
St Gregory's Cft NTHTN L30 70 B5
St Helen's Cl CL/PREN CH43 2 A5
St Helens Linkway
RAIN/WH L35 119 H5
STHEL WA9 103 H6
Saint Helens Rd ORM L39 53 K1
PR/KW L34 102 B6
St Helens Rd
GOL/RIS/CUL WA3 93 J3
ORM L39 45 K6
PR/KW L34 117 K1
RNFD/HAY WA11 87 J3
St Hilary Brow WAL/NB CH45 111 F3
St Hilary Dr WAL/NB CH45 111 F2
St Hilda's Dr FROD/HEL WA6 187 F6
St Hilda St ANF/KKDL L4 * 97 G5
St Hugh's Cl CL/PREN CH43 2 A5
St Ives Gv CLB/OSW/ST L13 114 D4
St Ives Rd CL/PREN CH43 130 D3
St Ives Wy HLWD L26 155 J3
St James Cl BRSC L40 54 C2
FROD/HEL WA6 187 F6
GR/UP/WCH CH49 128 E5
WD/CROXPK L12 114 E1
St James Dr BTL L20 4 C3
St James Mt RAIN/WH L35 118 E5
St James Pl TOX L8 132 D2
Saint James Rd RAIN/WH L35 118 E5
St James Rd BIRK CH41 130 C1
CLVPS L1 132 D2
HUY L36 116 E6
PR/KW L34 102 A6
WAL/NB CH45 95 H5
St James St CLVPS L1 132 C2
STHP PR8 27 J2
St Jerome's Wy NTHTN L30 70 B5
St John Av WARRS WA4 162 A1
St John's Av WLT/FAZ L9 82 D6
St John's Brow RUNC WA7 * 11 F3
St John's Cl HOY CH47 127 J1
St Johns Ct STHP PR8 * 33 K5
St John's La CLVPS L1 9 F3
St John's Pl CSBY/WL L22 80 E2
St John's Rd BTL L20 96 D4
CSBY/WL L22 80 E2
HUY L36 117 F6
PS/BROM CH62 184 D2
STHP PR8 27 G6
WAL/NB CH45 110 E2
St John's St RUNC WA7 11 F3
St John's Ter BTL L20 * 96 D4
St John St BIRK CH41 2 E5
ECCL WA10 103 F4
NEWLW WA12 106 A2
St Josephs Cl HUY L36 100 C6
WARRW/BUR WA5 141 F4
St Josephs Crs VAUX/LVPD L3 9 G1
St Jude's Cl HUY L36 * 100 C6
St Katherines Wy WARR WA1 17 H4
St Kevin's Dr KKBY L32 72 D5
St Kilda Cl EP CH65 203 G2
St Kilda's Rd MOR/LEA CH46 128 E2
St Laurence Cl BIRK CH41 2 E3
St Laurence Dr BIRK CH41 2 E4
St Laurence Gv KKBY L32 * 84 E3
St Lawrence Cl TOX L8 133 F5
St Lawrence Rd
FROD/HEL WA6 200 E2
St Leonard's Cl NTHTN L30 70 A5
St Lucia Rd WAL/EG CH44 111 K2
St Luke's Av GOL/RIS/CUL WA3 92 E3
St Luke's Church Rd FMBY L37 48 C5
St Lukes Cl DV/KA/FCH L14 115 K1
St Lukes Ct ANF/KKDL L4 97 J3
St Luke's Crs WDN WA8 139 G5
St Luke's Dr FMBY L37 48 C3
St Luke's Gv CHTN/BK PR9 23 G6
CHTN/BK PR9 15 K5
NTHTN L30 70 A5
St Luke's Rd CHTN/BK PR9 15 K5
CSBY/BLUN L23 68 E5
ECCL WA10 12 A5
St Luke's Wy FROD/HEL WA6 186 E6
HUY L36 100 C6
St Margaret's Av
WARRN/WOL WA2 123 K6
St Margarets Gv NTHTN L30 81 K1
St Margaret's Rd HOY CH47 127 F2
St Marks Crs GTS/LS CH66 202 D3
St Mark's Gv NTHTN L30 69 K5
St Mark's Rd HUY L36 117 F6
St Mark's St RNFD/HAY WA11 89 K5
St Martins Dr GTS/LS CH66 202 B1
St Martins Gv KKBY L32 84 E3
St Martins La RUNC WA7 178 C6
St Martin's Ms EV L5 113 G3
St Marys Ar ECCL WA10 * 13 H6
St Mary's Av ANF/KKDL L4 * 97 J3
WGNW/BIL/OR WN5 77 F5
St Marys Cl BTL L20 4 C4
WARRS WA4 162 B5
St Mary's Ct GOL/RIS/CUL WA3 93 J2
WLTN L25 154 D1
St Mary's Gdns STHP PR8 34 B2
St Mary's Ga BIRK CH41 3 H5
St Mary's Gv ANF/KKDL L4 * 97 J3
NTHTN L30 81 K1
St Mary's La ANF/KKDL L4 97 J3
St Mary's Pl ANF/KKDL L4 * 97 J3
St Mary's Rd ALL/GAR L19 153 J4
CSBY/WL L22 81 G3
HUY L36 116 E5
RUNC WA7 177 J4
WARRW/BUR WA5 141 G4
WDN WA8 10 D1
St Mary's St WAL/EG CH44 111 H3
WLTN L25 154 D1
St Mathews Cl ANF/KKDL L4 98 B3
HUY L36 117 F4
St Matthews Av LITH L21 81 K3
St Matthew's Cl HUY L36 * 117 F4
WARRS WA4 162 C4
St Matthews Gv ECCL WA10 102 E5
St Mawes Cl WDN WA8 157 K1
St Mawes Wy ECCL WA10 87 J5
St Mawgan Ct
WARRN/WOL WA2 124 B5
St Michael Rd ORM L39 52 D6
St Michael's Church Rd
AIG/SPK L17 152 C1
St Michael's Cl AIG/SPK L17 152 D1
CHTN/BK PR9 23 H2
WDN WA8 157 H4
St Michaels Ct HUY L36 116 E4
St Michael's Gv NPK/KEN L6 113 K3
NTHTN L30 69 K6
St Michaels Pk ORM L39 52 E6
PS/BROM CH62 151 G5
St Michael's Rd AIG/SPK L17 133 G6
CSBY/BLUN L23 68 C4
STHEL WA9 119 J4
WDN WA8 157 H4
St Monica's Cl WARRS WA4 162 C4
St Monica's Dr NTHTN L30 70 A5
St Nicholas' Dr NTHTN L30 70 A6
St Nicholas Gv STHEL WA9 * 104 B6
St Nicholas Pl VAUX/LVPD L3 8 A4
St Nicholas Rd
GOL/RIS/CUL WA3 93 H2
RAIN/WH L35 117 J6
WAL/NB CH45 110 D2
St Oswald's Av CL/PREN CH43 110 C6
St Oswalds Cl
WARRN/WOL WA2 * 123 H1
St Oswalds Ct NTHTN L30 * 70 C6
St Oswald's La NTHTN L30 70 C5
St Oswald's Ms CL/PREN CH43 110 C6
St Oswalds Rd AIMK WN4 91 F1
St Oswald's St
CLB/OSW/ST L13 114 E5
St Paschal Baylon Bvd
CHLDW L16 135 G1
St Patrick's Cl
NWD/KWIPK L33 * 72 D4
WDN WA8 158 B6
St Patrick's Dr NTHTN L30 * 70 A5
St Pauls Av WAL/EG CH44 112 A5
St Pauls Cl NWD/KWIPK L33 72 C4
RF/TRAN CH42 150 D1
St Pauls Gdns GTS/LS CH66 194 E2
St Pauls Ms RUNC WA7 * 10 E4
St Paul's Pas STHP PR8 14 D7
St Paul's Rd RF/TRAN CH42 150 E1
WAL/EG CH44 111 K5
WDN WA8 18 D5
St Paul's Sq STHP PR8 14 C7
VAUX/LVPD L3 8 C2
St Paul's St STHP PR8 14 C7
St Paul St ECCL WA10 12 D5
St Paul's Vls RF/TRAN CH42 150 D1
St Peter's Av FMBY L37 48 D1
St Peter's Cl FMBY L37 48 D1
HES CH60 167 K6
NWD/KWIPK L33 72 C4
St Peters Ct AIG/SPK L17 * 133 G5
St Peter's Ms RF/TRAN CH42 151 G2
St Peter's Rd RF/TRAN CH42 151 F2
STHP PR8 27 H4
WLT/FAZ L9 83 F4
St Peter's Wy CL/PREN CH43 129 K5
WARRN/WOL WA2 16 E2
St Philip's Av LITH L21 81 K3
St Richards Cl BTL L20 97 F4
St Seiriol Gv CL/PREN CH43 130 D3
St Stephen Rd
WARRW/BUR WA5 141 G4
St Stephen's Av
WARRN/WOL WA2 123 H4
St Stephens Cl HES CH60 181 H1
WLTN L25 135 K4
St Stephen's Gv NTHTN L30 70 A6
St Stephens Pl VAUX/LVPD L3 8 E1
St Stephen's Rd HTWN L38 59 F3
RF/TRAN CH42 150 A1
St Teresa's Rd ECCL WA10 12 A4
St Thomas Ct WDN WA8 * 157 K2
St Thomas's Dr NTHTN L30 70 A6
St Thomas' Vw EP CH65 6 B7
St Vincent Rd CL/PREN CH43 130 D3
WAL/EG CH44 111 K2
WARRW/BUR WA5 141 G4
St Vincent's Cl
WD/CROXPK L12 115 J1
St Vincent St VAUX/LVPD L3 9 H3
St Vincent's Wy STHP PR8 27 G3
St Werburgh's Sq BIRK CH41 3 F5
St Wilfrid's Dr WARRS WA4 163 H2
St William Rd CSBY/BLUN L23 69 J4
St Winifred Rd RAIN/WH L35 118 D2
WAL/NB CH45 95 H6
Saker St ANF/KKDL L4 97 H6
Salacre Cl GR/UP/WCH CH49 129 H5
Salacre Crs GR/UP/WCH CH49 129 H5
Salacre La GR/UP/WCH CH49 129 H4
Salacre Ter
GR/UP/WCH CH49 * 129 H4
Salcombe Dr CHTN/BK PR9 20 D6
WLTN L25 154 E4
Salem Vw CL/PREN CH43 130 E6
Salerno Dr HUY L36 116 D4
Saleswood Av ECCL WA10 102 C2
Salford Rd STHP PR8 33 J4
Saline Cl DV/KA/FCH L14 116 A1
Salisbury Av NTHTN L30 82 D2
WKBY CH48 146 B1
Salisbury Cl GTS/LS CH66 202 D3
Salisbury Dr PS/BROM CH62 151 G4
Salisbury Pk CHLDW L16 134 E3
Salisbury Rd AIMK WN4 * 79 F4
ALL/GAR L19 153 H5
BTL L20 4 C2
EV L5 113 J1
RNFD/HAY WA11 90 D2
WAL/NB CH45 95 G5
WAV L15 133 J2
Salisbury St BIRK CH41 2 D6
CHTN/BK PR9 28 D1
GOL/RIS/CUL WA3 92 B3
PR/KW L34 101 K6
RUNC WA7 10 D6
VAUX/LVPD L3 113 H4
WARR WA1 17 H3
WDN WA8 18 E3
Salisbury Ter WAV L15 134 A1
Salkeld Av AIMK WN4 78 E6
Sally's La CHTN/BK PR9 23 J3
Salop St ANF/KKDL L4 97 H5
Saltash Cl HLWD L26 155 H3
RUNC WA7 188 A1
Saltburn Rd WAL/NB CH45 110 D2
Saltergate Rd TOX L8 133 F5
Saltersgate GTS/LS CH66 202 D1
Salthouse Quay VAUX/LVPD L3 8 C6
Saltney St VAUX/LVPD L3 112 D3
Salton Gdns
WARRW/BUR WA5 142 B2
Saltpit La MGHL L31 62 C6
Saltwood Dr RUNC WA7 188 B2
Saltworks Cl FROD/HEL WA6 187 G5
Salvin Cl AIMK WN4 79 J6
Salvia Wy NWD/KWIPK L33 72 C4
Salwick Cl CHTN/BK PR9 20 C6
Samaria Av PS/BROM CH62 151 H4
Sambourn Fold STHP PR8 33 G4
Samphire Gdns STHEL WA9 105 F6
Samuel St STHEL WA9 103 F6
WARRW/BUR WA5 142 B5
Sanbec Gdns WDN WA8 138 C4
Sandalwood RUNC WA7 178 A4
Sandalwood Cl NPK/KEN L6 113 K2
WARRN/WOL WA2 123 K5
Sandalwood Dr
CL/PREN CH43 130 A5
Sandalwood Gdns STHEL WA9 104 A6
Sandbeck St TOX L8 132 E6
Sandbrook La MOR/LEA CH46 129 F1
Sandbrook Rd STHP PR8 33 J6
WLTN L25 135 H1
Sandcliffe Rd WAL/NB CH45 94 E5
Sandeman Rd ANF/KKDL L4 98 B4
Sanderling Rd NEWLW WA12 106 C1
NWD/KWIPK L33 73 F6
Sanders Hey Cl RUNC WA7 187 K2
Sanderson Cl
WARRW/BUR WA5 * 140 E3
Sandfield HUY L36 116 D5
Sandfield Av HOY CH47 108 B6
Sandfield Cl BEB CH63 * 150 C5
GOL/RIS/CUL WA3 93 F3
WD/CROXPK L12 115 G2
Sandfield Ct FROD/HEL WA6 200 E1
Sandfield Crs ECCL WA10 12 E6
Sandfield Pk HES CH60 167 H5
ORM L39 53 H3
Sandfield Pk East
WD/CROXPK L12 115 G1
Sandfield Pl BTL L20 4 C2
Sandfield Rd BEB CH63 150 C5
BTL L20 5 H6
ECCL WA10 87 H6
GR/UP/WCH CH49 148 E1
WAL/NB CH45 95 H6
WLTN L25 135 J5
Sandfields FROD/HEL WA6 200 E1
Sandfield Ter WAL/NB CH45 95 H6
Sandfield Wk
CLB/OSW/ST L13 115 F3
Sandford Dr MGHL L31 62 B5
Sandford St BIRK CH41 3 G3
Sandforth Cl WD/CROXPK L12 114 E2
Sandforth Ct
CLB/OSW/ST L13 * 114 E2
Sandforth Rd
WD/CROXPK L12 114 E2
Sandgate Cl SPK/HALE L24 173 G1
Sandham Gv HES CH60 168 C6
Sandham Rd SPK/HALE L24 174 B2
Sandhead St EHL/KEN L7 133 J1
Sandhey Rd HOY CH47 127 H1
Sandheys NSTN CH64 181 H6
Sandheys Av CSBY/WL L22 80 D2
Sandheys Cl ANF/KKDL L4 97 G6
Sandheys Dr CHTN/BK PR9 23 H4
Sandheys Gv CSBY/WL L22 80 D1
Sandheys Rd WAL/NB CH45 95 H6
Sandheys Ter CSBY/WL L22 80 D2
Sandhills HTWN L38 59 F4
Sandhills La EV L5 96 E6
The Sandhills MOR/LEA CH46 109 J4
Sandhills Vw WAL/NB CH45 110 D2
Sandhurst Cl FMBY L37 48 C4
LITH L21 81 G4
Sandhurst Dr AIN/FAZ L10 83 H1
Sandhurst Rd HLWD L26 155 K5
RAIN/WH L35 118 C2
Sandhurst St AIG/SPK L17 133 G6
WARRS WA4 143 J6
Sandhurst Wy MGHL L31 61 K2
Sandicroft Cl
GOL/RIS/CUL WA3 124 E2
Sandicroft Rd WD/CROXPK L12 99 K3
Sandilands Gv HTWN L38 59 F4
Sandino St TOX L8 132 D3
Sandirngham Dr AIG/SPK L17 133 G5
Sandiway BEB CH63 183 K1
HOY CH47 108 B6
HUY L36 117 F6
Sandiway Av WDN WA8 157 F2
Sandiways Av NTHTN L30 82 C1
Sandiways Rd WAL/NB CH45 110 E1
Sandlea Pk WKBY CH48 146 B1
Sandlewood Gv
NWD/KWIPK L33 72 E5
Sandling Dr GOL/RIS/CUL WA3 92 B1
Sandon Cl RAIN/WH L35 118 D3
Sandon Crs NSTN CH64 191 K4
Sandon Gv RNFD/HAY WA11 75 H3
Sandon Pl WDN WA8 19 K1
Sandon Rd STHP PR8 27 G6
WAL/EG CH44 111 K3
Sandon St CSBY/WL L22 80 E2
TOX L8 9 K7
Sandon Wy EV L5 112 D1
Sandown Cl RUNC WA7 187 F1
Sandown La WAV L15 134 A1
Sandown Park Rd AIN/FAZ L10 71 H6
Sandown Rd WAV L15 134 A1
Sandpiper Cl
GR/UP/WCH CH49 128 E3
NEWLW WA12 106 C1
Sandpiper Gv HLWD L26 * 155 H2
Sandpipers Ct CSBY/BLUN L23 80 D1
Sandra Dr NEWLW WA12 106 D2
Sandridge Rd PEN/TH CH61 148 C6
WAL/NB CH45 95 H6
Sandringham Av CSBY/WL L22 81 F3
FROD/HEL WA6 199 J6
HOY CH47 127 H1
Sandringham Cl HOY CH47 * 127 H2
NWD/KWIPK L33 72 D4
PS/BROM CH62 * 151 F4
Sandringham Ct CHTN/BK PR9 15 F3
Sandringham Dr STHEL WA9 120 A1
WAL/NB CH45 95 G5
WARRW/BUR WA5 141 K5
Sandringham Gdns EP CH65 203 H1
Sandringham Ms HOY CH47 * 127 H1
Sandringham Rd
CLB/OSW/ST L13 114 C1
CSBY/WL L22 81 F3
FMBY L37 48 E4
MGHL L31 * 71 F1
STHP PR8 33 J4
WDN WA8 138 E5
Sandrock Cl WAL/NB CH45 95 H6
Sandrock Rd WAL/NB CH45 95 H6
Sands Rd CALD/MH L18 134 A5
Sandstone Cl RAIN/WH L35 118 E6
Sandstone Dr RAIN/WH L35 118 B2
WKBY CH48 147 F1
Sandstone Ms WDN WA8 138 D5
Sandstone Rd East
CLB/OSW/ST L13 114 E3
Sandstone Rd West
CLB/OSW/ST L13 114 D3
Sandstone Wk HES CH60 168 A6
Sandwash Cl RNFD/HAY WA11 75 J5
Sandway Crs NG/CROX L11 98 E3
Sandy Brow La
NWD/KWIPK L33 85 K4
Sandy Ct GOL/RIS/CUL WA3 93 H2
Sandy Gn WLT/FAZ L9 83 F4
Sandy Gv CLB/OSW/ST L13 114 D1
Sandy Knowe WAV L15 * 134 B1
Sandy La BRSC L40 46 D4
BRSC L40 31 H1
CLB/OSW/ST L13 114 D1
GOL/RIS/CUL WA3 93 H1
GOL/RIS/CUL WA3 92 A3
HES CH60 168 A4
HTWN L38 59 G4
LITH L21 81 G4
MGHL L31 71 K4
MGHL L31 62 A2
NSTN CH64 192 B3
ORM L39 63 F1
PEN/TH CH61 147 K4
RNFD/HAY WA11 88 A3
RUNC WA7 188 D1
RUNC WA7 176 E6
SKEL WN8 55 K4
WAL/NB CH45 110 E1
WARRN/WOL WA2 123 H4
WARRS WA4 162 C3
WARRW/BUR WA5 141 H5
WDN WA8 140 C3
WDN WA8 138 D5
WKBY CH48 146 C3
WLT/FAZ L9 82 E5
Sandy La North PEN/TH CH61 147 K3
Sandy La West
WARRN/WOL WA2 123 G4
Sandy Moor La RUNC WA7 178 C2
Sandymount Dr BEB CH63 * 170 B1
WAL/NB CH45 95 G6
Sandy Rd LITH L21 81 G3
Sandyville Gv ANF/KKDL L4 98 C5
Sandyville Rd ANF/KKDL L4 98 B5
Sandy Wy BRSC L40 31 J3
CL/PREN CH43 130 D4
Sanfield Cl ORM L39 45 H5
Sangness Dr STHP PR8 28 B4
Sankey Mnr
WARRW/BUR WA5 * 141 F3
Sankey Rd MGHL L31 71 G2
RNFD/HAY WA11 89 J6
Sankey St CLVPS L1 9 G7
GOL/RIS/CUL WA3 92 B3
NEWLW WA12 106 A2
STHEL WA9 104 B3
WARR WA1 16 B5
WDN WA8 158 B5
Sankey Wy WARRW/BUR WA5 141 K4
Santon Av CLB/OSW/ST L13 114 C2
Santon Dr GOL/RIS/CUL WA3 93 F3
Sanvino Av STHP PR8 33 K4
Sapphire Dr NWD/KWIPK L33 72 D4
Sapphire St CLB/OSW/ST L13 114 D6
Sarah's Cft NTHTN L30 70 B6
Sark Av EP CH65 203 F2
Sark Rd CLB/OSW/ST L13 114 D3
Sarsfield Av
GOL/RIS/CUL WA3 92 E3
Sartfield Cl CHLDW L16 135 F1
Sarum Rd WLTN L25 135 H2
Sarus Ct RUNC WA7 178 A1
Satinwood Cl AIMK WN4 78 E6
Satinwood Crs MGHL L31 71 K6
Saughall Massie La
GR/UP/WCH CH49 129 F4
Saughall Massie Rd
WKBY CH48 127 J6
Saughall Rd MOR/LEA CH46 128 D2
Saunby St ALL/GAR L19 172 B1
Saunders Av RAIN/WH L35 117 K3
Saundersfoot Cl
WARRW/BUR WA5 122 E5
Saunders Rd RAIN/WH L35 117 K3
Saunders St CHTN/BK PR9 15 F1
Saunderton Cl
RNFD/HAY WA11 90 B4
Savannah Pl
WARRW/BUR WA5 141 K2
Saville Av WARRW/BUR WA5 142 C2
Saville Rd CLB/OSW/ST L13 115 F5
MGHL L31 62 A4
Savon Hook FMBY L37 49 H4
Savoylands Cl AIG/SPK L17 152 D1
Sawdon Av STHP PR8 28 B3
Sawley Av GOL/RIS/CUL WA3 92 E2
Sawley Cl RUNC WA7 178 D6
Sawpit La HUY L36 117 F5
Sawyer Dr AIMK WN4 79 J6
Saxby Rd DV/KA/FCH L14 116 A1
Saxon Cl NPK/KEN L6 113 K2
WARRS WA4 162 A6
Saxonia Rd ANF/KKDL L4 97 K3
Saxon Rd CSBY/BLUN L23 68 E6
HOY CH47 127 H1
MOR/LEA CH46 109 K6
RUNC WA7 11 H5
STHP PR8 27 G2
Saxon Ter WDN WA8 19 F2
Saxon Wy GTS/LS CH66 202 D3
NWD/KWIPK L33 72 D3
Saxony Rd EHL/KEN L7 113 J5
Sayce St WDN WA8 18 E2
Scafell Av WARRN/WOL WA2 123 J4
Scafell Cl PS/BROM CH62 184 A4
Scafell Lawn NTHLY L27 136 D6
Scafell Rd RNFD/HAY WA11 88 D4
Scaffold La HTWN L38 59 J1
Scape La CSBY/BLUN L23 69 F4
Scargreen Av NG/CROX L11 98 D2
Scarisbrick Av LITH L21 81 J4
STHP PR8 14 D4
Scarisbrick Cl MGHL L31 62 C4
Scarisbrick Crs NG/CROX L11 98 B2
Scarisbrick Dr NG/CROX L11 98 B2
Scarisbrick New Rd STHP PR8 27 K2
Scarisbrick Pl NG/CROX L11 98 B3
Scarisbrick Rd NG/CROX L11 98 B3
RNFD/HAY WA11 75 G2
Scarisbrick St CHTN/BK PR9 15 F5
ORM L39 45 J5
Scarsdale Rd NG/CROX L11 98 D4
Scarth Hill La ORM L39 53 J3
Scarth Pk SKEL WN8 56 E6
Sceptre Cl NEWLW WA12 106 A2
Sceptre Rd NG/CROX L11 99 G2
Sceptre Wk NG/CROX L11 * 99 G2
Scholars Green La
LYMM WA13 165 G1
Scholar St EHL/KEN L7 133 H2
Scholes La ECCL WA10 102 C6
Scholes Pk ECCL WA10 102 D6
Schomberg St NPK/KEN L6 113 J4
School Av FMBY L37 49 F2
NSTN CH64 192 A3
School Brow WARR WA1 17 F3
WGNW/BIL/OR WN5 77 H4
School Cl MOR/LEA CH46 109 K5
NTHLY L27 135 K2
ORM L39 * 53 G4
STHP PR8 27 J5
School Dr WGNW/BIL/OR WN5 77 H4
The Schooles ECCL WA10 102 D6
Schoolfield Cl
GR/UP/WCH CH49 148 E1
Schoolfield Rd
GR/UP/WCH CH49 148 E1
School Hl HES CH60 167 K6
School House Gn ORM L39 45 K6
School House Gv BRSC L40 38 D4
School Houses SKEL WN8 * 56 D5
School La AIMK WN4 78 B6
AIN/FAZ L10 83 G2
BEB CH63 150 C6
BRSC L40 54 E2
BRSC L40 39 F4
CHNE CH2 198 B6
CL/PREN CH43 110 C6
CLVPS L1 8 E5
FMBY L37 49 F2
FROD/HEL WA6 201 F2
GTS/LS CH66 184 C6
HOY CH47 127 G2
HUY L36 117 G1
LITH L21 81 H4
MGHL L31 71 K4
NSTN CH64 181 G6
ORM L39 51 H2
PEN/TH CH61 147 J5
PR/KW L34 85 F5
PS/BROM CH62 151 G4
RAIN/WH L35 119 H6

RUNC WA7 ... 177 J5
SKEL WN8 ... 55 K4
WAL/EG CH44 ... 110 E3
WDN WA8 ... 139 K2
WLTN L25 ... 154 D2
School Rd *EP* CH65 ... 6 B4
HTWN L38 ... 59 F3
WARRN/WOL WA2 ... 123 J6
School St *AIMK* WN4 ... 79 J4
GOL/RIS/CUL WA3 ... 92 B3
NEWLW WA12 ... 106 B2
RNFD/HAY WA11 ... 89 J5
WARRS WA4 ... 16 E7
School Ter *GOL/RIS/CUL* WA3 * ... 92 B3
School Wy *SPK/HALE* L24 ... 173 G2
WDN WA8 ... 139 J6
Schooner Cl *RUNC* WA7 ... 188 C1
Schwartzman Dr *CHTN/BK* PR9 ... 21 K5
Science Rd *SPK/HALE* L24 ... 173 H1
Scilly Cl *EP* CH65 ... 203 G2
Scone Cl *NG/CROX* L11 ... 99 G2
Scorecross *STHEL* WA9 ... 103 K5
Score La *CHLDW* L16 ... 115 G6
Scoresby Rd *MOR/LEA* CH46 ... 110 B4
The Score *STHEL* WA9 ... 119 J1
Scorpio Cl *DV/KA/FCH* L14 ... 116 A2
Scorton St *NPK/KEN* L6 ... 114 A2
Scotchbarn La *PR/KW* L34 ... 118 A1
Scoter Rd *NWD/KWIPK* L33 ... 84 E1
Scotia Av *PS/BROM* CH62 ... 151 H4
Scotia Rd *CLB/OSW/ST* L13 ... 114 E3
Scotland Pl *VAUX/LVPD* L3 ... 9 F1
Scotland Rd *VAUX/LVPD* L3 ... 113 F4
WARR WA1 ... 16 D4
Scott Av *HUY* L36 ... 136 D1
RAIN/WH L35 ... 118 B4
WDN WA8 ... 18 A3
Scott Cl *ANF/KKDL* L4 ... 97 H6
MGHL L31 ... 62 B6
Scott Dr *ORM* L39 ... 45 K4
Scotton Av *GTS/LS* CH66 ... 194 E4
Scott Rd *GOL/RIS/CUL* WA3 ... 92 E2
Scotts Av *STHEL* WA9 ... 119 J4
Scotts Pl *BIRK* CH41 ... 130 C2
Scotts Quays *BIRK* CH41 ... 112 A6
Scott St *BTL* L20 ... 4 C1
CHTN/BK PR9 ... 23 J6
WAL/NB CH45 ... 111 H2
WARRN/WOL WA2 ... 16 E2
The Scythes
GR/UP/WCH CH49 ... 128 D5
NTHTN L30 ... 70 E5
Scythia Cl *PS/BROM* CH62 ... 151 H3
Seabank Av *WAL/EG* CH44 ... 111 J2
Seabank Rd *CHTN/BK* PR9 ... 15 F2
HES CH60 ... 180 D1
WAL/NB CH45 ... 95 J6
Seabury St *WARRS* WA4 ... 143 K6
Seacole Cl *TOX* L8 ... 133 G3
Seacombe Dr *GTS/LS* CH66 ... 195 H6
Seacombe Prom
WAL/EG CH44 ... 112 A3
Seacombe Vw *WAL/EG* CH44 ... 112 A5
Seacroft Cl *DV/KA/FCH* L14 ... 116 A1
Seacroft Crs *CHTN/BK* PR9 ... 20 E6
Seacroft Rd *DV/KA/FCH* L14 ... 116 A1
Seafield *FMBY* L37 ... 49 G3
Seafield Av *CSBY/BLUN* L23 ... 69 G5
HES CH60 ... 180 D1
Seafield Cottages
ALL/GAR L19 * ... 153 K5
Seafield Rd *BTL* L20 * ... 4 C2
PS/BROM CH62 ... 151 G3
STHP PR8 ... 33 J3
Seaford Cl *RUNC* WA7 ... 178 C4
Seaford Pl *WARRN/WOL* WA2 ... 123 G3
Seafore Cl *MGHL* L31 ... 61 K3
Seaforth Dr *MOR/LEA* CH46 ... 129 F2
Seaforth Rd *LITH* L21 ... 81 H5
Seaforth V North *LITH* L21 ... 81 H4
Seaforth V West *LITH* L21 ... 81 H5
Seagram Cl *WLT/FAZ* L9 ... 83 F3
Sealand Av *FMBY* L37 ... 48 D3
Sealand Cl *FMBY* L37 ... 48 D3
WARRN/WOL WA2 ... 143 H1
Sea La *RUNC* WA7 ... 177 G3
Sealy Cl *BEB* CH63 ... 170 C4
Seaman Rd *WAV* L15 ... 133 K2
Seaport St *TOX* L8 ... 133 F3
Sea Rd *WAL/NB* CH45 ... 95 F5
Seascale Av *ECCL* WA10 ... 102 D5
Seath Av *STHEL* WA9 ... 104 C1
Seathwaite Cl *CSBY/BLUN* L23 ... 68 C6
RUNC WA7 ... 187 H2
Seathwaite Crs
NWD/KWIPK L33 ... 72 C5
Seaton Cl *WD/CROXPK* L12 ... 100 A2
Seaton Gv *STHEL* WA9 ... 119 F1
Seaton Pk *RUNC* WA7 ... 178 D2
Seaton Pl *SKEL* WN8 ... 56 A2
Seaton Rd *RF/TRAN* CH42 ... 131 F5
WAL/NB CH45 ... 111 G1
Seaton Wy *CHTN/BK* PR9 ... 20 D6
Seattle Cl *WARRW/BUR* WA5 ... 141 J2
Sea Vw *HOY* CH47 ... 127 G2
NSTN CH64 ... 191 K5
Seaview Av *PEN/TH* CH61 ... 148 A5
PS/BROM CH62 ... 184 E1
WAL/NB CH45 ... 111 G2
Sea View La *PEN/TH* CH61 ... 148 A5
Sea View Rd *BTL* L20 ... 4 B3
Seaview Rd *WAL/NB* CH45 ... 111 G1
Seawood Gv *MOR/LEA* CH46 ... 128 E2
Secker Av *WARRS* WA4 ... 162 C1
Secker Cl *WARRS* WA4 ... 162 C1
Second Av *CL/PREN* CH43 ... 129 J3
CSBY/BLUN L23 * ... 68 E5
RAIN/WH L35 ... 118 D3
RUNC WA7 ... 177 J5
WLT/FAZ L9 ... 83 F4
Sedbergh Av *AIN/FAZ* L10 ... 71 F6
Sedbergh Gv *RUNC* WA7 ... 187 H2
Sedbergh Rd *WAL/EG* CH44 ... 111 F2
Sedburgh Gv *HUY* L36 ... 116 B4
Sedburn Rd *KKBY* L32 ... 85 F4
Seddon Cl *ECCL* WA10 ... 102 B2
Seddon Pl *SKEL* WN8 ... 56 A2
Seddon Rd *ALL/GAR* L19 ... 153 K5
ECCL WA10 ... 102 D4
Seddons Ct *PR/KW* L34 ... 117 K1
Seddon St *CLVPS* L1 ... 8 E6
ECCL WA10 ... 88 C4
Sedgefield Rd *MOR/LEA* CH46 ... 129 H1
Sedgemoor Rd *NG/CROX* L11 ... 98 C2
Sedgewick Crs
WARRW/BUR WA5 ... 121 J1
Sedley St *ANF/KKDL* L4 ... 113 K1
Sedum Gv *NWD/KWIPK* L33 ... 72 C4
Seeds La *WLT/FAZ* L9 ... 83 F4
Seeley Av *BIRK* CH41 ... 130 D2
Seel Rd *HUY* L36 ... 117 F5
Seel St *CLVPS* L1 ... 9 F6
Sefton Av *LITH* L21 ... 81 J4
WDN WA8 ... 139 F6
Sefton Cl *KKBY* L32 ... 72 B6
Sefton Coastal Footpath
CSBY/BLUN L23 ... 68 A3
CSBY/WL L22 ... 80 C1
Sefton Dr *AIN/FAZ* L10 ... 83 H1
CSBY/BLUN L23 ... 69 H2
KKBY L32 ... 72 B6
MGHL L31 ... 70 D1
TOX L8 ... 133 H4
Sefton Fold Dr
WGNW/BIL/OR WN5 ... 77 G4
Sefton Fold Gdns
WGNW/BIL/OR WN5 ... 77 G4
Sefton Gdns *ORM* L39 ... 53 H6
Sefton Gv *AIG/SPK* L17 ... 133 H5
Sefton La *MGHL* L31 ... 70 E1
Sefton Mill Ct *SFTN* L29 * ... 70 C2
Sefton Mill La *SFTN* L29 ... 70 C2
Sefton Moss La *NTHTN* L30 ... 70 A6
Sefton Moss Vls *LITH* L21 ... 81 J3
Sefton Park Rd *TOX* L8 ... 133 G3
Sefton Rd *AIMK* WN4 ... 78 E3
BTL L20 ... 82 A6
FMBY L37 ... 48 E3
LITH L21 ... 81 J3
PS/BROM CH62 ... 151 F3
WAL/NB CH45 ... 95 H6
WLT/FAZ L9 ... 97 J1
Sefton St *LITH* L21 ... 81 J4
NEWLW WA12 ... 105 K2
STHP PR8 ... 27 J3
VAUX/LVPD L3 ... 132 C3
Sefton Vw *CSBY/BLUN* L23 ... 69 G5
Sefton Vls *BTL* L20 * ... 5 J2
Segar's La *ORM* L39 ... 34 D5
STHP PR8 ... 33 K4
Selborne *RAIN/WH* L35 ... 118 B5
Selborne Cl *TOX* L8 ... 133 F2
Selborne St *TOX* L8 ... 133 F2
Selbourne Cl
GR/UP/WCH CH49 ... 129 J6
Selby Cl *ECCL* WA10 ... 12 B7
RUNC WA7 ... 178 D1
Selby Dr *FMBY* L37 ... 49 H3
Selby Gn *GTS/LS* CH66 ... 194 E4
Selby Gv *HUY* L36 ... 117 H3
Selby Pl *SKEL* WN8 ... 55 K2
Selby Rd *WLT/FAZ* L9 ... 82 D5
Selby St *WAL/NB* CH45 ... 111 H2
WARRW/BUR WA5 ... 142 B4
Seldon St *EHL/KEN* L7 * ... 113 K5
Selina Rd *ANF/KKDL* L4 ... 5 K6
Selkirk Av *AIMK* WN4 ... 78 C5
PS/BROM CH62 ... 184 B2
WARRS WA4 ... 143 K6
Selkirk Cl *GTS/LS* CH66 * ... 194 C4
Selkirk Dr *ECCL* WA10 ... 87 J6
Selkirk Rd *CLB/OSW/ST* L13 ... 114 D5
Sellar St *ANF/KKDL* L4 ... 97 G6
Selsdon Rd *CSBY/WL* L22 ... 80 D1
Selsey Cl *EHL/KEN* L7 ... 133 G1
Selside Wk *NTHLY* L27 ... 136 D6
Selston Cl *BEB* CH63 ... 170 C3
Selworthy Dr *WARRS* WA4 ... 144 C6
Selworthy Gn *CHLDW* L16 ... 135 F3
Selworthy Rd *STHP* PR8 ... 26 E4
Selwyn Cl *NEWLW* WA12 ... 91 G6
WDN WA8 ... 139 J6
Selwyn St *ANF/KKDL* L4 ... 97 G4
Senator Point
NWD/KWIPK L33 * ... 85 G3
Seneschal Ct *RUNC* WA7 ... 187 H1
Sennen Cl *RUNC* WA7 ... 188 A2
Sennen Rd *KKBY* L32 ... 84 E3
Sentinel Wy *NTHTN* L30 ... 82 E3
Sephton Dr *ORM* L39 ... 45 K4
September Rd *NPK/KEN* L6 ... 114 A2
Serenade Rd *NWD/KWIPK* L33 ... 72 E3
Sergeant Rd *WD/CROXPK* L12 ... 99 J6
Sergeant York Loop
WARRW/BUR WA5 ... 141 J3
Sergrim Rd *HUY* L36 ... 116 D4
Serin Cl *NEWLW* WA12 ... 106 C2
Serpentine Rd *WAL/EG* CH44 ... 111 J2
The Serpentine South
CSBY/BLUN L23 ... 68 B5
The Serpentine *ALL/GAR* L19 ... 153 H3
CSBY/BLUN L23 ... 68 B5
ORM L39 ... 53 H5
Servia Rd *LITH* L21 ... 81 J4
Servite Cl *CSBY/WL* L22 ... 80 D1
EP CH65 ... 195 J3
Sessions Rd *ANF/KKDL* L4 ... 97 G5
Seth Powell Wy *HUY* L36 ... 116 C1
Settrington Rd *NG/CROX* L11 ... 98 D4
Seven Acre Rd *CSBY/BLUN* L23 ... 69 J4
Seven Acres La *PEN/TH* CH61 ... 148 D5
Sevenoaks Av *STHP* PR8 ... 33 H4
Sevenoaks Cl *EV* L5 ... 113 G2
Sevenoaks Gv *RAIN/WH* L35 ... 136 E2
Seventh Av *WLT/FAZ* L9 * ... 83 G4
Severn Cl *STHEL* WA9 ... 120 A1
WARRN/WOL WA2 ... 124 A5
WDN WA8 ... 140 A6
WGNW/BIL/OR WN5 ... 77 G5
Severn Rd *AIMK* WN4 ... 79 K4
NWD/KWIPK L33 ... 72 E3
RAIN/WH L35 ... 118 D4
Severn St *BIRK* CH41 ... 111 G6
EV L5 ... 113 H1
Severnvale *EP* CH65 ... 195 K6
Severs St *NPK/KEN* L6 ... 113 J3
Sewell St *PR/KW* L34 ... 117 K1
RUNC WA7 ... 11 G4
Sextant Cl *RUNC* WA7 ... 188 C1
Sexton Av *STHEL* WA9 ... 105 F3
Sexton Wy *DV/KA/FCH* L14 ... 115 J5
Seymour Dr *GTS/LS* CH66 ... 195 H3
MGHL L31 ... 62 C4
WARR WA1 ... 143 K2
Seymour Pl West
WAL/NB CH45 ... 95 H5
Seymour Rd *DV/KA/FCH* L14 ... 115 H6
LITH L21 ... 81 J4
Seymour St *BTL* L20 ... 4 C7
RF/TRAN CH42 ... 131 G5
VAUX/LVPD L3 ... 9 H3
WAL/NB CH45 ... 95 H5
Shacklady Rd *NWD/KWIPK* L33 ... 73 F5
Shackleton Cl
WARRW/BUR WA5 ... 142 A1
Shackleton Rd *MOR/LEA* CH46 ... 110 B3
Shadewood Crs *WARRS* WA4 ... 163 G1
Shadwell Cl *EV* L5 ... 112 D2
Shadwell St *EV* L5 ... 112 D2
Shaftesbury Av *STHP* PR8 ... 34 C1
WARRW/BUR WA5 ... 160 B1
Shaftesbury Gv *STHP* PR8 ... 27 H6
Shaftesbury Rd
CSBY/BLUN L23 ... 68 E5
STHP PR8 ... 34 C1
Shaftesbury St *TOX* L8 ... 132 D3
Shaftesbury Ter
CLB/OSW/ST L13 * ... 114 E4
Shaftesbury Wy
WARRW/BUR WA5 ... 105 K6
Shaftsbury Av
NWD/KWIPK L33 ... 72 C4
Shaftway Cl *RNFD/HAY* WA11 ... 90 E4
Shakespeare Av *KKBY* L32 ... 84 C2
RF/TRAN CH42 ... 150 E2
Shakespeare Cl *NPK/KEN* L6 ... 113 J3
Shakespeare Gv
WARRN/WOL WA2 ... 123 H5
Shakespeare Rd *NSTN* CH64 ... 181 K6
STHEL WA9 ... 119 J4
WAL/EG CH44 ... 111 K5
WDN WA8 ... 18 C1
Shakespeare St *ALL/GAR* L19 ... 153 K6
BTL L20 ... 4 B1
STHP PR8 ... 27 J2
Shakspeare Cl *NPK/KEN* L6 ... 113 J3
Shalcombe Cl *HLWD* L26 ... 155 K4
Shaldon Cl *KKBY* L32 ... 85 F3
Shaldon Gv *KKBY* L32 ... 85 F3
Shaldon Rd *KKBY* L32 ... 85 F4
Shalford Gv *WKBY* CH48 ... 146 E1
Shallacres *EP* CH65 ... 195 J2
Shallcross Ct *NPK/KEN* L6 ... 113 J3
Shallcross Pl *NPK/KEN* L6 ... 113 J3
Shallmarsh Cl *BEB* CH63 ... 150 C6
Shallmarsh Rd *BEB* CH63 ... 150 C6
Shalom Ct *AIG/SPK* L17 ... 133 K4
Shamrock Rd *BIRK* CH41 ... 130 C2
Shand St *ALL/GAR* L19 ... 172 B1
Shanklin Cl *WARRW/BUR* WA5 ... 140 D3
Shanklin Rd *WAV* L15 ... 114 D6
Shannon Gv *WDN* WA8 ... 157 K1
Shannons La *PR/KW* L34 ... 100 C4
Shannon St *BIRK* CH41 ... 111 F6
Shard Cl *NG/CROX* L11 ... 84 A6
Shard St *STHEL* WA9 ... 104 C6
Sharon Park Cl *WARRS* WA4 ... 163 H2
Sharpeville Cl *ANF/KKDL* L4 ... 97 F6
Sharples Crs *CSBY/BLUN* L23 ... 69 G6
Sharp St *WARRN/WOL* WA2 ... 16 E1
WDN WA8 ... 18 D3
Sharwood Rd *NTHLY* L27 ... 136 C5
Shavington Av *CL/PREN* CH43 ... 130 C6
Shawbury Av *BEB* CH63 ... 150 C4
Shawbury Gv *WARR* WA1 ... 124 C6
Shaw Cl *GTS/LS* CH66 ... 195 H5
ORM L39 ... 35 H3
Shaw Crs *FMBY* L37 ... 49 H1
Shawell Ct *WDN* WA8 ... 159 F1
Shaw Entry *RAIN/WH* L35 ... 137 K2
Shaw Hill St *CLVPS* L1 * ... 8 E3
Shaw La *GR/UP/WCH* CH49 ... 147 K1
RAIN/WH L35 ... 118 A3
Shaw Rd *SPK/HALE* L24 ... 155 G6
Shaws Aly *CLVPS* L1 ... 8 E7
Shaw's Av *STHP* PR8 ... 27 H6
WARRN/WOL WA2 ... 142 E1
Shaws Dr *HOY* CH47 ... 127 J1
Shaws Garth *ORM* L39 ... 35 H3
Shaw's Rd *STHP* PR8 ... 27 H6
Shaw St *AIMK* WN4 ... 79 G4
BIRK CH41 ... 2 D7
ECCL WA10 ... 13 J4
HOY CH47 ... 127 G2
NPK/KEN L6 ... 113 H4
RNFD/HAY WA11 ... 90 D5
RUNC WA7 ... 10 C5
STHEL WA9 ... 13 J6
Shawton Rd *CHLDW* L16 ... 134 E1
Shearman Cl *PEN/TH* CH61 ... 168 A1
Shearman Rd *PEN/TH* CH61 ... 167 K1
Sheen Rd *WAL/NB* CH45 ... 95 J6
Sheepfield Cl *GTS/LS* CH66 ... 195 F2
Sheerwater Cl *WARR* WA1 ... 143 J2
Sheffield Cl
WARRW/BUR WA5 ... 141 K4
The Sheilings
GOL/RIS/CUL WA3 ... 93 G3
Sheil Rd *NPK/KEN* L6 ... 114 A3
Shelagh Av *WDN* WA8 ... 18 D2
Sheldon Cl *BEB* CH63 ... 170 C4
Sheldon Rd *WD/CROXPK* L12 ... 99 H5
Sheldrake Gv *NSTN* CH64 ... 191 K4
Shelley Cl *HUY* L36 ... 117 F6
Shelley Ct *KKBY* L32 ... 84 C3
Shelley Dr *ORM* L39 ... 45 H5
Shelley Gv *ALL/GAR* L19 ... 153 K6
STHP PR8 ... 23 H6
WARRS WA4 ... 143 J5
Shelley Pl *RAIN/WH* L35 ... 118 B4
Shelley Rd *WDN* WA8 ... 158 B1
WDN WA8 ... 18 C1
Shelley St *BTL* L20 ... 4 C1
STHEL WA9 ... 119 K5
Shelley Wy *WKBY* CH48 ... 146 C3
Shellfield Rd *CHTN/BK* PR9 ... 23 J2
Shellingford Rd
DV/KA/FCH L14 ... 116 A3
Shellway Rd *CHNE* CH2 ... 197 F6
Shelmore Dr *TOX* L8 ... 132 D5
Shelton Cl *CLB/OSW/ST* L13 ... 114 E5
WDN WA8 ... 140 A6
Shelton Dr *STHP* PR8 ... 33 G5
Shelton Rd *WAL/NB* CH45 ... 111 G1
Shenley Cl *BEB* CH63 ... 150 E5
Shenley Rd *WAV* L15 * ... 134 D1
Shenley Wy *CHTN/BK* PR9 * ... 21 G6
Shenstone St *EHL/KEN* L7 ... 113 K6
Shenton Av *RNFD/HAY* WA11 ... 89 G5
Shepherd Cl
GR/UP/WCH CH49 ... 128 D5
Shepherds Fold Cl *TOX* L8 ... 133 F3
Shepherd's La *ORM* L39 ... 44 B6
Shepherd St *NPK/KEN* L6 ... 9 K2
Sheppard Av *CHLDW* L16 ... 135 H1
Shepperton Cl *WARRS* WA4 ... 162 C5
Shepsides Cl *GTS/LS* CH66 ... 195 F6
Shepston Av *ANF/KKDL* L4 ... 97 J4
Shepton Rd *GTS/LS* CH66 ... 202 C1
HUY L36 ... 116 D1
Sherborne Av *WLTN* L25 ... 155 G3
Sherborne Cl *RUNC* WA7 ... 178 E2
Sherbourne Rd *EP* CH65 ... 196 C6
Sherbourne Wy
WARRW/BUR WA5 ... 121 K1
Sherbrooke Cl
DV/KA/FCH L14 ... 115 J2
WD/CROXPK L12 ... 115 J3
Sherburn Cl *WLT/FAZ* L9 ... 83 G3
Sherdley Park Dr *STHEL* WA9 ... 119 K1
Sherdley Rd *STHEL* WA9 ... 103 H6
Sherford Cl *NTHLY* L27 ... 136 C5
Sheridan Av *GOL/RIS/CUL* WA3 ... 92 E4
Sheridan Pl
WARRN/WOL WA2 ... 123 G2
Sheri Dr *NEWLW* WA12 ... 106 D3
Sheriff Cl *EV* L5 ... 113 G3
Sheringham Cl
GR/UP/WCH CH49 ... 129 H2
STHEL WA9 ... 104 B2
Sheringham Rd
WARRW/BUR WA5 ... 141 F3
Sherlock Av *RNFD/HAY* WA11 ... 90 D4
Sherlock La *WAL/EG* CH44 ... 111 G5
Sherman Dr *RAIN/WH* L35 ... 119 F6
Sherrat St *SKEL* WN8 ... 55 K4
Sherringham Rd *STHP* PR8 ... 27 F5
Sherry Ct *AIG/SPK* L17 * ... 133 K4
Sherry La *GR/UP/WCH* CH49 ... 148 D1
Sherwell Cl *WAV* L15 ... 114 E6
Sherwood Av *AIMK* WN4 * ... 79 H5
CSBY/BLUN L23 ... 68 E4
ORM L39 ... 53 G3
PEN/TH CH61 ... 147 K4
Sherwood Cl *RAIN/WH* L35 ... 118 D2
WDN WA8 ... 157 H2
Sherwood Ct *HUY* L36 ... 117 F5
WD/CROXPK L12 ... 99 K2
Sherwood Crs
WARRW/BUR WA5 ... 121 J1
Sherwood Dr *BEB* CH63 ... 150 D4
RAIN/WH L35 ... 118 B5
SKEL WN8 ... 57 F2
Sherwood Gv *FROD/HEL* WA6 ... 199 H6
HOY CH47 ... 128 A2
Sherwood Rd *CSBY/BLUN* L23 ... 68 D4
HOY CH47 ... 128 A1
WAL/EG CH44 ... 111 J4
Sherwood's La *AIN/FAZ* L10 ... 83 J3
Sherwood St *VAUX/LVPD* L3 ... 112 D3
Sherwyn Rd *ANF/KKDL* L4 ... 98 A6
Shetland Cl *WARRN/WOL* WA2 ... 124 A3
WDN WA8 ... 139 K6
Shetland Dr *EP* CH65 ... 203 G2
PS/BROM CH62 ... 171 G5
Shevington Cl *STHEL* WA9 ... 104 A6
WDN WA8 ... 139 K6
Shevington's La
NWD/KWIPK L33 ... 72 D4
Shewell Cl *RF/TRAN* CH42 ... 131 G5
Shiel Rd *WAL/NB* CH45 ... 95 G6
Shiggins Cl *WARRW/BUR* WA5 ... 142 A3
Shillingford Cl *WARRS* WA4 ... 162 D6
Shimmin St *EHL/KEN* L7 ... 113 J6
Ship St *FROD/HEL* WA6 ... 186 E6
Shipton Cl *ALL/GAR* L19 ... 153 J3
CL/PREN CH43 ... 149 H2
WARRW/BUR WA5 ... 141 J1
WDN WA8 ... 138 C6
Shirdley Av *KKBY* L32 ... 84 E4
Shirdley Crs *STHP* PR8 ... 33 J6
Shirdley Wk *KKBY* L32 ... 84 E4
Shirebourne Av
RNFD/HAY WA11 ... 88 E4
Shireburn Rd *FMBY* L37 ... 40 C6
Shire Gn *STHEL* WA9 ... 120 A1
The Shires *ECCL* WA10 ... 12 D7
Shirley Dr *WARRS* WA4 ... 163 F1
Shirley Rd *ALL/GAR* L19 ... 153 K3
Shirley St *WAL/EG* CH44 ... 112 A4
Shirwell Gv *STHEL* WA9 ... 120 A3
Shobdon Cl *WD/CROXPK* L12 ... 99 K1
Shones Cft *NSTN* CH64 ... 192 B4
Shop La *MGHL* L31 ... 62 D4
Shop Rd *PR/KW* L34 ... 100 C1
Shore Bank *PS/BROM* CH62 ... 151 H3
Shore Dr *PS/BROM* CH62 ... 151 H5
Shorefields *PS/BROM* CH62 ... 151 G3
Shorefields Village *TOX* L8 ... 132 E6
Shoreham Dr
WARRW/BUR WA5 ... 141 H6
Shore Rd *BIRK* CH41 ... 3 G2
LITH L21 ... 81 G6
STHP PR8 ... 33 F3
WKBY CH48 ... 146 D4
Short Cl *NEWLW* WA12 ... 105 J2
Shortfield Rd
GR/UP/WCH CH49 ... 129 H5
Shortfield Wy
GR/UP/WCH CH49 * ... 129 H5
Short St *GOL/RIS/CUL* WA3 * ... 92 C2
NEWLW WA12 ... 105 J2
RNFD/HAY WA11 ... 90 D5
WDN WA8 ... 158 B6
Shortwood Rd
DV/KA/FCH L14 ... 115 K4
Shorwell Cl *WARRW/BUR* WA5 ... 140 D2
Shrewsbury Av *AIN/FAZ* L10 ... 71 F6
CSBY/WL L22 ... 68 E6
Shrewsbury Cl *CL/PREN* CH43 ... 130 C3
Shrewsbury Dr
GR/UP/WCH CH49 ... 129 H3
Shrewsbury Rd *ALL/GAR* L19 ... 153 K5
CL/PREN CH43 ... 130 C2
HES CH60 ... 168 A4
WAL/NB CH45 ... 111 F2
WKBY CH48 ... 146 B2
Shrewsbury St *WARRS* WA4 ... 143 G6
Shrewton Rd *WLTN* L25 ... 135 H2
Shropshire Cl *NTHTN* L30 ... 70 D5
WARR WA1 ... 144 D3
Shropshire Gdns *ECCL* WA10 ... 12 E7
Shropshire Rd *CHNE* CH2 ... 196 E6
Sibford Rd *WD/CROXPK* L12 ... 115 H2
Sibley Av *AIMK* WN4 ... 79 J5
Siddall St *ECCL* WA10 ... 88 C4
Siddeley Dr *NEWLW* WA12 ... 105 K2
Siddeley St *AIG/SPK* L17 ... 133 H6
Sidgreave St *ECCL* WA10 ... 12 D6
Siding La *RNFD/HAY* WA11 ... 65 K6
Sidings Ct *WARR* WA1 ... 17 F3
The Sidings *RF/TRAN* CH42 ... 150 E1
Sidlaw Av *STHEL* WA9 ... 104 D2
Sidlaw Cl *GTS/LS* CH66 ... 194 D3
Sidmouth Cl *ECCL* WA10 ... 87 K5
WARRW/BUR WA5 ... 141 F5
Sidney Av *WAL/NB* CH45 ... 95 G5
Sidney Gdns *RF/TRAN* CH42 ... 131 H5
Sidney Pl *EHL/KEN* L7 ... 113 J6
Sidney Powell Av *KKBY* L32 ... 84 B1
Sidney Rd *BTL* L20 ... 5 H6
CHTN/BK PR9 ... 23 H5
NSTN CH64 ... 182 A6
RF/TRAN CH42 ... 131 H5
Sidney St *BIRK* CH41 ... 3 G3
ECCL WA10 ... 12 B4
Sidney Ter *RF/TRAN* CH42 ... 131 H6
Sidwell St *ALL/GAR* L19 ... 153 K6
Signal Works Rd *WLT/FAZ* L9 ... 83 H3
Silcock St *GOL/RIS/CUL* WA3 ... 92 B2
Silcroft Rd *KKBY* L32 ... 84 D3
Silkstone Cl *ECCL* WA10 ... 12 B6
EHL/KEN L7 ... 133 G1
Silkstone Crs *RUNC* WA7 ... 178 A6
Silkstone St *ECCL* WA10 ... 12 B6
Silsden Av *GOL/RIS/CUL* WA3 ... 93 J3
Silver Av *RNFD/HAY* WA11 ... 89 K6
Silverbeech Av *CALD/MH* L18 ... 134 C5
Silverbeech Rd *WAL/EG* CH44 ... 111 J4
Silver Birch Gv *AIMK* WN4 ... 79 F4
Silverbirch Wy *GTS/LS* CH66 ... 202 D3
Silver Birch Wy *MGHL* L31 ... 61 K2
Silverbrook Rd *NTHLY* L27 ... 135 K2
Silverburn Av *MOR/LEA* CH46 ... 109 J6
Silverdale Av *CLB/OSW/ST* L13 ... 114 C2
Silverdale Cl *FROD/HEL* WA6 ... 201 F2
HUY L36 ... 136 B1
Silverdale Dr *LITH* L21 ... 82 A3
Silverdale Gv *RNFD/HAY* WA11 ... 88 D3
Silverdale Rd *BEB* CH63 ... 150 E4
CL/PREN CH43 ... 130 D5
NEWLW WA12 ... 106 B1
WARRS WA4 ... 162 A1
Silverlake Cl *WLT/FAZ* L9 ... 97 J2
Silverlea Av *WAL/NB* CH45 ... 111 H2
Silver Leigh *AIG/SPK* L17 ... 152 E2
Silverlime Gdns *STHEL* WA9 ... 102 D6
Silverne Dr *EP* CH65 ... 202 E1
Silverstone Dr *HUY* L36 ... 136 A1
Silverstone Gv *MGHL* L31 ... 61 K2
Silver St *WARRN/WOL* WA2 ... 16 D2
Silverthorne Dr *CHTN/BK* PR9 ... 23 H4
Silverton Rd *AIG/SPK* L17 ... 153 F3
Silverwell Rd *NG/CROX* L11 ... 84 C6
Silvester St *EV* L5 ... 112 E2
Simkin Av *WARRS* WA4 ... 143 J5
Simms Av *STHEL* WA9 ... 104 C2
Simm's Rd *NPK/KEN* L6 ... 114 B1
Simnel Cl *WLTN* L25 ... 135 J3
Simonsbridge *WKBY* CH48 * ... 146 E5
Simons Cl *RAIN/WH* L35 ... 137 F1
Simon's Cft *NTHTN* L30 ... 69 K6
Simonside *WDN* WA8 ... 157 H1
Simons La *FROD/HEL* WA6 ... 200 E3
Simonstone Gv *STHEL* WA9 ... 104 B6
Simonswood La
NWD/KWIPK L33 ... 85 F1
ORM L39 ... 63 K4
Simpson St *BIRK* CH41 ... 2 E4
CLVPS L1 * ... 132 C2
Sim St *VAUX/LVPD* L3 ... 9 H1
Sinclair Av *RAIN/WH* L35 ... 118 B2
WARRN/WOL WA2 ... 123 H5
WDN WA8 ... 18 B3
Sinclair Cl *RAIN/WH* L35 ... 118 B1
Sinclair Dr *CALD/MH* L18 ... 134 C3
Sinclair St *ALL/GAR* L19 ... 153 K6
Sineacre La *ORM* L39 ... 64 E6
Singleton Av *RF/TRAN* CH42 ... 131 F6
RNFD/HAY WA11 ... 89 G6
Singleton Dr *PR/KW* L34 ... 100 D2
Singleton Rd *EP* CH65 ... 195 J5
Sirdar Cl *EHL/KEN* L7 ... 133 G1
Sir Howard St *EHL/KEN* L7 * ... 9 K7
Sir Howard Wy *TOX* L8 * ... 9 K7
Sir Thomas St *CLVP* L2 ... 8 D3
Siskin Cl *NEWLW* WA12 ... 106 C2
Siskin Gn *WLTN* L25 ... 135 H5
Sisters Wy *BIRK* CH41 ... 2 D4
Six Acre Gdns *WARRS* WA4 ... 160 D6
Six Acre La *WARRS* WA4 ... 160 D6
Sixth Av *WLT/FAZ* L9 ... 83 H4
Skeffington *RAIN/WH* L35 ... 118 A5
Skelhorne St *VAUX/LVPD* L3 ... 9 G4
Skelmersdale Rd *ORM* L39 ... 55 G6
Skelton Cl *RNFD/HAY* WA11 ... 88 D4
Skelton St *AIMK* WN4 ... 78 E3
Skerries Rd *ANF/KKDL* L4 ... 113 J1
Skiddaw Cl *RUNC* WA7 ... 187 K3
Skiddaw Rd *PS/BROM* CH62 ... 171 G3
Skipton Av *CHTN/BK* PR9 ... 21 F5
Skipton Cl *RUNC* WA7 ... 177 J4
Skipton Dr *GTS/LS* CH66 ... 195 F5
Skipton Rd *ANF/KKDL* L4 ... 97 K6
HUY L36 ... 117 H4
Skirving Pl *EV* L5 ... 113 F1
Skirving St *EV* L5 ... 113 F1
Skye Cl *EP* CH65 ... 203 G2
WDN WA8 ... 139 K6
Sky Lark Ri *STHEL* WA9 ... 104 E2

Slackey La CHTN/BK PR9 24 A1
Slag La GOL/RIS/CUL WA3 93 G1
RNFD/HAY WA11 90 A4
Slaidburn Crs CHTN/BK PR9 20 D6
GOL/RIS/CUL WA3 92 A1
Slate La SKEL WN8 55 J3
Slater Pl CLVPS L1 9 F6
Slater St CLVPS L1 9 F6
WARRS WA4 17 G7
Slatey Rd CL/PREN CH43 130 E3
Sleaford Rd DV/KA/FCH L14 116 B2
Sleepers Hl ANF/KKDL L4 97 H6
Slenna Cl NTHLY L27 135 K3
Slessor Av WKBY CH48 127 J6
Slim Rd HUY L36 116 E3
Slingsby Dr GR/UP/WCH CH49 129 H5
Slutchers La WARR WA1 142 D6
Small Av WARRN/WOL WA2 123 J5
Small Crs WARRN/WOL WA2 123 J5
The Smallholdings MGHL L31 * 62 E4
Small La BRSC L40 37 J1
ORM L39 52 D2
Small La North ORM L39 44 B1
Small La South ORM L39 44 A6
Smallridge Cl PEN/TH CH61 * 167 J1
Smallshaw Cl AIMK WN4 91 F1
Smallwoods Ms HES CH60 * 167 J4
Smeaton St ANF/KKDL L4 97 G4
Smilie Av MOR/LEA CH46 109 G6
Smith Av BIRK CH41 130 E1
Smith Crs WARRN/WOL WA2 143 G1
Smithdown Gv EHL/KEN L7 133 F1
Smithdown La EHL/KEN L7 113 J6
Smithdown Pl WAV L15 134 B4
Smithdown Rd EHL/KEN L7 133 H2
Smith Dr BTL L20 82 B6
WARRN/WOL WA2 143 G1
Smithfield St CLVP L2 8 D2
STHEL WA9 104 A3
Smithford Wk RAIN/WH L35 136 E2
Smithills Cl GOL/RIS/CUL WA3 125 F2
Smith Pl EV L5 113 F1
Smith Rd WDN WA8 18 B5
Smith St EV L5 97 G6
PR/KW L34 * 118 A1
SKEL WN8 55 K4
STHEL WA9 104 C6
WARR WA1 16 E4
Smithy Cl FMBY L37 49 H1
NSTN CH64 192 B5
WDN WA8 138 B3
Smithy Gn FMBY L37 49 G1
Smithy Hey WKBY CH48 146 D1
Smithy Hl BEB CH63 182 B1
Smithy La BRSC L40 37 G5
BRSC L40 31 H1
FROD/HEL WA6 199 K4
GTS/LS CH66 195 F3
NSTN CH64 193 H1
ORM L39 62 D1
ORM L39 43 J5
WDN WA8 138 B4
Smithystone Cl WAV L15 134 B2
Smock La AIMK WN4 78 B5
Smollett St BTL L20 81 H5
EHL/KEN L7 * 113 K5
Smugglers Wy WAL/NB CH45 94 E5
Smyth Rd WDN WA8 158 E1
Snab La NSTN CH64 192 A5
Snabwood Cl NSTN CH64 191 K4
Snaefell Av CLB/OSW/ST L13 114 C2
Snaefell Gv CLB/OSW/ST L13 114 C2
Snaefell Ri WARRS WA4 162 B4
Snape Gn STHP PR8 36 B1
Snave Cl LITH L21 81 J6
Snoballey BRSC L40 37 F5
Snottesbrook Gn NG/CROX L11 98 D2
Snowberry Cl WDN WA8 139 K5
Snowberry Crs
WARRW/BUR WA5 142 A6
Snowberry Rd DV/KA/FCH L14 115 K1
Snowden Rd MOR/LEA CH46 128 D1
Snowdon Cl GTS/LS CH66 194 D3
WARRW/BUR WA5 141 F3
Snowdon Gv STHEL WA9 104 A6
Snowdon La EV L5 112 E2
Snowdon Rd RF/TRAN CH42 150 C1
Snowdrop Av BIRK CH41 130 C1
Snowdrop Cl RUNC WA7 187 J3
Snowdrop Ms LITH L21 81 J5
Snowdrop St EV L5 97 F6
Soane Cl AIMK WN4 79 J6
Soho Pl VAUX/LVPD L3 113 G4
Soho St VAUX/LVPD L3 113 G4
Solar Rd WLT/FAZ L9 82 E5
Solly Av RF/TRAN CH42 150 D1
Solomon St EHL/KEN L7 113 K5
Solway Cl AIMK WN4 79 F5
WARRN/WOL WA2 124 B3
Solway Gv RUNC WA7 187 G2
Solway St East TOX L8 133 G2
Solway St West TOX L8 133 G2
Soma Av LITH L21 81 K3
Somerford Rd DV/KA/FCH L14 115 K3
Somerset Dr STHP PR8 41 J1
Somerset Pl NPK/KEN L6 114 B2
Somerset Rd BTL L20 5 H2
CSBY/WL L22 80 D1
PEN/TH CH61 167 J1
WAL/NB CH45 110 E2
WKBY CH48 127 H6
Somerset St STHEL WA9 104 B3
Somerset Wy WARR WA1 144 A1
Somerton St WAV L15 133 K1
Somerville Cl BEB CH63 183 J1
NSTN CH64 191 K4
Somerville Crs EP CH65 6 E7
Somerville Gv CSBY/WL L22 80 E1
Somerville Rd CSBY/WL L22 80 E1
WDN WA8 157 J3
Sommer Av WD/CROXPK L12 * 98 E6
Sonning Av LITH L21 81 H2
Sonning Rd ANF/KKDL L4 98 B3
Sorany Cl CSBY/BLUN L23 69 J3
Sorbus Cl CHNE CH2 198 D6
Sorogold St STHEL WA9 104 A2
Sorrel Cl CL/PREN CH43 130 A4
WARRN/WOL WA2 124 E5
Sougher's La AIMK WN4 78 E3
South Albert Rd AIG/SPK L17 133 G5
Southampton Wy RUNC WA7 188 D1
South Av PR/KW L34 117 J2
WARRN/WOL WA2 142 E1
WARRS WA4 162 B2
South Bank CL/PREN CH43 130 E6
South Bank Rd ALL/GAR L19 153 J4
EHL/KEN L7 114 B5
South Bank Ter RUNC WA7 10 C3
South Barcombe Rd
CHLDW L16 135 F2
South Boundary Rd
NWD/KWIPK L33 85 G3
Southbourne Rd
WAL/NB CH45 110 D2
Southbrook Rd NTHLY L27 135 K2
South Cantril Av
WD/CROXPK L12 99 K6
South Chester St TOX L8 132 D3
South Cloughton Rd BIRK CH41 2 D5
Southcroft Rd WAL/NB CH45 110 D2
South Dl WARRW/BUR WA5 141 G4
Southdale Rd RF/TRAN CH42 150 D1
WARR WA1 143 K2
WAV L15 134 A1
Southdean Rd DV/KA/FCH L14 116 B1
South Dr GR/UP/WCH CH49 129 H4
HES CH60 168 A6
PEN/TH CH61 147 K6
WAV L15 134 A1
WD/CROXPK L12 115 F2
Southern Crs TOX L8 132 D4
Southern Rd SPK/HALE L24 173 K3
STHP PR8 14 C7
Southern's La RNFD/HAY WA11 75 H3
Southern St WARRS WA4 162 B2
Southey Cl WDN WA8 18 A3
Southey Gv MGHL L31 71 G3
Southey Rd ECCL WA10 102 E5
Southey St BTL L20 4 C1
WAV L15 133 K2
South Ferry Quay
VAUX/LVPD L3 132 C3
Southfield Rd GTS/LS CH66 195 F3
WLT/FAZ L9 82 C5
Southfields Av
WARRW/BUR WA5 141 G3
South Front RAIN/WH L35 137 H1
Southgate Cl WD/CROXPK L12 99 J2
Southgate Rd
CLB/OSW/ST L13 115 F4
South Gv CALD/MH L18 153 K2
TOX L8 133 F5
South Heath Rd RUNC WA7 176 C6
South Hey Rd PEN/TH CH61 167 H1
South Highville Rd
CHLDW L16 134 E3
South Hill Gv CL/PREN CH43 130 E6
TOX L8 133 F5
South Hill Rd CL/PREN CH43 130 E5
TOX L8 132 E6
South Hunter St CLVPS L1 9 J6
South John St CLVP L2 8 D4
STHEL WA9 * 104 A2
Southlands Av
WARRW/BUR WA5 141 G6
Southlands Ct RUNC WA7 * 10 C7
South La WDN WA8 139 K4
South Lane Entry WDN WA8 140 A4
South Manor Wy WLTN L25 155 F2
South Meade MGHL L31 61 K6
Southmead Gdns
ALL/GAR L19 154 B4
Southmead Rd ALL/GAR L19 154 B4
South Mossley Hill Rd
ALL/GAR L19 153 H2
Southney Cl MGHL L31 84 A1
South Pde KKBY L32 84 D1
RUNC WA7 176 A6
SPK/HALE L24 173 K3
WKBY CH48 146 B1
South Park Ct WAL/EG CH44 112 A4
South Park Rd KKBY L32 72 B6
South Parkside Dr
WD/CROXPK L12 99 G6
South Park Wy BTL L20 5 G6
South Pier Rd EP CH65 196 C2
EP CH65 7 F1
Southport New Rd
CHTN/BK PR9 25 F1
Southport Old Rd FMBY L37 41 H4
Southport Rd BRSC L40 36 D5
BTL L20 5 J5
CSBY/BLUN L23 69 H2
FMBY L37 41 G6
MGHL L31 61 K3
ORM L39 45 J5
ORM L39 43 J5
STHP PR8 28 D5
Southport St STHEL WA9 104 E2
Southridge Rd PEN/TH CH61 148 D6
South Rd ALL/GAR L19 153 G5
CSBY/WL L22 80 E3
DV/KA/FCH L14 115 H4
EP CH65 196 B6
RF/TRAN CH42 150 B1
SPK/HALE L24 174 A1
WKBY CH48 146 B2
WLT/FAZ L9 83 G5
South Station Rd WLTN L25 135 J4
South St STHEL WA9 103 F6
TOX L8 133 F4
South Sudley Rd ALL/GAR L19 153 H2
South Ter ORM L39 53 J1
South Vw CSBY/WL L22 * 81 F3
HUY L36 117 H5
PS/BROM CH62 151 J6
TOX L8 * 133 F5
South Vls WAL/NB CH45 95 H6
Southward Rd
RNFD/HAY WA11 91 F4
Southway WDN WA8 157 J3
RUNC WA7 177 H6
SKEL WN8 56 D5
South Wy WAV L15 134 C1
Southway Av WARRS WA4 162 C4
Southwell Cl GOL/RIS/CUL WA3 92 D3
Southwell Pl TOX L8 132 D4
Southwick Rd RF/TRAN CH42 131 H6
Southwold Crs
WARRW/BUR WA5 140 E3
Southwood Av RUNC WA7 178 B3
Southwood Cl KKBY L32 85 F4
Southwood Rd AIG/SPK L17 152 C1
Southworth Av
WARRW/BUR WA5 142 C1
Southworth La
WARRN/WOL WA2 107 K6
Southworth Rd NEWLW WA12 107 F1
Sovereign Cl GOL/RIS/CUL WA3 93 F4
RUNC WA7 178 C5
Sovereign Ct
GOL/RIS/CUL WA3 124 E3
Sovereign Rd NG/CROX L11 99 G2
Sovereign Wy BIRK CH41 111 K6
NG/CROX L11 99 G2
Spa Fold BRSC L40 55 G1
Spa La BRSC L40 55 H1
Spark La RUNC WA7 177 J4
Sparks La PEN/TH CH61 148 E5
Sparling St CLVPS L1 132 C2
Sparrow Hall Cl WLT/FAZ L9 * 98 D1
Sparrow Hall Rd NG/CROX L11 98 D1
Sparrowhawk Cl HLWD L26 155 H2
RUNC WA7 177 K6
Spawell Cl GOL/RIS/CUL WA3 93 F2
Speakman Av NEWLW WA12 91 G6
Speakman Rd ECCL WA10 88 A5
Speakman St RUNC WA7 10 C3
Speedwell Cl
GOL/RIS/CUL WA3 93 F3
HES CH60 * 168 C5
Speedwell Dr HES CH60 168 C5
Speedwell Rd BIRK CH41 130 C2
Speke Bvd SPK/HALE L24 173 G1
Speke Church Rd
SPK/HALE L24 173 G2
Speke Hall Av SPK/HALE L24 173 F1
Speke Hall Rd WLTN L25 154 D4
Spekeland Rd EHL/KEN L7 133 H1
Speke Rd ALL/GAR L19 154 A6
WDN WA8 156 E4
Speke Town La SPK/HALE L24 173 G1
Spellow La ANF/KKDL L4 97 H5
Spence Av BTL L20 82 A6
Spencer Av MOR/LEA CH46 110 A6
Spencer Cl HUY L36 * 136 C1
WDN WA8 157 K2
WDN WA8 * 18 A2
Spencer Gdns STHEL WA9 104 B5
Spencer Pl BTL L20 82 A4
CHTN/BK PR9 * 15 H5
Spencer's La MGHL L31 71 J6
ORM L39 34 E6
SKEL WN8 56 D5
Spencer St NPK/KEN L6 113 H3
Spennymoor Ct RUNC WA7 177 H6
Spenser Av RF/TRAN CH42 150 E2
Spenser Rd NSTN CH64 191 K1
Spenser St BTL L20 4 C2
Spicer Gv KKBY L32 84 D1
Spice St WLT/FAZ L9 82 E6
Spindle Cl NPK/KEN L6 113 H3
Spindle Hillock AIMK WN4 78 C5
Spindus Rd SPK/HALE L24 173 F2
Spinnaker Cl RUNC WA7 188 C1
The Spinnakers ALL/GAR L19 153 G4
Spinners Dr STHEL WA9 104 D5
Spinners Pl WARR WA1 17 G2
Spinney Av WDN WA8 157 F2
Spinney Cl NWD/KWIPK L33 85 H3
ORM L39 53 H2
STHEL WA9 120 A3
Spinney Crs CSBY/BLUN L23 68 C3
Spinney Dr GTS/LS CH66 202 B1
Spinney Gn ECCL WA10 102 C2
Spinney Rd NWD/KWIPK L33 85 H3
The Spinney BEB CH63 170 D2
FMBY L37 41 G6
HES CH60 181 H2
NSTN CH64 191 J1
PR/KW L34 101 J6
RNFD/HAY WA11 75 G2
STBRV L28 100 A6
WKBY CH48 146 E1
Spinney Vw NWD/KWIPK L33 85 J3
Spion Kop AIMK WN4 79 F6
Spire Gn WLT/FAZ L9 82 D5
Spires Gdns WARRN/WOL WA2 107 G6
The Spires ECCL WA10 102 C1
Spital Heyes BEB CH63 170 D2
Spital Rd BEB CH63 170 D2
PS/BROM CH62 171 F3
Spitfire Rd SPK/HALE L24 154 C5
Spofforth Rd EHL/KEN L7 133 J1
Spooner Av LITH L21 81 K4
Sprainger St VAUX/LVPD L3 112 D3
Sprakeling Pl BTL L20 82 B4
Spray St ECCL WA10 12 D3
Spreyton Cl WD/CROXPK L12 99 G3
Sprig Cl WLT/FAZ L9 83 G3
Spring Av GTS/LS CH66 195 F3
Springbank Cl RUNC WA7 186 E1
Spring Bank Rd ANF/KKDL L4 113 K2
Springbourne FROD/HEL WA6 201 G3
Springbourne Rd AIG/SPK L17 152 C1
Springbrook Cl ECCL WA10 102 C1
Spring Cl NWD/KWIPK L33 * 73 F4
STHP PR8 27 H2
Spring Ct RUNC WA7 10 E4
Springcroft NSTN CH64 181 H6
Springdale Cl MOR/LEA CH46 110 A6
WD/CROXPK L12 99 G6
Spring Fld RNFD/HAY WA11 66 A5
Springfield VAUX/LVPD L3 9 G1
Springfield Av FROD/HEL WA6 199 J6
GOL/RIS/CUL WA3 92 A3
LITH L21 81 K3
WARR WA1 143 J1
WARRS WA4 144 A6
WKBY CH48 127 K6
Springfield Cl BRSC L40 46 D1
FMBY L37 48 C3
GR/UP/WCH CH49 149 F1
Springfield La ECCL WA10 87 H6
Springfield Pk RNFD/HAY WA11 90 B4
Springfield Rd ECCL WA10 102 E5
ORM L39 62 D2
WDN WA8 157 F3
Springfield Sq ANF/KKDL L4 97 H5
Springfield St WARR WA1 16 B5
Springfield Wy
WD/CROXPK L12 99 J5
Spring Gdns GTS/LS CH66 195 F3
MGHL L31 71 H1
Spring Gv WD/CROXPK L12 115 G1
Springhill Av PS/BROM CH62 184 A1
Springhill Ct WAV L15 134 B3
Spring La GOL/RIS/CUL WA3 124 D1
Spring Meadow
KIRK/FR/WAR PR4 25 K3
Springmeadow Rd
WLTN L25 135 H4
Springmount
GOL/RIS/CUL WA3 93 F4
Springpool STHEL WA9 104 B6
Springs Cl BTL L20 * 5 G3
Springside Cl HUY L36 116 C1
Spring St RF/TRAN CH42 131 J6
WDN WA8 18 D7
Spring V WAL/NB CH45 94 E6
Spring Vls CL/PREN CH43 * 130 E5
Springville Rd WLT/FAZ L9 * 83 F4
Springwell Rd BTL L20 81 K4
Springwood Av ALL/GAR L19 154 A3
WLTN L25 154 C4
Springwood Gv KKBY L32 84 E4
Springwood Wy
PS/BROM CH62 151 F3
Spruce Cl GOL/RIS/CUL WA3 93 G4
RF/TRAN CH42 131 G5
WARR WA1 144 D2
Spruce Gv STBRV L28 100 B6
Spruce Wy FMBY L37 48 C2
Sprucewood Cl NPK/KEN L6 113 K2
Spunhill Av GTS/LS CH66 195 F6
Spur Cl NG/CROX L11 99 G2
Spurgeon Cl EV L5 113 H2
Spurling Rd
WARRW/BUR WA5 121 K1
Spurrier's La MGHL L31 72 C1
Spurstow Cl
CL/PREN CH43 130 C6
The Spur CSBY/BLUN L23 68 E6
Spymers Cft FMBY L37 41 G5
Square La BRSC L40 38 E6
The Square BRSC L40 37 F5
LYMM WA13 145 K6
Squires Av WDN WA8 18 C3
Squires Cl
NFD/HAY WA11 90 A5
Squires St EHL/KEN L7 113 J6
Squirrel Gn FMBY L37 40 C6
Stable Cl GR/UP/WCH CH49 128 D5
The Stables CSBY/BLUN L23 * 69 H4
The Stackfield WKBY CH48 127 K6
Stadium Ct PS/BROM CH62 171 H3
Stadium Rd PS/BROM CH62 171 G2
Staffin Av EP CH65 203 F3
Stafford Cl HUY L36 117 G3
Stafford Gdns EP CH65 6 C4
Stafford Moreton Wy
MGHL L31 * 62 A6
Stafford Rd ECCL WA10 103 F4
STHP PR8 27 H6
WARRS WA4 162 B1
Staffordshire Cl EV L5 113 G1
Stafford St SKEL WN8 55 K3
VAUX/LVPD L3 9 H2
Stag Rd SPK/HALE L24 154 B5
Stainburn Av NG/CROX L11 98 D2
Stainer Cl NEWLW WA12 91 G6
WD/CROXPK L12 115 K2
Staines Cl WARRS WA4 162 D6
Stainmore Cl
GOL/RIS/CUL WA3 125 K1
Stainton Cl HLWD L26 155 H3
RNFD/HAY WA11 88 E3
Stairhaven Rd ALL/GAR L19 153 J2
The Stakes MOR/LEA CH46 109 J4
Stalbridge Av CALD/MH L18 134 A4
Staley Av CSBY/BLUN L23 69 G6
Staley St BTL L20 81 K5
Stalisfield Av NG/CROX L11 98 E3
Stalisfield Gv NG/CROX L11 98 E3
Stalisfield Pl NG/CROX L11 98 E3
Stalmine Rd WLT/FAZ L9 97 J1
Stamford Ct LYMM WA13 145 K6
Stamfordham Dr ALL/GAR L19 153 K3
Stamfordham Gv
ALL/GAR L19 154 A4
Stamfordham Pl ALL/GAR L19 154 A4
Stamford Rd STHP PR8 27 J4
Stamford St EHL/KEN L7 114 A5
EP CH65 195 K4
Stanbury Av BEB CH63 151 F5
Standale Rd WAV L15 134 A1
Standard Pl RF/TRAN CH42 131 J6
Standard Rd NG/CROX L11 99 G1
Standedge Wy
DV/KA/FCH L14 116 A1
Standen Cl ECCL WA10 12 D4
Stand Farm Rd
WD/CROXPK L12 99 K2
Standhouse La ORM L39 53 G3
Standish Av
WGNW/BIL/OR WN5 77 H4
Standish Ct WDN WA8 157 J3
Standish Dr
RNFD/HAY WA11 75 H2
Standish St ECCL WA10 13 J3
VAUX/LVPD L3 8 E2
Stand Park Av NTHTN L30 82 C1
Stand Park Cl NTHTN L30 * 82 C1
Stand Park Rd CHLDW L16 134 E3
Stand Pkwy NTHTN L30 82 B1
Standring Gdn ECCL WA10 102 D5
Standside Pk SKEL WN8 55 K5
Stanfield Av EV L5 113 H2
Stanfield Dr BEB CH63 170 B2
Stanford Av WAL/NB CH45 95 H6
Stanford Crs WLTN L25 155 G3
Stangate MGHL L31 61 K5
Stanhope Dr HUY L36 116 C4
PS/BROM CH62 171 F4
Stanhope St ECCL WA10 12 E1
TOX L8 132 C3
Stanier Wy EHL/KEN L7 114 A6
Staniforth Pl CHLDW L16 115 H6
Stanlawe Rd FMBY L37 40 E5
Stanlaw Rd EP CH65 6 E6
Stanley Av BEB CH63 150 B3
RNFD/HAY WA11 75 F2
STHP PR8 27 G5
WAL/NB CH45 110 D1
WARRS WA4 162 E1
WARRW/BUR WA5 140 E2
Stanley Bank Rd
RNFD/HAY WA11 89 K4
Stanley Bank Wy
RNFD/HAY WA11 89 J5
Stanley Bungalows
PR/KW L34 * 100 C1
Stanley Cl ANF/KKDL L4 97 F6
WAL/EG CH44 112 A5
WDN WA8 158 D1
Stanley Ct BRSC L40 38 E4
RF/TRAN CH42 131 J6
Stanley Crs PR/KW L34 117 J1
Stanley Gdns WLT/FAZ L9 82 C6
Stanley La PS/BROM CH62 184 C2
Stanley Pk LITH L21 81 J2
Stanley Park Av North
ANF/KKDL L4 97 K4
Stanley Park Av South
ANF/KKDL L4 97 K5
Stanley Pl WARRS WA4 * 162 E1
Stanley Prec BTL L20 5 F6
Stanley Rd BIRK CH41 111 F6
BTL L20 4 E1
CSBY/WL L22 81 F3
EP CH65 196 B2
EV L5 97 F6
FMBY L37 40 E5
HOY CH47 127 F3
HUY L36 116 E5
LITH L21 81 J5
MGHL L31 71 F3
PS/BROM CH62 151 F3
SKEL WN8 57 J6
Stanley St ALL/GAR L19 172 B1
CHTN/BK PR9 14 E4
CLVP L2 8 D4
EHL/KEN L7 114 C4
NEWLW WA12 * 106 A2
ORM L39 45 K6
RUNC WA7 11 F3
WAL/EG CH44 112 A5
WARR WA1 16 D6
Stanley Vls RUNC WA7 * 10 C7
Stanley Wy SKEL WN8 56 A2
Stanlowe Vw ALL/GAR L19 153 G5
Stanmore Pk
GR/UP/WCH CH49 128 C6
Stanmore Rd WAV L15 134 C3
Stannanought Rd SKEL WN8 57 G5
Stanner Cl WARRW/BUR WA5 122 D5
Stanney Cl NSTN CH64 191 K2
PS/BROM CH62 184 B4
Stanney La EP CH65 6 C7
Stanney Mill La CHNE CH2 203 K2
Stanney Mill Rd CHNE CH2 203 K1
Stanney Woods Av EP CH65 203 G2
Stannyfield Cl CSBY/BLUN L23 69 J3
Stanny Field Dr CSBY/BLUN L23 69 J3
Stansfield Av MGHL L31 62 D6
WARR WA1 143 J3
Stansfield Dr WARRS WA4 163 F4
Stanstead Av
WARRW/BUR WA5 141 G6
Stanton Av LITH L21 81 H2
Stanton Cl NTHTN L30 70 A4
RNFD/HAY WA11 90 B5
Stanton Ct NSTN CH64 191 K1
Stanton Crs KKBY L32 84 B1
Stanton Rd BEB CH63 170 A2
CALD/MH L18 * 134 A4
WARRS WA4 144 C6
Stanwood Cl ECCL WA10 102 B2
Stanwood Gdns RAIN/WH L35 118 A4
Stapehill Cl CLB/OSW/ST L13 115 F5
Stapeley Gdns HLWD L26 155 K5
Staplands Rd DV/KA/FCH L14 115 H5
Stapleford Ct GTS/LS CH66 195 J1
Stapleford Rd WLTN L25 135 K3
Staplehurst Cl WD/CROXPK L12 99 J2
Stapleton Av
GR/UP/WCH CH49 128 E5
RAIN/WH L35 118 E3
SPK/HALE L24 173 J2
WARRN/WOL WA2 143 G1
Stapleton Cl RAIN/WH L35 118 E3
WLTN L25 135 J2
Stapleton Ct FROD/HEL WA6 201 F2
Stapleton Rd FMBY L37 48 D5
RAIN/WH L35 118 D2
Stapley Cl RUNC WA7 10 B6
Starbeck Dr GTS/LS CH66 194 E3
Starkey Gv WARRS WA4 * 143 J5
Star La LYMM WA13 145 H5
Starling Cl RUNC WA7 178 C6
Starling Gv WD/CROXPK L12 99 K4
Star St TOX L8 132 D3
Startham Av
WGNW/BIL/OR WN5 77 G6
Starworth Dr PS/BROM CH62 151 H4
Statham Av LYMM WA13 145 H6
WARRN/WOL WA2 123 J5
Statham Cl LYMM WA13 145 J6
Statham Dr LYMM WA13 145 J6
Statham La LYMM WA13 145 G4
Statham Rd BRSC L40 55 J1
CL/PREN CH43 129 K1
SKEL WN8 55 K2
Statham Wy ORM L39 53 J1
Station Ap BRSC L40 38 E4
HOY CH47 127 K1
MOR/LEA CH46 109 J5
ORM L39 * 45 K6
Station Av FROD/HEL WA6 199 J5
GTS/LS CH66 195 F2
Station Cl NSTN CH64 192 A2
Station Gn GTS/LS CH66 195 F2
Station Ms AIMK WN4 78 C6
KKBY L32 * 72 B6
Station Rd AIMK WN4 78 B6
BEB CH63 149 K6
BIRK CH41 111 F6
CHNE CH2 198 B4
CHTN/BK PR9 21 J6
EP CH65 6 E3

HES CH60 180 E1
HOY CH47 127 G3
HUY L36 116 C5
MGHL L31 72 A6
MGHL L31 61 J1
NSTN CH64 181 H6
ORM L39 45 K5
ORM L39 43 H5
PEN/TH CH61 166 D1
PEN/TH CH61 149 H6
PR/KW L34 117 K2
RAIN/WH L35 118 E4
RNFD/HAY WA11 90 B5
RUNC WA7 10 C4
STHEL WA9 104 C6
STHP PR8 33 J4
WAL/EG CH44 111 G3
WARRS WA4 162 D1
WARRW/BUR WA5 140 E6
WLTN L25 135 J4
Station Rd North
WARRN/WOL WA2 124 C5
Station Rd South
WARRN/WOL WA2 124 C6
Station St RAIN/WH L35 * 118 E4
Station Wy HUY L36 117 G5
Station Yd WARR WA1 * 143 K1
Statton Rd CLB/OSW/ST L13 115 F6
Staveley Av BRSC L40 38 E5
Staveley Rd ALL/GAR L19 153 J3
SKEL WN8 56 A2
STHP PR8 33 K5
Stavert Cl NG/CROX L11 99 F2
Staverton Pk KKBY L32 84 B2
Stavordale Rd MOR/LEA CH46 129 H1
Steble St TOX L8 132 E4
Steel Av WAL/NB CH45 111 J1
Steel Ct EV L5 112 E2
Steel St WARR WA1 143 H2
Steeplechase Cl WLT/FAZ L9 83 F3
Steeple Ct NSTN CH64 191 K2
The Steeple WKBY CH48 146 E5
Steeple Vw NWD/KWIPK L33 72 D4
Steers Cft STBRV L28 99 K5
Stein Av GOL/RIS/CUL WA3 93 F3
Steinberg Ct VAUX/LVPD L3 112 E3
Steley Wy PR/KW L34 117 K2
Stella Prec LITH L21 * 81 H5
Stenhills Crs RUNC WA7 11 G5
Stephens Gdns GTS/LS CH66 194 E3
Stephens La CLVP L2 * 8 D3
Stephenson Ct EHL/KEN L7 * 114 A6
Stephenson Rd
CLB/OSW/ST L13 * 114 E5
NEWLW WA12 106 C3
Stephenson Wy FMBY L37 49 H2
WAV L15 114 C6
Stephen St WARR WA1 17 J2
Stephen Wy RAIN/WH L35 * 118 D2
Stepney Gv ANF/KKDL L4 97 J4
Sterling Wy EV L5 113 F1
Sterndale Cl EHL/KEN L7 133 G1
Sterrix Av LITH L21 81 K1
Sterrix Gn LITH L21 81 K1
Sterrix La NTHTN L30 81 K1
Stetchworth Rd WARRS WA4 162 A2
Steve Biko Cl TOX L8 133 G2
Stevenage Cl STHEL WA9 103 H6
Steven Dr BEB CH63 170 B2
Stevenson Crs ECCL WA10 12 B4
Stevenson Dr BEB CH63 170 B2
Stevenson St WAV L15 134 A1
Stevens Rd HES CH60 168 C6
Stevens St STHEL WA9 103 F5
Steventon RUNC WA7 178 D1
Steward Ct RAIN/WH L35 118 B2
Steward's Av WDN WA8 18 A3
Stewart Av BTL L20 5 J3
Stewart Cl PEN/TH CH61 167 K2
Stewerton Cl
GOL/RIS/CUL WA3 92 A1
Stile Hey CSBY/BLUN L23 69 J4
Stiles Rd NWD/KWIPK L33 72 E3
The Stiles ORM L39 45 J6
Stillington Rd TOX L8 133 F5
Stiperstones Cl GTS/LS CH66 194 C3
Stirling Av CSBY/BLUN L23 69 F6
Stirling Cl WARR WA1 144 D2
Stirling Crs STHEL WA9 119 K1
Stirling Dr AIMK WN4 78 C5
Stirling La WLTN L25 155 G4
Stirling Rd SPK/HALE L24 173 G2
Stirling St WAL/EG CH44 111 H5
Stirrup Cl WARRN/WOL WA2 124 C4
Stockbridge La HUY L36 116 C1
Stockbridge Pl EV L5 113 J1
Stockbridge St EV L5 113 J2
Stockdale Cl VAUX/LVPD L3 * 8 D1
Stockdale Dr
WARRW/BUR WA5 141 F1
Stockham Cl RUNC WA7 177 K5
Stockham La RUNC WA7 178 A6
Stockley Crs ORM L39 64 E1
Stockmoor Rd NG/CROX L11 98 D2
Stockpit Rd NWD/KWIPK L33 85 J1
Stockport Rd WARRS WA4 144 C6
Stocks Av STHEL WA9 104 C2
Stocks La WARRW/BUR WA5 140 E4
Stockswell Rd WDN WA8 137 J5
Stockton Crs NWD/KWIPK L33 72 C3
Stockton Gv STHEL WA9 119 F1
Stockton La WARRS WA4 162 D2
Stockton Wood Rd
SPK/HALE L24 173 H2
Stockville Rd CALD/MH L18 135 F5
Stoddart Rd ANF/KKDL L4 97 J3
Stoke Cl PS/BROM CH62 184 B4
Stoke Gdns EP CH65 6 E7
Stoker Wy WLT/FAZ L9 82 D6
Stokesay CL/PREN CH43 130 A3
Stokesay Ct EP CH65 196 D6
The Stokes Ct
GOL/RIS/CUL WA3 92 E3
Stokesley Av KKBY L32 84 B1
Stokes St GOL/RIS/CUL WA3 125 G2
Stoke St BIRK CH41 * 2 B1
Stoke Wk EP CH65 6 E6
Stonebank Dr NSTN CH64 192 B3
Stonebarn Dr MGHL L31 62 A4
Stone Barn La RUNC WA7 187 J1
Stonebridge La AIN/FAZ L10 83 K5
Stoneby Dr WAL/NB CH45 95 G6
Stonechat Cl GOL/RIS/CUL WA3 93 F3
NTHLY L27 136 B5
RUNC WA7 187 H2
Stonecrop CALD/MH L18 135 F4
Stonecrop Cl
GOL/RIS/CUL WA3 124 E3
RUNC WA7 187 J3
Stonecross Dr RAIN/WH L35 119 F6
Stone Cross Dr WDN WA8 138 D4
Stone Cross La North
GOL/RIS/CUL WA3 92 D4
Stone Cross La South
GOL/RIS/CUL WA3 92 D5
Stonedale Crs NG/CROX L11 99 F1
Stonedale Pk NG/CROX L11 * 98 E1
Stonefield Rd DV/KA/FCH L14 115 K3
Stonefont Cl WLT/FAZ L9 97 J2
Stonegate Dr TOX L8 132 E5
Stonehaven Cl CHLDW L16 135 G1
Stonehaven Dr
WARRN/WOL WA2 124 C4
Stone Hay RAIN/WH L35 117 K6
Stonehey Dr WKBY CH48 146 D2
Stonehey Rd KKBY L32 84 D3
Stonehill Av ANF/KKDL L4 113 K1
BEB CH63 151 F5
Stonehills Ct RUNC WA7 11 J4
Stonehills La RUNC WA7 11 J5
Stonehill St ANF/KKDL L4 113 K1
Stonehouse Ms CALD/MH L18 134 E6
Stonehouse Rd
WAL/NB CH45 110 E2
Stonelea RUNC WA7 178 A3
Stoneleigh Cl STHP PR8 33 J5
Stoneleigh Gdns WARRS WA4 163 J2
Stoneleigh Gv RF/TRAN CH42 150 E3
Stone Pit Cl GOL/RIS/CUL WA3 93 F2
Stoneridge Ct
CL/PREN CH43 * 129 K1
Stone Sq BTL L20 82 B6
Stone St VAUX/LVPD L3 112 D3
Stoneville Rd CLB/OSW/ST L13 114 E4
Stoney Brow SKEL WN8 57 K3
Stoneycroft CLB/OSW/ST L13 115 F3
Stoneycroft Cl
CLB/OSW/ST L13 114 E2
Stoneycroft Crs
CLB/OSW/ST L13 114 E2
Stoney Hey Rd WAL/NB CH45 95 G6
Stoney Holt RUNC WA7 178 B5
Stoneyhurst Av AIN/FAZ L10 71 F6
Stoney La RAIN/WH L35 118 B3
Stonham Cl GR/UP/WCH CH49 129 F4
Stonyfield NTHTN L30 70 B4
Stonyhurst Cl RNFD/HAY WA11 88 E4
Stonyhurst Rd WLTN L25 154 E2
Stopford St TOX L8 132 E5
Stopgate La NG/CROX L11 98 B2
NWD/KWIPK L33 73 F3
WLT/FAZ L9 98 B1
Store St BTL L20 97 F4
Storeton Cl CL/PREN CH43 130 D6
Storeton La PEN/TH CH61 168 C1
Storeton Rd RF/TRAN CH42 150 A1
Stormont Rd ALL/GAR L19 153 J4
Storrington Av NG/CROX L11 98 E2
Storrington Heys NG/CROX L11 99 F1
Storrsdale Rd CALD/MH L18 153 J1
Stour Av RAIN/WH L35 118 E4
Stourcliffe Rd WAL/EG CH44 111 G4
Stour Ct EP CH65 6 C1
Stourport Cl
GR/UP/WCH CH49 * 128 D5
Stourton Rd KKBY L32 84 D3
STHP PR8 33 J5
Stourton St WAL/EG CH44 111 J5
Stourvale Rd HLWD L26 * 155 J4
Stowe Av AIN/FAZ L10 83 H1
Stowe Cl WLTN L25 154 E4
Stowell St EHL/KEN L7 9 J6
Stowford Cl WD/CROXPK L12 99 G3
Strada Wy VAUX/LVPD L3 9 J1
Stradbroke Cl
GOL/RIS/CUL WA3 93 H4
Strafford Dr BTL L20 5 J3
Straight Length
FROD/HEL WA6 200 B2
Straight Up La CHTN/BK PR9 24 A5
Straker Av EP CH65 195 J3
Strand Av AIMK WN4 79 G5
Strand Rd BTL L20 4 B5
HOY CH47 127 G2
Strand St VAUX/LVPD L3 8 C5
The Strand AIMK WN4 79 G5
CLVP L2 8 B4
Strange Rd AIMK WN4 78 C6
Stratford Cl STHP PR8 33 G3
Stratford Rd ALL/GAR L19 153 G3
NSTN CH64 191 J3
Strathallan Cl HES CH60 167 J3
Strathcona Rd WAL/NB CH45 111 H1
WAV L15 133 K2
Strathearn Rd HES CH60 180 E1
Strathlorne Cl RF/TRAN CH42 131 J6
Strathmore Av AIMK WN4 79 F4
Strathmore Dr
CSBY/BLUN L23 69 F6
Strathmore Gv STHEL WA9 120 A1
Strathmore Rd NPK/KEN L6 114 A3
Stratton Cl CALD/MH L18 154 B1
RUNC WA7 188 A1
WAL/NB CH45 111 J1
Stratton Dr STHEL WA9 119 F1
Stratton Pk WDN WA8 138 E4
Stratton Rd KKBY L32 84 B2
WARRW/BUR WA5 141 J4
Strauss Cl TOX L8 133 G3
Strawberry Cl
GOL/RIS/CUL WA3 124 E3
Strawberry Cross
CH/BCN CH1 * 202 E3
Strawberry Dr GTS/LS CH66 202 E3
Strawberry Gn GTS/LS CH66 203 F3
Strawberry Rd NG/CROX L11 98 C3
Streatham Av CALD/MH L18 134 A4
Street Hey La NSTN CH64 183 J5
The Street BIRK CH41 111 F6
Stretford Cl NWD/KWIPK L33 72 D4
Stretton Av
GOL/RIS/CUL WA3 * 92 E4
STHEL WA9 104 D2
WAL/EG CH44 111 G3
WGNW/BIL/OR WN5 77 H4
Stretton Cl CL/PREN CH43 130 B6
PS/BROM CH62 184 B4
WD/CROXPK L12 100 A2
Stretton Dr CHTN/BK PR9 23 H5
Stretton Wy HUY L36 117 H6
Strickland Cl WARRS WA4 163 F4
Strickland St ECCL WA10 13 J2
Stringer Crs WARRS WA4 143 H5
Stringhey Rd WAL/EG CH44 111 J2
Strokes Cl HLWD L26 155 K2
Stroma Av EP CH65 203 F3
Stroma Rd CALD/MH L18 153 J2
Stromness Cl
WARRN/WOL WA2 124 D4
Stroud Cl GR/UP/WCH CH49 128 D6
Stuart Av MOR/LEA CH46 109 K6
WLTN L25 155 F4
Stuart Cl MOR/LEA CH46 129 H1
Stuart Crs
WGNW/BIL/OR WN5 77 G4
Stuart Dr DV/KA/FCH L14 115 J4
WARRS WA4 162 E1
Stuart Gv BTL L20 97 F4
Stuart Rd BTL L20 5 K5
CSBY/WL L22 81 F1
ECCL WA10 87 K5
MGHL L31 72 A6
RF/TRAN CH42 131 G6
RUNC WA7 178 A1
Stuart Rd North BTL L20 5 K4
Stubbs La CL/PREN CH43 130 B6
Stub La BRSC L40 46 A1
Studholme St BTL L20 96 E6
Studland Rd WLT/FAZ L9 98 C1
Studley Rd WAL/NB CH45 110 E1
Sturdee Rd CLB/OSW/ST L13 115 F6
Sturgess Cl ORM L39 45 K4
Sturgess St NEWLW WA12 105 K2
Suburban Rd NPK/KEN L6 114 A1
Sudbrook Cl
GOL/RIS/CUL WA3 * 93 F3
Sudbury Cl WLTN L25 155 G1
Sudbury Rd CSBY/WL L22 80 C1
Sudell Av MGHL L31 62 D5
Sudell La MGHL L31 62 B1
Sudley Gra AIG/SPK L17 153 F2
Sudworth Rd WAL/NB CH45 95 G6
Suez St NEWLW WA12 106 A2
WARR WA1 16 C5
Suffield Rd ANF/KKDL L4 97 F5
Suffolk Av EP CH65 195 J4
Suffolk Cl WARR WA1 144 C3
Suffolk Pl WDN WA8 157 H4
Suffolk Rd STHP PR8 34 C1
Suffolk St BTL L20 5 G2
CLVPS L1 9 F6
RUNC WA7 10 B3
Suffton Pk KKBY L32 84 B2
Sugar La PR/KW L34 100 D2
Sugar Stubbs La
CHTN/BK PR9 25 G1
Sugnall St EHL/KEN L7 9 J6
Sulby Av CLB/OSW/ST L13 114 C2
WARRS WA4 142 E6
Sulby Cl STHP PR8 27 G4
Sulgrave Cl CHLDW L16 115 G6
Sullington Dr NTHLY L27 136 B3
Sullivan Av GR/UP/WCH CH49 129 G5
Sullivan's Wy STHEL WA9 103 K5
Sumley Cl RNFD/HAY WA11 89 G6
Summercroft Cl
GOL/RIS/CUL WA3 92 B4
Summerfield PS/BROM CH62 171 F3
Summerfield Av ECCL WA10 102 B2
WARRW/BUR WA5 123 F5
Summerford Cl
RF/TRAN CH42 131 H6
Summerhill Dr MGHL L31 71 J2
Summer La RUNC WA7 177 J4
WARRS WA4 189 G1
Summers Av BTL L20 5 J2
Summer Seat BTL L20 4 B5
VAUX/LVPD L3 112 E3
Summers Rd VAUX/LVPD L3 132 C4
Summer St SKEL WN8 56 B1
Summertrees Av
GR/UP/WCH CH49 128 E5
Summertrees Cl
GR/UP/WCH CH49 128 E5
Summertrees Rd
GTS/LS CH66 202 C1
Summerville Gdns
WARRS WA4 162 E2
Summer Wy BTL L20 5 F1
Summerwood PEN/TH CH61 148 A4
Summerwood La ORM L39 44 A2
The Summit WAL/EG CH44 111 J2
Summit Wy WLTN L25 135 G6
Sumner Av ORM L39 51 H1
Sumner Cl EV L5 112 E2
RAIN/WH L35 119 F6
Sumner Gv NWD/KWIPK L33 72 E4
Sumner Rd CL/PREN CH43 130 C1
FMBY L37 49 F2
Sumner St RNFD/HAY WA11 89 K5
Sunbeam Rd
CLB/OSW/ST L13 114 E4
Sunbeam St NEWLW WA12 106 C2
Sunbourne Rd AIG/SPK L17 152 C1
Sunbury Dr STHP PR8 33 H5
Sunbury Gdns WARRS WA4 162 D4
Sunbury Rd ANF/KKDL L4 97 K6
WAL/EG CH44 111 J4
Sunbury St ECCL WA10 * 102 E5
Suncroft Cl WARR WA1 144 D2
Suncroft Rd HES CH60 168 C6
Sundale Av RAIN/WH L35 118 B2
Sundew Cl WLT/FAZ L9 82 C4
Sundridge St TOX L8 * 133 F5
Sunfield Cl GTS/LS CH66 195 G6
Sunfield Rd MOR/LEA CH46 109 K5
Sunflower Cl STHEL WA9 104 E6
Sunlight St NPK/KEN L6 114 A2
Sunloch Cl WLT/FAZ L9 83 G3
Sunningdale MOR/LEA CH46 129 H1
Sunningdale Av WDN WA8 157 G2
Sunningdale Cl HUY L36 116 C6
WARRW/BUR WA5 121 K1
Sunningdale Dr BEB CH63 183 J1
CSBY/BLUN L23 68 D3
PEN/TH CH61 148 D6
Sunningdale Gdns FMBY L37 48 E2
Sunningdale Rd
WAL/NB CH45 95 F5
WAV L15 134 A1
Sunningdale Wy NSTN CH64 191 K5
Sunny Bank BEB CH63 150 C5
GR/UP/WCH CH49 129 G3
Sunnybank Av
CL/PREN CH43 130 A5
Sunnybank Cl NEWLW WA12 106 C1
Sunny Bank Rd CHLDW L16 134 E2
Sunnydale RAIN/WH L35 119 F4
Sunnyfields ORM L39 46 A6
Sunnygate Rd ALL/GAR L19 * 153 H3
Sunnymede Dr MGHL L31 62 B4
Sunny Rd CHTN/BK PR9 23 J3
Sunnyside EP CH65 6 E2
ORM L39 53 G6
STHP PR8 27 G4
TOX L8 133 F4
WARRW/BUR WA5 141 F3
Sunnyside La RUNC WA7 178 D1
Sunnyside Rd AIMK WN4 78 E3
CSBY/BLUN L23 68 D6
Sunrise Cl ALL/GAR L19 153 J4
Sunsdale Rd CALD/MH L18 * 134 B4
Sunset Cl NWD/KWIPK L33 73 F4
Superior Cl NTHLY L27 136 B4
Surby Cl CHLDW L16 135 F1
Surlingham Gdns STHEL WA9 119 G1
Surrey Av GR/UP/WCH CH49 129 F4
Surrey Dr WKBY CH48 146 D3
Surrey St BTL L20 5 G2
CLVPS L1 8 E7
RUNC WA7 10 D5
WAL/EG CH44 111 G4
WARRS WA4 143 G6
Surridge KNUT WA16 165 K6
Susan Dr WARRW/BUR WA5 140 E4
Susan Gv MOR/LEA CH46 128 E1
Susan St WDN WA8 158 D1
Sussex Cl BTL L20 5 G2
PEN/TH CH61 167 J1
Sussex Gv STHEL WA9 104 A3
Sussex Rd CHTN/BK PR9 15 H5
MGHL L31 71 G2
STHP PR8 28 B1
WKBY CH48 127 H6
Sussex St BTL L20 5 H3
CSBY/WL L22 * 80 D1
WDN WA8 19 J1
Sutch La BRSC L40 39 H5
Sutcliffe St NPK/KEN L6 113 K4
Sutherland Ct RUNC WA7 11 F4
Sutherland Dr
PS/BROM CH62 184 A3
Sutherland Rd PR/KW L34 118 A1
Sutton Av NSTN CH64 191 K3
Sutton Cswy FROD/HEL WA6 187 H5
Sutton Cl PS/BROM CH62 184 B4
Sutton Fold STHEL WA9 104 B5
Sutton Hall Dr GTS/LS CH66 194 D3
Sutton Hall Gdns GTS/LS CH66 194 D3
Sutton Heath Rd STHEL WA9 119 G1
Sutton Moss Rd STHEL WA9 104 D4
Sutton Oak Dr STHEL WA9 104 A4
Sutton Park Dr STHEL WA9 104 A6
Sutton Rd FMBY L37 48 E4
STHEL WA9 104 B4
WAL/NB CH45 95 H6
Suttons La FMBY L37 50 A3
WDN WA8 18 E6
Sutton St CLB/OSW/ST L13 114 C2
RUNC WA7 11 G5
WARR WA1 17 F6
Sutton Wy EP CH65 6 A6
GTS/LS CH66 195 H5
Sutton Wood Rd
SPK/HALE L24 173 H2
Swainson Rd AIN/FAZ L10 83 H4
Swale Av RAIN/WH L35 118 E4
Swaledale Av RAIN/WH L35 119 F4
Swaledale Cl PS/BROM CH62 184 B2
WARRW/BUR WA5 141 G2
Swalegate MGHL L31 62 A5
Swale Rd EP CH65 195 K2
Swallow Cl
GOL/RIS/CUL WA3 * 125 H3
NTHLY L27 136 C4
NWD/KWIPK L33 72 D2
WD/CROXPK L12 99 K2
Swallow Ct ECCL WA10 12 A5
Swallowfield Gdns
WARRS WA4 162 E6
Swallow Flds WLT/FAZ L9 98 D1
Swallowhurst Crs
NG/CROX L11 98 E3
Swanage Cl WARRS WA4 162 D1
Swan Av STHEL WA9 104 E3
Swan Cl GTS/LS CH66 202 A1
Swan Crs WAV L15 134 C1
Swan Delph ORM L39 53 G3
Swanfield Wk
GOL/RIS/CUL WA3 92 A1
Swan Gdns STHEL WA9 119 G1
Swan Hey MGHL L31 * 71 H2
Swan La ORM L39 62 C1
Swanpool La ORM L39 53 G3
Swan Rd NEWLW WA12 105 J1
Swansea Cl ALL/GAR L19 153 J5
Swanside Av DV/KA/FCH L14 115 J4
Swanside Rd DV/KA/FCH L14 115 J4
Swanston Av ANF/KKDL L4 97 J4
Swan St CLB/OSW/ST L13 114 D4
Swan Wk MGHL L31 71 H2
Sweden Gv CSBY/WL L22 * 80 E2
Sweet Brier Ct STHEL WA9 120 B5
Sweetfield Gdns GTS/LS CH66 195 G2
Sweetfield Rd GTS/LS CH66 195 G2
Sweeting St CLVP L2 8 C4
Swift Cl WARRN/WOL WA2 124 A4
Swift Gv WD/CROXPK L12 99 K1
Swift's Cl NTHTN L30 70 A5
Swift's Fold SKEL WN8 55 K5
Swift's La NTHTN L30 70 A5
Swift St ECCL WA10 13 H2
Swinbrook Gn NG/CROX L11 98 D3
Swinburne Cl CHLDW L16 135 G1
Swinburne Rd ECCL WA10 12 A2
Swindale Av
WARRN/WOL WA2 123 H4
Swindale Cl TOX L8 133 G2
Swinden Cl RUNC WA7 * 178 C3
Swinderby Dr MGHL L31 72 A6
Swindon Cl EV L5 97 F6
GR/UP/WCH CH49 128 D5
Swindon St EV L5 97 F6
Swinford Av WDN WA8 159 F1
Swisspine Gdns STHEL WA9 102 E6
Swiss Rd NPK/KEN L6 114 A4
Sword Wk NG/CROX L11 99 G2
Swynnerton Wy WDN WA8 139 G4
Sybil Rd ANF/KKDL L4 97 J6
Sycamore Av CSBY/BLUN L23 69 G3
GOL/RIS/CUL WA3 92 B2
GR/UP/WCH CH49 128 E3
HLWD L26 155 H5
NEWLW WA12 106 C2
RNFD/HAY WA11 89 K6
WDN WA8 158 C1
Sycamore Cl ECCL WA10 102 D1
GR/UP/WCH CH49 128 E2
WLT/FAZ L9 98 A2
Sycamore Dr GTS/LS CH66 202 D2
LYMM WA13 145 J5
RUNC WA7 187 K3
SKEL WN8 56 A3
Sycamore Gdns ECCL WA10 88 B5
Sycamore Gv FMBY L37 48 C4
Sycamore La
WARRW/BUR WA5 141 J3
Sycamore Pk CALD/MH L18 154 A1
Sycamore Ri
GR/UP/WCH CH49 147 K1
Sycamore Rd CSBY/WL L22 81 F1
HUY L36 116 E6
RF/TRAN CH42 131 G5
RUNC WA7 177 F5
Sydenham Av AIG/SPK L17 133 H4
Sydney St RUNC WA7 176 A6
WLT/FAZ L9 82 D5
Syers Ct WARR WA1 143 H1
Sylvan Ct WLTN L25 154 D2
Sylvandale Gv
PS/BROM CH62 171 F3
Sylvania Rd ANF/KKDL L4 97 J3
Sylvia Cl AIN/FAZ L10 84 A5
Sylvia Crs WARRN/WOL WA2 123 K6
Synge St WARRN/WOL WA2 143 F2
Syren St BTL L20 96 E5
Syston Av RNFD/HAY WA11 89 F5
Sytch Cft NSTN CH64 191 K1

T

Tabby Nook KIRK/FR/WAR PR4 25 K4
Tabley Av WDN WA8 157 J1
Tabley Cl CL/PREN CH43 130 C6
Tabley Gdns STHEL WA9 119 F1
Tabley Rd WAV L15 133 J2
Tabley St CLVPS L1 8 E7
Tace Cl TOX L8 132 E2
Tadgers La FROD/HEL WA6 186 A6
Tadlow Cl FMBY L37 48 C4
Taggart Av CHLDW L16 134 E3
Tagus Cl TOX L8 133 G3
Tagus St TOX L8 133 G3
Tailor's La MGHL L31 71 H1
Talaton Cl CHTN/BK PR9 20 D6
Talbot Av BEB CH63 169 G4
NSTN CH64 192 A3
Talbot Cl ECCL WA10 12 E4
GOL/RIS/CUL WA3 125 G4
NSTN CH64 192 A3
Talbot Ct CL/PREN CH43 130 D5
HUY L36 116 D6
Talbot Dr STHP PR8 14 E6
Talbot Gdns NSTN CH64 192 A3
Talbot Rd CL/PREN CH43 130 D5
GTS/LS CH66 195 J6
Talbot St AIMK WN4 * 79 J5
GOL/RIS/CUL WA3 92 B3
STHP PR8 14 D7
Talbotville Rd
CLB/OSW/ST L13 115 G6
Talgarth Wy WLTN L25 135 H2
Taliesin St EV L5 113 F2
Talisman Cl RUNC WA7 178 C6
Talisman Wy BTL L20 4 B2
Talland Cl HLWD L26 155 H2
Tallarn Rd KKBY L32 84 A1
Tall Trees STHEL WA9 103 K5
Talman Gv AIMK WN4 79 J6
Talton Rd WAV L15 133 J2
Tamar Cl NPK/KEN L6 113 J3
Tamar Gv MOR/LEA CH46 128 E2
Tamarisk Gdns STHEL WA9 102 E6
Tamar Rd RNFD/HAY WA11 90 B5
Tamerton Cl CALD/MH L18 154 B1
The Tamneys SKEL WN8 56 B4
Tamworth St ECCL WA10 12 C4
Tanar Cl BEB CH63 170 D2
Tanat Dr CALD/MH L18 134 C5
Tancred Rd ANF/KKDL L4 97 J6
WAL/NB CH45 111 G2
Tanfields SKEL WN8 56 B4
Tan House La
WARRW/BUR WA5 122 A2
WDN WA8 19 H3
Tanhouse Rd CSBY/BLUN L23 69 J4
SKEL WN8 56 E5
Tankersley Gv
WARRW/BUR WA5 141 H4
Tanner's La GOL/RIS/CUL WA3 92 C3
WARRN/WOL WA2 16 C3
Tannery La NSTN CH64 191 K1
WARRW/BUR WA5 140 D6
Tanning Ct WARR WA1 16 E5
Tansley Cl WKBY CH48 147 F1
Tanworth Gv MOR/LEA CH46 109 F6
Tapley Pl CLB/OSW/ST L13 114 D5

Taplow Cl *WARRS* WA4 162 D5
Taplow St *ANF/KKDL* L4 113 K1
Tapton Wy *CLB/OSW/ST* L13 114 C6
Tarbock Rd *HUY* L36 116 D6
SPK/HALE L24 173 J1
Tarbot Hey *MOR/LEA* CH46 128 D1
Target Rd *HES* CH60 167 F5
Tariff St *EV* L5 113 F2
Tarleswood *SKEL* WN8 56 B4
Tarleton Cl *HLWD* L26 155 H3
Tarleton Rd *CHTN/BK* PR9 23 J5
Tarleton St *CLVPS* L1 8 E4
Tarlscough La *BRSC* L40 31 H6
Tarlswood *SKEL* WN8 56 B4
Tarlton Cl *RAIN/WH* L35 118 C2
Tarnbeck *RUNC* WA7 178 B6
Tarn Brow *ORM* L39 53 G2
Tarn Cl *AIMK* WN4 79 G4
Tarn Ct *WARR* WA1 144 E2
Tarn Gv *RNFD/HAY* WA11 88 E3
Tarn Rd *FMBY* L37 48 D2
Tarnway *GOL/RIS/CUL* WA3 93 G4
Tarporley Cl *CL/PREN* CH43 130 C6
Tarporley Rd *GTS/LS* CH66 195 H5
Tarran Dr *MOR/LEA* CH46 109 H5
Tarran Rd *MOR/LEA* CH46 109 H5
Tarran Wy East
MOR/LEA CH46 109 H5
Tarran Wy North
MOR/LEA CH46 109 H5
Tarran Wy South
MOR/LEA CH46 109 H5
Tarran Wy West
MOR/LEA CH46 109 H4
Tarvin Cl *CHTN/BK* PR9 21 G6
EP CH65 6 E7
GOL/RIS/CUL WA3 93 F4
RUNC WA7 187 F1
STHEL WA9 119 K3
Tarvin Rd *FROD/HEL* WA6 200 C6
PS/BROM CH62 184 C3
Tasker Ter *RAIN/WH* L35 118 E3
Tasman Cl *WARRW/BUR* WA5 141 K1
Tasman Gv *STHEL* WA9 103 G6
Tate Cl *WDN* WA8 * 157 J1
Tate St *ANF/KKDL* L4 97 H5
Tatlock Cl *WGNW/BIL/OR* WN5 77 H4
Tatlock St *EV* L5 112 E3
Tattersall Rd *LITH* L21 81 H4
Tattersall Wy *EHL/KEN* L7 114 C5
Tatton Ct *WARR* WA1 * 144 C1
Tatton Dr *AIMK* WN4 78 E4
Tatton Rd *RF/TRAN* CH42 2 D7
WLT/FAZ L9 82 D5
Taunton Av *STHEL* WA9 120 B2
Taunton Dr *AIN/FAZ* L10 83 H1
Taunton Rd *HUY* L36 117 H5
WAL/NB CH45 110 E1
Taunton St *WAV* L15 133 K1
Taurus Pk *WARRW/BUR* WA5 122 D3
Taurus Rd *DV/KA/FCH* L14 116 A3
Tavener Cl *BEB* CH63 183 K2
Tavington Rd *HLWD* L26 155 K2
Tavistock Dr *STHP* PR8 33 H3
Tavistock Rd *WAL/NB* CH45 110 E1
WARRW/BUR WA5 141 F5
Tavlin Av *WARRW/BUR* WA5 123 F6
Tavy Rd *NPK/KEN* L6 113 J3
Tawd Rd *SKEL* WN8 56 E5
Tawd St *ANF/KKDL* L4 97 G5
Tawny Ct *RUNC* WA7 177 H6
Taylor Av *ORM* L39 46 A6
Taylor Cl *STHEL* WA9 104 C5
Taylor Rd *RNFD/HAY* WA11 90 E5
Taylors Cl *WLT/FAZ* L9 97 H2
Taylor's La *WARRW/BUR* WA5 159 H1
Taylors Rw *RUNC* WA7 11 J5
Taylor St *BIRK* CH41 3 G2
EV L5 113 F2
SKEL WN8 55 J4
STHEL WA9 104 C5
WARRS WA4 161 K2
WDN WA8 19 G1
Teakwood Cl *NPK/KEN* L6 113 K2
Teal Cl *ORM* L39 53 G3
RNFD/HAY WA11 88 E5
WARRN/WOL WA2 124 A4
Teal Gv *GOL/RIS/CUL* WA3 125 H4
HLWD L26 155 H2
Teals Wy *HES* CH60 167 H5
Teasville Rd *CALD/MH* L18 135 F5
Tebay Cl *MGHL* L31 62 D5
Tebay Rd *PS/BROM* CH62 171 G5
Teck St *EHL/KEN* L7 113 J5
Tedburn Cl *WLTN* L25 135 K5
Tedbury Wk *KKBY* L32 84 D4
Tedder Av *CHTN/BK* PR9 23 J6
Tedder Sq *WDN* WA8 157 J3
Teddington Cl *WARRS* WA4 162 D6
Teehey Cl *BEB* CH63 150 C5
Teehey Gdns *BEB* CH63 150 C5
Teehey La *BEB* CH63 150 C5
Tees Cl *ANF/KKDL* L4 97 F4
Tees Ct *EP* CH65 195 K2
Teesdale Cl *WARRW/BUR* WA5 141 G2
Teesdale Rd *BEB* CH63 170 A1
RNFD/HAY WA11 90 B4
Tees Pl *ANF/KKDL* L4 97 F4
Tees St *ANF/KKDL* L4 97 F4
Teilo St *TOX* L8 133 F4
Telary Cl *EV* L5 112 E2
Telegraph Rd *PEN/TH* CH61 167 G1
WKBY CH48 147 H5
Telford Cl *CL/PREN* CH43 130 E5
WDN WA8 138 C5
Telford Dr *STHEL* WA9 104 D6
Telford Rd *EP* CH65 7 H7
Tempest Hey *CLVP* L2 8 C3
Temple Ct *CLVP* L2 8 D4
GOL/RIS/CUL WA3 125 G1
Temple La *CLVP* L2 8 D3
Templemore Av *CALD/MH* L18 134 B6
Templemore Rd
CL/PREN CH43 130 D5
Temple Rd *RF/TRAN* CH42 150 B1
Temple St *CLVP* L2 8 D4
Templeton Crs *WD/CROXPK* L12 99 F4
Templeton Dr
WARRN/WOL WA2 124 C4
Tenbury Cl *WARRW/BUR* WA5 122 A6
Tenbury Dr *AIMK* WN4 78 E5
Tenby Av *LITH* L21 81 H2
Tenby Cl *WARRW/BUR* WA5 123 F5
Tenby Dr *MOR/LEA* CH46 129 G2
RUNC WA7 177 G3
Tenby St *EV* L5 113 J1
Tennis St *ECCL* WA10 12 B2
Tennis St North *ECCL* WA10 12 C1
Tennyson Av *RF/TRAN* CH42 * 150 E2
Tennyson Dr *ORM* L39 45 H5
WARRN/WOL WA2 123 J5
Tennyson Rd *EP* CH65 6 A6
HUY L36 136 D1
WDN WA8 18 C1
Tennyson St *BTL* L20 4 C1
STHEL WA9 119 J5
Tennyson Wy *KKBY* L32 84 C2
Tensing Cl *WARRW/BUR* WA5 141 J1
Tensing Rd *MGHL* L31 62 B6
Tenterden St *EV* L5 * 113 F3
Tenth Av *WLT/FAZ* L9 83 G4
Terence Av *WARR* WA1 143 J2
Terence Rd *CHLDW* L16 134 E3
Terminus Rd *HUY* L36 116 B2
PS/BROM CH62 171 F2
Tern Cl *NWD/KWIPK* L33 72 D2
WDN WA8 139 G5
Ternhall Rd *WLT/FAZ* L9 98 D1
Tern Wy *ECCL* WA10 102 C6
MOR/LEA CH46 109 F6
Terrace Rd *WDN* WA8 158 B6
Terret Cft *STBRV* L28 100 B6
Tetbury St *BIRK* CH41 2 C6
Tetchill Cl *GTS/LS* CH66 202 B1
RUNC WA7 178 C5
Tetlow St *ANF/KKDL* L4 97 H5
Tetlow Wy *ANF/KKDL* L4 97 H5
Teversham *SKEL* WN8 56 B3
Tewit Hall Cl *SPK/HALE* L24 173 H2
Tewit Hall Rd *SPK/HALE* L24 173 H2
Tewkesbury *SKEL* WN8 * 56 A3
Tewkesbury Cl *GTS/LS* CH66 202 C3
WD/CROXPK L12 99 K1
WLTN L25 155 F1
Tewkesbury Rd
GOL/RIS/CUL WA3 92 C3
Teynham Crs *NG/CROX* L11 98 D3
Thackeray Cl *TOX* L8 * 132 E3
Thackeray Gdns *NTHTN* L30 82 A3
Thackeray Pl *TOX* L8 132 E3
Thackeray Sq *TOX* L8 132 E3
Thackeray St *TOX* L8 132 E3
Thackray Rd *ECCL* WA10 102 E5
Thames Cl *WARRN/WOL* WA2 123 K5
Thamesdale *EP* CH65 6 B7
Thames Gdns *EP* CH65 195 K6
Thames Rd *STHEL* WA9 120 A1
Thames Side *EP* CH65 196 A6
Thames St *TOX* L8 133 G3
Thanet *SKEL* WN8 56 B3
Thatto Heath Rd *STHEL* WA9 103 F6
Thealby Cl *SKEL* WN8 56 A3
Thelwall La *WARRS* WA4 143 J6
Thelwall New Rd *WARRS* WA4 144 A6
Thelwall Rd *GTS/LS* CH66 195 H5
Thelwall Viad *LYMM* WA13 145 F4
Thermal Rd *PS/BROM* CH62 171 F1
Thetford Rd
WARRW/BUR WA5 141 F3
Thewlis St *WARRW/BUR* WA5 142 B4
Thickwood Moss La
RNFD/HAY WA11 75 G4
Thingwall Av *DV/KA/FCH* L14 115 H5
Thingwall Dr *PEN/TH* CH61 148 D5
Thingwall Gra *PEN/TH* CH61 148 E5
Thingwall Hall Dr
DV/KA/FCH L14 115 H5
Thingwall La *DV/KA/FCH* L14 115 H4
Thingwall Rd *PEN/TH* CH61 148 C5
WAV L15 134 C1
Thingwall Rd East
PEN/TH CH61 148 D4
Third Av *AIN/FAZ* L10 83 H4
CL/PREN CH43 129 J3
CSBY/BLUN L23 * 68 E5
RUNC WA7 177 J5
WLT/FAZ L9 83 G4
Thirlmere Av *AIMK* WN4 79 H5
CL/PREN CH43 129 K3
FMBY L37 49 G3
LITH L21 82 A3
RNFD/HAY WA11 88 E3
SKEL WN8 57 K6
WARRN/WOL WA2 123 J4
Thirlmere Cl *FROD/HEL* WA6 201 G1
MGHL L31 62 C5
Thirlmere Dr *LITH* L21 82 A3
STHP PR8 33 H6
WAL/NB CH45 111 H2
Thirlmere Gn *EV* L5 113 J2
Thirlmere Ms *HTWN* L38 * 59 G3
Thirlmere Rd *EP* CH65 203 G1
EV L5 113 J2
GOL/RIS/CUL WA3 92 D2
HTWN L38 59 G3
NSTN CH64 191 K3
Thirlmere Wk *NWD/KWIPK* L33 72 C5
Thirlmere Wy *WDN* WA8 157 G3
Thirlstane St *AIG/SPK* L17 133 G6
Thirsk *SKEL* WN8 56 A3
Thirsk Cl *RUNC* WA7 187 F1
Thistledown Cl *AIG/SPK* L17 133 F6
Thistleton Av *BIRK* CH41 130 C1
Thistleton Ms *CHTN/BK* PR9 15 H3
Thistlewood Rd *EHL/KEN* L7 114 C5
Thistley Hey Rd *KKBY* L32 84 E1
Thomas Cl *ALL/GAR* L19 153 K6
EP CH65 203 F1
Thomas Ct *RUNC* WA7 177 J6
Thomas Dr *DV/KA/FCH* L14 115 G5
RAIN/WH L35 117 J3
Thomas La *DV/KA/FCH* L14 115 H4
Thomasons Bridge La
WARRS WA4 161 H5
Thomas St *BIRK* CH41 3 G6
GOL/RIS/CUL WA3 92 B3
RUNC WA7 11 F3
WDN WA8 18 C6
Thomaston St *EV* L5 113 G1
Thomas Winder Ct *EV* L5 * 113 F1
Thompson Av *ORM* L39 46 A6
Thompson St *AIMK* WN4 79 J5
BIRK CH41 131 H5
ECCL WA10 103 F4
GOL/RIS/CUL WA3 125 G2
Thomson Rd *LITH* L21 81 H4
Thomson St *NPK/KEN* L6 113 K3
Thorburn Cl *PS/BROM* CH62 151 G3
Thorburn Crs *PS/BROM* CH62 151 G3
Thorburn Rd *PS/BROM* CH62 151 G3
Thorburn St *EHL/KEN* L7 113 K6
Thorley Cl *WAV* L15 114 E6
Thornaby Gv *STHEL* WA9 119 F1
Thornbeck Av *HTWN* L38 59 F4
Thornbeck Cl *WD/CROXPK* L12 99 K2
Thornbridge Av *BRSC* L40 38 E6
LITH L21 82 A3
Thornbrook Cl *WD/CROXPK* L12 99 H6
Thornbury *SKEL* WN8 56 B3
Thornbury Av
GOL/RIS/CUL WA3 93 F4
Thornbury Rd *ANF/KKDL* L4 98 A6
Thornbush Cl
GOL/RIS/CUL WA3 93 F2
Thorncliffe Rd *WAL/EG* CH44 111 G4
Thorn Cl *RUNC* WA7 177 F6
WARRW/BUR WA5 141 G6
Thorncroft Dr *PEN/TH* CH61 168 B1
Thorndale Rd *CSBY/WL* L22 80 E1
Thorndyke Cl *RAIN/WH* L35 119 G6
Thorne Dr *GTS/LS* CH66 194 E5
Thornes Rd *NPK/KEN* L6 113 K4
Thorness Cl
GR/UP/WCH CH49 * 147 K1
Thorneycroft Dr *WARR* WA1 17 G3
Thorneycroft St *BIRK* CH41 130 D1
Thornfield Cl
GOL/RIS/CUL WA3 92 D3
Thornfield Hey *BEB* CH63 170 C3
Thornfield Rd *CSBY/BLUN* L23 69 H3
WLT/FAZ L9 82 C6
Thornham Av *STHEL* WA9 104 A5
Thornham Cl
GR/UP/WCH CH49 129 H2
Thornhead La
WD/CROXPK L12 115 H1
Thornhill *ORM* L39 53 F4
Thornhill Rd *AIMK* WN4 78 B5
WAV L15 134 B2
Thornhills *WDN* WA8 138 A6
Thornholme Crs *NG/CROX* L11 98 E4
Thornhurst *KKBY* L32 84 D4
Thornleigh Av *PS/BROM* CH62 184 C4
Thornleigh Dr *GTS/LS* CH66 195 H3
Thornley Rd *LYMM* WA13 145 H6
MOR/LEA CH46 128 C2
Thorn Rd *ECCL* WA10 102 E2
RUNC WA7 177 F6
WARR WA1 143 K1
Thorns Dr *GR/UP/WCH* CH49 147 K1
The Thorns *MGHL* L31 61 K5
Thornton *WDN* WA8 * 157 K3
Thornton Av *BEB* CH63 150 C3
BTL L20 82 A5
Thornton Cl *AIMK* WN4 78 E5
Thornton Common Rd
BEB CH63 169 H6
Thornton Crs *HES* CH60 181 G1
Thorntondale Dr
WARRW/BUR WA5 141 F2
Thornton Gv *BEB* CH63 150 B3
Thornton Rd *BEB* CH63 150 C3
BTL L20 5 F1
CHLDW L16 115 J6
CHTN/BK PR9 23 H6
EP CH65 7 H7
WAL/NB CH45 111 G1
WARRW/BUR WA5 141 J5
Thornton St *BIRK* CH41 130 D1
LITH L21 81 J5
Thorntree Cl *AIG/SPK* L17 133 F6
Thorntree Gn *WARRS* WA4 163 G6
Thornwood *SKEL* WN8 56 B3
Thornwood Cl *NPK/KEN* L6 113 K2
Thornwythe Gv *GTS/LS* CH66 195 H5
Thornycroft Rd *WAV* L15 133 J3
Thoroughgood Cl *BRSC* L40 46 D1
Thorpe *SKEL* WN8 56 B3
Thorpe Bank *RF/TRAN* CH42 150 E3
Thorstone Dr *PEN/TH* CH61 147 K4
Thorsway *RF/TRAN* CH42 150 E1
WKBY CH48 146 E3
Threadneedle Ct *STHEL* WA9 104 D5
Three Butt La
WD/CROXPK L12 114 D1
Three Oaks Cl *BRSC* L40 47 H1
Three Pools *CHTN/BK* PR9 24 A2
Three Sisters Rd *AIMK* WN4 79 G2
Three Tuns La *FMBY* L37 49 F2
Threlfalls La *CHTN/BK* PR9 23 H3
Threlfall St *TOX* L8 133 F5
Thresher Av
GR/UP/WCH CH49 * 128 D5
The Threshers *NTHTN* L30 * 70 E5
Throne Rd *NG/CROX* L11 99 G2
Thurcroft Dr *SKEL* WN8 56 A3
Thurlby Cl *AIMK* WN4 79 J5
Thurlow *GOL/RIS/CUL* WA3 93 F4
Thurne Wy *WLTN* L25 135 H3
Thurnham St *NPK/KEN* L6 114 A2
Thursby Cl *KKBY* L32 84 E3
STHP PR8 33 H6
Thursby Crs *KKBY* L32 84 E3
Thursby Rd *PS/BROM* CH62 171 G3
Thursby Wk *KKBY* L32 84 E3
Thurstaston Rd *HES* CH60 167 J4
PEN/TH CH61 147 J5
Thurston *SKEL* WN8 56 A3
Thurston Cl *WARRW/BUR* WA5 142 A3
Thurston Rd *ANF/KKDL* L4 113 K1
Thynne St *WARR* WA1 16 B6
Tibbs Cross La *WDN* WA8 120 B6
Tichbourne Wy *NPK/KEN* L6 9 K1
Tickle Av *STHEL* WA9 104 B2
Tidal La *WARR* WA1 143 J1
Tideswell Cl *EHL/KEN* L7 133 G1
Tide Wy *WAL/NB* CH45 94 E5
Tilbey Dr *FROD/HEL* WA6 200 D1
Tilbrook Dr *STHEL* WA9 120 B1
Tilbury Pl *RUNC* WA7 188 C1
Tilcroft *SKEL* WN8 56 A3
Tildsley Crs *RUNC* WA7 186 C1
Tilley St *WARR* WA1 16 E3
Tillotson Cl *TOX* L8 132 D4
Tilman Cl *WARRW/BUR* WA5 141 J1
Tilney St *WLT/FAZ* L9 82 D5
Tilstock Av *PS/BROM* CH62 151 G3
Tilstock Cl *HLWD* L26 155 K1
Tilstock Crs *CL/PREN* CH43 149 J2
Tilston Av *WARRS* WA4 143 K5
Tilston Cl *NG/CROX* L11 98 B2
Tilston Rd *KKBY* L32 84 B1
WAL/NB CH45 111 G1
WLT/FAZ L9 98 B1
Timberscombe Gdns
WARR WA1 144 D3
Time Pk *RAIN/WH* L35 118 B2
Timmis Cl
WARRN/WOL WA2 124 C4
Timmis Crs *WDN* WA8 18 C2
Timms Cl *FMBY* L37 41 F6
Timms La *FMBY* L37 41 F6
Timon Av *BTL* L20 5 J2
Timor Av *STHEL* WA9 103 G5
Timperley Av *WARRS* WA4 143 K5
Timperley St *WDN* WA8 * 18 E4
Timpron St *EHL/KEN* L7 133 H1
Timway Dr *WD/CROXPK* L12 99 J5
Tinas Wy *GR/UP/WCH* CH49 129 H4
Tinling Cl *PR/KW* L34 118 A1
Tinsley Av *STHP* PR8 28 B4
Tinsley Cl *HLWD* L26 155 H1
Tinsley's La *STHP* PR8 28 C6
Tinsley St *ANF/KKDL* L4 97 J6
WARRS WA4 143 J6
Tintagel *SKEL* WN8 55 K3
Tintagel Cl *RUNC* WA7 188 B1
Tintagel Rd *NG/CROX* L11 84 C6
Tintern Av *AIMK* WN4 79 J6
Tintern Cl *WARRW/BUR* WA5 * 122 E5
Tintern Dr *FMBY* L37 49 H3
MOR/LEA CH46 129 F1
Tiptree Cl *WD/CROXPK* L12 99 K1
Titchfield St *EV* L5 112 E3
Tithebarn Cl *HES* CH60 * 167 K6
Tithebarn Dr *NSTN* CH64 181 G5
Tithebarn Gv *WAV* L15 134 B2
Tithe Barn La *KKBY* L32 84 C2
Tithebarn La *MGHL* L31 71 K4
Tithebarn Rd *AIMK* WN4 90 B1
CSBY/BLUN L23 69 G4
PR/KW L34 100 D1
STHP PR8 28 B1
STHP PR8 15 K6
Tithebarn St *CLVP* L2 8 C3
SKEL WN8 * 57 K6
Titherington Wy *AIG/SPK* L17 133 J3
The Tithings *RUNC* WA7 177 H4
Tiverton Av *SKEL* WN8 56 A3
WAL/EG CH44 111 H3
Tiverton Cl *HUY* L36 117 H5
WDN WA8 138 B6
Tiverton Rd *HLWD* L26 155 H5
Tiverton Sq *WARRW/BUR* WA5 141 F5
Tiverton St *WAV* L15 133 K1
Tobermory Cl *RNFD/HAY* WA11 89 K6
Tobin Cl *EV* L5 112 E3
Tobin St *WAL/EG* CH44 111 K3
Tobruk Rd *HUY* L36 116 D3
Todd Rd *STHEL* WA9 13 J6
Todd's La *CHTN/BK* PR9 21 K5
Toft Cl *WDN* WA8 18 A2
Toft St *EHL/KEN* L7 114 A5
Toftwood Av *RAIN/WH* L35 119 F6
Tokenspire Pk
NWD/KWIPK L33 * 85 G4
Toleman Av *BEB* CH63 151 F6
Toll *BIRK* CH41 3 H5
WAL/EG CH44 111 J5
Toll Bar Rd *WARRN/WOL* WA2 123 G4
Tollemache Rd *BIRK* CH41 130 B1
Tollemache St *WAL/NB* CH45 95 J4
Tollerton Rd *WD/CROXPK* L12 114 D1
Tollgate Crs *BRSC* L40 38 C6
Tollgate Rd *BRSC* L40 46 B1
Tolpuddle Rd *WLTN* L25 135 G6
Tolpuddle Wy *ANF/KKDL* L4 97 F5
Tolver St *ECCL* WA10 13 H4
Tomlinson Av
WARRN/WOL WA2 143 G1
Tom Mann Cl *VAUX/LVPD* L3 9 F2
Tonbridge Cl *SPK/HALE* L24 173 G1
Tonbridge Dr *AIN/FAZ* L10 71 G6
Tongbarn *SKEL* WN8 56 A3
Toothill Cl *AIMK* WN4 79 G4
Top Acre Rd *SKEL* WN8 56 E6
Topaz Cl *BTL* L20 5 K7
Topcliffe Gv *WD/CROXPK* L12 100 A2
Topgate Cl *HES* CH60 168 B5
Topham Dr *WLT/FAZ* L9 82 E1
Topping Ct *GOL/RIS/CUL* WA3 124 D3
Top Rd *FROD/HEL* WA6 201 G4
Topsham Cl *WLTN* L25 135 K5
Torcross Cl *CHTN/BK* PR9 20 D6
Torcross Wy *HLWD* L26 155 H3
WLTN L25 135 K5
Tordelow Cl *NPK/KEN* L6 113 J3
Toronto Cl *HUY* L36 116 D1
Toronto St *WAL/EG* CH44 112 A4
Torquay Dr
WGNW/BIL/OR WN5 77 H1
Torr Dr *PS/BROM* CH62 171 J6
Torridon Gv *GTS/LS* CH66 195 J6
Torrington Dr *HLWD* L26 155 H5
PEN/TH CH61 148 E5
Torrington Rd *ALL/GAR* L19 153 J4
WAL/EG CH44 111 G3
Torrisholme Rd *WLT/FAZ* L9 98 B2
Torr St *EV* L5 113 G1
Torus Rd *CLB/OSW/ST* L13 114 E3
Tor View Rd *WAV* L15 134 B3
Torwood *CL/PREN* CH43 130 A2
Tothale Turn *NTHLY* L27 136 C5
Totland Cl *WARRW/BUR* WA5 140 D2
Totnes Av *HLWD* L26 155 J2
Totnes Dr *CHTN/BK* PR9 20 D6
Totnes Rd *NG/CROX* L11 84 B6
Tourer Ter *BRSC* L40 37 F5
Tourney Gn *WARRW/BUR* WA5 122 A5
Towcester St *LITH* L21 81 J5
Tower Buildings
CHTN/BK PR9 * 15 G2
Tower End *FMBY* L37 40 C6
Tower Gdns *VAUX/LVPD* L3 8 B4
Tower Hl *ORM* L39 46 A6
RF/TRAN CH42 131 G6
Tower Hill Rd *SKEL* WN8 67 J2
Tower La *LYMM* WA13 165 G1
RUNC WA7 178 B6
Tower Nook *SKEL* WN8 67 J2
Tower Prom *WAL/NB* CH45 95 J4
Tower Quays *BIRK* CH41 * 3 F1
Tower Rd *BIRK* CH41 3 F1
RF/TRAN CH42 * 131 G6
Tower Rd North *HES* CH60 167 J3
Tower Rd South *HES* CH60 167 K4
Towers Av *MGHL* L31 62 A5
Towers Rd *CHLDW* L16 134 D3
The Towers
RF/TRAN CH42 * 150 C1
Tower St *VAUX/LVPD* L3 132 C4
Tower Wy *WLTN* L25 135 H6
Tower Whf *BIRK* CH41 3 F1
Towneley Ct *WDN* WA8 18 C2
Town End Cl *ORM* L39 53 H1
Townfield Av *AIMK* WN4 91 G1
Townfield Cl *CL/PREN* CH43 130 B6
Townfield Gdns *BEB* CH63 150 E4
Townfield La *BEB* CH63 150 E4
CL/PREN CH43 130 C6
FROD/HEL WA6 201 F2
Townfield Rd *RUNC* WA7 * 178 B3
WARRN/WOL WA2 * 123 G2
WKBY CH48 146 C1
Townfields *AIMK* WN4 79 F6
Townfield Vw *RUNC* WA7 178 B3
Town Green La *ORM* L39 53 G5
Town Hl *WARR* WA1 16 D4
Town La *BEB* CH63 150 D5
NSTN CH64 192 A3
SPK/HALE L24 174 E4
STHP PR8 28 A5
Town Lane (Kew) *STHP* PR8 27 K4
Town Meadow La
MOR/LEA CH46 109 F6
Town Rd *RF/TRAN* CH42 131 G6
Town Rw *WD/CROXPK* L12 99 F6
Townsend Av *NG/CROX* L11 98 C2
Townsend La *CLB/OSW/ST* L13 98 B6
NPK/KEN L6 114 A1
Townsend St *BIRK* CH41 110 E6
EV L5 112 D1
Townsend Vw *LITH* L21 81 J1
NG/CROX L11 98 C2
Townsfield La
WARRN/WOL WA2 123 G2
Townshend Av *PEN/TH* CH61 148 A6
Town Sq *RUNC* WA7 * 177 J6
Town Vw *CL/PREN* CH43 2 B6
Town Wk *RUNC* WA7 * 177 J6
Towson St *EV* L5 113 H1
Toxteth Gv *TOX* L8 133 F5
Toxteth St *TOX* L8 132 E4
Tracy Dr *NEWLW* WA12 106 E2
Trafalgar Av *WAL/EG* CH44 111 K2
Trafalgar Ct *WDN* WA8 158 B5
Trafalgar Dr *BEB* CH63 170 C1
Trafalgar Rd *STHP* PR8 27 F4
WAL/EG CH44 111 J2
Trafalgar St *ECCL* WA10 12 B3
Trafalgar Wy *NPK/KEN* L6 9 K1
Trafford Av *WARRW/BUR* WA5 142 B1
Trafford Crs *RUNC* WA7 187 F1
Tragan Dr *WARRW/BUR* WA5 140 E6
Tramway Rd *AIG/SPK* L17 133 H6
Trans Pennine Trail *CLVP* L2 8 D5
MGHL L31 70 E3
NG/CROX L11 98 B3
TOX L8 133 G4
WDN WA8 175 H2
WLT/FAZ L9 82 E6
WLTN L25 135 G2
Trap Hl *FMBY* L37 48 C3
Trapwood Cl *ECCL* WA10 102 D2
Travandon Cl *AIN/FAZ* L10 * 84 A5
Travanson Cl *AIN/FAZ* L10 84 A5
Travers' Entry *STHEL* WA9 120 E1
Traverse St *STHEL* WA9 104 A2
Travis St *WDN* WA8 18 E3
Treborth St *TOX* L8 133 F4
Trecastle Rd *NWD/KWIPK* L33 73 F5
Tree Bank Cl *RUNC* WA7 176 D5
Treen Cl *CHTN/BK* PR9 20 E5
Treesdale Cl *STHP* PR8 27 G3
Tree Tops *NSTN* CH64 191 K4
Treetops Cl *WARR* WA1 143 J2
Treetops Dr *BIRK* CH41 110 D6
Treetop Vls *CHTN/BK* PR9 * 23 H1
Trefoil Cl *GOL/RIS/CUL* WA3 124 E2
Treforris Rd *WAL/NB* CH45 95 F6
Trefula Pk *WD/CROXPK* L12 114 E1
Trelawney Cl *WLTN* L25 135 J3
Tremore Cl *WD/CROXPK* L12 99 G4
Trenance Cl *RUNC* WA7 188 A2
Trendeal Rd *NG/CROX* L11 84 C6
Trent Av *DV/KA/FCH* L14 115 K5
MGHL L31 62 D5
Trent Cl *BRSC* L40 39 F4
RAIN/WH L35 118 D4
STHEL WA9 120 A2
WD/CROXPK L12 99 H2
WDN WA8 139 G5
Trentdale *EP* CH65 196 A6
Trentham Av *CALD/MH* L18 134 A4
Trentham Cl *WDN* WA8 139 G5
Trentham Rd *KKBY* L32 84 B2
WAL/EG CH44 111 J4
Trentham St *RUNC* WA7 10 B2
Trent Rd *AIMK* WN4 79 K4
RAIN/WH L35 118 D4
WGNW/BIL/OR WN5 77 F5
Trent St *EV* L5 112 E1
Trent Wy *HES* CH60 181 G1
LITH L21 81 H2
Tresham Dr *WARRS* WA4 163 F3
Tressel Dr *STHEL* WA9 119 J4
Tressell St *WLT/FAZ* L9 97 H2
Trevelyan St *WLT/FAZ* L9 97 H2
Treviot Cl *NWD/KWIPK* L33 72 C3
Trevor Dr *CSBY/BLUN* L23 69 G6

Trevor Rd BRSC L40 38 D5
STHP PR8 33 J5
WLT/FAZ L9 82 D5
The Triad BTL L20 4 E3
Trident Pk RUNC WA7 * 177 H6
Trimley Cl GR/UP/WCH CH49 129 F4
Tring Cl GR/UP/WCH CH49 129 H2
Trinity Ct GOL/RIS/CUL WA3 125 H2
Trinity Gdns AIMK WN4 78 E5
FROD/HEL WA6 187 F6
STHP PR8 14 D7
Trinity Gv CSBY/BLUN L23 80 C1
Trinity La BIRK CH41 3 F3
Trinity Ms CHTN/BK PR9 15 H4
Trinity Pl BTL L20 5 G5
WDN WA8 18 E5
Trinity Rd BTL L20 4 E6
HOY CH47 127 G2
WAL/EG CH44 111 H2
Trinity St BIRK CH41 2 C3
STHEL WA9 104 A1
Trinity Wk VAUX/LVPD L3 9 H1
Trispen Cl HLWD L26 155 H3
Trispen Rd NG/CROX L11 99 H1
Trispen Wk NG/CROX L11 * 99 H1
Triumph Wy SPK/HALE L24 154 C5
Triam Rd BTL L20 4 C3
Troon Cl BEB CH63 183 K2
RNFD/HAY WA11 89 K6
WD/CROXPK L12 115 J1
Trossach Cl WARRN/WOL WA2 124 A5
Trotwood Cl WLT/FAZ L9 83 G3
Troutbeck Av MGHL L31 62 C5
NEWLW WA12 105 J1
WARRW/BUR WA5 142 C1
Troutbeck Cl
GR/UP/WCH CH49 148 D1
RUNC WA7 187 K2
Troutbeck Gv RNFD/HAY WA11 88 E1
Troutbeck Rd AIMK WN4 79 H4
CALD/MH L18 134 E4
Trouville Rd ANF/KKDL L4 98 A6
Trowbridge St VAUX/LVPD L3 9 H4
Trueman Cl CL/PREN CH43 129 K1
Trueman St VAUX/LVPD L3 8 E2
Truman Cl WDN WA8 138 E6
Trumans La GTS/LS CH66 195 F2
Trundle Pie La ORM L39 44 A5
Truro Av CHTN/BK PR9 20 E6
NTHTN L30 70 C5
Truro Cl GTS/LS CH66 202 D3
RNFD/HAY WA11 89 G4
RUNC WA7 188 B1
WARR WA1 144 A1
Truro Rd WAV L15 134 B3
Truscott Rd BRSC L40 38 D5
Tudor Av BEB CH63 170 C2
WAL/EG CH44 112 A5
Tudor Cl EHL/KEN L7 9 K5
GTS/LS CH66 202 D3
RNFD/HAY WA11 75 F1
WARRS WA4 163 F1
Tudor Ct WARRS WA4 * 162 D2
Tudor Gra GR/UP/WCH CH49 128 E6
Tudor Rd CSBY/BLUN L23 68 E6
RF/TRAN CH42 131 H6
RUNC WA7 178 A2
STHP PR8 33 H3
WLTN L25 155 F4
Tudor St NPK/KEN L6 113 K4
Tudor Vw NWD/KWIPK L33 72 D4
Tudorville Rd BEB CH63 150 E6
Tudorway HES CH60 168 B5
Tue La WDN WA8 138 A3
Tuffins Cnr NTHLY L27 136 A4
Tulip Av BIRK CH41 130 C1
Tulip Gv WARRW/BUR WA5 142 B6
Tulip Rd RNFD/HAY WA11 90 E5
WAV L15 134 B2
Tulketh St STHP PR8 15 F5
Tullimore Rd CALD/MH L18 153 H2
Tullis St ECCL WA10 12 C7
Tulloch St NPK/KEN L6 113 K4
Tully Av NEWLW WA12 105 J2
Tumilty Av BTL L20 5 J2
Tunbridge Cl
WARRW/BUR WA5 141 H1
Tunnel Rd BIRK CH41 3 H5
EHL/KEN L7 133 G1
Tunnel Top North WARRS WA4 189 F3
Tunstall Cl GR/UP/WCH CH49 129 F4
Tunstall St EHL/KEN L7 133 H2
Tunstall's Wy STHEL WA9 120 B3
Tupelo Cl WD/CROXPK L12 99 K1
Tupman St TOX L8 132 E4
Turmar Av PEN/TH CH61 148 E5
Turnacre DV/KA/FCH L14 115 J4
FMBY L37 41 H5
Turnall Rd WDN WA8 157 G4
Turnberry SKEL WN8 55 K3
Turnberry Cl HUY L36 116 C6
LYMM WA13 145 H5
MOR/LEA CH46 109 F6
WD/CROXPK L12 115 K1
Turnberry Wy CHTN/BK PR9 21 G6
Turnbridge Rd MGHL L31 62 A4
Turner Av BTL L20 82 B5
Turner Cl TOX L8 133 F6
WDN WA8 138 C6
Turner Gv NWD/KWIPK L33 72 D3
Turner St BIRK CH41 2 C7
Turner's Vw NSTN CH64 181 J5
Turney Rd WAL/EG CH44 111 G3
Turnill Dr AIMK WN4 79 G6
Turning La STHP PR8 35 J1
Turnpike Rd ORM L39 52 E3
Turnstone Av NEWLW WA12 106 C1
Turnstone Cl WD/CROXPK L12 99 J2
Turnstone Dr HLWD L26 155 H2
Turret Hall Dr
GOL/RIS/CUL WA3 93 F3
Turret Rd WAL/NB CH45 111 G1
Turriff Dr BEB CH63 183 K3
Turriff Rd DV/KA/FCH L14 116 A2
Turrocks Cl NSTN CH64 191 K4
Turrocks Cft NSTN CH64 191 K4
Turton Cl GOL/RIS/CUL WA3 124 E2
Turton St EV L5 * 113 F1
GOL/RIS/CUL WA3 92 B3
Tuscan Cl WDN WA8 139 G4
Tuson Dr WDN WA8 138 E5
Tutor Bank Dr NEWLW WA12 106 D2
Tweed Cl NPK/KEN L6 114 A3
Tweedsmuir Cl
WARRN/WOL WA2 124 C3
Tweed St BIRK CH41 111 G6
Twenty Acre Rd
WARRW/BUR WA5 141 K1
Twickenham Dr HUY L36 116 C6
MOR/LEA CH46 110 A4
Twigden Cl AIN/FAZ L10 83 J3
Twig La HUY L36 116 C3
MGHL L31 62 B6
Twist Av GOL/RIS/CUL WA3 92 D3
Twistfield Cl STHP PR8 27 G2
Two Acre Gv GTS/LS CH66 202 D2
Two Butt La RAIN/WH L35 118 C2
Twomey Cl EV L5 112 E3
Twyford Av LITH L21 81 J2
Twyford Cl MGHL L31 * 62 C6
WDN WA8 139 G4
Twyford La WDN WA8 139 J3
Twyford St NPK/KEN L6 113 K1
Tyberton Pl WLTN L25 155 F5
Tyburn Cl BEB CH63 170 B3
Tyburn Rd BEB CH63 170 B3
Tyndall Av CSBY/WL L22 81 G3
Tyne Cl ANF/KKDL L4 97 G5
STHEL WA9 119 F1
WARRN/WOL WA2 124 A5
Tynemouth Cl EV L5 113 J2
Tynemouth Rd RUNC WA7 188 B1
Tynesdale EP CH65 196 A6
Tynron Gv CL/PREN CH43 130 A4
Tynville Rd WLT/FAZ L9 83 F4
Tynwald Cl CLB/OSW/ST L13 114 D2
Tynwald Crs WDN WA8 138 E4
Tynwald Dr WARRS WA4 162 B4
Tynwald Hl CLB/OSW/ST L13 114 D3
Tynwald Pl CLB/OSW/ST L13 114 D3
Tynwald Rd WKBY CH48 146 B1
Tyrer Gv PR/KW L34 102 A6
Tyrer Rd NEWLW WA12 106 C4
ORM L39 45 K4
Tyrer's Av MGHL L31 62 A2
Tyrers Cl FMBY L37 49 F3
Tyrer St BIRK CH41 111 F6
CLVPS L1 * 9 F4

U

Uldale Cl NG/CROX L11 98 E3
STHP PR8 33 H6
Uldale Wy NG/CROX L11 98 E3
Ullapool Cl GTS/LS CH66 194 C3
Ullet Rd TOX L8 133 F5
Ullswater Av CL/PREN CH43 129 K3
RNFD/HAY WA11 88 D3
WARRN/WOL WA2 123 J4
Ullswater Cl NWD/KWIPK L33 72 C5
Ullswater Gv RUNC WA7 187 G2
Ullswater Rd EP CH65 203 G1
GOL/RIS/CUL WA3 92 D2
Ullswater St EV L5 113 J1
Ulster Rd CLB/OSW/ST L13 115 F4
Ultonia St ALL/GAR L19 172 B1
Ulverscroft CL/PREN CH43 130 C5
Ulverston Av
WARRN/WOL WA2 123 H4
Ulverston Cl MGHL L31 62 C5
RNFD/HAY WA11 89 K5
Ulverston Lawn NTHLY L27 136 C5
Umbria St ALL/GAR L19 172 B1
Underbridge La WARRS WA4 161 H5
Undercliffe Rd
CLB/OSW/ST L13 114 E3
Underhill Rd ECCL WA10 12 B7
Underley St EHL/KEN L7 133 H2
The Underway RUNC WA7 177 J5
Underwood Dr EP CH65 203 F1
Unicorn Rd NG/CROX L11 99 G1
Unicorn Wy BIRK CH41 3 H7
Union Bank La WDN WA8 119 K6
Union Ct CLVP L2 8 D4
Union St CHTN/BK PR9 15 F3
ECCL WA10 13 G2
RF/TRAN CH42 131 J6
RUNC WA7 11 G5
VAUX/LVPD L3 8 B3
WAL/EG CH44 111 K3
Unit Rd STHP PR8 33 K4
Unity Gv PR/KW L34 85 F6
University Rd BTL L20 5 G5
Unsworth Av GOL/RIS/CUL WA3 92 E2
Unsworth Ct
WARRN/WOL WA2 * 124 B6
Upavon Av
GR/UP/WCH CH49 * 128 C6
Upchurch Cl TOX L8 132 E5
Upland Cl ECCL WA10 102 E5
Upland Dr AIMK WN4 79 J5
Upland Rd ECCL WA10 102 D5
GR/UP/WCH CH49 129 G3
Uplands Cl ECCL WA10 102 D5
Uplands Rd PS/BROM CH62 170 E4
The Uplands RUNC WA7 177 J6
Upper Aughton Rd STHP PR8 27 H2
Upper Baker St NPK/KEN L6 113 J4
Upper Beau St VAUX/LVPD L3 113 G3
Upper Beckwith St BIRK CH41 130 E1
Upper Brassey St BIRK CH41 130 D1
Upper Bute St EV L5 113 G3
Upper Duke St CLVPS L1 9 G7
Upper Essex St TOX L8 132 E4
Upper Flaybrick Rd
CL/PREN CH43 130 B2
Upper Frederick St CLVPS L1 8 E7
Upper Hampton St TOX L8 132 E2
Upper Harrington St TOX L8 132 D3
Upper Hill St TOX L8 132 D3
Upper Hope Pl EHL/KEN L7 * 9 J6
Upper Huskisson St TOX L8 132 E3
Upper Main St TOX L8 132 D4
Upper Mann St TOX L8 132 D3
Upper Mersey Rd WDN WA8 158 B6
Upper Mersey St EP CH65 6 E1
Upper Newington CLVPS L1 9 G5
Upper Park St TOX L8 132 E4
Upper Parliament St TOX L8 132 D2
Upper Pitt St CLVPS L1 9 F7
Upper Pownall St CLVPS L1 8 E7
Upper Raby Rd NSTN CH64 182 B5
Upper Rice La WAL/EG CH44 111 J2
Upper Stanhope St TOX L8 132 D2
Upper Warwick St TOX L8 132 E3
Upper William St
VAUX/LVPD L3 112 D3
Uppingham SKEL WN8 55 K4
Uppingham Av AIN/FAZ L10 83 H1
Uppingham Rd
CLB/OSW/ST L13 114 D2
WAL/EG CH44 111 F2
Upton Av STHP PR8 33 H3
Upton Barn MGHL L31 62 A5
Upton Bridle Pth WDN WA8 138 E5
Upton By-Pass
GR/UP/WCH CH49 129 F4
Upton Cl GOL/RIS/CUL WA3 92 E3
GR/UP/WCH CH49 129 G4
SPK/HALE L24 * 173 K2
Upton Ct GR/UP/WCH CH49 129 G3
Upton Dr WARRW/BUR WA5 141 G4
Upton Gra WDN WA8 138 C5
Upton Gn SPK/HALE L24 * 173 K2
Upton La WDN WA8 138 D5
Upton Park Dr
GR/UP/WCH CH49 129 H3
Upton Rd GR/UP/WCH CH49 129 H5
GTS/LS CH66 195 G5
MOR/LEA CH46 129 F1
Upton Rocks Av WDN WA8 138 D5
Upwood Rd GOL/RIS/CUL WA3 92 E4
Ure Ct EP CH65 195 K2
Urmson Rd WAL/NB CH45 111 H2
Urmston Av NEWLW WA12 91 G6
Ursula St BTL L20 97 F4
Utkinton Cl CL/PREN CH43 130 C6
Utting Av ANF/KKDL L4 97 K5
Utting Av East NG/CROX L11 98 C4
Uxbridge St EHL/KEN L7 133 G1

V

Vahler Ter RUNC WA7 11 H4
Vale Av WARRN/WOL WA2 142 E1
Vale Ct WARRS WA4 189 F4
Vale Crs STHP PR8 41 J1
Vale Cft SKEL WN8 67 J1
Vale Dr WAL/NB CH45 95 J6
Vale Gdns EP CH65 6 B7
FROD/HEL WA6 199 J5
Vale Gv KKBY L32 85 F2
Vale Ldg WLT/FAZ L9 * 97 J2
Valencia Gv PR/KW L34 102 C6
Valencia Rd WAV L15 134 B1
Valentia Rd HOY CH47 127 F3
Valentine Gv AIN/FAZ L10 83 H2
Valentine Rd NEWLW WA12 105 K2
Valentines Wy WLT/FAZ L9 83 F2
Vale Owen Rd
WARRN/WOL WA2 123 K6
Valerian Rd BIRK CH41 130 C2
Valerie Cl AIN/FAZ L10 84 A5
Vale Rd CSBY/BLUN L23 68 E5
EP CH65 6 B7
WLTN L25 154 C1
Valescourt Rd
WD/CROXPK L12 115 G2
Valiant Cl WARRN/WOL WA2 124 B5
WD/CROXPK L12 100 A3
Valiant Wy BIRK CH41 131 J5
Valkyrie Rd WAL/NB CH45 111 G2
Vallance Rd ANF/KKDL L4 98 A6
Valleybrook Gv BEB CH63 170 D3
Valley Cl AIN/FAZ L10 83 J2
CSBY/BLUN L23 69 J5
Valley Ct WARRN/WOL WA2 124 B6
Valley Dr GTS/LS CH66 195 G4
Valley Rd AIN/FAZ L10 83 K4
ANF/KKDL L4 113 J1
BIRK CH41 110 D5
KKBY L32 84 C2
PS/BROM CH62 171 F5
Valley Vw GTS/LS CH66 195 G4
NEWLW WA12 106 B4
Vanbrugh Crs ANF/KKDL L4 98 A6
Vanbrugh Rd ANF/KKDL L4 98 A5
Vancouver Rd NTHLY L27 136 B4
Vanderbilt Av WLT/FAZ L9 82 E3
Vanderbyl Av
PS/BROM CH62 170 D3
Vandries St VAUX/LVPD L3 112 D3
Vandyke St TOX L8 133 H2
Vanguard Ct
GOL/RIS/CUL WA3 125 F3
Vanguard St EV L5 113 H1
Vanguard Wy BIRK CH41 131 J6
Vardon St BIRK CH41 2 D1
Varley Rd ALL/GAR L19 153 H2
STHEL WA9 104 A1
Varlian Cl BRSC L40 54 C2
Varthen St EV L5 113 J1
Vaudrey Dr WARR WA1 144 C2
Vaughan Cl FMBY L37 48 D1
Vaughan Rd STHP PR8 27 H3
WAL/NB CH45 95 J5
Vaughan St BIRK CH41 130 C1
Vaux Crs BTL L20 82 A6
Vauxhall Cl
WARRW/BUR WA5 141 G5
Vauxhall Rd VAUX/LVPD L3 112 E4
Vaux Pl BTL L20 5 H1
Venables Cl BEB CH63 170 D4
Venables Dr BEB CH63 170 C3
Venice St EV L5 113 H1
Venmore St EV L5 113 H1
Venns Rd WARRN/WOL WA2 143 G1
Ventnor Cl
WARRW/BUR WA5 140 E2
Ventnor Rd WAV L15 134 A1
Verbena Cl RUNC WA7 187 J3
Verdala Pk CALD/MH L18 * 154 A1
Verdi Av LITH L21 81 H5
Verdi St LITH L21 81 G6
Verdi Ter LITH L21 81 G6
Vere St TOX L8 * 132 D4
Vermont Av CSBY/BLUN L23 68 E5
Vermont Cl NWD/KWIPK L33 72 C2
WARRW/BUR WA5 141 K2
Vermont Rd
CSBY/BLUN L23 68 E5
Vermont Wy BTL L20 4 E3
Verney Crs ALL/GAR L19 153 K3
Verney Crs South
ALL/GAR L19 153 K3
Vernon Av GTS/LS CH66 184 D5
WAL/EG CH44 111 K5
Vernon Rd CHTN/BK PR9 23 J5
Vernon St CLVP L2 8 D2
STHEL WA9 13 K4
WARR WA1 16 E6
Verona St EV L5 113 H1
Veronica Wy GTS/LS CH66 195 G2
Verulam Cl TOX L8 133 F2
Verulam Rd
CHTN/BK PR9 23 K2
Verwood Cl PEN/TH CH61 148 A4
Verwood Dr
WD/CROXPK L12 100 A2
Veryan Cl HLWD L26 155 J2
Vescock St EV L5 113 F3
Vesta Rd ALL/GAR L19 172 C1
Vesuvian Dr ALL/GAR L19 154 A6
Vesuvius Pl EV L5 113 F1
Viaduct St NEWLW WA12 106 A2
Vicarage Cl BRSC L40 54 B2
CALD/MH L18 153 J1
FMBY L37 48 D1
RF/TRAN CH42 150 A2
SPK/HALE L24 175 F4
Vicarage Dr
RNFD/HAY WA11 89 K4
Vicarage Gdns BRSC L40 38 D4
Vicarage Gv WAL/EG CH44 111 J2
Vicarage Hl FROD/HEL WA6 199 K5
Vicarage La BRSC L40 54 D2
CHTN/BK PR9 21 J4
FROD/HEL WA6 201 F2
FROD/HEL WA6 199 K5
Vicarage Lawn WLTN L25 135 K4
Vicarage Pl PR/KW L34 117 J1
Vicarage Rd AIMK WN4 91 G1
FMBY L37 48 D1
RNFD/HAY WA11 89 K4
WDN WA8 18 D5
Vicarage Wk ORM L39 45 J6
Vicar Rd NPK/KEN L6 98 A6
Viceroy St EV L5 113 H1
Vickers Rd WDN WA8 176 B1
Victoria Av CSBY/BLUN L23 68 D5
DV/KA/FCH L14 115 H5
HES CH60 180 E1
RNFD/HAY WA11 88 D3
WARRS WA4 163 F1
WARRW/BUR WA5 140 E3
WAV L15 134 A1
WDN WA8 158 B1
Victoria Bridge Rd STHP PR8 15 G6
Victoria Cl AIG/SPK L17 133 K6
Victoria Ct STHP PR8 27 G3
WAV L15 134 B1
Victoria Dr RF/TRAN CH42 151 F2
WKBY CH48 146 B1
WLT/FAZ L9 82 C5
Victoria Falls Rd NTHLY L27 136 C5
Victoria Flds
RF/TRAN CH42 131 F5
Victoria Gdns
CL/PREN CH43 130 E5
Victoria Gv WDN WA8 139 F6
Victoria La CL/PREN CH43 130 E5
Victoria Mt CL/PREN CH43 130 E5
Victoria Pde WAL/NB CH45 95 J4
Victoria Pk SKEL WN8 55 J4
Victoria Park Rd
RF/TRAN CH42 150 C1
Victoria Pl RAIN/WH L35 118 E4
WAL/EG CH44 112 A5
WARRS WA4 162 B2
Victoria Rd AIG/SPK L17 153 F1
AIMK WN4 78 C5
BEB CH63 150 C5
CLB/OSW/ST L13 114 C1
CSBY/WL L22 81 F3
EP CH65 6 C4
FMBY L37 40 B6
HTWN L38 60 A4
HUY L36 117 F5
NEWLW WA12 106 C1
NSTN CH64 192 B3
ORM L39 53 G2
RF/TRAN CH42 131 F5
RUNC WA7 10 E5
WAL/NB CH45 95 G5
WARRS WA4 162 C2
WARRW/BUR WA5 140 E5
WDN WA8 18 C6
WKBY CH48 146 B2
Victoria Rd West
CSBY/BLUN L23 68 E5
Victoria Sq ECCL WA10 13 G4
WDN WA8 18 D5
Victoria St BRSC L40 38 E4
CHTN/BK PR9 15 F3
CLVP L2 8 D4
ECCL WA10 13 G2
PS/BROM CH62 151 G6
RAIN/WH L35 118 E4
RNFD/HAY WA11 75 G2
WARR WA1 17 F4
WDN WA8 18 E5
Victoria Ter RAIN/WH L35 118 E4
WAV L15 134 B3
Victoria Wy FMBY L37 40 D6
STHP PR8 14 B5
Victor St WAV L15 133 J1
Victory Av CHTN/BK PR9 23 J6
Victory Cl NTHTN L30 82 B3
Vienna St EV L5 113 H1
Viennese Rd WLTN L25 * 135 J2
Viewpark Cl CHLDW L16 135 G2
View Rd RAIN/WH L35 118 E5
Viking Cl LITH L21 81 H4
STHP PR8 27 H3
Village Cl RUNC WA7 177 K5
SKEL WN8 55 K5
WAL/NB CH45 110 E1
WARRS WA4 144 D5
Village Ct AIG/SPK L17 152 D1
Village Green Ct
CL/PREN CH43 * 129 K1
Village Moor AIN/FAZ L10 83 H1
Village Nook AIN/FAZ L10 * 83 H1
Village Rd CL/PREN CH43 130 D5
HES CH60 167 K6
WKBY CH48 146 D2
Village St NPK/KEN L6 113 H3
RUNC WA7 178 D3
The Village BEB CH63 151 F6
Village Vw
WGNW/BIL/OR WN5 77 H4
Village Wy HTWN L38 59 F3
SKEL WN8 55 K5
WAL/NB CH45 110 E2
Villa Gloria Cl ALL/GAR L19 153 H3
Villars St WARR WA1 17 G5
Villas Rd MGHL L31 63 F5
Villiers Crs ECCL WA10 87 G6
Villiers Rd PR/KW L34 85 G5
Vincent Cl
WARRW/BUR WA5 141 J1
Vincent Ct CLVPS L1 9 F7
Vincent Rd LITH L21 81 K2
RAIN/WH L35 118 D3
Vincent St CLB/OSW/ST L13 114 D6
ECCL WA10 13 H4
Vine Crs WARRW/BUR WA5 141 F3
The Vineries WLTN L25 135 F6
Vine Rd GTS/LS CH66 202 D3
Vineside Rd
WD/CROXPK L12 115 H2
Vine St EHL/KEN L7 133 F1
RUNC WA7 10 D5
WDN WA8 18 D5
Vine Ter WDN WA8 * 157 F1
Vineyard St ALL/GAR L19 154 B6
Vining Rd RAIN/WH L35 118 B1
Vining St TOX L8 * 132 E3
Viola St BTL L20 96 E4
Violet Cl GOL/RIS/CUL WA3 124 E3
Violet Rd BIRK CH41 130 C2
LITH L21 81 J5
Violet St AIMK WN4 91 G1
WDN WA8 18 C6
Virgil St ECCL WA10 12 C4
EV L5 113 F3
Virginia Av MGHL L31 62 A4
Virginia Gdns
WARRW/BUR WA5 141 J1
Virginia Gv MGHL L31 62 B4
Virginia Rd WAL/NB CH45 95 H4
Virginia St STHP PR8 15 G6
VAUX/LVPD L3 * 8 B2
Virgin's La CSBY/BLUN L23 69 G2
Viscount Rd
WARRN/WOL WA2 124 A5
Vista Av NEWLW WA12 106 A1
Vista Rd NEWLW WA12 106 A1
RUNC WA7 176 D5
Vista Wy NEWLW WA12 106 A1
Vitesse Rd SPK/HALE L24 154 C5
Vittoria Cl BIRK CH41 2 D3
Vittoria St BIRK CH41 2 D3
Vivian Av WAL/EG CH44 112 A5
Vivian Dr STHP PR8 27 H5
Vixen Gv WDN WA8 138 E5
Voelas St TOX L8 133 F3
Vogan Av CSBY/BLUN L23 69 H6
Volunteer St ECCL WA10 13 F3
FROD/HEL WA6 187 F6
Vose Cl WARRW/BUR WA5 142 A3
Vronhill Cl TOX L8 133 F3
Vulcan Cl CL/PREN CH43 130 C1
NEWLW WA12 106 C4
WARRN/WOL WA2 124 B4
Vulcan St ALL/GAR L19 172 B1
BTL L20 4 B3
CHTN/BK PR9 15 G5
VAUX/LVPD L3 112 D3
Vyner Cl CL/PREN CH43 130 B3
Vyner Pk CL/PREN CH43 130 B3
Vyner Rd WAL/NB CH45 111 F2
Vyner Rd North
CL/PREN CH43 130 A2
WLTN L25 135 H4
Vyner Rd South
CL/PREN CH43 130 A3
WLTN L25 135 H4
Vyrnwy St EV L5 97 H6

W

Waddicar La MGHL L31 71 K5
Waddington Cl
GOL/RIS/CUL WA3 * 93 G3
WARRN/WOL WA2 124 B6
Wadebridge Rd AIN/FAZ L10 83 K5
Wadeson Rd ANF/KKDL L4 98 B3
Wadham Pk BTL L20 96 E4
Wadham Rd BTL L20 96 E4
Wagon La RNFD/HAY WA11 90 A5
Waine Gv RAIN/WH L35 118 C2
Waine St RNFD/HAY WA11 89 J5
STHEL WA9 104 B1
Wainwright Cl EHL/KEN L7 * 133 G1
Wainwright Gv ALL/GAR L19 153 K5
Wakefield Dr MOR/LEA CH46 109 K3
Wakefield Rd GTS/LS CH66 202 C2
NTHTN L30 82 D1
Wakefield St
GOL/RIS/CUL WA3 92 B4
VAUX/LVPD L3 9 G1
Walby Cl GR/UP/WCH CH49 149 F1
Walden Cl WARRS WA4 144 C6
Walden Rd DV/KA/FCH L14 115 G4
Waldgrave Pl WAV L15 115 F6
Waldgrave Rd WAV L15 114 E6
Waldron Cl VAUX/LVPD L3 8 D1
Walford Cl BEB CH63 170 B3
Walford Rd AIMK WN4 79 H6
Walker Av STHEL WA9 119 K4

Walker Cl FMBY L37 49 F3
Walker Dr BTL L20 81 K4
Walker Ms RF/TRAN CH42 131 G6
Walker Pl RF/TRAN CH42 131 G6
Walker Rd LITH L21 81 H4
Walker's Cft WAL/NB CH45 111 F2
Walkers La GTS/LS CH66 195 F3
STHEL WA9 119 J4
WARRW/BUR WA5 141 F6
Walker St HOY CH47 127 G2
NPK/KEN L6 113 J4
PS/BROM CH62 * 151 G5
RF/TRAN CH42 131 G6
WARRN/WOL WA2 16 B3
Walker Wy WLT/FAZ L9 82 C5
The Walk SPK/HALE L24 173 F3
STBRV L28 * 100 C6
STHP PR8 27 H2
Wallace Av HUY L36 117 F3
Wallace Dr HUY L36 117 F3
Wallace St WDN WA8 18 D3
WLT/FAZ L9 82 D5
Wallacre Rd WAL/EG CH44 110 E3
Wallasey Bridge Rd
BIRK CH41 111 F6
Wallasey Rd WAL/EG CH44 111 F3
Wallasey Village
WAL/EG CH44 110 E2
Wallcroft NSTN CH64 193 H2
Wallcroft St SKEL WN8 56 A5
Waller Cl ANF/KKDL L4 97 G6
Waller St BTL L20 81 H5
Wallgate Rd WLTN L25 135 G3
Wallgate Wy WLTN L25 135 G3
Wallingford Rd
GR/UP/WCH CH49 129 G4
Wallis St WARRS WA4 142 E6
Wallrake HES CH60 167 K6
Wallsend Ct WDN WA8 138 D6
Walmer Ct STHP PR8 27 G4
Walmer Rd CSBY/WL L22 81 F3
STHP PR8 27 H4
Walmesley Dr RNFD/HAY WA11 75 H4
Walmesley Rd ECCL WA10 87 H6
Walmsley St EV L5 112 E2
NEWLW WA12 106 D1
WAL/EG CH44 111 J2
WDN WA8 19 H3
Walney Rd WD/CROXPK L12 98 E5
Walnut Av WLT/FAZ L9 98 A2
Walnut Cl WARR WA1 144 D2
Walnut Gv GTS/LS CH66 202 D2
MGHL L31 71 K6
STHEL WA9 103 K5
Walnut St STHP PR8 27 K3
Walpole Av RAIN/WH L35 118 B4
Walpole Gv WARRN/WOL WA2 123 J5
Walpole Rd RUNC WA7 186 E1
Walro Ms CHTN/BK PR9 23 J2
Walsham Gdns STHEL WA9 119 G1
Walsh Cl EV L5 112 E3
NEWLW WA12 91 H6
Walsh Rd DV/KA/FCH L14 115 G5
Walsingham Ct WAL/EG CH44 111 K4
Walsingham Dr RUNC WA7 178 C3
Walsingham Rd CHLDW L16 115 J6
WAL/EG CH44 111 K4
WARRW/BUR WA5 141 G4
Walter Beilin Ct AIG/SPK L17 * 133 K4
Walter Gv STHEL WA9 104 D6
Walters Green Crs
GOL/RIS/CUL WA3 92 A1
Walter St AIMK WN4 * 79 J5
EV L5 112 D2
WARR WA1 143 H2
WDN WA8 19 J1
Waltham Ct RUNC WA7 178 D1
Waltham Rd NPK/KEN L6 114 A1
Waltho Av MGHL L31 62 C6
Walton Av WARRW/BUR WA5 141 F4
Walton Breck Rd ANF/KKDL L4 97 H6
Walton Gra WLT/FAZ L9 98 B2
Walton Hall Av ANF/KKDL L4 97 K3
Walton Heath Rd WARRS WA4 162 A2
Walton La ANF/KKDL L4 97 H6
Walton Lea Rd WARRS WA4 161 J4
Walton New Rd WARRS WA4 162 A3
Walton Pk WLT/FAZ L9 97 J1
Walton Park Gdns
ANF/KKDL L4 97 J3
Walton Rd ANF/KKDL L4 97 G5
ECCL WA10 88 A5
GOL/RIS/CUL WA3 125 G2
WARRS WA4 162 B3
Walton St BIRK CH41 * 3 F5
CHTN/BK PR9 15 G3
RUNC WA7 10 E5
Walton V WLT/FAZ L9 82 D5
Walton Village ANF/KKDL L4 97 H3
Wambo La WLTN L25 135 K4
Wandsworth Rd NG/CROX L11 98 D4
Wandsworth Wy WDN WA8 158 A6
Wango La AIN/FAZ L10 83 H2
Wanishar La ORM L39 43 J6
Wansfell Pl WARRN/WOL WA2 123 G4
Wantage Vw HUY L36 135 K1
Wapping CLVPS L1 8 D7
Wapping Quay VAUX/LVPD L3 132 B2
Wapshare Rd NG/CROX L11 98 C4
Warbler Cl HLWD L26 155 G1
Warbreck Av WLT/FAZ L9 82 D4
Warbreck Moor WLT/FAZ L9 82 E4
Warbreck Rd WLT/FAZ L9 82 D5
Warburton Hey RAIN/WH L35 118 D3
Warburton St WARRS WA4 162 C2
Ward Av FMBY L37 48 D3
Ward Cl WARRW/BUR WA5 122 B6
Warden St ANF/KKDL L4 97 G5
Wardgate Av WD/CROXPK L12 99 J2
Ward Gv RF/TRAN CH42 150 E3
Wardour St WARRW/BUR WA5 142 B3
Ward Rd CSBY/BLUN L23 68 B3
Ward St ECCL WA10 13 G3
PR/KW L34 101 K6
VAUX/LVPD L3 9 G3
Ware Cl AIMK WN4 79 J6
Wareham Cl RNFD/HAY WA11 90 B4
WARR WA1 144 B1
Wareing Rd WLT/FAZ L9 83 F5
Waresley Crs WLT/FAZ L9 98 C1
Wargrave Ms NEWLW WA12 106 C4
Wargrave Rd NEWLW WA12 106 C2
Warham Rd ANF/KKDL L4 98 A6
Waring Av RF/TRAN CH42 150 C1
STHEL WA9 105 F3
WARRS WA4 143 J4
Warkworth Cl WDN WA8 138 B6
Warmington Rd
DV/KA/FCH L14 115 G4
Warner Dr ANF/KKDL L4 98 A5
Warnerville Rd
CLB/OSW/ST L13 115 F6
Warnley Cl WDN WA8 138 C6
Warpers Moss Cl BRSC L40 39 F4
Warper's Moss La BRSC L40 39 F3
Warren Ct FROD/HEL WA6 201 G3
GTS/LS CH66 195 G6
STHP PR8 27 F2
Warren Cft RUNC WA7 178 B6
Warrender Dr CL/PREN CH43 130 C1
Warren Dr CL/PREN CH43 129 K3
GTS/LS CH66 195 H2
NEWLW WA12 107 F1
WAL/NB CH45 95 F5
WARRS WA4 162 B3
Warren Gn FMBY L37 48 D1
Warren Hey BEB CH63 170 C4
Warren House Rd CSBY/WL L22 80 C1
Warrenhouse Rd
NWD/KWIPK L33 73 F5
Warren La WARR WA1 144 C1
Warren Rd CHTN/BK PR9 23 J5
CSBY/BLUN L23 68 B4
HOY CH47 127 F2
WARRN/WOL WA2 123 K6
WARRS WA4 162 B4
Warren St VAUX/LVPD L3 9 H4
The Warren GR/UP/WCH CH49 129 J4
Warren Wy HES CH60 167 H4
Warrington Av EP CH65 203 F1
Warrington New Rd
STHEL WA9 13 K6
Warrington Old Rd STHEL WA9 13 J6
Warrington Rd AIMK WN4 91 G1
GOL/RIS/CUL WA3 124 E4
LYMM WA13 145 F6
NEWLW WA12 92 B5
RAIN/WH L35 119 F4
RUNC WA7 * 177 H4
WARRS WA4 161 J5
WARRW/BUR WA5 140 E5
WDN WA8 139 J2
WDN WA8 19 G4
Warrington St BIRK CH41 131 H5
Warton Cl WARRW/BUR WA5 141 H6
Warton St BTL L20 81 H5
Warton Ter BTL L20 81 H5
Warwick Av AIMK WN4 91 J1
CSBY/BLUN L23 68 E6
NEWLW WA12 106 D3
WARRW/BUR WA5 142 C2
WARRW/BUR WA5 140 E2
Warwick Cl CL/PREN CH43 2 C6
HUY L36 117 G4
NSTN CH64 191 K4
STHP PR8 27 J4
Warwick Ct EP CH65 203 J1
Warwick Dr WAL/NB CH45 111 J1
WKBY CH48 146 D3
Warwick Gv RUNC WA7 177 J4
Warwick Rd BTL L20 5 H3
GR/UP/WCH CH49 129 G3
HUY L36 117 G4
Warwick St ECCL WA10 12 A6
STHP PR8 27 J3
TOX L8 132 D3
Wasdale Av MGHL L31 62 D5
RNFD/HAY WA11 88 E3
Wasdale Rd AIMK WN4 79 F1
WLT/FAZ L9 82 D6
Washbrook Av
CL/PREN CH43 * 129 K1
Washbrook Cl ECCL WA10 102 D1
Washbrook Wy ORM L39 53 J1
Washington Cl WDN WA8 138 E6
Washington Dr
NWD/KWIPK L33 72 C3
WARRW/BUR WA5 141 J3
Washington Pde BTL L20 4 E3
Washington Rd NTHLY L27 136 C5
Wash La WARRS WA4 162 D1
Washway La ECCL WA10 88 D4
Wasley Cl WARRN/WOL WA2 124 B4
Wastdale Ct MOR/LEA CH46 109 G6
Wastdale Dr MOR/LEA CH46 109 G6
Wastdale Ms MOR/LEA CH46 109 G6
Wastle Bridge Rd HUY L36 116 E2
Watchyard La FMBY L37 49 G2
Waterbridge Ct WARRS WA4 162 C3
Waterbridge Ms RUNC WA7 177 K3
Waterdale Crs STHEL WA9 104 B6
Waterdale Pl STHEL WA9 104 B6
Waterfall Dr ANF/KKDL L4 97 J2
Waterfield Cl BEB CH63 150 C6
Waterfoot Av STHP PR8 33 H6
Waterford Dr NSTN CH64 192 B2
Waterford Rd CL/PREN CH43 130 B4
NTHLY L27 135 K3
Waterford Wy RUNC WA7 188 B1
Waterfront WARRS WA4 188 E1
Watergate La WLTN L25 154 E1
Watergate Wy WLTN L25 154 E1
Waterhouse Cl NPK/KEN L6 113 K2
Waterhouse St EV L5 * 113 H3
Waterland La STHEL WA9 104 D3
Water La CHTN/BK PR9 21 G6
RAIN/WH L35 137 G5
Waterloo Cl CSBY/WL L22 80 E3
EP CH65 6 E5
Waterloo Pl BIRK CH41 3 G6
Waterloo Rd CSBY/WL L22 81 F3
RUNC WA7 10 C3
STHP PR8 27 F5
WAL/NB CH45 95 H4
WDN WA8 158 B5
Waterloo St ECCL WA10 13 F5
WAV L15 134 B1
Watermead Dr RUNC WA7 188 E2
Waterpark Cl CL/PREN CH43 149 J2
Waterpark Dr STBRV L28 99 K5
Waterpark Rd CL/PREN CH43 149 K2
Watersedge FROD/HEL WA6 187 G5
Watersedge Apartments
WAL/NB CH45 * 95 J4
Waterside NTHTN L30 70 B4
STHEL WA9 13 K3
WARRS WA4 162 C3
Waterside Ct STHEL WA9 13 K3
Waterside Dr FROD/HEL WA6 187 F5
Waterside La WDN WA8 157 H6
Waterside Pk HUY L36 116 D6
Waterstone Cl NG/CROX L11 99 F2
Water St BIRK CH41 3 H4
CLVP L2 8 C4
CSBY/BLUN L23 69 J3
CSBY/WL L22 * 80 E3
ECCL WA10 13 F5
NEWLW WA12 106 C1
PS/BROM CH62 151 G5
RUNC WA7 10 E3
VAUX/LVPD L3 8 B4
WAL/EG CH44 111 J3
WDN WA8 158 B5
Water Tower Rd NSTN CH64 181 K5
Waterway Av NTHTN L30 70 E6
Waterways WARRW/BUR WA5 142 A3
Waterworks Dr NEWLW WA12 107 F1
Waterworks La GTS/LS CH66 184 B6
WARRN/WOL WA2 107 H6
Waterworks Rd ORM L39 46 A5
Waterworks St BTL L20 5 G4
Watery La FROD/HEL WA6 201 H4
STHEL WA9 104 C5
WARRN/WOL WA2 122 E1
Watford Rd ANF/KKDL L4 97 K6
Watkin Cl NTHTN L30 82 E2
Watkins Av NEWLW WA12 105 K2
Watkinson St CLVPS L1 132 C2
Watkinson Wy WDN WA8 138 E2
WDN WA8 19 G3
Watkin St WARRN/WOL WA2 142 E2
Watling Av LITH L21 81 H2
Watling Wy RAIN/WH L35 118 C2
Watmough St EV L5 113 G3
Watson Av AIMK WN4 79 H6
GOL/RIS/CUL WA3 92 A2
Watson St BIRK CH41 2 E2
Watton Beck Cl MGHL L31 62 D5
Watton Cl WARRS WA4 144 B6
WD/CROXPK L12 100 A3
Watts Clift Wy STHEL WA9 13 J6
Watts Cl NWD/KWIPK L33 73 F5
Watts La BTL L20 82 B5
Wauchope St WAV L15 133 K1
Wavell Av CHTN/BK PR9 23 K6
WDN WA8 157 H3
Wavell Cl CHTN/BK PR9 23 K6
Wavell Rd HUY L36 116 E3
Waverley SKEL WN8 55 K4
Waverley Av WARRS WA4 162 C3
Waverley Dr PR/KW L34 117 F2
Waverley Gv RF/TRAN CH42 150 B1
Waverley Rd AIG/SPK L17 133 H5
CSBY/BLUN L23 68 D6
GOL/RIS/CUL WA3 92 E2
HOY CH47 127 H2
Waverley St BTL L20 4 D4
STHP PR8 14 D4
Waverton Av CL/PREN CH43 149 H1
Waverton Rd GTS/LS CH66 195 H4
Wavertree Av
CLB/OSW/ST L13 114 C6
WDN WA8 18 C3
Wavertree Bvd EHL/KEN L7 114 B6
Wavertree Bvd South
EHL/KEN L7 114 C6
Wavertree Ct GTS/LS CH66 195 J2
Wavertree Gn WAV L15 134 B2
Wavertree Nook Rd WAV L15 115 G6
Wavertree Rd EHL/KEN L7 113 K6
Wavertree V WAV L15 133 J2
Wayfarers Dr NEWLW WA12 106 E3
Wayford Ms FROD/HEL WA6 186 E6
Waylands Dr WLTN L25 154 E4
Wayside Cl LYMM WA13 164 E1
Wayville Cl CALD/MH L18 153 J1
Waywell Cl WARRN/WOL WA2 124 B4
Weald Dr GTS/LS CH66 194 D3
Weardale Rd WAV L15 133 K3
Wearhead Cl
GOL/RIS/CUL WA3 92 B4
Weasdale Cl STHEL WA9 104 B6
Weaste La WARRS WA4 163 J1
Weates Cl WDN WA8 139 K6
Weaver Av BRSC L40 39 F4
NWD/KWIPK L33 72 E3
RAIN/WH L35 118 D4
Weaver Crs FROD/HEL WA6 187 G6
Weaver Gv STHEL WA9 104 E2
Weaver La FROD/HEL WA6 186 E5
Weaver Rd EP CH65 196 B6
FROD/HEL WA6 187 G6
RUNC WA7 186 D1
Weaverside Av RUNC WA7 187 J3
Weavers La MGHL L31 71 J3
Weaver St WLT/FAZ L9 97 H2
Webb Cl EHL/KEN L7 114 A6
Webb Dr WARRW/BUR WA5 121 K1
Webber Rd NWD/KWIPK L33 85 G2
Webb St EHL/KEN L7 133 J1
STHEL WA9 104 B4
Webster Av BTL L20 5 J2
WAL/EG CH44 111 K2
Webster Ct WARRW/BUR WA5 122 B5
Webster Dr KKBY L32 84 D4
Webster Rd EHL/KEN L7 133 J2
Websters La GTS/LS CH66 202 D1
Webster St LITH L21 81 J5
VAUX/LVPD L3 8 E2
Weddell Cl WARRW/BUR WA5 142 A2
Wedge Av RNFD/HAY WA11 89 K6
Wedgewood Gdns STHEL WA9 118 D1
Wedgewood St EHL/KEN L7 114 A5
Wedgwood Dr WDN WA8 139 G5
Wednesbury Dr
WARRW/BUR WA5 141 G3
Weedon Av NEWLW WA12 91 G6
Weightman Gv WLT/FAZ L9 82 D5
Weir La WARR WA1 144 D3
Weir St WARRS WA4 161 K2
Welbeck Av CALD/MH L18 134 A4
NEWLW WA12 106 D3
Welbeck Ct CSBY/WL L22 * 80 E2
Welbeck Rd AIMK WN4 79 G4
STHP PR8 27 G3
Welbeck Ter STHP PR8 27 G3
Welbourne SKEL WN8 55 K4
Welbourne Rd CHLDW L16 115 G6
Weld Blundell Av MGHL L31 61 K3
Weld Dr FMBY L37 48 D1
Weldon Dr ORM L39 53 K1
Weldon St ANF/KKDL L4 97 H3
Weld Pde STHP PR8 27 G3
Weld Rd CSBY/BLUN L23 68 D6
STHP PR8 27 F2
Welfield Pl TOX L8 133 F5
Welford Av CL/PREN CH43 149 J1
GOL/RIS/CUL WA3 92 D4
Welland Cl HLWD L26 155 H6
Welland Rd AIMK WN4 79 K4
BEB CH63 * 150 C6
Wellbank Dr HLWD L26 155 K2
Wellbrae Cl GR/UP/WCH CH49 128 E4
Wellbrook Cl RUNC WA7 188 B2
SPK/HALE L24 * 173 J1
Wellbrooke Cl AIMK WN4 79 H6
Wellbrook Gn SPK/HALE L24 * 173 J2
Well Brow Rd ANF/KKDL L4 97 J3
Well Cl NSTN CH64 192 B5
Wellcroft Rd HUY L36 116 E3
Wellcross Rd SKEL WN8 67 K1
Weller St TOX L8 132 E4
Weller Wy TOX L8 133 F5
Wellesbourne Pl NG/CROX L11 98 E3
Wellesbourne Rd NG/CROX L11 98 E2
Wellesley Av EP CH65 6 E5
Wellesley Cl NEWLW WA12 91 G6
Wellesley Gv BEB CH63 151 F5
Wellesley Rd TOX L8 133 F5
WAL/EG CH44 111 H3
Wellesley Wk EP CH65 6 E5
Well Farm Cl WARR WA1 144 C1
Wellfarm Cl WLT/FAZ L9 98 B2
Wellfield RNFD/HAY WA11 75 H5
RUNC WA7 188 D2
WDN WA8 139 F5
Wellfield Av KKBY L32 84 D2
Wellfield La BRSC L40 54 C3
Wellfield Rd WLT/FAZ L9 97 J1
Wellfield St WARRW/BUR WA5 142 B3
Wellgreen Rd WLTN L25 135 G2
Wellington Av WAV L15 133 J2
Wellington Cl AIN/FAZ L10 71 F6
BEB CH63 151 F5
EP CH65 6 E4
SKEL WN8 57 G5
WARRN/WOL WA2 124 B5
Wellington Flds WAV L15 133 J3
Wellington Ga SPK/HALE L24 174 E3
Wellington Gv WAV L15 * 133 K1
Wellington Rd BEB CH63 151 F5
CL/PREN CH43 130 D5
EP CH65 6 C6
LITH L21 81 H4
TOX L8 132 E5
WAL/NB CH45 95 G5
WAV L15 133 K2
Wellington Rd North EP CH65 6 E5
Wellington St ALL/GAR L19 153 K6
CSBY/WL L22 80 E2
NEWLW WA12 106 A2
RUNC WA7 10 D3
STHP PR8 14 C6
WARR WA1 17 F5
WDN WA8 158 B5
Wellington Ter ECCL WA10 13 F2
RF/TRAN CH42 2 E7
TOX L8 133 F4
Well La BEB CH63 150 C5
BTL L20 5 G4
CHLDW L16 135 G2
GR/UP/WCH CH49 128 D6
HES CH60 181 F1
NSTN CH64 192 A4
RF/TRAN CH42 150 D1
WARRW/BUR WA5 141 G6
WLTN L25 135 G2
Well Lane Gdns BTL L20 5 G4
Wells Av WGNW/BIL/OR WN5 77 G3
Wells Cl GTS/LS CH66 202 C3
WARR WA1 144 A1
Wells St WAV L15 134 A2
Wellstead Cl WAV L15 134 B1
Wellstead Rd WAV L15 134 B2
Wellswood Rd GTS/LS CH66 195 H2
Welsby Cl WARRN/WOL WA2 124 B4
Welshampton Cl GTS/LS CH66 202 B1
Welshpool Cl
WARRW/BUR WA5 122 D4
Welton Av GR/UP/WCH CH49 129 G4
Welton Cl SPK/HALE L24 173 J2
Welton Gn SPK/HALE L24 173 J2
Welton Rd PS/BROM CH62 171 F3
Welwyn Av STHP PR8 33 K3
Welwyn Cl STHEL WA9 119 G1
WARRS WA4 144 B6
Wembley Gdns WLT/FAZ L9 82 C5
Wembley Rd CALD/MH L18 134 C4
CSBY/BLUN L23 * 69 G6
Wendell St TOX L8 133 H2
Wendover Av AIG/SPK L17 133 H6
Wendover Cl CL/PREN CH43 130 A5
RNFD/HAY WA11 90 B4
Wendron Rd NG/CROX L11 * 84 C6
Wenger Rd WDN WA8 139 G4
Wenlock Cl WARR WA1 143 K1
Wenlock Dr HLWD L26 155 H4
Wenlock Gdns GTS/LS CH66 202 D1
Wenlock La GTS/LS CH66 202 D1
Wenlock Rd ANF/KKDL L4 97 K6
RUNC WA7 187 K3
Wenning Av MGHL L31 62 C5
Wennington Rd CHTN/BK PR9 28 C1
Wensley Av HLWD L26 155 H4
Wensleydale WLT/FAZ L9 82 D4
Wensleydale Av
PS/BROM CH62 184 B2
RAIN/WH L35 119 F4
Wensleydale Cl MGHL L31 61 K5
WARRW/BUR WA5 141 G1
Wensley Rd GOL/RIS/CUL WA3 93 F4
WLT/FAZ L9 82 D4
Wentworth Av WAL/NB CH45 95 H6
WARR WA1 144 A2
Wentworth Cl CL/PREN CH43 130 A5
STHP PR8 33 J5
WDN WA8 139 F4
Wentworth Dr BEB CH63 183 J2
EV L5 113 H3
Wentworth Gv HUY L36 116 B5
Wentworth Rd AIMK WN4 78 E4
Wernbrook Cl CL/PREN CH43 130 A5
Wernbrook Rd
ANF/KKDL L4 98 A6
Wervin Cl CL/PREN CH43 149 H1
Wervin Rd CL/PREN CH43 149 H1
KKBY L32 84 C2
Wesley Av RNFD/HAY WA11 90 D4
WAL/NB CH45 111 J2
Wesley Cl NSTN CH64 191 J2
Wesley Gv WAL/EG CH44 112 A4
Wesley Hall Gdns
STHEL WA9 119 F1
Wesley St CSBY/WL L22 80 E3
STHP PR8 14 E6
Wessex Cl WARR WA1 144 C2
West Albert Rd AIG/SPK L17 133 G5
West Av GOL/RIS/CUL WA3 92 C2
WARRN/WOL WA2 142 E1
WARRS WA4 162 B2
Westbank Av WAL/NB CH45 95 J6
Westbank Dock WDN WA8 158 A6
West Bank Dock Est
WDN WA8 157 J6
West Bank Rd EHL/KEN L7 114 C5
Westbank Rd RF/TRAN CH42 131 F6
West Bank St WDN WA8 158 B6
Westbourne Av CSBY/BLUN L23 69 J3
Westbourne Gdns STHP PR8 27 F3
Westbourne Gv WKBY CH48 146 B1
Westbourne Rd CL/PREN CH43 2 B6
STHP PR8 26 E3
WAL/EG CH44 111 F3
WARRS WA4 162 A4
WKBY CH48 146 B1
Westbrook Av PR/KW L34 117 H1
WARRS WA4 162 C1
Westbrook Centre
WARRW/BUR WA5 122 C6
Westbrook Crs
WARRW/BUR WA5 122 B5
Westbrook Rd
MOR/LEA CH46 128 D2
WLTN L25 135 K4
Westbrook Wy
WARRW/BUR WA5 122 A6
West Brow Gdns
CL/PREN CH43 129 K1
Westbury Cl AIG/SPK L17 152 D2
WARR WA1 143 K1
WLTN L25 155 G3
Westbury St BIRK CH41 131 H5
Westcliffe Ct WDN WA8 139 G5
Westcliffe Rd STHP PR8 27 F2
WD/CROXPK L12 98 E6
West Cl CL/PREN CH43 130 A4
PR/KW L34 102 C6
Westcombe Rd ANF/KKDL L4 98 A6
Westcott Rd ANF/KKDL L4 113 K1
Westcott Wy CL/PREN CH43 130 A5
Westdale Rd RF/TRAN CH42 150 D1
WARR WA1 143 K2
WAV L15 134 A1
Westdale Vw WAV L15 134 A1
West Derby Rd
CLB/OSW/ST L13 114 C1
NPK/KEN L6 113 K3
West Derby St VAUX/LVPD L3 9 K3
West Derby Village
WD/CROXPK L12 99 F6
West Dr GR/UP/WCH CH49 129 H4
HES CH60 168 A6
NSTN CH64 191 J3
WARRW/BUR WA5 141 J5
West End Gv RNFD/HAY WA11 89 J5
West End Rd RNFD/HAY WA11 89 J5
Westenra Av EP CH65 195 J3
Westerhope Wy WDN WA8 138 E6
Western Av HUY L36 116 B4
PS/BROM CH62 171 F1
SPK/HALE L24 173 H2
Western Dr ALL/GAR L19 153 H4
Westerton Rd
WD/CROXPK L12 115 J1
Westfield Av AIMK WN4 79 F5
DV/KA/FCH L14 115 J5
Westfield Crs RUNC WA7 10 B7
Westfield Dr WD/CROXPK L12 99 J2
Westfield Ms RUNC WA7 10 B6
Westfield Rd BIRK CH41 111 K6
RUNC WA7 10 A7
WLT/FAZ L9 82 B5
Westfield St ECCL WA10 12 E6
Westfield Wk KKBY L32 84 A1
West Flt Ho BIRK CH41 * 111 H6
Westford Rd WARRS WA4 161 K2
Westgate SKEL WN8 55 K4
West Ga WDN WA8 157 G4
Westgate Rd BEB CH63 170 D1
WAV L15 * 134 B4
West Gv HES CH60 167 K5
West Hall Ct KNUT WA16 165 K6
Westhaven Crs ORM L39 53 G5
Westhay Crs
GOL/RIS/CUL WA3 125 J2
Westhead Av
GOL/RIS/CUL WA3 93 F3
NWD/KWIPK L33 84 E1
Westhead Cl NWD/KWIPK L33 85 F2
Westhead Wk NWD/KWIPK L33 84 E1
West Heath Gv LYMM WA13 145 H5
Westhill STHP PR8 * 14 C7
Westhouse Cl BEB CH63 183 K2
West Huskisson Dock BTL L20 * 96 D4
West Hyde LYMM WA13 145 H6
West Kirby Rd MOR/LEA CH46 128 D4
West Knowe CL/PREN CH43 * 130 C5
Westland Dr
WARRN/WOL WA2 124 A5
Westlands Cl NSTN CH64 182 A6

West La FMBY L37 41 F5
KNUT WA16 165 K5
LYMM WA13 165 K4
RUNC WA7 177 H6
Westleigh Pl STHEL WA9 120 A2
West Lodge Dr WKBY CH48 127 F6
West Mains SPK/HALE L24 174 B2
West Meade MGHL L31 61 K5
Westminster Av NTHTN L30 70 B5
Westminster Cl WARRS WA4 163 H1
WDN WA8 157 G3
Westminster Dr
PS/BROM CH62 184 A1
RNFD/HAY WA11 90 E4
STHP PR8 33 G4
Westminster Gv EP CH65 6 D3
PR/KW L34 117 G2
Westminster Pl WARR WA1 16 D4
Westminster Rd BTL L20 97 F4
EP CH65 6 D2
WAL/EG CH44 111 H3
Westmoreland Pl EV L5 113 F2
Westmoreland Rd STHP PR8 27 K2
WAL/NB CH45 95 J6
Westmorland Av NTHTN L30 69 K6
WDN WA8 18 E1
Westmorland Dr VAUX/LVPD L3 8 D1
Westmorland Pl EV L5 * 113 F2
Westmorland Rd HUY L36 116 E5
West Oakhill Pk
CLB/OSW/ST L13 114 E5
Westonby Ct AIMK WN4 79 J6
Weston Crs RUNC WA7 186 C1
Weston Gv HLWD L26 155 K5
MGHL L31 71 G3
Weston Point Dock
RUNC WA7 175 K6
Weston Point Expy
RUNC WA7 176 B4
Weston Rd RUNC WA7 176 B6
West Orchard La WLT/FAZ L9 83 G3
Westover Rd MGHL L31 62 A6
WARR WA1 143 J2
West Park Cl SKEL WN8 55 K5
West Park Dr GTS/LS CH66 202 D3
West Park Rd ECCL WA10 12 B7
West Quay Rd
WARRN/WOL WA2 123 F4
West Rd BTL L20 97 H1
CL/PREN CH43 130 A4
DV/KA/FCH L14 115 G5
EP CH65 196 B6
RUNC WA7 176 A6
Westry Cl MOR/LEA CH46 128 C1
West Side STHEL WA9 104 A3
West Side Av RNFD/HAY WA11 89 K5
West St ECCL WA10 103 F4
PR/KW L34 117 J1
STHP PR8 14 D5
WAL/NB CH45 * 111 H2
WARRN/WOL WA2 142 E2
West V NSTN CH64 191 K3
West Vw HUY L36 117 H5
RNFD/HAY WA11 * 75 G3
WARRN/WOL WA2 124 C6
West View Av HUY L36 117 H5
Westview Cl CL/PREN CH43 130 A5
West View Cl HUY L36 117 G5
West View St BIRK CH41 131 J5
Westward Ho WKBY CH48 146 E5
Westward Vw AIG/SPK L17 133 F6
CSBY/WL L22 80 C1
West Wy MOR/LEA CH46 109 J6
RUNC WA7 * 177 H5
Westway CL/PREN CH43 130 A5
GR/UP/WCH CH49 128 E5
HES CH60 180 E1
HTWN L38 59 F3
MGHL L31 62 A5
WAV L15 134 C1
Westwick Pl HUY L36 116 B4
Westwood RUNC WA7 178 B4
Westwood Cl STHP PR8 28 B4
Westwood Ct NSTN CH64 181 K5
Westwood Gv WAL/EG CH44 111 G3
Westwood Rd CALD/MH L18 153 K3
CL/PREN CH43 129 K3
Westy La WARRS WA4 143 H5
Wetherby Av WAL/NB CH45 110 E2
Wetherby Cl NEWLW WA12 91 H6
Wetherby Ct HUY L36 116 C2
Wetherby Wy GTS/LS CH66 194 E4
Wethersfield Rd
CL/PREN CH43 130 B5
Wetstone La WKBY CH48 146 D2
Wexford Av SPK/HALE L24 174 E3
Wexford Cl CL/PREN CH43 130 B5
Wexford Rd CL/PREN CH43 130 C5
Wexwood Gv RAIN/WH L35 118 A5
Weybourne Cl
GR/UP/WCH CH49 129 H2
Weybridge Cl WARRS WA4 162 D4
Weyman Av RAIN/WH L35 118 A4
Weymoor Cl BEB CH63 170 B3
Weymouth Av STHEL WA9 104 D4
Weymouth Cl CHLDW L16 135 G1
RUNC WA7 188 D1
Weymouth Rd
WARRW/BUR WA5 121 K1
Whaley La PEN/TH CH61 148 C5
Whalley Av ECCL WA10 88 B4
RNFD/HAY WA11 75 G3
Whalley Ct NTHTN L30 70 A5
Whalley Dr FMBY L37 49 G3
ORM L39 53 G5
Whalley Gv WDN WA8 139 J6
Whalley Rd RF/TRAN CH42 2 D7
Whalleys Rd SKEL WN8 56 D1
Whalley St TOX L8 * 132 E5
WARR WA1 17 G3
Wharfdale Cl
WARRW/BUR WA5 141 H2
Wharfedale RUNC WA7 188 A1
Wharfedale Av
RF/TRAN CH42 150 A1
Wharfedale Dr
PS/BROM CH62 184 C2
RAIN/WH L35 119 F4
Wharfedale Rd WAL/NB CH45 111 F1
Wharfe La GTS/LS CH66 195 K2
Wharford La RUNC WA7 178 D2
Wharf Rd NEWLW WA12 105 J3
Wharfside Ct WARRS WA4 162 D3
Wharf St PS/BROM CH62 151 G6
WARR WA1 17 G6
WARRS WA4 16 E6
Wharmby Rd RNFD/HAY WA11 90 D5
Wharncliffe Rd
CLB/OSW/ST L13 114 E4
Wharton Cl
GR/UP/WCH CH49 128 E3
Wharton St STHEL WA9 103 K4
Whatcroft Cl RUNC WA7 187 G1
Wheatacre SKEL WN8 56 A5
Wheat Cft WARRW/BUR WA5 141 K3
Wheat Croft Cl
WARRW/BUR WA5 141 K3
Wheatcroft Rd CALD/MH L18 153 K1
Wheatear Cl NTHLY L27 136 B5
Wheatfield Cl GTS/LS CH66 195 F6
MOR/LEA CH46 129 G2
NTHTN L30 70 E6
Wheatfield Rd WDN WA8 138 B4
Wheatfield Vw LITH L21 81 J1
Wheat Hill Rd HUY L36 136 B2
Wheatland Cl STHEL WA9 120 A3
Wheatland La WAL/EG CH44 111 K4
Wheatland Rd HES CH60 168 C6
Wheatlands RUNC WA7 177 H4
Wheat La BRSC L40 39 G6
Wheatley Av BTL L20 82 B6
NEWLW WA12 91 H6
Wheatsheaf Av STHEL WA9 120 B1
Wheeler Dr MGHL L31 72 A6
Wheelwrights Whf BRSC L40 36 D5
Whelan Gdns STHEL WA9 119 G1
Wheldon Rd WDN WA8 156 E5
Wheldrake Cl GTS/LS CH66 194 E4
Whernside WDN WA8 157 H1
Whetstone Hey GTS/LS CH66 195 G4
Whetstone La BIRK CH41 2 D5
Whickham Cl WDN WA8 138 E6
Whimbrel Av NEWLW WA12 106 C2
Whimbrel Cl RUNC WA7 187 J2
Whimbrel Pk HLWD L26 155 H2
Whinbury Ct STHEL WA9 120 A3
Whinchat Av NEWLW WA12 106 C1
Whinchat Cl
GOL/RIS/CUL WA3 93 F4
Whinchat Dr
GOL/RIS/CUL WA3 125 H4
Whinfell Gv RUNC WA7 187 H2
Whinfell Rd WD/CROXPK L12 115 F2
Whinfield Rd CSBY/BLUN L23 69 H3
WLT/FAZ L9 82 C5
Whinhowe Rd NG/CROX L11 99 F3
Whinmoor Cl CL/PREN CH43 130 A3
Whinmoor Rd AIN/FAZ L10 83 K4
WD/CROXPK L12 115 G2
Whinney Gv East MGHL L31 71 F3
Whinney Gv West MGHL L31 71 F3
Whiston La HUY L36 117 G3
Whitbarrow Rd LYMM WA13 145 H5
Whitburn Cl AIMK WN4 78 C5
Whitburn Rd NWD/KWIPK L33 73 F5
Whitby Av CHTN/BK PR9 21 F5
WAL/NB CH45 110 E2
WARRN/WOL WA2 123 K5
Whitby La CH/BCN CH1 202 E4
Whitby Rd EP CH65 6 C6
RUNC WA7 10 E7
Whitby St NPK/KEN L6 114 B1
Whitchurch Cl WARR WA1 143 K1
Whitchurch Wy RUNC WA7 187 G1
Whitcroft Rd NPK/KEN L6 114 B4
Whitebeam Av GTS/LS CH66 202 D2
Whitebeam Cl
NWD/KWIPK L33 72 E3
RUNC WA7 178 B4
Whitebeam Dr
WD/CROXPK L12 99 H2
Whitebeam Gdns STHEL WA9 118 E1
Whitebeam Wk
GR/UP/WCH CH49 147 J1
Whitechapel CLVPS L1 8 E3
White Clover Sq LYMM WA13 165 H1
Whitecroft Av
GOL/RIS/CUL WA3 93 F2
Whitecroft Rd GTS/LS CH66 202 C1
Whitecross Rd
WARRW/BUR WA5 142 B4
Whiteeside Cl
GR/UP/WCH CH49 129 H5
Whitefield Av ANF/KKDL L4 97 G5
Whitefield Cl
GR/UP/WCH CH49 129 J6
HTWN L38 59 F5
Whitefield Dr KKBY L32 84 A1
Whitefield La RAIN/WH L35 136 D3
Whitefield Rd ECCL WA10 12 A1
NPK/KEN L6 113 K3
WARRS WA4 162 A3
WLT/FAZ L9 82 D6
Whitefields CHNE CH2 198 C6
Whitefield Wy NPK/KEN L6 113 J3
Whitefriars ECCL WA10 102 C2
Whitegate Cl PR/KW L34 100 D1
Whitegates Cl NSTN CH64 183 F6
Whitegates Crs NSTN CH64 193 F1
Whitehall Cl ANF/KKDL L4 97 F4
Whitehall Pl FROD/HEL WA6 200 E1
Whitehart Cl ANF/KKDL L4 97 K4
Whitehaven Cl STHP PR8 33 H6
Whitehaven Rd EV L5 113 H1
Whitehedge Rd ALL/GAR L19 153 J4
Whitehey Rd SKEL WN8 56 A5
Whitehorn Dr STBRV L28 100 B5
Whitehouse Av FMBY L37 49 G2
White House Cl
RNFD/HAY WA11 90 A5
White House Dr WARR WA1 144 D2
Whitehouse Expy RUNC WA7 187 J2
White House La BRSC L40 30 B6
Whitehouse La FMBY L37 49 G2
HES CH60 168 D4
Whitehouse Rd
CLB/OSW/ST L13 115 F5
Whitehouse V RUNC WA7 * 188 E2
Whitelands Mdw
GR/UP/WCH CH49 129 F4
Whiteledge Rd SKEL WN8 66 D1
Whiteleggs La LYMM WA13 165 H2
Whiteley's La BRSC L40 54 C3
White Lodge Av HUY L36 116 D4
White Lodge Cl
PS/BROM CH62 184 B2
White Lodge Dr AIMK WN4 79 J5
Whitely Gv NWD/KWIPK L33 73 F3
White Meadow Dr
CSBY/BLUN L23 69 H3
Whitemere Ct EP CH65 * 6 D1
White Moss Rd SKEL WN8 55 J6
White Moss Rd South
SKEL WN8 56 A6
Whiterails Dr ORM L39 45 H5
Whiterails Ms ORM L39 45 G5
White Rock St NPK/KEN L6 113 K3
Whitesands Rd LYMM WA13 145 H5
Whiteside Av RNFD/HAY WA11 89 H6
Whiteside Cl EV L5 113 F2
Whiteside Rd RNFD/HAY WA11 90 A5
Whitestock SKEL WN8 56 A5
Whitestone Cl PR/KW L34 100 C3
White St CLVPS L1 9 F7
WARR WA1 16 B5
WARRS WA4 162 B2
WDN WA8 176 D1
Whitethorn Av
WARRW/BUR WA5 141 G4
Whitewell Dr
GR/UP/WCH CH49 129 G3
Whitewood Cl AIMK WN4 79 F3
Whitewood Pk WLT/FAZ L9 83 G5
Whitfield Av WARR WA1 143 J2
Whitfield Ct RF/TRAN CH42 131 G5
Whitfield Gv RNFD/HAY WA11 89 K5
Whitfield La HES CH60 168 A4
Whitfield St RF/TRAN CH42 131 G5
Whitford Rd RF/TRAN CH42 131 F5
Whitham Av CSBY/BLUN L23 81 G1
Whithorn St EHL/KEN L7 133 J1
Whitland Rd NPK/KEN L6 114 B4
Whitledge Gn AIMK WN4 79 F4
Whitledge Rd AIMK WN4 79 F4
Whitley Av WARRS WA4 143 K5
Whitley Cl RUNC WA7 176 C5
Whitley St VAUX/LVPD L3 112 D3
Whitlow Av GOL/RIS/CUL WA3 92 A2
Whitman St WAV L15 133 K2
Whitmoor Cl RAIN/WH L35 119 G6
Whitney Pl WLTN L25 155 F1
Whitney Rd WLTN L25 135 K6
Whitstable Pk WDN WA8 138 D5
Whitstone Cl CALD/MH L18 154 B1
Whitstone Dr SKEL WN8 57 F6
Whittaker Av
WARRN/WOL WA2 123 K5
Whittaker Cl
CLB/OSW/ST L13 * 114 D6
Whittier St TOX L8 133 H2
Whittle Av RNFD/HAY WA11 89 K6
WARRW/BUR WA5 141 H2
Whittle Cl EV L5 113 G1
Whittle Dr ORM L39 45 J4
Whittle Hall La
WARRW/BUR WA5 141 G3
Whittle St ECCL WA10 103 F4
EV L5 113 G1
Whittlewood Cl
GOL/RIS/CUL WA3 125 J2
Whittlewood Ct
NWD/KWIPK L33 72 E5
Whitwell Cl WARRW/BUR WA5 140 D2
Whitworth Cl
GOL/RIS/CUL WA3 125 G4
Wholesome La BRSC L40 30 B5
Wicket Cl NG/CROX L11 84 C6
Wickham Cl WAL/EG CH44 111 K5
Wicklow Cl GTS/LS CH66 194 D3
Wicks Crs FMBY L37 48 C1
Wicks Gdns FMBY L37 48 E2
Wicks Gn FMBY L37 48 C2
Wicks Green Cl FMBY L37 48 C1
Wicks La FMBY L37 48 C2
Wicksten Dr RUNC WA7 11 H5
Widdale Av RAIN/WH L35 * 119 F4
Widdale Cl WARRW/BUR WA5 141 G2
Widgeons Covert BEB CH63 182 A2
Widmore Rd WLTN L25 135 K5
Widnes Rd WARRW/BUR WA5 140 D6
WDN WA8 18 D4
The Wiend BEB CH63 151 F6
RF/TRAN CH42 150 C2
Wigan Rd AIMK WN4 79 G6
ORM L39 45 K6
SKEL WN8 56 B5
WGNW/BIL/OR WN5 77 J2
Wiggins La BRSC L40 31 F2
Wight Cl EP CH65 203 G2
Wightman Av NEWLW WA12 91 H6
Wightman St NPK/KEN L6 113 K4
Wight Moss Wy STHP PR8 28 A4
Wigmore Cl GOL/RIS/CUL WA3 125 J1
Wignall Cl KKBY L32 * 84 D4
Wignalls Meadow HTWN L38 59 F4
Wigston Cl STHP PR8 33 H5
Wilberforce Rd ANF/KKDL L4 97 K4
Wilbraham Pl EV L5 113 F2
Wilbraham St BIRK CH41 3 G5
EV L5 113 F2
STHEL WA9 120 C4
Wilburn St ANF/KKDL L4 97 H4
Wilbur St STHEL WA9 104 C6
Wilcock Cl EV L5 113 F2
Wilcock Rd RNFD/HAY WA11 91 F3
Wilcote Cl WDN WA8 139 H5
Wilcove SKEL WN8 56 D1
Wild Arum Cl GOL/RIS/CUL WA3 93 F3
Wildbrook Dr BIRK CH41 110 D5
Wildcherry Gdns STHEL WA9 102 D6
Wilderspool Cswy
WARRS WA4 142 E6
WARRS WA4 16 D7
Wilderspool Crs WARRS WA4 162 A2
Wilde St VAUX/LVPD L3 * 9 G3
Wilding Av RUNC WA7 11 G4
Wild Pl BTL L20 82 B4
Wildwood Gv WARR WA1 144 A2
Wilfer Cl EHL/KEN L7 133 H1
Wilfred Owen Dr BIRK CH41 130 B2
Wilkes Av MOR/LEA CH46 110 B4
Wilkie St WAV L15 133 K2
Wilkinson Av WARR WA1 143 J3
Wilkinson Cl WDN WA8 158 B6
Wilkinson St BIRK CH41 2 C6
WARRN/WOL WA2 143 F2
Wilkinson Street Ms EP CH65 6 D2
Wilkinson St North EP CH65 6 D2
Wilkin St ANF/KKDL L4 * 97 G6
Willan St CL/PREN CH43 130 E5
Willard St BTL L20 82 A5
Willaston Dr HLWD L26 155 K5
Willaston Rd ANF/KKDL L4 97 K4
BEB CH63 182 E1
MOR/LEA CH46 109 H6
NSTN CH64 182 E5
Willedstan Av CSBY/BLUN L23 69 F6
William Brown St
VAUX/LVPD L3 9 F2
William Ct NSTN CH64 182 A5
William Harvey Cl NTHTN L30 70 C6
William Henry St BTL L20 4 D7
VAUX/LVPD L3 113 G4
William Jessop Wy
VAUX/LVPD L3 8 A2
William Morris Av BTL L20 82 B6
William Moult St EV L5 113 F2
William Penn Cl
WARRW/BUR WA5 * 141 F5
William Rd RNFD/HAY WA11 89 J6
William Roberts Av KKBY L32 84 B1
Williams Av BTL L20 5 K1
NEWLW WA12 91 H6
Williamson Ct HLWD L26 155 K2
WLTN L25 * 155 F2
Williamson Sq CLVPS L1 8 E4
Williamson St CLVPS L1 8 E4
Williams St PR/KW L34 117 K1
William St BIRK CH41 3 G4
ECCL WA10 * 13 G4
WAL/EG CH44 112 A5
WDN WA8 158 D1
Williams Wy FROD/HEL WA6 200 D1
William Wall Rd LITH L21 81 J1
Willingdon Rd CHLDW L16 115 J6
Willington Av PS/BROM CH62 184 B4
Willink Rd RNFD/HAY WA11 89 F4
Willis Cl RAIN/WH L35 117 K5
Willis La RAIN/WH L35 117 K5
Willis St WARR WA1 17 H2
Williton Rd CHLDW L16 135 F4
Willmer Rd ANF/KKDL L4 97 K6
RF/TRAN CH42 2 C7
Willoughby Cl
WARRW/BUR WA5 122 C6
Willoughby Dr ECCL WA10 102 D5
Willoughby Rd CSBY/WL L22 81 F2
DV/KA/FCH L14 115 J5
WAL/EG CH44 111 F3
Willow Av HUY L36 136 B1
KKBY L32 72 B6
NEWLW WA12 106 D1
RAIN/WH L35 117 K4
WDN WA8 158 C1
Willowbank Cl HUY L36 116 C2
Willow Bank Est
NEWLW WA12 107 F2
Willowbank Rd
PS/BROM CH62 151 G5
RF/TRAN CH42 131 G6
Willow Brook ORM L39 35 J3
Willowbrow Rd BEB CH63 182 E4
Willow Cl LYMM WA13 145 K5
RUNC WA7 176 E6
Willow Ct TOX L8 * 133 F5
Willow Crs BRSC L40 39 F3
WARR WA1 144 A1
WARRS WA4 * 160 D4
Willowcroft Rd
WAL/EG CH44 * 111 J5
Willowdale NEWLW WA12 106 E2
Willowdale Rd CALD/MH L18 134 A4
WLT/FAZ L9 97 J1
Willowdale Wy GTS/LS CH66 202 D3
Willow Dr SKEL WN8 56 A4
WARRS WA4 162 C2
Willow End BRSC L40 39 F5
Willowfield Gv AIMK WN4 91 F1
Willow Gn ORM L39 45 K6
WLTN L25 135 G5
Willow Gv AIMK WN4 79 K4
CHNE CH2 198 B6
FMBY L37 49 F1
GOL/RIS/CUL WA3 92 B2
GTS/LS CH66 202 E2
MOR/LEA CH46 128 E2
RAIN/WH L35 118 A2
STHP PR8 23 G6
WAV L15 134 B1
Willowhey CHTN/BK PR9 23 H2
Willow Hey MGHL L31 71 H2
SKEL WN8 56 B4
Willow La BEB CH63 182 E4
Willow Lea CL/PREN CH43 130 C5
Willow Moss Cl
MOR/LEA CH46 110 A5
Willow Pk GR/UP/WCH CH49 128 D5
Willow Rd ECCL WA10 102 E2
NEWLW WA12 106 E1
RNFD/HAY WA11 90 D4
WAV L15 133 K1
The Willows FROD/HEL WA6 201 F1
STHEL WA9 * 120 A3
STHP PR8 * 27 K3
WAL/NB CH45 94 E6
WARRW/BUR WA5 141 G4
Willow Tree Av STHEL WA9 120 B3
Willow Wk SKEL WN8 56 D1
Willow Wy CSBY/BLUN L23 69 F4
NG/CROX L11 84 C5
Wills Av MGHL L31 62 A5
Willsford Av MGHL L31 72 A6
Wilmcote Gv STHP PR8 33 H5
Wilmere La WDN WA8 139 F3
Wilmot Av WARRW/BUR WA5 141 G3
Wilmot Dr GOL/RIS/CUL WA3 92 A4
Wilmslow Av GTS/LS CH66 195 H4
Wilmslow Crs WARRS WA4 144 C5
Wilmslow Dr GTS/LS CH66 195 H4
Wilne Rd WAL/NB CH45 * 111 G1
Wilsden Rd WDN WA8 157 G2
Wilsford Cl GOL/RIS/CUL WA3 92 C2
Wilson Av WAL/EG CH44 112 A3
Wilson Cl ECCL WA10 12 D5
WARRS WA4 144 C6
WDN WA8 19 K1
Wilson Gv ALL/GAR L19 153 K5
Wilson La GOL/RIS/CUL WA3 125 G2
Wilson Patten St WARR WA1 16 B6
Wilson Rd HUY L36 117 F5
WAL/EG CH44 * 112 A3
Wilsons La EP CH65 195 K6
LITH L21 81 J3
Wilson St GOL/RIS/CUL WA3 125 G2
WARRW/BUR WA5 142 D2
Wilstan Av BEB CH63 150 C6
Wilstone Cl NPK/KEN L6 113 H3
Wilton Gv CLB/OSW/ST L13 114 E5
Wilton La GOL/RIS/CUL WA3 93 H6
Wilton Rd HUY L36 116 D5
RF/TRAN CH42 151 F2
Wiltons Dr PR/KW L34 100 C2
Wilton St AIMK WN4 78 E3
WAL/EG CH44 111 H3
Wiltshire Cl WARR WA1 144 C3
Wiltshire Gdns ECCL WA10 103 H3
Wimbald Cl WLTN L25 135 K4
Wimbledon St WAL/NB CH45 111 H2
WAV L15 133 K2
Wimborne Cl DV/KA/FCH L14 116 B1
Wimborne Pl DV/KA/FCH L14 116 B2
Wimborne Rd DV/KA/FCH L14 116 B2
Wimborne Wy PEN/TH CH61 148 A4
Wimbourne Av PEN/TH CH61 148 D6
Wimbrick Cl MOR/LEA CH46 129 G1
ORM L39 53 H1
Wimbrick Ct
MOR/LEA CH46 * 129 G1
Wimbrick Crs ORM L39 53 H2
Wimbrick Hey MOR/LEA CH46 129 G1
Wimpole St EHL/KEN L7 113 K5
Winchester Av AIMK WN4 79 F6
AIN/FAZ L10 71 G6
CSBY/WL L22 80 D1
EP CH65 7 G7
WARRW/BUR WA5 141 K4
Winchester Cl WLTN L25 154 E4
Winchester Dr WAL/EG CH44 111 G2
Winchester Pl WDN WA8 157 H3
Winchester Rd NPK/KEN L6 114 A1
RNFD/HAY WA11 90 D2
Winchfield Rd WAV L15 134 A3
Windbourne Rd AIG/SPK L17 152 C1
Windermere Av
RNFD/HAY WA11 88 D3
WARRN/WOL WA2 123 J4
WDN WA8 139 G6
Windermere Cl NSTN CH64 192 A2
Windermere Crs STHP PR8 33 J6
Windermere Dr MGHL L31 62 C5
NWD/KWIPK L33 72 C5
RNFD/HAY WA11 66 B5
WD/CROXPK L12 99 G4
Windermere Rd
CL/PREN CH43 129 K3
EP CH65 203 G1
HTWN L38 59 G3
RNFD/HAY WA11 90 A5
Windermere St EV L5 113 J1
WDN WA8 139 G5
Windermere Ter TOX L8 * 133 G4
Windfield Cl NWD/KWIPK L33 73 F3
Windfield Gdns GTS/LS CH66 195 G2
Windfield Gn ALL/GAR L19 172 C2
Windfield Rd ALL/GAR L19 172 C1
Windle Ash MGHL L31 62 A5
Windle Av CSBY/BLUN L23 69 H5
Windlebrook Crs ECCL WA10 87 J5
Windle City ECCL WA10 88 C5
Windle Ct GOL/RIS/CUL WA3 * 124 E3
NSTN CH64 181 K5
Windle Gv ECCL WA10 87 K5
Windle Hall Dr ECCL WA10 88 B4
Windlehurst Av ECCL WA10 88 B5
Windlehurst Cottages
ECCL WA10 * 88 B5
Windleshaw Rd ECCL WA10 12 B1
Windle St ECCL WA10 12 E2
Windle V ECCL WA10 12 C2
Windmill Av CSBY/BLUN L23 69 G4
ORM L39 45 K6
Windmill Cl NWD/KWIPK L33 * 72 D4
WARRS WA4 162 B5
Windmill Gdns STHEL WA9 104 B1
Windmill Hts SKEL WN8 57 J5
Windmill Hill Av East
RUNC WA7 178 C4
Windmill Hill Av North
RUNC WA7 178 B2
Windmill Hill Av South
RUNC WA7 178 C3
Windmill Hill Av West
RUNC WA7 178 B3
Windmill La WARRS WA4 179 F6
WARRS WA4 162 B5
WARRW/BUR WA5 141 F4
Windmill St RUNC WA7 11 G4
Window La ALL/GAR L19 172 B1
Windrows SKEL WN8 56 B4
Windscale Rd
WARRN/WOL WA2 124 C5
Windsor Av LITH L21 81 H3
NEWLW WA12 106 D3
Windsor Cl BRSC L40 38 E6
GR/UP/WCH CH49 128 E6
NTHTN L30 70 C4
PS/BROM CH62 151 F4
Windsor Ct BTL L20 82 B6
STHP PR8 27 F3
WARRS WA4 * 162 D2
Windsor Dr EP CH65 195 K6
RNFD/HAY WA11 91 F4
WARRS WA4 144 A6
Windsor Gv RUNC WA7 176 E5
Windsor Ms PS/BROM CH62 * 151 G4
Windsor Park Rd AIN/FAZ L10 71 H6
Windsor Rd AIMK WN4 91 G1
BTL L20 82 B6
CHTN/BK PR9 15 J5
CLB/OSW/ST L13 114 B1

ECCL WA10 12 A5
FMBY L37 48 E4
GOL/RIS/CUL WA3 92 D3
HUY L36 116 B4
MGHL L31 71 F1
RAIN/WH L35 118 A3
SKEL WN8 57 J5
WDN WA8 139 F5
WGNW/BIL/OR WN5 77 J4
WLT/FAZ L9 82 D5
Windsor St BIRK CH41 2 C6
TOX L8 132 E2
WAL/NB CH45 95 H4
WARRW/BUR WA5 142 B3
Windsor Vw TOX L8 133 G2
Windus St ECCL WA10 12 D5
Windward Dr SPK/HALE L24 172 E1
Windways GTS/LS CH66 195 G2
Windy Arbor Cl RAIN/WH L35 117 K6
Windy Arbor Rd RAIN/WH L35 137 F1
Windy Bank PS/BROM CH62 151 F5
Windy Bank Av
GOL/RIS/CUL WA3 93 F3
Windy Harbour Rd STHP PR8 34 A2
Wineva Gdns CSBY/BLUN L23 69 G6
Winfield Wy WDN WA8 19 F3
Winford St WAL/EG CH44 111 K4
Winfrith Cl BEB CH63 170 B3
Winfrith Dr BEB CH63 170 B3
Winfrith Rd
WARRN/WOL WA2 124 C6
WLTN L25 135 K5
Wingate Av STHEL WA9 119 F1
Wingate Cl CL/PREN CH43 * 130 B5
Wingate Rd AIG/SPK L17 153 F1
NWD/KWIPK L33 72 E5
PS/BROM CH62 184 B2
Wingfield Cl SFTN L29 70 A1
Wingrave Wy NG/CROX L11 99 F4
Winhill WLTN L25 135 H5
Winifred La ORM L39 53 F4
Winifred Rd AIN/FAZ L10 84 A4
Winifred St EHL/KEN L7 113 K6
WARRN/WOL WA2 17 F1
Winkle St TOX L8 * 132 E4
Winmarleigh St WARR WA1 16 B5
Winmoss Dr NWD/KWIPK L33 72 E4
Winnard St GOL/RIS/CUL WA3 92 C1
Winnington Rd HOY CH47 127 F5
Winnipeg Dr NTHLY L27 136 B4
The Winnows RUNC WA7 177 G4
Winsford Cl RNFD/HAY WA11 90 E4
Winsford Dr
WARRW/BUR WA5 105 J6
Winsford Gv GTS/LS CH66 195 F6
Winsford Rd CLB/OSW/ST L13 114 D1
Winsham Cl KKBY L32 84 D3
Winsham Rd KKBY L32 84 D3
Winskill Rd NG/CROX L11 98 E4
Winslade Ct ANF/KKDL L4 97 K3
Winslade Rd ANF/KKDL L4 97 K4
Winslow Cl RUNC WA7 178 C5
Winslow St ANF/KKDL L4 97 H5
Winstanley Cl
WARRW/BUR WA5 141 K4
Winstanley Rd AIMK WN4 78 A2
CSBY/WL L22 81 F1
NSTN CH64 191 K4
PS/BROM CH62 151 G4
SKEL WN8 56 B5
Winster Dr NTHLY L27 136 D6
The Winsters SKEL WN8 56 B4
Winston Av NEWLW WA12 106 B2
STHEL WA9 105 F3
Winston Crs STHP PR8 28 B5
Winston Dr CL/PREN CH43 129 K4
Winstone Rd DV/KA/FCH L14 116 A3
Winston Gv MOR/LEA CH46 129 F1
Winterburn Crs
WD/CROXPK L12 99 H6
Winter Gv STHEL WA9 105 F2
Winterhey Av WAL/EG CH44 111 H5
Winterlea Dr HLWD L26 155 K5
Winter St NPK/KEN L6 113 J4
Winthrop Pk CL/PREN CH43 130 B4
Winton Cl WAL/NB CH45 95 G5
Winton Gv RUNC WA7 * 178 C4
Winton Rd GOL/RIS/CUL WA3 93 F6
Winwick La
GOL/RIS/CUL WA3 107 K3
Winwick Link Rd
WARRN/WOL WA2 123 H1
Winwick Park Av
WARRN/WOL WA2 123 G2
Winwick Quay
WARRN/WOL WA2 123 G4
Winwick Rd NEWLW WA12 106 E3
WARRN/WOL WA2 16 D1
Winwick St WARR WA1 16 D4
Winwick Vw
WARRW/BUR WA5 105 H4
Wirral Cl BEB CH63 170 B2
Wirral Country Pk WKBY CH48 146 D4
Wirral Crs NSTN CH64 192 A4
Wirral Gdns BEB CH63 170 B2
Wirral Mt WAL/NB CH45 111 F2
WKBY CH48 146 E1
Wirral Vw ALL/GAR L19 153 G5
Wirral Vls WAL/NB CH45 110 E1
Wirral Wy CL/PREN CH43 129 K4
NSTN CH64 193 G2
NSTN CH64 181 F4
PEN/TH CH61 166 D1
WKBY CH48 146 C1
Wisenholme Cl RUNC WA7 187 H3
Wisteria Wy STHEL WA9 104 E6
Witham Cl NTHTN L30 70 D5
Witham Rd SKEL WN8 55 K4
Withburn Cl
GR/UP/WCH CH49 129 F4
Withensfield WAL/NB CH45 111 H1
Withen's La WAL/NB CH45 111 H2
Withens Rd MGHL L31 62 B4
The Withens STBRV L28 100 B6
Withers Av WARRN/WOL WA2 143 G1
Wither's La KNUT WA16 164 D6
Withert Av BEB CH63 150 C3
Witherwin Av WARRS WA4 162 D4
Withington Rd SPK/HALE L24 174 A2
WAL/EG CH44 111 J4
Withins Fld HTWN L38 59 F4
Withins La FMBY L37 50 B6
Withins Rd RNFD/HAY WA11 90 D3
Within Wy SPK/HALE L24 175 F4
Withnell Cl CLB/OSW/ST L13 115 F5
Withnell Rd CLB/OSW/ST L13 115 F5
Withy Cl FROD/HEL WA6 201 F1
Withycombe Rd
WARRW/BUR WA5 141 F5
Witley Av MOR/LEA CH46 109 J6
Witley Cl MOR/LEA CH46 109 J6
Witney Cl GR/UP/WCH CH49 128 D6
Witney Gdns WARRS WA4 162 E5
Wittenham Cl
GR/UP/WCH CH49 * 129 G5
Wittering La HES CH60 167 H6
Wittom Rd CLB/OSW/ST L13 114 B1
Witton Wy RNFD/HAY WA11 75 H2
Witt Rd WDN WA8 18 C6
Wivern Pl RUNC WA7 11 G3
Woburn Av NEWLW WA12 106 D3
Woburn Cl CLB/OSW/ST L13 114 D3
RNFD/HAY WA11 90 E4
Woburn Dr WDN WA8 138 C4
Woburn Hl CLB/OSW/ST L13 114 D3
Woburn Pl RF/TRAN CH42 * 150 E1
Woburn Rd WAL/NB CH45 111 H1
WARRN/WOL WA2 123 G3
Wokefield Wy ECCL WA10 102 D1
Wokingham Gv HUY L36 136 B1
Wolfe Cl WARRS WA4 163 F3
Wolfenden Av BTL L20 82 B6
Wolferton Cl
GR/UP/WCH CH49 129 J2
Wolfe St TOX L8 132 D4
Wolfrick Dr BEB CH63 170 D4
Wolfson Sq AIMK WN4 78 E5
Wollaton Dr STHP PR8 28 C4
Wolmer St AIMK WN4 79 F5
Wolseley Rd ECCL WA10 12 D2
Wolsey Cl AIMK WN4 79 F4
Wolsey St BTL L20 96 E4
Wolstenholme Sq CLVPS L1 9 F6
Wolverham Rd EP CH65 196 B6
Wolverton SKEL WN8 56 B5
Wolverton Dr RUNC WA7 178 C4
Wolverton St NPK/KEN L6 114 A1
Woodacre Gv GTS/LS CH66 195 J1
Woodacre Rd GTS/LS CH66 195 H1
Woodale Cl WARRW/BUR WA5 141 F5
Woodall Dr RUNC WA7 11 F7
Wood Av BTL L20 5 K1
Woodbank Cl CHLDW L16 135 G1
Woodbank Pk CL/PREN CH43 130 B5
Woodbank Rd EP CH65 203 F1
WARRW/BUR WA5 141 H5
Woodberry Cl CL/PREN CH43 130 A5
NWD/KWIPK L33 72 E3
Woodbine St EV L5 97 F6
Woodbourne Rd
DV/KA/FCH L14 115 H3
Woodbridge Av HLWD L26 155 G1
Woodbrook Av WLT/FAZ L9 82 C5
Woodburn Bvd BEB CH63 150 D3
Woodburn Dr HES CH60 180 E1
Woodchurch Ct
CL/PREN CH43 131 F6
Woodchurch La GTS/LS CH66 195 H4
RF/TRAN CH42 150 A1
Woodchurch Rd
CL/PREN CH43 149 H2
CLB/OSW/ST L13 114 E3
GR/UP/WCH CH49 148 E2
Wood Cl BIRK CH41 2 E2
Woodclose GTS/LS CH66 184 D6
Wood Cl KKBY L32 84 C1
Woodcote Av EP CH65 203 F1
Woodcote Bank
RF/TRAN CH42 150 E4
Woodcote Cl NWD/KWIPK L33 73 F5
WARRN/WOL WA2 123 K6
The Woodcotes
PS/BROM CH62 184 A1
Woodcot La HES CH60 167 J4
Woodcroft SKEL WN8 56 B5
Woodcroft Dr PEN/TH CH61 167 K3
Woodcroft Gdns WARRS WA4 162 D5
Woodcroft La BEB CH63 150 D3
Woodcroft Rd WAV L15 133 J2
Woodcroft Wy STHEL WA9 * 120 A3
Woodedge AIMK WN4 79 F6
Woodend PEN/TH CH61 167 K1
Woodend Av CSBY/BLUN L23 69 F3
MGHL L31 71 F2
SPK/HALE L24 155 F6
Wood End La NSTN CH64 193 F5
Woodend La SPK/HALE L24 173 H1
Woodend Rd EP CH65 195 J3
Woodene Cl KKBY L32 85 F4
Woodfall Cl NSTN CH64 192 B3
Woodfall Gv NSTN CH64 192 B3
Woodfall La NSTN CH64 192 A3
Woodfarm Hey STBRV L28 100 A5
Woodfield Av BEB CH63 150 D3
Woodfield Crs AIMK WN4 91 F1
Woodfield Rd BEB CH63 170 C2
ORM L39 53 G2
PEN/TH CH61 167 J1
WLT/FAZ L9 82 C6
Woodfield Rd North EP CH65 6 D4
Woodford Av
GOL/RIS/CUL WA3 92 E4
Woodford Cl RUNC WA7 186 E1
WARRS WA4 144 B6
Woodford Rd DV/KA/FCH L14 115 J3
ECCL WA10 87 K5
PS/BROM CH62 151 G3
Woodgate NTHLY L27 135 K3
Woodger St ALL/GAR L19 153 K6
Wood Gn CL/PREN CH43 * 129 K1
PR/KW L34 117 J1
Woodgreen Rd
CLB/OSW/ST L13 114 E3
Wood Gv CLB/OSW/ST L13 114 D5
Woodhall Av WAL/EG CH44 111 K3
Woodhall Cl
WARRW/BUR WA5 141 H1
Woodhall Rd CLB/OSW/ST L13 114 E4
Woodham Gv NSTN CH64 192 A4
Woodhatch Rd RUNC WA7 187 K2
Woodhead Rd
PS/BROM CH62 151 H5
Woodhead St
PS/BROM CH62 151 G4
Wood Heath Wy
PS/BROM CH62 171 J6
Woodhey Gv BEB CH63 150 E4
Woodhey Rd ALL/GAR L19 153 H3
BEB CH63 150 E4
Woodhouse Cl ANF/KKDL L4 97 G6
GOL/RIS/CUL WA3 125 H4
Woodin Rd RF/TRAN CH42 151 F3
Woodkind Hey BEB CH63 170 C3
Woodland Av BRSC L40 36 D2
HOY CH47 108 B6
LYMM WA13 165 H1
NEWLW WA12 * 107 F2
WDN WA8 18 B1
Woodland Dr AIMK WN4 79 G4
GR/UP/WCH CH49 129 H6
LYMM WA13 165 G1
WAL/NB CH45 95 J6
Woodland Gv
RF/TRAN CH42 150 E3
Woodland Rd ANF/KKDL L4 98 B5
EP CH65 203 F1
GR/UP/WCH CH49 129 H6
HLWD L26 155 H4
LITH L21 81 F4
MGHL L31 71 K5
RF/TRAN CH42 150 E3
WKBY CH48 147 F1
Woodlands Cl CHTN/BK PR9 15 K2
FMBY L37 48 D3
NSTN CH64 191 J1
ORM L39 54 A1
Woodlands Dr PEN/TH CH61 168 C1
WARRS WA4 144 C6
Woodlands La WKBY CH48 146 E2
Woodlands Pk NEWLW WA12 91 H5
WD/CROXPK L12 114 E2
Woodlands Rd AIG/SPK L17 153 F1
FMBY L37 48 D3
HUY L36 116 B5
NSTN CH64 191 J1
PEN/TH CH61 148 A6
RNFD/HAY WA11 89 F4
WLT/FAZ L9 83 G5
The Woodlands BIRK CH41 2 D6
BRSC L40 39 G6
GR/UP/WCH CH49 129 G3
PR/KW L34 102 B6
STHP PR8 33 J4
Woodland Vw
CSBY/BLUN L23 69 H2
GTS/LS CH66 194 E1
Wood La FMBY L37 50 E4
GR/UP/WCH CH49 128 E4
HUY L36 117 H5
NSTN CH64 181 H5
NTHLY L27 136 C4
PR/KW L34 117 H1
RUNC WA7 187 J3
WAL/NB CH45 110 E1
WARRS WA4 162 D3
Wood Lea WD/CROXPK L12 99 J2
Woodlea Cl CHTN/BK PR9 21 G6
PS/BROM CH62 184 A2
Woodlee Rd WLTN L25 135 K5
Woodleigh Cl MGHL L31 61 K2
Woodley Fold
WARRW/BUR WA5 141 G5
Woodley Park Rd SKEL WN8 56 D1
Woodley Rd MGHL L31 71 F3
Woodmoss La STHP PR8 29 H5
Woodpecker Cl
GOL/RIS/CUL WA3 125 H3
GR/UP/WCH CH49 128 E4
WD/CROXPK L12 99 K4
Woodpecker Dr HLWD L26 155 H1
Woodridge RUNC WA7 178 B4
Wood Rd HLWD L26 155 H4
Woodrock Rd WLTN L25 154 E1
Woodrow SKEL WN8 56 A5
Woodruff St TOX L8 132 E5
Woods Cl ORM L39 51 H1
Woodside Av AIMK WN4 79 F1
FROD/HEL WA6 201 G2
MOR/LEA CH46 128 E2
RNFD/HAY WA11 88 C3
STHP PR8 33 H6
Woodside Cl WD/CROXPK L12 99 F5
Woodside Ferry Ap BIRK CH41 3 J3
Woodside La LYMM WA13 165 J2
Woodside Rd PEN/TH CH61 148 B5
RNFD/HAY WA11 90 D4
WARRW/BUR WA5 141 G3
Woodside St EHL/KEN L7 113 K6
Woodside Wy NWD/KWIPK L33 72 E4
Wood's La AIMK WN4 79 H5
Woodsome Cl EP CH65 203 F2
Woodsome Dr EP CH65 203 F2
Woodsorrel Rd BIRK CH41 130 C2
WAV L15 134 C2
Wood Sorrel Wy
GOL/RIS/CUL WA3 93 F3
Woodstock Av NEWLW WA12 106 D3
Woodstock Dr STHP PR8 34 B1
Woodstock Gdns WARRS WA4 162 E5
Woodstock Gv WDN WA8 157 J1
Woodstock Rd WAL/EG CH44 111 G4
Woodstock St EV L5 113 F2
Wood St ALL/GAR L19 153 K5
BIRK CH41 3 F2
CLVPS L1 9 F5
GOL/RIS/CUL WA3 92 C3
HOY CH47 * 127 G2
LITH L21 81 J4
PR/KW L34 117 K1
PS/BROM CH62 151 G6
STHEL WA9 104 A1
WARR WA1 17 J3
WDN WA8 19 G1
Woodthorn Cl WARRS WA4 178 E1
Wood V STHEL WA9 119 G1
Woodvale Cl CL/PREN CH43 129 K1
WARRN/WOL WA2 124 A6
Woodvale Ct CHTN/BK PR9 21 K6
Woodvale Dr
GOL/RIS/CUL WA3 93 F2
Woodvale Rd GTS/LS CH66 195 G3
STHP PR8 41 J1
WD/CROXPK L12 99 K2
WLTN L25 154 E1
Woodview PR/KW L34 100 D2
Woodview Av
WAL/EG CH44 111 K5
Woodview Crs WDN WA8 157 F3
Woodview Rd WDN WA8 157 F3
Wood View Rd WLTN L25 135 G4
Woodville Av
CSBY/BLUN L23 68 E6
Woodville Pl WDN WA8 157 J2
Woodville Rd RF/TRAN CH42 131 F5
Woodville St ECCL WA10 13 J3
Woodville Ter NPK/KEN L6 113 K2
Woodward Rd
NWD/KWIPK L33 73 H5
RF/TRAN CH42 151 F3
Woodway GR/UP/WCH CH49 128 E5
Woodyear Rd
PS/BROM CH62 171 G6
Woolacombe Av STHEL WA9 120 A2
Woolacombe Cl WARRS WA4 143 G6
Woolacombe Rd
CHLDW L16 135 F3
Wooler Cl MOR/LEA CH46 128 D1
Woolfall Cl HUY L36 116 B3
Woolfall Crs HUY L36 116 B3
Woolfall Heath Av HUY L36 116 C2
Woolfall Ter LITH L21 81 H5
Woolhope Rd ANF/KKDL L4 97 K3
Woolley Cl FROD/HEL WA6 187 G5
Woolmer Cl
GOL/RIS/CUL WA3 125 K1
Woolmoore Rd
SPK/HALE L24 155 F5
Woolston Grange Av
WARR WA1 144 D1
WARRN/WOL WA2 124 E5
Woolston Rd RNFD/HAY WA11 90 B4
Woolton Bvd WLTN L25 154 E2
Woolton Cl AIMK WN4 78 E4
Woolton Ct GTS/LS CH66 195 H1
Woolton Hill Rd WLTN L25 135 F5
Woolton Mt WLTN L25 135 H6
Woolton Pk WLTN L25 135 H6
Woolton Park Cl WLTN L25 135 H6
Woolton Rd ALL/GAR L19 153 K5
WAV L15 134 B2
WLTN L25 135 G4
Woolton St WLTN L25 154 E1
Worcester Av
CLB/OSW/ST L13 * 98 B6
CSBY/WL L22 80 D1
GOL/RIS/CUL WA3 * 92 C3
Worcester Cl ECCL WA10 12 E7
WARRW/BUR WA5 141 J4
Worcester Dr
CLB/OSW/ST L13 98 B6
Worcester Dr North
CLB/OSW/ST L13 98 B6
Worcester Rd BTL L20 5 H2
CL/PREN CH43 130 A1
Worcester St EP CH65 6 E2
Worcester Wk EP CH65 6 E2
Wordsworth Av
RF/TRAN CH42 150 E2
STHEL WA9 119 J4
WARRS WA4 142 E6
WDN WA8 18 A3
Wordsworth Cl ORM L39 45 H5
Wordsworth Ct KKBY L32 84 B3
Wordsworth St BTL L20 4 B1
TOX L8 133 H2
Wordsworth Wk WKBY CH48 146 C3
Wordsworth Wy GTS/LS CH66 202 C2
HUY L36 117 F6
Worrow Cl NG/CROX L11 99 F2
Worrow Rd NG/CROX L11 99 F2
Worsborough Av
WARRW/BUR WA5 141 J4
Worsley Av WARRS WA4 143 J5
Worsley Brow STHEL WA9 104 C5
Worsley Rd WARRS WA4 162 A2
Worsley St GOL/RIS/CUL WA3 92 B3
RNFD/HAY WA11 89 J5
WARRW/BUR WA5 142 C2
Worthing Cl STHP PR8 27 G4
Worthing St CSBY/WL L22 80 C1
Worthington Cl RUNC WA7 177 K6
Worthington St TOX L8 132 C3
Wortley Rd AIN/FAZ L10 83 H3
Wotton Dr AIMK WN4 79 J6
Wray Av STHEL WA9 120 B3
Wrayburn Cl EHL/KEN L7 133 H1
Wrekin Cl WLTN L25 154 E3
Wrekin Dr AIN/FAZ L10 83 H1
Wrenbury Cl CL/PREN CH43 * 149 J1
Wrenbury St EHL/KEN L7 114 A5
Wren Cl GOL/RIS/CUL WA3 125 H3
RUNC WA7 187 K1
Wrenfield Gv AIG/SPK L17 152 D1
Wren Gv HLWD L26 155 H2
Wrenshot La KNUT WA16 165 K6
Wrexham Cl
WARRW/BUR WA5 122 E5
Wright Crs WDN WA8 176 D1
Wrights Gn WARRS WA4 * 163 F5
Wrights La WARRW/BUR WA5 159 G1
WARRW/BUR WA5 121 J4
Wrights Ter STHP PR8 27 J4
WAV L15 134 B2
Wright St AIMK WN4 78 E3
CHTN/BK PR9 15 F4
EV L5 113 F2
WAL/EG CH44 111 K3
Wrigley Rd RNFD/HAY WA11 90 D5
Wrigleys Cl FMBY L37 41 F6
Wrigleys La FMBY L37 41 F6
Wroxham Cl FROD/HEL WA6 199 J5
GR/UP/WCH CH49 129 H4
Wroxham Dr
GR/UP/WCH CH49 129 H5
Wroxham Rd
WARRW/BUR WA5 141 F3
Wroxham Wy
GR/UP/WCH CH49 * 129 H4
Wryneck Cl ECCL WA10 102 D6
Wrynose Rd PS/BROM CH62 171 G5
Wulstan St EV L5 97 F6
Wyatt Gv AIMK WN4 79 J6
Wycherley Rd
RF/TRAN CH42 131 G6
Wycherley St PR/KW L34 * 117 K1
Wychwood
GR/UP/WCH CH49 129 G4
Wychwood Av LYMM WA13 145 H6
Wycliffe Rd ANF/KKDL L4 98 A6
GTS/LS CH66 195 J6
RNFD/HAY WA11 90 D4
Wycliffe St RF/TRAN CH42 * 150 E1
Wye Cl RF/TRAN CH42 131 J6
Wyedale EP CH65 196 A6
Wyedale Rd RNFD/HAY WA11 90 B5
Wye St EV L5 113 H1
Wyke Cop Rd CHTN/BK PR9 29 G4
Wykeham St ANF/KKDL L4 97 F6
Wykeham Wy
ANF/KKDL L4 97 F6
Wyke La CHTN/BK PR9 29 G3
Wyken Gv
RNFD/HAY WA11 89 F6
Wyke Rd RAIN/WH L35 118 A2
Wyke Wood La
CHTN/BK PR9 30 A3
Wyllin Rd NWD/KWIPK L33 85 F1
Wylva Av CSBY/BLUN L23 69 H6
Wylva Rd ANF/KKDL L4 113 J1
Wyncroft Cl EP CH65 195 K6
WDN WA8 157 H4
Wyncroft Rd WDN WA8 157 H4
Wyncroft St TOX L8 133 F5
Wyndale Cl
CALD/MH L18 134 C6
Wyndcote Rd
CALD/MH L18 134 C4
Wyndham Av DV/KA/FCH L14 116 A5
Wyndham Crs GTS/LS CH66 202 C1
Wyndham Rd WAL/NB CH45 110 D2
Wyndham St ANF/KKDL L4 97 H3
Wynne Rd ECCL WA10 12 D2
Wynnstay Av MGHL L31 62 B4
Wynnstay St TOX L8 133 F3
Wynstay Rd HOY CH47 127 H1
Wynwood Pk HUY L36 116 C6
Wyre Rd EV L5 97 H6
Wyrescourt Rd
WD/CROXPK L12 115 H2
Wyresdale Av ECCL WA10 88 B4
STHP PR8 28 A3
Wyresdale Rd WLT/FAZ L9 82 E4
Wyrevale Gv AIMK WN4 79 H6
Wysall Cl RNFD/HAY WA11 89 G6
Wyswall Cl HLWD L26 155 H2
Wythburn Crs
RNFD/HAY WA11 88 E3
Wythburn Gv RUNC WA7 187 H2
Wyvern Rd MOR/LEA CH46 129 F1

Y

Yanwath St TOX L8 133 G2
Yarcombe Cl HLWD L26 155 J2
Yardley Av WARRW/BUR WA5 142 C1
Yardley Dr BEB CH63 170 C4
Yardley Rd NWD/KWIPK L33 85 H2
Yarmouth Rd
WARRW/BUR WA5 141 F3
Yarrow Av MGHL L31 62 D5
Yates Cl WARRW/BUR WA5 141 K4
Yates' Ct PR/KW L34 117 K2
Yates St TOX L8 132 D4
Yeadon SKEL WN8 56 D4
Yeald Brow LYMM WA13 145 G6
Yellow House La STHP PR8 14 E7
Yelverton Cl HLWD L26 155 J2
Yelverton Rd ANF/KKDL L4 98 A6
RF/TRAN CH42 131 G6
Yeoman Cottages HOY CH47 127 H3
Yeoman Wy GTS/LS CH66 202 C2
Yeovil Cl WARR WA1 144 B1
Yew Bank Rd CHLDW L16 134 E2
Yewdale SKEL WN8 56 C4
Yewdale Av RNFD/HAY WA11 88 E2
Yewdale Dr GTS/LS CH66 202 D2
Yewdale Pk CL/PREN CH43 130 E5
Yewdale Rd AIMK WN4 79 F2
WLT/FAZ L9 97 K1
Yew Tree Av NEWLW WA12 106 A1
STHEL WA9 120 A1
Yewtree Cl GR/UP/WCH CH49 148 D1
NSTN CH64 192 A2
Yew Tree Cl LYMM WA13 145 K5
WD/CROXPK L12 115 J1
Yew Tree Ct
GOL/RIS/CUL WA3 * 125 J2
Yew Tree Gn MGHL L31 72 A5
Yew Tree La WARRS WA4 163 H6
WD/CROXPK L12 115 J1
Yewtree La WKBY CH48 127 G6
Yewtree Rd CALD/MH L18 134 E6
Yew Tree Rd BEB CH63 170 A1
HUY L36 136 A1
MOR/LEA CH46 109 K5
ORM L39 45 K5
WLT/FAZ L9 97 H1
WLTN L25 155 F3
Yew Tree Wy
GOL/RIS/CUL WA3 92 C3
Yew Wy MOR/LEA CH46 109 K6
Yorkaster Rd CALD/MH L18 153 K2
York Av AIG/SPK L17 133 J3
CSBY/BLUN L23 68 E5
STHP PR8 27 H2
WAL/EG CH44 111 K4
WARRW/BUR WA5 141 F2
WKBY CH48 146 C3
York Cl ECCL WA10 12 E3
FMBY L37 41 F5
NTHTN L30 70 C4
York Cottages WLTN L25 135 J5
York Ct WARRS WA4 * 162 D2
York Dr WARRS WA4 163 F1
York Gdns STHP PR8 27 H2
York Mnr FMBY L37 * 49 F2
York Pl RUNC WA7 10 E5

York Rd AIMK WN4 91 H1
CSBY/BLUN L23 69 F5
EP CH65 6 D5
FMBY L37 49 F2
HUY L36 117 G4
MGHL L31 71 G3
STHP PR8 27 G3
WAL/EG CH44 111 K5
WARRS WA4 163 F1
WDN WA8 157 H3
York Rd South AIMK WN4 91 H1
Yorkshire Gdns ECCL WA10 12 E7
York St ALL/GAR L19 172 B1
CLVPS L1 8 E6
CSBY/WL L22 80 E3
GOL/RIS/CUL WA3 92 B2
PS/BROM CH62 151 J6
RUNC WA7 10 D5
WARRS WA4 16 E7
WLT/FAZ L9 97 H2
York Ter CHTN/BK PR9 15 H3
EV L5 113 G1
York Vls ANF/KKDL L4 * 97 H6
York Wy ALL/GAR L19 172 C2
Youatt Av RAIN/WH L35 118 A3
Youens Wy DV/KA/FCH L14 115 J3
Yoxall Dr NWD/KWIPK L33 72 C3
Yvonne Cl AIMK WN4 79 J4

Z

Zander Gv WD/CROXPK L12 100 A2
Zante Cl EV L5 113 G1
Zara Ct RNFD/HAY WA11 90 B4
Zenith Wk WLTN L25 135 H2
Zetland Rd BIRK CH41 2 D6
CALD/MH L18 * 134 A4
WAL/NB CH45 95 F6
Zetland St CHTN/BK PR9 15 J5
Zig Zag Rd WAL/NB CH45 111 H1
WD/CROXPK L12 115 H2
Zircon Cl LITH L21 81 K3

Index - featured places

59 Rodney Street (NT) CLVPS L1 9 H7
Abbey Farm Caravan Park BRSC L40 46 C3
Abbey Lane Industrial Estate BRSC L40 46 C2
Abbey Sefton Hospitals CSBY/WL L22 81 F2
Abbeystead Medical Centre WAV L15 134 C2
Abbotsfield Road Industrial Park STHEL WA9 120 C2
Abbots Lea Special School CALD/MH L18 135 F5
ABC Cinema STHP PR8 14 E5
Abercromby Health Centre EHL/KEN L7 133 F1
Abingdon Medical Centre ANF/KKDL L4 98 A4
The Academy of St Francis of Assisi NPK/KEN L6 114 A3
Acorn Business Centre NWD/KWIPK L33 85 G2
Acorns Primary School EP CH65 195 J4
Ainsdale CE Primary School STHP PR8 33 K5
Ainsdale Clinic STHP PR8 33 K6
Ainsdale Hope CE High School STHP PR8 33 J3
Ainsdale Sand Dunes National Nature Reserve STHP PR8 40 E1
Aintree Davenhill Primary School AIN/FAZ L10 83 G1
Aintree Industrial Estate WLT/FAZ L9 82 E6
Aintree Osteopathic Clinic WLT/FAZ L9 83 F4
Aintree Racecourse Retail & Business Park WLT/FAZ L9 83 F2
AK Business Park CHTN/BK PR9 28 D1
Alban Retail Park WARRN/WOL WA2 123 G5
Albert Dock Village VAUX/LVPD L3 8 B7
Albert Road Medical Centre WDN WA8 19 F1
Alder Root Golf Club WARRN/WOL WA2 106 D6
Alexandria Industrial Estate WDN WA8 18 B6
Alicia Hotel AIG/SPK L17 133 H5
Allanson Street CP School STHEL WA9 104 B3
Allerton Cemetery WLTN L25 154 C4
Allerton Health Centre WAV L15 134 B4
Allerton Park Golf Club CALD/MH L18 154 A1
Allerton Remedial Clinic AIG/SPK L17 133 K4
All Saints Catholic Primary School ANF/KKDL L4 113 K1
All Saints CE Primary School RUNC WA7 10 D3
All Saints High School KKBY L32 84 D2
All Saints RC Primary School GOL/RIS/CUL WA3 92 C3
All Saints Upton Primary School WDN WA8 138 A6
Alsop High School ANF/KKDL L4 97 J3
Alt Bridge Secondary Support Centre HUY L36 117 F3
Alternative Medical Centre ECCL WA10 13 F4
Andersons Industrial Estate WDN WA8 18 D7
The Andrew Collinge Academy VAUX/LVPD L3 9 H3
Anfield Cemetery ANF/KKDL L4 97 J5
Anfield Community Comprehensive School ANF/KKDL L4 97 K5
Anfield Crematorium ANF/KKDL L4 97 J5
Anfield J & I School ANF/KKDL L4 113 K1
Anfield Medical Centre ANF/KKDL L4 97 K6
Appleton Thorn Trading Estate WARRS WA4 163 J6
Archbishop Beck Catholic High School Sports College WLT/FAZ L9 82 D5
Archbishop Blanch CE High School EHL/KEN L7 113 J6
Arden College CHTN/BK PR9 15 G5
Argyle Health Centre BIRK CH41 3 F5
Argyle Lawn Tennis Club CHTN/BK PR9 23 G3
Arncot CP School ANF/KKDL L4 97 H4
Arrowe Country Park GR/UP/WCH CH49 148 C2
Arrowe Hill Primary School GR/UP/WCH CH49 129 H6
Arrowe Park Hospital GR/UP/WCH CH49 148 D2
Ashfield Special School CHLDW L16 135 F3
Ashley Business Centre PR/KW L34 117 K1
Ashley Retail Park WDN WA8 19 F5
Ashley School WDN WA8 157 J2
Ashton Grange Industrial Estate AIMK WN4 79 G3
Ashton-in-Makerfield Golf Club AIMK WN4 90 D1
Ashton Leisure Centre AIMK WN4 79 F5
Ashton Medical Centre AIMK WN4 79 F4
Ashton Town AFC AIMK WN4 79 J5
Ashurst Health Centre SKEL WN8 56 D1
Ashurst Primary School RNFD/HAY WA11 89 G5
Ashville FC WAL/NB CH45 110 D3
Ashworth Hospital MGHL L31 62 E5
Asmall Primary School ORM L39 45 H4
Astmoor Industrial Estate RUNC WA7 177 J2
Astmoor Primary School RUNC WA7 177 J3
Aston by Sutton Primary School RUNC WA7 188 B5
Atherton House School CSBY/BLUN L23 68 E5
Atkinson Art Gallery STHP PR8 14 E5
Atlanta Swimming STHP PR8 27 H3
Auckland College AIG/SPK L17 133 G6
Aughton Christ Church Primary School ORM L39 53 G2
Aughton St Michaels CE Primary School ORM L39 53 F4
Aughton Town Green Primary School ORM L39 53 G5
Austin Rawlinson Sports Centre SPK/HALE L24 173 K2
Avalon School WKBY CH48 146 D3
Balmoral Lodge Hotel CHTN/BK PR9 15 H2
Bankfield School WDN WA8 157 J2
Bank Quay Trading Estate WARR WA1 142 C5
Banks Health Centre CHTN/BK PR9 21 J5
Banks Road Primary School ALL/GAR L19 172 C1
Barlows Primary School WLT/FAZ L9 83 G4
Barnston Primary School HES CH60 168 C6
Barrow Hall Community Primary School WARRW/BUR WA5 140 E2
Baycliff Road Health Centre WD/CROXPK L12 99 J6
BBC North & BBC Radio Merseyside CLVPS L1 8 D5
Beach Road Primary School LITH L21 81 H4
The Beacon CE Primary School EV L5 113 G2
Beacon Country Park SKEL WN8 57 H4
Beacon Park Golf & Country Club SKEL WN8 57 G3
Beacon School SKEL WN8 57 G5
Beamont Junior School WARRN/WOL WA2 143 F2
The Beatles Story VAUX/LVPD L3 8 B7
Beaufort Park CP School TOX L8 132 E4
Beaufort Park School TOX L8 132 E5
Bebington High Sports College BEB CH63 150 E5
Bechers Business Centre NTHTN L30 82 D1
Bedford Primary School BTL L20 5 H6
Beechenhurst School CALD/MH L18 134 E4
Beechwood CP School HUY L36 116 C1
Beechwood Primary School RUNC WA7 187 G2
Belair Industrial Estate CSBY/BLUN L23 69 G6
Bellerive High School TOX L8 133 G4
Belle Vale Health Centre WLTN L25 135 J3
Belle Vale Shopping Centre WLTN L25 135 J3
Belle Vale Swimming Pool WLTN L25 135 K3
The Belvedere School TOX L8 133 G5
Best Western Fir Grove Hotel WARRS WA4 143 K6
Best Western Royal Clifton Hotel STHP PR8 14 D5
Best Western Stutelea Hotel CHTN/BK PR9 15 H1
Bewsey Business Centre WARRW/BUR WA5 16 A2
Bewsey Lodge Primary School WARRW/BUR WA5 142 B2
BICC Athletic Club RAIN/WH L35 118 B2
Bickerstaffe CE Primary School ORM L39 64 E2
Bidston Avenue Primary School CL/PREN CH43 130 B2
Bidston Golf Club WAL/EG CH44 110 C4
Bidston Industrial Estate WAL/EG CH44 110 D4
Bigdale Medical Centre NWD/KWIPK L33 73 F6
Bigham Road Medical Centre NPK/KEN L6 114 A4
Billinge Chapel End Parish Council WGNW/BIL/OR WN5 77 H4
Billinge Chapel End Primary School WGNW/BIL/OR WN5 77 H5
Billinge Clinic WGNW/BIL/OR WN5 77 G5
Binns Road Industrial Estate EHL/KEN L7 114 C5
Birchley St Marys RC Primary School WGNW/BIL/OR WN5 77 G5
Birchwood CE Primary School GOL/RIS/CUL WA3 125 H3
Birchwood Community High School GOL/RIS/CUL WA3 125 F4
Birchwood Golf Club GOL/RIS/CUL WA3 125 F1
Birchwood Medical Centre GOL/RIS/CUL WA3 125 G4
Birchwood One Business Park GOL/RIS/CUL WA3 125 G4
Birkdale Cemetery STHP PR8 34 A2
Birkdale High School STHP PR8 34 A2
Birkdale Primary School STHP PR8 27 J4
Birkdale RC Cemetery STHP PR8 34 A3
Birkdale Trading Estate STHP PR8 27 G5
Birkenhead High School CL/PREN CH43 130 D4
Birkenhead High School for Girls CL/PREN CH43 130 D4
Birkenhead Park CC CL/PREN CH43 130 E3
Birkenhead Park RUFC BIRK CH41 130 D2
Birkenhead Preparatory School CL/PREN CH43 130 D4
Birkenhead Priory & Museum BIRK CH41 3 J5
Birkenhead School CL/PREN CH43 130 C4
Birkenhead Sixth Form College BIRK CH41 130 C2
Birleywood Health Centre SKEL WN8 67 F1
Bishop David Sheppard CE Primary School CHTN/BK PR9 23 K6
Bishop Martin CE Primary School SKEL WN8 57 F6
WLTN L25 154 D1
Blackbrook St Marys Catholic Primary School RNFD/HAY WA11 89 H5
Black Cat Industrial Estate WDN WA8 18 B7
Black Horse Hill Infant School WKBY CH48 127 J6
Black Horse Hill Junior School WKBY CH48 127 J6
Blacklow Brow Primary School HUY L36 116 D6
Blackmoor Park Infant School WD/CROXPK L12 115 H1
Blackmoor Park Junior School WD/CROXPK L12 115 H2
Black Moss School SKEL WN8 55 K3
Bleak Hill Primary School ECCL WA10 87 J5
Blessed Sacrament RC Infant School WLT/FAZ L9 82 E5
Blessed Sacrament RC Junior School WLT/FAZ L9 82 E5
Blowick Business Centre CHTN/BK PR9 28 D1
Blueberry Park CP School DV/KA/FCH L14 116 A1
Blueberry Park Primary School DV/KA/FCH L14 115 J2
The Blue Coat School WAV L15 134 B3
Blue Planet Aquarium EP CH65 203 H2
Blundells Hill Golf Club RAIN/WH L35 118 D6
Boaler Street Industrial Estate NPK/KEN L6 113 J4
Boat Museum EP CH65 7 F1
Bold Business Centre STHEL WA9 105 F6
Bold Hotel CHTN/BK PR9 15 F3
Bold Industrial Estate WDN WA8 139 H4
Bold Industrial Park STHEL WA9 121 F1
Bold Street Medical Centre WARR WA1 16 C6
Booker Avenue J & I School CALD/MH L18 153 J2
Bootle CC BTL L20 5 G7
Bootle Golf Club LITH L21 82 B2
Bootle High School NTHTN L30 70 D5
Bootle Leisure Centre BTL L20 4 E1
Bootle Stadium Sports Centre BTL L20 5 K3
Borough Cemetery ECCL WA10 88 A4
WDN WA8 139 F6
Borron Road Industrial Estate NEWLW WA12 106 C1
Botanic Estate EHL/KEN L7 114 B6
Botanic Gardens Museum CHTN/BK PR9 23 K3
Bousfield Health Centre ANF/KKDL L4 97 G6
Bowers Business Park WDN WA8 19 G5
Bowring Community Sports College HUY L36 116 B4
Bowring Park Golf Club HUY L36 116 B6
The Bowry Health Centre STHEL WA9 103 F5
Brackenwood Golf Club BEB CH63 169 K1
Brackenwood Infant School BEB CH63 150 E6
Brackenwood Junior School BEB CH63 150 D6
Bradshaw Community Primary School WARRS WA4 163 G1
Breckfield Community Comprehensive School EV L5 113 H2
Breckfield Primary School EV L5 113 J1
Bridgehouse Clinic BEB CH63 150 C5
Bridge Industrial Estate SPK/HALE L24 154 E6
Bridgewater High School WARRS WA4 162 C5
Bridgewater Upper School WARRS WA4 162 C4
Brindley Arts Centre RUNC WA7 10 E4
The British Lawnmower Museum STHP PR8 27 J2
Britonwood Trading Estate NWD/KWIPK L33 85 G4
Broadgreen Community Comprehensive School CLB/OSW/ST L13 115 F5
Broadgreen High School CLB/OSW/ST L13 115 F5
Broadgreen Hospital DVKH/FCH L14 115 H5
Broad Green JMI School CLB/OSW/ST L13 115 F5
Broad Oak Primary School STHEL WA9 104 E2
Broad Square Community Primary School NG/CROX L11 98 D5
Broadway Community High School ECCL WA10 102 E5
Bromborough Golf Club BEB CH63 183 J1
Bromborough Pool Primary School PS/BROM CH62 151 J6
Brook Acre Primary School WARRN/WOL WA2 124 A6
Brookdale Primary School GR/UP/WCH CH49 129 F6
Brookfield Community Primary School SKEL WN8 55 K3
Brookfield High School KKBY L32 84 C3
Brookfields School WDN WA8 158 E1
Brook House Business Centre WKBY CH48 146 C1
Brookhurst Primary School BEB CH63 183 K1
Brook Lodge Primary School RNFD/HAY WA11 75 G1
Brookside Primary School GTS/LS CH66 195 H5
STBRV L28 100 B6
Brookvale Primary School RUNC WA7 188 A2
Brookvale Recreation Centre RUNC WA7 188 B1
Broomfield County Junior School WARRS WA4 162 D4
Broughton Hall High School Technology College WD/CROXPK L12 115 J2
The Brow Community Primary School RUNC WA7 177 J4
Bruche Community Primary School WARR WA1 143 K2
Brunswick Business Park VAUX/LVPD L3 132 C5
Burscough Bridge Methodist Primary School BRSC L40 38 D4
Burscough CC BRSC L40 39 F5
Burscough Health Centre BRSC L40 38 E4
Burscough Industrial Estate BRSC L40 38 B4
Burscough Primary School BRSC L40 39 F4
Burscough Priory Science College BRSC L40 38 D4
Burscough Sports Centre BRSC L40 38 E4
Burtonwood Cemetery WARRW/BUR WA5 121 J1
Burtonwood Community Primary School WARRW/BUR WA5 105 J6
Burtonwood Industrial Centre WARRW/BUR WA5 105 J6
Business Development Centre STHEL WA9 13 K3
Business Resource Centre NWD/KWIPK L33 85 H3
Byrchall High School NEWLW WA12 91 G2
Byrne Avenue Recreation Centre RF/TRAN CH42 150 E2
Cabinet War Rooms CLVP L2 8 C3
Cables Retail Park PR/KW L34 117 K1
Calday Grange Grammar School WKBY CH48 146 E2
Calderstones School CALD/MH L18 134 D5
Caldy Golf Club WKBY CH48 147 F5
Camberley Medical Centre WLTN L25 155 F3
Cambridge House Hotel CHTN/BK PR9 23 G4
Cambridge Road Primary School EP CH65 6 E5
Cammell Laird's Sports Club RF/TRAN CH42 151 F2
Campanile Hotel RUNC WA7 10 D4
Campion Catholic High School EV L5 113 G3
Canalside Industrial Estate EP CH65 7 G2
Canning Road Industrial Estate CHTN/BK PR9 28 D1
Cansfield High School AIMK WN4 79 F5
Capenhurst Grange Special School GTS/LS CH66 202 B1
Capitol Trading Estate NWD/KWIPK L33 85 J1
Cardinal Heenan Catholic High School WD/CROXPK L12 115 H2
Cardinal Newman RC High School WARR WA1 143 J4
Carleton House Preparatory School CALD/MH L18 134 A6
Carlton Lawn Tennis Club STHP PR8 27 G5
Carmel College ECCL WA10 102 D4
Carr Lane Industrial Estate HOY CH47 127 H2
Carr Mill Primary School RNFD/HAY WA11 89 F2
Castlefields Health Centre RUNC WA7 177 K3
Castleview Primary School RUNC WA7 177 G5
Castleway Primary School MOR/LEA CH46 110 A3
Catalyst Science Discovery Centre WDN WA8 158 B6
Cathcart Street Primary School BIRK CH41 2 D2
Causeway Medical Centre WARRS WA4 142 E6
Cavendish Medical Centre BIRK CH41 130 E2
Cavendish Special School RUNC WA7 186 E2
Cavern Club CLVP L2 8 D4
Cedar Cross Medical Centre RAIN/WH L35 117 K4
Centec Business Centre AIN/FAZ L10 84 A6
Central Library VAUX/LVPD L3 9 F2
Chadwick Court Industrial Centre VAUX/LVPD L3 112 D4
Chaigley School WARRS WA4 144 D5
Chalon Way Industrial Estate ECCL WA10 13 H7
Chapelfield Clinic WDN WA8 157 G2
Chapel Street Clinic WDN WA8 18 D6
Charles Wootton Centre of Further Education TOX L8 133 G2
Cherryfield Primary School KKBY L32 84 D4
Cherry Tree Community School LYMM WA13 164 D1
Cheshire Oaks High School EP CH65 203 G1
Cheshire Oaks Outlet Village EP CH65 203 J1
Chesnut Lodge School WDN WA8 157 K2

Chesterfield High School Sports College CSBY/BLUN L23 ... 69 H5
Childer Thornton Primary School GTS/LS CH66 ... 194 E1
Childrens Centre ORM L39 ... 54 A2
Childwall CE Primary School CHLDW L16 ... 134 E4
The Childwall Golf Club NTHLY L27 ... 136 B2
Childwall School WAV L15 ... 134 D1
Childwall Valley Primary School WLTN L25 ... 135 H2
Chinese Arch CLVPS L1 ... 9 G7
Christ Church CE Primary School BTL L20 ... 5 G3
EP CH65 ... 203 F1
MOR/LEA CH46 ... 129 F1
WARRN/WOL WA2 ... 124 C6
Christian Fellowship School EHL/KEN L7 ... 133 G1
Christ the King Catholic High School & Sixth Form Centre STHP PR8 ... 27 J5
Christ the King RC Primary School PS/BROM CH62 ... 171 G6
Chromolyte Industrial Estate STHP PR8 ... 27 J2
Church Drive Primary School PS/BROM CH62 ... 151 G5
Churchill Industrial Estate WLT/FAZ L9 ... 83 F3
Church Road Medical Centre BEB CH63 ... 170 C1
Church Square Shopping Centre ECCL WA10 ... 13 G5
Church Street Industrial Estate WARR WA1 ... 17 F5
Churchtown Medical Centre CHTN/BK PR9 ... 23 J3
Churchtown Primary School CHTN/BK PR9 ... 23 K3
Cineworld CLB/OSW/ST L13 ... 114 D5
ECCL WA10 ... 13 F5
RUNC WA7 ... 177 J6
Cinnamon Brow CE Primary School WARRN/WOL WA2 ... 124 B4
The Citadel ECCL WA10 ... 13 G5
Claremont Medical Centre MGHL L31 ... 70 E1
Claremont Special School WAL/NB CH45 ... 111 F1
Claremount School MOR/LEA CH46 ... 110 A6
Clarence House School FMBY L37 ... 40 E5
Clatterbridge Hospital BEB CH63 ... 169 K4
Claughton Medical Centre CL/PREN CH43 ... 130 D2
Clayton Square Shopping Centre CLVPS L1 ... 9 F4
Cleveland Business Park BIRK CH41 ... 2 C1
Clifford Holroyde Centre of Expertise DV/KA/FCH L14 ... 115 H4
Clinic for the Handicapped WARRN/WOL WA2 ... 16 C3
Clock Face Country Park STHEL WA9 ... 120 D4
Cobbs Brow Community School SKEL WN8 ... 56 C2
The Cobbs Infant School WARRS WA4 ... 162 D3
Cockhedge Centre WARR WA1 ... 16 E4
Cole Street Primary School BIRK CH41 ... 2 B5
Collins Industrial Estate STHEL WA9 ... 89 F6
Commercial Business Centre RAIN/WH L35 ... 118 E4
Common Ground Sign Dance Theatre CLVPS L1 ... 8 E5
Community Care for Health WDN WA8 ... 18 D5
Concourse Shopping Centre SKEL WN8 ... 56 D4
Constance Industrial Estate WDN WA8 ... 158 B5
Copplehouse Medical Centre AIN/FAZ L10 ... 83 K4
Corinthian Community Primary School CLB/OSW/ST L13 ... 115 F3
Corner House Clinic WKBY CH48 ... 146 C1
Cornerstones School WARRS WA4 ... 162 E1
Cornerways Medical Centre HUY L36 ... 116 C2
Corpus Christi Catholic Primary School RNFD/HAY WA11 ... 75 G2
County Sessions House VAUX/LVPD L3 ... 9 G2
Cowley Language College ECCL WA10 ... 88 A5
Craighurst JMI School WLTN L25 ... 135 H2
Craven Business Centre BIRK CH41 ... 2 D4
Crawford Village Primary School SKEL WN8 ... 67 G4
Croft Business Park PS/BROM CH62 ... 171 F3
Cromdale Way Community Hall & Health Centre WARRW/BUR WA5 ... 141 F3
Cronton CE Primary School WDN WA8 ... 138 B3
Crosby Baths CSBY/BLUN L23 ... 80 C1
Crosby High School CSBY/BLUN L23 ... 69 F3
Cross Clinic LYMM WA13 ... 145 K6
Crossens CC CHTN/BK PR9 ... 24 B1
Cross Farm Primary School NTHLY L27 ... 136 C5
Cross Hall High School Adult Education Centre ORM L39 ... 46 B6
Crowland Street Industrial Estate CHTN/BK PR9 ... 28 C1
Crowne Plaza Hotel VAUX/LVPD L3 ... 8 A3
Crow Orchard Primary School SKEL WN8 ... 56 B3
Croxteth Community Comprehensive School NG/CROX L11 ... 84 B6
Croxteth Community Primary School NG/CROX L11 ... 99 H1
Croxteth Country Park WD/CROXPK L12 ... 99 H3
Croxteth Family Health Centre NG/CROX L11 ... 99 G1
Croxteth Hall WD/CROXPK L12 ... 99 H4
Croxteth Sports Centre NG/CROX L11 ... 99 G1
Cunard Building VAUX/LVPD L3 ... 8 B4
Dallam Community Primary School WARRW/BUR WA5 ... 123 F6
Dalweb Industrial Park CHTN/BK PR9 ... 25 G2
Daresbury Park Business Park WARRS WA4 ... 178 E5
Daresbury Primary School WARRS WA4 ... 179 G3
Dawpool CE Primary School PEN/TH CH61 ... 147 J5
Deacon Trading Estate NEWLW WA12 ... 106 A3
De La Salle RC High School NG/CROX L11 ... 99 F3
De La Salle School ECCL WA10 ... 102 E1
The Dell Primary School RF/TRAN CH42 ... 151 G2
Delph Side Primary School SKEL WN8 ... 56 D5
Derby Lane Medical Centre CLB/OSW/ST L13 ... 114 E4
Devaney Medical Centre CL/PREN CH43 ... 2 A7
De Vere Daresbury Park WARRS WA4 ... 179 F5
Devonshire Park Primary School RF/TRAN CH42 ... 150 B1
Deyes High School MGHL L31 ... 62 B6
Deysbrook Medical Centre WD/CROXPK L12 ... 99 G6
Diamond Business Park RNFD/HAY WA11 ... 75 J5
Dibbinsdale Local Nature Reserve BEB CH63 ... 170 D6
Dinas Lane Medical Centre HUY L36 ... 116 C3
The District CE Primary School NEWLW WA12 ... 106 A2
Ditton CE Primary School WDN WA8 ... 157 F2
Ditton Medical Centre WDN WA8 ... 157 H2
Dovecot Health Clinic DV/KA/FCH L14 ... 115 K3
Dovecot JMI School DV/KA/FCH L14 ... 116 A4
Dovedale County Infant School CALD/MH L18 ... 134 B4
Dovedale Junior School CALD/MH L18 ... 134 B4
Downholland Haskayne CE Primary School ORM L39 ... 51 G2
Drug Dependency Clinic CLVPS L1 ... 9 H5
WDN WA8 ... 18 D6
Duke Street Cemetery STHP PR8 ... 27 K3
Dunkirk Trading Estate CH/BCN CH1 ... 202 B6
Dunnys Sports Club WLT/FAZ L9 ... 97 J1
Eagle Sports Club WARRW/BUR WA5 ... 141 H5
Earle Road Medical Centre EHL/KEN L7 ... 133 H1
Eastcroft Park CP School NWD/KWIPK L33 ... 72 E4
East Gillbrands Industrial Estate SKEL WN8 ... 56 C6
Eastham Country Park PS/BROM CH62 ... 171 J6
Eastham Lodge Golf Club PS/BROM CH62 ... 184 D1
Eastside Industrial Estate STHEL WA9 ... 104 A3
Eastway Primary School MOR/LEA CH46 ... 109 J6
Eaton Road Medical Centre WD/CROXPK L12 ... 115 G2
Eaves Primary School STHEL WA9 ... 120 A1
Eccleston Lane Ends Primary School PR/KW L34 ... 102 B6
Eccleston Medical Centre ECCL WA10 ... 87 J6
Eccleston Mere Primary School ECCL WA10 ... 102 C2
Eccleston Park Golf Club RAIN/WH L35 ... 118 D1
Edge Hill College of Higher Education ORM L39 ... 54 A1
Edge Hill Enterprises WLT/FAZ L9 ... 83 G5
Edge Hill Enterprise Training Centre WLT/FAZ L9 ... 83 H5
Edge Hill Health Centre EHL/KEN L7 ... 114 A6
Edge Hill University (Ormskirk Campus) ORM L39 ... 54 A2
Edge Lane Medical Centre EHL/KEN L7 ... 113 K6
Edge Lane Retail Park CLB/OSW/ST L13 ... 114 D5
Edwards Lane Industrial Estate SPK/HALE L24 ... 154 E5
Egremont Medical Centre WAL/EG CH44 ... 111 K3
Egremont Primary School WAL/EG CH44 ... 111 K3
Elaine Norris Sports Centre VAUX/LVPD L3 ... 112 E3
Elimu Academy TOX L8 ... 133 G2
Elleray Park School WAL/NB CH45 ... 95 G6
Ellergreen Medical Centre NG/CROX L11 ... 98 D3
Ellesmere Port Business Centre EP CH65 ... 6 C5
Ellesmere Port Catholic High School EP CH65 ... 195 J6
Ellesmere Port Clinic EP CH65 ... 6 C7
Ellesmere Port Golf Centre GTS/LS CH66 ... 194 E1
Ellesmere Port Hospital EP CH65 ... 202 E1
Ellesmere Port Stadium EP CH65 ... 196 D6
The Elms Special School STBRV L28 ... 100 B5
Eltham Green Clinic GR/UP/WCH CH49 ... 148 E1
Elton Primary School CHNE CH2 ... 198 B5
Emmaus Primary School WD/CROXPK L12 ... 99 K2
English Martyrs Catholic Primary School LITH L21 ... 81 J3
Epic Leisure Centre EP CH65 ... 6 D7
Eric Moore Health Centre WARRN/WOL WA2 ... 16 C3
Ernest Cookson Special School WD/CROXPK L12 ... 115 F1
Erskine Street Industrial Estate NPK/KEN L6 ... 9 K2
Estuary Business Park SPK/HALE L24 ... 173 F1
Europa Pool BIRK CH41 ... 2 E4
Evelyn Primary School PR/KW L34 ... 102 A6
Evelyn Street Primary School WARRW/BUR WA5 ... 142 B5
Everite Road Industrial Estate WDN WA8 ... 157 G4
Everton FC (Goodison Park) ANF/KKDL L4 ... 97 H5
Everton Park Sports Centre EV L5 ... 113 G2
Everton Road Health Clinic NPK/KEN L6 ... 113 H3
Everyman Theatre VAUX/LVPD L3 ... 9 J5
Express Industrial Estate WDN WA8 ... 157 F4
Expressway Business Park RF/TRAN CH42 ... 131 J6
FACT-Foundation for Art & Creative Technology CLVPS L1 ... 9 G6
Fairfield High School WDN WA8 ... 139 G6
Fairfield Hospital RNFD/HAY WA11 ... 88 B1
Fairfield J & I School WDN WA8 ... 158 C1
Fairfield Medical Centre NPK/KEN L6 ... 114 A4
Fairfield RFC RF/TRAN CH42 ... 150 E1
Fairlie CP School SKEL WN8 ... 56 D2
Fairway Trading Estate WDN WA8 ... 157 K4
Faith House Yoga & Natural Health Centre WAL/NB CH45 ... 95 H5
Faith Primary School VAUX/LVPD L3 ... 113 G4
Falcongate Industrial Estate BIRK CH41 ... 111 H6
Family Health Centre KKBY L32 ... 84 B1
Farnborough Road J & I School STHP PR8 ... 34 B1
Farnworth CE Primary School WDN WA8 ... 139 F5
Fazakerley High School AIN/FAZ L10 ... 83 J4
Fazakerley Primary School AIN/FAZ L10 ... 83 J4
Fazakerley Sports Centre AIN/FAZ L10 ... 83 J3
Fearnhead Cross Medical Centre WARRN/WOL WA2 ... 124 B5
Fender Primary School GR/UP/WCH CH49 ... 129 K6
Fernhill Sports Centre BTL L20 ... 82 A5
Ferries Industrial Estate RF/TRAN CH42 ... 131 J6
Fingerprints of Elvis VAUX/LVPD L3 ... 8 B6
Fir Tree Drive South Medical Centre WD/CROXPK L12 ... 99 K2
Fishwicks Industrial Estate RNFD/HAY WA11 ... 90 E3
STHEL WA9 ... 104 B5
Fleet Lane Industrial Estate STHEL WA9 ... 104 C3
Fleming Industrial Estate WARR WA1 ... 17 F4
Floral Pavilion Theatre WAL/NB CH45 ... 95 J4
Florence Melly Community Primary School ANF/KKDL L4 ... 98 A3
Fordton Leisure Centre WARRN/WOL WA2 ... 123 G4
Forefield Infant School CSBY/BLUN L23 ... 69 H5
Forefield Junior School CSBY/BLUN L23 ... 69 G5
Forest Hills Hotel & Leisure Complex FROD/HEL WA6 ... 200 E3
The Forge Shopping Centre WARRS WA4 ... 162 B2
Formby Clinic FMBY L37 ... 49 F3
Formby AFC FMBY L37 ... 49 F2
Formby Business Park FMBY L37 ... 49 J2
Formby CC FMBY L37 ... 41 F6
Formby Golf Club FMBY L37 ... 40 D6
Formby Hall Golf & Country Club FMBY L37 ... 41 J3
Formby High School FMBY L37 ... 48 E1
Formby Junior Sports Club FMBY L37 ... 41 G6
Formby Ladies Golf Club FMBY L37 ... 40 D6
Formby Lawn Tennis Club FMBY L37 ... 41 F6
Formby Point & Squirrel Nature Reserve FMBY L37 ... 48 A5
Four Acre Lane Shopping Centre STHEL WA9 ... 119 K3
Foxfield School MOR/LEA CH46 ... 128 E1
Fox Wood School GOL/RIS/CUL WA3 ... 125 G4
Freight Terminal Buildings (Euro-Rail) LITH L21 ... 81 F5
Freshfield Primary School FMBY L37 ... 49 G1
Freshlea Private Clinic FMBY L37 ... 48 D4
Frodsham CE Primary School FROD/HEL WA6 ... 201 F2
Frodsham Golf Club FROD/HEL WA6 ... 200 E4
Frodsham Science & Technology College FROD/HEL WA6 ... 200 E1
Funland STHP PR8 ... 14 D3
Fylde Road Industrial Estate CHTN/BK PR9 ... 23 K1
Gallagher Industrial Estate BIRK CH41 ... 111 H5
Garston CE Primary School ALL/GAR L19 ... 154 A5
Garston Industrial Estate ALL/GAR L19 ... 172 B1
Garston Leisure Centre ALL/GAR L19 ... 153 K5
Garston Sports Centre ALL/GAR L19 ... 153 K4
Garswood Primary School AIMK WN4 ... 78 B5
Garswood United FC AIMK WN4 ... 78 A4
Garven Place Clinic WARR WA1 ... 16 B5
Gateacre Community Comprehensive School WLTN L25 ... 135 H4
Gateworth Industrial Estate WARRW/BUR WA5 ... 142 A6
Gayton Primary School HES CH60 ... 181 F1
Gemini Business Park WARRW/BUR WA5 ... 123 F4
Gilded Hollins Primary School LEIGH WN7 ... 93 K2
Gillmoss Industrial Estate NG/CROX L11 ... 84 A5
Gillmoss Medical Centre NG/CROX L11 ... 84 B6
Gilmour Infant School ALL/GAR L19 ... 153 J4
Gilmour Junior School ALL/GAR L19 ... 153 J4
Glenburn Sports College SKEL WN8 ... 56 C5
Golborne Clinic GOL/RIS/CUL WA3 ... 92 C2
Golborne CP School GOL/RIS/CUL WA3 ... 92 B3
Golborne High School GOL/RIS/CUL WA3 ... 92 D2
Golden Square Shopping Centre WARR WA1 ... 16 C5
Golden Triangle Industrial Estate WDN WA8 ... 157 H5
Gorse Covert Primary School GOL/RIS/CUL WA3 ... 125 K1
Gorsewood Primary School RUNC WA7 ... 178 D6
Gorsthills Primary School GTS/LS CH66 ... 195 F6
Grain Industrial Estate TOX L8 ... 132 D5
Granada Television VAUX/LVPD L3 ... 8 C6
The Grand National Experience WLT/FAZ L9 ... 82 E2
The Grange Comprehensive School RUNC WA7 ... 11 J7
The Grange Country Club NSTN CH64 ... 182 A3
The Grange Infant School RUNC WA7 ... 11 J6
The Grange Junior School RUNC WA7 ... 11 J6
Grange Park Golf Club ECCL WA10 ... 102 E4
Grange Primary School NTHTN L30 ... 70 B4
The Grange Shopping Precinct BIRK CH41 ... 2 E5
Grange Valley Primary School RNFD/HAY WA11 ... 90 C6
Grappenhall CC WARRS WA4 ... 163 F2
Grappenhall Clinic WARRS WA4 ... 144 A6
Grappenhall Hall School WARRS WA4 ... 163 G2
Grappenhall Heys Primary School WARRS WA4 ... 162 E4
Grappenhall Sports Club WARRS WA4 ... 162 E2
Greasby Health Centre GR/UP/WCH CH49 ... 128 E6
Greasby Infant School GR/UP/WCH CH49 ... 147 K1
Greasby Junior School GR/UP/WCH CH49 ... 148 A2
Great Crosby RC Primary School CSBY/BLUN L23 ... 69 G5
Great Homer Street Medical Centre EV L5 ... 113 G2
Great Meols Primary School HOY CH47 ... 108 C6
Great Sankey High School WARRW/BUR WA5 ... 140 E1
Great Sankey Primary School WARRW/BUR WA5 ... 141 H4
Great Sutton Health Centre GTS/LS CH66 ... 195 G4
Greenbank High School STHP PR8 ... 27 F6
Greenbank Primary School CALD/MH L18 ... 134 A4
Green Lane Medical Centre CLB/OSW/ST L13 ... 114 C2
Green Lane Special School WARR WA1 ... 144 A1
Greenleas School WAL/NB CH45 ... 110 C1
Greenoaks Farm Industrial Estate WDN WA8 ... 19 H3
Green Oaks Shopping Centre WDN WA8 ... 19 F3
Green Park Primary School MGHL L31 ... 61 K5
Greenways Special School ALL/GAR L19 ... 153 G4
Gresford Medical Centre DV/KA/FCH L14 ... 115 K4
Grove House Hotel WAL/NB CH45 ... 94 E6
Grove Street Primary School PS/BROM CH62 ... 151 F4
Guardian Medical Centre WARRW/BUR WA5 ... 142 C3
Guardian Street Industrial Estate WARRW/BUR WA5 ... 16 A3
Guinea Gap Baths & Recreation Centre WAL/EG CH44 ... 112 A4
Gulliver's World Theme Park WARRW/BUR WA5 ... 122 E6
Guys Industrial Estate BRSC L40 ... 46 B1
Gwladys Street Community Primary School ANF/KKDL L4 ... 97 J5
Halebank CE Primary School WDN WA8 ... 175 H1
Hale CE Primary School SPK/HALE L24 ... 175 F4
Hale Road Industrial Estate WDN WA8 ... 157 H6
Halewood CE Primary School HLWD L26 ... 155 K2
Halewood Community Comprehensive School HLWD L26 ... 155 H4
Halewood Health Centre HLWD L26 ... 155 J4
Halewood Sports Centre HLWD L26 ... 155 K4
Hall Green Clinic SKEL WN8 ... 57 K6
Hall Street Medical Centre ECCL WA10 ... 13 H5
Hallwood Park Primary School RUNC WA7 ... 187 H1
Halsall St Cuthberts CE Primary School ORM L39 ... 43 K2
Halsnead Community Primary School RAIN/WH L35 ... 117 K5
Halton General Hospital RUNC WA7 ... 187 J1
Halton High School RUNC WA7 ... 188 B2
Halton Lodge Primary School RUNC WA7 ... 177 G5
Halton School RUNC WA7 ... 177 J4
Hanson Road Business Park WLT/FAZ L9 ... 83 F6
The Hardshaw Shopping Centre ECCL WA10 ... 13 G5
Harold Magnay Special School WLTN L25 ... 135 G5
Hartley Trading Estate WLT/FAZ L9 ... 82 E6
Haslemere Industrial Estate AIMK WN4 ... 79 F1
Hatton Garden Industrial Estate CLVP L2 ... 8 D2
Hatton Hill Primary School LITH L21 ... 81 J1
Hawthorne Business Park WARRW/BUR WA5 ... 142 C1
Haydock CC RNFD/HAY WA11 ... 90 B5
Haydock English Martyrs Catholic Primary School RNFD/HAY WA11 ... 90 C4
Haydock High School RNFD/HAY WA11 ... 90 B5
Haydock Lane Industrial Estate RNFD/HAY WA11 ... 90 D3
Haydock Medical Centre RNFD/HAY WA11 ... 90 C5
Haydock Park Golf Club NEWLW WA12 ... 92 A6
Haydock Park Racecourse AIMK WN4 ... 91 H2
Hayfield School GR/UP/WCH CH49 ... 129 H3
Hazel Business Park RNFD/HAY WA11 ... 75 K5
Heath Road Medical Centre RUNC WA7 ... 176 E5
The Heath Specialist Technical College RUNC WA7 ... 176 E6
Heatwaves Leisure Centre STBRV L28 ... 100 B5
Hebrew Cemetery CLB/OSW/ST L13 ... 114 C2
DV/KA/FCH L14 ... 115 G5
EHL/KEN L7 ... 114 A5
WLT/FAZ L9 ... 97 J2
Helsby Cemetery FROD/HEL WA6 ... 200 A5
Helsby Health Centre FROD/HEL WA6 ... 199 J6
Helsby High School FROD/HEL WA6 ... 200 A4
Hesketh Centre (Hospital) CHTN/BK PR9 ... 15 H1

Hesketh Golf Club CHTN/BK PR9 ....23 G3
Heswall FC HES CH60 ....168 C6
Heswall Golf Club HES CH60 ....181 F2
Heswall Health Centre HES CH60 ....167 K4
Heswall Preparatory School HES CH60 ....167 J3
Heswall Primary School PEN/TH CH61 ....168 A4
Heygarth Primary School PS/BROM CH62 ....184 B2
Heygreen Community Primary School WAV L15 ....133 K1
Higher Bebington Junior School BEB CH63 ....150 B5
Higher Side Community Comprehensive School RAIN/WH L35 ....118 B4
Highfield Medical Centre WDN WA8 ....158 A1
Highfield School CL/PREN CH43 ....130 B3
Highfield Special School HLWD L26 ....155 K4
High Legh CP School KNUT WA16 ....165 K6
Hilbre High School WKBY CH48 ....127 J6
Hillbark Hotel WKBY CH48 ....147 H3
The Hillcrest Hotel WDN WA8 ....138 E4
Hillside Community Primary School SKEL WN8 ....57 F5
Hillside Golf Club STHP PR8 ....27 F6
Hillside Health Centre SKEL WN8 ....56 E4
Hillside High School BTL L20 ....5 K5
Hillside Primary School CL/PREN CH43 ....130 A4
FROD/HEL WA6 ....200 A4
Hill Street Business Centre TOX L8 ....132 C3
Hillview Primary School RUNC WA7 ....187 H3
Hinderton School GTS/LS CH66 ....195 J6
Historic Warships BIRK CH41 ....111 K6
HM Customs & Excise National Museum VAUX/LVPD L3 ....8 A6
HM Prison BTL L20 ....82 C6
WLT/FAZ L9 ....83 G5
Holland Business Park BRSC L40 ....55 J1
Holland Moor Primary School SKEL WN8 ....57 G6
Holly Lodge Girls College CLB/OSW/ST L13 ....114 E1
Hollywood Superbowl CLB/OSW/ST L13 ....114 D6
Holy Angels Catholic Primary School KKBY L32 ....84 B1
Holy Cross Catholic Primary School VAUX/LVPD L3 ....8 E1
Holy Cross RC Primary School BIRK CH41 ....110 E6
ECCL WA10 ....13 J4
Holy Family Catholic High School CSBY/BLUN L23 ....69 H3
Holy Family Catholic Primary School CHTN/BK PR9 ....23 G6
Holy Family RC Primary School WDN WA8 ....138 C3
WLTN L25 ....155 G2
Holy Name RC Primary School WLT/FAZ L9 ....83 H4
Holy Rosary RC Junior School AIN/FAZ L10 ....71 G6
Holy Rosary RC Primary School AIN/FAZ L10 ....71 F6
Holy Spirit Primary School STHEL WA9 ....104 E2
The Holy Spirit RC Aided Primary School RUNC WA7 ....177 G5
Holy Spirit RC Primary School NTHTN L30 ....70 A6
Holy Trinity CE Primary School CHTN/BK PR9 ....15 G3
HOY CH47 ....127 H2
Holy Trinity RC Primary School ALL/GAR L19 ....154 A6
Homoeopathic Medical Centre CLB/OSW/ST L13 ....114 E4
Hood Manor Medical Centre WARRW/BUR WA5 ....141 K4
Hope School NTHLY L27 ....136 A2
Hope Street Natural Health Centre CLVPS L1 ....9 J7
Hope Valley Community Primary School EV L5 ....97 H6
Hornspit Medical Centre NG/CROX L11 ....98 E5
Hotel Ibis CLVPS L1 ....8 D7
Houghwood Golf Club RNFD/HAY WA11 ....76 E2
Howley Quay Industrial Estate WARR WA1 ....17 H4
Hoylake Business Centre HOY CH47 ....127 H1
Hoylake Cottage Hospital HOY CH47 ....127 H1
Hoylake Golf Club HOY CH47 ....127 G3
Hoylake RFC HOY CH47 ....127 G2
Hudson Primary School MGHL L31 ....71 G2
Hugh Baird College of Further Education BTL L20 ....5 F7
Hugh Baird College of Technology BTL L20 ....5 F7
Hulmes Bridge Business Centre ORM L39 ....44 A1
Hunts Cross JMI School WLTN L25 ....155 F5
Hunts Cross Shopping Park SPK/HALE L24 ....154 D5
Hurlston Hall Country Caravan Park BRSC L40 ....45 G1
Hurlston Hall Golf Club BRSC L40 ....45 G1
Huyton Leisure Centre HUY L36 ....116 C6
Huyton & Prescot Golf Club HUY L36 ....117 G2
Huyton with Roby CE Primary School HUY L36 ....116 D4
IKEA Store Warrington WARRW/BUR WA5 ....122 C4
Innkeeper's Lodge ALL/GAR L19 ....153 H3
CLB/OSW/ST L13 ....115 F3
GOL/RIS/CUL WA3 ....93 F5
Interactive College CLVP L2 ....8 D3
Interchange Motorway Industrial Estate HUY L36 ....117 G6
International Business Centre WARRW/BUR WA5 ....122 C5
Irby CC PEN/TH CH61 ....148 A3
Irby Primary School PEN/TH CH61 ....148 B4
Irwin Road Health Centre STHEL WA9 ....104 B6
Isle of Man Ferry Terminal VAUX/LVPD L3 ....8 A3
Islington House Medical Centre VAUX/LVPD L3 ....9 K1
Job's Ferry PS/BROM CH62 ....171 J4
John Street Medical Centre GOL/RIS/CUL WA3 ....92 B3
Jubilee Medical Centre NG/CROX L11 ....99 G3
Junction 1 Retail Park WAL/EG CH44 ....110 D4
Kensington CP Infant School EHL/KEN L7 ....113 K5
Kensington CP Junior School EHL/KEN L7 ....113 K5
Kensington Industrial Estate CHTN/BK PR9 ....15 H6
Kensington Medical Centre NPK/KEN L6 ....113 J4
Kerfoot Business Park WARRN/WOL WA2 ....142 D1
Kew Medical Centre STHP PR8 ....28 B4
Kew Retail Park STHP PR8 ....28 D3
Kew Woods Primary School STHP PR8 ....28 B4
The King David High School WAV L15 ....134 D2
King David Primary School WAV L15 ....134 D2
King Edward Industrial Estate VAUX/LVPD L3 ....8 A1
Kingfisher Business Park LITH L21 ....81 J4
King George V College STHP PR8 ....28 B2
Kingsbury School ORM L39 ....45 H6
Kings Business Park PR/KW L34 ....117 G2
Kings Gap Court Hotel HOY CH47 ....127 F3
Kingsley Community School TOX L8 ....133 F2
Kings Meadow Primary School STHP PR8 ....33 K6
Kingsmead School HOY CH47 ....127 H1
Kingsway Industrial Park VAUX/LVPD L3 ....113 F3
Kingsway Primary School WAL/EG CH44 ....111 J5
Kingsway Surgery CSBY/WL L22 ....81 F1
Kingswood College at Scarisbrick School BRSC L40 ....36 E3
Kirby-Liverpool Municipal Golf Club KKBY L32 ....84 A3
Kirkby CE Primary School KKBY L32 ....72 C6
Kirkby Sports Centre KKBY L32 ....84 B3
Kirkdale St Lawrence CE Primary School ANF/KKDL L4 ....97 F5
Kirkfield Hotel NEWLW WA12 ....106 E1
Knotty Ash Primary School DV/KA/FCH L14 ....115 H3
Knowsley Business Park PR/KW L34 ....85 G6
Knowsley Central Primary Support Centre HUY L36 ....117 F3
Knowsley Community College HUY L36 ....116 E5
KKBY L32 ....84 C1
Knowsley Community College (Roby Campus) HUY L36 ....116 C5
Knowsley Hey School HUY L36 ....117 F4
Knowsley Industrial Park NWD/KWIPK L33 ....85 F5
Knowsley Medical Centre PR/KW L34 ....100 D2
Knowsley Northern Primary Support Centre NWD/KWIPK L33 ....72 E5
Knowsley Village Primary School PR/KW L34 ....100 C3
Lady Lever Art Gallery PS/BROM CH62 ....151 G5
Ladymount RC Primary School PEN/TH CH61 ....167 K2
Lairdside Technology Park BIRK CH41 ....131 J5
Lakeside School NTHLY L27 ....136 A2
Lancaster House Medical Centre ECCL WA10 ....13 F3
Lance Lane Medical Centre WAV L15 ....134 B2
Lander Road Primary School LITH L21 ....81 K5
Landgate Industrial Estate AIMK WN4 ....79 F1
The Landgate School AIMK WN4 ....79 F2
Landican Cemetery GR/UP/WCH CH49 ....148 E2
Landican Crematorium GR/UP/WCH CH49 ....148 E3
Langbank Medical Centre NG/CROX L11 ....98 D4
Langham Street Industrial Estate ANF/KKDL L4 ....97 H5
Lansbury Bridge School STHEL WA9 ....104 C2
Larkfield Primary School CHTN/BK PR9 ....23 J2
Latchford CE Primary School WARRS WA4 ....16 E7
Latchford Medical Centre WARRS WA4 ....143 H6
Lathom High School SKEL WN8 ....56 B2
Lathom Park CE Primary School BRSC L40 ....47 G3
Lathom Road Health Centre HUY L36 ....116 E4
Laurel Business Centre EHL/KEN L7 ....114 B5
Lawson House Hotel & Conference Centre RUNC WA7 ....176 D5
Lea Green Business Park STHEL WA9 ....119 H3
Leamington Community School NG/CROX L11 ....98 B3
Leasowe Castle Hotel MOR/LEA CH46 ....109 J3
Leasowe Golf Club MOR/LEA CH46 ....109 K3
Leasowe Millennium Centre MOR/LEA CH46 ....110 A4
Leasowe Primary School MOR/LEA CH46 ....110 B3
Leasowe Recreation Centre MOR/LEA CH46 ....110 A4
Lee Park Golf Club WLTN L25 ....136 A5
Legh Vale Primary School RNFD/HAY WA11 ....90 A5
Library & Rainford Gallery ECCL WA10 ....13 G4
Lifeboat House HOY CH47 ....127 F2
Linacre Primary School BTL L20 ....81 K6
Linaker Primary School STHP PR8 ....27 J2
Lincoln Road Health Centre STHP PR8 ....27 H6
Lingham Primary School MOR/LEA CH46 ....109 H6
Lingholme Health Centre ECCL WA10 ....13 F4
Lingley Mere Business Park WARRW/BUR WA5 ....141 F1
Liscard Primary School WAL/NB CH45 ....111 J2
Lister Drive Infant School CLB/OSW/ST L13 ....114 C3
Lister Drive Junior School CLB/OSW/ST L13 ....114 C3
Litherland High School LITH L21 ....82 A1
Litherland Moss Primary School LITH L21 ....82 A2
Little Digmoor Primary School SKEL WN8 ....66 D1
Little Sutton CE Primary School GTS/LS CH66 ....194 D3
Little Theatre BIRK CH41 ....2 C5
CHTN/BK PR9 ....15 F4
Liver Industrial Estate WLT/FAZ L9 ....98 A1
Liverpool Anglican Cathedral CLVPS L1 ....132 D2
Liverpool College CALD/MH L18 ....134 A5
Liverpool Community College CLB/OSW/ST L13 ....114 D1
CLVPS L1 ....9 G7
EHL/KEN L7 ....133 F1
EV L5 ....113 F1
VAUX/LVPD L3 ....112 E4
Liverpool CC ALL/GAR L19 ....153 G3
Liverpool Empire Theatre CLVPS L1 ....9 F3
Liverpool FC (Anfield) ANF/KKDL L4 ....97 J6
Liverpool FC Museum ANF/KKDL L4 ....97 J6
Liverpool Hope University VAUX/LVPD L3 ....9 J1
Liverpool Hope University College CHLDW L16 ....134 E3
Liverpool Hope University Education Deanery CHLDW L16 ....134 E3
Liverpool Institute for Performing Arts CLVPS L1 ....9 H7
Liverpool Institute of Higher Education CHLDW L16 ....134 E3
Liverpool Intermodal Freeport Terminal BTL L20 ....4 A4
Liverpool John Lennon International Airport SPK/HALE L24 ....173 H3
Liverpool John Moores University AIG/SPK L17 ....153 G2
CLVPS L1 ....9 H7
EHL/KEN L7 ....114 B5
Liverpool Marriott Hotel CLVPS L1 ....9 F3
SPK/HALE L24 ....172 E1
Liverpool Museum VAUX/LVPD L3 ....9 F2
Liverpool Playhouse Theatre CLVPS L1 ....9 F4
Liverpool St Helens RUFC RNFD/HAY WA11 ....87 H4
Liverpool University Botanic Gardens (Ness Gardens) NSTN CH64 ....192 B5
Liverpool University Dental Hospital VAUX/LVPD L3 ....9 K3
Liverpool Womens Hospital TOX L8 ....133 F1
Lockett Business Park AIMK WN4 ....79 H4
Locking Stumps Primary School GOL/RIS/CUL WA3 ....124 E2
Longbarn CP School WARRN/WOL WA2 ....124 D6
Long Lane CP School WARRN/WOL WA2 ....123 H6
Long Lane Medical Centre WLT/FAZ L9 ....98 D1
Longmoor Community Primary School WLT/FAZ L9 ....82 E5
Longton Lane Community Primary School RAIN/WH L35 ....118 D2
Longton Medical Centre RAIN/WH L35 ....118 D4
Longview Community Primary School HUY L36 ....116 E1
Lordsgate Township CE Primary School BRSC L40 ....38 E5
Lourdes Hospital CALD/MH L18 ....134 A5
Loushers Lane Special School WARRS WA4 ....162 C1
Lower Lee Special School WLTN L25 ....135 F5
Lowfield Industrial Estate STHEL WA9 ....119 H2
Lowton Business Park GOL/RIS/CUL WA3 ....93 H3
Lowton Community Sports College GOL/RIS/CUL WA3 ....93 J3
Lowton J & I School GOL/RIS/CUL WA3 ....93 H4
Lowton St Marys CE Primary School GOL/RIS/CUL WA3 ....93 J3
Lowton West Primary School GOL/RIS/CUL WA3 ....92 D3
Lunts Heath Primary School WDN WA8 ....139 G4
Lydiate Primary School MGHL L31 ....62 A3
Lyme Community Primary School NEWLW WA12 ....105 K1
Lymm Golf Club LYMM WA13 ....145 J4
The Lymm Hotel LYMM WA13 ....145 J5
Lymm RFC LYMM WA13 ....165 F2
The Lyndale School PS/BROM CH62 ....184 C2
Lyon Industrial Estate STHEL WA9 ....120 B3
Mab Lane JMI School STBRV L28 ....99 K6
Mackets Primary School WLTN L25 ....155 G2
Maghull Health Centre MGHL L31 ....62 A6
Maghull High School MGHL L31 ....71 F2
Malvern Primary School DV/KA/FCH L14 ....115 K5
Manor Farm Medical Centre HUY L36 ....117 F6
The Manor House Primary School FROD/HEL WA6 ....187 F6
Manor Industrial Estate WARRS WA4 ....17 K7
Manor Primary School CL/PREN CH43 ....129 K2
Mansfield Primary School EP CH65 ....195 J6
Marble Place Shopping Centre STHP PR8 ....14 E5
The Margaret Thompson Medical Centre SPK/HALE L24 ....174 B1
Maricourt Catholic High School MGHL L31 ....71 H1
Marine FC CSBY/BLUN L23 ....68 D6
Marshside Primary School CHTN/BK PR9 ....20 C6
Marshside RSPB Reserve CHTN/BK PR9 ....20 A6
Martlew Day Hospital RAIN/WH L35 ....118 E2
Maryland Health Centre CLVPS L1 ....9 J6
Massey Hall School WARRS WA4 ....164 A1
Maternity & Child Welfare Clinic STHEL WA9 ....104 D2
Matthew Arnold Primary School TOX L8 ....133 F6
Mayflower Industrial Estate FMBY L37 ....49 G4
Meadow Bank Special School AIN/FAZ L10 ....83 J3
Meadow Community Primary School GTS/LS CH66 ....202 C1
Meadow Lane Industrial Park EP CH65 ....7 F3
Meadowside School GR/UP/WCH CH49 ....148 D1
Megabowl NTHTN L30 ....70 D6
Melling Primary School MGHL L31 ....72 A5
Mendell Primary School PS/BROM CH62 ....171 G5
Meols Cop High School STHP PR8 ....28 C2
Meols Cop Retail Park CHTN/BK PR9 ....28 C3
Merchant Taylors Junior School for Girls CSBY/BLUN L23 ....69 F6
Merchant Taylors School CSBY/BLUN L23 ....69 F6
Merchant Taylors School for Girls CSBY/BLUN L23 ....68 E5
Mere Brow CE Primary School KIRK/FR/WAR PR4 ....25 K3
Merefield Special School STHP PR8 ....33 H5
Mersey Ferries Terminal VAUX/LVPD L3 ....8 B5
Mersey Park Primary School RF/TRAN CH42 ....131 H6
Merseyside Maritime Museum & International Slavery Museum VAUX/LVPD L3 ....8 A6
Merseyside Police Headquarters CLVPS L1 ....8 D6
Mersey Valley Golf & Country Club WDN WA8 ....140 A2
Mersey View FROD/HEL WA6 ....200 E2
Mersey View Special School AIG/SPK L17 ....153 F2
Merton Bank Primary School STHEL WA9 ....104 A1
Met Quarter (under development) CLVPS L1 ....8 E4
Metropole Hotel STHP PR8 ....14 D6
Metropolitan Cathedral of Christ the King VAUX/LVPD L3 ....9 J4
Middlefield Primary School SPK/HALE L24 ....173 K2
Millbrook Business Centre RNFD/HAY WA11 ....75 K6
Millbrook Primary School KKBY L32 ....72 C6
Millfields Primary School PS/BROM CH62 ....184 B3
Mill Green Special School NEWLW WA12 ....106 E2
Millingford Industrial Estate GOL/RIS/CUL WA3 ....92 C3
Mill Lane Industrial Estate CHNE CH2 ....196 E6
Millstead Special School WAV L15 ....134 B1
Mill Street Medical Centre ECCL WA10 ....13 F3
Miriam Health Centre BIRK CH41 ....130 C1
Model Village STHP PR8 ....14 C4
Monksdown Primary School NG/CROX L11 ....98 E4
Moore Primary School WARRS WA4 ....160 D6
Moore RUFC WARRS WA4 ....160 E5
Moorfield Primary School WDN WA8 ....139 J6
Moorfoot Road Industrial Estate STHEL WA9 ....104 D1
Moor Lane Business Centre WDN WA8 ....18 C6
Moorside Primary School SKEL WN8 ....57 G6
Moreton Medical Centre MOR/LEA CH46 ....129 F1
Mornington Business Centre CLVPS L1 ....9 H7
Mosscroft Primary School HUY L36 ....117 G4
Moss Industrial Estate GOL/RIS/CUL WA3 ....93 J2
Mosslands School WAL/NB CH45 ....110 E3
Moss Lane Sports Centre LITH L21 ....82 A2
Mossley Hill Hospital AIG/SPK L17 ....133 K5
Mossock Hall Golf Club ORM L39 ....63 J3
Mosspits J & I School WAV L15 ....134 C3
Mostyn House School NSTN CH64 ....191 G1
Mount Carmel Preparatory School ORM L39 ....53 H3
Mount Primary School WAL/NB CH45 ....95 G5
The Mount-St Marys Preparatory School CSBY/BLUN L23 ....68 C6
Much Woolton Catholic Primary School WLTN L25 ....154 E1
Multibowl PS/BROM CH62 ....171 F2
Murdishaw Health Centre RUNC WA7 ....178 C6
Murrayfield Hospital PEN/TH CH61 ....149 G6
Museum of Liverpool (due to open 2010) VAUX/LVPD L3 ....8 B5
National Conservation Centre CLVPS L1 ....8 E3
National Discovery Park VAUX/LVPD L3 ....8 D5
National Museums & Galleries Merseyside CLVPS L1 ....9 F3
National Wildflower Centre CHLDW L16 ....115 K6
Natural Health Clinic PR/KW L34 ....117 K1
Neptune Theatre CLVPS L1 ....8 E5
Neston CC NSTN CH64 ....191 H1
Neston High School NSTN CH64 ....182 A6
Neston Medical Centre NSTN CH64 ....191 K1
Neston Primary School NSTN CH64 ....191 K2
Neston Recreation Centre NSTN CH64 ....182 A6
Netherfield Family Health Clinic EV L5 ....113 G2
Netherley Health Centre NTHLY L27 ....136 B4
Netherley Sports Centre NTHLY L27 ....136 A4
Netherton Industrial Estate NTHTN L30 ....82 C3
Netherton Moss Primary School NTHTN L30 ....70 B6
New Brighton Primary School WAL/NB CH45 ....95 J5
New Brighton RUFC MOR/LEA CH46 ....109 K3
Newfield Special School CSBY/BLUN L23 ....69 J4
New Heys Comprehensive School CALD/MH L18 ....154 A2
New Hutte CP School HLWD L26 ....155 H5
New Lodge Industrial Estate NWD/KWIPK L33 ....85 G3
New Mersey Retail Park SPK/HALE L24 ....154 C6
New Park Primary School NPK/KEN L6 ....113 K4

New Solar School WAL/NB CH45 110 C2
Newstead Abbey TOX L8 133 H2
Newstead Vocational Education Centre KKBY L32 84 D3
Newton Bank Preparatory School NEWLW WA12 106 E1
Newton Community Hospital NEWLW WA12 106 B4
Newton Health Clinic NEWLW WA12 106 B1
Newton-le-Willows Cemetery NEWLW WA12 106 D3
Newton-le-Willows Community High School NEWLW WA12 91 J6
Newton-le-Willows High School NEWLW WA12 91 J6
Newton-le-Willows Primary School NEWLW WA12 106 C2
Newton-le-Willows Sports Club NEWLW WA12 106 C1
New Way Business Centre BIRK CH41 111 K5
Nicol Mere School AIMK WN4 79 F4
Nine Tree Primary School STBRV L28 100 A4
The Norman Pannell School NTHLY L27 136 B4
Norris Green Family Health Clinic NG/CROX L11 98 C4
North Cheshire Trading Estate CL/PREN CH43 149 H3
North Clinic CL/PREN CH43 130 D2
Northcote Primary School WLT/FAZ L9 97 J2
Northern CC CSBY/BLUN L23 69 G3
North Meols Lawn Tennis Club CHTN/BK PR9 23 J4
North Mersey Business Centre NWD/KWIPK L33 73 H5
North Mersey Community Hospital WLT/FAZ L9 83 G5
North Park Health Centre BTL L20 4 D1
Northway Community Primary School MGHL L31 62 C4
Northway Primary School WAV L15 115 F6
North Western Hall CLVPS L1 9 G3
North Wirral Coastal Park MOR/LEA CH46 109 H3
Norton Priory Museum & Gardens RUNC WA7 178 A2
Norton Priory Recreation Centre RUNC WA7 178 A3
Norwood Primary School CHTN/BK PR9 23 G6
Notre Dame Catholic College ANF/KKDL L4 97 G6
Nugent House School WGNW/BIL/OR WN5 77 G5
Nutgrove Methodist Primary School STHEL WA9 103 F6
Nye Bevan Swimming Pool SKEL WN8 56 D4
Oak Cottage Medical Centre HUY L36 116 E6
Oakdene Primary School RAIN/WH L35 118 E5
Oakfield Primary School WDN WA8 157 F3
Oak Remedial Clinic WD/CROXPK L12 99 J1
The Oaks Community Primary School EP CH65 196 C6
Oakwood Avenue Primary School WARR WA1 143 G2
Odeon Cinema CALD/MH L18 134 C5
CLVPS L1 9 F3
NTHTN L30 70 D6
PS/BROM CH62 171 F3
Old Boston Trading Estate RNFD/HAY WA11 91 F3
Oldershaw School WAL/NB CH45 111 G2
Old Foundry Estate WDN WA8 18 E6
Old Hall Farm Business Park CHTN/BK PR9 28 D2
Old Parkonians RFC CL/PREN CH43 130 D6
Old Rockerrians RFC CL/PREN CH43 149 J3
Old Swan Health Centre CLB/OSW/ST L13 114 E5
Ormskirk Business Park ORM L39 45 K5
Ormskirk CE Primary School ORM L39 45 K5
Ormskirk College ORM L39 45 J5
Ormskirk CC ORM L39 53 K1
Ormskirk & District General Hospital ORM L39 53 K1
Ormskirk Golf Club BRSC L40 46 E4
Ormskirk Rugby Union FC ORM L39 45 J5
Ormskirk School ORM L39 46 B6
Orrets Meadow School MOR/LEA CH46 129 G1
Our Lady Immaculate Catholic Primary School AIMK WN4 78 C3
Our Lady Immaculate RC Primary School EV L5 113 G1
Our Lady Mother of the Saviour Catholic Primary School RUNC WA7 187 K1
Our Lady of Compassion RC Primary School FMBY L37 49 G2
Our Lady of Good Help RC Primary School WAV L15 134 B1
Our Lady of Lourdes RC Primary School MOR/LEA CH46 110 B3
STHP PR8 27 H6
Our Lady of Mount Carmel RC Primary School TOX L8 132 E4
Our Lady of Perpetual Succour RC Primary School WDN WA8 156 E3
Our Lady of Pity Primary School GR/UP/WCH CH49 148 A1
Our Lady of the Assumption Primary School WLTN L25 135 J3
Our Lady of Walsingham RC Infant School NTHTN L30 82 B1
Our Lady of Walsingham RC Junior School NTHTN L30 82 B1
Our Lady Queen of Peace Catholic High School BRSC L40 56 B1
Our Lady Queen of Peace RC Primary School LITH L21 81 H1
Our Lady RC Primary School WARRS WA4 143 H6
Our Lady & St Edwards RC Primary School BIRK CH41 130 E1
Our Lady & St Philomenas Catholic Primary School WLT/FAZ L9 98 C1
Our Lady & St Swithins Catholic Primary School NG/CROX L11 84 B6
Our Ladys Bishop Eton RC Primary School CALD/MH L18 134 D4
Our Ladys Catholic Infant School EP CH65 195 K6
Our Ladys RC Junior School EP CH65 195 K6
Our Ladys RC Primary School PR/KW L34 101 K6
Our Lady Star of the Sea RC Primary School LITH L21 81 H5
The Oval Sports Centre BEB CH63 151 F4
Overchurch J & I School GR/UP/WCH CH49 129 G3
Overdale Primary School KKBY L32 72 E5
Overpool Cemetery EP CH65 195 J2
Oxton CC CL/PREN CH43 130 C5
Paddington House Hotel WARR WA1 143 K2
Padgate Business Centre WARR WA1 143 K1
Padgate Community High School WARRN/WOL WA2 124 B5
Padgate Medical Centre WARRN/WOL WA2 124 C6
Palacefields Primary School RUNC WA7 187 K1
Palace Theatre WARR WA1 16 D5
Palatine Industrial Estate WARRS WA4 143 F6
Palmerston Special School WLTN L25 135 F6
Parish CE Primary School ECCL WA10 13 H3
Park Brow Primary School KKBY L32 85 F3
Parkdale Industrial Estate WARR WA1 17 G6
Parkfield Medical Centre PS/BROM CH62 151 F3
Parkgate Primary School NSTN CH64 181 H6
Park High Lower School BIRK CH41 130 D2
Park House Medical Centre PR/KW L34 117 K1
Park Industrial Estate AIMK WN4 78 D6
Parklands High School SPK/HALE L24 173 K2
Parklands Primary School GTS/LS CH66 195 G3
Park Medical Centre WKBY CH48 146 B1
Park Pool ORM L39 45 J6
Park Primary School WAL/EG CH44 111 H4
The Park Primary School RUNC WA7 177 K4
Park Road Community Primary School WARRW/BUR WA5 141 F3
Park Road Sports Centre TOX L8 132 E4
Park View Primary School HUY L36 116 C3
Parliament Street North Waterfront Business Area VAUX/LVPD L3 132 B2
Parliament Street South Waterfront Business Area TOX L8 132 D2
Parr Hall WARR WA1 16 C6
Parr Industrial Estate STHEL WA9 104 C3
Parr Swimming Baths STHEL WA9 104 A2
Pasture Road Health Centre MOR/LEA CH46 109 J6
Patterdale Lodge Medical Centre NEWLW WA12 106 A2
Peatwood Medical Centre KKBY L32 84 E4
Peninsula Business Park MOR/LEA CH46 110 A5
Penketh Business Park WARRW/BUR WA5 141 J5
Penketh Community Primary School WARRW/BUR WA5 140 E5
Penketh County High School WARRW/BUR WA5 141 G4
Penketh Health Clinic WARRW/BUR WA5 141 F5
Penketh South Community Primary School WARRW/BUR WA5 141 G6
Penketh Swimming Baths WARRW/BUR WA5 141 F4
Penkford School NEWLW WA12 105 J3
Penlake Industrial Estate STHEL WA9 120 C1
Pennington Flash Country Park LEIGH WN7 93 K1
Penpoll Industrial Estate BTL L20 81 K5
Penpoll Trading Estate BTL L20 81 K5
Pensby Clinic PEN/TH CH61 168 A2
Pensby High School for Boys PEN/TH CH61 167 J2
Pensby Infant School PEN/TH CH61 167 K2
Pensby Junior School PEN/TH CH61 167 K2
Pensby Park Primary School PEN/TH CH61 167 H2
Pensby Recreation Centre PEN/TH CH61 148 D6
Peterhouse School CHTN/BK PR9 23 K2
Peter Lloyd Leisure Centre CLB/OSW/ST L13 114 D2
Pewithall Primary School RUNC WA7 176 E6
Philharmonic Hall CLVPS L1 9 J6
Phoenix Medical Centre ECCL WA10 13 F4
Phoenix Primary School EHL/KEN L7 114 C5
Picture House Cinema WLTN L25 154 D1
Pinehurst Primary School Infant Department ANF/KKDL L4 98 A6
Pinehurst Primary School Junior Department ANF/KKDL L4 98 A6
Pinfold Primary School BRSC L40 36 D6
Pinners Brow Retail Park WARRN/WOL WA2 16 D2
Plantation Business Park PS/BROM CH62 171 H3
Plantation Primary School HLWD L26 155 J3
Platts Lane Industrial Estate BRSC L40 46 E1
Plaza Cinema CSBY/WL L22 80 E2
Pleasant Street Primary School VAUX/LVPD L3 9 H5
Pleasureland STHP PR8 14 A4
Plessington Catholic Technology College BEB CH63 151 F4
Pontville School ORM L39 53 H2
Poole Hall Industrial Estate GTS/LS CH66 185 J6
Port Arcades EP CH65 6 D5
Portland Primary School BIRK CH41 130 D1
Port of Liverpool LITH L21 81 F5
Port of Liverpool Building VAUX/LVPD L3 8 C5
Poulter Road Medical Centre WLT/FAZ L9 82 E4
Poulton Lancelyn Primary School BEB CH63 170 C3
Poulton Park Golf Club WARRN/WOL WA2 124 C3
Poulton Primary School WAL/EG CH44 111 G4
Premier Travel Inn AIMK WN4 91 G1
CLB/OSW/ST L13 114 E1
GOL/RIS/CUL WA3 92 C4
GR/UP/WCH CH49 129 F5
GTS/LS CH66 194 D1
HES CH60 168 B6
HUY L36 116 B5
NTHTN L30 70 E5
PS/BROM CH62 171 G4
RAIN/WH L35 119 G6
RNFD/HAY WA11 89 F3
RUNC WA7 188 C3
STHEL WA9 119 H4
STHP PR8 14 C2
VAUX/LVPD L3 8 C7
WARR WA1 144 E3
WARRN/WOL WA2 123 G3
WLT/FAZ L9 82 E2
Prenton Golf Club RF/TRAN CH42 150 A3
Prenton High School for Girls RF/TRAN CH42 150 C2
Prenton J & I Schools CL/PREN CH43 149 K2
Prenton Preparatory School CL/PREN CH43 130 E6
Prescot AFC PR/KW L34 101 K6
Prescot Leisure Centre PR/KW L34 118 A2
Prescot Medical Centre PR/KW L34 117 K1
Prescot Museum PR/KW L34 117 J1
Prescot Primary School PR/KW L34 118 B1
Prescot School PR/KW L34 101 J6
Presfield Special School CHTN/BK PR9 23 J2
Price Street Business Centre BIRK CH41 2 B1
Priestley Business Centre WARRW/BUR WA5 142 C4
Priestley College WARRS WA4 143 F6
Prince Edwin Adult Centre EV L5 113 G3
Princes Park Health Centre TOX L8 133 G3
Princess Drive Medical Centre DV/KA/FCH L14 116 A1
Princes Special School TOX L8 133 F2
The Priory CE Primary School BIRK CH41 2 C2
The Priory Medical Centre NPK/KEN L6 114 A2
Pump House Museum BIRK CH41 3 H3
Pyramid WARR WA1 16 B6
Pyramids Shopping Centre BIRK CH41 2 E5
Quality Hotel GTS/LS CH66 194 C3
SKEL WN8 67 H2
Quay Business Centre WARRN/WOL WA2 123 G4
Queen Elizabeth II Law Courts VAUX/LVPD L3 8 C5
Queenscourt Hospice STHP PR8 28 B3
Queens Dock Business Centre VAUX/LVPD L3 132 C2
Queens Drive Family Health Clinic ANF/KKDL L4 97 J2
Queens Park CE/URC Primary School ECCL WA10 12 B3
Queens Park Community Leisure Centre ECCL WA10 12 D4
Queen Square Bus Station CLVPS L1 8 E3
Queensway Business Centre WDN WA8 158 B6
Racecourse Retail Park WLT/FAZ L9 83 F1
Radio City CLVPS L1 9 F4
Radisson SAS Hotel VAUX/LVPD L3 8 B2
Radnor Medical Centre NPK/KEN L6 114 B2
Raeburn Primary School PS/BROM CH62 184 A1
RAF Burtonwood WARRW/BUR WA5 141 H2
Rainbow Medical Centre STHEL WA9 104 C6
Rainford CE Primary School RNFD/HAY WA11 75 G3
Rainford Health Centre RNFD/HAY WA11 75 H3
Rainford High Technology College RNFD/HAY WA11 75 H1
Rainford Industrial Estate RNFD/HAY WA11 75 J5
Rainhill Clinic RAIN/WH L35 118 E4
Rainhill High School RAIN/WH L35 119 G5
Range High School FMBY L37 48 D5
Ravenhead Retail Park STHEL WA9 103 J4
Ravenscroft Primary School NWD/KWIPK L33 72 D4
Record Business Park WARRN/WOL WA2 142 D1
Rectory CE Primary School AIMK WN4 78 C4
Redbridge High School AIN/FAZ L10 83 J3
Redcourt St Anselms School CL/PREN CH43 130 D4
Redgate Primary School FMBY L37 49 G3
Red Lion Shopping Centre MGHL L31 62 B6
Reginald Road Industrial Park STHEL WA9 120 D1
Renacres Hall Hospital ORM L39 35 K4
Rice Lane J & I Schools WLT/FAZ L9 82 D6
Richard Evans Community Primary School RNFD/HAY WA11 89 J5
Ridgeway High School CL/PREN CH43 130 A5
Rimrose Valley Country Park CSBY/BLUN L23 81 H1
Ringtail Industrial Estate BRSC L40 46 B1
Risley Moss Nature Park GOL/RIS/CUL WA3 125 K3
Rivacre Business Centre GTS/LS CH66 195 H4
Rivacre Valley Country Park GTS/LS CH66 195 H1
Rivacre Valley CP School GTS/LS CH66 195 H2
Riverhill Hotel CL/PREN CH43 130 D6
Riverside Bowl WAL/NB CH45 95 H4
Riverside Holiday Park CHTN/BK PR9 25 H2
Riverside Primary School WAL/EG CH44 112 A4
Riverside Retail Park WARR WA1 17 F6
Riverside Trading Estate WARRW/BUR WA5 160 A2
Rivington Primary School ECCL WA10 12 C1
R L Hughes Primary School AIMK WN4 79 F6
Robins Lane Community Primary School STHEL WA9 104 A5
Robson Street Clinic WARR WA1 17 H3
Roby Medical Centre HUY L36 116 A5
Roby Mill CE Primary School SKEL WN8 57 K2
Roby Park Primary School HUY L36 116 B4
Rocket Trading Centre DV/KA/FCH L14 115 G6
Rock Ferry High School RF/TRAN CH42 150 E3
Rock Ferry Medical Centre RF/TRAN CH42 131 J6
Rock Ferry Primary School RF/TRAN CH42 150 E1
Rock Retail Park BIRK CH41 3 H7
Rodney Fertility Clinic CLVPS L1 9 H6
Roscoe Junior School CLB/OSW/ST L13 98 D6
Rosebank BIRK CH41 2 D3
Roseheath Primary School HLWD L26 155 J4
Rosehill Business Park CHTN/BK PR9 15 K6
Rossmore Primary School GTS/LS CH66 195 F2
Rother Drive Business Park EP CH65 195 K2
Rowan Park Special School LITH L21 82 A1
The Royal Birkdale Golf Club STHP PR8 26 E6
Royal College of Nursing CLVP L2 8 C4
Royal Court Theatre CLVPS L1 9 F3
The Royal Hotel CSBY/WL L22 80 E3
Royal Liver Building VAUX/LVPD L3 8 B4
Royal Liverpool Childrens Hospital (Alder Hey) DV/KA/FCH L14 115 G3
Royal Liverpool Golf Club HOY CH47 127 F3
Royal Liverpool University Hospital EHL/KEN L7 9 K3
NPK/KEN L6 113 J5
Royal School for the Blind WAV L15 134 A2
Roy Castle International Centre for Lung Research VAUX/LVPD L3 9 K2
Rudston J & I School CHLDW L16 134 E1
Ruffwood School NWD/KWIPK L33 72 D6
Runcorn AFC RUNC WA7 11 G4
Runcorn County Court RUNC WA7 177 J5
Runcorn Golf Club RUNC WA7 176 D6
Runcorn Rowing Club RUNC WA7 187 G3
Runcorn Ski Slope RUNC WA7 178 A6
Runcorn Swimming Pool RUNC WA7 11 F3
Runnymede St Edwards School WD/CROXPK L12 115 F2
Rutherford Medical Centre WAV L15 134 C3
Sacred Heart Catholic College CSBY/BLUN L23 69 F6
Sacred Heart Catholic Primary School WARRW/BUR WA5 142 B4
Sacred Heart RC Primary School EHL/KEN L7 113 J5
MOR/LEA CH46 109 K6
SAE Institute CLVP L2 8 C4
St Aelreds RC Technology College NEWLW WA12 106 D1
St Agnes RC Primary School HUY L36 117 F6
St Aidans CE Primary School WGNW/BIL/OR WN5 77 H4
St Aidans RC Primary School HUY L36 117 F4
St Albans RC Primary School WAL/EG CH44 111 G3
WARRW/BUR WA5 16 A2
St Alberts RC Primary School STBRV L28 100 A4
St Aloysius RC Primary School HUY L36 116 C3
St Ambrose Barlow Catholic College NTHTN L30 70 D4
St Ambrose RC Primary School SPK/HALE L24 174 B3
St Andrews CE Primary School BEB CH63 150 E5
WARRN/WOL WA2 123 J4
St Andrews Maghull CE Primary School MGHL L31 62 B6
St Andrews RC Primary School WLTN L25 155 G4
St Annes CE Primary School CLB/OSW/ST L13 114 D4
St Annes RC Primary School EHL/KEN L7 133 G1
HUY L36 116 D6
ORM L39 53 H1
RF/TRAN CH42 150 E3
STHEL WA9 104 B6
St Anns CE Primary School RAIN/WH L35 118 E4
WARRN/WOL WA2 143 F1
St Anselms College CL/PREN CH43 130 D3
St Anthony of Padua RC Primary School CALD/MH L18 134 A5
St Anthony's Shopping Centre EV L5 113 G2
St Augustine of Canterbury RC High School RNFD/HAY WA11 89 H6
St Augustines Catholic Primary Sch WARRS WA4 143 J5
St Augustines RC Primary School RUNC WA7 177 K3
St Austins RC Primary School ALL/GAR L19 153 J4
STHEL WA9 102 E6
St Barnabas CE Primary School WARRW/BUR WA5 142 C4
St Bartholomews RC Primary School RAIN/WH L35 119 G6
St Basil RC Primary School WDN WA8 137 K6
St Bedes Catholic High School ORM L39 53 H1
St Bedes RC J & I School WDN WA8 18 D1
St Benedicts College ALL/GAR L19 154 A5
St Benedicts RC Primary School NTHTN L30 70 C4
WARRN/WOL WA2 143 G2
St Benets Chapel & Presbytery Cemetery FROD/HEL WA6 200 D3
St Bernards RC Primary School EP CH65 196 C6
St Berteline CE Primary School RUNC WA7 178 B5
St Bridgets Catholic Primary School WARRN/WOL WA2 124 B4
St Bridgets CE Primary School WKBY CH48 146 C2

St Brigids RC Primary School *DV/KA/FCH* L14 .... 100 A6
St Catherines Centre for Girls *RNFD/HAY* WA11 .... 89 H5
St Catherine's Hospital *RF/TRAN* CH42 .... 131 G6
St Catherines RC Primary School *GOL/RIS/CUL* WA3 .... 93 F3
St Cecilias RC Infant School *CLB/OSW/ST* L13 .... 114 C2
St Chads Catholic High School *RUNC* WA7 .... 177 G6
St Charles RC Primary School *AIG/SPK* L17 .... 152 D1
St Christophers Catholic Primary School *SPK/HALE* L24 .... 173 J1
St Clares RC Primary School *WAV* L15 .... 133 J2
St Clements RC Primary School *RUNC* WA7 .... 10 D7
St Cleopas CE Primary School *TOX* L8 .... 132 E5
St Columbas RC Primary School *HUY* L36 .... 116 E2
St Cuthberts Catholic High School *STHEL* WA9 .... 104 D4
St Cuthberts RC Primary School *CLB/OSW/ST* L13 .... 114 D4
St Dominics RC J & I School *DV/KA/FCH* L14 .... 116 B1
St Edmund Arrowsmith Catholic High School
AIMK WN4 .... 91 F1
RAIN/WH L35 .... 118 B2
St Edmund of Canterbury Catholic High School *DV/KA/FCH* L14 .... 116 B1
St Edmunds Catholic Primary School *SKEL* WN8 .... 56 B4
St Edmund's & St Thomas Catholic Primary School *CSBY/WL* L22 .... 80 E2
St Edwards RC Primary School *RUNC* WA7 .... 11 G3
St Elizabeths Catholic Primary School *LITH* L21 .... 81 K5
St Elphin Fairfield CE Primary School *WARR* WA1 .... 17 G2
St Finbars Catholic Primary School *TOX* L8 .... 133 F6
St Francis De Sales Catholic Junior Mixed School *ANF/KKDL* L4 .... 97 G4
St Francis de Sales RC Infant School *ANF/KKDL* L4 .... 5 K7
St Francis of Assisi Catholic Primary School *SKEL* WN8 .... 57 F6
St Francis of Assisi RC Primary School *ALL/GAR* L19 .... 153 K5
St Francis Xaviers College *WLTN* L25 .... 135 F5
St George of England High School *BTL* L20 .... 82 A5
St George's Hall *CLVPS* L1 .... 9 F3
St Georges Medical Centre *WAL/NB* CH45 .... 95 H6
St Georges Primary School *WAL/NB* CH45 .... 110 E2
St Georges RC Primary School *MGHL* L31 .... 71 G2
St Gerrards RC Primary School *WDN* WA8 .... 18 E5
St Gregorys Catholic Primary School *MGHL* L31 .... 62 A3
St Gregorys RC High School *WARRW/BUR* WA5 .... 142 A4
St Gregorys RC JMI School *NTHLY* L27 .... 136 B4
St Helens AFC *STHEL* WA9 .... 104 D6
St Helens College *ECCL* WA10 .... 13 F5
St Helens Community College *NEWLW* WA12 .... 106 B1
St Helens Crematorium *ECCL* WA10 .... 87 K4
St Helens Cricket Club *ECCL* WA10 .... 12 C1
St Helens Hospital *STHEL* WA9 .... 104 A4
St Helens Retail Park *STHEL* WA9 .... 13 K6
St Helens RLFC (Knowsley Road Stadium) *ECCL* WA10 .... 102 E2
St Helens Theatre Royal *ECCL* WA10 .... 13 H5
St Hildas CE High School *AIG/SPK* L17 .... 133 J4
St Hughs JMI School *WAV* L15 .... 133 J2
St James CE Primary School *BRSC* L40 .... 54 E1
St James Primary School *RNFD/HAY* WA11 .... 90 D5
St James RC Primary School
School *BTL* L20 .... 4 C2
SKEL WN8 .... 56 D1
St Joan of Arc RC Primary School *BTL* L20 .... 4 B1
St John Bosco High School *NG/CROX* L11 .... 98 E2
St John Bosco RC Primary School *MGHL* L31 .... 61 K5
St John Fisher J & I School *WDN* WA8 .... 19 K1
St John Fisher RC Primary School *PR/KW* L34 .... 100 C1
St John's Beacon *CLVPS* L1 .... 9 F4
St Johns Catholic J & I School *BEB* CH63 .... 150 E4
St Johns Catholic Primary School *BRSC* L40 .... 46 E1
St Johns CE Primary School
BRSC L40 .... 39 F4
CHTN/BK PR9 .... 21 F6
CSBY/WL L22 .... 80 E2
St Johns Primary School *ANF/KKDL* L4 .... 97 G5
St Johns RC Primary School *SKEL* WN8 .... 56 E4
St John's Shopping Centre *CLVPS* L1 .... 9 F4
St John Stone Catholic Primary School *STHP* PR8 .... 41 K1
St John Vianney RC Primary School *STHEL* WA9 .... 119 G1
St Josephs Catholic Primary School *WARRW/BUR* WA5 .... 141 F4
St Josephs RC Primary School
GR/UP/WCH CH49 .... 129 H4
HUY L36 .... 117 F4
KKBY L32 .... 84 D2
WAL/EG CH44 .... 111 K5
St Julie RC Primary School *ECCL* WA10 .... 102 C1
St Julies Catholic High School *WLTN* L25 .... 154 D1
St Laurence Medical Centre *KKBY* L32 .... 84 E2
St Laurences RC Primary School
School *BIRK* CH41 .... 2 E3
KKBY L32 .... 84 E2
St Lawrence CE Primary School *ANF/KKDL* L4 .... 97 G4
St Leos RC Primary School *RAIN/WH* L35 .... 118 A5
St Lukes CE Primary School
FMBY L37 .... 48 D4
GOL/RIS/CUL WA3 .... 93 F4
St Lukes Halsall CE Primary School *CSBY/BLUN* L23 .... 68 E4
St Lukes RC Primary School
FROD/HEL WA6 .... 201 F1
RAIN/WH L35 .... 118 B3
St Malachys RC Primary School *TOX* L8 .... 132 D4
St Margaret Marys RC J & I School *DV/KA/FCH* L14 .... 115 K4
St Margarets Anfield CE Primary School *NPK/KEN* L6 .... 114 A2
St Margarets CE High School *AIG/SPK* L17 .... 152 E2
St Margarets CE Primary School *TOX* L8 .... 132 E2
St Margarets CE Primary School (Infant Department) *WARRN/WOL* WA2 .... 123 J5
St Margarets CE Primary School (Junior Department) *WARRN/WOL* WA2 .... 123 J6
St Marie RC Primary School *NWD/KWIPK* L33 .... 73 F6
St Marks Catholic Primary School *HLWD* L26 .... 155 K3
St Marks CE Primary School *BRSC* L40 .... 36 B1
St Martins Catholic Primary School *RUNC* WA7 .... 188 D1
St Mary of the Angel RC Primary School *GTS/LS* CH66 .... 195 G3
St Mary & St Paul's CE Primary School *RAIN/WH* L35 .... 117 K3
St Marys Catholic College *WAL/NB* CH45 .... 110 E1
St Marys Catholic Junior School *NEWLW* WA12 .... 106 B1
St Marys Catholic School *NEWLW* WA12 .... 106 C1
St Marys CE Primary School
PS/BROM CH62 .... 184 C2
RUNC WA7 .... 177 K5
WD/CROXPK L12 .... 99 F6
St Marys' Market *ECCL* WA10 .... 13 H6
St Marys RC Primary School
BRSC L40 .... 36 E2
CSBY/BLUN L23 .... 69 F1
St Mary & Thomas CE Primary School *ECCL* WA10 .... 12 E4
St Matthews Catholic Primary School *ANF/KKDL* L4 .... 98 B5
St Michael & All Angels RC Primary School *GR/UP/WCH* CH49 .... 149 G1
St Michael in the Hamlet Primary School *AIG/SPK* L17 .... 133 G6
St Michael Jubilee Golf Club *WDN* WA8 .... 157 K4
St Michaels Catholic Primary School
School *NPK/KEN* L6 .... 113 K3
WDN WA8 .... 157 H4
St Michaels CE High School *CSBY/BLUN* L23 .... 68 D3
St Monicas RC Primary School *BTL* L20 .... 5 J1
St Monica's RC Primary School *WARRS* WA4 .... 162 C4
St Nicholas Catholic Primary School *VAUX/LVPD* L3 .... 9 J5
St Nicholas CE Primary School *CSBY/BLUN* L23 .... 68 C6
St Oswalds Catholic Infant School *CLB/OSW/ST* L13 .... 114 E4
St Oswalds Catholic Junior School *CLB/OSW/ST* L13 .... 114 E5
St Oswald's CE Primary School *CL/PREN* CH43 .... 110 C6
St Oswalds CE Primary School *NTHTN* L30 .... 70 C6
St Oswalds RC J & I School *AIMK* WN4 .... 79 G6
St Oswalds RC Primary School *WARR* WA1 .... 143 H1
St Paschal Baylon RC Primary School *CHLDW* L16 .... 135 G1
St Patricks Catholic Primary School *TOX* L8 .... 132 E3
St Patricks RC Primary School *CHTN/BK* PR9 .... 23 J3
St Paul of the Cross Catholic Primary School *WARRW/BUR* WA5 .... 105 J6
St Pauls RC Primary School *CL/PREN* CH43 .... 129 J2
St Peter & St Pauls Catholic Primary School *RNFD/HAY* WA11 .... 88 E4
St Peter & Paul RC Primary School *WAL/NB* CH45 .... 95 G5
St Peters CE Primary School
AIMK WN4 .... 78 E3
FMBY L37 .... 41 G6
HES CH60 .... 167 K6
St Peter's CE Primary School *NEWLW* WA12 .... 106 D1
St Peters RC Primary School
CL/PREN CH43 .... 129 K5
WARR WA1 .... 144 B2
St Philips CE Primary School
LITH L21 .... 81 K3
STHP PR8 .... 15 H7
St Philip Westbrook CE Primary School *WARRW/BUR* WA5 .... 122 B6
St Richards Catholic Primary School *SKEL* WN8 .... 55 J4
St Robert Bellarmine RC Primary School *LITH* L21 .... 82 A4
St Saviours CE Aided Primary School *CL/PREN* CH43 .... 130 D6
St Saviour's RC J & I School *GTS/LS* CH66 .... 195 H6
St Sebastians Primary School *EHL/KEN* L7 .... 114 B5
St Silas CE Primary School *TOX* L8 .... 133 F4
SS Pauls & Timothys RC Infant School *WD/CROXPK* L12 .... 99 G6
SS Peter & Paul Catholic School *NWD/KWIPK* L33 .... 72 E4
SS Peter & Paul RC High School *WDN* WA8 .... 158 A1
St Stephens Catholic Primary School *WARRN/WOL* WA2 .... 123 H4
St Stephens CE Primary School *CHTN/BK* PR9 .... 21 K6
St Teresa of Lisieux Catholic Infant School *NG/CROX* L11 .... 98 D3
St Teresas Catholic Primary School
School *ECCL* WA10 .... 12 B4
SKEL WN8 .... 57 K4
St Teresas RC Infant & Nursery School *STHP* PR8 .... 27 H3
St Theresas Primary School *STHEL* WA9 .... 120 A4
St Thomas Becket School *HUY* L36 .... 117 G4
St Thomas CE Primary School
AIMK WN4 .... 79 H6
GOL/RIS/CUL WA3 .... 92 C2
MGHL L31 .... 62 B3
WARRS WA4 .... 162 C2
St Thomas of Canterbury Catholic Primary School *ECCL* WA10 .... 88 A5
St Thomas of Canterbury RC School *CSBY/WL* L22 .... 81 F3
St Thomas the Martyr CE Primary School *SKEL* WN8 .... 57 K6
St Vincent de Paul Catholic Primary School *CLVPS* L1 .... 9 F7
St Vincents Catholic Primary School *WARRW/BUR* WA5 .... 141 F6
St Vincents School for the Blind & Partially Sighted *WD/CROXPK* L12 .... 115 J1
St Weburgh CE Primary School *WARRS* WA4 .... 162 A1
St Werburghs RC Primary School *BIRK* CH41 .... 2 D7
St Wilfrids Catholic Primary School *AIMK* WN4 .... 79 J5
St Wilfrids CE Aided Primary School *WARRS* WA4 .... 163 G2
St Wilfrids RC High School *LITH* L21 .... 81 K4
St William of York RC Primary School *CSBY/BLUN* L23 .... 69 J4
St Winefrides RC Primary School *NSTN* CH64 .... 192 A2
Sandbrook Primary School *MOR/LEA* CH46 .... 129 G1
Sandfield Medical Centre *ECCL* WA10 .... 12 E6
Sandfield Park Special School *WD/CROXPK* L12 .... 115 F2
Sandhills Business Park *EV* L5 .... 112 E1
Sandon Industrial Estate *VAUX/LVPD* L3 .... 112 D1
Sandringham Medical Centre *TOX* L8 .... 133 G5
Sandy Lane Health Centre *SKEL* WN8 .... 55 K4
Sankey Bridge Industrial Estate *WARRW/BUR* WA5 .... 141 K5
Sankey Medical Centre *WARRW/BUR* WA5 .... 141 F2
Sankey Valley Country Park *WARRW/BUR* WA5 .... 122 D6
Sankey Valley Industrial Estate *NEWLW* WA12 .... 106 B3
Sankey Valley St James Primary School *WARRW/BUR* WA5 .... 141 K3
Savio High School *NTHTN* L30 .... 82 B3
Scarisbrick Hotel *STHP* PR8 .... 14 D4
School of Good Shepherd *ANF/KKDL* L4 .... 97 H4
Seabank Medical Centre *WAL/NB* CH45 .... 95 H6
Seacombe Ferry Terminal *WAL/EG* CH44 .... 112 B5
Seaforth Health Clinic *LITH* L21 .... 81 H4
Sefton Business Park *NTHTN* L30 .... 82 D3
Sefton CC *AIG/SPK* L17 .... 133 H5
Sefton Lane Industrial Estate *MGHL* L31 .... 70 D1
Sefton Park Medical Centre *WAV* L15 .... 133 J3
Sefton Road Health Clinic *LITH* L21 .... 81 J3
Senate Business Park *NTHTN* L30 .... 82 C3
Shaw Hall Caravan Park *BRSC* L40 .... 37 F5
Sherdley Business Park *STHEL* WA9 .... 103 K5
Sherdley Park Golf Club *STHEL* WA9 .... 103 J6
Sherdley Primary School *STHEL* WA9 .... 120 A1
Shorefields Community Comprehensive School *AIG/SPK* L17 .... 133 G5
Shorefields Technology College *AIG/SPK* L17 .... 133 F6
Shoreside Primary School *STHP* PR8 .... 33 H5
Shorrocks Hill Country Club *FMBY* L37 .... 48 B4
Showcase Cinemas *NG/CROX* L11 .... 98 E1
Silverdale Medical Centre *HES* CH60 .... 167 K5
Simms Cross CP School *WDN* WA8 .... 18 C4
Simonswood Industrial Park *NWD/KWIPK* L33 .... 73 G3
Simonswood Primary School *NWD/KWIPK* L33 .... 84 E1
Sir Alfred Jones Memorial Hospital *ALL/GAR* L19 .... 153 K5
Sir Thomas Boteler High School *WARRS* WA4 .... 143 H6
Skelmersdale & Ormskirk College (Northway Centre) *SKEL* WN8 .... 56 C4
Skelmersdale & Ormskirk College (Westbank Centre) *SKEL* WN8 .... 56 C5
Skelmersdale Sports Centre *SKEL* WN8 .... 56 E6
Skelmersdale United FC *SKEL* WN8 .... 55 J5
Skypark Industrial Park *SPK/HALE* L24 .... 173 G2
Slaidburn Industrial Estate *CHTN/BK* PR9 .... 23 J1
Small Business Centre *VAUX/LVPD* L3 .... 132 C4
Smithdown CP School *EHL/KEN* L7 .... 133 G1
Smithy Heritage Centre *ECCL* WA10 .... 87 K6
SMM Business Park *BIRK* CH41 .... 111 J6
Somerville Primary School *WAL/EG* CH44 .... 111 J4
Southbank Tennis Club *STHP* PR8 .... 28 B3
Southdene Medical Centre *KKBY* L32 .... 85 F3
Southern Primary Support Centre *WLTN* L25 .... 155 G3
South Lancashire Industrial Estate *AIMK* WN4 .... 79 G3
Southmead Community Primary School *RAIN/WH* L35 .... 118 A5
Southport & Ainsdale Golf Club *STHP* PR8 .... 33 J3
Southport & Birkdale CC *STHP* PR8 .... 27 F4
Southport Business Centre *CHTN/BK* PR9 .... 15 F4
Southport Business Park *STHP* PR8 .... 27 H4
Southport College of Further Education *CHTN/BK* PR9 .... 15 G4
Southport Crematorium *STHP* PR8 .... 28 E5
Southport FC *STHP* PR8 .... 28 B2
Southport Flower Show Site *STHP* PR8 .... 14 B5
Southport & Formby District General Hospital *STHP* PR8 .... 28 B3
Southport & Formby Hospital *CHTN/BK* PR9 .... 15 F4
Southport General Infirmary *STHP* PR8 .... 28 A2
Southport Girls FC *STHP* PR8 .... 28 C1
Southport Landing Area *STHP* PR8 .... 26 E1
Southport Municipal Golf Club *CHTN/BK* PR9 .... 22 E3
Southport Old Links Golf Club *CHTN/BK* PR9 .... 23 K4
Southport Pier *STHP* PR8 .... 14 B1
Southport RFC *STHP* PR8 .... 27 F6
Southport Sailing Club *STHP* PR8 .... 14 D1
Southport Swimming Baths *STHP* PR8 .... 14 B5
South Sefton Business Centre *BTL* L20 .... 4 D6
South Wallasey Neighbourhood College *WAL/EG* CH44 .... 111 H5
South Wirral High School *PS/BROM* CH62 .... 184 A3
Speke Family Health Clinic *SPK/HALE* L24 .... 173 K2
Speke Hall Industrial Estate *SPK/HALE* L24 .... 173 G2
Speke Hall (NT) *SPK/HALE* L24 .... 172 E3
Sphynx Tennis Club *STHP* PR8 .... 28 B3
The Sporting Edge Track *ORM* L39 .... 54 A2
Springfield Special School *KKBY* L32 .... 84 D4
Springwell Park Primary School *BTL* L20 .... 82 A6
Springwood Crematorium *WLTN* L25 .... 154 C3
Springwood Heath Primary School *ALL/GAR* L19 .... 154 B3
The Stables Business Centre *CLB/OSW/ST* L13 .... 98 C6
Stadt Moers Country Park *RAIN/WH* L35 .... 117 J5
Stanlaw Abbey Primary School *EP* CH65 .... 203 H1
Stanley High School Specialist Sports College *CHTN/BK* PR9 .... 23 H1
Stanley Medical Centre *EV* L5 .... 113 F1
Stanley School *PEN/TH* CH61 .... 148 D5
Stanney Mill Industrial Estate *CHNE* CH2 .... 203 K2
Stanney Mill Industrial Park *CHNE* CH2 .... 196 E6
Stanney Ten Industrial Estate *CHNE* CH2 .... 203 K1
Stanney Woods Country Park *EP* CH65 .... 203 F2
Stanton Road Primary School *BEB* CH63 .... 170 B2
Statham Primary School *LYMM* WA13 .... 145 H5
Station Road Industrial Estate *WARRS* WA4 .... 162 E1
Stockbridge Village Health Centre *STBRV* L28 .... 100 A5
Stockton Heath Community Primary School *WARRS* WA4 .... 162 B2
Stockton Heath Medical Centre *WARRS* WA4 .... 162 B2
Stockton Wood Community Primary School *SPK/HALE* L24 .... 173 H2
Stonebridge Business Park (under development) *NG/CROX* L11 .... 83 K6
Stone Cross Business Park *GOL/RIS/CUL* WA3 .... 92 C4
Stopgate Medical Centre *WLT/FAZ* L9 .... 98 B2
Storrsdale Medical Centre *CALD/MH* L18 .... 134 C6
The Strand Medical Centre *BTL* L20 .... 4 E2
Strand Shopping Centre *BTL* L20 .... 4 E3
Streatham House School *CSBY/BLUN* L23 .... 68 D5
Sudley House *CALD/MH* L18 .... 153 G1
Sudley Infant School *AIG/SPK* L17 .... 153 F1
Sudley Junior School *AIG/SPK* L17 .... 153 F2
Summerhill Primary School *MGHL* L31 .... 71 H1
Sunnymede School *STHP* PR8 .... 14 B7
Sutton CC *STHEL* WA9 .... 120 A1
Sutton Community Leisure Centre Track *STHEL* WA9 .... 119 J1
Sutton Green Primary School *GTS/LS* CH66 .... 194 E4
Sutton Hall Golf Club *RUNC* WA7 .... 187 K4
Sutton High School *GTS/LS* CH66 .... 195 H4
Sutton High Sports College *STHEL* WA9 .... 119 K1
Sutton Manor Community Primary School *STHEL* WA9 .... 119 J5
Sutton Oak CE Primary School *STHEL* WA9 .... 104 C5
Sycamore Lane Community Primary School *WARRW/BUR* WA5 .... 141 J4
Sylvester Primary School *HUY* L36 .... 117 F6
Tanhouse Industrial Estate *WDN* WA8 .... 19 H5
Tanning Court Industrial Estate *WARR* WA1 .... 16 E6
Tate Gallery *VAUX/LVPD* L3 .... 8 B7
Taylor Street Industrial Estate *EV* L5 .... 113 F2
Thatto Heath Community Primary School *STHEL* WA9 .... 103 G5
Theatre & Floral Hall *CHTN/BK* PR9 .... 14 E2
Thelwall Community Junior School *WARRS* WA4 .... 144 C6
Thelwall Infant School *WARRS* WA4 .... 144 B6
Thelwall New Road Industrial Estate *WARRS* WA4 .... 144 B5
Thelwall New Road Surgery *WARRS* WA4 .... 144 A6
Thingwall Primary School *PEN/TH* CH61 .... 148 D5
Thingwall Recreation Centre *PEN/TH* CH61 .... 148 E5
Thistle Hotel *RNFD/HAY* WA11 .... 91 G3
VAUX/LVPD L3 .... 8 B3
Thomas Gray Infant School *BTL* L20 .... 4 C2
Thomas Gray Primary School *BTL* L20 .... 4 D1
Thornton Crematorium *CSBY/BLUN* L23 .... 69 K2
Thornton Hall Hotel *NSTN* CH64 .... 182 A2
Thornton Hough Primary School *BEB* CH63 .... 169 H6
Thornton Primary School *CSBY/BLUN* L23 .... 69 J3
Three Sisters Racing Circuit *AIMK* WN4 .... 79 H2
Titanic Memorial *VAUX/LVPD* L3 .... 8 A4
Tower College *RAIN/WH* L35 .... 119 F6
Tower Hill Health Centre *NWD/KWIPK* L33 .... 72 E4
Townfield Primary School *CL/PREN* CH43 .... 130 B6
Town Lane Infant School *BEB* CH63 .... 150 D5
Toxteth Community College *TOX* L8 .... 9 K7
Toxteth Park Cemetery *TOX* L8 .... 133 J3
Toxteth Sports Centre *TOX* L8 .... 132 E3

Tranmere Oil Terminal
RF/TRAN CH42 ...... 131 K6
Tranmere Rovers FC (Prenton Park)
RF/TRAN CH42 ...... 150 B1
Transport Museum BIRK CH41 ...... 3 H2
Travelodge LYMM WA13 ...... 164 C5
PS/BROM CH62 ...... 184 C4
RNFD/HAY WA11 ...... 90 D4
VAUX/LVPD L3 ...... 132 C4
Trentham Road Medical Centre KKBY L32 ...... 84 A2
Trident Industrial Estate
GOL/RIS/CUL WA3 ...... 125 G1
Trident Retail Park
RUNC WA7 ...... 177 H6
Trinity Primary School
SKEL WN8 ...... 56 A4
The Trinity RC Primary School VAUX/LVPD L3 ...... 112 E3
Triumph Trading Park
SPK/HALE L24 ...... 154 D5
Twelve Quays Ferry Terminal
BIRK CH41 ...... 112 B6
Twig Lane Clinic HUY L36 ...... 116 C3
Unity Theatre CLVPS L1 ...... 9 H6
University Hospital Aintree
WLT/FAZ L9 ...... 83 G4
University of Liverpool Sports Centre EHL/KEN L7 ...... 9 K5
Upper Parliament Medical Centre EHL/KEN L7 ...... 133 G1
Upton CC GR/UP/WCH CH49 ...... 129 G4
Upton Hall School FCJ
GR/UP/WCH CH49 ...... 129 G4
Upton Medical Centre
WDN WA8 ...... 138 A6
Ursuline RC Primary School
CSBY/BLUN L23 ...... 68 C6
Uveco Business Centre
BIRK CH41 ...... 111 H6
Valewood Primary School
CSBY/BLUN L23 ...... 68 E4
Valley Medical Centre
ANF/KKDL L4 ...... 97 G6
CHLDW L16 ...... 135 F2
Valley Road Business Park
WAV L15 ...... 134 C1
VAT House & HM Customs & Excise VAUX/LVPD L3 ...... 132 B3
Vauxhall Business Centre
VAUX/LVPD L3 ...... 112 E4
Vauxhall Health Centre
EV L5 ...... 113 F3
Vernon Sangster Sports Centre ANF/KKDL L4 ...... 97 J6
Victoria Central Hospital
WAL/EG CH44 ...... 111 H4
Victoria Park Arena
WARRS WA4 ...... 17 J6
Victoria Road Primary School
RUNC WA7 ...... 10 D6
Victoria Trading Estate
RAIN/WH L35 ...... 118 E4
The Village Hotel & Leisure Club PS/BROM CH62 ...... 170 E1
RAIN/WH L35 ...... 137 F1
RNFD/HAY WA11 ...... 74 D5
WARR WA1 ...... 142 D6
Village Medical Centre
WLTN L25 ...... 154 D1
Villa Medical Centre
CL/PREN CH43 ...... 149 K3
Virgin Cinemas EHL/KEN L7 ...... 114 D6
Vittoria Medical Centre
BIRK CH41 ...... 2 D2
Vue Cinema BIRK CH41 ...... 3 F4
EP CH65 ...... 203 J2
Vulcan Industrial Estate
NEWLW WA12 ...... 106 D4
Vyner Primary School
CL/PREN CH43 ...... 110 D6
Wade Deacon High School
WDN WA8 ...... 158 B1
Wakefield Industrial Estate
NTHTN L30 ...... 70 D6
Walker Art Gallery
VAUX/LVPD L3 ...... 9 F2
Wallasey Golf Club
WAL/NB CH45 ...... 94 D6
Wallasey RFC WAL/NB CH45 ...... 110 D2
Wallasey School
MOR/LEA CH46 ...... 110 A4
Walton Hall WARRS WA4 ...... 161 K5
Walton Hall Golf Club
WARRS WA4 ...... 161 J4
Walton Hall Medical Centre
ANF/KKDL L4 ...... 97 J4
Walton Hospital WLT/FAZ L9 ...... 97 H2
Walton Lea Crematorium
WARRS WA4 ...... 161 K4
Walton Medical Centre
ANF/KKDL L4 ...... 97 H3
Walton Progressive School
WLT/FAZ L9 ...... 97 H2
Walton St Mary CE Primary School ANF/KKDL L4 ...... 97 H3
Walton Sports Centre
ANF/KKDL L4 ...... 97 K3
Walton Village Medical Centre
ANF/KKDL L4 ...... 97 J4
Wargrave House School
NEWLW WA12 ...... 106 C4
Wargrave Primary School
NEWLW WA12 ...... 106 C4
Warren Golf Club
WAL/NB CH45 ...... 95 F6
Warrington Business Centre
WARR WA1 ...... 16 D4
Warrington Business Park
WARRN/WOL WA2 ...... 123 J6
Warrington Bus Interchange
WARR WA1 ...... 16 C4
Warrington Central Trading Estate WARRN/WOL WA2 ...... 16 B2
Warrington Collegiate
WARR WA1 ...... 16 C6
WARRN/WOL WA2 ...... 123 H6
Warrington Community Health Care
WARRN/WOL WA2 ...... 123 F1
Warrington Golf Club
WARRS WA4 ...... 162 B6
Warrington Hospital
WARRW/BUR WA5 ...... 142 C3
Warrington Museum & Library
WARR WA1 ...... 16 C6
Warrington New Town CC
WARRW/BUR WA5 ...... 141 K4
Warrington Sports Club
WARRS WA4 ...... 161 K4
Warrington Town AFC
WARRS WA4 ...... 162 D1
Warrington Wolves RLFC (Halliwell Jones Stadium)
WARRN/WOL WA2 ...... 16 C2
Waterfront Business Area
VAUX/LVPD L3 ...... 132 B2
Watergate North Primary School AIN/FAZ L10 ...... 83 J3
Watergate School WLTN L25 ...... 154 E1
Waterloo FC
CSBY/BLUN L23 ...... 68 C4
Waterloo Primary School
CSBY/WL L22 ...... 81 F2
Wavertree Athletics Centre
WAV L15 ...... 134 A2
Wavertree CE Primary School
WAV L15 ...... 134 A2
Wavertree CC WAV L15 ...... 134 A1
Wavertree Health Clinic
WAV L15 ...... 134 B3
Wavertree Retail Park
EHL/KEN L7 ...... 114 A6
Wavertree Technology Park
EHL/KEN L7 ...... 114 C6
Wavertree Town Hall
WAV L15 ...... 134 B2
Wavertree Trading Estate
WAV L15 ...... 133 K2
Weatherhead High School & Media Arts College
WAL/EG CH44 ...... 111 F4
Weatherstone Business Centre NSTN CH64 ...... 192 D1
Weaver Industrial Estate
ALL/GAR L19 ...... 172 B2
Weaver Park Industrial Estate
FROD/HEL WA6 ...... 187 G5
Weaver Vale Primary School
FROD/HEL WA6 ...... 187 F5
Wellesbourne Primary School
NG/CROX L11 ...... 98 D3
Wellington Employment Park (under development)
EV L5 ...... 112 E1
Wellington Street Industrial Estate WDN WA8 ...... 18 C7
Well Lane Primary School
RF/TRAN CH42 ...... 131 H6
Wesley House
ECCL WA10 ...... 13 H4
West Bank Primary School
WDN WA8 ...... 176 C1
Westbourne School
WAL/NB CH45 ...... 111 J1
Westbrook Medical Centre
WARRW/BUR WA5 ...... 122 C6
Westbrook Old Hall Primary School WARRW/BUR WA5 ...... 142 A1
West Cheshire College
EP CH65 ...... 6 B5
West Derby Cemetery
NG/CROX L11 ...... 98 E1
West Derby Comprehensive School CLB/OSW/ST L13 ...... 114 E2
West Derby Golf Club
WD/CROXPK L12 ...... 115 J1
West End Primary School
ORM L39 ...... 45 J4
Westfield Primary School
RUNC WA7 ...... 10 B6
West Gillbrands Industrial Estate SKEL WN8 ...... 56 A6
West Kirby Foot Health Clinic
WKBY CH48 ...... 146 C1
West Kirby Grammar School
WKBY CH48 ...... 127 F6
West Kirby Health Centre & Swimming Pool
WKBY CH48 ...... 146 B1
West Kirby Primary School
WKBY CH48 ...... 127 F5
West Kirby Residential School
WKBY CH48 ...... 126 E6
West Kirby Sailing Club
WKBY CH48 ...... 146 C3
West Lancashire Golf Club
CSBY/BLUN L23 ...... 68 B3
West Lancashire Yacht Club
STHP PR8 ...... 14 D1
Westminster Industrial Park
EP CH65 ...... 195 J3
Westminster Medical Centre
ANF/KKDL L4 ...... 97 G4
Westminster Primary School
EP CH65 ...... 6 D2
Westminster Retail Park
EP CH65 ...... 7 F2
Westminster Road Swimming Pool ANF/KKDL L4 ...... 97 G6
Weston Point Primary School
RUNC WA7 ...... 176 B6
Weston Primary School
RUNC WA7 ...... 186 D1
West Park RFC ECCL WA10 ...... 102 D4
Westside Industrial Estate
STHEL WA9 ...... 104 A3
West Tower Country House Hotel ORM L39 ...... 52 D5
Westvale Health Centre
KKBY L32 ...... 84 B1
Westvale Primary School
KKBY L32 ...... 84 A1
Wheathill Industrial Estate
NTHLY L27 ...... 136 A3
Wheatland Business Park
WAL/EG CH44 ...... 111 K5
Whetstone Lane Health Centre BIRK CH41 ...... 2 D6
Whiston Health Centre
RAIN/WH L35 ...... 117 K4
Whiston Hospital
RAIN/WH L35 ...... 118 B3
Whiston Willis Primary School
RAIN/WH L35 ...... 118 B4
Whitby Heath Primary School
EP CH65 ...... 196 A6
The Whitby High School
GTS/LS CH66 ...... 202 E2
Whitefield CC
CHLDW L16 ...... 115 K6
Whitefield Primary School
NPK/KEN L6 ...... 113 J3
Whiteledge Centre SKEL WN8 ...... 56 D5
White Thorn Special School
WLT/FAZ L9 ...... 83 F3
Widnes Crematorium
WDN WA8 ...... 138 E6
Widnes CC WDN WA8 ...... 139 G5
Widnes Golf Club WDN WA8 ...... 18 B1
Widnes Public Baths
WDN WA8 ...... 18 D4
Widnes & Runcorn Sixth Form College WDN WA8 ...... 138 D4
Widnes Vikings RLFC (Halton Stadium) WDN WA8 ...... 18 B4
Wildfowl & Wetlands Trust Martin Mere BRSC L40 ...... 31 G6
Willaston Primary School
NSTN CH64 ...... 193 G1
William Beamont Community High School & Specialist Sports College
WARRN/WOL WA2 ...... 123 H6
William Gladstone CE Primary School LITH L21 ...... 81 H4
William Stockton Primary School EP CH65 ...... 6 B4
Willowbank Holiday Home & Touring Park STHP PR8 ...... 41 H1
Willow Grove School
AIMK WN4 ...... 79 K4
Willow Tree Primary School
STHEL WA9 ...... 120 B3
Wilson Business Centre
HUY L36 ...... 117 G6
Windlehurst Community Primary School
ECCL WA10 ...... 88 B5
Windmill Animal Farm
BRSC L40 ...... 31 G3
Windmill Hill Primary School
RUNC WA7 ...... 178 B3
Windmill Shopping Centre
WDN WA8 ...... 19 F3
Windsor Community Primary School TOX L8 ...... 132 E3
Wingate Medical Centre
NWD/KWIPK L33 ...... 73 F6
Winstanley Industrial Estate
WARRN/WOL WA2 ...... 123 H6
Winwick CE Primary School
WARRN/WOL WA2 ...... 123 H1
Winwick Parish Leisure Centre
WARRN/WOL WA2 ...... 123 H1
Wirral Business Centre
BIRK CH41 ...... 111 J6
Wirral Business Park
GR/UP/WCH CH49 ...... 129 G6
Wirral Country Park
NSTN CH64 ...... 193 F2
PEN/TH CH61 ...... 166 D2
Wirral Grammar School for Boys BEB CH63 ...... 170 A1
Wirral Grammar School for Girls BEB CH63 ...... 170 A1
Wirral Hospital
BEB CH63 ...... 169 K4
Wirral International Business Park PS/BROM CH62 ...... 171 H3
Wirral Ladies Golf Club
CL/PREN CH43 ...... 130 B3
Wirral Metropolitan College
PS/BROM CH62 ...... 171 J6
Wirral Museum BIRK CH41 ...... 3 H4
Wirral Stroke & Head Injury Clinic CL/PREN CH43 ...... 149 J2
Wirral Tennis & Sports Centre
CL/PREN CH43 ...... 110 D5
Wolverham Primary School
EP CH65 ...... 7 F6
Woodchurch CE Primary School GR/UP/WCH CH49 ...... 148 E1
Woodchurch High School Specialist Engineering College GR/UP/WCH CH49 ...... 129 K6
Woodchurch Leisure Centre
GR/UP/WCH CH49 ...... 129 K6
Woodchurch Road Primary School RF/TRAN CH42 ...... 131 F5
Woodcote Hotel
GTS/LS CH66 ...... 184 C6
Woodend Industrial Estate
SPK/HALE L24 ...... 155 F6
Woodfall Infant School
NSTN CH64 ...... 192 B3
Woodfall Primary School
NSTN CH64 ...... 192 B3
Woodland Primary School
SKEL WN8 ...... 56 E3
Woodlands Industrial Estate
NEWLW WA12 ...... 91 H5
Woodlands Infant School
GTS/LS CH66 ...... 202 D1
Woodlands Junior School
GTS/LS CH66 ...... 202 D2
Woodlands Primary School
BIRK CH41 ...... 2 E7
FMBY L37 ...... 48 D2
Woodside Business Park
BIRK CH41 ...... 3 J2
Woodside CP School
RUNC WA7 ...... 177 H6
Woodside Ferry Landing Stage
BIRK CH41 ...... 3 K2
Woodslee Primary School
PS/BROM CH62 ...... 171 F3
Woodvale Airfield
FMBY L37 ...... 41 F3
Woolston CE Primary School
WARR WA1 ...... 144 B1
Woolston Community High School WARR WA1 ...... 144 A2
Woolston Community Primary School
WARR WA1 ...... 144 B2
Woolton Golf Club
WLTN L25 ...... 154 E3
Woolton House Medical Centre WLTN L25 ...... 154 D1
Woolton Infant & Junior School WLTN L25 ...... 135 J6
Woolton Swimming Pool
WLTN L25 ...... 154 D1
World of Glass
ECCL WA10 ...... 13 G6
Yew Tree Trading Estate
RNFD/HAY WA11 ...... 90 C3

Acknowledgements

Schools address data provided by Education Direct.

Petrol station information supplied by Johnsons

Garden centre information provided by

Garden Centre Association Britains best garden centres

Wyevale Garden Centres 

The statement on the front cover of this atlas is sourced, selected and quoted from a reader comment and feedback form received in 2004